LAW OF COPYRIGHT

LAW OF COPYRIGHT

Second Edition

JATINDRA KUMAR DAS
Professor of Law and Head, Department of Law
Dean, Faculty of Law
University of Calcutta, Kolkata

PHI Learning Private Limited
Delhi-110092
2025

*In fond memory of **Shri Asoke K. Ghosh** (October 1942–February 2024), Founder Chairman and Managing Director of PHI Learning, whose vision endlessly inspires.*

The Legacy Continues... .

Published by Pushpita Ghosh, PHI Learning Private Limited, Rimjhim House, 111, Patparganj Industrial Estate, Delhi-110092 and Printed by Syndicate Binders, A-20, Hosiery Complex, Noida, Phase-II Extension, Noida-201305 (N.C.R. Delhi).

₹1350.00

LAW OF COPYRIGHT, Second Edition
Jatindra Kumar Das

ISBN-978-81-948002-0-0 (Print Book)
ISBN-978-81-948002-1-7 (e-Book)

The export rights of the book are vested solely with the publisher.

Where the mind is without fear and the head is held high;
Where knowledge is free;
Where the world has not been broken up into fragments
by narrow domestic walls;
Where words come out from the depth of truth;
Where tireless striving stretches its arms
towards perfection;
Where the clear stream of reason has not lost its way
into the dreary desert sand of dead habit;
Where the mind is led forward by thee into ever-widening
thought and action—
Into that heaven of freedom, my Father,
let my country awake.

RABINDRANATH TAGORE
Geetanjali: Song Offerings

Contents

Preface

As the title of the book indicates, it deals with the law relating to copyright for the copyright governance of the country. When the first edition of the book was published in 2015, there was no readable and dependable book for the general reader interested to be acquainted with the changing features of the law of copyright immediate after the enactment of the Copyright (Amendment) Act 2012. Since the publication of this book, the Supreme Court of India and High Courts have delivered a large number of judicial decisions on the subject. The author has surveyed all such Courts decisions and analysed them and inserted them in appropriate places of the book. It presents not only the provisions of the Copyright Act 1957 in the form of a normative, but points out the changes made thereon by formal amendments as well as conflicts of law which have been settled by judicial interpretations. Thus, in *Myspace Inc.* v. *Super Cassettes Industries Ltd.*,[1] the Delhi High Court held that Sections 79 and 81 of Information Technology Act 2000 and Section 51(a)(ii) of Copyright Act 1957 have to be read harmoniously. The Court further observed:

> Accordingly, proviso to Section 81 of Information Technology Act, does not preclude affirmative defence of safe harbor for an intermediary in case of copyright actions. Section 51(a)(ii) of Copyright Act, in case of internet intermediaries contemplates actual knowledge and not general awareness. Additionally, to impose liability on an intermediary, conditions under Section 79 of Information Technology Act, have to be fulfilled.

Over the last century and a half or so, the proposition that copyright is rooted entirely in a property paradigm, has been applied increasingly and its logic has been extended with ever greater force. In *Common Cause* v. *Union of India*,[2] the scope of ambit of cable television network has been examined by the Apex Court and observed: "No cable operator shall carry or include in his cable service any programme in respect of which copyright subsists under the Copyright Act 1957 unless he has been granted a licence by owners of copyright under that Act in respect of such programme." Again, in *Ferani Hotels Pvt. Ltd.* v. *The State Information Commissioner*,[3] the Supreme Court held there would be no such infringement if there is reproduction of any work in a certified copy made or supplied in accordance with any law for the time being in force. Section 52 of the Copyright Act 1957 permits certain activities which do not amount to infringement. In *Super Cassettes Industries Ltd.* v. *Shreya Broadcasting Pvt. Ltd.*,[4] the Delhi High Court held that in this "exception list" important are reproduction

1. 2017 (69) PTC 1 (Del): 236 (2017) DLT 478.
2. (2018) 13 SCC 440: 2017 (2) SCALE 169.
3. 2018 (5) CHN (SC) 238: 2018 (13) SCALE 672.
4. 258 (2019) DLT 116: 2019 III AD (Delhi) 552.

of literary, dramatic, musical or artistic works for educational purposes, e.g., research, review, etc., and reporting in newspapers, magazines and periodicals, etc.

The law of copyright protects the author of the copyright work from an unlawful reproduction or exploitation of his/her work by others and recognises the maximum exploitation of the creativity by providing several rights. The Chapter 1 of the book provides a detail outline of the theoretical foundations of law of copyright and explains whether copyright is property or not. As law of copyright is a branch of intellectual property law, this chapter also explains the expanded meaning intellectual property and its impact on copyright law, nature and meaning of copyright, general principles, special features and justifications for providing copyright to authors. The Chapter 2 of the book discusses the origin and development of law of copyright at international level and its utility in India. It presents the rudiment principles of various international conventions and treaties on the law of copyright which are applicable in India. Similarly, the Chapter 3 of the book demonstrates the origin and development of law of copyright in England, America and India. The Chapter 4 deals with the works in which copyright subsists. The discussions in this chapter are a necessary supplement to the earlier discussion on the theoretical foundations and origin and development of law of copyright in India.

The Chapter 5 provides an outline of the law of copyright relating to author of work, ownership of copyright, transfer of ownership of copyright as well as recognised rights of copyright owner. This chapter acquaints the reader with different facets of right of copyright owner. It is a matter of fact that copyright is a statutory right and this terms and conditions of copyright is provided in the Copyright Act 1957. The Chapter 6 examines the terms of copyright, licencing of copyright, international copyright and registration of copyright. Special rights are given to broadcasting organisations and performers under Section 37 and 38 inter alia of the Act. These rights are referred to as "neighbouring rights" under international conventions. The concept of neighbouring rights gained importance with technological developments. The Chapter 7 demonstrates the rights of broadcasting organisations and performers. Internet has been characterised as the largest threat to copyright protection since its inception, therefore, Chapter 8 deals with the protection of copyright in internet. The remaining two chapters, namely, Chapters 9 and 10, deal with the certain issues relating to infringement, defences and enforcement of copyright. The term "copyright" has been explained in the book in Chapter 1 and its various facets have been demonstrated in rest of the chapters where it has been shown that various judicial decisions have clarified the true picture of this statutory right.

This second edition should not only be useful to the law students (LL.B./B.A.LL.B including Hon's and LL.M. students), but also useful to the researchers, academicians, jurists, lawyers, judges as well as members of civil society.

JATINDRA KUMAR DAS

Table of Cases

1

Theoretical Foundations of Law of Copyright

ABSTRACT

Law of copyright as a branch of private law under intellectual property regime offers protection of original expression and seeks to balance between two conflicting interests of the private creator and the public. Thus, this branch of law protects the author of the copyright work from an unlawful reproduction or exploitation of his/her work by others and recognises the maximum exploitation of the creativity by providing several rights and their modes to assignment and licensing of the rights. This chapter discusses the concept, nature and meaning of copyright, general principles, special features as well as justifications for providing copyright to authors.

COPYRIGHT AS PROPERTY

Over the last century and a half or so, the proposition that copyright is rooted entirely in a property paradigm, has been applied increasingly and its logic has been extended with ever greater force. Consequently, we take for granted that copyrights are property; property rights are freely alienable; and the grantee of a property right stands in the position of the original holder. However, an examination of eighteenth-century sources shows that the concept of copyright as a form of property was neither the only, nor even the dominant, paradigm in circulation at the time.[1] In fact the author of a copyrighted work under copyright laws has been given little power and less money and the intermediaries own the copyrights, and are able to structure licenses so as to maximise their own revenue while shrinking their pay-outs to authors.

1. For detail discussion see Jatindra Kumar Das, "Law and Practice of Intellectual Property in Contemporary India," in Sabuj Kumar Chaudhuri (ed.) *Cross-Cutting Research in Social Sciences*, (UGC-Human Resource Development Centre, University of Calcutta, 2019) pp. 224–246; Jessica Litman, "What We Don't See When We See Copyright as Property," 77(3) *Cambridge Law Journal* (2018) pp. 536–558; Simon Stern, "Copyright as a Property Right? Authorial Perspectives in Eighteenth-Century England," 8 *UC Irvine Law Review* (2018) pp. 461–506.

The word "property" is derived from the Latin word "proprius" which means "one's own" and "what cannot be shared with others". In this sense, with pre-choice and eventual acquisition of thing, it becomes one's own, a part of one's embodied self. The most important feature of property is that the owner of the property may use it as he wishes and nobody else can lawfully use his property without his authorization. It is commonly agreed that people may own real property and tangible objects. Thus, under property law certain rights or interests in movable and immovable property are protected. As science developed, the need for publication of knowledge became inevitable. This was necessitated that some form of protection to be given to the creator. The work of an author therefore becomes the subject matter of the copyright law[2] and an owner of a copyright indisputably has a right akin to the right of property.[3] Copyright expansionists have long argued that "copyright as property" supplies an appropriate and economically efficient template for copyright. Conversely, copyright critics have seen property talk about copyright as the root of copyright's recent expansion.[4]

The idea of "property" casts a long shadow within copyright law, and thus, the question has persisted whether all understandings of property law are applicable in the law of copyright.[5] Admitting certain variations it can be said that while under property law possession is the root of title and the nature of property is tangible and is of indefinite duration,[6] the same under copyright law is for limited period and intangible in nature. Under the property law, adverse possession ensures title[7] while under copyright law a manuscript is the author's property and thus even if in the hands of anybody the manuscript is found, it still would be the author's property.[8] The scholars of copyright law continuously investing a considerable amount of

2. *See*, *Achla Sabharwal* v. *A. Saptrishi Films*, 258 (2019) DLT 663: 2019 (78) PTC 437 (Del); *Saregama India Limited* v. *Eros Digital FZ LLC*, 246 (2018) DLT 138: 2017 (72) PTC 550 (Del); *Institute for Inner Studies* v. *Charlotte Anderson*, 2014 (1) MIPR 129: 2014 (57) PTC 228; *Dabur India Limited* v. *Shree Baidyanath Ayurved Bhawan Pvt. Ltd.*, 193 (2012) DLT 558: 2012 (51) PTC 441 (Del); *Frito-Lay India* v. *Radesh Foods*, 2009 (40) PTC 37 (Del); *Rajesh Masrani* v. *Tahiliani Design Pvt. Ltd.*, AIR 2009 Delhi 44: 2009 (39) PTC 21 (Del).
3. *See*, *Entertainment Network (India) Ltd.* v. *Super Cassettes Industries Ltd.*, 2008 (37) PTC 353 (SC): (2008) 13 SCC 30.
4. *See*, Henry E. Smith, "Property as the Law of Things" 125 *Harvard Law Review* (2012) pp. 1691–1726; Julie E. Cohen, "Copyright as Property in the Post-Industrial Economy: A Research Agenda" *Wisconsin Law Review* (2011) pp. 141–165; Y. Barzel, *Economic Analysis of Property Rights*, (Cambridge University Press, 1997); T. Miceli, *Economics of the Law: Torts, Contracts, Property, Litigation*, (Oxford University Press, New York, 1997).
5. *See*, Helena Howe (Ed.), *Concepts of Property in Intellectual Property Law*, (Cambridge University Press, 2013); Simon Douglas and Ben McFarlane, "Defining Property Rights" in James Penner and Henry E. Smith (Ed.), *Philosophical Foundations of Property Law* (Oxford University Press, 2013) p. 240; Henry E. Smith, "Intellectual Property as Property: Delineating Entitlements in Information," 116(8) *Yale Law Journal* (2007) pp. 1742–1822.
6. *See*, Abraham Bell and Gideon Parchomovsky, "A Theory of Property," 90(3) *Cornell Law Review* (2005) pp. 531–615; R.C. Ellickson, "Property in Land". 102 *Yale Law Journal* (1993) pp. 1315–1400; R. Epstein, "Past and Future: The Temporal Dimension in the Law of Property" 64 *Washington University Law Quarterly* (1986) pp. 667–722; C.M. Rose, "Possession as the Origin of Property", 53 *University of Chicago Law Review* (1985) pp. 73–88; R. Epstein, "Possession as the Root of Title", 85 *Georgia Law Review* (1979) pp. 1221–1243.
7. Constance E. Bagley and Gavin Clarkson, "Adverse Possession for Intellectual Property: Adapting an Ancient Concept to Resolve Conflicts Between Antitrust and Intellectual Property Laws in the Information Age" 16 *Harvard Journal of Law and Technology* (2003) pp. 227–393.
8. Augustine Birrell, *Seven Essays on the Law and History of Copyright in Books* (Cassell and Company Limited, London, 1899) at p. 1.

skill, labour and judgment in drawing the variations between property law and copyright law.[9] Again, property law's "right" actively enables the exclusive use of the "res" and operates within the domain of positive liberty, while copyright law's "right" disables others from copying the expression and operates as a form of negative liberty. In spite of these variations, it is prudent to note that copyright is a property right as wrestling with the variations is one of the defining and foundational features of the law relating to copyright. The fact that copyright is subject to statutory restriction, but this restriction does not diminish its status as an inherent property right.[10] It is precisely for this reason that copyright's exclusive right to copy is heavily dependent on its correlative—"the duty not to copy"—for its disabling function, without which the right becomes functionally infructuous.[11]

In *Daily Calendar Supplying Bureau* v. *United Concern*,[12] the Court held: "copyright is property, and, therefore, a suit seeking relief of infringement of a copyright is a suit of a civil nature." However, law relating to copyright also provides criminal remedies for infringement of copyright besides civil remedies. In *Ramesh Suri* v. *Custodian*,[13] it was observed: Copyright is a right of property which is transmissible by assignment, by testamentary disposition, or by the operation of law as personal or movable property and other interests in copyright may also be created. The owner is entitled to come to the court for the protection of that property even though he does not show or prove actual damage. Explaining the concept property, the Calcutta High Court in *Tata Motors Limited* v. *The State of West Bengal*,[14] held that the word "property" connotes everything which is subject of ownership, corporeal or incorporeal, tangible or intangible, visible or invisible, real or personal; everything that has an exchangeable value or which goes to make up wealth or estate or status. Thus, the Court further observed:

> Property includes not only real and personal property but also incorporeal rights such as patents, copyrights, leases, chooses in action and every other thing of exchangeable value which a person may have, "profit a prendre", such as a right to catch fish in another's tank, the carcass of an animal belonging to a person.

As a result of expansion of law relating to copyright, computer software and databases came within the scope and ambit of copyright protection.[15] Since the inception, computer software and databases so developed was property. Thus, scientific knowledge was transformed into a form of property which is called intellectual property. While technological developments

---

9. Mark A. Lemley, "Property, Intellectual Property and Free Riding" 83 *Texas Law Review* (2005), pp. 1031–1075. *See also*, G. Calabresi and A. D. Melamed, "Property Rules, Liability Rules, and Inalienability: One View of the Cathedral," 85 *Harvard Law Review* (1972) pp. 1089–1128.
10. *See*, Paul Clement, Viet Dinh and Jeffrey Harris, *The Constitutional and Historical Foundations of Copyright Protection* (Center for Individual Freedom, Alexandria, 2012) p. 2.
11. *See*, Shyamkrishna Balganesh, "The Obligatory Structure of Copyright Law: Unbundling the Wrong of Copying", 125 *Harvard Law Review* (2012) pp. 1664–1690.
12. AIR 1967 Mad 381: (1964) ILR 2 Mad 666.
13. 1981 RLR 9: 1980 (18) DLT 454.
14. (2012) 3 CALLT 1 (HC).
15. *See*, *Star India Private Limited* v. *Department of Industrial Policy*, and Promotion, 2018 (14) SCALE 651: (2019) 2 SCC 104; *Microsoft Corporation* v. *Indus Valley Partners (India) Pvt. Ltd.*, 2014 (2) MIPR 373: 2014 (143) DRJ 191; *Burroughs Wellcome (India) Ltd.* v. *Uni-Sole Pvt. Ltd.*, 1998 (3) Bom CR 481: 1997 (3) Mh Lj 914. *See also*, Annemarie Beunen, *Protection for Databases: The European Database Directive and its Effects in Netherlands, France and United Kingdom* (Wolf Legal Publishers Leiden, 2007); Mark J. Davison, *The Legal Protection of Databases* (Cambridge University Press, Cambridge, 2003).

have had a radical impact upon our social, economic and cultural lives, they have also led to certain problems. In the field of computer software and databases, a massive investment of time and money is required for the creation of a computer programme. However, such software may be easily reproduced by pirating the original thereby saving the expense of both time and money. In the absence of some kind of protection, we may reach a stage where no one will be willing to create software since the returns do not even equal the investment.

Copyright provides protection of literary works which include novels, short stories, poems; dramatic works; musical works whether serious or light, songs, choruses, operas; artistic works whether two dimensional or three dimensional, maps and technical drawings, photographic works, motion pictures, sound recordings, computer programmes, etc.[16] Copyright provides an incentive for creative expression of author. As a matter of fact, copyright protects the commercial value of productive effort, the individual's mind intended to protect all intellectual property capable of extensive reproduction. The object of copyright is to protect the author of the copyright work from an unlawful reproduction or exploitation of his work by others.[17] Copyright is vital to maintaining the democratic character of public discourse in civil society. It supports an independent market-based sector of authors and publishers as the government administrators and private patrons do not meddle with their expressive content.[18] Copyright has a special role in the context of development, particularly since the 1950s when the political map of the world changed considerably. During this period, several states progressively became independent and other states were newly created. In such a scenario, developing countries had to cope with the enormous problems of educating the vast masses of their people through copyright protection.[19]

The critical issue in copyright law as a branch of intellectual property law is how to balance the tension between the copyright proprietor's desire to resist access of the copyrighted works only to those willing to pay for such access and public's interest in freely using the protected work. Thus, copyright law as a branch of intellectual property law is the breeding grounds of a system that seeks to balance between two conflicting interests of the private creator and the public. The balance is provided by the doctrine of "fair dealing"[20] and provisions for "non-voluntary licences"[21] in specific institutions. These doctrines allow copyright of a copyrighted work in certain situations, without deeming the copier an infringer. Thus, copyrighted materials may be copied within the broad limits of statutorily recognised "fair dealing". "Fair dealing" focuses on personal use or use which is not directly for profit. The balancing factor in favour

16. *See, International Confederation of Societies of Authors* v. *Aditya Pandey*, 2016 (9) SCALE 89: (2017) 11 SCC 437; *Twentieth Century Fox Film Corporation* v. *Zee Telefilms Ltd.*, MIPR 2012 (2) 377: 2012 (51) PTC 465 (Del).
17. *See, UTV Software Communication Ltd.* v. *1337X to and Ors.*, 2019 (78) PTC 375 (Del); *PEE PEE Publisher and Distributors (P) Ltd.* v. *Neena Khanna,* 2009 (40) PTC 515 (Del); *J.B. Khanna and Company* v. *S. Asad,* 2008 (5) Mh Lj 1469: MIPR 2008 (3) 19; *Time Warner Entertainment Company* v. *RPG Netcom,* AIR 2007 Delhi 226: 2007 (34) PTC 668 (Del).
18. Shahid Ali Khan, *Socio-Economic Benefits of Intellectual Property Protection in Developing Countries* (WIPO, Geneva, 2000).
19. WIPO, *Intellectual Property Reading Material* (Indiana University, 1995) p. 189.
20. *Star India Pvt. Ltd.* v. *Piyush Agarwal*, 2014 (58) PTC (Del) 169; *Super Cassettes Industries Ltd.* v. *Mr. Chintamani Rao*, 2012 (49) PTC 1 (Del).
21. Compulsory licences (Section 31, 31A, 31B) and statutory licences (Section 31C and 31D) are often referred to as non-voluntary licences.

of public interest is seen in the way in which the copyright legislation permits such types of acts in relations to copyright work. For example, while Section 52 of the Copyright Act, 1957 permits, *inter alia,* fair dealing of the work for the purposes of research or private use, Section 31B provides compulsory license for the benefit of the disabled and Section 31 for the published works withheld from public.

The main motivation for copyright protection is to encourage the creative activities in the form of property.[22] Newly emerging copyright industries are economically flourishing and obviously have a tremendous impact on the growth of national economy.[23] For last few centuries, the utility of copyright has been realised by all developed nations. It is, thus, an established fact that the role of copyright is *sine qua non* in the economic development of a nation and by exploiting copyright property, a number of prosperities can be achieved by all nations. In the recent past, new technologies, like internet, computer software, and databases have dramatically altered the shape of intellectual property throughout the world. Hence, protection and promotion of intellectual property is inevitable for the continuation of creative activities or inventions and for the economic and technological achievement of a nation.

EXPANDED MEANING OF INTELLECTUAL PROPERTY AND ITS IMPACT ON COPYRIGHT

The copyright is a branch of intellectual property like patent, trademarks,[24] designs, farmers and plant breeder's rights etc.[25] As the meaning of the phrase "intellectual property" has been expanded gradually, the meaning of the "copyright" has also been expanded time and again. The "copyright" is an intellectual property, as such, upon assignment, the ownership of right over the copyright would be vested on the assignee or the purchaser for value. Now the question is: Where would go the copyright of the copyrighted works on the death of owner? In such a case, the said copyrighted property as well as the rights flowing there from would definitely pass on to the legal heirs.[26] But in *ICSAC* v. *Aditya Pandey*,[27] the Apex Court further held that in assignment, normally, ownership of copyright of work is transferred but in case of licence another person is allowed to use work by author. Reading of various provisions of Copyright Act, 1957 leaves no doubt that though each of seven sub-clauses of

22. W.R. Cornish, *Intellectual Property: Patents, Copyright, Trademarks and Allied Rights* (Sweet and Maxell, London, 1995) p. 258.
23. For various issues on intellectual property, *see*, J.K. Das, "The TRIPS Agreement and Intellectual Property Rights" 16(6) *International Trade Law and Regulation* (Sweet and Maxwell, London, 2010) pp. 166–174; J.K. Das, *Intellectual Property Rights* (Kamal Law House, Kolkata, 2008); Ronan Deazley, *Rethinking Copyright: History, Theory, Language* (Edward Elgar Publishing Ltd., 2008); W.R. Cornish, *Intellectual Property: Cases and Materials* (Sweet and Maxwell, London, 1999); Holyook and Torremans, *Intellectual Property Law* (Butterworths, London, 1995); David I. Brainbridge, *Intellectual Property Law: Cases and Materials* (Pitman Publishing, London, 1995).
24. For a critical discussion *see* Lisa P. Lukose, "Non-Traditional Trademarks: A Critique" 57(2) *Journal of the Indian Law Institute* (2015) pp. 197–215.
25. *See*, Sanjit Kumar Chakraborty, "Contestation Over the Ownership, Use and Control of Plant Genetaic Resources: Rethinking Plant Intellectual Property Rights from Indian Perspective," 60(4) *Journal of the Indian Law Institute* (2018) pp. 369–388.
26. *See, Deepak Kumar Sanyal* v. *Naba Kanta Bardoloi*, MIPR 2018 (3) 44.
27. (2017) 11 SCC 437: 2016 (9) SCJ 423.

Clause (a) of Section 14 relating to literary, dramatic or musical work, are independent of one another, but reading these sub-clauses independently cannot be interpreted to mean that, right of producer of sound recording, who also comes under definition of author under Section 2(d)(v) of Copyrights Act, and has a right to communicate his work to public under Section 14(e)(iii) of Act is lost.

In fact, the term "intellectual property"[28] denotes the rights over an intangible object of the person whose mental efforts created it. Thus, it refers to creations of the mind, such as inventions, literary and artistic works, and symbols. Copyright, patents, trademarks, designs, geographical indications or any other similar intangible property under any law for the time being in force are instances of such intellectual property. Intellectual property plays a monumental role in furthering the economic interests of a country. The technology developed, research made or invention done in a country is protected which in turn strengthens the economy of that country since the other countries must buy the products from the country inventing, researching and developing the new things or products.[29] In this regard, after the American independence, the *Constitution of the United States of America* under Article 1 Section 8(8) vested in the Congress the power to grant to authors and inventors exclusive rights over their works in order to "promote the progress of Science and useful Arts" by securing for limited times to authors and inventors the exclusive right to their respective writings and discoveries. Copyright was seen not merely as a matter of legislative grace designed to incentives productive activity, but as a broader recognition of individuals' inherent property right in the fruits of their own labour.[30]

In *Mazer* v. *Stein,*[31] the US Supreme Court explaining the link between intellectual property rights and economic benefit to the society held that the economic philosophy behind Clause 8 empowering the Congress to grant patents and copyrights is the conviction that encouragement of individual efforts by personal gain through the talents of authors and inventors in science and useful arts is the best way to advance public welfare. Thus, intellectual property attracts foreign currency and enhances export.[32] The term "industrial property" was used in the 1883 *Paris Convention for the Protection of Industrial Property*.[33] The law of confidence and

---

28. For various issues on intellectual property, *see*, J.K. Das, "The TRIPS Agreement and Intellectual Property Rights" 16(6) *International Trade Law and Regulation* (Sweet and Maxwell, London, 2010) pp. 166–174; J.K. Das, *Intellectual Property Rights* (Kamal Law House, Kolkata, 2008); Ronan Deazley, *Rethinking Copyright: History, Theory, Language* (Edward Elgar Publishing Ltd., 2008); W.R. Cornish, *Intellectual Property: Cases and Materials* (Sweet and Maxwell, London, 1999); Holyook and Torremans, *Intellectual Property Law* (Butterworths, London, 1995); David I. Brainbridge, *Intellectual Property Law: Cases and Materials* (Pitman Publishing, London, 1995).
29. *See*, J.K. Das, New Dimensions of Intellectual Property Rights in India" 3(2) *Pragyaan: Journal of Law* (2013) pp. 11–33 at p. 11.
30. *See*, Paul Clement, Viet Dinh and Jeffrey Harris, *The Constitutional and Historical Foundations of Copyright Protection* (Center for Individual Freedom, Alexandria, 2012).
31. 347 US 201: 219 (1954).
32. For commercial exploitation of intellectual property, *see*, Hilary E. Pearson and Clifford G. Miller, *Commercial Exploitation of Intellectual Property* (Blackstone Press, 1990); John Adams, *Merchandising Intellectual Property* (Butterworths, London, 1987).
33. The *Paris Convention* entered into force in 1884. India is a party to the *Paris Convention.* It was revised several times, the latest being in 1967 at Stockholm, Sweden. For the full text of the *Paris Convention, see*, Alfredo Ilardi, *International Encyclopedia of Intellectual Property Treaties* (Oxford University Press, London, 2004).

passing off was also included within the term "industrial property". The Convention protected mainly three classes of "industrial properties" such as patents, trademarks and industrial designs within the territory of member states. Thus, Article 1(2) of the *Paris Convention* stated:

> The protection of industrial property has as its object patents, utility models, industrial designs, trademarks, service marks, trade names, indications of service or appellations of origin and the repression of unfair competition.

When other right such as copyright was added to "industrial property", the phrase used to describe the entirety of rights is "intellectual property". Thus, in modern times, however, "intellectual property" has acquired a compendious meaning, including all the rights enumerated in Article 1(2) of the *Paris Convention* as well.

The intellectual property is traditionally divided into two categories: (i) industrial property; and (ii) copyright. Industrial property includes inventions in all fields of human endeavour, scientific discoveries, industrial designs, trademarks, service marks, commercial names and designations, protection against unfair competitions, and all other rights resulting from intellectual activity in the industrial activity in the industrial, scientific, literary or artistic fields. Protection of public interest is one of the objects of intellectual property rights. Public interest implies non-interference with others' rights, which is an essential requirement of every civilised society. The society takes the responsibility to protect individual property so that it gets something in return, which is worth making the effort. This is evident from the nature of protection extended to individual property. The balancing of interests of the individual and the society is the foundation of all intellectual property laws. This is reflected from features such as limited term of protection to different types of intellectual property, depending upon the nature and scope of the right conferred upon the owner. The provision of fair dealing or research exemption to promote growth of knowledge, and limitations like provisions for compulsory and statutory licensing, government use to facilitate access to the products of knowledge at affordable costs are also intended to promote public interest. The protection of creators' rights is a fundamental social principle recognised by the United Nations through the 1948 *Universal Declaration of Human Rights* (UDHR). Article 27 of UDHR[34] runs as follows:

> Everyone has the right to the protection of the moral and material interests resulting from any scientific, literary or artistic production of which he is the author.

The modern jurisprudential approach with regard to ownership of author's copyright in literary and musical works is recognition of two rights: author's economic right[35] as well as moral right.[36] Even after lawful transfer of the former, ownership of the latter remains with author and it is protected under law against any distortion or mutilation. The reputation and honour of the creator or author is as much a property right as was enumerated under the

---

34. For commentaries on the Article 27 of UDHR *see* Olli Vilanka, *Article 27 of the Universal Declaration of Human Rights and Internet*, (University of Stockholm, 2014).
35. *See, Chancellor* v. *Rameshwari Photocopy Services*, MIPR 2017 (1) 39: 233 (2016) DLT 279; *PVR Pictures Ltd.* v. *Studio,* 2009 (41) PTC 70 (Del); *Amar Nath Sehgal* v. *Union of India,* 117 (2005) DLT 717: 2005 (30) PTC 253 (Del); *Garware Plastics and Polyester Ltd.* v. *Telelink,* AIR 1989 Bom 331: 1989 (2) Bom CR 433.
36. *See, Luxembourg Brands* v. *G.M. Pens International Pvt. Ltd.*, 2019 (77) PTC 68 (Del): 254 (2018) DLT 603; *Pine Labs Pvt. Ltd.* v. *Gemalto Terminals India Pvt. Ltd.*, 2011 (48) PTC 248 (Del).

Berne Convention.[37] It is in this sense that literary and artistic works of an author or creator are protected as a human right under Article 27 of *Universal Declaration of Human Rights.* The same position with respect to the protection of the honour and reputation of the creator or author was upheld by the Apex Court of India in *Entertainment Network (India) Ltd.* v. *Super Cassettes Industries Ltd.*[38] This protection is recognised to encourage creativity in the field of art, literature, music and aesthetic activity. If the author's copyright is distorted or mutilated, his honour, respect and reputation can be seriously affected. Hence, in every case of mutilation or distortion, the protection of the Court by way of injunction is called for.[39]

The expanded meaning of intellectual property is discernible from Article 2(viii) of the *Convention Establishing the World Intellectual Property Organization 1967* (WIPO Convention).[40]

The Convention does not seek to define intellectual property, but gives the following list of the subject matter protected by intellectual property rights:

1. literary, artistic and scientific works;
2. performances of performing artists, phonograms and broadcasts;
3. inventions in all fields of human endeavour;
4. scientific discoveries;
5. industrial designs;
6. trademarks, service marks, and commercial names and designations;
7. protection against unfair competition and all other rights resulting from intellectual activity in the industrial, scientific, literary or artistic fields.

In a similar vein, the World Trade Organization (WTO) has offered its own meaning that: "intellectual property rights are rights given to people over the creation of their minds". It goes on to state that "Creators can be given the right to prevent others from using their inventions, designs or others creations". These rights are known as "intellectual property rights". However, this is a very general meaning of intellectual property which excludes "ideas" from the ambit of the definition. Under the WTO regime, the Agreement on Trade Related

---

37. The *Berne Convention for the Protection of Literary and Artistic Works, 1886* was adopted on September 6, 1886. India is a party to Convention. The contracting States formed themselves into a Union known as "Berne Union" to ensure the protection of the rights of the authors of work in such States forming the "Union". The Convention underwent several revisions, the latest being in 1971 at Paris. *See*, Shahid Ali Khan, "Role of the Berne Convention in the Promotion of Cultural Creativity and Development: Recent Copyright Legislation in Developing Countries", 28 *Journal of the Indian Law Institute* (1986) pp. 424–440. The leading works on *Berne Convention* are, Sam Ricketson, *The Berne Convention for the Protection of literary and Artistic Works: 1886–1986* (Kluwer Law International, 1987); Wilhelm Nordemann, *International Copyright and Neighbouring Rights Law* (Aspen Publishers, 1990); Melville B. Nimmer and Paul Edward Geller, Nimmer and Geller, *International Copyright Law and Practice* (Matthew Bender, 1988).
38. (2008) 13 SCC 30: 2008 (37) PTC 353 (SC).
39. *Saregama India Ltd.* v. *Puneet Prakash Mehra*, 2011 (1) CHN 341: MIPR 2010 (3) 175.
40. The Convention was signed at Stockholm, Sweden, on 14 July 1967 and entered into force on 26 April 1970. As of October 2014, the WIPO Convention has 188 contracting Parties. The seven UN member states that have not ratified the WIPO Convention are: East Timor, Marshall Islands, Federated States of Micronesia, Nauru, Palau, Solomon Islands, South Sudan.

Aspects of Intellectual Property Rights (TRIPS Agreement)[41] provides for the following rights as intellectual property rights:

1. Copyright and related works.
2. Rights of traders in their trademarks.
3. Rights of manufacturers and producers for geographical indications in relation to such productions and produce.
4. Rights of designers for their distinctive industrial designs.
5. Rights of inventors to be granted patents for their inventions.
6. Rights of computer technologists or their layout designs of integrated circuits.
7. Rights of businessmen to protect their undisclosed information on technology and management, i.e., trade secrets/confidential information or simply, know-how.

Since TRIPS Agreement came into force, it has received a growing level of criticism from developing countries, academics and non-governmental organizations.[42] Some of this criticism is against the WTO as a whole, but many advocates of trade liberalization also regard TRIPS Agreement as bad policy. TRIPS Agreement's wealth concentration effects (moving money from people in developing countries to copyright and patent owners in developed countries) and its imposition of artificial scarcity on the citizens of countries that would otherwise have had weaker intellectual property laws are common bases for such criticisms. Despite these criticisms, in the contemporary era the phrase "intellectual property" has acquired compendious meaning. Intellectual property comprises all those things which emanate from the exercise of the human brain, such as inventions, creations, poems, designs, etc. Thus, intellectual property right means the legal rights which may be asserted in respect of a product of human intellect. The fruits of intellect would exist even if they enjoyed no legal protection. In *Sasken Communication Technologies Ltd.* v. *Joint Commissioner*,[43] it was observed:

---

41. TRIPS Agreement is one of the most important commercial treaties in modern history. Consisting of seven Parts and seventy three Articles, it lays down the basic principles, standards of enforcement, acquisition and maintenance, dispute prevention and settlement, transitional arrangements, as well as institutional arrangements of intellectual property rights. India is a party to the TRIPS Agreement which came into force with effect from January 1, 1995. For TRIPS Agreement, *see*, J.K. Das, "TRIPS Agreement and Intellectual Property Rights: An Indian Perspective" 6 *International Trade Law and Regulation*, Thomson Reuters (Legal) Limited, London, (2010) pp. 165–173; S.K. Verma, "Enforcement of Intellectual Property Rights: TRIPS Procedure and India" 46 *Journal of the Indian Law Institute* (2004) pp. 183–206; C. Niranjan Rao, "Patents for Biotechnology Inventions in TRIPS," 37 *Economic and Political Weekly* (2002) pp. 2126–2129; Sudip Chaudhury, "TRIPS Agreement and Amendment of Patents Act in India", 37 *Economic and Political Weekly* (2002) pp. 3354–3360; Nilima Chandiramani, "Legal Factors in TRIPS" 37 *Economic and Political Weekly* (2002) pp. 200–203; V.K. Ahuja, "GATT, TRIPS and India", 50 *India Quarterly* (1994) pp. 1–14; Suman Sahai, "Indian Patent Act and TRIPS", 28 *Economic and Political Weekly* (1993) pp. 1495–1497; S.R. Sen, "Innovation, TRIPS and Future Trends", 28 *Economic and Political Weekly* (1993) pp. 1918–1919; M.D. Nair, "TRIPS and Public Health: The Doha Declaration" 7(3) *Journal of Intellectual Property Rights,* (2002) pp. 241–244; T. Ramappa, *Intellectual Property Rights under WTO: Tasks Before India,* (Wheeler Publishing, New Delhi, 2000); M. Blakeney, *Trade Related Aspects of Intellectual Property Rights* (Sweet and Maxwell, London, 1996).
42. *See*, Mywish K. Maredia, "Application of Intellectual Property Rights in Developing Countries: Implications for Public Policy and Agricultural Research Institutes" (WTO, Geneva, 2001).
43. [2011] 33 STT 507: (2012) 55 VST 89 (Karn).

> Intellect is not property by itself. Through intellect, you can create intellectual property. It is that intellectual property that will become "goods" once put on a medium for sale. Intellectual property does not exist in the mind of the technician. What exists in his mind is the intellect. Using that intellect, a technician creates or develops "goods". It is that goods which is called intellectual property when put on a medium for sale. Therefore when a technician creates or develops an intellectual property, there is no element of transfer involved. When such intellectual property is put on a medium for sale, it is capable of being transferred. If transfer takes place, then, it constitutes sale of goods.

However, the above stated definition of intellectual property is general in nature and its associated rights are problematic. The general definition excludes, for instance, the most basic product of the mind "ideas" which are not generally protected as intellectual property. Thus, copyright exists in order to provide creators with an incentive to produce creative expression. This incentive is in turn meant to operate through copyright's promise of a set of "exclusive rights" in relation to the expression, which vest with the creator automatically upon creation in a fixed medium of expression and endure for a limited period of time. However, it may be submitted that the traditional explanation for protecting only expression emphasises the welfare losses from monopoly of an "idea". The author is both a user of "ideas" developed by others and a creator of "new ideas".[44] At the other extreme, confidential information[45] is conventionally viewed as a type of intellectual property, even though it is difficult to see how a secret, for instance, a marital secret such as a lesbian affair, constitutes a "product of the mind", although it may certainly have commercial value. Despite all these shortcomings, it is a matter of fact that the WIPO Convention and TRIPS Agreement have expanded the scope and ambit of the protection of intellectual property. Consequently, a large number of copyright protections have been expanded, for example, protection of computer software and database,[46] protection of rights of broadcasting organisation,[47] performer's rights under copyright law.

NATURE AND MEANING OF COPYRIGHT

Nature of Copyright

Copyright is a creation of statute under private property law regime that subsists in certain specified types of creative works.[48] In India the statutory law on copyright is contained in the Copyright Act, 1957 which has been amended from time to time. The latest amendment

44. William M. Landes and Richard A. Posner, "An Economic Analysis of Copyright Law" 18 *Journal of Legal Studies* (1989) pp. 325–363.
45. D.S. Sengar, "Protection of Trade Secrets and Undisclosed Information: Law and Litigation" 53 *Journal of the Indian Law Institute* (2011) pp. 254–276.
46. For detail discussion *see* Atul Singh, "Data Protection: India in the Information Age" 59(1) Journal of the Indian Law Institute" 59(1) *Journal of the Indian Law Institute* (2017) pp. 78–101.
47. *See*, Noppanun Supasiripongchai, "The Protection of Performer's Rights under the Copyright Law in Thailand: The Proposed Reform in the Light of the Prospective Free Trade Agreements with the United States and European Union," 2(4) *Intellectual Properties Rights* (2014) pp. 1–19.
48. *See*, J.K. Das, "Legal Protection of Creativity under Copyright Law: An Overview" in Shiv Sahai Singh (Ed.), *The Law of Intellectual Property Rights*, (Deep and Deep Publications Pvt. Ltd., New Delhi, 2004) pp. 224–235.

was the Copyright (Amendment) Act, 2012.[49] Unlike the Designs Act and the Trademarks Act which draw from pre-existing common law rights, in the case of the Copyright Act, "except under the provisions of the Act, there cannot be a copyright under the common law." Section 16 of the Copyright Act, 1957 makes it clear that there shall be no copyright except as provided in the Act.[50] It is also a settled position in law that no copyright can subsist in an idea and there cannot be any infringement in respect of any idea.[51] Further, copyright[52] is a property right that subsists[53] in certain specified types of creative works conferred by statute to an author[54] of an original literary, dramatic, musical and artistic work; sound recordings and cinematography films. Thus, copyright law covers the broad range of literary and artistic expression, including books, poetry, song, dance, dramatic works, computer programs, movies, sculpture, and paintings. In *Syndicate of the Press of the University of Cambridge* v. *B.D. Bhandari*,[55] the Delhi High Court observed that if a person writes a book on mathematics adopting his own innovative methods in making the subject easily understandable, such a work would be the result of his or her creative thinking and would become a subject matter of copyright protection.

The law of copyright protects the expressed ideas of an author's creativity by recognizing the exclusive right in his creation and enforces such right through effective mechanism. Thus, ideas themselves are not copyrightable, but the author's particular "expression" of an idea is protectable. A work must exhibit a modicum of "originality" and be fixed in a tangible medium of expression to receive protection. The "durability" of copyright protection is limited

---

49. *See, Novex Communication Pvt. Ltd.* v. *Lemon Tree Hotels Ltd.*, 2019 II AD (Delhi) 644; *India TV Independent News Service Pvt. Ltd.* v. *Yashraj Films Pvt. Ltd.*, MIPR 2013 (1) 104: 2013 (53) PTC 586 (Del).
50. *See, Gulf DTH FZ LLC* v. *Dishtv India Limited*, 2016 VIII AD (Delhi) 266; *Tekla Corporation* v. *Survo Ghosh*, 2014 (210) DLT 666: 2014 AIR (Del) 121; *Super Cassettes Industries Ltd.* v. *Mr. Chintamani Rao*, 2012 (49) PTC 1 (Del); *Time Warner Entertainment Company.* v. *RPG Netcom*, AIR 2007 Del 226: 2007 (34) PTC 668 (Del); *Manjeh Cine Productions* v. *A. Sundaresan*, AIR 1975 Mad 22: (1975) ILR 2 Mad. 353.
51. *Deepak Printers* v. *Forward Stationary Mart*, (1976) 17 GLR 338.
52. For the law of copyright, *see*, W.R. Cornish, *Intellectual Property* (Universal Law Publishing Co., New Delhi, 2001); David Bainbridge. *Intellectual Property*, (Pearson Education, New Delhi, 2002); P. Narayana, *Intellectual Property Law* (Eastern Law House, Kolkata, 2001); D.C. Chawhan, "Intellectual Property Rights have Assumed A Significant Importance", 27 (2 and 3) *Indian Bar Review* 2001, pp. 61–72. Section 14 of the Copyright Act, 1957 deals with the meaning of "copyright" which provides it is an "exclusive right." A copyright owner has exclusive right: (i) to copy the work; (ii) to issue copies of the work to the public; (iii) to rent or lend the work to the public; (iv) to perform, show or play the work in public; (v) to broadcast the work or include it in a cable programme; (vi) to make an adaptation of the work or do any of the above in relation to an adaptation.
53. Section 13 of the Copyright Act, 1957 provides for the works in which copyright subsists. According to Section 13(1) "copyright shall subsist throughout India in the following classes of works, that is to say (a) original literary, dramatic, musical and artistic works (b) cinematograph films and (c) sound recording."
54. According to Section 2(d) of the Copyright Act, 1957 "author means (i) in relation to a literary or dramatic work, the author of the work; (ii) in relation to a musical work, the composer; (iii) in relation to an artistic work other than a photograph, the artist; (iv) in relation to a photograph, the person taking the photograph; (v) in relation to a cinematograph film or sound recording, the producer; and (vi) in relation to any literary, dramatic, musical or artistic work which is computer generated, the person who causes the work to be created."
55. 185 (2011) DLT 346.

that copyright law confers and protects only against copying of protected expression. The ownership of a valid copyright protects a copyright holder from unauthorised copying, public performance, and display, and it entitles the holder to make derivative works and to control sale and distribution of the work subject to the fair dealing[56] of the material for certain purposes such as criticism, comment, news reporting, teaching including multiple copies for classroom use, scholarship, research, etc.

The copyright is given against the copying of defined types of cultural, informational and entertainment products. Classically, these have been "literary and artistic works"—the creations of authors, playwrights, composers, artists and film directors. The advent of modern technology beginning with the printing press changed the situation radically. Mass reproduction of copies from the originals facilitated commercial exploitation and making a business of piracy. Hence, the need for protection of the original[57] creativity of authors came to be recognised by the law of copyright. Thus, referring Section 13 of the Copyright Act 1957 the Bombay High Court in *Maroti* v. *State of Maharashtra*,[58] has classified that there are three classes of works in which copyright subsists which, *inter alia*, includes original literary, dramatic, musical and artistic works, cinematograph films, and also sound recording. The significant revolutions that took place in the last century were the invention of computers, internet and digital technology. In the contemporary era, the range of copyright has been complicated by the addition of certain analogous rights given to performers and the producers of sound recordings, films, broadcasters and other entrepreneurs.[59] The Copyright Act, 1957 confers copyright on (i) original literary, dramatic, musical and artistic works, (ii) cinematographic films and (iii) sound recordings. The Act empowers copyright holder(s) to do or authorise the doing of a number of activities. The important among these are:

1. to reproduce the work in material form;
2. to publish the work;
3. to perform the work in public or communicate it to the public;

---

56. Section 51 of the Copyright Act, 1957 identifies the varieties of acts, which infringes copyright and other rights of the owner created by the Act. Accordingly copyright of a work shall be infringed when any person without a proper licence from the owner: (a) does anything, the exclusive right to do which is conferred upon the owner by the Act; (b) permits to use any place for the performance of a copyrighted work in public for profit, unless he was not aware or had no reasonable grounds for believing that such performance would be an infringement of copyright; (c) makes infringing copies for sale or hire, or selling or letting them for hire; (d) distributes infringing copies either for the purposes of trade or to such an extent as to affect prejudicially, the owner of copyright; (e) by way of trade exhibits in public; (f) imports infringing copies, except for the private and domestic use of the importer.
57. Originality is the foundational concept of copyright law. According to Section 13 of the Copyright Act, 1957 original literary, dramatic, musical and artistic works are eligible for protection. *See*, *Vinod Kumar Gupta* v. *State of U.P.*, 2019 (106) ACC 378; *Govindan* v. *Gopalakrishnan,* AIR 1995 Mad. 391; *N.T. Raghnnathan* v. *AIR Ltd.,* AIR 1971 Bom. 48; *J.N. Bagga* v. *AIR Ltd.,* AIR 1969 Bom. 302; *R.G. Anand* v. *Delux Films,* AIR 1978 SC 1613; *Deepak Printers* v. *Forward Stationary Mart,* 17 *Guj. L Rep.* 338. For contemporary issues on copyright law, *see*, S.K. Verma and Raman Mittal (Ed.), *Intellectual Property Rights: A Global Vision*, (Indian Law Institute, New Delhi, 2004) pp. 176–277.
58. 2018 ALLMR (Cri) 4460.
59. Sometimes these rights are called "related" or "neighbouring" rights as distinct from "authors" rights. The traditional norms for the protection of copyright in the works were amended periodically to suit technological changes through the Copyright Act, 1957 in 1984, 1994, 1999 and 2012. *Also see*, *Star India Pvt. Ltd.* v. *Piyush Agarwal,* 2013 (1) MIPR 201: 2013 (54) PTC 222.

4. to produce, reproduce, perform or publish any translation of the work;
5. to make any cinematographic film or a record in respect of the work;
6. to make any adaptation of the work;
7. to do, in relation to a translation or an adaptation of the work, any of the acts specified to the work in sub clauses to (a) to (e) of Section 14 of the Act.

The above mentioned rights are "exclusive" in the sense that the creator (or right holder) alone has the right to enjoy these to the exclusion of others. The author by virtue of his creation becomes the "owner" of the copyright in the work. However, there can be exceptions to this as in the following two cases:

1. The creator may be employed by someone and having been employed to create a work, the rights belong to the employer, not the creator(s), and
2. The creator may transfer his copyright by a document in writing to another person. This is known as assignment.

Copyrights provide protection for original works of authorship. The word "original" means that it should not be copied from other works or alternatively it should be the outcome of independent efforts. The types of creations addressed by copyright range from traditional works of art, including literature, music and visual art, to such modern forms of artistic expression as sound recordings, motion pictures and even computer software. Copyright protection arises automatically, as soon as the work has been fixed in tangible form. Authors may register their works with the Copyright Office, however, and obtain certain procedural and substantive advantages during copyright enforcement. The copyright law affords authors the exclusive right to reproduce, adapt, and publicly distribute, perform, and display the protected work, subject to certain limitations such as the fair dealing privilege. A variety of more specialised rights are provided to certain types of works or in certain specific situations. The term of copyright is ordinarily the life of the author plus seventy years in US[60] and sixty years in India provided under Section 22 of the Copyright Act, 1957. Thus, the essence of copyright is to confer certain exclusive rights on the owner to deal with the work in certain ways. Copyright protects the particular form of expression but not the ideas and thoughts on which the expression is based. Others are free to write about the same subject matter or theme. Traditionally, copyright has embraced literary, dramatic, artistic and musical works, as well as sound recordings, films, sound and television broadcasts and published editions

---

60. *See*, the US Copyright Act, 1976. US Congress has supplemented the federal copyright statute with some related statures. The Audio Home Recording Act, 1971 established a royalty payment system for manufacturers of digital audio home recording devices. The Semiconductor Chip Protection Act, 1984 provides copyright-like rights for the circuitry designs of semiconductor chips. Also notable is the Digital Millennium Copyright Act, 1998 which prohibits the circumvention of anti-piracy measures built into computer software and limits the copyright infringement liability of Internet service providers. A number of intellectual property rights originating from state law are conveniently taken up alongside the federal copyright law. The right of publicity gives individuals control over the commercial use of their identities. In addition, the common law has also developed principles for protecting individuals who submit ideas to others from the uncompensated use of that idea. *See*, Robert P. Merges, Pater S. Menell and Mark A. Lemley, *Intellectual Property in the New Technological Age* (Aspen Law and Business, New York, 2000).

of works. However, in recent times, the range of copyright has expanded, e.g., the word "literary" has been stated to include computer software and electronic databases, artistic works have extended to technical drawings, sound recordings and films have included videos and CDs. More recently, performers' rights have been recognised and moral rights regime has been installed within the framework of the copyright system.

The grant of copyright is a limited monopoly. It is limited in the "scope" of the rights granted and in terms of "time". In India, copyright on a literary work is provided for the lifetime of the author plus sixty years after his death. In case of joint authorship, the sixty years period is calculated from the beginning of the calendar year following the year in which the last (surviving) author dies. Copyright with respect to photographs, cinematographic works and sound recordings spans for 60 years of its first publication. In order to strike a balance between the society's need for access to knowledge and the need to rewarding creators, limited uses of copyright protected works are permitted without author's consent. These are called "fair dealing"/"fair use" of copyright. Section 52 of the Copyright Act, 1957 permits certain activities which do not amount to infringement. Important in this "exception list" are reproduction of literary, dramatic, musical or artistic works for educational purposes, e.g., research, review, etc., and reporting in newspapers, magazines and periodicals, etc.[61]

It emerges from the foregoing discussion that the law of copyright is a statutory right under private law regime and origin of any copyright rests solely on the statutory system that confers on the holder of a copyright the exclusive right to use, license or sell any copyrighted work. All the requirements that are needed to generate a copyright derive from statute, for example, an original work fixed in a tangible medium, etc. Denying the private nature of copyright law, it has been argued that the law of copyright differs sharply from the law that governs land, houses, chattels and goods, in which common law largely created the exclusive rights of use, and the limitations thereon, even if they are subject to statutory modification. Therefore, law relating to copyright is not private law in nature. In response to this argument, it can be said that so far as the private law is concerned it defines, regulates, enforces, and administers relationships among individuals, associations, and corporations. Thus, private law is administered between citizen and citizen, or that is concerned with the rights in cases where both the person in whom the right inheres and the person upon whom the obligation rests are private individuals. In this sense, copyright law is private law.[62] It is needless to mention that the parties to a copyright infringement dispute are private that is one of the important elements of a private law. Besides, the reasoning for recognition of copyright law as private law is usually concerned with the duties that one party owes to another as a result of their particular interactions. It is a matter of fact that the private law regularly invokes a backward and looking analysis based on conduct that has already occurred. Thus, private law is a conception of relational duties and rights. It is commonly agreed that a relational duty is a duty owed by an individual to persons or classes of persons, while a general duty is a duty simply to act in a certain way, for example, duty towards sovereign. Remedies for infringement of violations of

---

61. *See, Super Cassettes Industries Ltd.* v. *Shreya Broadcasting Pvt. Ltd.*, 258 (2019) DLT 116: 2019 III AD (Delhi) 552; *E. Tech Projects Private Limited* v. *The State of Chhattisgarh*, 2018 (8) FLT 347; *Chancellor* v. *Rameshwari Photocopy Services*, 2017 (69) PTC 123 (Del): 235 (2016) DLT 409.
62. *See,* Julie E. Cohen, "Copyright's Public Private Distinction" 55 *Case Western Reserve Law Review* (2005) pp. 963–970.

relational rights and its corresponding relational duties typically involve a bilateral structure. These remedies involve payments from the infringer to the infringed party.[63] All these elements of a private law are present in copyright law.

It has also been argued that copyright law is not a private law on the ground that it involves situations in which the state imposes sanctions through the criminal law or in which it seeks to exercise the powers of taxation or eminent domain, which necessarily lodge only in public bodies or private individuals who are authorised to act on their behalf.[64] But this reasoning does not cease the private nature of copyright law as most of the remedies for infringement of copyright are of civil nature, for example, Injunction, Accounts of Profits, Damages, Anton Piller Order,[65] John Doe Order,[66] etc. It is true that in certain exceptional cases criminal remedies are granted for infringement of copyright, while arrest and detention are also granted in civil execution proceedings under the Code of Civil Procedure, 1908.[67] This provision of the Code is not a ground for loosing civil nature of the Code. Likewise criminalisation of copyright law is not a ground for losing private nature of copyright law.

Meaning of Copyright

Dictionary Meaning

According to the *Oxford Dictionary*, copyright is an exclusive right given by law for a certain term of years to authors, composer, etc. (or his assignee) to print, publish and sell copies of his original work.[68] The word "copy" is presumed to date back to 1485 AD (approximate date) and was used to connote a manuscript or other matter prepared for printing. The word copyright is derived from the expression "copier of words" first used in the context, according to the *Oxford Dictionary*, in 1586. The *Wharton's Law Dictionary* defines copyright as an

---

63. *See,* Andrew S. Gold, "A Moral Rights Theory of Private Law" 52 *William and Mary Law Review,* (2011) pp. 1873–1931.
64. *See,* Richard A. Epstein, "Unifying Copyright: An Instrumentalist's Response to Shyamkrishna Balganesh" 125 *Harvard Law Review* (2012) pp. 120–132.
65. The first use of *Anton Piller order* was made by Templemen J. in *EMI* v. *Pandit* [(1975) 1 All ER 481], to prevent the offending evidences from being destroyed. However, it was only after the case of *Anton Piller KG* v. *Manufacturing Processes Ltd.* [(1976) 1 All ER 776], that it gained recognition and popularity. The purpose of the order was explained in *Yousuf* v. *Salamon* [(1980) 3 All ER 405], where Lord Denning observed that the order intends to prevent the dander of destruction of evidence. *See*, Souvik Bhadra and Arka Majumdar, "Anton Piller Order in UK and Its Possible Implications in India." 12 *Journal of Intellectual Property Rights* (2007) pp. 488–426.
66. The term "John Doe Order" (or "John Doe Injunction") is used to describe as an injunction sought against someone whose identity is not known at the time of filing of the suit. It is basically a simple *ex-parte* interim injunction with the added benefit that the plaintiff is given liberty to add to the array of parties, infringers who have been identified after the filing of the suit. These orders are an exception to the general rule which requires the defendant to be identified prior to the filing of a suit. *See,* Juhi Gupta, "John Doe Copyright Injunctions in India" 18 *Journal of Intellectual Property Rights* (2013) pp. 351–359; Nathaniel Jurist Gleicher, "John Doe Subpoenas: Toward a Consistent Legal Standard", 118 *Yale Law Journal* (2008) pp. 320–368.
67. Sections 55 to 59 and Rules 30, 32, 37 to 39, Order 21 of the Code of Civil Procedure, 1908 deal with arrest and detention of the judgment-debtor.
68. A.S. Hornby, *Oxford Advanced Learner's Dictionary of Current English,* (Oxford University Press, 2011).

incorporeal right being the exclusive privilege of printing, re-printing, selling, and publishing of own original work.[69] More elaborately, the *Webster's New World Dictionary* (3rd edition) defines copyright as: "the exclusive right to the publication, production, or sale of the rights to a literary, dramatic, musical, or artistic work, or to the use of a commercial print or label, granted by law for a specified period of time to an author, composer, artist, distributer, etc." Thus, if a man wrote anything on the paper or parchment of another, the writing should belong to the owner of the blank material. The meaning thereby is that the mechanical operation of writing by the scribe deserved to receive satisfaction. In this sense, copyright is the right in literary property as recognised and sanctioned by law. An intangible incorporeal right granted to the author or originator of certain literary or artistic production whereby he is invested for a specified period with the sole and exclusive privilege of multiplying copies of the same and publishing and selling them.

Section 14 of the Act

The expression "copyright" has not been defined in Section 2 of the Copyright Act, 1957 but the meaning of the expression has been given in Section 14 of the Act. According to Section 14, copyright is an "exclusive right subject to the provisions of this Act", to do or authorise the doing of any number of prescribed acts in relation to: (i) literary, dramatic or musical works, (ii) computer programme and databases (iii) artistic work, (iv) cinematograph film, and (v) sound recording.[70] Thus, in *Rediff.Com India Ltd.* v. *E-Eighteen.Com Ltd.*,[71] the Delhi High Court held that Section 14 of the Copyright Act states that copyright is an exclusive right, subject to the provisions of the Act, to do or authorise the doing of the acts enumerated in the said section, in respect of a work or any substantial part thereof. For example, in case of a cinematograph film, copyright means the exclusive right to make a cinematograph film and to do or authorise the doing of any of the acts mentioned therein.[72] In *Pepsi Co. Inc.* v. *Hindustan Coca Cola*,[73] it was held that a copy can either be of the whole work or a substantial part of the work. The essential elements of the plaintiffs commercial in cinematograph film have been copied by the defendants in their television commercials and this act constitute infringement of copyright.

More specifically in *R.G. Anand* v. *Delux Films*,[74] the Apex Court held that in order to bring in an action within the four corners of Section 14 and to show infringement of copyright, it must be shown that there is a reproduction in material form of a work or substantial part thereof in respect of which there is an exclusive right. The phrase "substantial part" means

69. A.R. Lakshmanan, *Wharton's Law Dictionary* (Universal Law Publishing Co., New Delhi, 2013).
70. *See*, *Indian Performing Right Society Ltd.* v. *Aditya Pandey*, MIPR 2011 (3) 19; *Microfibres Inc.* v. *Girdhar*, MIPR 2009 (2) 229: 2009 (40) PTC 519 (Del); *Entertainment Network (India) Ltd.* v. *Super Cassettes Industries Ltd.*, JT 2008 (7) SC 11: 2008 (9) SCALE 69; *Gramophone Company of India Ltd.* v. *Birendra Bahadur Pandey*, AIR 1984 SC 667: (1984) 2 SCC 534; *Indian Performing Right Society Ltd.* v. *Eastern Indian Motion Pictures Association*, AIR 1977 SC 1443: (1977) 2 SCC 820.
71. MIPR 2013 (2) 333: 2013 (55) PTC 294 (Del).
72. *See*, *Sanjay Kumar Gupta* v. *Sony Pictures Networks India P. Ltd.*, AIR 2018 Delhi 169: 2018 (75) PTC 562 (Del); *Motorola Inc.*, v. *Deputy C.I.T.* [2005] 95 ITD 269 (Delhi): (2005) 96 TTJ (Delhi) 1; *Eastern India Motion Pictures Association* v. *Indian Performing Right Society Ltd.*, AIR 1974 Cal 257.
73. 94 (2001) DLT 30.
74. AIR 1978 SC 1613: (1978) 4 SCC 118.

the essential or material part of the work or leading features of the work.[75] Thus, Section 14 explains the meaning of copyright in relation to different categories of works.[76] In *Consim Info Pvt. Ltd.* v. *Google India Pvt. Ltd.*,[77] the Madras High Court held that under Section 14 of the Copyright Act, 1957, the owner of the copyright has a right to protect his interests and initiate proceedings against any infringement irrespective of where the infringing activities take place.

Section 14(a) enumerates what shall be a copyright which is an exclusive right, subject to the provisions of the Act, to do or authorise the doing of the acts provided in Clauses (i) to (vii) in respect of a work or any substantial part thereof in the case of a literary, dramatic or musical work, not being a computer programme.[78] The meaning of copyright in the case of a computer programme is provided under Section 14(b). While Section 14(c) deals with the meaning of copyright in the case of an artistic work, Section 14(d) deals with cinematograph film and Section 14(e) with sound recording. The Copyright (Amendment) Act, 2012[79] in connection with Section 14 relating to "meaning of copyright" provides the right of "commercial rental" to cinematograph films and sound recordings by amending the word "hire" to "commercial rental" in the existing provision relating to cinematograph films [clause (d)(ii)] and sound recording [clause (e) (ii)] with identical language providing for the right 'to sell or give on commercial rental or offer for sale or for such rental, any copy of the film' or 'sound recording'.

In *Saregama India Ltd.* v. *Suresh Jindal,*[80] explaining the meaning of copyright in different categories of works under Copyright Act, 1957, the Calcutta High Court observed:

> The expression "dramatic work", "literary work", "musical work" all has different and distinct meaning and connotation under the said Act. From the definitions contained in Sections 2(h), 2(o) and 2(p) with regard to "dramatic work", "literary work", "musical work" respectively, it clearly appears that "dramatic work" is in the nature of physical manifestation of such recitation of choreographic work or entertainment but does not include a cinematograph film. It would, therefore, mean that when someone does those acts as mentioned in Section 2(h) physically and live and is not a photographic imprint thereof it would mean dramatic work. The meaning of the expression "literary work" as in Section 2(o) is all encompassing and includes all kinds of literary work including computer programmes, tables and compilations including computer data base. Section 2(p) makes it clear that musical work is the music itself and the graphical notation of such music but does not include any words or any action intended to be sung, spoken and performed with the

---

75. *Ladbroke (Football) Ltd.* v. *William Hill (Football) Ltd.* (1964) 1 WLR 273; *Led Builders* v. *Eagle Home Property Ltd.*, 35 IPR 215.
76. *V.T. Thomas alias Toms* v. *Malayala Manorama Company Limited*, AIR 1988 Ker 291: ILR 1988 (2) Kerala 205.
77. 2011 (45) PTC 575. *See also*, *STAR India Private Limited* v. *Department of Industrial Policy*, 2018 (2) CTC 113; *Super Cassettes Industries Ltd.* v. *Myspace Inc.*, 2011 (47) PTC 49 (Del); *International Business Corporation* v. *Bhagirath Dolkheria*, (2009) 155 PLR 34; *Dhodha House* v. *S.K. Maingi* (2006) 9 SCC 41; *Exphar SA* v. *Eupharma Laboratories Ltd.* (2004) 3 SCC 688.
78. *Eastern Book Company* v. *D.B. Modak*, AIR 2008 SC 809: (2008) 1 SCC 1.
79. Act No. 27 of 2012. Came into force on 21-6-2012, *vide* S.O. 1393 (E), dated 20th June, 2012, published in the Gazette of India, Extra., II, Section 3(ii), No. 1164, 20th June, 2012. For detail discussion on the amendment see *Novex Communication Pvt. Ltd.* v. *Lemon Tree Hotels Ltd.*, 2019 II AD (Delhi) 644; *Phonographic Performance Ltd.* v. *HT Media Ltd.*, 2017 (70)PTC211(Del).
80. AIR 2006 Cal 340: 2007 (34) PTC 522 (Cal).

music. Therefore, the statute has made a distinction between musical work and a song may or may not be without music. But even a song is sung which has music it will not become a musical work under the said section.

While Section 14 which enumerates the rights that subsist in various classes of works, Section 13 provides that copyright, in case of literary or musical work, means *inter alia*: (a) the right to perform or cause the performance of the work in public and (b) to make or authorise the making of a cinematograph film or a record in respect of the work. It also provides that copyright in case of cinematograph film means, among other rights, the right of exhibiting or causing the exhibition in public of the cinematograph film that is of causing the film in so far as it consists of visual images to be seen in public and in so far it consists of sounds to be heard in public. The meaning of copyright, for each category of work, is quite extensive, especially when we note (as we do in the next sections) that the definitions of most *genres* of work is inclusive rather than exhaustive and that copyright protection extends to all kinds of work including those which represent "originality at vanishing point."[81] Thus, in *Shyam Lal Paharia* v. *Gaya Prasad Gupta*,[82] the Allahabad High Court observed that: "In modern complex society provisions have to be made for protecting every man's copyright, whether big or small whether involving a high degree of originality, as in a new poem or picture, or only originality at the vanishing point as in a law report." In connection to the musical works in copyright the Delhi High Court in *Indian Performing Right Society Ltd.* v. *Aditya Pandey,*[83] observed:

> The fact that music and words are combined together for the purposes of performance or recording does not cause the separate and distinct copyrights to merge intellectual property rights (IPRS) says that the exclusive rights accruing to literary works and musical works include under Section 14(a)(iii), (a) the right to perform the work in public and (b) the right to communicate the work to the public. Section 2(ff) which includes the substance of the definition of the old Section 2(q), thus implies that the Act takes into account the fact that literary and musical works would be communicated to the public by sound recording or film. This, according to IPRS, highlights the impact of Section 13(4) of the Act, which mandates separate existence of copyright despite the incorporation of literary works or musical works in sound recordings or films. IPRS disputes synergy's contentions and says that if the mandate of the Act, is that use of a sound recording precludes need for a license for the use of the "underlying works", this "exclusive right" would not have been granted in the case of lyrics or musical compositions, as it has been granted for films [Section 14(d)(iii)] and sound recordings [Section 14(e)(iii)] and the exclusive right for lyrics and musical compositions [Section 14(a)(iii)], would have stopped at the right to perform the work in public (i.e. the live acoustic performance) and/or would have excluded the communication to the public right of lyrics and musical compositions in respect of use of the said "underlying works", as part of sound recordings or films.

However, an analysis of the meaning of copyright as given in Section 14 of the Copyright Act, 1957 it appears that the expression "copyright" means the right to copy and to commercially exploit the same. In terms of Section 17 of the Act normally the author of a work shall be the first owner of the copyright therein. In case any work is made at the

81. *V. Govindam* v. *E.M. Gopalkrishna Kone*, AIR 1955 Mad. 391.
82. AIR 1971 All 192.
83. MIPR 2011 (3) 19: 2011 (47) PTC 392 (Del).

instance of another upon receiving valuable consideration the persons at whose instance the work is made will be the first owner of the copyright.[84] There is copyright in translation of a work.[85] Thus, translation of a work into another language without consent of author/owner will be an infringement.[86] In *Star India Private Limited* v. *Department of Industrial Policy and Promotion*,[87] the Supreme Court held that transient or incidental storage of a work or performance purely in technical process of electronic transmission or communication to public was not an act that would constitute infringement of copyright. In its reasoning the Court observed that copyright was meant to protect proprietary interest of owner, which in present case was a broadcaster, in "work", i.e. original work, its broadcast or its re-broadcast by him. Interest of end user or consumer was not focus of Copyright Act 1957 at all.

In *Entertainment Network (India) Ltd.* v. *Super Cassettes Industries Ltd.*,[88] the Apex Court held that where there are more applicants than one seeking a compulsory license for translation of a work or for reproduction of the work or for publication of an unpublished work, then the Copyright Board (Appellate Board)[89] make grant the compulsory license to such one of the applicants, as in the opinion of the Board, would best serve the interest of the general public. But common property are not the subject of copyright.[90] In *Indian Express Newspapers (Bom.) Pvt. Ltd.* v. *Jagmohan*,[91] the Bombay High Court observed:

> No doubt the central theme of the articles published by the second plaintiff and that of the drama and movie is the same, though the emphasis in the drama and the movie is more on human bondage, particularly of Indian women. The articles published by Ashiwini Sarin also contain an autobiographical account of the part actually played by him in the affair. He has presented the whole affair in his own style. But that at the most would give the plaintiff's copyright in respect of these articles. There cannot, however, be a copyright in an event which has actually taken place. There is a distinction between the materials upon which one claiming copyright has worked and the product of the application of his skill, judgment, labours and literary talent to these materials. Ideas, information, natural phenomena and events on which an author expends his skill, labour, capital, judgment and literary talent are common property and are not the subject of copyright.

In *Institute for Inner Studies* v. *Charlotte Anderson*,[92] the Court examined the issue relating to legal sustainability of the copyright claim in the "Pranic Healing Techniques" in literary works. In this case, the plaintiff's claim of copyright in the "Pranic Healing Techniques" is premised on the three grounds: (i) the plaintiff's ownership over the copyright titles in the books written by master, trade literature, CD Roms, etc.; (ii) the plaintiff's claim of copyright in the material stated in the books and thereby seeking the prohibitory orders on the performance of "Pranic Healing Techniques" in form imparting teachings, performing Asanas

84. *Saregama India Ltd.* v. *Suresh Jindal*, AIR 2006 Cal 340: 2007 (34) PTC 522 (Cal).
85. *Blackwood and Sons Ltd.* v. *A.N. Parasuraman*, AIR 1959 Mad 410.
86. *Barbara Taylor Bradford* v. *Sahara Media Entertainment Ltd.*, (2004) ILR 1 Cal 15: 2004 (28) PTC 474 (Cal).
87. (2019) 2 SCC 104: 2018 (14) SCALE 651.
88. MIPR 2008 (2) 129: 2008 (37) PTC 353 (SC).
89. Substituted by the Finance Act 2017 (7 of 2017), section 160(a) for "Copyright Board," [w.e.f. 26 May, 2017].
90. *Zee Telefilms Ltd.* v. *Sundial Communications Pvt. Ltd.*, 2003 (5) Bom CR 404: 2003 (27) PTC 457 (Bom).
91. MIPR 2008 (2) 129: 2008 (37) PTC 353 (SC).
92. 2014 (1) MIPR 129: 2014 (57) PTC 228.

or implementing the techniques by performance of the "Pranic Healing Techniques" in action by the defendants on the strength of the copyright claim in the compilation of the exercises which as per the plaintiff is the original compilation of the plaintiffs; (iii) the plaintiff's claim of the copyright in the "Pranic Healing Techniques" and exercises as the works of choreography which finds place of protection under the head of dramatic works under the law of copyright and the performance of the "Pranic Healing Techniques" physically should be prevented by the court on the above grounds. The Court on the aforementioned basis held that the plaintiff's claim that the defendants by reproducing the books written by the master, trade literature of the plaintiffs coupled with the performance of the said exercises or "Pranic Healing Techniques" is infringing the plaintiff's copyright in the works of the plaintiffs.

However, in *Tekla Corporation* v. *Survo Ghosh*,[93] the defendant argued that in our legal framework of copyright, the defence of "misuse of copyright" by the holder thereof is not available, neither to an action for infringement of copyright nor to an action for damages for infringement of copyright. Answering affirmatively, the court observed that no holder of copyright in any work, misusing the said work shall have copyright therein during that misuse i.e., during the misuse of a copyrighted work, the work affords its owner no copyright rights and a copyright owner can regain those rights only by ending the practices that constitute misuse. The principle behind denying damages for infringement during the period of misuse is stated to be that since during that time there is no copyright, there would be no infringement and resultantly no damages. Examining Section 14 of the Copyright Act, *inter alia,* in *John Wiley and Sons Inc.* v. *Prabhat Chander kumar Jain*,[94] the court observed:

> The rights conferred under Section 14 of the Act are subject to the provisions of the Act and the rights under Section 14 of the Act can be limited or circumscribed by the owner as per his/her desire in the manner provided in subsequent chapters relating to assignment and transmission. A careful reading of the Section further makes it clear that the owner by exercising the right to licence further demarcates the rights and imposes conditions and limitations by way of a period wise licence or territory wise licence exclusive or non-exclusive, etc. Licencing is a mode of maximum exploitation of the rights under the Act by imposing conditions and limitations upon the rights.

Negative Duty

Despite the above stated clear formulation, sometimes judges and jurists speak of copyright as a kind of "negative right."[95] It is a general principle of law of copyright that it provides an exclusive legal or statutory right to the original author on his creation of work and also it imposes a "negative duty" on others that prohibits from using or getting benefit from the work without the consent of the author.[96] While it is common to speak of copyright in terms of the "right" that it confers on creators, this right invariably corresponds to a duty that they

---

93. 2014 (210) DLT 666: AIR 2014 Del 121.
94. 2010 (4) RCR (Cri) 151: 2010 (170) DLT 701.
95. *See*, *Commissioner of Income Tax* v. *Samsung Electronics Co. Ltd.*, (2011) 245 CTR (Kar) 481: [2012] 345 ITR 494 (KAR); *Frito-Lay India* v. *Radesh Foods,* MIPR 2009 (3) 525: 2009 (40) PTC 37 (Del); *Burroughs Wellcome (India) Ltd* v. *Uni-Sole Pvt. Ltd.*, 1999 PTC 188.
96. *See*, Anjaneya Reddy and Lalitha Aswath, "Understanding Copyright Laws: Infringement, Protection and Exceptions," 2(1) *International Journal of Research in Library Science* (2016) pp. 48–53 at p. 50.

impose on others. This duty thus forms the "analytic reflex" of the right in question. When right is considered an "analytic reflex" of duty, the entire justification of the relationship rests on the reason for considering the defendant to be under a duty and right is then immediately attributed to anyone who would benefit from the performance of that duty.[97] Jeremy Waldron was perhaps the first to identify the functional and normative importance of duties to the analysis of intellectual property law when he noted that "the point of focusing on duties is more than merely analytic" because "legal duties are hard things for people to have since they constrain conduct and in that sense limit freedom."[98] Thus, copyright imposes a "duty not to copy". The above admonition is perhaps most true of copyright law, and yet copyright law continues to be discussed, analysed, and understood almost entirely in terms of its "right". Thus, in *Dabur India Limited* v. *Shree Baidyanath Ayurved Bhawan Pvt. Ltd.,*[99] the Delhi High Court observed:

> In essence the copyright is a negative right of preventing copying of physical material in the field of art, literature, etc.

Further, in *Dassault Systems K.K.* v. *Director of Income Tax,*[100] it was observed that copyright is a negative right in the sense that it is a right prohibiting someone else to do an act, without authorization of the same, by the owner. It may be submitted that the phrase "copyright is a negative right" which is both inaccurate and misleading. Copyright imposes a negative duty on others, that is, prohibits others from exploiting the work of the author for their own benefit without the consent or license of the author. The general principle, therefore, is that the copyrighted works cannot be used without the authorization of the owner of the rights. It bears reiteration that the set of rights subsumed under the rubric "copyright" is primarily defined in affirmative and positive sense. Copyright constitutes property rights *in rem* and *in personam,* violation of which can be redressed under the provisions of the Copyright Act, 1957.

Justice Holmes, a prominent spokesman of realist school of thought, readily thought of copyright as a duty-imposing legal regime.[101] While Justice Holmes never used the word "duty" to describe copyright, he was clearly conceptualizing copyright's "right" entirely in terms of the obligations (that is, the restraints, prohibitions, and restrictions) that it imposes on others. Copyright law was thus to Justice Holmes about the duty not to copy original expression, no more and no less. Commencing the analysis of copyright law with the duty not to copy as a functional and normative matter in *White-Smith Music Publishing Co.* v. *Apollo Co.,*[102] Justice Holmes observed:

> The right to exclude [in copyright] is not directed to an object in possession or owned, but is *in vacuo*, so to speak. It restrains the spontaneity of men where but for it there would

97. *See*, John C.P. Goldberg, "Introduction: Pragmatism and Private Law" 125 *Harvard Law Review* (2012) pp. 1640–1663.
98. *See*, Jeremy Waldron, "From Authors to Copiers: Individual Rights and Social Values in Intellectual Property", 68 *Chicago Kent Law Review* (1992) pp. 841–887.
99. 193 (2012) DLT 558: 2012 (51) PTC 441 (Del).
100. (2010) 229 CTR (AAR) 105: [2010] 188 TAXMAN 223 (AAR).
101. Harry W. Jones, "Law and Morality in the Perspective of Legal Realism", 61 *Columbia Law Review* (1961) pp. 799–809.
102. 209 US 1 (1908).

be nothing of any kind to hinder their doing as they saw fit. It is a prohibition of conduct remote from the persons or tangibles of the party having the right. It may be infringed a thousand miles from the owner and without his ever becoming aware of the wrong.

Statutory Right

It is also important to note that copyright is a statutory right and it is not a natural right or common law right.[103] In *Krishika Lulla* v. *Shyam Vithalrao Devkatta*,[104] the Supreme Court held that in India copyright is a statutory right recognized and protected by the Copyright Act, 1957. Thus, in *Crocs Inc.* USA v. *Aqualite India Limited*,[105] the Delhi High Court held that copyright is a statutory right and no copyright exists outside the statute. Thus, in India, the remedies for the infringement of a copyright are also statutory within the four corners of the Copyright Act, 1957.[106] Therefore, copyright does not exist outside any statute enacted by the competent authority. All the rights that the copyright holder gets are created by the statute namely the Copyright Act, 1957 and therefore, they are governed by the provisions of the Act.

Copyright in any work does not exist independently of the Act. Section 16 of the Act precludes from claiming any other right except as provided under the Act. Section 16 of the Act reads as thus: "No copyright except as provided in this Act. No person shall be entitled to copyright or any similar right in any work, whether published or unpublished, otherwise than under and in accordance with the provisions of this Act or of any other law for the time being in force, but nothing in this section shall be construed as abrogating any right or jurisdiction to restrain a breach of trust or confidence." In this connection the in *Gramophone Company of India Ltd.* v. *Super Cassettes Industries Ltd.*,[107] the Delhi High Court observed:

> Section 16 provides that no copyright can be acquired in respect of any work except in accordance with the provisions of the Act. Therefore, copyright is a statutory right. Only those rights which the Copyright Act creates; to the extent it creates, and; subject to the limitations that the Act imposes, vest in the owner of the copyright in the work, whether it is a primary work such as a literary, dramatic or musical work, or a derivate work such as a sound recording or cinematograph film. No right, which the Copyright Act does not expressly create can be inferred or claimed under the said Act.

Thus, Section 16 makes it amply clear that no person is entitled to copyright "or any similar right in any work" "otherwise than under and in accordance with the provisions of this Act or of any other law for the time being in force". No customary rights in the nature of copyright may, therefore, be pleaded. At the same time, this Section does not abrogate "any right or jurisdiction to restrain a breach of trust or confidence". In *Phonographic Performance Ltd.* v. *Music Broadcast (P) Ltd.*,[108] the Bombay High Court observed:

---

103. *See, Super Audio Madras Private Limited* v. *Entertainment Network India Private Limited*, 2011-1-LW611; *R.G. Anand* v. *Delux Films*, AIR 1978 SC 1613: (1978) 4 SCC 118.
104. (2016) 2 SCC 521: 2016 (4) SCJ 498.
105. 2019 (78) PTC 100 (Del).
106. *See, Micolube India Limited* v. *Rakesh Kumar*, MIPR 2012 (2) 200: 2012 (50) PTC 161 (Del); *Tobu Enterprises (P) Ltd.* v. *Joginder Metal Works*, AIR 1985 Delhi 244: (1985) ILR 2 Delhi 638; *Calico Printers Association* v. *Savani*, AIR 1939 Bom 10.
107. 2010 (44) PTC 541 (Del).
108. 2004 (7) LJSOFT 22: 2004 29 PTC 282.

It is thus clear from the perusal of Section 16 of the Act that all the rights that can be claimed by the copyright holder are the rights given to him by the Act and therefore, there is no question of one provision of the Act being narrowly construed or not being given its natural meaning, because it is likely to encroach upon some supposed rights of the copyright holder.

Thus, in *Time Warner Entertainment Company.*, v. *RPG Netcom,*[109] it was held that the plaintiff cannot claim copyright and sue for infringement of copyrights *de hors* the Act because copyright exists and can be only in accordance with the provisions of the Act or under any law which was in force at the time when the Act was enacted. Common law rights under copyright law were held to be abrogated by Section 31 of the erstwhile Copyright Act, 1911.

GENERAL PRINCIPLES GOVERNING COPYRIGHT

Copyright is a monopoly of limited duration wholly regulated by the Copyright Act, 1957. Under the present law, an author has no other title to his or her published or unpublished works than that given by statute.[110] A copyright work consists of two elements: the corporeal and the incorporeal—the physical work (e.g., paper, printing, record, diskette) and the thoughts, ideas, sentiments, conceptions, which constitute the invisible creation of the mind. The former is simply a channel of communication, a vehicle of conveyance, for the latter. The exclusive right of using and transferring property is a necessary consequence of the recognition of the right of property itself. It is the peculiarity of copyright that only by the reproduction can it have any value to its owner. By publication alone can the authors secure the reward of their labour. Without this, their toil is without fruit, their property without value.

Since the authors give to the readers the means of intellectual improvement and/or enjoyment contained in a work, it is just that they should reap the pecuniary benefits of their ingenuity and labour. The authors make no gain, if, the next moment after their works come out, they may be pirated upon worse paper, and in worse print, and in cheaper volumes. The authors may not be deprived of any profit, but lose the expense they have incurred. In many ways, copyright is perhaps the most important branch in the field of intellectual property.[111] Following governing principles of copyright law are worth mentioning:

1. There is a total absence of formal requirements for obtaining copyright protection. Copyright is absolutely automatic. No registration is required nor is any deposit to be made. Copyright subsists from the moment the work is created or produced. Even the international symbol of "(c)" is not a prerequisite for protection under the law. Obviously, this conferment of a legal right without any administrative work or expense to be incurred has created a very convenient and efficient system of

109. AIR 2007 Del 226: 2007 (34) PTC 668 (Del).
110. *See*, Section 16 of the Copyright Act, 1957.
111. For new dimension of law of copyright see Ralph Oman, "Computer Software as Copyrightable Subject Matter: Oracle V. Google, Legislative Intent, and the Scope of Rights in Digital Works," 31 *Harvard Journal of Law and Technology* (2018) pp. 639–652; Joseph P. Fishman, "Music as a Matter of Law," 131(7) *Harvard Law Review* (2018) pp. 1861–1923.

protection for the creators of intellectual works.[112] Indeed, this characteristic of copyright becomes even more significant when protection is sought, as it has now become common, internationally. Thus, a copyright, however, unlike a trade mark is a right created under the Copyright Act 1957 as is evident from Section 16 thereof.[113]

2. The copyright law does not grant a monopoly in the true sense of the word. Monopolies were frowned upon by the English common law; even today they are not encouraged but tolerated under stringent requirements. Copyright confers a limited monopoly.[114] It prohibits copying and not independent creation by others. There is no infringement even if two works resemble each other closely if the two authors had produced their identical works independently of each other.
3. The duration of copyright is much longer than the term protection for patents (20 years) and industrial designs (16 years). As a general rule, the maximum duration of copyright in case of literary work is the author's lifetime plus 60 years. In the case of films, records, television and sound broadcasts, photographs and published editions, the term of protection is 60 years or less.[115]
4. The prerequisites for copyright protection are less onerous than those under the allied fields of patents, industrial designs and trademarks. To gain copyright protection, a work must be original and have some literary merit that will contribute to the information, instruction, or entertainment of persons other than the owner. With respect to originality, the principle seems to be that if a person claims to be the owner of an intellectual production, on the ground that it is the creation of his or her own mind, it is obvious that person's claim will founder when there is an entire absence of originality, when the production is a mere copy of something else. In the celebrated decision of *Peterson* J. in *University of London Press Ltd.* v. *University Tutorial Press Ltd.,*[116] it was pointed out that the copyright law was not concerned with the originality of ideas, but with the expression of thought. In the ultimate analysis, what this means is that the work must not be copied from another work. The word "original" therefore, does not mean that the work must be an expression of inventive thought. The case was concerned with the copyright in examination question papers. The court held that they were original because they had originated from the examiners and had not been copied.
5. With respect to literary merit, commercial value and usefulness to society are not relevant considerations in determining the owner's exclusive rights. Copyright may exist in a work that has no commercial value. A person may own a useless lawnmower which may be collecting rust in the garden shed, a car which may not be roadworthy, or a sterile waste so worthless that he or she cannot give it away; yet it belongs to the owners, and the law will aid the owner in preventing another from appropriating it, or otherwise unlawfully using it. The same is true of intellectual property. A book may be void of literary qualities, a painting devoid of any theme, a

---

112. *See, Eastern Book Company* v. *D.B. Modak,* (2008) 1 SCC 1: 2007 (14) SCALE 191.
113. *See, Gramophone Company of India Ltd.* v. *D.B. Pandey,* AIR 1984 SC 667: 1984(2) ECC 142.
114. *See, Entertainment Network (India) Ltd.* v. *Super Cassette Industries Ltd.,* 2008 (4) ALD 47 (SC).
115. *See,* Section 22 of the Copyright Act, 1957.
116. (1916) 2 Ch. 601.

piece of sculpture without art excellence. Yet the owner may value it. It is immaterial for what purpose the work has been produced.

6. The next special point is that copyright consists of a bundle of rights, each of which is independent of others. The combination of ways in which copyright owners may assign their rights is almost endless. There may thus be a multiplicity of rights all stemming from the original work but all different and all capable of separate assignment. In *Arun Chadha* v. *Oca Productions Private Limited*,[117] the Delhi High Court held that sub-clause (b) of the Copyright Act, 1957 provides for remedies for protection of honour and reputation of the author. The bundle of rights and remedies provided by Section 57 is in tune with the modern development in law relating to protection of copyright of the author.
7. Original authorship is the basic concept of copyright in works. The Copyright Act, 1957 expressly requires in Section 13 that for copyright to subsist in a literary, dramatic, musical or artistic work, the work must be "original." There is no such specific requirement in the Act for subsistence of copyright in sound recordings, cinematograph films, television and radio broadcasts, and published editions of works. Nevertheless, in these cases, it seems that the subject matter must not be a pure copy or repetition of a sound recording, film, broadcast or published edition previously made.
8. The word "original" used in Section 13 of the Copyright Act, 1957 does not, in this connection, mean that the work must be the expression of original or inventive thought; the originality required relates to the expression of thoughts.[118] A mere copyist does not obtain copyright in his copy.[119] Works like abridgement, compilation, translation, etc. are, however, original even though the author has drawn on knowledge common to him and others,[120] or has used already existing material. The word "original" is not prefixed with cinematograph films and sound recordings as they are derivative works.
9. Copyright protection extends to expressions and not to ideas, procedures, methods of operation or mathematical concepts as such.[121] What is protected is not original thought or information, but the original expression of thought or information in some concrete form as the author is both a user of ideas developed by others and a creator of new ideas. Consequently, it is only an infringement if the defendant has made an unlawful use of the form in which the thought or information is expressed. The defendant must, to be liable, have made a substantial use of this form; he is not liable if he has taken from the work the essential idea, however original, and expressed the idea in his own form, or used the idea for his own purposes.[122] Ideas

---

117. 193 (2012) DLT 135: 2013 (53) PTC 401 (Del).
118. *See*, *Krishika Lulla* v. *Shyam Vithalrao Devkatta*, (2016) 2 SCC 521: 2016 (4) SCJ 498; *Ladbroke Football Ltd.* v. *William Hill (Football) Ltd.* (1964) IWL R 273; *Macmillan and Co. Ltd.* v. *Cooper K and J* (1923) 40 TLR 186; *University of London Press Ltd.* v. *University Tutorial Press Ltd.* (1916) 2 Ch. 601.
119. *Walter* v. *Lane* (1900) AC539; *Leslie* v. *Young J.* (1894) AC 335.
120. *Rupendra Kashyap* v. *Jiwan Publishing House*, 1996 PTC 439 (Del).
121. Article 9 (2), TRIPS Agreement.
122. *Hollinrake* v. *Truswell* (1894) 3 Ch. 420.

may, however, be protected under other laws like doctrine of unjust enrichment, quasi-contract or breach of trust or confidence.

10. Law relating to copyright is designed to afford protection to the owner of copyright in various kinds of works (viz., literary, dramatic, musical and artistic) and subject matter other than works (viz., sound recordings, cinematograph films, television and sound broadcasts and published editions of works). Since many of these works are made under commission (e.g., computer programs, architects' plans, advertising copies, portraits, paintings, photographs, and so on) issues frequently arise regarding ownership of copyright.[123]
11. Ownership falls in two broad categories: ownership by statue and ownership by assignment or transfer.[124] The Copyright Act 1957 seeks to maintain a balance between the interest of the owner of the copyright in protecting his works on the one hand and the interest of the public to have access to the works, on the other. The extent to which the owner is entitled to protection in regard to his work for which he has obtained copyright and the interest of the public is a matter which would depend upon the statutory provisions.[125]
12. One of the fundamental principles of copyright law is that a person who creates a work owns the copyright in that work. However, this principle providing for initial ownership to the author is not absolute. It is qualified in three specific instances, viz., employed journalists, commissioned works and works made by employees. The rationale of these exceptions is to be found in the recognition of economic exploitation interest in the sense that without a reallocation of the initial ownership, the employer or commissioner "might not commit the resources and facilities necessary to enable the author to create the work".

SPECIAL FEATURES OF COPYRIGHT

Besides the general principles governing copyright, certain special features of copyright have been recognised. Copyright is intangible, provides certain rights, exclusive, exhaustive, flourishing public domain, territorial in nature, commercial exploitation and having limited duration.[126] These special features need detailed deliberation.

Copyright is an Intangible Property

Copyright can be owned by the person who has produced it by his own strives with his labour, skill, judgement, mind and creativity. Therefore, copyright is intangible in nature. Software

---

123. *See*, Section 17 of the Copyright Act, 1957.
124. *See, ICSAC* v. *Aditya Pandey*, (2017) 11 SCC 437: 2016 (9) SCJ 423.
125. *See, Entertainment Network (India) Ltd.* v. *Super Cassettes Industries Ltd.*, 2008 (4) ALD 47 (SC).
126. For critical discussions see Maria A. Pallante, "The Next Great Copyright Act," 36(3) *The Columbia Journal of Law and the Arts* (2013) pp. 315–344; Lawrence Liang, "Exceptions and Limitations in Indian Copyright Law for Education: An Assessment," 3(2) *The Law and Development Review* (2010) pp. 197–240; Barton Beebe, "An Empirical Study of Us Copyright Fair Use Opinions, 1978–2005," 156(3) *University of Pennsylvania Law Review* (2008) pp. 549–624.

is a copyrightable property and it is an article of value. Copyright law does not address the tangible material object in which the creation of the mind has been embodied. It instead creates more abstract proprietary interests in the intangible. For example, a reader sends a letter to the co-authors of this text, offering a critique of our efforts. We are entitled to retain the document sent through the mails—the tangible pieces of paper on which the correspondence was physically written. However, the words of the letter constitute a work of authorship. Reproduction of that letter without the author's permission may implicate the copyright laws. Ironically, although copyright law concerns abstract creations, it does insist that the intellectual creation be embodied in something tangible at least once. In *Tata Consultancy Services* v. *State of Andhra Pradesh*,[127] the Apex Court rightly observed:

> Indian law does not recognize or make a distinction between tangible property and intangible property. A 'goods' may be a tangible property or an intangible one. It would become goods provided it has the attributes thereof having regard to: (a) utility; (b) capable of being bought and sold; (c) capable of transmitted, transferred, delivered, stored and possessed. If a software whether customized or non-customized satisfies these attributes, the same would be goods.

While copyright works must be fixed in tangible form to be protected; the patent law requires the inventions be "reduced to practice"; trademarks must, sooner or later, be subject to actual use in the market place.[128] These principles ensure that abstract ideas remain free from copyright rights. Copyright is instead allowed for the embodiment of that idea in a particular work of authorship. Thus, copyright is property and every person has the right to property. The Article 300A of the Constitution of India guarantees right to property and provides that "No person shall be deprived of his property save by the authority of law."[129] The term property is wide enough which includes not only real and personal property but also incorporeal rights such as patents, copyrights, leases, choses in action and every other thing of exchangeable value which a person may have.[130] This Constitutional principle is applicable to tangible property as well as to intangible intellectual property and bars a person from being deprived of his property save in the manner prescribed by law. The Constitution Bench of the Supreme Court in *K.T. Plantation Pvt. Ltd.* v. *State of Karnataka*,[131] observed:

> The expression "Property" in Article 300A which proclaims that no person can be deprived of his property save by authority of law meaning thereby that a person cannot be deprived of his property merely by an executive fiat without any specific legal authority or without the support of law made by a competent legislature, is confined not to land alone, but includes intangibles like copyrights and other intellectual property and embraces every possible interest recognised by law.

---

127. AIR 2005 SC 371: (2005) 1 SCC 308. *See also*, *Infotech Software Dealers Association* v. *Union of India* [2010] 29 STT 132: (2010) 34 VST 133 (Mad).
128. *See*, Breyer, "The Uneasy Case for Copyright: A Study of Copyright in Books, Photocopies, and Computer Programs," 84 *Harvard Law Review* (1970) pp. 281–351; Tyerman, "The Economic Rationable for Published Books: A Reply to Professor Breyer," 18 *UCLA Law Review* (1971) pp. 1100–1125; Breyer, "Copyright: A Rejoinder", 20 *UCLA Law Review* (1972) pp. 75–83.
129. Inserted by the Constitution (44th Amendment) Act, 1978, w.e.f. 20. 06. 1979.
130. *See*, *Shrirur Mutt* v. *Commissioner*, (1952) 1 MLJ 557; *Dwarkadas* v. *Sholapur Co.*, AIR 1951 Bom. 86.
131. (2011) 9 SCC 1.

Copyright Provides Bundle of Rights

It has persistently been asked: Is property a bundle of rights? In a similar manner it may also be asked: Is a diamond a collection of carbon atoms?[132] A diamond does consist of carbon atoms, but there is a lot more to a diamond. The concept of bundle of rights treats property in atom-counting fashion. It sees property as a bundle of sticks but misses the trees, not to mention the forest. The bundle picture treats property as a collection of rights or, metaphorically, of sticks. The exclusion of others leads to a characteristic structure of property. The use of boundaries, the sweeping of uses behind them, and the use of on/off proxies for violation, all stem from the transaction cost savings of employing shortcuts over the complete or full set of maximally articulated rights. That sticks come in standardised clumps, like fee simple, defeasible fee, life estate, future interests, easements, and so on which look more like happenstance on the bundle view.[133]

Likewise, copyright provides a bundle of rights which are recognised under any copyright statute. Thus, the copyright is a bundle of rights given by the law to the creators of literary, dramatic, musical and artistic works and the producers of cinematograph films and sound recordings. The rights provided under Copyright law include the rights of reproduction of the work, communication of the work to the public, adaptation of the work and translation of the work. The scope and duration of protection provided under copyright law varies with the nature of the protected work. In *Deshmukh* v. *Avinash Vishnu Khandekar*,[134] the Bombay High Court observed:

> Copyright is a bundle of rights as enumerated in Section 14 of the Copyright Act, 1957 and, therefore, there was no need to provide for various rights retained by the author in the agreement.

The bundle of copyrights which are conferred by the Copyright Act, 1957 can broadly be classified into four groups: (i) economic rights, (ii) moral rights or author's special rights, (iii) performers' rights, and (iv) broadcast reproduction rights. Section 14 of the Copyright Act, 1957 enumerates the following basic economic rights: (i) the reproduction right;[135] (ii) the distribution right; (iii) the adaptation right;[136] (iv) the public performance

---

132. There are divergent views on the issue whether copyright provides really bundle of rights see Jane B. Baron, "Rescuing the Bundle-of-Rights Metaphor in Property Law" 82(1) *University of Cincinnati Law Review* (2014) pp. 57–101; Alina Ng, "Literary Property and Copyright," 10(7) *Northwestern Journal of Technology and Intellectual Property* (2012) pp. 531–577; Henry E. Smith, "Property Is Not Just a Bundle of Rights," 8(3) *Econ Journal Watch* (2011) pp. 279–291; Harsh Kumar, "Employer's Copyright vis-à-vis Author's Right: An Unresolved Legal Dilemma," 10 Journal of Intellectual Property Rights (2005) pp. 112–118.
133. *See,* Anna Di Robilant, "Property: A Bundle of Sticks or a Tree?" 66(3) *Vanderbilt Law Review* (2013) pp. 869–932; Henry E. Smith, "Property Is Not Just a Bundle of Rights" 8(3) *Econ Journal Watch* (2011) pp. 279–291; Denise R. Johnson, "Reflections on the Bundle of Rights" 32 *Vermont Law Review* (2007) pp. 247–272.
134. 2005 (3) Mh Lj 387: 2006 (32) PTC 358 (Bom).
135. *See, Ferani Hotels Pvt. Ltd.* v. *The State Information Commissioner*, 2018 (5) CHN (SC) 238: 2018 (13) SCALE 672.
136. *See, Dassault Systems K.K.* v. *Director of Income Tax*, (2010) 229 CTR (AAR) 105: [2010] 188 TAXMAN 223 (AAR).

right;[137] (v) the rental right; (vi) the cable casting right;[138] and (vii) the broadcasting right.[139] Besides these, there are four categories of rights recognised as the "moral rights"[140] or "author's special rights"[141]: (i) the right to be identified as the author of a work; (ii) the right of an author of a work, the "integrity right"; (iii) a general right, that every person has, not to have a work falsely attributed to him; and (iv) right against piracy.

In reference to bundle of rights in copyright in *UTV Software Communication Ltd.* v. *1337X to and Ors.*,[142] the Delhi High Court observed that Indian Copyright Act, 1957 confers a bundle of exclusive rights on the owner of a "work" and provides for remedies in case the copyright is infringed. Effective copyright protection promotes and rewards human creativity and is, in modern society, an indispensable support for intellectual, cultural and economic activity. Copyright law promotes the creation of literary, artistic, dramatic and musical works, cinematograph films and sound recordings by providing certain exclusive rights to their authors and creators. Section 2(y) of the Copyright Act defines "work" as including a cinematograph film, which is defined under Section 2(f). Section 14 specifies the exclusive rights of the owners. Section 2(ff) defines "communication to the public". Interpreting all these provisions the Court concludes thus:

> Making any work available for being seen or heard by the public whether simultaneously or at places chosen individually, regardless of whether the public actually sees the film, will constitute communication of the film to the public. The intent was to include digital copies of works, which would include within its scope digital copies of works being made available online (as opposed to the physical world). Communication can be by various means such as directly or by display or diffusion. In this context, definition of "broadcast" is also relevant which identifies communication to public by wireless diffusion or by wire. Thus, making available of a film for streaming or downloads in the form of digital copies on the internet is within the scope of "communication to the public".

While economic rights are available to every owner of copyright, the moral rights are available to the author alone. In *PEE PEE Publisher and Distributors (P) Ltd.* v. *Neena Khanna,*[143] the Delhi High Court held that the moral rights are only relating to right to paternity, integrity and rights against the distortion and mutilation. The said rights do not advert into the question of economic right or gives any room for withdrawal of the work at the instance of the author. In *Ramesh Sippy* v. *Shaan Ranjeet Uttamsingh,*[144]the ad-interim relief sought is basically based on the claim of the plaintiff that he is the owner of the copyright in the cinematograph film Sholay and that he is the author of the said film and therefore entitled to claim moral rights under Section 57 of the Copyright Act, 1957. However, the entire material on record clearly shows that the plaintiff has no copyright in the said film. The court held that the defendant is the owner of the copyright in the said film Sholay and

---

137. *See, Eastern India Motion Pictures Association* v. *Indian Performing Right Society Ltd.*, AIR 1974 Cal 257.
138. *See, Common Cause* v. *Union of India*, (2018) 13 SCC 440: 2017 (2) SCALE 169.
139. *See, Swapnil Tripathi* v. *Supreme Court* of India, AIR 2018 SC 4806: (2018) 10 SCC 639.
140. *See, PEE PEE Publisher and Distributors (P) Ltd.* v. *Neena Khanna*, 2009 (40) PTC 515 (Del).
141. *See, Amar Nath Sehgal* v. *Union of India*, (2005) ILR 1 Delhi 236: 2005 (30) PTC 253 (Del).
142. 2019 (78) PTC 375 (Del).
143. 2009 (40) PTC 515 (Del).
144. 2013 (3) ABR 1228: MIPR 2013 (2) 125.

that since he is the author of the said film, he is entitled to claim moral rights. Accordingly, he gets the first ownership of the economic rights under Section 14 of the Act except for the exceptions carved out in Section 57 and is also vested with the "moral rights" or "author's special right" in the "work" as per Section 57 of the Act.

In addition to the economic and moral rights, Sections 37 and 38 of the Copyright Act, 1957 recognise certain analogous rights which are incidental to copyrighted works. They are the performers' rights and the broadcaster's rights often termed as "neighbouring rights" under international conventions. The Copyright (Amendment) Act, 1994 has recognised limited rights for the performers in their live performances for a period of fifty years from the year following the performance. According to Section 37 every broadcasting organization shall have a special right to be known as "broadcast reproduction right" in respect of its broadcasts every broadcasting organisation shall have a special right to be known as in respect of its broadcasts. The term "broadcast" has been defined in Section 2(dd) to mean communication to the public by any means of wireless diffusion, whether in any one or more of the forms of signs, sounds or visual images; or by wire, and includes a re-broadcast.

Thus, in *ICC Development (International) Ltd.* v. *New Delhi Television Ltd.*,[145] broadcasting rights are independent of the copyrights granted under the Act and such rights of rebroadcast are given exclusivity under Section 37 which provides that with respect to the rebroadcast no one has a right to use the audio and visual recording except in accordance with the license which is taken from the owner of the original audio and visual recording. The Copyright (Amendment) Act, 1994 has also introduced a special right known as Broadcast Reproduction Right (BRR) for the benefit of broadcasting organizations in respect of its broadcasts. In *ESPN Star Sports* v. *Global Broadcast News Ltd.*,[146] the broadcast reproduction right in respect of telecast of live event like a cricket match are a separate and distinct right as from the copyright and as such Section 61 of Copyright Act, which mandates impleadment of owner of copyright or host broadcaster as necessary party to proceedings, is not applicable to broadcast reproduction rights.

In relation to cinematograph films, the "bundle of exclusive rights" are those where the "visual portion and audible portion are synchronized". In *Indian Performing Right Society Ltd.* v. *Eastern Indian Motion Pictures Association*,[147] the Apex court described copyright in film as a "felicitous blend, a beautiful totality, a constellation of stars ... that ensemble which is the finished produced orchestrated performance by each of the several participants, although the components may, sometimes, in themselves be elegant entities." Thus, in *PVR Pictures Ltd.* v. *Studio 18*,[148] it was held that the bundle of copyrights does not only relate to the content of the film, it extends to the "doing" or "authorizing the doing" of: (i) making copies of the films or photographs of the images; (ii) sell, or offer for sale any copy of the film, regardless of whether such copy has been sold or hired earlier; (iii) give on hire, or offer for hire, any copy of the film regardless of whether such copy has been sold or given on hire earlier; (iv) to communicate the film to the public. The "bundle of exclusive rights", thus has the

145. (2012) 193 DLT 279: 2012 (132) DRJ 291.
146. MIPR 2008 (3)257: 2008 (38) PTC 477 (Del).
147. 1977 3 SCR 206.
148. 2009 (41) PTC 70: 2009 (111) DRJ 436.

widest content. In films, it includes making copies, which can extend to any medium, film prints, VCDs, DVDs, HDDs format, video cassettes, or any other form enabled through technologies. It includes licensing for communication of the film, a part of it or the songs, to the public.

Right to Exclude is a Feature

The right to exclude is one of the special features of copyright. Thus, copyright law grants "authors" (including artists, architects, choreographers, cinematographers, etc.) a number of exclusive rights in their works of authorship—the right to reproduce, adapt, publicly distribute, publicly display and publicly perform the work, or authorise others to do each of these things.[149] Section 14 of the Copyright Act, 1957 defines "copyright" to mean the "exclusive right subject to the provisions of the Act".

Contrasting cinematograph film and sound recording on the one hand and literary, dramatic, musical and artistic work on the other in *Adai Mehra Production Pvt. Ltd.* v. *Mr. Sumeet P. Mehra*,[150] the Bombay High Court observed that in the latter case the owner of the copyright has exclusive right to reproduce the work in any material form. This is absent and excluded insofar as the former case (cinematograph film or sound recording). The exclusive right in the former is to copy the recording of a particular film or sound recording. It is, therefore, clear that production by another person of even the same cinematographic film does not constitute infringement of a copyright in a cinematograph film. It is only when actual copy is made of a film by a process of duplication, i.e., by using mechanical contrivance. Copyright law confers the right to exclude others from exploiting the protected intangible subject matter. It does not affirmatively provide a marketing right that allows an author. Similarly, public distribution of copyrighted works of authorship and of products bearing trademarks may be subject to laws governing defamation and obscenity, among others.

In *ICC Development (International) Ltd.* v. *Ever Green Service Station*,[151] the official sponsors companies of the events were: (i) Pepsi, (ii) Hero Honda, (iii) LG Electronics, (iv) South African Airway, (v) Hutch-Orange, (vi) Standard Bank-South Africa, (vii) Toyota-South Africa, (viii) South African Breweries and (ix) MTN and in return such companies were given exclusive rights to associate themselves and their brands with the event. The entire advertisement or publicity value is the exclusive property of the plaintiff, who in turn has authorised its sponsors to enjoy these rights. The plaintiff and sponsors have the right to commercially exploit the "*in personam*" of the Event and to derive the maximum commercial benefit of being associated with it. The sponsors have been given the exclusive rights to organise schemes and contests that offer tickets to the World Cup as prizes. The plaintiff has undertaken to the sponsors not to authorise or permit any third party to associate itself with the event or in any manner use the indicia, marks, logo or the commercial "identity" or "*in personam*" of the event.

---

149. *See*, Henry E. Smith, "Intellectual Property as Property: Delineating Entitlements in Information," 117 *Yale Law Journal Pocket* (2007) pp. 1742–1822.
150. 2013 (3) ABR 1273.
151. 102 (2003) DLT 723: 2003 (26) PTC 228 (Del).

Principle of Exhaustion of Rights

Copyright is ordinarily subject to the doctrine of exhaustion. This doctrine of exhaustion is that the owner of copyright who consents for the marketing of the copyrightable work cannot use that right to prevent the person whom he consented for marketing or publishing. To this extent, the right is said to be exhausted by the first consensual marketing.[152] In *Chancellor* v. *Rameshwari Photocopy Services*,[153] the Delhi High Court held that the principle of exhaustion encapsulated in the Explanation to Section 14[154] provides that a copy once sold is deemed to be a copy already in circulation within the meaning of Section 14(a)(ii) and thus issuing such copy would not amount to infringement. But that the principle of exhaustion does not enlarge the scope of the right of a purchaser to 'issue copies of the work to the public' to include making of copies of the copyrighted work.

Exhaustion of rights is linked to the distribution right. The right to distribute objects (making them available to the public) means that such objects (or the medium on which a work is fixed) are released by or with the consent of the owner as a result of the transfer of ownership. In this way, the owner is in control of the distribution of copies since he decides the time and the form in which copies are released to the public. Content-wise the distribution of rights are to be understood as an opportunity to provide the public with copies of a work and put them into circulation, as well as to control the way the copies are used. The exhaustion of rights principle thus limits the distribution right, by excluding control over the use of copies after they have been put into circulation for the first time. In *Warner Brothers Entertainment Inc.* v. *Mr. Santosh V.G.*,[155] the Delhi High Court observed:

> The doctrine of exhaustion of copyright enables free trade in material objects on which copies of protected works have been fixed and put into circulation with the right holder's consent. The "exhaustion" principle in a sense arbitrates the conflict between the right to own a copy of a work and the author's right to control the distribution of copies. Exhaustion is decisive with respect to the priority of ownership and the freedom to trade in material carriers on the condition that a copy has been legally brought into trading. Transfer of ownership of a carrier with a copy of a work fixed on it makes it impossible for the owner to derive further benefits from the exploitation of a copy that was traded with his consent. The exhaustion principle is thus termed legitimate by reason of the profits earned for the ownership transfer, which should be satisfactory to the author if the work is not being exploited in a different exploitation field.

Once the copyright holder has sold a physical product to which its copyright is attached, he cannot prohibit the subsequent resale of that product. Any copyright in that specific physical product are said to have been "exhausted" by this first sale. The exhaustion doctrine allows, *inter alia*, law students to purchase used casebooks at the campus bookstore without further compensation to the book's authors and without fear of infringement liability.[156] However, in

152. This doctrine was best formulated in *Consten and Grunding* v. *Commission* (1966) ECR 299.
153. MANU/DE/3285/2016.
154. Explanation to Section 14, Copyright Act 1957 provides: "For the purposes of the Section, a copy which has been sold once shall be deemed to be a copy already in circulation."
155. MIPR 2009 (2) 175.
156. *Betts* v. *Willmott* (1871) LR 6 Ch. App 239.

John Wiley and Sons Inc. v. *Prabhat Chander Kumar Jain,*[157] the Court was concerned with the importation of the cinematograph works and came to the conclusion that the doctrine of exhaustion of rights will be confined to literary works only and will be inapplicable to the cinematograph works as the explanation appended to Section 14 is confined to literary works only.

Concept of Territoriality

Copyright law is not unified around the world, therefore, there is no global copyright. Copyright, chiefly in literary, musical, artistic and audio-visual works must secure and enforce these rights within the particular jurisdiction where they desire protection. Further, the reach of a copyright extends only so far as the nation or region recognizing the right. Copyright recognised in India under the Copyright Act, 1957 cannot be the basis of infringement litigation in Japan. The copyright laws of the United States are nonetheless linked through a modest number of international agreements that, together, comprise the international copyright regime. In *Penguin Books Ltd.* v. *India Book Distributors,*[158] wherein the Court held that import of Britain published books from USA without seeking licence from exclusive licencee amounts to infringement of copyright. The reasoning of the court is as under:

> Copyright law is a territorial concept and each nation has its own laws. In America it may not be possible to place restrictions on the resale of books. But sale within the United States obviously cannot abrogate the effect of the laws of the particular place where they are imported... An importer would be subject to the law of the particular country to which he happens to take the books. The importer cannot disregard the laws of other countries.

The foundational treaties, the *Berne Convention* (concerning copyright)[159] and the *Paris Convention* (concerning patent and trademark),[160] established the basic principle of national treatment. The requirement that signatories treat nationals of other signatory states no worse than their own citizens in intellectual property matters. More recently, *the World Trade Organization's* Agreement on Trade-Related Aspects of Intellectual Property Rights[161] (TRIPS Agreement) required its signatories to provide minimum substantive standards of copyright protection and enforcement.

---

157. 170 (2010) DLT 701: 2010 (44) PTC 675 (Del).
158. 1984 26 DLT 316 (DB).
159. *Berne Convention for the Protection of Literary and Artistic Works, 1886.* The Convention was adopted on September 6, 1886; the Contracting States formed themselves into a Union known as "Berne Union" to ensure the protection of the rights of the authors of such work in States forming the "Union". India is party to this Convention. The Convention met with several revisions and the latest being in 1971 at Paris.
160. *Paris Convention for the Protection of Industrial Property 1883.* The Convention protected mainly three classes of properties, namely, patents, trademarks and industrial designs that is only industrial property in the territory of member States. The Convention entered into force in 1884 with the member States. It was revised several times the latest being in 1967 at Stockholm. For the text of *Paris Convention, see,* Alfredo Ilardi, *International Encyclopedia of Intellectual Property Treaties* (Oxford University Press, London 2004).
161. *Agreement on Trade Related Aspects of Intellectual Property Rights* (TRIPS Agreement), April 15, 1994, Annex 1C 3 *International Legal Material* (1994) p. 1197.

Balancing Concept of Public Domain

Throughout history, one important idea lawmakers have concerned themselves is balancing the "public interest" with "individual rights". For example, the public's right to access knowledge should not be limited by the individual author's right to restrict access. With the application of copyright law, this delicate balance is achieved. Thus, copyright provides an incentive for creative expression of author.[162] The concept "public domain" balances between two conflicting interests of the creator and the public.[163] The goal of the copyright system is to give the monopoly only for as long as necessary to provide an incentive. After that the work falls into the public domain where anybody can use it, transform it, adapt it, build on it, republish it as he wish. It has been asked time and again: what is the public domain?[164]

A number of attempts have been made to define "public domain", but no definition is universally accepted.[165] Some authors surveying various definitions and providing their own definition[166] while some definitions are more obviously normative than others.[167] An examination of all these definitions shows as follows:

> The public domain provides the range of uses of information that any person is privileged to make absent individualized facts that make a particular use by a particular person unprivileged. If information is not protected by an exclusive right, or if a given use of otherwise protected information is privileged (through the fair use doctrine, for example), then it is in the public domain.

The term "public domain" refers to "creative materials" that are not protected by intellectual property laws. Things in the public domain can be appropriated by anyone without liability for infringement. In the context of copyright, the term indicates that the materials which are in public domain are "public property" and available for anyone to use for any purpose. Although copyright creating proprietary interests, it also account for the rights of consumers and other members of the user community. In today's copyright law, the facts and ideas in an author's work proceed immediately into the public domain. In other work, by confining the property right tightly to the "original expression" stemming from the unique personality of an individual author the law seems to accomplish a number of things simultaneously.[168]

Thus, the information arising from a cricket match is public property and that the score updates were being disseminated in public interest. However, in *Star India Pvt. Ltd.* v. *Piyush*

162. *See*, Arunabha Banerjee and Aniket Deepak Agrawal, "Morality of Copyright—A Critique in View of the '3 Idiots' Controversy" 16(5) *Journal of Intellectual Property Rights* (2011) pp. 394–401.
163. *See*, Robin J. Allan, "After Bridgeman: Copyright, Museums, and Public Domain Works of Art," 155 *University of Pennsylvania Law Review* (2007) pp. 961–989.
164. *See*, Julie E. Cohen, "Copyright, Commodification and Culture: Locating the Public Domain" in Lucie Guibault and P. Bernt Hugenholtz (Ed.), *The Future of The Public Domain* (2006) p. 121.
165. Steven J. Horowitz, "Designing the Public Domain" 122(5) *Harvard Law Review* (2009) pp. 1489–1510.
166. *See*, Christine D. Galbraith, "Remembering the Public Domain", 84(1) *Denver University Law Review* (2006) pp. 135–142; Anupam Chander and Madhavi Sunder, "The Romance of the Public Domain", 92 *California Law Review* (2004) pp. 1331–1373; Tyler T. Ochoa, "Origins and Meanings of the Public Domain", 28 *University of Dayton Law Review* (2003) pp. 215–267.
167. *See*, Yochai Benkler, Free as the Air to Common Use: First Amendment Constraints on Enclosure of the Public Domain, 74 *New York University Law Review* (1999) pp 354–446.
168. *See*, James Boyle, *The Public Domain*, (Yale University Press, 2008) p. 32.

Agarwal,[169] it was held that "news" or "noteworthy information" arising from a cricket match is very different from the ball-by-ball or minute-by-minute information. The dissemination of the ball-by-ball or minute-by-minute updates at a premium cannot be exonerated under the freedom of speech and expression as guaranteed under Article 19(1)(a) of the Constitution of India. Meanwhile, all noteworthy information arising from a cricket match constitute "news", and the "reporting" of such noteworthy information would be protected under Article 19(1)(a). In *Tata Press Limited* v. *Mahanagar Telephone Nigam Limited,*[170] the Apex Court held:

> Examined from another angle, the public at large has a right to receive the 'commercial speech'. Article 19(1)(a) not only guarantees freedom of speech and expression, it also protects the rights of an individual to listen, read and receive the said speech... The protection of Article 19(1)(a) is available to the speaker as well as to the recipient of the speech.

Out of recognition that one person's incentive can form another's limitation, various copyright doctrines strive to maintain a flourishing public domain.[171] Thus, in *Syndicate of the Press of the University of Cambridge* v. *B.D. Bhandari,*[172] the court held that the term "public domain" and "fair dealing" are distinct from each other and once a work comes within the ambit of "public domain" then there is no question of involvement of the fair dealing doctrine because the term "public domain" means there is no copyright protection is available at all to the concerned work. The term "public domain" may be used to connote the information becoming freely available to the public.

In *Star India Pvt. Ltd.* v. *Piyush Agarwal,*[173] the Delhi High Court held that the information emanating from a cricket match, enters the public domain at different moments of time. Thus, the information becomes freely available to the public at different moments of time. To elucidate through an example, the outcome of the first ball bowled in a cricket match, enters the public domain *instantly qua* the spectators in the stadium. The same information enters the public domain after a delay of a few seconds (or micro-seconds) subject to the time-lag in transmission of such information over a live telecast through television or radio. As a corollary, the information has still not entered the public domain qua the persons who do not have any access to a source of contemporaneous information, i.e., television or radio.

Free from the proprietary interests of others, the public domain provides a body of works that supports further creative expression, promotes effective communication, and ultimately allows each of us to experience our culture. In explaining "public domain" doctrine, we may cite the decision of the Apex Court in *Eastern Book Company* v. *D.B. Modak.*[174] In this case, the plaintiff claimed copyright over the judgments published in its journals and sought a temporary injunction against the defendants who were allegedly copying the judgments published by the plaintiff and republishing under their own name. Observing that plaintiff company could not claim copyright in a judgment under the heading "literary work" because it had already entered the public domain, the Apex Court only granted an injunction limited to the head notes, footnotes and editorial notes authored by the plaintiff and allowed the defendant to sell their CD-ROMs with the text of judgments.

---

169. *See*, MIPR 2013 (1) 201: 2013 (54) PTC 222 (Del).
170. *See*, AIR 1995 SC 2438: (1995) 5 SCC 139.
171. Jessica Litman, "The Public Domain", 39(4) *Emory Law Journal* (1990) pp. 965–1023.
172. *See*, 185 (2011) DLT 346.
173. MIPR 2013 (1) 201: 2013 (54) PTC 222 (Del).
174. AIR 2008 SC 809: (2008) 1 SCC 1.

There have been long debates as to whether the public domain is simply whatever is left over after various tests of legal protection under Copyright Act, 1957? Is it the mere "background," the "negative" of whatever may be protected? Or is there something about the public domain, some compelling public policy or legal principle, which gives it a life of its own that would tend to attribute positive aspects to it that would make it something of the form instead of just the background? Whatever it may be, there are three common ways under which a work can be attributed as a work in "public domain":

1. Section 13 of the Indian Copyright Act, 1957 provides for the works in which copy right subsists. Section 14 further provides that no person shall be entitled to copyright or any similar right in any work, whether published or unpublished, otherwise than under and in accordance with the provisions of this Act or any other law for the time being in force. Thus, whenever a work is created by an author, he gets copyright therein automatically by virtue of Section 13 of the Act and certain rights are granted to such a copyright owner as stipulated in Section 14 of the Act. A more lenient requirement applies to the copyright law, where the protected work of authorship must be original to the author and display a "modicum of creativity."[175] These standards ensure that copyright do not extract subject matter from the public domain.[176]
2. The owner of a copyrightable work may deliberately place it in the public domain. Therefore, Section 21 of the Indian Copyright Act, 1957 provides that an author may relinquish his copyright by giving a notice to this effect to the registrar of copyright if he wishes so.
3. The limited duration of copyright also contributes to the public domain. Section 22 of the Indian Copyright Act, 1957 provides that the copyright in a work shall subsist within the lifetime of the author until [sixty years][177] from the beginning of the calendar year next following the year in which the author dies. When these rights expire, the subject matter is no longer proprietary and becomes free for others to use as the subject matter will enter into the public domain.

Commercial Exploitation of Copyright

The important aspect of copyright is that it can be commercially exploited. The copyright can be owned by the person who has created it by his own strives with his intellect, labour, skill, judgment and mind. It has been observed that copyright is vital for economic development. Hence people who wish to progress sometimes use the copyright of others as of their own. This use of property causes damage and injury to the person whose copyright has been so

---

175. Copyrightable work shall maintain a minimum standard of creativity besides "sweat of the brow", i.e. sufficient expenditure of labour, skill and capital to make product original. *See*, *Eastern Book Company* v. *D.B. Modak,* AIR 2008 SC 809: (2008) 1 SCC 1.
176. *See*, *Jones* v. *London Borough of Tower Hamlets* (2001) RPC 407; *Designers Guild Ltd.* v. *Russell Willams (Textiles) Ltd.* (2001) FSR 113; *Gadget Shop Ltd.* v. *Bug. Com. Ltd.,* (2001) FSR 383.
177. Substituted by Copyright (Amendment) Act, 1992, Section 2, for "fifty years" [w.e.f. 28-12-1991]. Section 3 of the amending Act declared that copyright shall not subsist by virtue of this Act in any work in which copyright did not subsist immediately before the commencement of this Act.

used. This is the commercial exploitation of copyright. In other words, the unauthorised use of another's copyright by a person is called the commercial exploitation of copyright. Similarly, if a famous person's persona or any individual aspect of his personality is used by another for commercial exploitation or gain, without such person's authorisation or license, the act of using the said persona, or attributes of such personality constitute infringement of the famous person's right of publicity.[178]

The Copyright Act 1957 granted the right of commercial exploitation of the work for which the copyright has been granted. The Section 30 of the Act provides for granting licences by owners of copyright for publishing the work for commercial purpose, while Section 31 provides for granting compulsory licence in works withheld from public. However, in *Chancellor* v. *Rameshwari Photocopy Services*,[179] the Delhi High Court distinguished commercial purpose from the use of copyrighted work for the purpose of teaching/studies. In *Super Cassettes Industries Ltd.* v. *Music Broadcast Pvt. Ltd.*,[180] the Supreme Court held that the Appellants of the present case were interested in the commercial exploitation of a work, of which they were not "owners" of the copyright. To succeed in their claim for a compulsory licence in their favour, they must, firstly, establish that "the work was withheld from the public", because of the "owner's" refusal to republish the work, etc.; secondly, the owner's refusal was on grounds, which were "not reasonable" in law. Whether the owner was withholding the republication on grounds, which were unreasonable or not, was a question, which could only be decided upon affording a complete hearing to the owner of the work. By conceding a power to grant *Ad hoc* compulsory license during the pendency of the proceeding, under Section 31, would not only render the final inquiry into the question, a futile exercise in a case where the owner has reasons other than inadequacy of monetary compensation. The power under Section 31 to grant a compulsory license meant for avoiding the withholding of the republication or refuses to allow the performance in public of some "work" – is, essentially, for the benefit of the public. Commercial benefit to "publisher" is incidental. But the right of commercial exploitation is subject to reasonable restrictions under Section 52 of the Copyright Act 1957.

Section 52 of the Act provides that there are certain acts shall not constitute an infringement of copyright which are called fair use/fair dealing.[181] In *Rupendra Kashyap* v. *Jiwan Publishing House*,[182] the court held that if a publisher publishes a book for commercial exploitation and in doing so infringes a copyright, the defence under Section 52(1)(a)(i) of the Copyright Act, 1957 would not be available to such a publisher though the book published by him may be used or be meant for use in research or private study. Similarly, in *Syndicate of The Press of The University of Cambridge* v. *B.D. Bhandari*,[183] it was argued that the work

---

178. *See*, David Herlihy and Yu Zhang, "Music industry and copyright protection in the United States and China," 1(4) *Global Media and China* (2016) pp. 390–400; Lydia Pallas Loren, "The Evolving Role of 'For Profit' Use in Copyright Law: Lessons from the 1909 Act," 26 (2) *Santa Clara High Technology Law Journal* (2010) pp. 255–284.
179. 2017 (69) PTC 123 (Del): 2016 (235) DLT 409.
180. MANU/SC/0408/2012.
181. *See*, Niva Elkin-Koren and Orit Fischman-Afori, "Rulifying Fair Use," 59 *Arizona Law Review* (2017) pp. 161–200.
182. 1996 (38) DRJ 81: 1996 PTC 439 (Del).
183. 185 (2011) DLT 346.

was copied by the respondent purely as a commercial exploitation in mind for the purpose of its business, which act was not protected under Section 52(1)(h) Copyright Act, 1957. It was a business venture, which could not be denied by the respondent as the guides were published with a view to selling them and to earn profits. This commercial exploitation took the matter out of the ambit of "fair dealing" contemplated in Section 52(1)(h) of the Act. But the court held that the book of appellant was prescribed textbook for University and on one hand, respondents wanted to bring out all comprehensive guidebook to help the students in all courses of English and not limiting it to Grammar alone, purpose of this guidebook produced by respondents would be materially different.

Even a person himself can exploit his own copyright. Thus, it is seldom that the author of a copyright work himself exploits the work for monetary benefit. In *ICC Development (International) Ltd.* v. *New Delhi Television Ltd.*,[184] defendant is running news channels and not a sport channel. Presenting special programmes is a part of its right to report this event in which people of this country are greatly interested and to carry out its review. Therefore, there can be no valid objection to the defendant presenting special programmes with respect to ICC World Cup, 2012. But, if the defendant carries an advertisement immediately before, during or immediately at the end of such programmes and the footage of the plaintiffs is used in the programme, that, the court viewed, would amount to commercial exploitation of the work which is not protected either under Article 19(1)(a) of the Constitution nor under Section 37 and/or 52 of the Copyright Act, 1957.

In *Anil Gupta* v. *Kunal Dasgupta*,[185] the court held that for an idea/concept to be a subject matter of confidential communication it must have at least some attractiveness as a television programme and should be capable of being realised in actuality. Thus, the concept of "Swayamvar" as evolved by the plaintiff was capable of being used for commercial exploitation as a reality show for match making on television programme and, therefore, that confidential communication which the plaintiff had given to the defendant has been breached by the defendant by making "Shubh Vivah" a reality show based on match making. Breach of trust or confidence gives a broader right then breach of copyright. Therefore, injunction can be issued by the Court.

The period of commercial exploitation of copyright varies from one class of copyrightable work to another class. For example, "design" and "artistic work". In *Micolube India Limited* v. *Rakesh Kumar*,[186] the issue was whether the monopoly rights granted under the Design Act for a limited period can be extended by switching over the rights to Copyright Act? By answering the question in negative and applying Section 15 of the Copyright Act which clearly debars the same, the Delhi High Court observed:

> The Statement of Objects and Reasons of the Designs Bill, 1999 provided that the intent was to ensure that the law does not unnecessarily extend protection beyond what is necessary to create the required incentive for design activity while removing impediments to the very use of available designs. The definition of "design" has been amplified to incorporate therein

184. 193 (2012) DLT 279: 2012 (132) DRJ 291.
185. AIR 2002 Delhi 379: 97 (2002) DLT 257.
186. 199 (2013) DLT 740: 2013 (55) PTC 1 (Del). *See also*, *Mattel, Inc.* v. *Mr. Jayant Agarwalla*, MIPR 2008 (3) 298: 2008 (38) PTC 416 (Del); *Microfibres Inc.* v. *Girdhar & Co.*, 128 (2006) DLT 238: 2006 (32) PTC 157 (Del).

the composition of line and colours so as to avoid overlapping with the Copyright Act regarding definition of "design" in respect of "artistic work".

Furthermore, the legislative intent is also to be kept in mind which is to provide protection for a certain period of time for commercial exploitation. Thus, nature of protection is quite different for an artistic work under the Copyright Act which is for the lifetime of the author/ creator + 60 years. This is not so in the case of commercial exploitation as under the Designs Act and the Patent Act the period is much lesser. In the present case, the configuration was made only with the object of putting it to industrial/commercial use.

The Delhi High Court clarifying the above stated proposition of law in *Microforms Inc.* v. *Girdhar*,[187] held that Copyright Act in general protects the artistic work, but the idea behind excluding certain designs from the protection under the Copyright Act, although otherwise the same design might have been so entitled to protection, appears to be to avoid any hindrance being caused to the manufacture and sale of industrial articles which in the absence of a provision similar to Section 15 could not be achieved. The intention of the Legislature appears to be very clear that wherever any artistic work has to be in a commercial exploitation by the owner of the copyright the same should be excluded from the protection under the Copyright Act and should be provided protection under the Designs Act.

The copyright is a valuable asset that may be exploited in a number of ways. It may be assigned, whereby the ownership in the whole or part of the right is transferred, or licences may be granted in respect of it. As with assignments, licences may be in respect of the whole or part of the right. For example, the owner of the copyright in a dramatic work might grant a licence to a number of theatre companies to perform the work in public for five years, each company being restricted geographically in terms of where it might make the performance. Licences may be exclusive or non-exclusive. An exclusive licence grants the rights governed by the licence to the licensee who can perform those rights to the exclusion of everyone else including the owner. For example, the copyright owner may grant exclusive licence to publish, produce and sell the copyrighted work. A non-exclusive licence is appropriate where the owner of the copyright wishes to grant licences to numerous licensees, a good example being in the case of computer software. The Andhra Pradesh High Court in *Commissioner of Income Tax* v. *Samsung Electronics Co. Ltd.*,[188] held that right to make a copy of the software and storing the same in the hard disk of the designated computer and taking backup copy would amount to copyright work under section 14(1) of the Copyright Act, 1957 and the payment made for the grant of the licence for the said purpose would constitute royalty.

Sometimes a sole licence is appropriate. This grants permission to perform the particular acts to only one licensee but, unlike the exclusive licence, the owner retains the right to perform the acts himself. Other forms of exploiting copyright include using it as security for loan, such as by way of a mortgage or other charge. Alternatively, it may be acquired as an investment, by paying a capital sum in return for an assignment, the person acquiring it will hope to receive income from it over a number of year by granting licences. In *Dassault Systems K.K.* v. *Director of Income Tax*,[189] it was held that the transfer of rights in or over copyright or the conferment of the right of use of copyright implies that the transferee/licensee

---

187. 128 (2006) DLT 238: 2006 (32) PTC 157 (Del).
188. (2012) 345 ITR 494 (KARN): (2011) 245 CTR (Kar) 481.
189. (2010) 229 CTR (AAR) 105: [2010] 188 TAXMAN 223 (AAR).

should acquire rights either in entirety or partiality co-extensive with the owner/transferor who divests himself of the rights he possesses *pro tanto*. That is what follows from the language employed in the definition of "royalty" read with the provisions of the Copyright Act, 1957, viz., Section 14 and other complementary provisions. Explaining the concept commercial exploitation under Copyright Act the court observed:

> It seems to us that reproduction and adaptation envisaged by Section 14(a)(i) and (vi) can contextually mean only reproduction and adaptation for the purpose of commercial exploitation. Copyright being a negative right, it would only be appropriate and proper to test it in terms of infringement. What has been excluded under Section 52(aa) is not commercial exploitation, but only utilizing the copyrighted product for one's own use. The exclusion should be given due meaning and effect; otherwise, Section 52(aa) will be practically redundant. In fact, as the law now stands, the owner need not necessarily grant licence for mere reproduction or adaptation of work for one's own use. Even without such licence, the buyer of product cannot be said to have infringed the owner's copyright. When the infringement is ruled out, it would be difficult to reach the conclusion that the buyer/licensee of product has acquired a copyright therein.

Enforcement of Copyright

There is a perception in copyright industries that infringement of copyright is an often phenomena for which a strong enforcement machinery is required.[190] In this connection, the Agreement on Trade Related Aspects of Intellectual Property Rights (TRIPS Agreement) provides a detail scheme for enforcement of intellectual property rights including copyright.[191] The Copyright Act, 1957 provides for right holders dual legal machinery for enforcing their rights.[192] The owner of copyright has two kinds of remedies available for enforcement of the copyright: (i) administrative remedies and (ii) judicial remedies. Administrative remedies consisting of remedies followed by the Registrar of Copyright, the Appellate Board[193] and the Custom Authorities under the Customs Act, 1962.[194] Judicial remedies provide civil remedies and criminal remedies. The judicial remedies include imprisonment and/or monetary fines—depending upon the gravity of the crime. Sometimes remedies also include seizure, forfeiture and destruction of infringing copies and the plates used for making such copies.

The Copyright (Amendment) Act, 1984 has made copyright infringement a cognizable

---

190. For detail discussion see Peter Mezei and István Harkai, "Enforcement of Copyrights Over the Internet: A Review of the Recent ECJ Case Law," 21 (4) *Journal of Internet Law* (2017) pp. 13–28; Ben Depoorter, Francesco Parisi and Sven Vanneste, "Problems with the Enforcement of Copyright Law: Is there a Social Norm Backlash?" 12(3) *International Journal of the Economics of Business* (2005) pp. 361–369.
191. *See*, Carlos M. Correa, *Trade Related Aspects of Intellectual Property Rights* (Oxford University Press, 2007); L.T.C. Harms, *The Enforcement of Intellectual Property Rights: A Case Book* (World Intellectual Property Organization).
192. For judicial approach on enforcement of copyright see *SAP Aktiengesellschaft* v. *Appsone Consulting India (P) Ltd.*, 2015 (151) DRJ 679; *Foundry Visionmongers Ltd.* v. *Satyanayana Reddy S.*, 2015 (64) PTC 108 (Del); *Indian Heritage Society* v. *Meher Malhotra*, 2014 (59) 501 (Del).
193. Substituted by the Finance Act 2017 (7 of 2017), section 160(a) for "Copyright Board," [w.e.f. 26 May, 2017].
194. *See*, Micheal Blackeney (Ed.), *Border Control of Intellectual Property Rights* (Sweet and Maxwell, London 2004).

non-bailable offence. Under the provisions of the Act, any person who knowingly infringes or abets the infringement of copyright is considered as an offender and is punishable with a minimum of six months imprisonment which may extend to three years and a fine between fifty thousand and two lakh rupees. The 1994 Amendment has incorporated a special penal provision for knowingly using an infringing computer software. The punishment provided for this act is imprisonment for a term of seven days to a maximum of three years and a fine between fifty thousand and two lakh rupees. In case the infringing copy of the computer software is used not for pecuniary gain or in the course of trade or business, the imprisonment can be relaxed and fine can be maximum of fifty thousand rupees.[195]

JUSTIFICATIONS FOR PROVIDING COPYRIGHT TO AUTHORS

Initially in England, copyright was granted in favour of the *Stationer's Company* and provided that the exclusive right of printing company to print and sale books in perpetuity. This right is known as "Copyright", the right to make copies.[196] However, the *Statute of Anne of* 1709 changed the entire philosophy. The sole right and liberty of printing books that the *Statute of Anne* conferred was given to authors and their assigns in place of printing press. Since that time (1709) the copyright is an exclusive right of an author.[197] In the vast body of court decisions, legislations, and commentaries on copyright law, one can find references to a great many jurists justifications for its existence. All justifications for copyright protection must contend with a fundamental difference between ideas and tangible property that can occupy only one place at any given time. This means that possession of a physical thing is necessarily "exclusive"—if I have it, you don't. Ideas do not have this characteristic of excludability. The fact that the possession and use of idea is critical to copyright theory as because of traditional concept of economic justifications for tangible property do not fit in copyright concept. A number of jurists have therefore turned elsewhere to justify exclusive rights on ideas. Over the period of human history, numerous jurists have been put forth to explain copyright protection. The principal basis for such protection is the labour theory. Nonetheless, other jurists, most notably the jurists of economic incentive theory, personality theory and social requirements theory, have been justifying the understanding, development and scope of copyright protection in their own way.

Labour Theory

John Locke and *Immanuel Kant* are two predominant jurists who justify exclusive rights under "copyright" within the theory of labour. The theoretical underpinnings of copyright law are based heavily on the work of *John Locke*, one of the enlightenment thinkers who most

195. *See*, S.K. Verma, "Enforcement of Intellectual Property Rights: TRIPS Procedure and India", 46 *Journal of Indian Law Institute* (2004) pp. 183–206.
196. Dennis W.K. Khong, "The Historical Law and Economics of the First Copyright Act" 2(1) *Erasmus Law and Economics Review* (2006) pp. 35–69 at p. 38.
197. The *Statute of Anne* came into force in 1710 (The bill was first presented to the Parliament on 12 December 1709, and received the royal assent on 5 April 1710). *See*, Lionel Bently and Brad Sherman, *The Making of Intellectual Property: The British Experience* (Cambridge University Press, 1999).

influenced the founders. The foundational premise of *Locke's* theory is that all people have a natural right of property in their own bodies.[198] Because people own their bodies, *Locke* reasoned that they also owned the labour of their bodies and, by extension, the fruits of that labour. This approach dominate the theoretical literature that springs from the propositions that a person who labours upon resources that are "held in common" has a natural property right to the fruits of his or her efforts, and that the state has a duty to respect and enforce that natural right. This concept is widely thought to be especially applicable to the field of copyright, where labour seems to contribute so importantly to the value of finished products.[199]

According to *John Locke,* though the earth and all inferior creatures are common to all men, yet every man has a "property" in his own "person". This nobody has any right to but himself. The "labour" of this body and the "work" of his hands, we may say, are properly his. "Whatsoever, then, he removes out of the state that Nature hath provided and left it in, he hath mixed his labour with it, and joined to it something that is his own, and thereby makes it his property. It being by him removed from the common state Nature placed it in, it hath by this labour something annexed to it that excludes the common right of other men. For this "labour" being the unquestionable property of the labourer, no man but he can have a right to what that is once joined to, at least where there is enough, and as good left in common for others. Thus, *Locke*'s theory of labour can be applied to copyright "if ideas are fixed in a tangible property".[200]

Applying the labour theory, *Immanuel Kant* argues that it is the "natural obligation" to respect the author's ownership of his works. On the other hand, it is the "natural right" of the author to control the use of his work and to be rewarded for it[201] is one of the significant underpinnings of the copyright jurisprudence. Thus, according to natural right philosophers, every man has a natural right over the results of his labour and so the author who has put in effort to produce to work shall have a right to enjoy the fruits of his labour and object to any unauthorised modification or other attack on the integrity of the work.[202] Admitting the utility of labour theory of copyright, the Supreme Court of India in *Gramophone Company of India Ltd.* v. *D.B. Pandey,*[203] observed:

> An artistic, literary or musical work is the brain-child of an author, the fruit of his labour and, so, considered to be his property. So highly is it prized by all civilized nations that it is thought worthy of protection by national laws and international conventions relating to copyright.

---

198. John Locke, *Liberty of the Press* (Cambridge University Press, 1695, Re-print in 1997).
199. Justin Hughes, "The Philosophy of Intellectual Property" 77(2) *Georgetown Law Journal* (1988) pp. 287–366.
200. John Locke, *Two Treatises of Government* (Third Edition, 1698). *See also*, Robert P. Merges, Peter S. Menell and Mark A. Lemley. *Intellectual Property in the New Technological Age* (Aspen Publishers, New York, 2000) at p. 3.
201. *See*, Immanual Kant, "Of the Injustice of Counterfeiting Books" in *Essays and Treatises on Moral, Political and Various Philosophical Subjects* (Richardson ed., 1798) at pp. 229–230.
202. Peter Drahos, *A Philosophy of Intellectual Property,* (Dartmouth Publications, Aldershot, 1996) at p. 9. *See also*, Alfred Yen, "Restoring the Natural Law: Copyright as Labor and Possession", 51 *Ohio State Law Journal* (1990) pp. 517–559.
203. AIR 1984 SC 667: 1984(2)ECC142.

Similarly, the Madras High Court, while explaining the basis of protection to the work of intellectual creation in *Sulamanglam R. Jayalakshmi* v. *Meta Musical*[204] observed: "The primary function of copyright law is to protect the fruits of man's work, labour, skill or test from annexation by the other people." Thus, in *Rediff. Com India Ltd.* v. *E-Eighteen Com Ltd.*,[205] the Delhi High Court held that since the plaintiff incurred substantial expense of labour, skill and money to create a "Dial", the plaintiff is the owner of the copyright in the "Dial". Hence, the plaintiff is entitled to protection of his rights in the said work, and the defendant cannot exploit the same by resort to some slight modification of the basic design of the "Dial". On the question of justification for providing copyright to author, the Apex Court in *Eastern Book Company* v. *D.B. Modak*,[206] observed:

> The copyright protection finds its justification in fair play. When a person produces something with his skill and labour, it normally belongs to him and the other person would not be permitted to make a profit out of the skill and labour of the original author and it is for this reason the Copyright Act, 1957 gives to the authors certain exclusive rights in relation to the certain work referred in the Act. The object of the Act is to protect the author of the copyright work from an unlawful reproduction or exploitation of his work by others.

Personality Theory

The main alternative to a labour justification is a "personality theory" that describes property as an expression of the self. This theory, however, that more familiar civil rights doctrines, specifically rights of expression and privacy, also can provide a foundation for personality theory in copyright law. Personality theory of justification has developed a relationship between property and personality and justifies the copyright of authors. The proposition underlying the personality perspective is that to achieve proper self-development—to be a person—an individual needs some control over resources in the external environment. The necessary as assurances of control take the form of property rights. Most people possess certain objects they feel are almost part of themselves. These objects are closely bound up with personality because they are part of the way we constitute ourselves as continuing personal entities in the world. *Hegel* had developed the "personality" concept in his *Philosophy of Right*[207] and maintained that "property for personality". *Hegel* concludes that the person becomes a real self only by engaging in a property relationship with something external. Such a relationship is the goal of the person. *Hegel* says:

> The person has for its substantive end the right of placing its will in any and everything, which thing is thereby mine; [and] because that thing has no such end in itself, its destiny and should take on my will. [This constitutes] mankind's absolute right of appropriation over all things.[208]

The personality theory of right developed a relationship between property and personality. For the protection of personality the recognition of property right is required and there is

204. AIR 2000 Mad. 454.
205. 2013 (55) PTC 294: 2013 (202) DLT 657.
206. (2008) 1 SCC 1.
207. G.W.F. Hegel, *Philosophy of Right*, (Batoche Books, Kitchener, 2001).
208. *See*, Robert P. Merges, Peter S. Menell and Mark A. Lemley, *Intellectual Property in the New Technological Age* (Aspen Publishers, New York, 2000) at p. 8.

no difference between tangible property and intangible property. Therefore, copyright is a justified right and an essential property right for the protection of personality. According to personality theorists, private property rights should be recognised when and only when they would promote human flourishing by protecting or fostering fundamental human needs or interests. The first step in the application of this perspective to copyright as property is identification of the specific needs or interests one wishes to promote.[209] A wide variety of interests might be deemed fundamental, each of which arguably could be advanced by a system of property rights. Thus, peace of mind, self-reliance, self-realization as a social being, security and leisure, responsibility and citizenship are some of the interests which help to develop personality.[210] But, following are some interests essentially can be protected for development of personality:

1. Privacy. Property rights may be necessary to provide persons "refuge[s] from the general society of mankind"—places where they can either be alone or enjoy intimacy with others.[211]
2. Identity. Selfhood may be thought to depend upon the ability to project a continuing life plan into the future, which in turn is fostered by connection to and responsibility for property.[212]
3. Self-realization as an Individual. Ownership of property may be necessary to enable a person to assert his or her will and to be recognised as a free agent by others.[213]
4. Benevolence. Property rights may be thought essential to enable a person to express ideas of what is beautiful or to enact benevolent wishes.[214]

The above stated four interests (privacy, individual self-realization, identity, and benevolence) provide support to develop the system of copyright property rights. It is a matter of fact that copyright property rights have economic value and may be bought and sold, gained and lost, they may contribute to their owners' abilities to avoid guilt, become autonomous, engage in independent political action, etc. The personality based guidelines for crafting copyright property rights thus found in some combination of the interests of privacy, individual self-realization, identity and benevolence.

Economic Incentive Theory

Copyright law provides an author with more than a right to profit from a creative work. The owner of a copyright also holds the exclusive rights to authorise (or enjoin) any reproductions, derivative works, or public performances of his/her copyrighted material. Thus, one of the

---

209. *See*, William W. Fisher, "Theories of Intellectual Property" 1 *Chinese Intellectual Property Review* (2002) pp. 1–29 at p. 20.
210. *See*, Gregory S. Alexander, *Commodity and Propriety* (University of Chicago Press, 1997); Carol Rose, *Property and Persuasion* (Westview Press, Boulder, 1994); Richard N. Current (Ed.), *The Political Thought of Abraham Lincoln* (Bobbs-Merrill, Indianapolis, 1967).
211. *See*, Jeremy Waldron, *The Right to Private Property* (Harvard University Press, 1978) at p. 296.
212. *See*, Margaret Jane Radin, *Reinterpreting Property* (University of Chicago Press, 1993).
213. *See*, Jeremy Waldron, *The Right to Private Property* (Harvard University Press, 1978) at pp. 302–303.
214. *See*, Thomas Hill Green, *Lectures on the Principles of Political Obligation* (University of Michigan Press, 1967) at p. 220.

predominant justifications of copyright protection is the economic incentive of theory. According to this theory the copyright is often justified on the ground that it stimulates investment of time and money in the creation of new works.[215] Most authors' works of copyright rely on the income they derive from the publication of their works for their livelihoods. If such investment is not adequately protected, any person will misappropriate the fruits resulting from such investment. This acts as a disincentive to the author to engage in such initiatives. On the other hand, if such investment of labour and skill is rewarded it will stimulate creativity. Therefore, it is necessary to provide adequate reward to the author through copyright. The Supreme Court of America recognises the economic incentive philosophy of copyright protection in number of landmark cases.[216] Justice Stewart[217] described the basic purpose of the Copyright Act in America as follows:

> The limited scope of the copyright holder's statutory monopoly, like the limited duration required by the Constitution, reflects a balance of competing claims upon the public interest: creative work is to be encouraged and rewarded, but private motivation must ultimately serve the cause of promoting broad public availability of literature, music, and the other arts. The immediate effect of our copyright law is to secure a fair return to an "author's" creative labour. But the ultimate aim is, by this incentive, to stimulate artistic creativity for the general public good. "The sole interest of the United States and the primary object in conferring the monopoly," this Court has said, "lies in the general benefits derived by the public from the labours of authors."

In *Harper* v. *Nation Enterprises,*[218] the question before the US Supreme Court was whether the defendant's unauthorised publication of quotations from President Gerald Ford's unpublished manuscript was a fair use of the work. In concluding the Court's analysis focused on the effect that characterizing the defendant's actions as a form of fair use would have on copyright's incentive structure. The idea of "incentives" provided the Court with a rhetorical framework internal to the copyright system by which to justify its decision, rather than a meaningful basis with which to understand the very functioning of that system. The Court found it wholly unnecessary to ask whether extending copyright's entitlement to the defendant's actions was necessitated by its idea of incentives. Similarly, the court held in *Eldred* v. *Ashcroft,*[219] that copyright law serves public ends by providing individuals with an

---

215. *See*, Carlos Correa Jorge E. Viñuales, "Intellectual Property Rights as Protected Investments: How Open are the Gates?" 19(1) *Journal of International Economic Law*, (2016) pp. 91–120; William M. Landes and Richard A. Posner, *The Economic Structure of Intellectual Property Law* (Harvard University Press, 2003) at p. 13; Justin Hughes, *Fair Use Across Time*, 50 *Ucla Law Review*, (2003) pp. 775–800; Joseph P. Liu, "Copyright and Time: A Proposal", 101 *Michigan Law Review,* (2002) pp. 409–481.
216. *Mazer* v. *Stein* 347 US 201 (1954). The court observed: "The copyright law, like the patene statutes, makes reward to the owners secondary consideration."... However, it is "intended definitely to grant valuable, enforceable rights to authors, publishers, etc., without burdensome requirements: 'to afford greater encouragement to the production of literary [or artistic] works of lasting benefit to the world." The economic philosophy behind the clause empowering Congress to grant patents and copyrights is the conviction that it is the best way to advance public welfare through the talents of authors and inventors in "Science and useful Arts." Sacrificial days devoted to such creative activities deserve rewards commensurate with the services rendered. *See also, Sony Comp. of America* v. *Universal City Studio, Inc.,* 464 US 417 (1984).
217. *Twentieth Century Music Corp.* v. *Aiken,* 422 US 151 (1975).
218. 471 U.S. 539 (1985).
219. 537 U.S. 186, 212 n. 18 (2003).

incentive to pursue private ones and in *Campbell* v. *Acuff-Rose Music*,[220] that the licensing of derivatives is an important economic incentive to the creation of originals.

As in America the underlying idea of copyright protection is of economic benefit of author, the Constitution (Article 1, Section 8, Clause 8) expressly provides the power to congress to grant copyrights to author. This is the best way to advance public welfare through the talents of authors and inventors in "Science and useful Arts".[221] Thus, in *Feist Publications, Inc.* v. *Rural Telephone Service Company*,[222] the Supreme Court of America held that the primary objective of copyright is not to reward the labour of authors, but to promote the progress of "Science and useful Arts". To this end, copyright assures authors the right to their original expression but encourages others to build freely upon the ideas and information conveyed by a work. Thus, central to the economic incentive theory is the recognition that while copyright's exclusive rights framework provides creators with an economic incentive to create, it also entails large social costs, and that creators therefore need to be given just enough incentive to create in order to balance the system's benefits against its costs.

Social Requirements Theory

Social requirements theory is another theoretical justification for providing copyright to authors. According to this theory, law protects copyright in the interest of society. Therefore, it is in the interest of the society that authors should be encouraged to create more, as well as publish their works, since new works are additions to the cultural stock of society. Copyright law with its market monopoly benefits assures the author with economic reward which would instigate him to create and publish more and more works. The legal protection of copyright provides an incentive to the creation and dissemination of works to the benefit of the author as well as the society as a whole.

This justification has been approved by the Delhi High Court in *Smt. Mannu Bhandari* v. *Kala Vikas Pictures Pvt. Ltd.*,[223] where it has been recognised that the object of any culture is excellence of arts and literature. Quality of creative genius of artists and authors determine the maturity and vitality of any culture. Art needs wealthy environment and adequate protection. The protection which law offers is thus not the protection of artist or author alone. Enrichment of culture is of vital interest to each society; copyright law protects this social interest. In this case, the Delhi High Court described the social requirements justification of copyright as thus:

> The hallmark of any culture is excellence of arts and literature. Quality of creative genius of artists and authors determine the maturity and vitality of any culture. Art needs healthy environment and adequate protection. The protection which law offers is thus not the protection of the artist or author alone. Enrichment of culture is of vital interest to each

---

220. 510 U.S. 569, 593 (1994).
221. *See*, Michael Adelman, "Constructed Languages and Copyright: A Brief History and Proposal for Divorce" 27(2) *Harvard Journal of Law and Technology* (2014) pp. 544–562.
222. 499 US 340 (1991). *See*, *Eastern Book Company* v. *D.B. Modak*, AIR 2008 SC 809: 2007 (14) SCALE 191; *Eastern Book Company* v. *Navin J. Desai*, AIR 2001 Delhi 185; *Franz Xaver Huemer* v. *New Yash Engineers*, AIR 1997 Delhi 79: 1996 RLR 280.
223. AIR 1987 Delhi 13: (1986) ILR Delhi 191. *See also*, *P.P. Prabhakar* v. *Secretary, Government of India*, 1986 (2) Crimes 570: 29 (1986) DLT 248; *A.S. Ahluwalia* v. *General Manager, Delhi Telephones*, 29 (1986) DLT 143.

> society. Law that protects this social interest under Section 67 of the Copyright Act. 1957 is one such example of legal protection. Section 57 lifts authors' status beyond the material gains of copyright and gives it a special status... This is a statutory recognition of the intellectual property of the author and special care with which the intellectual property is protected. Under Section 57, the author shall have a right to claim the authorship of the work. He has also a right to restrain the infringement or to claim damages for the infringement. These rights are independent of author's copyright and the remedies open to the author under Section 55. In other words, Section 57 confers additional rights on the author of a literary work as compared to the owner of a general copyright. The special protection of the intellectual property is emphasized by the fact that the remedies of a restraint order or damages can be claimed "even after the assignment either wholly or partially of the said copyright." Section 57 thus clearly overrides the terms of the Contract of assignment of the copyright. To put it differently, the contract of assignment would be read subject to the provisions of Section 57 and the terms of contract cannot negate the special rights and remedies guaranteed by Section 57. The Contract of Assignment will have to be so construed as to be consistent with Section 57. The assignee of a copyright cannot claim any rights or immunities based on the contract which are inconsistent with the provisions of Section 57.

What is the substance of the protection of special rights guaranteed by Section 57? Sub-clause (a) of Clause (1) of the Section 57 prohibits any distortion or mutilation of the author's work. The words "other modification" appearing in the sub-clause (a) will have to be read *ejusdem generis* with the words "distortion" and "mutilation." The modification should not be so serious that the modified form of the work looks quite different work from the original. "Modification" in the sense of the perversion of the original, may amount to distortion or mutilation.[224] But, there can be a modification implicate such as where "A" is changed to "B", both being quite distinct. Sub-clause (a) thus provides inviolability to an intellectual work. Sub-clause (b) provides for remedies for protection of honour and reputation of the author. The bundle of rights and remedies provided by Section 57 is in true with the modern development in law relating to protection of intellectual property of the author and the international agreements and treaties in that regard.[225] Recognising the social utility of copyright the Supreme Court in *Entertainment Network (India) Ltd.* v. *Super Cassettes Industries Ltd.*[226] observed:

> The copyright recognizes the monopoly in favour of the author which requires protection from unlawful reproduction by others so as to encourage creativity. It also recognizes the social requirement and public interest to encourage author.

Copyright protection of author is being justified in all countries although different countries give varying emphasis to each of them. The principal basis for copyright protection in United States is the economic incentive theory, while continental countries give weight to labour theory and personality theory. The Indian practice is based on both labour theory and social requirement theory.

---

224. *A.S. Ahluwalia* v. *General Manager, Delhi Telephones,* 29 (1986) DLT 143.
225. *Sohan Singh* v. *State,* 29 (1986) DLT 200.
226. 2008 (13) SCC 30: 2008 (4) ALD 47 (SC).

2

Origin and Development of Law of Copyright at International Level and Its Utility in India

ABSTRACT

A large number of international instruments define the scope and ambit of copyright. The law relating to copyright was recognised as conventional law through the 1886 *International Convention for the Protection of Literary and Artistic Works.* Subsequently, a large number of treaties and conventions were adopted at international level to determine the scope and ambit of copyright law. Thus, it can be seen that the concept of copyright has been evolved over centuries at international level. In India it is also well-settled that a statute should be interpreted in the light of the international treaties and conventions. This chapter demonstrates the origin and development of law relating to copyright at international level and its utility in India.

ORIGIN AND DEVELOPMENT

A continuous surge is felt to develop international uniform rules for safeguarding the rights of the owner of intellectual property including copyright at international level. The first multilateral international convention on intellectual property is the International Convention for the Protection of Industrial Property commonly known as "Paris Convention" that was adopted in 1883 to which India is a signatory.[1] Under the Paris Convention, convention countries form

1. *See*, Ruth L. Okediji, Kristin Brandl, Izzet Darendeli and Ram Mudambi, "Foreign Actors and Intellectual Property Protection Regulations in Developing Countries," 50 (5) *Journal of International Business Studies* (2019) pp. 826–846; "Does Intellectual Property Need Human Rights?," 51 *International Law and Politics* (2018) pp. 1–68; M. W. Peng, D. Ahlstrom, S. Carraher, and W. Shi, "An Institution-Based View of Global IPR History", 48 (7) *Journal of International Business Studies* (2017) pp. 893–907; *Telefonaktiebolaget LM Ericsson (PUBL)* v. *Competition Commission of India*, 2016 (66) PTC 58 (Del): (2016) 4 Comp LJ 122 (Del); Jonathan Franklin, *International Intellectual Property Law* (American Society of International Law, 2013); *Reckitt Benkiser India Ltd.* v. *Wyeth Ltd.*, AIR 2013 Delhi 101: 198 (2013) DLT 521; *Ten XC Wireless Inc* v. *Mobi Antenna Technologies*, 2011 (48) PTC 426 (Del): 187 (2012) DLT 632.

a union for protection of industrial property. The basis of the union is equal treatment of nationals and residents of the convention countries.[2]

Copyright protection at the international level began by the middle of the nineteenth century on the basis of bilateral treaties. A number of such treaties providing for mutual recognition of rights were concluded but they were neither comprehensive enough nor of a uniform pattern. In 1886, the International Convention for the Protection of Literary and Artistic Works commonly known as "Berne Convention" was adopted to recognise and regulate the rights of the copyright owners. This was the first international convention on copyright which was revised several times at Berlin in 1908; at Rome in 1928; at Brussels in 1948; at Stockholm in 1967; at Paris in 1971, to meet the various challenges posed by the technological developments.[3]

The aim of the Berne Convention, as indicated in its preamble, is "to protect, in as effective and uniform a manner as possible, the rights of authors in their literary and artistic works". In 1952, the Universal Copyright Convention was adopted which was revised at Paris in 1971. Since its inception in 1886, the Berne Convention has been the primary instrument of international copyright law. The community of nations sets the international standards for moral rights protection of the author under the Berne Convention.[4] The author of "literary works" is a natural person, the actual author who composes or writes such "literary work". Such natural person (author or composer) is also the first owner of copyright under the Indian laws. In this regard, Indian copyright laws stand on the same footing as copyright laws in most countries of the world where the concept stems out of the Berne Convention.[5]

In 1967, the "Convention Establishing the World Intellectual Property Organisation" was adopted by which WIPO was established. The overall objective of WIPO is to maintain and increase respect for intellectual property throughout the world, in order to favour industrial and cultural development by stimulating creative activity and facilitating the transfer of technology and the disseminating of literary and artistic works. In 1996, WIPO adopted two treaties on copyright, Performances and Phonogram Treaty. Thus, there are two international covenants entered into by the countries who are members of World Intellectual Property Organisation which are known as WIPO Copyright Treaty 1996 (WCT) and WIPO Performance and Phonograms Treaty 1996 (WPPT).[6] The Provisions of these treaties are fully applicable in digital environment.

---

2. *See*, *Three-N-Products Private Limited* v. *Emami Limited,* MIPR 2008 (3) 319: 2009 (41) PTC 689 (Cal).
3. The world's first copyright law was the Statute of Anne, enacted in England in 1709. Legislation based on the Statute of Anne gradually appeared in other countries, such as the Copyright Act, 1790 in the United States, but copyright legislation remained uncoordinated at an international level until the 19th century. In 1886, however, the Berne Convention was introduced to provide mutual recognition of copyright between nation states, and to promote the development of international standards for copyright protection. The Berne Convention does away with the need to register works separately in each individual country, and has been adopted by almost all the nations of the world (over 140 of the approximately 190 nation states of the world). *See*, Sam Ricketson and Jane Ginsburg, *International Copyright and Neighbouring Rights: The Berne Convention and Beyond* (Oxford University Press, 2006).
4. *See*, *Chancellor* v. *Rameshwari Photocopy Services*, 2016 (68) PTC 386 (Del): 233 (2016) DLT 279; *Arun Chadha* v. *Oca Productions Private Limited*, 193 (2012) DLT 135: 2013 (53) PTC 401 (Del).
5. *Ramesh Sippy* v. *Shaan Ranjeet Uttamsingh*, 2013 (3) ABR 1228: MIPR 2013 (2) 125.
6. *Super Cassetes Industries Ltd.* v. *Myspace Inc.*, MIPR 2011 (2) 303: 2011 (48) PTC 49 (Del).

In addition to the aforesaid treaties, three more treaties were also adopted in the field of neighbouring rights: Rome Convention for the Protection of Performers, Producers of Phonograms and Broadcasting Organizations, 1961 (Rome Convention), Convention for the Protection of Producers of Phonograms Against Unauthorized Duplication of their Phonograms, 1971 (Geneva Phonograms Convention) and Convention Relating to the Distribution of Programme Carrying Signals Transmitted by Satellite, 1974 (Brussels Satellite Convention). Apart from this, in 1994, Agreement on Trade Related Aspects of Intellectual Property Rights (TRIPS Agreement) was adopted.[7] The TRIPS Agreement requires members to grant specific rights to performers, phonogram producers and broadcasting organisations. It mandates the members to give performers the right to communicate their performances to the public or broadcast them by wireless means, to fix their unfixed performances, and to reproduce fixations.[8] The Beijing Treaty on Audiovisual Performances, 2012 desires to develop and maintain the protection of the rights of performers in their audiovisual performances in a manner as effective and uniformly as possible.[9]

BERNE CONVENTION 1886

Origin and Its Revisions

As stated above, the first international convention on the law of copyright was the *Berne Convention for the Protection of Literary and Artistic Works, 1886.*[10] The convention was adopted and signed initially by ten countries; it has now a membership of 136 states, more than half of whom are developing countries. The universality of the *Berne Convention* is evident from the fact that its membership extends to a number of states in all continents. States at present party to this convention include those in Africa (38 States), in America (26 States), in Asia and the Pacific (26 States) including of course, India, and in Europe (46 States).

The *Berne Convention* has been revised several times in order to improve the international system of protection which the convention provides. Changes have been effected in order to cope with the challenges of accelerating development of technologies in field of utilisation of authors' works; in order to recognise new rights as also to allow for appropriate revisions of established ones. An additional Act was included in 1896. The first major revision, however, took place in *Berlin* in 1908, twenty-two years after the initial formulation of the *Berne Convention* in 1886. This was followed by the revisions in 1928, 1948, 1967 and 1971.

---

7. *See*, I. Botoy, "From the Paris Convention to the TRIPS Agreement," 7(1) *Journal of World Intellectual Property* (2004) pp. 115–130.
8. *See*, C. Deere, *The Implementation Game: The TRIPS Agreement and the Global Politics of Intellectual Property Reform in Developing Countries* (Oxford University Press, Oxford, 2008).
9. *See*, Christophe Geiger, Daniel Gervais and Martin Senftleben, "The Three-Step Test Revisited: How to Use the Test's Flexibility in National Copyright Law" 12 *Program on Information Justice and Intellectual Property* (2013) pp. 1–44.
10. Berne Convention for the Protection of Literary and Artistic Works, Berne, September 9, 1886, came into force on December 5, 1887. India ratified on April 1, 1928. For the text of the Convention, *see*, Alfredo Ilardiand and Michael Blakency, *International Encyclopedia of Intellectual Property Treaties* (Oxford University Press, 2004).

These revisions have successively helped to enrich the contents of the convention.[11] After the 1971 revision of the *Berne Convention* an analogous principle of the Section 14(d)(iii) of the Copyright Act 1957 is found embedded in Article 14 of the Berne Convention. Explaining Article 14 of the Convention and Section 14(d)(1), in *Thiagarajan Kumararaja* v. *Capital Film Works (India) Pvt. Ltd.*,[12] the Madras High Court held thus:

> A remake of the film or its versions which are, substantially similar to the original cinematograph film cannot come within the ambit of the right to copy a film, which is provided for under Section 14(1)(d)(i) of Copyright Act, 1957.

The revised 1971 Berne Convention contains special provisions concerning developing countries; that developing countries for certain works and under certain conditions, depart from the minimum standards of protection with regard to the right of translation and the right of reproduction of copyrighted works. More specifically permits developing countries to grant non-exclusive and non-transferable compulsory licences to translate works for the purpose of teaching, scholarship/research and to reproduce works for use in connection with systematic instructional activities. The purpose of the *Stockholm* revision of 1967 was to cater to the rapid technological developments as well as the needs of developing countries, and to introduce administrative and structural changes. For the first time, the right of reproduction of the work was expressly accorded to authors. As for the preferential provisions for developing countries worked out in *Stockholm,* these were further taken up at the *Paris Revision Conference* in 1971, where new compromises were worked out. The substantive provisions of the *Stockholm Act* (other than the appendix) which had also never entered into force were, however, adopted by the *Paris Revision Conference* in fact as they had been worked out and included in the *Stockholm Act.*

Each revision has added to and embellished the convention. Briefly, the additional *Act of 1896*, extended the duration of the right of translation to the normal term; it also took a step towards protection of architectural works. The *Berlin Act* of 1908 added choreographic works and entertainments in dumb show, photographic and similar works, works of applied art, cinematographic works as well as derivative works (translations, adaptations, etc.) to the list of protected works. The *Rome Act of 1928* further extended the enumeration of protected works to include lectures, addresses, sermons and other works of an oral nature. It also recognised the right of broadcasting as also the so-called moral rights. The *Brussels Act* of 1948 reinforced protection of works of applied art; extended the right of authors of dramatic and musical works to cover "any communication to the public of the performance of their works", the right of broadcasting was to cover any communication to the public by wire or by re-broadcasting of the broadcast of the work; obliged member states to provide for a term of protection covering fifty years after the death of the author; and included a provision for *droit de suite* (an interest in the sale of original works or manuscripts subsequent to the initial or first transfer). In India, Section 2(ff) of the Copyright Act 1957 defines the term "communication to the public" which in conformity of aforementioned developments.[13]

---

11. For detail discussion see Marvin Ammori, "The Uneasy Case for Copyright Extension," 16 *Harvard Journal of Law and Technology* (2002) pp. 287–285.
12. 2018 (73) PTC 365 (Mad): MIPR 2018 (1) 227.
13. *See*, Shahid Ali Khan, "Role of the Berne Convention in the Promotion of Cultural Creativity and Development: Recent Copyright Legislation in Developing Countries", 28 *Journal of the Indian Law Institute* (1986) pp. 424–440.

Thus, in *Thiagarajan Kumararaja* v. *Capital Film Works (India) Pvt. Ltd.*,[14] the Madras High Court held thus:

> Section 2(ff) of the 1957 Act which defines the expression 'communication to the public' expounds, that it involves making of any work available for being seen or heard or otherwise enjoyed by the public directly or by any means of display or diffusion other than by issuing copies of such work, regardless of whether any member of the public actually sees, hears or otherwise enjoys the work so made available. In other words, the provision only protects the right of the owner of the film to make the work accessible to the public via various modes, which are adverted to in that behalf. This right does not include the right to make changes to the work so that it is understood by a section of the society, as it would involve translation of literary or dramatic works without issuance of a licence or assignment of the right in the work.

Object and Purpose

While it was almost universally recognised that authors and other creators, should be afforded the necessary protection for their intellectual creations, there was also a consciousness that the developing countries had genuine problems in gaining greater and easier access to works protected by copyright, particularly for their technological and educational needs, from the developed countries, both in respect of formal and non-formal educational programmes. Solutions had to be found for meeting the immense and urgent needs of educational material in developing countries. The necessity for setting up of an international arrangement for permitting the developing countries a greater degree of access to protected works, while respecting the rights of authors, gathered momentum. Meanwhile, the advance of technology made the extension of the geographical scope of the intentional conventions and multilateral agreements to an increasingly larger number of countries, more attractive.

The purpose of the *Berne Convention* as indicated in its preamble is "to protect, in as effective and uniform a manner as possible, the rights of authors in their literary and artistic works". Article 1 lays down that the countries to which the convention applies constitute a Union for protection of the rights of authors in their literary and artistic works. The basic principles of the convention include "national treatment" according to which works originating in one of the member states are to be given the same protection in each of these states as the latter grant to works of their own nationals; also the principle of automatic protection, according to which such national treatment is not dependent on any formality; in other works protection is granted automatically and is not subject to the formality of registration, notice or deposit.[15] Thus, the "national treatment" implies that any discrimination against foreign products has to be made at the national borders, i.e., the customs borders and once foreign goods cross the national border, they are required to be treated equally with domestically produced goods.

---

14. 2018 (73) PTC 365 (Mad): MIPR 2018 (1) 227. *See* also *Fresh Trading Ltd.* v. *Deepend Fresh Recovery Ltd.*, (2015) EWHC 52 (Ch); Pine Labs Pvt. Ltd. v. Gemalto Terminals India Pvt. Ltd., 2011 VIII AD (Delhi) 380: 2011 (48) PTC 248 (Del.); *PVR Pictures Ltd.* v. *Studio 18*, MIPR 2009 (3) 153: 2009 (41) PTC 70.
15. *See*, *Novartis AG* v. *Union of India,* AIR 2013 SC 1311: 2013 (54) PTC 1 (SC); *P.B. Samant* v. *Union of India*, AIR 1994 Bom 323: 1994 (4) Bom CR 491; *Bishnu Krishna Shrestha* v. *Union of India* [1987] 168 ITR 815 (Cal): [1987] 67 STC 209 (Cal).

Keeping in view of this principle in *Karan Dileep Nevatia* v. *Union of India*,[16] the Bombay High Court held that the Government of India and also the States of India are bound to treat the imported goods on equal terms with domestically produced goods, once the customs duty has been paid on the imported goods and they have crossed the Customs border and there can be no discrimination between them of any nature whatsoever.

Standard

The *Berne Convention*[17] contains a non-limitative (illustrative and not exhaustive) list of such works, which include any original production in the literary, scientific and artistic domain, whatever may be the mode or form of its expression. Derivative works, that is those based on other pre-existing works, such as translations, adaptations, arrangements of music and other alterations of a literary or artistic work, receive the same protection as original works. The protection of some categories of works is optional. It is a matter for legislation in the countries of the Union to determine the protection to be granted to official texts of a legislative, administrative and legal nature and to official translations of such texts, as well as to works of folklore. It is also a matter for national legislation to determine the extent of the application of the law to works of applied art and industrial designs and models as well as the conditions under which lectures, addresses and other works of the same nature which are delivered in public may be reproduced by the press, broadcast, communicated to the public by wire and made the subject of public communication, when such use is justified by the informatory purpose.

Protection under the convention is to operate for the benefit of the author and his successors in title. For some categories of works, however, such as cinematographic works, ownership of copyright is a matter for legislation in the country where protection is claimed. Authors of works are protected, in respect of both their unpublished and published works if they are nationals or residents of a member country, furthermore, if, not being nationals or residents of a member country, they first publish their works in a member country or simultaneously in a non-member and member country. One of the important provisions is the one that covers works or expressions of what is called "folklore". Without mentioning the word, the Convention provides that any member country may give protection to unpublished works where the identity of the author is unknown, but where there is every ground to presume that the author is a national of that country, by designating, through the national legislation, the competent authority which should represent the author of unknown identity and protect and enforce his rights in the countries party to the Convention. By providing for the bringing of actions by authorities designated by the state, the Berne Convention offers to countries whose folklore is a part of their heritage, a possibility of protecting it.

---

16. 2010 (1) Bom CR 588: 2010 (172) ECR 1 (Bombay).
17. The leading works on *Berne Convention* are, Sam Ricketson, *The Berne Convention for the Protection of literary and Artistic Works: 1886–1986* (Kluwer Law International, 1987); Wilhelm Nordemann, *International Copyright and Neighbouring Rights Law* (Aspen Publishers, 1990); Melville B. Nimmer and Paul Edward Geller, Nimmer and Geller, *International Copyright Law and Practice* (Matthew Bender, 1988).

Certain minimum standards of protection have been prescribed relating to the right of authors and the duration of protection. The exclusive rights granted to authors under the convention include the right of translation, the right of reproduction in any manner or form (which includes any sound or visual recording), the right to perform dramatic, dramatico-musical and musical works, the right to broadcasting and communicating to the public by wire, the right of public recitation, the right of making adaptations, arrangements or other alterations of a work and the right of making the cinematographic adaptation and reproduction of a work. The so-called *droit de suite* (concerning original works of art and original manuscripts) is optional and applicable only if legislation in the country to which the author belongs so permits. Independent of the author's economic rights, the Convention provides for the right of the author to claim authorship of his work and to object to any distortion, mutilation or other modification of, or other derogatory action in relation to, the work which would be prejudicial to his honour or reputation ("moral rights"). In *Amar Nath Sehgal* v. *Union of India*,[18] the Delhi High Court elucidated the origin of the authors' moral rights as it stands in the Copyright Act, 1957. The Court held that under Berne Convention the community of nations set the international standards for moral rights protection of the author. Article 6bis of the Berne Convention enjoins the members of the Berne Union to provide legal recognition for the moral rights of attribution and integrity in a work in which copyright exists. Article 6bis of *Berne Convention* reads:

1. Independent of the author's economic rights, and even after the transfer of the said rights, the author shall have the right to claim authorship of the work and to object to any distortion, mutilation or other modification of, or other derogatory action in relation to, the said work, which would be prejudicial to his honour or reputation.
2. The rights granted to the author in accordance with the preceding paragraph shall, after his death, be maintained, at least until the expiry of the economic rights, and shall be exercisable by the persons or institutions authorised by the legislation of the country where protection is claimed. However, those countries whose legislation, at the moment of their ratification of or accession to this Act, does not provide for the protection after the death of the author of all the rights set out in the preceding paragraph may provide that some of these rights may, after his death, cease to be maintained.
3. The means of redress for safeguarding the rights granted by this Article shall be governed by the legislation of the country where protection is claimed.

The modern jurisprudential approach with regard to ownership of author's copyright in literary and musical works, is recognition of two rights—author's economic right and moral right. Even after lawful transfer of former, the ownership of later remains with author and it is protectable under law against any distortion or mutilation. Reputation and honour of creator/author is like property and human right. In *Entertainment Network India Ltd.* v. *Super Cassettes Industries Ltd.*,[19] the Supreme Court recognised the Berne Convention for the Protection of

18. 117 (2005) DLT 717: 2005 (30) PTC 253 (Del). *See also*, *Amar Nath Sehgal* v. *Union of India*, 117 (2005) DLT 717: 2005 (30) PTC 253 (Del).
19. 2008 (9) SCALE 69: (2008) 13 SCC 30.

Literary and Artistic Works and also Article 27 of the Universal Declaration of Human Rights. This protection is recognised to encourage creativity in the field of art, literature, music and aesthetic activity. If the author's copyright is distorted and mutilated, his honour, respect and reputation are seriously affected. Hence any case of mutilation or distortion is made out, protection of the Court by way of injunction is called for, otherwise not.[20]

As a sort of counter-balance to the minimum standards of protection, there are also provisions in the *Berne Convention* limiting the strict application of the rules regarding exclusive rights. These provide for the possibility of using protected works in particular cases without having to obtain the authorisation of the owner of the copyright and without having to pay any remuneration for such use. Such exceptions include reproduction in certain special cases, quotations and use of works by way of illustration for teaching purposes, etc. The minimum standards of protection provided for in the *Berne Convention* also relate to the duration of protection which shall be the life of the author and 50 years after his death. There are exceptions to this basic rule for certain categories of works. For cinematographic works, the term is 50 years after the work has been made available to the public, or, if not made available, then 50 years after the making of such work. For photographic works and works of applied art, the minimum term of protection is 25 years from the making of the work. A majority of countries in the world have legislated for life plus a 50-year term of protection, since it is felt that this could provide the incentive necessary to stimulate creativity, and constitute a fair balance between the interests of the authors and the needs of society.

The Berne Convention does not explicitly mention computer programs in its illustrative list of copyright works. However, as per TRIPS Agreement, member states should recognise computer programs (software) as literary works. Article 2(7) of the Berne Convention makes the protection of works of applied art dependant on domestic legislation, i.e., the extent to which protection may be granted and the conditions under which such works will be protected is dependent on the statute of the particular country where the work originated. Works enumerated in Article 2 of the Berne Convention are mere illustrations of the kinds of works to which copyright might extend. These illustrations are not exhaustive. Therefore, works such as computer programs that exhibit utilitarian characteristics and also contain expressive elements can be brought under the ambit of work of applied art. However, Article 7(4) of the Berne Convention exempts, inter alia, the works of applied art from the general term of protection and sets up a minimum term of only 25 years from the making of the work. As Article 2(7) makes the protection of works of applied art dependent on domestic legislations, the term of protection may be applicable accordingly with respect to different countries. In *Research in Motion Limited* v. *Data Infosys Limited*,[21] the Delhi High Court observed:

> Both India and Canada are signatories to the Berne Convention and thus works first published in Canada are entitled to protection in India as well. Such protection is available under Section 40 of the Copyright Act 1957 and by virtue of the International Copyright Order passed by the Indian Government, where under the works first published in the convention countries mentioned in the Schedule to the Copyright order are protected and all the provisions of the Copyright Act, except in Chapter VIII relating to the rights of

---

20. *Saregama India Ltd.* v. *Puneet Prakash Mehra*, 2011 (1) CHN 341: MIPR 2010 (3) 175.
21. 193 (2012) DLT 698: 2012 (50) PTC 560 (Del).

> broadcasting organisations and of all performers, apply to any work first made or published in such countries in like manner as if the work was first published in India. Therefore, all the software products of the plaintiff are entitled to protection in India as literary works and the plaintiff is entitled to take action for infringement of its copyright in such literary works and obtain relief from the Court as provided under the Copyright Act.

After the Second World War, with the break-up of colonial structures, and the birth of a number of newly independent countries, the lurking question was whether it was fair and workable to ask the developing countries as such to take on obligations under the convention that were agreed upon by developed countries, without taking into consideration the special situations in the developed countries, without taking into consideration the special situations in the developing ones. Especially the newly independent developing countries faced a difficult situation with regard to access to works of the mind. It seemed not very logical to expect them to take on heavy international commitments in respect of books and material required for educational needs. At the same time, it did not seem normal and was in fact even undesirable to have these countries outside the international copyright system, as absence of protection in their case was not likely to foster or encourage national creativity. There was certainly a challenge then posed to international copyright itself and this was, in a manner, sorted out through the give and take that culminated in the special provisions concerning developing countries that were incorporated in an appendix which now forms an integral part of the convention. However, Indian Courts are applying the provisions of the *Berne Convention* in appropriate cases. In *M/s. WD-40 Manufacturing Company* v. *M/s. Khemchand Enterprises,*[22] the Delhi High Court held that:

> By virtue of Berne Convention, to which India is a signatory, plaintiff's copyrights are further protected and enforceable in India... Gradually due to the excellent quality of the plaintiff's products demand for plaintiff's said goods grew in other countries of the world and today plaintiff's said goods under the said trademarks and Can Design are in demand and sold in large quantities in the major countries of the world including India. The list containing the details of the plaintiff's worldwide Trade Registration are placed on record...The plaintiff has obtained registrations of its said trademarks and Can Design in various countries of the world, details whereof is on record. Copies of plaintiff's few trademarks registration certificates issued by the concerned authorities of different countries, viz. Australia, Canada, China, CTM, Cyprus, Hong Kong, Korea, New Zealand, Northern Cyprus, and United States of America are also placed on record.

Special Facilities

The *Revision Conference* convened in *Paris* in 1971 was predominantly concerned with finding solutions in order to support the universal effect of the convention and to establish an appropriate basis for its operation, particularly in relation to the increasing number of developing countries which had to face serious problems in their economic, social and cultural development. The revision in 1971 aimed at harmonizing the individual interests of the author with the more general interest of the global community. The appendix to the *Paris Act (1971)* of the *Berne Convention* provides for special faculties open to developing countries

22. 186 (2012) DLT 672: 2013 (53) PTC 523 (Del).

concerning translation and reproduction of works of foreign origin. The convention's existing exceptions to the author's exclusive rights including those of reproduction and translation rights are remarkable. According to it, countries which are regarded as developing countries in conformity with the established practice of the *General Assembly* of the *United Nations* may, under certain conditions, depart from some of the minimum standards of protection provided for in the convention. This exceptional regime concerns two rights, the right of translation and the right of reproduction.[23]

The *Berne Convention* provides, in respect of developing countries, for the possibility of granting non-exclusive and non-transferable compulsory licences in respect of: (i) translation for the purpose of teaching, scholarship or research; and (ii) reproduction for use in connection with systematic instructional activities, of works protected under the convention; the term systematic instructional activities include systematic out-of-school or non-formal education. These licences could be granted under certain conditions to any national of a developing country which has duly availed itself of one or both of the faculties provided for in the appendix for grant of such compulsory licences in respect of translation and/or reproduction of works of foreign origin. They may be granted, after the expiry of certain time limits and after compliance with certain procedural steps, by the competent authority of the developing country concerned. They have to be applied for from the authority designated in the developing country as being competent to grant such licences. They must provide for compensation in favour of the owner of the right. In other words, the payment to be made by the compulsory licensee must be consistent with standards of royalties normally in vogue in respect of licences freely negotiated between persons in two countries concerned. The possibility that the appendix provides for granting a compulsory licence, if authorization is desired, may favourably influence negotiation and may lead to increased scope for voluntary licensing.

In conclusion it can be said that the minimum copyright term is the life of the author plus 50 years of all works except photographs and cinema. The Berne Convention provided that members should recognise and enforce a limited subset of the "moral rights". The Berne Convention also empowered member countries to adopt exceptions to the mandated copyright protections; which defines the freedom of member countries to create exceptions or limitations to authors' rights to control reproductions of their works. Besides, the Berne Convention provided that member countries' discretion to create more specific exceptions. The Berne Convention establishes three fundamental principles: (i) Principle of National treatment—this requires member countries to give the residents of other member countries the same rights under the copyright laws as they give to their own residents; (ii) Principle of independence of protection—this provides that each member country must give foreign works the same protection they give to domestic works, even when the foreign works would not be shielded under the copyright laws of the countries where they originated;

23. It is worth noting what the Convention does not cover: (1) it gives not right over the distribution and so does not address the vexed question whether copyright should be available to prevent parallel importation; (2) it attempts no legal regulation of collecting societies; (3) save in the case of films, it has nothing to say about initial entitlement to the ownership of copyright, or about other aspects of property rights, (4) the only aspect of remedies covered relates to the seizure of infringing copies and (5) it does not touch the now significant issue of the transmission of works held in digitised form.

(iii) Principle of automatic protection—this principle forbids member countries from requiring persons from other Berne Convention member countries with legal formalities as a prerequisite for copyright protection.[24]

UNIVERSAL COPYRIGHT CONVENTION 1952

Universality of the Convention

The Berne Convention suffered from two weaknesses. First, it lacked universality; and second, the Berne Convention provided for high level of protection which prevented some countries from joining the Union.[25] The Universal Copyright Convention which was first signed in Geneva on 6 September 1952 and subsequently it was revised in Paris in 1971.[26] The Universal Copyright Convention is one of the two principal international conventions protecting copyright; the other is the Berne Convention. The Universal Copyright Convention was developed by United Nations Educational, Scientific and Cultural Organization as an alternative to the Berne Convention for those states which disagreed with aspects of the Berne Convention, but still wished to participate in some form of multilateral copyright protection. These states included developing countries and the Soviet Union as well as the United States and most of Latin America. The former two thought that the strong copyright protections granted by the Berne Convention overly benefited Western developed copyright-exporting nations, whereas the latter two were already members of the Buenos Aires Convention, a Pan-American copyright convention that was weaker than the Berne Convention. The Berne Convention states also became party to the UCC, so that their copyrights would exist in non-Berne convention states.[27] Commenting on the Universal Copyright Convention 1952 *Joseph S. Dubin* observed:[28]

> The Universal Copyright Convention, adopted at Geneva on September 6, 1952, is a landmark in the field of copyright law. It creates no new law of copyright, but in harmonizing existing national systems, on a simplified reciprocal national treatment basis, it represents the culmination of more than five years of preparatory work. It represents a contract, through a plan of copyright, between groups of countries until then radically opposed to one another.

Through the 1971 revision, three basic rights were included to the Universal Copyright Convention: the reproduction right, the broadcasting right and the public performance right. According to this Convention, each contracting state is called upon to undertake to provide for the adequate and effective protection of the right of authors and other copyright proprietors in literary, scientific and artistic works including writings, musical, dramatic and cinematograph

24. Universal Copyright Convention, Geneva Act, September 6, 1952, came into force on September 16, 1955. India ratified on January 21, 1958. *See*, Paul Goldstein, *International Copyright: Principles, Law, and Practice*, (Oxford University Press, New York, 2001).
25. Arpad Bogsch, *The Law of Copyright and the Universal Convention* (Sijthoff Leyden Bowker, 1972) at p. 4.
26. Universal Copyright Convention was revised at, commonly known as Paris Act adopted on July 24, 1971 and came into force on July 10, 1974. India ratified the Convention on April 7, 1988.
27. *See*, *Lamba Brothers Pvt. Ltd.* v. *Lamba Brothers,* AIR 1993 Delhi 347: 1994 (28) DRJ 168.
28. Joseph S. Dubin, "The Universal Copyright Convention," 42(1) *California Law Review* (1954) pp. 89–119 at p. 89.

works and paintings, engraving and sculpture. The rights are to include the exclusive right to authorise reproduction by means of public performance and broadcasting. Each contracting state is required to adopt such measures as are necessary to ensure the application of the Convention. The Convention is not in any way to affect the provision of the Berne Convention for the protection of literary or artistic works or membership in the Union created by that Convention. The Universal Copyright Convention is not applicable to the relationships among countries of the Berne Union in so far as it relates to the protection of works having as their country of origin, within the meaning of the Berne Convention, a country of the Berne Union. The provision of Universal Copyright Convention applies, however, only to works that (i) were first published outside the country requiring the observance of the formalities, and (ii) were not authored by one of that country's nationals. In contrast to Berne Convention, formalities such as registration are permitted under the UCC in order to bring an infringement suit.

Applicability of Universal Copyright Convention in India

India is a signatory to the Universal Copyright Convention.[29] Thus, in *Ziff-Davis Inc.* v. *Dr. D.K. Jain,*[30] the Delhi High Court held that India being signatory to the Universal Copyright Convention and the Berne Convention and by virtue of the International Copyright Order, 1991, under the provisions of the said treaties, the plaintiff's said work is subject to the copyright protection in India under Copyright Act, 1957. Further, in *Chancellor Masters* v. *Orient Longman Private Limited,*[31] the Court observed that in the event of any unauthorised use being made of the work in any country not a party to the Copyright Union and/or the Universal Copyright Convention, the Author and the Publisher shall share any payment received in the proportion of sixty per cent to the Author and forty per cent to the Publisher.

The rights of the authors of member countries of the Universal Copyright Convention are protected under Indian Copyright Act, 1957 and India and the USA are signatories to the Universal Copyright Convention.[32] Therefore, in *Microsoft Corporation* v. *Mr. Ganesh Wakode,*[33] the Delhi High Court is of the view that plaintiffs are entitled to a decree of permanent injunction. Similarly, in *Microsoft Corporation* v. *Rajendra Pawar,*[34] the Delhi High Court held that the plaintiffs' works are created by authors of member countries and originate from and are first published in the said member countries. Plaintiffs' works are, thus, protected

29. *See Gramophone Company of India Ltd.* v. *Birendra Bahadur Pandey,* AIR 1984 SC 667: (1984) 2 SCC 534.
30. 1998 (18) PTC7 39 (Del).
31. 103 (2003) DLT 139: 2003 (26) PTC 186 (Del). *See also, Pepsi Foods Ltd.* v. *Bharat Coca-Cola Holdings Pvt. Ltd.* (1999) ILR Delhi 193: 81 (1999) DLT 122; *Taprogge Gesellschaft MBH* v. *IAEC India Ltd.,* AIR 1988 Bom 157; *Superintendence Company of India (P) Ltd.* v. *Krishan Murgai,* AIR 1980 SC 1717: (1981) 2 SCC 246.
32. *See, Weider Publications* v. *Shri Pushpendra Srivastav,* 2013 AD 1 (Delhi) 501: 2013 (53) PTC 275 (Del); *Microsoft Corporation* v. *Nimesh,* 2012 (51) PTC 205 (Del); *Microsoft Corporation* v. *S. Purohit,* 186 (2012) DLT 451: MIPR 2011 (3) 313; *Microsoft Corporation* v. *Prem Tiwari,* 2011X AD (Delhi) 129; *Microsoft Corporation* v. *M/s. G-Net Technologies,* 2012 (49) PTC 97 (Del); *Microsoft Corporation* v. *Mr. David Raju Polamuri,* 184 (2011) DLT 687: MIPR 2011 (3) 309.
33. 2013 (54) PTC 282 (Del).
34. 2008 (36) PTC 697 (Del).

in India under Section 40 of the Copyright Act, 1957 read with the International Copyright Order, 1999. It is thus the case of that the plaintiff that being the owner of the copyright in the aforesaid literary works within the meaning of Section 17 of the Copyright Act, 1957 is entitled to all exclusive rights flowing from such ownership as set out in Section 14 of the said Act. In connection to the applicability of the Universal Copyright Convention and Barne Convention the Delhi High Court in *ITC Limited* v. *Arora Offset Printers*,[35] observed:

> As per the plaint, the original and artistic works in the appellant's 'MANGALDEEP' packaging is also subject matter of protection under Section 2(c) of the Copyright Act, 1957 and the copyright therein is exclusively owned by the appellant herein. The packaging has instant recognition amongst the members of trade and public. The colour combination used by the appellant and the various aspects of the packaging are unique to the appellant and are identified as such. The conceptualization, arrangement and depiction of the pictorial and the artistic design of the appellant's packaging are an original artwork created for and on behalf of the appellant. Further, India being a member of the Berne Convention as well as the Universal Copyright Convention provides protection to all works irrespective of whether there is a claim of copyright on the work or not.

ROME CONVENTION 1961

Recognition of Neighbouring Rights

Special rights are recognised for broadcasting organisations and performers in the *Rome Convention for the Protection of Performers, Producers of Phonograms and Broadcasting Organizations*, 1961 (Rome Convention). These are referred to as "neighbouring rights". The concept of neighbouring rights gained importance with technological developments. Unauthorised duplication or reproduction of sound recordings of musical performances became a matter of concern for phonogram industry. The Diplomatic Conference in Rome in 1928 passed a resolution asking governments to consider the possibility of adopting measures to safeguard the interests of performers and producers of phonograms. Drafts were prepared for an annexure to the Berne Convention that would deal with the rights of performers, phonogram, producers and broadcasting organisations.[36] Thus, the Rome Convention provides for the protection of "neighbouring rights" of entertainment industries. Following are the achievements of the Rome Convention:

1. At that time neither sound recordings nor films could be routinely copied so as to produce a version just as good. Likewise, broadcasting frequencies were strictly limited, and extensions by cabling and by satellite relay lay in the future. Broadcasters had some copyright interests of their own, but *vis-à-vis* performers and record producers they were major users. It was a considerable achievement that the convention went as far as it did; and no surprise that it attracted relatively few adherents. The convention requires that each member state to apply national treatment in respect of the rights which it accords to performers, record produces and broadcasting organisations.[37]

---

35. 2017 (72) PTC 425 (Del).
36. *See*, Alka Chawla, *Law of Copyright: Comparative Perspective* (LexisNexis, 2013) at p. 20.
37. Rome Convention, Articles 2, 3. The Convention was adopted in Rome on October 26, 1961.

2. In addition, member states must offer those from other states who are protected by the *Convention* certain minimum rights. In the case of records (phonograms), these include an exclusive right to authorise all reproductions, direct or indirect; and also a right to equitable remuneration (which under national law could alternatively be paid to performers) for the use of records in broadcasts and public playing.[38]
3. Broadcasters are to have exclusive rights over fixation, reproduction, re-broadcasting and public communication.[39] These two industries, however, withstood pressure from the often unionised performers (actors and musicians alike) that they also should have rights to "authorise or prohibit" equivalent acts. Performers acquired only the "possibility of preventing" various specified acts, a distinction which was thought to allow, in particular, to continue its approach of only protecting performers by criminal sanctions.[40]
4. The convention guaranteed protection for a term of 20 years, from fixation, performance or broadcast as appropriate.[41]

The structure of the principal provisions of the Rome Convention is somewhat similar to the Berne Convention. (i) Like the Berne Convention, the Rome Convention makes such national treatment subject to certain minima of protection.[42] (ii) Thus, it is also based on the principle of national treatment.[43] National treatment is defined separately in respect of performers,[44] producers of phonograms and broadcasting organisations.[45] (iii) The Rome Convention permits exceptions for private use, etc.[46] (iv) The Rome Convention lays down a minimum term of protection of 20 years.[47] However, unlike the Berne Convention, the Rome Convention contains the principle of reciprocity in respect of certain rights expressed by reservations which any member state can make at any time.[48]

Applicability of Rome Convention in India

India is a signatory to the Rome Convention; therefore, to fulfil the international obligation, the International Copyright Order, 1999 was issued by the Central Government.[49] Now question arises whether the Rome Convention is applicable in arbitration cases in India. Notwithstanding the law of matrix contract in a case being governed by laws of India and despite arbitration agreement appearing to be governed, in the absence of any contrary indication, by governing law clause in matrix contract, arbitration did not appear to have been governed thereby. If there is an express choice of law to govern the contract as a whole, the arbitration agreement

38. *Ibid.*, Article 5.
39. *Ibid.*, Articles 6, 13.
40. *Ibid.*, Article 4.
41. *Ibid.*, Article 14.
42. *See*, Rome Convention, 1961, Article 7 (for performers), Article 10 (for phonogram producers), Article 13 (for broadcasting organizations).
43. *Ibid.*, Article 4.
44. *Ibid.*, Article 5.
45. *Ibid.*, Article 6.
46. *Ibid.*, Article 15.
47. *Ibid.*, Article 14.
48. *Ibid.*, Article 16.
49. *Entertainment Network (India) Ltd.* v. *Super Cassettes Industries Ltd.*, MIPR 2008 (2) 129: 2008 (37) PTC 353 (SC).

will also normally be governed by that law: whether or not the seat of the arbitration is stipulated, and irrespective of the place of the seat. It is, however, only "in exceptional cases, (that) the parties' express choice of a governing law for the main contract may be held not to apply to the arbitration agreement, where there are, as a matter of construction, contrary indications. In *Coal India Limited* v. *Canadian Commercial Corporation*,[50] the Calcutta High Court observed:

> If there is no express choice of law, and no choice of the seat of the arbitration, the applicable law of the main contract will be determined in accordance with the principles in the Rome Convention, and the arbitration agreement will be governed by the law so determined. If there is no express choice of the law to govern either the contract as a whole or the arbitration agreement, but the parties have chosen the seat of the arbitration, the contract will frequently (but not necessarily) be governed by the law of that country on the basis that the choice of the seat is to be regarded as an implied choice of the law governing the contract. In each of these cases, the main contract and the arbitration agreement will be governed by the same law.

Again, question arises how the Rome Convention is to be interpreted in India? It is a general principle of law in India as she is a signatory to the international copyright treaties including the Rome Convention and hence the provisions have to be read in consonance with the treaty obligations. In *Super Cassettes Industries Ltd.* v. *Entertainment Network*,[51] the issue was whether an infringer is entitled to be considered for the grant of compulsory licences without stopping the illegal broadcast of sound recording of the appellant? The Apex Court held that infringer is entitled for compulsory licence if completely stops illegal broadcasting. The Court in its reasoning the Berne Convention referred in which there are specific provisions of compulsory license and equitable remuneration to performers or producers of phonograms.

In *Super Cassettes Industries Limited* v. *Bathla Cassette Industries Pvt. Ltd.*,[52] the statutory license is an authorisation given by law to use a work protected by copyright in a specific manner and under certain conditions, against payment of an author's fee. The Berne Convention allows national legislations to introduce statutory licenses for broadcasting the work in a way that does not affect the moral rights of the author, and against equitable remuneration [Article 11 bids 2 and 3]; the possibility of introducing statutory licenses is also covered by the Berne Convention in respect of reproduction in certain special cases [Article 9(2)] and recording of musical works [Article 13(1)], subject to specified conditions. Thus, the Berne Convention did allow National Legislations to introduce statutory licences such as Section 52(1)(j) of the Indian Copyright Act, 1957. To make the Indian law of copyright in conformity with international law of copyright, the Indian Copyright Act 1957 has been amended in 1984, 1992, 1994, 1999 and 2012. Thus, in *Saregama Ltd.* v. *The New Digital Media*,[53] the Calcutta High Court observed:

> The 1994 Amendment was a major one which harmonized the provisions of the Copyright Act, 1957 with the Rome convention, 1961 by providing protection to the rights of performers, producers of phonograms and broadcasting organizations. It also introduced the concept of registration of copyright societies for collective management of the rights in each category of copyright works.

---

50. AIR 2012 Cal 92: (2012) 2 Cal LT 409 (HC).
51. AIR 2004 Delhi 326: 112 (2004) DLT 549.
52. 107 (2003) DLT 91: 2003 (27) PTC 280 (Del).
53. 2018 (73) PTC 329 (Cal): 2018 (3) CHN (CAL) 147.

TRIPS AGREEMENT 1994

Background of TRIPS Agreement

The Agreement on Trade Related Aspects of Intellectual Property Rights (TRIPS Agreement) is an international agreement administered by the World Trade Organization (WTO) that sets down minimum standards for many forms of intellectual property regulation as applied to nationals of other WTO members.[54] It was negotiated at the end of the Uruguay Round of the General Agreement on Tariffs and Trade (GATT) in 1994. The TRIPS Agreement is the most comprehensive multilateral agreement to set detailed minimum standards for the protection and enforcement of intellectual property rights, and aims at harmonising national intellectual property systems. All members of the World Trade Organization (WTO) are bound by the obligations under the TRIPS Agreement. India is one of the founding members of the GATT and thus a member of the WTO from its inception from January 1, 1995, and is bound by the obligations under TRIPS Agreement like all other members of the WTO.[55] Specifically, TRIPS Agreement requires WTO members to provide copyright rights, covering content producers including performers, producers of sound recordings and broadcasting organisations. TRIPS Agreement also specifies enforcement procedures, remedies, and dispute resolution procedures.

When the General Agreement on Tariffs and Trade (GATT) as negotiated in 1986, one of the principal concerns of industrialised countries in the matter of intellectual property was to stop piracy[56] and counterfeiting of intellectual property goods, which were alleged to be taking

54. Agreement on Trade-Related Aspects of Intellectual Property Rights, Marrakech, April 15, 1994, came into force January 1, 1995. Membership in TRIPS Agreement coincides with membership in the World Trade Organization except for least developed countries, which were granted a grace period; observer governments of the World Trade Organization are marked observer in the table below. India ratified it on January 1, 1995. *See*, Peter K. Yu, Data "Exclusivities and the Limits to TRIPS Harmonization," 46 *Florida State University Law Review* (2019) pp. 18–68; Peter K Yu, "The Objectives and Principles of the Trips Agreement," 46(4) *Houston Law Review* (2009) pp. 979–1046.
55. *See*, Alice Maxwell, "Plainly Justifiable? The World Trade Organization's Ruling on the Validity of Australia's 'Plain Packaging' Under Article 20 of the TRIPS Agreement," 14(1) *Asian Journal of WTO and International Health Law and Policy* (2019) pp. 115–145; *Novartis AG* v. *Union of India*, AIR 2013 SC 1311: 2013 (54) PTC 1 (SC); S.K. Verma and Raman Mitta (Ed.), *Intellectual Property Rights: A Global Vision* (The Indian Law Institute, New Delhi, 2004); Jayshree Watal, *Intellectual Rights in the WTO and Developing Countries* (Oxford University Press, Watal, 2001); T. Ramappa, *Intellectual Property Rights under WTO* (Wheeler, New Delhi, 2000).
56. The mandate for negotiations on Trade-Related Intellectual Property Rights (TRIPS Agreement) including Trade in Counterfeiting Goods in the Punta del Este Declaration in 1986 was :

    "[T]o reduce the distortions and impediments to international trade, and taking into account the need to promote effective and adequate protection of intellectual property rights, and to ensure that measures and procedures to enforce intellectual property rights, do not themselves become barriers to legitimate trade, the negotiations shall aim to clarify GATT provisions and elaborate, as appropriate new rules and disciplines.

    Negotiations shall aim to develop a multilateral framework of principles, rules and disciplines dealing with international trade in counterfeit goods ...."

    For the text of the *Punta de Este Declaration, see,* 25 *International Legal Material* 1623 at 1626 (1986). On the definition of piracy, *see*, J.H. Reichman, "Intellectual Property in International Trade: Opportunities and Risks of a GATT Connection" 22(4) *Vanderbilt Journal of International Law* (1989) pp. 747–891; *see also*, D. Peter Harvey, "Efforts Under GATT, WIPO and Other Multinational Organizations Against Trade mark Counterfeiting" 15 *European Intellectual Property Review* (1993) pp. 446–451; Daniel Gervais, *The TRIPS Agreement Drafting History and Analysis*, (Sweet and Maxwell, London, 2003).

place at a large scale in developing and newly industrialised countries. The agenda set for negotiations of intellectual property rights gave enough vent to this concern and aimed at not only to set new rules on intellectual property rights but also to ensure that they are enforced. The lack of enforcement powers in the WIPO (World Intellectual Property Organization) conventions, however, was considered to be the main reason behind the United State efforts in GATT-related solution. On enforcement, it pinpointed five areas of insufficient activity in developing countries: inadequate police support and insufficient possibilities of border seizure; obstacles to access to courts and authorities; stringent rules of evidence; lack of preliminary protection and insufficient deterrent criminal law provisions.

Consequently, when the negotiations went underway, emphasis was two-pronged: (i) to lay down the norms of substantive protection, and (ii) to prescribed rules on the enforcement of those rights. The final version of the agreement on Trade-Related Aspects Intellectual Property Rights (TRIPS Agreement) thus carried both these aspects along. Whereas Parts I and II contain norms of substantive protection, Part III (and to some extent Part IV) incorporate provisions on enforcement. The aim of the provisions on enforcement is to ensure the undisturbed exercise of the intellectual property rights, which find their place in the substantive provisions. All TRIPS Agreement members (i.e. WTO members) are required to give effect to these provisions under their national laws. The TRIPS Agreement has, thus, harmonised the law on the protection and enforcement of intellectual property rights. As in the case of substantive standards, the United States standards were made the basis on enforcement measures.

Copyright Related Scheme in TRIPS Agreement

Articles 9 to 14 of the TRIPS Agreement deal with the law related to copyright and related rights. Article 9 of the TRIPS Agreement provides that "Members shall comply with Articles 1 to 21 and the Appendix of the *Berne Convention* (1971)". For the first time in an international instrument, the basic dichotomy of this branch of the law appears: "copyright protection shall extend to expressions and not to ideas, procedures, methods of operation or mathematical concepts as such".[57] TRIPS Agreement makes the Berne principle restricting the extent of exceptions in national legislation to the reproduction right.[58] As to term, there is a new minimum of fifty years from the making of a work, where term is not measured by reference to a natural person's life.[59] Computer programs are required to be protected as literary works under the *Berne Convention*; and so are some compilations of data. A rental right is introduced for computer programs, and tentatively for films.[60]

The TRIPS Agreement has its own code of obligations relating to performers, sound-recording producers and broadcasting organisations. Performers must be provided with an exclusive right covering fixation, reproduction, wireless broadcasting and public communication of actual performances. It must last for 50 years from the performance.[61] Similarly, sound recording producers must have an exclusive right in the direct or indirect reproduction of their

57. *Ibid.*, Article 9(2).
58. *Ibid.*, Article 13.
59. *Ibid.*, Article 12.
60. *Ibid.*, Article 11.
61. *Ibid.*, Article 14(1), (5).

phonograms, and likewise (subject to certain limitations) to the rental of copies; it must at least for 50 years from fixation.[62] The TRIPS Agreement also provides that the broadcasting organisations themselves must have an exclusive right over fixation, reproduction and re-broadcasting of their (wireless) broadcasts, and a right of public communication in the case of television broadcasts; or else equivalent rights must be given to copyright owners of material broadcast. The minimum term is 20 years from the broadcast.[63]

The TRIPS Agreement also provides that phonogram producers must receive the "right to authorize or prohibit the direct or indirect reproduction of their phonograms." Broadcasting organizations must receive the right to fix and reproduce fixations of broadcasts as well as to rebroadcast them by wireless means and to communicate television broadcasts to the public. However, the Agreement allows members to provide for conditions, limitations, exceptions and reservations to the extent permitted by the Rome Convention.[64]

Enforcement Aspect of TRIPS Agreement

Part III of the TRIPS Agreement provides for "Enforcement of Intellectual Property Rights" containing a total of 21 Articles (Article 41–61) divided into five sections: General Obligations (Article 41); Civil and Administrative procedures and Remedies (Articles 42–49); Provisional Measures (Article 50); Special Requirements Related to Border Measures (Article 51–60); and Criminal Procedures (Article 61). Together these provisions are aimed at first, on the measures that the holders of intellectual property rights may require from the judicial, administrative and customs authorities to take against infringements and threatened infringements of their rights, and second, the procedures by which such measures may be obtained. These measures may be civil as well as criminal in nature to terminate and restrain infringements of intellectual property rights. Different provisions of the TRIPS Agreement, detail these procedures and measures. Article 41 of TRIPS Agreement sets out the general obligations of WTO members with regard to the domestic enforcement of intellectual property rights. Paragraph 1 of the Article 41 reads:

> Members shall ensure that enforcement procedures as specified in this Part are available under their national laws so as to permit effective action against any act of infringement of intellectual property rights covered by this Agreement, including expeditious remedies to prevent infringements and remedies which constitute a deterrent to further infringements. These procedures shall be applied in such a manner as to avoid the creation of barriers to legitimate trade and to provide for safeguards against their abuse.[65]

This provision lays down that WTO members have to ensure that enforcement procedures as specified in this part are available under their law so as to permit effective action against

62. *Ibid.*, Article 14(2), (3), (5).
63. *Ibid.*, Article 14(3), (5).
64. *Ibid.*, Article 14(6) adds "However, the provision of Article 18 of the Berne Convention (1971) shall also apply, *mutatis mutandis,* to the rights of performers and producers of phonograms in phonograrns."
65. The two copyright treaties concluded by WIPO on 20 December 1996 provide the similar provisions: WIPO Copyright Treaty Article 14, and WIPO Performances and Phonograms Treaty Article 23. For more on these treaties, *see*, Jorg Reinbothe, Maria Martin-Prat and Silke Von Lewinski, "The New WIPO Treaties: A First Resume" 19 *European Intellectual Property Review* (1997) pp. 171–176.

any of infringement of intellectual property rights covered by this agreement. It is up to the members to decide about the exact measures and to ensure their effectiveness in practice. Moreover, in giving effect to these procedures, the members are not obliged "to put in place a judicial system for the enforcement of intellectual property rights distinct from that for the enforcement of laws in general", neither should it affect their capacity to enforce their laws in general.[66] They need not specifically allocate the resources for the enforcement of intellectual property rights. This provision, thus, accepts the different legal systems for enforcement among the members, which also finds its mention in the preamble to the TRIPS Agreement. Hence, the effectiveness of the enforcement measures depends to a large extent on national legislature and practice that should not be subjected to pressure from outside.

The enforcement procedure as prescribed under TRIPS Agreement should be "fair and equitable", "not unnecessarily complicated or costly, or entail unreasonable time limits or unwarranted delays".[67] Further provisions have tried to give content to these terms. Accordingly, decisions on the merits of the case should preferably be in writing and reasoned[68] and be made available to the parties without delay. The courts must base their decision on evidence only in respect of which parties were offered the opportunity to be heard. There should be an opportunity for review by a judicial authority of final administrative decisions, and subject to the jurisdictional provisions in national laws.[69] Thus, Article 64 of the TRIPS Agreement provides for a mechanism for resolution of disputes between the members of the WTO. In case of a dispute, a panel of specially appointed trade experts interprets the provisions of the Agreement and issues a report. The panel's decision may be subjected to appeal before the WTO Appellate Body. If a party to the decision fails to abide by a decision, the other party can impose trade sanctions on the member in breach, upon authorisation by the Dispute Settlement Body. The dispute resolution mechanism in the TRIPS Agreement is strong and effective as was proved in the case of India herself. Article 65 (sub-articles 1 and 2) of the TRIPS Agreement allowed India to delay the application of the provisions of the Agreement for a period of 5 years, that is, till January 1, 2000; Sub-article 4 allowed India to delay for a further period of five years, that is, till January 1, 2005, the application of the provision relating to product patent, in respect of all articles excluded by the Patent Act, 1970, which included pharmaceuticals and agricultural chemical products. But, Article 70 (Sub-articles 8 and 9) enjoined that in the meanwhile it should provide for a means by which applications for patents for inventions in respect of pharmaceutical and agricultural chemical products could be filed and also for the grant of "exclusive marketing rights"[70] for such products.[71]

---

66. Paragraph 5 of the Article 41 of the TRIPS Agreement.
67. *Ibid.*, Paragraph 2.
68. *Ibid.*, Paragraph 3.
69. *Ibid.*, Paragraph 4.
70. For various issues on "exclusive marketing rights", *see*, *UCB Farchim SA* v. *Cipla Ltd.*, MIPR 2010 (1) 278: 2010 (42) PTC 425 (Del); *F. Hoffmann-LA Roche Ltd.* v. *Cipla Ltd.*, MIPR 2009 (2) 1: 2009 (40) PTC 125 (Del); *Hetero Drugs Ltd.* v. *Wockhart Ltd.*, MIPR 2007 (1) 403: 2007 (34) PTC 173 (SC); *Glaxo Smith Kline Plc* v. *Controller of Patents and Designs*, 2006 (3) CHN 577; *Novartis AG* v. *Mehar Pharma*, 2005 (3) Bom CR 191: 2005 (30) PTC 160 (Bom); *Intas Laboratories Pvt. Ltd.* v. *Novaritis A.G.*, 2005 (1) CTC 27.
71. *Novartis A.G.* v. *Union of India,* AIR 2013 SC 1311: 2013 (54) PTC 1 (SC).

Impact of TRIPS Agreement in India

TRIPS Agreement, *inter alia,* has influenced the copyright policy of several countries, including a number of developing countries and has been drawn upon in the preparation of copyright legislation, providing a balance between the needs and interests of authors, publishers, other copyright owners, as well as those of the general public. The conventional rights, effectively implemented, could serve as an incentive to one's national authors and their assigns (the publishers) to create and disseminate knowledge. It is something the society necessarily accepts if it wishes to encourage intellectual creativity, to ensure the progress of the sciences, the arts and of knowledge in general, to promote the industry using authors' works and to render it possible to distribute such works in an organised manner among the widest possible circle of interested persons. India has been following specific common law methods for enforcement.

After the entry into force of the TRIPS Agreement, India has given effect to its different provisions through amending the existing intellectual property laws or legislating new ones. In this process, it has amended its *Copyright Act, 1957* (in 1994 and subsequently, in 1999 and 2012) and the *Patents Act, 1970* (by the Patents (Amendment) Act, 2005); replaced the *Trade and Merchandise Marks Act, 1958* with the new *Trade Marks Act, 1999;* and enacted the *Geographical Indications of Goods (Registration and Protection) Act, 1999; the Integrated Circuits Layout Design Act, 2000;* and the *Plant Varieties and Farmers' Right Act, 2001.* Besides these specific intellectual property laws, some other general laws also provide enough scope for the enforcement of intellectual property. The Indian Penal Code makes counterfeiting an offence (Section 483), which is punishable with imprisonment and fine.[72] The *Specific Relief Act, 1963* provides the relief by way of injunction interim as well as permanent for the activity infringing the right of the owner.

In *Novartis A.G.* v. *Union of India,*[73] the Apex Court held that the TRIPS Agreement is the most comprehensive multilateral agreement to set detailed minimum standards for the protection and enforcement of intellectual property rights, and aims at harmonising national intellectual property systems. All members of the World Trade Organization (WTO) are bound by the obligations under the TRIPS Agreement. India is one of the founding members of the GATT and thus a member of the WTO from its inception from 1 January 1995, and is bound by the obligations under TRIPS Agreement like all other members of the WTO. Regarding the utility of the TRIPS Agreement, in *Navigators Logistics Ltd.* v. *Kashif Qureshi,*[74] the Delhi High Court observed:

> Article 39 of the Trade Related Aspects of Intellectual Property Rights (TRIPS Agreement) signed by India imposed an obligation on contracting states to provide means to protect secret information that has commercial value from disclosure without the consent of the persons who have maintained the secrecy of such information.

---

72. *See*, Section 89 of the Trade and Merchandise Marks Act, 1958. The penal laws, however, have been found inadequate and ineffective to deal with the infringement of intellectual property cases. *See also*, N.S. Gopalakrishnan, *Intellectual Property and Criminal Law* (Bangalore, National Law School of India University, 1994).
73. AIR 2013 SC 1311: 2013 (54) PTC 1 (SC).
74. 2018 (76) PTC 564 (Del): 254 (2018) DLT 307.

WIPO COPYRIGHT TREATY 1996 (WTC) AND WIPO PERFORMANCES AND PHONOGRAM TREATY 1996 (WPPT): INTERNET TREATIES

During 1970s and 1980s, a number of important new technological developments took place—reprography, video technology, compact cassette systems facilitating "home taping", satellite broadcasting, cable television, the increase of the importance of computer programs, computer generated works and electronic databases, etc.[75] The most astonishing feature of the emergence of new technologies is the enabling dissemination of knowledge in a hitherto unprecedented manner. These scientific break-through and technological developments have created a corresponding demand for strengthening and harmonising legal protection. Situated against this backdrop, the preparation of new binding international norms began in two forums, at GATT in the framework of the Uruguay Round negotiations resulting in WTO and at WIPO.

The 1980s and 1990s saw the digital revolution sweeping the world and advent of the Internet over the worldwide Web. After the adoption of TRIPS Agreement under the auspices of WTO, the preparation of new copyright and neighbouring right norms in the WIPO Committee was intensified to deal with specially those problems that were not covered by TRIPS Agreement. On 20 December 1996, representatives of approximately 120 countries participated in a Diplomatic Conference to discuss the challenges posed to the copyright system by the Internet. The Conference at it's eighth session adopted the WIPO Copyright Treaty 1996 (WTC)[76] together with WIPO Performances and Phonograms Treaty, 1996 (WPPT) in order to achieve the above objectives. The WCT came into force on 6 April 2002 and the WPPT came into force on 20 May 2002. These two treaties are together known as "Internet Treaties".[77] The WTC deals with the protection for the authors of literary and artistic works. The WPPT extends copyright like protection to performers and producers of phonograms.

The WCT and WPPT are intended to address the issue of copyright protection on the Internet, the world wide communication system possible by advancements in digital technologies. The WCT and WPPT address the issue in three ways, namely, (a) by clarifying the existing provisions in the Berne Convention and in the International Conventions for the Protection of Performers, Producers of Phonograms and Broadcasting Organisations, 1961 (Rome Convention) and in some cases, reaffirming the interpretations already generally adopted, (b) giving new interpretations to the existing provisions widening their scope, and (c) adding new provisions on rights and obligations.

---

75. *Tata Consultancy Services* v. *State of Andhra Pradesh*, AIR 2005 SC 371: (2005) 1 SCC 308; *O.R.G. Systems* v. *Collector of Central Excise*, AIR 1998 SC 2662: (1998) 6 SCC 56.
76. WIPO Copyright Treaty, Geneva, December 20, 1996, came into force March 6, 2002. India has not ratified so far. *See*, R.V. Vaidyanatha Ayyar, "Interest or Right? The Process and Politics of a Diplomatic Conference on Copyright," 1(1) *Journal of World Intellectual Property* (1998) pp. 3–35; Jorg Reinbothe, Maria Martin-Prat and Silke Von Lewinski, "The New WIPO Treaties: A First Resume" 19 *European Intellectual Property Review* (1997) pp. 171–176.
77. *See*, Zakir Thomas, "Overview of Changes to the Indian Copyright Law", 17 *Journal of Intellectual Property Rights* (2012) pp. 324–334.

WIPO Copyright Treaty 1996 (WTC)

As stated above the World Intellectual Property Organization Copyright Treaty, (WIPO Copyright Treaty or WCT), is an international treaty on copyright law adopted by the member states of the World Intellectual Property Organization (WIPO) in 1996. The WCT is closely connected to the 1971 Paris Act of the Berne Convention. The WCT of 1996 is a special agreement to the Berne Convention and requires compliance with the Berne Convention. This treaty makes explicit that computer programs are protected as literary works under the Berne Convention. It also states that compilations of data for which the selection or arrangement of the contents are sufficiently original are protected as compilations. The WCT obligates the contracting parties to comply with Articles 1 to 21 and the Appendix of the Berne Convention. Article 1 of the WCT states that it is a "special agreement within the meaning of Article 20 of the Paris Act, and that nothing in the Treaty is to derogate from the contracting parties existing obligations under the Berne Convention". The WCT further requires contracting parties, when creating exceptions to the rights granted under the Treaty, to abide generally by the formula that Article 9(2) of the Berne Convention Paris Act prescribes for limitations of the reproduction right.[78] The Treaty also requires contracting states to protect against circumvention of encryption technologies for copyrighted works, and against interference with electronic rights management information.[79] It also requires effective remedies to enforce rights under the Treaty.[80]

The WCT provides for certain new rights:

1. It provides for right of distribution for authors of literary and artistic works.[81] Under the Berne Convention, such a right was granted explicitly only in respect of cinematographic work.
2. It provides a qualified exclusive right of authorising commercial rental to the public in respect of computer programs, cinematographic works and works embodied in phonograms of the originals or copies of their work in order to strengthen the right of reproduction of authors.[82]
3. Authors of literary and artistic works shall enjoy the exclusive right of authorising any communication to the public of their works, by wire or wireless means, including making available to the public of their works in such a way that members of the public may access these works from a place and at a time individually chosen by them.[83]

---

78. WIPO Copyright Treaty 1996, Article 10. Agreed statement concerning Article 10: "It is understood that the provisions of Article 10 permit Contracting Parties to carry forward and appropriately extend into the digital laws which have been considered acceptable under the Berne Convention. Similarly these provisions should be understood to permit contracting parties to devise new exceptions and limitations that are appropriate in the digital network environment. It is also understood that Article 10(2) neither reduces nor extends the scope of applicability of the limitations and exceptions permitted by the Berne Convention."
79. *Ibid.*, Article 12.
80. *Ibid.*, Article 14 (2).
81. *Ibid.*, Article 6.
82. *Ibid.*, Article 7.
83. *Ibid.*, Article 8.

The WCT expands on three aspects of protectable subject matter under the 1971 Berne Convention Paris Act that had assumed significance in the contemporary digital environment:

1. Computer programs are protectable as literary works within the meaning of Article 2 of the Berne Convention Paris Act.[84]
2. Compilations of data or other material which by reason of the selection or by arrangement of their contents constitute intellectual creations, are protected as such.[85]
3. Copyright protection extends to expressions and not to ideas, procedures, methods of operation or mathematical concepts as such.[86]

Thus, the WCT provides additional protections for copyright deemed necessary due to advances in information technology since the formation of previous copyright treaties before it. It ensures that computer programs are protected as literary works (Article 4), and that the arrangement and selection of material in databases is protected (Article 5). It provides authors of works with control over their rental and distribution in Articles 6 to 8 which they may not have under the Berne Convention alone. It also prohibits circumvention of technological measures for the protection of works (Article 11) and unauthorised modification of rights management information contained in works (Article 12).

WIPO Performances and Phonogram Treaty 1996 (WPPT)

WIPO Performances and Phonograms Treaty, 1996 (WPPT) was adopted in order to achieve the same objectives of WIPO Copyright Treaty (WCT).[87] WPPT was formulated at the same diplomatic conference as the WCT and it responds to many of the same issues presented by new electronic media for disseminating creative productions. The provisions of the WPPT relating to the digital agenda cover the following issues:

1. Certain terms like performer, phonogram, fixation, producer of a phonogram, publication, broadcasting and communication to public are defined.[88]
2. Rights applicable to storage and transmission of performances and phonograms in digital systems.[89]
3. Limitations on and exception to rights in a digital environment.[90]
4. Technological measures of protection and rights management information.[91]

Thus, the provisions of the WPPT relating to the "digital agenda" cover certain definitions, rights applicable to storage and transmission of performances and phonograms in digital systems, limitations on and exceptions to rights in a digital environment, technological

84. *Ibid.*, Article 4. The scope of the protection for computer programs under Article 4, read with Article 2, is consistent with Article 2 of the Berne Convention and similar to Article 10 of TRIPS Agreement.
85. *Ibid.*, Article 5. This is similar to Article 10 of TRIPS Agreement.
86. *Ibid.*, Article 5. This is similar to Article 10 (2) of TRIPS Agreement.
87. The WPPT entered into force on May 20, 2002.
88. WIPO Performances and Phonograms Treaty 1996, Article 2.
89. *Ibid.*, Articles 7 to 10.
90. *Ibid.*, Article 16.
91. *Ibid.*, Articles 18, 19.

measures of protection and rights management information. The definitions cover more or less the same terms as those which are defined in Article 3 of the Rome Convention: "performers", "phonogram", "producer of phonograms", "publication", "broadcasting"; more, in the sense that the WPPT also defines "fixation" and "communication to the public", and less, in the sense that it does not define "reproduction" and "rebroadcasting".

Under Article 17 of the WPPT, the "term of protection to be granted to performers shall last, at least, until the end of a period of 50 years computed from the end of the year in which the performance was fixed in a phonogram." This term seems to differ from the term provided for in Article 14.5 of the TRIPS Agreement, which also refers to the year when the performance took place as an alternative starting point for the calculation of the term. The term of protection of phonograms differs also in substance from the term provided for in the TRIPS Agreement. Under Article 14.5 of the Agreement, the 50 year term is always computed from the end of the year in which the fixation was made, while under Article 17(2) of the WPPT, the term is calculated from the end of the year in which the phonogram was published, and it is only in case of absence of publication that it is calculated as under the TRIPS Agreement. Since publication normally takes place after fixation, the term under the Treaty, in general, is somewhat longer.

Harmonisation of WCT and WPPT with Indian Copyright Law

The most important feature of the WCT and the WPPT is that it includes provisions necessary for the adaptation of international norms on the protection of works, performances and phonograms to the situation created by the use of digital technology, particularly of global digital networks like the Internet. India has been a party to the negotiations concluding WIPO Copyright Treaty, 1996 (WCT) and WIPO Performances and Phonogram Treaty, 1996 (WPPT).[92] To harmonise the Copyright Act, 1957 with WIPO "Internet treaties", WCT and WPPT, the Copyright (Amendment) Act, 2012 has been enacted by the Government of India. The Amendment Act goes much beyond the "Internet treaties" and has introduced many changes in the Copyright Act, 1957.[93] Many provisions of these treaties like right of communication to the public have been available in the Indian copyright law since the 1994 amendment. The 2012 amendments can be categorised into (i) Amendments to rights in artistic works, cinematograph films and sound recordings; (ii) WCT and WPPT related amendments to rights; (iii) Author-friendly amendments on mode of assignment and licences to streamline business parties; (iv) Amendments to facilitate access to works further sub-classified into: (a) Grant of compulsory licences, (b) Grant of statutory licences, (c) Administration of copyright societies, (d) Access to copyrighted works by the disabled, and (e) Relinquishment of copyright; (v) Strengthening enforcement and

92. For detail analysis of the Treaties, *see*, Ayyar R.V.V., "The Process and Politics of a Diplomatic Conference on Copyright" 1(1) *Journal of World Intellectual Property*, (1998) pp. 3–35.

93. The Delhi High Court in *UTV Software Communication Ltd.* v. *1337X to and Ors.* [2019 (78) PTC 375 (Del)] observed that Copyright Act 1957 was amended in 2012 to partially implement obligations under the 1996 WIPO Internet Treaties (WIPO Copyright Treaty and the WIPO Performances and Phonograms Treaty), in light of the substantial developments in technology with the aim of protecting copyright in the digital context.

protecting against Internet piracy including WTC and WPPT related provisions; (vi) Reform of copyright board.[94]

In India the Copyright (amendment) Acts of 1984, 1994, 1999 and 2012 has been introduced certain changes to fulfil the obligations under the WCT and WPPT and Agreement on Trade Related Aspects of Intellectual Property Rights (TRIPS Agreement). Explaining the importance of WCT and WPPT the Supreme Court of India in *Star India Private Limited* v. *Department of Industrial Policy and Promotion*,[95] observed:

> WIPO Copyright Treaty 1996 (WCT) and WIPO Performances and Phonograms Treaty 1996 (WPPT) have set the international standards in these spheres. The WCT and the WPPT were negotiated in 1996 to address the challenges posed to the protection of copyrights and related rights by digital technology, particularly with regard to the dissemination of protected material over digital networks such as the Internet. The member countries of the WIPO agreed on the utility of having the Internet treaties in the changed global technical scenario and adopted them by consensus. In order to extend protection of copyright material in India over digital networks such as internet and other computer networks in respect of literary, dramatic, musical and artistic works, cinematograph films and sound recordings works of performers, it is proposed amend the Copyright Act 1957 to harmonise with the provisions of the two WIPO Internet Treaties, to the extent considered necessary and desirable. The WCT deals with the protection for the authors of literary and artistic works such as writings, computer programmes; original databases; musical works; audiovisual works; works of fine art and photographs. The WPPT protects certain "related rights" which are the rights of the performers and producers of phonograms.

BEIJING TREATY ON AUDIOVISUAL PERFORMANCES, 2012

The Beijing Treaty on Audiovisual Performances was adopted on 26 June 2012 by the Diplomatic Conference on the Protection of Audiovisual Performances of the World Intellectual Property Organization (WIPO). According to WIPO "the new treaty brings audiovisual performers into the fold of the international copyright framework in a comprehensive way, for the first time." The treaty is a multilateral treaty which regulates copyright for audiovisual performances. According to WIPO, "the new treaty brings audiovisual performers into the fold of the international copyright framework in a comprehensive way, for the first time" referring to the clauses dedicated to protecting their works on the Internet. It addresses the issue of the copyright system discriminating against certain groups of performers, as the previous treaties, such as WIPO Performances and Phonograms Treaty, focused more on the sound than visual aspects. WIPO states that the treaty boosts the economic rights and moral rights of audiovisual performers (the performers' rights). The expanded economic rights give them an opportunity to share the income collected by producers from internationally distributed audiovisual works. The moral rights address issues such as lack of attribution or distortion of their work.[96]

---

94. *See*, Zakir Thomas, "Overview of Changes to the Indian Copyright Law", 17 *Journal of Intellectual Property Rights* (2012) pp. 324–334.
95. (2019) 2 SCC 104: 2018 (14) SCALE 651.
96. For detail discussion *see* Daniel Gervais, "The Protection of Performers Under US Law in Comparative Perspective,"5(1) *IP Theory* (2015) pp. 116–133; Silke von Lewinski, "The Beijing Treaty on Audiovisual Performances," 6 *Max Planck Institute for Intellectual Property and Competition Law* (2012) pp. 539–546; Aaron X. Fellmeth, "The Beijing Treaty on Audiovisual Performances," 51(6) *International Legal Materials* (2012) pp. 1211–1222.

UTILITY OF INTERNATIONAL COPYRIGHT LAW IN INDIA

The Problem

Copyright has been recognised under international law as well as domestic law. In India, copyright subsists both in published and unpublished work. An owner of copyright can get protection in India in his unpublished work if on the date of making of the work he is a citizen of India or domiciled in India.[97] In the case of a published work, the work has to be first published in India. If the work is first published outside India, then the author on the date of publication should be a citizen of India. In case the author is dead on the date of publication, then on the date of his death he should have been citizen of India. If the work is a work of joint authorship then the conditions have to be satisfied by all the authors. All these issues of copyright law have been recognised under international law, but norms may vary from country to country. In *Macmillan & Co. Ltd.* v. *Cooper*,[98] the court held that the importance of copyright protection had become most apparent after the invention of the printing press by Johannes Gutenberg in 1436, which made duplication of the books very fast as compared to manual writing by authors. However, the norms of copyright were not universal as copyright traditions of common law and civil law countries were different. The countries, therefore, made an effort for harmonisation of laws and started entering into bilateral, regional and international conventions.

Theoretical Dichotomy and Indian Approach

There has been a theoretical dichotomy on the issue of enforcement of international law/ international copyright law in India for a long time. In this connection, the main questions which arise: How does India apply the rules of international law within the framework of national legal order? And how is the conflict between a rule of international law and a rule of national law to be solved? In a conflict between a rule of international law and that of a national law, a large number of states follow the theory that rules of international law cannot without express municipal adoption operate as a part of municipal law. In the *Constitutions* of certain states, relevant international legal standards concerning human rights, even if not specifically mentioned, have at least theoretically the same status as the domestically enacted law via the incorporation provision. Even so the specific content of international standards incorporated by general reference may be subject to the vagaries of interpretation, especially where customary norms are concerned. On the contrary, certain states show considerable flexibility in the procedure whereby they give effect within their territories the rules of international law. Thus, *Constitutions* of many countries include provisions that give domestic legal status to international conventional or customary law in general.[99]

---

97. Section 13(2)(ii), Copyright Act 1957.
98. (1924) 40 TLR 186 at p. 187.
99. For example, *Constitution of Argentina* (Article 31 establishing treaties as part of the supreme law of nation); the position is same in the *US Constitution* (Article VI); *Constitution of Honduras* (Article 16 establishing international treaties as part of the domestic law and with supremacy over conflicting domestic law).

According to Article 253, the *Constitution of India* confers on the Parliament the capacity to legislate, irrespective of the scheme of distribution of powers, to implement a treaty or a decision made at an international conference.[100] Article 253 provides: "Legislation for giving effect to international agreements—Notwithstanding anything in the foregoing provisions of this Chapter, Parliament has power to make any law for the whole or any part of the territory of India for implementing any treaty, agreement or convention with any other country or countries or any decision made at any international conference, association or other body."[101] Article 253 contains *non-obstante* clause, thus, operates notwithstanding anything contained in Article 245 and Article 246 (distribution of legislative powers). Article 245 of the *Constitution* empowers the Parliament not only to make laws for the whole or any part of the territory of India but also indicates that no law made by the Parliament shall be deemed to be invalid on the ground that it would have extra-territorial operation. Clause (1) of Article 246 of the *Constitution of India* confers exclusive legislative power upon the Parliament with respect to any of the matters enumerated in List I in the Seventh Schedule whereas in terms of Clause (2) thereof, the Legislature of any State also has the power to make laws with respect to any of the matters enumerated in List III in the Seventh Schedule, subject of course to the legislative competence of the Parliament as contained in Clause (1) but notwithstanding anything contained in Clause (3) thereof. The power of the State Legislature in terms of Clause (3) of Article 246 is subject to Clauses (1) and (2) in relation to the matters enumerated in List II in the Seventh Schedule.[102]

Article 246 confers power on the Parliament to enact laws with respect to matters enumerated in List I of the Seventh Schedule to the *Constitution*.[103] Entries 10 to 21 of List I of the Seventh Schedule pertain to international law. In making any law under any of these entries, the Parliament is required to keep Article 51 in mind. It would be useful to refer to Entry 14 of List I of the Seventh Schedule which read as under: "Entering into treaties and agreements with foreign countries and implementing of treaties, agreements and conventions with foreign countries." It is thus obvious that entering into a treaty obligation and its performance are two different stages covered by different wings of the Government. Entering into a treaty is the executive act performed by the head of the state whereas its implementation is the legislative function, if in a given case, a law is required to implement the treaty. In *Maganbhai Ishwarbhai Patel* v. *Union of India*,[104] the Apex Court observed:

> As was observed by Lord Atkin in *Attorney General for Canada* v. *Attorney General for Ontario*,[105] the position may be summed up thus: there is a distinction between (i) the formation and (ii) the performance of the obligation. The first is an executive act, the second a legal act if a law is required. The performance then has not force apart from a

100. *See*, *Government of NCT of Delhi* v. *Union of India*, (2018) 8 SCC 501: 2018 (8) SCALE 72; *Vishaka* v. *State of Rajasthan and Others*, AIR 1997 SC 3011: 1997 (5) SCALE 453.
101. *See*, *Justice K.S. Puttaswamy* v. *Union of India*, AIR 2017 SC 4161: (2017) 10 SCC 1; *Union of India* v. *Azadi Bachao Andolan* (2003) 263 ITR 706 (SC): (2003) Supp. 4 SCR 222; *Union of India* v. *Azadi Bachao Andolan*, 2003 (8) SCALE 287: (2004) 10 SCC 1; *N. Nagendra Rao* v. *State of Andhra Pradesh*, AIR 1994 SC 2663: (1994) 6 SCC 205; *Rosiline George* v. *Union of India*, 1993 (4) SCALE 230: (1994) 2 SCC 80; *Maganbhai Ishwarbhai* v. *Union of India*, AIR 1969 SC 783: (1970) 3 SCC 400.
102. *State of W.B.* v. *Kesoram Industries*, 2004 (1) SCALE 425: (2004) 10 SCC 201.
103. *Binod Kumar* v. *State of Jharkhand*, JT 2011 (4) SC 114: 2011 (4) SCALE 109.
104. AIR 1969 SC 783: (1970) 3 SCC 400.
105. (1937) A.C. 326.

> law that is to say unless Parliament assents to it and Parliament then accords its approval to the first executive act. The treaties created by executive action bind the contracting parties and, therefore, means must be found for their implementation within the law.[106]

Article 253 of the *Constitution* provides that while giving effect to an international treaty, the Parliament assumes the role of the State Legislature and once the same is done the power of the state is denuded.[107] Article 51 of the *Constitution* directs that the state shall endeavour to, *inter alia*, foster respect for international law and treaty obligations in the dealings of organised peoples with one another.[108] Notwithstanding the fact that great care with which the various entries in the three lists have been framed: on some rare occasions it may be found that one or the other field is not covered by these entries. The makers of our Constitution have, in such a case, taken care by conferring power to legislate on such residuary subjects upon the Union Parliament including taxation by reason of Article 248 of the Constitution. The Supreme Court in the *State of West Bengal* v. *Kesoram Industries Ltd.*,[109]

> It can be seen that Article 253 contains non-obstante clause. Article 253, thus, operates notwithstanding anything contained in Article 245 and Article 246. Article 246 confers power on the Parliament to enact laws with respect to matters enumerated in List I of the Seventy Schedule to the Constitution. Entries 10 to 21 of List I of the Seventh Schedule pertain to International Law. In making any law under any of these entries, parliament is required to keep Article 51 in mind.

However, the *Constitution* does not say that international law as such shall be part of or superior to the domestic law of India. As stated above, there is a theoretical dichotomy between rules of international law and rules of national law. At opposing extremes are the theories of "dualism" and "monism". According to the "dualism", international law and the internal law of states are totally separate legal systems. Being separate systems, international law would not as such form part of the internal law of a state. To the extent that in particular instances, rules of international law may apply within a state they do so by virtue of their adoption by the internal law of the state, and apply as part of that internal law and not as international law. Such a view avoids any question of the supremacy of one system of law over the other since they share no common field of application; each is supreme in its own sphere. On the other hand, according to "monism", the two systems of law are part of one single legal structure, the various national systems of law being derived by way of delegation from the international legal system. Since international law can thus be seen as essentially part of the same legal order as municipal law, and as superior to it, it can be regarded as incorporated in municipal law, giving rise to no difficulty of principle in its application as international law within states.[110] These differences in theories are not resolved by the practice of states or by such rules of international law as may apply in this situation. International developments, for

---

106. *Sarabjit Rick Singh* v. *Union of India*, 2007 (14) SCALE 263: (2008) 2 SCC 417; *Suman Sood* v. *State of Rajasthan*, AIR 2007 SC 2774: (2007) 5 SCC 634; *Rosiline George* v. *Union of India*, 1993 (4) SCALE 230: (1994) 2 SCC 80.
107. *See*, *Binod Kumar* v. *State of Jharkhand*, JT 2011 (4) SC 114: 2011 (4) SCALE 109; *S. Jagannath* v. *Union of India*, AIR 1969 SC 783: (1997) 2 SCC 87; *Union of India* v. *Harbhajan Singh Dhillon*, AIR 1972 SC 1061: (1971) 2 SCC 779; *State of Gujarat* v. *Vora Fiddali Badruddin Mithibarwala*, AIR 1964 SC 1043: (1964) 6 SCR 461.
108. *People's Union of Civil Liberties* v. *Union of India*, AIR 1997 SC 568: (1997) 1 SCC 301.
109. AIR 2005 SC 1646: (2004) 10 SCC 201.
110. Sir Robert Jennings and Sir Aurthur Watts (Ed.), *Oppenheim's International Law* (Pearson Education, New Delhi, 1996) Vol. 1, pp. 53–54.

example, the increasing role of individuals as subjects of international law, have tended to make the distinction between national law and international law less clear and more complex than was formerly supposed at a time when the field of application of international law could be regarded as solely the relations of states amongst themselves.

As in other common law, countries following the theory of "dualism" between international and domestic law, international law does not automatically become part of the domestic law of India.[111] However, in line with developments in the status of international law all over the world, general principles of international law are recognised as part of the domestic law of India and are observed in dealings within the domestic sphere. Although it is not yet conclusively settled, strong opinion is the first step towards the recognition of human rights among such general principles of international law binding on all nations. As regards international treaties and other instruments in general, they do not, *ipso facto*, become part of domestic law in the absence of supportive domestic legislation. In *Gramophone Company* v. *Birendra Bahadur Pandey,*[112] the Apex Court held that there can be no question that nations must march with the international community and the municipal law must respect rules of international law even as nations respect international opinion. The comity of Nations requires that rules of international law may be accommodated in the municipal law even without express legislative sanction provided they do not run into conflict with Acts of Parliament. But when they do run into such conflict, the sovereignty and the integrity of the Republic and the supremacy of the constituted legislatures in making the laws may not be subjected to external rules except to the extent legitimately accepted by the constituted legislatures themselves.

The doctrine of incorporation also recognises the position that the rules of international law are incorporated into and considered to be part of the national law, unless they are in conflict with an Act of Parliament. Comity of Nations or no, municipal law must prevail in case of conflict. National courts cannot say "yes" if Parliament has said "no" to a principle of international law. National courts will endorse international law except when it conflicts with national law. National courts being organs of the national State and not of international law must perforce apply national law if international law conflicts with it. But the Courts are under an obligation within legitimate limits, to so interpret the municipal statute as to avoid confrontation with the comity of Nations or the well-established principles of international law. But if conflict is inevitable, the latter must yield. Further, the Apex Court in *State of West Bengal* v. *Kesoram Industries,*[113] observed:

> It is true that the doctrine of "Monism" as prevailing in the European countries does not prevail in India. The doctrine of "Dualism" is applicable. But, where the municipal law does not limit the extent of the statute, even if India is not a signatory to the relevant International Treaty or Covenant, the Supreme Court in a large number of cases interpreted the statutes keeping in view the same.

Judicial Approach in India

The Courts in India have been giving effect to treaties and international instruments, irrespective of whether India is a party to them or not, if such treaties or instruments are not inconsistent

---

111. *Bhavesh Jayanti Lakhani* v. *State of Maharashtra*, 2009 (11) SCALE 467: (2009) 9 SCC 551.
112. AIR 1984 SC 667: (1984) 2 SCC 534.
113. 2004 (1) SCALE 425: (2004) 10 SCC 201.

with any domestic law. Explaining the utility of international Conventions at domestic level in *T.N. Godavarman Thirumalpad* v. *Union of India*,[114] the Apex Court observed that in the absence of any inconsistency between the domestic law and the international Conventions the rule of judicial construction in that regard must be had of international Conventions and norms even in construing the domestic law. Similarly, in *Apparel Export Promotion Council* v. *A.K. Chopra*,[115] the Apex Court observed that the international instruments cast an obligation on India and Courts are under an obligation to give due regard to international conventions and norms for construing domestic laws, more so, when there is no inconsistency between them and there is a void in domestic law. The Apex Court in numerous cases emphasised that the core principle embodied in the international Conventions and instruments and as far as possible give effect to the principles contained in those international instruments.[116] This principle of law was also laid down by the Apex Court in *Vishaka* v. *State of Rajasthan*.[117] The Apex Court observed:

> The international conventions and norms are to be read into them in the absence of enacted domestic law occupying in the field where there is no inconsistency between them. It is now an accepted rule of judicial construction that regard must be had to international conventions and norms for construing domestic law....

Citing the above case in *Pee Pee Publisher* v. *Neena Khanna*,[118] the Delhi High Court held that it is well-established principle of law that the international law can be relied upon in the cases where the municipal law is silent on the subject and which is not inconsistent with the municipal law. Where there is a conflict between municipal law and international law, the municipal law shall have prevailed. Applying the same principle, the Court further observed that even if there is a right of retraction or withdrawal exist in the international law, the same cannot substitute or supplant the express provisions of Section 57 of the Copyright Act, 1957 which does not recognise any such right. *Krishna* v. *Union of India*,[119] was concerned with an issue involving interpretation of Section 31 of the Copyright Act, 1957. In this case the court citing Apex Court's principle as laid down in *Chairman, Railway Board* v. *Mrs. Chandrima Das*,[120] held that a statute should be interpreted in the light of the international treaties and conventions. Thus, the Court has applied the norms of international laws and in particular the international covenants to interpret domestic legislation. In *Kesavananda Bharati* v. *State of Kerala*,[121] the Apex Court has categorically held:

> That there would be no inconsistency in the use of international norms to the domestic legislation, if by reason thereof the tenor of domestic law is not breached and in case of any such inconsistency, the domestic legislation should prevail.

---

114. (2002) 10 SCC 606.
115. AIR 1999 SC 625: (1999) 1 SCC 759.
116. *See, D.K. Basil* v. *State of West Bengal*, AIR 1997 SC 610: (1997) 1 SCC 416; *People's Union for Civil Liberties* v. *Union of India*, AIR 1997 SC 1203: (1997) 3 SCC 433; *Sheela Barse* v. *Secretary, Children's Aid Society*, AIR 1987 SC 656: (1987) 3 SCC 50; *Mackninnon Mackenzie* v. *Audrey D' Costa*, AIR 1987 SC 1281: (1987) 2 SCC 469.
117. AIR 1997 SC 3011: (1997) 6 SCC 241. *See also, Karma Dorjee* v. *Union of India*, AIR 2017 SC 113: (2017) 1 SCC 799.
118. 2010 LawSuit (Del) 4161.
119. 2010 LawSuit (Del) 2136.
120. 2000 Cr LJ 1473.
121. AIR 1973 SC 1461. (1973) 4 SCC 225.

3

Origin and Development of Law Relating to Copyright at National Level: England, America and India

ABSTRACT

Law of copyright was originated and developed at national level under private law regime. The English Statute of Anne of 1709 is the first copyright statute in the World. Following the Statute of Anne, the Congress of the United States of America in 1790 passed a series of copyright statutes. Indian copyright law has grown out of English common law. The Copyright Act, 1957 which is the current statute in India has followed the principles of English copyright law. The 1957 Act has been amended from time to time. The Copyright (Amendment Act) 2012 was enacted bringing changes to copyright law in India. These aspects are the subject matter of the present chapter.

ORIGIN AT NATIONAL LEVEL

The origin of law of copyright[1] at national level can be traced back to a period prior to the advent of printing technology. Probably during second century, the Roman jurist *Gaius* (A.D. 130–180) held that where an artist had painted upon a *tabula*, has a superior right over it[2] and this opinion was adopted in the *Code of Justinian* in the sixth century.[3] The right of an artist

1. For origin of copyright law, *see*, Mike Schuster, David Mitchell and Kenneth Brown, "Sampling Increases Music Sales: An Empirical Copyright Study," 56(1) *American Business Law Journal* (2019) pp. 177–229; Justin Hughes "A Short History of Intellectual Property in Relation to Copyright" 33 *Cardozo Law Review* (2012) pp. 1293–1340; Ronan Deazley, *Rethinking Copyright: History, Theory, Language* (Edward Elgar Publishing Ltd., 2006); L.R. Patterson, *Copyright in Historic Perspective—Overview*, (Vanderbilt University, 1968); Augustine Birrell, *Seven Essays on the Law and History of Copyright in Books*, (Cassell and Company Limited, London, 1899).
2. *See*, Frederic J. Haskin, "First Use of Anesthetics" *Salt Lake Tribune*, Newspaper, Utah, April 19, 1926 at p. 6. *See also*, *The Chehalis Bee-Nugget*, Newspaper, Washington, October 15, 1926 at p. 10.
3. *Code of Justinian* known as in Latin term *Corpus Juris Civilis* or *Codex Justinianus* means "Body of Civil Law" which is the collections of laws and legal interpretations developed under the sponsorship of the Byzantine emperor Justinian-I from 529 to 565 A.D.

as recognised by the Roman jurist *Gaius* was applied in a drawing upon wood in *Finnian* v. *Columba,*[4] the first record of a copyright case of sometime around A.D. 560. In this case, *Columba* copied the manuscript at the scriptorium under *Saint Finnian,* intending to keep the copy. But, *Saint Finnian* disputed his right to keep the copy. The Statute of the University of Paris, 1223 provided for duplication of texts for the use within the University.[5] Thus, the Statute provided that the "booksellers of the University" should produce duplicate copies of the texts authorised for the use of the University, and there is indication that payment was made by the University to scholars for the annotation and proofreading of such texts. Before the late fifteenth century, works of literature were mainly religious and were written by scholarly monks who would work painstakingly for considerable periods of time preparing their gloriously illuminated books. Obviously, because of the massive human labour and skill required to produce such works, plagiarism of books was usually a viable consideration. Additionally, there was not a market for books due to the general illiteracy of the population at large.

However, two inventions in the late fifteenth century changed everything in the world. *Johannes Gutenberg* (1398–1468) invented mechanical movable type printing started the printing revolution and which is widely regarded as the most important event of the modern period. Between 1450 and 1455, *Gutenberg* printed several texts although his technique of making movable type remains unclear. Similarly, *William Caxton* (1415–1492) set up a printing press at Westminster in 1476 and the first book known to have been produced there was the *Geoffrey Chaucer's Canterbury Tales*. It could be claimed that printing has had a greater impact on civilisation than any other single invention. Naturally, with the advent of the printing press, printed books were cheaper than hand-copied books and also pirating another's book could be comparatively easy.[6] However, it was virtually impossible for anyone centuries ago when the printing press was first invented to predict that an extremely complex set of laws would have to be developed to protect both creators of published and unpublished works. As a result of advent of printing technology, mass reproduction of copies from originals facilitated commercial exploitation and making a business of piracy.

Paradoxically, during 17th and 18th centuries in France and England there was a controversy as to whether authors were entitled to an exclusive right of multiplying copies of their works as property or as privilege. The reason why these questions were asked both in France and England was that certain rights over things amounting in the aggregate to a more or less complete exclusion of others than the owner from participating, save by consent, in their enjoyment had in the western world become recognised as property. Thus, in 1899 *Augustine Birrell* in his lecture as *Quain Professor of Law* at University College, London observed:[7]

---

4. *See*, Richard Rogers Bowker, *Copyright: Its History and Its Law,* (Houghton Mifflin Company, Boston and New York, 1912) at p. 3.
5. *See*, J.K. Das, "Legal Framework for Copyright Protection: Its Philosophical Justifications and Practical Implications on Indigenous Peoples" 33–34 *Banaras Law Journal* (2003–2004) pp. 157–180 at p. 159.
6. Dennis W.K. Khong, "The Historical Law and Economics of the First Copyright Act" 2(1) *Erasmus Law and Economics Review* (2006) pp. 35–69 at p. 37.
7. Augustine Birrell, *Seven Essays on the Law and History of Copyright in Books* (Cassell and Company Limited, London, 1899) at p. 1.

> The origin of property, of exclusive ownership, is one of the subjects about which our predecessors in title loved to discourse at large after a fashion more ingenious than historical. Occupancy and Labour are the mythical parents of Property, but we shall be less wrong in assuming that the pedigree was invented to account for the fact of possession than in attributing the fact of possession to the virtues of the pedigree. But whatever was its origin, the Western World has throughout its long history shown an ever increasing disposition to recognise the right of individuals to the exclusive possession of certain things, and these rights it has clustered together, recognised, venerated, worshipped, under the word property.

Whenever a man conceives an idea of a literary work and he thinks over it, he elaborates it and finally he clothes it in words capable of communicating it to other minds, it becomes a property. Thus, the manuscript of the completed work is material property, which belongs to the author just as much as the desk on which he wrote it. He can lend it to different persons if he chooses who might pay him for the pleasure of reading it. A manuscript is the author's property and thus even if in the hands of anybody the manuscript is found, it still would be the author's property. Today, in France, as in certain other European countries, it is a criminal act not simply to manufacture or sell, but also to possess, a counterfeit goods, regardless of where one purchased it.[8]

DEVELOPMENT IN ENGLAND

Royal Charter and Licencing

During the first half of the sixteenth century the piracy was flourished. Hence, in 1542 the *Stationers' Company* requested for granting a *Royal Charter* with greater power to control printing under the pretext of assisting the crown in regulating the press. Unfortunately, this attempt went unheeded. However, subsequently it was realised that the crown was unable to prevent abuses in printing seditious material, and in 1557, Queen Mary Tudor granted a *Royal Charter* in favour of the *Stationers' Company* for regulating the press. Thus, first "copyright" was granted in England by the *Royal Charter* in 1557.[9] The Crown by the *Royal Charter* consolidated the new printing business in the hands of the *Stationers' Company.*[10] It gave to the printers of this company, and not to the authors, the exclusive right to control the printing and sale of books, forever. The *Royal Charter* conferred these copyrights upon royal publishers who would not publish books considered politically or religiously objectionable by the Crown. Thus, it was prohibited to print a book contrary to any law, decree, patent, or company regulation, and extensive enforcement powers were given to the Company.[11] The *Licensing Act, 1662* was enacted as a punitive instrument for controlling printing presses. Thus, the 1662 Act was an "Act for preventing abuses in printing seditious, treasonable and

8. Barton Beebe, "Intellectual Property Law and the Sumptuary Code" 123(4) *Harvard Law Review* (2010) pp. 809–889 at p. 817.
9. Dennis W.K. Khong, "The Historical Law and Economics of the First Copyright Act" 2(1) *Erasmus Law and Economics Review* (2006) pp. 35–69 at p. 38.
10. For critical discussion on the Stationers' Company, *see*, Cyprian Blagden, *The Stationers' Company: A History* (Stanford University Press, 1977).
11. Ronan Deazley, "The Myth of Copyright at Common Law", 62 *Cambridge Law Journal* (2003) pp. 106–133.

unlicenced books and pamphlets, and for regulating of printing and printing presses."[12] Under the Act,[13]

> Legislative authority was given to the Rules and Ordinances of the Stationers' Company whereby the activities of printers, booksellers, and bookbinders were controlled. Sanction was afforded the ancient custom of the Company whereby the entrance of a book or copy in the Register was deemed to vest a perpetual copyright in the stationer who entered it; and protection was provided for the printing privileges of the two universities and the monopolies granted by royal letters patent to the Company or to individuals.

However, the existence of this privately arranged copyright was criticised by a Royal Commission in 1583, although by no means copyright of the *Stationers' Company* arose spontaneously. It started as "a licence to print" in the early seventeenth century.[14] *John Locke's* critique is an attack on the monopoly of the "dull wretches" of the *Stationers' Company*, and on pre-publication censorship and licensing policy. The *Licensing Act, 1662*, in the words of Lord Macaulay, "is condemned, not as a thing essentially evil, but on account of the petty grievances, the exactions, the jobs, the commercial restrictions, the domiciliary visits, which were incidental to it," [15] while the *Liberty of the Press*[16] was a letter of *John Locke* opposing the renewal of the licensing under the Act. In his letter, *John Locke* strongly argued for recognition of freedom of expression and social exchange, economic equality, common equity as well as recognition of authors' rights. He also puts forth his view about the kinds of authorial rights that should be granted, and distinguishes between these rights and the general right to property. Raymond Astbury explained *John Locke's* view thus:[17]

> In his Memorandum, though Locke spelt out in detail the ill-effects on the book trade, and on authors and readers, of the monopoly system and the powers, and the abuse of power, of the Stationers' Company, most of his complaints reveal directly or by implication his concern for the intellectual, economic, and social freedoms of the individual...and he linked [his] statement to an implied defence of the right to communicate new philosophical and scientific truths.

Statute of Anne

As a result of above stated criticism as well as *John Locke's* thought provoking arguments, the exclusive rights of the *Stationers' Company* ended in 1695, when the Parliament refused to renew the licence of the company by the ending of the Licensing Act which was an important

12. *See*, Lior Zemer, *The Idea of Authorship in Copyright* (Ashgate Publishing Ltd., 2007) at p. 125.
13. *See*, Lior Zemer, "The Making of A New Copyright Lockean" 29(3) *Harvard Journal of Law and Public Policy* (2006) pp. 891–947 at p. 11. *See also*, Dennis W. K. Khong, "The Historical Law and Economics of the First Copyright Act," 2(1) *Erasmus Law and Economics Review* (2006) pp. 35–69.
14. Mark Rose, *Authors and Owners: The Invention of Copyright*, (Harvard University Press, 1993) at p. 14. *See also*, Peter W. M. Blayney, The Stationers' Company and the Printers of London, 1501–1557 (Cambridge University Press, 2014)
15. Lord Macaulay, *The History of England from the Accession of James II* [Charles H. Firth (Ed.), 1913] at p. 2482.
16. John Locke, *Liberty of the Press* (1695, Cambridge University Press, Reprint in 1997).
17. *See*, Raymond Astbury, "The Renewal of the Licensing Act in 1693 and Its Lapse in 1695," Downloaded from http://library.oxfordjournals.org/at Calcutta University on December 29, 2014. *See also*, 33 *The Library* (5th Series, 1978) pp. 296–322.

event in the history of copyright.[18] Eventually, it became apparent that a stronger and surer copyright law was desirable and this was responded to by the Parliament through the passing of the Copyright Act, 1709, popularly known as *Statute of Anne* (the world's first copyright statute).[19] This Act introduced for the first time the concept of the author of a work being the owner of its copyright, and laid out fixed terms of protection. Thus, the *Statute of Anne* vested in authors of books a monopoly over their works, much to the surprise of the publishers. Unlike the rights granted to publishers by *Royal Charter*, the statutory right was limited to only 14 years, renewable for an additional 14 years by the author. The statute contained a complex system of registration, notice, and deposit requirements as well as strict compliance with those requirements was required by the English courts for many years. The Preamble of the *Statute of Anne* recognised the importance of copyright as a means of disseminating knowledge and information. It reads thus:

> An Act for the Encouragement of Learning, by Vesting the Copies of Printed Books in the Authors or Purchasers of such Copies, during the Times therein mentioned. Whereas Printers, Booksellers, and other Persons, have of late frequently taken the Liberty of Printing, Reprinting, and Publishing, or causing to be Printed, Reprinted, and Published Books, and other Writings, without the Consent of the Authors or Proprietors of such Books and Writings, to their very great Detriment, and too often to the Ruin of them and their Families.

Thus, the *Statute of Anne* established the right of authors' ownership of copyright and a fixed term of protection of copyrighted works such as fourteen years, and renewable for fourteen more if the author was alive upon expiration. The *Statute* prevented a monopoly on the part of the booksellers and created a "public domain" for literature by limiting terms of copyright and by ensuring that once a work was purchased the copyright owner no longer had control over its use. While the *Statute* did provide for an author's copyright, the benefit was minimal because in order to be paid for a work an author had to assign it to a bookseller or publisher.[20] John Feather,[21] described the *Statute's* purpose and effect as an attempt by the *Stationers' Company* to retain as much of its power and privileges in a changed world. However, many scholars expressed different views. Ronan Deazley,[22] emphasised that the motivation of *Statute* was to provide a balance between the author, the bookseller, and the reading public that was designed to maximise the production and dissemination of useful books. The right and liberty of printing books that the *Statute* conferred was given to authors and their assigns, and also provided basic mechanism of spreading knowledge through the grant of a property right in the work. Despite the controversy among the scholars, the *Statute*

---

18. For detail discussion, *see*, Karen Nipps, "Cum Privilegio: Licensing of the Press Act of 1662," 84(4) *The Library Quarterly: Information, Community, Policy* (2014) pp. 494–500; W. S. Holdsworth, "Press Control and Copyright in the 16th and 17th Centuries," 29(8) *Yale Law Journal* (1920) pp. 841–858.
19. The *Statute of Anne* came into force in 1710 (The bill was first presented to the Parliament on 12 December 1709, and received the royal assent on 5 April 1710). *See*, Lionel Bently and Brad Sherman, *The Making of Intellectual Property: The British Experience* (Cambridge University Press, 1999).
20. *See*, Rachel Ralston, Craig Fellenstein and Jaclyn Vassallo (Ed.), *Patents, Copyrights, and Trademarks: A Look Back The History of Copyrights*, (Pearson, 2005); Mark Rose, *Authors and Owners: The Invention of Copyright* (Harvard University Press, 1992).
21. John Feather, *A History of British Publishing* (Routledge, London, 1988) pp. 74–75.
22. Ronan Deazley, "The Myth of Copyright at Common Law", 62 *Cambridge Law Journal* (2003) pp. 106–133.

is commonly known for embodying the moment at which authors were recognised as the proper focal point of copyright protection and for establishing authors' legal rights and their ability to bargain for better terms in the marketplace.

Engraving Copyright and Beyond

The process of enlargement of copyright protection had begun in the eighteenth century. In this process, the engravers had succeeded their rights under copyright law.[23] Hence, the Engraving Copyright Act, 1734 was enacted. Given the role of the engraving process in the copperplate printing, a copyright extension to cover this new use of engraving seems one explanation why the request was in the form of copyright. However, the 1734 Act protected only those engravings that involved original designs and thus, implicitly, made a distinction between artists and mere craftsmen. Soon, however, Parliament was persuaded to extend protection to all engravings. Hence, the Engraving Copyright Act was re-enacted in 1766, 1777 and 1836. These Acts conferred exclusive rights, for a period of 14 years, on persons inventing and designing engravings and similar works and define "engravings" as any etching, lithograph, woodcut, print or similar work, but not photographs. Engravings were the first form of artistic work to be granted copyright protection. The recognition of the engraving right under copyright law from literature to the visual arts proved to be a vital step in maintaining artistic quality.[24]

During the above stated process of enlargement, the Calico Printers' Act, 1787 was passed for the encouragement of the arts of designing and printing linens, cottons, calicoes, and muslins, by vesting the properties thereof in the designers, printers and proprietors for a limited time.[25] The Act gave protection against the printing, working or copyright of an original pattern for certain types of textile. But it lasted only for two months from publication. The textile designs secured some very temporary protection by statutes which were the precursor of the present registered design system.[26] Subsequently, in 1798 and 1814 sculptures were protected under copyright, in 1833 copyright right was given in dramatic works and in 1842 the same was extended to musical works. As the technical possibilities for reproducing artistic works were increased, the Fine Arts Copyright Act, 1862 was enacted and extended for providing protection to paintings, drawings and photographs. In the late nineteenth and beginning of twentieth century, a number of international conventions were adopted on copyright law.[27] The Berne Convention, 1886 had introduced a multinational equal system of

---

23. *See*, R. Anthony Reese, "Copyrightable Subject Matter in the 'Next Great Copyright Act,'" 29(3) *Berkeley Technology Law Journal* (2014) pp. 1489–1533; Davit Hunter, "Copyright Protection for Engravings and Maps in Eighteenth-Century Britain" 9 *The Library* (1987) pp. 128–147.
24. *See*, Kathy Bowrey, "Art, Craft, Good Taste and Manufacturing: The Development of Intellectual Property Laws" 15(1) *Law in Context*, (1997) pp. 78–104.
25. *See*, Brad Sherman and Lionel Bently, *The Making of Modern Intellectual Property Law* (Cambridge University Press, 2004) at p. 63.
26. Ronan Deazley, *On the Origin of the Right to Copy* (Hart Publishing, Portland, 2001) at p. 115
27. They include: *Rome Convention for the Protection of Performers, Producers of Phonograms and Broadcasting Organisations, 1961; Geneva Convention for the Protection of Producers of Phonograms against Unauthorised Duplication of their Phonograms, 1971; Brussels Convention Relating to the Distribution of Programme Carrying Signals Transmitted by Satellite, 1974.*

copyright protection, under which either the personal connection of the author with a member state, or first publication in a member state, was to secure copyright in the other.[28] These changes were reflected in the Copyright Act, 1911. This Act is the first English copyright umbrella legislation which brought the various copyrights within a single text, and at the same time the rights were extended even in unpublished works on a statutory footing.

Post Second World War Period

In the post second world war period, there have been constant activities for copyright protection at international as well as domestic level. Hence, the Copyright Act, 1956 was enacted. The Act expanded copyright law in the UK and was passed in order to bring UK copyright law in line with international copyright law and technological developments.[29] The 1956 Act was most notable for adding three new forms of copyright—"in cinematograph films, broadcasts and the typographical format of published editions"—to the copyright in sound recordings.[30] Besides, Section 2 of the 1956 Act provides: "Copyright shall subsist, subject to the provisions of this Act, in every original literary, dramatic or musical work which is unpublished, and of which the author was a qualified person at the time when the work was made, or, if the making of the work extended over a period, was a qualified person for a substantial part of that period."

By the 1970s it was realised that if copyright was to survive the impact of modern technology-photocopying, audio and video taping and computing each on small-scale and large-adaptations of law and practice would be needed. Subsequently, the Copyright, Designs and Patents Act, 1988 was enacted. Just as technological leaps began to demand international adjustments to copyright law, so the same bounds produced repercussions for national systems. By the 1988 Act, the UK put itself in a position to ratify the 1971 Paris Revisions of Berne Convention. The very substantial in scope, embodied in the 1988 Act, is largely placed outside the frame of copyright and in the separate folds of registered and unregistered design right.[31]

---

28. *See*, Sam Ricketso, *The Berne Convention of the Protection of Literary and Artistic Works 1886–1986* (Kluwer International, Boston, 1987), The *Berne Convention for Protecting of Literary and Artistic Works, 1886* (last revised at Paris in 1971) have established an international regime for Copyright protection. The Preamble and Article 1 of the Convention state that protection of copyright shall operate to the benefit of the authors and successors in title. Besides the term of protection was extended to 50 years beyond the lifetime of the author and the nature and scope of the rights available too were enlarged to cover the advances in technology. Apart from the *economic rights*, *moral rights* too were provided to the author with respect to his work. There are also a number of other international conventions and treaties dealing with specific categories of copyright protection. *The Berne Convention for the Protection of Literary and Artistic Works* of September 9, 1886 completed at Paris on May 4, 1896, revised at Berlin on November 13, 1908 completed at Berne on March 20, 1914, revised at Rome on June 2, 1928 at Brussels on June 26, 1948 at Stockholm on July 14, 1967 and at Paris on July 24, 1971 and amended on September 28, 1979.
29. *See*, Mayer Brown, *Copyright Guide* (2013).
30. Michael Coyle, *The History of Copyright* (2002).
31. *See*, Hazel Carty and Keith Hodkinson, "Copyright, Designs and Patents Act 1988" 52(3) *The Modern Law Review* (Blackwell Publishing, 1989) pp. 369–379.

DEVELOPMENT IN AMERICA

Constitutional Right

The history of American copyright law originated with the introduction of the printing press to England in the late fifteenth century. As the number of presses grew, authorities sought to control the publication of books by granting printers a near monopoly on publishing in England. It is a principle of American law that an author of a work may reap the fruits of his or her intellectual creativity for a limited period of time. Copyright is a form of protection provided by the laws of the United States for original works of authorship, including literary, dramatic, musical, architectural, cartographic, choreographic, pantomimic, pictorial, graphic, sculptural, and audiovisual creations.[32]

The Constitution of the United States of America under Clause 8 of Section 8 of the Article 1 vested Congress power to grant to authors and inventors exclusive rights over their works. This Constitutional provision provides thus: "Congress has the power to promote the Progress of Science and useful Arts, by securing for limited Times to Authors and Inventors the exclusive Right to their respective Writings and Discoveries". The purpose of this provision is to advance a culture of creativity, which the government believes benefits society at large; otherwise, what's the incentive to create if everyone owns it?[33]

The 1790 Act

Akin to English approach in protecting copyright, the American approach[34] has developed parallel means of protecting authors through recognising a property right similar to the English statutory right. Following the English *Statute of Anne* of 1709 the US Congress in 1790 passed a series of copyright statutes,[35] the general goal of these statutes has been to establish an incentive for authors to create, by providing them an avenue for obtaining remuneration. The public's interest in ready access to information and art rests on one side, on the other rests the need to incentives creators. The ultimate goal is not author remuneration, however, but

---

32. Lyman Ray Patterson and Stanley W. Lindberg. *The Nature of Copyright: A Law of Users' Rights* (University of Georgia Press, Athens, 1991).
33. *See*, Lawrence B. Solum, "Congress's Power to Promote the Progress of Science: *Eldred* v. *Ashcroft*" 36 *Loyola of Los Angeles Law Review* (2002) pp. 1–82.
34. Copyright on the Continent, and particularly in France, similarly developed parallel means of protecting authors: a property right similar to the English statutory right, based on a decree by the Revolutionary government in January 1791 and on a series of moral rights established in judicial decisions. These rights have only relatively recently been embodied in statutory form. *See*, generally, Raymond Sarraute, "Current Theory on the Moral Right of Authors and Artists Under French Law", 16 *American Journal of Comparative Law* (1968) at p. 465; Stephen Breyer, "The Uneasy Case for Copyright: A Study of Copyright in Books, Photocopies, and Computer Programs", 84 *Harvard Law Review* (1970) at pp. 281–351.
35. Most of the United States passed State copyright laws modeled on the *Statute of Anne* shortly after gaining their independence. For the controversy between State copyright law and Federal copyright law in US, *see*, Dane S. Ciolino, "Why Copyrights are Not Community Property?" 1 *The ICFAI Journal of Intellectual Property Rights* (2002) at pp. 45–66.

the advancement and dissemination of culture and knowledge. One of the first Acts of the US Congress was the Copyright Act, 1790 (the 1790 Act). Examining the impact of *Statute of Anne* in the US, Oren Bracha[36] stated that "arrival of the *Statute of Anne* in the United States at the end of the eighteenth century was a clear case of a legal regime that was lifted from one legal culture and transferred to another where the legal, social, and cultural context was quite different."

In the US, the 1790 Act, like the *Statute of Anne,* granted protection for authors for 14 years, and allowed renewal: "if, at the expiration of the said term, the author or authors, or any of them, be living ... the same exclusive right shall be continued to him or them, his or their executors, administrators or assigns, for the further term of fourteen years." The 1790 Act allowed copyrights to be registered with the local district court and notice to be published in local newspapers. Like its predecessors, it was limited to books. Private individuals not engaged in the business of creating and disseminating works of authorship probably had little awareness or understanding of copyright law, but they had little need, because they were at very little risk of committing copyright infringement. As Justice Brewer wrote in an 1888 decision:[37]

> The effect of a copyright is not to prevent any reasonable use of the book which is sold... I may use that book for reference, study, reading, lending, copying passages from it at my will. I may not duplicate that book, and thus put it upon the market, for in so doing so I would infringe the copyright. But merely taking extracts from it, merely using it, in no manner infringes on the copyright.

Thus, the 1790 Act granted American authors the right to print, re-print, or publish their work for a period of fourteen years and to renew for another fourteen. The law was meant to provide an incentive to authors, artists, and scientists to create original works by providing creators with a monopoly.[38] At the same time, the monopoly was limited in order to stimulate creativity and the advancement of "science and the useful arts" through wide public access to works in the "public domain". However, a series of amendments and court decisions throughout the nineteenth century progressively expanded the scope of the 1790 Act, adding prints, musical compositions, dramatic works, photographs, artistic works, and sculpture. The Act granted to the authors of "any map, chart, book, or books" the "sole right and liberty of printing, reprinting, publishing and vending".[39]

Subsequently, by the Acts of Legislature—enacted on 3rd March 1891, 3rd March 1893 and 2nd March 1895—foreign authors, whose books have been first printed in the United States, and who observe certain conditions and formalities as to the deposit of copies, and so forth, have the same exclusive rights as American authors the duration of which is for a period of 28 years from the date of publication, and for a further period of 14 years, if at the

36. Oren Bracha, "The Adventures of the Statute of Anne in the Land of Unlimited Possibilities: The Life of a Legal Transplant" 25 *Berkeley Technology Law Journal* (2010) pp. 1427–1473 at p. 1427. *See also*, Oren Bracha, *Owning Ideas: A History of Anglo-American Intellectual Property* (Harvard Law School, 2005) pp. 12–129.
37. *Stover* v. *Lathrop*, 33 F. 348, 349 (C.C.D. Colo. 1888).
38. Mark Rose, *Authors and Owners: The Invention of Copyright,* (Harvard University Press, 1993).
39. Lawrence B. Solum, "Congress's Power to Promote the Progress of Science: Eldred v. Ashcroft" 36 *Loyola of Los Angeles Law Review* (2002) p. 4; Done S. Ciolino, "Why Copyrights are not Community Property?" *The ICFAI Journal of Intellectual Property Rights,* 1 (2002) pp. 45–66.

expiration of the 28 years the author is still living, or if there is then still living a widow, or a child, or children of the author.[40]

The 1790 Act is interesting for historical reasons, and was repeatedly revised in a number of times. Some of these revisions reflected changes in the idea of copyright (e.g., the 1831 change which added musical compositions to the protected list), while others reflected changes in technology as well as ideology (e.g., the 1865 addition of photographs). Also, in 1831 the initial term of fourteen years' protection (a descendant of the Statute of Anne) was extended to 28 years, with a potential 14 year renewal. Thus, under 1831 revision the term of protection of copyrighted works was extended and the Congress claimed that it extended the term in order to give American authors the same protection as those in Europe. The extension applied both to future works and those current works whose copyright had not expired.

Folsom v. *Marsh*[41] case brought before the Massachusetts Circuit Court in 1841, the owner and editor of a multi-volume collection of George Washington's letters sued Charles Upham for using hundreds of pages of the letters, in their entirety, in a volume on the life of Washington. Justice William Story found that Upham had infringed the owner's copyright in publishing some 350 pages of Washington's letters in his 866-page book. Justice Story held that Upham's work was:

> a selection of the entire contents of particular letters, from the whole collection or mass of letters of the work of the plaintiffs ... [and] that these letters are the most instructive, useful and interesting to be found in that large collection.

Explaining the nature of the infringement, Story said, "It is certainly not necessary, to constitute an invasion of copyright, that the whole of a work should be copied, or even a large portion of it, in form or in substance. If so much is taken, that the value of the original is sensibly diminished, or the labours of the original author are substantially to an injurious extent appropriated by another, that is sufficient, in point of law, to constitute a piracy protanto". The court's definition of what constituted a "justifiable use of the original materials" formed the basis of the "fair use" doctrine.[42] Put another way, Story said that, "the question of piracy, often depend[s] upon a nice balance of the comparative use made in one of the materials of the other; the nature, extent, and value of the materials thus used; the objects of each work; and the degree to which each writer may be fairly presumed to have resorted to the same common sources of information, or to have exercised the same common diligence in the selection and arrangement of the materials."

In *Stowe* v. *Thomas,*[43] Harriet Beecher Stowe sued F.W. Thomas, publisher of a German-language periodical, *Die Freie Presse,* in 1853. Thomas translated *Uncle Tom's Cabin* into

---

40. Augustine Birrell, *Seven Essays on the Law and History of Copyright in Books*, (Cassell and Company Limited, London, 1899) p. 36.
41. 9 F. Cas. 342 (C.C.D. Mass. 1841). *See*, Edward Samuels, *The Illustrated Story of Copyright* (St. Martin's Press, New York, 2000).
42. For various issues on fair use, *see*, Elizabeth Rosenblatt, "Fair Use as Resistance," 9 *UC Irvine Law Review* (2019) pp. 377–402; Cathay Smith, "Creative Destruction: Copyright's Fair Use Doctrine and the Moral Right of Integrity," 47 *Pepperdine Law Review* (2019) pp. 1–48; A.O. Rourke Maurke, "Toward a Doctrine of Fair Use in Patent Law," 100 *Columbia Law Review* (2000) pp. 1177–1250; Wendy J. Gordon, "Fair Use as Market Failure: A Structural and Economic Analysis of Betamex case and its Predecessors" 82 *Columbia Law Review* (1982) pp. 1600–1657
43. 23 F. Cas. 201 (C.C.E.D. Pa. 1853).

German and sold it in the United States without the author's permission. Judge Robert Grier of the Third Circuit Court of Appeals explained in the decision that once an author published her or his work, "and given his thoughts, sentiments, knowledge or discoveries to the world, he can have no longer an exclusive possession of them." With regard to translations, he continued, "the same conceptions clothed in another language cannot constitute the same composition; nor can it be called a transcript or 'copy' of the same book."

In *Burrow-Giles Lithographic Co.* v. *Sarony,*[44] Saucy was an up-and-coming photographer in the late 1800s, when the technology was even mysterious. In 1882, after months of effort, he convinced a young but famous playright, Oscar Grouch, to agree to pose for a photograph. Saucy takes great pains to arrange the backdrop, drapes, Grouch's outfit, and other visual aspects of the photograph in order to produce "a useful, new, harmonious, characteristic and graceful picture ... entirely from his own original mental conception." He toils over ways in which to pose the great author. He contemplates the various lighting options and the effects of light on his subject's face and frills. He finally produces a scene, and a photograph, which he believes worthy of the playright's reputation and his own aspirations. A lithograph company soon makes and sells 85,000 copies of the photo without Saucy's permission. Despite the lithograph company's argument that the 1865 addition of photographs by Congress was unconstitutional, the US Supreme Court would have good reason to uphold the lower court's finding for the plaintiff, Saucy.

The 1909 Act

In America, the Copyright Act, 1909 (the 1909 Act) was most significant as the Act generally broadened the scope of copyright protection. Protection for literary works was expanded from books to include "all writings", reaching works in progress, and speeches, among other new matter.[45] The 1909 Act is the last Act that maintained distinction between pre-publication and post-publication rights and this dichotomy is still significant with respect to the immense body of protected works that originally were governed by the 1909 Act. Since the enactment of the 1909 Act the American copyright law came to distinguish between the English copyright of an author to his unpublished creations, and the statutory copyright that might be secured upon publication. However, it was very difficult to interpret the 1909 Act which led to numerous attempts to reform it.

In *Williams and Wilkins Co.* v. *United States,*[46] Williams and Wilkins, publishers of specialised medical journals, sued the National Library of Medicine (NLM) and the National Institutes of Health (NIH) charging that the agencies had infringed copyright by making unauthorised photocopies of articles featured within their publications and distributing them to medical researchers. This was an important copyright law decision by the federal Court of Claims, later affirmed by a *per curiam* opinion from an evenly divided United States Supreme Court, with only eight justices voting (Harry Blackmun took no part in the decision of this case). The decision held that it was a fair use for libraries to photocopy articles for use by patrons engaged in scientific research. This decision, written by Judge Oscar Davis, has been

44. 111 U.S. 53 (1884).
45. *See*, Keller and Cunard, *Copyright Law: A Practitioner's Guide* (Practicing Law Institute, 2005).
46. 487 F. 2d 1345 (Ct. Cl. 1973).

cited as part of the trend in which the courts will take a cautious approach to copyright law issues raised by the advent of new technology. Rather than enforce the rights of the author articles by placing a prohibition on such copying, the Court in this case held that this was not prohibited by the law as written, leaving it to the United States Congress to address the issue through legislation. The US Court of Claims held that medicine, and medical research would be harmed by finding an infringement, and since the Copyright Act was under revision by Congress, it was better to allow the status quo to continue in the interim. In the decision, Judge Oscar Davis stated:

> the court holds, based on the type and context of use by NIH and NLM as shown by the record, that there has been no infringement, that the challenged use is 'fair' in view of the combination of all of the factors involved in consideration of 'fair' or 'unfair' use enumerated in the opinion, that the record fails to show a significant detriment to plaintiff but demonstrates injury to medical and scientific research if photocopying of this kind is held unlawful, and that there is a need for congressional treatment of the problems of photocopying.

The 1976 Act

The Copyright Act, 1976 (the 1976 Act) was enacted by the US Congress for two primary reasons. First, technological developments and their impact on what might be copyrighted, how works might be copied, and what constituted an infringement needed to be addressed. Second, the revision was undertaken in anticipation of Berne Convention adherence by the US. It was felt that the statute needed to be amended to bring the US into accord with international copyright law, practices, and policies. The 1976 Act expanded both the scope and duration of protection. All written works became protectable once they were "fixed in a tangible medium of expression", even if they were unpublished. Thus, the 1976 Act abandoned the distinction between pre-publication and post-publication rights of an author.[47]

The 1976 Act was modified in 1980 to expressly incorporate computer programs into the Copyright Act for the first time. In US one can get six exclusive legal rights with a copyright under the Copyright Act. These rights are right to reproduction, right to distribute, right to digital transmission, right to public performance, derivatives rights and right to public display.[48] In *Encyclopedia Britannica Educational Corp.* v. *Crooks,*[49] the *Encyclopedia Britannica* sued the Board of Cooperative Educational Services, a consortium of public school districts, for systematically taping educational programmes that were broadcast on public television stations and making copies available to member schools. The court found that the actions of the school board would have a detrimental effect on the market of the commercially produced programmes and that the use was not a fair use. The 1976 Act was modified again in 1988, when the United States finally ratified the *Berne Convention.* The 1988 amendments abolished the requirement of notice and certain other formalities.

47. For comparative analysis of copyright law in America, see generally, Arthur R. Miller and Michael H. Davis, *Intellectual Property Patents, Trademarks, and Copyright: In a Nutshell,* (West Publishing Co., Minnesota, 1983).
48. *See,* Siva Vaidhyanathan, *Copyrights and Copywrongs: The Rise of Intellectual Property and How It Threatens Creativity* (New York University Press, New York, 2001).
49. 58 F. Supp. 1247 (1983).

The doctrine of fair use limits the scope of the copyright monopoly in furtherance of its utilitarian objective. In American copyright law, one of the most hotly contested skirmishes revolves around the concept of "fair use", despite the gradual marginalisation of this doctrine, it continues to stand as "the oldest, broadest, and most important" limitation on the rights held by copyright owners. Section 107 of the 1976 Act carved out an exception to copyright infringement for "fair use/uses". These uses include reproduction of a work for the purpose of "criticism, comment, news reporting, teaching…, scholarship, or research". The celebrated four-factor test imposed as a mandatory part of an inquiry into fair use by Act of 1976 is thought by many to reflect Congressional approval of this exercise in obscurantism.[50] Fair use, while originally developed as a common law doctrine, in 1994 in *Campbell* v. *Acuff-Rose Music, Inc.*,[51] the US Supreme Court held that a copyright owner's statutory rights when enforcement of those rights "would stifle the very creativity which copyright law is designed to foster." In this case four factors the court encouraged to look to are:

(i) the purpose and character of the use,
(ii) the nature of the copyrighted work,
(iii) the amount and substantiality of the original portion used, and
(iii) the effect on the market for the original.

On the issue whether the secondary use is "transformative" the courts have developed a variety of definitions of "transformation", the narrowest being that a work must be a parody and the broadest that a work must manifest a different purpose than the original.[52] In 2013 in *Cariou* v. *Prince*,[53] the Second Circuit held that a series of photographic collages described as "appropriation art" qualified as fair use despite the fact that both the collage and the original photographs served similar expressive purposes, albeit in very different manners. The court adopted the broadest definition of transformation to date, which, though formally reliant on the language in *Campbell*,[54] relaxed the requirements for transformativeness such that a work need only show "new expression, meaning, or message".

The 1988 Act

Through the 1994 WTO Agreement on Trade-Related Aspects of Intellectual Property Rights (TRIPS Agreement), the United States has sought an international intellectual property regime that advances private interests, most notably those of pharmaceutical companies. TRIPS Agreement was successful in providing such standards, with the result that increased revenue flowed back to countries exporting intellectual property, particularly the United States.[55] In 1998, Congress enacted the *Sonny Bono Copyright Term Extension Act* which affords protection

50. Pierre N. Leval, "Toward a Fair Use Standard" 103 *Harvard Law Review* (1990) pp. 1105–1136.
51. 510 U.S. 569 (1994).
52. *See*, "Recent Cases" 127 *Harvard Law Review* (2014) p. 1228.
53. 714 F.3d 694 (2d Cir. 2013).
54. *Campbell* v. *Acuff-Rose Music, Inc.*, 510 U.S. 569 (1994).
55. *See*, Donald P. Harris, "TRIPS' Rebound: An Historical Analysis of How the TRIPS Agreement Can Ricochet back against the United States" 25 *Northwestern Journal of International Law and Business* (2004–2005) pp. 99–164.

against the circumvention of copy protection technologies as well as other provision.[56] Thus in the US copyright protection extends to protect just about anything that can be expressed in tangible form, and side by side new norms have been evolved to solve the problems in the digital context. The conflict led to the creation of technology capable of circumventing the technological measures applied by authors for the protection of their works which nevertheless resulted in the unauthorised use of the works. The *Digital Millennium Copyright Act, 1998* was also enacted in the US to protect technological measures applied by copyright owners to safeguard their works.

In *CleanFlicks* v. *Soderbergh*,[57] CleanFlicks provides edited versions of DVD movies to home viewers who wish to avoid objectionable content. On 6 July 2006, CleanFlicks lost a court case, *CleanFlicks* v. *Soderbergh*, against a group of directors and motion picture studios who claimed that CleanFlicks infringed their exclusive right of distribution. The Court rejected CleanFlicks' fair use defence, finding that CleanFlicks' edits were non-transformative and that public benefits were not outweighed by "the intrinsic value of the right to control the content of the copyrighted work which is the essence of the law of copyright."

Copyright Office

In America, the Copyright Office became a separate department of the Library of Congress in 1897. Today the Copyright Office is an important service unit of the Library of Congress. The mission of the Copyright Office is to promote creativity by administering and sustaining an effective national copyright system. The Copyright Office examines all applications and deposits presented for the registration of original and renewal copyright claims to determine their acceptability for registration under the provisions of the copyright law and Copyright Office regulations. The Office also records documents related to copyright ownership. In addition, the Office maintains a directory of service provider agents for notification of claims of infringement as required by Section 512(c) of the Copyright Act.[58] The Copyright Office records the copyright facts of all works registered in the Copyright Office as well as the copyright facts of all works deposited but not registered in the Office to comply with the copyright law, thus providing effective reference access to all information of record relating to registrations, deposits, recorded assignments, and other documents. The Office also maintains records of all documents related to copyright ownership that are submitted for recordation. As a service unit of the Library of Congress, the Copyright Office is part of the legislative branch of government. The Copyright Office provides public information and reference services concerning copyrights and recorded documents. The Copyright Office also serves as an advisor to the Library on all copyright issues.

56. For various copyright issues in internet, see generally, Roas Julia-Barcelo, "On-line Internationally Liability Issues: Comparing US and EU Legal Frameworks" 22 *European Intellectual Property Review* (2000) pp. 105–112; Simon Fitzpatirick, "Copyright Imbalance: US and Australian Response to the WIPO Digital Copyright Treaty" 22 *European Intellectual Property Review* (2000) pp. 214–228.
57. 433 F. Supp. 2d 1236 (D. Colo. 2006).
58. For critical discussion on Section 512(c) of the US Digital Millennium Copyright Act see Kristelia A. Garcia, "Copyright Arbitrage," 107 *California Law Review* (2019) pp. 199–266; Emily M. Asp, "Section 512 of the Digital Millennium Copyright Act: User Experience and User Frustration," 103 *Iowa Law Review* (2018) pp. 751–783.

DEVELOPMENTS IN INDIA

Law relating to copyright in India has grown out of English common law and statutory law. As stated above *Statute of Anne*, the first Copyright Act in England as well as world over, was passed in 17th century which provided that the author of any book already printed will have the sole right of printing such book for a term mentioned therein. Thereafter, the Copyright Act, 1814 was enacted, and then the Copyright Act, 1842 which repealed the two earlier Acts of 1709 and 1814. The Copyright Acts of 1847 and 1911 in England had codified and consolidated the various earlier Copyright Acts on different works and thereafter the Copyright Act, 1956 was enacted. In India, the first Copyright Act was enacted in 1914. This was nothing but a copy of the English Copyright Act, 1911 with suitable modifications to make it applicable to the then British India. The Copyright Act, 1957 which is the current statute in India, has followed and adopted the principles and provisions contained in the English Copyright Act, 1956 along with introduction of many new provisions.[59]

The Copyright Act, 1847

In fact, in India too modern copyright law emerged consequent to the spread of printing technology. It is true that while the history of printing of books in India goes back to 1557, that of copyright law is only little more than a hundred and fifty years old. This was because the early printing activities were mostly non-commercial and Christian missionaries driven up. But once commercial publishing picked up, need for a copyright to protect the interest of authors and publishers were felt. This led to the enactment of the Copyright Act, 1847 for India.[60] Thus, law relating to copyright begins in India when *East India Company* extended the Copyright Act, 1847 to the territories under its control. Its preamble recites several doubts which exist or which "may exist" concerning recognition and enforcement of copyright as a part of the common law or administration of justice on the basis of "justice, equity and good conscience" or as regards the application of British statutes to territories then administered by the *East India Company*.

The term of copyright was for the lifetime of the author plus seven years post-mortem. But in no case the total term of copyright was to exceed the period of forty-two years. The government was empowered to licence publication of the book if the owner of copyright upon the death of the author refused to allow its publication. Unauthorised printing of copyright work for (or as a part of attempt of) "sale hire, or exportation", or "for selling, publishing or exposing to sale or hire" constituted infringement. Suit or action for infringement was to be instituted in the "highest local court exercising original civil jurisdiction". The Act provided specifically that under a contract of service copyright in "any encyclopaedia, review, magazine, periodical work or work published in a series of books or parts" shall vest in the "proprietor, projector, publisher or conductor". Infringing copies were deemed to be copies of the proprietor of copyrighted work. Registration of copyright with the Home Office was mandatory for the enforcement of rights under the Act; but the proviso to Section 14 specifically reserved the

59. *See*, J.K. Das, New Dimensions of Intellectual Property Rights in India" 3(2) *Pragyaan: Journal of Law* (2013) pp. 11–33 at p. 14.
60. Tharini Kala, *How Copyright Works in Practice* (Bombay, 1996) at p. 2.

subsistence of copyright in the author, and his right to sue for its infringement to the extent available in law other than the 1847 Act.[61]

At the time of introduction of Copyright Act, 1847 in India, copyright law had already been under the process of development in Britain for over a century and the provisions of the 1847 enactment reflected the learnings from deliberations during this period. Thus, in its very first avatar, copyright had arrived in India as a modern law that was both abstract (encompassing "all works" of literature and art) and forward looking (in the way that it sought to accommodate both existing and new forms of subject matter). As a result, many of the philosophical debates over the nature of "literary property" that had animated the initial years of copyright development in Britain were conspicuous by their absence in the subcontinent.

The Copyright Act, 1914

In India, the first Copyright Act was passed in 1914. This was nothing but a copy of the Copyright Act, 1911 of United Kingdom with suitable modifications to make it applicable to the then British India. The above stated Act of 1847 was replaced by the Indian Copyright Act, 1914 that was based on English Copyright Act, 1911. The major changes made by the 1914 Act were (i) it introduced criminal sanctions for copyright infringement (Sections 7 to 12) and (ii) it modified the scope of the term of copyright; under Section 4 the "sole right" of the author to "produce, reproduce, perform or publish a translation of the work shall subsist only for a period of ten years from the date of the first publication of the work".[62] The author, however, retained his/her "sole rights" if within the period of ten years he/she published or authorised publication of his/her work a translation in any language in respect of that language. So far as the first change is concerned, it has been criticised that the property rights with criminal sanctions can probably be understood as a part of general colonial legal and political policies which sought to protect, generally, right to property over rights to personal freedom. The modification of term of copyright for translation rights had adverse impact and disadvantageous to the authors and a boon to publishers.[63] This Act has been elaborated by judicial decisions like, *Macmillan* v. *R.C. Cooper.*[64]

---

61. The question whether or not India, as a civilised nation had prior to the colonisation any notions or institutions for legal protection of creative artists has not even been asked so far; this makes even tentative approaches to answers quite ambitious at this state. Legal and social historians of ancient and medieval India have yet to attend to this aspect. See generally, Upendra Baxi, "Copyright Law and Justice in India" 28 *Journal of the Indian Law Institute* (1986) pp. 497–540; Tushar Kanti Saha, "Copyright Law in Changing World", 8 *Journal of Intellectual Property Rights* (2003) pp. 23–31.
62. *See*, Report of the Joint Select Committee, *The Gazette of India Extraordinary* (1956), Part 2, Section 2, p. 907.
63. In the *Joint Select Committee of the Indian Parliament* in 1956 Mr. R.D. Sinha argued that: "Most of the novels by Sarat Chandra Chatterjee ... were translated in Hindi, while the author was yet alive. The author's novels, in translation sold thousands of copies, but the author did not get a pie out of the sale-proceeds... Something like this happened in the case of *Gurudeva (Tagore)*. Publisher in Hindi and other languages were making good money out of the translations of his works, but the poet, revered by the nation, was in his extremely old age touring the country for money to support the Shanti-Niketan". *See*, Report of the Joint Select Committee, *The Gazette of India Extraordinary*, (1956), Part 2, Section 2, p. 907.
64. AIR 1924 PC 75.

In the post Second World War era, a number of important new technological developments took place. For a while, the international copyright community followed the strategy of "guided development" by study and discussion, rather than trying to establish new international norms. This means that guidance was provided to governments by various international bodies as to how to respond to the challenges thrown by these new technologies in the field of intellectual property law. This guidance policy did create an impact on the national legislations. Therefore, after independence in 1947 and adoption of the Constitution of India in 1950, a need was felt to consolidate the law on copyright keeping in mind the technological developments and international conventions. To harmonise the technological developments and international conventions the Indian Copyright Act, 1957 was passed replacing the Copyright Act, 1914. In *Indian Performing Rights Society Limited* v. *East India Motion Picture Associations*,[65] Krishna Iyer, J. observed:

> The creative intelligence of man is displayed in multiform ways of aesthetic expression but it often happens that the economic system so operate that the priceless divinity which we call artistic or literary creativity in man is exploited and masters, whose works are invaluable are victims of piffling payments. World opinion in defence of human rights to intellectual property led to international conventions calculated to protect work of art. India responded to his universal need by enacting the Copyright Act of 1957.

The Copyright Act, 1957

Legislative Scheme of the 1957 Act

The Copyright Act, 1957 is the current statute, has followed and adopted the principles and provisions contained in the English Copyright Act of 1956 along with introduction of many new provisions. The 1914 Act was continued with minor modifications till the Copyright Act, 1957 was brought into force on 24 January 1958. There were a number of factors for enacting the 1957 Act. First, it was clear that continued existence of the 1911 Act through the 1914 Act was unbecoming to "the changed Constitutional status of India". Second, the 1914 Act did not accord with the 1948 *Brussels Act* of the *Berne Convention* and the 1952 *Universal Copyright Convention*. Third, new "and advanced method of communications" rendered modernisation of the law necessary. Fourth, the need for an "independent self-contained law" was also felt in the light of the experience of the "working" of the 1911 Act, and more importantly, of "the growing public consciousness of the rights and obligations of the author."[66] The 1957 Act explicitly states that there shall be no copyright in any work, except as according to the provisions of the Act.[67]

The 1957 Act, as it emerged, was not in any sense a replication of the English legislative proposals. In this sense, the 1957 Act was the first truly Indian legislation after well over two

---

65. AIR 1977 SC 1443: (1977) 2 SCC 820.
66. The Statement of objects and reasons to the bill, *see*, *The Gazette of India, Extraordinary*, Pt. 2, Section 2 p. 907 (1956).
67. Copyright Act, 1957, Section 16: "No person shall be entitled to copyright or any similar right in any work, whether published or unpublished, otherwise than under and in accordance with the provisions of this Act or of any other law for the time being in force, but nothing in this section shall be construed as abrogating any right or jurisdiction to restrain a breach of trust or confidence."

centuries of the subjection to the "imperial" law. The Act was not sufficiently far-sighted; it, for example, does not protect the right of the performers adequately. In many respects (as demonstrated later), it is drafted in ways which make it meaningful only to judges and lawyers and sometimes not even to them. But the fact remains that the country had its *own* law of copyright for the first time in contemporary history; and, for weal or woe, it represented the law-policy choices made by its independent legislature. This then is the net historical significance of the 1957 Act. In what follows, we explore the principal features of the law and administration of the Act for the past twenty-three years.

The general scheme and the principal features of the 1957 Act are as follows. Chapter I, III, IV and V deal with copyright and its ownership; Chapter XI with infringement; Chapter IX with international copyright; Chapter X with registration of copyright; Chapter XII to XIV with civil and criminal remedies and Chapters II, VI, VII and X with powers and functions of the registrar of copyrights and the Appellate Board.[68] A short special Chapter VIII deals with the rights of broadcasting authorities. The Act is divided into fifteen Chapters and contains seventy-nine Sections. In addition, the government has enacted copyright rules under Section 78 of the Act. The rules deal with mattes of procedure primarily in matters like applications of licences for translations, performing rights societies, relinquishment and registration of copyright and related matters. In addition to the Act and the rules, we must note that the government is empowered to make an order directing that any or all the provisions of the 1957 Act may apply to copyright in foreign works and in works of certain international organisations. The orders are to be laid before Parliament and subject to modification by it. The orders have to be published in the government gazette.

The 1957 Act makes certain administrative arrangements for implementation. It creates, for the first time, two distinct institutions: the Copyright Office and the Appellate Board.[69] The Copyright Office is headed by a registrar of copyrights and the office is under the superintendence and direction of the Government of India. The Ministry of Education and Social Welfare is the administrative ministry overseeing the Copyright Office. A principal function of the office is to maintain, in all relevant particulars, a register of copyrights (contemplated by the bill to be mandatory, but rendered optional by the Act as it emerged); to entertain and deal with applications for compulsory licences and to inquire into complaints of importation of infringing copies. The registrar performs judicial functions in relation to these tasks; and an appeal is provided from his decision to the Appellate Board.[70]

The board has a number of essential functions under the Act. All of them involve determination of claims of rival rights and liabilities; the *Joint Select Committee on the Bill* was right to insist that the board should be headed by a chairman who is or has been a "Judge of the Supreme Court or a High Court" or is so qualified to be a High Court judge. The principal functions of the board are to consider and determine:

68. Substituted by the Finance Act 2017 (7 of 2017), section 160(a) for "Copyright Board," [w.e.f. 26 May, 2017].
69. Substituted by the Finance Act 2017 (7 of 2017), section 160(a) for "Copyright Board," [w.e.f. 26 May, 2017].
70. Substituted by the Finance Act 2017 (7 of 2017), section 160(a) for "Copyright Board," [w.e.f. 26 May, 2017].

(i) Whether any literary, dramatic, musical or artistic work, or records, are issued in "sufficient quantities" within the meaning of Section 3.[71]

(ii) Whether the term of copyright is shorter in any other country as compared to the term provided under the Act.[72]

(iii) Application for licences to produce and publish a translation of literary or dramatic work in any language.[73]

(iv) Complaints that certain copyrighted works are unreasonably withheld from public.[74]

(v) Objections to tariff of fees, charges and royalties announced by performing rights societies.[75]

(vi) Rectification of the register of copyrights.[76]

In relation to items (i) and (ii) above, the Act declared that the decision of the board shall be "final". The board as well as the registrar are empowered, by Section 74, with certain powers of civil courts (in respect of summoning witnesses, ordering discovery of documents, receiving and examine evidence, etc.) and every order either by the registrar or the board for payment of any money is rendered executable in the same way as if it was the decree of a civil court.[77] The board is required to circuit in ones in various parts of India; and individuals may file proceedings in the appropriate zones where they voluntarily reside or carry on business or work for personal gain.

Amendments to the 1957 Act

In order to keep pace with the fast technological developments in the area of copyright and also to abide by its international obligation, the Government of India amended the Copyright Act, 1957 in 1983, 1984, 1992, 1994, 1999 and 2012. Thus, in *Star India Private Limited* v. *Department of Industrial Policy and Promotion*,[78] the Supreme Court observed the Copyright Act, 1957 was enacted to amend and consolidate the law relating to copyrights in India. To meet with the national and international requirements and to keep the law updated, the Act has been amended several times since then, once each in the years 1983, 1984, 1992, 1994, 1999 and 2012. The salient features of these amendments are discussed below.

The 1983 Amendment

India is a member of the Barn Convention 1886[79] and the Universal Copyright Protection 1952.

71. Copyright Act 1957, Section 6(a).
72. *Ibid.*, Section 6(b).
73. *Ibid.*, Section 32.
74. *Ibid.*, Section 31.
75. *Ibid.*, Sections 33–36.
76. *Ibid.*, Section 70.
77. *Ibid.*, Section 76.
78. (2019) 2 SCC 104: 2018 (14) SCALE 651. See also, *Saregama Ltd.* v. *The New Digital Media*, 2018 (73) PTC 329 (Cal): (2018) 1 CALLT 190 (HC).
79. *See, Berne Convention for the Protection of Literary and Artistic Works, 1886. See*, Paul Adward Geller, "Copyright Protection in Barne Union: Analyzing the Issues", 13 *Columbia Law Journal* (1989) p. 439; Sam Ricketon, The *Berne Convention for the Protection of Literary and Artistic Works: 1886–1986* (University of London, 1987); Paul Adward Geller, "Copyright Protection in Berne Union: Analyzing the Issues", 13 *Columbia Law Journal* (1989) p. 439.

Therefore, the Government of India confirming the provisions of these two conventions enacted the Copyright Act, 1957. Subsequently, these two Conventions were revised at Paris in 1971. These revised Conventions provide for certain additional facilities to enable the developing countries to grant compulsory licences for translation and reproduction of works of foreign origin required for the purposes of teaching, scholarship or research or for purposes of systematic instructional activities.[80]

Hence, the Copyright (Amendment) Act, 1983[81] introduced new Sections 32A and 32B for issuing "compulsory licences" for publication of copyrighted foreign works in any Indian language for the purposes of systematic instructional activities at a "low price" with the permission of the Appellate Board[82] on certain conditions. The other crucial change affected by the amendment, through the insertion of Section 19A, in the teeth of heavy opposition by copyright industries, relates to the conferral of power in the Appellate Board,[83] upon a due complaint to it, to order revocation of the assigned copyright either where the terms are "harsh" or where the publication of the work is unduly delayed; the board is also competent to issue certificates of royalties recoverable by the owner.

In addition, the 1983 Amendment Act provides for power in the Appellate Board[84] to publish unpublished Indian works, and for the protection of "oral works" under Section 31A. The 1983 Amendment also defined "Indian Work" under Section 2(l) to mean a literary, dramatic or musical work—(i) the author of which is a citizen of India; or (ii) which is first published in India; (iii) the author of which, in the case of an unpublished work is, at the time of the making of the work, a citizen of India. Under Section 2(dd) of the 1983 Amendment a new concept was introduced defining "broadcast" as communication to the public to mean: (i) by any means of wireless diffusion whether in any one or more of the forms of signs, sounds or visual images; or (ii) by wire and includes rebroadcast. Section 2(ff) is introduced defining "Communication to the public" as communication to the public in whatever manner, including communication through satellite; and Section 2(g) is amended stating "delivery" as including "broadcast". Section 2(m) defines "infringing copy" and includes the infringement right to the "broadcasting right" of Government of which the Government is declared as sole owner, unless licence is given.[85]

The 1984 Amendment

The Copyright (Amendment) Act, 1984,[86] following in the wake of vociferous concern about piracy of copyrighted works, provides for stringent punishments for piracy and effective procedures to inhibit it. The Members of Parliament while considering the Copyright

80. Statement of Objects and Reasons of the Copyright (Amendment) Bill, 1983.
81. *See*, Amendment Act 23 of 1983.
82. Substituted by the Finance Act 2017 (7 of 2017), section 160(a) for "Copyright Board," [w.e.f. 26 May, 2017].
83. Substituted by the Finance Act 2017 (7 of 2017), section 160(a) for "Copyright Board," [w.e.f. 26 May, 2017].
84. Substituted by the Finance Act 2017 (7 of 2017), section 160(a) for "Copyright Board," [w.e.f. 26 May, 2017].
85. *See*, *Ramakrishna Dish Antenna System* v. *The Deputy Superintendent of Police,* AIR 1989 AP 295: 1989 (2) ALT 212.
86. Amendment Act 65 of 1984.

(Amendment) Bill, 1984 to amend the Copyright Act, 1957 discussed the problem of piracy as it has a serious impact on the right of reproduction of authors. The Members were of the opinion that there was an urgent need of taking sufficient anti-piracy measures.

In Statement of Objects and Reasons annexed to the Copyright (Amendment) Act, 1984, it was stated:

> Mainly there are three types of piracy: piracy of printed word; of sound recordings and of cinema films. The object of pirates in all such cases is to make money and avoid payment of legitimate taxes and royalty. In respect of books, it is estimated that 400–500 titles are pirated every year in India and on each of the pirated titles, the loss to the government in the form of tax evasion amounts approximately to ₹ 11,000/-. The emergence of new techniques of recordings, fixation and reproduction of audio programs combined with the advent of video technology has greatly helped pirates. It is estimated that losses to the film's producers and other owners of copyright, amount to several crores of rupees. The loss to government in terms of tax evasion also amounts to crores of rupees. In addition, because of the video boom in the country, there are reports that uncertified video films are exhibited on a large scale. A large number of video parlours have also sprung up and they exhibit such films by charging fee from their clients.[87]

The Copyright (Amendment) Act, 1984 was mainly introduced with the objective to discourage and prevent the widespread piracy prevailing in video films and records. In Section 2(ff), in the explanation clause it has been provided that for the purpose of Copyright Act, video films shall also be deemed to be work produced by a process analogous to cinematography.[88] Thus, the 1984 amendment also took note of technological advances, for example, "video film" was added to the definition of "cinematograph film",[89] and "computer programs" to the definition of "literary work",[90] and a new definition of "duplicating equipment" under Section 2(hh),[91] was also inserted. According to Section 2(hh) "duplicating equipment" means any mechanical contrivance or evidence used or intended to be used for making copies of any work. The 1984 Amendment Act also provided for enhanced punishment in cases of continuing convictions and also declared offences of infringement of copyright as an economic offence so that the period of limitation as provided in the Criminal Procedure Code is not applicable to these offences. The Amendment Act made infringement of copyright, a cognisable and non-bailable offence. By making punishment for such offences more stringent[92] the 1984 Amendment Act made the Copyright Act, 1957 more dynamic.

The 1992 Amendment

Gurudev Rabindranath Tagore died in the year 1941 and copyright in his published works, which stood vested in Visva Bharati, was to expire on 31st December, 1991. There had been numerous demands for according extended protection to his works in view of their national importance. While it was not considered feasible and appropriate to extend the term of copyright in respect of one author alone, the Government reviewed the whole question of what should

87. Statement of Objects and Reasons annexed to the Copyright Amendment Bill, 1984 (19-8-1984).
88. *Coalbelt Cinema Exhibitors* v. *State of West Bengal*, 97 CWN 1085 (1993).
89. *See*, Copyright Act, 1957, Section 2(f)
90. *Ibid.*, Section 2(0).
91. *Ibid.*, Section 2(hh).
92. Chapter XIII, dealing with offences.

be the appropriate term of copyright and decide to extend the term of copyright generally in all works protected by the Copyright Act, 1957 from fifty to sixty years.[93] Ultimately the Copyright (Amendment) Act, 1992 was enacted with retrospective effect. Section 2 of the Copyright (Amendment) Act, 1992 provides that in Chapter V of the Copyright Act, 1957 (principal Act) for the words "fifty-years", wherever they occur, the words "sixty years" shall be substituted. Hence, in post amended Section 22 of the principal Act provides that the copyright shall subsist in any literary, dramatic, musical or artistic work published within the lifetime of the author until [sixty years][94] from the beginning of the calendar year next following the year in which the author dies. Further, Section 3 of the 1992 amending Act declared that copyright shall not subsist by virtue of this Act in any work in which copyright did not subsist immediately before the commencement of this Act.

The 1994 Amendment

This amendment was introduced after the addition of the TRIPS Agreement under international law. Thus, the Copyright (Amendment) Act, 1994 has brought the Indian copyright law in conformity with the TRIPS Agreement. The 1994 Amendment Act under Section 2(o) defines "literary work" to include (among others) computer programs, tables and compilations including computer databases. Thus, the 1994 Amendment Act shows that copyrights with regard to the data work, data basis, computer work, etc., are specifically covered under the Copyright Act.[95]

In *Burlington Home Shopping Pvt. Ltd.* v. *Rajnish Chibber*, the issue was whether a database consisting of compilation of mailing addresses of customers can be subject matter of a copyright. Citing the 1994 Amendment Act, the Delhi Court held that a computer database is a collection of information stored on computer media and it will be protected by copyright. The Statement of Objects and Reasons of the Copyright (Amendment) Act, 1994 clearly stipulates that the amendments were made "to protect the interest of authors, assignors or licensors in regard to the assignment of copyright and the issue of licenses"; "to extend more effective protection to owners of copyright" and "to simplify and improve the law relating to copyright and related rights, in the interests of the general public, and in particular of the users as well as the owners of the rights.[96] Thus, the amendment provided for the assignment of copyright by an author or artist to protect the interests of both assignor and assignee and also for protection of computer programs, cinematograph films and sound recordings. A new Chapter VII dealing with copyright societies, seeking to promote effective administration of rights of the authors, composers and other creative artists and a definition of "reprography" under Section 2(x) were also inserted. According to Section 2(x), "reprography" means the making of copies of a work, by photocopying or similar means. The 1994 Amendment Act introduced protection for performers by giving them a right to reproduce their live performances by way of sound or visual recordings, etc., under Chapter VIII.

---

93. *See*, Statement of Objects and Reasons of the Copyright (Amendment) Act, 1992.
94. Substituted by Copyright (Amendment) Act, 1992, Section 2, for "fifty years" [w.e.f. 28-12-1991].
95. *B.N. Firos* v. *State of Kerala*, AIR 2006 Ker 279: 2007 (34) PTC 98 (Ker).
96. *Gramophone Company of India Ltd.* v. *Mars Recording Pvt. Ltd.*, AIR 2001 SC 2885: (2002) 2 SCC 103.

The 1999 Amendment

The Copyright Act, 1957 required only minor changes to comply with the obligations under the Agreement on Trade-Related Aspects of Intellectual Property Rights (TRIPS Agreement) through the amendment made in the year 1999. The Copyright (Amendment) Act, 1999 increased the protection of performers from 25 to 50 years required by the Article 14 of the TRIPS Agreement. Since 15 January 1999 the Section 38(2) of the Copyright Act, 1957 provides that "The performer's right shall subsist until fifty years[97] from the beginning of the calendar year next following the year in which the performance is made". Through the 1999 Amendment Act under Section 14(b)(ii) rental right was introduced in case of computer programs to strengthen the right of reproduction of authors of computer programmes. Under Section 40A, a new provision was inserted which gave power to the Central Government to apply Chapter VI of the Act dealing with the rights of broadcasting organisation and of performers to broadcasting organisations and performers of certain other countries, which, fulfilled the conditions, specified therein.

Section 42A was added through the 1999 Amendment Act whereby power was given to the Central Government to restrict the rights of foreign broadcasting organisation and performers if it appears to the government that such a foreign country does not give or has not undertaken to give adequate protection to rights of broadcasting organisation or performer of our country.[98] The obligation under Article 11 of the TRIPS Agreement, Article 7 of WCT and Article 9 of WPPT is to provide for "commercial rental" rights for computer programme and cinematograph film. This right was introduced in 1994 in Section 14 using the word "hire". However, keeping in view the possibility of interpreting this term to include non-commercial hire and lending by libraries and educational institutions, the term "hire" in Section 14(b) for computer programme was replaced with the term "commercial rental" in the 1999 Amendment.

The 2012 Amendment

The Copyright (Amendment) Act, 2012[99] has been enacted by the Government of India bringing changes to the Copyright Act, 1957. The amendments make Indian copyright law at par with the Internet Treaties, WIPO Copyright Treaty (WCT) and WIPO Performances and Phonograms Treaty (WPPT).[100] The amendment has made some changes that clarify the rights in artistic works, cinematograph films and sound recordings. The Amendment has introduced affirmative performer's rights by amending the present Section 38. Broadly the amendments strengthen the rights of the authors, streamline the process of assignment and grant of licences, facilitate better access to works, and extend fair use provisions, in general and in particular to the Internet. The changes made in the provisions of assignment and licensing and in copyright

---

97. Subs. by Act 49 of 1999, Section 4, for "twenty five years".
98. *B.N. Firos* v. *State of Kerala*, AIR 2006 Ker 279: 2007 (34) PTC 98 (Ker); *Mr. Sudhir Bhatia* v. *M/s Midas Hygiene Industries (P) Ltd.*, 94 (2001) DLT 639.
99. Act No. 27 of 2012. Came into force on 21-6-2012, *vide* S.O. 1393(E), dated 20th June, 2012, published in the Gazette of India, Extra., II, Section 3(ii), No. 1164, 20th June, 2012. *See*, Arathi Ashoke, "Technology Protection Measures and the Indian Copyright (Amendment) Act, 2012: A Comment", 17 *Journal of Intellectual Property Rights* (2012), pp. 521–531.
100. *See*, T.C. James, "Indian Copyright Law and Digital Technology", 7 *Journal of Intellectual Property Rights* (2002) pp. 423–435.

societies are expected to streamline business practices but has an underlying concern about protecting authors' interests. There are also welcome reforms to administration of copyright societies and the Appellate Board.[101] These changes made by the 2012 Amendment Act are discussed below.

Cinematograph Films

The 2012 Amendment Act has amended the definition of "cinematograph film" under Section 2(f). The previous definition of "cinematograph films" is simplified by omitting a few words that elaborated visual recordings. Since the words are omitted from the definition of cinematograph films, a new definition for "visual recording" is inserted by a new Sub-Section 2(xxa).[102] The amended definition reads: "cinematograph film means any work of visual recording on any medium." The Act introduces a definition of "visual recording" in Sub-Section 2(xxa) to mean "recording in any medium, by any method including storing of it by electronic means, of moving images or representations thereof, from which they can be perceived, reproduced or communicated by any method".

Section 14(d) relates to the exclusive rights in a cinematograph film. The existing sub-clause (i) provides the right to make a copy of the film, including a photograph of any image forming part thereof. This sub-clause has been amended through the 2012 Amendment Act to extend the rights of the author to include the "storing" of the work in any medium by electronics or other means. The cinematograph films were considered as commissioned works prior to the amendment of 2012 and, therefore, the producer was considered as the first owner of copyright not only with respect to the film but even with respect to literary, dramatic, musical or artistic works incorporated in the film.[103] The 2012 Amendment Act has added a proviso to Section 17 whereby, the authors of literary, dramatic, artistic and musical works continue to have copyright in their work irrespective of the fact that their work is incorporated in the film. The rights of such authors can be assigned only for the purpose of exhibition in the film as the right of exhibition of film in a cinema hall vests with the producer. But, their right to claim an equal share of royalty and consideration payable if their work is communicated to public, not as part of cinematograph film in a cinema hall but by some other means, cannot be assigned to anyone except their heirs or the copyright society registered for collection and distribution of royalty.[104] If such assignment takes place, then it will be void.

Prior to 2012, any performer lost his right as a performer once his performance was incorporated in the film.[105] A new section 38A[106] is inserted by the 2012 Amendment Act whereby performer in a film is given special rights and therefore he becomes entitled to royalty in case of commercial use of his performance. However, only those performers are covered by this clause whose performance is not casual and incidental in the film.

---

101. Substituted by the Finance Act 2017 (7 of 2017), section 160(a) for "Copyright Board," [w.e.f. 26 May, 2017].
102. Inserted by the Copyright (Amendment) Act, 2012 [w.e.f. 21-6-2012], Section 2(vi). Section 2(vi). *See also, Vinod Kumar Gupta* v. *State of U.P.*, 2019 (106) ACC 378.
103. Copyright Act, 1957, Section 17(b).
104. *Ibid.*, Section 18(9).
105. *Ibid.*, Section 38(4).
106. Inserted by the Copyright (Amendment) Act, 2012 [w.e.f. 21-6-2012], Section 27.

WPPT and WCT Related Amendments

The 2012 Amendment Act to Section 14 relating to "meaning of copyright" provides the right of "commercial rental" to cinematograph films and sound recordings by amending the word "hire" to "commercial rental" in the existing provision relating to cinematograph films [clause (d)(ii)] and sound recording [clause (e) (ii)] with identical language providing for the right "to sell or give on commercial rental or offer for sale or for such rental, any copy of the" film or sound recording. The obligation under Article 11 of the TRIPS Agreement, Article 7 of WCT and Article 9 of WPPT is to provide for "commercial rental" rights for computer programme and cinematograph film. Therefore, the 2012 Amendment Act has introduced a definition of the term "commercial rental" in Section 2(fa)[107] of the Act as below: "Commercial rental" does not include the rental, lease or lending of a lawfully acquired copy of a computer programme, sound recording, visual recording or cinematograph film for nonprofit purposes by a non-profit library or non-profit educational institution.

Explanation—For the purposes of this clause, a "non-profit library or non-profit educational institution" means a library or educational institution which receives grants from the Government or is exempted from payment of tax under the Income Tax Act, 1961.[108]

The term "commercial rental" is inserted with the objective of expressly clarifying that this right is not applicable to non-commercial activities of giving on "hire" including the activities of libraries and educational institutions. The 2012 Amendment Act substitutes the word "hire" with commercial rental, but has deleted the words "regardless of whether such copy has been sold or given on hire on earlier occasions". This deletion in the case of both cinematograph films and sound recordings brings in the doctrine of first sale exhaustion to these works. It may be recalled that the doctrine of first sale exhaustion was applicable only to the literary, dramatic and artistic works before the amendment.

Compulsory Licences

Section 31 of the Copyright Act, 1957 deals with compulsory licences of works withheld from public. This section provides that if the owner of copyright in any "Indian work"[109] has refused to republish or allow the republication or has refused the performance in public of the work and withheld the work from the public or has refused to allow communication to the public by broadcast of the work recorded in sound recording, the Appellate Board[110] may, on the basis of a complaint received and after such inquiry as it may deem necessary, direct the Registrar of Copyrights to grant to the complainant, a licence. Applicability of this section is amplified from "Indian work" to "any work". "Explanation" relating to the definition of "Indian work" is also omitted.[111] The word "complainant" is replaced with the words "such

107. *Ibid.*, Section 2(ii).
108. Copyright Act, 1957, Section 2(fa).
109. *Ibid.*, Section 2(l).
110. Substituted by the Finance Act 2017 (7 of 2017), section 160(a) for "Copyright Board," [w.e.f. 26 May, 2017].
111. Explanation to Section 31 of the Copyright Act, 1957 omitted by the Copyright (Amendment) Act, 2012 [w.e.f. 21-6-2012]. Before omission, the explanation stood as under:

"Explanation. In this sub-section, the expression "Indian work" includes—

(i) an artistic work, the author of which is a citizen of India; and

(ii) a cinematograph film or a sound recording made or manufactured in India."

person or persons who, in the opinion of the Appellate Board[112], is or are qualified to do so." Sub-section (2) is omitted so as to enable the Appellate Board to grant compulsory licence to more than one person.[113]

By virtue of the 2012 Amendment, compulsory licences can be obtained for "any work" withheld from the public and not just "Indian works" and the licence can be granted to such persons as the Board may decide. Section 31A relates to compulsory licences in unpublished "Indian works". The section has been amended to allow compulsory licences to any unpublished work or any work published or communicated to the public where the work is withheld from the public in India and in cases where the author is dead or unknown or the owner cannot be traced. Special provisions have been provided for compulsory licensing of the works for the disabled by inserting Section 31B[114] by the 2012 Amendment Act.

Statutory Licences for Cover Versions and Broadcasters

A new Section 31C[115] as introduced by the 2012 Amendment Act provides for statutory licence to any person desiring to make a cover version of a sound recording in respect of any literary, dramatic or musical work. This is not totally a new provision for statutory licence for cover version as it is, but a replacement of Section 52(1)(j) as it stood before the amendment. The person making the sound recording shall give to the owner prior notice of his intention in the prescribed manner, provide the copies of all covers or labels with which the version is supposed to be sold, and pay in advance the royalty at the rate fixed by the Appellate Board[116]. Such sound recordings can be made only after the expiration of 5 years after publication of the original sound recording. There is a requirement of payment of a minimum royalty for 50,000 copies of the work during each calendar year.

In *Shumita Deb* v. *Saregama India Limited,*[117] the Karnataka High Court held that with regard to cover version, the Section 31C of the Copyright Act applies to third parties who want to make a sound recording and it is not applicable to the present case as the first defendant appears to be owner of copyright. With regard to Section 31C of the Copyright Act, the learned counsel for the respondent argued that the said Section is not applicable because the CD that the defendants have released is not a cover version. These being the circumstances, the plaintiff cannot claim an order of temporary injunction. A perusal of the impugned order shows that the court below has rightly come to conclusion that there is no case for granting temporary injunction. When the discretion appears to have been exercised properly, the appellate court should not interfere. Therefore he argued for dismissing the appeal. Thus, the

112. Substituted by the Finance Act 2017 (7 of 2017), section 160(a) for "Copyright Board," [w.e.f. 26 May, 2017].
113. Sub-section (2) of the Section 31 of the Copyright Act, 1957 omitted by the Copyright (Amendment) Act, 2012 [w.e.f. 21-6-2012]. Before omission, Sub-section (2) stood as under:
"(2) Where two or more persons have made a complaint under sub-section (1), the licence shall be granted to he complainant who in the opinion of the Copyright Board would best serve the interests of the general public."
114. Inserted by the Copyright (Amendment) Act, 2012 [w.e.f. 21-6-2012], Section 18.
115. *Ibid.*
116. Substituted by the Finance Act 2017 (7 of 2017), section 160(a) for "Copyright Board," [w.e.f. 26 May, 2017].
117. 2019 (1) AKR 485.

Court the trial court has come to right conclusion that a case for grant of temporary injunction does not exist. The reasons given by trial court cannot be disturbed even though it is possible to take other view by upholding the plaintiff's case. Therefore, the High Court concluded that these two appeals should be dismissed.

Through the 2012 Amendment Act, a new Section 31D has been inserted under which a provision has been made for the grant of a statutory licence for broadcasting of literary and musical works and sound recordings, subject to payment at such rate that may be fixed by the Appellate Board.[118] A new Section 31D provides for statutory licence for broadcasting of literary and musical works and sound recordings. It provides that any broadcasting organisation desiring to broadcast a work including sound recording may do so. The broadcasting organisation shall give prior notice to the right holders, pay royalty as fixed by the Appellate Board[119] in advance. The names of the authors and principal performers shall be announced during the broadcast. The broadcasting organisation shall maintain records of the broadcast, books of account and render to the owner such records and books of account.

The above amendment has been brought in to facilitate access to the works for the growing broadcasting industry. At present, the access to copyright works by broadcasters was dependent on voluntary licensing. As a result unreasonable terms and conditions were being set by the copyright societies and owners. There are divergent views by the courts in interpreting the existing compulsory licensing provisions under Section 31. There were litigations pending before various High Courts as well as the Copyright Board regarding the nature of licence and the rate of royalties to be paid when works particularly songs were used for broadcasting. Automatic licence or non-voluntary licence such as the proposed statutory licence ensuring adequate return to the owner of works was the best solution to make access easy for broadcasting industry.

Moral Rights of Authors and Performers

The Copyright Act, 1957 provided for moral rights to authors under Section 57 titled "author's special rights", though it did not use the term "moral rights" in the Act. The legal heirs of the author have been granted the right to paternity and right to integrity even after the expiry of the term of copyright. Moral rights of performers are introduced by newly inserted Section 38B[120] through the 2012 Amendment Act. A new Section 38B grants performers moral rights on their performances as follows:

The performer of a performance shall, independently of his right after assignment, either wholly or partially of his right, have the right,—

(a) to claim to be identified as the performer of his performance except where omission is dictated by the manner of the use of the performance; and

(b) to restrain or claim damages in respect of any distortion, mutilation or other modification of his performance that would be prejudicial to his reputation.

---

118. Substituted by the Finance Act 2017 (7 of 2017), section 160(a) for "Copyright Board," [w.e.f. 26 May, 2017].

119. Substituted by the Finance Act 2017 (7 of 2017), section 160(a) for "Copyright Board," [w.e.f. 26 May, 2017].

120. *See*, Copyright (Amendment) Act, 2012, Section 27.

The explanation clause to this provision clarifies that mere removal of any portion of a performance for the purpose of editing, or to fit the recording within a limited duration, or any other modification required for purely technical reasons shall not be deemed to be prejudicial to the performer's reputation.

Assignment of Rights

Section 18(1) provides that the owner of a copyright in any work or prospective owner of a future work may assign the copyright. The 2012 Amendment Act introduced a proviso to this sub-section 1 which clarifies that in the case of future work, assignment will come into force only when the work comes into existence. A second proviso has also been inserted in this sub-section by providing that no such assignment shall apply to any mode of exploitation that did not exist or was not known in commercial use when the assignment was made. Another proviso provides that the author of a literary or musical work incorporated in a cinematograph film or sound recording shall not assign the right to receive royalties in any form other than as a part of the film or sound recording.[121]

Section 19 of the Act relates to the mode of assignment. The sub-section (3) has been amended to provide that the assignment shall specify the "other considerations", besides royalty, if any, payable. Therefore, it is not necessary that only monetary compensation by way of royalty could lead to assignment. The amendment has inserted a new sub-section (8) to provide that any assignment of copyright in any work contrary to that of the terms and conditions of the rights already assigned to a copyright society in which the author of the work is a member, shall be deemed to be void. A new sub-section (9) provides that no assignment of copyright in any work to make a cinematograph film or sound recording shall affect the right of the author of the work to claim royalties in case of utilization of the work in any form other than as part of cinematograph film or sound recording.[122]

Section 19A relates to disputes with respect to assignment of copyright. This section provides that on receipt of a complaint from an aggrieved party, the Copyright Board may hold inquiry and pass orders as it may deem fit, including an order for the recovery of any royalty payable. Second proviso is amended to provide that pending disposal of an application for revocation of assignment, the Copyright Board may pass any order as it deems fit regarding implementation of the terms and conditions of assignment.[123]

Fair Dealing Provisions

Section 52 of the Act enumerates the acts that will not be infringement of copyright. These are popularly known as fair use clauses. Certain amendments have been made to extend these provisions in the general context. The existing clause (1) (a) of this section provides fair use to "literary, dramatic, musical or artistic works" only. This clause has been amended to provide fair dealing with any work, not being a computer program, for the purposes of private and personal use. With 2012 amendment, the fair use provision has been extended to cinematograph and musical works. Fair dealing on the above lines has been extended by amendment to bring

121. *Ibid.*, Section 9.
122. *Ibid.*, Section 9(ii).
123. *Ibid.*, Section 10(i).

in the word "any work" to reproduction in the course of judicial proceedings;[124] reproduction or publication of any work prepared by secretariat of a legislature;[125] in certified copies supplied as per law.[126]

The 2012 amendment Act introduced a new clause 52(1)(w) provides that the making of a three dimensional object from a two dimensional work, such as a technical drawing, for industrial application of any purely functional part of a useful device shall not constitute infringement. This provision should help reverse engineering of mechanical devices. A new clause 52(zc) has been introduced to provide that importation of literary or artistic works such as labels, company logos or promotional or explanatory material that is incidental to products or goods being imported shall not constitute infringement. This clause supports the parallel import provisions embedded in the Trade Marks Act, 1999. Clauses (zb) and (zc) provide for fair dealing in the use of disabled persons.[127]

The Information Technology Act, 2000 and Its Impact on Law of Copyright

The Copyright (Amendment) Act 1999 has defined "literary work" under Section 2(o) of the Copyright Act 1957. According to Section 2(o) "literary work" includes computer programmes, tables and compilations including computer (databases). Thus, electronic data is a subject matter of copyright. To supplement this development of law of copyright, the Information Technology Act, 2000[128] was enacted to provide legal recognition for transactions carried out by means of electronic data interchange and other means of electronic communication, commonly referred to as "electronic commerce", which involve the use of alternatives to paper-based methods of communication and storage of information, to facilitate electronic filling of documents with the Government agencies. This 2000 Act was enacted pursuant to the United Nations Commission on International Trade Law (UNCITRAL), which had adopted the Model Law on Electronic Commerce in 1996. The General Assembly of United Nations by its Resolution[129] had recommended that all states should give favourable considerations to the said Model when they enact or revise their laws. The Model Law provided for equal legal treatment of users of electronic communication and paper-based communication.[130]

The 2000 Act provides for legal recognition of electronic records[131] and digital signatures.[132] It enables conclusion of contracts and the creation of rights and obligations through electronic medium. It has also provided for a regulatory regime to supervise the

124. Copyright Act, 1957, Section 52(1)(d).
125. *Ibid.*, Section 52(1)(e).
126. *Ibid.*, Section 52(1)(f).
127. Inserted by the Copyright (Amendment) Act, 2012 [w.e.f. 21-6-2012], Section 32.
128. Act of 21 of 2000. Came into force on 17th October, 2000, *vide*, G.S.R. 788(E), dated 17th October, 2000.
129. Resolution No. 51/162, dated 30th January, 1992.
130. *See*, Statement of Objects and Reasons to the Information Technology Bill, 2000.
131. The Information Technology Act, 2000, Sections 2–14.
132. *Ibid.*, Sections 3 and 15. Section 2(c) of the Information Technology Act, 2000 reads: "electronic record" means data, record or data generated, image or sound stored, received or sent in an electronic form or micro film or computer generated micro record.

certifying authorities issuing digital signature certificates.[133] The 2000 Act also attempts to facilitate electronic governance.[134] Offences have been specified[135] and civil and criminal liabilities for contravention of the provisions of the Act have also been provided for.[136] The 2000 Act provides for situations[137] where online service providers will not be held liable. The 2000 Act clarifies that the service providers will not be held liable for any third party information or data made available by them if he proves that the offence or contravention was committed without his knowledge or that he had exercised all due diligence to prevent the commission of such offence or contravention. The Information Technology Act, 2000 enacted by Indian Parliament is the first legislation, which contains provisions of data protection.[138]

In *State* v. *Mohd. Afzal*,[139] the Delhi High Court observed that the last few years of the 20th Century saw rapid strides in the field of information and technology. The expanding horizon of science and technology threw new challenges for the ones who had to deal with proof of facts in disputes where advanced techniques in technology was used and brought in aid. Storage, processing and transmission of date on magnetic and silicon medium became cost effective and easy to handle. Conventional means of records and data processing became out dated. Law had to respond and gallop with the technical advancement. He who sleeps when the sun rises misses the beauty of the dawn. Law did not sleep when the dawn of information and technology broke on the horizon. World over, statutes were enacted. Rules relating to admissibility of electronic evidence and its proof were incorporated. In England this positive mandate was statutorily enacted and the prosecution had to show by positive and affirmative evidence that it was safe to rely upon the document produced by a computer from out of its memory. Thus, in India by way of amendment in 2000 (Act. No. 21 of 2000) to the Evidence Act, 1872, following was inserted:

> The expression "Certifying Authority", "digital signature", "Digital Signature Certificate", "electronic form", "electronic records", "information", "secure electronic records", "secure digital signature" and "subscriber" shall have the meanings respectively assigned to them in the Information Technology Act, 2000.

The protection to computer software is derived out of two acts, the Copyright Act, 1957 and the Information Technology Act, 2000. While the Copyright Act grants protection to the computer program as it is granted to other forms of copyrighted work, the technological and complex nature of the computer programs calls for technically effective protection. The Indian Copyright Act, 1957 accords a special status to computer software as compared to other forms of copyrighted work. The Copyright Act regards the computer programs as literary works and in addition to the general exclusive rights provided to other literary works, it grants extraordinary exclusive rights to the owners of the computer programs like right to sell or offer for sale, and the right to give on commercial rental or offer for commercial

---

133. *Ibid.*, Sections 17–39.
134. *Ibid.*, Sections 4–10.
135. *Ibid.*, Sections 65–78.
136. *Ibid.*, Sections 43–47.
137. *Ibid.*, Sections 79.
138. *See*, Shiv Shankar Singh, "Privacy and data Protection in India: A Critical Assessment" 53 *Journal of the Indian Law Institute* (2011) pp. 663–667.
139. 107 (2003) DLT 385: 2003 (71) DRJ 178.

rental. The Copyright Act has also exempted computer programs from "fair dealing exception" (i.e. private use for research, criticism or review of that work or any other work) which is available in case of other copyright works. The Information Technology Act provides for punishment for tampering with the "source code" of a computer program but this protection applies to computer source codes "which are required to be kept or maintained by law for the time being in force". Hence, the protection accorded by the Information Technology Act is only for source code of computer programs of government agencies and the "source code" of computer programs of private users still stand unprotected.[140]

In *Sharat Babu Digumarti* v. *Govt. of NCT of Delhi*,[141] the Supreme Court held that in case of conflict between Information Technology Act 2000 and Copyright Act 1957 the later will prevail over former and referred the Section 81 of the IT Act which has overriding effect except in cases of copyright and patents. Thus Section 81 provides: "The provisions of this Act shall have effect notwithstanding anything inconsistent therewith contained in any other law for the time being in force. Provided that nothing contained in this Act shall restrict any person from exercising any right conferred under the Copyright Act 1957 or the Patents Act 1970." The Court further explained:

> Section 67 clearly stipulates punishment for publishing, transmitting obscene materials in electronic form. The said provision read with Section 67A and 67B is a complete code relating to the offences that are covered under the IT Act. Section 79 is an exemption provision conferring protection to the individuals. Section 81 also specifically provides that the provisions of the Act shall have effect notwithstanding anything inconsistent therewith contained in any other law for the time being in force. All provisions will have their play and significance, if the alleged offence pertains to offence of electronic record. The IT Act is a special enactment. It has special provisions. Section 292 of the Indian Penal Code makes offence sale of obscene books, etc. but once the offence has a nexus or connection with the electronic record the protection and effect of Section 79 cannot be ignored and negated. It is a special provision for a specific purpose and the Act has to be given effect to so as to make the protection effective and true to the legislative intent. This is the mandate behind Section 81 of the IT Act. The additional protection granted by the IT Act would apply.

In *Myspace Inc.* v. *Super Cassettes Industries Ltd.*,[142] the issue was: does the Section 51 of Copyright Act, 1957 is to be interpreted in case there is a conflict with Section 81 of the Information Technology Act 2000? Does proviso to Section 81 of IT Act, override "safe harbour" granted to intermediaries under Section 79 of IT Act and that is there any possibility of harmonious reading of Sections 79 and 81 of IT Act and Section 51 of Copyright Act? The Delhi High Court held that both under Copyright Act 1957 and Information Technology Act 2000 "actual" knowledge and not just suspicion is essential to fasten liability. Copyright Act does not specifically mention or define internet intermediaries nor does it lay down any special protection except as provided for under Section 52 of Act. Thus, Appellant falls within Section 2(1)(w) of IT Act, and qualifies as an intermediary/Internet service provider because it acts as a "conduit"/portal for information where users can upload and view content. It acts

---

140. For critical discussion on relation between Copyright Act and Information Technology Act, *see*, *B.N. Firos* v. *State of Kerala*, (2018) 9 SCC 220: 2018 (5) SCALE 155.
141. AIR 2017 SC 150: (2017) 2 SCC 18.
142. 2017 (69) PTC 1 (Del): 236 (2017) DLT 478.

as a service provider by allowing users to upload, stream, share and view content which it hosts. MySpace clearly places an embargo on its users from uploading content in which they do not possess relevant rights and at same time gives content owners option of notifying them in event that they find content hosted on its website is without due license.

It claims immunity from liability, as an intermediary following due diligence as well complying with provisions of Section 79 of IT Act.[143] Under circumstances, it is difficult to conceive how one would pose a barrier in applicability of other. Further true intent of Section 79 of IT Act, is to ensure that in terms of globally accepted standards of intermediary liabilities and to further digital trade and economy, an intermediary is granted certain protections. Section 79 of IT Act, is neither an enforcement provision nor does it list out any penal consequences for non-compliance. It sets up a scheme where intermediaries have to follow certain minimum standards to avoid liability; it provides for an affirmative defence and not blanket immunity from liability. Section 79 provides an affirmative defence to an intermediary as long as it complies with associated conditions. Also Sections 79 and 81 of IT Act, and Section 51(a)(ii) of Copyright Act, have to be read harmoniously. Thus, the Court further observed:

> Accordingly, proviso to Section 81 of IT Act, does not preclude affirmative defence of safe harbor for an intermediary in case of copyright actions. Section 51(a)(ii) of Act, in case of internet intermediaries contemplates actual knowledge and not general awareness. Additionally, to impose liability on an intermediary, conditions under Section 79 of IT Act, have to be fulfilled.[144]

143. For interpretation of Section 79 of the Information Technology Act 2000, see, *Christian Louboutin SAS* v. *Nakul Bajaj*, 2018 (76) PTC 508 (Del): 253 (2018) DLT 728.
144. See, *Myspace Inc.* v. *Super Cassettes Industries Ltd.*, 2017 (69) PTC 1 (Del): 236 (2017) DLT 478.

4

Works in Which Copyright Subsists

ABSTRACT

Section 13 of the Copyright Act, 1957 stipulates the works in which copyright subsists. However, the concept of "originality" is a debatable issue in determining subsistence of copyright. Similarly, idea and expression dichotomy, copyright in common property and actual events, determination of literary work including computer software and databases, dramatic, musical and artistic works, cinematograph films and sound recording are certain controversial issues that are determined and re-determined by the courts from time to time. Besides these, the question remains open for consideration whether copyright subsists beyond Section 13? This Chapter demonstrates aforementioned issues.

STATUTORY SCHEME

Works in which copyright subsists have been controversial over time. Section 13 of the Copyright Act, 1957 enumerates six categories of works are eligible for protection. Accordingly all "original" literary, dramatic, musical and artistic works as well as cinematographic films and sound recordings are eligible for protection under the Act.[1] However, in the case of a cinematograph film and a sound recording, such protection is not available if a substantial part of it is an infringement of copyright in any other work.[2] This limitation has been placed to safeguard the rights of authors in individual works from being appropriated and exploited illegitimately. Further, the Section states that the copyright in a cinematograph film or a record shall not affect the separate copyright in any individual work, in respect of which

1. *See, Vinod Kumar Gupta* v. *State of U.P.*, 2019 (106) ACC 378; *Novex Communication Pvt. Ltd.* v. *Lemon Tree Hotels Ltd.*, 2019 II AD (Delhi) 644; *Gurukrupa Mech Tech Pvt. Ltd.* v. *State of Gujarat,* (2018) 4 GLR 3324; *ICSAC v. Aditya Pandey*, (2017) 11 SC C437: 2016 (9) SCALE 89; *Institute for Inner Studies* v. *Charlotte Anderson*, 2014 (1) MIPR 129: 2014 (57) PTC 228; *Adai Mehra Production Pvt. Ltd.* v. *Mr. Sumeet P. Mehra,* 2013 (3) ABR 1273; *Syndicate* v. *B.D. Bhandari,* 185 (2011) DLT 346; *Rupalli R. Shah* v. *Adani Wilmer Ltd.*, 2012 (52) PTC 305 (Bom); *Anil Kumar* v. *State of Punjab,* 2012 (51) PTC 159 (P&H); *Radio Today Broadcasting Ltd.* v. *Indian Performing Rights Society Ltd.*, 2009 (39) PTC 431 (Cal).
2. Copyright Act 1957, Section 13(3). *See, Super Cassettes Industries Limited* v. *Mr. Chintamani Rao*, 2012 (49) PTC 1 (Del). Justine Pila, "Copyright and Its Categories of Original Works," 30(2) *Oxford Journal of Legal Studies* (2010) pp. 229–254.

or a substantial part of which the film or sound record is made.[3] This enables the author of individual works, i.e., literary, dramatic, artistic and musical work to realise his rights in the work as he chooses. His control over the work is not automatically lost with the incorporation of his work into a film or a record. Section 13 of the Copyright Act, 1957 is reproduced below:

"Section 13: Works in which copyright subsists—(1) Subject to the provisions of this section and the other provisions of this Act, copyright shall subsist throughout India in the following classes of works, that is to say—

(a) Original literary, dramatic, musical and artistic works;
(b) Cinematograph films; and
(c) [Sound recording][4].

(2) Copyright shall not subsist in any work specified in sub-section (1) other than a work to which the provisions of section 40 or section 41, apply, unless,—

(i) in the case of a published work, the work is first published in India, or where the work is first published outside India the author is at the date of such publication, or in a case where the author was dead at that date, was at the time of his death a citizen of India;
(ii) in the case of an unpublished work other than [work of architecture][5], the author is at the date of the making of the work a citizen of India or domiciled in India; and
(iii) in the case of [work of architecture][6], the work is located in India,

EXPLANATION—In the case of a work of joint authorship, the conditions conferring copyright specified in this sub-section shall be satisfied by all the authors of the work.

(3) Copyright shall not subsist—

(a) in any cinematograph film if a substantial part of the film is an Infringement of the copyright in any other work;
(b) in any [sound recording][7] made in respect of a literary, dramatic musical work, If in making the [sound recording][8], copyright III such work has been infringed.

(4) The copyright in a cinematograph film or a [sound recording][9] shall not affect the separate copyright in any work in respect of which or a substantial part of which, the film, or, as the case may be, the [sound recording][10] is made.

(5) In the case of [work of architecture][11], copyright shall subsist only III the artistic character and design and shall not extend to processes or methods of construction."

---

3. *Ibid.*, Section 13(4). *See*, *Indian Performing Right Society Ltd.* v. *Aditya Pandey*, MIPR 2012 (2) 140: 2012 (50) PTC 460 (Del).
4. Substituted by Act 38 of 1994, Section 2, for "record" (w.e.f. 10-5-1995).
5. Substituted by Act 38 of 1994, Section 2, for "architectural work of art" (w.e.f. 10-5-1995).
6. Substituted by Act 38 of 1994, Section 2, for "architectural work of art" (w.e.f. 10-5-1995).
7. Substituted by Act 38 of 1994, Section 2, for "record" (w.e.f. 10-5-1995).
8. Substituted by Act 38 of 1994, Section 2, for "record" (w.e.f. 10-5-1995).
9. Substituted by Act 38 of 1994, Section 2, for "record" (w.e.f. 10-5-1995).
10. Substituted by Act 38 of 1994, Section 2, for "record" (w.e.f. 10-5-1995).
11. Substituted by Act 38 of 1994, Section 2, for "architectural work of art" (w.e.f. 10-5-1995).

Section 38 of the Copyright Act, 1957 enumerates another two categories of works which are to be eligible for protection, namely, video film and a performer's performance. What are the rights which can be the subject matters of a copyright under the Act are contained in Sections 13 and 38.[12] Thus, a conjoint reading of Sections 13 and 38 shows that a copyright subsists in eight classes of works, i.e., literary work, dramatic work, musical work, artistic work, a cinematograph film including video film, a sound recording, and a performer's performance.[13] This position of law was upheld by the Bombay High Court in *Wellington Cinema* v. *The Performing Right Society,*[14] where the Court held that the performing right of the author does not expire with the incorporation of his work into a sound record, unless it is expressly assigned. But in *Eastern India Motion Pictures Association* v. *Indian Performing Right Society Ltd.,*[15] the Calcutta High Court held that the performing rights of the author of a musical work stands defeated upon permission of it to be incorporated into a film. This decision severally hampers the right of thc author in realising their genuine public performance rights as recognised by the Act. Unfortunately the Supreme Court too confirmed this holding.[16] Thus, today if the music composer or lyricist agrees to incorporate his work in a cinematograph film, the author is not in a position to enjoy the public performance right as long as his work is shown to the public as part of the film. Thus, his right to collect royalty when the film was shown in the theatre, Cable TV, internet, etc. are lost by this decision. The Calcutta High Court continued this anomaly when it abided by the wrong precedent set by the Superior Court in a similar issue in *Eastern India Motion Pictures* v. *Performing Right Society Ltd.*[17] The objective of copyright is not to create monopoly in ideas but to prevent unlawful reproduction and dealing with the manner and material form in which "ideas are expressed".[18] In *Eastern Book Company* v. *D.B. Modak,*[19] the Supreme Court goes on to hold that,

> The primary objective of copyright is not to reward the labour of authors, but to promote the progress of science and useful arts. To this end, copyright assures authors the right to their original expression but encourages others to build freely upon the ideas and information conveyed by a work.

What is protected is the expression of thought, the form, formulation, order, plan or arrangement of presentation as testifying to the investment by the author of mental faculties, skills, competence, craftsmanship, knowledge, labour and capital in the production of any work, in other words, the requirement of originality is an elliptical way of expressing the idea that the work should not be a substantial copy of another work; it should not amount to piracy of another's skill, competence, craftsmanship, labour and capital.[20] In this sense,

---

12. *See, Sanjay Kumar Gupta* v. *Sony Pictures Networks India P. Ltd.,* AIR 2018 Delhi 169: 2018 (75) PTC 562 (Del).
13. *Star India Pvt. Ltd.* v. *Piyush Agarwal,* MIPR 2013 (1) 201: 2013 (54) PTC 222 (Del).
14. AIR 1937 Bom 472: 1937 (39) BOM LR 654.
15. AIR 1974 Cal 257.
16. *Indian Performing Right Society Ltd.* v. *Eastern Indian Motion Pictures Association,* AIR 1977 SC 1443: (1977) 2 SCC 820.
17. AIR 1978 Cal 477.
18. *See, R.G. Anand* v. *Delux Films,* AIR 1978 SC 1613: (1978) 4 SCC 118; *N.T. Raghunathan* v. *All India Reporter Ltd.,* AIR 1971 Bom 48; *J.N. Bagga* v. *All India Reporter Ltd.,* AIR 1969 Bom 302: 1969 (71) BOM LR 409; *V. Govindam* v. *E.M. Gopalkrishna Kone,* AIR 1955 Mad 391.
19. AIR 2008 SC 809: (2008) 1 SCC 1.
20. *See, Deepak Printers* v. *Forward Stationary Mart,* (1976) 17 GLR 338.

copyright law protects the author against dishonest and wilful misappropriation or theft of the author's efforts. There is copyright in translation of a work.[21] However, the syllabi issued in a circular by the Board of Secondary Education of the State, containing guidelines of authors and publishers of textbooks cannot be taken as original work being the product of labour, skill and capital of some men engaged by the Board.[22] The work of a cine artist, his performance as an actor in a cinematograph film does not fall within the definition of "cinematograph film" to be found in Section 2(f), and hence, is not protected under this Act. It is the cinematograph film that enjoys protection along with its sound track.[23]

There are four categories of works eligible for copyright protection under the umbrella of "original" under Section 13 of the Act. The first sight, the requirement of originality seems not to attach to films and records; but this omission is infelicitously made good by the language of clause (3)[24] of the Section 13. Literary, dramatic and cinematograph works are defined inclusive by the Act whereas artistic, musical works and sound recording are exhaustively defined by Section 2. These differences in the way in which the definition clause has defined different category of works have led (as we shall note later) to some crucial differences in respect of the range of copyright protection. The requirement of "originality" in Indian law, as elsewhere, does not refer to ideas but rather to the manner and material forms of their expression.[25] The objective of copyright, it has been stressed in India, is not to "create monopoly in ideas"; rather, the protection aims at prevention of unlawful reproduction of dealing with the manner and material form in which ideas are expressed. Consequently, "originality" also refers not to "novelty" or "creativity" in ideas but only to the manner and material form of their presentation. What is protected is the expression of thought—the form, formulation, order, plan or arrangement of presentation—as testifying to the investment by the author of mental faculties, skills, competence, craftsmanship, knowledge, labour and capital in the production of any work. In other words, the requirement of originality is an elliptical way of expressing the idea that the work should not be a substantial copy of another work; or, more colourful (but less precisely) it should not amount to piracy of another's skill, competence, craftsmanship labour and capital. In a sense, copyright law protects the author against dishonest and wilful misappropriation or theft of the author's works.

THE WORD "ORIGINAL" IN SECTION 13

The word "original" in Section 13 of the Copyright Act, 1957 is prefixed to literary, dramatic, musical and artistic works and not to cinematograph films and sound recordings as they are works made by making use of literary, dramatic, musical and artistic works. A narrow copyright

21. *See, M/s. Blackwood and Sons Ltd.* v. *A.N. Parusuraman,* AIR 1959 Mad 410.
22. *Nag Book House* v. *State of West Bengal,* AIR 1982 Cal 245: 87 CWN 107.
23. *Fortune Films International* v. *Dev Anand,* AIR 1979 Bom 17: 1978 (80) BOM LR 263.
24. According to clause (3) of the Section 13 if a substantial part of the film is an infringement of copyright in any other work, and if a record made in respect of literary, dramatic or artistic work infringes such work, then no copyright shall subsist in such film or record. *See, John Wiley and Sons Inc.* v. *International Book Store,* 2010 (43) PTC 496 (Del).
25. *See, R.G. Anand* v. *Delux Films,* AIR 1978 SC 1613: (1978) 4 SCC 118; *N.T. Raghunathan* v. *All India Reporter Ltd.,* AIR 1971 Bom 48.

protection is accorded to a film and sound recordings than for literary, dramatic or artistic work.[26] Thus, the requirement of originality is absent for claiming copyright in cinematograph films and sound recordings. The position in the case of literary, dramatic musical or artistic works seems to be different.[27] In *Music Broadcast Private Ltd.* v. *Indian Performing Right Society Ltd.*,[28] the Bombay High Court observed:

> A sound recording must be distinguished from, on the one hand, the material objects on which the sound is recorded, and, on the other hand, the underlying musical composition, or dramatic or literary work that is recorded and transposed into aural form by the sound recording. Clearly, a sound recording copyright vest no proprietary rights in the material object as such.

It undoubtedly is the policy of the law to protect the "original author", and to secure to him the benefit of any enrichment unjustly made by the piracy of his work.[29] But the word "original" is not defined by the legislatures in UK, USA and India. *Black's Law Dictionary*[30] defines originality as "the quality or state of being the product of independent creation and having a minimum degree of creativity." It further says that although "originality is a requirement for copyright protection but this is a lesser standard than that of novelty in patent law." However, the courts are often faced with the facts where they have to determine whether the literary, dramatic, musical and artistic works are original or not. The judiciary thus formulated tests to determine originality of work as and when the cases appeared before them. With the concept of "originality" an inference drawn that originality plays a vital role in the copyright law and nothing else can defeat it. Only original works has to be protected as an intellectual property. The sole reason behind being anyone can copy a work but it is hard to find original ideas into expressions. Nevertheless, the concept of "originality" is a foundational concept of copyright law in England, America and India which need detail deliberation.[31]

Concept of Originality in England

English courts have interpreted the concept of "originality" in a number of copyright cases and laid down the standard of originality for the purpose of copyright law.[32] The issue of

26. *See, Maroti* v. *The State of Maharashtra*, 2018 ALLMR (Cri) 4460; *Urmi Juvekar Chiang* v. *Global Broadcast News Limited,* MIPR 2007 (2) 223: 2008 (36) PTC 373 (Bom).
27. *See, Dart Industries Inc.* v. *Techno Plast*, 2016 (67) PTC 457(Del): 233 (2016) DLT 1; *Star India Private Ltd.* v. *Leo Burnett (India) Private Limited,* 2003 (27) PTC 81 (Bom): 2003 (2) Bom CR 655. *See also, Zee Entertainment Enterprises Ltd.* v. *Mr. Gajendra Singh*, MIPR 2007 (3) 299: 2008 (36) PTC 53 (Bom).
28. MIPR 2011 (3) 84: 2011 (47) PTC 587 (Bom).
29. *Super Cassettes Industries Limited* v. *Bathla Cassette Industries Pvt. Ltd.*, 107 (2003) DLT 91: 2003 (27) PTC 280 (Del); See also *Gramophone Company of India Ltd.* v. *Super Cassette Industries Ltd.*, 2010 (44) PTC 541 (Del): ILR (2010) Supp. (5) Delhi 656.
30. (7th ed.).
31. For detail discussion see Palash Soni, "Judicial Approach to the Concept of 'Originality'," 4(1) *The World Journal on Juristic Polity* (2018) pp. 2394–5044; Andreas Rahmatian, "Originality in UK Copyright Law: The Old 'Skill and Labour' Doctrine under Pressure," 44(1) *International Review of Intellectual Property and Competition Law* (2013) pp. 4–34.
32. For example, *Macmillan Publishers Ltd.* v. *Thomas Reed Publications Ltd.* (1993) FSR 455; *Ladbroke (Football) Ltd.* v. *Willian Hill (Football) Ltd.* (1964) 1 WLR 273; *Macmillan & Co. Ltd.* v. *K & J Cooper* (1923) 93 LJPC 113: 1924 PC 75.

"originality" was examined in detailed in *University of London Press Ltd.* v. *University Tutorial Press Ltd.,*[33] in 1916. This case involved a situation where the University of London assigned to the plaintiff, the copyright in examination papers set by it for school matriculation examinations. The defendants published a number of these papers without permission. The publications of the defendants, however, included criticisms and model answers. One of the issues in this case was what is "originality"?

The Court examined the scope of copyright ability under the Copyright Act, 1911. Section 1(1) of the Act which provided that copyright is available in "every original literary, dramatic, musical and artistic work. Thus, for the plaintiff to successfully get a relief he must be able to establish that his work was "original" and that if felt within "literary", "dramatic", or "artistic" work. The court went into an attempt to find a definition of literary work. It looked into the 1842 Act which protected "books". The Court commented that the purpose of the 1911 Act was to restrict the scope of copyright ability, since many things which had no pretensions of literary style had acquired copyright, (under the 1842 Act), such as list of fox hands and hunting days, and trade catalogues, the words "literary works", "cover work" which are expressed in printing or writing, irrespective of the question whether the quality or the style is high. The word "literary" refers to any written or printed matters. Papers set by examiners are literary work. The court then went into the definition of "originality" and held that an "original" work must not be copied from another work, but that it should originate from the author. The implication of this is that the constituent parts of the work themselves need not be new in any sense and that the work as a whole can be made up from commonplace and pre-existing materials. In this case Paterson J. went further to lay down that:

> The word 'original' does not in this connection mean that the work must be an expression of original or inventive thought. Copyright Acts are not concerned with the originality of ideas, but with the expression of thought, and, in the case of a 'literary work', with the expression of thought in print or writing. The originality that is required relates to the expression of the thought. But the Act does not require that the expression must be in an original or novel form, but the work must not be copied from another work—that it should originate from the author. In the present case it was not suggested that any of the [examination] papers were copied. [The examiners] proved that they had thought out the questions which they set, and that they had made notes of memoranda for future questions and drew on those notes for the purposes of the questions which they set. The papers which they prepared originated from themselves, and were, within the meaning of the Act, original.[34]

Thus, the *University of London Press* evolved the principle that the word "original" requires only that the work should not be copied but should originate from author. In certain cases, English Courts equated "originality" with the degree of skill, labour and judgement that went into the creation of the work. This approach is called "sweat of the brow" approach. In *Ladbroke (Football) Ltd.* v. *William Hill (Football) Ltd.*, the court held that the requirement of originality means that the product must originate from the author in the sense that it is

33. For example, *Macmillan Publishers Ltd.* v. *Thomas Reed Publications Ltd.* (1993) FSR 455; *Ladbroke (Football) Ltd.* v. *Willian Hill (Football) Ltd.* (1964) 1 WLR 273; *Macmillan & Co. Ltd.* v. *K & J Cooper* (1923) 93 LJPC 113: 1924 PC 75.

34. *Ibid.*, at pp. 608–609. This concept has been followed subsequently in *Ladbroke (Football) Ltd.* v. *Willian Hill (Football) Ltd.* (1964) 1 WLR 273; in *Duriròn Company Inc* v. *Hugh Jennings & Co. Ltd.*, (1984) FSR 1.

the result of a substantial degree of skill, industry or experience employed by him. Further, in *LB (Plastics) Ltd.* v. *Swish Products Ltd.,*[35] the Court held that the question of originality depended upon the amount of labour, skill and judgement expended on the creation of the work.[36] Hence, the requirement for "skill, labour and judgement" is another test to be used to determine whether the thing concerned is "original". The abovementioned English "sweat of the brow" approach has become a standard all over the World in the process of judicial determination regarding whether a work is copyrightable or not. In *Syndicate of the Press of the University of Cambridge* v. *Chancellor Masters and Scholars of the University of Oxford,*[37] the Delhi High Court rightly summaries the English position on the issue of originality as thus:

> Although a number of interpretations have been given to the term, there are certain points on which agreement seems to have been firmly established. Primary among these points are two basic concepts, First that the work must not be merely a copy of a previous work, and secondly that the work is the result of the investment of individual skill, judgment or labour.

However, over the time it has been criticised that this English "sweat of the brow" approach has failed to include "the creativity" the most importation criteria to determine "originality" in copyright law. On close examination of the English copyright law it shows that the concept "originality" does not require novelty or a high degree of inventiveness, and athletes devote time, effort, skill and labour to refining their performances. Thus, in *Infopaq International* v. *Danske Dagblades Forenig,*[38] it was held that the English test of originality might need to be slightly reshaped, at least to the extent that a work can no longer be exclusively dependent on skill and labour. Under the 'author's own intellectual creation' test, a production which is solely dictated by its technical function does not embed the modicum of creativity and individuality required to be original. The choreographed sports reflect their author's personality, and endow free and creative choices notwithstanding the operation of the game rules and the goal of winning a competition.[39]

Concept of Originality in America

The question of originality, the threshold standard of qualification for copyright protection, is at the core of copyrightability in the United States of America too. The originality is the Constitutional requirement under the copyright clause of the American Constitution and is

35. (1979) RPC 551.
36. *See also*, *Biotrading and Financing* v. *Biohit Ltd.* (1998) FSR 109. In this case the *Court of Appeal* said that the question is whether sufficient independent labour, skill and judgement had been expanded in the creation and this is a matter of fact. *See also*, *Guid* v. *Eskandar Ltd.* (2201) FSR 645.
37. 185 (2011) DLT 346.
38. [2009] ECR I-6569.
39. For critical discussion, *see*, Khanuengnit Khaosaeng, Wands, Sandals and the Wind: Creativity as a Copyright Exception 36(4) European Intellectual Property Review (2014) pp. 238–249 at p. 239; R. Keith Sawyer, *Explaining Creativity: The Science of Human Innovation* (Oxford University Press, 2012) at p. 3; Andreas Rahmatian, *Copyright and Creativity: The Making of Property Rights in Creative Works* (Edward Elgar, 2011) 199; Lawrence Lessig, *Free Culture: How Big Media uses Technology and the Law to Lock Down Culture and Control Creativity* (The Penguin Press, 2004) at p. 199.

a *sine qua non* of the copyrightability. The Courts in the America have also interpreted the concept "originality" in a liberal sense in copyright law initially. Nevertheless, controversy has arisen over the limits of "originality" itself recently as soon as the Court held that for copyright protection a "minimal degree of creativity"[40] is required.

In 1903, *Bleistein* v. *Donaldson Lightographing Co.,*[41] the US Supreme Court held, however, that copyright was not limited to the fine arts and that it was outside both copyright law and the competence of courts to attempt to assess the artistic merits of original creations. The Court articulated a broad concept of originality, refusing to weigh the creative or artistic merits of lithographs against their more mundane commercial functions. As long as the work fits the statutory category of copyrightable matter and as long as the claimant originated it, there is no bar to copyrightability. A work has originality if it is "one man's alone".

In 1951, Justice Frank in *Alfred Bell & Co.* v. *Catalda Fine Arts, Inc.,*[42] observed that "original" in reference to a copyrighted work means that the particular work "owes it origin to the author". No large measure of novelty is necessary. The Court held that copyrightability of reproductions is based on the fact that the copyist has originated the reproduction, if nothing else. Although the underlying subject matter is not, of course, protected—since others are free to copy the original—the copyist is protected against those who might attempt to gain a "free ride" by simply reproducing the reproduction instead of investing the effort required to copy the original. Subsequently, the US Supreme Court in *Twentieth Century Music Corp.* v. *Aiken,*[43] held that the objective of copyright law is to encourage creativity. Therefore, immediate effect of the copyright law is to secure a fair return for an author's creative labor. But the ultimate aim is, by this incentive, to stimulate artistic creativity for the general public good.

In the United States, the judicial trend, to trace out the elements of originality in a given work was to focus on the "sweat of the brow" test or the industriousness. However, there has been a consistent shift from this approach towards a test based on "creativity". In 1991, in *Feist Publications, Inc.* v. *Rural Telephone Service Co.,*[44] there is a glaring example of this shift wherein the Supreme Court of the United States was categorically observed that "as a constitutional matter, copyright protects only those constituent elements of a work that possess more than a *de minimis quantum* of creativity. The Court further held that the originality requirement in copyright law is the Constitutional mandates some minimal degree of creativity and an author who claims infringement must prove the existence of intellectual production, of thought, and conception. Thus, in US there is a respectable body of judicial opinion holding that some kind of creative or artistic quality must present for copyright protection.

---

40. *See, Feist Publications* v. *Rural Telephone Service Co.*, 499 US 340 (1991). For detail discussion, *see,* Eleonora Rosati, "Why Originality in Copyright is not and Should not be a Meaningless Requirement," 13(8) *Journal of Intellectual Property Law and Practice* (2018) pp. 597–598; Teresa Scassa, "Original Facts: Skill, Judgment, and the Public Domain," 51 *McGIll Law Journal* (2006) pp. 253–278; Howard B. Abrams, "Originality and Creativity In Copyright Law," 55(2) *Law and Contemporary Problems* (1992) pp. 1–44.
41. 188 US 239 23 S. Ct 298: 47 L. Ed. 460 (1903).
42. 191 F. 2d 99: 102 (2nd Cir. 1951).
43. 422 U.S. 151 (1975).
44. 499 U.S. 340 (1991).

Concept of Originality in India

Development of the Concept in India

Skill, Judgment and Labour Approach

The Indian judiciary also analysed the concept of "originality" in a number of cases[45] on copyright law. The approaches of the Indian Courts are almost same with the English and American Courts. However, the Indian judiciary relying on the decisions of English and American Courts developed the concept of originality in India for copyright law. In *Macmillan Company*[46] case the Court held that the word original does not mean that the work must be the expression of original or invented thoughts. But the work must not be copied from other works. Any new and original plan arrangement or compilation of material will entitle the author to copyright therein whether the materials themselves be old or new. That whatever by his own skill, labour and judgments writes a new work may have a copyright therein unless it be directly copied or evasively imitated from another's work. This decision was primarily based on the *University of London Press* case of England. In this case the court examined the definition of "originality" and held that an "original" work must not be copied from another work, but that it should originate from the author. *Paterson J.* went further to lay down that:

> The word 'original' does not in this connection mean that the work must be an expression of original or inventive thought. Copyright Acts are not concerned with the originality of ideas, but with the expression of thought, and, in the case of a 'literary work', with the expression of thought in print or writing. The originality that is required relates to the expression of the thought. But the Act does not require that the expression must be in an original or novel form, but the work must not be copied from another work—that it should originate from the author. In the present case it was not suggested that any of the [examination] papers were copied. [The examiners] proved that they had thought out the questions which they set, and that they had made notes of memoranda for future questions and drew on those notes for the purposes of the questions which they set. The papers which they prepared originated from themselves, and were, within the meaning of the Act, original.

Subsequently, Madras High Court in *C. Cunniah and Co.* v. *Balraj and Co.*[47] case evolved the principle that the use of original skill or labour is essential to acquire copyright in a work. In this case, the appellants are a firm of merchants carrying on business in Madras city in pictures, picture frames, etc. In 1932, one Shri T.M. Subramanian drew a picture of Lord Balasubramaniyan and gave it the title of Mayur Priya. On July 13, 1938, he assigned the copyright in this picture to the appellant firm. The appellant firm got this picture registered in 1952. The appellants' case is that the picture "Bala Murugun" painted and sold by the respondent is a colourable imitation of the picture "Mayur Priya" in which the appellant's firm owns the copyright. They held that it is well-established that, in order to obtain copyright,

---

45. See, *Marico Ltd.* v. *Jagit Kaur*, 2018 (74) PTC 384 (Del): 248 (2018) DLT 623; *Fateh Singh Mehta* v. *O.P. Singhal,* AIR 1990 Raj 8: 1989 WLN (UC) 522; *R.G. Anand* v. *Delux Films,* AIR 1978 SC 1613: (1978) 4 SCC 118; *Mishra Bandhu Karyalaya* v. *Shivratanlal Koshal,* AIR 1970 MP 261: ILR [1973] MP 88; *C. Cunniah and Co.* v. *Balraj and Co.,* AIR 1961 Mad 3: (1960) 1 MLJ 53; *Macmillan Company Ltd.* v. *K. & J. Cooper,* AIR 1924 PC 75.
46. *Macmillan Company Ltd.* v. *K. & J. Cooper,* AIR 1924 PC 75: 1924 (26) BOM LR 292.
47. AIR 1961 Mad 111.

production for literary, dramatic, musical and artistic works, the subject dealt with need not to be original, nor the ideas expressed be something novel. What is required is the expenditure of original skill or labour in execution and not originally of thought. Thus, though pictorial representation of Lord Balasubramanyan in a human form is a subject which is common to everyone, still, if a picture of Lord Balasubramanyan drawn by an artist made of conventional ideas as to his posture, his form, the ornaments he wears, the vahanam he uses and other matters, the picture produced is still the result of skill, and labour of the artist and it certainly entitles him to claim copyright in the production of his labour.

Again, the Madhya Pradesh High Court in *Mishra Bandhu Karyalaya* v. *Shivratanlal Koshal*[48] held that originality and registration is *sine qua non* for the right to copyright in any work. In this case the Court has observed that under the Copyright Act, 1957, it appears that under Sections 13 and 45, the registration of book with the Registrar of Copyright is a condition. A copyright in a book now is only seemed if it is an original compilation and has been duly registered according to the provision of the 1957 Act. Once it is so registered, the author is deemed to acquire property rights in the book. The right arising from the registration of the book can be the subject matter of civil or criminal remedy, so that, without it, the author can have no rights, nor remedies in spite of the fact that his work is an original work.

Under the Indian Copyright Act, 1957, copyright subsists only on "original literary, dramatic, musical and artistic" work. This requirement of originality does not refer to an idea, but to the manner and material form of their expression.[49] In other words, the requirement of originality is an elliptical way of expressing the idea that the work should not be a substantial copy of another work; it should not amount to piracy of another's skill, competence, craftsmanship, labour and capital.[50] The extent or amount of originality in expression or material form may be very small, but that small amount is protected by law.[51] In this sense, copyright law protects the author against dishonest and wilful misappropriation or theft of the author's efforts. In *Marico Ltd.* v. *Jagit Kaur*,[52] the Delhi High Court observed:

> Copyright registration can only be granted to original artistic works. Registration of copyright cannot be granted to works which are a reproduction or imitation of other original works. If any person has obtained registration of copyright of a work which is not an original work under Section 13 of the Copyright Act, such a registration or entry made in the register would be an entry wrongly made.

In *R.G. Anand* v. *Delux Films*,[53] the Supreme Court went on to analyse the concept of originality while deciding whether the film named "New Delhi" infringed the copyright in the play "Hum Hindustani". There were considerable similarities between the play and the film as the central theme of both was based on the evils of provincialism. The Plaintiff, the author of the play had alleged the film as an adaptation of the play and as such an infringement of his copyright in the play. The Supreme Court while deciding the case observed thus:

---

48. AIR 1970 MP 261: 1970 (15) MPLJ 475.
49. *See*, *STAR India Private Limited* v. *Department of Industrial Policy*, 2018 (2) CTC 113; *R.G. Anand* v. *Delux Films*, AIR 1978 SC 1913: (1978) 4 SCC 118; *N.T. Raghunathan* v. *All India Reporter Ltd.*, AIR 1971 Bom 48; *J.N. Bagga* v. *All India Reporter Ltd.*, AIR 1969 Bom 302: 1969 (71) BOMLR 409; *V Govindam* v. *E.M. Gopalkrishna Kone,* AIR 1955 Mad 391.
50. *See*, *Deepak Printers* v. *Forward Stationary Mart* (1976) 17 GLR 338.
51. *See*, *V. Govindam* v. *E.M. Gopalkrishna Kone,* AIR 1955 Mad 391.
52. 2018 (74) PTC 384 (Del): 248 (2018) DLT 623.
53. AIR 1978 SC 1613: (1978) 4 SCC 118.

> An idea, principle, theme or subject matter or historical or legendary facts being common property cannot be the subject matter of copyright of a particular person. It is always open to any person to choose an idea as a subject matter and develop it in his own manner and give expression to the idea by treating it differently from others. Where two writers write on the same subject, similarities are bound to occur because the central idea of both are the same, but the similarities and coincidences by themselves cannot lead to the irresistible in Prince of plagiarism or piracy. Take for instance the great poet and dramatist Shakespeare, most of whose plays are based on Greek-Roman and British mythology or legendary stories like Merchant of Venice, Hamlet, Romeo and Juliet, Julius Ceaser, etc. But the treatment of the subject by Shakespeare in each of his dramas is so fresh, so different, so full of poetic exuberance, elegance and erudition and so novel in character as a result of which the end product becomes an original in itself. In fact, the power and passion of his expression, the uniqueness, eloquence and excellence of his style and pathos and bathos of the dramas become peculiar to Shakespeare and leaves precious little of the original theme adopted by him. It will thus be preposterous to level a charge of plagiarism against the great play right. In fact, throughout his original thinking, ability and incessant labour Shakespeare has converted an old idea into a new one, so that each of his dramas constitutes a masterpiece of English Literature. It has been rightly said that 'every drama of Shakespeare is an extended metaphor'.[54]

Thus, the defendant's work ceases to be an original one only if he adopts not only the idea in the copyright work but also the manner, arrangement, situation to situation, scene to scene with minor changes here and there. Here since the film had a broader perspective and because of the dissimilarities in scenic arrangement and presentation, the Court reasoned the film as original work and non-violative of copyright in the play. Because, the law protects originality of expression but not originality of the central idea, not merely because of the balancing of two conflicting polices. The two polices are as follows: The first is that the law must protect originality of artistic work, thereby allowing artists to reap the fruits of their labour and stopping unscrupulous pirates from enjoying those fruits. The second policy is that the protection must not become an over protection, thus, curbing down future artistic activity. If mere plots and characters were to be protected by copyrights, no original artist could write anything "original" at all, on a similar plot or on similar characters.[55]

New Dimension

It is clear from the above discussion that the Supreme Court of India has found many occasions to reiterate that the test of originality in India is same as in the UK which is based on the "skill, judgment and labour."[56] Recently, in 2004 in *CCH Canadian Ltd.* v. *Law Society*

---

54. This proposition of law has been applied subsequently in *M. Radhakrishnan* v. *Surabhi Publications*, MIPR 2017 (1) 125: 2016 (3) KLJ 321; *Narendra Mohan Singh* v. *Ketan Mehta*, 2015 (64) PTC 260 (Bom); *Shuhaib Hameed* v. *James Albert*, 2015 (3) KHC 343; *Twentieth Century Fox Film Corporation* v. *Zee Telefilms Ltd.*, 2012 (51) PTC 465 (Del): MIPR 2012 (2) 377.
55. *Barbara Taylor Bradford* v. *Sahara Media Entertainment* (2004) ILR 1 Cal 15: 2004 (28) PTC 474 (Cal).
56. *See*, J.K. Das, "New Dimensions of Intellectual Property Rights in India", 3(2) *Pragyaan: Journal of Law* (2013) pp. 11–33. *See also, Navigators Logistics Ltd.* v. *Kashif Qureshi*, 2018 (76) PTC 564 (Del): 254 (2018) DLT 307; *Tech Plus Media Private Ltd.* v. *Jyoti Janda*, 2014 (60) PTC 121 (Del); *Syndicate* v. *B.D. Bhandari*, 2011 (47) PTC 244 (Del): 185 (2011) DLT 346; *Indiana Gratings* v. *Anand Udyog Fabricators*, 2009 (39) PTC 609 (Bom); *Tech Plus Media Private Ltd.* v. *Jyoti Janda*, 2008 (38) PTC 308 (Del); *Reckeweg and Co. Gmbh.* v. *Adven Biotech Pvt. Ltd.*, 2008 (38) PTC 308 (Del).

of Upper Canada,[57] the Supreme Court of Canada has noticed the competing views on the meaning of "original" in copyright law wherein some courts have held that a work which has originated from an author and is more than a mere copy of a work, is sufficient to give copyright. Thus, in *Eastern Book Company* v. *D.B. Modak,*[58] the Indian Supreme Court has adopted a new approach and similar to the Canadian approach unlike the English "Sweat of brow" approach. In this case, the Apex Court categorical to observe:

> Copyrighted material is that what is created by the author by his own skill, labour and investment of capital, may be it is a derivative work which gives a flavour of creativity.

In *Emergent Genetics India Pvt. Ltd.* v. *Shailendra Shivam,*[59] the Delhi High Court observed that it will be obvious that the elucidation of a DNA or protein sequence is a task frequently calling for very substantial independent skill, labour, and so on. If so, the statutory requirement of originality is satisfied. It might be objected that the sequence cannot be original because it is copied from nature, but this would be to ignore well-established law. A work may be original and copyright although derived from antecedent material, provided further independent skill, useful labour, knowledge or judgment have been bestowed on its creation.

In *Syndicate* v. *B.D. Bhandari,*[60] the Court examined two issues: Firstly, whether the appellant's work satisfies the "originate from the author" test coupled with the requirement of "skill, judgment and labour" and secondly, whether the grammar sentences and exercises in question are copyrightable expressions evolved upon the un-copyrightable ideas pertaining to the knowledge of grammatical constructs of the English language. The Court observed that while structuring the book, the author had given equal importance to the practice exercises, which form integral part of the book. Even additional exercises are included for further practice of particular areas of grammar. Some messages given to the teachers as well who could usefully made use of the book for supplementing and supporting their class room teachers. Thus, it has originated from the author and is nobody's case that the author has copied these exercises from other source. It also satisfies the test of "skill, judgment and labour".

On the issue of subsistence of copyright in relation to the nomenclature of drugs in *Dr. Reckeweg* v. *Adven Biotech Private Ltd.,*[61] the court examine the listing of the medicines in a particular fashion, the description and the curative effect compilation in a brochure. But in this case finding the plaintiffs to have failed to demonstrate how they had employed any skill, judgment and labour in describing the curative elements, let alone any creativity and in the absence of any averment as to the uniqueness of such description or intellectual creativity, it was *prima facie* held that no copyright can subsist therein.

The Indian courts time and again held that question paper set for examination is copyrightable. Thus, in *Rupendra Kashyap* v. *Jiwan Publishing House,*[62] it was held that a question paper set for the purpose of conducting examination of CBSE can form subject matter of copyright. It was also held that as per Section 17 of the Copyright Act, 1957 first owner of

---

57. 2004 (1) SCR 339 (Canada).
58. AIR 2008 SC 809: (2008) 1 SCC 1.
59. 2011 (125) DRJ 173: 2011 (47) PTC 494 (Del).
60. 2011 (47) PTC 244 (Del): 185 (2011) DLT 346.
61. (2008) 38 PTC 308 (Del).
62. 1996 (38) DRJ 81. *See also, Agarwala Publishing House* v. *Board of Higher Secondary and Intermediate Education*, AIR 1967 All 91; *Jagdish Prasad Gupta* v. *Parmeshwar Prasad Singh*, AIR 1966 Pat 33.

the copyright would be the author of the said work, viz., papers setters and merely because the paper was set for the CBSE, the CBSE does not become the owner thereof. In *Krishika Lulla* v. *Shyam Vithalrao Devkatta*,[63] the issue was whether the respondent has copyright in the title "Desi Boys" which he has given to the synopsis of the story? The Apex Court opined that a title of a work has been considered to be not fit to be the subject of copyright law as will be apparent from the cases considered later. A title by itself is in the nature of a name of a work and is not complete by itself, without the work.[64] The Court in its justification observed:

> In India copyright is a statutory right recognized and protected by the Copyright Act, 1957. It must therefore be first seen if the title "Desi Boys" can be the subject of copyright. On a plain reading of Section 13, copyright subsists in inter-alia an original literary work. In the first place a title does not qualify for being described as "work". It is incomplete in itself and refers to the work that follows. Secondly, the combination of the two words "Desi" and "Boys" cannot be said to have anything original in it. They are extremely common place words in India. It is obvious, therefore, that the title "Desi Boys", assuming it to be a work, has nothing original in it in the sense that its origin cannot be attributed to the Respondent.

Originality and Derivative Work

A derivative work consists of a contribution of original material to a pre-existing work so as to recast, transform or adapt the pre-existing work. This would include a new version of a work in the public domain and abridgement adaptation, arrangement, dramatization or translation.[65] In *Navigators Logistics Ltd.* v. *Kashif Qureshi*,[66] the Delhi High Court held that a derivative work being a collection or sequencing of already existing information and did not satisfy the standard of creativity required to qualify as a work in which copyright subsists. Therefore, the standard of creativity required to qualify as a work in which copyright subsists is higher than the standard required in cases of primary works. Literary works are either: "primary or prior works" or "secondary or derivative works". Derivative works are based on existing subject matter. Work is defined in Section 2(y) which would be a literary, dramatic, musical or artistic work; a cinematograph film; and a sound recording. Under Section 2(o), literary work would include computer programmes, tables and compilations including computer databases. In *Pearson India Education Service Pvt. Ltd.* v. *New Rubric Solutions*,[67] the Karnataka High Court held that creation of the work which has resulted from little bit of skill, labour and capital are held to be sufficient for a copyright in derivative work of an author.

The Copyright Act, 1957 generally gives copyright owners exclusive rights to reproduce the copyrighted work, to prepare derivative works, to distribute copies or phono-records of the work, to perform the copyrighted work publicly, or to display the copyrighted work publicly. The important aspect here is that what is protected is the expression of the idea, and not the

---

63. (2016) 2 SCC 521: 2016 (4) SCJ 498.
64. The Apex Court has referred to several judgments to uphold that title of a work is not copyrightable work such as *Kanungo Media (P) Ltd.* v. *RGV Film Factory*, 2007 (34) PTC 591 (Del): (2007) ILR 1 Del 112; *E.M. Forster* v. *A.N. Parasuran*, AIR 1964 Mad. 331: (1964) ILR 2 Mad 258; *Hogg* v. *Maxwell* (1866–67) LR 2 Ch. App. 307.
65. *American Express Bank Ltd.* v. *Ms. Priya Puri*, [2006 (110) FLR 1061]: (2006) IIILLJ 540 Del.
66. 2018 (76) PTC 564 (Del): 254 (2018) DLT 307. *See also*, *Reckeweg* v. *Adven Biotech Pvt. Ltd.*, 2008 (38) PTC 308 (Del).
67. AIR 2016 Kant 25: ILR 2016 KARNATAKA 2766.

idea itself. For example, a description of a machine could be copyrighted, but this would only prevent others from copying the description; it would not prevent others from writing a description of their own or from making and using the machine.[68] Now question arises: Whether the expenditure of skill, labour and capital in the production of a derivative literary work from pre-existing material in the public domain, by an author of such work, is enough to confer copyright protection in respect of such derivative work? Subject to the provisions of Section 13 of the Copyright Act, 1957 and the other provisions of the Act, there shall be a copyright throughout India in original literary work, dramatic, musical and artistic works, cinematograph films and sound recording, subject to the exceptions provided in Sub-sections (2) and (3) of Section 13. For copyright protection, all literary works have to be original as per Section 13 of the Act.

Thus, in *Rupalli R Shah* v. *Adani Wilmer Ltd.*,[69] the Bombay High Court rightly observed: "In many cases, a work is derived from an existing work. Whether in such a derivative work, a new copyright work is created, will depend on various factors, and would one of them be only skill, capital and labour expended upon it to qualify for copyright protection in a derivative literary work created from the pre-existing material in the public domain, and the required exercise of independent skill, labour and capital in its creation by the author would qualify him for the copyright protection in the derivative work. Or would it be the creativity in a derivative work in which the real position will depend upon the amount and value of the corrections and improvements, the independent skill and labour, and the creativity in the end-product is such as to create a new copyright work to make the creator of the derivative work the author of it, and if not, there will be no new-copyright work and then the original author will remain the author of the original work and the creator of the derivative work will have been the author of the alterations or the inputs put therein, for their nature will not have been such as to attract the protection under the law of copyright." In *Hawkins Cookers Limited* v. *Khaitan Pressure Cooker Pvt. Ltd.*,[70] the Calculate High Court held that "copyright is that which is created by the author or it is a derivative work which gives a creativity". In Gurukrupa Mech Tech Pvt. Ltd. v. State of Gujarat,[71] the Gujrat High Court has explained the originality requirement in derivative work thus:

> The originality requirement in derivative work is that it should originate from the author by application of substantial degree of skill, industry or experience. Precondition to copyright is that work must be produced independently and not copied from another person. Where a compilation is produced from the original work, the compilation is more than simply a rearranged copyright of original, which is often referred to as skill, judgment and or labour or capital. The copyright has nothing to do with originality or literary merit. Copyrighted material is that what is created by the author by his skill, labour and investment of capital, maybe it is derivative work.

In connection to the legal position of derivative work the Supreme Court in *Academy of General Education, Manipal* v. *B. Malini Mallya,*[72] observed:

68. *Bayer Corporation* v. *Cipla, Union of India*, 162 (2009) DLT 371: 2009 (41) PTC 634 (Del).
69. 2012 (52) PTC 305 (Bom).
70. AIR 2015 Call 50: 2015 (64) PTC 232 (Cal).
71. (2018) 4 GLR 3324.
72. AIR 2009 SC 1982: (2009) 4 SCC 256.

> The Copyright Act is not concerned with the original idea but with the expression of thought. Copyright has nothing to do with originality or literary merit. Copyrighted material is that what is created by the author by his own skill, labour and investment of capital, maybe it is a derivative work which gives a flavour of creativity. The copyright work which comes into being should be original in the sense that by virtue of selection, coordination or arrangement of pre-existing data contained in the work, a work somewhat different in character is produced by the author. On the face of the provisions of the Copyright Act, 1957, we think that the principle laid down by the Canadian Court would be applicable in copyright of the judgments of the Apex Court. We make it clear that the decision of ours would be confined to the judgments of the courts which are in the public domain as by virtue of Section 52 of the Act there is no copyright in the original text of the judgments. To claim copyright in a compilation, the author must produce the material with exercise of his skill and judgment which may not be creativity in the sense that it is novel or non-obvious, but at the same time it is not a product of merely labour and capital. The derivative work produced by the author must have some distinguishable features and flavour to raw text of the judgments delivered by the court. The trivial variation or inputs put in the judgment would not satisfy the test of copyright of an author.[73]

For the purposes of the Copyright Act, 1957, Section 14(1) enumerates what shall be a copyright which is an exclusive right, subject to the provisions of the Act, to do or authorise the doing of the acts provided in Clauses (i) to (vii) in respect of a work or any substantial part thereof in the case of a literary, dramatic or musical work, not being a computer program. Section 2(k) defines the "government work" which would be a work which is made or published by or under the direction or control of amongst others, any Court, Tribunal or other judicial authority in India.[74] By virtue of this definition, the judgments delivered by the Supreme Court would be a government work. Under Section 17(d), the Government shall, in the absence of any agreement to the contrary, be the first owner of the copyright in a government work. In the absence of any agreement to the contrary, the government shall be the first owner of the copyright in the judgments of the Supreme Court, the same being a government work under Section 2(k). Section 52(1) expressly provides that certain acts enumerated therein shall not constitute an infringement of copyright and Sub-clause (iv) of Clause (q) excludes the reproduction or publication of any judgment or order of a Court, Tribunal or other judicial authority, unless the reproduction or publication of such judgment or order is prohibited by the Court, the Tribunal or other judicial authority from copyright.[75] The judicial pronouncements of the Apex Court would be in the public domain and its reproduction or publication would not infringe the copyright. The reproduction or publication of the judgments delivered by the Supreme Court by any number of persons would not be infringement of a copyright of the first owner thereof, namely, the Government, unless it is prohibited. The question, therefore, is whether by introducing certain inputs in a judgment delivered by a court it becomes "original copy-edited judgment" and the person or authority or company who did so could claim to have embodied the originality in the said judgment and the judgment takes the colour of original judgment having a copyright therein of its publisher.

---

73. *See also, Eastern Book Company* v. *D.B. Modak*, AIR 2008 SC 809: (2008) 1 SCC 1. *See also, Rediff. Com India Ltd.* v. *E-Eighteen.Com Ltd.*, 2013 (55 PTC 294 (Del): 202 (2013) DLT 657; *Syndicate* v. *B.D. Bhandari*, 2011 (47) PTC 244 (Del): 185 (2011) DLT 346.
74. *Academy of General Education, Manipal* v. *B. Malini Mallya*, AIR 2009 SC 1982: (2009) 4 SCC 256; *Eastern Book Company* v. *D.B. Modak*, AIR 2008 SC 809: (2008) 1 SCC 1.
75. *Gramophone Company of India Ltd.* v. *Birendra Bahadur Pandey*, AIR 1984 SC 667: (1984) 2 SCC 534.

In *Eastern Book Co.* v. *Navin. J. Desai,*[76] the Delhi High Court examined the nature of copyright in judgments of court and the requirement of "originality" to claim copyright protection of a literary work. In this case, the plaintiff is the publisher of the CD-ROM on SCC Online-Supreme Court Case Finder and Supreme Court Cases Full Text. The plaintiff claimed copyright on these works as compilation. In addition to this, they also claimed copyright on the head-notes of the cases and in the copy-edited full text of the cases as published by them. The copyright claim of the plaintiff on the full text of the judgments is on the ground that the judgments are copy-edited before publication. This includes correcting typographic errors, paragraph numbering, inclusion of comas and full stops, adding citation of cases, footnotes, etc. which involves skill, labour and judgment necessary to constitute original literary work. The plaintiff alleged infringement of copyright by their competitors. "THE LAWS" and "GRAND JURIX"—whereby they copied the full text of the judgments and a number of head-notes from the plaintiff's CD-ROM SCC Online. It was contended by the defendants that their work is different from that of the plaintiff's since many new items like legislation, rules, etc. are included in addition to the full text of the cases and head-notes. The defendant also contended that there is no copyright on the full text of the judgments of courts and the modification made by the plaintiff in the form of copy-editing is trivial to claim copyright.

Regarding the question whether judgments have copyright protection the Delhi High Court[77] after examining Sections 17(d), 2(k) and 52(q) concluded that there is no copyright in judgments and they are in public domain once published. This seems to be the reality of the situation[78] *de hors* a literal interpretation of the provisions of the Copyright Act, 1957. Judgment of a court as per Section 13(a) is a literary work and as per Section 2(d) the judge who wrote the judgment could be the author of such work. According to Section 17 the author of the work is the first owner of copyright except in cases specifically exempted under that Section. If one examines Section 17(d),[79] in case of government works, the ownership of copyright in such works will be with the government unless there is an agreement to the contrary. Section 2(k)[80] makes it clear that the judgments are government works. Thus, it gives an impression that the government would like to retain the copyright over the judgments unless there is an agreement to the contrary.

Section 14(a) of the Act defines the bundle of exclusive rights enjoyed by the owner of copyright in literary work. This includes reproduction right including storing of it in any electronic medium, issue of copies, communication to public, conversion into cinematograph film or sound recording, translation, adaptation of the work, etc. Thus, in case of judgments, the

---

76. 2001 PTC 57 (Del).
77. *Eastern Book Company* v. *Navin. J. Desai,* 2001 PTC 57 (Del).
78. The Allahabad High Court in *S.K. Dutt* v. *Law Book Co.,* AIR 1954 All 570 at p. 573 make the following passing observation "Decision reported in law reports are "Common Property" for commentators on the law, and they must per necessity have to have recourse to them because without reference to them no commentator can give his readers a correct idea of the law".
79. Section 17(d) reads: "in case of a government work, the government shall in the absence of any agreement to the contrary be the first owner of copyright therein".
80. Setion 2(k) reads: "government work means a work which is made or published by or under the direction of control of (i) the Government or any department of the Government; (ii) any Legislature in India; (iii) any Court, Tribunal or other judicial authority in India".

government, it could be argued, owns all these right for a period of 60 years from publication.[81] All these rights are not taken away by Section 52(q) as understood and interpreted by the court in this case. If one examines Section 52(q)(iv),[82] it is only reproduction and publication of the judgments without the permission of the government who is the owner of copyright as per the Act that is exempted from the act of infringement. The Section also recognises the right of the court to prohibit the publication of judgments. It appears that this provision was included in the Act on public interest to ensure that judgments are available to the public through different sources and to prevent anyone from monopolising the exclusive right to reproduce and publish the judgments including the government.

Historically also the government never exercised the copyright even though there existed a debate regarding the copyright of judgments on the crown.[83] Thus, the court is correct in concluding that any one is free to reproduce or publish the same without permission of the government. But in case of all other purposes, the copyright as per the Act seems vested with the government for a period of 60 years and persons who are interested in enjoying these rights need to take permission from the government to avoid infringement. Even though this is the legal position it is evident from the practice that the government is not going to enforce these rights and ensure that monopoly is not going to be created in these rights. This appears to be the reason why the court concluded after referring to Section 52(1)(q) that in judgments none has copyright and are in public domain even though the statutory provisions gives a different impression.

On the question of copyright on the copy-edited full text of the judgment, the Delhi High Court after examining Indian[84] and US[85] cases concluded thus:

> Changes consisting of elimination, changes of spelling, elimination or addition of quotations and corrections of typographical mistakes are trivial and hence no copyright exists therein[86] ... Materials in which no one has a copyright is available to all. Every man can take what is useful from them, improve, add and give to the public the whole comprising the original work with his additions and improvements. Under the law of copyright, the plaintiffs cannot ask the court to restrain the defendants from making this material available to public. I am, therefore, of the opinion that the judgment/orders published by the plaintiff in their law reports "Supreme Court Cases" is not their original literary work but has been composed of, compiled and prepared from and reproduction of the judgments of the Supreme Court

81. Section 28 reads: "In case of government work, where government is the first owner of the copyright therein copyright shall subsist until sixty years from the beginning of the calendar year next following the year in which the work is first published".
82. Section 52(1)(q)(iv) reads: "The following acts shall not constitute an infringement of copyright, namely, ... any judgment or order of a court. Tribunal or other judicial authority, unless the reproduction or publication of such judgment or order is prohibited by the court, the Tribunal or other judicial authority as the case may be".
83. For a detailed analysis, *see*, Ann Monotti. "Nature and Basis of Crown Copyright in Official Publications" 14, *European Intellectual Property Review* (1992) 305 at 309–311; Paul Von Nessen. "Law Reporting: Case for Deregulation", 48(4) *Modern Law Review* (1985) 412–433; Copinger and Skone James (Ed.), *Copyright* (Sweet and Maxwell, London, 1999) pp. 573–574.
84. *See*, *S.K. Dutt* v. *Law Book Co.,* AIR 1954 All 570.
85. *See*, *Bellsouth Advertising and Publishing Corp.* v. *Donnelles Information Publ. Inc.*, 33 IPR 587; *Feist Publication Inc.* v. *Rural Telephone,* 499 US 340 (1991); *Matthew Bender* v. *West Publication Co.*, 47 IPR 228 (1999–2000).
86. *See*, *Star India Pvt. Ltd.* v. *Piyush Agarwal*, 2014 (58) PTC 169 (Del).

> of India open to all. I am also of the opinion that merely correcting certain typographical or grammatical mistakes in the raw source and by adding commas, full stops and by giving paragraph numbers to the judgment will not make their work original literary work entitled to protection under the Copyright Act....[87]

The court is correct in reaching this conclusion having regard to the copyright law even though the efforts taken by the plaintiff to make the judgment more readable goes unrewarded. The attempt of the plaintiff seems to protect the investment made by him using copyright law. But the consequence would be to extend a new monopoly over the judgments that too for a period of life and 60 years after the death of the author. This would in effect have enabled the plaintiff to convert the property of the government to his private property for a longer period than one envisaged by law. This can also prevent others from reproducing and using unless the user shows that he has taken it from the original judgment of courts, which is practically impossible to access. For example, if a law professor wanted to produce a book on cases and materials on copyright law practically, he will be prevented from taking the judgments from any of the reports without permission. If permission is denied, he has to travel from court to court to get the copy of the original judgments or seek a compulsory licence. The situation can be further worsened if a publisher collects the unreported cases of the courts, publish the same and claim copyright over it. It is to avoid these situations that Section 52(q) was included in the Act. This is the reason why the court refused to accept the contention of the plaintiff regarding copyright protection in the copy-edited judgment. This is also the reason why courts follow the *principle of triviality* to reject copyright protection. Even though the requirement of originality is very low for claiming copyright protection if the changes made in terms of intellectual input are very little the policy of the law is not to extend copyright protection. It is also clear that the concern of the copyright law is to emphasis on the intellectual input in the work while extending copyright protection. The protection of investment is incidental to this and not to be the primary purpose based on the *sweat of the brow* theory. The court in the present case held that there is no copyright infringement by the defendant in the case of taking full text of the judgment. The decision of the court is a welcome one. This seems to be the reason why the division bench of the Delhi High Court refused to interfere with the order.[88]

Regarding head-notes the court concluded that unlike copy-editing there could be copyright protection if the parties can show that there is originality intellectual input in the creation of the head-notes.[89] This, according to the court, is based on facts and circumstances of each case. Since there are thousands of head notes in these works and the defendant undertook to ensure that the copyright in the head-notes of the plaintiff would not be infringed, the court did not pass any orders as to whether the defendant has infringed the copyright of the plaintiff. The Delhi High Court in *Pepsi Co. Inc.* v. *Hindustan Coca Cola,*[90] incidentally examined the question whether copyright subsists in slogans and words. In this case, the plaintiff has registered the slogan "YEH DIL MANGE MORE" under the Copyright Act. It was, *inter alia,* argued that the use of the phrase by the defendant in their advertisements violates the copyright

87. *Eastern Book Company* v. *Navin J. Desai,* 2001 PTC 57 (Del).
88. *Eastern Book Company* v. *Navin J. Desai,* 2001 PTC 243: AIR 2001 Delhi 185. *See also, N. Rangaswamy* v. *Godrej and Boyce Manufacturing Co. Ltd.,* 2003 (26) PTC 408 (Mad).
89. *Eastern Book Company* v. *Navin J. Desai,* AIR 2001 Delhi 185: 2001 PTC 57 (Del).
90. 2001 PTC 699 (Del): 94 (2001) DLT 30.

of the plaintiff. The court after examining the definition of literary and artistic works under the Act, English cases[91] on copyright protection of words and the observation of Copinger[92] applied the principles of triviality and held:

> In view of the aforesaid it appears that the advertising slogans are prima facie not protectable under the Copyright Act. They may be protected under the law of passing off in case the plaintiff makes out a case... However it is admitted position that defendants have not used the phrase/slogan "YEH DIL MANGE MORE" in relation to their product. It is used in a mocking manner only in the course of comparative advertising. This itself would not prima facie amount to infringement of copyright.

Copyright is purely a creation of the statute under the Copyright Act, 1957. What rights the author has in his work by virtue of his creation, are defined in Sections 14 and 17 of the Act. These are exclusive rights, but subject to the other provisions of the Act. In the first place, the work should qualify under the provisions of Section 13, for the subsistence of copyright. Although the rights have been referred to as exclusive rights, there are various exceptions to them which are listed in Section 52. In *Eastern Book Company* v. *D.B. Modak,*[93] the Supreme Court examined two important issues:

(a) What shall be the standard of originality in the copy-edited judgments of the Supreme Court which is a derivative work and what would be required in a derivative work to treat it the original work of an author and thereby giving a protected right under the Copyright Act, 1957 to the author of the derivative work? and
(b) Whether the entire version of the copy-edited text of the judgments published in the appellants law report SCC would be entitled for a copyright as an original literary work, the copy-edited judgments having been claimed as a result of inextricable and inseparable admixture of the copy-editing inputs and the raw text, taken together, as a result of insertion of all SCC copy-editing inputs into the raw text, or whether the appellants would be entitled to the copyright in some of the inputs which have been put in the raw text?

In this case the appellants, the publishers of law report by name "Supreme Court Cases" (SCC), claimed copyrights in the copy cited judgments published by the alleged infringement of the same by the respondent in their publication "Grand Jurix". According to the appellants their report consists of various inputs to make the judgments user-friendly by correcting the mistakes, adding cross references, footnotes, proper paragraph numbering, standardise formatting of the text, verification of the reference, etc. These constitute considerable skill, labour and expertise including substantial capital expenditure on infrastructure, staff, equipment, etc. This is sufficient to treat the reported judgment "original literary work" for copyright protection. It was, *inter alia,* alleged that the defendants literary copied the copy-edited judgment. According to the respondent there is no copyrights protection for the copy cited judgments since the input is substantial to constitute an "original" literary work. The

---

91. *See*, *Sinanide* v. *La Maison*, 139 *The Law Times* 356; *Kirk* v. *J & R Flemine Ltd.* (1929) Ch. D. 44; *Francis Das & Hunter Limited* v. *Twentieth Century Fax Corporation Ltd.* (1940) AC 112.
92. *See*, Copinger and Skone James, *Copyright*, Sweet and Maxwell (14th ed., Vol. 1), Paras. 21.20 and 21.35.
93. AIR 2008 SC 809: (2008) 1 SCC 1.

lower Court denied injunction on the ground that the inputs of the appellant is trivial in nature and inadequate to constitute originality to claim copyright protection the copy cited judgment. The Supreme Court considered the copy cited judgment as derivative work and examined the standard of originality required for the derivative work to be considered for copyright protection. Reading the standard of originality after examining English,[94] US[95] and Indian[96] cases the Supreme Court opined:

> The originality requirement in derivative work is that it should originate from the author by application of substantial degree of skill, industry or experience. Precondition to copyright is that work must be produced independently and not copied from another person. Where a compilation is produced from the original work, the compilation is more than simply a re-arranged copyright of original, which is often referred to as skill, judgment and/or labour or Capital. The copyright has nothing to do with originality or literary merit. Copyrighted material is that what is created by the author by his skill, labour and investment of capital, maybe it is derivative work. The courts have only to evaluate whether derivative work is not the end-product of skill, labour and capital which is trivial or negligible but substantial. The courts need not go into evaluation of literary merit of derivative work or creativity aspect of the same.[97]

Thus, the courts in England, America and India, have elaborated the concept of "originality" and laid down some standard criteria for determination of originality. These criteria do not include requirements of novelty, ingenuity, or aesthetic merit, and there is no intention to enlarge the standard of copyright protection to require them.[98] The requirement of "originality" in Indian law, as elsewhere, does not refer to ideas but rather to the manner and material forms of their expression.[99] The objective of copyright, it has been stressed in India, is not to "create monopoly in ideas"; rather, the protection aims at prevention of unlawful reproduction of dealing with the manner and material form in which ideas are expressed. Consequently, "originality" also refers not to "novelty" or "creativity" in ideas but only to the manner and material form of their presentation. What is protected is the expression of thought—the form, formulation, order, plan or arrangement of presentation—as testifying to the investment by the author of mental faculties, skills, competence, craftsmanship, knowledge, labour and capital in the production of any work.

---

94. *Ladbroke (Football) Ltd.* v. *Willim Hill (Football) Ltd.*, [1964] 1 WLR 273 (HL); *Designers Guild Ltd.* v. *Russell Williams (Textiles) Ltd.*, [2000] 1 WLR 2416 (HL); *University of London Press Limited* v. *University Tutorial Press Limited* [1916] 2 Ch 601.
95. *Feist Publications Inc.* v. *Rural Telephone Service Co. Inc.*, 18 USPQ 2d. 1275; *Matthew Bender and Co., Inc.* v. *West Publishing Co.,* 158 F.3d 674; *Key Publications, Inc.* v. *Chinatown Today Publishing Enterprises, Inc.*, MANU/EG/0443/1991: 945 F. 2d. 509.
96. *Gopal Das* v. *Jagannath Prasad,* AIR 1938 All 266; *V. Govindam* v. *E.M. Gopalakrishna Kone,* AIR 1955 Mad 391; *C. Cunniah S. Co.* v. *Balraj S. Co.,* AIR 1961 Mad 111; *Agarwala Publishing House* v. *Board of High School and Intermediate Education,* AIR 1967 All 91.
97. *Eastern Book Company* v. *D.B. Modak,* AIR 2008 SC 809: (2008) 1 SCC 1.
98. *See*, J.K. Das, "Legal Framework for Copyright Protection: Its Philosophical Justifications and Practical Implications on Indigenous Peoples", This paper was presented at national seminar on "Enforcement of Copyright Law", Organized by the Department of Law, Osmania University, Hyderabad and sponsored by the Ministry of HRD, New Delhi on January 10 and 11, 2004 and published in 33–34 *Banaras Law Journal* (2003–2004) pp. 157–180 at p. 159.
99. *R.G. Anand* v. *Delux Films,* AIR 1978 SC 1613: (1978) 4 SCC 118.

IDEA AND EXPRESSION DICHOTOMY

The Dichotomy

It is often said that copyright subsists in the "expression of an idea" and not the "idea" itself. Like most generalisations, there is some truth in this statement, but the reality is rather more sophisticated. Thus, there is a controversy: Is there any difference between ideas and expression?[100] There are numerous judicial decisions where "ideas" have been held not to have copyright protection. For instance, the "ideas" or "concept" for the format of "Opportunity Knocks", taken in isolation, was held not to be the subject of copyright. But in other cases, both the "idea" and its "expression" converged to make them inseparable. An example of this difficulty arises with computer software and copyright. It is, of course, entirely possible to "express" an original program in a completely different computer code, yet both the original program and the "copy" may embody the same "ideas" as to structure of "look" and "feel". Thus, the law of copyright does not protect "ideas", but they deal with the particular "expression" of the ideas fixed in intangible thing. Where an idea ends and the expression begins is a very difficult question, which depends on the facts of each case. In *Institute for Inner Studies* v. *Charlotte Anderson*,[101] the Delhi High Court observed:

> There are the cases where the courts have to draw the line between the ideas and expression of an idea by themselves by indulging into the depth enquiry into the work in order to identify first as to what may constitute idea in a particular work and what is an expression of idea where the originality resides in order to delineate the scope of the protection of work and dissecting it from the ideas. Such a kind of enquiry by courts in copyright cases is more commonly known as idea and expression dichotomy.

ILLUSTRATION

It is the general principle of copyright law that copyright protection extends to expressions and not to ideas. Thus, in *R.G. Anand* v. *Delux Films*,[102] the Apex Court held: "there is no copyright in ideas or schemes or systems or methods; it is confined to their expression." Mr. Vashisht Narayan discloses an idea to Mr. Upendra Bhabha with an implicit understanding that Mr. Upendra Bhabha will use the idea of Mr. Narayan and in returned Mr. Bhabha will pay Mr. Narayan. The question is whether Mr. Narayan be protected under

---

100. For critical discussions on idea and expression dichotomy, *see*, Ed Barker and Iona Harding, "Copyright, the Ideas/Expression Dichotomy and Harmonization: Digging Deeper into SAS," 7(9) *Journal of Intellectual Property Law and Practice* (2012) pp. 673–679; Abraham Drassinower, A Rights-Based View of the Idea/Expression Dichotomy in Copyright Law" 16(1) *Canadian Journal of Law and Jurisprudence* (2003) pp. 3–21; Fred Anthony Rowley, "Dynamic Copyright Law" Its Problems and A Possible Solution," 11(2) *Harvard Journal of Law and Technology* (1998) pp. 481–528; Richard H. Jones, "The Myth of the Idea/Expression Dichotomy in Copyright Law," 10 (3) Pace Law Review (1990) pp. 551–507.
101. 2014 (57) PTC 228(Del): MIPR 2014 (1) 129.
102. AIR 1978 SC 1613: (1978) 4 SCC 118. *See also*, *Dabur India Limited* v. *Shree Baidyanath Ayurved Bhawan Pvt. Ltd.*, 193 (2012) DLT 558, 2012 (51) PTC 441 (Del); *Vipul Amrutlal Shah* v. *Shree Venkatesh Films Pvt. Ltd.*, MANU/WB/0181/2009; *Urmi Juvekar Chiang* v. *Global Broadcast News Limited*, MIPR 2007 (2) 223: 2008 (36) PTC 373 (Bom); *Barbara Taylor Bradford* v. *Sahara Media Entertainment Ltd.* (2004) ILR 1 Cal 15: 2004 (28) PTC 474 (Cal).

copyright law? In this case Mr. Narayan will be protected under the common law doctrine of "unjust enrichment" but not under the law of copyright.

However, the courts in certain occasions to deal with almost similar to the above situation held that when an idea is converted into a concept, it becomes copyrightable. In *Anil Gupta* v. *Kunal Dasgupta*,[103] the plaintiffs conceived the idea of producing reality TV programme of match-making to the point of actual spouse selection in which real everyday ordinary persons would participate before TV audience. The Delhi High Court held that "the interlocutory injunction could be issued to restrain the breach of confidentiality of the theme, concept or scripts, else the same could be catastrophic for television industry".

The economic rationale behind the idea and expression dichotomy is explained by Landes and Posner as follows:[104]

> If an author of spy novels copies a portion of an Ian Fleming novel about James Bond, he is an infringer. If, inspired by Fleming, he decides to write a novel about a British secret agent who is a bon vivant, he is not an infringer. If an economist reprints Professor Coase's article on social cost without permission, he is an infringer; but if he expounds the Coase's Theorem in his own words, he is not. In the case of the novel, the reason for the limited protection is easily seen.[105] The novelist creates the novel by combining stock characters and situations (many of which go back to the earliest writings that have survived from antiquity) with his particular choice of words, incidents, and *dramatis personae.* He does not create the stock characters and situations, or buy them. Unlike the ideas for which patents can be obtained, they are not new and the novelist acquires them at zero cost, either from observation of the world around him or from works long in the public domain. Most works of fiction that anyone would want to copy are intended for a mass audience—which means they *must* use stock characters and situations in order to be understood. To give the author of a work embodying such characters or situations ("expression") a copyright would increase the cost of expression of later authors without generating offsetting benefits. What passes for "ideas" in the case of most expressive writing normally is not comparable to the sort of inventions, costly to develop, that receive protection under the patent laws. An alternative to distinguishing between ideas and expression, therefore, would be to confine copyright protection to original works, or to a work insofar as it was original.

Just as patent protection extends to any useful, non-obvious, novel, application of an idea, and, as trade mark applies to any appropriated and used device for indicating origin of goods and services; copyright protection centres fundamentally upon the original expression of an idea, whether literary, artistic, commercial, or otherwise. The expression is the key because only the expression is protected under copyright law.[106] The law of copyright is the extension of the right of speech and expression, which means if an individual has freedom of "speech and expression", then he must naturally get a right to protect an intellectual idea which is being expressed and fixed in any tangible property.

---

103. AIR 2002 Delhi 379: 97 (2002) DLT 257. *See also*, Zee *Telefilms Ltd. and Film and Shot* v. *Sundial Communications Pvt. Ltd.*, 2003 (3) Mh Lj 695: 2003 (27) PTC 457 (Bom).
104. William M. Landes and Richard A. Posner, "An Economic Analysis of Copyright Law", 18(2) *The Journal of Legal Studies* (1989) p. 325.
105. *See*, Richard A. Posner, *Law and Literature: A Misunderstood Relation* (Harvard University Press, Cambridge, Massachusetts, 1988).
106. *Gopal Das* v. *Jagannath Prasad*, AIR 1938 All 266.

Thus, copyright law is a branch of law of expression. This has been recognised in England in *Bailey* v. *Taylor*,[107] where the Court of Chancery held that the basic idea of a romantic novel is not protected by copyright but the words "expressing" the story are protected. In England freedom of speech and discussion is not based on any Constitutional declaration or statute or common law, but based on ordinary rule of law. Hence, freedom of speech and discussion consists with the right of a citizen to speak or write subject to the common law of: (a) defamation, (b) sedition, (c) blasphemy, (d) obscenity, or (e) contempt of Court; or the provisions of any statute, such as the Official Secrets Acts, 1911–1939; the Public Order Act, 1936.

Article-1, Section-8, Clause-8 of *The Constitution of the United States of America* provides that: "The Congress shall have Power ... To promote the Progress of Science and useful Arts, by securing for limited Times to Authors and Inventors the exclusive Right to their respective Writings and Discoveries." This is the Patent and Copyright Clause. Under this clause, *Congress* has the power to enact any legislation consistent with the intent of the Constitution to provide copyright protection. *Congress* has enacted the *Copyright Act, 1976* under which all intellectual ideas became protectable once they were "fixed in a tangible medium of expression". The most significant doctrine limiting the copyright ability of works is the "idea–expression" dichotomy, which is codified in Section 102(b) of the Act of 1976 which reads thus: "In no case does copyright protection for an original work of authorship extend to any idea, procedure, process, system, method of operation, concept, principle, or discovery regardless of the form in which it is described, explained, illustrated, or emobodied in such work." The First Amendment to the Constitution of the United States (1791) lays down that: "The Congress shall make no laws ... abridging the freedom of speech or of the press...." On this clause, the US Supreme Court has observed that:

> The safeguarding of these rights to the ends that man may speak as they think on matters vital to them and that falsehoods may be exposed through the process of education and discussion in essential to free government.[108]

The First Amendment, therefore, provides two democratic freedoms, namely, (i) freedom of speech and (ii) freedom of press. The combined effect of these two freedoms produces a third type of freedoms, namely, freedom of expression. In *Abrams*[109] case the US Supreme Court held that freedom of speech and expression predicates freedom of the intellect to entertain unorthodox or even ideas hateful to the prevailing climate of opinion. The freedom of expression is not confined to any particular field of human interest. It can be exercised not only for religious purposes but for political, economic, scientific news or informational ends as well.[110]

Article 19(1)(a) of the *Constitution of India* recognises the right to "freedom of speech and expression".[111] The Apex Court has interpreted the concept of freedom of speech and

---

107. (1825) Russ and M 73, Court of Chancery, *See also*, *Corelli* v. *Gray* (1913)30 TLR 116, Court of Appeal.
108. *Whitney* v. *California* (1927) 278 US 357.
109. *Abrams* v. *US* (1919) 250 US 616 (630).
110. *Douglas* v. *Jeanette* (1943) 319 US 310 (88).
111. *Douglas* v. *Jeanette* (1943) 319 US 310 (88).

expression in a number of cases[112] and held that the right of expression means that the right to express one's convictions and opinions freely, by word of mouth, writing, printing, picture, or electronic media, or in any other manner. It would thus include not only the freedom of the press, but the expression of one's ideas by any visible representation, such as by gestures and the like. Expression, naturally-presupposes a second party to whom the ideas are expressed or communicated. In short, freedom of expression includes the freedom of propagation of ideas, their publication and circulation and the right to answer the criticism levelled against such views, the right to acquire and import ideas and information about matters of common interest. The copyright law provides the protection of expression of ideas of an author. Thus, the concept of "expression" is one of the fundamental aspects of copyright law, which is supported by the doctrine of the rule of law in England, and by the Constitutional guarantees in America and in India. The fundamental rule of copyright law is that there is no copyright in an idea but the expression of an idea is protected.[113] Article 9(2) of TRIPS Agreement states that "Copyright protection shall extend to expressions and not to ideas, procedures, methods of operation or mathematical concepts as such." Article 2 of WCT, 1996 uses the same language and is therefore consistent with TRIPS Agreement. The Indian Copyright Act, 1957 does not have a similar provision but the Indian courts have time and again held that there is no copyright in an idea or ideas, the copyright vests in the expression of an idea.

Indian Judiciary on Idea and Expression Dichotomy

It is a debatable issue whether copyright law is law of idea or law of expression[114]. What is protected in copyright law is not original thought or information, but the original expression of thought or information in some concrete form as the author is both a user of ideas developed by others and a creator of a new ideas. In *R.G. Anand* v. *Delux Films,*[115] the plaintiff, a playwright, dramatist and producer of stage plays wrote a play entitled *Hum Hindustani* based

---

112. Article 19 of the *Universal Declaration of Human Right, 1948*: "Everyone has the right to freedom of opinion and expression; this right includes freedom to hold opinions without interference and to seek, receive and impart information and ideas through any media and regardless of frontiers." *See also*, Article 19(2) of the *International Covenant on Civil and Political Rights, 1966.* India has ratified ICCPR in 1979. Since then ICCPR is binding law in India. *The Constitution of Japan*: Article 21 says, "Freedom of Assembly, association speech and press and all other forms of expression are *guaranteed.* No other forms of expression are guarantee. No other forms of expression are guaranteed. No censorship shall be maintained, nor shall the secrecy of any means of communication be violated."

113. *See*, *Dart Industries Inc.* v. *Techno Plast*, 2017 II AD (Delhi) 602: 2016 (67) PTC 457 (Del); *M. Radhakrishnan* v. *Surabhi Publications*, MIPR 2017 (1) 125: 2016 (3) KLJ 321; *OK Play India* v. *Mayank Aggarwal*, 2016 (67) PTC 665 (Del): 233 (2016) DLT 234; *Jyoti Kapoor* v. *Kunal Kohli*, 2015 (63) PTC 347 (Bom): 2015 (6) BomCR 54; *Life Insurance Corporation* v. *Professor Manubhai D. Shah,* AIR 1993 SC 171: (1992) 3 SCC 637; *Hamdard Dawakhana* v. *Union of India,* AIR 1960 SC 554: [1960] 2 SCR 671; *Romesh Thappar* v. *State of Madras,* AIR 1950 SC 124: [1950] 1 SCR 594.

114. *See*, Nicholas Caddick, Gillian Davies and Gwilym Harbottle, *Copinger* and *Skone James on Copyright* (Sweet and Maxwell, 2016); Lionel Bently and Brad Sherman, *Intellectual Property Law* (Oxford University Press, 2014) at p. 184; Andreas Rahmatian, *Copyright and Creativity*: *The Making of Property Rights in Creative Works* (Edward Elgar, 2011) at p. 199; Leslie A. Kurtz, "Speaking to the Ghost: Idea and Expression in Copyright," 47 (5) University of Miami Law Review (1993) pp. 1221–1261 at p. 1224.

115. AIR 1978 SC 1613: (1978) 4 SCC 118.

on the idea of provincialism and parochialism. The defendants made the film *New Delhi* which portrays three main themes: (1) Two aspects of provincialism, viz. the role of provincialism in regard to marriage and in renting out accommodation; (2) evils of a caste ridden society; and (3) evils of dowry. After the release of the film there were comments in the newspaper that the picture was very much like the play. The Apex Court observed that:

> …a close perusal of the script of the film clearly shows that all the three aspects mentioned above are integral parts of the story and it is very difficult to divorce one from the other without affecting the beauty and the continuity of the script of the film. Further, it would appear that the treatment of the story of the film is in many respects different from the story contained in the play. On a close and careful comparison of the play and the picture, but for the central idea (provincialism which is not protected by copyright), from scene to scene, situation to situation, in climax to anti-climax, pathos, bathos, in texture and treatment and support and presentation, the picture is materially different from the play.

The Apex Court further laid down the following propositions[116] which have been followed by the different High Courts in various cases:

1. There can be no copyright in an idea, subject matter, themes, and plots or historical or legendry fact and violation of the copyright in such cases is confined to the form, manner and arrangement and expression of the idea by the author of the copyrighted work.[117]
2. Where the same idea is being developed in a different manner, it is manifest that the source being common, similarities are bound to occur. In such a case the courts should determine whether or not the similarities are on fundamental or substantial aspects of the mode of expression adopted in the copyrighted work. If the defendant's work is nothing but literal imitation of the copyrighted work with some variation here and there it would amount to violation of the copyright. In other words, in order to be actionable the copy must be a substantial and material one which at once leads to the conclusion that the defendant is guilty of an act of piracy.[118]
3. One of the surest and the safest tests to determine whether or not there has been violation of copyright is to see if the reader, spectator or the viewer after having read or seen both the works is clearly of the opinion and gets an unmistakable impression that the subsequent work appears to be a copy of the original.[119]
4. Where the theme is the same but is presented and treated differently so that the subsequent work becomes a completely new work, no question of violation of copyright arises.[120]
5. Where however apart from the similarities appearing in the two works there are also material and broad dissimilarities which negate the intention to copy the original and

---

116. *R.G. Anand* v. *Delux Films*, AIR 1978 SC 1613: (1978) 4 SCC 118.
117. *See, Roderick John Andrew Mackenzie* v. *Himalayan Heli Services Pvt. Ltd.*, 2019 (77) PTC 379 (Del); *Maddock Films Private Limited* v. *Shiboprasad Mukherjee*, 2017(4) CHN (CAL) 614.
118. *See, Gurukrupa Mech Tech Pvt. Ltd.* v. *State of Gujarat*, (2018) 4 GLR 3324.
119. *See, Khaidem Jacko Meitei* v. *Union of India*, 2018 (4) GLT 107.
120. *See, Zee Entertainment Enterprises Ltd.* v. *Sony Pictures Networks India Pvt. Ltd.*, AIR 2017 Bom 221: 2017 (70) PTC 300 (Bom).

the coincidences appearing in the two works are clearly incidental no infringement of the copyright comes into existence.[121]

6. As a violation of copyright amounts to an act of piracy, it must be proved by clear and cogent evidence after applying the various test laid down by the case law.[122]
7. Where however, the question is of the violation of the copyright of stage play by a film producer or a director, the task of the plaintiff becomes more difficult to prove piracy. It is manifest that unlike a stage play, a film has much broader perspective, wider field and a bigger background where the defendants can be introducing a variety of incidents to give a colour and complexion different from the manner in which the copyrighted work has expressed the idea. Even so, if the viewer after seeing the film gets a totality of impression that the film is by and the large a copy of the original play, violation of the copyrighted might be said to be proved.[123]

The idea-expression dichotomy in copyright law has also been discussed in the Bombay High Court in *Zee Telefilms Ltd.* v. *Sundial Communications Pvt. Ltd.*[124] In this case, the issue was relating to the protection of the television serial where it was alleged that the plaintiff developed the original concept for the serial "Krish Kanhaiyya". The concepts generated are expressed through concept notes, character sketches, detailed plots and episodes, main story lines that are put down in writing. This written expression of the original concept was registered with Film Writers Association. This was discussed with the defendant for production and broadcast in Zee Television channel. But since there was no positive response from the defendant, the plaintiff decided to give the script to Sony Entertainment Television. The plaintiff then came to know that the defendants are producing a serial based on the same concept. They also registered the title with the Motion Picture Association and started advertising promotional materials. Knowing this Sony refused to sign the contract with the plaintiff. The defendants started broadcasting the serial "Kanhaiyya" based on the same concept. The present suit by the plaintiff is for breach of confidence and infringement of copyright. The defendants contended that though the concept had some similarity their production was substantially different from that of the plaintiff. They also argued that they received a similar script from another person at the same time and they decided to accept that instead of the one given by the plaintiff. The court after examining the facts found that there were existed a relationship of confidentially between the parties though there was no written agreement and the defendant violated the same. It was evident from the fact that the plaintiff registered their detailed written concept with the Film Writers Association. But it was not clear whether the practice was to keep this in confidence by the association till the film was produced. If it was not so it was difficult to appreciate how the principles of confidentiality could be applied to this case since the story was available to the members for examination. On the issue of copyright infringement, the court after examining the script of the plaintiff and the first episode of the defendant applied the test laid down in *R.G. Anand*[125]

121. *See, M. Radhakrishnan* v. *Surabhi Publications*, 2016 (3) KLJ 321: MIPR 2017 (1) 125.
122. *See, Narendra Mohan Singh* v. *Ketan Mehta,* 2015 (64) PTC 260 (Bom).
123. *See, Institute for Inner Studies* v. *Charlotte Anderson,* 2014 (57) PTC 228 (Del): MIPR 2014 (1) 129.
124. 2003 (27) PTC 475 (Bom.): 2003 (5) Bom CR 404.
125. *See, R.G. Anand* v. *Deluxe Films*, AIR 1978 SC 1613: (1978) 4 SCC 118.

and concluded that there was infringement of copyright. The justification of the court is as follows:

> Having considered two works involved in this case not hypocritically and with meticulous scrutiny but by the observations and impressions of the average viewer, we find that striking similarities in two works cannot in the light of the materials placed on record be said to constitute mere chance. We feel that the only inference that can be drawn from the material available on record is unlawful copying of the plaintiff's original work. The ... Lord Krishna in child form is removed from the serial of the defendants, their programme would become meaningless. In order to find out similarity in the two concepts what is to be seen in the substances, the foundation, the kernel and the test as to whether the reproduction is substantial is to see if the rest can stand without it. If it cannot, then even if many dissimilarities exist in the rest, it would nevertheless be a substantial reproduction liable to be restrained....[126]

It appears that the court is giving more emphasis to the substantial similaritics in the concept rather than in the form in which the parties express it. Though the court following the ration in *R.G. Anand* held that idea/concept is not protected under copyright, the decision seems to be influenced by the similarity of the concept of both the parties. It is true that, *R.G. Anand* stressed on the impression of the viewers as the surest test to find out substantial copying of the expression. But the court qualified it with the necessity of looking into the similarities and dissimilarities in the form in which the idea/concept is expressed. The Supreme Court also cautioned that when the concept is same, there are bound to be similarities. In such cases it was laid down in. *R.G. Anand* that "the court should determine whether or not the similarities are on fundamental or substantial aspects of the *mode of expression adopted* in the copyrighted work". This is clearly to ensure that the idea is not protected if the similarities are essential for the expression of the idea. It appears that it is the failure of the *Zee Television* court to appreciate this part of the ratio in *R.G. Anand* that resulted in the above observation giving an impression that the concept of Lord Krishna is protected and not the form in which it was presented by the plaintiff. The court seems to be influenced by the economic rational applied by the Delhi High Court in *Anil Gupta* v. *Kunal Das Gupta.*[127]

In *Anil Gupta* v. *Kunal Dasgupta,*[128] the plaintiff conceived the idea of producing reality television programme based on the concept of *Swayamvar,* i.e., woman herself selecting a groom from a variety of suitors. This was a novel concept, which was disclosed by the plaintiff to the defendant under a strict confidential agreement. The plaintiff sent a concept note to the defendant for the purpose of production of the TV serial. Later, the plaintiff came to know about the defendant's plan of launching a reality show, *Shubh Vivah,* plaintiff filed a suit for copyright violations of the concept of reality show. The court held:

> An idea per se has no copyright. But if the idea is developed into a concept fledged with adequate details, then the same is capable of protection under the Copyright Act. The court cited with approval *Fraser* v. *Thomas Television* [(1983) All ER 101] where the court observed, "I accept that to be capable of protection the idea must be sufficiently developed, so that it would seem to be a concept which has at least some attentiveness for a television programme and which is capable of being realized as an actuality.

---

126. The justification has been applied in *XYZ Films LLC* v. *UTV Motion Pictures*, 2016 (67) PTC 81 (Bom): MIPR 2016 (3) 59; *Interlude Technologies* v. *Popular Entertainment Network Ltd.*, 2009 (40) PTC 485 (Del).
127. AIR 2002 Delhi 379: 97 (2002) DLT 257.
128. AIR 2002 Delhi 379: 97 (2002) DLT 257.

The Calcutta High Court in *Barbara Taylor Bradford* v. *Sahara Media Entertainment Ltd.*,[129] explained the idea-expression dichotomy. They pointed out that the law protected originality of expression and not originality of the central idea due to the balancing of two conflicting policies. The first policy was that the law must protect originality of work, thereby allowing the authors reap the fruits of their labour and stopping unscrupulous pirates from enjoying those fruits. The second policy was that must not become an over protection, thus, curbing future creativity. If mere plots and characters were to be protected by copyright, an author could not write anything "original" at all, on a similar plot or on a similar character. The Calcutta High Court justifying this balancing approach observed:

> If in plaintiffs play hero has inherited a fortune from his uncle subject to the condition that if he dies unmarried the money will go to his cousin, the Villain. The Villain shoots him but makes it look like an accident. The hero defeats the machination of the Villain by bribing a beggar girl out of the streets to marry him before his death can ensue.
>
> In defendant's play the hero has inherited a fortune from his father subject to the condition that if he dies marry before the age of twenty five or else the money will go to his cousin, the Villain. The Villain induces to pass his time drinking and gambling so as to forget the condition. The family lawyer finds the hero on the eve of his twenty fifth birthday and persuades him to go home. On his way home, the hero meets a beggar girl and out of compassion gives her shelter for night. The next day the lawyer turns up with a special marriage licence and insists on immediate marriage. The hero marries the beggar girl.
>
> If one were asked to decide whether the defendant's play infringes the copyright the plaintiff's play, quite a natural reaction would be, to place emphasis on the basic theme of both the plays, that is, if a marriage does not take place within a specific time the good person loses everything and the bad person takes everything. This is the Common theme of both the plays.
>
> The existence of common characters cannot also be denied. Both the plays show a cousin as the Villain. In both the plays the beggar girl happens to take the morsel out of the villain's mouth at the very last moment. In both the plays the subject-matter is inherited fortune. One would thus conclude, that the substance of the play of the plaintiff has been reproduced by the defendant and he is therefore copying it. A substantial part of the plaintiff's work has been adopted, not merely adapted, by the defendant.[130] One would assume that the conclusions hereby made are quite mime with the dicta in *R.G. Anand's* case *(supra)*. The defendant's action is no more than an act of piracy where the basic artistry of the plaintiff has been copied.

One would feel secure in this conclusion. One would happily pass appropriate orders of relief by way of injunction. One would feel confident but one would go thereby utterly wrong copyright law. The Calcutta High Court went on to explain the rationale behind the basic copyright law which is, that you can borrow the idea of another author, but not the expression. The Court raised various questions like way is it that the theme of a play, like the marriage of an heir contingent to a beggar girl does not create a copyright? Why is it that the plot by itself is usually not the subject-matter of a copyright? Why is it that identical characters, like a villain cousin and the devising ancestor wishing his legatee to marry young, do not create

129. (2004) ILR 1 Cal 15: 2004 (28) PTC 474 (Cal).

130. For the application of the test of copying "substantial part" see *Novex Communication Pvt. Ltd.* v. *Lemon Tree Hotels Ltd.*, 2019 II AD (Delhi) 644; *Lyca Productions* v. *J. Manimaran*, 2018 (73) PTC 525 (Mad): 2018 (3) CTC 605.

copyright? The court then went on to give answers to these questions and observed that the answer is two-fold.

> The first answer is that these characters are common, no doubt, but too common. Therefore, there is no protection given by the law to the first writer who is not really the first writer at all. The above idea of the risk of a fortune being lost to others, the other Idea, of, say, two persons looking alike, are not the subject of the authors original literary work. The second reason for not giving protection in this regard is even more important. If plots and ordinary prototype characters were to be protected by the copyright law, then soon would come a time in the literary world, when no author would be able to write anything at all without infringing copyright. Fathers, mothers, revenge, lust, sudden coming into fortune, Count of Monte Cristo [*sic*] themes, beggar girl marrying rich boy, rich girl marrying poor boy, and one thousand such theme, characters and plots would become the subject-matter of copyright and an intending author, instead of concentrating upon the literary merit of his expression, would be spending his life first determining whether he is infringing the copyright of the other authors who have written on this topic. The law of copyright was intended at granting protection and not intended for stopping all literary works altogether by its application.
>
> Again the law cannot become this lax. It would pave the way to plagiarism and the labours of the authors would be freely picked up by unscrupulous' persons. They would utilise the fruits or [*sic*] originality, not author the work themselves. Therefore, even if the plot is copied, the person who copies it, be it consciously or unconsciously, must also weave into the plot sufficient creations of his own imagination and literary skill, to make the work his own and not a copy of the work which might have inspired him in the first place.
>
> The question is how does one distinguish between a copy of an idea or a plot, which is permitted, and the copy of an expression of the author, which is protected and which is his or her own?[131] Where does an idea end and expression begin? These are the questions which are the most difficult to answer or even to explain. The best answer is that there are no final answers yet, and there is no hope that there will be any final answers ever. These are situation of legal assessment. Just as there is no mathematical formula for finding out when it is just and convenient to appoint a receiver, similarly, although at a more refined level of intellectual operation, there is no final and exact way of determining what is a copy, or what is a copy of the expression, or what is a copy of the idea, or what is a copy of the idea only. This is why copy has never been attempted to be defined in any of the copyright Acts.

The Bombay High Court in *Urmi Juvekar Chiang* v. *Global Broadcast News Ltd.*,[132] held, it is often stated that there is no copyright in ideas. There are two aspects to this statement, the first namely, that it is not the concern of copyright enactments to protect ideas unless and until the ideas have found expression in the form of a work of a category recognized as deserving of protection and the second aspect is the corollary of the first, that once the ideas have been expressed in the form of a work, it is the form of expression which is the subject of protection, not the ideas, which themselves may be freely extracted from the work and absorbed and used by others to produce their own works, so long as the form of expression of the work is not also taken. In this respect, however, it is to be noted that the form of expression of a literary work does not mean only the text in which that work is written, it may include the selection and arrangement in a particular order of incidents, whether factual or fictional.[133]

---

131. The distinguish between a copy of an idea or a plot has been discussed by Delhi High Court in *Twentieth Century Fox Film Corporation* v. *Zee Telefilms* Ltd., 2012(51) PTC 465 (Del): MIPR 2012 (2) 377.
132. MIPR 2007 (2) 223: 2008 (36) PTC 373 (Bom).
133. *See*, *Vipul Amrutlal Shah* v. *Shree Venkatesh Films Pvt. Ltd.*, MIPR 2009 (3) 134.

The same considerations apply to literary works whose principal purpose is to communicate news, and indeed it is often stated that there is no copyright in news. This is perhaps not an accurate way of applying the general principle referred to above. The fact that the content of a literary work is news does not prevent that work from being capable of protection by copyright. But again, what is protected is the form of expression of that content. The information itself, as information stripped of its particular form of expression, may be freely used, as with any other literary work. In the instant case, the plaintiff had given shape to her idea by expressing it in a detailed concept note and the production plan relating to the programme "Work in Progress". This had been substantially reproduced by the defendant channel, namely CNN IBN in its show titled as "Summer Showdown". For determining whether there was substantial reproduction or not the court applied the "average viewer test". According to this test, the two works are not to be compared with hypercritical and meticulous scrutiny but from the standpoint of the observations and impressions of an average viewer.[134]

Merger of Idea and Expression

The merger of ideas and expression are permissible in cases where there are only a few ways of expressing an idea, so that protecting expression fully would, as a practical matter, prevent anyone but the author from using the idea. Thus, in *Dart Industries Inc.* v. *Techno Plast*,[135] the Delhi High Court held that in India the law has recognized the shift of idea expression merger, and mandates that not every effort or industry, or expending of skill, results in copyrightable work, but only those which create works that are somewhat different in character, involve some intellectual effort, and involve a certain degree of creativity. This standard of originality is now applicable in respect of the plaintiffs' claim to copyright of its drawings. Thus, there are further limitations in the law of copyright such as the idea expression merger. The Section 39A of the Copyright Act 1957 provided under the proviso of the Section that copyright protection available to performers in addition to performer's rights. The proviso reads: "Provided that where copyright or performer's right subsists in respect of any work or performance that has been broadcast, no licence to reproduce such broadcast shall take effect without the consent of the owner of rights or performer, as the case may be, or both of them." In *Akuate Internet Services Pvt. Ltd.* v. *Star India Pvt. Ltd.*,[136] it was held that all those limitations that apply to copyrights (such as no protection to ideas or facts or underlying information, the idea expression merger doctrine, etc.) would apply in the case of copyrighted works which are also the subject of broadcast rights. In *Emergent Genetics India Pvt. Ltd.* v. *Shailendra Shivam*,[137] court explained the circumstances when idea expression merges and observed:

> The evolution of the "idea-expression merger" doctrine shows that when there is only one or there are very few ways of expressing a particular idea, then it (the expression) merges with the idea.

---

134. *See*, *XYZ Films LLC* v. *UTV Motion Pictures*, 2016 (67) PTC 81 (Bom): MIPR 2016 (3) 59.
135. 2017 II AD (Delhi) 602: 2016 (67) PTC 457 (Del).
136. MIPR 2013 (3) 1.
137. 2011 (47) PTC 494 (Del): 2011 (125) DRJ 173.

The Delhi High Court in *Mattel, Inc.* v. *Jayant Aggarwalla,*[138] applied the doctrine of merger to deny copyright protection of games. The plaintiff in this case claimed copyright in their word board game marketed as "SCRABBLES". It was alleged that the defendant produced a web-based game similar to that of "SCRABBLES" using the red, pink, blue and light blue titles, use of identical pattern of arrangement of coloured tiles and use of a star pattern on the central quire. The defendant denied the allegations and argued based on the doctrine of merger that there was no copyright in the alleged elements in the game since they were ideas of playing game expressed in the work and could not be separated. Accepting this, the court observed:

> Furthermore, and most importantly, the application of the doctrine of merger would mean that the colour scheme on such a board can be expressed only in a limited number of ways; if the plaintiffs' arrangements were to be avoided, it is not known whether the idea of such a word game could be played at all. Similarly, the reasoning in *Allen* and *Atari* as far as copyright ability of rules of a game are concerned apply squarely in this case. This doctrine of merger is applicable with respect to games as (according to those decisions) "they consist of abstract rules and play ideas". By way of illustration, the arrangements of colours, values on the board, the collocation of lines, value for individual alphabetical titles, etc., have no intrinsic meaning, but for the rules. If these rules which form the only method of expressing the underlying idea are to be subject to copyright, the idea in the game would be given monopoly, a result not intended by the law makers who only wanted expression of idea to be protected.[139]

The court refused injunction to the plaintiff. The clarity of this observation deserves appreciation since the court is correct in maintaining the balance between laws dealing with different forms of intellectual property. It is evident that the attempt of the plaintiff is to get protection through the copyright law for an item that falls under the patent or design law. It has become a normal practice, as seen from many reported cases from various high courts, for the plaintiff who failed to take protection under design or patent to claim copyright protection. It is laudable that this judgment has relied on fundamental principles of copyright law to arrest this unhealthy trend to extend monopoly.

In *Institute for Inner Studies* v. *Charlotte Anderson,*[140] the court held that originality in copyright sense would mean the hard work, labour and skill extended truly by author in relation to creativity and not in relation to innovation done in respect of deriving some principle or method. If one has to find out what can be idea and what can be an expression of an idea, it can be said that the way the author has described the art is not an idea but the expression of an idea and therefore the manner of performing the art should also be given protection due to the unique expression of art or principle of science mentioned in a book and the idea is merely the plot of the book which is the book on scientific principle/art but the manner indicated in a book for performing the art is unique to the author and thus deserve protection. The Court further observed:

> The idea expression problem has been evolved firstly by the courts in US and recently has also been recognized by the courts in UK. India is still in the process of accepting the said proposition as the courts are in the process of facing the factual situations wherein the

138. MIPR 2008 (3) 298: 2008 (38) PTC 416 (Del).
139. *Mattel, Inc.* v. *Mr. Jayant Agarwalla,* MIPR 2008 (3) 298: 2008 (38) PTC 416 (Del).
140. 2014 (1) MIPR 129; 2014 (57) PTC 228.

dividing line between idea and expression is blurred though some cases in India shed some light on the subject by quoting the international cases relating to idea expression problems but do not clearly spell out the problem relating to idea and expression in so many words as laid down in the said judgments[141] in US and in UK.

NO COPYRIGHT IN COMMON PROPERTY AND ACTUAL EVENTS

When a thing is common property, so that anyone can make use of it who likes, it is said to be *publici juris*.[142] Therefore, common property cannot be the subject-matter of copyright of a particular person.[143] Similarly, there cannot be a copyright in an event which has actually taken place.[144] In *Zee Telefilms Ltd.* v. *Sundial Communications Pvt. Ltd.,*[145] the Bombay High Court held that common property are not the subject of copyright. Similarly, in *Indian Express Newspapers (Bom.) Pvt. Ltd.* v. *Jagmohan Mundhara,*[146] the Court observed:

> No doubt the central theme of the articles published by the second plaintiff and that of the drama and movie is the same, though the emphasis in the drama and the movie is more on human bondage, particularly of Indian women. The articles published by Ashwani Sarin also contain an autobiographical account of the part actually played by him in the affair. He has presented the whole affair in his own style. But that at the most would give the plaintiffs copyright in respect of these articles. There cannot, however, be a copyright in an event which has actually taken place. There is a distinction between the materials upon which one claiming copyright has worked and the product of the application of his skill, judgment, labours and literary talent to these materials. Ideas, information, natural phenomena and events on which an author expends his skill, labour, capital, judgment and literary talent are common property and are not the subject of copyright.

In the above case, the Bombay High Court following the principle as laid down by the Apex Court in *R.G. Anand* v. *Delux Films*[147] held that there is no copyright in an actual event. In this case Ashwani Sarin, an investigative journalist took upon himself the challenging task of exposing the widespread prevalence of flesh trade in the State of Madhya Pradesh. For the sake of conducting research and writing articles, he made himself a participant in the flesh trade and bought a woman by the name of Kamla from village Shivpuri in Madhya Pradesh for ₹2,300/-. Well-known playwright Vijay Tendulkar wrote a play first and then a story about it for a film. The journalist and the newspaper proprietors filed a suit against the playwright and the film producer complaining that the film was an infringement of their copyright in the newspaper stories. The court held:

---

141. *See, Feist Publications Inc* v. *Rural Telephone Services Company*, 1991 499 US 340; *Kleeneze Ltd.* v. *D.R.G. (U.K.) Ltd.*, 1984 FSR 399; *L.B. (Plastics) Ltd.* v. *Swish Products Ltd.*, 1979 RPC 551; *Ladbroke (Football) Ltd.* v. *William Hill (Football) Ltd.*, 1964 1 WLR 273; *Kenrick* v. *Lawrence,* 1890 25 QBD 99.
142. *See, P.M. Palani Mudaliar* v. *Jansons Exports*, 2018 (73) PTC 260(Mad): AIR 2017 Mad 105.
143. *See, M. Radhakrishnan* v. *Surabhi Publications*, 2016 (3) KLJ 321: MIPR 2017 (1) 125; *Narendra Mohan Singh* v. *Ketan Mehta*, 2015 (64) PTC 260 (Bom).
144. *See, J.B. Khanna and Company* v. *S. Asad*, 2008 (5) MhLJ 1469: MIPR 2008 (3) 19.
145. 2003 (5) Bom CR 404: 2003 (27) PTC 457 (Bom).
146. AIR 1985 Bom 229.
147. AIR 1978 SC 1613: (1978) 4 SCC 118. In *R.G. Anand* v. *Delux Films* [AIR 1978 SC 1613: (1978) 4 SCC 118] the Supreme Court also held that there is no copyright in an actual event.

> There is a distinction between the materials upon which one claiming copyright has worked and the product of the application of his skill, judgment, labours and literary talent to these materials. Ideas, information, natural phenomena and events on which an author expends his skill, labour, capital, judgment and literary talent are common property and are not the subject of copyright. The form, manner or arrangement of a drama and movie are materially different from a newspaper article and by very nature of the media there is fundamental and substantial dissimilarity in the mode of expression of the idea in a newspaper article and in a stage play or in a movie. *Prima facie,* therefore, the claim in respect of infringement of copyright appears to be misconceived.[148]

It may be noted that in this case the film producer did not merely take ideas from the writings of Sarin but he made a cinematograph film on the very autobiographical account of the journalist retaining even the name of the principal character Kamla. Moreover, a plain reading of Section 17 proviso (a) of the Copyright Act, 1957 shows that the right to make a cinematograph film from the work vests with the author. In this case, the film producer has enriched himself at the cost of the labour, skill and intellect of the journalist without paying him his due. It is submitted that the reporting of current events is different from stories dug out by the journalists after continuous investigation by intellect and creativity and therefore, need to be distinguished from actual events, in which there is no copyright. This was not simply information in public domain or news *simplicities* but a course of biographical events resulting in a real non-fiction story that has to be protected under copyright law.

ORIGINAL LITERARY WORK

Definition of Literary Work

An original literary work is a subject matter of copyright protection. The Copyright Act, 1957 does not define "literary work" except to state under Section 2(0) that, "it includes computer programs, tables and compilations including computer data bases." The definition of literary work is inclusive and the inclusion contains compilations.[149] The "computer" and "computer programmes" are defined in Sections 2(ffb) and 2(ffc), respectively but "Computer database" is not defined by the Copyright Act. However, a definition of computer database is given in the Information Technology Act, 2000. Explanation to Section 43 of the Act states that computer data-base|| means a representation of information, knowledge, facts, concepts or instructions in text, image, audio, video that are being prepared or have been prepared in a formalised manner or have been produced by a computer, computer system or computer network and are intended for use in a computer, computer system or computer network.[150] The Berne Convention[151] gives a collective definition of the expression "literary and artistic work" thus:

---

148. *Indian Express Newspapers (Bom.) Pvt. Ltd.* v. *Jagmohan Mundhara,* AIR 1985 Bom 229.
149. *See, Navigators Logistics Ltd.* v. *Kashif Qureshi*, 2019I AD (Delhi) 418: 2018 (76) PTC 564 (Del).
150. Information Technology Act, 2000, Section 43(j), Explanation (ii). *See also, Gagan Harsh Sharma* v. *The State of Maharashtra*, 2019 ALLMR (Cri) 595: 2019 Cri LJ 1398.
151. Article 2 of the Berne Convention for the Protection of Literary and Artistic Works, 1886 (Latest revision in Paris in 1971).

> It shall include every production in the literary, scientific and artistic domain, whatever may be the mode or form or its expression, such as books, pamphlets and other writings; lectures, addresses, sermons and other works of the same nature; and entertainments in dumb show; musical compositions with or without words; cinematographic works to which are assimilated works expressed by a process analogous to cinematography; works of drawing, painting, architecture, sculpture, engraving and lithography; photographic works to which are assimilated works expressed by a process analogous to photography; works of applied art; illustrations, maps, plans, sketches and three-dimensional works relative to geography, topography, architecture or science.

Literary works are of two kinds: (a) primary or prior works: These are the literary works not based on existing subject-matter and, therefore, would be called primary or prior works; and (b) secondary or derivative works: These are literary works based on existing subject-matter. Since such works are based on existing subject-matter, they are called derivative works or secondary works.[152] Both kinds of works have to be original according to Section 14(a).

The dictionary[153] meaning of the word "literary" is, "well versed in or connected with literature". A literary work means any work, other than a dramatic or musical work, which is written, spoken or sung. A literary work should provide some element of either information and instruction or pleasure in the form of literary enjoyment. But to qualify as a literary work, there is certainly no need for the work to have any intrinsic literary merit. For example, examination papers, tables, compilations and computer programs are literary works. Peterson, J. in *University of London Press* v. *University Tutorial press*[154] observed that any work which is expressed in print or writing irrespective of the question whether the quality or style is high is literary work. The courts in India have also adopted this view and thereby held that[155] the literary merit or quality is not a pre-requisite for a work to be a literary work under the Copyright Act, 1957.

Scope and Ambit of Definition

The aforementioned definitions of literary work literary work provided in the Copyright Act, 1957 and the Berne Convention have been supplemented by the Information Technology Act, 2000 provide a wide definition of "literary work". This wide definition encouraged the courts to include mundane compilations of information. Thus, the Indian Courts have clearly ruled that the inclusive definition of literary work in the Copyright Act, 1957 enlarges its scope to include all works expressed in writing whether they have any literary merit or not. For copyright to subsist in a literary work, it must be more than *de minimis*. Single words will not attract copyright protection.[156]

---

152. *See, Rupalli R Shah* v. *Adani Wilmer Ltd.*, 2012 (52) PTC 305 (Bom); *Eastern Book Company* v. *D.B. Modak,* AIR 2008 SC 809: (2008) 1 SCC 1.
153. *See*, Bernard S. Cayne (Ed.), *You're listening to a sample of the Audible audio edition. Learn more. The New Lexicon Webster's Dictionary of the English Language* (Lexicon Publication, 1957).
154. [1916] 2 Ch_601 at 608.
155. *See, Rupendra Kashyap* v. *Jiwan Publishing House,* 1996 (38) DRJ 81:1996 PTC 439 (Del).
156. *See SAP AG* v. *Jayanth Kumar*, 2015 (61) PTC 474 (Del); Sap *Aktiengesellschaft* v. *Rohit Sharma*, 2014 (60) PTC 395 (Del).

In *Exxon Corporation* v. *Exxon Insurance Consultants International Ltd.*,[157] the claimant was a multinational oil company. It decided to choose a new corporate name, and after considerable research and consultation in word "*Exxon*" was decided upon. The claimant contended that the word "*Exxon*", being first used by it, was *original,* that it was literary because it was expressed in litters and that it was a work being the result of considerable research and effort. Therefore, the claimant argued that the word "*Exxon*" was an "original literary work". However, it was held that the word "*Exxon*" was not to be a literary work. Since "*Exxon*" is both original, being an invented word, and conveys information about the source of the goods to which it applies, it is arguable that the "*Exxon*" decision was actually taken on public interest grounds. There has been a long-standing judicial reluctance to endow single words with copyright protection largely because simple words or phrases as the basic building blocks of language should be available for public use. Also, if words have commercial value, such as "*Exxon*" itself does, they may well be protected as trademarks or by an action in passing-off, and dual protection would be undesirable.

Thus, mere slogans like *Yeh Dil Mange More* being trivial are not subject matter of protection as "original literary work". This decision was given by the Delhi High Court in *Pepsi Co. Inc.* v. *Hindustan Coca Cola.*[158] In this case, the court further observed that the defendant had not used the phrase/slogan *Yeh Dil Mange More* in relation to their product and hence no protection could be claimed under the *Trade & Merchandise Marks Act 1958* for these words. Moreover, the defendant used it only in a mocking manner in a competitive advertisement. However, the Copyright Board (Appellate Board)[159] misread the judgment and ordered that slogans were copyrightable in *Enercon Systems Pvt. Ltd.* v. *Registrar of Copyright*[160] and *Kamdhenu Ispat Ltd.* v. *Registrar of Copyright.*[161] Again, in *Godfrey Phillips India Ltd.* v. *Dharampal Satyapal Ltd.,*[162] the Delhi High Court held that the slogan "*Shauq Badi Cheez Hai*", being combination of common words, would not fall within the scope of "Artistic/literary work" under the Copyright Act. Slogan "*Shauq Badi Cheez Hai*" does not appear to be an outcome of great skill, inasmuch as, it uses the short stereo type combination of words. In fact, both the slogans, that is, "*Shauq Badi Cheez Hai*" and "*Swad Badi Cheez Hai*" are commonly spoken in Hindi language in day-to-day life. That apart, the slogans, are not copyrightable.

In *Macmillan* v. *Cooper*[163] it was held that copyright could exist in notes to North's translation of Plutarch's life of Alexander. As to the text, the Privy Council held that there was not a sufficient investment of knowledge, judgment, labour or literary skill to entitle

157. (1981) 3 All ER 241.
158. 94 (2001) DLT 30.
159. Substituted by the Finance Act 2017 (7 of 2017), section 160(a) for "Copyright Board," [w.e.f. 26 May, 2017].
160. 2008 (37) PTC 599 (CB).
161. 2010 (44) PTC 345 (CB).
162. (2012) 191 DLT 109: 2012 (51) PTC 251 (Del).
163. AIR 1924 PC 75. In *Mary P. Marshall* v. *Ram Narain Lal,* AIR 1934 All 922: 1934 AWR (H.C.) 3255, the Allahabad High Court preferred a quantitative criterion of "abridgement". It ruled that an abridgement should not be a "substantial reproduction" of the original. *See also, Santra Publication* v. *Jibesh Guha,* 2012 (1) CHN 383: MIPR 2012 (1) 201; *Dabur India Ltd.* v. *K.R. Industries,* AIR 2008 SC 3123: (2008) 10 SCC 595.

the appellants to copyright in the text. At the same time, the Privy Council also refused to characterise both the appellants' and respondents' work as "abridgements". Copying of certain passages or reduction of bulk would not, by itself, constitute abridgement. For, a true abridgement is a literary work in its own right. To constitute an abridgement, it was held, there should be "a statement designed to be complete and accurate of the thoughts, opinions and ideas" of the author in the "much more compressed language of the abridger". The court further observed:

(i) To constitute a true and equitable abridgement, the entire work must be preserved in its precise import and exact meaning, and then the act of abridgement is an exertion of the individuality employed in moulding and transferring a large work into a small compass, thus rendering it less expensive and more convenient both to the time and use of the reader.
(ii) Independent labour must be apparent and the restriction of the size of the work by copying some of its parts and omitting others confers no title to the authorship, and the result will not be an abridgement.
(iii) To abridge in the legal sense of the word is to preserve the substance, the essence of the work in language suited to such a purpose, language substantially different from that of the original.
(iv) To make such an abridgement requires the exercise of mind, labour skill and judgment brought into play and the result is not mere copying.
(v) Thus, literary taste and skill requisite to compile properly and effectively is important. Mere process of selecting passages from works is not enough; the skill manifested in making or arranging selection is important. One may have borrowed much of the material from others, but if they are combined in a different manner, i.e., are original, one has a copyright them.

Similarly, in *Macmillan* v. *Suresh Chandra Deb*[164] it was decided that there existed copyright in selection of songs and poems in *Palgrave's Golden Treasury*. Copyright in selection may exist when there is evidence that the author has done "extensive reading, careful study and comparison" and has exercised "taste and judgment in selection". This is a more certain test than the other also enunciated in this case, namely, that two men may make same selection but that it "must be by resorting to the original author". As regards compilations, Indian courts have held that a compilation which may be derived from "a common source falls within the ambit of literary work". Mere similarity between two compilations would not automatically constitute infringement. That determination (or whether, in terms of the 1914 Act, there has been a "colourable imitation") will have to be decided as a question of fact in the circumstances of each case.[165] Head notes in law reports have posed problems in India as elsewhere; but Indian courts have held them to be copyrightable, even though in many cases the substance of the head notes does no more than verbatim reproduce certain passages from the texts of judicial decisions.[166] However, recently the Supreme Court of India in *Eastern*

164. ILR (1890)17 Cal. 951.
165. *Kartar Singh* v. *Lodha Singh,* AIR 1933 Lah. 777.
166. *V. Govindam* v. *E.M. Gopalkrishna Kone,* AIR 1955 Mad. 391.

Book Company v. *D.B. Modak,*[167] held that judicial pronouncements of the apex court being in public domain, its reproduction or publication would not infringe copyright.

Ultimately, the determining standards of *Cooper*[168] and *Deb*[169] continue to guide assessment of how far copyright can exist in works of this nature which manifest the vanishing point of originality. The controversial question is whether a translation of a literary work is "literary work" or not? The word "translation" has not been defined in the *Copyright Act, 1957.* The expression translation as defined in *Black's Law Dictionary* means: "the reproduction in one language of a book, document or speech in another language." According to *Oxford Dictionary,* "translate" means to interpret, explain, also "to express one thing in terms of another" and "translation" means the action or process of turning from one language into another; also the product of this, a version in a different language, the expression or rendering of something in another medium or form, transformation, alteration or change. On the other hand the language of the Act might suggest a laudable policy of promoting wider diffusion of Indian works in one language into other Indian languages, a consideration which might have appeared distinctive to India as compared with the UK. There might also have been the desire to promote the growth of publication industry in numerous Indian languages. Therefore, in *Blackwood* v. *Parasuraman,*[170] it was held that a translation of literary work is itself a literary work and is entitled to copyright protection if it is original and the author has expended sufficient labour and skill on it. It was further held that if copyright subsists in the original work, then reproduction or publication of the translation without the consent or licence of the owner of the copyright in the original will constitute infringement. Thus, translation of a work into another language can be an infringement.[171] However, in *Entertainment Network (India) Ltd.* v. *Super Cassettes Industries Ltd.*,[172] the Apex Court held that where there are more applicants than one seeking a compulsory license for translation of a work or for reproduction of the work or for publication of an unpublished work, then the Copyright Board (Appellate Board)[173] make grant the compulsory licence to such one of the applicants, as in the opinion of the Board, would best serve in the interest of the general public.

However, historical facts are not copyrightable. A book on history is designed to convey information to the readers. There can be no copyright in the information as such but if the manner of its presentation is unique to its author, it is an "original literary" work. In *Ravencraft* v. *Herbert,*[174] it was held that a historical work is not to be judged by precisely the same standards as a work of fiction. Historical work would have another purpose as well; to add to the knowledge possessed by the reader and in the process to increase the sum total of human experience and understanding. The author of a historical work must have attributed to him an intention that the information thereby imparted may be used by the reader, because knowledge

---

167. AIR 2008 SC 809: (2008) 1 SCC 1.
168. *Macmillan* v. *Cooper,* AIR 1924 PC 75.
169. *Macmillan* v. *Suresh Chandra Deb,* ILR (1890)17 Cal. 951.
170. AIR 1959 Mad 410. *See also, Apple Computer Inc.* v. *Computer Edge* (1984) FSR 481.
171. *Barbara Taylor Bradford* v. *Sahara Media Entertainment Ltd.* (2004) ILR 1 Cal 15: 2004 (28) PTC 474 (Cal).
172. MIPR 2008 (2) 129: 2008 (37) PTC 353 (SC).
173. Substituted by the Finance Act 2017 (7 of 2017), section 160(a) for "Copyright Board," [w.e.f. 26 May, 2017].
174. 1980 RPC 193.

would become sterile if it could not be applied. Therefore, it is reasonable to suppose that the law of copyright will prohibit the wider use to be made of a historical work. The knowledge built upon an historical work can, however, be extracted. Such an extraction of knowledge from historical work can claim copyrighting in itself.

In *Agarwala Publishing House* v. *Board of Higher Secondary and Intermediate Education*,[175] a Gazette notification vesting the copyright in the questions papers prepared for the examinations conducted by the Board with the Board and forbidding the publication of it without the permission of the Board was challenged. The petitioner, who was a publisher, contended that copyright could not be claimed in question papers as it was not an "original literary" work. The Allahabad High Court while dismissing the contention of the petitioner observed thus:

> The literary works referred to in Section 13 of the Indian Copyright Act 1957 are not confined to works of literature in the commonly understood sense, but must be taken to include all works expressed in writing, whether they have any literary merit or not. This is clear from the definition given in Section 2(0) of the Act, which states that literary work includes tables and compilations. And the word original used in Section 13 does not imply any originality in ideas but merely means that the work in question should not be copied from some other work but should originate from the author, being the product of his labour and skill.

Accordingly various Courts in the country have held that copyright can subsist in law books and reports, gazettes, grammar books, maps, almanacs and encyclopedias, guide books and compilations,[176] examination papers,[177] ready-recknors of prices of commodities at given rate of mathematical calculations[178] and works of religious preachers or compilation of discourse or teaching,[179] letters,[180] catalogues, dictionaries,[181] research thesis and dissertation.[182] Thus every original work irrespective of its literary merit can be protected as a literary work under the Copyright Act. In *Fateh Singh Mehta* v. *O.P. Singhal,*[183] the Rajasthan High Court held that "literary work" includes "dissertation" submitted by a student. In *Satsang* v. *Kiron Chandra Mukhopadhyay,*[184] the Calcutta High Court held that writings, sermons and sayings of a religious preacher fall within the definition of "literary work". In *Sulamangalam R. Jayalakshmi* v. *Meta Musicals,*[185] the lyrics written by a *swami* were held to be "literary work".

Secondary or Derivative Literary Work

There are two classes of literary work, viz., primary or prior works and secondary or derivate work. The primary work is the literary work not based on existing subject matter. The derivate

175. AIR 1967 All 91.
176. *V. Govindam* v. *E.M. Gopalkrishna Kone*, AIR 1955 Mad. 391.
177. *Jagdish Prasad Gupta* v. *Parmeshwar Prasad Singh*, AIR 1966 Pat. 33: 1966 Cri LJ 54; *Agarwala Publishing House* v. *Board of High School and Intermediate Education U.P.*, AIR 1967 All 9.
178. *Shyam Lal Paharia* v. *Gaya Prasad Gupta,* AIR 1971 All 192.
179. *Satsang* v. *Kiron Chandra,* AIR 1972 Cal 533: (1974) ILR 1 Cal 498.
180. *Walter* v. *Lane* (1900) AC 539.
181. *Lamba Brothers Pvt. Ltd.* v. *Lamba Brothers,* AIR 1993 Delhi 347: 1994 (28) DRJ 168.
182. *Fateh Singh Mehta* v. *O.P. Singhal,* AIR 1990 Raj 8: 1989 WLN (UC) 522.
183. AIR 1990 Raj 8: 1989 WLN (UC) 522.
184. AIR 1973 Cal 533: (1974) ILR 1 Cal 498.
185. AIR 2000 Mad 454: 2000-3-LW38.

work is literary work based on existing subject matter.[186] In many cases we can find only derived work. Compilation is the good example for derivate work. A question arises whether in such a derivate work a new copyright is created. The decisions of courts clearly indicate that copyright subsists in such work. The creation of such new right is depending upon various factors, and would one of them be only skill, capital and labour expended upon it to qualify for copyright protection in a derivative literary work created from the pre-existing material in the public domain, and the required exercise of independent skill, labour and capital in its creation by the author would qualify him for the copyright protection in the derivate work. If it is not the case, copy right would not subsist.[187] Thus, in *Institute for Inner Studies* v. *Charlotte Anderson*,[188] the Court observed:

> The problems often arises in the cases where the protection is sought for the derivative nature of the works or in cases where the work contains the historical facts collated from history or ancient times or in cases where work consists of methods of construction, any theorems, principles which are common place or scientific principles or experiments touching the patents which are sought to be protected under the guise of original works of authorship.

In *Blueberry Books* v. *Bharti Goyal*,[189] the Court observed: "Section 16 of the Copyright Act 1957 provides that no copyright can be acquired in respect of any work except in accordance with the provisions of the Act. Therefore, copyright is a statutory right. Only those rights which the Copyright Act creates; to the extent it creates, and; subject to the limitations that the Act imposes, vest in the owner of the copyright in the work, whether it is a primary work such as a literary, dramatic or musical work, or a derivate work such as a sound recording or cinematograph film. No right, which the Copyright Act does not expressly create can be inferred or claimed under the said Act." Thus, the Court recognises that a derivate work is copyrightable such as a sound recording or cinematograph film. But Copyrights Act 1957 does not define the term "derivate work". The word "work" is defined in Section 2(y) which would be a literary, dramatic, musical or artistic work; a cinematograph film; and a sound recording. Further, under Section 2(o), "literary work" would include computer programs, tables and compilations including compute computer databases. However, it is not clear from the definitions of "work" or "literary work" what exactly derivative work is?

In *Eastern Book Co.* v. *D.B. Modak.*[190] Appellants, the publishers of law report by name "Supreme Court Cases" (SCC), claimed copyright in the copy-edited judgments published by them and alleged infringement of the same by the respondent in their publication "Grand Jurix". According to the appellants, their report consists of various inputs to make the judgments user-friendly by correcting the mistakes, adding cross references, footnotes, proper paragraph numbering, standardised formatting of the text, verification of the references, etc. These constitute considerable skill, labour and expertise including substantial capital expenditure on infrastructure, staff, equipment, etc. This is sufficient to treat the reported judgment "original

---

186. *Eastern India Motion Pictures Association* v. *Indian Performing Right Society Ltd.*, AIR 1974 Cal 257.
187. *See*, *Maroti* v. *The State of Maharashtra*, 2018 ALLMR (Cri) 4460; *Nagpur Distilleries Pvt. Ltd.* v. *Karmaveer Shankarrao Kale*, 2017 (5) ABR 140; *Thiagarajan Kumararaja* v. *Capital Film Works*, AIR 2017 Mad 32; Krishika Lulla v. Shyam Vithalrao Devkatta, (2016) 2 SCC 521: 2015 (10) SCALE 718.
188. 2014 (57) PTC 228 (Del): MIPR 2014 (1) 129.
189. AIR 2019 Delhi 84: 2019 II AD (Delhi) 233.
190. AIR 2008 SC 809: 2008 (1) SCC 1.

literary work" for copyright protection. It was, *inter alia,* alleged that the defendants literally copied the copy-edited judgment of the appellant violating their copyright in the copy-edited judgment. According to the respondent, there is no copyright protection for the copy-edited judgments since the input is insubstantial to constitute an "original" literary work. The lower court denied injunction on the ground that the inputs of the appellant is trivial in nature and inadequate to constitute originality to claim copyright protection in the copy-edited judgment.[191] The Supreme Court considered the copy-edited judgment as a derivative work and examined the standard of originality required for the derivative work to be considered for copyright protection. Regarding the standard of originality after examining English[192] and Indian cases[193] and referring to Section 52(1)(q) of the Indian Copyright Act 1957 the Supreme Court observed:[194]

> The judicial pronouncements of the Apex Court would be in the public domain and its reproduction or publication would not infringe the copyright. That being the position, the copy-edited judgments would not satisfy the copyright merely by establishing amount of skill, labour and capital put in the inputs of the copy-edited judgments and the original or innovative thoughts for the creativity are completely excluded. Accordingly, original or innovative thoughts are necessary to establish copyright in the author's work .... To secure a copyright for the judgments delivered by the court, it is necessary that the labour, skill and capital invested should be sufficient to communicate or impart to the judgment printed in SCC some quality or character which the original judgment does not possess and which differentiates the original judgment from the printed one.

Thus, the Supreme Court treated the reported judgment of the "Supreme Court Cases" (SCC) as derivative works. The general principles laid down by the court seem to be correct that the application of the same to the facts has created confusion. The reason is the failure of the court to find out the correct subject matter of protection and the application of the test of originality laid down by it to the subject matter in its totality. Though the court stated in the beginning without any analysis that the reported judgment is a "derivative work", it is evident from the observations that the court on many occasions treated it as a "compilation" to determine the standard of originality. It is important to note that though the court quoted from the House of Lords judgment in *Ladbroke (Football)*[195] regarding the importance of applying the test of originality to the whole of the work it is disappointing to note that the same was not applied to the facts of this case. It is equally disappointing to note that the court did not make any sincere effort to determine what constitutes a derivative work and whether reported judgment fell under this category.

---

191. *Eastern Book Co.* v. *Navin J. Desai,* 2001 PTC 57 (Del).
192. *Ladbroke (Football) Ltd.* v. *William Hill (Football) Ltd.,* [1964] I WLR 273 (HL); *Walter and Another* v. *Lane,* [1900] AC 539 (HL); *Designers Guild Ltd.* v. *Russell Williams (Textiles) Ltd.,* [2000] I WLR 2416 (HL); *University of London Press Limited* v. *University Tutorial Press Limited,* [1916] 2 Ch 60 I; *Kelly* v. *Morris* (1866) LR I Eq. 697 and *Parry* v. *Moring and Gollancz,* Cop Cas (1901–1904) 49.
193. *Gopal Das* v. *Jagannath Prasad and Another,* AIR 1938 All 266; *V. Govindam* v. *E.M. Gopalakrishna Kane and Another,* AIR 1955 Mad 391; *C. Cunniah & Co.* v. *Balraj & Co.,* AIR 1961 Mad III; *Agarwala Publishing House* v. *Board of High School and Intermediate Education and Another,* AIR 1967 All 91; *Gangavishnu Shrikisondas* v. *Moreshvar Bapuji Hegishte and Others,* ILR 13 Bom 358; *Rai Toys Industries and Others* v. *Munir Printing Press,* 1982 PTC 85 and *Macmillan and Another* v. *Suresh Chandra Deb,* ILR 17 Cal 952.
194. *Eastern Book Co.* v. *D.B. Modak,* AIR 2008 SC 809: 2008 (1) SCC 1.
195. *Ladbroke (Football) Ltd.* v. *William Hill (Football) Ltd.,* [1964] I WLR 273 (HL).

Regarding reported judgments, the observation of the court is pertinent. It is the admitted position that the report in the Supreme Court Cases (SCC) of the judgments of the Supreme Court is a derivative work in public domain. It is to be noted that there is no express provision in the Indian Copyright Act defining derivative work. In this context it is worth looking into Berne Convention for the Protection of Literary and Artistic Work and law in US to find out whether the above classification could be the basis for analysis for treating reported judgments as derivative work of original judgments of the court. According to article 2(3) of the Berne Convention, a derivative work means:[196]

> Translations, adaptations, arrangements of music and other alterations of a literary or artistic work shall be protected as original works without prejudice to the copyright in the original work.

It is clear that the obligation is to protect translations, adaptations or other alterations as original work without prejudice to the copyright in the original work. In addition to this, the Berne Convention, as per Articles 14[197] and 14bis[198] also recognises adaptation of a literary or artistic work into cinematograph film as original work. This is reflected in the definition of derivative work in the copyright law of United States. Section 101 defines derivate work as follows:[199]

> A work based upon one or more pre-existing works, such as a translation, fictionalization, motion picture version, condensation, or any other form in which a work may be recast, transformed or adapted. A work consisting of editorial versions, annotation, elaboration, or other modifications which, as a whole, represent an original work of authorship is a derivative work.

These provisions make it clear that a derivative work is based on a "pre-existing work" and not based on an "existing subject matter" as stated by the Supreme Court. It may be noted that the Supreme Court made it clear that there is no copyright protection for the subject matter as such and it is the manner of expression of the subject matter that attracts protection.[200] Similarly, the existing work must get transformed to be treated as a whole to form a derivative work. In *American Express Bank Ltd.* v. *Priya Puri*,[201] the Court held that the copyright can be claimed in derivative work only in the following manner:

---

196. *Ibid.*, para. 38.
197. Article 14 reads: "(1) Authors of literary or artistic works shall have the exclusive right of authorizing: (i) the cinematographic adaptation and reproduction of these works, and the distribution of the works thus adapted or reproduced;...."
198. Article 14bis (1) reads: "Without prejudice to the copyright in any work which may have been adapted or reproduced, a cinematographic work shall be protected as an original work. The owner of copyright in a cinematographic work shall enjoy the same rights as the author of an original work, including the rights referred to in the preceding Article."
199. Title 17 USC $ 101.
200. *See, Rupalli R Shah* v. *Adani Wilmer Ltd.*, 2012 (52) PTC 305 (Bom). *See also*, *R.G. Anand* v. *Delux Films,* (AIR 1978 SC 1613 at 1627) where the Apex Court observation: "There can be no copyright in an idea, subject matter, themes, plots or historical or legendary facts and violation of the copyright in such cases *is confined to the form, manner and arrangement and expression of the idea by the author of the copyrighted work* .... It is always open to any person to choose an idea as a subject matter and develop it in his own manner and give expression to the idea by treating it differently from others".
201. (2006) III LLJ 540 Del: 2006 (110) FLR 1061.

> A derivative work consists of a contribution of original material to a pre-existing work so as to recast, transform or adapt the pre-existing work. This would include a new version of a work in the public domain and abridgement adaptation, arrangement, dramatization or translation. A collective work will qualify for copyright by reason of the original effort expended in the process of compilation, even if no new matter is added. In determining whether a work based upon a prior work is separately copyrightable as a derivative or collective work, the Courts may not properly consider whether the new work is a qualitative improvement over the prior work. However, in order to qualify for a separate copyright as a derivative or collective work, the additional matter injected in a prior work or the matter of rearranging or otherwise transforming a prior work, must constitute more than a minimal contribution.

In this context if one examines the scheme of the Indian Copyright Act 1957, one could see the same reflected in section 14 and the related definitions in Section 2. Section 14 recognises the right to make translation, cinematograph film and adaptation of the literary work. It is also made clear that the translated or adapted work will enjoy independent copyright. The term adaptation is also defined.[202] In case of literary works, it is made clear that this includes conversion into dramatic work by way of performance, abridgment of the work or *use of the work involving its re-arrangement or alteration.* This is in accordance with the provisions of the Berne Convention. It is clear that to treat a work as a derivative work there must be substantial change in the character of the derivative work based on an existing work. The transformation as a whole must be considered to treat it as a derivative work. It is evident that the Supreme Court failed to examine these provisions before it made the broad classification and treated the reported judgment as derivative work. The judgment as reported by the SCC in no way could be treated as a derivative work since it is not an adaptation of the original judgments of the court as understood in our law. There is no re-arrangement or alteration of the original judgments as envisaged in our Act to make the reported judgments original, adapted work or derivative work. It is the failure of the court to examine the content of the derivative work as envisaged in the Berne Convention and incorporated in our law that led to the conclusion that the reported judgments are derivative works. This also resulted in the court that wrongly applying the standard of originality and concluding that some changes made in the judgment deserve protection while the other changes do not. The approach is wrong since if it is a derivative work the transformation as a whole must be considered to determine whether it is original or not to provide independent protection. It is quite unfortunate that the judgment of the Supreme Court resulted in wrong interpretation of the law and it is expected that the court will use the next opportunity to rectify this though one is not sure when this is going to happen given the conditions in India.

Textbooks or guidebooks, by their very nature, are "derivative works". Thus, it will be permissible to publish a guide book if it qualifies the proper description of a guide book and

202. According to Section 2(a): "adaptation" means: (i) in relation to a dramatic work, the conversion of the work into a non-dramatic work; (ii) in relation to a literary work or an artistic work, the conversion of the work into a dramatic work by way of performance in public or otherwise; (iii) in relation to a literary or dramatic work, any abridgement of the work or any version of the work in which the story or action is conveyed wholly or mainly by means of pictures in a form suitable for reproduction in a book, or in a newspaper, magazine or similar periodical; (iv) in relation to a musical work, any arrangement or transcription of the work; and (v) in relation to any work, any use of such work involving its re-arrangement or alteration.

becomes a derivative work of the author who has produced such guide book. A guide book, by its very nature, is "derivative work". A derivative work qualifies to become original when such work is a result of skill, labour, capital and a minimum degree of creativity.[203] Clarifying this proposition of law, the Court in *Syndicate of the Press of the University of Cambridge* v. *Chancellor Masters*,[204] observed:

> A derivative work qualifies to become original when such work is a result of skill, labour, capital and a minimum degree of creativity. That is sufficient to acquire original creativity. Once we examine the appellant's work applying this test, we are convinced that the work of the appellant qualifies the test of "minimum degree of creativity". The "originality" with regard to a new work that is a primary work does not emanate from creativity. Creativity is inherent in a new work.

Compilation of Literary Work

Even prior to the *Copyright (Amendment) Act,* 1994, the scope and ambit of copyright protection in case of a compilation of literary work was settled by Courts in various cases. The question whether a plaintiff is entitled to copyright depends on whether it is an "original literary" work.[205] The 1994 Copyright Amendment Act defined literary work under Section 2(o). Literary work is defined in Section 2(o) as including computer programmes, tables and compilations including computer databases. In *Navigators Logistics Ltd.* v. *Kashif Qureshi*,[206] the Delhi High Court held that the definition of literary work is inclusive and the inclusion contains compilations. But, the question which thus arises is, whether all compilations are literary work in which copyright can subsist? Answering to this question in *Gurukrupa Mech Tech Pvt. Ltd.* v. *State of Gujarat*,[207] the Gujarat High Court held that as regards compilation, originality is a matter of degree depending on the amount of skill, judgment or labour that has been involved in making the compilation. The Court in its reasoning observed:

> The word 'original' does not demand original or inventive thought, but only that the work should not be copied but should originate from the author. In deciding, therefore, whether a work in the nature of a compilation is original, it is wrong to consider individual parts of it apart from the whole. For many compilations have nothing original in their parts, yet the sum total of the compilation may be original. In such cases the courts have looked to see whether the compilation of the unoriginal material called for work or skill or expense. If it did, it is entitled to be considered original and to be protected.

Prior to the 1994 amendment Court held that "literary work" includes a compilation.[208] These words are used to describe any work which can be expressed in print or writing irrespective of whether it has any excellence of quality or style of writing. The word "original"

---

203. *See, Institute for Inner Studies* v. *Charlotte Anderson*, 2014 (57) PTC 228 (Del): MIPR 2014 (1) 129; *Rediff.Com India Ltd.* v. *E-Eighteen.Com Ltd.*, 2013 (55) PTC 294 (Del): 202 (2013) DLT 657.
204. 185 (2011) DLT 346: 2011 (47) PTC 244 (Del).
205. *See*, K.N. Chandrasekharan Pillai, "Copyrightability of Supreme Court Judgment" 50 *Journal of the Indian Law Institute* (5008) pp. 94–97.
206. 2019 IAD (Delhi) 418: 2018 (76) PTC 564 (Del). *See also*, *Maroti* v. *The State of Maharashtra*, 2018 ALLMR (Cri) 4460.
207. (2018) 4 GLR 3324.
208. *See, Ladbroke (Football) Ltd.* v. *William Hill (Football) Ltd.*, 1964 WL 19516 (HL): [1964] 1 All E.R. 465.

does not demand original or inventive thought, but only that the work should not be copied but should originate from the author.[209] Now question arises: whether a work in the nature of a compilation is original? In this context, it has to be remembered that many compilations may have nothing original in their parts, yet the sum total of the compilation may be original. In such cases, the courts have looked to see whether the compilation of the not-original material called for work or skill or expense. If it did, it is entitled to be considered original and to be protected against those who wish to steal the fruits of the work or skill or expense by copying it without taking the trouble of compiling it themselves. Hence, the protection given by such copyright is in no sense a monopoly, for it is open to a rival to produce the same result if he chooses to evolve it by his own labours.[210]

Thus, directories, catalogues, and the like have been held to be original and to acquire copyright if the work that goes into their making has been sufficient.[211] In *G.A. Cramp and Sons Ltd.* v. *Frank Smythson Ltd.*,[212] it was held to have no copyright, where the work of compilation was not "substantial", but "negligible". The arrangement of the material is one of the factors to be considered. The Court observed:

> There was no evidence that any of these tables was composed specially for the respondents' diary. There was no feature in them which could be pointed out as novel or specially meritorious or ingenious from the point of view of the judgment or skill of the compiler. It was not suggested that there was any element of originality or skill in the order in which the tables were arranged.

Therefore, in each case, it is a question of degree whether the labour or skill or ingenuity or expense involved in the compilation is sufficient to warrant a claim to originality in a compilation. In *Macmillan and Co.* v. *K. and J. Cooper*,[213] an abridgement of an author's work which in fact was not an abridgement but a collection of detached passages from the author's work joined together, was held not to be an abridgement of the original work of the author but merely a selection of scripts taken from the author's work printed in the form of a narrative. The Judicial Committee observed:

> ... it is the produce of the labour, skill and capital of one man which must not be appropriated by another, not the elements, the raw material if one may use the expression, upon which the labour and skill and capital of the first have been expended. To secure copyright for this product it is necessary that the labour, skill and capital expended should be sufficient to impart to the product some quality or character which the raw material did not possess, and which differentiates the product from the raw material.

In *G.A. Cramp and Sons Ltd.* v. *Frank Smythson Ltd.*,[214] both the parties were publishers of pocket diaries. The question for consideration was whether the appellants, in respect of their inserting certain tables in their diary of 1942, had infringed any copyright that the respondents had in a collection of tables included in their pocket diary known as "Litublue". Seven of the tables in the appellants' diary had been copied from the respondents' diary. The question was whether having regard to its nature and subjects, the compilation to be found

209. *University of London Press Ltd.* v. *University Tutorial Press Ltd.*, [1916] 2 Ch. 601, 608.
210. *Kelly* v. *Morris* (1886) L.R. 1 Eq. 697, 701.
211. *H. Black Lock and Co. Ltd.* v. *C. Arthur Pearson Ltd.*, [1915] 2 Ch. 376: 31 T.L.R. 526.
212. [1944] A.C. 329.
213. AIR 1924 PC 75.
214. (1944 A.C. 329).

in the respondents' diary which had thus been copied and made use by the appellants, could be regarded as the subject matter of copyright. It was held that the impugned compilation fell short of "displaying the qualities requisite to attract copyright". The Court observed:

> Under Section 1(1) of the Copyright Act of 1911, copyright subsists in 'every original literary work' and this expression includes compilation. The existence of sufficient originality is a question of fact and degree.

Similarly, in *S.K. Dutt* v. *Law Book Co.*,[215] the plaintiff alleged that the copyright in his work "Indian Partnership Act, by Mukerji and Dutt" had been infringed by the second defendant in his publication entitled: "Law Book Company's Commentaries of Law and Practice of Partnership and Private Companies in India." It was observed that in order to construe infringement of a man's copyright, there must be sufficient infringement of the work. Fair dealing by any one has been kept out of the mischief of the *Copyright Act*. It was further observed:

> Several persons may originate similar works in the same general form without anyone infringing the law in regard to copyright. The infringement comes in only when it can be shown that someone has, instead of utilising the available sources to originate his works, appropriated the labours of another by resorting to a slavish copy of mere colourable imitation thereof. The 'animus furandi', that is, an intention to take from another for purposes of saving labour, is one of the important ingredients to be found against a defendant before he can, in a suit under the Copyright Act, be demnified.

Further, in *Mohini Mohan Singh* v. *Sitanath Basak*,[216] the plaintiff was the author of a book entitled: "Adarshalipi-o-Saral-Barna-Parichaya" which was first published in 1902 and had run into several editions. In 1919, the defendant published two books in which, according to the allegations of the plaintiff, his copyright had been infringed by the defendant. It was observed that the question whether a colourable imitation had been made of the work of another must necessarily be a question of fact. A mere similarity is not enough as it may be due to chance, both works having been taken from a common source. It was observed: "Though similarity is to a large extent inevitable and each one of the points of similarity may not be worth anything, a conglomeration of so many points of similarity which, in the opinion of the defendant's own expert, constitutes a strange coincidence, points to the defendants having copied from the plaintiff's book." *Govindan* v. *Gopalakrishna*[217] was a case of compilation. It was held that though in the case of "compilation", the amount of originality will be very small but even that small amount is protected by law and no man is entitled to steal or appropriate for himself the result of another's brain, skill or labour even in such works. On the defence, plea of common source it was held:

> A person relying on it must show that he went to the common source from which he borrowed, employing his skill, labour and brains and that he did not merely do the work of the copyist, by copying away from another work.

In *Shyam Lal Paharia* v. *Gaya Prasad Gupta*,[218] the Allahabad High Court examined the various cases on the issue of compilation work and developed various principles enunciated in

215. AIR 1954 All 570: ILR (1954) 1 All 289.
216. AIR 1931 Cal 233.
217. AIR 1955 Mad 391.
218. AIR 1971 All 192.

these cases[219] may be briefly summarised as follows: (i) A compilation which may be derived from a common source falls within the ambit of literary work; (ii) A work of compilation of a nature similar to that of another will not by itself constitute an infringement of the copyright of another person's work written on the same pattern; (iii) The question whether an impugned work is a colourable imitation of another person's work is always a question of fact and has to be determined from the circumstances in each case; (iv) The determining factor in finding whether another person's copyright has been infringed is to see whether the impugned work is a slavish imitation and copy of another person's work or it bears the impress of the author's own labours and exertions.

From the statements of the authorities and the trend of judicial opinion, it is clear that a compilation of previous works developed by any one by devoting time, money, labour and skill although the sources may be commonly situated, amounts to a "literary work" of the author who has a copyright. Thus, a compilation derived from a common source falls within ambit of literary work. A work of compilation of a nature similar to that of another will not by itself constitute an infringement of the copyright of another person's work written on the same pattern. The question whether a work is a colourable imitation of another person's work is always a question of fact. The determining factor is to see whether the impugned work is a slavish imitation and a copy of another person's work or it bears the impress of the author's own labours and exertions.

Whether Copyright Subsists in Supreme Court and High Courts Judgments

The Supreme Court or High Courts Judgments are in public domain. Thus, Section 17(d) of the Copyright Act, 1957 states that unless otherwise stated, the first owner of any government work is the government itself. According to Section 2(k) of the Act, government work means a work which is made or published by or under the direction or control of "(i) the Government or any department of the Government; (ii) any Legislature in India; (ii) any Court, Tribunal or other judicial authority in India." By virtue of this definition, the judgments delivered by the Supreme Court or High Courts would be a government work.[220] Further, Section 52(q)(iv) of the Act provides that the reproduction or publication of any judgment or order of a court, Tribunal or other judicial authority unless otherwise prohibited by the court permissible and exempts the same from the realm of infringement. Thus, effect of these copyright provisions impels that a judgment of the court is a matter within the public domain, i.e., not subject to copyright regulations and can be utilised by anyone.

In *N.T. Raghunathan* v. *All India Reporter (AIR) Ltd.*,[221] the Bombay High Court held that head notes in case reporters prepared by the plaintiff was copied by the defendant and the defendant not only had copied the idea but also the comparison of the ideas and the form in

---

219. *Waterlow Directors Ltd.* v. *Reed Information Service Ltd.*, 1992 FSR 409; *William Hill (Football) Ltd.* v. *Ladbroke (Football)*, 1980 RPC 539; *Khemraj Shrikrishandas* v. *Garg and Co.*, AIR 1975 Delhi 130: ILR 1975 Delhi 251; *Shyam Lal Paharia* v. *Gaya Prasad*, AIR 1971 All 182; *Govindan* v. *Gopalakrishna*, AIR 1955 Mad 391.
220. *See*, *Eastern Book Company* v. *D.B. Modak*, AIR 2008 SC 809: (2008) 1 SCC 1.
221. AIR 1962 Bom. 48.

which they were expressed in the plaintiff's digest. In this case, the AIR publications, besides usual publications of Supreme Court or High Courts Judgments, along with their points of law and head notes, also printed the bare head notes of unreported judgments as "Notes of Unreported Cases" or "NUC". The head notes of the judgments reported in these journals were being directly taken by another journal known as Madras Weekly Notes. Accordingly, a suit for copyright infringement was field in the matter. The High Court, in consideration of the broad issue, compared the fact situation in this case to that of the case of *Sweet* v. *Benning*,[222] and affirmed UK English Court's dictum laid down therein.[223] Thus, initially disputes regarding copyrightability of law reporters were limited only to the protection granted to its constituent parts like head notes, marginal notes, etc., and not to the entire reporter itself.

Recently, the Apex Court examined the issue: whether copyright subsists in Supreme Court judgments?[224] Although the Supreme Court Judgments are in public domain, in *Eastern Book Company* v. *D.B. Modak,*[225] M/s. Eastern Book Company claimed copyright in the copy-edited judgments of the Supreme Court published by them. Their interim injunction against the despondences was rejected on 17-1-2001 by the Delhi High Court. The earlier stay was vacated. However, before the single judge, the respondents concealed that the appellants have copyright in the head notes and as such they undertook not to copy these head notes in their CD ROMs.

Aggrieved by this order, the appellants approached the Division Bench of the Delhi High Court which, however, did not agree with the submission of the appellants that by making certain corrections in the judgments or putting paragraph numbers or arranging the said judgments in a particular manner while printing, the appellants can claim that the copy-edited judgments become their original literary work. The Division Bench accordingly held that the reading of the judgment and searching important portion thereof and collecting sentences from various places for the purpose of making head-notes would involve labour and skill. Accordingly, an order of injunction was granted by the Division Bench as far as footnotes and editorial comments, etc. are concerned. The Division Bench also held that the appellants are not the author of the Supreme Court judgments and by merely making certain corrections therein or giving paragraph numbers the corrector of a judgment does not change and it does not become materially different from the original judgment.[226] The Division Bench applying the traditional English "sweat of brow" theory held:

> sufficient expenditure of labour, skill and capital to make product original.

It is clear that the opinion of the Division Bench of the Delhi High Court that no person should claim copyright in the text of the judgment by mere putting certain inputs to make it user-friendly. And M/s. Eastern Book Company appealed to the Apex Court. A Division Bench of the Supreme Court comprising B.N. Agrawal and P.P. Naolekar, JJ. declared:

---

222. (1855) 139 All ER 838.
223. *Macmillan and Co.* v. *K. and J. Cooper*, AIR 1924 PC 75.
224. *See*, Anu Tiwari and Shruti Rajan, "Proprietory Rights or Common Property?—The Dilemmas of Copyright Protection of Case—Law Reporters", 11 *Journal of Intellectual Property Rights* (2006), pp. 33–42.
225. AIR 2008 SC 809: 2008 (1) SCC 1.
226. That judgment of the Division Bench of the Delhi High Court is reported as 2002 (25) PTC 641 (Del): AIR 2001 Delhi 185.

> The editor who inserts para numbering must know how legal argumentation and legal discourse is conducted and how a judgment of a court of law must read... Setting of paragraphs by the appellants of their own in the judgment entailed the exercise of the brain work, reading and understanding of subject of disputes, different issues involved, statutory provisions applicable and interpretation of the same and then dividing them in different paragraphs so that chain of thoughts and process of statement of facts and the application of law relevant to the topic discussed is not disturbed, would require full understanding of the entire subject of the judgment. Making paragraphs in a judgment could not be called a mechanical process. It requires careful consideration, discernment and choice and thus it can be called a work of an author. Creation of paragraphs would obviously require extensive reading, careful study of subject and the exercise of judgment to make paragraph which has dealt with particular aspect of the case, and separating intermixing of a different subject. Creation of paragraphs by separating them from the passage would require knowledge, sound judgment and legal skill. In our opinion, this exercise and creation thereof has a flavour of minimum amount of creativity.
>
> The said principle would also apply when the editor has put an input whereby different judges' opinion has been shown to have been dissenting or partly dissenting or concurring, etc. It also requires reading of the whole judgment and understanding the questions involved and thereafter finding out whether the Judges have disagreed or have the dissenting opinion or they are partially disagreeing and partially agreeing to the view on a particular law point or even on facts. In these inputs put in by the appellants in the judgments reported in SCC, the appellants have a copyright and nobody is permitted to utilize the same.

Thus, the Supreme Court held that M/s. Eastern Book Company could not claim copyright in a judgment under the heading "literary work". But the Court only granted an injunction limited to the headnotes, footnotes and editorial notes in judgment. In this context, it is worthwhile to remember that the copyrightability of headnotes was already almost accepted by parties and courts. It is interesting to note that in a decision rendered more than a year prior to the present decision, the Kerala High Court declined to consider the copyrightability of each fragment of a judgment. It declared that judgment is a composite piece and when its headnotes, etc. are copyrightable the whole judgement should be copyrightable. Thottathil B. Radhakrishnan, J. in *M/s. Infoseek Solutions* v. *M/s. Kerala Law Times,*[227] observed:

> I find considerable support in the decision of the Division Bench of the Delhi High Court in Eastern Book Company's case (supra) holding that the work of preparing head-notes, editorial notes, etc., even by collecting sentences from the text of the judgment, involves labour and skill and that originality and creativity in preparation of head-notes are also available. However, for the reasons stated in the preceding paragraphs, with respect, I am unable to concur with the views of the learned single Judge and the Division Bench of the Delhi High Court in Eastern Book Company's case (supra), in so far as they relate to copyright over the published version of the text of the judgment, as reported and published as reports. In my view, a law report is a composite document and its head-notes, editorial comments, footnotes, setting, layout, presentation, etc. and even the skill and labour involved in choosing as to whether a judgment should be reported, lead to the reporter and publisher acquiring copyright over such report, as a composite document including the text of the judgment as to published by the reporter. No distinction exists between head-notes, etc. on the one hand and the main text on the other, while considering the question as to whether a report has a copyright over the publication.

227. AIR 2007 Ker 1: 2007 (34) PTC 231 (Ker).

In the operative part of the judgment,[228] the Supreme Court also declares:

> The high Court has already granted interim relief to the plaintiff-appellants by directing that though the respondent-defendants shall be entitled to sell their CD-ROMS with the text of the judgments of the Supreme Court along with their own headnotes, editorial notes, if any, they should not in any way copy the headnotes of the plaintiff-appellants; and that the defendant-respondents shall also not copy the footnotes and editorial notes appearing in the journal of the plaintiff-appellants. It is further directed by us that the defendant-respondents shall not use the paragraphs made by the appellants in their copy-edited version for internal references and their editor's judgment regarding the opinions expressed by the Judges by using phrases like concurring, "partly dissenting", etc. on the basis of reported judgments in SCC.

The Kerala High Court decision was obviously not referred to or discussed. It seems that the Supreme Court's ruling falls short of affording total copyrightability to the copy-edited versions of the Supreme Court judgments. But leaving headnotes, editorial notes, paragraph making and addition of "dissenting", "concurring", etc. What is left is the "original" version emerging from the Court which is already in the public domain. So reading the two judgments, one gets the feeling that inputs for improving the readability and understandability of judgments alone may have copyright ability. In practical terms, the Kerala High Court decision helps to resolve disputes in as much as it tends to treat the improved version as composite one distinct from the "original" instead of treating the different fragments of the improved version as new additions. Irrespective of one's agreement with either of these views, it is certain that the fallout of these decisions would be positive. The legal fraternity could hope to get more sophisticatedly a noted version of cases with innovations as the publishers may try to achieve copyrightability of case reports in future. Those reporters who are not competent and competitive may stop publishing raising the possibility of avoiding replication and confusion.

However, in *Tech Plus Media Pvt. Ltd. v. Jyoti Janda*,[229] the Delhi High Court held that laying down that to claim copyright in a compilation, the author must produce the material with exercise of his skill and judgment which may not be creativity in the sense that it is novel or non-obvious but at the same time it is not a product of merely labour and capital. The Court further clarified that the exercise of skill and judgment required to produce the work must not be so trivial that it could be characterized as a purely mechanical exercise. Thus, the Court held that copy edited judgments would not satisfy the copyright merely by establishing amount of skill, labour and capital put in the inputs of the copy edited judgments as the original or innovative thoughts for the creativity are completely excluded.

Future Work and Industrial Drawing

As discussed above, Section 13 of the Copyright Act 1957 provides subsistence of copyright in literary, dramatic, musical, artistic works, cinematograph films, and sound recording. Besides these categories of works whether copyright subsists in future work as well as in industrial

228. *Eastern Book Company* v. *D.B. Modak,* AIR 2008 SC 809: 2008 (1) SCC 1.
229. 2014 (60) PTC 121 (Del): 2014 Indlaw (Del) 2834. *See also, CNH Industrial (India) Pvt. Ltd.* v. *Tirth Agro Technology Pvt. Ltd.*, 2019 (78) PTC 35 (Del).

drawing have been controversial over time. An attempt has been made in the following pages to discuss these controversial issues.

Copyright in Future Work

Can copyright subsist in future literary, dramatic, musical, artistic works, cinematograph films or sound recording? Sections 13 of the Copyright Act 1957 has not clarified the issue, but Section 18 of the Act stated that owner of the copyright in a future work may assign the copyright. In *Saregama Ltd.* v. *The New Digital Media,*[230] the Calcutta High Court held that the owner of the copyright or the prospective owner of the copyright in a future work may assign the copyright to any person either wholly or partially for the whole of the copyright or any part thereof and once an assignment is made the assignee for the purpose of the said Act is treated as the owner of the copyright.

In *Vithalbhai Pvt. Ltd.* v. *Union Bank of India,*[231] the Supreme Court held that a person having even a contingent right in a property may sue for a declaration. However, in *Gangappa Gurupadappa Gugwad Gulbarga* v. *Rachawwa,*[232] plaintiff had a contingent right and no vested interest, and therefore it was a question whether he was entitled to a simple declaration. Again in *Bhagwati Prasad Sah* v. *Bhagwati Prasad Sah,*[233] the Supreme Court observed that in the pre-emptive tenement (the tenement by the ownership of which the preemptor wants to exercise his right of pre-emption), the preemptor should have vested ownership and not a mere expectancy of inheritance of a reversionary right, or any other kind of contingent right, or any interest which falls short of full ownership. Therefore, subsistence of copyright in future work is a debatable issue.

Keeping in view of contingent right, the question whether an injunction could be granted preventing infringement of a film that was not in existence came for consideration before the Delhi High Court in *Time Warner Entertainment Co.* v. *RPG Net Com.*[234] In this case, the plaintiff field a suit for injunction for preventing the broadcasting of existing and future films of the plaintiff by the defendants. The single judge granted injunction preventing the defendants from broadcasting the films listed in the plaint but refused to grant injunction for the future films not yet produced by the plaintiff. On appeal to the division bench, it was argued by the plaintiff that since it was argued by the plaintiff that since there was a provision for the assignment for the future copyright in the film there was also the possibility of preventing infringement of the copyright of such future works. This was countered by the defendant stating that even though there was a provision for the assignment of copyright of future works this would come into force only after the work was created and not before. Hence the relief of infringement was available only after the work was created and not before.

---

230. (2018) 1 WBLR (Cal) 329: (2018) 1 CALLT 190 (HC). *See also, Novex Communication Pvt. Ltd.* v. *Lemon Tree Hotels Ltd.*, 2019 II AD (Delhi) 644; *Asianet Communications Ltd.* v. *SUN T.V. Network Limited*, 2017 (69) PTC 348 (Mad): 2017 (1) CTC 709; *Maganlal Savani* v. *Multi Screen Media Pvt. Ltd.*, 2016 (68) PTC 373 (Bom): MIPR 2017 (1) 112; *K.M. Varghese* v. *CBS Publisher*, 2016 (66) PTC 295 (Del).
231. AIR 2005 SC 1891: (2005) 4 SCC 315.
232. AIR 1971 SC 442: (1970) 3 SCC 716.
233. [1964] 5 SCR 105.
234. 2007 (34) PTC 668 (Del) (DB).

After referring to Sections 13, 14, 16, 17, 18, and 55 of the Copyright Act, the Court accepted the arguments of the defendant and held:

> Reading of the above provision of the Act and keeping in mind the object and purpose behind the Act, it cannot be said that any right to claim infringement in a future work exists in any person before a cinematograph film is completed. It is only upon completion of the film that the purchaser/author of the film becomes first owner within the meaning of Section 17 read with Section 2(d)(v) of the Act. As stated before, a prospective owner can enter into an agreement to assign rights in a film to a third person but the said rights are effective only after the film is completed and not before. Likewise, right to claim infringement on the basis of copyright under Section 55 of the Act has been given to an owner as defined in Section 17 of the Act and not to a prospective owner. In view of the above, it cannot be said that films which have not been conceived or after being conceived are under production can become subject-matter of an infringement action relating to cinematographic film under Section 55 of the Act. Existing owner of cinematographic films cannot under the Act get obvious interim injunction order for cinematographic film of which they may become owners in future. The Act itself does not postulate and give any such right to the applicants-plaintiffs.

The reasoning of the Court is correct and it goes with the basic philosophy of copyright law that only expressions of the ideas are protected and not ideas. It also supports the basic principle that copyright is infringed only if there is substantial copy of the protected work and to find this out the work must be in existence in one or other medium. Thus, existence of the work is a pre-requisite for the owner to take the benefit of the provisions of the Act.

Copyright in Industrial Drawing

According to Section 15(1) of the Copyright Act, 1957, copyright shall not subsist in under this Act in any design which is registered under the Design Act, 2000.[235] The Section 15(2) further clarifies that where a design, capable of being registered under the Designs Act, is not so registered, copyright (in such design) shall cease as soon as any article to which the design has been applied is reproduced more than 50 times by an industrial process by the owner of the copyright or with his licence, by any other person. Thus, the Copyright Act, 1957 by Section 15 specifically excludes copyrights in designs which are capable of being registered under the Designs Act, 2000.[236] This exclusion is understandable. What is not so readily understandable is the fact that by necessary implication it is legally permissible to register or claim a copyright in a trademark, which is also capable of registration as a trademark, receiving thus deal protection. Since the registration of copyright is relatively a simple and expeditious process as compared with trademarks, the office of the registrar of copyrights is inundated with registration applications for copyright in marks as "literary" or "artistic"

---

235. For detail discussion, *see*, *Gurukrupa Mech Tech Pvt. Ltd.* v. *State of Gujarat*, (2018) 4 GLR 3324; *IPEG Inc.* v. *Kay Bee Engineers*, AIR 2016 Guj 104: 2016 (66) PTC 305 (Guj); *Jagdamba Impex* v. *Tristar Products Private Ltd.*, 2014 (59) PTC 149 (Del): 2014 (143) DRJ 298; *Micolube India Limited* v. *Rakesh Kumar*, 2013 (55) PTC 1 (Del): 199 (2013) DLT 740.
236. Section 15(2) of the Copyright Act 1957 runs: "(2) Copyright in any design, which is capable of being registered under the Designs Act, 2000, but which has not been so registered, shall cease as soon as any article to which the design has been applied has been reproduced more than fifty times by an industrial process by the owner of the copyright or, with his license, by any other person."

works.[237] Besides, concurrent registration of both trademark and copyright in relation to the same matter often causes understandable, but avoidable, judicial confusion where, for example, standards apt for judging passing-off action for marks tend to rub off to the determination of copyright infringement in the same proceedings.[238] Thus, in *Holland Company LP* v. *S.P. Industries*,[239] the Court observed:

> A conjoint reading of Section 2(d) of Designs Act, 2000, Section 14(c) and 15(2) of the Copyright Act, 1957, makes it amply clear that where a design of an article is prepared for the industrial production of an article, it is a design and registrable under Designs Act and under Section 14(c), the author of such design can claim copyright, however, since such a design is registrable under the Designs Act, and if such design has been used for production of articles by an industrial process for more than 50 times by the owner of the copyright, or, by any other person with his permission, then such person ceases to have copyright in such design.

In *Devendra Somabhai Naik* v. *Accurate Transheat Pvt. Ltd.*,[240] the Gujarat High Court examined whether an application can be filed before the Copyright Board (Appellate Board)[241] to cancel the registration of copyright of an artistic work on the ground that as per Section 15(2) of the Act the artistic design has been reproduced as an industrial design more than 50 times. In this case, the respondent filed an application before the copyright board (appellate board) to delete the registration of the artistic work since the appellant manufactured the design of the artistic work more than 50 times. It was contended by the appellant before the board that the artistic work was not a design capable of registration under the Design Act and even if it was a design, the manufacture of the article out of the design was not a "reproduction" as per Section 15(2) of the Act. This was rejected by the board and was approved by the court. As to the interpretation of Section 15(2) the Court observed:

> When the law says that the Copyright shall cease as soon as an article to which the design has been applied has been reproduced more than fifty times, then the logical and intelligible interpretation would be that any article has been produced for more than fifty times applying the said design. Application of the design for manufacturing or creating an article would not mean that the design has been reprinted and has been posted on the body of the machine. The word 'application' in the present context would mean that the knowledge has been derived, the said design and that knowledge has been applied for manufacturing a particular machine. We cannot have dogmatic approach in the present matter when the law clearly says that the Copyright shall cease as soon as any article to which design has been applied has been reproduced more than fifty times. In the present matter indisputably after applying the design a machine has been manufactured at least 170 times every year. The logical conclusion would be that the Copyright shall cease to have the effect. The Board was absolutely justified in directing deletion/cancellation of the said registration.[242]

---

237. *See*, Upendra Baxi, "Copyright Law and Justice in India" 28 *Journal of the Indian Law Institute* (1986) 496–540 at p. 509.
238. *See*, e.g., *Khemraj* v. *Garg & Co.*, AIR 1975 Delhi 135. The case upheld both the passing-off action in the mark as well as infringement of copyright. The latter, received scant attention. And standards for determination got mixed up. For example the doctrine of 'fading memory' is apt for the former, but unknown to the latter, domain of law.
239. 2017 (71) PTC 630 (Del): MIPR 2017 (3) 237.
240. 2005 (31) PTC 172 (Guj.).
241. Substituted by the Finance Act 2017 (7 of 2017), section 160(a) for "Copyright Board," [w.e.f. 26 May, 2017].
242. *Devendra Somabhai Naik* v. *Accurate Pvt. Ltd.*, 2005 (31) PTC 172 (Guj.) at 174.

The decision is in keeping with the intention of the legislature to avoid dual protection for the same category of intellectual property. The issue whether an industrial drawing capable of protection under the Design Act could claim copyright protection under the Copyright Act was again considered by the Delhi High Court in *Dart Industries Inc.* v. *Techno Plast.*[243] Following the earlier cases[244] and section of the Copyright Act the court reiterated the law thus:[245]

> ... The underlying message is that copyright in an industrial design is governed by the Design Act 2000. If a design is registered under that Act it is not eligible for protection under the Copyright Act. In such cases after the design is registered under the Design Act, the protection given is not copyright protection by a true monopoly based on statute inasmuch as such designs were never protected by the common law. Exception may be in those cases where copyright had come into existence in respect of artistic drawing and subsequently those drawings were used as models or patterns to be multiplied by any industrial process. There, if the drawing becomes capable of registration as a design it would not result in copyright being forfeited.[246] However, if the intended industrial use of the work was contemporaneous with its coming into existence, Section 15 of the Copyright Act would apply.

Regarding the coexistence of copyright and design right, the court added:

> I may hasten to clarify that it is not suggested that if any design is registered, copyright under no circumstance exists in the drawings. Section 15 lays down that no registration of a design under the Design Act, the copyright shall not subsist in that design and not in the drawings. Therefore, it is possible that when the moulded plastic article of novel shape is made from a working drawing, as in the instant case, the drawing may qualify as an original work entitled to copyright protection and at the same time, a registered design for the shape of the article would be protected under the Design Act. If an unauthorized copy is made of the article, it may constitute an indirect copy of the drawing and therefore may infringe the copyright.

It appears that the court is wrong in making this observation which seems self-contradicting. If the intention of Parliament as reflected in Section 15 of the Copyright Act is to prevent dual protection of the artistic work capable of industrial application, the above observation of the court defeats this. The distinction the court is trying to make between the word "design" used in Section 15 and the word "drawing" seems to be artificial. It is the drawing (artistic work) that is converted into external features through industrial process to claim protection under the Design Act. If the drawing and the design are one and the same providing protection for the "drawing" under the Copyright Act and "external shape" made out of it under the Design Act as suggested by the court would result in over protection. The reason being after the protection under the Design Act is over (maximum of 15 years), the owner could claim monopoly for the design through the Copyright Act as artistic work (drawing) for a period of life and 60 years of the author. The argument of the owner would be that the infringer is depicting his two-dimensional work into three-dimensional violating the reproduction right under Section 14(c)(i) in the artistic work in the drawing of the design.

---

243. 2007 (35) PTC 129 (Del).
244. *See*, *Samsonite Corp.* v. *Vijay Sales,* 1998 PTC (18) 372 and *Microfiber Inc.* v. *Girdhar & Co.,* 2006 (32) PTC 157 (Del).
245. *Dart Industries Inc.* v. *Techno Plast and Others,* 2007 (35) PTC 129 (Del) at p. 153.
246. *See*, *Warner Brother* v. *Roadrunner,* 1988 FSR 292.

This is what Parliament wanted to prevent through Section 15. Hence the reasoning of the court seems faulty and against the basic principles of separating the protections under different intellectual property laws. It is satisfying to note that the court did not apply this reasoning to the facts of this case and refused injunction.

Keeping in view the above legal dichotomy the question which is required to be examined: What is the nature of the Section 15 of the Copyright Act, 1957? Clarifying the issue in *Kiran Shoes Manufacturers* v. *Registrar of Copyright*,[247] the court held that if a particular artistic work is capable of treating as design, and is meant for the use of goods and can be registered under the Designs Act, its registration under the Copyright Act as artistic work is not permissible. It would mean that even an artistic work which is commercially exploited in relation to goods in the manner provided under the Designs Act, it ceases to be a work which would get protection under the Copyright Act. Similarly, in *Holland Company Lp.* v. *S.P. Industries*,[248] the court held that as per Section 15 of the Copyright Act, 1957 upon the application for registration as a design being made, the copyright if any therein is deemed to have been surrendered/abandoned. In *Polymer Papers Ltd.* v. *Gurmit Singh*,[249] the court further observed that the claim of copyright in the industrial drawings and designs which were being used for manufacturing purposes is not maintainable. One important issue always arises is whether the copyright in the design is capable of registration within the meaning of Section 15(2) of the Copyright Act. Following the principle laid down in *Samsonite Corporation* v. *Vijay Sales*,[250] the Delhi High Court in *Aga Medical Corporation* v. *Faisal Kapadi*,[251] held that when two enactments deal with the same subject and the provisions are in pan material, they have to be interpreted harmoniously. Here the position is, the Copyright Act which is later in point of time would impliedly incorporate into that Act the provisions of the Designs Act.

On the question of scope and durability of the protection, the Delhi High Court relying on the ruling in *Microfibres Inc.* v. *Girdhar*,[252] held subsequently in *Servewell Products Pvt. Ltd.* v. *Dolphin*,[253] that there is lesser copyright protection, in the case of industrial designs. In its reasoning the court observed that a perusal of the Copyright Act, Designs Act and the Preamble and Statement of Objects and Reasons of the Designs Act makes it clear that the legislative intent was to grant a higher protection to pure original artistic works such as paintings, sculptures, etc., and lesser period of protection to design activity commercial in nature. The period of copyright would be the author's life span plus 60 years. However, the legislature has allocated a lesser time span for the protection available to a registered design as only being 15 years. Thus, commerce and art have been treated differently by the legislature and any activity which is commercial in nature has been granted lesser period of protection. Paradoxically, pure artistic works have been granted a longer protection. Thus, the operation

247. 2012 (50) PTC 14: 2012 (129) DRJ 105.
248. 2014 LawSuit (Del) 1878.
249. 2002 25 PTC 327.
250. 73 (1998) DLT 732.
251. 2003 (26) PTC 349: 2003 (103) DLT 321.
252. 2006 (32) PTC 157. *See also*, *Dart Industries Inc*, v. *Techno Plast*, 2007 (141) DLT 777, 2007 (35) PTC 129.
253. 2010 (43) PTC 507: 2010 (117) DRJ 16.

of Section 15(2) of the Copyright Act does not exclude from the ambit of copyright protection either the original "artistic work" upon which the design is based or the design which by itself is an artistic work.

Computer Software

There are two principal modes of protection of software—copyright protection and patent protection prevalent in most of the countries. Copyright protection is the most common means to protect computer programs because writing of a code is similar to any type of literary work.[254] Under Copyright Act, 1957, computer programs are considered as "literary work".[255] Thus, the Copyright Act covers a wide array of works including literary, music, videograph, computer programs etc.[256] Thus, the software programs are "computer programs" within the meaning of Section 2(ffc) of the Copyright Act 1957 and are included in the definition of a "literary work" as per Section 2(o) of the Act.[257] Hence, the law surrounding computer software copyright is on a collision course with computer science. One of the main reasons for this is that legal terms of art in copyright case law do not reflect accepted computer science terminology.[258] For example, the cases have coined phrases like "structure, sequence, and organization" and "program structure", but neither term accurately reflects computer science reality.[259] Thus, the question arises what is computer software?

What is Computer Software?

Software is a computer program. It comprises instructions to make the hardware work. There are two types of software, namely, "system software" which control the working of the computer and "application software" such as a word processing program, database, etc., which perform the functional tasks that we use computers for. In addition, there is also "network software" which enables groups of computers to communicate and "language software" which provides the tools with which one writes a program.[260] There is also "packaged software" which is sold through retail outlets.[261] In *Tata Consultancy Services* v. *State of Andhra Pradesh,*[262] the Apex Court observed:

---

254. *See*, J.K. Das, "Copyright Protection for Computer Softwares and Databases: From Sweat of the Brow to Modicum of Creativity" 3(2) *Indian Journal of Law and Justice* (2012) pp. 57–80.
255. Copyright Act 1957, Section 2(o).
256. *See*, *STAR India Private Limited* v. *Department of Industrial Policy*, 2018 (2) CTC 113; *Dart Industries Inc.* v. *Techno Plast*, 2017 II AD (Delhi) 602: 2016 (67) PTC 457 (Del).
257. *See*, *Microsoft Corporation* v. *Manish Poddar*, 240 (2017) DLT 595.
258. Yogesh Pai, "Copyright Protection for Computer Programs,"48(3) *Journal of the Indian Law Institute* (2006) pp. 359–399; Nancy F. DuCharme, "Copyright Protection for Computer Software in Great Britain and the United States: A Comparative Analysis," 3(2) *Computer and High Technology Law Journal* (1987) pp. 257–282.
259. *See*, Marci A. Hamilton, "Computer Science Concepts in Copyright Cases: The Path to a Coherent Law" 10(2) *Harvard Journal of Law and Technology* (1997) pp. 2040–2280.
260. *See*, *Indian Aluminium Company* v. *Commissioner of Income Tax*, (2017) 291 CTR (Cal) 196: (2016) 384 ITR 386 (Cal).
261. *Commissioner of Customs* v. *Hewlett Packard India Sales (P) Ltd.*, 2007 (10) SCALE 535: (2007) 8 SCC 404.
262. 2001 (2) SCALE 417: (2001) 4 SCC 629.

> Software is an essentially classic form of intellectual property. The value of the tapes on which it is sold is much lesser than the value of the software programme itself; that the software programme is always transferred onto the hardware and then the tapes are useless; that, therefore, the licensee/payer is paying for the programme and not for the tapes or discs; these discs are different from music cassettes and video tapes, music reels, etc. because the programme on the discs is separable and is always transferred to the hardware, whereas in the case of music cassettes, etc. though they may be separable and can be transferred to another cassette or tape this is not generally done and the music or movie always remains on the tangible property on which it was stored when sold; that there are other methods by which a software programme can be installed, like, the programme directly keying in the programme can be installed, like, the programme directly keying in the programme through the console keyboard; that what is transferred is the right to use the programme (which is a set of instructions) and not the tape on which it is stored; that though software has a physical component, these physical components are merely tangential incidents of a computer programme, they do not change the programmes' clearly intangible character.

Thus, software comprises not only the actual software but also switching operations of hardware components according to a particular program and the action which translates other program expressed in a programming language into their final form. It also includes other kinds of program that complement the hardware to ease the carrying out of a new program.[263]

In *Amway India Enterprises* v. *Deputy Commissioner of Income Tax*,[264] the Delhi High Court held that a computer software includes any computer program recorded on any disk, tape, perforated media or other information storage device. Therefore, computer software is a tangible asset by itself. In *Abdulgafar A. Nadiadwala* v. *Assistant Commissioner of Income Tax*,[265] the Bombay High Court held that Sections 10A and 10B of the Income Tax Act deal with export incentives and exempt income from export of articles and things and computer software. These Sections define "computer software" to imply any computer program recorded on any disc, tape, perforated media or any other information storage device. Thus, there is an overwhelming authority that even intangible rights, etc., once recorded on a tape or disc, can be considered goods and merchandise.

In *Associated Cement Companies Ltd.* v. *Commissioner of Customs*,[266] the Apex Court examined whether drawings and designs could be considered goods. The Court ruled that a mere technical device or information technology may be an intangible asset but the moment the information of device is put on media, whether on paper or cassettes or diskettes or any other thing, it becomes chattel. Computer software may be explained to comprise the following three elements:

1. "Computer program": implying a set of instructions expressed in words, codes, schemes or in any other form, including a machine readable medium, capable of causing a computer to perform a particular task or achieve a particular result.[267]

---

263. *See*, S.K. Verma, "IP Protection of Software and Software Contracts in India: A Legal Quagmire" 17 *Journal of Intellectual Property Rights* (2012) pp. 284–295.
264. [2008] 301 ITR 1 (Delhi): (2008) 114 TTJ (Delhi) 476. *Commissioner of Income Tax* v. *Arawali Constructions Co. (P.) Ltd.*, (2002) 177 CTR (Raj) 79: [2003] 259 ITR 30 (Raj).
265. (2004) 188 CTR (Bom) 232: [2004] 267 ITR 488 (Bom).
266. AIR 2001 SC 862: (2001) 4 SCC 593.
267. *See*, *Tata Consultancy Services* v. *State of Andhra Pradesh*, AIR 2005 SC 371: (2005) 1 SCC 308; *O.R.G. Systems* v. *Collector of Central Excise*, AIR 1998 SC 2662: (1998) 6 SCC 56.

2. "Program Description": implying a comprehensive procedural presentation in verbal, schematic or other form, in sufficient detail to determine a set of instructions constituting a corresponding computer program.
3. "Supporting Material": implying a material other than a computer program or a program description, created for aiding the understanding or application of a computer program, i.e., problem descriptions and user instructions.[268]

Thus, "computer software" including computer program, drawings, designs, broadcasting of signals and are "goods" and tangible assets by themselves. The cost of developing a program is far greater than that involved in duplicating it. This acts as an incentive to pirates to opt for unauthorised duplication at the cost of the original a program. Quite arguably, then, the production of such program will only be undertaken where the creator can recover all his costs and even make some kind of profit by spreading the cost over sale of number of copies of the work with protection from unauthorised duplication.

TRIPS Agreement and Computer Software

The Agreement on Trade-Related Aspects of Intellectual Property Rights marks a significant development over existing international copyright law in clarifying that computer program should be protected as literary works. Article 2 of the *Berne Convention* defined "literary and artistic works" to mean every production in the literary, scientific or artistic domain, whatever may be the mode or form of its expression.[269] The Article being merely illustrative of what could constitute literary or artistic works, the non-inclusion of specific works led to a debate whether computer program were included in the definition. Article 10 of TRIPS Agreement clarified that computer program are eligible for protection under copyright law as:

Article 10: Computer Programs and Compilations of Data:

1. Computer programs, whether in source or object code, shall be produced as literary works under the *Berne Convention* 1971.
2. Compilation of data or other material, whether in machine readable or other form, which by reason of the selection or arrangement of their contents constitute intellectual creations shall be protected as such. Such protection, which shall not extend to the data or material itself, shall be without prejudice to any copyright subsisting in the data or material itself.

Article 10.1 of the TRIPS Agreement specified that computer programme are to be protected as literary works, therefore, the shorter term of protection of 25 years applicable to works of applied art under the *Berne Convention* [Article 7(4)] was explicitly excluded. Article 2(5) of the *Berne Convention* recognises the protection of collections of literary or artistic works which, by reason of their selection and arrangement of their contents, constitute intellectual creations without prejudice to the copyright in each of the works forming part of such collections. According to the World Intellectual Property Organization (WIPO) Guide to

---

268. WIPO, Model Provisions on Protection of Computer Software (1978), *see*, P.M. Dhar, "Intellectual Property in Computer Programs: Weakness of the Indian Copyright Act, 1957," 28 *Journal of the Indian Law Institute* (1986) pp. 487–496.
269. *See*, Jayshree Watal, *Intellectual Property Rights in the WTO and Developing Countries* (Oxford University Press, New York, 2001).

the *Berne Convention,* the creator of such a collection is required to bring to bear an element of creativity in such a work. In other words, a telephone directory that simply lists names and addresses with no creative selection or arrangement cannot be protected under this provision. Article 10.2 of the TRIPS Agreement elaborates upon this provision of the *Berne Convention* to include: (i) databases or other compilations of data or other material, (ii) material in both machine-readable and other form, (iii) compilations of non-copyrightable material.[270]

Copyright Act, 1957 and Computer Software

Subject to the provisions of Section 13 and the other provisions of the Indian Copyright Act, 1957 there shall be a copyright throughout India in "original literary work", dramatic, musical and artistic works, cinematograph films and sound recording, subject to the exceptions provided in Sub-sections (2) and (3) of Section 13.[271] For copyright protection, all literary works have to be original as per Section 13 of the Act. However, there are two classes of literary works: (a) primary or prior works, and (b) secondary or derivative works. Primary or prior works are the literary works not based on existing subject-matter, therefore, would be called primary or prior works. Secondary or derivative works are literary works based on existing subject-matter; since such works are based on existing subject-matter, they are called derivative work or secondary work. For the purposes of the Act, Section 14(1) enumerates what shall be a copyright which is an exclusive right, subject to the provisions of the Act, to do or authorise the doing of the acts provided in Clauses (i) to (vii) in respect of a work or any substantial part thereof in the case of a literary, dramatic or musical work, not being a computer program.[272]

The Copyright (Amendment) Act, 1994 has included "computer programmes" and also added "databases" within the definition of literary works.[273] Section 2(o) defines "literary work" to include (among others) computer programs, tables and compilations including computer databases. Section 2(y) defines "work" as meaning any of the following works namely: (i) a literary, dramatic, musical or artistic work, (ii) a cinematographic film, (iii) sound recording. Under Section 14, literary work is one of the items wherein exclusive rights can be claimed so as to amount to copyright. Under Section 17(c) if a work is made in the course of other's employment under a contract of service or apprenticeship it is the employer who is the first owner of the copyright therein in the absence of any agreement to the contrary.[274] As per Section 2(ffc), a computer program means a set of instructions expressed in works, codes, and schemes or in any other form, including a machine readable medium, capable of causing

---

270. *See* The Chancellor v. Rameshwari Photocopy Services, 2017 (69) PTC 123 (Del): 235 (2016) DLT 409; *Foundry Visionmongers Limited* v. *Parish Tekriwal*, 2017 (69) PTC 360 (Bom).
271. *See, Vinod Kumar Gupta* v. *State of U.P.*, 2019 (106) ACC 378; *Exxon Mobil Corporation* v. *P.K. Sen*, 2018 (76) PTC 263 (Cal).
272. *See, New Delhi Television* v. *ICC Development*, 2013 (53) PTC 71 (Del): 195(2012) DLT61.
273. For discussion on Copyright (Amendment) Act 1984, see, *Novex Communication Pvt. Ltd.* v. *Lemon Tree Hotels Ltd.*, 2019 II AD (Delhi) 644; *Star India Private Limited* v. *Department of Industrial Policy*, (2019) 2 SCC 104: 2018 (14) SCALE 651; *Kajal Agarwa* v. *The Managing Director*, 2018 (5) CTC 185: (2018) 5 MLJ 818.
274. *Burlington Home Shopping Pvt. Ltd.* v. *Rajnish Chibber and Another,* 1996 PTR 40: (1995) 15 PTC 274.

a computer to perform a particular result. Thus copyright subsists in a computer program including databases provided sufficient effort or skill has been expended to give it a new or original character. But it must be written down, recorded or otherwise reduced to a material form. However, it has been argued that computer programs and databases are not "original literary works" rather compilation of various works; therefore, these works are not protectable under copyright law.[275]

Post-1994 Amendment Development on Computer Software

Doctrine of Sweat of the Brow: Its Contemporary Relevance

During post Copyright (Amendment) Act, 1994 a large number of cases have been decided by Indian Courts. Indian law has recognised that computer programs, tables and compilations including computer databases are entitled to copyright protection.[276] However, that would not end the debate. The law mandates that the work claiming protection ought to be original. Copyright law does not also grant the author of a literary work protection on ideas and facts.[277] It is the creative expression of an idea or fact which gets rewarded by law, through copyright monopoly for a specified period. The law does not, however protect every expression, but grants such recognition and protection to expressions that are "original". This standard is incorporated by Section 13, in respect of every class of work. A literary work, in order to qualify as work in which copyright can subsist, must therefore be original. The standard for judging "originality" has undergone a radical change from the time a work was deemed original if it was the product of the "Sweat of the Brow" as it was enunciated in *University of London Press*.[278] The underlying notion of the "Sweat of the Brow" doctrine was that copyright was

---

275. *Gurleen Kaur* v. *State of Punjab* (2010) ILR 1 P and H 52; *Eastern Book Company* v. *D.B. Modak,* AIR 2008 SC 809: (2008) 1 SCC 1.
276. Section 2(o) of the Copyright Act 1957 defines "literary work" to include (among others) computer programmes, tables and compilations including computer databases. Section 2(y) defines "work" as meaning any of the following works namely: (i) a literary, dramatic, musical or artistic work, (ii) a cinematographic film, (iii) sound recording. Under Section 14, literary work is one of the items wherein exclusive rights can be claimed so as to amount to copyright. *See, B.N. Firos* v. *State of Kerala,* (2018) 9 SCC 220: 2018 (5) SCALE 155; *Barbara Taylor Bradford* v. *Sahara Media Entertainment Ltd*., 2004 (28) PTC 474 (Cal): (2003) 47 SCL 445 (Cal); *O.R.G. Systems* v. *Collector of Central Excise*, AIR 1998 SC 2662: (1998) 6 SCC 56.
277. *Baker* v. *Seldon,* [1879] 101 US 99; *Nichols* v. *Universal Pictures Corporation*, 45 F.2d (2d Cir. 1930); *R.G. Anand* v. *Delux Films*, AIR 1978 SC 1613: (1978) 4 SCC 118.
278. The Chancery Court in *University of London Press Limited* v. *University Tutorial Press Limited,* [1916] 2 Ch 60 I observed thus: "Assigning that they are "literary work", the question then is whether they are original. The word "original" does not in this connection mean that the work must be the expression of original or inventive thought. Copyright Acts are not concerned with the originality of ideas, but with the expression of thought, and, in the case of "literary work", with the expression of thought in print or writing. The originality which is required relates to the expression of the thought. But the Act does not require that the expression must be in an original or novel form, but that the work must not be copied from another work—that it should originate from the author. In the present case it was not suggested that any of the papers were copied. Professor Lodge and Mr. Jackson proved that they had thought out the questions which they set, and that they made notes or memoranda for future questions and drew on those notes for the purposes of the questions which they set. The papers which they prepared originated from themselves, and were, within the meaning of the Act, original."

a reward for the hard work that went into compiling facts.[279] The classic formulation of the doctrine was as follows:

> The right to copyright a book upon which one has expended labour in its preparation does not depend upon whether the materials which he has collected consist or not of matters which are publici juris, or whether such materials show literary skill or originality, either in thought or in language, or anything more than industrious collection. The man who goes through the streets of a town and puts down the names of each of the inhabitants, with their occupations and their street number, acquires material of which he is the author.[280]

In *Burlington Home Shopping Pvt. Ltd.* v. *Rajnish Chibber,*[281] the Delhi High Court examined the issue regarding the protection of computer databases. In this case the plaintiff was doing the business of mail order service. One of the major investments for the success of the business is the compilation of the list of the customers. The plaintiff has developed a list of customers' database over a period of three years prior to the institution of the suit by investing considerable amount of money and time and kept it as a trade secret. The defendant, a previous employee of the plaintiff, but not connected with the work of the compilation of the customers' database, recently started mail order service business. According to the plaintiff, the defendant managed to get a copy of the plaintiff's customers' database and was using it for establishing relationship with the plaintiff's customers. It was contended by the plaintiff that this amounted to infringement of copyright in the database and violation of the trade secret. He, therefore, prayed for a permanent injunction restraining the defendant from infringing the copyright and confidentiality. The defendant denied the allegations and argued that the plaintiff had no copyright on the database on the ground that the address of customers included in the database were collection of facts from common source. According to the defendant, he developed his own database and the utilisation of it did not amount to any infringement of the copyright of the plaintiff. The court examined the question whether a compilation of addresses in computer database from the common source is a literary work for the purpose of copyright protection. After quoting from various provisions[282] of the Indian *Copyright Act*, foreign authorities[283] and case laws from India[284] and abroad,[285] *R.C. Lahoti J.* concluded thus:

---

279. For critical examination of the doctrine of "sweat of the brow" and its application in copyright law, *see*, Andreas Rahmatian, "Originality in UK Copyright Law: The Old ''Skill and Labour'' Doctrine Under Pressure," 44(1) *IIC-International Review of Intellectual Property and Competition Law* (2013) pp. 4-34; Nehaluddin Ahmad and Saurabh Chaturvedi, "Originality Requirement and Copyright Regime of Music: A Comparative Overview of Indian Perspective", 22(2) *Information and Communications Technology Law* (2013) pp. 132–145; Cristin Fenzel, "Still Life with "Spark" And "Sweat": The Copyrightability of Contemporary Art in the United States and the United Kingdom," 24(2) *Arizona Journal of International and Comparative Law* (2007) pp. 541–584.
280. *See, Jeweler's Circular Publishing Co.* v. *Keystone Publishing Co.*, 281 F. 83 (CA2 1922) at 88.
281. 1996 PTR 40: (1995) 15 PTC 274.
282. The court referred to Sections 2(o), 2(y), 14 and 17(c) of the Copyright Act 1957.
283. The court quoted from Laddie, Prescot and Vitoria, *The Modern Law of Copyright, 1980; Copinger and Skone James on Copyright,* 1991; David Bainbridge, *Software Copyright Law* (1996).
284. *Govindan* v. *Gopalakrishnan,* AIR 1955 Mad 391; *Shyam Lal Paharia* v. *Gaya Prasad,* AIR 1971 All 182.
285. *Waterlow Directors Ltd.* v. *Reed Information Service Ltd.*, 1992 FSR 409 and *William Hill (Football) Ltd.* v. *Labroke (Football) Ltd.*, 1980 RPC 539.

> From the above statement of the authorities and the trend of judicial opinion it is clear that a compilation of addresses developed by any one by devoting time, money, labour and skill though the sources may be commonly situated amounts to a 'literary work' wherein the author has a copyright.[286]

It appears from Section 2(0)[287] of the Copyright Act, 1957 that computer database is specifically included as a compilation to treat it as a literary work. But it is only "original" literary work that is protected under Section 13[288] of the Act. In case of compilations, the originality is not on the materials but on the manner of organisation of the material since in some cases the materials as such can enjoy separate copyright protection. It is the well-established law of copyright that facts are not copyrightable and are to be left open in the public domain as common source for free use by the public for creation of new works since they are considered to be the basic building blocks. Thus, in cases of compilation of facts the question is whether there is any originality in the manner of organisation of the facts for copyright protection. So the important question in this case was not whether the database was a compilation but whether the one created by the plaintiff would qualify the test of "originality" for the purpose of copyright protection. Instead of examining this question, it appears that the court has followed the "Sweat of the Brow" doctrine for the purpose of extending copyright protection for compilations of facts. The court, thus, relied on the time, money and labour of the plaintiff in collecting the information, which by itself is uncopyrightable, for the purpose of extending copyright protection. Even though the court used the word "skill", it appears it has not inquired about the amount of skill used by the plaintiff in the manner of organisation of the compilation. Thus, the court focused on the slavish imitation by the defendant to make out a clear case of infringement.[289] The court in this process has not dealt with the basic question of the requirement of originality for the purpose of extending copyright protection to compilation as a literary work. This seems to be the trend followed by the Indian courts even in earlier cases.

The "sweat of the brow" doctrine had numerous flaws, the most glaring being that it extended copyright protection in a compilation beyond selection and arrangement, the compiler's original contributions, to the facts themselves. Under the doctrine, the only defence to infringement was independent creation. A subsequent compiler was "not entitled to take one word of information previously published", but rather had to "independently work out the matter for himself, so as to arrive at the same result from the same common sources of information". The Supreme Court in *Eastern Book Co.* v. *D.B. Modak,*[290] relied on the US[291] and Canadian[292] judgments and observed thus:

---

286. *Burlington* v. *Rajnish,* 1996 PTR 40 at 46.
287. Section 2(0) reads: "literary work includes computer programmes, tables and compilations including computer databases".
288. Section 13(1) reads "Subject to the provisions of this section and the other provision of this Act, copyright shall subsist throughout India in the following classes of works, that is to say,—(a) original, literary, dramatic, musical and artistic works..." (emphasis supplied).
289. 1996 PTR 40 at 46.
290. AIR 2008 SC 809: 2008 (1) SCC 1.
291. *See, Feist Publications Inc.* v. *Rural Telephone Service Co. Inc.,* 18 USPQ 2d. 1275; *Matthew Bender & Co. Inc.* v. *West Publishing Co.,* 158 F.3d 674 (2nd Cir. 1998); *Key Publications, Inc.* v. *Chinatown Today Publishing Enterprises, Inc.,* 945 F.2d.509.
292. *CCH Canadian Ltd.* v. *Law Society of Upper Canada,* 2004 (I) SCR 339 (Canada).

> The sweat of the brow approach to originality is too low a standard which shifts the balance of copyright protection too far in favour of the owner's right, and fails to allow copyright to protect the public's interest in maximizing the production and dissemination of intellectual works. On the other hand, the creativity standard of originality is too high. A creative standard implies that something must be novel or non-obvious—concepts more properly associated with patent law than copyright law. By way of contrast, a standard requiring the exercise of skill and judgment in the production of a work avoids these difficulties and provides a workable and appropriate standard for copyright protection that is consistent with the policy of the objectives of the Copyright Act.

Modicum of Creativity Theory and Abolition of Doctrinal Tension

In order for derivative work to be entitled to copyright protection, one must show that there is a modicum of originality in the selection and arrangement of such facts. Thus, for copyright protection the existence of some modicum of creativity is required. To qualify for copyright protection, a work must be the product of both independent origination and a "modicum of creativity."[293] In *Shree Nath Heritage Liquor Pvt. Ltd.* v. *Allied Blender and Distillers Pvt. Ltd.*,[294] the Delhi High Court held that to establish copyright infringement, the right holder must show: (i) the owner of the work, (ii) copyright ability of the work, (iii) the work should be original, (iv) the work should have a "modicum of creativity", (v) the work should be protectable expression, (vi) the copying of the work by the defendant.

Whenever a work has been originated from an author and is more than a mere copy of the original work, would be sufficient to generate copyright. In *Gurukrupa Mech Tech Pvt. Ltd.* v. *State of Gujarat*,[295] the Gujarat High Court observed that this approach is consistent with the "sweat of the brow" standards of originality. The creation of the work which has resulted from little bit of skill, labour and capital are sufficient for a copyright in derivative work of an author. However, the rudiment principles applicable in interpreting the doctrine of "originality" in copyright law has undergone considerable change from the previously applicable "sweat of the brow" doctrine spelt out in University of London Press[296] to the "modicum of creativity" doctrine in held in *Fiest Publication Inc.* v. *Rural Telephone Service*.[297] The Supreme Court of Canada in *CCH Canadian Ltd.* v. *Law Society of Upper Canada*,[298] held that the work must be original in the sense that by virtue of selection, co-ordination or arrangement of pre-existing data contained in the work, a work somewhat different in character is produced by the author. These two positions i.e. the sweat of the brow on the one hand, and "modicum of creativity" were extreme; it preferred a higher threshold than the doctrine of "sweat of the brow" yet, not as high as "modicum of creativity." Thus, in *Dart Industries Inc.* v. *Techno Plast*,[299] the Delhi High Court Observed:

---

293. *See*, Howard B. Abrams, "Originality and Creativity In Copyright Law," 55(2) *Law and Contemporary Problems* (1992) pp. 1–44 at p. 42.
294. 2015 (63) PTC 551 (Del): 221 (2015) DLT 359.
295. (2018) 4 GLR 3324. *See also*, *Hawkins Cookers Limited* v. *Khaitan Pressure Cooker Pvt. Ltd.*, AIR 2015 Cal 150: 2015 (64) PTC 232 (Cal).
296. *University of London Press Limited* v. *University Tutorial Press Limited*, [1916] 2 Ch 60 I.
297. (1991) 199 US 340.
298. (2004) SCC 13.
299. 2017 II AD (Delhi) 602: 2016 (67) PTC 457 (Del).

> Therefore in India too, the law has recognized the shift, and mandates that not every effort or industry, or expending of skill, results in copyrightable work, but only those which create works that are somewhat different in character, involve some intellectual effort, and involve a certain degree of creativity.

A higher criterion of "Modicum of Creativity" theory was deemed necessary after the decision of the American Supreme Court in *Fiest Publication Inc.* v. *Rural Telephone Service.*[300] In this case the court had examined whether the white pages of a telephone directory could claim copyright protection as compilation. The court while rejecting the "Sweat of the Brow" doctrine followed in earlier cases emphasised the need to demonstrate originality for the protection of copyright in compilation. It was categorically stated that facts as such were not copyrightable. The observation of the court is quite pertinent, as follows:

> This, then, resolves the doctrinal tension: Copyright treats facts and factual compilations in a wholly consistent manner. Facts, whether alone or as part of a compilation are not original and therefore may not be copyrighted. A factual compilation is eligible for copyright if it features an original selection or arrangement of facts. In no event may copyright extend to the facts themselves.

Since there was no originality in the organisation of the name and address of the customers in the telephone directory the court held that the white pages were not entitled to copyright protection.[301] It is true that the court has not laid down the standard of originality or creativity required to be satisfied in compilation for the purposes of determining copyright. It appears that it has been left to the lower courts to find out the originality or creativity based on the facts of each case. The application of the Feist's ratio by the US lower courts for extending protection to maps[302] and numbers[303] is indicative of this. Had the Indian Courts examined these decisions, the court could have set the law in the proper direction. It is also interesting to examine whether the act of making a single copy or storing it in electronic means and using the information in it for business purpose amounts to infringement of copyright or can be treated as a fair dealing for private purpose. According to Section 14 of the Indian Copyright

---

300. (1991) 199 US 340. The US Supreme Court in *Feist Publications Inc.* v. *Rural Telephone Service Co. Inc.,* 499 US 340 (1991) observed thus: "The *sine qua non* of copyright is originality. To qualify for copyright protection, a work must be original to the author. *See, Harper & Row* at 547–549. Original, as the term is used in copyright, means only that the work was independently created by the author (as opposed to copied from other works), *and that it possesses at least some minimal degree of creativity.* M. Nimmer & D. Nimmer, *Copyright* at 2.01[A], [B] (1990) (hereinafter Nimmer). *To be sure, the requisite level of creativity* is *extremely low; even a slight amount will suffice.* The vast majority of works make the grade quite easily, as they possess some creative spark, "no matter how crude, humble or obvious" it might be. *ld.* at 1.08[C][I]. *Originality does not signify novelty;* a work may be original even though it closely resembles other works so long as the similarity is fortuitous, not the result of copying. To illustrate, assume that two poets, each ignorant of the other, compose identical poems. Neither work is novel, yet both are original and, hence, copyrightable...."
301. The court observed: "The selection, coordination, and arrangement of Rural's white pages do not satisfy the minimum constitutional standards for copyright protection. As mentioned at the outset, Rural's white pages are entirely typical. Persons designing telephone service in Rural's service area fill out an application and Rural issues them a telephone number. In preparing its white pages, Rural simply takes the data provided by its subscribers and lists in alphabetically by surname. The end product is a garden-variety white pages directory, devoid of even the slightest trace of creativity." 499 US 340 (199) at p. 362.
302. *See, Mason* v. *Montgomery Data, Inc.,* 967 F. 2d 135 (5th Cir. 1992).
303. *See, CCC Information Service* v. *Maclean Hunte Reports,* 44 F.3d 61 (2d Cir. 1994).

Act 1957, the act of reproduction including the storing in electronic means, distribution, communication to public, translation, etc., are the rights of the copyright owner. It is the exercise of these rights without the authorisation of the owner that constitutes infringement of copyright. Strictly speaking, even making a single copy or storing it in personal computer may amount to infringement of the reproduction right of the owner. But keeping in mind the public interest, the Copyright Act permitted limited use of copyrighted materials without permission of the owner of copyright. One such use is the fair dealing of literary work for private use[304] under Section 52 of the Copyright Act. It is true that the Act has not defined fair dealing and the courts find it difficult to lay down precise standards. On an examination of the case law from various jurisdictions, it is clear that the most important test is to find out whether the use is likely to harm the potential market or the value of the copyrighted work.[305]

It is generally understood that making a single copy for private use is within the ambit of fair use. The US Supreme Court has examined the issue of copying the entire work for private use in *Sony Corp.* v. *Universal City Studios Inc.*,[306] and concluded that it falls within the scope of fair use. It is clear from the facts of the present case that the copy possessed by the defendant was copied from the plaintiff. It was not the allegation of the plaintiff that the defendant was reproducing the work and distributing it so as to affect his potential market in exercising the reproduction right. It was the use of the information in the work by the defendant to compete in the business of mail order service of the plaintiff that forced him to file this suit. It is needless to emphasise that the object of copyright is not to protect information and recognise exclusive use of it. On the contrary, the purpose of copyright protection is to facilitate the dissemination of information. In this context, it appears difficult to appreciate the conclusion of the court that the act of the defendant amounts to infringement of copyright. In this regard the observation of the US Supreme Court in *Sony Corp.* case is worth noting:

> Even unauthorised uses of a copyrighted work are not necessarily infringing. An unlicensed use of the copyright is not an infringement unless it conflicts with one of the specific exclusive rights conferred by the copyright statute.[307]

It is the trade secret law that safeguards the confidential business information and copyright law cannot be pressed into use for this purpose. Even though the Delhi High Court referred to some literature on the trade secret law, it has not applied it to the facts of the case. It appears from the facts of the case that reliance on the principles of trade secret protection would be of little help to the court in giving relief to the plaintiff. This seems to be the reason for giving relief under copyright. Unfortunately, the court has not examined these issues. It is hoped that it will examine these issues when the case comes up for final disposal.

The Supreme Court of India has also recognised the above shift to "Modicum of Creativity" theory from the "Sweat of the Brow" and in *Eastern Book Company* v. *D.B. Modak*,[308] following the approach adopted by the Canadian Supreme Court in *CCH Canadian*

---

304. Section 52(1)(a) reads: "a fair dealing with a literary, dramatic, musical or artistic work, not being a computer program, for the purpose of (1) private us…."
305. *See*, for example *Civic Chandran* v. *Ammini Amma,* 1996 PTR 142; *Hubbard* v. *Vosper.* (1972) 2 WLR 389; *Sony Corporation* v. *Universal City Studios, Inc.*, 464 US 417 (1984).
306. 464 US 417. In this case the court examined whether home video taping for time shifting constitutes infringement of copyright.
307. *Sony Corp.* v. *Universal City Studios Inc.*, 464 US 417.
308. AIR 2008 SC 809: 2008 (1) SCC 1.

Ltd. v. *Law Society of Upper Canada.*[309] The Indian Supreme Court also rejected the "Sweat of the Brow" doctrine, (which conferred copyright on works merely because time, energy, skill and labour was expended, that is, originality of skill and labour), and held that the work must be original "in the sense that by virtue of selection, co-ordination or arrangement of pre-existing data contained in the work, a work somewhat different in character is produced by the author". Recently, the Supreme Court of India noticed that the two positions: (i) the "Sweat of the Brow" on the one hand, and (ii) "Modicum of Creativity" were extreme positions. The Apex Court preferred a higher threshold than the doctrine of "Sweat of the Brow" but not as high as "Modicum of Creativity". Since then the test of "originality" applying the creativity requirement has been followed by Indian Courts to grant copyright. In *Servewell Products Pvt. Ltd.* v. *Dolphin,*[310] the Delhi High Court had observed:

> The Supreme Court has recognized the shift in *Eastern Book Company* v. *D.B. Modak*, following the approach laid down by the *Canadian Supreme Court in CCH Canadian Ltd.* v. *Law Society of Upper Canada* (2004) SCC 13, rejected the "sweat of the brow doctrine" (which conferred copyright on works merely because time, energy, skill and labour was expended), and held that the work must be original "in the sense that by virtue of selection, co-ordination or arrangement of pre-existing data contained in the work, the work somewhat different in character, is produced by the author.

Thus, in India, the test for creativity establishes a higher threshold than the "sweat of the brow" doctrine, but not as high as "modicum of creativity". The Indian law mandates that not every effort or industry, or expending of skill, results in copyrightable work, but only those which create works that are somewhat different in character, involve some intellectual effort, and involve a minimum degree of creativity. Even before the Indian Copyright (Amendment) Act, 1984, in the UK[311] and in the USA,[312] computer databases and computer programs were afforded copyright protection. Thus, copyright is capable of subsisting in a scientific record consisting of a series of letters or other characters symbolising the sequential structure of DNA, proteins and similar constructs found in molecular biology, provided the recorded sequence is of sufficient length. This view may seem somewhat surprising at first blush, but it is submitted that it is rather difficult to see how any other can be sustained, consistent with the language of the Copyright Act and well-established principles of copyright law. Any sense

---

309. (2004) SCC 13: 2004 (1) SCR 339 (Canada). The Canadian Supreme Court in *CCH Canadian Lid.* v. *Law Society of Upper Canada,* 2004 (I) SCR 339 observed thus: "I conclude that the correct position falls between these extremes. For a work to be "original" within the meaning of the *Copyright Act,* it must be more than a mere copy of another work. At the same time, it need not be creative, in the sense of being novel or unique. What is required to attract copyright protection in the expression of an idea is an exercise of skill and judgment. By skill, I mean the use of one's knowledge, developed aptitude or practiced ability in producing the work. By judgment, I mean the use of one's capacity for discernment or ability to form an opinion or evaluation by comparing different possible options in producing the work. This exercise of skill and judgment will necessarily involve intellectual effort. The exercise of skill and judgment required to produce the work must not be so trivial that it could be characterized as a purely mechanical exercise. For example, any skill and judgment that might be involved in simply changing the font of a work to produce "another" work would be too trivial to merit copyright protection as an "original" work".
310. 2010 (43) PTC 507 (Del).
311. *Sega Enterprises Ltd.* v. *Richards and Anr.,* 1983 FSR 73.
312. *Apple Computer, Inc.* v. *Franklin Computer Corporation*, 714 F. 2d 1240, 1253 (3d Cir. 1983).

of surprise would appear to arise not from the legal principles but from the dramatically novel set of scientific facts to which they are applied. It will often be the case that such sequences will be held in the form of computer databases.

In *Emergent Genetics India Pvt. Ltd.* v. *Shailendra Shivam,*[313] the plaintiff sought for permanent injunction restraining defendants from selling "tomato seeds" under trademark "ANUPAMA". However, Court allowed application of plaintiff's for ad-interim temporary injunction and granted such relief, ex-parte. Hence, this case for vacation for ad-interim temporary injunction. The issue was whether, in absence of copyright protection, Plaintiff could claim injunction on ground that its trade secret, and confidential information had been unauthorised misappropriated by defendants? The Delhi High Court observed:

> Quality of confidence highlights that trade secrets were legal concept with sufficient effort or through illegal acts rivals might access trade secrets. However, if trade secret or information owner proved that reasonable efforts were made to keep information confidential, information remains trade secret and was legally protected. If, trade secret owners could not establish reasonable efforts to protect confidential information, they risk losing quality of confidentiality of information even if its information was obtained by rivals without permission. It was noticed by Court that suit and documents were bereft in materials about nature and quality of information which was confidential and precise developments, which plaintiffs' seeds offer to public. This aspect was crucial, because if information and techniques were neither unique, nor novel, but were merely documentation, or compilation of existing material, or existing techniques, freely available, or widely practised, there was no question of confidentiality. However, plaintiff did not claim exclusivity in respect of any particular technique or process. Thus, seeds in question were in respect of commercial crop would not in any manner detract from circumstance that nature of protection sought, that confidentiality, affects all classes of seeds. Therefore, Plaintiff was unable to establish, prima facie, its claim for copyright protection in databases, claimed by it. It was also found that it had not shown that information, which it claims to be exclusive was capable of protection, qualifying as "confidential information". So, ex-parte injunction granted at an earlier stage of proceeding, had to be vacated.

The Delhi High Court justified its above decision by explaining Sections 2(o), 2(y) and 14 of the Copyright Act 1957. The Court stated: "Indian law has recognized that compilation of databases is entitled to copyright protection. However, that would not end the debate." The law mandates that the work claiming protection ought to be original. Copyright law does not also grant the author of a literary work protection on ideas and facts.[314] It is the creative expression of an idea or fact which gets rewarded by law, through copyright monopoly for a specified period. The law does not, however protect every expression, but grants such recognition and protection to expressions that are "original". This standard is incorporated by Section 13, in respect of every class of work. A literary work, in order to qualify as work in which copyright can subsist, must therefore be original. However, mere labour (sweat of the brow) or investment of manpower and resources, is not a substitute for originality. Sequences obtained from nature (e.g., the sequence for a gene) cannot per se, be original. The microbiologist or scientist involved in gene sequencing "discovers" facts. There is no independent creation of a "work", essential for matching the originality requirement. Such a scientist merely copies

313. 2011 (125) DRJ 173.

314. *Baker* v. *Seldon*, [1879] 101 US 99; *Nichols* v. *Universal Pictures Corporation*, 45 F.2d (2d Cir. 1930); *R.G. Anand* v. *Delux Films*, AIR 1978 SC 1613: (1978) 4 SCC 118.

from nature-genetic sequence that contains codes for proteins. Therefore, there is no minimum creativity. So long as a researcher constructs a DNA sequence based on a sequence discovered in nature, there is no independent creation, no minimum creativity and thus no originality.[315]

In *Dr. Reckeweg and Co.* v. *Adven Biotech Pvt. Ltd.*,[316] the Court held that a work, in order to be called original must contain at least a "Modicum of Creativity". In that sense there must be intellectual originality and creativity. The level of such creativity, of course, would vary from case to case to render the work copyrightable. It noted that the originality requirement is not particularly stringent. A compiler may settle upon a selection or arrangement that others have used; novelty is not required. Originality requires only that the author make the selection or arrangement independently (i.e., without copying that selection or arrangement from another work), and that it display some minimal level of creativity. Presumably, the vast majority of compilations will pass this test, but not all will. There remains a narrow category of works in which the creative spark is utterly lacking or so trivial as to be virtually non-existent. Such works are incapable of sustaining a valid copyright. Dealing with the question of copyright in compilations, the Court held that there could be no copyright on facts, which form the compilation, but only on the arrangement of those facts, if a minimal level of creativity could be established. Similarly, copyright could subsist on the manner of expression of facts only if such "Modicum of Creativity" were established. In this regard, the Court observed:

> To this end, copyright assures authors the right to their original expression, but encourages others to build freely upon the ideas and information conveyed by a work. This principle, known as the idea-expression or fact-expression dichotomy, applies to all works of authorship. As applied to a factual compilation, assuming the absence of original written expression, only the compiler's selection and arrangement may be protected; the raw facts may be copied at will. This result is neither unfair nor unfortunate. It is the means by which copyright advances the progress of science and art.

Law mandates that not every effort or industry, or expending of skill, results in copyrightable work, but only those which create works that are somewhat different in character, involve some intellectual effort, and involve a certain degree of "Modicum of Creativity".[317]

In *Sap Aktiengesellschaft* v. *Sadiq Pasha Proprietor*,[318] defendant illegally obtained/installed licence and was using pirated/infringing software products belonging to Plaintiffs, as Plaintiff had not granted any valid licence. The issue was whether, there was infringement of copyright of software program of plaintiff and therefore whether plaintiff was entitled for injunction against defendants. The software programs developed and marketed by plaintiff are "computer programmes" within the meaning of Section 2(ffc) of the Indian Copyright Act, 1957 and are also included in the definition of a "literary work" as per Section 2(o) of the Copyright Act. It is also alleged that both India and Germany are signatories of the Berne Convention, Universal Copyright Convention and WTO's TRIPS Agreement and,

---

315. *Mattel, Inc. and Ors.* v. *Mr. Jayant Agarwalla and Ors.*, MIPR 2008 (3) 298: 2008 (38) PTC 416 (Del); *Dr. Reckeweg and Co. Gmbh. and Anr.* v. *Adven Biotech Pvt. Ltd.*, 2008 (38) PTC 308 (Del); *Servewell Products Pvt. Ltd.* v. *Dolphin*, 2010 (43) PTC 507 (Del).
316. 2008 (38) PTC 308 (Del).
317. *Chancellor Masters and Scholars of The University of Oxford* v. *Narendera Publishing House*, MIPR 2008 (3) 402: 2008 (38) PTC 385 (Del).
318. 179 (2011) DLT 709: 2011 (46) PTC 335 (Del).

therefore, rights of the Plaintiff companies are protected in India under Copyright Act. In this case,[319] the Delhi High Court held that as per Section 51 of the Copyright Act, copyright work could be infringed when any person without licence granted by owner of copyright or registrar in contravention of conditions of licence does anything, of which exclusive right to do was conferred upon the owner of copyright. However, as per evidence on record it was proved that no licence was issued by plaintiffs to use software as it was not found in database maintained by plaintiff company. Therefore, defendant could not claim that software found loaded on his hardware was licensed software and was not pirated version. Using pirated versions of software, copyright of which vested in Plaintiff companies, Defendant infringed their copyright in those software. Moreover, defendant was using software for purpose of imparting training in SAP R/3 or any other program and defendant had not have any education licence agreement with plaintiffs, therefore he had no right to impart training in program to any person. Hence, defendant had infringed copyright of Plaintiffs by using pirated software R/3 and by imparting training using aforesaid software. Thus, defendant could restrain from using any pirated/unlicenced software of Plaintiff company including R/3. The Delhi High Court observed:

> Section 51 of the Copyright Act, to the extent it is relevant, provides that copyright in a work shall be deemed to be infringed when any person without a licence granted by the owner of the copyright or the Registrar of Copyrights under the Act or in contravention of the conditions of a licence so granted or of any condition imposed by a competent authority under the Act does anything, the exclusive right to do which is by the Act is conferred upon the owner of the copyright.[320] Section 14 of the Copyright Act, to the extent it is relevant, provides that copyright means the exclusive rights subject to the provisions of the Act, to do or authorize the doing of specified acts in respect of a work or any substantial part thereof, which in the case of a computer programme would include to reproduce the work in any material form including the storing of it in any medium by electronic means. It has come in evidence that no license has been issued by the Plaintiffs to use the above referred software. Had any such license been issued and had the same been valid, it would have been found in the database maintained by the plaintiff company. In any case, the defendant has not come forward to claim that the software found loaded on his hardware was licensed software and was not by pirated version. Therefore, by using pirated versions of the software, copyright of which vest in the plaintiff companies, the defendant infringed their copyrights in those software.[321]

Computer Databases

Like the computer programmes, tables and compilations, the computer databases have been included in the definition of "literary work" under Section 2(o) of the Copyright Act, 1957[322]

---

319. *Sap Aktiengesellschaft* v. *Sadiq Pasha Proprietor,* 179 (2011) DLT 709: 2011 (46) PTC 335 (Del).
320. For detail dissuasion, *see, Novex Communication Pvt. Ltd.* v. *Lemon Tree Hotels Ltd.*, 2019 II AD (Delhi) 644; *Maroti* v. *The State of Maharashtra*, 2018 ALLMR (Cri) 4460; *Myspace Inc.* v. *Super Cassettes Industries Ltd.*, 2017 (69) PTC 1 (Del): 236 (2017) DLT 478; *Nethaji* v. *State*, 2015 (1) MLJ (Crl) 450; *Bablu Alam* v. *State of Chhattisgarh*, 2014 CriLJ 4835.
321. *See, Microsoft Corporation* v. *G.V. Rao*, MIPR 2009 (2) 67.
322. For detail discussion, *see, Novex Communication Pvt. Ltd.* v. *Lemon Tree Hotels Ltd.*, 2019 II AD (Delhi) 644; *Navigators Logistics Ltd.* v. *Kashif Qureshi*, 2018 (76) PTC 564 (Del): 254 (2018) DLT 307; *B.N. Firos* v. *State of Kerala*, (2018) 9 SCC 220: 2018 (5) SCALE 155.

and thus computer databases are protectable as literary work.[323] This is in the contrast to US approach as laid down in *Feist Publications, Inc.* v. *Rural Telephone Service Co.*,[324] where the US Supreme Court excluded the protection of white pages of a telephone directory on the ground that copyright law only protects works involving creativity, judgement or skill but not labour. To qualify for protection as a "literary work", however, a program should be original. The Indian courts in a number of cases have attributed the same meaning to "originality" as under British law.[325]

The Copyright (Amendment) Act, 1999 included "databases" in the definition of "literary work" in the Section 2(0) of the principal Act (Copyright Act, 1957). But the Copyright Act, 1957, does not define databases. Prior to the amendment of 1999, the Delhi High Court had an occasion to deal with databases in *Burlington Home Shopping Private Ltd.* v. *Rajnish Chibber.*[326] In this case the plaintiff, a mail order service developed a compilation of list of customers' database over a period of three years. Rajnish, a previous employee of Burlington managed to get a copy of the plaintiff's database. On comparison of the data made available by the plaintiff with the data available on the floppies seized from the custody of the defendant, it was found that a substantial number of entries were comparable word by word, line by line and even space by space. In some of the entries, the notations of commas and full stops (punctuation marks) were comparable. In a good number of entries, spelling mistakes occurring in the plaintiff's data were to be found in the data compilation of the defendant as well. These provided an intrinsic, irrefutable circumstantial evidence of defendant having indulged into slavish imitation of plaintiff's compilation making out a clear case of infringing of copyright as the compilation of list of clients/customers developed by a person by devoting time, money, labour and skill amounts to a literary work wherein the author has a copyright.

In this case,[327] the question arose whether a data base consisting of compilation mailing addresses of customers can be subject matter of a copyright whether the defendant can be said to have committed infringement of the plaintiff's copyright. Section 2(o) of the Copyright Act, 1957 defines "literary work" to include (among others) computer programs, tables and compilations including computer databases. Section 2(y) defines "work" as meaning any of the following works namely: (i) a literary, dramatic, musical or artistic work, (ii) a cinematographic film, (iii) sound recording. Under Section 14, literary work is one of the items wherein exclusive rights can be claimed so as to amount to copyright. Under Section 17(c) if a work is made in the course of other's employment under a contract of service or apprenticeship, it is the employer who is the first owner of the copyright therein in the absence of any agreement to the contrary. The court held that if the defendant was permitted to make use of plaintiff's database it was sure to cause an injury to the plaintiff, which would be incapable of being estimated in terms of money. The balance of convenience was also on the side of the plaintiff. The court focused on the question whether there was infringement by the defendant or not. It did not deal with the basic question of the requirement of originality for the purpose of extending copyright protection to compilation as literary work. The court made

323. *Burlington Home Shopping Pvt. Ltd.* v. *Rajnish Chibber* (1996) PTR 40 (Del): 61 (1995) DLT 6.
324. 499 US 340 (1991).
325. *R.G. Anand* v. *Delux Films,* AIR 1978 SC 1613: (1978) 4 SCC 118.
326. (1996) PTR 40 (Del): 61(1995) DLT 6. *See*, D.S. Sengar, "Protection of Trade Secrets and Undisclosed Information: Law and Litigation" 53 *Journal of the Indian Law Institute* (2011) pp. 254–274.
327. *Burlington Home Shopping Private Ltd.* v. *Rajnish Chibber* (1996) PTR 40 (Del.): 61 (1995) DLT 6.

reference to many foreign judgments but did not take cognisance of the *Feist Publication Inc.* v. *Rural Telephone Services.*[328] Subsequently, the Information Technology Act, 2000 was enacted which defines the "data" as well as "computer database". Expression "data" is defined in Section 2(o) of the Act as follows:

> Data means a representation of information, knowledge, facts, concepts or instructions which are being prepared or have been prepared in a formalised manner, and is intended to be processed, is being processed or has been processed in a computer system or computer network, and may be in any form (including computer printouts magnetic or optical storage media, punched cards, punched tapes) or stored internally in the memory of the computer.[329]

The Explanation to the Section 43 of the Information Technology Act, 2000 defines[330] the "computer database" thus:

> Computer database means a representation of information, knowledge, facts, concepts or instructions in text, image, audio, video that are being prepared or have been prepared in a formalised manner or have been produced by a computer, computer system or computer network and are intended for use in a computer, computer system or computer network.[331]

In fact, the Information Technology Act, 2000 (IT Act) enacted by the Indian Parliament is the first legislation, which contains provisions on data protection. The IT Act doesn't provide for any definition of personal data and, the definition of "data" would be more relevant in the field of cyber-crime.[332] Further, the IT Act defines certain key terms with respect to data protection, like access,[333] Computer,[334] Computer network,[335] Computer resource,[336] Computer system,[337] Computer database,[338] Data,[339] Electronic form,[340] Electronic record,[341] Information,[342] Intermediary,[343] Secure system,[344] and Security procedure.[345] The idea behind

---

328. 499 US 340 (1991). *Also see*, *G.A. Cramps and Sons Ltd.* v. *Frank Smythson Ltd.* (1944) AC 329.
329. *See*, *Amit Kumar Jadaun* v. *State of U.P.*, 2019 (142) RD 280: *Chandrasekar* v. *State*, 2018 (3) MLJ (Crl) 548; *K. Ramajayam* v. *The Inspector of Police*, 2016 CriLJ 1542: 2016 (4) RCR (Criminal) 390.
330. *See*, Explanation (ii) of Section 43. *Also see*, Hughes, *Copyright and Databases*, Essays in Copyright Law (1990) p. 68; *Lea G. Databases and Copyright* (1993) 9 CLSR 68.
331. *See Gulshan* v. *State*, 257 (2019) DLT 296: 2019 II AD (Delhi) 545; *Gagan Harsh Sharma* v. *The State of Maharashtra*, 2019 ALLMR (Cri) 595: 2019 CriLJ 1398; *Amit Kumar Jadaun* v. *State of U.P.*, 2018 (105) ACC 443: 2018 (130) ALR 877.
332. In *Shantaram* v. *The State of Maharashtra* (2019 (3) ABR 513: 2019 (2) ALLMR 375) the Bombay High Court observed: "Justice B.N. Shrikrishna, Former Hon'ble Judge of Supreme Court, is appointed to prepare a draft of personal Data Protection Bill, 2018, which will protect right to privacy and steps are likely to be taken to see that the data of criminal activity of a person is erased after particular period from the relevant records of the agencies."
333. Information Technology Act, 2000, Section 2(1)(a). The Act came into force on 17th October, 2000, *vide*, G.S.R. 788(E), dated 17th October, 2000.
334. *Ibid.*, Section 2(1)(i).
335. *Ibid.*, Section 2(1)(j).
336. *Ibid.*, Section 2(1)(k).
337. *Ibid.*, Section 2(1)(l).
338. *Ibid.*, Section 43, Explanation (ii).
339. *Ibid.*, Section 2(1)(o).
340. *Ibid.*, Section 2(1)(r).
341. *Ibid.*, Section 2(1)(t).
342. *Ibid.*, Section 2(1)(v).
343. *Ibid.*, Section 2(1)(w).
344. *Ibid.*, Section 2(1)(ze).
345. *Ibid.*, Section 2(1)(zf).

the aforesaid section is that the person who has secured access to any such information shall not take unfair advantage of it by disclosing it to the third party without obtaining the consent of the concerned party. "Third party information" is defined to mean "any information dealt with by an intermediary in his capacity as an intermediary", and it may be arguable that this limitation also applies to "data" and "communication". Section 79 provides that an intermediary shall not be liable for any third party information, data, or communication link made available or hasted by him: except in the conditions provided in sub-section (2) and (3) thereof. The IT Act doesn't provide any definition of personal data. Furthermore, the definition of "data" would be more relevant in the field of cyber-crime. Data protection consists of a technical framework of security measures designed to guarantee that data are handled in such a manner as to ensure that they are safe from unforeseen, unintended, unwanted or malevolent use.

Thus, the Information Technology Act, 2000 incorporates the defence of safe harbour for the intermediaries. It defines an intermediary under Section 2(1)(w), as including ISPs. The Act, under Section 79, creates a safe harbour for all intermediaries from liability for any third-party data, information or communication link that is made available by the ISP. Such exemption applies when the function of ISPs is limited to providing a communication system over which third party information is transmitted or temporarily stored. However, copyright is not included in the activities to be covered under the Act, so is generally inapplicable to this batch of matters. Consequently, while dealing with Section 79 and the issue of extent of knowledge of an intermediary for it to act and take down content, the Supreme Court in *Shreya Singhal* v. *Union of India*,[346] the Supreme Court has held that the requisite knowledge which obligates an intermediary to act is when it receives a Court order directing the blocking of access. Mere receipt of notice does not obligate the intermediaries to act and take down content. Subsequently, a Division Bench of the Delhi Court in *Myspace Inc.* v. *Super Cassettes Industries Ltd.*,[347] has held that though Section 79 grants a measured privilege to an intermediary, yet that does not mean that the rights guaranteed under the Copyright Act are curtailed in any manner. All that Section 79 does is to regulate the liability in respect of intermediaries, while the copyright Act grants and controls rights of a copyright owner.

ORIGINAL DRAMATIC WORK

An original dramatic work is the product of human intellect that qualifies for copyright under Section 13 of the Copyright Act, 1957.[348] Section 2(h) defines "dramatic work" to include any piece for recitation, choreographic work or entertainment in dumb show, the scenic arrangement or acting form of which is fixed in writing or otherwise but does not include a cinematograph film. It is interesting to note that the definition insists for fixation of the work "in writing or otherwise", a requirement not insisted in any other works like, literary, musical,

346. AIR 2015 SC 1523: (2015) 5 SCC 1
347. 236 (2017) DLT 478: MIPR 2017 (1) 274.
348. *See*, *Twentieth Century Fox Film Corporation* v. *Zee Telefilms Ltd.*, 2012 (51) PTC 465 (Del): MIPR 2012 (2) 377; *Academy of General Education* v. *B. Malini Mallya*, 2009 (2) KCCRSN 58: MIPR 2008 (1) 373; *Gramophone Company of India Ltd.* v. *Birendra Bahadur Pandey*, AIR 1984 SC 667: (1984) 2 SCC 534; *Smt. Somavanti* v. *The State of Punjab*, AIR 1963 SC 151: (1963) 2 SCR 774.

artistic, cinematograph film, sound recording mentioned in Section 2(y).[349] In *Institute for Inner Studies* v. *Charlotte*,[350] the Delhi High Court observed that the essential feature of a dramatic work is that it capable of being physically performed. However, not all works which are capable of being performed are dramatic works. However, not all works which are capable of being performed are dramatic works. It is possible, in one sense, to perform a literary work (for example, by reciting a poem), or a musical work (for example, by singing a song) or an artistic work (for example, by creating a tableau vivant with human actors), but that possibility does not make such a work a dramatic work. To constitute a work a dramatic work something more is necessary than mere capability of performance in this sense. Thus, a work which was intended to be sung by a singer in character costume but without action would not, it is thought, be a dramatic work. Similarly, the assemblage of a scene to be viewed or to be subject of a photograph, even if incorporating human actors, does not constitute a dramatic work, as it lacks the necessary element of action. The Court further observed:

> However, in order for a work to constitute a dramatic work there must be sufficient certainty of its subject matter in the case of a play or a screenplay, this presents little problem, since what knits the separate incidents together so that they can be performed as an entity is the structure of the work, or the plot, which comprises the setting, the characters, and their inter-relationship and development.

Under the definition to be found in Section 2(h), only for a dramatic work of any of the three types specified, i.e., (i) piece for recitation, (ii) choreographic work or (iii) entertainment in a dumb show would be included, and then further only where the scenic arrangement or acting form of which (in the three types) is fixed in writing or otherwise. When this requirement is satisfied then the work under consideration will amount to a "dramatic work" which will be protected by the provision contained in the Copyright Act. The definition of "dramatic work" to be found in Section 2(h), however, is an inclusive definition. On the other hand, the definition expressly excludes a cinematograph film by the closing words of Section 2(h). In *Fortune Films International* v. *Dev Anand*,[351] the Bombay High Court observed:

> The performance by an artiste in a cinematograph film cannot be equated to any of the five categories of "artistic work" (namely, a painting, a sculpture, a drawing, an engraving or a photograph) in Section 2(c). A cinematograph film was expressly excluded in the definition of a dramatic work in Section 2(h). In view of the definitions of "artistic work", "dramatic work" and "cinematograph film" in Section 2(f), it would appear that the Copyright Act, 1957, does not recognise the performance of an actor as a "work" (defined by Clause (y) of Section 2), which is protected by the Copyright Act.

Further, in *Saregama India Ltd.* v. *Suresh Jindal*,[352] the Calcutta High Court held that the expressions "dramatic work", "literary work" and "musical work" have different and distinct meaning and connotation under the said Act. From the definitions contained in Sections 2(h), 2(o) and 2(p) with regard to "dramatic work", "literary work" and "musical work", respectively, it clearly appears that "dramatic work" is in the nature of physical manifestation of such recitation of choreographic work or entertainment but does not include a cinematograph film.

---

349. *See, Novex Communication Pvt. Ltd.* v. *Lemon Tree Hotels Ltd.*, 2019 II AD (Delhi) 644; *Lyca Productions v. J. Manimaran*, 2018 (73) PTC 525 (Mad): 2018 (3) CTC 605.
350. 2014 (57) PTC 228 (Del): MIPR2014(1)129.
351. AIR 1979 Bom 17: 1978 (80) Bom LR 263.
352. AIR 1979 Bom 17: 1978 (80) Bom LR 263.

It would, therefore, mean that when someone does those acts as mentioned in Section 2(h) physically and live and is not a photographic imprint, thereof, it would mean dramatic work.

In *Academy of General Education* v. *Smt. B. Malini Mallya*,[353] the Karnataka High Court held that from the meaning given to the expression "dramatic work" in Section 2(h) of the Copyright Act, 1957, it is clear that it includes any piece of recitation, choreography work, the scenic arrangement or acting form of which is fixed in writing or otherwise. Therefore, if the recitation part of the dramatic work is fixed in writing and so also the scene arrangements as well as the acting part comes within the expression "dramatic work". Dramatic works are also treated as dramatic literature. In *Norowzian* v. *Arks Ltd.*,[354] the court held that the definition of dramatic work is at large and the term must be given its natural and ordinary meaning. Thus, a dramatic work is a work of action with or without words or music which is capable of being performed before an audience. A film is, of course, capable of being performed before an audience. Thus, there is an overlapping between dramatic works and films and three possibilities were identified in that a film could be: (i) a dramatic work in itself, (ii) a recording of a dramatic work and also a dramatic work in itself, (iii) a recording of something which is not a dramatic work.

An interesting issue camp up in *Indian Express Newspapers (Bombay) Pvt. Ltd.* v. *Jagmohan Mundhara,*[355] where the defendants made a stage play and a movie based on the central theme of certain series of articles published by the plaintiff, namely purchase of a woman by the name *Kanta* by a journalist to highlight the flesh trade flourishing in some parts of the country. The article published contained an autobiographical account of the part actually played by the author in the affair. In the film, the emphasis was on human bondage particularly of Indian women. The Court held that stage play on the movie was not as infringement of the copyright in the article.

ORIGINAL MUSICAL WORK

The Section 2(p) of the Copyright Act 1957 has defined a "musical work" which means a work consisting of music and includes any graphical notation of such work but does not include any words or any action intended to be sung, spoken or performed with the music. It is pertinent to note that Section 2(y) of the Act defines "works" which, *inter alia*, means a literary, dramatic, musical or artistic work. Further, Section 13 of the Act has classified three classes of works in which copyright subsists which, *inter alia*, includes original literary, dramatic, musical and artistic works, cinematograph films, and also sound recording.[356] Thus, original musical works are one of the subject matters of copyright protection. Section 2(p) of the Copyright Act, 1957 defines "musical work", but the word "music" is not defined. A common understanding of the word "music" would exclude a live musical concert.[357] But, in *Super Cassettes Industries Pvt. Ltd.* v. *Trimurti Films Pvt. Ltd.*,[358] the Bombay High Court held that the definition of the term

353. 2009 (2) KCCRSN 58: MIPR 2008 (1) 373.
354. (2000) FSR 363.
355. AIR 1985 Bom. 229.
356. *See, Ilaiyaraja* v. *B. Narsimhasn*, 2015 (63) PTC 358 (Mad): 2015 (3) CTC 622; *Star India Pvt. Ltd.* v. *Piyush Agarwal*, 2014 (58) PTC 169 (Del).
357. *See, Gypsy Pegasus Ltd.* v. *State of Gujarat*, 2018[15] GSTL 305.
358. 2018 (1) BomCR 156: 2018 (4) ALLMR 541.

"musical work", as defined in Section 2(p), means any combination of melody and harmony or either of them, printed, reduced to writing or otherwise graphically produced or reproduced.

The definition of "musical work" contained in the Copyright Act 1957, as originally enacted, limited the definition of a musical work to the composer's recorded graphical notation. Hence, the Copyright (Amendment) Act, 1984 introduced the aforementioned new definition. According to the un-amended definition, fixation of music was essential before it could be protected. There are a numbers of examples from the Indian classical music and the music industry wherein it can be shown that the composer of music and performer of music are the same person, such a person improvises within the framework of a highly developed discipline on a pre-selected traditional theme without fixation of his composition on a piece of paper. The un-amended definition insisted for the requirement of fixation and also linked to "melody and harmony". This was based on the English law and seems to be influenced by the way in which western music is understood.[359]

Western classical music is created by composers who conventionally record their compositions in writing on paper, using an elaborate, well-established system of musical notation. Performers who can read the notation then perform their works. Personal contact between composer and performer is not necessary and, even before the era of sound recordings, a composer's works could be performed long after his death. This composer-performer dichotomy has become the paradigm in the conceptualisation of music as a form of copyrighted work, and of the different rights arising out of its creation and use, but it does not precisely fit the Indian situation. Indian civilisation gave birth to the only other classical form of music that has reached heights of sophistication comparable to that of West, but on altogether different principles. Here the same persons both compose and perform simultaneously, improvising, within the framework of a highly developed discipline, on pre-selected traditional themes ("ragas") as they sing or play on musical instruments.[360]

The author in relation to a "musical work" is the "composer" under Section 2(d)(ii) and the composer in relation to musical work means under Section 2(ffa) the person who composes the music regardless of whether he records it on any form of graphical notation. A combined reading of Sections 2(p) and 2(ffa) makes it very clear that the legislature has not only protected "musical work" in graphical notation but also taken care to protect traditional Indian musical compositions which may involve graphical notations.

ILLUSTRATION

In an occasion the music composer Mr. A.R. Rahaman played music on the lyrical composition of Mr. Sameer along with Ms. Kavita Krishnamurty who singing song and Ms. Bipasha Basu dances on the song in the stage. In this occasion, words of song are a "literary work" where lyricist Mr. Sameer has the copyright. Music is the "musical work" where composer Mr. A.R. Rahaman has the copyright. Ms. Kavita Krishnamurty, Ms. Bipasha Basu and all players of the musical instruments are the performers who have a right in their performances. In this complex situation generally all rights are assigned by the author, composer and performers to the manager of the occasion.

---

359. *See,* N. Gopalakrishnan and T.G. Agitha, *Principles of Intellectual Property*, Eastern Book Company (2009) p. 160.

360. *See,* Jagdish Sagar, "Entertainment Media and IP Rights: An Indian Perspective" in S.K. Verma and Raman Mittal, *Intellectual property Rights: A Global Version,* Indian Law Institute, New Delhi (2004).

Based on the new definition, the Delhi High Court in *Gramophone Co. Ltd.* v. *Super Cassettes Industries*[361] has looked into the content of a "musical work". Here the plaintiff had alleged that the sound records produced by the defendants were extracts of musical works in the film "*Hum Aapke Hai Kaun*" of which the plaintiff is the copyright owner. However, the Court concluded that since the musical works in the film has not been printed, written or graphically produced or reproduced, it did not fall within the definition of musical works and so the plaintiff could not claim copyright in the work. The Court viewed a musical work not as a mere combination of melody and harmony or either of them. It must necessarily also have been printed, reduced to writing or graphically produced or reproduced. Every musical composition has a structure or shape, i.e., the arrangement of individual elements so as to constitute a whole and that musical notation means a visual record of musical sound (heard or imagined) or a set of visual instructions for the performance of music. Its main elements are pitch (location of music on scale), duration, timbre, and volume. There are various systems of notations like verbal, alphabetical, numerical, graphic and tablatures. The Court further observed:

> Musical work is not merely a combination of melody and harmony or either of them. It must necessarily also have been "printed, reduced to writing or otherwise graphically produced or reproduced" ...[M]usical notation means a visual record of musical sound (heard or imagined) or a set of visual instructions for performance of music. Its main elements are pitch (location of musical sound on the scale), duration, timbre, and volume. There are various systems of notation like, verbal, alphabetical, numerical, graphic and tabulators. The words printed, reduced to writing or otherwise graphically produced or reproduced are thus not an empty formality.

In India "plagiarism" is not the same as "copyright infringement" provided by the Copyright Act, 1957. It has been successfully argued that remixes can be covered by the term "adaptation" which attracts its own copyright. "Adaptation of musical work" is protected under Section 14(a)(vi). Adaptation in relation to musical work is "any arrangement or transcription of the work" under Section 2(a)(iv). Transcription means "arrangement of a musical composition for some instrument or voice other than the original". In most cases of remixes the subsequent company borrowed songs from the original music company on payment of royalty. The result was that the music composers who had assigned their rights in the original music company did not get any share from the sale of remix song. This resulted in an unfair treatment of original music composers. This position has, however, been changed by introduction of Section 31C and deletion of Section 52(l)(j) by the Copyright (Amendment) Act, 2012.

In *Gypsy Pegasus Ltd.* v. *State of Gujarat*,[362] the issue before the Supreme Court was whether the musical concert organized by the appellant was for the purposes of promotion of cultural activities or for commercial purposes? The Court observed that a musical concert would not be a musical event as it is not a "musical work" and thus the definition of the term "musical work" contained in Section 2(p) of the Copyright Act, 1957 makes it clear that the common understanding of the word "music" would exclude a live musical concert. Thus, necessary exemption can apply to a non-taxable form of entertainment such as educational, cultural or charitable entertainment.

---

361. (1996) 16 PTC 252 (Del): 58(1995) DLT 99.
362. 2018 [15] GSTL 305.

ORIGINAL ARTISTIC WORK

What is Original Artistic Work?

Section 13 of the Copyright Act, 1957 provides that "original artistic works" are subject-matter of copyright protection and Section 2(c) of the Act provides a wide definition of the term "artistic work" covering a large number of areas of art like painting, sculpture, drawing, engraving, photograph, work of architecture, etc.[363] In *Makemy Trip (India) Private Limited* v. *Pravasi Guide Private Limited,*[364] the Delhi High Court held that apart from serving as a source identifier, the plaintiff's MakeMyTrip logo marks, including but not limited to the logos also constitute original artistic works within the meaning of the Copyright Act 1957.

In *ICC Development (International) Ltd.* v. *Ever Green Service Station,*[365] certain companies paid large sums of money for plaintiff's events and in return such companies were given exclusive rights to associate themselves and their brands with the event. "ICC Cricket World Cup South Africa 2003" is the trade name of the plaintiff. They have made enormous efforts and spent huge amounts of money in popularising the words: "ICC World Cup", "Cricket World Cup, 2003" and "ICC World Cup 2003". The plaintiff has created a distinct phrase "ICC World Cup South Africa 2003" logo and a mascot—"Dazzler". The logo denotes the black and white striped colours of the Zebra, which represents the harmonious co-existence of black and white population in South Africa. The Court held that the plaintiff is the copyright owner of artistic work in the aforesaid words and logo within the meaning of Section 2(c) of the Copyright Act, 1957.

The WIPO guide observes: "the category of visual arts covers virtually all artistic works whether in two dimensions (drawings, engravings, etc.) or in three (sculptures, statues, etc.) independent of their nature (figurative or abstract) and their intention (pure or commercial art).[366] While Section 2(c) of the Copyright Act, 1957 provides a wide definition of the term "artistic works", the Act did not protect storing of artistic work in electronic means until the 2012 amendment. The Copyright (Amendment) Act, 2012 has made certain changes that clarify the rights in artistic works. Section 14(c) relates to the exclusive rights of the author of an artistic work. Clause (i) of the Section 14(c) grants the right to reproduce the work in any material form. This clause is amended by Copyright (Amendment) Act, 2012 to provide that the right to reproduce the work in any material form includes "the storing of it in any medium by electronic or other means".[367] The clause has been redrafted, numbering as sub-

---

363. *See*, *Varsha Polymers* v. *Vajra Plastics Industry*, 2018 (5) KHC 861; *King Point Enterprises Co. Ltd* v. *Ali Asgar,* 206 (2014) DLT 24: 2013 (56) PTC 222 (Del); *Dr. Reddy's Laboratory Ltd.* v. *Reddy Pharmaceuticals Ltd.,* 2013 (56) PTC 372 (Del); *Living Media India Ltd.* v. *M. Hussain*, 202 (2013) DLT 39: 2013 (55) PTC 548 (Del).
364. 2019 (78) PTC 154 (Del): 2019I VAD (Delhi) 567.
365. 102 (2003) DLT 723: 2003 (26) PTC 228 (Del).
366. WIPO, *Guide to the Berne Convention for the Protection of Literary and Artistic Works* (Paris Act, 1971), p. 16.
367. Substituted by the Copyright (Amendment) Act, 2012, Section 5(i) for sub-clause (i) [w.e.f. 21-6-2012]. Sub-clause (i) of the Section 14(c), before substitution, stood as under: "(i) to reproduce the work in any material form including depiction in three dimensions of a two-dimensional work or in two dimensions of a three-dimensional work."

clauses the existing right of depiction in three dimensions of a two-dimensional work or in two dimensions of a three-dimensional work. The net effect of the amendment is the addition of the right of storing of the work in any medium by electronic or other means. Section 2(c) of the Copyright Act, 1957, defines "artistic work" to mean:[368]

(i) a painting, a sculpture, a drawing (including a diagram, map, chart or plan), an engraving or a photograph, whether or not any such work possesses artistic quality;
(ii) a [work of architectural][369] and
(iii) any other work of artistic craftsmanship.

ILLUSTRATION

As a result of wide publicity, involving huge expenditure a product under the trademark DICLOMOL has gained tremendous reputation in the business market and also in the public. The trademark DICLOMOL appears in a bold typeface on a coloured strip having a half arrow head at its one end. This configuration constitutes an original artistic work within the meaning of Section 2(c) of the Copyright Act, 1957. By virtue of prior adoption, long, continuous, extensive as well as owing to the large scale publicity, the trademark DICLOMOL is identified exclusively with the copyright owner and therefore the copyright owner has the exclusive right to use the said mark and the use of the said mark or any other mark deceptively similar by anyone else without the consent of the copyright owner would amount to violation of the copyright owner's legal rights.

A question may arise whether packaging is an artistic work. In *Sanjay Kapur* v. *Dev Agri Farms Pvt. Ltd.*,[370] the plaintiffs innovated a new way and manner of packaging their tea. The innovative features and element of the said packaging included packing tea in a soft paper packet shaped in a rectangular sided cuboid. This packet is slipped into a fabric sleeve and is closed at top by a traditional drawstring/dori. Answering affirmatively the court held that the packaging is innovative/creative and is an original artistic work under Section 2(c) of the Copyright Act, 1957 and is capable of protection.

In *Burroughs Wellcome (India) Ltd.* v. *Uni-Sole Pvt. Ltd.*,[371] the Bombay High Court held that an artistic work on a carton or a container of goods can become the subject matter of copyright. The Delhi High Court in *Dart Industries Inc.* v. *Techno Plast*,[372] held that the definition of artistic work has a very wide connotation as it is not circumscribed by any limitation of the work possessing any artistic quality. Even an abstract work, such as a few lines or curves arbitrarily drawn would qualify as an artistic work. It may be two dimensional or three dimensional. The artistic work may or may not have visual appeal. The rights to which a holder of an original artistic work is entitled are enumerated in Section 14(c) of the Copyright Act 1957.[373]

---

368. *See*, *Holland Company* v. *S.P. Industries*, 2014 LawSuit (Del) 1878; *Mohan Lal* v. *Sona Paint*, 2013 (55) PTC 61: 2013 (200) DLT 322.
369. Substituted by the Copyright (Amendment) Act, 1994, Section 2, for "architectural work of art" (w.e.f. 10-5-1995).
370. 2014 (59) PTC 93: 2014 LawSuit (Del) 4624.
371. 1999 (19) PTC 188 (Bom): 1998 (3) BomCR 481.
372. 2016 (67) PTC 457 (Del): 233 (2016) DLT 1.
373. *See*, *IPEG Inc.* v. *Kay Bee Engineers*, AIR 2016 Guj 104: 2016 (66) PTC 305 (Guj); *Ritika Private Limited* v. *Biba Apparels Private Limited*, 230 (2016) DLT 109: MIPR 2016 (2)166; *Midas Hygiene Industries Pvt. Ltd.* v. *Sudhir Bhatia*, 2015 (64) PTC 366 (Del): 225 (2015) DLT 178.

Original Painting as Artistic Work

The expression "painting" is used in the definition of "artistic work" under Section 2(c) of the Copyright Act 1957. But the painting cannot be protected under the Act unless it is found as an original work of the author. Thus, unless the author of a painting employs either skill in painting or work and labour in seeking to depict some actual object or abstract design, the work cannot be protected. In *Gurukrupa Mech Tech Pvt. Ltd.* v. *State of Gujarat*,[374] the Gujarat High Court held that in case of original work of art, copyright would exist and the author/holder would continue enjoying the longer protection granted under the Copyright Act in respect of the original artistic work. But whenever a design created from such a painting for the purpose of industrial application on an article so as to produce an article which has features of shape, or configuration or pattern or ornament or composition of lines or colours and which appeals to the eye would also be entitled design protection in terms of the provisions of the Designs Act. Clarifying this proposition of law, the Delhi High Court in *Dart Industries Inc.* v. *Techno Plast*,[375] held that a original painting is an original work of art such a painting will continue to enjoy the protection available to an artistic work under the Copyright Act. But whenever a design created from such a painting for the purpose of industrial application and the design is registered under the Designs Act, the Design would lose its copyright protection under the Copyright Act but not the original painting. In *Ritika Private Limited* v. *Biba Apparels Private Limited*,[376] the Court observed:

> Even if the artistic work such as a painting has been used as the basis for designing an industrially produced object for commerce, such as the furnishing in the present case, nevertheless the original painting would indeed enjoy full copyright protection, while the result of the industrial application of such painting, namely, the design used in the industrial production of the ultimate product shall enjoy lesser period of protection as stipulated under the Designs Act provided it is registered as a design under the Designs Act.

Similarly, in *Photoquip India Limited* v. *Delhi Photo Store*,[377] the Bombay High Court held that if the design is registered under the Designs Act, the design would lose its copyright protection under the Copyright Act but not the original painting. Thus, the Madras High Court in *Tractors and Farm Equipment Ltd.* v. *Standard Combines (Pvt.)* Ltd.,[378] distinguishing between the copyright protection available to original painting and the design derived from and founded upon original painting for the purpose of industrial production of furnishings observed that the design derived from original painting would only be covered by the limitations placed in Section 15 of the Copyright Act. The reason is that original painting is a part of original "literary work" under Section 2(o) of the Act. Thus, in *Microfibres Inc.* v. *Girdhar*,[379] it was held that an artistic work must be original to qualify protection under the Act. Thus, in *Brooke Bond India Ltd.* v. *Balaji Tea (India) Pvt. Ltd.*,[380] the Bombay High Court observed:

---

374. (2018) 4 GLR 3324.
375. 2017 II AD (Delhi) 602: 2016 (67) PTC 457 (Del).
376. 230 (2016) DLT 109: MIPR 2016 (2) 166.
377. 2015 (6) ABR 210: 2014 (60) PTC 563 (Bom).
378. MANU/TN/1935/2012.
379. 2009 (40) PTC 519 (Del): MIPR 2009 (2) 229.
380. MANU/TN/0623/1989.

> To qualify for copyright protection, an artistic work must be original, i.e., it must originate from the author. The work need not possess any artistic quality; but the author must have bestowed skill judgment and effort upon bestowed skill judgment and effort upon the work.

Further, a painting is an object and not an idea, therefore, it can only be done on some kind of surface. In an English case, *Merchandising Corporation of America* v. *Harpbond*,[381] it was held that facial make-up as such, however, idiosyncratic it might be as an idea, was not a painting within the meaning of Section 3 of the UK Copyright Act, 1956. The final product is to be taken into consideration in case of imparting a "painting". If a painting is imported into India, duty will necessarily have to be charged on the value of the final product. In India, the Customs Valuation Rules, 1988 are framed keeping in view the GATT protocol and the WTO agreement for the purpose of valuation under the 1988 Rules the concept of "transaction value" which was introduced. According to the 1988 Rules, "it is not the input alone but goods whose value has been enhanced by the said inputs". The final product at the time of import is either the magazine or the encyclopedia as the case may be. For example, paintings are also to be taxed. In *Associated Cement Companies Ltd.* v. *Commissioner of Customs*,[382] the Apex Court observed:

> Valuable paintings are worth millions. A painting or a portrait may be specially commissioned or an article may be tailor-made. This aspect is irrelevant since what is taxed is the final product as defined and it will be an absurdity to contend that the value for the purposes of duty ought to be the cost of the canvas and the oil paint even though the composite product, i.e., the painting, is worth millions.

Original Sculpture as Artistic Work

Copyright subsists in sculpture irrespective of its artistic quality. Section 2(C) of the Copyright Act 1957 provides that "artistic work" to mean a painting, a sculpture, a drawing, a work of architectural etc. Thus, sculpture is an artistic work and thus copyright subsists Thus, in respect of sculpture the work need not have an artistic quality, i.e., it is not required to meet any aesthetic standard. The only important factor is that it is original work. Section 2(za) of the Copyright Act, 1957 provides that "work" of sculpture" includes casts and models. In *Raj Rewal* v. *Union of India*,[383] it was held that a work of architecture, when transformed in a building or structure, has a very different connotation from most other works in which copyright subsists. All such other works in which copyrights subsists, are expressed in mediums which in themselves are of no value viz. a canvas or a record or tape or paper. A painting or a drawing or a photograph or a film or an audio recording are on mediums title wherein invariably vests in the owner of the copyrighted work expressed thereon. So is a sculpture, unless permanently attached to earth.

Besides the casts and models, how many other arts are covered in sculpture. According to *New Encyclopedia Britannica*, sculpture is the name of art that grows and changes, and

381. (1983) FSR 32.
382. AIR 2001 SC 862: (2001) 4 SCC 593. *See also*, *Union of India* v. *M/s Honda Siel Car India Limited*, 2012 (189) ECR 183 (Delhi); *Commissioner of Customs* v. *Gujarat Perstorp Electronics Ltd.* (2005) 7 SCC 118; [2005] Supp (2) SCR 389; *Tata Consultancy Services* v. *State of Andhra Pradesh*, AIR 2005 SC 371: (2005) 1 SCC 308.
383. 260 (2019) DLT 190.

is continually extending the range of its activities and evolving new kinds of objects. Thus, sculpture is the product of art of forming representations of things or abstract designs in the round or in relief by chiselling stone, craving wood, modelling clay, casting metal or similar processes. In *Pranda Jewelry Pvt. Ltd.* v. *Aarya 24 KT*,[384] the Bombay High Court observed that when a sculpture of an artist is cast in a certain material, the artist is not applying the features of its shape, configuration, etc. to the material, but reproducing the very sculpture in a three-dimensional form. When we copy a painting, whether in hand or by print, we are not applying the features of shape, configuration, etc. to the canvas or the paper, but reproducing the very painting which is the copyrighted work of the artist. The sculpture or the painting is an artistic work, even though it may not have any artistic qualify.

Original Drawing as Artistic Work

Drawing, another form of artistic work, is also a subject of copyright protection. The word drawing is not defined in the Act except that drawing of any kind whether or not it possesses any artistic quality would be covered by the term "artistic work". This means that even mechanical or engineering drawings are artistic work entitled to copyright protection. However, a drawing must originate with the author and not be copied from another work. Thus, in *Samsonite Corporation* v. *Vijay Sales*,[385] it was held that a drawing which is simply traced from another drawing is not an original artistic work, a drawing which is made without any copying from anything originates with the artist is protected under copyright law. This case was debated on the meaning of the word drawing and held:

> In English, to draw means literally to trace or delineate, implying that a drawing is an image represented purely in line and therefore monochromatic. In this sense, drawing is closely related to writing, since both involve graphic notation and significant linear configurations; indeed, the tools of drawing and writing have generally been identical. In other languages, however, the word for drawing-disegno (Italian) dressing (French)—includes the concept of design in a broader sense, the full range of visual composition.[386]

Thus, the Court held that the concept of projecting a drawing for the purpose of claiming copyright must be one satisfying the comprehensive meaning of the word "drawing". It is also stated that there is another aspect of drawing called perspective drawing. The drawing concerned has to give a sectional view, dimensions and the production details, including assembling. In *Binj Rajka Steel Tubes Ltd.* v. *State by Inspector of Police,*[387] the Madras High Court held that engineering drawing is an artistic work within the meaning of Section 2(c) of the Copyright Act, 1957. Further, in *AGA Medical Corporation* v. *Mr. Faisal Kapadi*,[388] the Delhi High Court held that as per the definition of artistic work, a drawing includes a diagram, map, chart or plan. A diagram, map, chart and plan are not necessarily the work of an artist but they are usually prepared by different technical hands well-versed in such job.

---

384. AIR 2015 Bom 157: 2015 (62) PTC 254 (Bom).
385. 73 (1998) DLT 732: 1998 (18) PTC 372 (Del). *See also*, *AGA Medical Corporation* v. *Faisal Kapadi*, 2003(26) PTC 349 (Del): 2003 II AD (Delhi) 351.
386. *See*, *AGA Medical Corporation* v. *Mr. Faisal Kapadi*, 103 (2003) DLT 321: 2003 (26) PTC 349 (Del).
387. MANU/TN/1319/2004.
388. 103 (2003) DLT 321: 2003 (26) PTC 349 (Del).

For instance, plans and maps are generally prepared by architects and draftsmen and not by an artist. An artist of course may prepare a painting, a sculpture and a drawing as well. Thus, drawings are artistic work within the meaning of Section 2(c) and the plaintiff has a copyright in the same within the meaning of Section 14.

In *Camlin Private Ltd.* v. *M/s National Pencil Industries,*[389] the Delhi High Court has held that in absence of proof that a human author actually invested labour and skill in producing a multicolumn design on a carton, no copyright may subsist in a mechanically reproduced printed carton. In this case the plaintiffs had alleged that the defendant copied the floral design in its printed carton/boxes and that it amounted to an infringement of his copyright in the artistic work. But since the floral design in the carton was found to be a mechanically produced one, the Court held that the plaintiff was not entitled to copyright. The Court reasoned that no skill and labour is expended upon the artistic carton as the same has been produced by mechanical action of a printing machine rather than the skill and labour of a natural person. In order to be covered by copyright law, any work in which copyright is claimed must originate from the author who must have expended his skill and labour and the work must be something, which has not been copied by the author from anyone else. Only then can it be said that it originated from the author. This decision thus negates the scope of works created by a mechanical process, unless proved to emanate from a human author's efforts, from receiving copyright protection. Thus it is clear that to claim protection under the Act, the work must fall within copyrightable subject matter as well as satisfy the test of originality.

In *John Richard Brady* v. *Chemical Process Equipments (P) Ltd.*,[390] some important and difficult issues relating to copyright in "industrial drawings" camp up for consideration before the Delhi High Court which the court had not at that stage to consider as it was only disposing of an interlocutory application for *ad interim* injunction pending disposal of the suit. In the suit, the plaintiff sought relief against the defendant on the grounds that the defendant had infringed his copyright in certain industrial drawings as well as that the defendant had committed breach of confidence in respect of information and know-how disclosed to it on conditions of confidence. The court held that the plaintiff had established a *prima facie* case to warrant an order of interim injunction. In the suit the plaintiff rested his claim on the basis that he was the owner of the artistic copyright in the drawing and as such exclusively entitled to reproduce the drawing, whether two dimensionally as drawing or three dimensionally as the objects represented by those drawings. Dealing with the question of infringement of copyright in the plaintiff's drawings by the defendant's object (fodder production unit) based on disclosures made by the plaintiff to the defendants, the court pointed out that this was to be tested on the visual appearance of the object and drawing in question and applying the test (called the lay-observer test) whereby it was tested whether it appeared, to persons who are not experts in relation to the object of that description, to be a reproduction. If to the lay-observer it did not appear to be reproduction, there is no infringement of the artistic copyright in the work in two dimensions. If it did appear to be so, to a lay-observer, there is infringement. In the present case, the court found that the defendants' machine satisfied this

389. AIR 1986 Del 444: 30 (1986) DLT 347.
390. AIR 1987 Del 372.

test and it was obvious to the eye that it was a mere three-dimensional reproduction of the plaintiff's industrial drawing. The lay-observer test applied by the court was derived from Clause (w) of Section 52(1) which provided that the Act shall not constitute an infringement of copyright if "the making of an object of any description in three dimensions of an artistic work in two dimensions, if the object would not appear, to persons, who are not experts in relation to object of that description, to be a reproduction of the artistic work". Clause (w) of Section 52(1) was omitted by the Copyright (Amendment) Act, 1994.[391] However, Copyright (Amendment) Act, 1012 reintroduced Clause (w) to Section 52(1) of the principal Act. New Clause (w) to Section 52(1) provides that the making of a three-dimensional object from a two-dimensional work, such as a technical drawing, for industrial application of any purely functional part of a useful device shall not constitute infringement. This provision should help reverse engineering of mechanical devices.[392]

Original Engraving as Artistic Work

Engravings were the first artistic works to receive statutory protection under the Engraving Copyright Act, 1735.[393] According to Section 1 of the Act, "every person who shall invent and design, engrave, etch, or work, in mezzotinto or chiaro-oscuro, or from his own works and investigation shall cause to be designed and engraved, etched, or worked, in mezzotinto or chiaro-oscuro, any historical or other print or prints, shall have the sole right and liberty of printing and reprinting the same for the term of fourteen years, to commence from the day of first publishing thereof, which shall be truly engraved with the name of the proprietor on each plate, and printed on every such print or prints." The process of enlargement of the concept of copyright had begun in the eighteenth century. The engraves had succeed their rights under copyright law.

In *Rameshwar Prasad* v. *Emperor*,[394] the Nagpur High Court held that in England that photography would be included under the Engraving Copyright Act, 1735 though it had not been invented till more than a century after the Act was passed; but it may be noted that in the very words of the Act, it is stated "or in any other manner copying prints and engravings", and photography would be one method of copying. Similarly, in *R. Swarup Reddy* v. *M/s. Kotak Mahindra Bank Ltd.*,[395] the Madras High Court held that Engraving Copyright Act, 1735 imposed a penalty for practically engraving, by etching or otherwise, or "in any other manner" copying prints and engravings, applied to copying by photography. Section 2(i) of the Copyright Act, 1957 defines engravings to include etchings, lithographs, wood-cuts,

---

391. Clause (w) of Section 52 (1) was omitted by the Copyright (Amendment) Act, 1994, Section 17 (w.e.f. 10-5-2012).
392. *See, Telemecanique and Controls (I) Limited* v. *Schneider Electric Industries SA*, 94 (2001) DLT 865.
393. For detail discussion on engraving history, *see*, N. Charney, *Art of Forgery: The Minds, Motives and Methods of the Master Forgers* (Pheidon Press, London, 2015); Hitesh Chopra and Sandeep Kumar, "Intellectual Property Protection and Rights: Historical and Current Prospective," 6(5) (2014) pp. 572–578; Ronan Deazley, Martin Kretschmer and Lionel Bently, *Privilege and Property Essays on the History of Copyright* (Open Book Publishers, Cambridge, 2010); L. Patterson, *Copyright in Historical Perspective* (Vanderbilt University Press, Nashville, 1968).
394. AIR 1931 Nag 177.
395. (2010) 1 MLJ 437.

prints and other similar works not being photographs. In *Super Cassetes Industries Ltd.* v. *Myspace Inc.*,[396] the Delhi High Court held that photograph copy is held to be a copy under the engravings.

Original Photograph as Artistic Work

Section 2(s) of the Copyright Act, 1957 defines a photograph to include photo-lithograph and any work produced by any process analogous to photography but does not include any part of a cinematograph film. In *George Jacob* v. *Nandakumar Moodadi*,[397] the Kerala High Court held that Section 2(s) of the Act defines "photograph" which includes photo-lithograph and any work produced by any process analogous to photography, but does not include cinematograph film. Section 2(m) of the Act defines "infringing copy" in relation to an artistic work as a reproduction thereof otherwise than in the form of cinematographic film. Further, in *Chancellor* v. *Rameshwari Photocopy Services*,[398] the Delhi High Court held that the Section 2(s) defines "photograph" as including photo-lithograph and any work produced by any process analogous to photography. Thus, the definition itself makes it clear that, in order to be eligible for protection, the work need not possess any artistic quality. But, it must be original.

To constitute an original artistic work neither original thought nor original research is essential and the standard of originality required is a low one. It is the original skill or labour in execution, and not originality of thought which is required. Accordingly photographs or images of deities in calendars[399] and even a picture of Mahatma Gandhi[400] produced by combining two other pictures of him were held entitled to copyright. In *Associated Publishers* v. *K. Bashyam,*[401] the defendant made a portrait of Mahatma Gandhi based on two photographs. The Madras High Court held that it was copyrightable as portrait was different from the photographs. The precise amount of knowledge, labour, judgment, skill or taste, which the artist must bestow upon his composition in order to acquire a copyright, is to be determined by a judicious analysis of facts and circumstances.

Original Work of Architecture

Section 2(b) of the Copyright Act, 1957 defines "work of architecture" to mean: "any building or structure having an artistic character or design or any model for such building or structure." Thus, the structure or the building does not form protectable subject matter under the Act unless it has an artistic character or design that is, as some aesthetic value.[402] However,

396. 2011 (48) PTC 49 (Del): MIPR 2011 (2) 303. *See also, Sadhna Agrawal* v. *State of Chhattisgarh*, 2017 Lab IC 617; *Devshree Bandhe* v. *Chhattisgarh State Power Holding Company Limited*, 2017 (5) CGLJ 340: 2017 Lab IC 1506.
397. 2014 Cri LJ 3421: 2014 (2) RCR (Criminal) 786.
398. 2016 (68) PTC 386 (Del): 233 (2016) DLT 279.
399. See, *Daily Calender* v. *United Concern*, AIR 1967 Mad 381: (1964) ILR 2 Mad 666; *Lallubhai Motira* v. *Laxmishankar Ambalal,* AIR 1945 Bom. 51: 1944 (46) Bom LR 679.
400. *Associated Publishers* v. *K. Bashyam,* AIR 1961 Mad. 114: (1961) ILR Mad 134.
401. AIR 1961 Mad. 114: (1961) ILR Mad 134.
402. *See*, Section 2(b) of the Copyright Act, 1957.

Section 13(5) clarifies that the process or method of construction does not form protectable subject matter. According to Section 13(5) in case of work of architecture, copyright shall subsist only in the artistic character or design and shall not extend to processes or method of construction. In the US, an Amendment to Copyright Act in 1990 extended protection to architectural works including protection for the overall form as well as the arrangement and composition of spaces and elements in the design but excluded protection for individual standard features. Creating a work of architecture is a long process. Thus, an architect designs and supervises the construction of a building. An architect first makes of a plan, which is treated as "drawing" or an "artistic work", which is protectable subject matter under Section 2(c) of the Copyright Act.

The Section 14 of the Copyright Act 1957 confers exclusive right in the owner of the copyright, in the case of artistic work, to communicate the work to the public and to include the work in any cinematographic film. However, in *Raj Rewal* v. *Union of India*,[403] the Delhi High Court held that the Section 52(1) (s), (t), (u), (v) and (w) constitutes, making of a photograph of or display of a work of architecture or inclusion in a cinematograph film of a work of architecture or a functional drawing of a work of architecture, not amounting to infringement of copyright so as not to prevent the owner of a property from letting others see his property and take photographs thereof. To that extent the Copyright Act discriminates between architectural works and their authors and other artistic works and in fact any other kind of works mentioned in the Copyright Act. In OK *Play India Limited* v. *Mayank Aggarwal*,[404] it was held that the definition of "artistic work" in Section 2(c) of the Copyright Act has a very wide connotation and includes a work of architecture or an abstract work such as a few lines or curves arbitrarily drawn.

In *Lucasfilm Ltd.* v. Ainsworth,[405] the English Court held that the fact that a work of architecture is functional design does not disqualify it from copyright protection. But, for obtaining the copyright protection of the "work of architecture", it must be original one. In *George Hensher Ltd.* v. *Restawile Upholstery (Lancs) Ltd.*,[406] the House of Lords held that copyright subsists irrespective of whether or not the work has artistic merit and artistic quality and that artistic merit in the work is irrelevant as a matter of statutory construction and that evaluation of artistic merit is not a task for which Judges have any training or general aptitude. In *Meikle* v. *Maufe*,[407] it was held that though the building owner is the owner of the plans prepared by the architect but the architect owns the copyright in the plan and also the design embodied in the owners building; the building owner may not therefore reproduce the plans or repeat the design in a new building without the architect's express or implied consent; on the contrary, the architect is free to repeat the building for another owner; the question, as has arisen herein, whether the building owner could not, without breach of copyright, do extensive repairs to the buildings or reconstruct the building which had been destroyed, was however left unanswered.

---

403. 260 (2019) DLT 190.
404. 2016 (67) PTC 665 (Del): 233 (2016) DLT 234.
405. [2011] UKSC 39:
406. [1974] 2 All ER 420: [1973] 3 All ER 414.
407. [1941] 3 All ER 144.

Original Work of Artistic Craftsmanship

Section 2(c) (iii) of the Copyright Act, 1957 provides that artistic work includes artistic craftsmanship. Thus, artistic craftsmanship is qualified for copyright protection as an "artistic work" under Section 13 of the Act. However, the term "artistic craftsmanship" has not been defined in the Act. The phrase artistic craftsmanship expressly refers to the quality of being artistic. There are two essential ingredients of this sub-clause. First, the work has to be of a craftsman and secondly it has to be of artistic value. In *Sartaj Singh Pannu* v. *Gurbani Media Pvt. Ltd.*,[408] it was held that the expression "artistic craftsmanship" in Section 2(c)(iii) of the Act reflects the production of durable handmade objects in a skilful way. It was never meant to and could not be interpreted to include the contribution by a Director to the making of a cinematograph film. Likewise he could not be an author, much less a joint author in relation to a literary or dramatic work or a musical work.

While dealing with artistic craftsmanship in *George Hensher Ltd.* v. *Restawile Upholstery (Laneo) Ltd.*,[409] the House of Lords dealt with the question whether the manufacturer of jars and shelties could claim their products to be artistic. It was observed that protection should have been sought under the Registered Designs Act, 1949 and not under the Copyright Act, 1956. It is not necessary to expatiate any further. In *Merlet* v. *Mothercare Plc.*,[410] it was held by the House of Lords that prototype of a cape for a mother and child was not a work of artistic craftsmanship. In *Re Ananda Expanded Italics*,[411] an interesting question came whether typefaces/fonts are artistic work and capable of registration as works under Copyright Act. The court held that Section 2 (c) of the Copyright Act, 1957 is wide enough to include any work that reflects artistic craftsmanship. Designing typefaces involve creativity and thus it involves artistic craftsmanship. In *Yonex Kabushiki Kaisha* v. *Phillips International*,[412] the court held that arrangement and colour scheme, logo of the packaging used as trademarks or appearance of the packaging constitute work of artistic craftsmanship and are subject matter of copyright protection. The label used in the packaging is an original artistic work within the meaning of Section 2(c) of the Act and therefore, is subject matter of copyright protection under Section 13 of the Act.

CINEMATOGRAPH FILM

Definition of Cinematograph Film

According to *Webster's English Dictionary*,[413] cinematograph film is "a camera for producing motion pictures so construed that a large number of separate exposures of frames are made in very rapid succession". It is also called *kinetograph* according to the above dictionary. Initially, there was no statuary provision dealing with cinematograph film before the Copyright Act,

---

408. 2015 (63) PTC 590 (Del): 220 (2015) DLT 527.
409. [1976] AC 64: 1975 RPC 31. *See*, *Samsonite Corporation* v. *Vijay Sales*, 73 (1998) DLT 732.
410. (1984) FSR 358.
411. (2002) 24 PTC 427.
412. MIPR 2007 (3) 228: 2007 (35) PTC 345 (Del).
413. *The New International Webster's Comprehensive Dictionary of the English Language* (1999 Edition).

1911 was enacted. During the time of 1908 revision of the text of Berne Convention, it was recognised that cinematograph films were a new art form and the Berne Convention and the Copyright Act, 1911 for the first time accorded such films' copyright. Like 1911 Act, Section 2(f) of the Copyright Act, 1957 defines "cinematograph film". Subsequently Article 2(1) of the Berne Convention was revised in Paris in 1971 which assimilated "works expressed by process analogous to cinematography" under "cinematographic works". It includes films or videotaped fixations of traditional dramatic works such as plays, comedies, documentary films, cartoons, regardless of the technical process employed.[414] According to Bogsch:[415]

> silent or sound motion pictures shall be protected irrespective of their destination (theatrical exhibition, television broadcasting, exhibition for a restricted group of spectators), person of their producers (producers of commercial films, amateurs, broadcasting organizations producing kinescopes), their genre (film dramas, documentaries, news-reel, etc.), length, mode of realization (filming of nature, cartoons) or technical process used (picture on transparent films, on electronic tapes, etc.).

Copyright protection in the film includes the sound track. The copyright in the entire film may cover portions of the film in the sense that the owner of the copyright in the film will be entitled to the right in portions of the film; but idea or concept cannot be extended to encompass an idea that there would be one owner of the cinematograph film and different owners of portions hereof in the sense of performers who have collectively played roles in the motion picture. In *Indian Performing Right Society Ltd.* v. *Eastern India Motion Picture Association*,[416] Krishna Iyer, J. observed:

> Cinematograph is a felicitous blend, a beautiful totality, a constellation of stars. Cinema is more than long strips of celluloid, more than miracles in photography, more than song, dance and dialogue and, indeed, more than dramatic story, exciting plot, gripping situations and marvellous acting. But it is that ensemble which is the finished product of orchestrated performance by each of the several participants, although the components may, sometimes, in themselves be elegant entities. Copyright in a cinema film exists in law, but Section 13(4) of the Act preserves the separate survival, in its individuality, of a copyright enjoyed by the 'work' notwithstanding its confluence in the film.

However, the 1957 definition of "cinematograph film" as provided under the Section 2(f) of the Copyright Act, 1957 was amended by Copyright (Amendment) Act, 1984. After the 1984 amendment the Madras High Court in *Entertaining Enterprises* v. *State of Tamil Nadu*,[417] held that the extended definition of a cinematograph film in Section 2(f) which includes any process analogous to cinematography, the video tape should also be taken to come within the definition of "cinematograph film". Again, the Copyright (Amendment) Act, 2012 amended the definition of "cinematograph film" and the previous definition of "cinematograph films"

---

414. WIPO, *Guide to the Berne Convention for Literary and Artistic Works.*
415. *See*, Arpad Bosch: *The Law of Copyright under the Universal Copyright Convention* 9 (3rd ed., 1968) at p. 9; *See also*, Pascal Kamina, *Authorship of Films and Implementation of the Term Directive*: *The Dramatic Tale of the Two Copyrights*, 16 *European Intellectual Property Review* (1994) at p. 319; Kirti Dahiya, "Cinematographic Lyricists Right to Royalty: Myth or Reality?" 16 *Journal of Intellectual Property Rights* (2011) pp. 335–340.
416. AIR 1977 SC 1443: [1977] 3 SCR 206. *See also*, *Fortune Films International* v. *Dev Anand*, AIR 1979 Bom 17: 1978 (80) Bom LR 263; *Ramesh Sippy* v. *Shaan Ranjeet Uttamsingh*, 2013 (55) PTC 95 (Bom): 2013 (4) BomCR 4; *Kajal Aggarwal* v. *The Managing Director*, 2012-1-LW 330: 2012 (1) CTC 812.
417. AIR 1984 Mad 278.

is simplified by omitting a few words that elaborated visual recordings. Since the words are omitted from the definition of cinematograph films a new definition for "visual recording" is inserted by a new Section 2(xxa).[418] Thus, "cinematograph film" according to Section 2(f) of the Copyright Act, 1957, as amended by the 2012 amendment means:

> any work of visual recording [...][419] and includes a sound recording accompanying such visual recording and "cinematograph" shall be construed as including any work produced by any process analogous to cinematography including video films.

This definition has to be read along with that of a drama work[420] and that of a photograph[421] both of which specifically exclude a film from its ambit. The definition brings into its fold any process, analogous to cinematography and so a video film shall also come within its ambit.[422] It can be in any medium or by any means. Thus even a digital fixation can be included within the definition. But the work of a cine-artist; his performance as an actor in a cinematograph film does not fall within the definition of a cinematograph film.[423] It is the cinematograph film that enjoys protection along with its sound track, rather than the performances. The right of the performer in the performance is now protected separately. The sound track associated with the film is a part of the cinematograph film which is the subject of copyright. Besides this it was held that video and television are both cinematograph films.[424] In *Eastern India Motion Pictures* v. *Performing Right Society Ltd.*,[425] the Calcutta High Court observed:

> A cinematograph film is to be taken to include the sounds embodied in any sound track associated with the film. The expression 'sound track associated with a cinematograph film' means any record of sounds which is incorporated in any print, negative, tape or other article, on which the film or part of it, in so far as it consists of visual images, is recorded, or which is issued by the maker of the film for use in conjunction with such an article.

In *Indian Performing Right Society Ltd.* v. *Aditya Pandey*,[426] the Delhi High Court held that the Section 13 of the Copyright Act 1957 recognises "cinematograph film" as a distinct and separate class of "work" and declares that copyright shall subsist therein throughout India. In *A.V. Meyyppan* v. *Commissioner of Commercial Taxes*,[427] the Madras High Court held that the copyrights in the cinematograph films have been considered as goods as the items are subject to sales tax by the State Legislature in terms of Entry 54 of List II of the Constitution and while so, Parliament cannot resort to Entry 97 of List I to levy service tax on the temporary transfer or permitting the use or enjoyment of the copyright. However, the first category of copyright, i.e., original literary, dramatic, musical and artistic works are out

418. Inserted by the Copyright (Amendment) Act, 2012 [w.e.f. 21-6-2012], Section 2(vi).
419. The words "on any medium produced through a process from which a moving image may be produced by any means" omitted by the Copyright (Amendment) Act, 2012 [w.e.f. 21-6-2012], Section 2(i).
420. Copyright Act, 1957, Section 2(h).
421. *Ibid.*, Section 2(s).
422. *Entertaining Enterprises, Madras* v. *State of Tamil Nadu,* AIR 1984 Mad. 278 at p. 290.
423. *Fortune Films* v. *Dev Anand,* AIR 1979 Bom. 17.
424. *See, Balwinder Singh* v. *Delhi Administration,* AIR 1984 Del 379; *Tulsidas* v. *Vasantha Kumari,* (1991) 1 LW (Mad) 220.
425. AIR 1978 Cal 477.
426. 2011 (47) PTC 392 (Del): MIPR 2011 (3) 19.
427. AIR 1969 Mad 284: [1967] 20 STC 115 (Mad).

of the service tax. In *Union of India* v. *Board of Control for Cricket in India*,[428] the issue before the Supreme Court was whether live telecast of cricket match amounts to production of cinematograph film conferring on author and its assignee same inviolable rights that provisions of the Copyright Act confer on copyright holder? It is a matter of fact that under Section 37 (Chapter VII) of the Copyright Act, 1957, it is argued that the telecast of the cricket matches is like production of a cinematograph film within the meaning of Section 2(f) of the Copyright Act. The Board of Control for Cricket in India (BCCI) as the organizer is the author of the copyright who has assigned the same to Star India Pvt. Ltd. There is a statutory curtailment of the said right under Section 3 of the Sports Act, 2007, the extent of which must be understood to be confined to the explicit contours of the said provision which cannot be readily and easily extended. Thus, any unwarranted extension would amount to an invasion of the copyright including broadcasting right.

Subsistence of Copyright in Cinematograph Film

The Section 13(1)(b) of the Copyright Act, 1957 provides that copyright subsists in cinematograph films[429] according to Section 14, "copyright" means the exclusive right subject to the provisions of the Act, to do or authorise the doing of anything (in the case of cinematograph films) to make a copy of the film, including a photograph of any image forming part thereof; to sell or give on hire, or offer for sale or hire, any copy of the film, regardless of whether such copy has been sold or given on hire on earlier occasions and to communicate the film to the public. Section 14(d) relates to the exclusive rights in a cinematograph film. The existing sub-clause (i) of Section 14(d) provides the right to make a copy of the film, including a photograph of any image forming part thereof. This sub-clause has been amended by the Copyright (Amendment) Act, 2012 to extend the rights of the author to include the "storing" of the work in any medium by electronics or other means. The inclusive language used in the amendments clarify that the right of reproduction extends to storage in the case of artistic works, cinematograph films and sound recordings. In the case of literary, dramatic and musical works, the existing Clause (a)(i) of Section 14 clarifies that the right to reproduce includes "storing of the work in any medium by electronic means".[430] The Copyright (Amendment) Act, 2012 extends this inclusive language on right of reproduction to artistic works, cinematograph films and sound recordings.

The author of a work of cinematograph film may obtain raw materials for the work from any or many sources but will only be entitled to copyright if these raw materials are converted, by use of his labour skill, capital and intelligence to create another material or work which is something different from the raw materials and has an element of novelty.[431] Thus,

---

428. (2018) 11 SCC 700: 2017 (8) SCJ 410.
429. *See, Raj Rewal* v. *Union of India*, 260(2019)DLT190; *Indian Performing Right Society Ltd.* v. *Vodafone Idea Ltd.*, (2019) 2 CALLT 436 (HC); *Navigators Logistics Ltd.* v. *Kashif Qureshi*, 2018 (76) PTC 564 (Del): 254 (2018) DLT 307; *Tandav Films Entertainment P. Ltd.* v. *Four Frames Pictures*, 2009 (41) PTC 515 (Del); *Abdulgafar A. Nadiadwala* v. *Assistant Commissioner of Income Tax* (2004) 188 CTR (Bom) 232: [2004] 267 ITR 488 (Bom); *Raj Video Vision* v. *K. Mohanakrishnan*, AIR 1998 Mad 294.
430. See *Sanjay Kumar Gupta* v. *Sony Pictures Networks India P. Ltd.*, AIR 2018 Delhi 169: 2018 (75) PTV 562 (Del).
431. (2018) 1 CALLT 190 (HC): 2018 (73) PTC 329 (Cal).

in *Saregama Ltd.* v. *New Digital Media*,[432] the Calcutta High Court has explained the law relating to subsistence of copyright in cinematograph films:

> When the film as whole is exhibited the individual owners of copyright in works who have permitted the film to be made cannot claim copyright but if a part of the film is segregated and the individual work is culled out and exhibited then the individual owner can assert his copyright. Now, suppose the producer of the film without taking permission of the owners of the copyrighted works exhibits the film, the film may not have any copyright at all as a substantial part of the film is infringement of other work or works.[433]

However, in *Thiagarajan Kumararaja* v. *Capital Film Works (India) Pvt. Ltd.*,[434] the Madraj High Court held that a remake of the film or its versions which are, substantially similar to the original cinematograph film cannot come within the ambit of the right to copy a film, which is provided for under Section 14(1)(d)(i) of Copyright Act, 1957. The Copyright Act, 1957 confers a separate copyright on a cinematograph film on the producer of the film. In *Sholay Media and Entertainment Pvt. Ltd.* v. *Parag Sanghavi*,[435] the plaintiffs' claim is that they are absolute and complete owner of the copyright in the film SHOLAY and its constituent parts including the script, screenplay, underlying music and lyrics, synchronized background score, artwork, characters, dialogues and has all exclusive rights under Section 14 of the Copyright Act, 1957. In this case the plaintiffs have also obtained registration of the marks Gabbar and Gabbar Singh with a view to protect the name and prevent its misappropriation by unscrupulous infringers. Thus, the Court held that the publicity material coupled with the impugned film, gives an overall impression that it is a remake of the film SHOLAY. The use of similar plot and characters in the impugned film coupled with use of the underlying music, lyrics and background score and even dialogues from the original film SHOLAY amounts to infringement of copyright in the film SHOLAY. Even if the impugned film is considered as an adaptation of the film SHOLAY, the same being without authorization of the copyright owner amounts to passing off as the plaintiffs are the owner of the names of characters and dialogues. Such use by the defendants was unauthorized and it is a deliberate act of the said defendants in order to gain profits. They are also guilty of infringement under Section 14(a) read with Section 55 of the Copyright Act, 1957. While passing the permanent injunction the Court observed:

> The defendants have distorted and mutilated the original copyright work of the plaintiffs. The defendants have also infringed the moral rights of the plaintiffs as under Section 57 of the Copyright Act, 1957. As the said defendants have similar name of characters under the music, lyrics and dialogues from the original work of the plaintiffs which was created by them for the first time and were author and owner of the same, the defendants are thus also guilty of passing off. They are not able to assign any valid reason for the same. Despite of statement made in the Court for change of the name of the movie, when the same was released, still it appears that the defendants' movie have similar name of the characters and they have used the lyrics and dialogues in material form in their movie. The movie was produced and released without authorisation from the owner and author i.e. plaintiffs.

---

432. *See, Performing Right Society Ltd.* v. *Eastern India Motion Picture Association*, AIR 1977 SC 1443: (1977) 2 SCC 820.
433. *See*, Section 13(3)(a), Copyright Act 2019.
434. 2018 (73) PTC 365 (Mad): MIPR 2018 (1) 227.
435. 2015 (64) PTC 546 (Del): 223 (2015) DLT 152.

its author under Section 2(d)(v) of the Act being the owner of the film at the time of its completion; that in the case of a lyric or music incorporated in the sound track of a cinematograph film, since under Section 2(f) of the Act, cinematograph film includes its sound track. Section 13(1)(b) confers copyright on the cinematograph film and Section 14(d)(ii) confers on the owner of copyright the right to cause the film in so far as it consists of visual images to be seen in public and in so far as it consists of songs to be heard in public, it is not necessary for the owner of the cinematograph film to secure the permission of the composer of the lyric or of the music incorporated in the sound track of a cinematograph film for exhibiting or causing the exhibition of the sound portion of the film in public or for causing the records of the sound track of the film to be heard in public. Section 14(1)(c)(ii) of the Act and all that Section 13(4) of the Act (when applicable) provide the rights created by Section 14(1)(a) and (b) shall co-exist with those created by Section 14(1)(c) and (d) of the Act, e.g., under Clause (a), the copyright in a literary work such as a novel entitles its author to make a cinematograph film in respect of the work, and to exercise the remaining rights created by Section 14(1)(a) of the Act. But once he has licensed someone to make, a cinematograph film, the licencee shall have the rights provided in Clauses (c) and (d) of Section 14(1) of the Act in respect of the film. Therefore, the Supreme Court in *Indian Performing Right Society Ltd.* v. *Eastern India Motion Pictures,*[436] clearly laid down that:

> When a cinematograph film producer commissions a composer of music or a lyricist for reward or valuable consideration for the purpose of making his cinematograph film or composing music or lyric therefore, i.e., the sounds for incorporation or absorption in the sound track associated with the film, which are included in a cinematograph film, he becomes the first owner of the copyright therein and no copyright subsists in the composer of the lyric or music so composed unless there is a contract to the contrary between the composer of the lyric or music on the one hand and the producer of the cinematograph film on the other.[437]

In *Star India Pvt. Ltd.* v. *Leo Burnett (India) Pvt. Ltd.*,[438] the Bombay High Court examined the interpretation of the right of making copies of the film granted under Section 14 of the *Copyright Act* to cinematograph film. In this case the plaintiff doing business on broadcasting produced a television serial *Kyun Ki Saas Bhi Kabhi Bahu Thi*. The serial consisting of 262 episodes was telecast from July 2000 onwards and became popular. The name of the characters in the serial also acquired a reputation and goodwill. It was alleged that the defendants produced a television commercial entitled *Kyun Ki Bahu Bhi Kabhi Saas Banegi* for their product *Time Detergent* by engaging the same stars using identical characters. Plaintiff alleged infringement of the copyright in the film by copying the film, characters and the story. It was contended by the defendants that they had not copied any part of the serial and they independently produced the advertisement having 30 seconds duration. They admitted that they used the same stars and their names in the serial but argued that there was no copyright on the characters or the theme in the film. As to the question whether independently making a film using the same characters and story resembling an existing film amounted

436. AIR 1977 SC 1443: (1977) 2 SCC 820.
437. *See*, *Saregama Ltd.* v. *The New Digital Media*, 2018 (73) PTC 329 (Cal): 2018 (3) CHN (CAL) 147; *Salim Khan* v. *Sumeet Prakash Mehra*, 2013(56)PTC1(Bom): 2013 (5) BomCR 556.
438. 2003 (27) PTC 81.

to copying of the film, the court after examining the meaning of the term "copy" and the difference between the rights given to literary works and film observed thus:

> As pointed earlier contrasting Section 14(d) and (e) on the one hand and Section 14(a), (b) and (c) on the other, in the latter case the owner of the copyright has exclusive right to reproduce the work in any material form. This is absent and excluded insofar as the former case (cinematograph film/sound recording). The exclusive right in the former is to copy the recording of a particular film/sound recording. It is, therefore, clear that production by another person of even the same cinematograph film does not constitute infringement of a copyright in the cinematograph film. It is only when actual copy is made of a film by a process of duplication, i.e., by using mechanical contrivance that it falls under Section 14(d)(i). The expression "to make a copy of the film" would mean to make a physical copy of the film itself and not another film which merely resembles the film.[439]

The court is correct in the above interpretation. The court further clarified the reason for this difference in approach thus:

> ...A narrow copyright protection is accorded to a film/sound recording than for literary, dramatic or artistic work. The reason perhaps could be that they have to be original to satisfy the test of copyrightability, whereas the requirement of originality is absent for claiming copyright in cinematograph film/sound recording.[440]

The reasoning seems to be wrong. A film consists of literary, dramatic, musical and artistic work. If one looks at the rights given to these works in Section 14 it is clear that there is a separate right to include these works in a film. Thus, the originality of the film is linked to the originality of the literary, dramatic, musical and artistic work included in the film. It is mandatory that before making a film the producer have to take permission to incorporate these works in the film popularly known as the synchronisation right. It is clear form Section 13(3)(a) that copyright shall not subsist in any cinematograph film if a substantial part of the film is an infringement of the copyright of any other work. Thus, once the producer takes the permission of the author of the works by assignment or licencing this right will be with the producer of the film. So, if any other person independently reproduces the same film, it will amount to infringement of the copyright (synchronisation right) of literary, dramatic, musical and artistic work incorporated in the film. The producer of the film has the right to prevent this. It is made clear by Section 13(4) that the copyright in a cinematograph film shall not affect the separate copyright in any work in respect of which or a substantial part of which, the film is made. This inter-relationship of rights seems to be the reason for the different wording of the rights for these works and film. In effect the producer enjoys the reproduction right and right of copy of the film.

In *Eastern India Motion Pictures* v. *Performing Right Society Ltd.*,[441] the Calcutta High Court examined the issue: Whether producer of cinematograph film can defeat right of composer of music or lyricist by engaging him? When cinematograph film producer commissions a composer of music or a lyricist for reward or valuable consideration for purpose of making his cinematograph film or composing music or lyric that sounds for incorporation or absorption in sound track associated with film which included in cinematograph film he becomes the first owner of copyright. Explaining Sections 14(1), 17 and 35 of Copyright Act, 1957 the

439. *Ibid.*, at p. 94.
440. *Ibid.*
441. AIR 1978 Cal 477.

Court held that the composers, lyricists and musicians have no copyright in the soundtrack of the film. Thus, no copyright subsists in composer of lyric or music so composed unless there is contract to contrary between composer of lyric or music on one hand and producer of cinematograph film on other hand. However, in *Indian Performing Right Society Ltd.* v. *Eastern Indian Motion Pictures Association,*[442] the Supreme Court held:

> The composer of a lyric of a musical work, however, retains the right of performing it in public for profit otherwise than as a part of the cinematograph film and he cannot be restrained from doing so. In other words, the author (composer) of a lyric or musical work who has authorised a cinematograph film producer to make a cinematograph film of his work and has thereby permitted him to appropriate his work by incorporating or recording it on the soundtrack of a cinematograph film cannot restrain the author (owner) of the film from causing the acoustic portion of the film to be performed or projected or screened in public for profit or from making any record embodying the recording in any part of the sound-track associated with the film by utilising such sound-track or from communicating or authorising the communication of the film by radio-diffusion as Section 14(1)(c) of the Act expressly permits the owner of the copyright of the cinematograph film to do all these things. In such cases, the author (owner) of the cinematograph film cannot be said to wrongfully appropriate anything which belongs to the composer of the lyric or musical work.

Permitted Use of Dress in Film

In the United States of America, under the trade-dress law, various product features are to be protected from imitation in the market. This protection suggests manufacturers to advertise their "brand names" through their products designs without fear of competitors passing off imitation goods as originals.[443] The US Supreme Court in *John H. Harland Co.* v. Clarke Checks, Inc.,[444] defines "trade dress" as the total image of a product which may include features such as size, shape, color, or color combinations, textures, graphics, or even particular sales techniques. Clarifying the distinction between trade-dress and trademark law the Court in *Duraco Prods.* v. *Joy Plastic Enters.*,[445] held that in the strictest sense, the term "trade-dress law" refers to the protections reserved for the designs or features on a product or on its packaging, while "trademark law" refers to the protections granted for words or phrases. However, the "functional" features on a product can never be protected under trade-dress law. The reason has also being explained by the Court in *Keds Corp.* v. *R. Renee Int'l Trading Corp.*,[446] where it was held that the functional shapes are not subject to appropriation by manufacturers. Nevertheless, if the functional feature or combination is also found to have acquired secondary meaning, the imitator may be required to take reasonable steps to minimize the risk of source confusion. Copying functional aspects required defendant to take special precautionary steps to ensure that buyers would not be misled as to source.[447]

---

442. AIR 1977 SC 1443: (1977) 2 SCC 820.
443. *See*, Mitchell M. Wong, Aesthetic Functionality Doctrine and the Law of Trade-Dress Protection," 83(4) *Cornell Law Review* (1998) pp. 1116–1167 at p. 1117.
444. 711 F.2d 966, 980 (11th Cir. 1983). *See also*, Two Pesos, Inc. v. Taco Cabana, Inc., 505 U.S. 763, 764 n.1 (1992).
445. 40 F.3d 1431, 1438–42 (3d Cir. 1994).
446. 888 F.2d 215, 221 (1st Cir. 1989).
447. *Fisher Stoves, Inc.* v. *All Nighter Stove Works, Inc.*, 626 F.2d 193, 195 (lst Cir. 1980).

Where central female protagonist of film is shown wearing a particular dress designed by a designer, producer of film, notwithstanding his defence that he has engaged some other costume designer who has supplied dress, is a necessary and proper party in a case alleging infringement of copyright was held in *Suneet Varma Design Pvt. Ltd.* v. *Jas Kirat Singh Narula*.[448] In this case the Delhi High Court examined the scope and application of the exception under section 52(1)(u)[449] of the Copyright Act. In this case the plaintiff, a renowned designer of international repute, designed a dress for women consisting of blue poncho and heavily embroidered trousers. The blue poncho and trousers consist of specific fabric cuts and original artistic embroidery. This design was presented in many fashion shows. The plaintiff noticed that this dress was used by the heroin of the film "Bunty Aur Bubli" and her picture wearing this dress was used in the advertisements of the film, the cover page of the CD and cassette of the songs, etc. The plaintiff filed the present suit against the dress designer and the producer of the film alleging infringement of her copyright in the said design. The present petition was filed by the producer of the film requesting the court to remove his name from the list of defendants on the ground that he had not violated the copyright of the plaintiff. It was contended by him that he engaged one of the defendants to design/identify suitable dress for the film and he purchased the alleged dress from a shop in Mumbai. It was also contended that the use of the dress in the film was not a violation of the copyright of the plaintiff since this was permissible under section 52(1)(u)(ii) of the Copyright Act. While rejecting the petition and declaring that the defendant was a necessary party to the suit, the court examined the scope of the exception provided under this section. Rejecting the argument of the defendant that the use of the dress in the film by the heroin was incidental to the film and not a violation of the copyright the court observed:[450]

> .... Many times, for a particular role to be played by an actor in a film, the costumes are designed in such a way as to bring out the character that particular actor is to play. The styling of the movie, therefore, is becoming as important as dialogue, screenplay or music. The audience look at an actor in the move and then notice what he/she is wearing. To promote particular dress used in a film, actors have started walking on the ramp-way during fashion shows. Bollywood has become integral to Indian fashion. In fact, in the award ceremonies, there are specific awards for best costumes in a film. Therefore, it cannot be presumed, *per se,* that for all kinds of clothes worn by the actors in film provisions of Section 52(1)(u)(ii) of the Copyright Act would be applicable. May be, this argument would be relevant for most of the dresses worn in a film, however, whether a particular dress/ costume in a film was only by way of background or incidental to the principal matter represented in the film will have to be viewed after the evidence is led.

It appears that the court made the above observation on the assumption that the dress is an artistic work protected under the Copyright Act. It is true that the parties did not contend that the dress is not an artistic work protected under the Copyright Act. But it is interesting to find out whether an industrial product like a designer dress would fall within the scope of artistic work as defined in the Copyright Act or an industrial design protected under the Design Act.

---

448. 2007 (34) PTC 81 (Del).
449. Section 52(1)(u) read: "the inclusion in a cinematograph film of—(i) any artistic work permanently situate in a public place or any premises to which the public has access; or (ii) any other artistic work, if such inclusion is only by way of background or is otherwise incidental to the principal matters represented in the film."
450. *Suneet Varma Design Pvt. Ltd.* v. *Jas Kirat Singh Narula*, MIPR 2007 (1) 175: 2007 (34) PTC 81.

An examination of the definition of design under section 2(d)[451] of the Design Act and Class 02 of the third schedule of the Design Rules classifying the designs to be protected under the Act, gives an impression that the design dress is covered under the Design Act. Class 02 of the schedule is for "Articles of clothing and haberdashery". Class 02-02 is specifically for "Garments" and the note makes it clear that this includes all sorts of garments. Since class 05 deals specifically with "textile piece goods, artificial and natural sheet materials", it is clear that the classification on "Garments" is intended to include readymade garments as well. There is no reason to doubt that design of the dress in issue is the "features of shape, configuration, pattern ... applied to any article whether in two dimensional or ... by any industrial process or means, whether manual, mechanical ... which in the finished article appeal to and are judged solely by the eye" as per the definition of the design in the Design Act. If that be the case needs to ask the question whether in the absence of a registration of the design under the Design Act the plaintiff is entitled to claim protection under the Copyright Act. The fact that the suit is filed under the Copyright Act gives an impression that the plaintiff has not registered the dress under the Design Act. It is also evident from the facts that the defendants purchased this dress from a shop in Mumbai. It is not clear whether this is the only piece available in the market or more numbers are available. If there are more than 50 pieces in the market it is clear from section 15 of the Copyright Act that the plaintiff cannot claim copyright protection for a design capable of registration under the Design Act but not registered. The Delhi High Court in an earlier case[452] made it clear the scope of the exception to the artistic work as defined in the Copyright Act given in the definition of design.

The aforementioned issue is required to be re-examined by the Court in India otherwise it would result in overprotection of the design in the dress leading to serious implications in the use of dress not only in the film but also for other purposes. In US the law relating to trade-dress protection is a judicial expression of two basic policy considerations. First, trade-dress law prevents suppliers of a product from monopolizing the indispensable features of the product. Thus, the rights holder of an invention or a design has to select only one specific form of intellectual property protection for the invention or design.[453] Second, the trade-dress law prevents from permanently securing designs that are more properly guarded by transitory species of intellectual-property law, such as patents or copyrights. Therefore a trade dress often encompasses not just a source indicator but also "a useful product feature (that should) not be unfairly monopolized."[454]

---

451. Section 2(d) read: "design" means only the features of shape, configuration, pattern, ornament or composition of lines or colours applied to any article whether in two dimensional or three dimensional or in both forms, by any industrial process or means, whether manual, mechanical or chemical, separate or combined, which in the finished article appeal to and are judged solely by the eye; but does not include any mode or principle of construction or anything which is in substance a mere mechanical device, and does not include any trade mark as defined in clause (v) of sub-section (I) of section 2 of the Trade and Merchandise Marks Act, 1958 or property mark as defined in section 479 of the Indian Penal Code or any artistic work as defined in clause (c) of section 2 of the Copyright Act, 1957.
452. *See*, *Microfiber Inc.* v. *Girdhar and Co.*, 2006 (32) PTC 157 (Del). *See also*, *Gopal Glass Works Ltd.* v. *Asst. Controller of Patents and Designs*, 2006 (33) PTC 434 (Cal); *Gopal Glass Works Ltd.* v. *IAG Company Ltd.*, 2006 (33) PTC 620 (Guj).
453. For detail discussion, *see*, Douglas R. Wolf, "The Doctrine of Elections: Has the Need to Choose Been Lost?," 9 (2) *Cardozo Arts and Entertainment Law Journal* (1991) pp. 439–474.
454. *See*, Christina Farmer, "Red in the Eye of the Beholder: The Case for Aesthetic Functionality," 28(4) *Berkeley Technology Law Journal* (2013) pp. 777–804 at p. 782.

SOUND RECORDING

The Concept and Issue

Sound recording was not a subject matter of copyright protection prior to the enactment of Copyright Act, 1911 which provided that copyright protection should be offered to "records", perforated rolls and other contrivances by means of which sounds may be mechanically protected. Thus, in 1937 explaining the concept "record" in musical work in *Wellington Cinema* v. *Performing Right Society Ltd.*,[455] the Bombay High Court held that on the maker of a record of a musical work, by means of which sounds are mechanically reproduced, presupposes that the making of the record was a lawful act, which means that the record was made with the consent of the owner of the copyright in the original work, if the owner of such copyright exists. The Copyright Act, 1957 originally contained the terms "record" and "recording". Copyright (Second Amendment) Act, 1994 has omitted the definition of "record" and substituted a new definition for "recording"; and the term "recording" has been substituted by "sound recording".

Thus, copyright subsists in sound recording under Section 13(1)(c) of the Copyright Act, 1957 in the sense that the owners of such copyrights enjoy different rights which are defined under Section 14(d). Thus, once a sound recording is made, it is only the producer, as the owner thereof, who can exploit it exclusively in the manner provided in Section 14(1)(e). However, those rights are confined to that particular sound recording and that sound recording alone. The owner of the sound recording can communicate the same to the public, *inter alia*, by broadcasting it or playing it in public places. The owners of the underlying musical and literary work embodied in such sound recording cannot interfere with these rights of the owner of sound recording. Thus, the Bombay High Court in *Music Broadcast Private Ltd.* v. *Indian Performing Right Society Ltd.*,[456] held that although Clauses (b) and (c) of Section 13 protects derivative works in a restricted field, whereas Clause (a) thereof protects original works in a broader field, it does not mean that the rights of an owner of a sound recording are, in any way, inferior to those of an owner of copyright in the original literary or musical work.

However, musical work used in a sound recording or film retains its separate identity as a copyright work, as made clear by Section 13(4) of the Act.[457] Therefore, despite the statutory recognition for copyright protection of sound recording a question which often arises is: Whether copyright subsists in sound recording like other works? Prior to examine this issue it is essential to examine the meaning of sound recording. According to Section 2(xx) of the Copyright Act, 1957 "sound recording" means:

> a recording of sounds from which such sounds may be produced regardless of the medium on which such recording is the method by which the sounds are produced.

Thus, the definition talks of "sound" not music, so that recording of non-musical sounds will come within the definition and a recording of a person reciting a passage from a book or a poem falls within the meaning of a sound recording. The definition is very wide in

---

455. AIR 1937 Bom 472: ILR 1937 Bom 724.
456. MIPR 2011 (3) 84: 2011 (47) PTC 587 (Bom).
457. *Tandav Films Entertainment P. Ltd.* v. *Four Frames Pictures and Ors.*, 2009 (41) PTC 515 (Del).

terms of storage media to take account of changes in technology. There is nothing to prevent several persons making recordings of the same thing at the same time and each having their own copyright. For example, if several persons make a sound recording of concord passing through the sound barrier, each will own the copyright in their own recording, and can sue for infringement if someone makes a copy of their recording without permission. The legal position has been clarified by the Court in *Indian Performing Right Society Ltd.* v. *Aditya Pandey*,[458]

> The Copyright Act 1957 recognizes three classes of work viz. (a) literary, dramatic, musical or artistic work; (b) cinematographic film and (c) sound recording. Whereas musical and literary works are original works, sound recording is a derivative work.

Section 13(2) of the Copyright Act, 1957 provides the general-rule in respect of all categories of work is that copyright does not subsist in any work, unless in the case of a published work, the work is first published outside India, the author is at the date of such publication, or in a case where the author was dead at that date, was at the time of his death, a citizen of India. In case of an unpublished work, the copyright subsists only when the author is at the date of the making of work is a citizen of India.[459] According to Section 13(2) of the Act copyright does not subsists in any sound recording made in respect of a literary, dramatic or musical work, if in making the sound recording, copyright in such work has been infringed. However, it is provided by Section 13(4) that copyright in a sound recording does not affect the separate copyright in any work in respect of which or a substantial part of which, the film or as the case may be, the sound recording is made. Further, under Section 14 of the Act exclusive right is recognised to do or authorise to do sound recording in respect of the work is copyright. Thus, copyright subsists in a sound recording.[460] The Supreme Court in *Entertainment Network (India) Ltd.* v. *Super Cassettes Industries Ltd.*[461] observed:

> Section 14 of the Act provides for the meaning of copyright. Clause (c) of Sub-section (1) of Section 14 talks about artistic work. For the purposes of the Act, "copyright" means the exclusive right, subject to the provisions of this Act, to do or authorize the doing of any act. The acts specified therein in respect of a work or any substantial part thereof and in the case of a sound recording, namely, (i) to make any other sound recording embodying it; (ii) to sell or give on hire, or offer for sale or hire, any copy of the sound recording, regardless of whether such copy has been sold or given on hire on earlier occasions; (iii) to communicate the sound recording to the public. **Explanation**—For the purposes of this Section, a copy which has been sold once shall be deemed to be a copy already in circulation.

In *Sholay Media and Entertainment Pvt. Ltd.* v. *Vodafone Essar Mobile Services*,[462] the issue was around the interpretation of the assignment deed executed between the parties in

---

458. 2012 (50) PTC 460 (Del): MIPR 2012 (2) 140.
459. *See, Maroti* v. *The State of Maharashtra*, 2018 ALLMR (Cri) 4460; *Navigators Logistics Ltd.* v. *Kashif Qureshi*, 2018 (76) PTC 564 (Del): 254 (2018) DLT 307; *Lyca Productions* v. *J. Manimaran*, 2018 (73) PTC 525 (Mad): 2018 (3) CTC 605.
460. *See, Saregama India Ltd.* v. *Puneet Prakash Mehra*, 2011 (1) CHN 341: MIPR 2010 (3) 175; *Saregama India Ltd.* v. *Suresh Jindal*, AIR 2006 Cal 340: 2007 (34) PTC 522 (Cal); *Gramophone Co. of India Ltd.* v. *Mars Recording Pvt. Ltd.*, AIR 2001 SC 2885: (2002) 2 SCC 103; *Gee Pee Films Pvt. Ltd.* v. *Pratik Chowdhury*, AIR 2002 Cal 33: 2002 (24) PTC 392 (Cal).
461. JT 2008 (7) SC 11: 2008 (9) SCALE 69.
462. 2011 [46] PTC 352 (Del.).

1978 when the existence of "digital rights",[463] i.e., making ringtones of sound recordings was not in contemplation. Hence, the court was called upon to adjudicate whether the plaintiff, which was the producer of the cinematographic film titled SHOLAY had assigned all rights in the nature of copyrights in the sound recording to the defendant and thus could the defendant in that case include the use of sound recording of the film on digital and/or mobile platform as well or whether the residual rights were retained by the plaintiff and thus defendant could not exploit such rights without plaintiff's permission. After examining the various provisions of the deed, the Bombay High Court came to the conclusion that the assignment could be interpreted both ways on a *prima facie* reading as the entire case revolved around the meaning of the expression "records" as used in the agreement. The assignor in this case had assigned rights to making of records and the expression records had been defined to include discs, tapes or any other device in which sound recording is embodied. While the plaintiff contended that expression device would include only a physical device like a disc or a tape and not a digital device the defendants argued otherwise. While the court abstained from giving any clear finding on this issue, and ordered the case to go for trial, the court seemed to be inclined in favour of defendant's view that the intention of the parties was to assign all rights in the sound recording and that in this scientific age the word device as used in the agreement should be interpreted to include digital device. Thus the court passed only interim orders, including payment of royalties and left main issues for trial.

Term of Copyright in Sound Recording

Under the Copyright Act, 1911 the term copyright was limited to fifty years from the date on which the original plate was made. However, rather than creating an entirely new type of copyright, the Act provided that such controversies were musical works.[464] Subsequently, the term of copyright protection has been increased to sixty years in the existing Copyright Act, 1957. Section 27 of the existing Act provides for the term of copyright in sound recording in the following terms: "In the case of a sound recording, copyright shall subsist until [sixty years][465] from the beginning of the calendar year next following the year in which the sound recording is published."

However, only because the term for holding copyright under the said provisions are different, the same would not mean that the right of the copyright owner in sound recording is somewhat inferior.[466] For a proper construction of the provisions, will it be necessary to keep in mind the difference between the right of the original work and right of sound recording? Should we also bear in mind that there are various forms of intellectual property rights. Section 16 provides that a right, *inter alia*, in respect of any work must be claimed only under and in accordance with the provisions of the Act unlike trademark and passing off rights can

---

463. For discussion on "digital rights," *see, Star India Pvt. Ltd.* v. *Haneeth Ujwal*, 2014 (60) PTC 504 (Del); *Sholay Media and Entertainment Pvt. Ltd.* v. *Vodafone Esssar Mobile Services Ltd.*, 2011 (46) PTC 352 (Del): 182 (2011) DLT 226.

464. Section 19(1), Copyright Act, 1911.

465. Substituted by Copyright (Amendment) Act, 1992, Section 2, "fifty years".

466. *Entertainment Network (India) Ltd.* v. *Super Cassettes Industries Ltd.*, 2008 (37) PTC 353 (SC): 2008 (9) SCALE 69.

be enforced even though they are not registered. It must also be noticed that whereas the term of a copyright in original literary, dramatic, musical and artistic works remains protected not only in the entire lifetime of the author but also until sixty years from the beginning of the calendar year next following the year in which the author dies, the term of copyright in sound recording subsists only for sixty years, but as indicated herein before, the same would not mean that the right of an owner of sound recording is in any way inferior to that of right of an owner of copyright on original literary work, etc.[467]

Derivative Works in Sound Recording

Derivative works are those which are based on existing works, such as translations, adaptations, compilations, guide books and new editions.[468] In the United States of America, under the Copyright Act 1976, a copyright owner has, *inter-alia*, right "to prepare derivative works based upon the copyrighted work."[469] The Act defines derivative works to mean "a work based upon one or more pre existing works, such as a translation, musical arrangement, dramatization, fictionalization, motion picture version, sound recording, art reproduction, abridgment, condensation, or any other form in which a work may be recast, transformed, or adapted. A work consisting of editorial revisions, annotations, elaborations, or other modifications which, as a whole, represent an original work of authorship, is a 'derivative work."[470] While an original prior work is protected under copyright law, a secondary or derivative works does not enjoy the same protection.[471] In *Super Cassettess Industries Limited* v. *Mr. Chintamani Rao*,[472] the Court held the sound recordings are derivative works, which are eventually derived from original literary, dramatic, musical and artistic works are impliedly included in Section 51(1)(a) and 52(1)(b) of the Copyright Act, 1957. That does not make copyright in sound recordings inferior. Merely because sound recordings are derivative works, it does not mean that such works can be used wherever the use of the underlying works is permitted by law. However, in *Saregama Ltd.* v. *New Digital Media*,[473] the Calcutta High Court observed:

> A sound recording has a "unitary" nature wherein the individual constituents are complete in themselves which enjoy independent copyrights. However, the vesting of such independent copyrights in such ingredients does not affect the unitary nature of a sound recording or its unitary use. Only when the use is not unitary, it results in the infringement of copyrights in underlying works/ingredients.

In *Indian Performing Right Society Ltd.* v. *Aditya Pandey*,[474] the issue was: what happens to the copyright in an underlying work (literary and musical works) when the derivative work

---

467. *Music Broadcast Private Ltd.* v. *Indian Performing Right Society Ltd.*, 2011 (113) Bom LR 3153: MIPR 2011 (3) 84.
468. For a critical analysis of the concept "derivative works" in sound recording, *see*, Pamela Samuelson, "The Quest for a Sound Conception of Copyright's Derivative Work Right," 101 *The Georgetown Law Journal* (2013) pp. 1505–1564.
469. 17 USC, Section 106(2) (Supp. II 2002).
470. Ibid., Section 101.
471. *See*, Michael Abramowicz, "A Theory of Copyright's Derivative Right and Related Doctrines "90 *Minnesota Law Review* (2005) pp. 317–388 at p. 324.
472. 2012 (49) PTC 1 (Del).
473. (2018) 1 WBLR (Cal) 329: 2018 (73) PTC 329 (Cal).
474. MIPR 2012 (2) 140: 2012 (50) PTC 460 (Del).

(sound recording) is exploited? Does he who obtains a permission from the copyright owner of the derivative work to broadcast by way of communicating to the public said derivative work, additionally requires a similar permission from the owner of the underlying works, i.e., the literary and musical works? Copyright Act, 1957 recognises three classes of works: (a) literary, dramatic, musical or artistic work; (b) cinematographic film and (c) sound recording. While musical and literary works are original works, sound recording is a derivative work. Section 13(4) of the Copyright Act, 1957 prescribes that copyright in a cinematographic film or a sound recording shall not affect the separate copyright in any work in respect of which or a substantial part of which, the cinematographic film or sound recording is made. Thus, Section 13(4) prescribes that the copyright subsisting in a derivative work (sound recording) shall not prejudice the copyright subsisting in original works (literary and musical).

The Copyright (Amendment) Act, 1994 introduced significant changes in the principal Act for protection of the performers by means of a special right, to be known as the "performer's right", in respect of the making of sound recordings or visual recordings of their live performances, and of certain related acts. Another change made was to replace the term "record" with "sound recording" as the former term had become outdated through association with an obsolescent technology of sound reproduction. Through Section 2(xx), "sound recording" was defined, to mean a recording of sounds from which such sounds may be produced regardless of the medium on which such recording is the method by which the sounds are produced; obviously to include piano rolls and mechanical instruments from which jingles are produced. The amended Act recognizes three classes of work viz. (a) literary, dramatic, musical or artistic work; (b) cinematographic film and (c) sound recording. While musical and literary works are original works, sound recording is a derivative work. It is significant to note that Section 13(4) of the unamended Act was retained in the post amendment, with the only difference being that Section 13(4) of the amended Act provided that the copyright subsisting in a sound recording shall not prejudice the copyright subsisting in literary and musical work, i.e., the only amendment incorporated in Section 13(4), on the subject was to replace the word "record" with the words "sound recording".

Version Recording

What is a version recording?[475] Whether there are exclusive copyrights in version recording? Version recording is a sound recording made of an already published song by using another voice or voices and with different musicians and arrangers. Version recording is thus neither copy, nor reproduction of the original recording.[476] The rights of the owner of copyright in version recordings includes the exclusive right to issue copies of the version recording under Section 14(e)(ii) and there is no limitation under the Copyright Act with regard to the format in which the version recording may be sold or hired. There is no limitation contained in the

475. *See,* Nawaneet Vibhaw and Abishek Venkataraman, "Recording of Different Version: An Indian Raga," 12 *Journal of Intellectual Property Rights* (2007) pp. 480–487; Jonathan G. Colombo, "The Right to Privacy in Verbal Communication: The Legality of Unauthorised Participant Recording" 35 *MsGill Law Journal* (1990) pp. 934–942.

476. *Gramophone Company of India Ltd.* v. *Super Cassettes Industries Ltd.*, MIPR 2010 (2) 349: 2010 (44) PTC 541 (Del); *Gramophone Company of India Ltd.* v. *Super Cassettes Industries Ltd.*, 1999 PTC 2 (Del).

Act which prohibits the exploitation of the version recordings by sale or hire of copies of the version recording, as a version recording through mobile telephones or through the internet.

In *Commissioner Central Excise* v. *Manaksia Limited,*[477] the Gujarat High Court observed that there is nothing in the Copyright Act from which it might be inferred that the Parliament intended to limit the statutory licence under Section 52(1)(j) to any particular mode of distributing copies of the version recording. However, the making copies of version recording and its sale must comply with the requirements of Section 52(1)(j) and Rule 21 of the copyright rules. Thus, it is clear that copyright subsists in version recording and the rights of the owner of copyright in version recordings includes the exclusive right to issue copies of the version recording [Section 14(e)(ii)]. Owner of the copyright in a sound recording cannot proceed to incorporate the sound recording or version recording in a cinematograph film without the express licence from the owners of the copyright in the literary, dramatic or musical works from which the sound recording is made. Making of copies of the version recording and its sale must comply with the requirements of Section 52(1)(j) of the Copyright Act and Rule 21 of the Copyright Rules.[478]

Similarly, in *Gramophone Company of India Ltd.* v. *Super Cassettes Industries Ltd.,*[479] the Delhi High Court observed that the person making the sound recordings is obliged to comply with the conditions contained in Section 52(1)(j)(i) and (ii) and the provisos set out after Section 52(1)(j)(ii). The said conditions would continue to bind the person making the version recording, irrespective of the format in which the version recording may be exploited as a version recording. Therefore, even if the copies of the version recordings are sold or hired, or offered for sale or hire over the Internet or mobile phones, the producer/owner of the copyright in the version recording is obliged to ensure that the spirit contained, inter alia, in Clause (ii) read with proviso (ii) of Section 52(1)(j) are complied with.

The purpose of Clause (ii) and proviso (ii) to Section 52(1)(j) is to ensure that the person making and marketing the version recordings, by resort to Section 52(1)(j) does not mislead or confuse the public as to their identity as version recordings. The purpose is to prevent any confusion in the minds of the public that what is being offered by the producer of the version recordings is his version recording, and not any other earlier sound recording or version recording of the same literary, dramatic or musical work(s). Therefore, when a person making a version recording sells or hires or offers for sale or hire his version recording as ring tones on mobile phones, in my view, it is essential for him to clearly state that the same is his version recording. It would not be enough for him to merely indicate the title of the song or other composition of which he has made the version recording for the purpose of identifying the same. Similarly, when the person making the version recording sells or hires or offers for sale or hire his version recording over the Internet along with the title/icon of the version recording, it should be clearly stated on the website concerned that the same is his version recording, and if a label/icon is displayed, the same should also conform with the requirements of Section 52(1)(j).

---

477. 2010 (179) ECR 148 (Gujarat).
478. *Commissioner Central Excise and Customs* v. *Manaksia Limited,* 2010 (179) ECR 148 (Gujarat); *Gramophone Co. of India Ltd.* v. *Super Cassettes Industries Ltd.*, 58 (1995) DLT 99: 1995 (33) DRJ 333; *Indian Performing Right Society Limited* v. *Eastern Indian Motion Picture Association,* AIR 1977 SC 1443: (1977) 2 SCC 820.
479. MIPR 2010 (2) 349: 2010 (44) PTC 541 (Del).

In *Super Cassettes Industries Ltd.* v. *Bathla Cassette Industries Pvt. Ltd.*,[480] the Court held "version recordings would really be such sound recordings where while being inspired by the original melody a distinct interpretation, different both in presentation, rhythm and orchestral arrangement emerges". Such a sound recording may enjoy the benefit of Section 52(1)(j) of the Copyright Act. On the issue of exclusive rights in version recording, the court held:

> By taking resources to the traditional reservoir of Indian Classical Rags and traditional folk music, compositions based thereon may result in a sound recording. Such a derivative by a contemporary composer/performer may not refer to the original source in their sound recording. In such a situation, the current composer cannot claim exclusive rights to such a sound recording, which are assertable against any other performer/sound recording based on such traditional repertoire. Thus no enforceable rights can be acquired by any contemporary musician in rendering/recording traditional compositions. Consequently, the traditional repertoire of Indian music which may not now enjoy copyright protection due to passage of time and being in the public domain, cannot be appropriated by any individual by virtue of a later and current sound recording by excluding other performers and/or composers. The tradition of Indian Classical and folk music is a valuable public heritage common to all adherents and cannot be purloined by a contemporary performer/composer by denying to others the benefit of the same.

In *Gramophone Co. of India Ltd.* v. *Mars Recording Pvt. Ltd.*,[481] question of law involved was whether an entity which seeks to make "version recording" or "cover versions of an earlier sound recording" requires the consent of the owner of the copyright. And whether "version recording" or "cover versions of an earlier sound recording" is an infringing copy. In this case, sound recording in respect of some musical cassettes had been previously made with consent of copyright owner. The contention put forth on behalf of the respondents that the present case is a case of "version recording" and they are referred to as "debased version"; a different singer, a different orchestra and a different studio only perpetuates and compounds the act of piracy and the case put forth on behalf of respondents does not find support in any literature. "Cover versions" or "version recordings" are fresh recordings made using a new set of musicians. While Section 30 of the Act refers to voluntary licences in which case the consent of the party is concerned. As opposed to this, there are two types of non-voluntary licences, namely, (a) compulsory licence, dealt with in Sections 31 and 31A of the Act; and (b) Statutory licences such as dealt with in Section 52(1)(j) of the Act. For the present case, we are not concerned with the first category of licences. The first condition of Section 52(1)(j) of the Act must be "with the consent of the owner" whereas the owner's consent is not a pre-requisite for the sound recording. Moreover, a combined reading of clause (iii) of the proviso to Section 52(1)(j) with Section 52(1)(j)(i) of the Act makes it further clear that the consent requirement is only for the first recording. A statutory licence of the nature contemplated under Section 52(1)(j) of the Act is considered to be in public interest and is recognised in most of the countries in the world and is resorted to as the appropriate from the licensing. Further, Section 2(m) of the Act clearly states that in respect of a literary, dramatic or musical work, it is a reproduction which amounts to an infringement while in the case of a cinematographic film, it is a copy of the film embodying the recording in any part

480. (2003) 27 PTC 280 (Del).
481. AIR 2001 SC 2885: (2002) 2 SCC 103.

of the sound track associated with the film. Similarly, in the case of a record, it is only such record which embodies the same recording. Thus the use of the words "records embodying the record" or the "record embodying the same record" clearly mean that it is only when the same signal has been kept, would there be a violation. If another signal is created, such as in the case of version recording, it is not an infringing copy within the meaning of Section 2(m).

In *Mars Recording Private Limited* v. *Saregama India Limited*,[482] the Karnataka High Court held that according to Section 52(1)(j) of the Copyright Act 1957 it would not be an infringement of a copyright in a sound recording, if the same has been made with the consent or by licence of the copyright owner. If a negotiated consent is not possible, a person becomes legally entitled to make a sound recording of such a copyrighted sound recording by recourse to the procedure prescribed and subject to the conditions that would apply. It is to be emphasized that it however, does not entitle the person to make a copy or a duplication of the sound recording. But is entitled to produce a "version recording", which is a fresh recording using a different set of performers, musicians and artistes and facilities. It would be a "sound alike" recording or a close imitation, of the original sound recording and would not be an infringement of the copyright.

---

482. MANU/KA/0151/2015. *See also, Star India Pvt. Ltd.* v. *Piyush Agarwal*, 2014 (58) PTC 169 (Del).

5

Author of Work, Owner of Copyright and Recognised Rights of Copyright Owner

ABSTRACT

Law relating to copyright is to protect the literary, dramatic, musical and artistic works, cinematograph films, sound recordings, broadcasting rights and/or performers' rights of authors and owners. This Chapter examines the meaning of work, publication of work, meaning of author, legal status of work of joint authorship, ownership of copyright, first owner of copyright, meaning of contract of service and contract for service, transfer of ownership of copyright such as assignment, relinquishment and licensing of copyright, various recognised rights of copyright owner, for example, exclusive economic rights, performer's and author's moral rights and neighbouring rights.

INTRODUCTION

The copyright law protects the author of the work from the possible fraudulent reproduction of the work without his permission. An author being a creator of a work, by using his talents, skill and knowledge must be in a position to enjoy the benefits of such creation. In such a case third parties, who have not played any part in such creation should not be given the benefits by its unlawful reproduction.[1] The basic principle of the copyright law is that the author is the first owner of copyright,[2] but the "owner of copyright" is the person who has plenary control over the work.

In *Commissioner of Income Tax* v. *Meenakshi Devi Avaru,*[3] the Karnataka High Court held that "ownership" is a plenary control over an object. An owner has three kinds of powers,

1. *See, Anant* v. *State of Maharashtra,* 2019 ALLMR (Cri) 1327; *Shyam Singh* v. *State,* 2016 (3) MLJ (Crl) 359; *Tekla Corporation* v. *Survo Ghosh,* 2014 AIR (Del) 121: 2014 (59) PTC 323; *S. Mahalingam* v. *Vasan Publications Pvt. Ltd.*, 2013-1-LW 776; *Visakha Chemicals* v. *Mala Ram*, 2006, (32) PTC 441 (Del); *Microforms Inc* v. *Girdhar and Co.,* 128 (2006) DLT 238: 2006 (32), PTC 157 (Del); *Glaxo Orthopedic* v. *Samrat Pharma*, AIR 1984 Delhi 265: 1984 RLR 291.
2. *See, CNH Industrial (India) Pvt. Ltd.* v. *Tirth Agro Technology Pvt. Ltd.*, 2019 (78) PTC 35 (Del); *Nitin Sethi* v. *Frontier Biscuit Factory Pvt. Ltd.*, 2007 (34), PTC 78 (Del).
3. [2019] 410 ITR 306 (KAR): (2019) 308 CTR (Kar) 83.

namely, possession, enjoyment and ownership. Similarly, in *Mohinder Pal* v. *State of H.P.*,[4] the Himachal Pradesh High Court rightly defines ownership as "a plenary control over an object". Copyright Act 1957 provides a detail scheme of law in determining "authorship", "owner of copyright" as well as assignment and relinquishment of ownership of copyright. The Act also provides a bundle of rights that the scope of which has been widen overtime.[5]

In *Super Cassettes Industries Ltd.* v. *Myspace Inc.*,[6] the Delhi High Court held that copyright is a bundle of rights which is meant to encourage creativity. The traditional concept of the copyright has undergone a drastic change as traditionally, the law relating to copyright was meant to encourage the original literary, books and also to help the poor authors. But, due to the advent of new technologies, its scope has extended manifolds. Now, the modern law of copyright encompasses musical works, cinematograph works, computer programs, performers' rights, broadcasting rights. The copyright has now become part of the business of the big organization more specifically in film industry where the major chunk of money is reaped out of the royalties arising out of the licencing and assignment of copyright in the respective works. One more stage of complexity has been attained by the copyright law due to emergence of the virtual world of the Internet.

In the following pages an attempt has been made to demonstrate the different facets of copyright law relating to the work of author, ownership of copyright and rights of copyright owner.

AUTHOR OF WORK

Meaning of Work

Copyright protection subsists in "works" of author fixed in any tangible medium of expression from which they can be perceived, reproduced or otherwise communicated, either directly or with the aid of a machine or device. Thus, for subsistence of copyright, it must qualify as a "work".[7] To make the copyright law more specific, the Section 2(y) of the Act defines "work" to mean any of the following works, namely—

1. a literary, dramatic, musical or artistic work;
2. a cinematograph film;
3. a sound recording.

The word "sound recording" was substituted by the Copyright (Amendment) Act, 1994 in the definition of the term "work" appearing in 2(y), for the word "record".[8] Recognising the

---

4. AIR 1995 HP 15: 1994 (2) Shim LC 337.
5. *See*, *Mallikarjun* v. *Principal Secretary*, 2019(2) AKR 812; *Madhusri Konar* v. *New Central Book Agency Pvt. Ltd.*, 2019 (1) CLJ (CAL) 75; *State of Kerala* v. *The Malayala Manorama Company Limited*, (2017) 98 VST 445 (Ker): 2017 (2) KLT 36.
6. MIPR 2011 (2) 303: 2011 (48) PTC 49 (Del).
7. *See*, *Kajal Agarwal* v. *The Managing Director*, (2018) 5 MLJ 818: 2018 (5) CTC 185; *International Confederation of Societies of Authors* v. *Aditya Pandey*, (2017) 11 SCC 437: 2016 (68) PTC 472 (SC); *Adai Mehra Production Pvt. Ltd.* v. *Sumeet P. Mehra*, 2014 (59) PTC 575 (Bom): 2013 (4) BomCR 313.
8. Substituted by the Copyright (Amendment) Act, 1994, Section 2 [w.e.f. 10–5–1995].

word "record" as "work" in *Rupalli R. Shah* v. *Adani Wilmer Ltd.*,[9] the Bombay High Court observed that a bare perusal of the definition "record" would show that any disc, tape, etc., or other device in which sounds are embodied so as to be capable of being reproduced therefrom, other than sound track associated with a cinematograph film, is a record. Thus, it was always understood that this is not just a definition of the act of making a record or recording but it was understood as a work independently capable of being recognised for the purposes of a copyright. However, this observation is not enough to provide the criteria for selecting a "work" for copyright protection. Now question arises what is the way of determining whether an act is a "work" or not? It is a well-recognised principle that in determining a "work" for copyright protection there must be some amount of skill, labour and brain that has been invested for its creation.[10]

In *Sanjay Kumar Gupta* v. *Sony Pictures Networks India P. Ltd.*,[11] the Delhi High Court held that under the Copyright Act 1957 it is only a literary work or dramatic work or artistic work or musical work or sound recording or cinematographic film or live shows/performers' rights (Sections 37 to 39A) which are the subject matter of a copyright. The expression "work" with respect to which copyright is granted is defined in Section 2(y) of the Act. Except such copyrights, statutorily no copyright can exist. Not only what is a copyright work is provided in Act, but what is the maximum entitlement of a copyright holder to exploit the copyright work and in which manner is also provided in Act and this is stated in Section 14. In *Kamal Kishor* v. *State of MP*,[12] the Madhaya Pradesh High Court observed:

> The "work" means a literary, dramatic, musical or artistic work, a cinematograph film or sound recording. The allegation relating to duplicate spark plug, by no stretch of imagination, falls within the ambit of "work", as defined in the Act. If the scheme of the Act is minutely examined, it is clear that it does not cover any other right, which may be even remotely relatable to a spark plug. In other words, the spark plug cannot be treated as an artistic work and, therefore, Copyright Act itself has no application in relation to allegation of possessing duplicate spark plugs.

In *Radio Today Broadcasting Ltd.* v. *Indian Performing Rights Society Ltd.,* the Calcutta High Court observed that copyright shall subsist in certain classes of works, namely, "original literary, dramatic, musical, and artistic works" and "cinematograph films" and "sound recordings". A "song", therefore, comprises a "bundle" of works, namely, "words" or "lyrics", "music" or "musical compositions". Whenever a singer performs these aforementioned works and the performance is recorded, a sound recording is created. Thus, lyrics are "literary works", within the meaning of Section 2(o) of the Copyright Act, 1957, and musical compositions are defined as "musical works" under Section 2(p) of the Copyright Act, 1957. Similarly, a "sound recording" is defined in Section 2(xx) for the purpose of copyright protection. Further, in *Saregama India Limited* v. *Mahal Pictures Private Limited,*[13] the Bombay High Court clarified

---

9. 2012 (52) PTC 305 (Bom).
10. *See, Gurukrupa Mech Tech Pvt. Ltd.* v. *State of Gujarat*, (2018) 4 GLR 3324; *Microforms Inc* v. *Girdhar*, 128 (2006) DLT 238: 2006 (32) PTC 157 (Del); *Star India Private Limited* v. *Leo Burnett (India) Private Limited*, 2003 (2) Bom CR 655: 2003 (27) PTC 81 (Bom); *R.G. Anand* v. *Delux Films*, AIR 1978 SC 1613: (1978) 4 SCC 118.
11. AIR 2018 Delhi 169: 2018 (75) PTC 562 (Del).
12. 2016 (I) MPJR 301: 2016 CriLJ 1640.
13. 2009 (39) PTC 431 (Cal). *See also*, *Indian Performing Right Society Ltd.* v. *Aditya Pandey*, MIPR 2012 (2) 140: 2012 (50) PTC 460 (Del).

that the term "work" includes the sound recording. In connection to the cinematograph film in *Shalimar Video Company* v. *Divya Exports,*[14] the Andhra Pradesh High Court held that "work" means the original film in the form of negative only, from which alone the required number of copies can be made. After making such copies from the original work, i.e., the negative "broadcasting" through different media like tape, disc, etc.

In *Fortune Films International* v. *Dev Anand,*[15] the Bombay High Court examined the issue whether the performance of a cine artiste in a cinematograph film would be "work" protected by the Copyright Act, 1957. In this case, the plaintiff was a cine artiste of a Hindi motion picture entitled "Darling Darling" produced by the first defendants. In the course of correspondence exchanged between the parties, it was inter alia provided that in consideration of his services to the producers he would be paid remuneration of ₹ Seven Lakh in certain amounts on or before the release of the picture in the territories of Delhi, U.P., Bengal, Nizam, Mysore, C.P., Tamil Nadu and Andhra Pradesh. It was further provided that the copyright in the cine artiste's work in the motion picture was to vest in the cine artiste till full payment of the agreed amount was made to him on which it would automatically vest in the producers. The plaintiff alleged that the producers were releasing the picture in the Bombay and overseas territories without full payment of the remuneration to him, and he sued to restrain the producers from doing so. Examining various provisions of the Copyright Act, 1957 the Court held that the performance by an artiste in a cinematograph film cannot be equated to any of the five categories of "artistic work" (namely, a painting, a sculpture, a drawing, an engraving or a photograph) in Section 2(c). A cinematograph film was expressly excluded in the definition of a dramatic work in Section 2(h). In view of the definitions of "artistic work", "dramatic work" and "cinematograph film" in Section 2(f), it would appear that the Copyright Act, 1957, does not recognise the performance of an actor as a "work" [defined by Clause (y) of Section 2], which is protected by the Copyright Act. Referring *Ramkishorilal* v. *Kamalnarayan,*[16] and *Indian Performing Right Society* v. *Eastern India Motion Picture Association,*[17] the Court further held:

> On a proper construction of the agreement the rights of the cine artiste are restricted to the seven territories which would mean that any injunction to which he is entitled must be restricted to the Bengal, Nizam, Tamil Nadu and Andhra Pradesh territories since the motion picture had been released in the other three.

Again question arises whether factual information in table containing information such as sunrise and sunset is "work" for copyright protection? In *G.A. Cramp and Sons Ltd.* v. *Frank Smythson Ltd.*,[18] the Court considered similar issue and said that the sun does in fact rise, and the moon set, at times which have been calculated, and the utmost that a table can do on such a subject is to state the result accurately. There is no room for judgment. The creation of a new table or compilation containing exclusively factual information may require a significant amount of work and effort in deriving that information, for example, by scientific observation and measurement. It seems unduly harsh to deny protection against another wishing to copy

14. 2011 (113) Bom LR 3472: MIPR 2011 (3) 228
15. AIR 1979 Bom 17: 1978 (80) Bom LR 263.
16. AIR 1963 SC 890: [1963] Supp 2 SCR 417.
17. AIR 1977 SC 1443: (1977) 2 SCC 820.
18. (1944) AC 329.

the information to save himself the trouble and expense of deriving the same information independently, particularly if his purpose is to produce a competing work. Of course, there may be copyright in the manner in which the information is presented, for example, in the design and layout of the table itself or in annotations, but that does not protect the information.

It is an often asked question that whether the application of sheer effort alone is sufficient to bestow copyright upon the resulting work. The US Supreme Court held "no" in *Feist Publications Inc.* v. *Rural Telephone Service Co. Inc.*,[19] in denying copyright protection to purely factual compilations, lying to rest the "sweat of the brow" doctrine. According to the "sweat of the brow" doctrine copyright was a reward for the hard work that went into compiling facts. In this case it was held that the white pages in a telephone directory were not protected by copyright because that section of the directory was the result of effort only and did not require the application of skill and judgment. It was basically a question of arranging names in alphabetical order and including address and telephone numbers. On the other hand, "yellow pages" in telephone directories could be copyright material because of the skill and judgment expended in selecting the classification system and the fact that other copyright materials such as advertisements were also included.

It is clear from the above discussion that it would be ridiculous to afford copyright protection to works that are trivial in the extreme or so small as to be entirely insignificant. However, a line has to be drawn separating works that are the proper subject matter of copyright from those that are not. The courts will often, though not always, use the principle *de minimis non curat lex,* that is, that the work which is insufficiently significant to be afforded copyright protection. Examining the copyright infringement of a work in *Smt. Somavanti* v. *State of Punjab,*[20] the Apex Court observed that the parts of a work which were so taken were neither substantial nor material parts and as it was impossible to say that damage had accrued to the plaintiff from such taking, his action must fail.

In *India TV Independent News Service Pvt. Ltd.* v. *Yashraj Films Pvt. Ltd.*,[21] the musical score and the lyrics limited to "*mera chain vain sab ujda*" were used in the advertisement. Hence, the issue was: whether the principle *de minimis non curat lex* would be defence for copyright infringement? The Delhi High Court held that *de minimis non curat lex* a valid defence for copyright infringement. The maxim "*de minimis*" means: (a) the law does not concern itself with trifles; (b) the law does not regard trifles; and (c) the law cares not for small things. Thus, applying "*de minimis*" as an adjective and giving it the meaning: trifling, unimportant or insufficient, the Court held that trifling, unimportant or insufficient violations would be treated as minor legal violations and hence would either be non-actionable or would be a good defence to an action for violation of a legal right.

Similarly, in *R.G. Anand* v. *Delux Films*,[22] the Apex Court held that the principle *de minimis non curat lex* applies to a supposed wrong in taking a part of dramatic works, as well as in reproducing a part of a book. However, in *Ram Narain Singh* v. *State of Bihar*,[23] the Patna High Court rightly observed:

---

19. 499 US 340 (1991).
20. AIR 1963 SC 151: [1963] 2 SCR 774.
21. MIPR 2013 (1) 104: 2013 (53) PTC 586 (Del).
22. AIR 1978 SC 1613: (1978) 4 SCC 118.
23. AIR 1978 Pat 136.

It was true that Courts of justice generally did not take trifling and immaterial infractions of law into account, yet use of maxim was not appropriate when extent of power conferred or liability imposed by statute was question of construction.

Publication of Work

Like the meaning of work, the publication of work is another controversial issue as the term "publication" has different meaning in different branches of law. For example, in the law of patent, it means the communication of information about the invention to any member of the public who is free in law and equity to use it as he pleases.[24] Under the law of defamation, it means communication of the defamatory matter to any person other than the person defamed.[25] In copyright law, it means making a work available to the public by issue of copies or by communicating the work to the public. Section 3 of the Copyright Act, 1957 defines the term "publication" as follows:

> For the purposes of this Act, 'publication' means making a work available to the public by issue of copies or by communicating the work to the public.

In *Raj Kumar Saraf* v. *Vaidya Nandram Gigraj Chamaria*,[26] the Delhi High Court held that Section 3 of the Copyright Act 1957 stipulates that for the purposes of the Act "publication" means making a work available to the public by issue of copies or by communicating the work to the public. Thus, the work can be made available to the public either by issuance of copies or by communicating the work to the public. Further, Section 2(ff) provides a definition for "communication to the public" as making any work available for being seen or heard or otherwise enjoyed by the public directly or by any means of display or diffusion other than by issuing copies of such work regardless of whether any member of the public actually sees, hears or otherwise enjoys the work so made available. For the purposes of Section 2(ff) communication through satellite or cable or any other means of simultaneous communication to more than one household or place of residence including residential rooms of any hotel or hostel shall be deemed to be communication to the public. Thus, the Act provided a more expansive definition of "communication to the public" in order to address various technological advances.[27]

It is clear from the above definition that there are two ways of publishing a work: (i) by issue of copies of the work,[28] or (ii) by communicating the work to the public. So far as the first way of publication is concerned to mean the "issue of copies of the work" to the public, it follows that a work cannot be orally published, and there can be no publication of the work whenever there exists a single example only. In case of cinematograph film, the single

24. *J.K. (Bombay) Ltd.* v. *Central Board of Direct Taxes* (1979) ILR Delhi 407: [1979] 118 ITR 312 (Delhi).
25. *See, Nagpur Distilleries Pvt. Ltd.* v. *Karmaveer Shankarrao Kale,* 2017 (5) ABR 140; *Narain Singh* v. *Hanuman Prashad,* 2000 (2) Civil CC: 2000 (1) Shim LC 205; *Narain Singh* v. *Hanuman Prashad,* 1997 (26) Civil CC (NULL); *Dinkar Rajaram Pole* v. *Ramrao Nandanwankar*; 1986 Mh LJ 691; *Sukhdeo* v. *Emperor,* AIR 1933 All 210: (1933) ILR 55 All 252.
26. 2013 (55) PTC 354 (Del). *See, Star India Private Limited* v. *Department of Industrial Policy and Promotion,* (2019) 2 SCC 104: 2018 (14) SCALE 651.
27. *See, UTV Software Communication Ltd.* v. *1337X to and Ors.,* 2019 (78) PTC 375 (Del).
28. *Associated Publishers* v. *K. Bashyam,* 1960-73-LW541: (1962) 1 MLJ 258.

film could be put on sale or hire or offer for sale or hire to constitute its publication. The writer of a literary work may permit his manuscript to be viewed or read by any number of persons without thereby publishing the work. Thus, the issue of copies for public distribution is publication of such copies. In India when the right is given to foreign book company under an exclusive licence what matters is the issue of copies in India for purposes of infringement. Whether they have already been published lawfully in America is of little consequence. The importation sale, and public distribution of American editions constitute infringement of copyright of the exclusive licensees.[29] The Appellate Board[30] has been authorised under Section 6 of the Act to decide if there has been sufficient quantities of the work issued to the public or not. Section 6 provides that if any question whether the copies of works are issued to the public in a manner sufficient to satisfy the reasonable requirement of the public or whether the records are issued to the public in sufficient quantities, it shall be decided finally by the Appellate Board[31] Constituted under Section 11 of the Act.

The second way of publishing a work is by communicating the work to the public. According to Section 2(ff) of the Copyright Act "communication to the public" means making any work available for being seen or heard or otherwise enjoyed by the public directly or by any means of display or diffusion other than by issuing copies of such work regardless of whether any member of the public actually sees, hears or otherwise enjoys the work so made available. For the purposes of this clause, communication through satellite or cable or any other means of simultaneous communication to more than one household or place of residence including residential rooms of any hotel or hostel shall be deemed to be communication to the public. In *Phonographic Performance Ltd.* v. *Music Broadcast (P) Ltd.*,[32] the Bombay High Court held that perusal of the definition "communication to the public" under Section 2(ff) shows that making any work available so that the work is seen or heard by the public by means of display or diffusion amount to communication to the public. In other words, broadcasting of a work is communication to the public. But the phrase "communication to the public" covers other means of communication than broadcast.

The concept "communication to the public" has also been explained more progressively by the Delhi High Court in *Super Cassettes Industries Ltd.* v. *Board of Film Certification*,[33] and held the publishing of a video film in respect of any work would take place when such work is made available to the public for being seen, heard or otherwise enjoyed by means of display or diffusion "regardless of whether any member of the public actually sees, hears or otherwise enjoys the work so made available". Besides, exhibition through satellite TV or cable or simultaneous communication to more than one user including residential rooms of any hotel or hostel shall be deemed "to be communication to the public". This is a marked change from the understanding of what could tantamount to "exhibition to the public". It is no longer confined to a place where the public is admitted like a cinema hall but it would include

29. *Penguin Books Ltd., England* v. *India Book Distributors,* AIR 1985 Delhi 29: 26 (1984) DLT 316.
30. Substituted by the Finance Act 2017 (7 of 2017), section 160(a) for "Copyright Board," [w.e.f. 26 May, 2017].
31. Substituted by the Finance Act 2017 (7 of 2017), section 160(a) for "Copyright Board," [w.e.f. 26 May, 2017].
32. 2004 (3) ALLMR 196: 2004 (29) PTC 282 (Bom).
33. MIPR 2010 (3) 342: 2011 (46) PTC 1 (Del).

residential rooms of any hotel or hostel. Consequently, a whole new dimension has been added to the legislative understanding of "public exhibition". The first publication of a work is another important criterion for determining the subsistence of copyright. Thus, copyright subsists in any work only if the work is first published in India or where it is first published outside India the author was a citizen of India at the time of publication. Section 5 deals with the issue—when a work deemed to be first published in India? According to Section 5 of the Copyright Act—

> ...a work published in India shall be deemed to be first published in India, notwithstanding that it has been published simultaneously in some other country, unless such other country provides a shorter term of copyright for such work; and a work shall be deemed to be published simultaneously in India and in another country if the time between the publication in India and the publication in such other country does not exceed thirty days or such other period as the Central Government may, in relation to any specified country, determine.

Meaning of Author

The concept "author" has been defined in Section 2(d) of the Copyright Act, 1957 to mean: (i) in relation to a literary or dramatic work, the author of the work;[34] (ii) in relation to a musical work, the composer;[35] (iii) in relation to an artistic work other than a photograph, the artist;[36] (iv) in relation to a photograph, the person taking the photograph;[37] (v) in relation to a cinematograph film or sound recording, the producer;[38] and (vi) in relation to any literary, dramatic, musical or artistic work which is computer-generated, the person who causes the work to be created.[39]

A work of an "author" is protected under Copyright Act subject to fulfilment of conditions laid down in the Act. It is also a fact that time and again the scope and ambit of the copyright protection has been expanded. Hence, the meaning of the word "author" has also been expanded.[40] Keeping in view of this expanding phenomena in *Entertaining Enterprises* v. *State of Tamil Nadu*,[41] the Madras High Court held that the definition of copyright was enlarged to include the exclusive right to communicate works by radio-diffusion, and a separate copyright was recognised in a cinematograph film apart from its various components, namely, story, music, etc. Section 2(d) of the Copyright Act defines an author in relation to a cinematograph film, as the owner of the film at the time of its completion.

In *Visakha Chemicals* v. *Mala Ram*,[42] the Delhi High Court held that Section 13 of the Copyright Act gives a clue as to how a copyright is acquired. It says that copyright shall subsist throughout India, *inter alia*, in case of original literacy, dramatic, musical and artistic works. Therefore, emphasis is on the originality. It is, therefore, that artistic work which is

---

34. *See, Raj Rewal* v. *Union of India*, 260 (2019) DLT 190.
35. *See, Lyca Productions* v. *J. Manimaran*, 2018 (73) PTC 525 (Mad): 2018 (3) CTC 605.
36. *See, Adai Mehra Production Pvt. Ltd.* v. *Sumeet P. Mehra*, 2014 (59) PTC 575 (Bom).
37. *See, Nagpur Distilleries Pvt. Ltd.* v. *Karmaveer Shankarrao Kale*, 2017 (5) ABR 140.
38. *See, Umesh Bharatbhai Thakkar* v. *State of Gujarat*, 2017 (4) RCR (Criminal) 948: 2017 CriLJ 3713.
39. *See, International Confederation of Societies* v. *Aditya Pandey*, (2017) 11 SCC 437: 2016 (9) SCALE 89.
40. *See*, Sherri Irvin, *Authors, Intentions and Literary Meaning* (Blackwell Publishing, 2006).
41. AIR 1984 Mad 278.
42. 2006 (32) PTC 441 (Del).

original in which copyrights can vest. According to Section 17 the author of the work shall be the first owner of the copyright therein and there is a relation between the definition of author under Section 2(d) and the first owner under Section 17. Thus, in *Glaxo Orthopedic* v. *Samrat Pharma*,[43] the Delhi High Court also held that the definition of word "author" and Section 17 lay emphasis on the fact that copyright vests in that person who is original creator of the work. In some cases, it may not be possible to be definite as to who was the original creator. In such cases, therefore, obviously the person who got registration earlier or who is established to be earlier user can be presumed to be the author or original creator of the artistic work. In *Jagdish Prasad Gupta* v. *Parmeshwar Prasad Singh*,[44] the Patna High Court held that person who sets question paper shall be author of work and first owner of copyright as per provision of law. The court observed:

> "Author" has been defined in Section 2(d) of the Copyright Act, 1957, and this expression means the author of the work in relation to a literary or dramatic work. The word "author", according to the dictionary, means originator or writer of a book of treatise. It is thus obvious that the persons who set these question papers were the authors of this work and according to Section 17, those authors were the first owners of the copyrights therein.

In *Navigators Logistics Ltd.* v. *Kashif Qureshi*,[45] the Court held that the Section 3 of the Copyright Act defines 'publication' as, making a work available to the public by issue of copies or by communicating the work to the public. It is not the case of the plaintiff that it has published the said list, for clause (i) of Section 13(2) to apply. For clause (ii) of Section 13(2) to apply, the author of the list has to be citizen of India or domiciled in India. The plaintiff claims ownership of copyright under Section 17 of the Act, presumably under clause (c) thereof. However, the plaintiff has not disclosed the name of the author, who was employed with the plaintiff. The plaintiff, which is a company, cannot be the author. In *Rupendra Kashyap* v. *Jiwan Publishing House Pvt. Ltd.*,[46] the Court observed:

> In the context of question papers for an examination, that the author of the examination paper is a person who has compiled the questions; the person who does this compiling, is a natural person, a human being, and not an artificial person; Central Board of Secondary Education is not a natural person--it would be entitled to claim copyright in the examination papers only if it establishes and proves that it has engaged persons specifically for purposes of preparation of compilation, known as question papers, with a contract that copyright therein will vest in Central Board of Secondary Education.

Author of Cinematograph Film and Sound Recording

According to Section 2(d)(v) of the Copyright Act, 1957 the author in cinematograph film and sound recording is the producer.[47] Further, the Section 2(uu) defines "producer", in relation to a cinematograph film or sound recording, as a person who takes the initiative and

---

43. AIR 1984 Delhi 265: 1984 RLR 291.
44. AIR 1966 Pat 33: 1966 Cri LJ 54.
45. 2019 IAD (Delhi) 418: 2018 (76) PTC 564 (Del).
46. 1994 (14) PTC 97 (Del): 1994 (28) DRJ 286.
47. Substituted by the Copyright (Amendment) Act, 1994, Section 2 for sub-clauses (v) and (vi) [w.e.f. 10-5-1995].

responsibility for making the work.[48] In *Gee Pee Films Pvt. Ltd.* v. *Pratik Chowdhury*,[49] the Calcutta High Court held:

> In order to be a producer, a person must take initiative as well as responsibility of the recording. The expenses of recording including hire charges of studio and remuneration of the musician will not bring the plaintiff within the purview of "producer" unless in addition to this, the plaintiff avers that it has also taken responsibility of such recording. The mere statement that a master tape of recording owned by the plaintiff was prepared and retained by it does not suggest that it has taken responsibility of such recording. If a person bears all the expenses for recording and keep the master tape thereof, such facts do not imply that he has also taken responsibility of the recording and thus cannot be held to be a producer. The word "responsibility" appearing in Section 2(uu) does not refer to financial responsibility, but means "consequential legal liability" for such recording.

Section 17 of the Act provides the law relating to first owner of copyright. Proviso (b) to Section 17 states that where a cinematograph film is made for valuable consideration at the instance of any person, such person shall, in the absence of any agreement to the contrary, be the first owner of the copyright.[50] In *Ramesh Sippy* v. *Shaan Ranjeet Uttamsingh*,[51] the Bombay High Court held that if the person who finances and takes the risk of making the work and directs others to do work for valuable consideration, such person is the owner within the meaning of the Copyright Act. Thus, based on the censor certificate itself, the firm Sippy films appears to be the owner of the copyright in the cinematograph of the film Sholay. According to Proviso (b) to Section 17 where a cinematograph film or sound recording is made in the course of the author's employment under a contract of service or apprenticeship, the employer is the first owner in the absence of any agreement of to the contrary.

Unfortunately, a distinction has been maintained in Section 2(d) between a literary, dramatic work, musical work, artistic work, photograph or a computer generated literary, dramatic, musical or artistic work on the one hand and a cinematograph film and sound recording on the other hand. However, this distinction is not carried to its logical end in the provisos to Section 17.[52] In such a case it appears to be a legislative mix up. Once the term "author" is defined by Section 2(d)(v) to mean only the "producer" in so far as a cinematographic film is concerned and once it is declared by Section 17 that such author (namely, the producer) is the first owner of the copyright in the film, there was no necessity to state in proviso (b) of Section 17 that in the absence of an agreement to the contrary, the producer will be the first owner. In respect of all works of art or music other than cinematographic film, the first ownership vests in the creator. But when they are created by the author while under a contract of employment with someone else the first ownership vests in such person who happens to be the employer.

In *Sree Gokulam Chit and Finance Company (P.) Ltd.* v. *Johny Sagariga Cinema Square*,[53] the Madras High Court held that in order to make this shift in ownership (from the

48. Inserted by the Copyright (Amendment) Act, 1994, Section 2 [w.e.f. 10-05-1995].
49. AIR 89 2002 Cal 33: 106 CWN 170.
50. *See,* Kirti Dahiya, "Cinematographic Lyricists Right to Royalty: Myth or Reality" 16 *Journal of Intellectual Property Rights* (2011) pp. 335–340.
51. 2013 (3) ABR 1228: MIPR 2013 (2) 125.
52. *See, Vinod Kumar Gupta* v. *State of U.P.*, 2019 (106) ACC 378; *Super Cassettes Industries Pvt. Ltd.* v. *Trimurti Films Pvt. Ltd.*, 2018 (1) BomCR 156: 2018 (4) ALLMR 541.
53. MIPR 2010 (2) 40: 2011 (46) PTC 513 (Mad).

author to the employer) very clear, the provisos under Section 17 are inserted. But in the case of a cinematographic film, the ownership does not shift in the first instance at all, in view of the fact that the producer himself is recognised as the author. In fact, Section 2(uu) of the Act, defines the term "producer" in relation to a cinematograph film, to mean a person who takes the initiative and responsibility for making the work. Such a person, despite not being the creator, is already recognised by Section 2(d)(v) to be its author. Omitting to take note of this, proviso (b) under Section 17 creates a confusion in so far as cinematographic film is concerned, providing a hunting ground for legal pundits.

Work of Joint Authorship

The question often arises: whether a work of a joint authorship is a "work" for the purpose of copyright protection? The term "work of joint authorship" has been defined under Section 2(z) of the Copyright Act, 1957 to mean "a work produced by the collaboration of two or more authors in which the contribution of one author is not distinct from the contribution of the other author or authors".[54] Thus, if there is intellectual contribution by two or more persons, pursuant to a pre-concerned join design, to the composition of a literary work then those persons have to be regarded as joint author. The works of joint authors are protected under the Act.[55] However, in *Nav Sahitya Prakash* v. *Anand Kumar*,[56] the Allahabad High Court held that one joint author cannot reproduce the work himself, or grant licence to others to reproduce it, without the consent of other author or authors, but may by himself take proceedings for infringement against third party.

Again, question arises: whether a partnership is a joint author? In *Ramesh Sippy* v. *Shaan Ranjeet Uttam Singh*,[57] it was argued that a partnership firm cannot be an owner of copyright and therefore cannot be a joint author. However, the respondent strongly argued in this case that under Section 17 of the Copyright Act, the author of a work shall be the first owner of the copyright except as provided in clauses (a), (b), (c), (cc), (d), (dd) and (e) of Section 17 of the Act. Therefore, the contention that the partnership firm cannot be the owner of the copyright is not correct. Relying on Section 2(z) of the Act, the respondent further submitted that in the case of a partnership firm, the partners who were the owners of the cinematograph film at the time of the completion of the film were the joint authors of the cinematograph film and thus the first owners of the copyright. The film will be the property or asset of the firm, and all the persons who were partners at the time when the film was completed would have joint or common interest in the film so completed. Therefore, the partnership property belongs to all the partners constituting the firm. In this case, the Bombay High Court rejected the submission of plaintiff that a partnership firm could not be owner of copyright and held that joint authorship was acknowledged in Section 2(z) of the Act, wherein "work of joint authorship" was defined to mean a work produced by collaboration of two or more authors in

54. *See*, *Novex Communication Pvt. Ltd.* v. *Lemon Tree Hotels Ltd.*, 2019 II AD (Delhi) 644; *Maroti* v. *State of Maharashtra*, 2018 ALLMR (Cri) 4460.
55. *See*, Navdeep Kour Sasan, "Rights of the Author: Possible Extensions under Copyright Law in India" 2(2) *International Journal of Innovation and Applied Studies* (2013), pp. 104–112
56. AIR 1981 All 200.
57. 2013 (3) ABR 1228: MIPR 2013 (2) 125.

which contribution of one author was not distinct from contribution of other author or authors. The concept that a partnership firm owned intellectual property rights was not alien to laws relating to intellectual property. If a partnership firm had been using trademark, unless there was evidence to contrary, it had to be *prima facie* presumed that it was the property of firm. Further, Section 13(2) of the Act, did not set out any pre-requisite for authorship. It only laid down certain conditions for subsistence of copyright and hence there are no other conditions.

In *Najma Heptulla* v. *Orient Longman Ltd.*,[58] the plaintiff, Maulana Azad, during his lifetime wrote the book *India Wins Freedom*. It is clear that Prof. Humayun Kabir, father of the defendant No. 6 was associated with the writing of the said book. According to defendant No. 6, the said book was composed and written by her father and he is the author thereof. The nearest relatives of Maulana Azad signed two documents which were identical, purported have given their consent to the arrangement which has been arrived at for the publication of the book, excluding 30 pages which were lying in sealed cover with Orient Longmen Ltd. On 2 September 1958, an agreement was entered into between Prof. Humayun Kabir and Orient Longman for the publication of the aforesaid book excluding 30 pages. In the said agreement, Prof. Kabir was stated to be the composer of the aforesaid book and it was mentioned that Maulana Azad had during his lifetime, dictated and given certain notes to Prof. Kabir and out of that material, Prof. Kabir had composed the book which had been approved by the late Maulana Azad. The Delhi High Court observed that where there was active and close intellectual collaboration and co-operation between the narrator and the writer resulted in the book. There was a pre-concerted joint design between the two in the writing of the book. The material for the book was supplied by the narrator with a clear understanding that the writer will describe those thoughts and conversation and write the same in the English language and in fact the writer had categorically stated in the preface of the book that his function was only to record narrator's findings and it would have been highly improper to let his views colour the narrative. The preface itself shows that Maulana Azad, along with Prof. Kabir read every word of the manuscript and made alternations, additions, omissions and corrections. It is Maulana Azad who decided as to which 30 pages of the book were not to be published and it is he who decided as to which of his views should be contained in the book. The court further observed that Prof. Kabir was not the sole author as 50% of the royalty of the book has been paid to the representatives of Maulana Azad. The court thereafter held that Maulana Azad and Prof. Kabir were the joint-authors of the said book.

Is there any distinction between work of joint authorship and collective work? Where a work produced by the collaboration of two or more authors in which the contribution of one author is distinct from the contribution of the other author or authors, it is a collective work. Thus a collective work is to be distinguished from a work of joint authorship which is a work produced by the collaboration of two or more authors in which the contribution of one author is not distinct from the contribution of the other author or authors. Thus, in *Macmillan* v. *Suresh C. Chander Deb*,[59] the Privy Council held that a work, containing particular selections and a particular arrangement on special lines, from the works of an author whose works were open to all was entitled to protection, as such a work involved the expenditure of skill, labour,

---

58. AIR 1989 Del 63: 1989 (16) DRJ 5.
59. AIR 1924 PC 75.

judgment and learning by the compiler. Apart from the fact therefore whether the collective work is entirely original (in the sense that nothing in it was produced in the same form and works before) or is a mere compilation being a collection of the works of several authors specially selected and arranged on special lines such work will always have a copyright of its own. But the owner of such a work must himself not have infringed the copyrights of any other owner whose works or part of whose works are included in such a collective work. That is to say the various works or parts whereof have been reproduced must be either such as have no copyright attached to them or the copyright of them must be secured by the owner.

In *Godfrey* v. *Lees*,[60] the plaintiff claimed that he is the joint author and joint owner of copyright in six musical works in the versions in which he performed with a pop group of which the defendants were members. It was held that the plaintiff had allowed the defendants to assume to their detriment that, subject to the arrangements they had reached with their recording and publishing companies, they were entitled to exploit the six works as their own. He had allowed them to labour under that assumption for fourteen years before asserting his rights. In the meantime, the defendants had worked hard to build their reputation and market the recordings. In the circumstances, Blackburne J. held that it would be unconscionable for the plaintiff to assert his legal rights and accordingly, he was stopped from revoking the implied licence.

OWNERSHIP OF COPYRIGHT

Copyright law provides a property right over human creativity recognising "ownership of copyright". Ownership is a right which avails against every one which is subject to the law conferring the right to put thing to user of indefinite nature.[61] Referring Holland in *Mohinder Pal* v. *State of H.P.*,[62] the Himachal Pradesh High Court rightly defined ownership as "a plenary control over an object". Similarly, referring Salmond[63] in *Nishikanta Roy* v. *Monmohon Sen Gupta*,[64] the Calcutta High Court further observed that ownership; in its most comprehensive signification, denotes the relation between a person and right that is vested in him that which a man owns in this sense is in all cases a right. As a corollary to the above, it can be said that the ownership extends to all classes of rights irrespective of the question whether such right is proprietary or personal or *in rem* or *in personam* or in *re propria* or in *re aliena*. For example, I may own a debt, or a mortgage or a share in a company or money in the public funds, or a copyright or a lease or a right of way, or a power of appointment. Every right is owned, and nothing can be owned except a right. Every man is the owner of the rights which are his.

---

60. [1995] EMLR 307.
61. T.C. James, "Copyright Law of India and the Academic Community" 9 *Journal of Intellectual Property Rights* (2004) pp. 207–225.
62. AIR 1995 HP 15: 1994 (2) Shim LC 337.
63. *See, Salmond's Jurisprudence* (7th Edition, Pages 277 to 279).
64. AIR 1973 Cal 529: (1974) ILR 1 Cal 46. *See also*, *Sudhir Kumar Chatterjee* v. *B.N. Sinha*, 1995 (2) BLJR 745; *Swadesh Ranjan Sinha* v. *Haradeb Banerjee*, AIR 1991 Cal 299: (1991) 1 Cal LT 223 (HC); *Balkrishan Gupta* v. *Swadeshi Polytex Ltd.*, AIR 1985 SC 520: (1985) 2 SCC 167; *Nishikanta Roy* v. *Monmohon Sen Gupta*, AIR 1973 Cal 529: (1974) ILR 1 Cal 46.

The owner of the copyright has been defined in Section 54 of the Copyright Act 1957. According to Section 54, the expression "owner of copyright" shall include- (a) an exclusive licensee; (b) in the case of anonymous or pseudonymous literary, dramatic, musical or artistic work, the publisher of the work, until the identity of the author or, in the case of an anonymous work of joint authorship, or a work of joint authorship published under names all of which are pseudonyms, the identity of any of the authors, is disclosed publicly by the author and the publisher or is otherwise to the satisfaction of the Appellate Board[65] by that author or his legal representatives.[66] In *Inception Media LLP* v. *Star India Pvt. Ltd.*,[67] the Bombay High Court held that a suit can only be brought by the "owner of copyright" which is defined in Section 54 of the Copyright Act, and the civil remedies of such an owner are set out in Section 55. The former says that the owner of a copyright includes an exclusive licensee. Thus, an exclusive licencee can be owner of copyright in the context of the agreement so requires.[68]

The Copyright Act, 1957 provides a detail scheme of law for determining the "owner of copyright" as well as assignment and relinquishment of ownership of copyright, etc.

Legislative Scheme

Chapter IV (Sections 17 to 21) of the Copyright Act, 1957 provides a detail scheme of law relating to ownership of copyright and the rights of the owner. Section 17 of the Act declares that subject to the provisions of this Act, "the author of a work shall be the first owner of a copyright". In *Blueberry Books* v. *Bharti Goyal*,[69] it was held that under Section 17 of the Copyright Act, the author of a work is the first owner of the copyright and assignment is possible under Section 18 and 19 of the Copyright Act by a deed in writing signed by the assignor. Accordingly, the "author" in relation to a work is the first owner of copyright in it. An "author" according to Section 2(d) of the Act means: (i) in relation to a literary or dramatic work, the author of the work; (ii) in relation to a musical work, the composer; (iii) in relation to an artistic work other than a photograph, the artist; (iv) in relation to a photograph, the person taking the photograph; (v) in relation to a cinematograph film or sound recording, the producer, and (vi) in relation to any literary, dramatic, musical or artistic work which is computer generated, the person who causes the work to be created. The Act also recognises joint authorship in cases where it is not possible to identify the separate contribution of different authors in a joint work.[70] In such circumstances, the co-authors will collectively be the first owners of copyright in the work.

Section 17, further places certain exceptions upon the general rule regarding ownership of copyright. Accordingly when a work is created during the course of employment of the author, for valuable consideration or under a contract of service or apprenticeship such

---

65. Substituted by the Finance Act 2017 (7 of 2017), section 160(a) for "Copyright Board," [w.e.f. 26 May, 2017].
66. *See, Managing Director* v. *Sradhananda Jena*, 2018 (4) Crimes 184 (Ori.). *See also, Amilal Ramkishan Dass* v. *Ashok Kumar Sethi*, 2019 (77) PTC 296 (Mad): (2018) 8 MLJ 160.
67. 2016 (65) PTC 149 (Bom): 2016 (5) BomCR 309.
68. *See, Modern Publishers* v. *Satish Kumar Gupta*, 2017 (69) PTC 198 (P and H).
69. AIR 2019 Delhi 84: 2019 II AD (Delhi) 233.
70. *See*, Section 2(z). *See, Najma Heptulla* v. *Orient Longman*, AIR 1989 Delhi 63: 1989 (16) DRJ 5.

employer, proprietor or person, who causes for the production of the work, becomes the first owner of copyright in the work.[71] Similarly, when a work is undertaken under the control of public undertakings or for the government or an international organization such undertaking, government or international organization becomes the first owner of copyright. Except in these circumstances, the author of a work becomes the first owner of copyright. Even in the above circumstances the author can retain the ownership through an agreement, between the parties at the time of commissioning of the work.

Thus, Section 17 does not deal with creation of copyright or its scope but only with its ownership. The same Section provides five categories of exceptions. The first three categories deal, generally speaking, with situations where the author of the work produces the work under contract of service, or apprenticeship or for valuable consideration. In all the three situations, the first owner of copyright is the person who commissions the work. However an agreement to the contrary is recognised, in which case the author herself can be the owner of copyright. The fourth situation is one where, in case of a government work, the government is declared to be the first owner of copyright, in the absence of an agreement to the contrary. Finally, for works to which provisions of Section 41[72] apply the ownership of copyright is vested in international organisations. Section 18 of the Copyright Act empowers the owner of a copy right to assign the same and Section 19 contemplates mode of assignment. Section 19A of the Act covers disputes which arise with regard to the assignment of a "Copyright" or the terms of an assignment of a "Copyright". Section 21 provides for transmission of copyright in manuscript by testamentary disposition while Section 21 provides for the right of the author to relinquish the copyright.

Section 17 of the Copyright Act reads thus:

> Subject to the provisions of this Act, the author of a work shall be the first owner of the copyright therein:
>
> Provided that—
>
> (a) in the case of a literary, dramatic or artistic work made by the author in the course of his employment by the proprietor of a newspaper, magazine or similar periodical

---

71. *See, Sanofi India Ltd.* v. *Universal Neutraceuticals Pvt. Ltd.*, 215 (2014) DLT 585: 2014 (60) PTC 593(Del); *Rediff.Com India Ltd.* v. *E-Eighteen.Com Ltd.*, 2013 (55) PTC 294 (Del): 202 (2013) DLT 657.
72. Section 41 reads: "Provisions as to works of certain international organizations—(1) Where—(a) any work is made or first published by or under the direction or control of any organization to which this section applies, and (b) there would, apart from this section, be no copyright in the work in India at the time of the making or, as the case may be, of the first publication thereof, and (c) either—(i) the work is published as aforesaid in pursuance of an agreement in that behalf with the author, being an agreement which does not reserve to the author the copyright, if any, in the work, or (ii) under section 17 any copyright in the work would belong to the organization there shall, by virtue of this section, be copyright in the work throughout India.
    (2) Any organisation to which this section applies which at the material time had not the legal capacity of a body corporate shall have and be deemed at all material times to have had the legal capacity of a body corporate for the purpose of holding, dealing with, and enforcing copyright and in connection with all legal proceedings relating to copyright.
    (3) The organisations to which this section applies are such organisations as the Central Government may, by order published in the Official Gazette, declare to be organisations of which one or more sovereign powers or the Government or Governments thereof are members to which it is expedient that this section shall apply."

under a contract of service or apprenticeship, for the purpose of publication in a newspaper, magazine or similar periodical, the said proprietor shall, in the absence of any agreement to the contrary, be the first owner of the copyright in the work in so far as the copyright relates to the publication of the work in any newspaper, magazine or similar periodical, or to the reproduction of the work for the purpose of its being so published, but in all other respects the author shall be the first owner of the copyright in the work;

(b) subject to the provisions of clause (a), in the case of a photograph taken, or a painting or portrait drawn, or an engraving or a cinematograph film made, for valuable consideration at the instance of any person, such person shall, in the absence of any agreement to the contrary, be the first owner of the copyright therein;

(c) in the case of a work made in the course of the author's employment under a contract of service or apprenticeship, to which clause (a) or clause (b) does not apply, the employer shall, in the absence of any agreement to the contrary, be the first owner of the copyright therein;

[73][(cc) in the case of address or speech delivered in public, the person who has delivered such address or speech or if such person has delivered such address or speech on behalf of any other person, such other person shall be the first owner of the copyright therein notwithstanding that the person who delivers such address or speech, or, as the case may be, the person on whose behalf such address or speech is delivered, is employed by any other person who arranges such address or speech or on whose behalf or premises such address or speech is delivered;]

(d) in the case of a Government work, Government shall, in the absence of any agreement to the contrary, be the first owner of the copyright therein;

[74][(dd) in the case of a work made or first published by or under the direction or control of any public undertaking, such public undertaking shall, in the absence of any agreement to the contrary, be the first owner of the copyright therein;

EXPLANATION—For the purposes of this clause and Section 28A, "public undertaking" means—

(i) an undertaking owned or controlled by Government; or

(ii) a Government company as defined in Section 617 of the Companies Act, 1956 (1 of 1956); or

(iii) a body corporate established by or under any Central, Provincial or State Act;]

(e) in the case of a work to which the provisions of Section 41 apply, the international organisation concerned shall be the first owner of the copyright therein.

[75][Provided that in case of any work incorporated in a cinematograph work, nothing contained to in Clauses (b) and (c) shall affect the right of the author in the work referred to in clause (a) of sub-section (1) of Section 13.]

First Owner of Copyright

The Section 17 of the Copyright Act 1957 deals with the law relating to the author is the first owner of copyright.[76] In *Nitin Sethi* v. *Frontier Biscuit Factory Pvt. Ltd.*,[77] it was held

73. Inserted by the Copyright (Amendment) Act, 1983, Section 8(a) [w.e.f. 9-8-1984].
74. Inserted by the Copyright (Amendment) Act, 1983, Section 8(b) [w.e.f. 9-8-1984].
75. Inserted by the Copyright (Amendment) Act, 2012, Section 17 [w.e.f. 21-6-2012].
76. *See, Kajal Agarwal* v. *Managing Director*, 2018 (5) CTC 185: (2018) 5 MLJ 818; *Microsoft Corporation* v. *Rajeev Trehan*, 2014 (213) DLT 238.
77. 2007 (34) PTC 78 (Del).

that an author is the first owner of copyright as per the Section 17 of the Act. There is a distinction between the author and the owner. Thus, though the author may be the first owner of copyright, the Provisos (a), (b), and (c) to Section 17 explain the position in respect of different situations. In *Lalgudi G. Jayaraman* v. *Cleveland Cultural Alliance*,[78] the Madras High Court observed: "It is clear from the language of Section 17 that as a matter of general rule, the author of a work, is the first owner of the copyright therein. It is only the exceptions to the general rule, which are spelt out in clauses (a) to (e) under the proviso to Section 17. Clause (a) of the proviso to Section 17 deals with literary, dramatic or artistic work. Clause (b) deals with photographs, paintings, portraits, engravings and cinematograph films. Clause (c) deals with a work to which clauses (a) and (b) will not apply. These clauses (a), (b) and (c) make persons other than the authors, as the first owners of the copyrights, under certain circumstances." Further, in *Ushodaya Enterprises Limited* v. *T.V. Venugopal*,[79] it was held that whoever is the first owner of the copyright is the owner of that copyright and his copyright shall subsist throughout India.

Explaining the legal position of Section 17 in *Novex Communication Pvt. Ltd.* v. *Lemon Tree Hotels Ltd.*,[80] the Delhi High Court observed: "It may be noted that though a person may be a creator of the work, if the person is creating a work on account of payment made to him by another person, then though the author creates the work, since the work is created on account of payment made by third person, in that case, it is the person who makes payment who would become the first owner of the copyright vide Section 17 of the Act." In *Microsoft Corporation* v. *Indus Valley Partners (India) Pvt. Ltd.*,[81] it was held that the plaintiff was the owner of copyright in its software programs developed and marketed by it and these software programs were "computer programs" within the meaning of Section 2(ffc) of the Copyright Act, 1957 which was included in the definition of "literary works" as per Section 2(o) of the Act. The owner of copyright in the literary works within the meaning of Section 17 of the Copyright Act is entitled to all the exclusive rights flowing from such ownership enumerated under Section 14 of the Copyright Act. However, this rule of first ownership is subject to a number of limitations. Thus, according to Section 17(c) of the Act if the author of the work is an employee of another or government or public undertaking or an international organisation then the employer is deemed to be the first owner of copyright. The fundamental principle of copyright law is that an author is the creator of the work and "owner of copyright" is the person who has plenary control over the work. Thus, in copyright law there is a distinction between "owner of copyright" and "first owner of copyright". The author is the first owner of copyright while the ownership of physical embodiment of the work is different from the ownership of copyright in the work.

ILLUSTRATION

Mr. M.F. Hussain made a painting of his daughter in which she is crying at the bank of river and presented it to Mr. Suresh Ambani, an industrialist of Mumbai. In this transaction, Mr. Hussain handed over mere physical ownership of the painting but not the copyright

78. MANU/ TN/ 2297/ 2008.
79. 2001 (4) ALD 723: 2001 (21) PTC 727.
80. 2019 II AD (Delhi) 644.
81. 2014 (2) MIPR 373: 2014 (143) DRJ 191.

in the painting. Although physical ownership has been transferred in this transaction, yet Mr. Ambani cannot make the copy of the painting for the purpose of any commercial interest. As soon as Mr. Ambani makes copies of the painting for commercial purpose, it will be an infringement of copyright of the painting of Mr. Hussain.

In *Pine Labs Pvt. Ltd.* v. *Gemalto Terminals India*,[82] "Fleet Program" was developed by "Pine Labs", which is the creator of the said program. The court held that according to Section 17 of the Copyright Act, "Pine Labs" would be the first owner of the copyright in this work. Section 18 of the Act, however, permits the copyright owner to assign the copyright either wholly or partially and either generally or subject to limitation and either for the whole term of the copyright or any part thereof. Section 19 of the Act stipulates the mode of assignment. Sub-section (1) thereof provides that in no uncertain term that assignment has to be in writing signed by the assignor or by his authorised agent. According to Section (2) of Section 19 of the Act, the assignment of the copyright, any such work is to identify such work and also specify the rights assigned and the "duration and territorial extent of such assignment". Thus, by agreement, the assignment can be for a limited duration and limited territory. But question arises: What happens if the agreement is silent on the duration and territorial extent of the assignment? Answer is provided by sub-section (5) and sub-section (6) of Section 19 of the Act. Sub-section (5) provides that if the period of assignment is not stated, it shall be deemed to be five years from the date of assignment and according to sub-section (6) if the territorial extent of assignment of the rights is not specified; it shall be presumed to extend within India. In the present case, as no duration or territorial extent is provided in agreement or any assignment deed, provisions of Section 19(5)(6) of Copyright would be attracted.

In *Nitin Sethi* v. *Frontier Biscuit Factory Pvt. Ltd.*,[83] the Delhi High Court held that there is a distinction between the author and the owner. Thus, though the author may be the first owner of copyright according to Section 17, the proviso explains the position in respect of different situations and assignment of copyright is permissible under Section 18 of the Copyright Act, 1957. The mode of assignment is provided under Section 19. In case of any dispute about the assignment of copyright, Section 19A comes into play and that is a matter to be considered by the Appellate Board.[84] Section 21 provides for the right of the author to relinquish the copyright. In *Blueberry Books* v. *Bharti Goyal*,[85] the suit was filed by the plaintiffs seeking a decree of declaration that the plaintiffs are the owners of the copyright in the work "Eight Science Olympiad Books Parts 1–8" as per the agreement. The defendants urges that the claim of the plaintiffs is based on an agreement of October 20, 2012 and other documents to claim exclusive rights on the copyright in question. It is urged that under Section 17 of the Copyright Act, the author of a work is the first owner of the copyright and assignment is possible under Section 18 and 19 of the Copyright Act by a deed in writing signed by the assignor. Hence, it is urged that the defendants being the original author is the original owner of the copyright and the issue revolves around the agreement

82. 2011 (8) AD (Del) 380: 2011 (48) PTC 248.
83. 2007 (34) PTC 78 (Del).
84. Substituted by the Finance Act 2017 (7 of 2017), section 160(a) for "Copyright Board," [w.e.f. 26 May, 2017].
85. AIR 2019 Delhi 84: 2019 II AD (Delhi) 233.

between the parties. Thus, the suit is based on statutory rights arising under the Copyright Act especially Sections 18 and 19 of the said Act. The Court held that Section 16 of the Act may be noticed. Section 16 provides that no copyright can be acquired in respect of any work except in accordance with the provisions of the Act. Therefore, copyright is a statutory right. Only those rights which the Copyright Act creates; to the extent it creates, and; subject to the limitations that the Act imposes, vest in the owner of the copyright in the work, whether it is a primary work such as a literary, dramatic or musical work, or a derivate work such as a sound recording or cinematograph film. No right, which the Copyright Act does not expressly create can be inferred or claimed under the said Act. Thus, no doubt, to explain as to how the copyright vests in the plaintiffs a narration of historical facts has been made. This narration of historical facts are ancillary and incidental to the rights which are sought to be agitated by the plaintiffs, namely, its copyright. Merely because some additional or ancillary issues are also arising in the course of adjudication of the controversy in the plaint, would not be sufficient to hold that the suit is barred.

First Owner of Copyright of Literary, Dramatic, Artistic Work [Section 17, Proviso (a)]

Under Clause (a) of the proviso to Section 17 of the Copyright Act, 1957 the proprietor of a Newspaper, magazine or periodical would become the first owner of the copyright in a literary, dramatic or artistic work, if it was made by the author "in the course of his employment under a contract of service or apprenticeship". Thus, the Proviso provides that if an author of literary, dramatic or artistic work is in contract of service or apprenticeship with a newspaper, magazine or periodical then the proprietor or employer is the first owner of copyright in so far as the copyright relates to publication of works in any newspaper, magazine or similar periodical. All other rights, for example, the right to make a cinematograph film, right to perform the work etc. vests with the author who created the work for the employer newspaper. However, this exception will not apply if the employee enters into an agreement with the employer whereby it is stated that the employee author will remain the first owner of copyright in respect of works created by him during the course of employment. In *B.N. Firos* v. *State of Kerala*,[86] the challenge made by Appellant before the court was founded on a claim of copyright in FRIENDS application software. Said claim, *ex facie*, was not tenable in light of provisions contained in Section 17(a) of Copyright Act, 1957. In this case it was entrusted by Microsoft to develop software for which it received due consideration from Microsoft. In present case the point for adjudication was claim of Appellant, as developer of application software, to be first author of said work so as to vest in him, which is a copyright under provisions of Section 17 of Act, a claim which was palpably unfounded both on basis of provisions of Section 17(a) of 1957 Act. The Apex Court declared that Microsoft is the first owner of copyright. The Court in its reasoning observed thus:

> Microsoft which had undertaken to make available the same to the first Respondent through the 4th Respondent free of cost. The invoice raised by the Appellant on Microsoft in this regard shows payment of remuneration by Microsoft to the Appellant. Therefore, under Section 17(a) of the Copyright Act, 1957 Microsoft is the first owner of the copyright.

86. (2018) 9 SCC 220: 2018 (8) SCJ 576.

The copyright is a bundle of rights and thus these rights can be split and exploited in different ways. One of the important and special aspects envisaged under Proviso (a) to Section 17 of the Act is that it recognises that there is a split copyright if the work is made by a journalist in the course of the employment under a contract of service. By split copyright we mean that so far as the copyright relates to the publication of a work in a newspaper, etc., or to the reproduction of work for the purposes of its being so published in the newspaper, etc., proprietor of the newspaper is the first owner of the copyright in the work; in all other respects the author is the first owner of the copyright in the work. The concept of split copyright may be explained through the following illustration.

ILLUSTRATION

> Mr. Gulzaar Nirmal is the author of an English novel "Tailorbird Warbler". Thus, Mr. Nirmal is the first copyright owner of the novel. In the capacity of copyright owner of the novel he can transfer different rights concerning the first owner of the novel. Therefore, Mr. Nirmal assigns the right of adaptation to Mr. Prakash Jha, a dramatist; the right to make film on the novel to Mr. Subhash Bhatt, a producer of film; the right to issue copies of the book by publishing to Mr. Anurag Deep, a publisher; and the right to translation to Mr. Balakrishnan for translation in Telgu and to Mr. Sukhbinder to translate in Punjabi. Thus, Mr. Nirmal splitting his copyright to exploit it in different ways.

Clearly, a film producer who makes a film without authorisation of journalist's story or report in a newspaper will be infringing the copyright of the journalist in the report or the story, unless it is a film not made "in respect of his work". In *Indian Express Newspapers (Bom.) Pvt. Ltd.* v. *Jagmohan*,[87] an investigative journalist working for the *Indian Express* newspaper publishers took upon himself the difficult task of exposing the widespread prevalence of trafficking in women in the state of Madhya Pradesh and the callous indifference of the state government towards the evil. To prove his point, he made himself a participant in the flesh-trade by actually buying a woman by the name Kamla from a village in Madhya Pradesh. He then on the basis of investigative journalism exposed the flesh-trade in Madhya Pradesh by writing his article in the newspaper giving a vivid account of how he went about the business of purchasing Kamla. Its publication caused a furor. Other sensational events followed and eventually Kamla mysteriously vanished from the women's home where she was kept never to be traced again. These formed the stories for three subsequent follow up reports in the same newspaper. These stories led to the making of a "cinematograph film"[88] on the basis of a script written by well-known playwright, Vijay Tendulkar. However, the journalist as well as the proprietor of the newspaper was portrayed in a defamatory manner. The film was named "Kamla". The movie was virtually a cinematographic transformation of the journalist's stories in the newspaper. The journalist and the proprietor of the newspaper filed a suit against the playwright and the film producer complaining that the film was an infringement of their copyright in the newspaper stories and the departures made in the film only made it worse by depicting them in a defamatory manner. They claimed permanent injunction and damages and took out notice of motions to restrain the defendants from exhibiting the film and for

87. AIR 1985 Bom 229.
88. For various issues on "cinematograph film", *see, Super Cassettes Industries Pvt. Ltd.* v. *Trimurti Films Pvt. Ltd.*, 2018 (1) Bom CR 156: 2018 (4) ALLMR 541; *Shuhaib Hameed* v. *James Albert*, 2015 (3) KHC 343.

an order for delivery of the infringing copies for destruction. The Bombay High Court held that *prima facie* the claim in respect of infringement of copyright was misconceived as the "cinematograph film" was based on common source and the treatment given in the movie to the subject was materially different.

Thus, in *Saregama Ltd.* v. *The New Digital Media*,[89] the Calcutta High Court held that when author of a lyric or a musical work parts with a portion of his copyright by authorising a film producer to make a cinematograph film in respect of his work and thereby to have his work incorporated or recorded on the sound track of a cinematograph film, the latter acquires by virtue of s. 14(1)(c) of the Copyright Act 1957, on completion of the cinematograph film, a copyright which gives him the exclusive right inter alia of performing the work in public i.e. to cause the film in so far as it consists of visual images to be seen in public and in so far as it consists of the acoustic portion including a lyric or a musical work to be heard in public without securing any further permission of the author (composer) of the lyric or a musical work for the performance of the work in public. The composer of a lyric or a musical work, however, retains the right of performing it in public for profit otherwise than as a part of the cinematograph film and he cannot be restrained from doing so. In *Exegesis Infotech (india) Pvt. Ltd.* v. *Medimanage Insurance Broking Pvt. Ltd.*,[90] the Bombay High Court clarified the proposition of law as has been laid down in Section 17 along with provisos (a) to (dd) thus:

> Section 17 declares that subject to the provisions of the Act the author of a work is the first owner of the copyright in it. Clauses (a) to (dd) contain the various provisos to this central rule. These deal with individual cases of different types of works created under diverse circumstances. For example, proviso (a) deals with the special case of a literary, dramatic or artistic work made by the author in the course of his employment by the proprietor of a newspaper, magazine or similar periodical under a contract of service or apprenticeship, for the purpose of publication in a newspaper, magazine or similar publication. The ordinary rule stated at the outset does not apply in such a case. Instead the proprietor of such newspaper, magazine, etc. is the owner of the copyright insofar as such copyright relates to the publication of the work in any newspaper, magazine or similar periodical, or to the reproduction of the work for the purpose of such publication, though in all other respects, the author continues to be the first owner of the copyright in the work. This special rule itself is subject to an exception, namely, there being any agreement to the contrary.

First Owner of Copyright in Case of Commissioned Works: [Section 17, Provisos (b)]

Under Clause (b) of the Proviso to Section 17 of the Copyright Act 1957, a person at whose instance a photograph is taken, or a painting or portrait is drawn or an engraving or a cinematographic film is made, "for valuable consideration", becomes the first owner of the copyright therein. Thus, a commissioned work is what is covered by the Proviso (b) to Section 17. This proviso enumerates some specific cases of commissioned worked where the first owner of copyright will be the person at whose instance the work is commissioned and not the author. The said proviso deals with a photograph or a painting or a portrait or an engraving or a cinematographic film made for valuable consideration. The Proviso (b) is subject to Proviso

89. 2018 (73) PTC 329 (Cal): (2018) 1 WBLR (Cal) 329.
90. 2016 (2) BomCR 303: 2015 (63) PTC 612 (Bom).

(b) of the Section 17. The fundamental rule given under proviso (a) to Section 17 is that where there is a contract for service, the author will be the first owner. Section 17 provides for the first owner of copyright, and it is provided that the author of a work shall be the first owner of the copyright therein. In respect of a cinematograph film provision is to be found in clause (b) of the Proviso to Section 17, which is in the following words:[91]

> "(b) subject to the provisions of clause (a), in the case of a photograph taken, or a painting or portrait drawn, or an engraving or a cinematograph film made, for valuable consideration at the instance of any person, such person shall, in the absence of any agreement to the contrary, be the first owner of the copyright therein."

In *Agi Music Sdn Bhd* v. *Ilaiyaraja*,[92] the Madras High Court observed that the Proviso (b) to Section 17 addresses painting, portrait, engraving or a cinematograph film made for valuable consideration at the instance of any person (in this case the producer), and states that such person (the producer) shall, in the absence of any agreement to the contrary with the creator of such painting, portrait, engraving or cinematograph film (that includes a sound recording), be the first owner of the copyright. In *Gee Pee Films Pvt.* v. *Pratik Chowdhury*,[93] the Calcutta High Court held that in case of a commissioned work for writing lyrics of the song or composing a music the author will be the first owner of copyright. However, the commissioner of work can protect his position by express agreement. In *Aamir Raza Husain* v. *Cinevistaas Limited*,[94] it was held that as in the present case it is declared that the relationship of both the parties was that of independent entities collaborating in the production. Therefore this is not a case of work made by anybody in the course of an employment under a contract of service or apprenticeship and hence Section 17, Proviso (c) of the Act has no application at all. Besides, since this is a joint venture, it cannot be said to be at the instance of an other for consideration and therefore, Section 17, Proviso (b) also will not apply.

When a person gets a work done by paying a valuable consideration to another, then the work is a commissioned work. An author may create a work at the instance of another person for valuable consideration. Examples are a person writing a report on a subject for a company, a composer composing a song for a film company, or a photographer taking a photo at the instance of another person or a painter drawing a portrait at the request of another person, all for valuable consideration. In such cases, in the absence of any agreement to the contrary, the person at whose instance the work is made is the owner of the copyright in the work. In case a person accepts a commission to design certain drawings for another person the equitable rights in the copyright passes from the designer to the person who has commissioned the work. Even if the equitable title in the copyright work did not pass to the person who commissioned the work there is an implied licence for him to use the drawings. In *Indian Performing Right Society Ltd.* v. *Eastern Indian Motion Pictures Association*,[95] the issue was whether producer of cinematograph film can defeat right of composer of music

91. *See*, *Fortune Films International* v. *Dev Anand*, AIR 1979 Bom 17: 1978 (80) Bom LR 263; *Gama Prasad Agarwalla* v. *Nabahash Goswami*, AIR 1967 Gau 70; *Bunny Reuben* v. *B.J. Panchal*, 2000 (4) Bom CR 680: 2000 (102 (1)) BomLR 512.
92. MANU/ TN/ 2435/ 2019.
93. AIR 89 2002 Calcutta 33: 106 CWN 170.
94. 2003 (27) PTC 425 (Bom): 2003 (105 (2)) BomLR 433.
95. AIR 1977 SC 1443: (1977) 2 SCC 820.

or lyricist by engaging him? The Court held that according to Proviso (b) of Section 17 when cinematograph film producer commissions composer of music or lyricist for sound track associated with film he becomes first owner of copyright unless contract to contrary exists. The Court further held that according to the Proviso (b) of Section 17 of the Copyright Act 1957 when a cinematograph film producer commissions a composer of music or a lyricist for reward or valuable consideration for the purpose of making his cinematograph film, or composing music or lyric therefore i.e. the sounds for incorporation or absorption in the sound track associated with the film, which as already indicated, are included in a cinematograph film, he becomes the first owner of the copyright therein and no copyright subsists in the composer of the lyric or music so composed unless there is a contract to the contrary between the composer of the lyric or music on the one hand and the producer of the cinematograph film on the other.

In *Pine Labs Pvt. Ltd.* v. *Gemalto Terminals India Pvt. Ltd.*,[96] the court held that equitable assignment exists in cases involving the agreement to assign future work and equitable assignment generally flows from contractual relations where work is commissioned. In case of actual assignment, the interest, whether absolute or partial, passes along with the beneficial interest. On the other hand, the agreement to assign or other vernacular for the same being 'assignment in equity' exists independent from the actual assignment. The said agreement is termed as 'equitable assignment' due to the reason that the said assignment is such which passes rights and interests in equity to the assignee with the assignor/author retaining beneficial rights.

In *Dabur India Limited* v. *Shree Baidyanath Ayurved Bhawan Pvt. Ltd.*,[97] in paragraph 12 of the plaint, a specific statement has been made by the plaintiff that the packaging which was adopted by the plaintiff is an original artistic work within the meaning of Section 2(c) of the Copyright Act, 1957, which is authored and created by Mr. Subhashish Dutta of Mudra India Ltd., an advertising agency at the instance of the plaintiff for consideration paid. Mr. Subhashish Dutta of Mudra India Pvt. Limited has given a no objection certificate dated 20 August 2010 in favour of the plaintiff. Being the commissioned work, the plaintiff is the owner of the copyright therein under the provisions of the Copyright Act, 1957 having exclusive right to use or reproduce features thereof in any material form. Any unauthorised copying, imitation and colourable reproduction thereof by any unauthorised person would constitute infringement of copyright of plaintiff therein under Section 51A of the Copyright Act, 1957 which is not only liable to be injuncted but also constitutes a cognizable offence under Sections 63 and 64 of the Copyright Act, 1957.

In *Indian Heritage Society* v. *Meher Malhotra*,[98] the court held that the present case is a clear threat to the rights of the plaintiff under the Copy Right Act. In this case the issue pertains to an Annual Day Event organised by the plaintiffs on 18-2-2011. It is stated that defendant No. 2 was assisting plaintiff No. 2 towards publication of the book comprising of the subject matter of the present suit. The book was to consist of photographs depicting different Asanas of Iyenger Yoga and their improvisations with the use of props, etc. meant to tackle different health issues. Justifying its decision, the court observed that according

96. 2010 (42) PTC 229 (Del).
97. 193 (2012) DLT 558: 2012 (51) PTC 441 (Del).
98. 2014 (57) PTC 438: 2013 (3) MIPR 245.

to the Section 17(b) in the case of a photograph taken, or a painting or portrait drawn, or an engraving or a cinematograph film made, for valuable consideration at the instance of any person, such person shall, in the absence of any agreement to the contrary, be the first owner of the copyright therein. Thus, it is apprehended that defendant No. 2 would misuse the photographs. Defendant No. 2, has failed and neglected to handover the necessary photographs to plaintiff No. 2 and has wrongly been and illegally demanding that in view of handing over of these compilations, she be allowed to join the teacher's training programme and stay at the Yoga Centre with a remuneration of at least ₹1,00,000/- for her to obtain a work permit.

First Owner of Copyright in Works made by Employee Authors: [Section 17, Proviso (c)]

Under Clause (c) of the Proviso to Section 17 of the Copyright Act 1957, an employer becomes the first owner of the copyright, in a work to which clauses (a) and (b) does not apply, if the work was made "in the course of his employment under a contract of service or apprenticeship" The Proviso reads: "(c) in the case of a work made in the course of the author's employment under a contract of service or apprenticeship, to which clause (a) or clause (b) does not apply, the employer shall, in the absence of any agreement to the contrary, be the first owner of the copyright therein." In *Quintessential Designs India Pvt. Ltd.* v. *Puma Sports India (Pvt.) Ltd.*,[99] the Madras High Court observed: "A perusal of proviso (c) to Section 17 only indicates that the author of a work shall be the first owner of the copyright therein provided that there must be an employer-employee relationship under a contract of service or apprentice." In *M/s. Vijay Solvex Ltd.* v. *Shree Hari Agro Industries Ltd.*,[100] the Rajasthan High Court held that a bare perusal of the provisions of Section 17 of the Copyright Act 1957 clearly reveals that ordinarily the author of the work is the first owner of the copyright. However, the said general rule is subject to certain exceptions made in the proviso. According to Proviso (c) in case a work is created in the course of employment or apprenticeship, then, in the absence of any agreement to the contrary, the first owner of the copyright shall be the employer and not the creator of the work. Thus, in *Quintessential Designs India Pvt. Ltd.* v. *Puma Sports India (Pvt.) Ltd.*,[101] the Madras High Court observed:

> A perusal of proviso (c) to Section 17 only indicates that the author of a work shall be the first owner of the copyright therein provided that there must be an employer-employee relationship under a contract of service or apprentice. In this case, admittedly, no amount is agreed to be paid by the defendants to the plaintiffs for the work done by them, and therefore, there is no question of claiming that the principal and agent relationship exists between the parties. As rightly contended by the plaintiffs, it is seen that the work done by them for the defendants, is on a principal to principal basis and not as an employment. Therefore, the contention of the defendants on this aspect, cannot be accepted.

In *Abhay Agarwal* v. *Puranmal Goods Private Limited*,[102] the issue was whether the Gulf Technical Printing Press's engagement by the 1st Plaintiff was a contract of service or apprenticeship? The Plaintiffs do not suggest that their relationship with Gulf Technical Printing

99. 2015 (64) PTC 17 (Mad).
100. AIR 2014 Raj 163: 2014 (58) PTC 602 (Raj).
101. 2015 (64) PTC 17 (Mad).
102. MANU/ MH/ 1321/ 2016.

Press was that of an employer or an employee. One can ordinarily understood a contract of service as indicating an element of servitude, i.e., an employer-employee relationship as distinct from a client-consultant relationship. It is for this reason that Ms. Ghone is compelled to invoke the Macleods Pharmaceuticals decision: she suggests that this kind of an agreement falls in some grey zone where though not a contract of service, yet because of a degree of control, the person creating the artwork did little more than a mechanical exercise, while all elements of creativity were the work of the client. In other words, the consulting press or agency merely delivered the kind of output that could commonly done by a computer or a robot today. Of this, there is no evidence in the Plaint at all; and even Macleods Pharmaceuticals cannot, be fairly read to suggest that every consultancy agreement is a contract of service, or that no proof of the exercise of a high degree of control is ever required. Thus, the Plaintiffs have established themselves to be the first owners of the copyright in question. This is because of the provisions of Section 17, and, specifically proviso (c) would operate: the 'author' would be the employee, and the work would have to be said to be one done in the course of his employment, thus making the employer-firm the first owner of copyright. The Court further observed:

> The first proviso speaks of a literary, dramatic or artistic work made by an author in the course of employment. That does not apply to the present case. The second proviso (b) speaks of, and this is important, not the general categories of literary works, dramatic works and artistic works, but of specific items such as a photograph, painting, portrait, engraving or a cinematograph film; i.e., a subset of the categories mentioned in clause (a). The present case falls in neither clause (a) nor clause (b), and both sides agree that it would be covered by clause (c) of the proviso.

The employer is not entitled to copyright in every work created by an employee except "those created in the course of employment". The meaning and scope of the words "those created in the course of employment" depends on the nature of the employment. In *Byrne* v. *Statist Co.*,[103] the court held that an employee was the owner of the copyright in a translation from Portuguese to English, which he made for employer in his own time for a separate fee since translations were not part of what he was normally, employed to do. In *Community for Creative Non-Violence* v. *Reid.*,[104] an artist and the organisation that hired him to produce a sculpture contest the ownership of the copyright in that work. In this case, the US Supreme Court held that the term employee for the purposes of determining authorship of the works interpreted according to general common law agency principles. Whenever a work prepared by an employee within the scope of his or her employment under the common law of agency principles and the work was done in the scope of employment, the employer (not the employee) is the copyright owner/author. The court identified certain factors that characterise an employer—employee relationship: (i) control by the employer over the work, (ii) control by the employer over the employee, and (iii) status of employee.

Employer is the proprietor of copyright of a work produced by the employee in the course of employment. In *V.T. Thomas and Other* v. *Malayala Manorama Co. Ltd.*,[105] the dispute was between a publishing house, Malayala Manorama Co. Ltd. and a reputed cartoonist, Toms.

103. (1914) KB 622.
104. 490 U.S. 730 (1989).
105. AIR 1989 Ker 49.

The term "author" occurring in Section 17(c) is defined under Section 2(d) of the Copyright Act, 1957. That term has to be understood in relation to a "work". Two different entities are visualised in the sub-section, the "author" and the "employer". It is impossible to imagine that in relation to any artistic work, the same person would simultaneously be the author and the employer. It is therefore unassumable that as regards the cartoons and caricatures produced by Toms, Manorama is the author. Toms is the person who clothes the idea in form. He is not a mere shorthand writer transcribing an author's stenographed words. Toms is the person who impregnates an idea; one who actually executes a design. It is Toms' hands which fix the picture upon the paper. Toms is therefore the author. The artistic works of an author made as employee, and while in the course of his employment, pass on to the employer in contingencies postulated, *inter alia* in Section 17(c). This process comes to an end in certain situations. The termination of the employment is one such situation. There has been such a situation in the present case. It would then follow that as regards the future productions of Toms, there is no inhibition arising out of the statutory sanction under Section 17(c). He is free to draw. He is independent to take his brush and draw the lines and create the figures. He can give life to his characters as he wishes; and he can present them in such media as he prefers.

In *M/s. Vogueserv International Pvt. Ltd.* v. *Rajesh Gosain*,[106] the Delhi High Court after referring to the provisions of Section 17(c) of the Copyright Act which provides that if a work is made in the course of other's employment under a contract of service, apprenticeship it is the employer who is the first owner of the copyright therein in the absence of any agreement to the contrary, a reference has been made as to what can be compilations to be included in literary works and such information would include a list of clients and their addresses.

ILLUSTRATION

> Mr. Amartya Sen teaches "Welfare Economics" at Harvard University and written a book on the subject he teaches. In this case, Mr. Sen is the Author of the book "Welfare Economics" and hence he is entitled to copyright but author is not the employer, i.e., the Harvard University. The legal reasoning is that Mr. Sen is employed to teach "Welfare Economics" and not to write book on the subject.

Thus, where employer is the proprietor of Newspaper, Magazine, Periodical or Journal, the proprietor has only the publishing rights in connection to the work, the other rights vest with the employee author of the work. However, the rights and duties of the proprietor and author are subject to any agreement to the contrary, if any.

Contract of Service and Contract for Services [Section 17, Provisos (a) and (c)]

Proviso (a) to Section 17 of the Copyright Act, 1957 stated that in case the author in the course of his employment under a "contract of service" the proprietor shall be the first owner of copyright while Proviso (c) to Section 17 of the Act provides that in case Provisos (a) and (b) does not apply in absence of any agreement to the contrary the employer shall be the first

106. 203 (2013) DLT 613: 2013 (55) PTC 480 (Del). *See also*, *Burlington Home Shopping Pvt. Ltd.* v. *Rajnish Chibber*, 1995 (35) DRJ 335: 61 (1996) DLT 6.

owner of copyright. Whether Provisos (a) and (c) distinguish between "contract of service" and "contract for service"?[107] Whether a particular arrangement is a contract of service or contract for services is often a complex question. Thus, in *Academy of General Education* v. *B. Malini Mallya*,[108] the contract of service, as distinguished from a contract for services, are the degree of control over the making of the work exercised by the employer and the extent of which the person doing the work is integrated into the business of the person for whom he does it. On the other hand, a "contract for services" is one between a person and an independent contractor who undertakes to perform specified services for that person. In *Diljeet Titus* v. *Alfred A. Adebare*,[109] the Delhi High Court held that the fundamental test to be applied is this: "Is the person who has engaged himself to perform these services performing them as a person in business on his own account". If the answer to that question is "yes", then the contract is a contract for services. If the answer is "no" then the contract is a contract of service.

Proviso (a) pointing out "contract of service" means not only the appointment of the workmen on a particular day or given number of days but something more than that. Once a relationship of employer and employee is established between the Corporation and the *badli* workman then there are certain terms in the contract of employment. If it is a contract of service what are the obligations of the employer to the workmen and vice versa? One of the obligations to the employer is to pay wages to the workmen for the days on which they worked. In *Mukunda* v. *Managing Director*,[110] the Karnataka High Court sought to produce a definition that reflects the modern concept of the contract of service thus:

> ... One feature which seems to run through the instance is that, under a contract of service, a man is employed as part of the business, and his work is done as an integral part of the business; whereas, under a contract for service, his work, although done for the business, is not integrated into it but is only accessory to it.

Explaining the distinction between "contract of service" and "contract for service" in *Akhil Raj Rajya Hand Pump Mistries* v. *State of Rajasthan*,[111] the Rajasthan High Court observed:

> It is often easy to recognise a contract of service when you see it, but difficult to say where the difference lies. A ship's master, a chauffeur and a reporter on the staff of a newspaper are all employed under a contract of service; but a ship's pilot, a taximan and a newspaper contributor are employed under a contract for service.

In *Architect Bruno Dias Souza* v. *Gustavo Renato Pinto*[112] the learned Counsel for the appellant argued that under Section 17 of the Copyright Act 1957, an Architect continues to

---

107. For various issues on "contract of service and contract for services," *see*, Simon Honeyball and David Pearce, "Contract, Employment and the Contract of Employment," 35 (1) *Industrial Law Journal* (2006) pp. 30–55; Robert C. Bird, "Employment as A Relational Contract," 8(1) *U. PA. Journal of Labor and Employment Law* (2005) pp. 149–217; S. Deakin, *The Contract of Employment: A Study in Legal Evolution* (Centre for Business Research, Cambridge, 2001).
108. ILR 2008 Karnataka 1074: 2009 (2) KCCRSN 58.
109. 2006 (32) PTC 609 (Del): 130 (2006) DLT 330.
110. ILR 1986 Karnataka 769: (1986) ILLJ 470 Kant.
111. (1994) IILLJ 631 Raj: 1994 (1) WLC 1.
112. 2018 (2) ALLMR 508: 2017 (5) Bom CR 351.

be the owner of the copyright in the drawings, irrespective whether the professional fees for engaging his services are paid or not. The learned Counsel also pointed out that there was a "contract for service" between the plaintiff and the defendant No. 1 and not a "contract of service." He further pointed out that under Section 19 of the Act, which prescribes the mode of assignment, the assignment of any such copyright has to be in writing. Thus, he tried to wriggle out of the effect of Section 19 and Proviso (a) to section 17 of the Copyright Act, saying that there was a "contract for services" between the plaintiff and the defendant No. 1 and not a "contract of service". But, the Bombay High Court held that the suit is not simplicities for damages, but also for injunction, restraining the respondents from misusing the drawings in future. In fact the respondents have no intention and shall not make use of the drawings as prepared by the appellant in future for any other project. In the result, the appeals are dismissed.

In *Lalgudi* G. *Jayaraman* v. *Cleveland Cultural Alliance*,[113] the Madras High Court held that in absence of an identity of minds, there was no contract at all. When there was no contract at all, there could not have been either a "contract of service" or even a "contract for services". 38. Once it is found that the first defendant failed miserably to prove that there was any kind of a contract between them and the plaintiffs (much less a contract of service), the proviso to Section 17 does not come into operation. If the proviso does not come into operation, the author of the work would continue to be the owner of the copyright. But, in this case the question whether there was a "contract of service" or a "contract for services" between the plaintiffs and the first defendant? The Court finds that the correspondence between the parties does not disclose any identity of minds between them, so as to show the existence of a contract. But the case on hand is a ballet, which can at the most come within the meaning of the expression "dramatic work" as defined under Section 2(h). Therefore, it is covered by Clause (a) and not by Clause (b) of the proviso to Section 17. Even if it is not covered by Clause (a), it would be covered by Clause (c). The payment of "valuable consideration" is not the sine qua non under Clause (a) or (c), but the creation of the work "in the course of employment under a contract of service or apprenticeship" is the sine qua non under Clauses (a) and (c).

In *Mr. Diljeet Titus* v. *Mr. Alfred A. Adebare*,[114] controversy was around the nature of relationship with which the parties got together to carry on their profession. In this case the plaintiff claimed that the defendants were only working for him and paid remuneration for the same in the form of fee. However, the plaintiff was in control of the professional business but, defendants claimed to have worked more in the nature of partnership with the plaintiff. In this background, plaintiff filed suit, alleging infringement of copyright against the defendants as the defendants took away the privileged information of the organisation. However, defendants claimed to be the owners of the copyright. The Delhi High Court held that no contract whereby the parties had a profit sharing arrangement in pursuance to the arrangement of partnership was there. The copyright existed not only in what was drafted and created but also in the list of clients and addresses designed by the organisation and the relationship between the plaintiff and the defendants was one of contracts of service. The court further observed:

113. MANU/ TN/ 2297/ 2008.
114. 130 (2006) DLT 330: 2006 (32) PTC 609 (Del).

> The test which emerges from the authorities, whether on the one hand the employee is employed as part of the business and his work is an integral part of the business, or whether his work is not integrated into the business but is only accessory to it, or, the work is done by him in business on his own account.

There has been considerable dispute as to whether an author is under a contract of service or contract for service. Only if the author is under a contract of service does the transfer of ownership of copyright takes place. The important case in this regard is the English decision in *University of London Press Ltd.* v. *University Tutorial Press Ltd.*[115] In this case, certain examiners who were not the staffs of the University were appointed for setting up question papers for a matriculation examination conducted by the University of London. One of the conditions of appointment was that the copyright arising out of the question paper should belong to the University. But when the dispute regarding the ownership of copyright arose, the Court held that, the copyright vested with the examiners, as they were not under a contract of service of the University. The Court relied on the fact that the examiners were paid in lumpsum and that they were free to prepare questions at their convenience, skill and judgement having regard to the syllabus. Though there were instructions issued by the University, they were found to be only regulations framed with a view to securing accuracy in the system of marking. Therefore, the Court held that there was no effective control exercised by the University over the examiners and so they were held to be owners of copyright, rather than the University. The Court pointed out that transfer of ownership of copyright in such cases could take place only through a written agreement.

This decision, which distinguishes a contract of service with a contract for service based on the nature of control exercised by the employer upon the author has been followed by the Indian Courts too in *Agarwala Publishing House* v. *Board of High School and Intermediate Education*[116] and *Jagdish Prasad Gupta* v. *Prameswar Prasad Singh.*[117] In *Gama Prasad* v. *Nabashah,*[118] this principle was extended to dramatic works too by the Assam High Court. In this case the plaintiffs were the office bearers of Nawgong Natya Samithy, an institution created with an objective of enriching Assamese literature and Art, by encouraging authors to write and compile dramas in Assamese language. The defendants wrote a drama named *Piyoli Phookan* at the instance of the Samithy. The Samithy printed and published the drama at its own expense. Later on when the defendants converted the drama into a film, the plaintiff sued for infringement. The court upon perusing the evidence could not find anything that underlined that the authors were in the course of employment or under a contact of service of the Samithy while writing the drama. It was held that the Samithy, was not the owner of the copyright in the drama.

First Owner of Copyright in case of Address or Speech Delivered in Public: [Section 17, Proviso (cc)]

According to Proviso (cc) to Section 17 of the Copyright Act, 1957, in the case of any address or speech delivered in public, the person who delivers the speech in public is the first

115. (1916) 2 Ch. 601.
116. AIR 1967 All 91.
117. AIR 1967 Pat 33: 1966 Cri LJ 54.
118. AIR 1967 Gau 91.

owner of copyright. Proviso (cc) was inserted by the Copyright (Amendment) Act, 1983.[119] Before the 1983 amendment, the position of law was different. In *Walter* v. *Lane,*[120] the issue involved was whether a person who makes notes of a speech delivered in public transcribes them and publishes in the newspaper a verbatim report of the speech, is entitled to the copyright protection. The House of Lords held that each reporter is entitled to report and each undoubtedly would have a copyright in his own published report. Subsequently, in *Macmillan* v. *K. and J. Cooper,*[121] the Bombay High Court held that a person who makes notes of a speech delivered in public and publishes in a newspaper is the "author" of the report and is entitled to the copyright protection. However, this principle of law has been altered by Proviso (cc), which was inserted by the Copyright (Amendment) Act, 1983. Again, according to Section 52(a)(iii) of the Act reporting of a lecture delivered in public is not an act amounting to infringement of Copyright. The Proviso (cc) to Section 17 reads thus:

> "(cc) in the case of any address or speech delivered in public, the person who has delivered such address or speech or if such person has delivered such address or speech on behalf of any other person, such other person shall be the first owner of the copyright therein notwithstanding that the person who delivers such address or speech, or, as the case may be, the person on whose behalf such address or speech is delivered, is employed by any other person who arranges such address or speech or on whose behalf or premises such address or speech is delivered."

It appears from the term "speech delivered in public" used in Proviso (cc) to Section 17 is that this proviso is not applicable to lectures delivered to a private audience. Now the question arises whether Section 14 and Proviso (cc) to Section 17 are free from any dichotomy in case of lectures and speeches delivered. Section 14 gives certain rights to the copyright owner which are commonly referred to as "exclusive economic rights"[122] of copyright owner. In *Microfibres Inc* v. *Girdhar and Co.,*[123] the Delhi High Court held that originality is an essential ingredient and the purpose of copyright law is to provide the owner of a copyright with specific exclusive economic rights. This is the reason that author/ creator of the work not made in course of employment is usually the first owner and has the exclusive right to reproduce, publish, publicly perform, broadcast and adapt the work. It is a settled law that to enjoy the rights of copyright owner the work must be "reduced to material form". Thus, a lecture if not reduced to writing or printing therefore is not a work as it has not been converted into a material form. If reduced to writing, then copyright subsists in the latter as literary work. A combined reading of Proviso (cc) to Section 17 and Section 14 shows that if a lecture is delivered in public the copyright subsists in the lecture even if it is not reduced to a material form. Whenever a lecture is delivered before private audience, one has to find out whether it is extempore or written down. In case it is extempore

---

119. Inserted by the Copyright (Amendment) Act, 1983 (Act 23 of 1984), Section 8(a) [w. e. f. 8-10-1984].
120. [1900] AC 539 (HL).
121. 1924 (26) Bom LR 292.
122. *See*, Arathi Ashok, "Economic Rights of Authors under Copyright Law: Some Emerging Judicial Trends," 15(1) *Journal of Intellectual Property Rights* (2010) pp. 46–54; Robert C. Bird and Lucille M. Ponte, "Protecting Moral Rights in the United States and the United Kingdom: Challenges and Opportunities under the U.K.'S New Performances Regulations," 24 *Boston University International Law Journal* (2006) pp. 213–282.
123. 128 (2006) DLT 238: 2006 (32) PTC 157 (Del). See also *R. Madhavan* v. *S. K. Nayar*, AIR 1988 Ker 39.

or oral and has not been converted to a material form, then copyright does not subsist but the person delivering the lecture may be protected by performer's rights in terms of Section 38.

In *Diljeet Titus* v. *Alfred A. Adebare*,[124] the court observed that the provisions of Sections 2(o), 14, 16 and 17 of the Copyright Act have to be read together. Section 2(o) provides for the definition of "literary work" while Section 14 deals with meaning of copyright. According to Section 16, no person shall be entitled for copyright except as provided in this Act and Section 17 provides that the author of the work shall be the first owner of the copyright. Thus, only if the defendants were the owner of the copyright would it have the right to make it public in view of the provisions of Section 14 of the Copyright Act.

TRANSFER OF OWNERSHIP OF COPYRIGHT

One of the primary objectives expressed by the Copyright Act 1957 is to make transfers of copyright ownership more transparent and unequivocally intentional. The Act provides that transfers of copyright ownership must be in writing and signed by the assignor or his or her duly authorised agent.[125] Besides this, the ownership of a copyright may be transferred in whole or in part by any means of conveyance or by operation of law, and may be bequeathed by will or pass as personal property by the applicable laws of interstate succession.[126] Thus, the transfer of exclusive rights is valid if the transfer is in writing and signed by the owner as copyright is a proprietary right of the owner. In *Commissioner of Income Tax* v. *Techno Shares and Stocks Limited*,[127] the Bombay High Court held that under the Copyrights Act 1957, a copyright can be transferred by assignment and interest in a copyright can also be transferred by way of a licence.

Further, in *Amar Nath Sehgal* v. *Union of India*,[128] the Court held that the rights recognised under copyright law which the author can exploit independently for economic benefit by exercising these rights. A copyright owner may exploit his work himself or license others to exploit any one or more of the rights for a consideration which may be in the form of royalty or a lump sum payment. Thus, copyright can be transferred like any other property. The owner of the copyright can thus assign it to anyone (Sections 18, 19, 19A), license it (Sections 30–32), make a testamentary disposition or relinquish the right (Section 21), the transfer can take place by operation of any law as in the case of any other property. Out of these, there are two popular ways that a copyright owner can transfer some or all of his or her copyright rights: (i) through a licence, or (ii) through an assignment.[129]

---

124. 2006 (32) PTC 609: 2006 (130) DLT 330.
125. Copyright Act 1957, Section 19(1).
126. For critical discussion on the issue "transfer of ownership of copyright," *see*, Glenda A. Gertz, "Copyrights in Faculty-Created Works: How Licensing Can Solve the Academic Work-Forhire Dilemma," 88 *Washington Law Review* (2013) pp. 1465–1493; Dotan Oliar, Nathaniel Pattison and K. Ross Powell, "Copyright Registrations: Who, What, When, Where, and Why," 92 *Texas Law Review* (2014) pp. 2212–2250; Alice Haemmerli, "Take It, It's Mine: Illicit Transfers of Copyright by Operation of Law," 63 *Washington and Lee Law Review* (2006) pp. 1011–1045; Paul Edward Geller, "Conflicts of Laws in Copyright Cases: Infringement and Ownership Issues," 51 *Journal of the Copyright Society of the USA* (2004), pp. 315–394.
127. 2009 (111) BomLR 3801: (2009) 225 CTR (Bom) 337.
128. 97 (2002) DLT 439: 2002 (63) DRJ 558.
129. *See, Saregama Ltd. v. The New Digital Media*, 2018 (73) PTC 329 (Cal): (2018) 1 WBLR (Cal) 329.

Transfer by Assignment of Copyright

Sections 18, 19 and 19A of the Copyright Act 1957 provide for the law relating to transfer by assignment of copyright. Sections 18 and 19 of the Act deal with assignment of copyright and royalty or other consideration payable to the owner for such assignment, while Section 19A provides for settlement of disputes with respect to assignment of copyright.[130] In *STAR India Private Limited* v. *Department of Industrial Policy*[131] the Madras High Court clarified that "Section 18 speaks of 'assignment of copyright' with Section 19 'mode of assignment'. These provisions are meant to protect the right of the copyright holder with specific reference to the royalty factor." Under these provisions of law, the owner of a copyright is entitled to assign his/her copyright. Copyright thus assigned may be in an existing work or in a future work. It may be assigned either wholly or partially, and either generally or with conditions and limitations for the whole or partial term of copyright.[132] In *Indian Performing Right Society Ltd.* v. *Vodafone Idea Ltd.*,[133] the Calcutta High Court observed that the sound recordings does not cover use of the musical works and unless tariffs are paid to the society for exploitation of such musical rights the defendant has no right to use such musical works. Thus, third proviso to Section 18 of the Act states that author of the literary or musical work included in the sound recording retain its right not to assign or waive the right to receive royalty to be shared on an equal basis with the assignee of copyright for any utilization of such work.

There is a distinction between assignment of copyright and licence of copyright. In *Saregama Ltd.* v. *The New Digital Media*,[134] the Calcutta High Court held that the main difference between assignment and licence is that in a licence the person granting permission (Licensor) retains an interest in the property being licensed, whereas in an assignment the assignor transfers his rights in the property being assigned. In other words when one gives a copyright assignment, he parts with his copyright and he does not own his copyright anymore and the other party does, unlike a copyright licence where the licensor retains ownership of his copyright and gives the other party permission to use some or all of his copyright rights. The Court further observed:

> In an assignment of copyright rights, the owner sells his or her ownership rights to another party and has no control over how the third party uses those rights. A copyright assignment is sometimes referred to as a sales agreement for copyright. The buyer (assignee) can then use the copyrighted work or do whatever he or she wants with it. A valid assignment of copyright must be in writing and signed by, or on behalf of, the copyright owner/assignor. The subject of the assignment must be clear as to what copyright is being assigned in which work(s).

In *Ajanta Limited* v. *Ajanta Transistor Clock Manufacturing Co.*,[135] the court opined that under Section 18 of the Copyright Act, 1957, "assignment" means an assignment in writing by

---

130. *See, Star India Private Limited* v. *Department of Industrial Policy*, (2019) 2 SCC 104: 2018 (14) SCALE 651.
131. 2018 (74) PTC 417 (Mad).
132. Section 18 of the Copyright Act, 1957. *See, Reoti Saran Sharma* v. *Numero Uno International*, 1995 PTR 132; *Godrej Soaps (P) Ltd.* v. *Dora Cosmetics Co.*, 2001 PTC 407 (Del.).
133. (2019) 2 CALLT 436 (HC).
134. 2018 (73) PTC 329 (Cal): (2018) 1 WBLR (Cal) 329.
135. 2014 (57) PTC 569 (Del): 2013 (138) DRJ 407.

act of the parties concerned. Further, in *Sulamangalam R. Jayalakshmi* v. *Meta Musicals,*[136] the Madras High Court observed that on a conspectus of the scheme of the Copyright Act, 1957, it is clear that a protectable copyright has been vested with the author of the literary or musical work and if it is assigned, the assignee will get the said right. In *Sree Gokulam Chit* v. *Johny Sagariga Cinema Square,*[137] the Madras High Court discussed the purpose of Sections 18 and 19 of the Act. In this case, the court observed that a careful reading of Sections 18 and 19 would show that the purpose of assignment is actually to enable the assignee to exploit the rights that the owner of the copyright has in (a) the literary, dramatic or musical work, (b) the computer program, (c) the artistic work, (d) the cinematograph film or (e) the sound recording. The court further held that an assignment serves two purposes. For the assignee, it confers the right of exploitation for a specified period in a specified territory. For the assignor, it confers the right to receive royalty. Thus, Calcutta High Court in *Saregama India Ltd.* v. *Suresh Jindal,*[138] observed:

> The owner of copyright in a work may assign copyright either wholly or partially for the whole or any part of such copyright to any person. The assignment of copyright may be a limited assignment both in content and period. An assignment does not automatically mean that it is an absolute assignment. The intention of the parties with regard to the nature and extent of the assignment is required to be gathered and ascertained from the agreement itself. If on a proper construction of the agreement, it appears that the assignment is for a limited duration then it cannot be contended that simply because an assignment of copyright has been made by giving absolute ownership with regard to the copyright it has to be for an unlimited period.

In *Sunil Aggarwal* v. *Kum Kum Tandon,*[139] the Delhi High Court held that Section 18 of the Copyright Act confers ownership rights in a copyright on the assignee. An agreement which contemplates that a future document of assignment is to be executed has been held to take effect as an equitable assignment. In *Reoti Saran Sharma* v. *Numero Uno International,*[140] the Delhi High Court also held that a mere agreement to assign does not operate to pass the property right but gives equitable rights. It operates as an equitable assignment of copyright as and when the work comes into existence. Thus, Section 18(1) provides that the owner of the copyright in an existing work may assign the copyright either wholly or partially and either generally or subject to limitations, to any person. The prospective owner of a future work may assign the copyright. The first proviso to this sub-section clarifies that in the case of future work, assignment will come into force only when the work comes into existence. This was the only limitation for the operation of the Section 18 until 2012 amendment to the Section which came into force on 21 June 2012. The Copyright (Amendment) Act, 2012 inserted three limiting provisos after the existing proviso in sub-section (1) of Section 18 which are as follows:

> Provided further that no such assignment shall be applied to any medium or mode of exploitation of the work which did not exist or was not in commercial use at the time when the assignment was made, unless the assignment is specifically referred to such medium or mode of exploitation of the work:

---

136. AIR 2000 Mad 454: 2000-3-LW 38.
137. MIPR 2010 (2)40: 2011 (46) PTC (Mad).
138. 2007 (34) PTC 522 (Cal).
139. 1995 II AD (Delhi) 627: 1995 (33) DRJ 599.
140. 1995 PTR 132.

> Provided also that the author of the literary or musical work included in a cinematograph film shall not assign or waive the right to receive royalties to be shared on an equal basis with the assignee of copyright for the utilization of such work in any form other than further communication to the public of the work along with the cinematograph film in a cinema hall, except to the legal heirs of the authors or to a copyright society for collection an distribution and any agreement to contrary shall be void:
>
> Provided also that the author of the literary or musical work included in the sound recording but not forming part of any cinematograph film shall not assign or waive the right to receive royalties to be shared on an equal basis with the assignee of copyright for any utilization of such work except to the legal heirs of the authors or to a collecting society for collection and distribution and any assignment to the contrary shall be void.

The Madras High Court in *S. M. Ashokan* v. *Raj Television Net Work Ltd.*,[141] rightly held that owner of copyright can assign either wholly or partly and either generally or subject to limitations and either for whole term of copyright or any part thereof. The second proviso has been inserted by 2012 amendment in Section 18 by providing that no such assignment shall apply to any mode of exploitation that did not exist or was not known in commercial use when the assignment was made. The third proviso provides that the author of a literary or musical work incorporated in a cinematograph film or sound recording shall not assign the right to receive royalties in any form other than as a part of the film or sound recording. The above amendments strengthen the position of the author if new modes of exploitation of the work come to exist. It may be recalled that in the eighties, there were mostly video cassette recorders which were played in closed environments, but with the advent of the Internet, new models of exploitation of the works came into existence. It is possible that with the advent of high speed bandwidths and Internet telephony, new modes of exploitation of the work not contemplated at the time of assigning of works, may yet arise.

The Section 18 deals with assignment of future work "... or the prospective owner of the copyright in a future work may assign to any person the copyright". First Proviso to Section 18(1) states that assignment in respect of future works comes into effect when the work is created. The second proviso to Section 18(1) imposed a limitation by stating that "... no such assignment shall be applied to any medium or mode of exploitation of the work which did not exist ..." It is relevant to state that the issue of the ownership of a new right—telecast right—introduced by the amendment to the Copyright (Amendment) Act, 1984 came up for consideration before the Bombay High Court in *Maganlal Savani* v. *Rupam Pictures (P) Ltd.*[142] In this case, the defendant who produced the film *Chupke Chupke* in 1973 assigned all the rights to the plaintiff. The defendant recently assigned the telecast right on another. The plaintiff filed the suit to prevent the assignment of the telecast right to the ground that the terms of assignment will include not only the existing rights but also the future rights. The terms of the agreement read as follows: "The Assignor hereby agree and undertake that the said picture shall not be "exploited" or distributed or exhibited commercially, non-commercially or in any other manner whatsoever ..." It was contended by the defendant that since the telecast right was not in existence at the time of assignment it was not possible to assign the same in 1973. Relying on the word "exploitation" used in the assignment, the court negated this and observed:

141. MIPR 2017 (1) 398: 2016-5-LW 881.
142. AIR 2000 Bom 416: 2000 (4) Bom CR 400.

> What is assigned to the first plaintiff is the exploitation, distribution and exhibition commercially or otherwise of the picture. In this context we have to give a wider meaning to the term 'exploitation'. Exploitation of a film takes in all the scientific and technological devices that may be invented in future also and the plaintiff could make use of those inventions. Given such an interpretation of the word "exploitation" the objection raised by the first plaintiff in conducting satellite telecasting of the picture 'Chupke Chupke' will *per se* be violative of the provisions of the agreement.

It appears that the court has failed to appreciate the scheme of the Copyright Act, 1957.[143] As per Section 17 of the Act, the author is the first owner of the copyright. The rights are expressly stated in Section 14 of the Act. Since copyright is a statutory right, it is made clear by Section 16 that only those rights expressly stated in the Act are entitled to be enjoyed by the owner. Thus, when a new right is recognised by the legislature, this will automatically go to the author. As per Sections 18 and 19, the rights can be transferred to another by assignment in writing and signed by the parties.[144] It is made further clear by Section 18(2) that the assignor will be the owner of the unassigned rights. Since there is no express provision stating that only existing rights can be assigned, it may be possible for the first owner to assign even future rights. But this must be expressly stated in the assignment or else the normal interpretation is that the owner transfers only existing rights. The amendments introduced to Section 19 in 1994 are indicative of this intention of the legislature. In case of doubt regarding the terms of the agreement, the intention of the parties are looked into to find out the meaning of the words. This is what the Madras High Court did in a similar situation and held that the future rights are not assigned. In the above context, the court should not have interpreted the word "exploitation" in the agreement without ascertaining whether the first owner had the intention to assign even the future possible rights. The interpretation given by the court is against the spirit of the Copyright Act and interest of the first owner of copyright.

Section 18(2) of the Copyright Act clarifies that where the assignee of a copyright becomes entitled to any right comprised in the copyright, the assignee as respects the rights so assigned, and the assignor as respects the rights not assigned, shall be treated for the purposes of this Act as the owner of copyright. Thus, in *Sholay Media and Entertainment Pvt. Ltd.* v. *Vodafone Esssar Mobile Services Ltd.*, the Delhi High Court held that where the assignee of a copyright becomes entitled to any rights comprised in any copyright, he becomes the owner of the copyright so assigned and in respect of the rights which are not assigned, the assignor is treated as the owner of the copyright.

ILLUSTRATION

Ms. Shobha De writes a novel "Postmodern" and assigned the right of publication of the "Postmodern" to a publisher Thomson and Thomson. Here only the right of publication has been transferred to Thomson and Thomson as an assignee. However, in this transaction the right to make drama, cinematograph film or translation to any other language from the "Postmodern" remains with the assignor Shobha De.

---

143. *See, Raj Video Vision* v. *K. Mohan Krishna,* AIR 1998 Mad. 294.
144. *See, Lahari Recording Co. P. Ltd.* v. *Jain Television*, 2017 (5) CTC 60: 2016 (67) PTC 59 (Mad); *Maganlal Savani* v. *Rupam Pictures (p) Ltd.*, AIR 2000 Bombay 416 : 2000 (20) PTC 556 (Bom)] and *Laxmi Video Theatre* v. *State of Haryana*, AIR 1993 SC 2328: (1993) 3 SCC 715; *P. Thulasidas* v. *K. Vasanthakumari*, 1991-1-LW 220.

In *Reddys Laboratory Ltd.* v. *Reddy Pharmaceuticals Ltd.*,[145] plaintiff claims that the logo "Dr. Reddy's" was an original artistic work within the meaning of Section 2(c) of the Copyright Act. The said work was formally assigned to the plaintiff by way of an assignment deed dated December 18, 2002 and the plaintiff claims to be the proprietor of the said copyright with the exclusive right to use the said logo. The plaintiff submits that the defendant, Reddy Pharmaceuticals Ltd., is a company that was initially carrying on the business of purchasing various pharmaceutical ingredients from the plaintiff and supplying them to other formulators since the year 1997 that the defendant, at no stage, was engaged in purchasing, with the purpose of creating or marketing its own finished dosage brands. Hence the activities of the defendant are purported to have been in the nature of distributorship/agency supplying the active pharmaceutical ingredients manufactured by the plaintiff to formulators without changing the packing or the label. Consequently, the plaintiff claims that the above-mentioned activities of the defendant were not detrimental to the plaintiff. The Court held that the plaintiff acquiesced to the adoption of the impugned trademark name by the defendants. Thus, there is considerable force in the plaintiff's argument that there was no cause for concern regarding the defendant encashing upon the goodwill of the plaintiff by adopting the impugned trademark/trade name, as long as it was not in the same line of business, i.e., marketing and sale of finished drug formulations.

The Section 19A of the Copyright Act 1957 deal with the disputes in respect to assignment of copyright. Clarifying the legal position under Section 19A in *Uday Chand Jindal* v. *Galgotia Pulblications Pvt. Ltd.*,[146] the Delhi High Court held that the statute has empowered the Copyright Board (Appellate Board)[147] to adjudicate the dispute with respect to assignment of copyright including revocation of assignment agreement. Thus, by virtue of Section 19A of the Copyright Act 1957, the Appellate Board[148] is the only body entrusted with the power to adjudicate disputes with respect to assignment of copyright including revocation of assignment agreement. Further, In *South Indian Music Companies Association* v. *Union of India*,[149] the Madras High Court held that under Section 19A, the Board hears disputes regarding assignment of copyright, which would encompass a private dispute between the parties.

Mode of Transfer of Assignment of Copyright

The Section 19 of the Copyright Act 1957 deals with the law relating to mode of assignment. According to Section 19(1) of the Copyright Act, 1957, an assignment has to be in writing and signed by the assignor or her duly authorised agent. To safeguard the interest of the authors, the Copyright (Amendment) Act, 1984 introduced additional requirements for a valid transfer of rights. It must also specify the rights transferred, the duration, territorial extent; rate of royalty payable, etc. Only an agreement complying with these formalities can have effect

145. 2013 (56) PTC 372: 2013 (56) PTC 372.
146. 2017 (72) PTC 492 (Del).
147. Substituted by the Finance Act 2017 (7 of 2017), section 160(a) for "Copyright Board," [w.e.f. 26 May, 2017].
148. Substituted by the Finance Act 2017 (7 of 2017), section 160(a) for "Copyright Board," [w.e.f. 26 May, 2017].
149. 2016 (67) PTC 99 (Mad): (2016) 3 MLJ 647.

before law. It is also stipulated that in case the period of assignment is not mentioned it will be presumed that the contract is only for five years.[150] Similarly if the territorial application of the right is not specified, it will be understood that the agreement applies only to India.[151] It is further made clear that if the assignee does not exercise the rights assigned to him within a period of one year from such assignment, the rights will revert back to the author unless otherwise expressly provided in the agreement.[152] The Act has thus tried to safeguard the author from the risks involved in a contract agreement.

In *K.M. Varghese* v. *CBS Publishers and Distributors*,[153] the Delhi High Court held that the Sections 19, 30 and 31A of the Act clearly stated the licence of the copyright has to be signed by the licensor. Thus, the court observed: "Section 19 of the Indian Copyright Act, 1957 provides that an assignment is only valid if it is in writing signed by the assignee or by his duly authorized agent. What is applicable to assignment under Section 19 of the Act, mutatis mutandis applies to grant of a licence and this is so specifically stated in Sections 30 and 30A of the Act. It is therefore the law that before a licensee claims rights in a copyright, the licence has to be by means of writing signed by the licensor." In *Adai Mehra Production Pvt. Ltd.* v. Sumeet P. Mehra,[154] the Bombay High Court pointed out that following are few essentials of a valid assignment:

1. No assignment of the copyright in any work shall be valid unless it is in writing signed by the assignor or by his duly authorised agent.[155]
2. The assignment of the copyright in any work shall, among other things,-indicate clearly the rights proposed to be assigned and the size of the work.[156]
3. The assignment of copyright in any work shall also specify the amount of royalty payable, if any, to the author or his legal heirs during the currency of the assignment and the assignment shall be subject to revision, extension or termination on terms mutually agreed upon by parties.[157]

The aforementioned essentials are certain prerequisites for the valid assignment prescribed by the Act for the determination of the valid assignment. In *Sree Gokulam Chit and Finance Company (P.) Ltd.* v. Johny Sagariga Cinema Squareand,[158] the Madras High Court observed that there are various essential ingredients of the valid assignment which can

---

150. Copyright Act, 1957, Section 19(5).
151. *Ibid.*, Section 19(6).
152. *Ibid.*, Section 19(4).
153. 2016 (66) PTC 295 (Del).
154. 2014 (59) PTC 575 (Bom): 2013 (4) Bom CR 313.
155. *See*, *S. Vijayaraghavan* v. *Sellappappa Keeran*, MANU/TN/1160/2011: *K.A. Venugopala Setty* v. *Dr. Suryakantha U. Kamath*, AIR 1992 Kant 1: 1992 (12) PTC 55 (Karn).
156. *See*, *K.M. Varghese* v. *CBS Publishers*, 2016 (66) PTC 295 (Del).
157. *See*, *Warner Bros. Entertainment Inc.* v. *Santosh V.G.*, MIPR 2009 (2) 175.
158. 2011 (46) PTC 513 (Mad): 2011 (3) CTC 747. Similarly, in *PEE PEE Publisher and Distributors (P) Ltd.* v. *Neena Khanna*, 2009 (40) PTC 515 (Del) the Delhi High Court laid down essential ingredients of the valid assignment that: (i) the assignment must be in writing; (ii) the assignment must identify the work and specify the assigned rights, duration and territorial extent; (iii) the assignment must provide for royalty payable to the author; (iv) the period if not stated in the assignment shall be deemed to be 5 years; (v) the territorial extent if not stated shall be deemed to be india; and (vi) if the assignee does not exercise the rights assigned within 1 year from the date of the assignment, the same shall be lapsed.

be briefly summarized as thus:(i) that the assignment, to be valid, should be in writing, signed by the assignor or his duly authorised agent; (ii) that the assignment should identify (a) the work (b) the rights assigned (c) the duration of assignment and (d) the territorial extent of the assignment; (ii) that the assignment should also specify the amount of royalty payable to the author during the currency of the assignment; (iv) that if the assignee does not exercise the rights assigned to him under any of the other Sub-sections of Section 9, within one year, the assignment would be deemed to lapse after the expiry of the period; (v) that if the period of assignment is not specified, it shall be 5 years; and (vi) that if the territorial extent of assignment is not specified, it should be presumed to extend within India.[159]

In *National Publishing House* v. *Amit Sachdeva,*[160] the Delhi High Court examine the importance of handwritten addition to otherwise standard form of contract to find out whether the agreement is an assignment or licence of copyright. The author of the book *Micro Economic Part-I and II* entered into an agreement with the publisher for the publication of the book. The agreement is a standard for contract in which it was stated that the copyright would be with the publisher. But the author made a handwritten addition into Clause 8 of the agreement dealing with copyright retaining the copyright with the author. There was also an arbitration clause in the agreement. Since there was breach of terms of the agreement, the author sent a letter of termination of the contract. Both the parties filed suits and pleaded and prayed for an injunction. Neither of the parties has disputed the existence of an arbitration clause. The only question for determination is whether the parties are entitled to interim relief. In this context, arguments centred on the legal rights of the parties vis-à-vis the tenure of the agreement. It was contended that although the contract clearly sets down the period of assignment as five years, Sub-Section (5) of Section 19 also prescribes that if the period of assignment is not stated, it shall be deemed to be five years from the date of its assignment. The court after examining the scope of Section 19 as well as terms of the agreement observed thus:

> Although some of the terms of the contract appear to indicate that the publisher had a right for a period of five years, the handwritten inclusion into Clause 8 should be given its full application. If this be so, there appears to be no manner of doubt, as subsequently clarified in the published version of the work that the Copyright vested with the author.

In *National Publishing House* v. *Amit Sachdeva,*[161] the issue before the Delhi High Court was where the agreement between the parties was one where there was no assignment in favor of the publisher and was more in the nature of conveying the license to print, the author is entitled to the relief prayed for? The Court held that the author has made out a convincing prima facie case Therefore, for the grant of the injunctions prayed for by him. The Copyright belongs to him and he should be left unfettered to enjoy the fruits of his labour/work. The publisher had contended, during the pendency of the Arbitration Proceedings, that nether of the parties should deal with the book any further. In this context, the court held that even if there is an arbitration clause in the agreement, it is not a bar for seeking remedy from normal courts. The court further observed:

---

159. *See, Warner Bros. Entertainment Inc.* v. *Santosh V.G.*, MIPR 2009 (2) 175. *ESPN Stars Sports* v. *Global Broadcast News Ltd.*, 2008 (36) PTC 492 (Del): MIPR 2008 (2) 75.
160. 2001 PTC 437 (Del): 90 (2001) DLT 697.
161. 2001 (21) PTC 437 (Del): 90 (2001) DLT 697.

> Although, this at first flush appeared to be conducive to the balancing of convenience, it subsequently appeared to me to be inopportune, since neither party would benefit from the status quo nor it would negate the rights, established prima facie, in favour of the author. The publisher can claim appropriate relief, inter alia, in the nature of rendition of accounts and damages in the context of subsequent publication carried out by the author. The publisher is not left without remedy. On the contrary, if the publication of the work is interdicted and frozen, it may render it outdated if the Arbitration Proceedings are protracted over some years. In this case, it is the author who would suffer irreparable injury.

In *Dorling Kindersley (India) Pvt. Ltd.* v. *Sanguine Technical Publishers*,[162] the respondent No. 4 entered into an agreement dated 15 January, 2007 for the assignment of the copyright in favour of the respondent No. 1. The said agreement dated 15 January, 2007 does not provide for any term or period for which the assignment would subsist. Therefore, as a matter of law, the assignment would subsist only for 5 years as per the applicability of the Section 19(5) of the Copyright Act. Accordingly, on the date of the retirement which was 13 February, 2012, the respondent No. 4 was the sole owner of the titles as the rights of the works under the agreement have reverted back to the respondent No. 4.

However, the Copyright (Amendment) Act, 2012 has added three more limitations to the ones already in existence with respect to assignment.[163] Thus, by 2012 amendment, the sub-section (3) of Section 19 has been amended to provide that the assignment shall specify the "other considerations", besides royalty, if any, payable. Therefore, it is not necessary that only monetary compensation by way of royalty could lead to assignment. The 2012 amendment has also inserted a new sub-section (8) to provide that any assignment of copyright in any work contrary to that of the terms and conditions of the rights already assigned to a copyright society in which the author of the work is a member, shall be deemed to be void. A new sub-section (9) provides that no assignment of copyright in any work to make a cinematograph film or sound recording shall affect the right of the author of the work to claim royalties in case of utilisation of the work in any form other than as part of cinematograph film. Also a new sub-section (10) has been inserted similar to sub-section (9) for sound recording. In *Indian Performing Right Society Ltd.* v. *Vodafone Idea Ltd.*,[164] the Court held that after amendment of Section 19 in 2012 the newly inserted sub-Sections namely, sub-Sections 8, 9 and 10 declare any assignment of copyright to any work contrary to the terms and conditions of the right already assigned to a copyright society in which the author of the work is a member shall be void.

ILLUSTRATIONS

1. Mr. Michael George producer of a film "Dinosaur" gives a right to remake the film to another person Mr. Rituparno Ray for school project in West Bengal under the right to education programme for certain consideration. The writer of the script Mr. Adams for the said film "Dinosaur" will get an equal share in the consideration paid by Mr. Ray to the producer. The right to get this type of share is newly recognised right by the Copyright (Amendment) Act, 2012 under Section 19(9).[165]

---

162. 2013 (3) Arb LR 52: 2013 (56) PTC 40.
163. Copyright (Amendment) Act, 2012, Section 9 (ii) [w.e.f. 21-6-2012].
164. (2019) 2 CALLT 436 (HC).
165. Section 19(9) of the Copyright Act, 1957 [as introduced by the Copyright (Amendment) Act, 2012, Section 9(ii)].

2. Mr. Anu Malik, a music composer, composed a music and assigns his rights to Mr. Shahid Parvez a producer of sound recording. Mr. Parvez sells the sound recording to Mr. Anand, a producer of a cinematograph film to be used in the film for ₹10 lakh. Mr. Malik and Mr. Parvez will have an equal share of the aforesaid amount of ₹10 lakhs. The legal reasoning here is that if a composer of music assigns his copyright to the producer of sound recording which does not form part of any cinematograph film then he will have a right to claim an equal share of royalties.[166]

The Copyright Act, 1957 also provides for transmission of copyright in manuscript by testamentary disposition.[167] In the absence of a contrary indication in the testamentary instrument(s), bequest of an unpublished literary, dramatic, musical or artistic work "shall be construed as including copyright in the work". The Copyright (Amendment) Act, 1984 provides for the settlement of disputes with respect to the assignment of copyright.[168] On a complaint by either party to an assignment, the Appellate Board[169] now stands empowered to decide disputes either in regard to the entire range of assignment or any terms of it. Upon due enquiry, the board is authorised to make two kinds of orders. First, the board may permit the revocation of assignment if it finds that their terms of assignment are "harsh" or when the publisher unduly delays publication of the assigned work. Second, the board may issue a "certificate of royalty due to the owner". Of course, the power of the board is "inclusive". It may thus pass other orders as well. But the situations calling for its intervention are otherwise well defined. Although the section enables both parties to make a complaint, it is unlikely, though conceivable, that the assignee, usually a copyright industry will come before the board protesting the whole assignment or any of its terms as harsh. Clearly, the other kinds of orders that the board is empowered to pass are such that only the assignor may invoke. Indeed, even the order of revocation or variation of a harsh assignment is more to be invoked by the assignor.

Understandably, there was an aggressive protest from the copyright industries during the consideration of Section 19A in Parliament; the industries felt, obviously, that such a legislative proposal was itself "harsh" on them. Clearly, this section by itself does not injure the interests of copyright industries; it only addresses the more crudely exploitative interests among such industries to keep away from unconscionable exercise of their dominance in the market. Thus, Section 19A relates to disputes with respect to assignment of copyright. This section provides that on receipt of a complaint from an aggrieved party, the Appellate Board[170] may hold inquiry and pass orders as it may deem fit, including an order for the recovery of any royalty payable. The Copyright (Amendment) Act, 2012 has amende second proviso is to provide that pending disposal of an application for revocation of assignment, the Appellate Board[171] may pass any order as it deems fit regarding implementation of the terms and conditions of assignment.[172]

166. Section 19(10) of the Copyright Act, 1957 [as introduced by the Copyright (Amendment) Act, 2012, Section 9(ii)].
167. *See*, Copyright Act 1957, Section 20.
168. *Ibid.*, Section 19A.
169. Substituted by the Finance Act 2017 (7 of 2017), section 160(a) for "Copyright Board," [w.e.f. 26 May, 2017].
170. Substituted by the Finance Act 2017 (7 of 2017), section 160(a) for "Copyright Board;" [w.e.f. 26 May, 2017].
171. Substituted by the Finance Act 2017 (7 of 2017), section 160(a) for "Copyright Board," [w.e.f. 26 May, 2017].
172. Inserted by the Copyright (Amendment) Act, 2012, Section 8 [w.e.f. 21-6-2013].

Despite having a detail provisions of law relating to mode of assignment, a large number of issues have been decided by the judiciary over the time. The question considered by the Bombay High Court in *Video Master* v. *Nishi Productions*[173] was whether the assignment of video rights would include the right for satellite broadcast as well. Nishi Productions, the producer of the film *Bees Saal Baad* assigned the video copyrights of the film to the plaintiff, Video Master. This included the right to exhibit, distribute, sell, offer for sale, lease, and let on hire or licence or otherwise exploit or to make copies or deal with video cassettes/videograms/discs/tapes and cable TV rights. According to the plaintiff, in view of this agreement, he has the exclusive ownership of the video copyright including the right to exhibit and broadcast the film in India by use of video format in any manner including cable TV. The plaintiff alleged that, based on a separate assignment from the first defendant, the other defendants were trying to broadcast the film through satellite TV (Zee TV) by making Betachem cassettes. This according to the plaintiff was an infringement of his video copyright on the film. In a suit for infringement, it was contended by the defendants that since there were different modes of communication to the public, such as, theatrical, terrestrial television broadcasting (Doordarshan), satellite broadcasting and video TV, the owner of the film had separate copyright in all these modes and he could assign it to different persons. Thus, the satellite broadcast copyright of the film was a separate right of the owner of the film and the video copyright assigned to the plaintiff would not include this. After examining various provisions in the *Copyright Act* and the terms of the agreements, the court rightly accepted this argument. The argument of the plaintiff that preparation of the Betachem cassettes for the purpose of satellite broadcasting infringed that his copyright was rejected by the court referring to the exception under Section 52(1)(z) of the Act to this effect.[174]

In *Raj Video Vision* v. *K. Mohan Krishna,*[175] the Madras High Court examined the issue of the ownership of new rights recognised by legislature on an existing work. The first defendant, the owner and producer of the Tamil film *Pasamalar* assigned all his rights except the rights for Hindi version in 1961 to *M/s. Azam & Co.* and from them in 1966 to the second defendant. They were enjoying the rights since then. On 6 January 1988 the first defendant entered into another agreement with *Raj Video*, the plaintiff, assigning the video rights in the film. On 10 March 1989, the second defendant sent a letter to the plaintiff requesting him not to use the video rights since he is the owner of all the rights including the video rights. This suit was filed by the plaintiff for the declaration of his video rights under the Copyright Act. It was argued by the defendant that by virtue of the assignment of all the rights in the film in 1961, even the future rights that accrued after the assignment would automatically go to the assignee who is the owner of the copyright. Since the author of the film, the producer, has no rights on the film after assignment, it was argued, could not claim the new rights. Rejecting this the court observed:

173. 23 IPLR 388(1998).

174. Section 52(1)(z) reads "the making of an ephemeral recording by a broadcasting organisation using its own facilities for its own broadcast by a broadcasting organisation of a work which it has the right to broadcast; and the retention of such recording for archival purposes on the ground of its exceptional documentary character."

175. AIR 1998 Mad. 294: 1998-2-LW718.

> The obvious reason is that in the year 1961 neither the assignors nor the assignees could have dreamt of telecasting or video rights for exploitation or exhibition or distribution or printing, transferring master cassettes, etc. However, the conclusion which can be arrived at is that when the producers themselves were not aware of their future rights accrued due to scientific advancements, it cannot be said they had already transferred the rights not in existence by way of assignment. The assignment cannot be made on rights not in existence and therefore it can be safely decided that the video rights of the film were not given to the assignee....

The significance of the need for clarity about the nature and content of the work in the terms of assignment of copyright for future work is highlighted by the decision of the Bombay High Court in *Zee Telefilm Ltd.* v. *Aalia Productions.*[176] *Zee* entered into a written contract with the defendant to produce a tele serial by name *India's Most Wanted* comprising of 104 episodes. The agreement clearly stated about the transfer of copyright in the film based on the concept/script/story, etc. as stated in Schedule II to the agreement to *Zee*. But Schedule II was never produced. After 65 episodes, the defendant stopped supplying the episodes. The defendants then produced a similar serial by name *Fugitive Most Wanted* and started telecast *Doordarshan*. The present suit was filed for infringement of copyright in the serial *India's Most Wanted* and to prevent the defendants from producing and telecasting the new serial and also transfer all the new episodes he produced to the plaintiff. The defendants contended that the nature and content of the work for which the agreement was entered into was vague and hence the agreement was not enforceable. It was further argued that the new serial was totally different from the serial *India's Most Wanted.* After examining the terms of the contract, the court accepted the argument of the defendants and observed:

> In the absence of Schedule II, concept/synopsis/story/script of the programme titled "India's Most Wanted" cannot be said to be specific and as a matter of fact becomes totally vague and uncertain.... There cannot be copyright in any concept or idea as such and in the absence of any definite and certain agreement between the parties about the structure and format of the programme since Schedule II in which it has been specified as per the agreement itself being not available, the plaintiffs cannot be said to have acquired copyright in whatever is produced or production is made by the defendants....

Again in the *Chancellor Masters* v. *Orient Longman Pvt. Ltd.*,[177] the Delhi High Court examined the nature of the negative covenant in the contract of assignment of copyright and held that it is not a restraint of trade. The plaintiff in this case entered into a contract with the third defendant to write a book to be published by the plaintiff. The book was first published in 1994 and revised in 2001 and 2002. He learnt that the third defendant had agreed to write a similar book for the first defendant and it was about to be released. The present suit is filed to restrain the defendants from doing so, based on the negative covenant in the contract of assignment. Clause 13 of the assignment read: "During the continuance of this Agreement the Author shall not without the consent in writing of the publisher prepare or edit for any other publisher any work that is an expansion, abridgement or revision of the work or of any part of it or publish or cause to be published any work on the same subject at or about the price the sale of which may reasonably be regarded as conflicting or likely to conflict with the sale of the work." It was also established that on comparison, the new work was similar to the earlier

176. 2000 (1) ALLMR 260: 2000 (2) Bom CR 251.
177. 103 (2003) DLT 139: 2003 (26) PTC 186 (Del).

work of the author. The defendant contented that the negative covenant in the contract was a restraint of trade. The court based on the ratio of the Supreme Court in *M/s. Gujarat Bottling Co. Ltd.* v. *Coca Cola Company,*[178] held that the terms were not a restraint of trade but were restrictions within the continuation of the contract.

In *National Publishing House* v. *Amit Sachdeva,*[179] the court examined the importance of handwritten addition to otherwise standard form contract to find out whether the agreement is an assignment or licence of copyright. The author of the book *Micro Economics Part I and II* entered into an agreement with the publisher for the publication of the book. The agreement is a "standard form contract" in which it was stated that the copyright would be with the publisher. But the author made a handwritten addition into Clause 8 of the agreement dealing with copyright retaining the copyright with the author. There was also an arbitration clause in the agreement. Since there was a breach of terms of the agreement, the author sent a letter terminating the contract. Both the parties filed suits and pleaded for interim relief. One of the contentions of the parties was regarding the nature of the agreement. It was contended by the publisher that the agreement is an assignment of copyright and on the other hand the author argued that the handwritten addition in the agreement makes it only a licence of right to publish. After examining Section 19 of the Act and the terms of the agreement the court concluded:[180]

> Although some of the terms of the contract appear to indicate that the publisher had a right for a period of five years, the handwritten inclusion into clause 8 should be given its full application. If this be so, there appears to be no manner of doubt, as subsequently clarified in the published version of the work, that the copyright vested with the author.

In a number of cases it has been seen the agreement merely amount to a publication agreement and could not be regarded as an assignment of copyright right.[181] Thus, it was contended[182] that since there is an arbitration clause in the agreement the parties are prevented from approaching the court for remedies on the ground of infringement and the publisher pleaded for an order of *status quo* till the disposal of arbitration. The court rejected this on the ground of balance of convenience and observed:

> Although, this at first flush appeared to be conducive to the balance of convenience, it subsequently appeared to be inopportune, since neither party would benefit from the *status quo* and it would negate the rights established *prima facie,* in favour of the author. The publisher can claim appropriate relief, *inter alia,* in the nature of rendition of accounts and damages in the context of subsequent publication carried out by the author. The publisher is not left without remedy. On the contrary if the publication of the work is interdicted and frozen it may render it outdated if the Arbitration proceedings are protracted over some years. In this case, it is the author who would suffer irreparable injury.

Thus, it is clear that even if there is an arbitration clause in the agreement it is not a bar for seeking remedy from normal courts.

---

178. AIR 1995 SC 2372: 1995 (5) SCC 545.
179. 90 (2001) DLT 697: 2001 PTC 437 (Del).
180. *See, National Publishing House* v. *Amit Sachdeva*, 90 (2001) DLT 697: 2001 PTC 437 (Del).
181. *See, China Cotton Exporters* v. *Beharilal Ramcharan Cotton Mills Ltd.*, AIR 1961 SC 1295: [1961]3 SCR 845; *William Butler Yeats* v. *Prof. Eric Dickinson*, AIR 1938 Lah 173; *Noorbhai Gulam Hussein Makali* v. *M. Allabux and Co.*, 42 Ind. Cas. (1917) 820.
182. *See, National Publishing House* v. *Amit Sachdeva*, 90 (2001) DLT 697: 2001 PTC 437 (Del).

Transfer by Licence Agreement

Section 30 of the Copyright Act 1957 provides provisions for transfer of copyright by granting of licenses. Thus the owner of copyright can transfer his rights in an existing or future work by way of a licence agreement. Explaining the scope and ambit of the "licence agreement" in copyright the Delhi High Court in *Novex Communication Pvt. Ltd.* v. *Lemon Tree Hotels Ltd.*,[183] observed: "A license is granted by the original owner of the copyright or by the assignee of the copyright. A licensee is not equal to the owner of the copyright. A licensee only has the right to use the copyright work as a licensee or if the license agreement so provides then to further license the work ahead including if the statutory licensee is a copyright society as per Section 33 of the Act." Section 30 of the Copyright Act provides that the owner of copyright in any existing work or prospective owner of copyright in any future work may grant any interest in the right by licence in writing signed by him or his duly authorised agent. In *Star India Private Limited* v. *Department of Industrial Policy*,[184] the Supreme Court held that the Copyright Act refers to the right to licence any interest in copyright by the author or his duly authorised agent.

The Copyright (Amendment) Act, 2012 has amended Section 30 by deleting the term "signed". Prior to the 2012 amendment, the licence deed had to be signed by the owner or prospective owner as the case may be. The requirement of signing has now been dispensed with.

Section 30 reads as under:

> "30. Licences by owners of copyright. The owner of the copyright in any existing work or the prospective owner of the copyright in any future work may grant any interest in the right by licence in [writing by him][32] or by his duly authorised agent:
>
> Provided that in the case of a licence relating to copyright in any future work, the licence shall take effect only when the work comes into existence.
>
> EXPLANATION—Where a person to whom a licence relating to copyright in any future work is granted under this Section dies before the work comes into existence, his legal representatives shall, in the absence of any provision to the contrary in the licence, be entitled to the benefit of the licence."

In *STAR India Private Limited* v. *Department of Industrial Policy*,[185] the Madras High Court clarified that under Section 30, a licence may be granted by the owner in favour of the licensee. Section 31D specifically mentions the requirement of the licence for broadcasting of literary and musical works and sound recording. Here again, it mandates a broadcasting organisation to pay the owner of the copyright the royalties and for that purpose maintain the accounts. Thus, even this provision speaks about the duty of the broadcasting agencies *vis* a *vis* the rights of the owner. In *Entertainment Network (India) Ltd.* v. *Super Cassettes Industries Ltd.*,[186] the Apex Court held that Section 30 provides for the licences by owners of copyright. It, in other words, deals with a situation where licence is granted on a voluntary basis. In *PVR Pictures Ltd.* v. Studio,[187] the Delhi High Court held that a licence in respect of any copyright, has to be in writing and the document should reflect the intention to grant

183. 2019 II AD (Delhi) 644.
184. (2019) 2 SCC 104: 2018 (14) SCALE 651.
185. 2018 (74) PTC 417 (Mad).
186. 2008 (37) PTC 353 (SC): (2008) 13 SCC 30.
187. 2009 (41) PTC 70 (Del).

the licence or assign the particular copyright. Similarly, in *Saregama India Ltd.* v. *Suresh Jindal*,[188] the Calcutta High Court held that a licence, in respect of any copyright, has to be in writing. Thus, the document in question must clearly reflect the intention to grant the licence or assign the particular copyright, as the case may be.

Where a person to whom a licence relating to copyright in any future work is granted under this Section dies before the work comes into existence, his legal representatives shall, in the absence of any provision to the contrary in the licence, be entitled to the benefit of the licence. Thus, where the original work is subject matter of copyright, it necessarily follows that the consent of the owner of that copyright must be obtained. In giving such consent, the owner may impose certain conditions which may restrict the public performance of records made from plate.[189] A joint owner of a copyright cannot, without the consent of the other joint owner, grant a licence or interest in it and the other joint owner aggrieved by such grant can sue the licence for infringement of the right. The joint owner guilty of such dealing will also be answerable to the other owners.[190] While in the case of an assignment, ownership of copyright is transferred, in the case of a licence; the licencee is only entitled to exploit the rights permitted according to the terms of the agreement. But to have effect before law, both the assignment and the licence agreement must be in writing and must be duly signed by the assignor or the licenser.[191] An oral assignment is neither permissible nor valid. Same is the case with a licence agreement. There also exists some confusion in distinguishing an assignment and a licence of rights, since the conditions regulating them are one and the same.

While an assignment deed transfers ownership of copyright, a licence agreement only allows the licencee to exploit the rights licenced. Mere usage of terminology, i.e., "assignment" or "licence" may not help to settle it, the House of Lords in *BBC* v. *Messenger*,[192] considered this. Here the Court held that although the term's "*licensor*" and "*Licensee*" are used throughout the agreement, upon the construction of the agreement it operated as an absolute assignment. So the distinction between an assignment and a licence is to be made looking into the real meaning of the agreement. The Punjab High Court followed this decision in *Dharam Dutt Dhawan* v. *Ram Lal Suri*,[193] to determine the case as that of a partial assignment. In this case, the appellant was the co-author of a Geometry textbook. He along with his co-author entered into an agreement with the respondent for printing and publishing the book. The dispute arose when the appellant in favour of another publisher revoked this agreement. The Court looked into the real meaning of the agreement and held it as one of partial assignments.

But in *Mishra Bandhu Karyalaya* v. *Shivratanlal Koshal*,[194] the Court adopted a different yardstick to distinguish an assignment from a licence. Here too the copyright owner entered into a publishing agreement with the defendant and revoked it for nonpayment of royalties. The defendant contended that because he has been assigned the publication right it couldn't be revoked. Here the Court held that, where the agreement between the author and his publisher

188. AIR 2006 Cal 340: 2007 (34) PTC 522 (Cal).
189. *See, Najma Heptulla* v. *Orient Longman Ltd.*, AIR 1989 Del 63: 36 (1988) DLT 31; *Wallington Cinema Co.* v. *Performing Rights Society Ltd.*, AIR 1937 Bom 472.
190. *Nav Sahitya Prakash* v. *Anand Kumar*, AIR 1981 All 200.
191. *See,* Sections 19 and 30 of the Copyright Act, 1957.
192. (1929) AC 151 (HL).
193. AIR 1953 Punj 279.
194. AIR 1970 MP 261: ILR (1973) MP 88.

contains no express terms as to copyright and where the consideration payable to the author is by way of royalties or a share of the profits instead of a sum of money paid down, the inference is that the copyright is not assigned, but that only a sole and exclusive licence is conferred upon the publisher. If the payment is in the form of a sum of money instead of payment of a share of profits, then the inference is that the agreement is one of an assignment rather than a licence. Here the Court solely relied on the consideration part of an agreement to distinguish a licence from an assignment. This again has confused the position regarding this. This can also not be considered to be an apt decision, as it is nowhere intended in the Act that an assignment is to be compensated in lump sum. In fact, the Act now visualises a part payment of profits as royalty during assignment as can be seen from Section 19. Going by this rationale, it prevents an assignor from insisting a likely share of the profit derived by the assignee from the assignment. This is also against the intention of the Act in rewarding the author.

In *Gramophone Company of India Ltd.* v. *Shanti Film Corporation*,[195] the Calcutta high Court examined the distinction between assignment and licensing of copyright. The *Shanti Films*, the owner of the film *Sharu* entered into an agreement with *Gramophone Company* for the production and distribution of the records of the film. According to the agreement, the owner was entitled to royalty as per the sale of the records. Based on the agreement, records were made and distributed. In 1995 the Gramophone Company noticed the publication of the cassettes of the film by the second defendant with the permission of *Shanti Films*. In a suit for infringement of copyright, it was argued by the plaintiff that since the defendant has assigned the copyright, for the production and sale of the records of the film to them, he had no further right to assign the same to the second defendant and the act of the second defendant thus constituted an infringement of the rights of the plaintiff. It was contended by the defendant that the agreement was not an assignment of right but only a licence to use the right. It was also contended that since no consideration was passed on to the defendant as royalty, the agreement should not be construed as an assignment looking into the words of the agreement. After referring to the cases on the distinction between assignment and licence the court observed:[196]

> The intention of the parties whether it was an assignment or a grant of permission to use should, in the normal course, be gathered from the writing itself and the words used therein. If the word 'assignment' is used then the assignment in the normal course be readily accepted. Payment of royalty in future on some given basis as consideration will not stand in the way of construing the intention to assign. In the event the writing contains covenants which indicate that assignor retains some right in spite of writing in relation to the copyright then the same may be either a partial assignment or a licence. In the even the grant is conditional then until fulfillment of the condition the assignment may not take effect. Similarly, if the assignor becomes entitled to any right on the happening of the particular thing then on the happening of such thing the assignor gets back such right. The assignment will take effect immediately. The most important thing, it appears to me, is the right of the recipient to deal with the copyright as owner thereof, i.e., right of the user or right to destroy the copyright at his own volition; any of which, if can be gathered, assignment can be readily accepted.

---

195. AIR 1997 Cal 63.
196. *See generally, Janathan Cape Ltd.* v. *Consolidated Press Ltd.*, 1994 (3) All ER 253; *Mishra Bandhu Karyalaya* v. *Shivratanlal Koshal*, AIR 1970 MP 261: 1970 MPLJ 475; *Chaplin* v. *Leslie Frewin (Publishers) Ltd.*, 1965 (3) All ER 764; *Savitri Devi* v. *Dwarka Prasad*, AIR 1939 All 305: (1939) ILR 61 All 275; *Messager* v. *British Broadcasting Co. Ltd.*, 1929 AC 151.

Transfer by Relinquishing Copyright

Section 21 of the Copyright Act 1957 declares the right of author to relinquish copyright and thus transfer of copyright is permitted by relinquishing copyright. The authors of literary, dramatic, musical or artistic works may relinquish copyright in their works, wholly or partially. The relinquishment can occur only by sending a notice in the prescribed form to the registrar of copyright who is under a duty to have it published in the official gazette (or in any other form).[197] The rights thus relinquished will cease to exist from the date of the notice. However, such relinquishment shall have no effect on the rights subsisting in favour of third persons. We do not know the number of philanthropic persons who have availed of the provisions of Section 21 of the Act described thus far. Not many authors normally know that the copyright in published or unpublished works generally subsists in them. In this situation, not many are likely to know that copyright can be relinquished by the simple device of a notice. The Section 21 reads thus:

> "21. Right of author to relinquish copyright—(1) The author of a work may relinquish all or any of the rights comprised in the copyright in the work by giving notice in the prescribed form to [the Registrar of Copyrights or by way of public notice][198] and thereupon such rights shall, subject to the provisions of sub-section (3), cease to exist from the date of the notice.
>
> (2) On receipt of a notice under sub-section (1), the Registrar of Copyrights shall cause it to be published in the Official Gazette and in such other manner as he may deem fit.
>
> [(2A) The Registrar of Copyrights—within fourteen days from the publication of the notice in the Official Gazette, post the notice on the official website of the Copyright Office so as to remain in the public domain for a period of not less than three years.][199]
>
> (3) The relinquishment of all or any of the rights comprised in the copyright in a work shall not affect any rights subsisting in favour of any person on the date of the notice referred to in sub-section (1)."

In *Syndicate* v. *B.D. Bhandari*,[200] the issue before the Delhi High Court was that whether the prescription of the book by Guru Nanak Dev University would mean that the owner, i.e., the appellant has relinquished its copyright by dedicating the same in public domain. Referring the Section 21 of the Copyright Act 1957 the Court held that the owner of the copyright can, thus, relinquish his rights by giving notice in the prescribed form to the Registrar of Copyrights. In the present case such notice given by the appellant manifests its intention to relinquish its copyright. It would naturally follow that merely because the book in question prescribed by the University for its students would not mean that the author is snatched of its

197. *See*, Francina Cantatore and Jane Johnston, "Moral Rights: Exploring the Myths, Meanings and Misunderstandings in Australian Copyright Law," 21(1) *Deakin Law Review* (2016) pp. 71–92; Navdeep Kour Sasan, "Rights of the Author: Possible Extensions under Copyright Law in India," 2(2) *International Journal of Innovation and Applied Studies* (2013) pp. 104–112.
198. Substituted by the Copyright (Amendment) Act, 2012 (Act 27 of 2012), Section 11(i) for "the Registrar of Copyrights" [w.e.f. 21-6-2012].
199. Newly substituted by the Copyright (Amendment) Act, 2012 (Act 27 of 2012), Section 11(ii) [w.e.f. 21-6-2012].
200. 2011 (47) PTC 244 (Del): 185 (2011) DLT 346.

copyright. Thus, in *Dhiraj Dharamdas Dewani* v. *Sonal Info Systems Pvt. Ltd.*,[201] the Bombay High Court held that the Section 21 of the Copyright Act provides for right of author to relinquish copyright where upon the said relinquishment is published in the official gazette by the Registrar.

One assumes, although the Copyright Act does not specify it, that relinquishment should be an act of free will and that like the requirement of consent in contract, it will be vitiated if it can be shown that the Act of relinquishment was a product of coercion, undue influence, fraud or misrepresentation. Indeed, since the mere giving of the notice produces cessation of copyright in whole or part, it might be desirable to provide an explanation to Section 21 clarifying that the act of relinquishment must be a product of free will of an author in sound mind: and that ordinarily the registrar should satisfy herself that this is the case before the cessation becomes operative. Although cases of relinquishment may be rare, the need to adequately protect the author relinquishing copyright justifies the suggested changes. Thus, Section 21 deals with the right of author to relinquish copyright. The author of the work may relinquish all or any of the rights comprised in the copyright in the work by giving notice in the prescribed form to the Registrar of Copyrights. The sub-section (2) mandated that the Registrar shall cause the notice to be published in the Official Gazette. This procedure is arguably cumbersome.

The Copyright (Amendment) Act, 2012 amended Sub-section 1 of Section 21 to facilitate relinquishment of copyright either by giving notice to the Registrar of Copyrights or by way of public notice. With this amendment, authors have the right to relinquish copyright through public notice. Sub-section 2 has also been amended to provide that in cases where Registrar receives such a notice, he shall, within 14 days of publication of the notice in the official gazette, post the notice on the official website of the Copyright Office so as to remain in the public domain for a period of not less than three years.

RECOGNISED RIGHTS OF COPYRIGHT OWNER

Copyright is not a common law right or a natural right and is purely a creation of statute. Thus, unless such copyright has roots in the statute, there is no such right. Further, copyright is not a positive right but an exclusionary right i.e. a right to prevent others from doing certain things. Save for what is provided in the statute, there is no other right.[202] One of the important features of the copyright law is that it specifically identifies the nature of the rights enjoyed by the owners of different categories of works of author. These rights are based on the possible mode of commercial exploitation of the subject matter of protection. Such modes of exploitation are depending upon the subject-matter. Thus, the nature and content of these rights differs which are based on the nature of a particular work.[203]

---

201. 2012 (52) PTC 458 (Bom): 2012 (114) BomLR 2251.
202. *See, Raj Rewal* v. *Union of India*, 260 (2019) DLT 190; *Chancellor* v. *Rameshwari Photocopy Services*, 2016 (68) PTC 386 (Del): 233 (2016) DLT 279.
203. *See, Novex Communication Private Ltd.* v. *National Restaurant Association of India*, 2018 (75) PTC 179 (Del): 249 (2018) DLT 18. *Gramophone Company of India Ltd.* v. *Super Cassettes Industries Ltd.*, MIPR 2010 (2) 349: 2010 (44) PTC 541 (Del); *Tobu Enterprises (P) Ltd* v. *M/s Joginder Metal Works*, AIR 1985 Delhi 244; (1985) ILR 2 Delhi 638; *R.G. Anand* v. *Delux Films*, AIR 1978 SC 1613: (1978) 4 SCC 118; *Calico Printers Association* v. *Savani*, 1939 (41) Bom LR 45.

In *Microfibres Inc.* v. *Girdhar and Co.*,[204] the court rightly observed: "the legislative intent is also to be kept in mind which is to provide protection for a certain period of time for commercial exploitation. Thus, nature of protection is quite different for an artistic work under the Copyright Act which is for the lifetime of the author/creator plus 60 years. This is not so in the case of commercial exploitation as under the Designs Act and the Patent Act the period is much lesser." Considering this variation, *inter alia*, the courts have also interpreted and expanded the nature and scope of the rights granted by the statute. The scheme of the Indian Copyright Act, 1957 with respect to different kinds of rights is as under:

1. Section 14 gives certain rights to the copyright owner which are commonly referred to as "exclusive economic rights" of copyright owner. Thus, the purpose of copyright law is to provide the owner of a copyright with specific exclusive economic rights.[205]
2. Section 37 specifies a special right called "broadcast reproduction rights" to every broadcasting organisation.[206]
3. Section 38A specifies performers' rights. The Copyright (Amendment) Act 2012 has given moral rights to the performers also.[207]
4. Section 57 specifies two special rights to authors, who are the first owners of copyright. These are called "author's moral rights".[208]

Thus, under the copyright law, owners of copyright have a large variety of rights with respect to the works owned by them. Broadly speaking, four classless of rights are conferred by the Copyright Act, 1957. These rights can be broadly classified into four groups: (i) exclusive economic rights of copyright owner, (ii) author's moral rights, (iii) broadcast reproduction rights and (iv) performers' rights. The "exclusive economic rights" of the copyright owner are those rights that help the authors to enjoy economic benefits. These rights could be transferred to anyone who has the capacity for commercial exploitation.[209] These rights includes reproduction rights, distribution rights, communication rights, public performance rights, translation rights, adaptation rights, etc., with respect to literary, dramatic and musical works and also commercial rental or lending rights with respect to computer programs, cinematograph film and sound recordings. Communication rights also include broadcasting and cable casting rights. With the development of technology, the scope of communication to public is also expanding with incredulous pace.

While exclusive economic rights of copyright owner are available to every owner of copyright, the moral rights are available to the author alone. The "author's moral rights" may be classified into four classes: (i) the right to be identified as the author of a work,

---

204. 2006 (32) PTC 157 (Del): 128 (2006) DLT 238. *See also*, *Micolube India Limited* v. *Rakesh Kumar*, 199 (2013) DLT 740; *Dart Industries Inc.* v. *Techno Plast*, 2007 (35) PTC 129 (Del): 2007 (35 PTC 285 (Del).
205. *See*, *Microfibres Inc* v. *Girdhar*, 2006 (32) PTC 157 (Del): 128 (2006) DLT 238; *R. Madhavan* v. *S. K. Nayar*, AIR 1988 Ker 39: 1987 KLJ 942.
206. *See*, *Kajal Agarwal* v. *The Managing Director*, 2018 (5) CTC 185: (2018) 5 MLJ 818.
207. *See*, *Sanjay Kumar Gupta* v. *Sony Pictures Networks India P. Ltd.*, AIR 2018 Delhi 169: 2018 (75) PTC 562 (Del).
208. *See*, *Super Cassette Industries* v. *Bathla Cassette Industries*, 107 (2003) DLT 91: 2003 (27) PTC 280 (Del).
209. *See*, *Anand Bhushan* v. *Union of India*, 2018 (75) PTC 106 (Del): 2018 VI AD (Delhi) 153

(ii) the right of an author of a work, the "integrity right",[210] (iii) a general right, that every person has, not to have a work falsely attributed to him, and (iv) right against piracy. Besides these economic and moral rights, the Act also recognises certain analogous rights, which emanates incidental to copyrighted works. They are the performers' rights and the broadcaster's rights, often termed as "neighbouring rights" under international conventions. Neighbouring rights are adjunct to those of the primary copyright holder. The Copyright (Amendment) Act, 2012 has inserted a new Section 38B[211] whereby moral rights have been ascribed to the performers too.

Exclusive Economic Rights of the Copyright Owner

Statutory Scheme

Section 14 of the Copyright Act, 1957 recognises exclusive economic rights. The Section provides that "copyright", means the exclusive right subject to the provisions of this Act, to do or authorise the doing of any of the acts, with respect to a work or any substantial part thereof as specified in Section 14 enumerated in sub-clauses (a) to (e). Naturally, exclusive economic rights under the Copyright Act are to be determined under Section 14 along with other provisions like Sections 51, 52, etc.[212] For example, in respect of a single sound recording, the owner of the copyright has the exclusive right to make any other sound recording embodying it including storing it in any medium be electronic or other means. In respect of the same sound recording, he also has the right to sell or give on commercial rental or offer for sale or for such rental, any copy of the sound recording. He also has the right to communicate the same sound recording to the public. Explaining the elements of Section 14, in *Tips Industries Ltd.* v. *Wynk Music Ltd.*,[213] the Bombay High Court observed:

> Section 14 of the Copyright Act provides the meaning of copyright for the purposes of this Act. It provides that for the purposes of this Act, copyright means the exclusive right to do or authorise doing of any of the acts given in sub sections (a) to (e) in respect of work or any substantial part thereof subject to the other provisions of the Act. The meaning of copyright in respect of sound recording is provided in Section 14(1)(e) of the Act. A bare perusal of Section 14(1)(e) of the Act would reveal that three broad categories of rights have been contemplated in respect of sound recordings. These three categories of rights are provided in Section 14(1)(e)(i), Section 14(1)(e)(ii) and Section 14(1)(e)(iii) of the Act. These three categories of rights are independent and distinct of each other.[214]

---

210. In *C. Golak Nath* v. *State of Punjab*, the Supreme Court observed that all private property is a system of monopolies and the right to monopolise lies at the foundation of the institution of property and in classifying *right in rem* puts private property along with personal integrity [right against injury to life, body and health (body or mental), personal liberty (free motion and locomotion)], Society and control of one's family and dependents.
211. Inserted by the Copyright (Amendment) Act, 2012 [w.e.f. 21-6-2012] Section 27.
212. *See, Holland L.P.* v. *A.D. Electro Stell Co. Pvt. Ltd.*, 2017 (70) PTC 512 (Del).
213. MANU/MH/0862/2019.
214. *See also, International Confederation of Societies of Authors* v. *Aditya Pandey*, (2017) 11 SCC 437: 2016 (68) PTC 472 (SC); *Entertainment Network (India) Limited* v. *Super Cassette Industries Limited*, 2008 (9) SCALE 69: (2008) 13 SCC 30; *Indian Performing Right Society Ltd.* v. *Aditya Pandey*, 2012 (50) PTC 460 (Del): MIPR 2012 (2) 140.

Thus, in *Super Cassettes Industries Limited* v. *Mr. Chintamani Rao*,[215] it was held that the right conferred by Section 14 is subject to the other provisions of the Act, which would include Section 52. Section 52 of the Act states that when a copyright in a work is infringed, it, *inter alia,* states that "copyright in a work shall be deemed to be infringed when any person, without a licence granted by the owner of the copyright or the Registrar of Copyrights under this Act, or in contravention of the conditions of a licence so granted or of any condition imposed by a competent authority under this Act. Further, in *Nazir Hussain* v. *Dookhmochan Thakur 'Door-Vadal'*,[216] it also held that infringement of copyright is of two types, direct and indirect. Clause (a) of Section 51 deals with direct infringement of copyright. This clause makes it an infringement of copyright if any person does anything, the exclusive right to do which is, by this Act conferred upon the owner of the copyright. What these exclusive economic rights of copyright owner are is provided by Section 14. Clause (b) of Section 51 deals with an indirect infringement. Section 14 defines the term "copyright". It means the exclusive right to do certain things which are specified in the Section.

In connection to Section 14 of the Copyright Act 1957 the Bombay High Court in *Music Broadcast Private Ltd.* v. *Indian Performing Right Society Ltd.*,[217] held that Section 14 stipulates the exclusive right to do or authorise the doing of the acts mentioned therein in respect of a work or any substantial part thereof. Rights which may be exercised in respect of each class of work are stipulated in Section 14. However, Section 14 does not indicate any order of priority between the different classes of works. Nor does it place any particular work above the others. It merely prescribes the rights that can be exercised in respect of each class of work. The nature and content of the rights vary according to the nature of the work. So they are separately specified in Section 14. In case of a literary, dramatic or musical work, the rights include the right:

1. to reproduce the work in any material form including the storing of it in any medium by electronic means;[218]
2. to issue copies of the work to the public not being copies already in circulation;[219]
3. to perform the work in public, or to communicate to the public;[220]
4. to make any cinematographic film or sound recording in respect of the work;[221]
5. to make any translation of the works;[222]
6. to make any adaptation of the work;[223] and
7. to do, in relation to a translation or an adaptation of the work, any of the acts specified in relation to the work in sub-clauses (i) to (vi) of Section 14(a).[224]

215. 2012 (49) PTC 1 (Del).
216. 1969 (17) BLJR 12.
217. MIPR 2011 (3) 84: 2011 (47) PTC 587 (Bom). *See also, Indian Performing Right Society Ltd.* v. *Aditya Pandey*, MIPR 2012 (2) 140: 2012 (50) PTC 460 (Del).
218. *See, Music Choice India Private Limited* v. *Phonographic Performance Limited*, MIPR 2010 (1) 162: 2010 (44) PTC 171 (Bom); *Bharati Cellular Ltd.* v. *Jai Distillers P. Ltd.*, AIR 2007 Bom 33: 2006 (33) PTC 220 (Bom).
219. *See, Adai Mehra Production Pvt. Ltd.* v. *Mr. Sumeet P. Mehra*, 2013 (3) ABR 1273; *Rupalli R. Shah* v. *Adani Wilmer Ltd.*, 2012 (52) PTC 305 (Bom); *Samsonite Corporation* v. *Vijay Sales*, 73 (1998) DLT 732.
220. *Satyam Infoway Ltd.* v. *Sifynet Solutions (P.) Ltd.*, AIR 2004 SC 3540: 2004 (28) PTC 566 (SC).
221. *Eastern Book Company* v. *D.B. Modak*, 101 (2002) DLT 205.
222. *Samsonite Corporation* v. *Vijay Sales*, 73 (1998) DLT 732.
223. *West Bengal Board of Secondary Education* v. *Standard Book Co.*, 70 CWN 1130.
224. Copyright Act 1957, Section 14(a).

As far as a computer program is concerned, in addition to the rights given to the literary work, the owner has the right to sell or give on commercial rental, or offer for sale or commercial rental any copy of the computer program. But this rental right is not available in respect of computer programs where the program itself is not the essential object of the rental. In the case of an artistic work, the rights are: (i) the right to reproduce the work in any material form including depiction in three dimensions of a two-dimensional work or in two dimensions of a three-dimensional work; (ii) to communicate the work to the public; (iii) to issue copies of the work to the public not being copies already in circulation; (iv) to include the work in any cinematographic film; (v) to make any adaptation of the work, and (vi) to do in relation to an adaptation of the work any of the acts specified above. In *Dy. Commissioner of Income Tax* v. *Metapath Software International Ltd.*,[225] the Delhi High Court pointed out that the term copyright has not been defined in the Act and therefore reliance can be placed on its definition as per Section 14 of the Copyright Act, 1957. The term copyright, in the case of computer software, means the exclusive right to do or authorise the doing of the following acts:

1. To reproduce the work in any material from including the storing of it in any medium by electronic means;[226]
2. To issue copies of the work to the public, not being copies already in circulation;[227]
3. To perform the work in the public, or communicate it to the public;[228]
4. To make any translation/adaptation of the work;[229]
5. To sell or give the software on hire.[230]

In the case of a cinematographic film and sound recordings are concerned, the owner has the right to make a copy of the film including a photograph of any image forming part thereof or storing of it in any medium by electronic or other means as the case may be; the right to sell or give on hire or offer for sale or hire, any copy of the film or sound recording, regardless of whether such copy has been sold or given on commercial rental or offer for sale or for such rental and the right to communicate the film or sound recording to the public.[231]

The exclusive economic rights of authors of literary, artistic, dramatic and musical works of artistic works and of cinematograph films, sound recording, and computer program are in certain respects similar; they are reproduced in Table 5.1.

As stated in Table 5.1, the exclusive economic rights include the right to reproduction, distribution or communication to public. In addition to this in case of computer programs, films and sound records, a rental right too is provided. The scope of some of these rights were examined by the courts and given expanded meaning to accommodate the new enjoyment of these rights due to technological changes.

---

225. [2006] 9 SOT 305 (Delhi).
226. *See, IPEG Inc.* v. *Kay Bee Engineers*, AIR 2016 Guj 104: 2016 (66) PTC 305 (Guj).
227. *See, Thiagarajan Kumararaja* v. *Capital Film Works (India) Pvt. Ltd.*, 2018 (73) PTC 365 (Mad); *Prince Rubber Industries* v. *K.S. Rubber Industries*, 1983 (3) PTC 34 (Del).
228. *See, Super Cassettes Industries* v. *Chintamani Rao*, 2012 (49) PTC 1 (Del).
229. *See, Managing Director* v. *Sradhananda Jena*, 2018 (4) Crimes 184 (Ori.).
230. *See, Commissioner of Income Tax* v. *Kiran Kapoor*, (2015) 274 CTR (Del) 343: [2015] 372 ITR 321 (Delhi); *Asstt. Commissioner of Income Tax* v. *Amadeus India (P) Ltd.*, [2001] 79 ITD 407 (Delhi).
231. Inserted by the Copyright (Amendment) Act 2012 [w.e.f. 21-6-2012] Section 5(ii).

Table 5.1 Exclusive Economic Rights

Column	*Subjects*	*Rights*
A.	Literary, dramatic or musical work, artistic work.	(i) Right to reproduce the work in any material form [Section 14(a)(i); (c)(i)]. (ii) Right to publish the work [Section 14(a)(ii); (c)(ii)]. (iii) Right to make any adaptation of the work [Section 14(a)(vii); (c)(vi)].
B.	Literary, dramatic or musical work [see also column (A)]	(i) Right to perform the work in public [Section 14(a)(iii)]. (ii) Right to produce, perform, or publish any translation of the work [Section 14(a)(vii)].
C.	Oral works	(i) Right to ownership of an address of speech delivered in public vests in the speaker [Section 17(cc)]. (ii) Right to make a cinematograph film or a record in respect of the work [Section 14(d)]. (iii) Right to communicate the work by radio diffusion or of public communication through amplifier [Section 14(a)(vi)].
D.	Artistic work (see also column A)	(i) Right to include the work in any cinematograph film [Section 14(b)(iv)].
E.	Cinematograph film	(i) Right to make a copy of the film [Section 14(d)(i)]. (ii) Right to sell or given on hire or offer for sale of hire any coy of the film [Section 14(d)(ii)]. (iii) Right to communicate the film to the public [Section 14(d)(iii)].
F.	Sound Records	(i) Right to make any other recording embodying the recording [Section 14(e)(i)]. (ii) Right to sell or given on hire, or offer for sale or hire any copy of the sound recording [Section 14(e)(ii)]. (iii) Right to communicate the sound recording to the public [Section 14(e)(iii)].
G.	In respect of all genres of work	(i) Right of total or partial assignment (Section 18), testamentary disposition (Section 20) and relinquishment (Section 21). (ii) Right to "paternity" (that is, "right to claim authorship of the work" despite assignment, total or partial). (iii) Right to "integrity" in works (that is, right to object to distortions, mutilations of work, which prejudice author's honour or reputation) (Section 57).
H.	Computer Program	(i) Similar right in case literary, dramatic or musical work [Section 14(b)(i)]. (ii) Right to sell or commercial rental Right [Section 14(b)(ii)].

Right to Reproduction of the Work in any Material Form

Right to reproduction of the work in any material form is one of the basic rights available to a copyright owner as recognised under Section 14 of the Copyrights Act, 1957. To "reproduce" means to produces again; to produce a copy. It may be an exact copy or an imitation. It is the action or process of bringing again before the mind in the same form. The word "reproduction" is a term of art and is used in commercial sense. Right to reproduce is not for the convenience of the user but for the purpose of distribution.[232] However, Section 14 used different terminology for recognising this right. The scope of this right also differs. While one can see the term "reproduction" is used in the case of literary, dramatic, musical and artistic works, it is the words "make any copy" and "make any sound recording" that are the terminology used in case of cinematograph film and sound recording to recognise this right. The Copyright Act, however, does not define the term "reproduction" or "copy". However, in connection to the copyright in *Gurukrupa Mech Tech Pvt. Ltd.* v. *State of Gujarat*,[233] the Gujarat High Court held that copyright exists even without it being registered for the purposes of its enforcement. The nature of copyright is also meant to be borne in mind. It subsists in any material form in which ideas are translated. Thus, the Supreme Court with respect to the reproduction into a three-dimensional medium in copyright in *Midas Hygiene Private Limited* v. *Sudhir Bhatia*,[234] observed:

> "It is the exclusive right of the holder of a Copyright in an original artistic work to reproduce the work in any material form. For example, a drawing of an imaginary futuristic automobile, which is an original artistic work, may be reproduced in the three-dimensional material form using an element, such as a metal sheet."

Concept of Right to Reproduction

In order to explain the meaning of term "reproduction" or "copy", the Bombay High Court in *Star India (P) Ltd.* v. *Leo Burnett India (P) Ltd.*,[235] discussed the following points some of which were: (1) What is the meaning of right to reproduce under Section 14(d) of the Copyright Act of 1957 with respect to the cinematograph film? (2) Is reproduction right of cinematograph film different from that granted in case of literary, dramatic, musical or artistic works? They, while explaining the meaning of the term "reproduction" and the "copy of the work", used in Section 14 with respect to the literary, dramatic, musical, artistic works or computer programs, on one hand and that for the cinematograph film and sound recording on the other, held that their extent varies in degree only, where one confers the exclusive right to reproduce the work in any mater form in case of the former category of works and in the latter to make copy of the respective works, which means making of the physical copy of the film itself. The scope of the right to reproduce a work, thus, depends upon the nature of the subject matter in question. As in case of literary works, the reproduction right stretches to a series of works, which are considered as literary works under Section 2(o) of the Copyright (Amendment) Act, 1994.

---

232. *State Bank of India* v. *Collector of Customs* (2000) 1 SCC 727: [2000] 1 SCR 137.
233. (2018) 4 GLR 3324. *See also*,
234. (2004) 3 SCC 90: 2004 (2) SCALE 231.
235. (2003) 27 PTC 81 Bom.

A question may arise whether an abridgement of a literary work is entitled for copyright protection? The owner of the copyright can prevent others from reducing the contents of the work and by simply omitting certain material and copying some, and then claiming copyright on it. As abridgement of the work involves a sense of judging the things, skill, labour, etc., every abridgement does not entitle the creator of the abridged work a copyright in that work. A genuine abridgement of the work amounts to the creation of an original work, which can entitle the author of that work with the copyright. It is well recognised in copyright law that copying certain passages and omitting others would not entitle the author of that work a copyright and a digest of any literary work is an abridgement. In *Raghunathan* v. *All India Reporter*,[236] the Bombay High Court held that a genuine abridgement of the literary work is an original work and is the subject matter of copyright abridgement amounts to the reproduction of an original work in a much more precise and concise way. An analysis of clauses (a), (b) and (c) to Section 14 of the Copyright Act, 1957 show that the right to reproduction constitutes only one of the bundles of rights accorded to a copyright owner of literary, dramatic, musical or artistic work. The "right to reproduction" is not given to the copyright owner of cinematograph films and sound recordings but the "right to make a copy" is given instead. The right to translation, right to adaptation, right to performance of work, etc., also involves reproduction in the generic sense of the term. Whether this difference is justified? Whether right to reproduction is an umbrella right or a residuary right? In case of artistic work, Section 14(c)(i) gave the right to reproduce the work in any material form to the copyright owner but the right to store the work in any medium by electronic means was not given. The Copyright (Amendment) Act, 2012 has removed this lacuna and included storing of work to the right of reproduction in case of artistic work also. However, in case of artistic works, the right is elaborated to include depiction in three dimensions of a two-dimensional work or in two dimensions of a three-dimensional work.[237]

ILLUSTRATION

Ms. Ritu Kumar draws designs of garments at Mumbai and exhibits the same at her showroom at Kolkata. Ms. Madhu Bala without obtaining permission from Ritu Kumar makes garments using these designs for commercial purpose. In this case Ms. Madhu Bala violated the copyright of Ms. Ritu Kumar in her designs as she has converted a two-dimensional work into three-dimensional work without licence from the copyright owner Ms. Ritu Kumar.

In *Indian Performing Right Society Ltd.* v. *Aditya Pandey*,[238] the Delhi High Court observed that the underlying words and music are necessarily and automatically reproduced upon reproduction of the sound recording, there was no reason for the Parliament to provide for a separate and distinct right under Section 14(a)(iv) (right to make cinematographic film or sound recording in respect of the work), when the right to reproduction under Section 14(a)(i) already existed. The legislative intent in providing for a separate exclusive right in making of a sound recording based on the lyrics and music makes it clear that the owner of the musical work and accompanying lyrics can continue to exercise its rights of reproduction in relation

236. AIR 1971 Bom. 48.
237. Inserted by the Copyright (Amendment) Act, 2012 [w.e.f. 21-6-2012] Section 14(c)(i).
238. MIPR 2011 (3) 19: 2011 (47) PTC 392 (Del).

to other reproductions, even after losing its copyright in making of a sound recording and its natural and consequent exploitation by way of communication to the public/broadcast. Thus, even on a harmonious reading of Section 14(a)(iii) and 14(e)(iii), the right in 14(a)(iii) can be effectively exercised in relation to other communications to the public of the musical works and lyrics other than that sound recording, in respect of which the rights have been transferred.

In *Periyar Self Respect Propaganda Institution* v. *Periyar Dravidar Kazhagam*,[239] the petitioner filed application challenging republication of works of X by respondents by contending that same amount to infringement of copyright of petitioner over said work. Thus, in this case, the issue was whether re-publication of works of X by respondents amounts to infringement of copyright of petitioner. The Madras High Court held that X was writer of re-published work. The work, in question, is a kind of article, published in newspapers mostly related to the then existed economic, political, social and religious topics. Therefore, unless X had expressly reserved his right of reproduction, no copyright will vest with anyone and reproduction of such articles cannot constitute infringement of copyright as per Section 52(1)(m) of the Copyrights Act, 1957.

The concept of reproduction has been discussed in the House of Lords decision of *Ladbroke (Football) Ltd.* v. *William Hill (Football) Ltd.*[240] In this case, the respondent was a well-known publisher of football booking coupons, which also contained the list of matches to be played. The respondent claims copyright in the coupon and alleged that the appellants have copied the coupon. While holding that the appellants have infringed the copyright of the respondents by copying not only the pieces of information in the coupon but also its style and arrangement Lord Reid observed:

> Broadly reproduction means copying, and does not include cases where an author or computer produces a substantially similar result by independent work without copying. If he does copy, the question whether he has copied a substantial part depends much more on the quality than on the quantity of what he has taken. One test may be whether the part, which he has taken, is novel or striking, or is merely a matter of commonplace arrangement of ordinary words or well-known data. So it may sometimes be a convenient shortcut to ask whether the part taken could by itself be the subject of copyright. But in my view, that is only a short cut, and the correct approach is first to determine whether the plaintiffs work as a whole is original and protected by copyright, and then inquires whether the part taken by the defendant is substantial.

Similarly, in *Francis Day and Hunter Ltd.* v. *Bron*,[241] the Court of Appeal held:

> In order to constitute a reproduction there must be both sufficient objective similarity between the two works and some casual connection between the work infringed and the infringer's work.

In determining whether piracy has been effected from the original work and substantially reproduced, adopted or copied in making cinematograph film, is subject of consideration in judicial and extra-judicial dicta.[242] Referring above decision[243] in *Barbara Taylor Bradford* v. *Sahara Media Entertainment Ltd.*,[244] the Calcutta High Court held that in copyright

239. MIPR 2010 (1) 5: 2009 (41) PTC 448 (Mad).
240. [1964] 1 All ER 465: [1964] 1 WLR 273.
241. (1963) Ch D 583.
242. *See, K. Marari* v. *Muppala Ranganayakamma*, MANU/ AP/ 0276/ 1987.
243. *See, Francis Day and Hunter Ltd.* v. *Bron*, (1963) Ch D 583.
244. 2004 (28) PTC 474 (Cal): [2003] 47 SCL 445 (Cal).

infringement appeal against infringement of copyright of book in question plaintiff filed without any *prima facie* basis similarities between original work and television serial alleged to be the copy of original work found to be sketchy, basic and spars law protects originality of expression such originality of artistic works must not become overprotection curbing down future artistic works if plots and characters allowed to be protected by copyright original artist could not write anything "original" at all appeal dismissed. But, the court held that a substantial reproduction of a copyrighted work is sufficient to make it a copy. In *Mohendra Chandra* v. *Emperor*,[245] the Calcutta High Court has clarified that a copy is that which comes to near the original, as to suggest that original to the mind of every person seeing it. Thus, there is no reproduction if there is no copying of the works and the defendant makes his own version.

Reproduction in case of literary, dramatic or musical works includes the reproduction of the work in any material form including the storage of it in any medium by electronic means. In *Microsoft Corporation* v. *Vijay Kaushik*,[246] the Court held that Section 14 of the Copyright Act, to the extent relevant, provides that copyright means the exclusive rights subject to the provisions of the Act, to do or authorise the doing of specified acts in respect of a work or any substantial part thereof, which in the case of a computer program would include to reproduce the work in any material form including the storing of it any medium by electronic means. Thus, even storage of the work in electronic means such as floppy discs, CD-ROMs or in computers shall be deemed to be a reproduction. This has been incorporated to guard the interest of right holders in the digital context. In the case of cinematograph films and sound recordings, the definition clause itself brings digital fixations within the scope of reproduction. But the term storage has not been defined. There is a possibility of including temporary storage also within reproduction right. This may create problems for the Internet users and service providers there by tilting the traditional balance of copyright law.

Right to Reproduction in Artistic Work

The right to reproduction of artistic work is recognised under Section 14 (c) of the Copyright Act 1957 as "to reproduce the work". Section 14(c) provides that "in the case of an artistic work, to reproduce the work in any material form including: (i) the storing of it in any medium by electronic or other means; or (ii) depiction in three-dimensions of a two-dimensional work; or (iii) depiction in two-dimensions of three dimensional work."[247] In *MRF Limited* v. *Metro Tyres Limited*,[248] the Delhi High Court held that the meaning of the right "to reproduce the work" in case of literary dramatic, musical work, computer programme and artistic work differs from the cinematograph film and sound recording. Thus, the Court citing *Star India Private Limited* v. *Leo Burnett (India) Pvt. Ltd.*,[249] the Bombay High Court contrasting Sections 14(d) and (e) on the one hand and Sections 14(a), (b) and (c) on the other, observed that in the latter case the owner of the copyright has exclusive right to reproduce the work in

245. AIR 1928 Cal 359.
246. MIPR 2011 (2) 362: 2011 (48) PTC 127 (Del).
247. Substituted by the Copyright (Amendment) Act, 2012 (Act 27 of 2012), Section 5(i), for sub-clause (i) [w.e.f. 21-6-2012].
248. MANU/ DE/ 2037/ 2019. *See also, IPEG Inc.* v. *Kay Bee Engineers*, AIR 2016 Guj 104: 2016 (66) PTC 305 (Guj).
249. (2003) 27 PTC 81 (Bom): 2003 (2) BomCR 655.

any material form. This is absent and excluded insofar as the former case (cinematograph film/ sound recording). The exclusive right in the former is to copy the recording of a particular film/sound recording. It is, therefore, clear that production by another person of even the same cinematographic film does not constitute infringement of a copyright in a cinematograph film. It is only when actual copy is made of a film by a process of duplication i.e. by using mechanical contrivance that it falls under section 14(d)(i).

Further, in *Raj Rewal* v. *Union of India*,[250] the Delhi High Court held that: (i) artistic work includes a work of architecture and the author thereof is the architect; (ii) vide Section 13(1)(a) of the Copyright Act, copyright subsists in such artistic work; Section 13(5) only clarifies that the said copyright subsists only in artistic character and design and does not extend to process and methods of construction; (iii) vide Section 14(c) of the Act, copyright in the case of artistic work confers in the architect, the exclusive right to reproduce the work in any form; (iv) the Copyright Act does not make any distinction between the medium on which the artistic works is executed. In *Dart Industries Inc*. v. *Techno Plast*,[251] the Court held that it is the exclusive right of the holder of a copyright in an original artistic work to reproduce the work in any material form. For example, a drawing of an imaginary futuristic automobile, which is an original artistic work, may be reproduced in the three-dimensional material form using an element, such as a metal sheet.

In *Polymer Papers Ltd.* v. *Gurmit Singh,*[252] the court considered the effect of Section 2(c) of the Copyright Act and Section 11 of the Designs Act to come to the conclusion that industrial drawings and designs in which copyright was claimed were for purposes of manufacturing of filter related machines or components and as such clearly fell within the meaning of "design" as defined in the Designs Act, 2000 and since the alleged designs had not been registered under the Designs Act, the plaintiff in the suit could not claim any copyright therein.

In *Microforms Inc.* v. *Girdhar and Co.*,[253] the court held that in order for the work of the plaintiff to qualify as an "artistic work", it must fall within the definition of Sub-section (c) of Section 2 of the Copyright Act. A reading of the said provision would show that attempt of the plaintiff can only be to bring it within the concept of "painting". The comparison with the painting of M.F. Hussain would be otiose as the work in question, in the present case, is not a piece of art by itself in the form of a painting. There is no doubt that labour has been put and there is some innovativeness applied to put a particular configuration in place. Such configuration is of the motifs and designs which by themselves would not be original. The originality is being claimed on the basis of the arrangement made. What cannot be lost sight of is the very objective with which such arrangements or works had been made. The objective is to put them to industrial use. An industrial process has to be done to apply the work or configuration to the textile. It is not something which has to be framed and put on the wall or would have any utility by itself. The two important aspects are the object with which it is made (which is industrial) and its inability to stand by itself as a piece of art. In fact, it has no independent existence of itself.

---

250. 260 (2019) DLT190.
251. 2016 (67) PTC 457 (Del): 233 (2016) DLT 1.
252. 2002 (25) PTC 327 (Del).
253. 128 (2006) DLT 238: 2006 (32) PTC 157 (Del).

In the case of artistic works, reproduction of the works in any material form, for example, photography, videography, etc., is sufficient to constitute reproduction under the Act. Apart from the material form, reproduction includes the depiction of a two-dimensional work into a three-dimensional one or vice-versa. The Delhi High Court in *Escorts Construction Equipment Ltd.* v. *Action Construction Equipment Ltd.*,[254] reiterated this position. The Court held an industrial drawing as an original artistic work and any conversion of it into a three-dimensional article as a reproduction of the drawing. Going by this decision, any reproduction of sculptures and other art objects into a two-dimensional one, i.e., paintings, sketches, photographs, etc., and any reproduction of a two-dimensional work vice-versa without proper authorisation becomes actionable under copyright law. A reproduction is also deemed to have taken place if there is substantial copying of an earlier work. No hard and fast rule can be laid to determine this substantiality component. It has to be tested upon the facts and circumstances of each case. It is to be noted that reproduction right of artistic work in digital format is not expressly protected.

Right to Reproduction in Cinematograph Film or Sound Recording

There are six categories of rights that have been enumerated in the Section 14 of the Copyright Act, 1957. In *Gurukrupa Mech Tech Pvt. Ltd.* v. *State of Gujarat*,[255] the Gujarat High Court held that the following six categories of rights become available to a bona fide owner of a copyright (i) right to reproduce the work, (ii) right to issue copies of the work, (iii) right to perform the work in public (iv) right to make a cinematograph film or sound recording, (v) right to translate the work, (vi) right to adapt or derive other works from it. The right to reproduction in case of cinematograph film or sound recording has a different footing from literary, dramatic, musical and artistic works. Therefore, contrasting Section 14(d) and (e) of the Copyright Act, 1957, on the one hand, and Section 14(a), (b) and (c) on the other, it may be concluded that in the latter case, the owner of the copyright has exclusive right to reproduce the work in "any material form". This is absent and excluded insofar as the former case (in case of cinematograph film or sound recording). The exclusive right in the former is to copy the recording of a particular cinematograph film or sound recording. It is, therefore, clear that production by another person of even the same cinematographic film does not constitute infringement of a copyright in a cinematograph film. It is only when actual copy is made of a film by a process of duplication, i.e., by using mechanical contrivance that it falls under Section 14(d)(i). The expression "to make a copy of the film" would mean to make a physical copy of the film itself and not another film which merely resembles the film.[256]

In *Star India Private Limited* v. *Leo Burnett (India) Private Limited*,[257] the Bombay High Court held that the making of another film is not included under Section 14(d)(i) and such other film, even though it resembles completely the copyrighted film, does not fall within the expression "to make a copy of the film". Therefore, if the film has been filmed or shot separately by a person and it resembles the earlier film, the subsequent film is not a copy

254. AIR 1999 Del 73: (1999) 19 PTC 36 (Del).
255. (2018) 4 GLR 3324.
256. *See,* J.K. Das, *Intellectual Property Rights* (Kamal Law House, Kolkata, 2008), pp. 155–170.
257. 2003 (2) Bom CR 655: 2003 (27), PTC 81 (Bom).

of the first film and, therefore, does not amount to infringement of whole of the copyright of the first film. The position in the case of literary, dramatic or artistic work seems to be different. A narrow copyright protection is accorded to a film or sound recordings than for literary, dramatic or artistic work. The reason perhaps could be that they have to be original to satisfy the test of copyrightability, whereas the requirement of originality is absent for claiming copyright in cinematograph films/sound recordings. Therefore, considering the terminology used in the Act, the facts on record and the cases discussed, it is clear that the defendants made their own film independently. The film of the defendants, therefore is not a copy, and therefore, would not amount to an infringement of the plaintiff's copyright in its film considering the language of Section 14(d) of the Copyright Act.

In *Indian Express Newspapers (Bombay) Pvt. Ltd.* v. *Jagmohan Mundhara*,[258] the Bombay High Court held that the form, manner or arrangement of a drama and movie are materially different from a newspaper article and by very nature of the media there is fundamental and substantial dissimilarity the mode of expression of the idea in a newspaper article and in a stage play or in a movie. Ideas, information, natural phenomena and events on which an author expends his skill, labour, capital, judgment and literary talent are common property and are not the subject of copyright. There is a distinction between the materials upon which one claiming copyright has worked and the products of the application of his skill, judgment, labour and literary talent to these materials. Ideas, information, natural phenomena and events on which an author expends his skill, labour, capital, judgment and literary talent are common property and are not the subject of copyright. In *R.G. Anand* v. *Deluxe Films*,[259] the Apex Court observed:

> There can be no copywriting in an idea, subject matter, themes, plots or historical or legendary facts and violation of the copyright in such cases is confined to the form, manner, arrangement and expression of the idea by the author of the author of the copyrighted work.

In *Twentieth Century for Film Corporation* v. *Sohail Maklai Entertainment Pvt. Ltd.*,[260] the issue was for determination of infringement of copyright in the script, screen, storyline and dialogues of the film, namely "Phone Booth". The plaintiff contended that defendant has infringed copyright in his film "Knock Out". The court following the principle laid down in *Sheldon* v. *Metro Goldwyn Pictures Corporation*[261] held that the test of concluding whether the second work is a pirated copy is the impression of the average viewer. The other test is that if those parts were removed from the copied work whether the remainder would become meaningless and hence what must be seen is the substance, the foundation, the kernel and the copied work and to see if the rest can stand without it. However, in *Indian Performing Rights Society* v. *Aditya Pandey*,[262] the court held that once a license is obtained from the owner or someone authorised to give it, in respect of a sound recording, for communicating it to the public, including by broadcasting, a separate authorisation or licence is not necessary from the copyright owner or author of the musical and/or literary work.

---

258. AIR 1985 Bom 229.
259. AIR 1978 SC 1613: [1979] 1 SCR 218.
260. 2010 (44) PTC 647 (Bom): 2010 (112) Bom LR 4216.
261. 1993 (81) F 2nd 49.
262. MIPR 2011 (3) 19: 2011 (47) PTC 392 (Del).

A sound recording is a derivative work being derived from the musical and literary work while the musical and literary works are the original works. The creator of the original musical and literary work ought therefore to be given precedence over the owner of the copyright in a sound recording. In *Music Broadcast Private Ltd.* v. *Indian Performing Right Society Ltd.*,[263] the Bombay High Court held that once a sound recording is made, it is only the producer, as the owner thereof, who can exploit it exclusively in the manner provided in Section 14(1)(e). Owner of the sound recording can communicate the same to the public, *inter alia*, by broadcasting it or playing it in public places. Owners of the musical and literary work embodied in such sound recording could not interfere with these rights of the owner of the sound recording qua that sound recording owners of copyright in the literary, dramatic and musical works can make or authorise the making of a new sound recording by utilising the same literary, dramatic or musical work which may earlier have been utilised for making an earlier sound recording. Owner of the copyright in the earlier produced sound recording cannot object to the making of such subsequent sound recordings or version recordings merely because he is the owner of the copyright in the earlier made sound recording. Unless a sound recording actually embodies a previous sound recording or a substantial part thereof, there is no copying or infringement of the copyright of the owner of a sound recording. The court justified its pronouncement with the following propositions:

1. The Act recognises only three classes of work, viz. (a) literary, dramatic, musical or artistic work; (b) cinematograph films and (c) sound recordings. Each class is independent of the other. Each class of work gives bundles of right to the owner thereof, which are independent of the other works. The rights therein can be exploited by the owner of the work in each class without the interference by the owners of the works is other classes.[264]
2. No class of work is inferior to the work in another class.[265]
3. In sound recordings and cinematograph films, the literary and musical work gets incorporated therein and thereupon independent copyrightable works, viz. sound recordings and cinematograph films come into existence and, therefore, rights under Section 14 in respect of each sound recording and cinematograph film come into existence which can be exploited by the owner of the sound recording or cinematograph film without interference from the owners of copyright in the underlying literary or musical works therein. The rights of a copyright holder in a sound recording or a cinematograph film include the right to make the work available to the public by other modes of communication as also by broadcast.[266]
4. The owner of a sound recording has, *inter alia*, the exclusive right of communicating the sound recording to the public. Though the exercise of such right has the effect of communicating the underlying works, viz. musical or literary to the public such

263. MIPR 2011 (3) 84: 2011 (47) PTC 587 (Bom).
264. *See, K. Bhagyalakshmi* v. *Deputy Commissioner of Income Tax*, (2014) 265 CTR (Mad) 545: [2014] 221 TAXMAN 225 (Mad).
265. *See, Music Broadcast Private Ltd.* v. *Indian Performing Right Society Ltd.*, 2011 (113) BomLR 3153: 2011 (47) PTC 592 (Bom).
266. *See, Entertainment Network (India) Limited* v. *Super Cassette Industries Limited*,: (2008) 13 SCC 30: 2008 (9) SCALE 69.

communication of underlying works being a part of sound recording does not amount to infringement of the copyright of communicating to the public, the underlying works.

The owner of a sound recording has an exclusive right to communicate the sound recording in any form and such communication in exercise of right under Section 14(1)(e)(iii) cannot amount to infringement of any underlying work in such sound recording.[267]

5. The owners of underlying works incorporated in a sound recording do not have the right of communicating the same to the public as a part of the sound recording.
6. The owner of a copyright in the underlying works retains the bundle of copyrights therein otherwise than as a part of the sound recording.
7. The right of public performance of an underlying work is different from the right to communicate the sound recording in which the musical or literary work is incorporated.[268]
8. The defendant, therefore, can claim licence fees only in respect of public performance of musical or literary works of its members or in respect of communication of such works otherwise than as a part of other copyright work, viz. sound recording or cinematograph film. In other words, the defendant cannot claim licence fees in respect of public broadcast or communicate to the public, musical or literary works as a part of a sound recording.[269]
9. Upon the owner of a copyright in musical and literary work permitting the making of a sound recording, his right to make or permit to be made another sound recording containing such work comes to an end.[270]

Right to Store a Work in Electronic Medium

Right to store a work in electronic medium is newly recognised economic right of an author under Copyright Act, 1957. The recent technological development like the Internet, DVD, CD-ROM, etc., have enabled the libraries and publishers of newspapers and magazines and so on to store the printed work in electronic medium. A question arises whether the storing in electronic medium is legal under copyright law? Section 14 of the Act clarifies that for the purpose of storing in electronic medium, the libraries and publishers also have to obtain permission from the author. Therefore, the Copyright (Amendment) Act, 1984 amended Section 14(1)(a)(i) which provided "to reproduce the work in any material form including the storing of it in any medium by electronic means".[271]

Recently, the Copyright (Amendment) Act, 2012 amended Section 52 of the Act to make the fair use defence available to all works including cinematograph films and sound recordings.

---

267. *See, Phonographic Performance Ltd.* v. *Music Broadcast (P) Ltd.*, 2004 (7) LJSOFT 22 : 2004 29 PTC 282.
268. *See, Gramophone Company of India Ltd.* v. *Super Cassette Industries Ltd.*, ILR (2010) Supp. (5) Delhi 656: 2010 (44) PTC 541 (Del.).
269. *See, Indian Performing Right Society Ltd.* v. *Eastern Indian Motion Pictures Association* AIR 1977 SC 1443: 1977 2 SCC 820.
270. *See, Music Broadcast Private Ltd.* v. *Indian Performing Right Society Ltd.*, 2011 (113) BomLR 3153: 2011 (47) PTC 592 (Bom).
271. Inserted by the Copyright (Amendment) Act, 1994 [w.e.f. 10-5-1995] Section 7.

The 2012 amendment replaced the words "literary, dramatic, musical or artistic work" used in Section 52(1)(a) and 52(1)(b) with the expression "any work".[272] The amendment provides that the works which are stored in an electronic medium for the purposes of fair use do not constitute infringing copies. To facilitate digitisation of libraries, a new clause (n) has been introduced to Section 52(1) identifying certain acts not to be infringement of copyright to enable the storage of a digital copy of a work if the library possesses a non-digital version of it. The newly substituted clause (n) runs thus:

> The storing of a work in any medium by electronic means by a non-commercial public library, for preservation if the library already possesses a non-digital copy of the work.

Explanation to Section 52(1)(a) clarifies that he storing of any work in any electronic medium for the purposes mentioned in this clause, including the incidental storage of any computer programme which is not itself an infringing copy for the said purposes, shall not constitute infringement of copyright.[273] The Copyright (Amendment) Act 2012 replaces the words "literary, dramatic, musical or artistic work" used in Section 52(1)(a) and 52(1)(b) with the expression "any work." The amendment does not seek to make a substantive change in the law as it was existed at before the amendment. The intention of this change was to provide that works which are stored in an electronic medium for the purposes of fair use do not constitute infringing copies and also to exclude the process of "caching" from the charge of infringement.[274] However, in *Taxmann Allied Services Pvt. Ltd.* v. *Casansaar Web Solution Pvt. Ltd.*,[275] the plaintiff has filed a suit for permanent injunction restraining infringement of copyright (in editorial comments/head notes to cases) and unfair competition and for damages etc. against the defendant. In this case the plaintiff also commenced the use of the on-line electronic medium for publishing and selling its publications (including case law reports on subscription basis). The Court held that the plaintiff has been able to make out a strong prima facie case for grant of ad interim injunction. Hence, the defendant is restrained from continuing with the infringement of plaintiffs copyright in its editorial comments/case Head-notes. They are directed to remove the existing infringing material from its website which may amount to infringement of plaintiffs copyright as claimed.

Right to Communication to Public

Under the Section 14 of the Copyright Act 1957 the "right to communication to public" maintains a relation between "public" and "any work or performance". While Section 14(d)(i) of the Act provides the a right to copy of a film, the Section 14(d)(iii) provides that communication to the public of a cinematograph film or any substantial part thereof is one such exclusive right. Thus, making any work available for being seen or heard by the public whether simultaneously or at places chosen individually, regardless of whether the public actually sees the film, will constitute communication of the film to the public. The intent was to include digital copies of works, which would include within its scope digital copies of

272. Inserted by the Copyright (Amendment) Act, 2012 [w.e.f. 21-6-2012] Section 32(i)(a).
273. *See, Super Cassettes Industries Ltd.* v. *Shreya Broadcasting Pvt. Ltd.*, 2019 III AD (Delhi) 552: 258 (2019) DLT 116.
274. *See, Super Cassettes Industries Limited* v. *Chintamani Rao*, 2012 (49) PTC 1 (Del).
275. 2016 (65) PTC 127 (Del).

works being made available online (as opposed to the physical world). Communication can be by various means such as directly or by display or diffusion. In this context, definition of "broadcast" is also relevant which identifies communication to public by wireless diffusion or by wire. In *UTV Software Communication Ltd.* v. *1337X*,[276] the Delhi High Court held that making available of a film for streaming or downloads in the form of digital copies on the internet is within the scope of "communication to the public". Further, in *Star India Private Limited* v. *Department of Industrial Policy*,[277] the Supreme Court held that Section 52(1)(b) of Copyright Act 1957 indicated that transient or incidental storage of a work or performance purely in technical process of electronic transmission or communication to public was not an act that would constitute infringement of copyright.

One of the important elements of the right to communication to public is the notion of public. However, the scope of the word "public" has not been defined by the Act. The word "public" generally means to general public and the performance or communication to a closed group however large in numbers may not constitute performance in public or communication to public. The Bombay High Court in *Garware Plastics* v. *Telelink*[278] was confronted with this question. Here the plaintiffs, copyright owners of various cinematograph films, the suit against the defendants who after obtaining videocassettes of the copyrighted films from the market displayed it in the cable TV network operated by them. By such display any person, whose TV set is connected to the network, by payment of nominal charges could access to the video-films shown by the defendants on their cable TV network. The court adopted the following three tests to find out whether viewers of the work could be treated as public. They are:

1. the character of the audience and whether it can be described as a private or domestic audience consisting of family members of the household;
2. whether the audience in relation to the owner of the copyright can be so considered; and
3. whether permitting such performance would in any way whittle down the protection given to the author of a copyrighted work under the Copyright Act resulting in the owner being deprived of monetary gains out of his intellectual property.

By following this test, the Court held that showing a video-film over a cable television network to various subscribers amounts to broadcasting video-films to the public. This is because the entire audience taken together cannot in any way be considered as members of common household or as family members. They are residents of different apartments or houses and are connected with each other only by cable. Thus, they can only be viewed as a portion of the public. This decision was also affirmed by a Division Branch of the Court in *Venkatesan* v. *Deputy Manager, Telecom*[279] by holding that showing a video film over a cable network amounts to broadcasting video-films to the public.

The scope of the right to communication to public in the context of development of broadcasting video-films to the public through cable was subject to the discussion of number of cases. The court expanded the rights to accommodate different methods of communication

276. 2019 (78) PTC 375 (Del).
277. (2019) 2 SCC 104: 2018 (14) SCALE 651.
278. AIR 1989 Bom. 331.
279. (1991) 1 LW 456.

through the advance technology on broadcasting. In *Video Master* v. *Nisi Productions*,[280] the issue was whether by receiving satellite signals on *dish antenna* owned by cable TV operator or private party and by relaying signals through media of cable to viewers-plaintiffs' copyrights are infringed? The court examines the role of antenna of cable TV operators or of society is that signals are received on dish antenna and carried further by cable without editing whatever programmes they receive. The court observed that Section 2(ff) of the Copyright Act, 1957 provides for communication to public in any manner including communication through the satellite. It is regardless as to whether any member of public sees or hears or otherwise enjoys the same or not. According to Section 14(d)(iii), copyrights exist in communication of the film to the public. Thus, the plaintiffs have with them copyrights for exhibition of the film on video by playback equipment or Cable TV rights. There are several ways of communication and each one is separately divisible and can exist in different persons at the same time. Different classes or species of communication are:

1. Theatrical rights, i.e., right to exhibit the cinematograph film in theatres;[281]
2. Terrestrial television broadcasting rights, i.e., the right to exhibit the film on terrestrial television (i.e., Doordarshan);[282]
3. Satellite broadcasting rights, i.e., the right to exhibit or communicate the film by satellite signals to the public with or without cable and through the satellite medium;[283]
4. Cable TV rights, i.e., the right to exhibit the film by a cable originated programme. Thus, the Court held that broadcasting cinematograph through the satellite does not amount infringement of plaintiffs' copyrights.[284]

The Copyright (Amendment) Act, 2012 has amended the definition of "communication to the public" inserting a new definition under Section 2(ff)[285] extending the right to performances as under:

> Section 2(ff) "communication to the public" means making any work or performance available for being seen or heard or otherwise enjoyed by the public directly or by any means of display or diffusion other than by issuing physical copies of it, whether simultaneously or at places and times chosen individually, regardless of whether any member of the public actually sees, hears or otherwise enjoys the work or performance so made available.

---

280. 1997 ARBLR 47 (Bom): (1987) 18 PTC 117.
281. *See, Video Master* v. *Nishi Productions,* 1998 (18) PTC 117 (Bom).
282. *See, Sivaji Productions* v. *Symphony Home Videos*, AIR 2017 Mad 65: 2018 (73) PTC 296 (Mad).
283. *See, A. Somasekhara Rao* v. *Javvadi Narendra Babu*, 2017 (71) PTC 136 (Mad).
284. *See, Ashwin Management Sawani* v. *Raj Enterprises*, 2014 (1) MhL J9: 2013 (6) ALLMR 272; *Sholay Media and Entertainment Pvt. Ltd.* v. *Indus Video Pvt. Ltd.*, 2014 (58) PTC 424 (Del).
285. Inserted by the Copyright (Amendment) Act, 2012 [w.e.f. 21-6-2012] Section 2(iii). Clause (ff), before substitution by the 2012 amendment, stood as under:

    2(ff) "'communication to the public' means making any work available for being seen or heard or otherwise enjoyed by the public directly or by any means of display or diffusion other than by issuing copies of such work regardless of whether any member of the public actually sees, hears or otherwise enjoys the work so made available.

    EXPLANATION—For the purposes of this clause, communication through satellite or cable or any other means of simultaneous communication to more than one household or place of residence including residential rooms of any hotel or hostel shall be deemed to be communication to the public."

EXPLANATION—For the purposes of this clause, communication through satellite or cable or any other means of simultaneous communication to more than one household or place of residence including residential rooms of any hotel or hostel shall be deemed to be communication to the public."

The 2012 amendment thus amends the definition by adding "or performance" after "work" and extending communication to the public simultaneously or at places and times chosen individually, which has significance for performers. It may be recalled that the right of "communication to public" was introduced in the 1994 amendment to extend the rights to Internet. These rights hitherto limited to authors have been extended to performers by the present amendment.

ILLUSTRATION

One Mr. Vasanth handed over the copyright work of Mr. Gopalacharya without obtaining permission of Mr. Gopalacharya forwarded to all his friends through an E-mail. In this case, Mr. Vasanth has infringed the right to communication to public of Mr. Gopalacharya.

In *Thiagarajan Kumararaja* v. *Capital Film Works (India) Pvt. Ltd.*,[286] the Madras High Court held that a close perusal of the definition of "communication to the public" under Section 2(ff) would show that it envisages making of any work or performance available for being seen or heard or otherwise enjoyed by the public directly or by means of display or diffusion other than by making physical copies of it, whether simultaneously or at places and times chosen individually, regardless of the fact whether any member of public actually sees or hears or otherwise enjoys the work or performance so made available. Thus, a remake of the film or its versions which are, substantially similar to the original cinematograph film cannot come within the ambit of the right to copy a film, which is provided for under Section 14(1)(d)(i) of Copyright Act, 1957. In *Sun TV Network Ltd.* v. *K.S. Talkies*,[287] it was held that in respect of satellite television broadcasting, direct to home broadcast, direct satellite service, terrestrial television broadcast and all other rights connected therewith including exhibition of the said film by means of wireless diffusion and by wire for communication and other means of communication to the public through television broadcast for the entire world. Thus, the words, broadcast, communication to the public, copy, copyright and licence shall have the same meaning as assigned to them under the Indian Copyright Act 1957.[288]

Explaining Section 2(ff) of the Act in *Thiagarajan Kumararaja* v. *Capital Film Works (India) Pvt. Ltd.*,[289] the Madras High Court held that the expression "communication to the public" involves making of any work available for being seen or heard or otherwise enjoyed by the public directly or by any means of display or diffusion other than by issuing copies of such work, regardless of whether any member of the public actually sees, hears or otherwise enjoys the work so made available. In other words, the provision only protects the right of the owner of the film to make the work accessible to the public via various modes, which are adverted to in that behalf. This right does not include the right to make changes to the work so that it is understood by a section of the society, as it would involve translation of literary or dramatic works without issuance of a licence or assignment of the right in the work.

286. 2018 (73) PTC 365 (Mad): MIPR 2018 (1) 227.
287. MANU/ TN/ 6462/ 2018.
288. *See, K. Bose Babu* v. *Gowri Productions*, 2018 (76) PTC 48 (Mad).
289. 2018 (73) PTC 365 (Mad): MIPR 2018 (1) 227.

Right to Issue Copies of the Work to the Public

Under the Section 14(a)(ii) and 14(c)(iii) of the Copyright Act, 1957, the owner of copyright has the exclusive right to issue copies of the work to the public not being copies already in circulation. In *T.T. Krishnamachari and Co.* v. *Union of India*,[290] the Madras High Court held that although the has not been re-produced in any material form; or to communicate the artistic work to the public; or to issue copies of the work to the public; or to include the work in any Cinematograph film; or adaptation of the work; or adaptation of the work; or conversion of the work into a dramatic work by way of performance in public. However, the logo was mainly used by group of companies in order to create impression among public. Logo had got some inherent goodwill and it was used by group companies in products to get maximum mileage of goodwill arising from such use. Nevertheless, on record the petitioners had contravened provision of Copyright Act 1957. Thus, in *SAP AG* v. *Jayanth Kumar*,[291] the Delhi High Court held that the copyright is an exclusive right to, *inter alia*, issue copies of the work to the public. Thus, any exercise of the said exclusive right which is exclusively vested in the plaintiffs, by any person, organization, company without the express consent and/or authorization of the plaintiffs, amounts to infringement of plaintiffs' exclusive rights. In connection to the nature of right under the Act, in *Music Broadcast Private Ltd.* v. *Indian Performing Right Society Ltd.*,[292] the Bombay High Court observed:

> Section 2(y) read with Section 13(1) indicates that the Act recognizes three classes of works viz. (a) original, literary, dramatic, musical and artistic work; (b) cinematograph films and (c) sound recording. Section 14 stipulates the exclusive right to do or authorize the doing of the acts mentioned therein in respect of a work or any substantial part thereof. The rights which may be exercised in respect of each class of work are stipulated in Section 14 which does not indicate any order of priority between the different classes of works. Nor does it place any particular work above the others.

Interpreting Clauses (a)(ii) and (c)(iii) of the Section 14 of the Copyright Act 1957 in *Lahari Recording Company Limited* v. *Music Master Audio Video Manufacturing Co. (P) Ltd.*,[293] the Madras High Court held that if an individual without the consent or licence of the owner of the copyright does or authorises the doing of an act to issue the copies of the work to the public not being copies already in circulation, or distribute infringing copies either for the purpose of trade or to such an extent as to effect prejudicially the owner of the copyright or to reproduce the work in any material form including the storing of it in any medium by electronic means, he will be infringing the copyright work as per Section 51 read with Section 14(a) and Section 14(c) of the Act. However, in *John Wiley and Sons Inc.* v. *Prabhat Chander Kumar Jain*,[294] the Delhi High Court clarified that it is the prerogative of the owner of the copyright to issue the copies of the work to the public if the same are not in circulation already. The words "already in circulation" clearly recognise the first sales doctrine whereby once the owner of copyright has exercised his right to issue the copies, the owner loses all future rights to control the subsequent sales of the same work. This position has already been

290. (2015) 83 VST 222 (Mad): 2015 [37] S.T.R.679 (Mad.).
291. 2015 (61) PTC 474 (Del).
292. 2011 (47) PTC 592 (Bom): 2011 (113) BomLR 3153.
293. MIPR 2008 (2) 341: 2008 (37) PTC 121 (Mad).
294. (2010) ILR 5 Delhi 510: 2010 (44) PTC 675 (Del).

clarified by Explanation to Section 14 which states: "For the purposes of this Section, a copy which has been sold once shall be deemed to be a copy already in circulation."

ILLUSTRATION

Mr. Washim has sold copies of his original literary work "Nikaah-a-Hind" in the market. Subsequently, Mr. Shamim started marketing with the pirated copies of Mr. Washim's "Nikaah-a-Hind." In this case Mr. Shamim infringed the right to reproduction of original literary work of Mr. Washim. However, Mr. Shamim did not infringe the right to issue copies of the work to the public.

There is a relation between two concepts: "issue copies of the work to the public" and "publication". Therefore, the former is complemented and supplemented by latter. The word "publish" has to be understood considering the extensive definition of the word "publication" as defined under Section 3 of the Copyright Act. According to Section 3 "publication" means: "making a work available to the public by issue of copies or by communicating the work to the public." Thus, in *Super Cassettes Industries Ltd.* v. *Board of Film Certification,*[295] the Delhi High Court held that the publishing of a video film in respect of any work would take place when such work is made available to the public for being seen, heard or otherwise enjoyed by means of display or diffusion "regardless of whether any member of the public actually sees, hears or otherwise enjoys the work so made available". The explanation to Section 2(ff) of the Act which was inserted by the 1984 amendment and later further amended in 1994 makes it clear that exhibition through satellite TV or cable or simultaneous communication to more than one user including residential rooms of any hotel or hostel shall be deemed "to be communication to the public". This is a marked change from the understanding of what could tantamount to "exhibition to the public". It is no longer confined to a place where the public is admitted like a cinema hall but it would include residential rooms of any hotel or hostel. Consequently, a whole new dimension has been added to the legislative understanding of "public exhibition".

In *Diljeet Titus* v. *Alfred A Adebare,*[296] the Court observed that the provisions of Sections 2(o), 14, 16 and 17 of the Copyright Act have to be read together. Section 2(o) provides for the definition of "literary work" while Section 14 deals with meaning of copyright. According to Section 16, no person shall be entitled for copyright except as provided in this Act and Section 17 provides that the author of the work shall be the first owner of the copyright. Thus, only if the defendants were the owner of the copyright would it have the right to make it public in view of the provisions of Section 14 of the copyright Act. A question often arises that if the defence of "misuse of copyright" can be taken by the holder of copyright during issuing copies of the work to the public. In *Tekla Corporation* v. *Survo Ghosh,*[297] the defendant argued that in our legal framework of copyright, the defence of "misuse of copyright" by the holder thereof is not available, neither to an action for infringement of copyright nor to an action for damages for infringement of copyright. Answering affirmatively, the court observed that no holder of copyright in any work, misusing the said work shall have copyright therein during that misuse, i.e., during the misuse of a copyrighted work, the work affords its owner

---

295. MIPR 2010 (3) 342: 2011 (46) PTC 1 (Del).
296. 2006 (32) PTC 609: 2006 (130) DLT 330.
297. 2014 (210) DLT 666: AIR 2014 Del 121.

no copyright rights and a copyright owner can regain those rights only by ending the practices that constitute misuse. The principle behind denying damages for infringement during the period of misuse is stated to be that since during that time there is no copyright, there would be no infringement and resultantly no damages.

Right to Make Adaptation of the Work

The Section 14 of the Copyright Act 1957 has given a separate economic status of the right to make adaptation of the work in order to presumably strengthen the basic right of reproduction of the author.[298] Sometimes the economic right of adaptation may also overlap with the moral right of integrity, which similarly empowers the authors to control changes in their work that "allows arrangement or transcription of the musical work".[299] The 1886 Berne Convention (as revised in Paris in 1971) under Article 14(3) makes it clear that copyright in an adaptation is without prejudice to the copyright in the original work. Article 12 of the Berne Convention provides that authors of literary and artistic works "shall enjoy the exclusive right of authorizing adaptations, arrangements and other alterations of their work". In case of artistic works, especially, the "works of architecture" as defined under Section 2(b)[300] of the Copyright Act 1957 which means any building or structure having character or design, or any model for such building or structure, the owner of the work such as building often alters the maps of the buildings from time to time so as to make the house more modern as per the trend in the property market or otherwise, that may frequently lead to conflict with the copyright of the author of the work, who in this case would be an architect.

Thus, in such works the question arises whether alteration is permissible to the owner of the work as against the author of the work? In order to protect the works of architecture and works relative to architecture against unauthorised reproduction by the owners of the work, and also resolve this issue of conflicting interests of the owner and the author, the UNESCO and the WIPO suggested a way-out so as to protect the owner from the act of infringement against the author on one hand, and protection of the economic interest of the author, which is as under:

> The author of the work of architecture should enjoy the exclusive right of authorizing alterations of that work, except where the alteration is of a kind that is of great importance to the owner of the building or other similar construction and that does not amount to a distortion, mutilation or other modification which would be prejudicial to the honour or reputation of the author of the work of architecture.

Recognising the importance of various principles laid down in the Berne Convention, the Bombay high Court in *Ramesh Sippy* v. *Shaan Ranjeet Uttam Singh*,[301] observed: "Indian copyright laws stand on the same footing as copyright laws in most countries of the world where the concept stems out of the Berne Convention." In *R.G. Anand* v. *Delux Films*,[302] the

---

298. *See, Holland Company LP* v. *S.P. Industries*, 2017 (71) PTC 630 (Del): 2017 VI AD (Delhi) 272; *OK Play India Limited* v. *Mayank Aggarwal*, 2016 (67) PTC 665 (Del): 233 (2016) DLT 234; *Photoquip India Limited* v. *Delhi Photo Store*, 2016 (4) ALLMR 327: 2015 (6) ABR 210.
299. *Saregama India Ltd.* v. *Puneet Prakash Mehra,* 2011 (1) CHN 341: MIPR 2010 (3)175.
300. Substituted for the words 'architectural works of art' by the Copyright (Amendment) Act, 1994).
301. 2013 (3) ABR 1228: MIPR 2013 (2) 125.
302. AIR 1978 SC 1613: (1978) 4 SCC 118.

Apex Court compared the Copyright Act, 1957 with the Copyright Act, 1911 and observed that the 1911 Act did not even contain a definition of adaptation while we have a much more extended definition of adaptation in the 1957 Act.

The Copyright Act, 1957 defines "adaptation" under Section 2(a) to mean:

(i) in relation to a dramatic work, the conversion of the work into a non-dramatic work;
(ii) in relation to a literary work or an artistic work, the conversion of the work into a dramatic work by way of performance in public or otherwise;
(iii) in relation to a literary or dramatic work, any abridgement of the work or any version of the work in which the story or action is conveyed wholly or mainly by means of pictures in a form suitable for reproduction in a book, or in a newspaper, magazine or similar periodical;
(iv) in relation to a musical work, any arrangement of transcription of the work; and
(v) in relation to any work, any use of such work involving its rearrangement or alteration.[303]

ILLUSTRATION

Indu Razdan writes an original novel in Kashmiri language—"Gul Gulshan Gulfaam" in 1991. Thus, he is the copyright owner of the novel. Subsequently, he assigns his right of making an adaptation to Vikram Sharma who converts the work of Indu Razdan "Gul Gulshan Gulfaam" into a drama to be performed in theatre. In this dramatic work, Vikram Sharma has a copyright in the drama as an original work but copyright in the novel to make a cinematograph film or sound recording or translation etc. remains with Indu Razdan.

This definition of adaptation gives ample scope for interpretation. Even though the rearrangement, alteration or conversion of a work into another format constitutes adaptation, to determine the precise amount of rearrangement or alteration needed to constitute adaptation is not an easy task. It is to be judged from the circumstances of each case.

Under Section 2(a) of the Copyright Act 1957 the copyright subsists in the adaptation of literary, dramatic and musical works and thus the copyright owner of any such work has the exclusive right to make any adaptation of it. However, in *Saregama India Limited* v. *Puneet Prakash Mehra*,[304] the Calcutta High Court held that re-arrangement as per Section 2(a)(iv) and (v) of the Copyright Act, 1957 involves re-arrangement in respect of the contract works embodied in producer's film and none else. Therefore, such rights extending to exploitation of sound track in another film is contrary to the terms agreed between the parties. In *Gramophone Company of India Limited* v. *Shanti Films Corporation*,[305] the Calcutta High Court held that by virtue of Section 14(a)(iv), (vi) and (vii), the company has exclusive right to make any adaptation of the literary, dramatic or musical works assigned to it and all that is done by the said agreement is to adapt the lyrics and music. Therefore, for all the said reasons, the interim order passed be continued. Thus, making of adaptation of any such work without authority of the copyright owner is an infringement.

303. Clause (v) has been inserted in the Act by the Copyright (Amendment) Act, 1994 [w.e.f. 21-6-2012] Section 2.
304. MIPR 2010 (2) 222.
305. AIR 1997 CAL 63.

In *Barbara Taylor Bradford* v. *Sahara Media Entertainment*[306] the Calcutta High Court examined various aspects of the Copyright Act. The plaintiff fielded a suit for infringement restraining the defendants from telecasting the serial "Karishma—the Miracle of Destiny". According to her, the serial was based on her book *A Women of Substance*. To establish this, she relied on a published interview of a journalist with the director of the serial where he told that the story was influenced and based on the book. But it was contended by the defendant that the story was not based on the book though the theme and some of the characters resemble to that in the plaintiff's book. There was substantial difference between the book and the serial was more than 200 episodes and first episode was schedule to be telecast on 12 May 2003. The single judge issued an *ex parte* order on 7 May 2003 but the same was vacated by the division bench on 12 May 2003 on the ground of suppression of facts. It was contented that a similar suit was filed before of the Bombay High Court and was withdrawn by the plaintiff and the same was not brought to the notice of the court. Against the judgment of the division bench, the plaintiff filed an appeal before the vacation judge of the Supreme Court on the evening of 12 May 2003 and the court granted an injunction preventing the telecast of the first episode. But before this could be communicated, the first episode was telecast. The high court then vacated the stay on 30 June 2003 and ordered the deposit of ₹25 lakh to pay the damages, if any, at the end. An important issue contended before the court was that the serial is an adaptation of the book. It was argued that since the words "rearrangement and alteration" included in the definition of adaptation in Section 2 is similar to that of English law it shall be interpreted to prohibit any kind of rearrangement or alteration following the precedents from England. Rejecting this, the court asserted:

> This type of statutory construction is not permissible. One is not permitted to impute to our Parliament both the fact of copying and the charge of copying badly. If Parliament has said something, may be following some Act somewhere else, may be unwisely, yet it is law made by Parliament and the plain words have to be given plain, fair and reasonable meaning.

Further, the Section 2(a)(v) of the Copyright Act, 1957 provides "in relation to any work, any use of such work involving its rearrangement or alteration". Now a question arises what the meaning of "alter" Is. In *Barbara Taylor Bradford* v. *Sahara Media Entertainment*,[307] the Calcutta High Court held: "Any reader having the time or wish to do so can think of numerous instances where the word 'alter' will fit both the slight change meaning and the large change meaning." Thus, the Karnataka High Court in *NRI Film Production Associates (P) Ltd.* v. *Twentieth Century Fox Film Corporation*,[308] interpreted the word "alter" thus:

> In our opinion, the large change meaning cannot be ascribed to the word "alter" in Section 2(a)(v) of the Copyright Act, 1957 because it renders the interpretation absurd. Minor changes, slight changes, not making the original something beyond recognizable possibilities, changes in some of the details, this would be the meaning that would fit the word alter in sub Section (v). In our opinion this sub-section might have a very good bearing when applied to copyright in computer programme and databases, but in relation to literary works, the sub-section does not bring in any very great change in law; one can at

306. (2004) ILR 1 Cal 15: 2004 (28) PC 474 (Cal).
307. (2004) ILR 1 Cal 15: 2004 (28) PC 474 (Cal).
308. ILR 2004 Karnataka 4530: 2005 (1) KCCR 126.

best say that the sub section would make it slightly, we repeat only slightly, easier for an author or authors to establish infringement, after its introduction, that it would have been before the introduction.

Right to Make Translation of the Work

Right to make translation by the author is a recognised right under Copyright Act, 1957. In *Blackwood and Sons Ltd.* v. *A.N. Parasuraman,*[309] the Madras High Court held that the right to translate vests with the author of the work. The translation of a literary work is itself a literary work and is entitled to copyright protection. Thus, a reproduction of that work in any other language, without the consent of the owner, would amount to infringement of the original work. Further, in *Cherian P. Joseph* v. *K. Prabhakaran Nair,*[310] the Court clearly laid down that the author has the exclusive right to publish the translation and no other person has the right to translate the author's works. More clearly, the Delhi High Court explained the scope and ambit of rights of author of the book in *PEE PEE Publisher and Distributors (P) Ltd.* v. *Neena Khanna,*[311] and observed: "The author of the book enjoys several rights under the copyright which include right to publish the work, right to communicate the work to the public, right to translate the work, right to abridge the work and many others as stated under the provisions of Section 14 of the Copyright Act, 1957." However, the right to translate the work is not a new right. The right to copyright in the translation springs from the terms of Section 1 of the Copyright Act, 1911. In 1959 in *Macmillan and Company* v. *Little Flower Company,*[312] the Madras High Court observed:

> The object of the provisions of Section 4(1) of the Copyright Act, 1911 was to confer on the author the sole right of translation for a period of ten years. If this was omitted to be exercised, the result would be that at the end of the ten-year period, the statutory right to copyright would not include the sole right of translation. But this does not mean that there is no copyright in the translation. The right to copyright in the translation springs from the terms of Section 1 of the Copyright Act, 1911, because the translation would be an original literary work.

Unfortunately, neither the Copyright Act, 1911 nor the Copyright Act, 1957 defined the term translation. According to the Shorter Oxford Dictionary "translate" means, "to interpret, explain, also to express one thing in terms of another". According to *Black's Law Dictionary*, "translation" means the reproduction in one language of a book, document or speech in another language. Thus, the right to make translation of the work means reproducing the work or expression of work in a language other than that of the original version. The author is given the exclusive economic right to do or authorise to do a translation under Section 14(a)(v), and Section 14(a)(vii) of the Copyright Act, 1957.[313] Thus, according to Section 14(a)(v) of the Act "to make any translation of the work"[314] is an exclusive economic right of an author. As regards a translation is concerned, the Act considers the works capable

309. AIR 1959 Mad 410.
310. AIR 1959 Mad 410.
311. AIR 1967 Ker. 234: 1967 (11) KLJ 14.
312. 2009 (40) PTC 515 (Del).
313. *See, Cherian P. Joseph* v. *K. Prabhakaran Nair,* AIR 1967 Ker. 234: 1967 (11) KLJ 14.
314. *Dhiraj Dharamdas Dewani* v. *M/s Sonal Info Systems Pvt. Ltd.*, 2012 (3) Mh Lj 888: MIPR 2012 (2) 235.

of independent protection. All the rights envisaged by Section 14 of the Act are independently available to the author of a translation of a work too, subject to the rights of the author of the parent work. This can be judged from the scope of rights given to this works in Section 14(a)(v), and Section 14(a)(vii).

ILLUSTRATION

Kashi Ka Assi, the original story in Hindi appeared in 2011 authored by Mr. Kashinath Singh. This had been translated into English and published in 2012 without obtaining the permission from the author. The result of this would be that for the term of copyright in the original Hindi work the right would include the sole right to translate into English, the language in which the translation took place, and though in the case of other stories no one was precluded from translating them into English with the permission of author. In case of this particular story, Kashi Ka Assi, such a translation could be the subject matter of injunction as an infringement of the copyright. This right is quite distinct from the right to copyright in the translation as an original literary work.

In *Rupalli R. Shah* v. *Adani Wilmer Ltd.*,[315] the Bombay High Court rightly observed: "For the purposes of the Act, Section 14(a) enumerates what shall be a copyright which is an exclusive right, subject to the provisions of the Act, to do or authorize the doing of the acts provided in clauses (i) to (vii) in respect of a work or any substantial part thereof in the case of a literary, dramatic or musical work, not being a computer programme." Thus, in order to translate a work protected by copyright, authorisation of the copyright owner is required but the translations also enjoy copyright without prejudice to the rights of the original author. In *Chancellor Masters and Scholars of the University of Oxford* v. *Narendra Publishing House*,[316] the Delhi High Court held that the plaintiff's books have not been pirated or reproduced verbatim/completely, and therefore, the defendants' actions do not amount infringement within Section 14(a)(v) and (vii).

ILLUSTRATION

Mr. Mayur translates a Hindi novel of Mr. Harivansh in Malayalam without authorisation from Mr. Harivansh. In this case, Mr. Mayur had to take prior permission for the translation from Mr. Harivansh as the original author of the novel. Hence, Mr. Mayur infringes the translation right of Mr. Harivansh.

In connection to a translation of a work in *Cherian P. Joseph* v. *K. Prabhakaran Nair*,[317] the issue was whether the defendant committed any offence punishable under Section 63 of the Copyright Act, 1957? The court held that "according to prosecution witnesses there was no consistent evidence to show that there were true translations of complainant's books and so there was no conclusive proof that there were translations." Section 63 of the Act postulates knowledge on the part of the accused that the Malayalam translations were really piratical reproductions of the complainant's books. It is true that the possibilities are that he must have known but in a case of an appeal against acquittal, unless there is clear and conclusive proof of the knowledge the accused cannot be found guilty of the offence.

---

315. 2012 (52) PTC 305 (Bom).
316. MIPR 2008 (3) 402: 2008 (38) PTC 385 (Del).
317. AIR 1967 Ker. 234: 1967 (11) KLJ 14.

PROBLEM

A translator hopes to persuade a foreign author to let him translate his latest novel into English with a view to publication. He translates a chapter and submits it as an unsolicited sample of his workmanship. The foreign author refuses the offer but subsequently relents and the translated work is duly published. In *Super Cassettes Industries Limited* v. *Bathla Cassette Industries,*[318] the court held that it would be absurd to say that the translator is not entitled to enjoy any copyright in the chapter in question on the ground that its translation was an act of infringement at the time when it was made.

Broadcast Reproduction Right

Under Section 37 of the Copyright Act, 1957, every broadcasting organisation has been given a broadcast reproduction right in respect of its broadcast.[319] The term "broadcast" has been defined in Section 2(dd)[320] of the Act to mean communication to the public by any means of wireless diffusion, whether in any one or more of the forms of signs, sounds or visual images; or by wire, and includes a re-broadcast.[321] From this definition, it is clear that the broadcasting right also include the right to communicate the work to the public. "Communication to the public" under Section 2(ff),[322] means "making any work or performance available for being seen or heard or otherwise enjoyed by the public directly or by any means of display or diffusion other than by issuing physical copies of it, whether simultaneously or at places and times chosen individually, regardless of whether any member of the public actually sees, hears or otherwise enjoys the work or performance so made available". An explanation is provided to show that the communication through the satellite or cable or any other means of simultaneous communication to more than one household or place of residence including residential rooms of any hotel or hostel shall be deemed to be communication to public.

In *Garware Plastic and Polyester Ltd.* v. *Telelink,*[323] the Bombay High Court while determining the question as to whether causing a video film to be shown over a cable television network by a person having no video copyright over such film amounted to broadcasting, resulting in the infringement of the copyright over the film? Or in other words, whether it amounts to the communication to public? In order to answer these questions, the court felt a need to discussed the term 'public' as against communication in private, which essentially depends upon the persons receiving the communication. The court held that in this case as the communication of the film over the cable television network was meant for the public having in view the nature of the audience of the Cable TV Network, thus amounted to infringement of the copyright. In *Star India Pvt. Ltd.* v. *Piyush Agarwal,*[324] the court held that the rebroadcast is the exact and identical audio and visual recording. It is when the original audio and visual recording is again broadcast, it is called a rebroadcast. Such rights of rebroadcast are given

318. 2003 (107) DLT 91: 2003 (27) PTC 280.
319. *See, Umesh Bharatbhai Thakkar* v. *State of Gujarat*, 2017 CriLJ 3713: 2017 (4) RCR (Criminal) 948; *Asia Industrial Technologies Ltd.* v. *Ambience Space Sellers Ltd.*, 1997 (99) Bom LR 613.
320. Inserted by the Copyright (Amendment) Act 1983, Section 3.
321. *ICC Development (International) Ltd.* v. *New Delhi Television Ltd.*, 193 (2012) DLT 279: 2012 (132) DRJ 291.
322. Substituted by the Copyright (Amendment) Act, 2012.
323. AIR 1989 Bom. 33.
324. MIPR 2013 (1) 201: 2013 (54) PTC 222 (Del).

exclusivity under the Act as per Section 37 and which provides that with respect to the rebroadcast also no one has a right to use the audio and visual recording except in accordance with the licence which is taken from the owner of the original audio and visual recording. Thus, broadcasting rights are independent of the copyrights granted under the Act. This legal preposition was upheld by a Division Bench of the Delhi Court in *ESPN Star Sports* v. *Global Broadcast News Ltd.*[325] In this case, the Court held that broadcast reproduction right in respect of telecast of live event like a cricket match are a separate and distinct right as from the copyright and as such Section 61 of Copyright Act, which mandates impleadment of owner of copyright or host broadcaster as necessary party to proceedings, is not applicable to broadcast reproduction rights.

In *Jak Communications Pvt. Ltd.* v. *Sun TV Network Limited*,[326] the Madras High Court held that Section 55 of the Copyright Act 1957 provides for civil remedies for infringement of copyright, while Section 37 deals with violation of copyright which is known as "Broadcast Reproduction Right." In terms of Section 39, no broadcasting reproduction right or performer's right shall be infringed and for such infringement, civil remedies are available under Section 55 of the Telecom Regulatory Authority of India Act 1997 (TRAI Act). Inasmuch as the suit is laid on the ground of infringement of copyright and piracy, the provisions of Section 14 of TRAI Act are not applicable and the suit is well within the provisions of Section 55 of the Copyright Act. It is a matter of fact that the Section 37 of the Copyright Act recognises the broadcast reproduction right as a special right while Section 39A directed for certain provisions to apply in case of broadcast reproduction rights. Further in case of providing civil remedies for infringement of copyright the "owner of copyright to be the party to the proceeding." Now question arises what is the criteria for application of the provisions. In *ESPN Star Sports* v. *Global Broadcast News Ltd.*,[327] the Delhi High Court observed thus:

> The mandate of Section 61 (1) applies in case of claims for infringement of broadcast reproduction right and the non-impleadment of the owner of the copyright is fatal to the maintainability of the suit. Similarly, the non-joinder of the owner of the copyright was held to render the suit liable to be rejected. However, we are unable to approve the view taken by the learned Single Judge. Section 39A of the Act relating to "other provisions applying to broadcast reproduction right and performer's right" has not expressly included Section 61 which deals with owners of the copyright to be made party to the proceedings. The inclusion of specific Sections of the Act in Section 39A and making them applicable to Broadcast Reproduction Right and Performer's Right clearly shows that the broadcast reproduction right is separate and distinct from copyright in a work. Thus, the Special Broadcast Reproduction Right conferred under Section 37 in Chapter VIII of the Act is a distinct and separate right conferred on every broadcasting organization and independent of the right of an owner of a copyright and the omission of Section 61 in Section 39A of the Act makes this position amply clear.

In *Akuate Internet Services Pvt. Ltd.* v. *Star India Pvt. Ltd.*,[328] the Court observed that the cricketing events (i.e. the matches) are organized by the BCCI on each occasion. It has granted exclusive broadcasting rights to Star to disseminate the information/content emanating

325. MIPR 2008 (3) 257: 2008 (38) PTC 477 (Del).
326. 2010-2-LW 936.
327. 2008 (38) PTC 477 (Del): MIPR 2008 (3) 257. *See also, Asianet Communications (P) Ltd.* v. *Surya T.V.*, 2016 (1) CTC 493: 2015-4-LW 595.
328. MIPR 2013 (3) 1.

from the event; other copyrights emanating from recording of the live event too have been assigned to Star. These include the right to record, reproduce, broadcast etc. the actual event with other related rights. Among these are "mobile distribution" rights, which is the bone of contention in these proceedings. The plaintiffs assert that these rights enable only Star, to the exclusion of all others to disseminate time sensitive match information, i.e. almost contemporaneous news such as the result of a ball bowled, milestones achieved by the player, the score, fall of a wicket, etc. through SMS alerts. The appellants (defendants) assert that once the event occurs, it is a "fact" over which no one can claim monopoly. The Court observed:

> If Parliament had intended to give protection to facts, "time sensitive information" or events (such as match information), there would have been conscious protection of those rights by express provision.

Performer's and Author's Moral Rights

In addition to the exclusive economic rights, moral rights are also available to the performer and author under Sections 38B and 57 of the Indian Copyright Act, 1957, respectively. The WIPO Copyright Treaty, 1996[329] (WCT) and WIPO Performances and Phonograms Treaty, 1996[330] (WPPT) together known as the "Internet treaties" address the challenges relevant to the dissemination of protected material over digital networks such as the Internet. The WCT deals with the protection for the authors of literary and artistic works while the WPPT extends copyright protection to performers and producers of phonograms. Many provisions in these treaties (like right of communication to the public) have been available in the Indian copyright law since the 1994 Copyright (Amendment) Act. The Copyright (Amendment) Act, 2012 was amended to harmonise the Copyright Act, 1957 with WCT and WPPT. Thus, the Copyright (Amendment) Act, 2012 introduced affirmative performer's rights by amending the Section 38 which had granted only negative rights by prohibiting certain acts in its sub-section (3) and (4). These sub sections have been omitted and a new Section 38A has been inserted which provides the performer's right as the exclusive right to do or authorise the doing of any of the acts in respect of the performance, without prejudice to the rights conferred on authors. To substantiate these rights, the 2012 amendment also introduced another new Section 38B which grants performers moral rights on their performances.

Performer's Moral Rights

According to Section 38B[331] Copyright Act, 1957, the performer of a performance shall, independently of his right after assignment, either wholly or partially of his right, have the right,— (a) to claim to be identified as the performer of his performance except where omission is dictated by the manner of the use of the performance; and (b) to restrain or claim damages in respect of any distortion, mutilation or other modification of his performance that would be prejudicial to his reputation. The Explanation clause to this provision clarifies that mere removal of any portion of a performance for the purpose of editing, or to fit the recording

329. Adopted in Geneva on December 20, 1996 and Entry into force on March 6, 2002.
330. Adopted in Geneva on December 20, 1996 and Entry into force on May 20, 2002.
331. Inserted by the Copyright (Amendment) Act, 2012 [w.e.f. 21-6-2012] Section 27.

within a limited duration, or any other modification required for purely technical reasons shall not be deemed to be prejudicial to the performer's reputation.

The Copyright Act, 1957 provided for moral rights to authors under Section 57 titled "author's special rights", though it did not use the term "moral rights" in the Act. The new Section 38B provides moral rights to performers and calls these rights "moral rights" in the title. Article 5 of WPPT covers the moral rights of performers and the amendment is in line with that Article. Moral rights have been extended to performers, considering the possibility of digital alteration of performances in a digital environment. However, some amount of alteration will be required for the purposes of editing. The explanation to the Section clarifies that editors are free to perform their tasks without the fear of legal consequences.[332]

It is a matter of fact that the Section 16 of the Copyright Act states that there is "no copyright except as provided in this Act." In *Star India Pvt. Ltd.* vs. *Piyush Agarwal*,[333] it was held that the Section 39A of the Act enumerates those provisions of it that apply to copyright would also apply, *mutatis mutandis* to the neighboring rights (e.g. Performer's rights, Broadcasting reproduction rights). However, the Section 16 is not enumerated under Section 39A of the Act. Moreover, the Copyright Act creates several rights besides copyright. These rights include the rights of broadcasting organisations under Section 37, the rights of performers under Sections 38 and 38A, and the moral rights of authors which are recognized under Section 57; which are all distinct from copyright.

Author's Moral Rights

One of the most noteworthy developments in copyright law over the past few decades has been the adoption of statutory moral rights regimes. However, the concept of moral rights was completely alien to the legal traditions of number of countries like the United States of America, the United Kingdom, Ireland, Australia, and New Zealand.[334] Recently, it has been the enactment of statutory moral rights that has changed the traditional conservative approach of copyright law. The copyright management information provisions of the Digital Millennium Copyright Act, 1998, or the Family Movie Act, 2005 are the examples of statutory moral rights protections in the United States of America. The Family Movie Act, 2005, which exempts from copyright and trademark infringement liability certain services and technologies that enable individuals to skip and mute audio and video content in motion pictures. The 2005 Act was enacted as a partial legislative intervention in the pending moral rights case of *Huntsman* v. *Soderbergh*.[335] Thus, the recognition of special moral rights as part of copyright law is significant, because it symbolises a fundamental break with the traditional conception of moral rights in common law countries.[336]

---

332. *See,* Navdeep Kour Sasan, "Rights of the Author: Possible Extensions under Copyright Law in India," 2(2) *International Journal of Innovation and Applied Studies* (2013) pp. 104–112.
333. 2013 (54) PTC 222 (Del): MIPR 2013 (1) 201.
334. *See,* Martin A. Roeder, The Doctrine of Moral Right: A Study in the Law of Artists, Authors and Creators, 53 *Harvard Law Review* (1940) pp. 554–578.
335. No. 02-M-1662 (MJW) (D. Colo. Aug. 29, 2002).
336. *See,* Cyrill P. Rigamonti, "Deconstructing Moral Rights" 47(2) *Harvard International Law Journal* (2006), pp. 353–412 at pp. 353–354.

In India, the Section 57 of the Copyright Act, 1957 recognises the author's moral rights. The term "moral right" is a translation of the French term "*droit moral*", and refers not to "moral" as advocated by the religious right, but rather to the ability of authors to control the eventual fate of their works. An author is said to have the "moral right" to control his/her work. The concept of moral rights thus relies on the connection between an author his/her creation. Moral rights protect the personal and perpetual, rather than purely monitory, value of a work to its creator. In other words, the moral rights is an aspect of a copyright law that seeks to protect the non-commercial, personal or spiritual interests of an author in his work. Moral rights are rights which protect the author's honour and reputation. This concept of copyright is inevitable, given that a copyright work, such as a book, a song or a painting, is a form of self-expression. The author writes to earn a living but he has to work within the limits of his/her character. The circulation of a work which no longer reflects the author's view subjects in to ridicule and embarrassment. Similarly, the author is not recognised and cannot therefore build up a reputation where a work is published without his name on it.[337] In *Amar Nath Sehgal* v. *Union of India*,[338] the Delhi High Court observed:

> The moral rights are recognized by the Court and thus the right of retraction is a moral right analogous to other ones, the Court should interpret which is a moral right as against the economic right.

Moral rights have a continuing relationship with the author and are thus different from economic rights in at least two ways: (i) economic rights can be transferred but moral rights remain with the author even after the transfer of economic rights, (ii) moral rights are perpetual in duration.[339] Moral rights in a work which passed into public domain are protected by the author's heirs and in their absence by the authors associations. Distinguishing author's moral rights from the economic rights the 1886 Berne Convention (Revised in 1971) provides legal recognition of the international standards for moral rights protection of the author. Thus, at international level even after the transfer of the author's economic rights, under Article 6bis of the Berne Convention, "the author shall have the right to claim authorship of the work and to object to any distortion, mutilation or other modification of, or other derogatory action in relation to, the said work, which would be prejudicial to his honour or reputation".[340] Article 6bis was introduced for the first time by the Rome Convention (1928), later extended by the Brussels Convention (1948), and repeated with amendments in the Stockholm (June 1967) and Paris Conventions (1971). Article 6bis confers on authors what is known as *droit moral* or moral rights as distinguished from the exclusive economic rights comprised in the copyright in a work and is of European origin. These moral rights are:

1. paternity right or the right to claim authorship of the work; and
2. integrity right or the right to object to "any distortion, mutilation or other modification of, or other derogatory action in relation to the said work which would be prejudicial to his honour or his reputation".

---

337. *See*, W.R. Cornish, *Intellectual Property: Patent, Copyright, Trademark and Allied Rights* (Second Indian Reprint, 2003); Akolda M. Tier, "Rights Conferred by Sudanese Copyright Protection Act, 1974" 38 *Journal of Indian Law Institute* (1996), pp. 331–347.
338. 2005 (30) PTC 253 (Del): 117 (2005) DLT 717.
339. Sachiv Kumar "Economic and Moral Rights of the Copyright Holder under Digital Environment: An Analysis" 1 *Rajiv Gandhi National University of Law Review* (2011) p. 311.
340. *Amar Nath Sehgal* v. *Union of India*, 2005 (30) PTC 253 (Del): 117 (2005) DLT 717.

These rights belong to an author independently of his exclusive economic rights and even after he transfers his rights. Section 57 of the Copyright Act, 1957 implements the provisions of 6bis of the Berne Convention. In *Arun Chadha* v. *Oca Productions Private Limited*,[341] the Court held that author of a work has the right to claim authorship of work in respect of any modification in relation to his work, if such modification is prejudicial to his honour or reputation. The British copyright law did not give specific recognition to these moral rights till 1988, when statutory provisions in this direction were incorporated in the UK Copyright, Designs and Patents Act, 1988 in pursuance of the recommendation of the Whitford Committee in 1977 which accepted that moral rights should be incorporated into British law to a reasonable extent. The UK Copyright, Designs and Patents Act, 1988 defines four distinct moral rights (the first two of which are in the fulfilment of the Berne obligation): (i) the right to be identified as author or director (the right of paternity); (ii) the right to object to derogatory treatment of a work (the right of integrity); (iii) the right against false attribution of a work; and (iv) the right to privacy in private photographs and films.

Though the Indian copyright law is based on the British copyright law, India took the step ahead of Britain in incorporating Section 57 in its first post-independence copyright legislation and thereby giving recognition to the moral rights of authors. However, it has been argued that a careful examination did not precede this bold step of the implications of the superimposition of a European concept of *droit moral* on a British mould statute. Under Section 57 "Author's special rights" is a special provision for the protection of special rights of the authors. The object of Section 57 is to put the intellectual property on higher footing than the normal objects of copyright. The language of Section 57 is of wide amplitude which speaks of "Author's special rights". It does not speak of publisher's or owner's special rights. Action "prejudicial to his honour or reputation" within the ambit of Section 57(1)(b) is also referable to the author only.[342] The Section 57 runs:

> Author's special rights—(1) Independently of the author's copyright and even after the assignment either wholly or partially of the said copyright, the author of a work shall have the right—
>
> (a) to claim authorship of the work; and
> (b) to restrain or claim damages in respect of any distortion, mutilation, modification or other act in relation to the said work [...][343] if such distortion, mutilation, modification or other act would be prejudicial to his honour or reputation:
>
> Provided that the author shall not have any right to restrain or claim damages in respect of any adaptation of a computer programme to which clause (aa) of sub-section 52 applies.
>
> EXPLANATION—Failure to display a work or to display it to the satisfaction of the author shall not be deemed to be an infringement of the rights conferred by this section.
>
> (2) The right conferred upon an author of a work by sub-section (1) [...][344] may be exercised by the legal representatives of the author.

---

341. 193 (2012) DLT 135: 2013 (53) PTC 401 (Del).
342. *Wiley Eastern Ltd.* v. *Indian Institute of Management,* 61 (1996) DLT 281: 1995 (35) DRJ 522.
343. The words "which is done before the expiration of the term of copyright" omitted by the Copyright (Amendment) Act, 2012 [w.e.f. 21-6-2012] Section 36(i).
344. The words "other than the right to claim authorship of the work" omitted by the Copyright (Amendment) Act, 2012, [w.e.f. 21-6-2012] Section 36(ii).

The Delhi High Court in *Mannu Bhandari* v. *Kala Vikas Pictures Pvt. Ltd.,*[345] considered a number of issues relating to author's moral rights. The issues for the consideration of court were: How far law protects creative aesthetic expression of an artist? Is the intellectual property of an artist governed by the same norms as commercial property? Where does the freedom (of expression) of author end, where does the director begin? What is the scope and width of Section 57 of the Copyright Act, 1957? The court held that any deed of assignment of copyright shall be subject to this special right of the author. In this case the plaintiff permitted the defendant to convert her novel into a film by assigning all her filming rights. Even after the assignment the plaintiff has sought to restrain the defendants from screening or exhibiting the film on grounds of distortion and mutilation. The Court, while deciding the case clarified Section 57 as overriding any terms of a contract of assignment of copyright. In other words, a contract of assignment was held subject to the provisions of Section 57. The terms of a contract of assignment cannot negate the special rights and remedies guaranteed by Section 57. Thus, Section 57 in effect elevates the author beyond the material gains of copyright.

The court further stated thus:

> Section 57 of the Copyright Act is one such example of legal protection. Section 57 lifts author's status beyond the material gains of copyright and gives it as special status. This is a statutory recognition of the intellectual property of the author and special care with which the intellectual property is protected. Under Section 57, the author shall have a right to claim the authorship of the work. He has also a right to restrain the infringement or to claim damages for the infringement. These rights are independent of author's copyright and the remedies open to author under Section 55. In other words, Section 57 confers additional rights on the author of a literary work as compared to the owner of a general copyright. The special protection of the intellectual property is emphasized by the fact that the remedy of a restraint order or damages can be claimed 'even after the assignment either wholly or partially of the said copyright. Section 57 thus clearly overrides the terms of the contract of assignment of the copyright. The contract of assignment would be read subject to the provisions of Section 57 and the terms of the contract cannot negate the special rights and remedies guaranteed by Section 57. The contract of Assignment will have to be so construed as to be consistent with Section 57. The assignee of a copyright cannot claim any rights or immunities based on the contract which are inconsistent with the provisions of Section 57.

In *Wiley Eastern Ltd.* v. *Indian Institute of Management,*[346] the court held that the words "Action prejudicial to his honour or reputation" under Section 57(1)(b) refers only to the author of the work and not to any other person related with the work in any manner. Section 57 is a special provision for the protection of the special rights of the author. The objective of the section is to put the intellectual property on higher footing than the normal objects of copyright. The scope of the moral right protection under Section 57 of the Copyright Act 1957 was considered by the Court in *Amar Nath Sehgal* v. *Union of India.*[347] The plaintiff in this case at the request of Government of India agreed to produce a piece of art—a bronze mural sculpture—140 feet span and 40 feet sweep on one of the walls of Vigyan Bhavan lobby in 1957. The theme of the mural was a delicate balance between the cultural and material aspects in national perspective and science of rural and modern India. The copyright of the mural was transferred to the Government of India. The mural was in the lobby till 1979

345. AIR 1987 Delhi 13: (1986) ILR Delhi 191.
346. 1995 PTR 53 (Del.).
347. 2005 (30) PTC 253 (Del): (2005) 117 DLT 717.

when it was pulled down and stored in the government stored at the time of renovation of the Vigyan Bhavan. This act of destruction of the mural was without the permission, consent or authorisation of the plaintiff. According to the plaintiff, the mural has become an important part of India's cultural heritage. Hence he requested the Government of India to reinstate the same in the same lobby. The government expressed its inability to put it back on the lobby though agreed to reinstate in some other place. Aggrieved by this, the plaintiff filed the present suit for the violation of moral rights under Section 57 of the Act and prayed for the injunction restraining further destruction, damages of ₹50 lakh and return of the mural for reconstruction.

It was clear from the letter from the Government of India dated 6 July 1991 to the plaintiff that the government was willing to display the mural in the Vigyan Bhavan Annex in any location as per the choice of the plaintiff. But it expressed the difficulty of assuring him to put it back in the lobby of Vigyan Bhavan.[348] It appears that the plaintiff was not happy with it and wanted the government to return his mural. It is also evident from the facts that though it was stated in the letter from the Government of India to the plaintiff that the mural was intact, the commissioner appointed by the court clearly stated that there was some destruction caused to the mural. So the precise question that needs consideration was whether failure to display the artistic work to the full satisfaction of the author and failure to preserve the work would amount to violation of the rights given under section 57 of the Act, It is clear from Section 57 that the author can claim remedy "if such distortion, mutilation, modification or other act would be prejudicial to his honour or reputation". The question in this case was whether the failure on the part of the Government of India to display the mural in the lobby of Vigyan Bhavan would fall under "other act prejudicial to his honour or reputation" and the failure to preserve the mural from destruction would fall under "distortion or mutilation prejudicial to his honour or reputation". It is clear from the facts that the artist is a very reputed person and his mural was well received by the public and became part of the cultural heritage of India. So the act of dismantling the mural and storing it is government store resulting in its destruction was a clear case which affected the reputation of the author.

It is unfortunate to note that to reach this conclusion the court referred to a host of authorities like *Berne Conventions*, Shakespeare's *Othello*, amendments introduced to Section 57, academic writings, chapter on art and Culture in the 10th Five Year Plan of India, international conventions protecting cultural heritage.[349] The court finally interpreted Section 57 thus:

> It has to be noted that as originally enacted, Section 57 of the Copyright Act, 1957 was very widely worded because of the fact that the words "would be prejudicial to his honour or reputation" which found mention in sub Clause (b) of sub Section (1) of Section 57 were not qualifying sub Clause (a) of sub Section (1) of Section 57, Further, the words "any other action" which found mention in sub Clause (b) implied that the action could be other than a claim for damages or a claim for injunction. Post amendment, as the section stands effective from 10 May 1995, the legislature has restricted the right of the author to claim damages or to seek an order of restrain. Further, proof of prejudice to the author's honour or reputation has been made the *sine qua non* for claiming damages.[350]

348. *Ibid.* at p. 258 (PTC).
349. *Ibid.* at pp. 265–266 (PTC).
350. *Ibid.* at p. 267 (PTC).

Since the court found it difficult to get a clear interpretation of Section 57 to decide the case it further observed:

> There would therefore be urgent need to interpret Section 57 of the Copyright Act, 1957 in its wider amplitude to include destruction of a work of art, being the extreme form of mutilation, since by reducing the volume of the author's creative corpus it affects his reputation prejudicially as being actionable under said section. Further, in relation to the work of an author, subject to the work attaining the status of a modern national treasure, the right would include an action to protect the integrity of the work in relation to the cultural heritage of the nation.[351]

The court finally concluded:

> It is held that the plaintiff has a cause to maintain an action under Section 57 of the Copyright Act, 1957 notwithstanding that the copyright in the mural stands vested in the defendants. It is further held that the defendants have not only violated the plaintiff's moral right of integrity in the mural but have also violated the integrity of the work in relation to the cultural heritage of the nation.[352]

A plain reading of Section 57 before and after amendment makes it clear that there are four categories of acts—distortion, mutilation, modification or other act—that constitute moral right violation. Before amendment it was only in case of "other act" thus there was a need to establish that it was prejudicial to the honour or reputation of the author. But after the amendment in all cases it is necessary to establish that it is prejudicial to the honour or reputation of the author. So it is very clear that once it is established that the honour or reputation of the author is affected irrespective of the nature of the act it would amount to violation of moral right. So there was no difficulty in this case to conclude that the act of dismantling and keeping it in storeroom resulting in destruction of the work was a violation of moral right of the plaintiff. Instead of doing this, the court seems to have interpreted the words "other acts" to mean remedies other than injunction and damages. But the interesting question that was not answered by the court is whether the failure to display the work to the satisfaction of the author would amount to violation of moral rights. It is to be noted that while the case was pending the section was amended and an explanation was added to exclude this from the category of "other acts". It appears that his was introduced keeping in mind the present case. But if the whole purpose for which a work was commissioned is to display it in a particular place and the work was created by the author with that intention, it is important to examine whether failure to display it in that manner results in violation of moral rights. It is also important to note that one of the rights conferred to the author in Section 14(1)(c) is to communicate the work to the public. This right includes the display of the work in public for viewing. As per the contract, this right has been transferred to the Government of India as part of the copyright. In this context, it is interesting to examine whether the author could think of a public display as part of the moral right. Instead of wasting the time and energy on finding the scope of moral right in cultural heritage, the court should have used the opportunity to examine this issue and decide the scope of the amendment.

The court in this case granted the following remedies:[353]

351. *Ibid.*
352. *Ibid.* at p. 268 (PTC).
353. *Ibid.*

1. A mandatory injunction directing the defendants to return to the plaintiff the remnants of the mural within two weeks from today.
2. Declaration is granted in favour of the plaintiff and against the defendants that all rights in the mural shall henceforth vest in the plaintiff the defendants would no right whatsoever in the mural.
3. Declaration is granted in favour of the plaintiff that he would have an absolute right to recreate the mural at any place and would have the right to sell the same.
4. Damages in the sum of ₹5 lakh are awarded in favour of the plaintiff and against the defendants. If not paid within one month from today, the damages shall carry simple interest at 9% p.a. from today till date of payment.
5. Costs shall follow in favour of the plaintiff and against the defendants.

One of the remedies provided under Section 57 is to restrain the owner of copyright from violating the moral right. The court concluded that the Government of India had violated the moral rights by dismantling the mural and keeping it in the storeroom. So the proper remedy was to direct the government to display the mural and to preserve the same at the expense of the Government of India. Of course given the facts and circumstances of the case, this needed the help of the author.[354] Instead the court directed the government to return the remnants of the mural to the author to prevent moral right violation. It appears that it was the failure of the court to examine the right of the author to display his work as moral rights that resulted in this conclusion. This forced the court to direct the return of the copyright in the mural to the author and gave him the absolute right to recreate the work and enjoy the copyright of the work. The net result is that the court accepted the fact that the author of the work has no moral right to demand the display of the work once it is transferred. It appears that in this case the court directed to return the work to the author since it is getting damaged. But in cases where the work is kept in a locked room without any damage, it is difficult to use this precedent to demand the return of the work along with the copyright on the ground of violation of moral rights. In such cases, the author may not have any remedy including the one granted in this case unless the right to display the work is recognised as moral right. In the light of the amendment introduced in Section 57, if the author wanted to ensure that his work is displayed, he must either retain his right to communication with him or make it clear in the contract transferring the copyright that his must be displayed.

In *Ramesh Sippy* v. *Shaan Ranjeet Uttam Singh*,[355] the issue before the Bombay High Court was whether the appellant had special rights as author in film. In this case, the appellant claimed to be author of and first owner of copyright in the film *Sholay*. He claimed to be entitled to author's special rights in the film and sought injunction restraining respondents from alienating, encumbering, disposing of or creating any interests and releasing 3-D version of *Sholay*. It was alleged by appellant that he had both copyright in film as unpublished work under Section 13(2)(ii) of Copyright Act, 1957 and author's special rights under Section 57 of Act. However, the Court observed that there was no material available to show that appellant contributed any finance. Further, for almost four decades, *Sholay* has been exhibited and distributed in different media and format and at no point did appellant object to any of this.

354. *See, Amar Nath Sehgal* v. *Union of India*, 2005 (30) PTC 253 (Del): 117 (2005) DLT 717.
355. MIPR 2014 (1) 32.

To the contrary, evidence was presented to show that when respondents asserted their rights in other legal proceedings, far from objecting, appellant supported its claim. Also observed that after release of *Sholay*, various entities dealt with rights and as many as twelve agreements were entered including assignment of video copyright and cable TV, Pay TV, Satellite, Broadcasting and Communication rights. But execution of these agreements was never disputed by appellant. Further, two public notices were issued by respondents asserting its exclusive ownership of copyrights in various films, including *Sholay*. There was no material to show that in forty years, appellant even once objected to these transactions, proposed assignments and assertions of copyright ownership by respondent. The Court also observed that authorship of work was to be determined when work came into existence whereas in the present case, on date of appellant's retirement, appellant could not have acquired any copyright in film as *Sholay* was not complete by then. Hence, Appellant was not able to make out *prima facie* case in his favour. Thus, authorship of any work can only be determined if the work comes into existence.

Release Share Right

Another aspect of moral rights is "release share right in original work". The Copyright (Amendment) Act, 1994 inserted a new Section 53A to the principal Act. According to Section 53A of the Act, when an original copy of a painting; sculpture, drawing or a manuscript of a literary, dramatic or musical work is resold at a price exceeding ₹10,000, the author is entitled to a share of ten per cent of the resale price, irrespective of the ownership of exclusive economic rights. This right subsists in the author and his heirs for the distribution for which the copyright subsists in them. The release share shall in no circumstances exceed ten per cent of the resale price. The parties themselves may fix the share or the Appellate Board[356] may do so. The Appellate Board may fix different shares for different kinds of works but cannot exceed ten per cent of the resale price. If any dispute arises regarding the right, then it shall be referred to the Copyright Board whose decision shall be final. Besides, Section 58[357] of the Copyright Act, 1957 provides that all infringing copies of any work in which copyright subsists or any of substantial part thereof, become the property of the owner of the copyright. He has a right to recover the possession of the infringing copies unsold and the price of copies sold. The infringing copies which have been sold being regarded as the property of the owner, he is entitled to the money in which they were actually sold.[358] Thus, moral rights are basic rights of artists that extend beyond ownership of economic control of works of authorship, to

356. Substituted by the Finance Act 2017 (7 of 2017), section 160(a) for "Copyright Board," [w.e.f. 26 May, 2017].

357. Section 58 reads: "Rights of owner against persons possessing or dealing with infringing copies—All infringing copies of any work in which copyright subsists, and all plates used or intended to be used for the production of such infringing copies, shall be deemed to be the property of the owner of the copyright, who accordingly may take proceedings for the recovery of possession thereof or in respect of the conversion thereof:

Provided that the owner of the copyright shall not be entitled to any remedy in respect of the conversion of any infringing copies, if the opponent proves—(a) that he was not aware and had no reasonable ground to believe that copyright subsisted in the work of which such copies are alleged to be infringing copies; or (b) that he had reasonable grounds for believing that such copies or plates do not involve infringement of the copyright in any work."

358. *Gopal Das* v. *Jagan Nath Prasad*, AIR 1938 All 266.

encompass protections of the "personality" of the author. They normally include (and often go beyond) the right to have one's name associated with one's work (right of attribution); and the right to protect one's works from distortion (right of integrity).[359]

Neighbouring Rights

Neighbouring rights were established in order to ensure that individuals auxiliary to the creation or production of musical content could have similar control over their creative endeavours to that which is granted to composers of musical works through copyright. These rights protect the performances of musical compositions embodied within phonographic recordings commonly transmitted to the public through radio or other such broadcasting services. The owner of these rights have the exclusive right to cause the sound recording to be heard in public, to cause the recording to be broadcasted, and to make secondary phonographs embodying the recording or any part of it. Thus these rights tend to be collectively administered in order to allow rights holders the ability neighbouring rights tend to be collectively administered in order to allow rights holders the ability.[360] These special rights are referred to as "neighbouring rights" under international conventions.

These special rights or "neighbouring rights" are given to broadcasting organisations and performers under Section 37 and 38 *inter alia* of the Copyright Act, 1957 in India too. The Copyright (Amendment) Act, 1994 introduced for the first time limited rights for the performers in their live performances for a period of fifty years from the year following the performance through Section 38. Substantial provisions of the Act which are applicable to the owners of copyright have also been extended to the performer's right with necessary variations and modifications. According to Section 2(qq)[361] a "performer"[362] includes an actor, singer, musician, dancer, acrobat, juggler, conjurer, snake charmer, and a person delivering a lecture or any other person whom makes a performance. Further, under Section 2(q), "performance"[363] includes any visual or acoustic presentation made live by one or more performers. Thus, any person who (a) makes a sound recording or visual recording of the performance; or (b) reproduces a sound recording or visual recording made without the performers consent; or (c) broadcasts the performance; or (d) communicates the performance to the public, without the consent of the performer, infringes his rights.[364] However, once the performer has consented

359. *See, Raj Rewal* v. Union of India, 260 (2019) DLT 190; *PEE PEE Publisher and Distributors (P) Ltd.* v. *Neena Khanna*, 2009 (40) PTC 515 (Del).
360. For detail discussion, see, James A. Hayes, "Copyright and Related Rights in Canada and Abroad: A View Towards a More Globally Unified System of Neighbouring Rights," 64 *Journal of Copyright Society of the USA* (2017) pp. 411–436; Rasmus Fleischer, "Protecting the Musicians and/or the Record Industry? On the History of 'Neighbouring Rights' and the Role of Fascist Italy," 5(3) *Queen Mary Journal of Intellectual Property* (2015) pp. 327–343.
361. Inserted by the Copyright (Amendment) Act, 1999, Section 2.
362. For various issues on performers' rights, *see*, WIPO, "Protection of Neighbouring Right's (Rights of Performers, Producers of Phonograms and Broadcasting Organisations): International Conventions in the Field of Neighbouring Rights" 28 *Journal of the Indian Law Institute* 1986 pp. 450–469; K. Ponnuswami, "Performing Right of the Intellectual Worker: Judicial Annihilation", 28 *Journal of the Indian Law Institute* (1986) pp. 470–486.
363. Copyright Act, 1957, Section 2(q).
364. *Ibid.*, Section 38(3).

to the incorporation of his performances into a film, his right ceases to operate in such performance.[365] This limitation imposed to save the film industry in fact defeats the object behind the protection of performer's right. The term of protection of performer's right is 50 years from the beginning of the next calendar year following the performance.[366] Performer's right too can be assigned or licenced with, freely. All the conditions applicable to transfer of copyright have to be followed this case too.[367] The consent required from the performer to incorporate his performance into a cinematograph film must also be in a similar format. It has to be in writing and duly signed. Although this is not expressly stated in the Act, the intention of the legislators to this effect is clear from Section 39A, which makes the conditions laid down in Section 19 applicable to performer's rights.

Like rights for the performers, the Copyright (Amendment) Act 1994 has introduced another special right known as Broadcast Reproduction Right (BRR) for the benefit of broadcasting organisations in respect of its broadcasts through Section 37. This right too like other rights mentioned earlier could be freely transferred by an assignment or a licence agreement. It subsists for a period of 25 years from the year of broadcast and enables the owner of it to prevent the unauthorised—(i) rebroadcast of the broadcast; (ii) communication of the broadcast to the public upon payment of charges; (iii) sound or visual recording of the broadcast and the reproduction of such sound or visual recording; and (iv) sale or hire to public or offering for such sale or hire.[368] The owner is entitled to take infringement action if any person unauthorisedly engages in such activities. The BRR can be infringed in three ways: (i) by unauthorised re-broadcast of the programme (or any substantial part thereof); or (ii) by causing it to be heard in public (whether in whole or in substantial part); or (iii) finally, by making a record, in whole or part, of the programme. It has been declared by Section 39, for the removal of doubts, that BRR shall not affect the copyright in any literary, dramatic or musical work which is broadcast by the authority or in any record recording such work. Provisions regarding assignment of BRR, licencing, infringement by importation of copies, civil remedies, and criminal sanctions and processes for infringement are made applicable, *mutatis mutandis,* to BRR.

The Copyright Act also places some limitations upon the exclusive rights envisaged by it. These are done to further the interests of the public in the maximum dissemination of works at reasonable prices. Further the scope of rights has been limited so as to exempt private usage of works, research and study purposes, etc. from the scope of infringement actions. These limitation can be seen in the provisions relating to compulsory licences and permissible use without licence envisage in the Act. While the compulsory licencing provisions (Sections 31 to 32A) entitle any person to apply for a compulsory licence to print, publish and translate the work if it is withheld from the public, Section 52 exempts certain acts from the scope of infringement of rights.[369]

---

365. *Ibid.*, Section 38(4).
366. *Ibid.*, Section 38(2).
367. *Ibid.*, Section 39(A).
368. *Ibid.*, Section 37.
369. For general discussion, *see*, Daniel Gervais, "The Protection of Performers under US Law in Comparative Perspective," 5(1) *IP Theory* (2019) pp. 116–133; Noppanun Supasiripongchai, "The Protection of Performer's Rights under the Copyright Law in Thailand: The Proposed Reform in the Light of the Prospective Free Trade Agreements with the United States and European Union," 2(4) *Intellectual Properties Rights: Open Access* (2014) pp. 1–19.

6

Term of Copyright, Licencing of Copyright, International Copyright and Registration of Copyright

ABSTRACT

The term of copyright is fixed by the statute for a limited period separately for different categories of works while a statute of copyright recognises licencing as a method of copyright transfer. Thus, owner of the copyright in any existing work or the prospective owner of the copyright in any future work may grant any interest in the right by licence. Under "international copyright" certain works of foreign authors/owners are accorded the same protection in India to which the Indian citizens are entitled while registration of copyright serves as a piece of evidence. Thus, the author or publisher of the work, or the owner of or other person interested in the copyright in any work may apply for registration. This chapter demonstrates major issues on aforementioned subjects.

INTRODUCTION

Copyright is not an absolute right; it is a right with limitations. But, how long should a copyright last? This question has troubled scholars and policymakers ever since the first copyright statute was enacted in England in 1709 and continues to do so today. The controversy continues because of fundamental differences of opinion concerning the basic philosophy and purposes of copyright law.[1] Nevertheless, there are certain statutory limitations on copyright as has been recognised in the Copyright Act 1957.[2] Thus, copyright does not continue for an indefinite period.[3] The sections 22 to 29 of the Act provide for a period of time, a duration for which the rights of a copyright owner exist and thereafter the work falls in public domain. Limited duration of copyright is true for all classes of works like literary, dramatic, musical, artistic

1. *See*, Tyler T. Ochoa, *Limits on Duration of Copyright: Theories and Practice* (Santa Clara University School of Law, 2010).
2. *See*, Zakir Thomas, "Overview of Changes to the Indian Copyright Law," 17 *Journal of Intellectual Property Rights* (2012) pp. 324–334.
3. *See*, *UTV Software Communication Ltd.* v. *1337X*, 2019 (78) PTC 375 (Del); *Prabhat Agri Biotech Ltd.* v. *Registrar of Plant Varieties*, MIPR 2017 (1) 349.

works, cinematograph films and sound recording.[4] In *Holland Company LP* v. *S.P. Industries*,[5] the Court has specifically held that the owner can relinquish it's copyright by dedicating the same in public domain as prescribed under Section 21 of the Act. But in a case where the owner neither relinquished nor entered in public domain its copyright, it cannot be said that the work has entered in public domain. In *Gramophone Company of India Ltd.* v. *Super Cassettes Industries Ltd.*,[6] the Delhi High Court rightly observed that as per Section 13(4) of the Act an owner's copyright in primary works remains unaffected by utilisation of the said works for making a sound recording. This is the position when owner's copyright in such primary works subsists. However, upon expiry of term of copyright in such primary works the same falls in public domain and becomes available for exploitation by others in all possible ways. Further, in *Syndicate* v. *Chancellor Masters*,[7] the Court held that the public domain is most often discussed in contrast to works whose use is restricted by copyright. Under modern law, most original works of art, literature, music, etc. are covered by copyright from the time of their creation for a limited period of time (which varies by country). When the copyright expires, the work enters the public domain. Sections 30 to 32B of the Act provide another limitation on copyright. These provisions of the Act deal with the law relating to licencing of copyright. The Act recognises licences as a method of copyright transfer. In *Raj Video Vission* v. *K. Mohankrishnan,*[8] it was held that when producers are not aware of their rights accrued to them due to scientific advancements, it cannot be said that they have already transferred the rights not in existence by way of assignments. Sections 40 to 43 of the Act recognise the international copyright. In the following sections an attempt has been made to discuss the law relating to terms of copyright, compulsory licencing, international copyright and registration of copyright.

TERMS OF COPYRIGHT

Copyright is a part of intellectual property rights like other forms of property interests.[9] Once a copyright is acquired, the entire bundle of rights may be assigned to others.[10] Alternatively, the owner may divide and transfer particular rights. Nonetheless, there are significant differences between ownership rules governing copyright and those governing other property interests in society that copyrights have limited duration, but other property rights are perpetual. In England the Statute of Anne, 1709 had provided exclusive copyright in favour of authors for a limited

4. *See*, *Star India Private Limited* v. *Department of Industrial Policy*, (2019) 2 SCC 104: 2018 (14) SCALE 651; *S.M. Ashokan* v. *Raj Television Net Work Ltd.*, MIPR 2017 (1) 398; 2016-5-LW 881; *Music Broadcast Limited* v. *Axis Bank*, 2016 (67) PTC 638 (Del).
5. 2017 (71) PTC 630 (Del): MIPR 2017 (3) 237.
6. MIPR 2010 (2) 349: 2010 (44) PTC 541 (Del).
7. 185 (2011) DLT 346.
8. AIR 1998 Mad 294.
9. *See*, *Crocs Inc.* v. *Bata India Ltd.*, 2019 (78) PTC 1 (Del); *Sun Pharma Laboratories Limited* v. *MNC Therapeutic Sciences Pvt. Ltd.*, 2019 (77) PTC 452 (Mad); *Dabur India Limited* v. *Shree Baidyanath Ayurved Bhawan Pvt. Ltd.*, 193 (2012) DLT 558: 2012 (51) PTC 441 (Del); *Frito-Lay India* v. *Radesh Foods*, 2009 (40) PTC 37 (Del); *Burroughs Wellcome (India) Ltd.* v. *Uni-Sole Pvt. Ltd.*, 1998 (3) Bom CR 481: 1997 (3) Mh Lj 914.
10. *See*, *Luxottica Group S.P.A.* v. *Mify Solutions Pvt. Ltd.*, 2019 (77) PTC 139 (Del): 254 (2018) DLT 472; *Maganlal Savani* v. *Uttam Chitra,* 2008 (3) Bom CR 624: MIPR 2008 (2) 95.

period of 14 years and which was extendable for another 14 years. However, the perpetual copyright had enjoyed by the Universities of Oxford and Cambridge and the Colleges of Eton, Winchester and Westminster in relation to certain works under the Copyright Act, 1775. The English Copyright, Designs and Patents Act, 1988 abolished the perpetual copyright of Universities and provides copyrights for limited duration for all.[11] In America, the copyright law also provides the limited duration of copyright.[12]

There is no universal copyright term even among the countries of the Berne Union. Article 7 of the Berne Convention 1886 (Revised in 1971) provides a floor limit of life term of author plus 50 years. Thus, according to Article 7(1) of the Berne Convention, "the term of protection granted by this Convention shall be the life of the author and fifty years after his death".[13] The term of protection subsequent to the death of the author shall run from the date of the death. Such term shall always be deemed to begin on the first of January of the year following the death. However, in any case, the term shall be governed by the legislation of the country where the protection is claimed. At the national level, the governments are free to provide a longer term of protection. For example, in England and United States of America, the period of protection of works is the lifetime of the author plus seventy years.

In India, the law relating to determining the period or duration for subsistence of copyright are given under Sections 22 to 29 of the Copyright Act, 1957. The rules for determining the duration of copyright depend on the nature of the work in question. Thus, Section 22 deals with the term of copyright in published literary, dramatic and musical or artistic work.[14] In the case of anonymous and pseudonymous works, term is provided under Section 23 and posthumous work under Section 24. Sections 26 and 27 deal with the term of copyright in cinematograph film and sound recording and such term is 60 years from the beginning of the calendar year next following the year in which the film or the sound recording is published.[15] This is also the period for government works,[16] works of public undertakings[17] and international organisations.[18]

Term of Copyright in Published Literary, Dramatic, Musical and Artistic Works [Section 22]

Section 22 of the Copyright Act, 1957 deals with the term of copyright in published literary, dramatic and musical or artistic work and stipulates that such term shall be [sixty years][19]

11. Schedule 1 of the English Copyright, Designs and Patents Act, 1988 provides that copyright least for the life of the author plus 70 years for literary, dramatic, musical and artistic works (the "original works") and films, and at least 50 years for sound recordings, broadcasts and cable programmes and 25 years for typographical arrangements of published editions.
12. *See*, Kevin A. Goldman, "Limited Times: Rethinking the Bounds of Copyright Protection," 157 *University of Pennsylvania Law Review* (2006) pp. 705–740.
13. *See*, *Novartis AG* v. *Union of India*, AIR 2013 SC 1311: (2013) 6 SCC 1.
14. *Microfibres Inc.* v. *Girdhar*, MIPR 2009 (2) 229: 2009 (40) PTC 519 (Del).
15. *Sulamangalam R. Jayalakshmi* v. *Meta Musicals,* AIR 2000 Mad 454: 2000-3-LW 38.
16. Copyright Act, 1957, Section 28.
17. *Ibid*., Section 28A.
18. *Ibid*., 1957, Section 29.
19. Substituted by the Copyright (Amendment) Act, 1992, Section 2 for "fifty years".

from the beginning of the calendar year next following the year beyond the lifetime of the author.[20] Further, the Explanation of Section 22 clarifies that in the case of a work of joint authorship, be construed as a reference to the author who dies last.[21] Thus, in *Shuddhananda Yoga Samaj* v. *Rajeswari Book Shop*,[22] it was argued that as per the Section 22 the copyright in the literary works of Yogi Shuddhananda Bharathi would commence to operate only from the date of his demise i.e., April 7, 1990. Thus, it will operate for a period of sixty years from April 7, 1990, which means, the copyright will subsist till April 6, 2050. Therefore, by operation of Section 22, copyright did subsist in the plaintiff (on the date of filing of the suit) qua the aforesaid work being literary work in the form of a book which goes by the title "Maha Kavi Dhante". The Court held that the proposition of law as has been argued on Section 22 of Copyright Act, is absolutely correct.

ILLUSTRATIONS

1. Mr. Amarnath Sehgal writes a Book on Environmental Law in 1990. The author Mr. Sehgal published the book in the year 1991 but he dies on 1 October 1992. The 60 year will be counted from 1 January 1993, i.e. the calendar year next following the years in which the author dies. The copyright in the work therefore, continues until 1 January 2053. Thereafter the work will be fall in public domain.
2. Before Copyright (Amendment) Act, 1992, the term of copyright in published literary, dramatic, musical and artistic works was (other than a photograph) published within the lifetime of the author until fifty years from the beginning of the calendar year next following the year in which the author dies. Thus, in *Khemraj Shrikrishandas* v. *Garg*,[23] the Delhi High Court held that Pandit Mani Ram died in 1905 as contended by the plaintiffs (or in 1909 as contended by the defendants), at all events, he died more than 50 years ago. Considered from any point of view, after 1960 copyright in the work or Panchang of Mani Ram, if any, could not subsist in the hands of his legal heirs.

In *Diamond Pocket Books Private Limited* v. *Prasad Nyas*,[24] the plaintiff filed the suit seeking a declaration that copyright to the works of late Shri Jai Shankar Prasad, who died on 15 November 1937 has come to an end 50 years from the beginning of the calendar year next following the year in which the author dies, in terms of Section 22 of the Copyright Act. The copyright thus came to an end on 15 January 1988. The right to reproduce the works of late Shri Jai Shankar Prasad in any material form got converted from an exclusive right into a public right, and in pursuance thereof any person could publish the works of late Shri Jai Shankar Prasad. In view of Section 22[25] of the Copyright Act, every person is entitled to publish the works of the said author as they have entered "public domain".

---

20. *See*, *Gramophone Company of India Ltd.* v. *Super Cassettes Industries Ltd.*, MIPR 2010 (2) 349: 2010 (44) PTC 541 (Del). *See also*, *Microforms Inc* v. *Girdhar*, 128 (2006) DLT 238: 2006 (32) PTC 157 (Del); *Sulamangalam R. Jayalakshmi* v. *Meta Musicals*, AIR 2000 Mad 454: 2000-3-LW 38; *Indian Performing Right Society Ltd.* v. *Eastern Indian Motion Pictures Association*, AIR 1977 SC 1443: (1977) 2 SCC 820; *Khemraj Shrikrishandas* v. *Garg*, AIR 1975 Delhi 130: (1975) ILR Delhi 251.
21. *Academy of General Education, Manipal* v. *B. Malini Mallya*, AIR 2009 SC 1982: (2009) 4 SCC 256.
22. 2018 (75) PTC 25 (Mad): 2018 (4) CTC 276.
23. AIR 1975 Delhi 130: (1975) ILR Delhi 251.
24. 1989 (2) DL 285: 1989 (17) DRJ 110.
25. Section 22 of the Copyright Act, 1957 states: "... copyright shall subsist in any literary, dramatic, musical or artistic work published within the lifetime of the author until sixty years from the beginning of the calendar year next following the year in which the author dies." Substituted by the Copyright (Amendment) Act, 1992 (Act 13 of 1992), Section 2, for "fifty years" [w.r.e.f. 28-12-1991].

Similarly, in *Kamlapati Khatri* v. *Sharda Prakashan*,[26] the plaintiff prayed for an injunction restraining the defendants from publishing literary work "BHUTNATH". Answering negatively, the court held that the literary work BHUTNATH is written by Shri Devki Nandan Khatri who died in the year 1913 and, according to the provisions of Section 22 of the Copyright Act, 1957, all the seven volumes of the work BHUTNATH except the epilogue at the expiry of 50 years from the date of the death of Shri Devki Nandan Khatri became "public domain".

A question may arise whether the copyright can be held by a company? Referring to Section 22 of the Copyright Act, 1957, in *Holland Company LP* v. *S.P. Industries*,[27] the court observed that since the stipulation "sixty years" refers to the death of the author, the copyright cannot be held by a Company. In this case, a distinction was also sought to be made out between a copyright and a design.

Term of Copyright in Anonymous and Pseudonymous Literary, Dramatic, Musical and Artistic Works [Section 23]

Section 23(1) of the Copyright Act, 1957 provides that in the case of a literary, dramatic, musical or artistic work (other than a photograph), which is published anonymously or pseudonymously, copyright shall subsist until sixty years from the beginning of the calendar year next following the year in which the work is first published. Where the identity of the author is disclosed before the expiry of the said period, copyright shall subsist until sixty years from the beginning of the calendar year following the year in which the author dies.[28]

ILLUSTRATIONS

1. Certain anonymously or pseudonymously works are published in the year 2000. The statutory period of 60 years will be counted from first January 2001 and thus the copyright will subsists until first January 2061. In this case, the relevant date is the date of publication of work.
2. Certain anonymously or pseudonymously works are published in the year 1990 but the identity of author was disclosed in the year 2000. The author died on 15 August 2002. The statutory period of 60 years will be counted from first January 2003 and thus the copyright will subsists until first January 2063. In this case, the protection is given for a longer duration than in case of Illustration 1. If identity of author is known, the relevant date is the day of the author's death.

In the case of an anonymous work of joint authorship, references to the author in Sub-section (1) of Section 23 shall be construed,

(a) where the identity of the authors is disclosed, as references to that author;
(b) where the identity of more authors than one is disclosed, as references to the author who dies last from amongst such authors.

---

26. 1987 (33) DLT 392.
27. 2014 (59) PTC 212: 2014 LawSuit (Del) 1878.
28. *See*, *Academy of General Education, Manipal* v. *B. Malini Mallya*, AIR 2009 SC 1982: (2009) 4 SCC 256.

ILLUSTRATION

An anonymous work of joint authorship was published in the year 1980 but the identity of one of the author's was disclosed in the year 1990 and other was disclosed in the year 1992. One of the authors died in the year 2000 and the other died in the year 2002. The statutory period of 60 years will be counted from first January 2003 and thus the copyright will subsists until first January 2063.

In the case of pseudonymous work of joint authorship, there may be a number of possibilities. The names of some of the authors may be pseudonymous while the name of some others may not be pseudonymous. Certain authors may have disclosed their identity while others may not have done so.[29] This action covers all such contingencies. In the case of pseudonymous work of joint authorship references to the author, in Sub-section (1) of Section 23 shall be construed—

1. where the names of one or more (but not all) of the authors are pseudonymous and his or their identity is not disclosed, as references to the author whose name is not a pseudonym, or, if the names of two or more of the authors are not pseudonyms, as references to such of those authors who dies last;
2. where the names of one or more (but not all) of the authors are pseudonyms and the identity of one or more of them is disclosed, as references to the author who dies last from amongst the authors whose names are not pseudonyms and the authors whose names are pseudonyms and are disclosed; and
3. where the names of all the authors are pseudonyms and the identity of one of them is disclosed, as references to the author whose identity is disclosed or if the identity of two or more of such authors is disclosed, as references to such of those authors who dies last.

The Explanation to Section 23 states that the identity of an author shall be deemed to have been disclosed, if either the identity of the author is disclosed publicly by both the author and the publisher or is otherwise established to the satisfaction of the Appellate Board[30] by that author.

ILLUSTRATION

A pseudonymous work of joint authorship was published in the year 1980 but the identity of one of the authors was disclosed in the year 1990 and other was disclosed in the year 1992. One of the authors died in the year 2000 and the other died in the year 2002. The term of the copyright would be until the expiry of 60 years beginning from the calendar year following the death of the "disclosed author" or the death of the "last of the disclosed authors". Thus, in this case the copyright will subsist until first January 2063.

Referring the anonymous and pseudonymous works in *Academy of General Education, Manipal* v. *B. Malini Mallya*,[31] the Apex Court held that a literary work with dramatic elements in it would also be literary work. Therefore, the main classification as literary work

---

29. *See, Academy* v. *B. Malini Mallya*, AIR 2009 SC 1982: (2009) 4 SCC 256.
30. Substituted by the Finance Act 2017 (7 of 2017), section 160(a) for "Copyright Board," [w.e.f. 26 May, 2017].
31. AIR 2009 SC 1982: 2009 (39) PTC 393.

and dramatic work cannot be construed to mean that dramatic work has nothing to do with literary work. The only difference in them is that the dramatic work (Plays) forms the text upon which the performance of the plays rests whereas a "literary work" enables one to read the printed words. Neither of the two can be produced without the imaginative skill of the author.

Term of Copyright in Posthumous Work [Section 24]

Section 24 of the Copyright Act, 1957 provides that in case of a literary, dramatic or musical work or an engraving in which copyright subsists at the date of the death of the author or, in the case of any such work of joint authorship, at or immediately before the date of the death of the author who dies last, but which, or any adaptation of which has not been published before that date, copyright subsists until 60 years from the beginning of the calendar year next following the year in which the work is first published or, where an adaptation of the work is published in any earlier year, from the beginning of the calendar year next following that year. For the purpose of Section 24, a literary, dramatic or musical work for an adaptation of any such work is deemed to be published if it has been performed in public or if any sound recording made in respect of the work have been sold to the public or have been offered for sale to the public. Thus, the copyright subsists until 60 years from the beginning of the calendar year next following the year in which the work is first published.

ILLUSTRATION

Mr. Amar Singh Badal authored a novel in the year 1960 but subsequently he dies on 31 August 1962. Thereafter, his heirs published his work in March 1963. The statuary requirements of 60 years begin from 1 January 1964 and therefore copyright will subsist until 1 January 2024. In this case the work is deemed to be published if: (i) it has been performed in public, or (ii) if any sound recording made in respect of the work have been sold to the public or have been offered for sale to the public.

Term of Copyright in Photographs [Section 25]

According to Section 25 of the Copyright Act, 1957 in the case of a photograph copyright subsists until 60 years from the beginning of the calendar year next following the year in which the photograph is published. The Copyright (Amendment) Act, 2012 has deleted Section 25[32] where by the term of 60 years was counted from the date of publication. After 2012 amendment, the term of protection is the same as literary work. Thus, the term of copyright in a photograph has been made at par with other artistic works, namely, until sixty years after the death of the author, by deleting "other than photographs" in Clause 22 and deleting Section 25 which provided for a special term for photographs (of sixty years from publication). This amendment is consequential to Article 9 of WCT regarding duration of protection of photographic works.

32. Copyright (Amendment) Act, 2012, Section 13 [w.e.f. 21-6-2012].

Term of Copyright in Cinematograph Films [Section 26], Sound Recordings [Section 27]

Section 26 of the Copyright Act, 1957 provides that in the case of a cinematograph film, copyright shall subsists until [sixty years] from the beginning of the calendar year next following the year in which the film is published. Explaining the term of copyright in cinematograph films under Section 26 of the Act in *AGS Entertainment Private Limited* v. *Union of India*,[33] it was held that copyright shall subsist until sixty years from the beginning of the calendar year next following the year in which the film is published. Similarly, according to Section 27 of the Act in the case of a [sound recording][34] copyright shall subsists until [sixty years][35] from the beginning of the calendar year next following the year in which the [sound recording][36] is published. Thus, in *Gramophone Company of India Ltd.* v. *Super Cassettes Industries Ltd.*,[37] the Delhi High Court held that Sections 26 and 27 deal with term of copyright in cinematograph film and sound recording and such term is 60 years from the beginning of the calendar year next following the year in which the film or the sound recording is published.

ILLUSTRATION

> Mr. Anurag Deep published a cinematograph film on 15 August 2000. On the same date, his friend Mr. A.R. Rahman published his sound recording. In both cases, the statutory period of 60 years begins from 1 January 2001 and the copyright will subsist until 1 January 2061.

Comparing Section 27 with Section 22 of the Act in *Entertainment Network (India) Ltd.* v. *Super Cassette Industries Ltd.*,[38] the Supreme Court held that whereas the term of a copyright in original literary, dramatic, musical and artistic works not only remains protected in the entire lifetime of the author but also until 60 years from the beginning of the calendar year next following the year in which the author dies, the term of copyright in sound recording subsists only for 60 years, but as indicated hereinbefore, the same would not mean that the right of an owner of sound recording is in any way inferior to that of right of an owner of copyright on original literary work, etc. The Court further observed:

> Only because the term for holding copyright under the said provisions are different, the same would not mean that the right of the copyright owner in sound recording is somewhat inferior.[39]

In *Kajal Agarwal* v. *The Managing Director*,[40] the Madras High Court held that as the respondent is the first owner of the copyright, he will have the exclusive right to communicate the cinematograph film to the public by virtue of Section 14 (i) (d) (iii). Thus, once the respondent becomes the first owner of the copyright, the right shall subsist for a period of 60

---

33. (2013) 262 CTR (Mad) 471: 2013 (4) CTC 473.
34. Substituted by the Copyright (Amendment) Act, 1994, Section 2, for "record" [w.e.f. 10-5-1995].
35. Substituted by the Copyright (Amendment) Act, 1992, Section 2, for "fifty years" [w.r.e.f. 28-12-1991].
36. Substituted by the Copyright (Amendment) Act, 1994, Section 2, for "record" [w.e.f. 10-5-1995].
37. MIPR 2010 (2) 349: 2010 (44) PTC 541 (Del).
38. 2008 (9) SCALE 69: (2008) 13 SCC 30. *See also, International Confederation of Societies of Authors* v. *Aditya Pandey*, (2017) 11 SCC 437: 2016 (9) SCALE 89.
39. *See also, Music Broadcast Private Ltd.* v. *Indian Performing Right Society Ltd.*, 2011 (47) PTC 592 (Bom): 2011 (113) BomLR 3153.
40. (2018) 5 MLJ 818: 2018 (5) CTC 185.

years as provided under Section 26 of the Copyright Act 1957. Thus, in *S.M. Ashokan* v. *Raj Television Net Work Ltd.*,[41] it was held that the owner of copyright can assign either wholly or partly and either generally or subject to limitations and either for whole term of copyright or any part thereof.

Term of Copyright in Works of Government, Public Undertakings and International Organisations [Sections 28, 28A and 29]

According to Sections 28 and 28A of the Copyright Act, 1957 where government or public undertaking is the first owner of copyright therein then [sixty years][42] will be counted from 1 January of the calendar year next following the year in which the work is first published. Further, Section 29 of the Act provides that in the case of a work of any international organisation copyright shall subsists until sixty years from the beginning of the calendar year next following the year in which the work is first published.

It emerges from the foregoing discussions that the general term for copyright in literary, dramatic, musical and artistic works, etc. is the author's life and sixty years thereafter. If there are joint authors, then the term is measured from the death of the longest living among those who qualify for copyright. The term of copyright varies according to the nature of the work. The copyright protection takes effect only from the date of publication of the work. In the case of literary, dramatic, musical and artistic works where the author is natural person the term of copyright is lifetime of the author plus sixty years. In all other cases, the term of copyright is sixty years. Thus, the copyright is a statutory right for a limited duration.[43] Comparing this limited duration of copyright with other branches of intellectual property, the Delhi High Court in *Mohan Lal* v. *Sona Paint*,[44] observed:

> ... the legislature has deliberately provided a lifespan for a design. Example is given by way of rights under the Copyright Act where the term of protection is the lifetime of the copyright holder plus sixty (60) years. Similarly, under the Patents Act where the term of protection is twenty (20) years from the date of application, and lastly, under the Designs Act, where the term of protection is ten (10) years, which is extendable by further (5) five years, and thus in all, a total of fifteen (15) years is provided as the statutory lifespan. It is only under the trademark law that the protection is initially granted for a period of ten (10) years with limitless renewals. In other words, except for the trade mark law, where protection can be in perpetuity, all other rights, have a statutory lifespan.

LICENCING OF COPYRIGHT

Chapter VI (Sections 30 to 32B) of the Copyright Act, 1957 deals with the aspect of licencing

41. MIPR 2017 (1) 398: 2016-5-LW 881.
42. Substituted by the Copyright (Amendment) Act, 1992, Section 2, for "fifty years" [w.r.e.f. 28-12-1991].
43. *Gramophone Company of India Ltd.* v. *Super Cassettes Industries Ltd.*, MIPR 2010 (2) 349: 2010 (44) PTC 541 (Del); *Tobu Enterprises (P) Ltd* v. *M/s. Joginder Metal Works*, AIR 1985 Delhi 244; (1985) ILR 2 Delhi 638; *R.G. Anand* v. *Delux Films*, AIR 1978 SC 1613: (1978) 4 SCC 118; *Calico Printers Association* v. *Savani*, 1939 (41) Bom LR 45.
44. MIPR 2013 (2) 156.

which is merely a permissive right and is a way of limiting the rights of the licence by the owner of the copyright. In *John Wiley and Sons Inc.* v. *Prabhat Chander Kumar Jain,*[45] the Delhi High Court held that a careful reading of the various sections makes it clear that the owner by exercising the right to licence further demarcates the rights and imposes conditions and limitations by way of a period wise licence or territory wise licence exclusive or non-exclusive, etc. Licencing is a mode of maximum exploitation of the rights under the Act by imposing conditions and limitations upon the rights.

Section 30 of the Copyright Act deals the law relating to licences by owners of copyright.[46] Thus, an author or the copyright owner has the authority to grant a licence with respect to his work. Where the licence is granted by an agent, it will be invalid unless the agent either had authority to grant it or was held out by the person entitled to grant it having authority to grant it. Besides, the Copyright Act provides for three kinds of non-voluntary licences: (a) compulsory licences—(i) compulsory licence in works withheld from public,[47] (ii) compulsory licence in unpublished or published works;[48] (ii) compulsory licence for the benefit of the disabled,[49] (b) statutory licences—(i) statutory licence for cover version,[50] (ii) statutory licence for broadcasting of literary and musical works and sound recording[51]; (c) licence after expiry of prescribed periods—(i) licence to produce and publish translations[52]; (ii) licence to produce and publish works for certain purposes[53]. Section 32B provides for the termination of licences issued under Sections 32 and 32A.

Compulsory Licences

Sections 31 to 32B of the Copyright Act, 1957 deal with the compulsory licencing provisions. These are incorporated to ensure the constant availability of copyrighted works in the market at reasonable prices. Section 31 enumerates the procedure for the issuance of a compulsory licence to republish copyrighted works, which are withheld from public. An application from such licence is to be made to the Appellate Board[54] and the Copyright Board after giving the owner of copyright a reasonable opportunity of being heard may direct the Registrar of Copyright to grant a compulsory licence. Section 31A deals with compulsory licences to publish unpublished works. Here the proposal to publish the work must be first advertised, before the application is made. Similarly, Section 32 allows any person or a broadcasting authority to approach the Appellate Board[55] for a licence to publish

45. 170 (2010) DLT 701: 2010 (44) PTC 675 (Del).
46. *See, Phonographic Performance Limited* v. *Lizard Lounge* (2009) ILR 2 Delhi 726: ILR (2009) Supp. (Delhi) 726.
47. Copyright Act 1957, Section 31.
48. *Ibid.*, Section 31A.
49. *Ibid.*, Section 31B.
50. *Ibid.*, Section 31C.
51. *Ibid.*, Section 31D.
52. *Ibid.*, Section 32.
53. *Ibid.*, Section 32A.
54. Substituted by the Finance Act 2017 (7 of 2017), section 160(a) for "Copyright Board," [w.e.f. 26 May, 2017].
55. Substituted by the Finance Act 2017 (7 of 2017), Section 160(a) for "Copyright Board," [w.e.f. 26 May, 2017].

translations of works or broadcasts after a limited period from the date of publication of the parent work. Further, Section 32A allows any person to approach the Appellate Board[56] to publish works of literary, scientific or artistic significance, if it is not made available within the country at reasonable rates.

The Section 31 of the Act deals with the compulsory licence in works withheld from public. Since a party can invoke Section 31 of the Act for obtaining a compulsory license from the Registrar of Copyrights by approaching the Appellate Board,[57] competing interests have been duly balanced by it. Thus, in *Anand Bhushan* v. *Union of India*,[58] the Court observed:

> The Act seeks to maintain a balance between the interest of the owner of the copyright in protecting his works on the one hand and the interest of the public to have access to the works on the other. The extent to which the owner is entitled to protection in regard to his work for which he has obtained copyright and the interest of the public is a matter which would depend upon the statutory provisions. Whereas the Act provides for exclusive rights in favour of owners of the copyright, there are provisions where it has been recognised that public has also substantial interest in the availability of the works. The provisions relating to grant of compulsory licence must be viewed having regard to the aforementioned competing rights wherefore an appropriate balance has to be struck.

Compulsory Licence in Works Withheld from Public (Section 31)

While discussing the scope of the law of licences of works in *International Confederation of Societies of Authors* v. *Aditya Pandey*,[59] the Supreme Court held that it is necessary to understand distinction between assignment of a copyright of a work and licence to use the work. In the assignment, normally, ownership of the copyright of the work is transferred but in the case of licence another person is allowed to use the work by the author. In *Music Choice India Private Limited* v. *Phonographic Performance Limited*,[60] the Bombay High Court held that grant of relief of compulsory license in respect works withheld from public is exclusively vested with the Copyright Board (Appellate Board)[61] and such a relief cannot be granted by the civil court. Section 31 of the Copyright Act, 1957 provides for compulsory licences of works withheld from public. This section provides that if the owner of copyright in any "Indian work" has refused to republish or allow the republication or has refused the performance in public of the work and withheld the work from the public or has refused to allow communication to the public by broadcast of the work recorded in sound recording, the Appellate Board[62] may, on the basis of a complaint received and after such inquiry as it may

56. Substituted by the Finance Act 2017 (7 of 2017), Section 160(a) for "Copyright Board," [w.e.f. 26 May, 2017].
57. Substituted by the Finance Act 2017 (7 of 2017), section 160(a) for "Copyright Board," [w.e.f. 26 May, 2017].
58. 2018 (75) PTC 106 (Del): 2018 VI AD (Delhi) 153.
59. (2017) 11 SCC 437: 2016 (9) SCALE 89.
60. 2010 (44) PTC 171 (Bom): 2010 (112) Bom LR 470.
61. The phrase "Appellate Board" has been substituted by the Finance Act 2017 (7 of 2017), section 160(a) for "Copyright Board" [w.e.f. 26 May, 2017].
62. Substituted by the Finance Act 2017 (7 of 2017), section 160(a) for "Copyright Board," [w.e.f. 26 May, 2017].

deem necessary, direct the Registrar of Copyrights to grant to the complainant, a licence.[63] The Copyright (Amendment) Act, 2012 has the enlarged the applicability of Section 31 which amplified from "Indian work" to "any work". "Explanation" relating to the definition of "Indian work" is also omitted. The word "complainant" is replaced with the words "such person or persons who, in the opinion of the Copyright Board, is or are qualified to do so". Sub-section (2) is omitted so as to enable the Copyright Board to grant compulsory licence to more than one person. By virtue of the Copyright (Amendment) Act, 2012, compulsory licences can be obtained for "any work" withheld from the public and not just "Indian works" and the licence can be granted to such persons as the Board may decide.

Section 31 reads:

> 31. Compulsory licence in works withheld from public. (1) If at any time during the term of copyright in [any work][64] which has been published or performed in public, a complaint is made to the Appellate Board[65] that the owner of copyright in the work—
>
> (a) has refused to republish or allow the republication of the work or has refused to allow the performance in pubic of the work, and by reason of such refusal the work is withheld from the public; or
>
> (b) has refused to allow communication to the public by [broadcast][66] of such work or in the case of [sound recording][67] the work recorded in such [sound recording],[68] on terms which the complainant considers reasonable;
>
> the Appellate Board,[69] after giving to the owner of the copyright in the work a reasonable opportunity of being heard and after holding such inquiry as it may deem necessary, may, if it is satisfied that the grounds for such refusal are not reasonable, direct the Registrar of Copyrights to grant to the complainant a licence to republish the work, perform the work in public or communicate the work to the public by [broadcast],[70] as the case may be, subject to payment to the owner of the copyright of such compensation and subject to such other terms and conditions as the Appellate Board[71] may determine; and thereupon the Registrar of Copyrights shall grant the [licence to such person or persons who, in the opinion of the Appellate Board,[72] is or are qualified to do so][73] in accordance with the directions of the Appellate Board,[74] on payment of such fee, as may be prescribed.

---

63. *See*, *Tekla Corporation* v. *Survo Ghosh*, 2014 LawSuit (Del) 1928.
64. Substituted by the Copyright (Amendment) Act, 2012, Section 16(1)(a), for "any Indian work" [w.e.f. 21-6-2012].
65. Substituted by the Finance Act 2017 (7 of 2017), section 160(a) for "Copyright Board," [w.e.f. 26 May, 2017].
66. Substituted by the Copyright (Amendment) Act, 1983, Section 2, for "radio-diffusion" [w.e.f. 9-8-1984].
67. Substituted by the Copyright (Amendment) Act, 1994, Section 2, for "record" [w.e.f. 10-5-1995].
68. Substituted by the Copyright (Amendment) Act, 1994, Section 2, for "record" [w.e.f. 10-5-1995].
69. Substituted by the Finance Act 2017 (7 of 2017), section 160(a) for "Copyright Board," [w.e.f. 26 May, 2017].
70. Substituted by the Copyright (Amendment) Act, 1983, Section 2, for "radio-diffusion" [w.e.f. 9-8-1984].
71. Substituted by the Finance Act 2017 (7 of 2017), section 160(a) for "Copyright Board," [w.e.f. 26 May, 2017].
72. Substituted by the Finance Act 2017 (7 of 2017), section 160(a) for "Copyright Board," [w.e.f. 26 May, 2017].
73. Substituted by the Copyright (Amendment) Act, 2012, Section 16(1)(b), for "licence to the complainant" [w.e.f. 21-6-2012].
74. Substituted by the Finance Act 2017 (7 of 2017), section 160(a) for "Copyright Board," [w.e.f. 26 May, 2017].

In *Phonographic Performance Ltd.* v. *Radio Mid Day (West) India Ltd.*,[75] the Delhi High Court held that the jurisdiction of the Copyright Board (Appellate Board)[76] can be invoked under Section 31(1)(b) of the Copyright Act by a complainant who considers that the owner of a copyright has offered unreasonable terms for the broadcast of a sound recording. When that happens, the Copyright Board (Appellate Board)[77] is required to give the copyright owner a reasonable opportunity of being heard before directing the complainant to pay compensation to him (and determining other terms and conditions) for the broadcast. As a part of the "reasonable opportunity of being heard" the Copyright Board (Appellate Board)[78] may hold such inquiry as it deems necessary. In Super *Cassettes Industries Ltd.* v. *Music Broadcast Pvt. Ltd.*,[79] the issue was whether the Copyright Board (Appellate Board),[80] exercising the jurisdiction under Section 31 of the Copyright Act, can grant Ad hoc compulsory licence by an interim order pending the adjudication of the issue in works withheld from public? The Supreme Court answered in the following manner:

> If the Copyright Board (Appellate Board) is satisfied that the grounds of refusal are not reasonable, the Copyright Board (Appellate Board) is authorised, by law, to take steps for the grant of a compulsory licence. The power under Section 31 to grant a compulsory licence meant for avoiding the withholding of the republication or refuses to allow the performance in public of some "work" is, essentially, for the benefit of the public. Unless, it is demonstrated that failure to imply such power to direct immediate republication or performance of a work in public would be detrimental to public interest, the power to grant Ad hoc compulsory license, cannot be implied.

Prior to 2012 amendment, compulsory licence could be obtained only by the complainant in Indian works withheld from the public. Post-2012 amendment, it may be granted in respect of any work, whether Indian or foreign, withheld from public. The scope of the Section 31 has thus been enlarged. Now question arises when jurisdiction of the Appellate Board[81] can be invoked. In connection to broadcast and sound recording, in *Phonographic Performance Ltd.* v. *Radio Mid Day (West) India*,[82] the Delhi High Court held that the jurisdiction of the Copyright Board (Appellate Board)[83] can be invoked under Section 31(1)(b) of the Copyright Act by a complainant who considers that the owner of a copyright has offered unreasonable terms for the broadcast of a sound recording. When that happens, the Copyright Board (Appellate Board) is required to give the copyright owner a reasonable opportunity of being heard before directing

75. 2010 (43) PTC 377 (Del): (2010) ILR 4 Delhi 603.
76. Substituted by the Finance Act 2017 (7 of 2017), section 160(a) for "Copyright Board," [w.e.f. 26 May, 2017].
77. Substituted by the Finance Act 2017 (7 of 2017), section 160(a) for "Copyright Board," [w.e.f. 26 May, 2017].
78. Substituted by the Finance Act 2017 (7 of 2017), section 160(a) for "Copyright Board," [w.e.f. 26 May, 2017].
79. (2012) 5 SCC 488: 2012 (5) SCALE 142.
80. Substituted by the Finance Act 2017 (7 of 2017), section 160(a) for "Copyright Board," [w.e.f. 26 May, 2017].
81. Substituted by the Finance Act 2017 (7 of 2017), section 160(a) for "Copyright Board," [w.e.f. 26 May, 2017].
82. 2010 LawSuit (Del) 3091. *See*, *Event and Entertainment Management Association* v. *Union of India*, 2011 (46) PTC 405: 2011 (182) DLT 100.
83. Substituted by the Finance Act 2017 (7 of 2017), section 160(a) for "Copyright Board," [w.e.f. 26 May, 2017].

the complainant to pay compensation to him (and determining other terms and conditions) for the broadcast. As a part of the "reasonable opportunity of being heard", the Copyright Board (Appellate Board) may hold such inquiry as it deems necessary. As regards the nature of inquiry is concerned, the court held that "the inquiry postulated is quasi-judicial and quasi-adversarial in nature". The reason behind it is that the Copyright Board (Appellate Board) is not a Court nor is it a Tribunal. Two facts are significant in this regard and they are that the Copyright Board (Appellate Board) does not have the powers of a civil court to summon and enforce attendance of a witness or to require the discovery or production of a document, nor does it pass a decree (it only passes a final decision). Therefore, when the Copyright Board (Appellate Board)[84] conducts an inquiry it does so with very limited powers. In *South Indian Music Companies Association* v. *Union of India*,[85] the Madras High Court observed:

> Section 31 of the Act deals with granting of compulsory licence in works withheld from public. Such a work ought to have been published or performed in public. Thus, it must have come into the public domain. A complaint can be made to the Board when the owner of copyright has refused to republish or allow the republication of the work or has refused to allow the performance in public of the work, and by reason of such refusal the work is withheld from the public and similarly when such a owner has refused to allow communication to the public by (broadcast) of such work or in the case of a (sound recording) the work recorded in such (sound recording) on terms which the complainant considers reasonable. When such a complaint is made, the Board after giving to the owner a reasonable opportunity of being heard and after holding such an enquiry, which is required, if it is satisfied that the grounds of such refusal are not reasonable, then direct the Registrar of Copyrights to grant the complainant a licence to republish the work, perform the work in public or communicate the work to the public by (broadcast), as the case may be, subject to adequate payment to the owner of the copyright by way of compensation.

The scope of Section 31 of the Copyright Act relating to compulsory licences was considered by the Delhi and Bombay High Courts in *Super Cassettes Industries Ltd.* v. *Entertainment Network (India) Ltd.*[86] and *Phonographic Performances Ltd.* v. *Music Broadcast (P) Ltd.*,[87] resulting in divergent interpretation. In both the cases, it is the denial of licence to the newly permitted private FM Radio stations to broadcast musical works by the owners that resulted in issue of compulsory licence by the copyright board (Appellate Board)[88] and further litigation. In *Super Cassettes Industries Ltd.* v. *Entertainment Network (India) Ltd.*,[89] the appellant is the producer of large number of music cassettes. The respondents who are operators of an FM Radio station by name Radio Mirchi started broadcasting the musical work without licence when the same was denied. The appellant filed a suit for infringement of copyright in their musical work and the suit was pending. The respondents pending litigation applied for compulsory licence to the copyright board (Appellate Board). The board issued the licence without examining all the evidence. On appeal, it was argued that since the appellant

84. Substituted by the Finance Act 2017 (7 of 2017), section 160(a) for "Copyright Board," [w.e.f. 26 May, 2017].
85. 2016 (67) PTC 99 (Mad): MIPR 2016 (2) 64.
86. 2004 (29) PTC 8 (Del): AIR 2004 Delhi 326.
87. 2004 (29) PTC 282 (Bom): 2004 (3) ALLMR 196.
88. Substituted by the Finance Act 2017 (7 of 2017), section 160(a) for "Copyright Board," [w.e.f. 26 May, 2017].
89. 2004 (29) PTC 8 (Del). AIR 2004 Delhi 326.

had already issued licence to two prominent broadcasters and the work is not withhold from the public, the board had no jurisdiction to issue compulsory licence in such cases. One of the questions examined by the court was whether the copyright board (Appellate Board) had power to issue compulsory licence to more than one person as per the scheme of the Act. After examining Section 31, the Court opined:

> When the licenses have already been granted to other broadcasters, who have substantial presence, then perhaps the application for grant of compulsory license will be treated differently, than in a situation where the artistic work has been totally withheld from the public. The legislature in its wisdom has used the expression "may" in Section 31(1). According to Section 31 it is not imperative for the Board to grant license to each and every complainant. In our considered view the license can be granted or denied on valid grounds. Section 31 itself envisages that the decision to grant or refuse a license should be made after holding such inquiry as it may deem necessary. While granting compulsory licenses the Board must take into consideration whether the work has been totally withheld from public or licenses have been granted to other broadcasters and to what extent public interest is served.[90]

It was argued by the respondent that once the work was in public by issue of licence to one person, the owner of the work couldn't deny licence to another on unreasonable grounds. Accepting this argument the court observed: We have carefully considered this aspect and we are in agreement with the respondent that once a copyright is taken in public domain then it becomes commercial right and refusal to grant licence has to be on reasonable ground.... Once the copyright is in the public domain, refusal has to be on reasonable and valid ground.... While making an order under Section 31(1) of the Act, the Board has to maintain a delicate balance private rights and the copyright *vis-à-vis* public interest.[91] It was also contented by the appellant that since the respondent was infringing the copyright of the appellant, they did not have the right to apply for compulsory licence under the Act. This was accepted by the court and directed the respondent to stop infringement. The case was sent back to the copyright board (Appellate Board)[92] for fresh reconsideration.

In *Phonographic Performance Ltd.* v. *Music Broadcast (P) Ltd.*,[93] the division bench of the Bombay High Court also considered the scope of Section 31. In this case, the respondent who was given a licence by the central government to start FM Radio station approached the appellants for licence to broadcast the music owned by them. Since the terms and conditions were very harsh, the respondents approached the copyright board (Appellate Board)[94] for compulsory licence under Section 31. The appellants argued before the board that since the musical works owned by them were already in the public through licence to other broadcasters, the board had no jurisdiction to issue compulsory licence under Section 31. It was also argued that the licence could be issued to only one person under the Section and the compensation must be fixed based on evidence. The board rejected all these arguments and issued compulsory

90. *Super Cassettes Industries Ltd.* v. *Entertainment Network (India) Ltd.*, 2004 (29) PTC 8 (Del) at pp. 34–35.
91. *Ibid.*, at p. 36.
92. Substituted by the Finance Act 2017 (7 of 2017), section 160(a) for "Copyright Board," [w.e.f. 26 May, 2017].
93. 2004 (29) PTC 282 (Bom). 2004 (3) ALLMR 196.
94. Substituted by the Finance Act 2017 (7 of 2017), section 160(a) for "Copyright Board," [w.e.f. 26 May, 2017].

licence and the compensation was fixed based on best judgment assessment. On appeal it was argued before the high court that the Section was not applicable to broadcasting of sound records since the music was available to the public. After examining the provision in detail, the court interpreted it thus:

> It is, thus, clear that really speaking clause (b) of sub-section (1) is in the nature of provision or exception to clause (a) of sub-section (1) of Section 31. The purpose of enacting clause (b) of sub-section (1) of Section 31 was to take out of the field of broadcasting from clause (a) and to deal with that field separately. Different treatment that has been given by the Legislature to the field of broadcasting is that refusal of the holder of the copyright to re-broadcast of the work need not result in withholding the work from public. In other words, even if the copyright holder in a work himself re-broadcast the work or is allowing others to broadcast the work, still a complaint can be made. The legislature has made its intention of dealing with the mode of communication, namely, broadcast differently and therefore, in our opinion, as the words of the provisions are clear there is no question of importing the concept of the refusal in withholding of the work from the public into the field of broadcast also, as the intention of the legislature in that regard is absolutely clear....[95]

Regarding the argument that Sub-section (2) of Section 31 limits the licence to one person only, the court further observed.

> So far as the provisions of sub-section (2) of Section 31 are concerned, in view of the clear wordings used in sub-section (1) of Section 31 and the intention of the legislature insofar as right to rebroadcasting is concerned, that any person who wishes to have a license and is willing to offer reasonable terms is entitled to a licence. Provisions of sub-section (2) of Section 31 will not apply to the cases covered by clause (b) of sub-section (1) of Section 31. Operation of sub-section (2) of Section 31 has to be restricted to the cases covered by clause (a) of Sub-section (1) of Section 31. To say that the Copyright Board is to select any one of the persons who have made complaints would mitigate against the principles underlying by clause (b) of sub-section (1) of Section 31... In our opinion, therefore, in order to make the scheme contained in Section 31 workable, operation of sub-section (2) of Section 31 will have to be restricted to the cases covered by clause (a) of sub-section (1) of Section 31 of the Act.

It appears that the courts in both the cases adopted a purposive interpretation to Section 31 rather than a literal one. On a plain reading of the Section, it is clear that compulsory licence could be issued only if the work is withheld from the public. It is to be remembered that these provisions were included in the Act when broadcasting was completely under the control of the government. But such an interpretation will defeat the whole purpose for which the government now permitted private radio stations. It is to facilitate simultaneous broadcast of the same musical works to the public that licence is issued to start private FM stations. This will be defeated if the owners of copyright in musical work deny licence or put unreasonable conditions for grant of licence. If they were allowed to get the benefit of the literal interpretation of Section 31, the broadcasters have no remedy under the copyright law if the owners deny licence to them. It is this factor that forced the Delhi High Court to interpret the word "may" in Section 31 and the Bombay High Court to adopt an interpretation separating the act of broadcast different from that of other communication to the public mentioned in Section 31 to find jurisdiction for the copyright board. It appears that there was a need to

95. *See, Phonographic Performance Ltd.* v. *Music Broadcast (P) Ltd.*, 2004 (29) PTC 282 (Bom) at p. 295.

amend the law introducing a specific provision to tackle such cases. However, the Finance Act 217 has substituted the "Copyright Board" by the Appellate Board[96]. It is expected that this will help to straighten the law rather than leaving it to judicial interpretation.

It is a matter of fact that if Section 31 of the Copyright Act 1957 is interpreted literally then it would defeat the object of the Act and create anomalous position. Therefore, in *Entertainment Network (India) Ltd.* v. *Super Cassettes Industries Ltd.*,[97] the Apex court held that while granting compulsory licenses the court has to strike a balance between rights of the owner of the copyright and the other person's right to get a compulsory license. In this case, the respondent is one of the leading music companies engaged in the production and/or acquisition of rights in sound recordings. It has copyright over a series of cassettes and CDs commonly known as T-series. It has copyrights in cinematographic films and sound recordings. Appellant M/s. Entertainment Network (India) Ltd. (ENIL) broadcasts under the brand name "Radio Mirchi". It is a leading FM radio broadcaster. Disputes and differences arose between Bennett Coleman & Co. Ltd., the holding company of the first respondent and Phonographic Performance Ltd. (PPL) as regards the playing of the songs of which copyrights belongs to the first respondent in their FM radio network. Appellant is a company which holds licence for running FM radio stations in various cities across India.

The core questions which, therefore, arise for consideration in these appeals are:

(i) Whether the Copyright Board (Appellate Board)[98] has jurisdiction under Section 31(1)(b) of the Copyright Act, 1957 to direct the owner of a copyright in any Indian work or a registered copyright society to issue compulsory licences to broadcast such as works, where such work is available to the public through radio broadcast?

(ii) Whether in any event such a compulsory license can be issued to more than one complainant in the light of Section 31(2)?

(iii) What would be the relevant considerations which the Copyright Board (Appellate Board)[99] must keep in view while deciding on;

  (a) Whether to issue a compulsory license to a particular person; and

  (b) The terms on which the compulsory license may be issued, including the compensation?

The Apex Court held that, by virtue of Section 31(1)(b), if the owner of copyright refuses to allow communication to the public a sound recording on terms which complainant considers reasonable then a complaint to the board made in this regard for issuance of compulsory licence is maintainable as it has jurisdiction to deal with the same. If a compulsory licence is granted only once covering every single part of the country, the same cannot lead to a conclusion that no other person can approach the Board. After examining the wording of the provisions and the international obligations, the court interpreted the provision thus:

96. Substituted by the Finance Act 2017 (7 of 2017), section 160(a) for "Copyright Board," [w.e.f. 26 May, 2017].
97. 2008 (37) PTC 353 (SC): (2008) 13 SCC 30.
98. Substituted by the Finance Act 2017 (7 of 2017), Section 160(a) for "Copyright Board," [w.e.f. 26 May, 2017].
99. Substituted by the Finance Act 2017 (7 of 2017), Section 160(a) for "Copyright Board," [w.e.f. 26 May, 2017].

> Significantly, in between the clauses (a) and (b), the word "or" has been used. It must be read disjunctively and not conjunctively. Even otherwise, reading the said provision conjunctively is not possible. Clause (a) refers to republication or allowing republication of the works etc., clause (b) refers to refusal to allow communication to the public in the case of broadcast or in case of sound recording.[100]

The court buttressed the argument by referring to the nature of rights recognised under Section 14 and also the use of the words "such work" and "public" in section 31. The court held that these provisions in the context of radio broadcast did not prohibit a person from approaching the Copyright Board (Appellate Board)[101] for compulsory licence even if the sound records are licenced to All India Radio.[102] The reasoning of the court is correct given the nature of the work and its possible dissemination to the public. If the intention of the legislature is to facilitate the multiple transmission of the work to the public, a restricted interpretation as argued by the respondents would have defeated the purpose. As reasoned by the court, it is evident that the amendment introduced in the Act aims at simultaneous communication of the work through different means and a refusal to give licence could attract the power under this section for issue of compulsory licence.

It was further contended by the respondent that "refusal" under this section demands failure on the part of the owner to give permission and if agreed to give permission based on a royalty fixed by the owner even though not agreeable to the user, could not be considered as refusal. Rejecting this, the court observed thus: [103]

> The meaning of a word must be attributed to the context in which it is used. For giving a contextual meaning, the text of the statute must be kept in mind. An act of refusal depends upon the fact of each case. Only because an offer is made for negotiation or an offer is, made for grant of licence, the same per se may not be sufficient to arrive at a conclusion that the owner of copyright has not withheld its work from public. When an offer is made on an unreasonable term or a stand is taken which is otherwise arbitrary, it may amount to refusal on the part of the owner of a copyright.

This interpretation also is in tune with the context in which the court was examining the issue. The court seems to have appreciated the danger of abuse of monopoly by the owner of copyright in case it refuses to recognise the power of Copyright Board (Appellate Board)[104] to interfere. In *Music Choice India Pvt. Ltd.* v. *Phonographic Performance Ltd.*,[105] the court held that the Copyright Act, 1957 did not prohibit the Copyright Board (Appellate Board)[106] from passing any interim order for determination of reasonable fees by way of royalty or compensation by the plaintiff as the Copyright Board (Appellate Board) have

---

100. *See, Entertainment Network (India) Ltd.* v. *Super Cassettes Industries Ltd.*, 2008 (37) PTC 353 (SC): (2008) 13 SCC 30 (at p. 385, PTC).
101. Substituted by the Finance Act 2017 (7 of 2017), section 160(a) for "Copyright Board," [w.e.f. 26 May, 2017].
102. *See, Entertainment Network (India) Ltd.* v. *Super Cassettes Industries Ltd.*, 2008 (37) PTC 353 (SC): (2008) 13 SCC 30 (at p. 386, PTC).
103. *Ibid.* (at p. 386, PTC).
104. Substituted by the Finance Act 2017 (7 of 2017), section 160(a) for "Copyright Board," [w.e.f. 26 May, 2017].
105. 2009 (39) PTC 597.
106. Substituted by the Finance Act 2017 (7 of 2017), section 160(a) for "Copyright Board," [w.e.f. 26 May, 2017].

the power to grant an interim compulsory licence under Section 31 of the Act. In *Super Cassettes Industries Limited* v. *Chintamani Rao*,[107] the plaintiffs, Super Cassettes and Yashraj Films have expressed their willingness to grant licence to the defendant India TV for use of their copyrighted works, namely, cinematograph films and sound recordings. In fact, other broadcasters are obtaining licences and it is only the defendant India TV which continues to use their copyrighted derivative works without obtaining any licence. Thus, the remedy for India TV lies in approaching the Copyright Board (Appellate Board)[108] under Section 31 of the Act. The defendant India TV cannot seek to bypass the said procedure and use the derivative copyright works of the plaintiffs, Super Cassettes and Yashraj Films without obtaining a valid licence. The court explained the procedure to obtain relief under Section 31 of the Act thus:

> Section 31 of the Act entitles any person to approach the Copyright Board (Appellate Board)[109] with a complaint, during the term of copyright in any Indian work (which includes, a cinematograph film or a sound recording made or manufactured in India), which has been published or performed in public, that the owner of the copyright in the work has, inter alia, refused to allow communication to the public by broadcast of such work [Section 31(1)(b)]. Upon such an application being made, the Copyright Board (Appellate Board), upon being satisfied, may direct the Registrar of Copyrights to grant to the complainant a licence to, *inter alia*, communicate the work to the public by broadcast on payment of compensation to the owner of the copyright.

In *Houghton Mifflin Company* v. *Rajinder Kumar Arya*,[110] the Delhi High Court confirmed a statutory mandate that the licence for publication or sale of copyright work could only be in writing in terms of mandate of Section 19 of the Act. The defendant had pleaded exchange of communications for grant of such licence for permission and consent. Negating the defendant's contention, the Court held that the same is not licence and hence any action pursuant thereto is infringement and to be restrained. The Court further opined that at best it could amount to an assurance by the plaintiff that in the event of a particular decision—(to enter or re-enter Indian market with special re-prints)—the defendant could be granted a licence.

In *Super Cassettes Industries Ltd.* v. *Music Broadcast Pvt. Ltd.*,[111] the issue was whether the Copyright Board (Appellate Board)[112], exercising the jurisdiction under Section 31 of the Copyright Act, can grant ad hoc compulsory licence by an interim order pending the adjudication of the issue in works withheld from public? The Apex Court observed that the Copyright Board (Appellate Board)[113], after giving to the owner of the copyright in the work a reasonable opportunity of being heard and after holding such inquiry as it may deem

107. *See*, 2012 (49) PTC 1: 2011 LawSuit (Del) 3245. *See also*, *Federation of Hotels and Restaurants Association of India* v. *Union of India*, 2011 (8) AD (Del) 720: 2011 (46) PTC 169.
108. Substituted by the Finance Act 2017 (7 of 2017), section 160(a) for "Copyright Board," [w.e.f. 26 May, 2017].
109. Substituted by the Finance Act 2017 (7 of 2017), section 160(a) for "Copyright Board," [w.e.f. 26 May, 2017].
110. 2010 (44) PTC 240 (Del): 171 (2010) DLT 211.
111. AIR 2012 SC 2144: (2012) 5 SCC 488.
112. Substituted by the Finance Act 2017 (7 of 2017), section 160(a) for "Copyright Board," [w.e.f. 26 May, 2017].
113. Substituted by the Finance Act 2017 (7 of 2017), Section 160(a) for "Copyright Board," [w.e.f. 26 May, 2017].

necessary, may, if it is satisfied that the grounds for such refusal are not reasonable, direct the Registrar of Copyrights to grant to the complainant a licence to republish the work, perform the work in public or communicate the work to the public by broadcast, as the case may be, subject to payment to the owner of the copyright of such compensation and subject to such other terms and conditions as the Copyright Board (Appellate Board)[114] may determine; and thereupon the Registrar of Copyrights shall grant the licence to the complainant in accordance with the directions of Copyright Board (Appellate Board), on payment of such fee as may be prescribed. Section 31 of the Copyright Act creates an exception to the principle of the right of the owner of the copyright. In substance, the Section deprives the "copyright" of the "owner" against his volition. In other words, by Section 31, the State is authorised, by its coercive powers, to deprive the owner of his copyright in a work, which is his property and the right to enjoy such property in the manner as the owner of the property pleases. Necessarily, in view of the constitutional mandate under Article 300A, such a deprivation can only be by the authority of law and it is too well entrenched a principle on the constitutional law that such a law could be only for a public purpose. The core of Section 31 is that the owner of a copyright has:

1. either refused to "republish" or "allow the republication" of his work or "refused to allow the performance in public" of the work;
2. by reason of such refusal the work is withheld from the public; and
3. the grounds for such refusal are not reasonable. It is in the abovementioned circumstances, if the Copyright Board (Appellate Board)[115] is satisfied that the grounds of refusal are not reasonable, the Copyright Board (Appellate Board) is authorised, by law, to take steps for the grant of a compulsory licence.

In the above cited case,[116] the appellants were interested in the commercial exploitation of a work, of which they are not "owners" of the copyright. In this case, the Apex Court held that to succeed in their claim for a compulsory licence in their favour, they must, firstly, establish that "the work is withheld from the public", because of the "owner's" refusal to republish the work, etc.; secondly, the owner's refusal is on grounds, which are "not reasonable" in law. Whether the owner is withholding the republication on grounds, which are unreasonable or not, is a question, which can only be decided upon affording a complete hearing to the owner of the work. If the author, on realising that repeated publication of the work might endanger his security, declines or refuses republication of the work, it cannot be said that the author (owner) unreasonably withheld republication. Such a refusal has nothing to do with the monetary considerations. Therefore, by conceding a power to grant ad hoc compulsory licence during the pendency of the proceeding, under Section 31, would not only render the final inquiry into the question, a futile exercise in a case where the owner has reasons other than inadequacy of monitory compensation. The power under Section 31 to grant a compulsory licence meant for avoiding the withholding of the republication or

---

114. Substituted by the Finance Act 2017 (7 of 2017), Section 160(a) for "Copyright Board," [w.e.f. 26 May, 2017].
115. Substituted by the Finance Act 2017 (7 of 2017), Section 160(a) for "Copyright Board," [w.e.f. 26 May, 2017].
116. *See, Super Cassettes Industries Ltd.* v. *Music Broadcast Pvt. Ltd.*, AIR 2012 SC 2144: (2012) 5 SCC 488.

refuses to allow the performance in public of some "work"—is, essentially, for the benefit of the public. Commercial benefit to "publisher" is incidental. Unless, it is demonstrated that failure to imply such power to direct immediate republication or performance of a work in public would be detrimental to public interest, the power to grant ad hoc compulsory licence, cannot be implied. No such detriment is demonstrated in this case.

Compulsory Licence in Unpublished or Published Works (Section 31A)

In connection to compulsory licence in unpublished or published works, Section 31A, of the Copyright Act, 1957 empowers the Appellate Board[117] to issue a compulsory licence in respect of an unpublished work or a translation thereof in the language, whose author is dead or unknown or cannot be traced or the owner of copyright in such work cannot be found.[118] The applicant prior to the filing of an application shall publish his proposal in a daily English newspaper. If the application is for translation of the work, then it has to be published in a daily newspaper of that language. In this connection, the Copyright Board after holding such inquiry as may be prescribed, direct the Registrar of Copyrights to grant to the applicant a licence to publish the work or a translation thereof in the language mentioned in the application subject to the payment of such royalty. The Registrar of Copyrights shall grant the licence to the applicant in accordance with the direction of the Copyright Board.[119]

Compulsory Licence for the Benefit of the Disabled (Section 31B)

Section 31B was introduced by the Copyright (Amendment) Act, 2012.[120] Special provisions have been provided for compulsory licencing of the works for the disabled by inserting Section 31B. According to Section 31B, any person for earning profit or doing business may apply to the Appellate Board[121] for a compulsory licence to publish any work if the two conditions are fulfilled: (i) publication of work is for the benefit of the disabled, (ii) copyright subsists in such a work and does not fall under Section 51(1)(zb) dealing with acts not amounting to infringement in case of the disabled. Section 31B imposed an obligation that the Copyright Board has to consider the application expeditiously and endeavour to dispose of the application within two months. It is also obligatory that the Copyright Board before granting the licence, it must hold an inquiry to determine that (a) compulsory licence needs to be issued to make the work available to the disabled, (b) the application is made in good faith, (c) credentials of the applicants are to the satisfaction of the Board. The compulsory licence issued under Section 31B must specify four things: (i) the means and format of publication, (ii) the time period for which compulsory licence may be exercised, (iii) number of copies is to be issued, and (iv) royalty to be paid to the copyright owner.

---

117. Substituted by the Finance Act 2017 (7 of 2017), section 160(a) for "Copyright Board," [w.e.f. 26 May, 2017].
118. *Super Cassettes Industries Ltd.* v. *Mr. Punit Goenka*, ILR (2009) Supp. (Delhi) 781: 2009 (41) PTC 1 (Del).
119. *Entertainment Network (India) Ltd.* v. *Super Cassettes Industries Ltd.*, 2008 (37) PTC 353 (SC): (2008) 13 SCC 30.
120. Inserted by the Copyright (Amendment) Act, 2012, Section 18 [w.e.f. 21-6-2012].
121. Substituted by the Finance Act 2017 (7 of 2017), section 160(a) for "Copyright Board," [w.e.f. 26 May, 2017].

Statutory Licences

Statutory Licence for Cover Version (Section 31C)

The Explanation to Section 31C of the Copyright Act 1957 provides that for the purposes of this Section "cover version" means a sound recording made in accordance with this section.[122] Prior to the Copyright (Amendment) Act, 2012, Section 52(1)(j) of the Copyright Act, 1957 dealt with production of cover versions. Section 52(1)(j) of the Act envisages a statutory licencing mechanism, whereby any person is free to make and publish a sound recording of a literary, dramatic or musical work already in circulation after paying the statutory royalty fixed by the Copyright Board (Appellate Board)[123] to the copyright owner. Thus, in *Mars Recording Private Limited* v. *Saregama India Limited*,[124] the Karnataka High Court observed that though the reference to a "statutory licence" is not to be found in the Copyright Act 1957 prior to its amendment in 2012, the procedure to secure such licence to make a sound recording as is contemplated under Section 52(1)(j)(ii) and the procedure to obtain, what is now defined as a "statutory licence for cover versions", under Section 31C of the Copyright (Amended) Act 1957, are identical—though with some variation as to particulars. Thus, Section 31C of the Act provide thus:

> Any person desirous of making a cover version, being a sound recording in respect of any literary, dramatic or musical work, where sound recordings of that work have been made by or with the licence or consent of the owner of the right in the work, may do so subject to the provisions of this section:
>
> Provided that such sound recordings shall be in the same medium as the last recording, unless the medium of the last recording is no longer in current commercial use.[125]

The person making the sound recordings shall give prior notice of his intention to make the sound recordings in the manner as may be prescribed, and provide in advance copies of all covers or labels with which the sound recordings are to be sold, and pay in advance, to the owner of rights in each work royalties in respect of all copies to be made by him, at the rate fixed by the Appellate Board[126] in this behalf: Provided that such sound recordings shall not be sold or issued in any form of packaging or with any cover or label which is likely to mislead or confuse the public as to their identity, and in particular shall not contain the name or depict in any way any performer of an earlier sound recording of the same work or any cinematograph film in which such sound recording was incorporated and, further, shall state on the cover that it is a cover version made under this section.[127] The person making such sound recordings shall not make any alteration in the literary or musical work which has not been made previously by or with the consent of the owner of rights, or which is not technically necessary for the purpose of making the sound recordings: Provided that such

---

122. Inserted by the Copyright (Amendment) Act, 2012 (Act 27 of 2012), Section 18 [w.e.f. 21-6-2012].
123. Substituted by the Finance Act 2017 (7 of 2017), section 160(a) for "Copyright Board," [w.e.f. 26 May, 2017].
124. MANU/KA/0151/2015.
125. Copyright Act 1957, Section 31C(1).
126. Substituted by the Finance Act 2017 (7 of 2017), section 160(a) for "Copyright Board," [w.e.f. 26 May, 2017].
127. *Ibid.*, Section 31C(2).

sound recordings shall not be made until the expiration of five calendar years after the end of the year in which the first sound recordings of the work was made.[128]

One royalty in respect of such sound recordings shall be paid for a minimum of fifty thousand copies of each work during each calendar years in which copies of it are made: Provided that the Appellate Board[129] may, by general order, fix a lower minimum in respect of works in a particular language or dialect having regard to the potential circulation of such works.[130] The person making such sound recordings shall maintain such registers and books of account in respect thereof, including full details of existing stock as may be prescribed and shall allow the owner of rights or his duly authorised agent or representative in inspect all records and books of account relating to such sound recording: Provided that if on a complaint brought before the Appellate Board[131] to the effect that the owner of rights has not been paid in full for any sound recordings purporting to be made in pursuance of this section, the Appellate Board[132] is, prima facie, satisfied that the complaint is genuine, it may pass in order ex-parte directing the person making the sound recording to cease from making further copies and, after holding such inquiry as it considers necessary, make such further order as it may deem fit, including an order for payment of royalty.[133] Thus, the concept "cover version" can be explained by following illustration.

ILLUSTRATIONS

Suppose a famous singer sings particular lyrics and which singing is accompanied by an orchestra which plays out music. This performance involves various works and use of all such works jointly results in a new copyright work called the sound recording which let us call the first sound recording. In such first sound recording there are a total of three copyrights which get amalgamated to create one consolidated work. The first copyright is in the lyrics created by the lyrics writer i.e. the literary work. The second copyright is in the musical work. The third copyright is in the performance by the performers viz. the singer and the persons comprising the orchestra.[134]

An interesting question that came up for consideration in *Super Cassettes Industries Ltd.* v. *Bathla Cassette Industries Pvt. Ltd.*[135] is whether sound records created based on Section 52(1)(j) be treated as original work having separate copyright. The plaintiff created a version recording to the song *Chalo Dildar Chalo* from the film *Pakeezah* after following the requirements under Section 52(1)(j) of the Copyright Act. The defendants attempted to create a version record of the same song following the same procedure. The present suit was to restrain the defendants from doing so on the ground that the version record created by the plaintiff was an original work. According to the plaintiff for the re-recording of the songs, they used sufficient independent skill and labour by engaging musicians, singers and

128. *Ibid.*, Section 31C(3).
129. Substituted by the Finance Act 2017 (7 of 2017), section 160(a) for "Copyright Board," [w.e.f. 26 May, 2017].
130. *Ibid.*, Section 31C(2).
131. Substituted by the Finance Act 2017 (7 of 2017), section 160(a) for "Copyright Board," [w.e.f. 26 May, 2017].
132. Substituted by the Finance Act 2017 (7 of 2017), section 160(a) for "Copyright Board," [w.e.f. 26 May, 2017].
133. *Ibid.*, Section 31C(5).
134. *See, Star India Pvt. Ltd.* v. *Piyush Agarwal*, 2014 (58) PTC 169 (Del).
135. 2003 (27) PTC 280 (Del): 107 (2003) DLT 91.

music conductors to create the original version record. The court rejected this without giving adequate reasons. Instead it questioned whether version recording using new singers would fall under Section 52(1)(j) an issue on which parties to the dispute did not have any disagreement. The court after stressing the condition in the section that "the recording should be without any change" opined:

> If a sound recording under Section 52(1)(j) is to be made there should be prior consent of the owner when a change as significant as the change of the singer is being contemplated. This is clearly indicated by the fact that the integrity of the original sound recording in question which is a vocal rendering is clearly affected by the substitution of the singer. Such a change may not be discernible to a lay listener as is indeed the finding after listening to and comparing the plaintiffs tape and the original work. However, to the owner of the sound recording, the vital substitution of the singer is clearly a change which cannot fall within a change necessary for adaptation of the work as neither a change has been made by the original owner of the work nor has permission been granted for the plaintiff's adaptation by the original owner.[136]

Both the parties in fact argued that version recording using different singers would fall under Section 52(1)(j). This is evident from the following observation of the court, thus:

> In other words the plea of the plaintiff and oddly enough the defendant to some extent, in the present case is that a close imitation of an existing recording using alternate performers' is not a copyright infringement. Sustenance for such action is sought to be derived from the Section 52(1)(j) of the Copyright Act.[137]

After referring to the re-recording of the Beatle's songs, the court gave the following meaning to version recording:

> Version recording would really be such sound recording where while being inspire by the original melody a distinct interpretation, different both in presentation, rhythm and orchestral arrangement emerges.... What is adapted in a version recording is the original melody, but the beat, the orchestral arrangement and indeed the end product is what can be called a substantially new arrangement. In such a version recording while the original melodic arrangement inspires the new creation yet it is a version unmistakably different and distinct from the original. Such a version recording, if made in India may enjoy the benefit of Section 52(1)(j) subject to satisfaction of the requirements of the said provision and Rule 21(2) but not a total copy though with different singers, as in the plaintiff recording....[138]

Based on the above reasoning the court concluded that since the recording of the plaintiff itself was an infringement, he could not complain about such recording by the defendants. So injunction was refused. Even though the observation is *obiter dicta* it is wrong for the following reasons.

The court seems to have missed the interpretation on the Delhi High Court in *Gramophone Co. of India Ltd.* v. *Super Cassettes Industries Ltd.*,[139] where it was observed that re-recording using different singers would fall within the scope of Section 52(1)(j).[140] The court also did

136. *Ibid.*
137. *Ibid.*, at p. 293 (PTC).
138. *Ibid.*, at p. 301.
139. 1995 PTR 64: 58 (1995) DLT 99.
140. Section 52(1)(j) reads: "The making of sound recordings in respect of any literary, dramatic or musical work, if (i) sound recording of that work have been made by or with the licence or consent of the owner of the right in the work...."

not correctly appreciate the objectives and scope of Section 52(1)(j). It is to be noted that the purpose of this Section is for the re-recording, i.e., making of sound recording of the literary, dramatic or musical work. The scope of this Section, thus, is not for making copies or re-recording of existing sound recording of these works using same set of persons as seems to have understood by the court. This provision enables a re-recording of the works literary, dramatic and musical work—without the consent of the owner of the works if conditions stipulated in the Section are followed. This presupposes that the person making re-recording has to engage musicians, singers and music conductors, etc., for this purpose. These persons could be the same set of persons who were used first to create the sound recording of the works or different set of persons. So change of persons for re-recording is envisaged under the Section itself. This is the practice followed by the industries from the very inception of the Section not only in our country but also in other countries where similar provisions exist. This is the reason why the parties did not question this. Any other interpretation will make the Section meaningless and redundant. It appears that the court has failed to appreciate this while trying to understand the meaning of version recording and its applicability to the scope of this Section. One of the conditions stipulated is on alteration of the work.[141]

It is clear from the words "adaptation of the work" that the alteration anticipated is in the literary, dramatic or musical work on which the sound recording is made and not on the persons performing the work for recording it. It is to be noted that the owner of the copyright has no right or control over the talent of the persons performing the work once the consent to perform is given. This means that the alteration envisaged with reference to a song is on its lyrics and musical composition. This is intended to protect the moral rights of the author. The provision permits only minimum changes which are required for the adaptation of the work for the purpose of re-recording. When a new set of persons are engaged for the purpose of re-recording of the songs they, in fact, perform the song, i.e., the lyric and musical composition without any change in these works. In fact they have no right to alter it and if they do it without permission it will amount to violation of the moral rights of the owner of the work. So change of singers cannot be treated as alteration affecting the reputation of the owner of the rights since this has nothing to do with the work. On the contrary, changes of performers are envisaged under the Section for achieving the objectives for which the Section is incorporated in the Act. The issue is not whether version recording as understood by the court is permitted under the Section but whether the act of engaging new set of persons for re-recording the work after satisfying the conditions are in conformity with the section.

In *Gramophone Co. of India* v. *Mars Recording Pvt. Ltd.*[142] the Karnataka High Court examined the scope of Section 52(j). In this case, the plaintiff-respondent intending to publish audio cassette of three songs owned by the *Gramophone Company* followed the procedure under Section 52(j) of the Act for a statutory licence. Accordingly, the plaintiff sent a notice with inland cards and demand draft of ₹1,500/- each towards royalty. After 15 days of the notice, the plaintiff not receiving any reply from the defendant produced the cassettes. Since the defendant started threatening civil and criminal action for infringement of copyright, the

141. Section 52(1)(j) Povisio (1) reads: "no alteration shall be made which have not been made previously by or with the consent of the owner of rights, or which are not reasonably necessary for the adaptation of the work for the purpose of making the sound recording."
142. 2000 PTC 171.

plaintiff filed the present suit to prevent any action by the defendant and the same was granted by the district court. In appeal the defendant argued that Section 52(j)(i) and (ii) must be read conjointly and the written consent of the owner of copyright is necessary for the purpose of producing the cassettes even after complying with the formalities under Section 52(j) of the Act. Rejecting this, the court correctly observed:

> I am of the opinion that the licence is deemed to have been granted and the person producing the cassette after the expiry of 15 days is not said to have infringed copyright. If Section 52(j)(i) and (ii) are read conjointly Section 52(j)(ii) becomes redundant and such narrow interpretation cannot be given to defeat the very object and purpose of Section 52(1)(j)(ii). From a perusal of Rule 21 it is clear that it is framed so as to enable a person intending to make a sound recording to obtain consent or licence from the copyright owner by complying with the requirements of sending a notice of such intention to the owner of copyright and to the Registrar of Copyright giving 15 days notice in defence of making the sound records and also paying the required amount and the rate of royalty is as fixed by the Copyright Board in this behalf.[143]

The Copyright (Amendment) Act, 2012 introduced a new Section 31C[144] which provides for statutory licence to any person desiring to make a cover version of a sound recording in respect of any literary, dramatic or musical work. This is not totally a new provision for statutory licence for cover version as it is, but a replacement of Section 52(1)(j) as it stood before the amendment. According to new Section 31C, the person making the sound recording shall give to the owner prior notice of his intention in the prescribed manner, provide the copies of all covers or labels with which the version is supposed to be sold, and pay in advance the royalty at the rate fixed by the Appellate Board[145]. Such sound recordings can be made only after the expiration of 5 years after publication of the original sound recording. There is a requirement of payment of a minimum royalty for 50,000 copies of the work during each calendar year.

Statutory Licence for Broadcasting of Literary and Musical Works and Sound Recording (Section 31D)

The Copyright (Amendment) Act, 2012 introduced a new Section 31D[146] which provides for statutory licence for broadcasting of literary and musical works and sound recordings. It provides that any broadcasting organisation desiring to broadcast a work including sound recording may do so. The broadcasting organisation shall give prior notice to the right holders, pay royalty as fixed by the Appellate Board[147] in advance. The names of the authors and principal performers shall be announced during the broadcast. The broadcasting organisation shall maintain records of the broadcast, books of account and render to the owner such records and books of account.

---

143. *Ibid.*, at pp. 122–123.
144. Inserted by the Copyright (Amendment) Act, 2012, Section 18 [w.e.f. 21-6-2012].
145. Substituted by the Finance Act 2017 (7 of 2017), section 160(a) for "Copyright Board," [w.e.f. 26 May, 2017].
146. Inserted by the Copyright (Amendment) Act, 2012, Section 18 [w.e.f. 21-6-2012].
147. Substituted by the Finance Act 2017 (7 of 2017), section 160(a) for "Copyright Board," [w.e.f. 26 May, 2017].

The above amendment has been brought in to facilitate access to the works for the growing broadcasting industry. At present, the access to copyright works by broadcasters was dependent on voluntary licencing. As a result, unreasonable terms and conditions were being set by the copyright societies and owners. There are divergent views by the courts in interpreting the existing compulsory licencing provisions under Section 31. There were litigations pending before various High Courts as well as the Copyright Board (Appellate Board)[148] regarding the nature of licence and the rate of royalties to be paid when works particularly songs were used for broadcasting. Automatic licence or non-voluntary licence such as the proposed statutory licence ensuring adequate return to the owner of works was the best solution to make access easy for broadcasting industry. In *South Indian Music Companies Association* v. *Union of India*,[149] it was arged in the Madras High Court that the Section 31D of the Copyright Act 1957 is violative of Article 19(1)(g) of the Constitution of India, as it provides for the royalties to be fixed for radio broadcasting by the Board directly. Thus, such a power cannot be termed as a reasonable restriction. Rejecting the contention the Court observed:

> Section 31D was introduced taking note of Article 11(2) and 13 of Berne Convention and Article 15(2) of the Rome Convention (for sound recordings) and Article 9(1) of the TRIPS Agreement. It was meant to support the development and growth of private radio broadcasting. The object is also to strike at the monopoly to the detriment of the general public. While doing so, the provisions also take care of the interest of the owner.

Licence after Expiry of Prescribed Periods

Licence to Produce and Publish Translations (Section 32)

Section 32 of the Copyright Act, 1957 deals with the provisions relating to licence to produce and publish translations. According to Section 32(1), any person may apply to the Appellate Board[150] for a licence to produced and publish a translation of a literary and dramatic work in any language [after a period of seven years from the first publication of the work].[151] The provisions of Section 32(1) apply in case of Indian works. However, Section 32 provides a detail framework of law in case of works which are not Indian.

Works Which are not Indian

Section 32(1A)[152] of the Copyright Act provides that where the work is not an Indian work, any person may apply to the Appellate Board[153] for a licence to produce and publish a translation, in printed or analogous form of reproduction, of a literary or dramatic work, in any language in general use in India after a period of three years from the first publication of

---

148. Substituted by the Finance Act 2017 (7 of 2017), section 160(a) for "Copyright Board," [w.e.f. 26 May, 2017].
149. 2016 (67) PTC 99 (Mad): MIPR 2016 (2) 64.
150. Substituted by the Finance Act 2017 (7 of 2017), Section 160(a) for "Copyright Board," [w.e.f. 26 May, 2017].
151. Inserted by the Copyright (Amendment) Act, 1983, Section 13 [w.e.f. 9-8-1984].
152. Inserted by the Copyright (Amendment) Act, 1983, Section 13 [w.e.f. 9-8-1984].
153. Substituted by the Finance Act 2017 (7 of 2017), Section 160(a) for "Copyright Board," [w.e.f. 26 May, 2017].

such work, if such translation is required for the purposes of teaching, scholarship or research. Where such translation is in a language not in general use in any developed country, such application may be made after a period of one year from such publication. In Section 32, "developed country" means a country which is not a developing country.[154] "Developing country" means a country which is for the time being regarded as such in conformity with the practice of the General Assembly of the United Nations.[155] The expression "purposes of teaching, research or scholarship" includes— (i) purposes of instructional activity at all levels in educational institutions, including Schools, Colleges, Universities and Tutorial Institutions and (ii) purposes of all other types of organised educational activity.[156]

The licence granted in respect of non-Indian work will not extend to the export of copies of the translation outside India and every copy of such translation should contain a notice to the effect that the copy is available for distribution only in India. However, the export of copies of translation in a language other than English, French or Spanish can be made by the Government to any country if such copies are sent to citizen of India residing outside India or to any association of such citizens outside India, or where such copies are meant to be used for purposes of teaching, scholarship or research, and not for any commercial purpose. The export is possible only when importing country has permitted it.[157] Such licence shall be granted on an application made in the prescribed form along with the prescribed fee and after holding inquiries. Such a licence shall not be exclusive licence and the licencee shall pay to the owner of copyright royalties in respect of copies of the translation of the work sold to the public. The rate of royalty shall be calculated by the Board in the prescribed manner.

Besides the above conditions, there are some more conditions which are to be fulfilled before a licence is granted to produce or publish the translation of the work. These conditions are:

1. A translation of the work has not been published by the owner of the copyright in the work or by any person authorised by him, [within seven years or three years or one year, as the case may be, of the first publication of the work],[158] or if a translation has been so published, it has been out of print.
2. The applicant has proved to the satisfaction of the Appellate Board[159] that he had requested and had been denied authorisation by the owner of the copyright to produce and publish such translation, or that [he was, after due diligence on his part unable to find][160] the owner of the copyright.
3. Where the owner of the copyright is not traceable the applicant has sent a copy of his request for such authorisation by registered air mail post to the publisher not less than two months before the application for the licence.

154. Explanation (a) to Section 32 of the Copyright Act, 1957.
155. Explanation (b) to Section 32 of the Copyright Act, 1957.
156. Explanation (d) to Section 32 of the Copyright Act, 1957.
157. Section 32(4) of the Copyright Act, 1957.
158. Inserted by the Copyright (Amendment) Act, 1983, Section 13 for "within seven years of the first publication of the work" [w.e.f. 9-8-1984].
159. Substituted by the Finance Act 2017 (7 of 2017), Section 160(a) for "Copyright Board," [w.e.f. 26 May, 2017].
160. Inserted by the Copyright (Amendment) Act, 1983, Section 13 for "he was unable to find" [w.e.f. 9-81984].

4. A period of six months in the case of an application relating to a non-Indian work (for translation in a language in general use in India) and nine months in the case of an application relating to non-Indian work (translation in a language not in general use in any developed country) must have elapsed from the date of making the request or from the date of sending the copy, as the case may be. It is also important to note that a translation of the work has not been published within the period of such six months or nine months, as the case may be.[161]
5. In the case of translation of a non-Indian work, the name of the author and the title of the particular edition of the work proposed to be translated are printed in all the copies of the translation and if the work is composed mainly of illustrations, the provisions of Section 32A are also complied with.
6. The Appellate Board[162] is satisfied that the applicant is competent to produce and publish a correct translation of the work and possesses the means to pay to the owner of the copyright the royalties payable to him.
7. The author has not withdrawn from circulation copies of the work.
8. An opportunity of being heard is given, wherever practicable, to the owner of the copyright in the work.

Grant of Licence to Broadcasting Authority

According to Section 32(5)[163] of the Copyright Act, 1957 in case of the non-Indian work any Broadcasting authority may apply to the Appellate Board[164] for a licence to produce and publish the translation of a work published in printed or analogous form of reproduction, or any text incorporated in audio-visual fixations prepared and published solely for the purpose of systematic instructional activities, for broadcasting such translation for the purposes of teaching or for the dissemination of the result of specialised, technical or scientific research to the experts in any particular field. The procedure to be followed is the same as that prescribed for Indian work with the necessary modifications. A licence in such a case will not be granted unless—

1. the translation is made from a work lawfully acquired,
2. the broadcast is made through the medium of sound and visual recordings,
3. such recording has been lawfully and exclusively made for the purpose of broadcasting in India by the applicant or by any other broadcasting agency, and
4. the translation and broadcasting of such translation are not used for any commercial purposes.[165]

---

161. Inserted by the Copyright (Amendment) Act, 1983, Section 13 [w.e.f. 9-8-1984].
162. Substituted by the Finance Act 2017 (7 of 2017), Section 160(a) for "Copyright Board," [w.e.f. 26 May, 2017].
163. Inserted by the Copyright (Amendment) Act, 1983, Section 13 [w.e.f. 9-8-1984].
164. Substituted by the Finance Act 2017 (7 of 2017), Section 160(a) for "Copyright Board," [w.e.f. 26 May, 2017].
165. Section 32(6) of the Copyright Act, 1957.

Licence to Reproduce and Publish Works for Certain Purposes (Section 32A)

Section 32 of the Copyright Act, 1957 deals with the provisions relating to licence to produce and publish translations, while Section 32A which was inserted by the Copyright (Amendment) Act, 1983 deals with licence to reproduce and publish works for certain purposes.[166] Section 32A provides that where, after the expiration of the "relevant period",[167] from the date of the first publication of an edition of a literary, scientific or artistic work—(a) the copies of such edition are not made available in India; or (b) such copies have not been put on sale in India for a period of six months, to the general public, or in connection with systematic instructional activities at a reasonable price by the owner of the right of reproduction or by any person authorised by him on this behalf, then any person may apply to the Appellate Board for a licence to reproduce and publish such work in printed or analogous forms of reproduction at the price at which such edition is sold or at a lower price for the purposes of systematic instructional activities. The Copyright Board, after holding prescribed inquiry and after giving the owner of copyright an opportunity of being heard wherever practicable, may grant to the applicant a licence, not being an exclusive licence, to produce and publish a reproduction of the work subject to the payment of royalties of such amount as it may determine in the prescribed manner. The licence granted shall not extend to the export of copies. Further, conditions similar to those applicable for the grant of licence to produce and publish translations under Section 32 are applicable here with some changes. In addition, some conditions which are required to be fulfilled are:

1. that the applicant undertakes to reproduce and publish the work at such price as may be fixed by the Copyright Board (Appellate Board)[168], being a price reasonably related to the price normally charged in India for works of the same standard on the same or similar subjects; and
2. that a reproduction of the work has not been published by the owner of the copyright within six month in the case of work of natural science, physical science or technology or three months in the case of any other work from the date of making the request to the owner of the copyright for authorisation, to reproduce and publish the work or sending a copy of the request to the publisher, as the case may be.

A licence to reproduce and publish the translation of a work under Section 32A shall not be granted unless such translation has been published by the owner of the right of translation or a person authorised by him, and the translation is not in a language in general use in India. However, a licence may be granted for the reproduction and publication, or translation into a

166. *See, Entertainment Network (India) Ltd.* v. *Super Cassettes Industries Ltd.*, 2008 (13) SCC 30: 2008 (37) PTC 353.
167. According to Explanation to Section 32A of the Copyright Act, 1957 'relevant period' means a period of (a) seven years for works relating to fiction, poetry, drama, music or art; (b) three years for works relating to natural science, physical science, mathematics or technology and (c) five years for any other work.
168. Substituted by the Finance Act 2017 (7 of 2017), section 160(a) for "Copyright Board," [w.e.f. 26 May, 2017].

language in general use in India, of any text incorporated in audio-visual fixations prepared and published solely for the purpose of systematic instructional activities.

Termination of Licences (Section 32B)

Termination of licence granted under Sections 32(1A) and 32A of non-Indian work has been recognised under Section 32B[169] of the Copyright Act 1957. Section 32B provides that where the Copyright Board has granted a licence to any person to produce and publish a translation of a non-Indian work in any language under Section 32(lA), if at any time after granting the licence the owner of the work or a person authorised by him has published a translation of the work in the same language which is substantially the same in content at a price reasonably related to the price charged in India for the translation of works of the same standard on the same or similar subject the licence granted will be terminated. A licence granted under Section 32A shall be terminated in the similar way with some necessary changes. The termination will not take effect until after the expiry of three months from the date of service of a notice in the prescribed manner on the person holding the licence by the owner of the right of translation intimating the publication. The licence holder will be permitted to sell or distribute copies of the translation produced before the termination of the licence takes effect until they are exhausted.

INTERNATIONAL COPYRIGHT

Copyright law is "territorial" and national in scope. Regardless of where the author lives or where the work was first published, the copyright protection accorded to a work depends on the national laws of the country in which the author seeks protection. In this sense, there is no such thing as an "international copyright" that will automatically protect an author's writings throughout the world. Protection against unauthorised use in a particular country depends on the national laws of that country. However, most countries offer protection to foreign works under certain conditions that have been greatly simplified by international copyright treaties and conventions. Under the Copyright Act, 1957 works of foreign authors/owners are accorded the same protection in India to which the Indian citizens are entitled under the Act.[170] Thus, "Chapter IX" (Sections 40–43) of the Copyright Act recognises the international copyright. In exercise of the powers by Section 40 of the Act and in suppression of the International Copyright Order, 1991, the Central Government framed the International Copyright Order, 1999. While the Act applies only to works first published in India irrespective of nationality of the author, Section 42 of the Act restricts the rights in works of foreign authors first published in India. In SAP *Aktiengesellschaft* v. *Appsone Consulting India (P) Ltd.*,[171] the plaintiff No.

169. Inserted by the Copyright (Amendment) Act, 1983, Section 14 [w.e.f. 9-8-1984].
170. According to Section 2(l) of the Copyright Act, 1957 "Indian work" means a literary, dramatic or musical work,—(i) the author of which is a citizen of India; or (ii) which is first published in India; or (iii) the author of which, in the case of an unpublished work, is, at the time of the making of the work, a citizen of India.
171. A 2015 (151) DRJ 679.

1's computer programs are "works" that has been first published and registered in Germany. Further, Copyright Registrations have also been obtained from the United States Copyright Office. The computer programs and the supplementary user instruction Manuals supplied by the plaintiffs are "original literary works" as contemplated under Section 2(o) and Section 13(1) of the Copyright Act 1957. The Delhi High Court held that the plaintiff No. 1's works are protected in India under Section 40 of the Act read in conjunction with the International Copyright Order 1999, by virtue of the fact that both India and Germany are signatories (hence members) to the Berne and Universal Copyright Convention, the said Conventions, on a reciprocal basis, recognize the copyright in a work created in any member country.

The Section 40 of the Copyright Act further extends copyright protection to foreign works.[172] According to Section 40 of the Act, the Government of India has the power to extend the benefits of all or any of the provisions of the Act to works first published in any foreign country. Thus, it may do by notification in the Gazette of India. The benefits granted to foreign works will not extend beyond what is available to the works in the country, and that too only on a reciprocal basis, i.e., to say the foreign country must grant similar protection to works entitled to copyright under the Act. The applicability of the Act to foreign works may extend either generally or limited to particular classes of works or particular classes of cases. The term of the copyright in India to the foreign work will not exceed that conferred by the foreign country. The enjoyment of the rights conferred by the Act may be subject to certain conditions and formalities. In applying provisions of the Act to foreign works, suitable exceptions and modifications may be made having regard to the law of foreign country. The protection granted will not apply to works made or first published before the commencement of the order granting the benefits.

In *Microsoft Corporation* v. *Ganesh Wakode*,[173] the plaintiff a Microsoft Corporation established under the laws of State of Washington, USA. Plaintiffs' software programs are popular, famous and renowned throughout the world. The products of plaintiff are distributed in India through various authorised distributors. The plaintiff upon receiving information of the defendants' infringing activities in India regarding unlicensed use of the plaintiffs' software program, immediately initiated an investigation and submitted a report to the court. Having heard and satisfied with the evidence as well as document placed on record, the Court is of the opinion that plaintiff in fact proved the facts stated in the complaint. Moreover, the software programs as developed and marketed by the plaintiffs are a "computer programme" within the meaning of Section 2(ffc) of the Copyright Act, 1957 and also included in the definition of a literary work as per Section 2(o) of the Copyright Act, 1957. The plaintiffs' work are also protected in India under Section 40 of the Copyright Act, 1957 read with the International Copyright Order 1999 as the rights of authors of member countries of the Berne and Universal Copyright Conventions are protected under Indian Copyright law. India and the USA are signatories to both the Universal Copyright Convention and the Berne Convention. Similarly,

---

172. *See, Holland Company LP* v. *S.P. Industries*, 2017 (71) PTC 630 (Del): MIPR 2017 (3)237; *Photoquip India Ltd.* v. *Delhi Photo Store*, MIPR 2014 (3) 149: 2014 (60) PTC 563 (Bom); *Microfibres Inc.* v. *Girdhar*, 2009(40) PTC 519 (Del): MIPR 2009 (2) 229, *Indiana Gratings Pvt. Ltd.* v. *Anand Udyog Fabricators Pvt. Ltd.*, 2009(39) PTC 609 (Bom); *John Richard Brady* v. *Chemical Process Equipments P. Ltd.*, AIR 1987 Delhi 372.
173. 2013 LawSuit (Del) 638.

in *Microsoft Corporation* v. *Indus Valley Partners (India) Pvt. Ltd.*,[174] the Court held that the plaintiffs computer programs are "works" that have been first published and registered in the USA, and as such also enjoy protection in India by virtue of Section 40 of the Copyright Act read with the International Copyright Order, 1999.

Section 41 of the Act gives copyright protection to works of international organisation. According to Section 41 works made or published by international organisations are entitled to such benefit are decided by the government and declared and published in the official Gazette. One or more sovereign powers, or the government or the governments thereof may be members of this organisation. If such organisation has not the legal capacity or a body corporate, will be deemed to have such capacity for the purpose of holding, dealing with, and enforcing copyright and in connection with all legal proceedings relating to copyright. In accordance with the provision of Section 41 of the Act, the Central Government has framed the Copyright (International Organisations) Order, 1958.

Section 42 of the Act provides that in case a foreign country does not give an adequate protection to Indian authors, the Government of India may by order deny protection to works first published in India whose author is a citizen of such foreign country and not domiciled in India. According to Section 43, any order made under Section 40 will be laid before parliament and will be subject to any modifications made by parliament. In *Microfibres, Inc.* v. *Girdhar*,[175] the plaintiff is a company incorporated under the laws of the USA and claims to have extensive international reputation with manufacturing bases and operations in several countries of the world and there are more than 250 brands of microfibres which are apparently sold in India. The plaintiff has claimed that the artistic work constitutes original artistic work as defined within the meaning of Section 2(c) of the Copyright act. The plaintiff also claims that it enjoys copyright protection in India as a consequence of the provisions of Section 40 of the Copyright Act and the Berne convention, Universal Copyright Convention read with Indian International copyright Order, 1999. Recognising the international copyright of the plaintiff, the Court observed:

> In exercise of the power conferred by Section 40 of the Copyright Act, the international Copyright Order 1999 was published in the Gazette of India dated 6-4-1999. Para 3 of the said order postulates that subject to the provisions of Para 4, 5 and 6, all provisions of the Copyright Act, except those in Chapter VIII and those other provisions which apply exclusively to the Indian works, shall apply to any work, first made or published in a country mentioned in Part I, II, III, IV or VI of the Schedule in like manner as if it was first published in India. The United States of America is mentioned at serial no. 56 of Part III.

Similarly, in *Yonex Kabushiki Kaisha* v. *Phillips International*,[176] the label has been created for the plaintiff by its employees, in the course of their employment with the plaintiff and both India and Japan being signatories to the Berne Convention as well as the Universal Copyright Convention. The Court held that the plaintiff's works are protected in India by virtue of Section 40 of the Copyright Act 1957, read in conjunction with the International Copyright Order 1999.

---

174. 2014 (2) MIPR 373: 2014 (143) DRJ 191.
175. 2006 (128) DLT 238: 2006 (32) PTC 157.
176. 2007 (35) PTC 345: 2007 (8) AD (Del) 413. *See also*, *John Wiley* v. *Prabhat Chander Kumar Jain*, 2010 (170) DLT 701: 2010 LawSuit (Del) 1325.

PROCEDURE FOR COPYRIGHT REGISTRATION: IS COPYRIGHT REGISTRATION MANDATORY?

Procedure

Sections 44 to 50A of the Copyright Act, 1957 provide provisions for registration of copyright while according to Sections 13 and 14 of the Copyright Act, 1957 which defines the copyright and its meaning do not require registration. Thus, it is a general question of copyright law whether copyright registration is mandatory?[177] According to Section 44 of the Act, there shall be at the Copyright Office a registrar in the prescribed form to be called the Register of Copyrights in which may be entered the names or titles of works and names and address of the author, publishers and owners of copyright and such other particulars and owners of copyright and such other particulars as may be prescribed. Section 45(1) of the Act further clarifies that the author or publisher of, or the owner of or other person interested in the copyright in, any work may make an application in the prescribed form accompanied by the prescribed fee to the Registrar of Copyrights for entering particulars of the work in the Register of Copyrights. In *Gurukrupa Mech Tech Pvt. Ltd.* v. *State of Gujarat*,[178] the Gujrat High Court observed:

> It is well settled that although under the Copyright Act 1957, there is a provision of registration, under Section 44 of the Act. It is not in doubt that the said procedure is an enabling provision and registration is not compulsory for the purpose of enforcing copyright. Section 44 of the Act provides for registration of work in which copyright exists but in order to claim copyright registration is not necessary. This is because registration is only to raise a presumption that the person shown in the certificate of registration is the author. This presumption is not conclusive, but no further proof is necessary unless there is a proof rebutting the contents of the said certificate.

In *Louis Vuitton Malletier* v. *Iqbal Singh*,[179] the suit was filed by the plaintiff is for permanent injunction restraining infringement of its trademark, passing off, dilution, rendition of accounts of profits, damages and delivery up. Disposing the application the Delhi High Court held that the plaintiff enjoys copyright over the above pattern, which is an artistic work within the meaning of the Indian Copyright Act 1957. The said work has a copyright registration with the Copyright Office of the United States of America.

Under Rule 16(3) of the Copyright Rules, 1958 an applicant making an application for registration of copyright is required to give notice of its application to all parties that may have an interest in the work to be registered. The person applying for registration of a Copyright shall simultaneously send a copy of the application to every other person interested in the copyright of the work. If this is not done, the registration is liable to be cancelled on this ground.[180] Commenting upon the nature of interest under Rule 16(3), the Copyright Board

---

177. *See, Tea Board, India v. ITC Limited,* (2019) 1 CALLT 538 (HC). *Madhavan* v. *Nayar*, AIR 1988 Ker 39; *Nav Sahitya Prakash* v. *Anand Kumar*, AIR 1981 All 2000; *Kumari Kanaka* v. *Sundararanjan*, (1972) Ker LR 536; *Mishra Bandhu* v. *Koshal*, AIR 1970 MP 261.
178. (2018) 4 GLR 3324. See also *Burroughs Wellcome (India) Ltd.* v. *Uni-sole Pvt. Ltd.*, 1999 (19) PTC 188 (Bom): 1998 (3) BomCR 481.
179. 258 (2019) DLT 760: 2019 (78) PTC 315 (Del).
180. *Kwality Ice-cream* v. *India Hobby Centre* (1993) PTC 29.

(Appellate Board)[181] opined that such interest of Interested Party referred to in Rule 16(3) of the Copyright Rules is not required to be proprietary and it may be any other interest. The underlying concept is to bring in anyone who has any interest in the subject matter and for that reason can help the Registrar in arriving at a proper decision.[182] Under Rule 16 read with Second Schedule of the Copyright Rules, 1958 an application for registration of copyright should be on Form IV accompanied by the prescribed fee. Persons who are permitted to make applications including the authors, publisher, owner or any other person interested in the copyright in any work.

Section 46 of the Copyright Act, 1957 provides that there shall be kept at the Copyright Office such indexes of the Register of Copyrights as may be prescribed. According to Section 47 of the Act, the Register of Copyrights and indexes thereof kept under this Act shall at all reasonable times be open to inspection, and any person shall be entitled to take copies of, or make extracts from, such register or indexes on payment of such fee and subject to such conditions as may be prescribed. Section 48 of the Act clarified that the Register of Copyrights is to be *prima facie* evidence of particulars entered therein. In *Surya Roshni Ltd.* v. *Metalman Industries Ltd.*,[183] the court held that in the matter of trademark, there cannot be infringement where colour is related to quality. Clearly functional and relates to Indian Standards Institute (ISI) specification standards and can be used by all the manufacturers.

Under Section 49 of the Act, corrections of entries in the Register of Copyrights are permissible. According to Section 50 the Appellate Board[184], on application of the Registrar of Copyrights or of any person aggrieved, shall order the rectification of the Register of Copyrights by—(i) the making of any entry wrongly omitted to be made in the register, or (ii) the expunging of any entry wrongly made in, or remaining on, the register, or (iii) the correction of any error or defect in the register. The expression "person aggrieved" used in Section 50, but it is not defined in the Copyright Act. Similarly, the expression "person aggrieved" is found in several statutes without having definition. A seven Judges Bench of the Apex Court in *Bar Council of Maharashtra* v. *M.V. Dabholkar*[185] held that the meaning of the words "person aggrieved" will have to be ascertained with reference to the purpose and the provisions of the statute. The Court further observed:

> Person aggrieved corresponds to the requirement of locus standi which arises in relation to judicial remedies.

Discussing the concept "person aggrieved" in *Ganga Vishnu Raheja Trustee* v. *Swami Satyanand Trust*,[186] the Copyright Board at New Delhi observed that in general principles applied under the copyright law in deciding who is a person aggrieved is applicable with suitable modifications. It was also observed that on careful scrutiny of the records none of the

181. Substituted by the Finance Act 2017 (7 of 2017), section 160(a) for "Copyright Board," [w.e.f. 26 May, 2017].
182. *See, Indi Brine Industries Ltd.* v. *Ram Niwas*, 2010 (43) PTC 608 (CB).
183. 2001 PTC 777 (Del).
184. Substituted by the Finance Act 2017 (7 of 2017), section 160(a) for "Copyright Board," [w.e.f. 26 May, 2017].
185. (1975) 2 SCC 702.
186. (2000) PTC 84 (Del) (CB). *See also, Raj Kumar Saraf, Proprietor Bindal Food Products* v. *Vaidya Nandram Gigraj Chamaria*, 2013 (55) PTC 354.

factors could be said to be present in the present case in favour of the appellant to give him a *locus standi* and to make him a "person aggrieved". Thus, it was held that the appellant cannot have any grievance and is not a "person aggrieved" within the meaning of the provisions of Section 50. Similarly, in *Kappy Plastic Industries* v. *Capital Plastic Industries*,[187] it was held that a person who is not the owner of copyright in the artistic work (trademark) sought to be expunged from the register is not a person aggrieved.

In *Hindustan Pencils Ltd.* v. *Alpha Cottage Industries,*[188] it was held that where similarities between the artistic works are fundamental and substantial in material aspects, then it amounts to violation of copyright. In *Marly Colling Tower Co.* v. *Paharpur Cooling Pvt. Ltd.*,[189] the issue was relating to obtaining registration of copyright fraudulently. In this case, the registrar rectified it by removal of entry. Where the registered proprietor of a copyright work has abandoned the copyright and he has been injuncted in a suit for infringement of copyright rectification under Section 50 of the Copyright Act, 1957 will be allowed. In *Herrington Construction and Finance Ltd.* v. *Eicher Goodearth Ltd.*,[190] rectification of drawing of a horse head Rookie Coin was refused on the ground that it was different from the coin and that the author had utilised labour and skill to bring out a new work. However, in *Hindustan Pencils Pvt. Ltd.* v. *Universal Trading Company*,[191] the registration of respondents' alleged artistic work was rectified on the ground of suppression of material facts before the Registrar and that they were not true owners of the copyright in the work. In *Vandana* v. *Vandana Saree Emporium*,[192] it was held that civil courts have no jurisdiction to rectify copyright register. Hence, when civil proceedings before courts or Trademarks Registry are pending there is nothing preventing the Copyright Board (Appellate Board)[193] from proceeding with rectification proceedings which is not *sub judice*.

Section 50A of the Copyright Act, 1957 provides that every entry made in the Register of Copyrights or the particulars of any work entered under Section 45, the correction of every entry made in such register under Section 49, and every rectification ordered under Section 50, shall be published by the Registrar of Copyrights in the Official Gazette or in such other manner as he may deem fit. In *Urmilacharan Gupta* v. *Charushila Sharan Gupta*,[194] it was held that the Copyright Board (Appellate Board)[195] in its discretion may permit a petitioner to file rectification proceedings in respect of a number of registrations in one application provided the different registrations are in the name of the same person or persons.

Section 45 Copyright Act, 1957 provides that the author or publisher of, or the owner of or other person interested in the copyright in any work "may" make an application to the registrar for entering the particulars in the registrar of copyrights. Thus, registration of

187. (1998) PTC 351 (Delhi) (CB).
188. 2001 PTC 504 (Goa).
189. (2000) PTC 647 (Cal) (CB).
190. (1997) PTC 75 (Thiru) (CB).
191. (1999) PTC 379 (CB).
192. (1983) PTC 119 (CB).
193. Substituted by the Finance Act 2017 (7 of 2017), section 160(a) for "Copyright Board," [w.e.f. 26 May, 2017].
194. (1983) PTC 84 (Del) (CB).
195. Substituted by the Finance Act 2017 (7 of 2017), section 160(a) for "Copyright Board," [w.e.f. 26 May, 2017].

copyright is the discretion of the author or publisher of, or the owner of or other person interested in the copyright in the work. The Berne Convention for the Protection of Literary and Artistic Works, 1986 of which India is a signatory and which has also been adopted in the TRIPS Agreement states in its Article 5(2) that enjoyment and exercise of the rights shall not be subject to any formality (of registration). In *Burroughs Welcome (India) Ltd.* v. *Uni-Sole Pvt. Ltd.*,[196] the Supreme Court has held that Section 44 of the Copyright Act, 1957 provides for registration of work in which copyright exists but in order to claim copyright registration is not necessary. This is because registration is only to raise a presumption that the person shown in the certificate of registration is the author. This presumption is not conclusive, but no further proof is necessary unless there is a proof rebutting the contents of the said certificate. Under Section 48 of the Registration Act, therefore, the act of registration is ex-facie prima facie evidence of the particulars incorporated in the certificate. There is no provision under the Act which deprives the author of his rights on account of non-registration of the copyright.

Nature of Registration

Although Sections 44 to 50A of the Copyright Act, 1957 provide provisions for registration, yet it is not expressly mentioned in any of these Sections that whether the registration is mandatory in nature? In *Rajesh Masrani* v. *Tahiliani Design Pvt. Ltd.*,[197] the Delhi High Court examined the issue whether registration is mandatory for claiming protection under Copyright Act or not ? The Court held that registration of the work is not mandatory nor is a condition precedent for maintaining a suit for damages for infringement of copyright. In a similar language, the Court in *Tahiliani Design Pvt. Ltd.* v. *Rajesh Masrani*[198] held that registration of copyright is not compulsory either for acquiring copyright or for enforcing the copyright by an action for infringement. Similarly, in *Godfrey Phillips India Ltd.* v. *Dharampal Satyapal Ltd.*,[199] the Court held that there is nothing in the Act to suggest that the registration is condition precedent to the subsistent of the copyright or acquisition of copyrights or ownership thereof or for reliefs of infringement of copyrights. Hence, the registration of copyright is not compulsory for the purpose of enforcing copyright by a party. The Kerala High Court in *R. Madhavan* v. *S.K. Nayar*[200] has taken the same view that Section 44 and 45 of the Copyright Act are only enabling provisions and do not affect the common law right to sue for infringement of copyright. Thus, in *Glaxo O.U.K. Limited* v. *Samrat Pharma*,[201] the Court observed:

---

196. 1999 PTC (19) 188.
197. AIR 2009 Delhi 44: 2009 (39) PTC 21 (Del). *See also*, *Microfibres, Inc* v. *Girdhar*, 2006 (128) DLT 238: 2006 (32) PTC 157.
198. 2008 (38) PTC 251 (Del). *See also*, *K.C. Bokadia* v. *Dinesh Chandra Dubey*, 1999 (1) MPLJ 33; *R. Madhavan* v. *S.K. Nayar*, AIR 1988 Ker 39: PTC (Suppl) (2) 221 (Ker) (DB)); *Nav Sahitya Prakash* v. *Anand Kumar*, AIR 1981 All 200; *Satsang* v. *Kiron Chandra Mukhopadhyay*, AIR 1972 Cal 533: (1974) ILR 1 Cal 498.
199. 191 (2012) DLT 109: 2012 (51) PTC 251 (Del).
200. AIR 1988 Kerala 39.
201. AIR 1984 Del 265: 1984 (4) PTC 66. *See also*, *Nav Sahitya Prakash* v. *Anand Kumar*, AIR 1981 All 200; *Kumari Kanaka* v. *Sundara Rajan* (1972) Ker LR 536.

> The relevant provisions regarding the registration of copy rights are sections 44 and 45 of the Copyright Act. Section 44 says that there shall be kept at the copyright Office register in the prescribed form to be called register of copyright. It is apparent from a plain reading of section 45 that it is discretionary with any author of any work to apply for the registration of copyrights and that registration as such does not confer any rights. There is no other provision at all in the Copyright Act which confers rights on account of registration of a copyright. Therefore, copyrights exist whether the registration is done or not and the registration is merely a piece of evidence as to when a certain author started claiming copyrights in some artistic or some other work.

However, according to the Bombay High Court, the registration of copyright is a compulsory in order to invoke the provisions of the Copyright Act or the remedies provided therein. This is according to the decision of the A.B. Chaudhuri J. in *Dhiraj Dharamdas Diwani* v. *Sonal Info Systems Pvt. Ltd.*[202] In this case, the Court justified that the word "may" in Section 45(1) of the Copyright Act, 1957 means that if anyone wants to invoke civil and criminal remedies provided in the Act, he must have registration. The word "may" used in Section 45 of the Act will have to be read as "shall" considering the scheme of the Act. To arrive in to the conclusion the court based on the rational on the decision of the Apex Court in *Exphar Sa* v. *Eupharma Laboratories,*[203] where the court stated that if a person does not want to register a copy he may omit to do so, but he will not be entitled to seek remedy under the Copyright Act, 1957 for want of registration. Similarly, in *Mishra Bandhu Karyalaya* v. *Shivratanlal Koshal,*[204] the Madhya Pradesh High Court held that registration copyright was mandatory. It may be humbly submitted that this view is not in conformity with Sections 13 and 14 of the Copyright Act, 1957. Therefore, the view is not rational.

In *Nandhini Deluxe* v. *Karnataka Co-Operative Milk Producers Federation Ltd.,*[205] the appellant had also obtained registration of copyright of 'NANDHINI' under Copyright Act, 1957. In this case the issue was whether appellant was entitled to seek registration of mark 'NANDHINI' in respect of goods in which it was dealt with and that whether such a registration in favour of appellant would infringe rights of respondent? The Apex Court held that in the present case not only visual appearance of two marks was different, they even related to different products. Further, manner in which they were traded by appellant and respondent respectively, it was difficult to imagine that, an average man of ordinary intelligence would associate goods of appellant as that of respondent. Hence, reasoning of High Court that goods belonging to appellant and respondent (though nature of goods was different) belonged to same class and, therefore, it would be impermissible for appellant to have registration of concerned trade mark in its favour, would be meaningless.

---

202. 2011 (114) Bom LR 2251: 2012 (2) Bom CR 842.
203. 2004 (3) SCC 688.
204. AIR 1970 MP 216.
205. AIR 2018 SC 3516: (2018) 10 SCC 639.

7

Rights of Broadcasting Organisation and of Performers (Neighbouring Rights)

ABSTRACT

The broadcast reproduction right is comparatively new in comparison to copyright protection for literary, dramatic, musical and artistic works as well as cinematographic films and sound recordings. The owner of copyright in a broadcast has the exclusive right. The rights of performers have developed in parallel with copyright and the exercise of these rights is very often linked with the exercise of copyright. These rights have been recognised for the benefit of various kinds of performers like actors, dancers, musicians, jugglers, acrobats and so on. These rights are somewhat analogous to broadcast reproduction right. This chapter is primarily devoted to an examination of the aforementioned aspects.

BACKGROUND

The law relating to exclusive broadcasting rights gives the developer sole rights to exploit his/her product,[1] while the law relating to performer's rights is in its formative stage and there is still no consensus on what the terms "performance," "perform" and "performer's" rights mean.[2] In *STAR India Private Limited* v. *Department of Industrial Policy*,[3] the Madras High Court held that rights of broadcasting organisation have been brought under Chapter

1. *See*, M. Sakthivel, "Is It Broadcast or Broadcasting?" 16 *Journal of Intellectual Property Rights* (2011) pp. 23–26; Divyanshu Sehgal and Siddharth Mathur, "Rights and Duties of Broadcasting Organisations: Analysis of WIPO Treaty on the Protection of Broadcasting Organisations," 16 *Journal of the Intellectual Property* Rights (2011) pp. 402–408; Sanjay Pandey, "Neighbouring Rights Protection in India", 9 *Journal of Intellectual Property Rights* (2004) pp. 356–370.
2. *See*, Sanhita Ambast, "Protecting Performers' Rights: Does India Needs Law Reform?" 13 *Journal of the Intellectual Property* Rights (2008) pp. 574–582; Shweta S. Deshpande, "Copyright Protection of Performers Rights," 28(3) DESIDOC *Journal of Library and Information Technology* (2008) pp. 66–68; Robert C. Bird and Lucille M. Ponte, "Protecting Moral Rights in the United States and the United Kingdom: Challenges and Opportunities under the U.K.'S New Performances Regulations," 24 *Boston University International Law Journal* (2006) pp. 213–282.
3. 2018 (74) PTC 417 (Mad).

VIII of the Copyright Act. However, this chapter does not deal with a "broadcast right" as such but only a "broadcast reproduction right." More specifically, in Lahari Recording Company Private Limited v. Sourabh Marketing,[4] the Karnataka High Court held that rights of broadcasting organisation and all performers are covered by Sections 37 to 39A of Chapter VIII. Further, in *Akuate Internet Services Pvt. Ltd.* v. *Star India Pvt. Ltd.*,[5] it was held that rights of broadcasting organisations have been recognised under the Section 37 of the Copyright Act 1957. Thus, Section 16 of the Act is limited by Section 39A which deals with "neighbouring" or "related rights." The provisions of the Act would apply *mutatis mutandis* to the neighbouring rights (e.g. Performer's rights, Broadcasting reproduction rights).

In *Syndicate* v. *B.D. Bhandari*,[6] the Delhi High Court held that the copyright and related rights protect the rights of authors, performers, producers and broadcasters, and contribute to the cultural and economic development of nations. Rights of broadcasting organisation and of performers are related rights of copyright and also called "neighbouring rights" of copyright. The English term "neighbouring rights" may be compared with the French words "Droits voisins" which means "near to the musical work". Neighbouring rights have developed parallel to the copyright and are also called "related rights" or "secondary rights". The oldest and best-known neighbouring rights are economic rights granted to persons who are not authors of a work but who contribute to its creation such as performers, producers, and broadcasting associations. Some countries also have privacy and publicity rights that complement copyright. For example, some countries prevent the public distribution of works that contain personally identifiable information, unless permission is granted by that person. However, the "related rights" or "secondary rights" under copyright law is no way inferior to the main right of author. In *ESPN Stars Sports* v. *Global Broadcast News Ltd.*,[7] the Delhi High Court observed that the neighbouring rights are adjunct to those of the primary copyright holder.

The concept of neighbouring rights originated from analogue technologies, it faces a substantial change in its scope in response to rapid developments in digital technologies which consist of computers, digital on-line communications, satellite communications and so on. Since digital technologies brought about new concepts like digital reproduction, on-line transmission, satellite broadcasting, public performance connected to computer network and the like, it is highly uncertain whether these new concepts fit into existing neighbouring rights system or whether amendments should be made to existing copyright statute. A classical case on the need of broadcasters' right in hi-tech era could be illustrated as the broadcasting organisation's entrepreneurial efforts can be thwarted not only by direct use of its broadcast but also by unauthorised use of a pre-broadcast programme carrying signal transmitted via a terrestrial or satellite telecommunications link and intended only for the broadcaster itself for use in its broadcast. An example would be a cricket match played in country A; the live coverage (picture and international sound) is sent simultaneously via a communications

4. ILR 2000 KARNATAKA 5057: 2001 (4) KarLJ 78.
5. MIPR 2013 (3) 1.
6. 185 (2011) DLT 346. *See*, *UTV Software Communication Ltd.* v. *1337X*, 2019 (78) PTC 375 (Del); *Akuate Internet Services Pvt. Ltd.* v. *Star India Pvt. Ltd.*, 2013 (3) MIPR 1: 2013 LawSuit (Del) 3251; *Phonographic Performance Limited* v. *Lizard Lounge* (2009) ILR 2 Delhi 726: ILR (2009) Supp. () Delhi 726; *Gramophone Co.* v. *Mars Recording Pvt. Ltd.*, AIR 2001 SC 2885: (2002) 2 SCC 103; *Gee Pee Films Pvt. Ltd.* v. *Pratik Chowdhury*, AIR 2002 Cal 33: 106 CWN 170.
7. MIPR 2008 (2) 75: 2008 (36) PTC 492 (Del).

satellite to the authorized broadcaster in country B; a competitor or cable operator in country B intercepts the satellite signal and uses it himself, probably even adding his own advertising.[8]

The Rome Convention, 1961,[9] the TRIPS Agreement, 1994[10] and the Beijing Treaty, 2012[11] recognise the (i) rights of broadcasting organisation, (ii) rights of performing artists and (iii) rights of producers of phonograms or sound recordings. In India, the Copyright Act, 1957 nowhere uses the term "neighbouring rights" or "related rights". However, the Copyright (Amendment) Act, 1994 incorporated Sections 37 and 38 providing special rights to broadcasting organisations and performers, respectively. The producer of phonograms were granted copyright in 1994 by including "sound recording" under Section 13 dealing with works in which copyright subsists and enumerating the rights of the producers of sound recordings in Section 14 of the Copyright Act. Section 37 ensures broadcasts reproduction right, however, Section 38 defines and explains performer's right. Section 39 of the Act identifies those instances when an act shall not amount to infringement of neighbouring rights (broadcasters' and performers' rights). Section 39A makes applicable other specific provisions of the Copyright Act, 1957. The Copyright (Amendment) Act, 2012 inserted a new Section 38A[12] giving exclusive rights to performers and Section 38B[13] granting moral rights to the performers for the first time. The 2012 amendment has deleted the old Section 39A which has been substituted by a new Section 39A.[14] This chapter discusses different facets of law relating to rights of broadcasting organisation and of performers.

RIGHTS OF BROADCASTING ORGANISATION

Concept of Broadcasting Organisation

The basis of international law on the protection of intellectual property rights can be traced back to the Berne Convention for the Protection of Literary and Artistic Works, 1886 (Berne Convention) that grants substantive rights to authors.[15] The Berne Convention particularly vests with authors the rights of reproduction,[16] translation,[17] adaptation,[18] and communication

8. *See*, Sanjay Pandey, "Neighbouring Rights Protection in India", 9 *Journal of Intellectual Property Rights* (2004) 356–370.
9. The Rome Convention for the Protection of Performers, Producers of Phonograms and Broadcasting Organizations, 1961.
10. Agreement on Trade Related Aspects of Intellectual Property Rights, 1994 (TRIPS Agreement).
11. Beijing Treaty on Audiovisual Performances, 2012.
12. Substituted by the Copyright (Amendment) Act, 2012, Section 27 [w.e.f. 21-6-2012].
13. Substituted by the Copyright (Amendment) Act, 2012, Section 27 [w.e.f. 21-6-2012].
14. Substituted by the Copyright (Amendment) Act, 2012, Section 28, for Section 39A [w.e.f. 21-6-2012].
15. *See*, Nehaa Chaudhari and Amulya Purushothama, "The Proposed Treaty for the Protection of Broadcasting Organizations: Old Wine in a New Bottle?," 11 *Indian Journal of Law and Technology* (2015) pp. 66–86; Atharva Sontakke and Himaja Bhatt, Scope of Rights of Broadcasting Organisations under Copyright Act, 1957, 1(1) *RGNUL Student Law Review* (2013) pp. 102–121.
16. The 1986 Berne Convention, Article 9.
17. *Ibid.*, Article 8.
18. *Ibid.*, Article 12.

to the public,[19] broadcasting and cable transmission[20] and the right of resale[21] of their works. However 'broadcast right' as a specific neighbouring right to copyright was first recognized and protected in international intellectual property law in the Rome Convention for the Protection of Performers, Producers of Phonograms and Broadcasting Organizations, 1961 (Rome Convention).[22] This Convention protects the rights of performers and producers of phonograms as well as the rights of broadcasting organisation with regard to the right to authorize rebroadcasting, fixation, reproduction and communication of their broadcasts, but not cable distribution of broadcasts.[23] Further it protected the right of performers to prevent public broadcasting or communication of their performances, right to fixation of their unfixed performances and right to reproduction of a fixed performance in certain cases.[24]

Broadcast reproduction rights are a special class of rights, recognised under Part VIII of the Copyright Act, 1957.[25] However, neither the Copyright Act nor the international conventions define the term "broadcasting organisation". But the word "broadcast" is defined in various international instruments and Indian Statute. Article 3(f) of the Rome Convention for the Protection of Performers, Producers of Phonograms and Broadcasting Organizations, 1961 defines the term "broadcasting" to mean the transmission by wireless means for public reception of sounds or of images and sounds.[26] The term "broadcasting" is also defined in WIPO Performance and Phonograms Treaty 1996 (WPPT). According to Article 2 of the WPPT "broadcasting" is a transmission by wireless means for public reception of sounds or images and sounds or the representations thereof; such transmission by satellite is also "broadcasting"; transmission of encrypted signals is "broadcasting" where the means for decrypting are provided to the public by the broadcasting organisation or with its consent. Subsequently, WIPO Standing Committee on Copyright and Related Rights in ninth session, 2003 held in Geneva defines "broadcasting" to mean:

> The transmission by wireless means for public reception of sounds, images or sounds and images, or of the representations thereof. Such transmission by satellite is also "broadcasting". Wireless transmission of encrypted signals is "broadcasting" where the means for decrypting are provided to the public by the broadcasting organization or with its consent. "Broadcasting" shall not be understood as including transmissions over computer networks or any transmissions where the time and place of reception may be individually chosen by members of the public.

Originally, the Copyright Act, 1957 used the term "radio-diffusion" which was substituted in 1983 by "broadcast". "Broadcast" according to Section 2(dd)[27] means communication to the public: (i) by any means of wireless diffusion, whether in any one or more of the forms of signs, sound or visual images; or (ii) by wire, and includes a re-broadcast. Thus, the broadcasting

---

19. *Ibid.*, Article 11.
20. *Ibid.*, Article 11.
21. *Ibid.*, Article 14.
22. *See*, Shyamkrishna Balganesh, "The Social Costs of Property Rights in Broadcast and Cable Signals" 22 *Berkeley Technology Law Journal* (2007) pp. 1309–1312.
23. The 1961 Rome Convention, Article 13.
24. *Ibid.*, Article 7.
25. Substituted by the Copyright (Amendment) Act, 2012, Section 28, for Section 39A [w.e.f. 21-6-2012].
26. *See*, *ESPN Stars Sports* v. *Global Broadcast News Ltd.*, MIPR 2008 (2) 75: 2008 (36) PTC 492 (Del).
27. Substituted by the Copyright (Amendment) Act, 1983, Section 3 [w.e.f. 9-8-1983].

can be by television, radio or cable. Explaining the word "broadcast" in *Sun Direct TV Pvt. Ltd.* v. *State of U.P.*,[28] the Allahabad High Court observed that the 1999 Chelliah Committee made recommendations on which the service tax was introduced in the budget of 1994–1995 through the Finance Act, 1994 under residuary entry 97 of List I of the Seventh Schedule of the Constitution of India. By the Constitutional (88th Amendment) Act, 2003, a new entry 92C was introduced in List I for the levy of tax on service. The broadcasting services were brought within the purview of service tax net with effect from July 16, 2001 by the Finance Act, 2001 under Section 65(105). Section 65(15) of the Act defines "broadcasting" and gives it binding to it in Clause C of Section 2 of the Prasar Bharati (Broadcasting Corporation of India) Act, 1990 and also includes programme selection, scheduling or presentation of sound or visual matter on radio or TV channel in India for public listening or viewing as the case may be, and in the case of broadcasting agency or organisation, having its head office situated in any place outside India, to include the activity of selling of time slot or obtaining sponsorship for broadcasting any form of communication or collecting the broadcasting charges, etc. The scope of the taxable services has been widened by the Finance Act to convert the service tax generally from broadcaster to the customer under Section 65(105)(zk), which defines "taxable service"; "taxable service", any service provided or to be provided to a client, by a broadcasting agency or client, or organisation in relation to broadcasting, in any manner...."

Broadcasting of any kind including paid commercials or news items, etc., are covered under the Prasar Bharati (Broadcasting Corporation of India) Act, 1990. The Prasar Bharati Corporation of India is a single unit with two distinct wings, viz., Radio and Television for ensuring commonality in overall approach in terms of entertainment, information and education. The Broadcasting Corporation was formed with specific objectives with emphasis of upholding unity and integrity of the country nurturing the democratic and social values and projecting the varied cultural traditions of different regions of the country. Clause C of Section 2 of the Act defines "broadcast" as follows:[29]

> Broadcasting means the dissemination of any form of communication like signs, signals, writing, pictures, images and sounds of all kinds by transmission of electromagnetic waves through space or through cables intended to be received by the general public either directly or indirectly through the medium of relay stations and all its grammatical variations and cognate expressions shall be construed accordingly.

In *Tata Sky Limited* v. *State of M.P.*,[30] the Madhya Pradesh High Court held that the broadcasting falls within the domain of the legislative competence of the Government of India under entry 92C of List I of the Seventh Schedule to the Constitution of India. Under Article 268A of the Constitution of India, taxes on services shall be charged by the Government of India and such taxes shall be collected and appropriated by the Government of India and the States. The State cannot by terming a service as "entertainment" levy tax under entry 62 of List II of the Seventh Schedule to the Constitution. The broadcasting is also defined in

28. (2013) 61 VST 481 (All).
29. *See*, *R. Muthukrishnan* v. *Union of India*, 2013 Writ LR 401; *Sun Direct TV Pvt. Ltd.* v. *State of U.P.*, (2013) 61 VST 481 (All); *Tata Sky Limited* v. *State of Punjab* (2011) 37 VST 1 (P&H): (2011) 37 VST 1 (P&H); *Dish T.V. India Limited* v. *State of Uttarakhand*, AIR 2009 Utr 31: (2009) 26 VST 649 (Uttarakhand).
30. (2012) 53 VST 30 (MP). *See also*, *Tata Sky Limited* v. *State of Uttarakhand* (2013) 62 VST 5 (Uttarakhand).

clause (c) of Section 2 of the Prasar Bharati (Broadcasting Corporation of India) Act, 1990 and also includes programme selection, scheduling or presentation of sound or visual matter on radio or television channel, i.e., in India for public listening or viewing as the case may be. Service tax is a value added tax, which in turn is a destination based consumption tax in the sense that it is on commercial activity and is not a charge on the business but on the consumer. Similarly, the entertainment tax is also on consumer. Thus, the field is being occupied by the Union and the State by defining entertainment so as to include "direct to home" (DTH) cannot tax DTH broadcasting services.

Under Section 67 of the Finance Act, 2001 the value of taxable service is the gross amount charged by the service provider or production of service. In *Dish T.V. India Limited* v. *State of Uttarakhand*,[31] the Uttarakhand High Court pointed out that the above definition of the word "broadcasting" has been adopted by the Finance Act, 2001 (with the following changes made vide Finance Act, 2003):

> "Broadcasting" has the meaning assigned to it in Clause C of Section 2 of the Prasar Bharati (Broadcasting Corporation of India) Act, 1990 (25 of 1990) and also includes programme selection, scheduling or presentation of sound or visual matter on a radio or a television channel that is intended for public listening or viewing, as the case may be; and in the case of a broadcasting agency or organisation, having its head office situated in any place outside India, includes the activity of selling of time slots or obtaining sponsorships for broadcasting of any programme or collecting the broadcasting charges on behalf of the said agency or organisation, by its branch office or subsidiary or representative in India or any agent appointed in India or by any person who acts on its behalf in any matter.

The Telecommunication (Broadcasting and Cable Services) Interconnection Regulations 2004, provides definition of expression "directed to home operator" in Regulation 2(k), as under:

> direct to home operator means an operator licensed by the central Government to distribute multi channel TV programmes in KU band by using a satellite system directly to subscriber's premises without passing through intermediary such as cable operator or any other distributor of TV channel.

It emerges from the foregoing discussion that the definition of broadcast includes rebroadcast. It is a matter of fact that rebroadcast is the exact and identical audio and visual recording. Whenever the original audio and visual recording is again broadcast that is called a rebroadcast. Such rights of rebroadcast are given exclusivity under Section 37 of the Copyright Act, 1957 which provides that with respect to the rebroadcast also no one has a right to use the audio and visual recording except in accordance with the licence which is taken from the owner of the original audio and visual recording. Thus, Section 37 in a way could be said to be duplication, if not otiose, inasmuch as, once really a combination of audio and visual recording creates a video recording such as cinematographic film which is broadcasted, there would come into existence a "cinematograph film" according to the provision of Section 2(f),[32] and a cinematograph film is also a subject matter of the copyright under

31. AIR 2009 Utr 31: (2009) 26 VST 649 (Uttarakhand).
32. Section 2(f) of the Copyright Act, 1957 provides that "cinematograph film" means any work of visual recording and includes a sound recording accompanying such visual recording and "cinematograph" shall be construed as including any work produced by any process analogous to cinematography including video films.

Section 13(1)(b)[33] of the Act. Thus, no one can broadcast or rebroadcast or communicate to the public or in any manner utilise the cinematograph film except with the consent of and the permission of the owner/author of the cinematograph film otherwise that would be an infringement by the broadcast or rebroadcast in terms of Section 51. Section 37, therefore, does not give any further protection to an audio-visual recording which is otherwise not protected and provided for in the other relevant provisions of the Act for a cinematographic film. Thus, using without licence, the cinematographic film such as video recording or the identical visual recording or audio recording or both, will amount to a clear violation of the performer's rights which have been created under Sections 38 and 38A of the Act. Therefore, the necessary licence under the Act will have to be taken from the performer or his assignee before such identical audio and/or visual recording of the performance of the performer is used.

Indian Broadcasting Organisations and their Importance

During the period of British India, broadcasting began in the month of July 1923 with programmes by the Radio Club of Bombay and other radio clubs privately owned stations. Thus, the private Indian Broadcasting Company Ltd. (IBC) was authorised to operate two radio stations, the Bombay Station began on 23 July 1927, and the Calcutta Station followed on 26 August 1927. As a result of liquidation of the IBC on 1 March 1930, on an experimental basis for two years, the government took over the broadcasting facilities beginning the Indian State Broadcasting Service (ISBS) on 1 April 1930. Subsequently, on 8 June 1936 the ISBS was renamed All India Radio. The word "Akashvani" was coined by M.V. Gopalaswamy after setting up the nation's first private radio station in his residence, "Vittal Vihar" (about 200 yards from All India Radio's current location in Mysore) in 1936.[34] In India the external broadcasting service began with a broadcast in Pushtu language on 1 October 1939. After Indian independence in 1947, the network of All India Radio had through only six stations (Delhi, Bombay, Calcutta, Madras, Lucknow, and Tiruchi). The Vividh Bharati Service was launched on 3 October 1957. Television broadcasting began in Delhi in 1959 as part of All India Radio, but was split off from the radio network as Doordarshan on 1 April 1976. FM broadcasting began on 23 July 1977 in Madras, and was expanded during the 1990s. Thus, the broadcasting industry started expanding at a first pace with the technological developments like satellite broadcasting, cable TV, FM radio, etc. Originally television broadcasting started with a monopoly government controlled TV channel but presently it has around 825 private channels. Besides, at present there are about 245 private FM stations operating in around 90 cities in India along with the state run All India Radio.

In *Secretary, Ministry of Information and Broadcasting* v. *Cricket Association of Bengal*,[35] the Apex Court has held that though several countries had enacted laws on the subject of broadcasting and telecasting, India has not made any law on the subject and the

33. According to Section 13(1)(b) of the Copyright Act, 1957 copyright shall subsists throughout India in cinematograph film too.
34. *Akashvani* means "celestial announcement"; the word, of Sanskrit origin, is often found in Hindu mythology. When the gods wished to say something, an *akashvani* occurred. Literally, *akash* means "sky" and *vani* means "sound" or "message".
35. AIR 1995 SC 1236: (1995) 2 SCC 161.

only enactment relevant in this behalf is the Indian Telegraph Act, 1885. The Apex Court has elaborately considered the system of telecasting and held:

> Telecasting is a system of communication either audio or visual or both. We are concerned in the present case with audio-visual telecommunication. The first stage in telecasting is to generate the audio-visual signals of the events or of the information which is sought to be communicated. When the event to be telecast takes place on the earth, necessarily the signal is generated on the earth by the requisite electronic mechanism such as the audio-visual recorder. This stage may be described as the recording stage. The events may be spontaneous, accidental, natural or organised. The spontaneous, accidental and natural events are by their nature uncontrollable. But the organised events can be controlled by the law of the land.[36]

The Apex Court further held that telecasting is of three types: (i) terrestrial, (ii) cable and (iii) satellite. The Apex Court has also considered whether there is any distinction between the system of print media and electronic media such as radio and television. The Court held that the electronic media such as television has a greater impact in the minds of the viewers and is also more readily accessible to all including the children. The Apex Court has also considered the importance and significance of the television in the modern world. The Apex Court held:

> The television is unique in the way in which it intrudes into our homes. The combination of picture and voice makes it an irresistibly attractive medium of presentation. Call it idiot box or by any other pejorative name, it has a tremendous appeal and influence over millions of people. Many of them are glued to it for hours on end each day. Television is shaping the food habits, cultural values, social mores and what not of the society in a manner no other medium has done so far. Younger generation is particularly addicted to it. It is a powerful instrument, which can be used for greater good as also for doing immense harm to the society. It depends upon how it is used. With the advance of technology, the number of channels available has grown enormously. National borders have become meaningless. The reach of some of the major networks is international; they are not confined to one country or one region. It is no longer possible for any government to control or manipulate the news, views and information available to its people.

Regulatory Framework of Broadcasting in India

The Indian Telegraph Act, 1885 and the Indian Wireless Telegraphy Act, 1933 provided the basis for regulatory framework of broadcasting in India. The Indian Telegraph Act, 1885 was enacted with an object to give power to the Government and to any company or person and specially empowered in this behalf, to place telegraph lines under or over property belonging whether to private persons or to public bodies. However, technological advancement resulted in growth of broadcasting industry but its regulatory framework did not take place in a coordinated manner. Hence, in recent time a large number of issues have been examined by the Courts in India. The important thing that arises for consideration is whether the Indian Telegraph Act, 1885 in its present form is capable of being interpreted in today's cyber age to include cyberspace within its ambit?

---

36. *See, also, Sunil Shantisarup Gupta* v. *Department of Legal Affairs*, MANU/ MH/2221/2016; *Mammootti* v. *Rajaji Mathew Thomas*, ILR 2006 (2) Kerala 707: 2006 (3) KLT 335; *Peoples' Union for Liberties* v. *Union of India*, AIR 1996 Cal 89: (1995) ILR 2 Cal 453.

In *Sun Direct TV Pvt. Ltd.* v. *State of U.P.*,[37] the Allahabad High Court held that in relation to entertainment through a direct-to-home (DTH) system any person having licence to provide DTH service, by the Central Government under Section 4 of the Indian Telegraph Act, 1885 and the Indian Wireless Telegraphy Act, 1933 and also includes the service provider of cable television signals and value added services, registered or licensed under the Cable Television Network (Regulation) Act, 1995.

In *Secretary, Ministry of Information and Broadcasting* v. *Cricket Association of Bengal*,[38] the Apex Court held that Section 4 of the Telegraph Act is the only Section which deals with granting of licence to television channels but that Section has no application. Thus, the Apex Court observed:

> The Indian Telegraph Act, 1885 is totally inadequate to govern an important medium like the radio and television, i.e., broadcasting media. The Act was intended for an altogether different purpose when it was enacted. This is the result of the law in this country not keeping pace with the technological advances in the field of information and communications. While all the leading democratic countries have enacted laws specifically governing the broadcasting media, the law in this country has stood still, rooted in the Telegraph Act of 1885.

Subsequently, in *Delhi Science Forum* v. *Union of India*,[39] the Apex Court while dealing with provision of licences to private companies as well as establishment, maintenance and working of such licences under the provisions of the Telegraph Act, 1885, applied the "wednesbury principle" and held that "as such the Central Government is expected to put such conditions while granting licences which shall safeguard the public interest and the interest of the nation. Such conditions should be commensurate with the obligations that flow while parting with the privilege which has been exclusively vested in the Central Government by the Act.

Keeping in view the above stated inadequacy of broadcasting law, the Parliament enacted the Cable Television Network (Regulation) Act, 1995. The regulation according to the statement of objects and reasons was enacted to regulate the haphazard mushrooming of cable television networks due to the availability of rights of foreign television networks via satellite. The regulation was considered necessary to ward off the "cultural invasion" unleashed by the predominantly western programmes beamed by the network.[40] Enactment of this legislation was also considered necessary in order to acquaint the programmers, cable operators and subscribers of their rights, responsibilities and obligations the regime of regulation is ushered in through the mechanism of registration. No person can operate a cable television network unless register as a cable operator. Persons operating cable networks before the commencement of the Act are permitted to continue the activity provided they apply for registration with in a period of 90 days from the commencement of the Act.[41]

---

37. (2013) 61 VST 481 (All).
38. AIR 1995 SC 1236: (1995) 2 SCC 161. *See also*, *Mammootti* v. *Rajaji Mathew Thomas,* ILR 2006 (2) Kerala 707: 2006 (3) KLT 335.
39. AIR 1996 SC 1356: 1996) 2 SCC 405.
40. *See*, *Mr. R. Basu* v. *National Capital Territory of Delhi,* 2007 Cri LJ 4254: 2007 (96) DRJ 7; *M. Arumugham* v. *The Senior Post Master,* 2000 (2) CTC 80; *K. Srinivasa Reddy* v. *Secretary to Government*, 1998 (1) ALD 277.
41. Section 3 of the Cable Television Network (Regulation) Act, 1995.

However, the 1995 Cable Television Network (Regulation) Act was amended through the Cable Television Networks (Regulation) Amendment Act, 2011. The prefatory note of the amendment Act records the statement of objects and reasons for amendment which are to the following effect:

1. The Cable Television Networks (Regulation) Act, 1995 was enacted for the purpose of regulating the operations of cable television networks in the country so as to bring uniformity in their operations, avoid undesirable programmes from being made available to viewers as well as to enable the optimal exploitation of the technology which had the potential of making available to the subscribers a vast pool of information and entertainment.[42]
2. The Telecom Regulatory Authority of India (TRAI), in its recommendations dated 5th August, 2010 on "Implementation of Digital Addressable Cable Systems in India" had, *inter alia*, recommended that "digitalisation with addressability be implemented on priority in cable TV services in Non-CAS areas" and, accordingly, recommended a time-frame comprising four phases for switch over from analogous system to the digital addressable system (DAS) in the cable TV sector. In view of the above-mentioned recommendations of the TRAI, the Central Government decided to introduce digitalisation with addressability in the cable TV services in a phased time bound manner on a pan India basis, leading to complete switch off of analogous TV services by the 31st December, 2014.[43]
3. For the implementation of DAS, certain amendments were required to be made in the aforesaid Act mandating all cable operators to provide programmes of all channels, including free-to-air (FTA) channels, in an encrypted form through DAS in a phased manner at specified areas from specified dates to be notified by the Central Government. It is also mandatory that any such notification should give at least six months' time to the cable operators for being able to install the necessary digital equipment for migration and educate the subscribers in this area. In order to protect the interest of consumers, it has been proposed to empower TRAI to specify a package of free-to-air channels, called basic service tier, which shall be offered by every cable operator to the consumers. It is also necessary that every cable operator should offer channels in the basic service tier on à la carte (individual) basis to consumers at a tariff fixed by TRAI.[44]
4. It has also been considered necessary to carry out certain amendments in the Act for rectifying certain deficiencies noticed during the operation of the Act for the last fifteen years. These, *inter alia*, include systemisation of registration of cable operators, providing right of way to cable operators and permission by public authorities, compulsory transmission of certain channels, inspection of cable network services, prescription of interference standards by the Central Government and empowering the TRAI to specify basic service tier and its tariff.[45]

---

42. *See*, *Cable Operators Welfare Association* v. *Union of India*, 2019 (2) KHC 807.
43. *See*, *Gulshan Kumar Ghai* v. *State of Uttarakhand*, AIR 2014 Utr 29.
44. *See*, *Sharad Traders* v. *State of U.P.*, 2011 (11) ADJ 732.
45. *See*, *All India Local Television Channel Owners Welfare Trust* v. *State of U.P.*, 2013 (5) ADJ 138.

Allahabad High Court in *All India Local Television Channel Owners Welfare Trust* v. *State of U.P.*,[46] has analysed the above amendment and observed that by the Cable Television Networks (Regulation) Amendment Act, 2011 in sub-clause (ii) to clause (g) of Section 2, the words "through video cassette recorders or video cassette players" have been omitted. Thus, by omission of words "through video cassette recorders or video cassette players" the exhibition by video has now gone out of purview of the Cable Television Networks (Regulation) Act, 1995. The provisions of Section 2(g) defines "programme" as any television broadcast including exhibition of films, features, drama, advertisement and serials through video cassette recorders or video cassette players. By deletion of the words "through video cassette recorders or video cassette players", the definition of programme has become wider. It is to be noted that Section 2(g) defines programme as any television broadcast including those mentioned in sub-clauses (i) and (ii). The definition being inclusive definition is wide enough. By amendment brought in Section 2(g), the definition of programme has been made more wide and not confined to through video cassette recorders or video cassette players.

In 1997, Parliament has enacted the Telecom Regulatory Authority of India Act, 1997 to provide for the establishment of Telecom Regulatory Authority of India (TRAI). Subsequently in the year 2000, the 1997 Act was amended and provision was made for establishment of the Telecom Disputes Settlement and Appellate Tribunal (TDSAT). A number of infrastructural service, which were at one time exclusively provided through governmental undertakings, are increasingly now being privatised and licensed out. State control has shifted from providing services to regulating them. The establishment of the Telecom Regulatory Authority of India Act, 1997 is an effort in this direction. In *MTNL* v. *Telecom Regulatory Authority*,[47] the Delhi High Court held that the statement of objections and reasons sets out that the Act is enacted for the establishment of Telecom Regulatory Authority of India to regulate the telecommunication services and for matters connected therewith. Even though this may be the statement of objects and reasons ultimately one has to look at the provisions of the said Act to see what functions and powers are given to the Authority.

In order to lend legitimacy to this quasi-judicial body, Section 4 of the Telecom Regulatory Authority of India Act, 1997 provides that the Chairperson of the authority shall be a person who is or has been a Judge of the Supreme Court or who is or has been a Chief Justice of a High Court. Members are to be chosen from amongst persons who have special knowledge and professional experience in telecommunication, industry, finance, accountancy, law, management and consumer affairs.[48] Besides, Section 5 confers the power of appointment on the central government and specially enjoys the government to satisfy itself that the person does not have financial or other interest as is likely to prejudice affect the performance of functions under the Act. Section 11 of the Act spells out a wide range of functions for the authority. Thus, in *Avishek Goenka* v. *Union of India*,[49] the Apex Court held that in terms of Section 11 of the Telecom Regulatory Authority of India Act, 1997, it is a statutory

46. 2013 (5) ADJ 138.
47. AIR 2000 Delhi 208: 84 (2000) DLT 70.
48. *See*, *Samy Fuel Service* v. *Union of India*, 2006 Writ LR 242.
49. AIR 2012 SC 2226: (2012) 5 SCC 275. *See also*, *Centre for Public Interest Litigation* v. *Union of India*, 2012 (2) SCALE 180: (2012) 3 SCC 1; *CPIL* v. *Union of India*, 2012 (1) CGBCLJ 209.

obligation upon the TRAI to recommend a regulatory regime which will serve the purpose of development, facilitate competition and promote efficiency, while taking due precautions in regard to safety of the people at large and the various other aspects of subscriber verification.

It emerges from the foregoing discussion that the Cable Television Networks (Regulations Act), 1995 and the Telecom Regulatory Authority of India Act, 1997 are the parliamentary legislations covering the field. The cable service having been notified as Telecommunication Service, the cable network has gone outside the purview of State Legislature and there is no legislative competence in the State since the field is already occupied by Parliamentary enactments. The Cable Television Networks (Regulation) Amendment Act, 2011 in Clause (g) in Sub-clause (i) of Section 2 the words "through video cassette recorders or video cassette players" having been omitted, the entire field is covered by Parliamentary enactments and no additional licence fee can be demanded from the television channels. Thus, there is no mechanism to fix the liability of payment of additional fee. Whether additional licence fee is payable by local TV channels or MSO or cable operators has not been provided for. Local television channels are not exhibiting anything on any television screen. They only send signals to the MSO hence, the local television channels cannot be held liable for payment of any additional licence fee.[50]

In *Common Cause* v. *Union of India*,[51] the scope of ambit of cable television network has been examined by the Apex Court. In this case precise contention of the Petitioner was, that there was no defined complaint redressed mechanism, with reference to violation of the code of conduct set out (for television programmes), and with reference to similar norms, prescribed for radio programmes. The Court held that there was indeed an existing mechanism i.e., a self-regulatory mechanism. However, that mechanism, was not known to the general public. Therefore same needs to be adequately published. This would enable complainants, to air their grievances, before the appropriate forum and to obtain a determination thereof, at the hands of the concerned Competent Authority, in the Ministry of Information and Broadcasting. The Central Government, having framed Rules in the nature of Cable Television Networks Rules, 1994, would be well advised, to frame similar Rules, in exercise of the power vested with it under Section 22 of the Cable Television Networks (Regulation) Act, 1995, to formalize the complaint redressal mechanism, including the period of limitation within which a complaint can be filed, and the concerned statutory authority which shall adjudicate upon the same, including the appellate and other redressal mechanisms, leading to a final conclusive determination. The Central Government, within the framework of Section 22 of the Cable Television Networks (Regulation) Act, 1995, deliberate on the issue, and take a conscious decision thereon, and to finalise a similar statutory framework for radio programmes, as well. In connection to the copyrighted matter the Apex Court further observed:

> No cable operator shall carry or include in his cable service any programme in respect of which copyright subsists under the Copyright Act, 1957 (14 of 1957) unless he has been granted a licence by owners of copyright under that Act in respect of such programme.

50. 2013 (5) ADJ 138.
51. (2018) 13 SCC 440: 2017 (2) SCALE 169.

International Protection for Broadcasting Organisations

Rome Convention

The International Convention for the Protection of Literary and Artistic Works commonly known as "Berne Convention" is silent to provide protection for broadcasting organisations or the cable operators. However, special rights are recognised for broadcasting organisations in the *Rome Convention for the Protection of Performers, Producers of Phonograms and Broadcasting Organizations*, 1961 (Rome Convention).[52] This Convention did not give the broadcasting organisations the right to control the wire diffusion of their programmes and did not also provide for consequences if the programmes broadcast by them violate the copyright of the content providers. According to Article 3(f) of the Rome Convention "broadcasting" means the transmission by wireless means for public reception of sounds or of images and sounds and "rebroadcasting" according to Article 3(g) means the simultaneous broadcasting by one broadcasting organisation of the broadcast of another broadcasting organisation. Thus, to broadcast is to cast or through forth something in all directions at the same time. A radio or television broadcast is a program that is transmitted over airwaves for public reception, by anyone with a receiver turned to the right signal channel. A broadcasting may be public, commercial, educational and so on. Public broadcasting is TV, radio, etc., funded by an official or governments, with no paid advertisements. Commercial broadcasting, on the other hand, is TV funded by paid advertisements and contain advertisements during the TV or radio times. Educational broadcasting is the one where the broadcasting of specific subject materials are educational. Live broadcast takes place where various types of media broadcast without any significant delay.[53]

In *Saregama Ltd.* v. *The New Digital Media*,[54] the Calcutta High Court held that the Indian Copyright (Amendment) Act 1994 was a major one which harmonized the provisions of the Copyright Act, 1957 with the Rome convention, 1961 by providing protection to the rights of performers, producers of phonograms and broadcasting organizations. The most significant provisions with objective consequences in the legislation of the states party to the Convention are those included in Article 12 which reads as under:

> If a phonogram published for commercial purposes, or a reproduction of such phonogram, is used directly for broadcasting or for any communication to the public, a single equitable remuneration shall be paid by the user to the performers, or to the producers of the phonograms, or to both. Domestic law may, in the absence of agreement between these parties, lay down the conditions as to the sharing of this remuneration.[55]

Article 12 thus imposes upon the broadcaster of phonograms published for commercial purposes the obligation to pay a "single equitable" remuneration for the (aural or audio-visual)

52. For commentaries, *see*, Richard Fentiman, "Commercial Expectations and the Rome Convention" 61 *Cambridge Law Journal* (2002) pp. 1–52.
53. *See*, S. Sivakumar and Lisa P. Lukose, *Broadcasting Reproduction Right in India: Copyright and Neighbouring Rights Issues* (Indian Law Institute, New Delhi, 2013) pp. 64–65.
54. 2018 (3) CHN (CAL) 147: 2018 (73) PTC 329 (Cal).
55. For application of Article 12, *see*, *Entertainment Network (India) Ltd.* v. *Super Cassette Industries Ltd.*, (2008) 13 SCC 30: 2008 (9) SCALE 69.

broadcasting. The single and equitable remuneration: (i) concerns phonograms published for commercial purposes (exclusively aural fixations of sounds offered to the public in reasonable quantity according to the definitions of the Rome Convention), (ii) is due in the case of broadcasting or any communication to the public, (iii) must be paid to the performers or the producers of phonograms or to both. A state can thus ratify the Rome Convention granting a right to an equitable remuneration only to the phonogram producers and not to the performers and vice versa. Moreover, no sharing rule is established between the performers and the phonogram producers both of whom are beneficiaries of this remuneration. Article 13 of the Rome Convention, however, provides certain rights to the broadcasting organisations are as follows:

1. The broadcasting organizations have the right to authorise or prohibit: (a) the rebroadcasting of their broadcasts; (b) the fixation of their broadcasts.
2. The broadcasting organisations also have the right of the reproduction: (i) of fixations, made without their consent, of their broadcasts; (ii) of fixations, made in accordance with the provisions of Article 15, of their broadcasts if the reproduction is made for purposes different from those referred to in those provisions.[56]
3. The communication to the public of their television broadcasts if such communication is made in places accessible to the public against payment of an entrance fee; it shall be a matter for the domestic law of the state where protection of this right is claimed to determine the conditions under which it may be exercised.

Thus, under Article 13 of the Rome Convention, broadcasting organisations have the right to authorise certain uses of their broadcasts (re-broadcasting, fixation, reproduction and communication to the public), but not cable distribution of broadcasts. The Rome Convention establishes possible exceptions for private use, reporting current events, ephemeral recordings and use for teaching and scientific purposes.[57]

Brussels Satellite Convention

Besides the Rome Convention, the Brussels Satellite Convention, 1974 also provides protections for broadcasting organisations. The Convention was adopted in the context of a perceived need to protect broadcasting organisations as regards the distribution of program-carrying signals transmitted by satellite. Although there were doubts as to whether such satellite transmissions would qualify as broadcasting under Rome Convention, the Satellite Convention provides protection against unauthorised distribution of satellite signals. The Convention also defines distribution as the operation by which a distributor transmits derived signals to the public and thus extending protection to cable distribution.[58] The fundamental obligation imposed in the Satellite Convention is to prevent the distribution of programme-carrying signals by any distributor for whom the signals passing through the satellite are not intended.[59] It is relevant to mention here that the Convention shifted the term of protection to national legislation. The

56. *See*, *South Indian Music Companies Association* v. *Union of India*, 2016 (67) PTC 99 (Mad): (2016) 3 MLJ 647.
57. Article 15 of the Rome Convention.
58. Brussels Satellite Convention, 1974, Articles 3 and 1(viii).
59. Brussels Satellite Convention, 1974, Article 2.

Brussels Satellite Convention permits certain restrictions on protection, such as, in the case of developing countries, where the program carried by the emitted signals is distributed solely for the purposes of teaching or scientific research.[60] Thus, it is clear from the Rome Convention and the Brussels Satellite Convention that broadcasting via satellites is also "broadcasting". However, WIPO's Standing Committee on Copyright and Related Rights, which is responsible for the broadcasting negotiations, is in the process of drafting a new treaty addressing the following issues:

1. What should be protected as the rights of broadcasting organisations?
2. Feasibility of opting for a technology neutral protection.
3. The issue of webcasting.
4. How should broadcast signals be protected?
5. Need of introducing anti-circumvention measures.
6. Creation of new rights including protection from foreign piracy.
7. What limitations and exceptions should there be?
8. How long should protection last?[61]

In India, in *STAR India Private Limited* v. *Department of Industrial Policy*,[62] the Madras High Court held that the Section 37(3) of the Copyright Act 1957 deals with acts constituting infringement of broadcast reproduction rights and thus the idea of the legislature was to provide a separate and distinct right to the broadcasting organizations to help them protect their rights in their broadcasts against third parties. But, satellite broadcasting rights are treated as separate rights and the said rights are recognized throughout the world as independent rights.[63]

TRIPS Agreement

The Rome Convention has not been revised since 1961 but some of its provisions are reflected in the TRIPS Agreement.[64] According to Article 14(3) of the 1994 TRIPS Agreement, broadcasting organisations have the right to control the fixation, reproduction, wireless rebroadcasting and communication to the public of broadcasts.[65] Article 14(3) of the 1994 TRIPS Agreement provides that broadcasting organisations shall have the right to prohibit the following acts when undertaken without their authorisation:

1. the fixation,
2. the reproduction of fixations, and
3. the rebroadcasting by wireless means of broadcasts, as well as the communication to the public of television broadcasts of the same.

---

60. Brussels Satellite Convention, 1974, Article 4(iii).
61. *See*, WIPO Background Brief: Protection of Broadcasting Organisations. Important developments in technology and marketplace have taken place in the broadcasting sector since the adoption of the Rome Convention in 1961. The process was initiated at the WIPO Worldwide Symposium on Broadcasters' Rights which was held in Manila in 1997.
62. 2018 (2) CTC 113.
63. *See*, *AA Associates* v. *Prem Goel*, AIR 2002 Del 142: 2002 (24) PTC 369 (Del); M/s. Video Master v. M/s. Nishi Productions, 1998 (18) PTC (Bom)117; *Raj Video Vision* v. *M/s. Sun TV*, 1994(2) Mad. LW 158.
64. Compare Article 14 of the TRIPS Agreement with Articles 7, 10, 13 and 15(1) of the Rome Convention.
65. Article 14(3) of the TRIPS Agreement follows Article 13 of the Rome Convention.

If any of the contracting states do not grant such rights to broadcasting organisations, they shall provide owners of copyright in the subject matter of broadcasts with the possibility of preventing the above acts, subject to the provisions of the Berne Convention (1971). The minimum term of protection granted under TRIPS Agreement shall last for at least 20 years from the end of the calendar year in which the broadcast took place. However, any member may, in relation to the rights to broadcasting organisations, provided for conditions, limitations, exceptions and reservations to the extent permitted by the Rome Convention.

Broadcasting Right under Indian Copyright Act

Broadcasting Right of the Copyright Owner: Section 14(a)(iii)

The Section 14(a)(iii) of the Copyright Act, 1957 provides that the copyright owner has the exclusive right to communicate his work to the public or authorise communication to public of his work or any substantial part thereof. Further, the Section 2(ff) of the Act defines "communication to public" which means making any work available for being seen or heard or otherwise enjoyed by the public directly or by any means of display. The Section 2(ff) reads as follows:

> "Communication to public" means making any work available for being seen or heard or otherwise enjoyed by the public directly or by any means of display or diffusion other than by issuing copies of such work regardless of whether any member of the public actually sees, hears or otherwise enjoys the work so made available.
>
> Explanation—For the purposes of this clause, communication through satellite or cable or any other means of simultaneous communication to more than one household or place of residence including residential rooms of any hotel or hostel shall he deemed to be communication to the public.[66]

The above definitions make it clear that making any work available for being seen or heard by the public whether simultaneously or at places chosen individually, regardless of whether the public actually sees the film, will constitute communication of the film to the public. In *UTV Software Communication Ltd.* v. *1337X*,[67] the Delhi High Court held that the intention of the adoption of this definition was to include digital copies of works, which would include within its scope digital copies of works being made available online (as opposed to the physical world). Communication can be by various means such as directly or by display or diffusion. In this context, definition of "broadcast" is also relevant which identifies communication to public by wireless diffusion or by wire. Thus, making available of a film for streaming or downloads in the form of digital copies on the internet is within the scope of "communication to the public."[68] However, performing literary or musical work in public does not only mean a musical performance in a public place as contended by the appellant, but also the broadcasting of the songs would involve communication of the music to the public who

---

66. Substituted by the Copyright (Amendment) Act, 2012 (Amendment) Act, 2012 (Act 27 of 2012), Section 2(iii) [w.e.f. 21-6-2012.
67. 2019 (78) PTC 375 (Del).
68. *See*, *Star India Private Limited* v. *Department of Industrial Policy*, (2019) 2 SCC 104: 2018 (14) SCALE 651.

have enjoyed by hearing. Communication via satellite which can be received by dish antenna or cable network will amount to communication to public. So showing a video film on cable network will amount to infringement of copyright. In Garware Plastics and *Polyster Ltd.* v. *Telelink*,[69] the Bombay High Court held that a broadcast can be a private broadcast if it is received in a private home, but the same broadcast becomes a public broadcast if received in a public place. Nevertheless, there are three criteria to be applied to determine whether a broadcasting film is communicating it to a section of public thus:

1. First, the viewers of a Cable TV network or those who receive such broadcast through a dish antenna to which their television sets are connected, are either residents of apartments in a building which has such a network or they may be residents of a locality which is covered by this facility.They can only be viewed as a portion of public.
2. This becomes apparent if one applies the second test, namely, the nature of the relationship between the owner of the copyright and the audience. The viewers cannot be considered as domestic viewers of the owner of the copyright i.e. the plaintiffs. They must be considered as members of the public.
3. The last test which has been applied in such cases is the test of ascertaining the character of the audience in view of the purpose of the Copyright Act. The Act is meant to protect the owner of the copyright against unauthorised performance of his work, thereby entitling him to earn monetary gain from his intellectual property. The audience which watches such video films would have otherwise paid for watching the film. In fact, the audience does pay the Defendants for watching the film. The author of the copyright is, therefore, directly affected as he is deprived of earnings from his intellectual property. The defendants by showing the film over a video TV network are broadcasting the film or communicating it to a section of the public.[70]

Thus, "communication to public" includes communication by TV, radio, cable, etc. Section 2(dd) of the Copyright Act further defines "broadcast" to mean communication to public: (i) by any means of wireless diffusion, whether in any one or more of the forms of signs, sounds or visual images; or (ii) by wire, and includes a re-broadcast.[71] Thus, the definition of broadcast includes rebroadcast. In *Indian Performing Right Society Ltd.* v. *Aditya Pandey*,[72] the Delhi High Court held that obviously rebroadcast is the exact and identical audio and visual recording. It is when the original audio and visual recording is again broadcast it is called a rebroadcast. Such rights of rebroadcast are given exclusivity under the Act as per Section 37 and which provides that with respect to the rebroadcast also no one has a right to use the audio and visual recording except in accordance with the licence which is taken from the owner of the original audio and visual recording. The broadcasting right thus encompasses the primary right to authorize the initial broadcast of work and also the secondary rights of rebroadcasting, the broadcasting organisation, therefore, must obtained the consent or licence from the copyright owner for the purposes of broadcasting their work.

In *Swapnil Tripathi* v. *Supreme Court of India*,[73] the petitioners sought for a declaration that Supreme Court case proceedings of "constitutional importance having an impact on the

69. AIR 1989 Bom 331: 1989 (2) Bom CR 433.
70. *See also, Indian Performing Right Society Ltd.* v. *Aditya Pandey*, MIPR 2011 (3) 19: 2011 (47) PTC 392 (Del).
71. *See, Asianet Communications (P) Ltd.* v. *Surya T.V.*, 2016 (1) CTC 493: 2015-4-LW 595.
72. MIPR 2012 (2) 140: 2012 (50) PTC 460 (Del).
73. AIR 2018 SC 4806: (2018) 10 SCC 639.

public at large or a large number of people" should be live streamed in a manner that is easily accessible for public viewing. It has been argued by citing Apex Court decision in *Naresh Shridhar Mirajkar* v. *State of Maharashtra*,[74] that citizens have a fundamental right to carry on their occupation under Article 19(1)(g) of the Constitution; that they also have a right to attend the proceedings in court under Article 19(1)(d); and that their right to freedom of speech and expression guaranteed under Article 19(1)(a) included their right to publish a faithful report of the proceedings which they have witnessed and heard in Court as journalists. The Court whilst considering the said argument went on to emphasise about the efficacy of open trials for upholding the legitimacy and effectiveness of the Courts and for enhancement of public confidence and support. The Apex Court granted the arguments of petitioners, but for limited purpose with strict court control. Thus the Court lays down guidelines to safeguard and limit the broadcasting and recording of its proceedings to ensure better access to justice. Any unauthorized usage of the live streaming and/or webcasts will be punishable as an offence under the Indian Copyright Act, 1957 and the Apex Court retains copyright over the broadcasted material with it and has the final say in respect of use of the coverage material.

Broadcast Reproduction Right: Section 37

As stated above TRIPS Agreement under Article 14(3) recognises rights of broadcasting organisations. India being the signatory to the TRIPS Agreement accordingly the Copyright Act, 1957 was amended through Copyright (Amendment) Act, 1994 so as to incorporate broadcast reproduction right under Section 37.[75] Before the 1994 amendment of the Copyright Act, the only broadcaster in India was Doordarshan (DD) which used to telecast free to air channels that could be captured by an antenna installed on rooftops and was connected to the television sets by a wire. It is relevant to mention here that even after the aforesaid amendment of the Copyright Act, the definition of "copyright" under Section 14 was not amended to include "Broadcast reproduction right", as has been the case in some countries such as the United States of America, United Kingdom and New Zealand, where Broadcast reproduction right had been specifically included within the meaning of copyright. Some countries such as France, Germany and India have given a special right known as "Broadcasting Reproduction Right" which is a related right and is different from copyright.[76]

Thus, unlike other countries the broadcasting rights by themselves were introduced in India for the first time by substituting Section 37 by the Copyright (Amendment) Act, 1994. It is true that the rights of free-to-air broadcasters have not been dealt with in a specific legislation unlike some other jurisdiction. It may, however, be of some importance to note that Chapter VII deals with Copyright society, the concept whereof was incorporated in the Act so as to enable an author to commercially exploit his intellectual property by a widespread dispersal in a regulated manner. As soon as the broadcasting organisation takes the licence

---

74. AIR 1967 SC 1: (1966) 3 SCR 744.
75. Substituted by the Copyright (Amendment) Act, 1994, Section 13 for Section 37. The amendment came into effect from May 10, 1995. *See*, *Super Cassettes Industries Limited* v. *Mr. Chintamani Rao*, 2012 (49) PTC 1 (Del).
76. *See*, *Umesh Bharatbhai Thakkar* v. *State of Gujarat*, 2017 (4) RCR (Criminal) 948: 2017 CriLJ 3713; *ESPN Star Sports* v. *Global Broadcast News Ltd.*, MIPR 2008 (3) 257: 2008 (38) PTC 477 (Del).

from the copyright owners and broadcasts the work, then the broadcasting organisation will have a right in its broadcast according to Section 37 of the Copyright Act, 1957. Thus, Section 37 confers a special right to every broadcasting organisation for its broadcasts, which is known as "broadcast reproduction right".[77] The broadcast reproduction right subsists until 25 years from the beginning of the calendar year next following the year in which the broadcast is made.[78] The owner of copyright in a broadcast has the exclusive right to rebroadcast the broadcast. It is a restricted act to rebroadcast the broadcast without the licence of the right owner.[79] The Act also provides that it is a restricted act to causes the broadcast to be heard or seen by the public on payment of any charges.[80] Making of sound recording or visual recording of the broadcast,[81] reproduction of such sound recording or visual recording,[82] and issue of copies to the public is subject to the condition recognised by the Copyright Act, 1957. Thus, during the continuance of the broadcast reproduction right if any person, without the licence of the owner of the right, i.e., the broadcasting organisation, does any of the following acts of the broadcast or any substantial part thereof, he shall be deemed to have infringed the broadcast reproduction right:

(a) rebroadcasts the broadcast; or
(b) causes the broadcast to be heard or seen by the public on payment of any charges; or
(c) makes any sound recording or visual recording of the broadcast; or
(d) makes any reproduction of such sound recording or visual recording where such initial recording was done without licence or, where it was licenced, for any purpose not envisaged by such licence; or
[(e) sells or gives on commercial rental or offer for sale or for such rental, any such sound recording or visual recording referred to in Clause (c) or Clause (d).][83]

Thus, Section 37 of the Copyright Act provides that every broadcasting organisation shall have broadcast reproduction rights in respect of its broadcast. In *Star India Pvt. Ltd.* v. *Haneeth Ujwal*,[84] the plaintiffs are the leading sports broadcaster in India and the exclusive licencee of media rights to various sporting events/properties. The Delhi High Court held that any hosting, streaming, making available for viewing and/or communication to the public of the "2014 India–England Series Matches", as broadcast on the plaintiffs' channels by any means on any platform including the Internet and mobile, by any of the named or unnamed defendant websites would be illegal and amount to violation of the broadcast reproduction rights of the plaintiff's protection under Section 37 of the Copyright Act, 1957.

---

77. *See*, Section 37(1) of the Copyright Act, 1957.
78. *See*, Section 37(2) of the Copyright Act, 1957.
79. *See*, Section 37(3)(a) of the Copyright Act, 1957.
80. *See*, Section 37(3)(b) of the Copyright Act, 1957.
81. *See*, Section 37(3)(c) of the Copyright Act, 1957.
82. *See*, Section 37(3)(d) of the Copyright Act, 1957.
83. Substituted by the Copyright (Amendment) Act, 2012, Section 25, for Clause (e) [w.e.f. 21-6-2012]. Clause (e), before substitution, stood as under: "(e) sells or hires to the public, or offer for sale or for such sale or hire, any such sound recording or visual recording referred to in clause (c) or clause (d)."
84. 2014 LawSuit (Del) 2711.

In *Asia Industrial Technologies* v. *Ambience Space Sellers Ltd.*,[85] the Bombay High Court deals with "Broadcast Reproduction Right". In this case it was argued that since the third plaintiffs are operating from countries which are not parties to the Berne Convention, they have no right to seek protection of Section 37 since the whole Act is inapplicable so far as the third plaintiffs are concerned. But the Court held that the right conferred under Section 37 is available to all broadcasting organisations, wherever they are situated, so long as the broadcast is available in India for viewing. Sub-section (1) of Section 37 clearly provides that every broadcasting organisation shall have a special right to be known as "broadcasting reproduction right" in respect of its broadcast. Under Sub-section (2), it is provided that the broadcast reproduction right shall subsist until 25 years from the beginning of the calendar year next following the year in which the broadcast is made. Sub-section (3) provides that any person who, without the licence of the owner of the right rebroadcasts the broadcast or causes the broadcast to be heard or seen by the public on payment of any charge or does any other acts mentioned in the said sub-section, shall be deemed to have infringed the broadcast reproduction right. The language of the section makes it very clear that the right is not confined only to Berne Convention countries. This is also clear from the fact that the International Copyright Order, 1991 exclude the application of Chapter VIII which deals with broadcast reproduction right.

The term "broadcast" has been defined in Section 2(dd) of the Copyright Act, 1957 to mean communication to the public by any means of wireless diffusion, whether in any one or more of the forms of signs, sounds or visual images; or by wire, and includes a rebroadcast. Further, Section 39 of the Act, to the extent it is relevant, provides that no broadcast reproduction right shall be deemed to be infringed by the use consistent with fair dealing, of excerpts of a performance or of a broadcast in the reporting of current events or for bona fide review, teaching or research. In *ICC Development (International) Ltd.* v. *New Delhi Television Ltd.*,[86] the Delhi High Court held that broadcasting rights are independent of the copyrights granted under the Copyright Act, 1957. In *ESPN Star Sports* v. *Global Broadcast News Ltd.*,[87] the court observed:

> The term "broadcast" has been separately defined under Section 2(dd), as a communication to the public. It is thus evident that there could be both copyright and broadcasting reproduction right which could separately co-exist. As an example, the copyright of cinematography film being broadcast on a satellite channel vests with the producer of the film whereas the broadcast reproduction right for the same vests with the broadcaster channel itself. The recording of such movie and unauthorised re-telecast by cable operators could thus result in violation of two separate rights. The first being the copyright which vests with the producer and second the broadcast reproduction right which vests with the broadcaster channel. These rights may vest with two different persons or even with the single person which is evident from the Act.

An examination of the definition of "copyright" under Section 14 and "broadcast reproduction right" under Section 37 of the Copyright Act, 1957 shows that there are two separate rights recognised under Sections 14 and 37. While Section 37 recognises "broadcast reproduction right", the definition of "copyright" under Section 14 did not provide any

85. 1998 (18) PTC 316: (1997) 99 Bom LR 613.
86. 193 (2012) DLT 279: 2012 (132) DRJ 291.
87. 2008 (36) PTC 492 (Del).

protection to the broadcasters. The statement of object and reasons itself provides that "Certain Rights akin to copyright are conferred on the broadcasting authorities in respect of programs broadcast by them." This sufficiently brings out the difference between the two rights in Copyright Act, 1957. The Copyright (Amendment) Act, 1994 extended such rights to all broadcasting organisations apart from more clearly crystallising the nature of such rights. The fact that such a distinction has been demonstrated by Section 51 of the Act which deals with acts constituting infringement of a copyright, while there is a separate Section 37(3) that deals with acts constituting infringement of broadcast reproduction rights.[88]

In *ESPN Stars Sports* v. *Global Broadcast News Ltd.*,[89] it was observed that broadcast reproduction rights are a special class of rights, recognised under Part VIII of the Copyright Act, 1957. Section 37(3) provides, in Clauses (a) to (e) acts deemed to be infringement of broadcast reproduction rights. The unauthorised telecast of footage belonging to the plaintiff, by the defendants, amounted to rebroadcast under Section 37(3)(a) and also reproduction of the event under Section 37(3)(d). Where the defendants in suit had not signed any licensed agreement with plaintiff's distributors and was not authorised to distribute channels over their cable operators and transmission of these channels was violative of Section 37(3) of Copyright Act and thus was not justified. Thus, the legislature intended to provide a separate and distinct right to the broadcasting organisations to help them in protecting their rights in their broadcasts against third parties. In *Phonographic Performance Ltd.* v. *Radio Mid Day (West) India Ltd.*,[90] the Delhi High Court observed:

> The jurisdiction of the Copyright Board [Appellate Board][91] can be invoked under Section 31(1)(b) of the Copyright Act, 1957 by a complainant who considers that the owner of a copyright has offered unreasonable terms for the broadcast of a sound recording. When that happens, the Copyright Board is required to give the copyright owner a reasonable opportunity of being heard before directing the complainant to pay compensation to him (and determining other terms and conditions) for the broadcast. As a part of the "reasonable opportunity of being heard" the Copyright Board may hold such inquiry as it deems necessary.

In *Raj Video Vision* v. *Sun TV*,[92] the Madras High Court held that copyright for broadcasting or telecasting the film through satellite, cable, wire wireless or through any other system or any other form, means and modes other than through Doordarshan terrestrial Primary Channel without restriction of geographical area is a separate right. Satellite right is new, separate and distinct species or right hitherto not visualised and this cannot be said to be included under the agreements relied upon by the plaintiff's in any event. In fact, cassettes are used for home TV, whereas "U" tapes are used for Satellite Transmission. *The Bombay High Court in Video Master* v. *Nishi Productions*,[93] pointed out the differences and clauses or species of the communication and held that theatrical rights include the right to exhibit the

88. *See*, *Star India Private Limited* v. *Department of Industrial Policy*, (2019) 2 SCC 104: 2018 (14) SCALE 651.
89. MIPR 2008 (2) 75: 2008 (36) PTC 492 (Del).
90. (2010) ILR 4 Delhi 603: 2010 (43) PTC 377 (Del).
91. Substituted by the Finance Act 2017 (7 of 2017), Section 160(a) for "Copyright Board," [w. e. f. 26 May, 2017].
92. TV 1994 (2) MLW 158.
93. 1998 (18) PTC 117.

cinematograph film in theatres, terrestrial rights is the right to exhibit the film on Doordarshan and satellite broadcasting rights is the right to exhibit and communicate the film by satellite signals to public with or without cable and through the satellite medium while the cable TV right is right to exhibit a film by cable originated programme.

Subsequently, in *AA Associates* v. *Prem Goel*,[94] the court held that satellite broadcasting rights are treated as separate rights and the said rights are recognised throughout the world as independent rights. A similar view has been taken in *Video Master* v. *Nishi Productions*.[95] In *ESPN Star Sports* v. *Global Broadcast News Ltd.*,[96] it was held that both copyright and broadcasting reproduction rights could separately co-exist and that the same may vest with two different persons or even with a single person.

Thus, in *ESPN Star Sports* v. *Global Broadcast News Ltd.*,[97] it was held that Sections 13 and 14 of the Copyright Act make it clear that copyright will subsist only in work. "Work" does not include "broadcast". As a result, there will only be a broadcasters right in the telecast of live events communicated to the public as provided under Section 37 of the Copyright Act, which is separate and distinct from copyright. Therefore, what emerges from the above is that the Broadcast Reproduction Right, which is different from Copyright, is with the Broadcasting Organization which is causing the broadcast to be communicated to the public under their logo by any means of wireless diffusion or by wire, i.e., the Appellants in the present case, as per the Definition of Broadcast under Section 2(dd) and the definition of the Communication to Public under Section 2(ff) of the Act. The Delhi High Court further observed:

> The Legislature itself by terming broadcast rights as those akin to copyright clearly brought out the distinction between the natures of two rights in Indian Copyright Act, 1957. This was a clear manifestation of the legislative intent to treat copyright and broadcasting reproduction rights as distinct and separate rights. Further, it is to be seen that the Amendment Act of 1994 while amending the Act not only extended such rights to all Broadcasting Organizations, but also clearly crystallised the nature of such rights. Hence, in our view, the contention of the respondent that the broadcast reproduction right as a special right, does not stand dehors copyright and that the two rights are not mutually exclusive, cannot be sustained as it is clearly seen from the legislative intent that the two rights though akin are nevertheless separate and distinct.

In *Neo Sports Broadcast Private Ltd.* v. *New Sanjay Cable Network*,[98] the plaintiff claims that its broadcast reputation rights embodied in Section 37 of the Copyright Act, 1957 so far as the telecast of the live events are concerned, and the copyrights subsisting by virtue of Section 14(1)(c), are infringed. The materials on record, particularly the Local Commissioner's report indicates that the Defendants were causing live broadcasts in the NEO Sports and NEO Cricket to be viewed by their clients. The court held that by virtue of Section 51(a), when anyone, without a licence granted by the owner of the copyright or in contravention of conditions of licence or of any license imposed by competent authority, does anything the exclusive right to which is conferred on the copyright owner, it amounts to infringement. However, the evidence on record shows that the infringement was only in one instance. In

94. AIR 2002 Delhi 142.
95. 1998 (18) PTC 117.
96. 2008 38 PTC 477.
97. MIPR 2008 (3) 257: 2008 (38) PTC 477 (Del).
98. 2010 (120) DRJ 611: 2011 (45) PTC 402 (Del).

the circumstances, ends of justice would be met with if decree for permanent injunction and reasonable or nominal costs are granted.

In *Star India Pvt. Ltd.* v. *Haneeth Ujwal*,[99] the plaintiffs have filed the suit for permanent injunction, accounts of profits, delivery up, damages, etc., against unknown "John Doe" defendants. The case of the plaintiffs is that they are leading sports broadcaster in India and the exclusive licencee of media rights to various sporting events/properties. It is stated in the plaint that having the Exclusive Television rights, the plaintiffs are broadcasting and communicating the live, delayed, highlights, clips and repeat telecast of the 2014 India-England Series matches in India through the Star Sports Channels of the plaintiffs. In this case, the court directed that any hosting, streaming, making available for viewing and/or communication to the public of the 2014 India–England Series Matches, as broadcast on the plaintiffs' channels by any means on any platform including the Internet and mobile, by any of the named or unnamed defendant websites would be illegal and amount to violation of the broadcast reproduction rights of the plaintiffs protected under Section 37 of the Copyright Act, 1957. In *Taj Television* v. *Rajan Mandal*,[100] it is recognised that the Indian Courts have power to pass orders against such unknown "John Doe" defendants in exercise of its inherent jurisdiction. In fact, Indian Courts have already passed restraint orders against such unknown "John Doe" or "Ashok Kumar" defendants in a number of previous cases.[101]

Broadcasting Freedom

Broadcasting freedom is recognised in the Article 19(2) of the *International Covenant on Civil and Political Rights*, 1966. According to Article 19(2) of the Covenant, everyone shall have the right to freedom of expression; this right shall include freedom to seek, receive and impart information and ideas of all kinds, regardless of frontiers, either orally, in writing or in print, in the form of art or through any other media of his/her choice. It is no doubt true that in a democratic framework, free flow of information to the citizens is necessary for proper functioning particularly in matters which form part of public record. Article 19(1)(a) of the Constitution of India which guarantees freedom of speech and expression to all citizen of India. In *Indian Express Newspapers (Bombay) Pvt. Ltd.* v. *Union of India*,[102] the Apex Court held that the expression "freedom of the press" has not been used in Article 19, but it is comprehended within Article 19(1)(a). In *Odyssey Communications Pvt. Ltd.* v. *Lokvidayan Sanghatana*,[103] the Apex Court examined the limitations of "freedom of speech and expression" under Article 19(1)(a) and held that the right of citizens to exhibit films on Doordarshan subject to the terms and conditions to be imposed by Doordarshan is a part of the fundamental right of freedom of expression guaranteed under Article 19(1)(a)which can be curtailed only under circumstances set out under Article 19(2).

In *Secretary, Ministry of Information and Broadcasting* v. *Cricket Association of Bengal*,[104] the Apex Court has further widened the scope and ambit of "freedom of speech and expression" and held that broadcasting is a means of communication and, therefore, a

---

99. 2014 LawSuit (Del) 2711.
100. [2003] FSR 22.
101. *See*, *Januki Kumari* v. *Ashok Kumar*, 2017 (71) PTC 200 (Del): 240 (2017) DLT 362.
102. AIR 1986 SC 872: (1985) 1 SCC 641.
103. AIR 1988 SC 1642: 1988 SCR (Supp.) (1) 486.
104. AIR 1995 SC 1236: (1995) 2 SCC 161.

medium of speech and expression. Hence in a democratic polity, neither any private individual, institution or organisation nor any government or government organisation can claim exclusive right over it. State monopoly on electronic media is not mentioned in Article 19(2). The broadcasting freedom is a Constitutional right under Article 19(1)(a). The government can impose restrictions on such a right only on grounds specified in the Article 19(2) of the Constitution and not on any other ground. State monopoly on electronic media is not mentioned in the Article 19(2).

In *ICC Development (International) Ltd.* v. *New Delhi Television Ltd.*,[105] the Delhi High Court deals with the rights of the news organisations in reporting the current sports events. The issue brought up in this case include Constitutional rights under Article 19(1)(a), statutory rights Sections 37 and 52 of the Copyright Act, 1957 and so on. The court held that reporting news and current events was a part of fundamental right of freedom of speech and expression, guaranteed under Article 19(1)(a) of the Constitution. But, since reasonable restrictions could always be placed on such a right in terms of Article 19(2) of the Constitution, and the validity of the Copyright Act, 1957, to the extent it protected the copyright and broadcast rights subjected to the exceptions and exemptions stipulated therein, had not been challenged. The court decided that the defendant could not use the footage of the plaintiff to give an unfair advantage to its advertisers, at the cost of official advertisers of the plaintiff, by carrying out advertisements in case the footage was used during the special/sponsored programmes.

Thus, broadcasting freedom involves and includes the right of the viewers and listeners who retain their interest in free speech. It has been held by the Supreme Court in *Secretary, Ministry of Information and Broadcasting* v. *Cricket Association of Bengal*,[106] that freedom of expression includes the right to receive information and ideas as well as freedom to impart them. The free speech interests of viewers and listeners in exposure to a wide variety of material can best be safeguarded by the imposition of programme standards, limiting the freedom of radio and television companies. Right of viewers is also a right under broadcasting freedom. In *Advocates Association Bangalore* v. *Union of India*,[107] the Karnataka High Court has classified broadcasting freedom into four facets: (a) freedom of the broadcaster, (b) freedom of the listeners/viewers to a variety of view and plurality of opinion, (c) right of the citizens and groups of citizens to have access to the broadcasting media, and (d) the right to establish private Radio/TV stations.

Access to Broadcasting

An important facet of the broadcasting freedom is access to broadcasting. It is the freedom of individuals and groups of individuals to have access to broadcasting media to express their views. The reason behind it is that the public is entitled to hear range of options held by different groups so that it can make sensible choices on political and social issues. In particular, these views should be exposed on television, the most important contemporary medium. It is intended that the interest of audience that justified the imposition of impartiality rules and positive programme standards upon the broadcasters.[108]

105. 193 (2012) DLT 279: 2012 (132) DRJ 291.
106. AIR 1995 SC 1236: (1995) 2 SCC 161.
107. MANU/ KA/ 0736 /2012.
108. *Secretary, Ministry of Information and Broadcasting* v. *Cricket Association of Bengal*, AIR 1995 SC 1236: (1995) 2 SCC 161.

There was a conflict between public access to the media and journalistic freedom in the field of electronic communication in the United States of America. This conflict emerged during the mid-1960s as groups of citizens sought to combat the presentation of views by an increasingly centralized press with a novel constitutional theory. In contrast to the traditional negative theory, based on the first amendment's prohibition of laws which abridge freedom of speech, the proponents of access urged a positive approach. Since the established media no longer provided an adequate outlet for dissonant minority views, the public needed access, a right of entry into the marketplace of ideas.[109] The decision in *Colombia Broadcasting System* v. *Democratic National Committee*,[110] of the Supreme Court of the United States of America is important on the issue of access to broadcasting. In this case, the issue was that CBS's refusal to sell advertising time to the plaintiffs for expressing controversial views violated First Amendment rights. The Court held that the general policy of refusing to sell any editorial advertising time did not violate the First Amendment or the Federal Communications Act of 1934. Thus, a broadcast licencee may refuse to accept editorial advertisements (advertorials) without violating either his statutory duty to serve the public interest or the first amendment. This case set the precedent that broadcasters were not required by the Constitution to accept editorials in the form of ads. One of the things that sets the United States apart from other countries is the wide range of freedoms its citizens enjoy. Among those freedoms, one of the most precious is the freedom of speech as expressed in the Constitution's First Amendment.

Statutory Licence for Broadcasting

The Copyright (Amendment) Act, 2012 inserted a new Section 31D to the Copyright Act, 1957 which provides for statutory licence for broadcasting of literary and musical works and sound recordings. It provides that any broadcasting organisation desiring to broadcast a work including sound recording may do so. The broadcasting organisation shall give prior notice to the right holders, pay royalty as fixed by the Copyright Board (Appellate Board)[111] in advance. The names of the authors and principal performers shall be announced during the broadcast. The broadcasting organisation shall maintain records of the broadcast, books of account and render to the owner such records and books of account. The 2012 amendment has been brought in to facilitate access to the works for the growing broadcasting industry. At present, the access to copyright works by broadcasters was dependent on voluntary licencing. As a result unreasonable terms and conditions were being set by the copyright societies and owners. There are divergent views by the courts in interpreting the existing compulsory licencing provisions under Section 31. There were litigations pending before various High Courts as well as the Copyright Board (Appellate Board)[112] regarding the nature of licence and the rate of royalties to be paid when works particularly songs were used for broadcasting. Automatic licence or non-voluntary licence such as the proposed statutory licence ensuring adequate return to the owner of works was the best solution to make access easy for broadcasting industry.

---

109. *See*, Roy L. Mason and Robert E. Ganz, "Columbia Broadcasting: Public Access to the Media Denied" 23(2) *Catholic University Law Review* (1973) pp. 339–358.
110. [1973] 94 US 412.
111. Substituted by the Finance Act 2017 (7 of 2017), Section 160(a) for "Copyright Board," [w.e.f. 26 May, 2017].
112. Substituted by the Finance Act 2017 (7 of 2017), Section 160(a) for "Copyright Board," [w.e.f. 26 May, 2017].

RIGHTS OF PERFORMERS

Background of Rights of Performers

The rights of performers, record producers and broadcasting organisations are referred to as neighbouring rights because they have developed in parallel with copyright, and the exercise of these rights is very often linked with the exercise of copyright. It is a matter of fact that the Copyright Act, 1957 creates several rights besides copyright. These rights include the rights of broadcasting organisations under Section 37, the rights of performers under Sections 38 and 38A, and the moral rights of authors which are recognised under Section 57; which are all distinct from copyright.[113] Copyrights for a long time did not extend to rights of performers like musicians, singers, actors, acrobats, etc. Thus, in 1979 in *Fortune Film International* v. *Dev Anand*,[114] the Bombay High Court held that performers did not have copyright in their performances. The performers had not been given a right to share the royalties received by the record producer or film producer as the case may be for public performance or broadcasting of records or films. In this way, the performers were put in a pitiable condition without any right in his performance under the Copyright Act, 1957. It is in the wake of livelihood threatening technological changes that the law intervened.

The modern technology resulted in the "technological unemployment" of the performers as once recorded, the performance can be repeated in public without the necessity of engaging the performer any more. The law had not shown concern to this "technological unemployment" in India until 1994. The Copyright Act, 1957 was amended in 1994; the amendment introduced the recognition of the rights of the performer through performer's rights. Section 38 of the Copyright Act confers rights to performers like actors, dancers, jugglers, acrobats, etc. Likewise, broadcasting rights were not given statutory protection. It was only through the same 1994 amendment that broadcast rights were afforded protection. The traditional understanding of copyrights, therefore, was altered in 1994. At international level the concerns of the performer's rights have been addressed in four major instruments: the Rome Convention 1961, TRIPS Agreement 1994, WPPT 1996 and Beijing Treaty 2012.

Rights of Performers at International Level

Rome Convention 1961

Under the Bern Convention, films were protected as cinematographic works at an early stage. However, before 1961 producers of sound recordings received no international protection against piracy. Performers had problems in the form of piracy of their recorded performances. During 1920s broadcasters began public broadcasting. Thus, there were three interests, separate from those of authors, which needed protection at an international level. The three parties involved would have to reach to a compromise, which took the form of the Rome Convention

---

113. *See, Star India Pvt. Ltd.* v. *Piyush Agarwal,* MIPR 2013 (1) 201: 2013 (54) PTC 222 (Del); *ESPN Star Sports* v. *Global Broadcast News Ltd.,* MIPR 2008 (3) 257: 2008 (38) PTC 477 (Del.); *AA Associates* v. *Prem Goel*, AIR 2002 Del 142: *M/s. Video Master* v. *M/s. Nishi Productions*, 1998 (18) PTC 117.
114. AIR 1979 Bom 17.

(The Rome Convention for the Protection of Performers, Producers of Phonograms and Broadcasting Organisations, 1961). The Rome Convention is based on the principle of national treatment, with minimum standards of protection.[115]

Thus, the Rome Convention responded to the new circumstance of ideas variously represented in easily reproduced units by covering performers of recordings under copyright. In this Convention performers (actors, singers, musicians, dancers and other persons who perform literary or artistic works) are protected against certain acts they have not consented to. Such acts are: (i) the broadcasting and the communication to the public of their live performance, (ii) the fixation of their live performance, (iii) the reproduction of such a fixation if the original fixation was made without their consent or if the reproduction is made for purposes different from those for which they gave their consent. Under Article 7, the Rome Convention recognised the following right:

1. The protection provided for performers by this Convention shall include the possibility of preventing:
   (a) the broadcasting and the communication to the public, without their consent, of their performance, except where the performance used in the broadcasting or the public communication is itself already a broadcast performance or is made from a fixation;
   (b) the fixation, without their consent, of their unfixed performance;
   (c) the reproduction, without their consent, of a fixation of their performance:
   (i) if the original fixation itself was made without their consent;
   (ii) if the reproduction is made for purposes different from those for which the performers gave their consent;
   (iii) if the original fixation was made in accordance with the provisions of Article 15, and the reproduction is made for purposes different from those referred to in those provisions.
2. (a) If broadcasting was consented to by the performers, it shall be a matter for the domestic law of the Contracting State where protection is claimed to regulate the protection against rebroadcasting, fixation for broadcasting purposes and the reproduction of such fixation for broadcasting purposes.
   (b) The terms and conditions governing the use by broadcasting organisations of fixations made for broadcasting purposes shall be determined in accordance with the domestic law of the Contracting State where protection is claimed.
   (c) However, the domestic law referred to in sub-paragraphs (1) and (2) of this paragraph shall not operate to deprive performers of the ability to control, by contract, their relations with broadcasting organisations.

---

115. *See*, W. Rumphorst, "Neighbouring Rights Protection of Broadcasting Organizations" 10 *E.I.P.R.* (1992) pp. 339–342; I.D. Thomas, "Revision of the Rome Convention: Is it Necessary and Timely?" 25 *Copyright Bulletin* (1991) pp. 32–35; R. Rembe, "Time for a Performer's Convention" 25 *Copyright Bulletin* (1991) pp. 25–31; A. Françon, "Should the Rome Convention on Neighbouring Rights be Revised?" 25 *Copyright Bulletin* (1991) pp. 20–24; A. Kerever, "Should the Rome Convention be Revised and if so, is this the Right Moment?" 25 *Copyright Bulletin* (1991) pp. 5–16; V.B. Labra, "The Rome Convention: A Three-Cornered Marriage (a love triangle?)" 25 *Copyright Bulletin* (1991) pp. 17–19.

Thus, according to the Rome Convention Performers are not given an exclusive right, but merely the possibility of preventing certain acts: broadcasting and the communication to the public of their performances, fixation of their unfixed performances and reproduction of a fixed performance in certain cases.[116] Producers of phonograms are given the right to prohibit reproduction of their phonograms.[117] Broadcasting organisations have the right to authorise certain uses of their broadcasts (rebroadcasting, fixation, reproduction and communication to the public), but not cable distribution of broadcasts.[118] A single equitable remuneration has to be paid by broadcasters or other users of a phonogram to the performers, producers, or both, but this right can be restricted or waived by Member Countries.[119] The Rome Convention establishes possible exceptions for private use, reporting current events, ephemeral recordings and use for teaching and scientific purposes.[120] Protection lasts for a minimum period of twenty years computed from the year in which the fixation of the phonogram is made, or the performance or the broadcast takes place.[121]

TRIPS Agreement

Following the Uruguay Round of Multilateral Negotiations under the General Agreement on Tariffs and Trade (GATT), the Agreement on Trade-Related Aspects of Intellectual Property Rights (TRIPS Agreement) was adopted and it came into force on January I, 1995. The TRIPS Agreement is the most comprehensive multilateral agreement to set detailed minimum standards for the protection and enforcement of intellectual property rights, and aims at harmonising national intellectual property systems. All members of the World Trade Organisation (WTO) are bound by the obligations under the TRIPS Agreement. India is one of the founding members of the GATT and thus a member of the WTO from its inception from 1 January 1995, and is bound by the obligations under TRIPS Agreement like all other members of the WTO.[122]

1. In respect of a fixation of their performance on a phonogram, performers shall have the possibility of preventing the following acts when undertaken without their authorisation: the fixation of their unfixed performance and the reproduction of such fixation. Performers shall also have the possibility of preventing the following acts when undertaken without their authorisation: the broadcasting by wireless means and the communication to the public of their live performance.[123]
2. Producers of phonograms shall enjoy the right to authorise or prohibit the direct or indirect reproduction of their phonograms.
3. Broadcasting organisations shall have the right to prohibit the following acts when undertaken without their authorisation: the fixation, the reproduction of fixations, and

116. Rome Convention, Article 7.
117. *Ibid.*, Article 10.
118. *Ibid.*, Article 13.
119. *Ibid.*, Articles 12 and 16.
120. *Ibid.*, Article 15.
121. *Ibid.*, Article 16.
122. *See*, *Novartis A.G.* v. *Union of India,* AIR 2013 SC 1311: 2013 (54) PTC 1 (SC).
123. *See*, *STAR India Private Limited* v. *Department of Industrial Policy*, 2018 (2) CTC 113; *ESPN Star Sports* v. *Global Broadcast News Ltd.*, MIPR 2008 (3) 257: 2008 (38) PTC 477 (Del.).

the rebroadcasting by wireless means of broadcasts, as well as the communication to the public of television broadcasts of the same. Where members do not grant such rights to broadcasting organisations, they shall provide owners of copyright in the subject matter of broadcasts with the possibility of preventing the above acts, subject to the provisions of the Berne Convention (1971).[124]

4. The provisions of Article 11 in respect of computer programs shall apply *mutatis mutandis* to producers of phonograms and any other right holders in phonograms as determined in a member's law. If on 15 April 1994 a member has in force a system of equitable remuneration of right holders in respect of the rental of phonograms, it may maintain such system provided that the commercial rental of phonograms is not giving rise to the material impairment of the exclusive rights of reproduction of right holders.
5. The term of the protection available under this Agreement to performers and producers of phonograms shall last at least until the end of a period of 50 years computed from the end of the calendar year in which the fixation was made or the performance took place. The term of protection granted pursuant to paragraph 3 shall last for at least 20 years from the end of the calendar year in which the broadcast took place.
6. Any member may, in relation to the rights conferred under paragraphs 1, 2 and 3, provide for conditions, limitations, exceptions and reservations to the extent permitted by the Rome Convention. However, the provisions of Article 18 of the Berne Convention (1971) shall also apply, *mutatis mutandis*, to the rights of performers and producers of phonograms in phonograms.[125]

Thus, under the TRIPS Agreement performers are given the possibility of preventing the unauthorised fixation, reproduction, wireless broadcasting and communication to the public of their performances.[126] Producers of phonograms are given the right to prohibit reproduction of their phonograms.[127] Broadcasting organisations have the right to control the fixation, reproduction, wireless rebroadcasting and communication to the public of broadcasts.[128] Member states are allowed to provide for conditions, limitations, exceptions and reservations to the extent permitted by the Rome Convention.[129]

Beijing Treaty on Audiovisual Performance, 2012

The 2012 Beijing Treaty on Audiovisual Performances[130] was adopted to strengthen the economic rights of film actors and other performers. The treaty potentially enables performers to share proceeds with producers for revenues generated internationally by audio-visual

---

124. *See, ESPN Star Sports* v. *Global Broadcast News Ltd.*, MIPR 2008 (3) 257: 2008 (38) PTC 477 (Del.).
125. *See, Gramophone Company of India Ltd.* v. *Birendra Bahadur Pandey*, AIR 1984 SC 667: (1984) 2 SCC 534.
126. Article 14(1) of the TRIPS Agreement follows Article 7 of the Rome Convention.
127. Article 14(2) of the TRIPS Agreement follows Article 10 of the Rome Convention.
128. Article 14(3) of the TRIPS Agreement follows Article 13 of the Rome Convention.
129. Article 14(6) of the TRIPS Agreement and Article 15(1) of the Rome Convention.
130. The treaty was adopted by the Diplomatic Conference on June 24, 2012.

productions. The treaty also provides performers moral rights to prevent lack of attribution or distortion of their performances. While the Rome Convention provided protection for audio performers, it only gave limited rights to audio-visual performers. The 1996 WPPT modernised international standards for sound performances. However, the audio-visual performers and their performances continued to be largely unprotected by international standards. The conclusion of the Beijing Treaty is an important milestone towards closing the gap in the international rights system for audio-visual performers and reflects the collaborative nature of the multilateral process.

Now question arises who the beneficiaries of the new Treaty are. Under the 2012 new Treaty audio-visual performers, i.e., actors and also any other performers (e.g. musicians, dancers) whose performances are incorporated in an audio-visual work (e.g. a film, a TV program) are the beneficiaries. According to Article 2(a) of the 2012 Beijing Treaty, "performers" are actors, singers, musicians, dancers, and other persons who act, sing, deliver, declaim, play in, interpret, or otherwise perform literary or artistic works or expressions of folklore. The Treaty grants performer's rights both for the offline and online exploitation of their performances (e.g., the distribution or rental of their performances, for instance, in DVDs, by making them available on the Internet, etc.). These rights would allow performers to be fairly remunerated when their performances are used. It also recognises performers' moral rights (i.e., the right to be identified, the right to object to distortions of the performance). Performers from countries ratifying or acceding to the Treaty will enjoy the minimum level of protection granted by the Treaty plus national treatment (i.e., their performances will also be protected when exploited by other contracting parties).[131]

Protection of Performer's Rights in India

Sections 38 and 39 of the Copyright Act 1957 as amended by the Copyright (Amendment) Act 1994 deal with the performer's right. While Section 38 discusses the meaning and duration of performer's rights, Section 39 deals with the acts not amounting to infringement of broadcast reproduction right or performer's right. Sections 38A, 38B and 39A have been inserted to the Copyright Act, 1957 by the Copyright (Amendment) Act, 2012. The new Section 38A deals with the exclusive right of performers while Section 38B provides for moral rights of the performers. Section 39A provides for certain provisions to apply in case of broadcast reproduction right and performer's right. These provisions need detail deliberation.

Meaning and Duration of Performer's Rights: Section 38

As stated above, the issue relating to performer's rights was discussed during the Uruguay Round of the WTO Agreement of Trade-related Aspects of Intellectual Property Rights (TRIPS Agreement) in 1994. Recognising the need to protect the rights to performers, Article 14 was incorporated into the TRIPS Agreement. In India the Copyright (Amendment) Act, 1994 was enacted to bring the Copyright Act, 1957 in conformity with the provisions of TRIPS Agreement. The definition of "performer" has been inserted by the 1994 amendment to the Copyright Act, 1957. Section 2(qq) of the Act defines "performer" to include an actor, a singer,

131. Article 3 of the Beijing Treaty on Audiovisual Performances, 2012.

a musician dancer, an acrobat, a juggler, a conjurer, a snake charmer, a person delivering a lecture or any other person who makes a performance.[132] A proviso has been added to the definition of performer in Section 2(qq) by the Copyright (Amendment) Act, 2012[133] which provides that in a cinematograph film, a person whose performance is casual or incidental in nature and, in the normal course of practice of the industry, is not acknowledged anywhere including the credits of the film, shall not be treated as a performer. This provision removes from the definition of performers a category of incidental performers in films, popularly called "extras" in Indian cinema.

The definition of "performance" has also been amended by the Copyright (Amendment) Act, 1994. According to Section 2(q) "performance", in relation to performer's right, means any visual or acoustic presentation made live by one or more performers. In *Star India Pvt. Ltd.* v. *Piyush Agarwal*,[134] the Delhi High Court observed that when a cricket match is played, there are various dramatis personae in the performance. So far as the visual recording is concerned, the performers essentially are the cricket players who play out the match. Also, and in a way, the umpires are also an integral part of the live performance, and thus they can also be said to be performers in the match. Though a cricket match is not specified under Section 2(q) or Section 2(qq), in view of the categorical language of these provisions, it cannot be doubted that a cricket match very much falls within the definition of expression "performance" and qua such performance the cricketers/players (as also umpires) would be performers.

In *Neha Bhasin* v. *Anand Raj Anand*,[135] it was argued that the plaintiff does not have a copyright in the song and also does not have any performer's rights. The Court held that it is essentially the reproduction of the performance through sound or visual recordings without the permission of the performer that is prohibited. While the definition of "performer" in Section 2(qq) of the Copyright Act, 1957 includes within its sweep a singer, Section 2(q) defines "performance", in relation to performer's right, to mean any visual or acoustic presentation made live by one or more performers. Every performance has to be live in the first instance whether it is before an audience or in a studio. If this performance is recorded and thereafter exploited without the permission of the performer then the performer's right is infringed.

Section 38 (1) of the Copyright Act, 1957 provides that where any performer appears or engages in any performance, he shall have a special right to be known as the "performer's right" in relation to such performance. Further, Section 38(2) provides that performer's right shall subsists until fifty years from the beginning of the calendar year next following the year in which the performance is made. A reading of Section 38 shows that there are two important expressions which are used, viz. a performer and the performance. Again, Section 13 provides that copyright shall subsist throughout India in literary, dramatic, musical and artistic work, cinematograph films and sound recording. In *Star India Pvt. Ltd.* v. *Piyush Agarwal*,[136] the Delhi High Court held that a conjoint reading of Sections 13 and 38 shows

---

132. *See*, *Indian Performing Right Society Ltd.* v. *Aditya Pandey*, MIPR 2012 (2) 140: 2012 (50) PTC 460 (Del); *Academy of General Edu., Manipal* v. *B. Malini Mallya,* AIR 2009 SC 1982: (2009) 4 SCC 256.
133. Inserted by the the Copyright (Amendment) Act, 2012, Section 2(iv) [w.e.f. 21-6-2012].
134. 2013 (1) MIPR 201: 2013 (54) PTC 222.
135. 132 (2006) DLT 196: 2006 (32) PTC 779 (Del).
136. 2013 (1) MIPR 201, 2013 (54) PTC 222.

that a copyright subsists in seven classes of works, i.e., literary work, dramatic work, musical work, artistic work, a cinematograph film including video film, a sound recording, and a performer's performance.

Acts Not Amounting to Infringement of Broadcast Reproduction Right or Performer's Right: Section 39

Section 39 of the Copyright Act, 1957 enumerates the circumstances when the broadcast reproduction right or performer's right does not get infringed. Section 39 was inserted in its present form by Copyright (Amendment) Act, 1994. This provision specifically provides exception to the broadcast reproduction right conferred by Section 37 or performer's right conferred by Section 38 of the Act. Section 37 was also inserted in the Act by the same amendment.[137] In *New Delhi Television Limited* v. *ICC Development (International) Limited*,[138] the Court held that no broadcast right is deemed to be infringed by the use, consistent with fair dealing, of excerpts of a broadcast when current events are reported. Thus, according to Section 39 no broadcast reproduction right or performer's right shall be deemed to be infringed by—

(a) the making of any sound recording or visual recording for the private use of the person making such recording, or solely for purposes of bona fide teaching or research; or

(b) the use, consistent with fair dealing, of excerpts of a performance or of a broadcast in the reporting of current events or for bona fide review, teaching or research; or

(c) such other acts, with any necessary adaptations and modifications, which do not constitute infringement of copyright under Section 52.

Thus, the scope and ambit of Section 39 is to be examined taking into consideration Section 52 of the Act. In *ESPN Star Sports* v. *Global Broadcast News*,[139] issue considered was with respect to the exception contained in Section 39 to the broadcast reproduction right. The Court held that the case of broadcast of cricket matches, although the visual recording of the cricket match becomes a cinematograph film, it does not become the film of any underlying copyrighted work but only of certain events. The court observed thus:

> Section 39 of the Act, to the extent it is relevant, provides that no broadcast reproduction right shall be deemed to be infringed by the use consistent with fair dealing, of excerpts of a performance or of a broadcast in the reporting of current events or for bona fide review, teaching or research. Section 52 of the Act, to the extent it is relevant, provides that a fair dealing with any work not being a computer programme, for the purpose of reporting of current events and current affairs, shall not constitute an infringement. Therefore, the legislature while recognizing copyright and broadcast rights as independent rights has permitted use of the work of another person for limited purposes, provided that such use does not travel beyond the fair dealing with the work.

Explaining Section 39 of the Copyright Act, 1957 in *ICC Development (International) Ltd.* v. *New Delhi Television Ltd.*,[140] the Delhi High Court observed that Section 39 of the

137. *Super Cassettes Industries Limited* v. *Mr. Chintamani Rao,* 2012 (49) PTC 1 (Del).
138. MIPR 2013 (1) 118: 2013 (53) PTC7 1 (Del).
139. 2008 (38) PTC 477 (Del): MIPR 2008 (3) 257.
140. 193 (2012) DLT 279: 2012 (132) DRJ 291.

Act, to the extent it is relevant, provides that no broadcast reproduction shall be deemed to be infringed by the use consistent with fair dealing, of excerpts of a performance or of a broadcast in the reporting of current events or for bona fide review, teaching or research. Section 52 of the Act, to the extent it is relevant, provides that a fair dealing with any work not being a computer program, for the purpose of reporting of current events and current affairs, shall not constitute an infringement. Therefore, the legislature while recognising copyright and broadcast rights as independent rights has permitted use of the work of another person for limited purposes, provided that such use does not travel beyond the fair dealing with the work.

In *New Delhi Television Limited* v. *ICC Development (International) Limited,*[141] the court held that no performer's right is deemed to be infringed by the use, consistent with fair dealing, of excerpts of a broadcast when current events are reported. With reference to clause (b) of Section 39 of the Copyright Act 1957, it has to be kept in mind that while reporting current events, consistent with fair dealing, use of excerpts of a performance or of a broadcast does not constitute infringement of the broadcast reproduction right or the performer's rights. Similarly, with reference to Section 52(1)(a)(iii) of the Copyright Act 1957, the reporting of current events and current affairs but as fair dealing do not constitute an infringement of the copyright held by the broadcaster or a performer. Thus, one has to first determine: whether the offending activity is by way of reporting or otherwise. If the offending activity is not reporting, that would be the end of the matter.

Exclusive Rights of Performers: Section 38A

The Copyright (Amendment) 2012 has introduced affirmative performer's rights by amending the present Section 38 of the Copyright Act, 1957 which had granted only negative rights by prohibiting certain acts in its sub section (3) and (4). These sub Sections have been omitted and a new Section 38A[142] has been inserted which provides the performer's right as the exclusive right to do or authorise the doing of any of the acts in respect of the performance, without prejudice to the rights conferred on authors. The new Section 38A reads as under:

> Section 38A. Exclusive right of performers—(1) Without prejudice to the rights conferred on authors, the performer's right which is an exclusive right subject to the provisions of this Act to do or authorize for doing any of the following acts in respect of the performance or any substantial part thereof, namely—
>
> (a) to make a sound recording or a visual recording of the performance, including—
>
> (i) reproduction of it in any material form including the storing of it in any medium by electronic or any other means;
>
> (ii) issuance of copies of it to the public not being copies already in circulation;
>
> (iii) communication of it to the public;
>
> (iv) selling or giving it on commercial rental or offer for sale or for commercial rental any copy of the recording;
>
> (b) to broadcast or communicate the performance to the public except where the performance is already broadcast.
>
> (2) Once a performer has, by written agreement, consented to the incorporation of his performance in a cinematograph film he shall not, in the absence of any contract to the contrary, object to the enjoyment by the producer of the film of the performer's right in the same film:

141. MIPR 2013 (1) 118: 2013 (53) PTC 71 (Del).
142. Inserted by the Copyright (Amendment) Act, 2012, Section 27 [w.e.f. 21-6-2012].

Provided that, notwithstanding anything contained in this subsection, the performer shall be entitled for royalties in case of making of the performances for commercial use.

Section 38A deals with what are the legal rights of a performer. In *Indian Singers Rights Association* v. *Night Fever Club and Lounge*,[143] the Delhi High Court held that the Copyright (Amendment) Act, 2012 inserted Section 38A which provides certain exclusive rights to performers. These exclusive rights include (i) the rights of fixation of performance (as sound/ video recordings) and subsequent communication to the public or commercial distribution of such recordings[144]; (ii) right of the broadcasting/communicating to the public, the performance at the first instance.[145]

Further, in *Kajal Agarwal* v. The *Managing Director*,[146] the Madras High Court observed that a reading of the Section 38A of the Copyright Act makes it very clear that once a performer by a written agreement consents to incorporate that performance in a cinematograph film, the performer thereafter cannot object to the producer's right in the cinematograph film, unless there is a contract to the contrary. Thus the appellant having consented to incorporate her performance as an actor in the cinematograph film produced by the respondent who is the author of it, the appellant cannot stop the respondent from enjoying their producer's right. The grant of performer's right will enable the performers to earn continued royalty in their performances which they were not entitled hitherto as they only had a negative right to prohibit "fixation" of their live performances. The negative right has now been converted into the positive rights listed above. The emphasised portion of the aforesaid Section shows that a performer's right is an exclusive right only for specified purposes as stated in clauses (a) and (b) of sub-section (1) of Section 38A. In terms of the language of this provision, basically, the performer's right would be making of a sound recording or visual recording of the performance; reproducing the sound recording and the visual recording; issuing copies of the recording or communicating the same to the public; and, selling or otherwise doing a commercial act including with respect to the copy of the recording. Clause (b) of Section 38A(1) is relevant inasmuch as a clue is provided in this clause which seems to indicate that with respect to a broadcast already made, qua the information which is disseminated through the first broadcast in public domain (as against the audio visual recording itself) the performer cannot claim a right, inasmuch as, Section 38A(1)(b) states that the entitlement of the performer with respect to his performance rights is to broadcast or communicate the performance to the public except where the performance is already broadcast. It is, therefore, a clear pointer to the fact that once a performance is already broadcast it may be possible to say that except with respect to the actual visual and audio recording of the performance itself, there may not be other rights with respect to the information contained in the performance which is already broadcast. Sub-section (2) of Section 38A states that once the rights of the performer and his performance have been incorporated in a cinematographic film, the performer cannot object to the commercial exploitation by the producer of the film of the performance rights in the same film. Explaining the nature and scope of Section 38A in *Star India Pvt. Ltd.* v. *Piyush Agarwal*,[147] the Delhi High Court observed:

143. 2016 (68) PTC 596 (Del): 2016 (68) PTC 596 (Del).
144. Copyright Act 1957, Section 38A(1) (a).
145. *Ibid.*, Section 38A(1) (b).
146. 2018 (5) CTC 185: (2018) 5 MLJ 818.
147. 2014 (58) PTC 169: 2012 LawSuit (Del) 3641.

A performer's right is an exclusive right only for specified purposes as stated in clauses (a) and (b) of sub-section (1) of Section 38A. Whenever a performance is already broadcast it may be possible to say that except with respect to the actual visual and audio recording of the performance itself, there may not be other rights with respect to the information contained in the performance which is already broadcast. Except to the extent of original sound recording and original visual recording of the performance, and the rights which flow there from, there is no other right of a performer or his assignee with respect to the audio and/or visual recording of the performance. The underlying content/information is not made a subject matter of a copyright, and thus if only the content or information contained in an audio recording and/or a visual recording is used for creating on information bank/data base, then, use of the information/content cannot/does not amount to infringement of the copyright either in the performance or in the audio and/or visual recording of the performance.

Moral Rights to Performers: Section 38B

Copyright confers both economic and moral rights on owner. Section 14 of the Copyright Act enlists the economic rights while Section 57 guarantees certain special rights to the author of copyright. The rights are identified based on the nature of commercial exploitation of a particular work they are subject matter specific. The special rights are called moral rights. The moral rights are independent and separate from economic rights. Thus, under the moral rights provisions, the author of a work has paternity right—right to claim authorship of the work and the integrity right—right to restrain or claim damages in respect of any distortion, mutilation, modification or other act in respect to the work, if such distortion, mutilation, modification or other act is prejudicial to his honour or reputation.[148]

One of the most important changes introduced by the Copyright (Amendment) Act, 2012 is the conferment of the moral rights of performers by inserting a new Section 38B. In *Neha Bhasin* v. *Anand Raj Anand*,[149] which was decided prior to 2012 amendment dealt with the issues relating to protection of performer's rights in the digital era and reminds us of the need to make Indian law compatible to the WIPO Performers and Phonogram Treaty, 1996 (WPPT) which was drawn up to protect the rights of performers in the digital age. The court also examined the issue whether performer is entitled to protection of her moral rights based on principle of equity and common law? In this case, by layering of sound using software the performer was used as a back-up vocalist. Since more layers included other singers, others were mentioned as lead singers and not the plaintiff. The court stated that commercial aspirations as the reasoning to it to propound moral rights of the performers—granted the performers moral right to equity since the current version of the Act does not provide for it. Thus, the plaintiff has a right in equity for being given proper credit for the song sung by her. If her voice is used and commercially exploited, she has the right to prevent it being attributed to somebody else. The court also observed that the question of giving appropriate credit for services rendered in the production of a film as an interim relief came up for consideration before the Supreme Court in the case of *Suresh Jindal* v. *Rizsoli Corriere Della Sera Prodzioni T.V.*,[150] In this case, the Supreme Court found that the appellant therein was

148. *See*, *Raj Rewal* v. *Union of India*, 260 (2019) DLT 190; *Uday Chand Jindal* v. *Galgotia Pulblications Pvt. Ltd.*, 2017 (72) PTC 492 (Del).
149. 2006 (32) PTC 779 (Del): 132 (2006) DLT 196.
150. 1991 Supp (2) SCC 3.

entitled to due acknowledgement being given to him as the appellant did "play some part in making the film possible" whether there was a concluded contract between them or not.

However, the Copyright (Amendment) Act, 2012 settles the matter forever by making provisions for moral right for performers in the statute itself. It is interesting to note that though the Copyright (Amendment) Act, 1994 uses the term "special rights" in respect of authors under Section 57, the 2012 amendment uses the term "moral rights" in respect of performers instead of special rights. The new Section 38B[151] grants performers moral rights on their performances as follows:

The performer of a performance shall, independently of his right after assignment, either wholly or partially of his right, have the right,—

(a) to claim to be identified as the performer of his performance except where omission is dictated by the manner of the use of the performance; and

(b) to restrain or claim damages in respect of any distortion, mutilation or other modification of his performance that would be prejudicial to his reputation.

The Explanation clause to this provision clarifies that mere removal of any portion of a performance for the purpose of editing, or to fit the recording within a limited duration, or any other modification required for purely technical reasons shall not be deemed to be prejudicial to the performer's reputation.

The Copyright Act, 1957 provided for moral rights to authors under Section 57 titled "author's special rights", though it did not use the term "moral rights" in the Act. The new Section 38B provides moral rights to performers and calls these rights "moral rights" in the title. Article 5 of WIPO Performance and Phonograms Treaty, 1996 covers the moral rights of performers and the amendment is in line with that article. Moral rights have been extended to performers, considering the possibility of digital alteration of performances in a digital environment. However, some amount of alteration will be required for the purposes of editing. The explanation to Section 38B clarifies that editors are free to perform their tasks without the fear of legal consequences.

Operational Regime of Broadcast Reproduction Right and Performer's Rights: Section 39A

As stated above, rights of broadcasting organisation and of performers (neighbouring rights) are no way inferior to the main right of author under the Copyright Act, 1957. Thus, Section 39A of the Copyright Act provides that Sections 18, 19, 30, 30A, 33, 34, 35, 36, 53, 55, 58, 63, 64, 65, 65A, 65B, 66 shall be, with necessary adaptations and modifications, apply in relation to the broadcast reproduction right in any broadcast and the performer's right in any performance as they apply in relation to copyright in a work. According to first proviso of Section 39A where copyright or performer's right subsists in respect of any work or performance that has been broadcast, no licence to reproduce such broadcast, shall be given without the consent of the owner of right or performer, as the case may be, or both of them. Further, the second proviso of Section 39A provides that the broadcast reproduction

151. Inserted by the the Copyright (Amendment) Act, 2012, Section 27 [w.e.f. 21-6-2012].

right or performer's right shall not subsist in any broadcast or performance if that broadcast or performance is an infringement of the copyright in any work. The broadcast reproduction right or the performer's right shall not affect the separate copyright in any work in respect of which, the broadcast or the performance, as the case may be, is made.

Thus, According to Section 18 of the Copyright Act, 1957, owner of neighbouring right (broadcast reproduction right or the performer's right) may assign rights under the work to any one provided that in the case of the assignment of copyright in any future work, the assignment shall take effect only when the work comes into existence. Under Section 19 the mode of assignment of neighbouring rights, which requires that no assignment of the copyright in any work shall be valid unless it is in writing signed by the assignor or by his duly authorised agent. The owner of the neighbouring rights in any existing work or the prospective owner of the neighbouring right in any future work may grant any interest in the right by licence in writing signed by him or by his duly authorised agent. However, in the case of a licence relating to neighbouring right in any future work, the licence shall take effect only when the work comes into existence under Section 30. Again, Section 53 regulates importation of copies in India of work having neighbouring right/copyright in them and Section 55 provide for civil remedies for infringement of neighbouring rights, e.g., injunction, damages, accounts, etc. Rights of owner against persons possessing or dealing with infringing copies; such infringing copies shall be deemed to be property of the owner of neighbouring right under Section 58. Similarly, Section 64 provides power of police to seize infringing copies of the work having neighbouring rights. Although Section 39A does not make applicable Section 63 of the Act, but Section 64 requires that the police officer may, if he is satisfied that an offence under Section 63 in respect of the infringement of copyright in any work has been, is being, or is likely to be, committed, seize without warrant, all copies of the work, and all plates used for the purpose of making infringing copies of the work, wherever found, and all copies and plates so seized shall, as soon as practicable, be produced before a Magistrate. Section 65 punishes possession of plates for the purpose of making infringing copies. It reads, person who knowingly makes, or has in his possession, any plate for the purpose of making infringing copies of any work in which copyright subsists shall be punishable with imprisonment, which may extend to two years and shall also be liable to fine. Section 66 deals with disposal of infringing copies or plates used, to be used for purpose of making infringing copies. Such materials are to be handed over to the owner of copyright-neighbouring rights.

In *Star India Pvt. Ltd.* v. *Piyush Agarwal*,[152] the Delhi High Court held that Section 39A of the Copyright Act, 1957 enumerates those provisions of the statute that apply to copyright would also apply, mutatis mutandis to the neighbouring rights (e.g. Performer's rights, Broadcasting reproduction rights). However, it is pertinent to note that Section 16 is not enumerated under Section 39A of the Act. Moreover, the Copyright Act creates several rights besides copyright. These rights include the rights of broadcasting organisations under Section 37, the rights of performers under Sections 38 and 38A, and the moral rights of authors which are recognised under Section 57; which are all distinct from copyright. Thus, it can be said that the Copyright Act, 1957 under Chapter VIII encompasses right as well as protection paraphernalia of neighbouring rights in India which is insufficient. It may be

152. MIPR 2013 (1) 201: 2013 (54) PTC 222 (Del).

relevant to note that Section 53A has not been made available to those holding neighbouring rights, which creates a presumption that in cases of neighbouring rights either there is no possibility of resale or such works have no economic value so that owners could get something during resale. In the realm of neighbouring rights in India, it could be seen that Chapter VIII has segregated the entire conceptual framework of neighbouring rights from the awesome enforcement of Copyright Act, 1957. This is so because Section 39A has identified provisions of the Copyright Act, which are applicable to neighbouring rights with suitable adaptations. An argument might be advanced that Section 39A has limited the scope of Copyright Act in relation to neighbouring rights. Similarly, Section 63 that elucidates the penal provision in relation to copyright infringement would have been ousted, but for clause (b) of Section 63 has become applicable to infringement of neighbouring rights (broadcasters' rights).[153]

153. *See also*, *STAR India Private Limited* v. *Department of Industrial Policy*, 2018 (2) CTC 113.

8

Protection of Copyright in Internet

ABSTRACT

Innovation and speed are the twin watchwords of a knowledge-based economy. The most astonishing feature of the emergence of new technologies is the enabling dissemination of knowledge in a hitherto unprecedented manner. These scientific break-through and technological developments through the Internet have created a corresponding demand for strengthening the legal protection machinery. Situated against this backdrop, legal protection of copyright in the Internet poses a singular range of legal issues. This chapter critically examines these advancements and their link with the law of copyright with special reference to the role of judiciary, and recommends reforms necessary in the developing context of India.

STATEMENT OF PROBLEM

The Internet is the greatest communication medium of the contemporary era. It brings the whole world to a mouse click of a computer, making innumerable sources and references available in matter of seconds. Copyright protection is provided to the authors of "original works" of literary, dramatic, musical, artistic, architectural and certain other intellectual works, both published and unpublished[1] while the Internet has been characterised as the largest threat to copyright protection since its inception.[2] The Internet is awash in information, a lot of it with varying degrees of copyright protection. Copyrighted works on the Internet include news stories, software, novels, screenplays, graphics, pictures, use Internet messages and even email. In fact, the frightening reality is that almost everything on the Internet is protected by copyright law. That can pose problems for the hapless surfer. In a modern world where information is a key factor and the information is available with the click of a mouse on a computer from the Internet, it's an era of expansion.[3]

1. *See*, *Novex Communication Pvt. Ltd.* v. *Lemon Tree Hotels Ltd.*, 2019 IIAD (Delhi) 644; *Institute for Inner Studies* v. *Charlotte Anderson*, MIPR 2014 (129) 1; *Bayer Corporation* v. *Cipla, Union of India*, MIPR 2009 (3) 467: 2009 (41) PTC 634 (Del); *Syndicate of Press of the University of Cambridge* v. *Kasturi Lan*, 2006 (32) PTC 487 (Del); *Macmillan and Co. Ltd.* v. *K. and J. Cooper*, AIR 1924 PC 75: 1924-19-LW 299.
2. *See*, Ejan Mackaay (Ed.), *The Electronic Superhighway: The Shape of Technology and Law to Come*, (Kluwer Law International, 1995).
3. *Mrs. Ishi Khosla* v. *Anil Aggarwal* (2007) ILR 1 Delhi 615: 2007 (34) PTC 370 (Del).

The Internet is a medium which provides audio-visual interactive facility for doing business. Merely because it is a more advanced or superior medium, it does not impinge on the determination of the issue whether the merchandiser is carrying on business at a particular place. Prior to the advent of electronic commerce (e-commerce) over the Internet, and even now, business was and continues to be done over telephone and fax. Merely because a person has embarked upon an e-commerce business model, the tests which apply for determination of issues, such as when and where the contract is made, or whether the vendor carries on business at the place where the merchandise may be sold, or service may be offered, would not change and would be the same as apply to communications over telephone and fax.[4] In *Yahoo, Inc.* v. *Akash Arora*,[5] the Delhi High Court takes note of the transcendental nature of the Internet business's wherein the Court observed that:

> As a matter of fact in a matter where services are rendered through the domain name in the Internet, a very alert vigil is necessary and a strict view is to be taken for its easy access and reach by anyone from any corner of the globe.

Thus, one of the significant technological revolutions took place in the last century was the invention of digital technology. The emergence of the Internet as a powerful and reliable platform for communication facilitated the creation of new works in the form of multimedia. Hence, these works are used not only for educational purposes but also for businesses. This led to the formation of new capital in the area of information creation and distribution for commercial gains in the global market, information technology industry is projected as one of the most powerful sources for capital formation and employment generation in the new century. The law relating to copyright proved to be one of the powerful legal instruments for the purpose of protecting capital investment in the area of cultural industries. It was also projected as a legal instrument that tried to maintain the delicate balance between the interest of owners of copyright and the general public. The traditional norms for the protection of copyright in the works were amended periodically to suit technological changes without sacrificing the public interest.[6]

However, questions have persisted about the implementation and utility of existing legal norms to control the misuse of the digital technology. It has been argued that in the context of digital technology existing legal norms seem inadequate to solve the problems posed by this new technology.[7] The most fundamental issues in the field of copyright and related rights are the determination of the scope and protection of rights of copyright owners in the digital era.[8] Besides, the right of reproduction of an author is another controversial issue in the digital era. In the digital context, the copyrighted works are stored in digital format and multiplied every time it is used or sent to another person. In some cases like browsing of materials in the web, transmission of materials, providing access by linking, etc., the works are reproduced for

---

4. *See*, J.H. Smith Grahm, *Internet Law and Regulation* (Sweet and Maxual, London, 2002).
5. 1999 (19) PTC 201: 78 (1999) DLT 285.
6. *See*, the amendments introduced to the Copyright Act, 1957 in 1984, 1994, 1999 and 2012.
7. Sinday A. Rosenzweig, "Don't Put My Article Online: Existing Copyright's New-use Doctrine to the Electronic Publishing Media and Beyond", 143 *University of Pennsylvania Law Review*, 639 (1994–1995).
8. *See*, Binu Poornamodan Cholayil, "Digital Rights Management and Fair Use in Copyright Law" 33(1–2) *Cochin University Law Review* (2009) p. 166.

a short period of time. The users may also download and store the material in the computer for the purpose of using it at their convenience. They may also transmit it to others for personal use. The question that arises is whether all forms of reproduction, whether temporary or permanent, form part of reproduction right in the digital context. The creators of content for the digital argue that all forms of reproduction whether temporary or permanent must be treated as reproduction even though there can be exception in some cases. On the other hand, the users of the work and the providers of access to these materials assert that reproduction in permanent found alone must be recognised as right of reproduction.[9]

The question is who will take the responsibility to monitor violations of rights in the Internet? Can the providers of the Internet service be held responsible for the violations that take place in the Internet of which he may or may not have any information? If so, to what extent? Do they have the responsibility to monitor the violation? Can they absolve the responsibility even if the violations are brought to their notice? Are their activities like providing access by linking including deep linking, system caching, framing, etc. violations of the right of reproduction? Similarly, the question of the liability of the users of the Internet is controversial in the contemporary era. Are the activities of browsing, downloading, storing and transmitting of works for any non-commercial purposes violation of the rights? Is this to be treated as fair use or use with implied licence? How should the right of authors be defined and what are the exceptions and limitations to be permitted to such rights? How are the rights of authors to be enforced and administered in this digital environment? Can the existing worldwide copyrights law adequately protect the interests of those who hold copyright or are changes to the existing rules required? These questions need detail deliberation.

VARIOUS CONCEPTS, ACTS AND USES IN THE INTERNET AND THEIR COPYRIGHT IMPLICATIONS

The activity of the Internet has raised many issues under the copyright law as copying transmission of information, via the Internet, takes place without any degradation and every copy is perfect. Under Section 13 of the Copyright Act, 1957, the word "original" is prefixed to "literary, dramatic, musical and artistic works". Thus, for benefit of copyright the protection the work of the author must be original. The expression "literary work" is defined in Section 2(o) to include computer programs, tables and compilations including computer data bases.[10] Therefore, in case of subsistence of copyright in literary, dramatic, musical and artistic works, the work has to be original.[11] The judiciary has formulated test to determine originality of a work. In *R.G. Anand* v. *Delux Films*,[12] the Apex Court held: "One of the surest and the safest tests to determine whether or not there has been a violation of copyright is to see if the reader, spectator or the viewer after having read or seen both the works is clearly of the opinion and gets an unmistakable impression that the subsequent work appears to be a copy

9. Nandan Kamat, *Law Relating to Computers Internet and E-Commerce*, Universal Law Publishing Co., New Delhi (2012).
10. Substituted by the Copyright (Amendment) Acts, 1994 and 1999. *See*, *Institute for Inner Studies* v. *Charlotte Anderson*, MIPR 2014 (129) 1.
11. *Rediff.Com India Ltd.* v. *E-Eighteen.Com Ltd.*, MIPR 2013 (2) 333: 2013 (55) PTC 294 (Del).
12. PTC (Supp) (1) 802 (SC): AIR 1978 SC 1613.

of the original." In *Eastern Book Company* v. *D.B. Modak*,[13] the Apex Court held that the word "original" does not mean that the work must be the expression of original or inventive thought. The word "original" does not demand original or inventive thought, but only that the work should not be copied but should originate from the author.

There is a conceptual dichotomy between a physical document and a document in the Internet. The physical document is normally a piece of paper, which exists in one space-time location only. It can be copied, in which case there are two documents, the "original" and a "copy". In case of the Internet activity, seven interim "copies" in whole or in part, may be made when transmitting computers will buffer each type data, as well the route, the receiving computer itself (in RAM), the web browser, the video decompression chief, and the video display board. These copies are in addition to the one that may be stored on the recipient computer's hard disk. In case of postal service the "original" packet is supplied while in case of the Internet service the "original" packet never arrives. Thus, copying is fundamental to all communications between computers.[14] The equivalent digital document, however, is simply a set of binary data, conveniently conceptualised as Is or Os. It is more accurate to say that it is "stored", rather than "exists in original and copied" and many well be stored in multiple locations.[15]

Before discussing any copyright issue on the Internet, it is essential to discuss various concepts, acts and uses of the Internet having copyright implications. Therefore, it is proposed to discuss in the following pages various concepts, acts, uses of the Internet and their copyright implications.

Internet, Internet Protocol and Domain Name System

The Internet is not a physical or tangible entity, but rather a giant network which interconnects innumerable smaller groups of linked computer networks. The Internet is a global system of interconnected computer networks that use the standard Internet protocol suite to serve several billion users worldwide. It is a "network of networks"[16] that consists of millions of private, public, academic, business, and government networks, of local to global scope, that are linked by a broad array of electronic, wireless and optical networking technologies. Thus, the Internet consists of thousands of smaller regional networks spread throughout the world. The Internet is referred as a physical part of the global network. It is a giant collection of cables and computers. No one "owns" the Internet, though there are companies that help out to manage different parts of the networks that tie everything together, there is no single governing

13. AIR 1978 SC 1613: 2008 (1) SCC 1. *See also*, *Twentieth Century Fox Film Corporation* v. *Zee Telefilms Ltd.*, MIPR 2012 (2) 377: 2012 (51) PTC4 65 (Del); *Mother Dairy Fruit* v. *Mallikarjuna Dairy Products Pvt. Ltd.*, 2012 (49) PTC 346 (Del); *Societe Des Produits Nestle* v. *Continental Coffee Ltd.*, MIPR 2012 (1) 135: 2012 (49) PTC 46 (Del).
14. *See*, Mark A. Lemley, Dealing with Overlapping Copyrights on the Internet, 221 *Dayton Law Review* (1997) pp. 547–555; Neal Kumar Katyal, "Criminal Law in Cyber-space" 149 *University of Pennsylvania Law Review*, (2001) pp. 1006–1013.
15. *See*, Krishna Kumar, *Cyber Laws Intellectual Property and E-Commerce Security* (Dominant Publishers and Distributors, 2001) at p. 69.
16. *See*, Rodney D. Ryder, *Intellectual Property and the Internet* (LexisNexis Butterworths, 2002).

body that controls what happens on the Internet. The networks within different countries sponsor the finance and manage according to the local procedure.[17] In *Stephen Koenig* v. *Arbitrator, National Internet Exchange of India*,[18] the Delhi High Court defines "internet" to mean connect or be connected to a computer network; a computer network consisting of or connecting a number of smaller networks, such as two or more local area networks connected by a shared communications protocol.

The Internet is a global collection of computer networks linking millions of public and private computers around the world. The Internet is now recognised as an international system, a communication medium that allows anyone from any part of the globe with access to the Internet to freely exchange information and share data. The Internet provides information about various corporations, products as also on various subjects like educational, entertainment, commercial, government activities and services. Every computer on the public Internet has a unique numeric address—similar to the uniqueness of a telephone number—which is a string of numbers that is difficult for most people to remember. This string is called the "IP address". IP stands for "Internet Protocol". In *Stephen Koeing* v. *Arbitrator NIXI*,[19] it was held that Internet Protocol (IP) is a standard that specifies the format and addressing scheme of packets of data sent over the internet or other network. To make it easier to find a given location on the Internet, the Domain Name System, or DNS, was invented. International registration of Domain Name System (DNS) is regulated by the Uniform Domain Name Dispute Resolution Policy (UDRP) of the World Intellectual Property Organisation.[20] The UDRP is a process established by the Internet Corporation for Assigned Names and Numbers (ICANN) for the resolution of disputes regarding the registration of Internet domain names.[21]

The Domain Name System (DNS) is the distributed set of databases residing in computers around the world that contain address numbers mapped to corresponding domain names, making it possible to send and receive messages and to access information from computers anywhere on the Internet. Many of the technical, operational, and management decisions regarding the DNS can have significant impacts on Internet-related policy issues such as copyright, privacy, Internet freedom, e-commerce, and cyber security. Registration of domain name is an administrative act, which involves a request to the domain name registry, payment of fee and allotment, if there is no prior user with the same domain name. Registration being ministerial act is not a pronouncement on the question of violation or infringement.[22] In *Raymond Limited* v. *Raymond Pharmaceutical Pvt. Ltd.*,[23] the Bombay High Court held that since inception of the domain name system, a domain name has been the identifier of an individual or entity operating within the world wide web comprising cyberspace. In *Stephen Koenig* v. *Arbitrator, National Internet Exchange of India*,[24] the court observed:

---

17. *See*, J.H. Smith Grahm, *Internet Law and Regulation* (Sweet and Maxual, London, 2002).
18. 2012 (49) PTC 304 (Del): 186 (2012) DLT 43.
19. 2015 (64) PTC 406 (Del): 224 (2015) DLT 407.
20. *See*, Guide to WIPO Uniform Domain Name Dispute Resolution Policy, Visit: http://www.wipo.int/amc.
21. Visit: http://en.wikipedia.org/wiki/Uniform_Domain-Name_Dispute-Resolution_Policy.
22. *Beiersdorf A.G.* v. *Ajay Sukhwani*, MIPR 2009 (1) 143: 2009 (39) PTC 38 (Del).
23. 2017 (69) PTC 79 (Bom).
24. 186 (2012) DLT 43: 2012 (49) PTC 304 (Del). *See also, Info Edge (India) Ltd.* v. *Sumanta Bhattacharya*, 2017 (71) PTC 454 (Del): 240 (2017) DLT 737.

> Among the serious problems of the Domain Name System ('DNS') is "cyber squatting" resulting from deliberate and fraudulent registration of domain names using well-known trademarks with the intention of selling them to the owners of those trademarks at a huge price. Cyber squatters could also sell these domain names to any other person for a price, thus "diluting" a well-known trademark or trade name. The problems of "cyber piracy", of "trademark dilution" and a host of other issues led to the formulation of the Uniform Domain Names Dispute Resolution Policy (UDRP) as a result of consultations between the World Intellectual Property Organisation (WIPO) and the Internet Corporation for Assigned Names and Numbers (ICANN), a non-profit organisation managing the DNS.

The DNS translates IP addresses into unique alphanumeric addresses called domain names that are easier to remember. If, for example, someone likes to visit the ICANN website, he can rather remember the IP address 192.0.34.163, or type www.icann.org. By associating a familiar string of letters—the domain name—with an IP address, the DNS makes it much easier for the Internet users to remember websites and email addresses. In the example above, the "icann.org" part of the address is called the domain name. The "www." part identifies the browser that someone is looking for the World Wide Web interface for that domain name. A domain name is an identity or name, which distinguishes the registrant from another. Internet allows universal access cutting across boundaries. Domain name therefore gives universal exclusivity. No two domain names can be exactly similar. Thus, a computer or device that is attached to the Internet has an address which is known as domain name. The same is established by using suffix "com" and registering with Network Solutions Inc. A domain name identifies a computer or a sub network of computers in the Internet. One way to establish a presence on the Internet is by placing a web page. In *Mars Incorporated* v. *Kumar Krishna Mukherjee*,[25] the Delhi High Court held:

> With the onset of information technology in modern times, registration of a website which is popularly known as domain name, a party owning a website has a right to protect the same if any person registers the website with a name which is inherently deceptive. In such cases either party is directed to change the name of the site or handover to its owner.

The original role of a domain name was no doubt to provide an address for computers on the internet. But the internet has developed from a mere means of communication to a mode of carrying on commercial activity. With the increase of commercial activity on the internet, a domain name is also used as a business identifier. Thus, the Apex Court in *Satyam Infoway Ltd.* v. *Sifynet Solutions Pvt. Ltd.*,[26] observed:

> The domain name not only serves as an address for internet communication but also identifies the specific Internet site. In the commercial field, each domain name owner provides information/services which are associated with such domain name. A domain name is easy to remember and use, and is chosen as an instrument of commercial enterprise not only because it facilitates the ability of consumers to navigate the internet to find websites they are looking for, but also at the same time, serves to identify and distinguish the business itself, or its goods or services, and to specify its corresponding online internet location. Consequently a domain name as an address must, of necessity, be peculiar and unique and where a domain name is used in connection with a business, the value of maintaining an exclusive identity becomes critical.

---

25. 2003 (26) PTC 60 (Del).
26. 2004 28 PTC 566 (SC). *See also*, *Times Internet Ltd* v. *Belize Domain Who is Service Ltd.*, 2011 (45) PTC 96.

In *Manish Vij* v. *Indra Chugh*,[27] the court recognises that every "domain name" is divided into levels. The "top level" domain name is a suffix which serves to place the within one of the broad category such as .com (for commercial), .edu (for educational), .gov (for government) .org (for organization), .net (network) etc. The "second level" domain name appears before the top level and serves as a trademark or trade name function. The prefix www. is a standard for all World Wide Web addresses. For example, user of the internet wishing to get information from Economic Times newspaper, has a reasonable expectation of reaching the Economic Times website by merely typing the address www.economictimes.com, into software programs that are used to navigate the World Wide Web, without actually knowing internet address of the newspaper. Thus, domain name indicates to a user information as to the content of a website. It shares many of the attributes of trademarks or trade names. Each domain name is unique. The "domain name" cannot be same irrespective of geographical distance, which may not so in case of trademarks or tradenames. The registered "domain name" may be used from anywhere in the world.

Obtaining fraudulent registration with intent to sell the domain name to the lawful owner of the name at premium is called "cyber squatting".[28] The Cyber squatters quickly sell the domain names to other non-related entities, thereby enabling passing off and diluting of famous trademarks or trade names. There can be no dispute that with the advancement of technology and communication through internet, domain names have attained as much legal sanctity, as the trade names. The services rendered at the internet are equally important for any business. The domain name is a valuable corporates asset entitled to protection like trade names and trademarks.[29]

Browsing on the Internet

A software program that permits one to access the internet via web addresses (URL—Uniform Resource Locator). In essence, it is like a picture frame that one uses to display photographs. The stuff you usually see at the top of the browser are simply controls that let you tailor what you want that specific browser to do. Thus, a browser is a program on your computer that enables you to search ("surf") and retrieve information on the World Wide Web (WWW), which is part of the Internet. The Web is simply a large number of computers linked together in a global network, that can be accessed using an address (URL, Uniform Resource Locator, e.g., "http://www.veths.no" for the Oslo Veterinary School), in the same way that you can phone anyone in the world given their telephone number. URLs are often long and therefore easy to type incorrectly. They all begin with http://, and many (but not all) begin with http://www. In many cases, the first part (http://, or even http://www.) can be omitted, and you will still be able to access the page. When browsing the World Wide Web (www) sites on the Internet, for example, the browser will make a "copy" of (download) the material into the

---

27. AIR 2002 Delhi 243: 97 (2002) DLT 1.
28. *See, Pfizer Products Inc.* v. *Mr. Altamash Khan,* 127 (2006) DLT 738: 2006 (32) PTC 208 (Del). *See also, Tata Sons Limited* v. *Aniket Singh*, 2016 (65) PTC 337 (Del); *Stephen Koeing* v. *Arbitrator NIXI*, 2015 (64) PTC 406 (Del): 224 (2015) DLT 407; *Oxigen Services India Pvt. Ltd.* v. *Oxigen24 Teleservices*, 2014 (58) PTC 160 (Del): 2014 iii AD (Delhi) 587.
29. *Rediff. Communication Limited* v. *Cyberbooth*, AIR 2000 Bom. 27.

local computer's memory. This is a necessary function of the technology currently available with which to browse. The flicking through and reading of a book are not within a copyright holder's exclusive rights. However, the unauthorised use of copyright work over the Internet leads to suspension of the service provider's activity. In India, the Copyright (Amendment) Act, 2012 has inserted Clause (b) to Section 52. The new clause (b) in Section 52 seeks to provide that transient and incidental storage of a work or performance purely in the technical process of electronic transmission or communication to the public shall not constitute an infringement of copyright.[30]

In *ACLU* v. *Reno*,[31] the United States District Court (Pennsylvania) described the nature of browsing on the Internet and held the World Wide Web (W3C) was created to serve as the platform for a global, online store of knowledge, containing information from a diversity of sources and accessible to the Internet users around the world. Though information on the Web is contained in individual computers, the fact that each of these computers is connected to the Internet through W3C protocols allows all of the information to become part of a single body of knowledge. It is currently the most advanced information systems developed on the Internet, and embraces within its data model most information in previous network information systems such as ftp, gopher, wais, and Usenet. The court further observed:

> The Web utilizes a "hypertext" formatting language called hypertext markup language (HTML), and programs that "browse" the Web can display HTML documents containing text, images, sound, animation and moving video. Any HTML document can include links to other types of information or resources, so that while viewing an HTML document that, for example, describes resources available on the Internet, one can "click" using a computer mouse on the description of the resource and be immediately connected to the resource itself. Such "hyperlinks" allow information to be accessed and organized in very flexible ways, and allow people to locate and efficiently view related information even if the information is stored on numerous computers all around the world.[32]

In *Eicher Goodearth Pvt. Ltd.* v. *Krishna Mehta*,[33] it was observed that a person browsing the website of the defendants will be well aware that the products shown therein are the products of the defendants. The defendants are not selling their products in the name of the plaintiff or in any other name which is identical to or similar to the name of the plaintiff. Thus, in *Myspace Inc.* v. *Super Cassettes Industries Ltd.*,[34] the Delhi High Court held that mere browsing or accessing content does not require registration. But, in *Glaxosmithkline Pharmaceuticals Ltd.* v. *Sarath Kumar Reddy G.*,[35] the plaintiffs claim that sometime in April, 2009, while browsing the website of the Registrar of Companies, it came to their knowledge that a company by the name of "GSK Life Sciences Private Limited" is using the acronym "GSK" as part of their trade name "GSK Life Sciences Limited". The Delhi High Court has granted permanent injunction restraining the Defendants, their

---

30. *See*, *Star India Private Limited* v. *Department of Industrial Policy*, (2019) 2 SCC 104: 2018 (14) SCALE 651.
31. Civil Action No. 96–963 et al. (June 11, 1996).
32. *See*, *Consim Info Pvt. Ltd.* v. *Google India Pvt. Ltd.*, 2011 (45) PTC 575 (Mad): 2010 (6) CTC 813; *Banyan Tree Holding (P) Limited* v. *A. Murali Krishna Reddy*, 2010 (42) PTC 361 (Del): MIPR 2009 (3) 247; *Banyan Tree Holdings Limited* v. *M. Murali Krishna Reddy*, 2008 (38) PTC 288 (Del).
33. 2015 (63) PTC 444 (Del): MIPR 2015 (2) 345.
34. 2017 (69) PTC 1 (Del): 236 (2017) DLT 478.
35. 2017 (69) PTC 160 (Del): 234 (2016) DLT 459.

companies, their directors, partners or proprietors as the case may be, their officers, servants, agents and representatives from using the name/ mark GSK as a part of their trade name/ trading style. The problem of placing "browsing" under fair dealing doctrine would be that some countries may not apply defensive doctrines such as fair dealing and implied licence. Article 10(2) of the WIPO Copyright Treaty, 1996 provides "Contracting Parties shall, when applying the Berne Convention, confine any limitations of or exceptions to rights provided for therein to certain special cases that do not conflict with a normal exploitation of the work and do not unreasonably prejudice the legitimate interests of the author." Thus, it would be better if international rules like those under WIPO Copyright Treaty include "browsing" illustratively either under "some special cases" in Article 10(2) or "non-commercial fair dealing" like "research and private study". The Court in United States in *Religious Technology Center* v. *Netcom On-Line Communication Services, Inc.*,[36] observed:

> Absent a commercial or profit-depriving use, digital browsing is probably a fair use; there could hardly be a market for licencing the temporary copying of digital works onto computer screens to allow browsing. Unless such a use is commercial, such as where someone reads a copyrighted work online and therefore decides not to purchase a copy from the copyright owner, fair use is likely. Until reading a work online becomes as easy and convenient as reading a paperback, copyright owner do not have much to fear from digital browsing and there will not likely be much market effect.
>
> Additionally, unless a user has reason to know, such as from the title of a message, that the message contains copyrighted materials, the browser will be protected by the innocent infringer doctrine, which allows the court to award no damages in appropriate circumstances. In any event, users should hardly worry about a finding of direct infringement; it seems highly unlikely from a practical matter that a copyright owner could prove such infringement or would want to sue such an individual.

Under the English Copyright, Designs and Patents Act, 1988, Internet online browsing amounts to reproduction. Section 17(6) of the 1988 Act states: "Copying in relation to any description of work includes the making of copies which are transient or are incidental to some other use of the work." In *Newspaper Licencing Agency Ltd.* v. *Meltwater Holding BV*,[37] the High Court of England and Wales determined the issue whether Public Relations Consultants Association Limited ("PRCA") and its members ("the End-Users") require a licence from the claimants in order lawfully to receive and use Meltwater News. Such a licence is known as a Web End-User Licence ("WEUL"). The court held that without a licence from the Publishers there is infringement of the Publishers' copyright by the End-Users in receiving and using Meltwater News. When an end-user receives an email containing Meltwater News, a copy is made on the end-user's computer and remains there until deleted. Further, when the end-user views Meltwater News via Meltwater's website on screen, a copy is made on that computer. However, it may be submitted that browsing creates merely ephemeral copy, which should not be considered a form of copyright infringement. Thus, this directive treats the Internet browsing as "reading" and "using" any literary work which does not implicate the copyright laws.

36. 907 F. Supp. 1361: 1995 U.S. Dist. Lexis 18173 (N.D. Cal. 1995).
37. [2010] EWHC 3099 (Ch).

Offline Web Browsing

The Internet access connects individual computer terminals, computers, mobile devices, and computer networks to the Internet, enabling users to access the Internet services (for example, email and the World Wide Web). The Internet Service Providers (ISPs) offer Internet access to the public through various technologies that offer a wide range of data signalling rates (speeds).[38] Besides, the Internet access requires three primary things: (i) a server computer that responds to requests across a computer network to provide, or help to provide, a network service. Servers can be run on a dedicated computer, which is also often referred to as "the server", but many networked computers are capable of hosting servers. In many cases, a computer can provide several services and have several servers running;[39] (ii) a client computer, which requires that electronic data stored on the server through web browser software. A client is a piece of computer hardware or software that accesses a service made available by a server. The server is often (but not always) on another computer system, in which case the client accesses the service by way of a network. The term applies to programs or devices that are part of a client;[40](iii) a communication link (usually phone lines) connecting the server computer to the client computer.[41] Offline web browsing essentially puts all three of these software and hardware requirements on single computer, i.e., client computer. The content from the server is downloaded and copied for storage on the client's hard drive.[42]

Offline web browsing arise unique questions in copyright law. The offline web browsing is a clear case of storage of data on the computer which is within the scope and ambit of the exclusive right of reproduction of the author. In *Entertainment Network (India) Ltd.* v. *Super Cassettes Industries Ltd.*,[43] the Delhi High Court held that there cannot be any doubt whatsoever that an artistic, literary or musical work is the brain-child of an author, the fruit of his labour and, so, considered to be his property. A copyright, however, unlike a trademark is a right created under the Copyright Act, 1957 as is evident from Section 16 thereof. When an author of a copyright and other claims a copyright, it is subjected to the provisions of the Act. The rights and obligations of the author ought to be found out within the four corners of the Act. It creates a monopoly in favour of the author. Copyright also creates a monopoly in favour of the copyright society. What requires protection is unlawful reproduction of the author's work by others. The Copyright (Amendment) Act, 2012 has extended fair use provisions to the digital environment. Thus, any deliberate storing of such works and unauthorised reproduction and distribution of such works is an infringement under Section 51 of the Act attracting civil and criminal liability. In this connection an explanation has been inserted by the new amendment to clause (1)(a) of Section 52 to clarify that storing of any work in any electronic medium for the specified purposes, including the incidental storage of a computer program which in itself is not an infringing copy, shall not be an infringement. Thus, in *Super Cassettes Industries Ltd.* v. *Shreya Broadcasting Pvt. Ltd.*,[44] the Delhi High Court held that the use of the copyright

38. Visit: http://en.wikipedia.org/wiki/Internet_access.
39. Visit: http://en.wikipedia.org/wiki/Server_(computing).
40. Visit: http://en.wikipedia.org/wiki/Client_(computing).
41. Visit: http://en.wikipedia.org/wiki/Telecommunications_link.
42. *See*, *Indian Performing Right Society Ltd.* v. *Vodafone Idea Ltd.*, (2019) 2 CALLT 436 (HC).
43. MIPR 2008 (2) 129: 2008 (37) PTC 353 (SC).
44. 258 (2019) DLT 116: 2019 III AD (Delhi) 552.

work of the plaintiff by the defendant was for the criticism or review of the copyright work. The same was in a way to enhance the programmes of the defendant. Hence the defendant cannot claim the benefit of Section 52(1)(a)(ii) of the Copyright Act.

Caching

In *Myspace Inc.* v. *Super Cassettes Industries Ltd.*,[45] the it was held that Section 52(1)(b) of the Copyright Act 1957 refer to transient and incidental storage. Transient means any work which is temporary or impermanent and incidental would mean something subordinate to something of greater importance. These include "cached" data, web cookies or any other like form of data, which is generated automatically to improve the performance of the core function. The caching is an automatic, intermediate and temporary storage of that information, performed for the sole purpose of making more efficient the information's onward transmission to other recipients of that service. The caching is also an "auxiliary memory from which high-speed retrieval is possible." Hosting and storing data does not qualify to be referred to as incidental or transient data. The nature of the data being uploaded is of a permanent type, one which is accessible whenever demanded or searched for. These are the major functions and any storage which is of a temporary form aiding in the better performance of the main function would be covered under Section 52(1)(b) and (c).

Caching involves storage of an entire site or other complete set of material from a source for a later use. In computer science, a cache is a component that transparently stores data so that future requests for that data can be served faster. The data that is stored within a cache might be values that have been computed earlier or duplicates of original values that are stored elsewhere. If requested data is contained in the cache (cache hit), this request can be served by simply reading the cache, which is comparatively fast. Otherwise (cache miss), the data has to be recomputed or fetched from its original storage location, which is comparatively slow. Hence, the greater the number of requests that can be served from the cache, the faster the overall system performance becomes.[46] Caching process used by browsers of storing "browsed" material in the browser computer's RAM.[47] Caching is of two kinds: (i) local caching[48] and (ii) proxy caching.[49] The idea behind cache-oblivious algorithms is efficient usage of processor caches and reduction of memory bandwidth requirements. Both

45. 2017 (69) PTC 1 (Del): 236 (2017) DLT 478.
46. Visit: http://en.wikipedia.org/wiki/Cache_(computing).
47. A computer's RAM is the memory used to store data and programs on a temporary basis. The RAM is compared to short-term memory, as it stores applications and information that is actively used while the system is on. In comparison, the hard drive, the long-term memory, stores all programs and information permanently, whether the computer is on or not. Visit http://www.technewsdaily.com/6287-what-is-ram.html.
48. The server stores objects in serialized form in the cache. When a cache client requests an object from the cache, the server sends it to the client over the network. The cache client then deserializes the object for use by the client application. To speed up the process of retrieving an object, enable local cache. Visit: http://msdn.microsoft.com/en-us/library/ee790983(v=azure.10).aspx.
49. Proxy cache referred to as a Web proxy cache, a function of a proxy server that caches retrieved Web pages on the server's hard disk so that the page can be quickly retrieved by the same or a different user the next time that page is requested. The proxy cache eases bandwidth requirements and reduces delays that are inherent in a heavily trafficked, Internet-connected network. Visit: http://www.webopedia.com/TERM/P/proxy_cache.html.

things are equally important for single-threaded algorithms, but especially crucial for parallel algorithms, because available memory bandwidth is usually shared between hardware threads and frequently becomes a bottleneck for scalability.[50] Catching carries certain disadvantages to the owner of the copyrighted material in print media because most catching is invisible to the user. Catching may result in the loss of control over access to information at a site. In print media version of information is in control of the copyright owner but in case of catching the control of version moves from the hands of the website controller to the Online Service Providers (OSP) of the end-user.

Although, the Copyright (Amendment) Act, 2012 has extended fair use provisions to the digital environment, any transient and incidental storage of any work through the process of "caching" has been provided exceptions as per the international practice is infringement or not is debatable issue. However, any deliberate storing of such works and unauthorised reproduction and distribution of such works is an infringement under Section 51 of the Copyright Act attracting civil and criminal liability. Exceptions under Section 52 have been extended to education and research purposes as works are available in digital formats and in the Internet.[51] In the United States there are four factors to be considered in determining whether it is a case of fair use. These factors are (a) the purpose and the character of the use, including whether such use is of a commercial nature or is for non-profit educational purposes; (b) the nature of the copyrighted work; (c) the amount and substantiality of the portion used in relation to the copyrighted work as a whole; and (c) the effect of the use upon the potential market for or value of the copyrighted work.[52] In India, fair use is determined on the same four factors.

Thus, in *M/s. Blackwood & Sons Ltd.* v. *A.N. Parasuraman,*[53] Madras High Court while determining fair use the purpose for which a copyrightable material was used was considered. The Apex Court in *R.G. Anand* v. *Deluxe Films,*[54] the opinion of the spectator or the reader after seeing or reading the works, i.e., nature of the copyrighted work was considered. Subsequently, in the *Chancellor Masters and Scholars of the University of Oxford* v. *Narendera Publishing House,*[55] where the quantum and value of the matter taken was considered as also the fourth factor, i.e., the effect on the market share of the prior work was considered. In *India TV Independent News Service Pvt. Ltd.* v. *Yashraj Films Pvt. Ltd.,*[56] the Delhi High Court held that *de minimis* a valid defence for copyright infringement. However, *Bridgeport Music Inc.* v. *Dimension Films,*[57] the Court in the United States adopted the bright-line rule and negated application of either *de minimis* or substantial similarity. A physical lifting of a mere two seconds of the plaintiff's sound recording for a rap song was held to be an infringement on the reason that a physical lifting lacked intellectual input, and thus the need for a bright-line rule. Its logic was that by not paying, the defendant was unjustly enriched, and secondly, there existed a market for sample licenses.

---

50. Visit: http://www.1024cores.net/home/parallel-computing/cache-oblivious-algorithms.
51. *See*, Copyright (Amendment) Act, 2012, Section 32(i), for clause (a).
52. *See*, *Ringgold* v. *Black Entm't Television Inc.*, 126 F. 3d 70 (2d Cir. 1997).
53. AIR 1959 Mad. 410.
54. AIR 1978 SC 1613: 1978 (4) SCC 118.
55. 2008 (38) PTC 385 (Del): MIPR 2008 (3) 402.
56. MIPR 2013 (1) 104: 2013 (53) PTC 586 (Del).
57. 401 F. 3d 647 (6th Cir. 2004).

In *Super Cassettes Industries Limited* v. *Mr. Chintamani Rao,*[58] the learned Counsel for the defendant India TV has also sought to place heavy reliance on the Copyright (Amendment) Bill, 2010 which, *inter alia*, proposes to amend Section 52 of the Copyright Act to make the fair use defence available to all works including cinematograph films and sound recordings. The proposed amendment replaces the words "literary, dramatic, musical or artistic work" used in Sections 52(1)(a) and 52(1)(b) with the expression "any work". It is argued that the amendment is clarificatory and does not seek to make a substantive change in the law as it exists at present. It is argued that the primary purpose of Clause 31 of the Bill is to provide that works which are stored in an electronic medium for the purposes of fair use do not constitute infringing copies. The purpose of the amendment is to exclude the process of "caching" from the charge of infringement. But, the court held that taking of plaintiff's copyright works by defendants was, *prima facie*, substantial and purpose of such copying of plaintiffs' copyright works, in no way, appeared to be for purpose of criticism or review of said works, or of any other works. Usage of said copyright works of plaintiff also could not be said to be for purpose of reporting current events, much less said usage could be described as a fair dealing of plaintiffs' copyright works. Plaintiffs had clearly made out, *prima facie*, a case in their favour for grant of interim protection.

Linking

Linking is perhaps the most effective information sharing tool on the Internet. Links are references to the Internet addresses, i.e., statements of locations without original contents, which fall under the categories of facts. There are three types of links that can be used in a web page: (i) relative link, (ii) site root relative link, and (iii) absolute link. A relative link points to a location that is relative to the current page. Having a link to "index.html" is a relative link that points to the "index.html" page in the same directory as the current page. Links can also be made to "./index.html" to go to "index.html" in the parent directory. A site root-relative link points to a location that is relative to the root directory of the site. They begin with a slash "/". Having a link to "/index.html" is a site root-relative link that points to the "index.html" page in the root directory of the site. One common use of this is to have all images in an image directory and then to link to images with links like "/images/mypic.jpg". An absolute link is simply one that includes the entire path to the file like "http://www.contoso.com/news/index.html". These are generally used for links that need to point to a different site than the one on which your page is located.[59]

A hyperlink is a location reference that the web browser interprets, often by underlining the text in blue, to "link" to another information resource when clicked. In HTML (HyperText Markup Language, the code used to write web pages), a hyperlink looks like this: link. "Deep linking" refers to the creation of hyperlinks to a page other than a website's homepage. For example, instead of pointing a link at http://www.chillingeffects.org, this site's "homepage", another site might link directly to the linking FAQ at http://www.chillingeffects.org/linking/faq. Some website owners complain that deep links "steal" traffic to their homepages or

58. 2012 (49) PTC 1 (Del).
59. Visit: http://blogs.msdn.com/b/xweb/archive/2010/04/26/different-types-of-hyperlinks.aspx.

disrupt the intended flow of their websites.[60] Deep linking, hyperlinking to another website's interior pages, was the subject of considerable controversy in the late 1990s and early 2000s because it allowed consumers to bypass a website's advertising-rich homepage. This could lead to significant financial losses in advertising revenue based on page impressions.

In *Shetland Times Ltd.* v. *Dr. Janathan Wills and Zet News Ltd.*,[61] the issue was whether "deeplinking" to internal or embedded pages of the Shetland Times' ("Times") website by the Shetland Times ("News") through the use of the plaintiff website's news headlines was an act of copyright infringement under the United Kingdom's Copyright Designs and Patents Act of 1988. The plaintiff (Times) sought, and received, an injunction precluding such deep linking. In granting the injunction, the court held only that the plaintiff had presented a *prima facie* case of copyright infringement under the Act because it could not be said that the websites at issue were not covered by the Act or that the Times's headlines which the News had used as linking text were not protected under the Act as "literary works". The News appealed this ruling and the matter settled before trial. As part of that settlement, the News agreed to link only through the Times/News website's front page and agreed to include a legend identifying the headlines as from The Shetland Times wherever such headlines were posted on the News' website.

In *Ticket Master* v. *Tickets.com,*[62] Ticketmaster sued its rival online ticket vendor, Tickets.com, for allegedly deep linking to copyrighted information from the Ticketmaster site in violation of Ticketmaster's rights. In this case the United States District Court for the Central District of California finding that deep linking did not violate the Copyright Act, 1976 because it did not involve direct copying. The decision permitted Tickets.com to place deep links to Ticketmaster. In *Perfect 10 Inc.* v. *Amazon.com,*[63] the United States Court of Appeals for the Ninth Circuit specifically addressed the copyright status of linking. The court held that Google's framing and hyperlinking as part of an image search engine constituted a fair use of Perfect 10's images because the use was highly transformative. The court pointed out that Google made available to the public the new and highly beneficial function of "improving access to [pictorial] information on the Internet". This had the effect of recognising that "search engine technology provides an astoundingly valuable public benefit, which should not be jeopardized just because it might be used in a way that could affect somebody's sales."

Links are facts, therefore, they should not be copyrightable. In *R.G. Anand* v. *Delux Films*,[64] the Supreme Court of India held that facts are not copyrightable and there is no copyright in an actual event too. In *Harper and Row, Publishers, Inc.* v. *Nation Enterprises*,[65] the American Supreme Court also held that the most fundamental axiom of copyright law is that "no author may copyright his ideas or the facts he narrates". Facts and discoveries, of course, are not themselves subject to copyright protection. At the same time, however, it is beyond dispute that compilations of facts are within the subject matter of copyright. Compilations were expressly mentioned in the Copyright Act of 1909, and again in the

60. Visit: http://www.chillingeffects.org/linking/faq.cgi.
61. 1997 F.S.R. (Ct. Sess. O.H.), 24 October 1996.
62. 54 U.S.P.Q. 2d 1344 (C.D. Cal. 2000).
63. 508 F. 3d 1146 (9th Cir. 2007).
64. AIR 1978 SC 1613: (1978) 4 SCC 118.
65. 471 U.S. 539, 556 (1985).

Copyright Act of 1976. Thus, in *Feist Publications Inc.* v. *Rural Telephone Service Co.*,[66] the American Supreme Court held that factual compilations must entail some originality as to the selection and arrangement of facts they contain. Referring this decision in the *Eastern Book Company* v. *D.B. Modak*,[67] the Supreme Court of India held that originality does not signify novelty; a work may be original even though it closely resembles other works so long as the similarity is fortuitous, not the result of copying. The Court further observed: "no one claim originality as to the facts. This is because facts do not owe their origin to an act of authorship." The distinction is one between creation and discovery is that in case of creation the first person to find and report a particular fact has not created the fact. In this case, he or she has merely discovered its existence. Factual compilations, on the other hand, may possess the requisite originality. The compilation author typically chooses which facts to include, in what order to place them, and how to arrange the collected data so that they may be used effectively by readers. These choices as to selection and arrangement, so long as they are made independently by the compiler and entail a minimal degree of creativity, are sufficiently original. Thus, if the compilation author clothes facts with an original collocation of words, he or she may be able to claim a copyright in this written expression.

In India, Copyright (Amendment) Act, 2012 inserted clause (c) to Section 52 of the Copyright Act, 1957 which provides that transient and incidental storage of a work or performance for the purposes of providing electronic links, access or integration, where such links, access or integration has not been expressly prohibited by the right holder, shall not constitute infringement. The new clause (c) of Section 52 while providing for fair use exemption for transient or incidental storage of works, also provides for the Internet service provider's liability when read with the addition of rights of storage and definition of infringement. A proviso has been added to this clause to provide a safe harbour as per international norms to the Internet service providers, as they are merely carriers of information provided by others. This is generally referred to as "notice and take down procedure".[68] If the person responsible for the storage of the copy has received a written complaint from the owner of copyright in the work, that the transient or incidental storage is an infringement, such person responsible for the storage shall refrain from facilitating such access for a period of twenty-one days or till he receives an order from the competent court refraining from facilitating access. In case no such order is received before the expiry of such period of twenty-one days, he may continue to provide the facility of such access.

E-Mail and Bulletin Board Service

In *Google India Private Limited.* v. *Visaka Industries Limited*,[69] the Haryana High Court observed that the intent of the Bulletin Board Service (BBS) operator was irrelevant and applied strict liability principle of the Copyright Act. The BBS operator was liable for direct infringement as a result of the defendant's system itself equipped unauthorized copies of

66. 499 U.S. 340 (1991).
67. AIR 2008 SC 809: (2008) 1 SCC 1.
68. *See*, *Myspace Inc.* v. *Super Cassettes Industries Ltd.*, 2017 (69) PTC 1 (Del): 236 (2017) DLT 478; *Super Cassetes Industries Ltd.* v. *Myspace Inc.*, 2011 (48) PTC 49 (Del): MIPR 2011 (2) 303.
69. 2017 (4) ALD 327: 2017 (1) ALT 620.

proprietary work and created them offered to the public. It was irrelevant that the suspect did not create infringing copies itself. An electronic mail (or e-mail) is the most frequently used service on the Internet. E-mail consists of messages which are sent and received using the Internet. E-mail is sent and received through electronic "post offices" known as mail servers. Thus, sending an e-mail can be described as sending a message or a letter to someone through the electronic medium, i.e., the computer.[70] Once a person enters the address of the recipient, compose your message, and click send, your e-mail software handles the delivery. To read own e-mail, one must retrieve it from the mail server. Like a postal address, an e-mail address specifies the destination of an electronic message. An Internet e-mail address looks like this: user name@ domain name. The user name is a unique name that identifies the recipient. The domain name is the address. Subject contains the main topic of the message in brief. Recipients see this in their summary of incoming e-mails. Attachment contains the names of files that you may be sending, for example, a word-processing document or a spreadsheet.[71] An e-mail has the following properties: (i) the user produces, sends, and usually also receives mail at a computer screen, a terminal, or a personal computer; (ii) the messages sent have a data structure, which can be handled by a computer. This structure can be more or less advanced: it can, for example, allow the user to ask his computer to find the last received letter from person *N* about the subject *XYZ*, or to find the outgoing message, to which a certain incoming message replies. The e-mail needs facilities to store messages. Messages are usually stored in personal mailboxes for senders and recipients, but some systems for group communication employ storage areas shared by several users.[72]

In all copyright infringement suits including suits relating to copyright infringement in Internet, the speedy services of summons to defendant is a controversial issue. According to Rule 9 of Order 5 of the Code of Civil Procedure, 1908 summons to defendant residing within the jurisdiction of the court shall be served through court officer or approved courier service. Summons can also be served by registered post, speed post, courier service, fax, message, e-mail service or by any other permissible means of transmission. Where the defendant is residing outside the jurisdiction of the court, the summons shall be served through an officer of the court within whose jurisdiction the defendant resides. The court shall treat refusal of acceptance as a valid service. Where summons is properly addressed, prepaid and duly sent by registered post acknowledgment due, there will be a presumption of valid service of summons even in the absence of an acknowledgement slip.[73] Speedy service of summons or notices is essential for speedy dispensation of justice. However, in various Courts, the statistical data indicates that, on account of delay in process of serving, arrears keep on mounting. In Delhi itself, the input indicates that fifty per cent of the arrears in Courts particularly in commercial cases are on account of delay in process serving. Keeping note of this fact, the Apex Court in *Central Electricity Regulatory Commission* v. *National Hydroelectric Power Corporation Ltd.*,[74] felt the necessity to avoid the delay in process serving and suggested that the service

---

70. Visit: www.lib.unc.edu/cws.
71. *See*, Olle Bälter, *Electronic Mail in a Working Context* (Stockholm 1998).
72. *See*, Jacob Palme, *Electronic mail* (Artech House, London, 1996).
73. *Subodh S. Salaskar* v. *Jayprakash M. Shah*, AIR 2008 SC 3086: (2008) 13 SCC 689; *Indu Bhushan* v. *Munna Lal*, JT 2007 (3) SC 171: 2007 (2) SCALE 514.
74. 2010 (7) SCALE 485: (2010) 10 SCC 280.

of notice/s may be effected by e-mail. Accordingly, the following directions were issued to expedite the service of summons and notices issued in matters before it:

1. In addition to normal mode of service, service of Notice(s) may be effected by e-mail for which the advocate(s) on-record will, at the time of filing of petition/ appeal, furnish to the filing counter a soft copy of the entire petition/appeal in PDF format;
2. The advocate(s) on-record shall also simultaneously submit e-mail addresses of the respondent(s) Companies/Corporation(s) to the filing counter of the Registry. This will be in addition to the hard copy of the petition/appeal;
3. If the Court issues notice, then, in that event alone, the Registry will send such an additional notice at the e-mail addresses of the respondent(s) Companies/ Corporation(s) via E-mail;
4. The Registry will also send Notice at the e-mail address of the advocate(s) for respondent(s) Companies/Corporation(s), who have filed caveat. Advocate(s) on-record filing caveat shall provide his/her e-mail address for effecting service; and
5. Within two weeks from today, Cabinet Secretariat shall also provide centralised e-mail addresses of various Ministries/Departments/Regulatory Authorities along with the names of the Nodal Officers, if already appointed, for the purposes of service.

The Apex Court further clarified that service of summons by e-mail is in addition to the modes of service mentioned in the existing Supreme Court Rules. This facility, for the time being, is extended to commercial litigation and to those cases where the advocate(s) on-record seeks urgent interim reliefs. The Court also directed for sending a copy of its order to all the High Courts for necessary action.

Electronic bulletin board systems are vital tools for computer-mediated communication among computer users. This system started in the late 1970s, as a means of communication for virtual community existing in Cyberspace where participants usually under pseudonames may send and receive public and private messages to each other on any topic, transfer software, play online games, etc.[75] Bulletin board is a development of the e-mail communication. Thus, a bulletin board is a surface intended for the posting of public messages, for example, to advertise items wanted or for sale, announce events, or provide information. Bulletin boards are often made of a material such as cork to facilitate addition and removal of messages, or they can be placed on computer networks so people can leave and erase messages for other people to read and see.[76] It is a computer system running software that allows users to connect and log into the system using a terminal program. Once logged in, a user can perform functions such as uploading and downloading software and data, reading news and bulletins, and exchanging messages with other users, either through e-mail, public message boards, and sometimes via direct chatting.[77] High quality digitised pictures, music, software are all capable of being uploaded and downloaded from bulletin boards. Illegal distribution of

75. Visit: http://gndec.ac.in/~librarian/sveri/dbit1504023.pdf.
76. Visit: http://en.wikipedia.org/wiki/Bulletin_board.
77. Visit: http://en.wikipedia.org/wiki/Bulletin_board_system.

copyright materials on computer bulletin boards has become a serious problem. The users who upload and download copyrighted materials without the permission of the copyright owners are infringements of copyright law except the cases mentioned in Section 52(1)(a) of the Copyright Act, 1957. Section 52(1) expressly provides that certain acts enumerated therein shall not constitute an infringement of copyright. The Copyright (Amendment) Act, 2012 extended the scope of Section 52 to ensure that introduction of new technology will also be covered under this new Section 52(1)(a). By the 2012 amendment, an explanation has been inserted to clause (1)(a) of Section 52 to clarify that storing of any work in any electronic medium for the specified purposes, including the incidental storage of a computer program which in itself is not an infringing copy, shall not be an infringement.

RIGHT OF REPRODUCTION IN INTERNET

The Concept

It is a matter of fact that the one of the important copyright implications by the transmission and use of works on the Internet is the exclusive right of reproduction of the author, i.e., "to reproduce the work in any material form including the storing of it in any medium by electronic means".[78] Section 14 of the Copyright Act, 1957 states that copyright is an exclusive right, subject to the provisions of the Act, to do or authorise the doing of the acts enumerated in the said section, in respect of a work or any substantial part thereof. The Act provides for "the exclusive rights flowing from such ownership as set out in Section 14."[79] Further, under Sections 14(i)(a) and (e), the right of reproduction of a literary, dramatic, musical work, sound recording in any medium by electronic means are recognised. The concept of reproduction has been discussed in the House of Lords decision of *Ladbroke (Football) Ltd.* v. *William Hill (Football) Ltd.*[80] In this case, the court held that copyright gives the exclusive right to do certain things including "reproducing the work in any material form", and reproduction includes reproduction of a substantial part of the work. Explaining the meaning of reproduction the court further observed:

> Broadly, reproduction means copying, and does not include cases where an author or compiler produces a substantially similar result by independent work without copying. And, if he does copy, the question whether he has copied a substantial part depends much more on the quality than on the quantity of what he has taken. One test may be whether the part which he has taken is novel or striking, or is merely a commonplace arrangement of ordinary words or well-known data. So it may sometimes be a convenient short cut to ask whether the part taken could by itself be the subject of copyright. But, in my view, that is only a short cut, and the more correct approach is first to determine whether the plaintiffs' work as a whole is "original" and protected by copyright, and then to inquire whether the part taken by the defendant is substantial.

78. Copyright Act, 1957, Sections 14(i)(a) and (e). *See, Rediff.Com India Ltd.* v. *E-Eighteen.Com Ltd.*, MIPR 2013 (2) 333: 2013 (55) PTC 294 (Del).
79. *See, Weider Publications* v. *Shri Pushpendra Srivastav,* 2013 1 AD (Delhi) 501: 2013 (53) PTC 275 (Del).
80. [1964] 1 All E.R. 465: (1964) 108 S.J. 135.

Thus, even a substantial reproduction of a copyrighted work is sufficient to make it a copy.[81] The Delhi High Court in *Escorts Construction Equipment Ltd.* v. *Action Construction Equipment Pvt. Ltd.*,[82] held that a reproduction is also deemed to have taken place if there is substantial copying of an earlier work. In *Mohendra Chandra* v. *Emperor*,[83] the Calcutta High Court has clarified that which comes to near the original, as to suggest that original to the mind of every person seeing it. Thus, there is no reproduction if there is no copying of the works and the defendant makes his own version, or goes to the common source if any.

It appears from the above discussion that the right of reproduction is one of the basic rights available to a copyright owner. To reproduce means to produce again, to produce a copy. It is the action or process of bringing again before the mind in the same form. In this sense, even storage of the work in electronic means such as floppy discs, CD-ROMs or in computers shall be deemed to be a reproduction. This has been incorporated to guard the interest of right holders in the digital context. In the case of cinematograph films and sound recordings, the definition clause itself brings digital fixations within the scope of reproduction. But the term storage has not been defined. There is a possibility of including temporary storage also within reproduction right. This may create problems for the Internet users and service providers thereby tilting the traditional balance of copyright law.

Again, the right of reproduction is at the core of Internet activity because any transmission of a work or an object of related rights pre-supposes the upholding of that work or object into memory of a computer or other digital device. In addition, when the work is the transmitted over networks, multiple copies are made in the memory of computers in the networks at numerous points. "Copies" in the digital environment are something else than what they are in the case of printed word. For example, a node computer may receive only a few packets of the total data, the other packets being passed through a different route and therefore a different node computer's RAM. Whether the law considers these partial images as a "copy" of the work? How can interim partial images of data stored in RAM be deemed a "copy" of a work, in the case where there is no point in time at which the entire work is available in a single RAM? It is therefore necessary to examine how the right of reproduction of authors is infringed by making of such copies by different computers in the network and others who access such works.

In *Star India Pvt. Ltd.* v. *Roy MA*,[84] plaintiffs are leading sports broadcaster in India and the exclusive licencee of media rights to various sporting events/properties. They are also the owners of a network of sports television channels and by virtue of necessary downlink permissions from the Ministry of Information and Broadcasting. The plaintiffs alleged that the defendant's websites carry infringing content. It is also alleged that a Uniform Resource Locator (URL) at which the cricket matches are available for viewing on the plaintiffs' website is http://starsports.com/cricket/index. In order to protect and enforce its exclusive rights, the plaintiffs engaged the services of a third party agency to monitor websites and gather evidence of their infringing activity. After carefully monitoring the activities of various websites for the past 3 (three) events for which the plaintiffs had exclusive rights, and in light of the evidence

81. *Keld Ellentoft India (P) Ltd.* v. *KE Burgmann*, 2003 (26) PTC 541 (Del).
82. AIR 1999 Del. 73.
83. AIR 1928 Cal. 359.
84. 2014 LawSuit (Del) 4442.

gathered against such websites, a list of 150 (one hundred and fifty) "Rogue Websites" has been prepared, whose primary business model appears to be providing illegal content for viewing and download. The court held that the plaintiffs have been able to make out a strong *prima facie* case for grant of ex-parte order. The balance of convenience also lies in favour of the plaintiffs and against the defendants. In case the interim orders are not passed, the plaintiffs would suffer irreparable loss and injury. In ad-interim orders, the court restrained defendant from hosting, streaming, broadcasting, rebroadcasting, retransmitting, exhibiting, making available for viewing and downloading, providing access to and/or communicating to the public (including to its subscribers and users), through the Internet, in any manner whatsoever, the plaintiffs' broadcast.

International Protection

The international law had no occasion to address the protection of rights on the Internet till recently. This is evident from the fact that the TRIPS Agreement has no provision to solve these problems.[85] Even though there was the possibility to interpret Article 9 of the Berne Convention dealing with reproduction right in the digital environment, there was considerable opposition having regard to the background in which this Article was introduced in Berne.[86] There is also no provision in the Berne Convention capable of interpretation that can afford protection to the communication to public or publications right of the author in digital context. Needless to say that there is hardly any provision to enforce the rights. The TRIPS Agreement even though dealt with general provisions dealing with enforcement of rights, the issue of protecting technological measures used to protect digital materials was not addressed.

These issues for the first time caught the attention of the international community in the WIPO Copyright Treaty, 1996 (WCT).[87] Though there was general agreement among nations to protect communication to public right, there were serious objections regarding the nature; and extend of reproduction right in digital format. The right of making available to the public the work in such a way that the members of the public may access the work from a place and at a time individually chosen by them was incorporated in the WCT to cover the Internet/

85. Agreement on Trade-Related Aspects of Intellectual Property Rights, Marrakech, April 15, 1994, came into force January, 1 1995. Membership in TRIPS Agreement coincides with membership in the World Trade Organization except for least developed countries, which were granted a grace period; observer governments of the World Trade Organization are marked observer in the table below. India ratified it on January 1, 1995.
86. Berne Convention for the Protection of Literary and Artistic Works, Berne, September 9, 1886, came into force on December 5, 1887. India ratified on April 1, 1928. For the text of the Convention, see, Alfredo Ilardiand and Michael Blakency, *International Encyclopedia of Intellectual Property Treaties* (Oxford University Press, 2004). The leading works on *Berne Convention* are, Ricketson, *The Berne Convention for the Protection of literary and Artistic Works: 1886–1986* (1987); Nordemann, *International Copyright and Neighbouring Rights Law (1990)*; Nimmer and Geller, *International Copyright Law and Practice* (1988).
87. WIPO Copyright Treaty, Geneva, December 20, 1996, came into force March 6, 2002. India has not ratified so far. See R.V. Vaidyanatha Ayyar, "Interest or Right? The Process and Politics of a Diplomatic Conference on Copyright," *Journal of World Intellectual Property* (1998) p. 3; Jorg Reinbothe, Maria Martin-Part and Silke Von Lewinski, "The New WIPO Treaties: A First Resume," 19 *European International Property Report* (1997) p. 171.

online communication of the works.[88] It was further made clear that providing mere physical facilities for enabling or making a communication does not in itself amount to communication with the meaning of this provision. This is to ensure protection for the service providers who provide mere physical facilities for Internet communication. Since there was no agreement to treat both temporary and permanent reproduction as part of reproduction right in digital format, no specific provision was included in the WCT in this regard. But considering the importance of this right in the digital context it was agreed to extend Article 9 of Berne Convention to digital environment and expressly stated that storage of works in digital form would constitute reproduction as understood in Berne. Agreed statement concerning Article 1(4) read:

> The reproduction right, as set out in Article 9 of the Berne Convention, and the exceptions permitted there under, fully apply in the digital environment, in particular to the use of works in digital form. It is understood that the storage of protected work in digital form in an electronic medium constitutes a reproduction within the meaning of Article 9 of the Berne Convention.

It was the failure of the international community due to the pressure from interest groups to reach consensus on the nature of the liability of service providers and users that lead this situation. This left the international norms regarding the rights of users of digital materials and the liability of the service providers unsettled. But it was agreed that all the exceptions and limitations recognised under the Berne Convention would be applicable to digital materials as well.[89] This gives freedom to nations to introduce appropriate provision in their domestic law to protect the interest of the users and service providers without sacrificing the interest of the owners. This will lead to different types of norms followed by different countries for a technology that has no territoriality putting the content providers and service providers into difficulties.

One of the major achievements of WCT is the provision regarding protection of right. It is obligatory on the part of nations to take adequate measures to protect the technological measures[90] and right management system.[91] Article 12 of the WCT provides thus:

> Contracting Parties shall provide adequate and effective legal remedies against any person knowingly performing any of the following acts knowing, or with respect to civil remedies having reasonable grounds to know, that it will induce, enable, facilitate or conceal an infringement of any right covered by this Treaty or the Berne Convention:

---

88. *See*, Zakir Thomas, "Overview of Changes to the Indian Copyright Law", 17 *Journal of Intellectual Property Rights* (2012) pp. 324–334.
89. See Article 10 read; "It is understood that the provisions of Article 10 permits Contracting Parties to carry forward and appropriately extend in to the digital environment limitations and exception in their national laws which have been considered acceptable under the Berne Convention. Similarly these provisions should be understood permit Contracting Parties to devise new exceptions and limitation that are appropriate in the digital network environment". It is also understood that Article 10(2) neither reduces not extends the scope of applicability of the limitation and exceptions permitted by the Berne Convention".
90. Article 11 read: "Contracting Parties shall provide adequate legal production and effective legal remedies against the circumvention of effective technological measures that are used by authors in connection with the exercise of their rights under this treaty or the Berne Convention and that restrict acts, in respect of their works. Which are not authorized by the authors concerned or permitted by law."
91. *See*, Article 12.

(i) to remove or alter any electronic rights management information without authority;

(ii) to distribute, import for distribution, broadcast or communicate to the public, without authority, works or copies of works knowing that electronic rights management information has been removed or altered without authority.

Article 19 of the WIPO Performances and Phonograms Treaty, 1996 (WPPT) contains nearly identical language. According to Article 19(2) of WPPT "rights management information" means information which identifies the performer, the performance of the performer, the producer of the phonogram, the phonogram, the owner of any right in the performance or phonogram, or information about the terms and conditions of use of the performance or phonogram, and any numbers or codes that represent such information, when any of these items of information is attached to a copy of a fixed performance or a phonogram or appears in connection with the communication or makes available of a fixed performance or a phonogram to the public. The workings of these provisions give sufficient flexibility to introduce appropriate provisions keeping in mind the interest of the users, manufactures of technology and that of the owners of work.[92]

United States Digital Act

The appropriate application of the reproduction right in the case of temporary copies in computer random access memory continues to be a subject of debate world over. Hence, the Digital Millennium Copyright Act, 1998[93] (DMCA) was enacted in the United States to supplement the copyright law that implements two treaties of the World Intellectual Property Organization (WIPO). These treaties are: the WIPO Copyright Treaty, 1996 and the WIPO Performances and Phonograms Treaty, 1996. It criminalises production and dissemination of technology, devices, or services intended to circumvent measures (commonly known as Digital Rights Management or DRM) that control access to copyrighted works. It also criminalises the act of circumventing an access control, whether or not there is actual infringement of copyright itself. In addition, the DMCA heightens the penalties for copyright infringement on the Internet. The DMCA is divided into five titles:

1. Title I, the "WIPO Copyright and Performances and Phonograms Treaties Implementation Act of 1998", implements the WIPO treaties.
2. Title II, the "Online Copyright Infringement Liability Limitation Act", creates limitations on the liability of online service providers for copyright infringement when engaging in certain types of activities. The Title two of the DMCA addresses the issue of Internet Service Providers (ISPs) responsibility for copyright infringement committed by their subscribers. The DMCA says that ISPs are not responsible for

92. For detail discussion see David Bainbridge, *Intellectual Property*, Person Education (Singapore Ptc. Ltd., 2003); W. R. Cornish, *Intellectual Property: Cases and Materials* (Sweet and Maxwell, London, 1999); W.R. Cornish, *Intellectual Property* (Sweet and Maxwell, London, 1996); Holyook and Torremans, *Intellectual Property Law* (Butterworths, London, 1995); David I. Brainbridge, *Intellectual Property Law: Cases and Materials* (Pitman Publishing, London, 1995).

93. Pub. L. No. 105-304, 112 Stat. 2860 (Oct. 28, 1998). *See*, *Super Cassetes Industries Ltd.* v. *Myspace Inc.,* MIPR 2011 (2) 303: 2011 (48) PTC 49 (Del).

the actions of their clients as long as they meet a number of provisions. They first have to meet one of the four definitions of an ISP as set out by the DMCA. Each of the four types has a different set of provisions the ISP must comply with. They then have to inform their users of and carry out a policy which says that people caught using their service for infringement multiple times will have their subscriptions to the service cancelled. Finally, this section of the DMCA gives the copyright holder a new right to call upon the courts to subpoena an ISP for the identification of an alleged copyright infringer.

3. Title III, the "Computer Maintenance Competition Assurance Act", creates an exemption for making a copy of a computer program by activating a computer for purposes of maintenance or repair.
4. Title IV contains six miscellaneous provisions, relating to the functions of the Copyright Office, distance education, the exceptions in the Copyright Act for libraries and for making ephemeral recordings, "webcasting" of sound recordings on the Internet, and the applicability of collective bargaining agreement obligations in the case of transfers of rights in motion pictures.
5. Title V, the "Vessel Hull Design Protection Act", creates a new form of protection for the design of vessel hulls.

Several judicial decisions of the United States courts have discussed a large number of issues on protection of right of reproduction on the Internet. In July 2002, *Edelman* v. *N2H2*[94] American Civil Liberties Union filed a suit on the behalf of Benjamin Edelman, a computer researcher at Berkman Centre for Internet and Society, seeking a declaratory judgment to affirm his first amendment rights when reverse engineering the censorware product of defendant N2H2 in case he intended to publish the finding. N2H2 filed a motion to dismiss, which the court granted. In *RealNetworks, Inc.* v. *DVD Copy Control Association, Inc.,*[95] the DVD Copy Control Association won a suit against RealNetworks for violating copyright law in selling its RealDVD software, allowing users to copy DVDs and store them on a hard drive. The DVD Copy Control Association claimed that Real violated the Digital Millennium Copyright Act by circumventing anti-piracy measures ARccOS Protection and RipGuard, as well as breaking Real's licencing agreement with the MPAA's Content Scrambling System. The United States District Court concluded that RealNetworks violated the anti-circumvention and anti-trafficking provisions of the Digital Millennium Copyright Act when the DVD copying software RealDVD bypasses the copy protection technologies of DVD.

In *Viacom Inc.* v. *YouTube, Google Inc.,*[96] Viacom sued YouTube, a video-sharing site owned by Google, alleging that YouTube had engaged in "brazen" and "massive" copyright infringement by allowing users to upload and view hundreds of thousands of videos owned by Viacom without permission. A motion for summary judgment seeking dismissal was filed by Google and was granted in 2010 on the grounds that the Digital Millennium Copyright Act's "safe harbor" provisions shielded Google from Viacom's copyright infringement claims. In 2012, on appeal to the United States Court of Appeals for the Second Circuit, it was

94. Civil Action No. 02-CV-11503-RGS (2003).
95. 641 F. Supp. 2d 913 (2009).
96. No. 07 Civ. 2103.

overturned in part. On April 18, 2013, District Judge Stanton again granted summary judgment in favour of defendant YouTube.

In *IO Group, Inc.* v. *Veoh Networks, Inc.*,[97] IO Group, Inc. on June 23, 2006 filed a complaint against Veoh Networks, Inc. in the United States District Court for California's Northern District. IO Group alleged that Veoh was responsible for copyright infringement by allowing videos owned by IO Group to be accessed through Veoh's online service without permission over 40,000 times between the dates June 1 and June 22. Veoh is a Flash video site relying on user contributed content. IO Group argued that since Veoh transcoded user uploaded videos to Flash format it became a direct infringer and the materials were under their direct control, thereby disqualifying them for the Digital Millennium Copyright Act safe harbor protection. The ruling judge disagreed with the argument, stating that "Veoh has simply established a system whereby software automatically processes user-submitted content and recasts it in a format that is readily accessible to its users. Veoh preselects the software parameters for the process from a range of default values set by the third party software.... But Veoh does not itself actively participate or supervise the uploading of files. Nor does it preview or select the files before the upload is completed. Instead, video files are uploaded through an automated process which is initiated entirely at the volition of Veoh's users." The Court has granted the Veoh's motion for summary judgment, on the basis of the Digital Millennium Copyright Act, holding that the defendant's video-sharing website complied and was entitled to the protection of the statute's "safe harbor" provision.

In *Vernor* v. *Autodesk, Inc.*,[98] referring the Digital Millennium Copyright Act, Timothy S. Vernor sued Autodesk in August 2007 alleging that Autodesk abused the Digital Millennium Copyright Act and disrupted his right to sell used software he bought at a garage sale. In May 2008, a federal district judge in Washington State dismissed Autodesk's argument that the software's licence agreement pre-empted the seller from his rights under the first-sale doctrine. In September 2010, the United States Court of Appeals for the Ninth Circuit reversed, holding that a software user is a licencee rather than an owner of a copy where the copyright owner (i) specifies that the user is granted a licence; (ii) significantly restricts the user's ability to transfer the software; and (ii) imposes notable use restrictions.

In *Lenz* v. *Universal Music Corp.*,[99] the United States District Court for the Northern District of California denied a motion to dismiss for failure to state a claim. Although the opinion is of limited precedential value—it was not scheduled for publication—the case has received substantial attention for its treatment of the fair use defence in the context of takedown notices under the Digital Millennium Copyright Act. Deciding the question of first impression, the court concluded that a copyright owner must determine whether a particular use is protected under fair use, in order to proceed under Section 512(c), which requires "a good faith belief that the use of the material in the manner complained of is not authorised by the copyright owner, its agent, or the law". District Judge Jeremy Fogel of San Jose, California ruled that copyright holders cannot order a deletion of an online file without determining whether that posting reflected "fair use" of the copyrighted material. The court held that a

97. 586 F. Supp. 2d 1132 (N.D. Cal. 2008).
98. 621 F.3d 1102 (9th Cir. 2010).
99. 572 F. Supp. 2d 1150, 1151 (N.D. Cal. 2008).

failure to consider fair use prior to issuing the takedown notice was sufficient to constitute a cause of action for misrepresentation.[100]

In *Flava Works, Inc.* v. *Gunter,*[101] the court denied the defendant safe harbour protection under Digital Millennium Copyright Act. The district court found that the defendant had knowledge of its users' infringing activity and also failed to prevent future infringing activity. As such the plaintiff's motion for preliminary injunction was granted. On appeal, however, the Seventh Circuit vacated the injunction, citing the standard set in *eBay Inc.* v. *MercExchange, L.L.C.,*[102] which states that courts should not rely on categorical rules as a standard for injunction.

In *Ouellette* v. *Viacom International Inc.,*[103] the court denied plaintiff's attempt to find liability for YouTube and Myspace's takedowns of the plaintiff's home-made videos. Despite potential fair use claims, the court found it impossible to use the Digital Millennium Copyright Act takedown provisions as a foundation for liability. The court found that the safe harbour provision serves to limit the liability of Internet service providers, not to create liability that could not otherwise be imposed under existing law independent of the Digital Millennium Copyright Act.

In *Sony Computer Entertainment America* v. *George Hotz,*[104] Sony sued Hotz over violating Section 1201 of the Digital Millennium Copyright Act as well as the Federal Fraud and Abuse Act due to facilitating consumers to jailbreak their Play Station 3 consoles. Hotz argued that because he had purchased the product, he had the right to do with it as he pleased. After three months, Sony and Hotz decided to settle out of court. This also included an injunction against George Hotz, barring him from hacking any more Sony products.

Indian Protection

Since the time of Copyright (Amendment) Act, 1984, a number of attempts have been made to make Indian Copyright Act, 1957 in tune with the digital technology. The Indian Copyright Act was amended a number of times to include computer program as literary work. But the major effort took place in the Copyright (Amendment) Act, 1994. After the amendment, the reproduction right of literary, dramatic or musical work includes storing of it in "any medium by electronic means".[105] The new definition sound recording[106] recognises recording of it in any medium. Thus, Section 2(xx) of the Copyright Act, 1957 provides "sound recording means a recording of sounds from which such sounds may be produced regardless of the

100. For detail discussion see Ayush Sharma, "Indian Perspective of Fair Dealing under Copyright Law: *Lex Lata or Lex Ferenda*?" 14 *Journal of Intellectual Property Rights* (2009) pp. 523–531; Giuseppina D'Agostino, "Healing Fair Dealing? A Comparative Copyright Analysis of Canada's Fair Dealing to UK Fair Dealing and US Fair Use," 53 McGill Law Journal (2008) pp. 309–363; Burrell Robert, "Reining in Law: Is Fair Use the Answer?", 4 *Intellectual Property Quarterly* (2001) pp. 361–388.
101. 689 F.3d 754 (7th Cir. 2012).
102. 547 U. S. 388 (2006).
103. 2012 WL 850921 (D. Mont. April 25, 2012).
104. No. CV11-0167 (N.D. Cal. Apr. 11, 2011).
105. *See*, Section 14(a)(ii) of the Copyright Act, 1957.
106. Inserted by the Copyright (Amendment) Act, 1994.

medium on which such recording is made or the method by which the sounds are produced". That will include digital medium as well. So the reproduction right recognised for these works in Section 14 will be applicable even to films and sound recordings in digital format. Only work left out is the artistic works since there is no specific mention of the right to storage of the work in the digital medium in Section 14(1)(c) similar to Section 14(1)(a)(i).

The right of making available recognised in the WCT in the context of digital technology is covered under the new definition of communication to public. According to new Section 2(ff) of the Copyright Act, 1957, "communication to the public means making any work or per-formance available for being seen or heard or otherwise enjoyed by the public directly or by any means of display or diffusion other than by issuing physical copies of it, whether simultaneously or at places and time chosen individually, regardless of whether any member of the public actually sees, hears or otherwise enjoys the work or performance so made available."[107] The Copyright (Amendment) Act, 2012 in connection to Section 14 regarding "meaning of copyright" provides the right of "commercial rental" to cinematograph films and sound recordings by amending the word "hire" to "commercial rental" in the existing provision relating to cinematograph films [clause (d)(ii)] and sound recording [clause (e)(ii)] with identical language providing for the right "to sell or give on commercial rental or offer for sale or for such rental, any copy of the" film or sound recording.

The obligation under Article 11 of the TRIPS Agreement, Article 7 of WCT and Article 9 of WPPT is to provide for "commercial rental" rights for computer program and cinematograph film. This right was introduced in 1994 in Section 14 using the word "hire". However, keeping in view the possibility of interpreting this term to include non-commercial hire and lending by libraries and educational institutions, the term "hire" in Section 14(b) for computer program was replaced with the term "commercial rental" in the 1999 Amendment. The term "hires" in Sections 14(d) and (c) with regard to a cinematograph film and sound recording, respectively, is now replaced with the term "commercial rental". Thus, the right of communication in Section 14 recognises the making available of the work regardless, of whether any member of the public actually sees, hears or otherwise enjoys the work so made available. This will enable the authors of all categories of work to protect the communication of the work through the Internet. The notion of publication of the work is also changed in the Act so as to enable publication through the new media. As per Section 3 of the Act, publication means making a work available to the public by issue of copies or by communicating the work to the public. This section read with the new definition of communication to public will enable the authors who publish the work through the Internet satisfy the requirement of publication to enjoy the benefits under the Act.

Section 37 of the Copyright Act provides that every broadcasting organisation shall have broadcast reproduction rights in respect of its broadcast. In *Star India Pvt. Ltd.* v. *Haneeth Ujwal*,[108] the plaintiffs are the leading sports broadcaster in India and the exclusive licencee of media rights to various sporting events/properties. The Delhi High Court held that any hosting, streaming, making available for viewing and/or communication to the public of the "2014 India–England Series Matches", as broadcast on the plaintiffs' Channels by any means

107. Inserted by the Copyright (Amendment) Act, 2012.
108. 2014 LawSuit (Del) 2711.

on any platform including the Internet and mobile, by any of the named or unnamed defendant websites would be illegal and amount to violation of the broadcast reproduction rights of the plaintiffs protected under Section 37 of the Copyright Act, 1957.

Thus, both reproduction and communication to public rights are now extended to substantially all kinds of works in digital format. But the Act has not deemed storage and it is a matter of interpretation to determine whether temporary and permanent reproduction will form part of this right. If temporary reproduction is included as part of reproduction right, the interest of users of digital materials and service providers of these materials will be affected. To overcome this corresponding changes there is nothing introduced in Section 52 dealing with permitted use of works without the permission of the owner. The activities of browsing, downloading, storing of digital materials for research or personal use may be treated as reproduction and the existing fair dealing provisions in Section 52 are inadequate to protect them particularly when the materials are in multimedia. Section 52(1)(a) covers only literary, dramatic, musical or artistic work. There is no provision permitting fair dealing or personal use of cinematograph film and sound recordings.

This is true in the case of temporary reproduction made by the service providers while routing the materials. Service providers providing link facilities including deep linking will be the worst affected since their activities will constitute reproduction. There is a need to introduce specific provision in Section 52 to permit these activities. The host providers will also be affected since they provide space for the purpose of storing materials for distribution through the Act. As of now they are liable if they have knowledge or reasonable ground to believing that the making available of the materials would be infringement of copyright.[109] The Information Technology Act, 2000 has in some cases added the responsibility of the service providers by mandating them to establish their innocence to escape liability.[110] The present provisions are inadequate to protect the interest of various kinds of service providers. In this context, it is important to note that no attempt was made in 1994 to introduce new provisions to protect the fair dealing rights of the users of digital materials that too on the Internet. So is the case with the liability of service providers. In *TV Independent News Service Pvt. Ltd.* v. *India Broadcast Live* (LLC),[111] the court has adopted a somewhat nuanced approach, at the same time, it noticed the absence of long arm statutes or provisions, in Indian law. That Parliament cannot be attributed the lack of awareness of such aspects is clear from provisions of the Information Technology Act, 2000. Sections 2(j)(k) and (1) contain definitions which are of the widest amplitude sufficient to accommodate the Internet and subsequent technologies.

The Copyright (Amendment) Act, 2012 has introduced provision relating to protect the electronic right management system and circumvention of technological measures. A new Section 65A has been introduced to provide for protection of technological measures used by a copyright owner to protect his rights on the work. Any person who circumvents an effective technological measure applied for protecting any of the rights, with the intention of infringing such rights, shall be punishable with imprisonment which may extend to two years and shall also be liable to fine. Another new Section 65B has also been introduced to provide protection of rights management information. Sub-section (1) provides, "Any person, who knowingly

109. *See*, Section 51(a)(ii).
110. *See*, Section 79 of the Information Technology Act, 2000.
111. 145 (2007) DLT 521.

(i) removes or alters any rights management information without authority, or (ii) distributes, imports for distribution, broadcasts or communicates to the public, without authority, copies of any work, or performance knowing that electronic rights management information has been removed or altered without authority, shall be punishable with imprisonment which may extend to two years and shall also be liable to fine." The proviso to the clause states that if the rights management information has been tampered with in any work, the owner of copyright in such work may also avail of civil remedies against the persons indulging in such acts. This amendment conforms to Article 12 of WCT and Article 19 of the WPPT relating to rights management information. The 2012 amendment has introduced a definition of "Rights Management Information" under Section 2(xa) of the Copyright Act, 1957. According to Section 2(xa) "Rights Management Information" means,

(a) the title or other information identifying the work or performance;
(b) the name of the author or performer;
(c) the name and address of the owner of rights;
(d) terms and conditions regarding the use of the rights; and
(e) any number or code that represents the information referred to in sub-clauses (a) to (d), but does not include any device or procedure intended to identify the user.

The case of the plaintiff in *Rediff.Com India Ltd.* v. *E-Eighteen.Com Ltd.*,[112] is that it is an online media company carrying on worldwide online business of providing news, communication, entertainment, stock market analysis and shopping services through the Internet. The plaintiff claims that the defendant company runs the website "www.moneycontrol.com"—a personal finance portal. In the month of May 2008, the plaintiff noticed on the Internet that the defendant had been infringing the plaintiff's copyright and passing it off as its own Dial, by displaying a deceptively similar Dial, similar to that of the plaintiffs, which was titled as "Mutual Fund Meter", to promote their business through the Internet on its website "moneycontrol.com". The plaintiff claims that by using a deceptively similar Dial to that of the plaintiffs Dial in the same line of business, i.e., imparting information relating to the capital markets, the defendant is infringing the plaintiff's copyright, as aforesaid. The plaintiff claims that it has suffered incalculable damage due to the aforesaid alleged infringement of its copyright detailed hereinabove. It was argued that the plaintiff's copyright in the literary-cum-artistic artwork as enumerated in Section 14 of the Copyright Act, 1957 has been infringing by the defendant company. Both in relation to literary and artistic works, clauses (a) and (c) of Section 14 grant the exclusive right to make any adaptation of the work of the owner of the copyright. By reference to the definition of the expression "adaptation" contained in Section 2(a) of the Act, it is claimed that the right to make adaptation only means "any use of such work involving its rearrangement or alteration".

The court held that a comparison of works of plaintiff with that of defendant, on whole, did not lead to inference or perception that two works were similar and that the dial adopted by the defendant is an "adaptation" of the plaintiff's work, also has no merit. Adaptation is defined in Section 2(a) to mean-in relation to a literary work or an artistic work, "the conversion of the work into a dramatic work by way of performance in public or otherwise";

---

112. MIPR 2013 (2) 333: 2013 (55) PTC 294 (Del).

in relation to literary or dramatic work, the same means, "any abridgement of the work or any version of the work in which the story or action is conveyed wholly or mainly by means of pictures in a form suitable for reproduction in a book, or in a newspaper, magazine or similar periodical report".[113] It also means in relation to any work, "any use of such work involving its re-arrangement or alteration". The copyright of the plaintiff in respect of its work aforesaid, is in its literary work, "How hot is the stock?" and the artistic work, i.e., the graphic representation of the Dial. The plaintiff has not claimed, and cannot claim, that its literary work or artistic work has been converted into a dramatic work. It cannot be claimed by the plaintiff that its literary work has been abridged by the defendant. The defendant's work cannot be labelled as use of the plaintiff's work involving its rearrangement or alteration. The plaintiff's work is not at all used by the defendant. For it to be an adaptation, falling in Section 2(a)(v) of the Act, the work of which it is claimed that an adaptation has been made, should itself be used with rearrangement or alteration.

Justification of Indian Protection

A close examination of clauses (a), (b) and (c) to Section 14 of the Copyright Act, 1957 shows that the right to reproduction constitutes only one of the bundles of rights accorded to a copyright owner of literary, dramatic, musical or artistic work.[114] The "right to reproduction" is not given to the copyright owner of cinematograph films and sound recordings but the "right to make a copy" is given instead. The right to translation, right to adaptation, right to performance of work etc. also involves reproduction in the generic sense of the term. Whether this difference is justified? Whether right to reproduction is an umbrella right or a residuary right? In case of artistic work, Section 14(c)(i) gave the right to reproduce the work in any material form to the copyright owner but the right to store the work in any medium by electronic means was not given.[115] The Copyright (Amendment) Act, 2012 has removed this lacuna and included storing of work in right of reproduction in case of artistic work also. However, in case of artistic works the right is elaborated to include depiction in three dimensions of a two dimensional work or in two dimensions of a three dimensional work.[116] Again question arises whether right to reproduction in Internet is sufficiently protected under the post 2012 amended Copyright Act 1957.

It is relevant to mention here that the Internet is the greatest communication medium of the contemporary era. It brings the whole world to a mouse click of a computer, making innumerable sources and references available in matter of seconds.[117] Copyright protection is provided to the authors of "original works" of literary, dramatic, musical, artistic, architectural

---

113. *See*, *Umesh Bharatbhai Thakkar* v. *State of Gujarat*, 2017 (4) RCR (Criminal) 948: 2017 Cri LJ 3713.
114. For various issues on copyright, see, Jatindra Kumar Das, "The TRIPS Agreement and Intellectual Property Rights" 16 (6) *International Trade Law and Regulation* (Sweet and Maxwell, London, 2010) pp. 166–174; Jatindra Kumar Das, *Intellectual Property Rights* (Kamal Law House, Kolkata, 2008).
115. *See*, *Super Cassettes Industries Pvt. Ltd.* v. *Trimurti Films Pvt. Ltd.*, 2018 (1) Bom CR 156.
116. Inserted by the Copyright (Amendment) Act, 2012 [w.e.f. 21.6.2012] Section 14(c)(i).
117. *See*, Mark A. Lemley, Dealing with Overlapping Copyrights on the Internet, 224 *Dayton Law Review* (1997) pp. 547–555; Neal Kumar Katyal, "Criminal Law in Cyber-space" 149 *University of Pennsylvania Law Review*, (2001) pp. 1006–1013.

and certain other intellectual works, both published and unpublished[118] while the Internet has been characterized as the largest threat to copyright protection since its inception.[119] The Internet is awash in information, a lot of it with varying degrees of copyright protection. Copyrighted works on the Internet include news stories, software, novels, screenplays, graphics, pictures, use Internet messages and even email. In fact, the frightening reality is that almost everything on the Internet is protected by copyright law. That can pose problems for the hapless surfer. In a modern world where information is a key factor and the information is available with the click of a mouse on a computer from the Internet, its an era of expansion.[120]

Internet is a medium which provides audio-visual interactive facility for doing business. Merely because it is a more advanced or superior medium, it does not impinge on the determination of the issue whether the merchandiser is carrying on business at a particular place. Prior to the advent of electronic commerce (e-commerce) over the Internet, and even now, business was and continues to be done over telephone and fax. Merely because a person has embarked upon an e-commerce business model, the tests which apply for determination of issues, such as-when and where the contract is made, or whether the vendor carries on business at the place where the merchandise may be sold, or service may be offered, would not change and would be the same as apply to communications over telephone and fax.[121] In *Yahoo, Inc* v. *Akash Arora*,[122] the Delhi High Court takes note of the transcendental nature of Internet business's wherein the Court observed that:

> "As a matter of fact in a matter where services are rendered through the domain name in the Internet, a very alert vigil is necessary and a strict view is to be taken for its easy access and reach by anyone from any corner of the globe."

Thus, one of the significant technological revolutions took place in the last century was the invention of digital technology. The emergence of Internet as a powerful and reliable platform for communication facilitated the creation of new works in the form of multimedia. Hence, these works are used not only for educational purposes but also for business. This led to the formation of new capital in the area of information creation and distribution for commercial gains in the global market, information technology industry is projected as one of the most powerful sources for capital formation and employment generation in the new century. The law relating to copyright proved to be one of the powerful legal instruments for the purpose of protecting capital investment in the area of cultural industries. It was also projected as a legal instrument that tried to maintain the delicate balance between the interest of owners of copyright and the general public. The traditional norms for the protection of copyright in the works were amended periodically to suit technological changes without sacrificing the public interest.[123]

---

118. *See*, *Myspace Inc.* v. *Super Cassettes Industries Ltd.*, 2017(69)PTC1(Del): MIPR2017(1)274; *Institute for Inner Studies* v. *Charlotte Anderson*, MIPR 2014 (129) 1; *Bayer Corporation* v. *Cipla, Union of India*, MIPR 2009 (3) 467: 2009 (41) PTC 634 (Del); *Syndicate of Press of the University of Cambridge* v. *Kasturi Lan*, 2006 (32) PTC 487 (Del); *McMillan and Co. Ltd.* v. *Kand J. Cooper*, AIR 1924 PC 75: 1924–19–LW 299.
119. *See*, Ejan Mackaay (ed.), *The Electronic Superhighway: The Shape of Technology and Law to Come*, (Kluwer Law International, 1995).
120. *Mrs. Ishi Khosla* v. *Anil Aggarwal*, (2007) ILR 1 Delhi 615: 2007 (34) PTC 370 (Del).
121. *See*, J. H. Smith Grahm, *Internet Law and Regulation* (Sweet and Maxual, London, 2002).
122. 1999 (19) PTC 201: 78 (1999) DLT 285.
123. *See*, the amendments introduced to the Copyright Act, 1957 in 1984, 1994, 1999 and 2012.

It has been argued that in the context of digital technology existing legal norms seem inadequate to solve the problems posed by this new technology.[124] The most fundamental issues in the field of copyright and related rights are the determination of the scope and protection of rights of copyright owners in the digital era.[125] Besides, the right of reproduction of an author is another controversial issue in the digital era. In the digital context the copyrighted works are stored in digital format and multiplied every time it is used or sent to another person. In some cases like browsing of materials in the web, transmission of materials, providing access by linking etc., the works are reproduced for a short period of time. The users may also download and store the material in the computer for the purpose of using it at their convenience. They may also transmit it to others for personal use. The question that arises is whether all forms of reproduction, whether temporary or permanent, form part of reproduction right in the digital context. The creators of content for the digital are argue that all forms of reproduction whether temporary or permanent must be treated as reproduction even though there can be exception in some cases. On the other hand the users of the work and the providers of access to these materials assert that reproduction in permanent fond alone must be recognized as right of reproduction.[126]

The question is who will take the responsibility to monitor violations of rights in Internet? Can the providers of Internet service be held responsible for the violations that take place in the Internet of which he may or may not have any information? If so, to what extent? Do they have the responsibility to monitor the violation? Can they absolve the responsibility even if the violations are brought to their notice? Are their activities like providing access by linking including deep linking, system caching, framing etc. are violations of the right of reproduction? Similarly, is the question of the liability of the users of the Internet is controversial in the contemporary era. Are the activities of browsing, downloading, storing and transmitting of works for any non-commercial purposes violation of the rights? Is this to be treated as fair use or use with implied licence? How the right of authors should be defined and what exceptions and limitations are to be permitted to such rights? How are the rights of authors to be enforced and administered in this digital environment? Can the existing worldwide copyrights law adequately protect the interests of those who hold copyright or are changes to the existing rules required?

Right to reproduction of the work in any material form is one of the basic rights available to a copyright owner as recognized under Section 14 of the Copyrights Act, 1957 which includes right to reproduction in Internet. To "reproduce" means to produces again; to produce a copy. It may be an exact copy or an imitation. It is the action or process of bringing again before the mind in the same form. The word "reproduction" is a term of art and is used in commercial sense. Right to reproduce is not for the convenience of the user but for the purpose of distribution.[127] However, Section 14 used different terminology for recognizing this right.

---

124. See Sinday A. Rosenzweig, "Don't Put My Article Online: Existing Copyright's New-use Doctrine to the Electronic Publishing Media and Beyond", 143 *University of Pennsylvania Law Review*, 639 (1994–95).
125. *See*, Binu Poornamodan Cholayil, "Digital Rights Management and Fair Use in Copyright Law" 33(1–2) *Cochin University Law Review* (2009) p. 166.
126. See Nandan Kamat, *Law Relating to Computers Internet and E-Commerce*, (Universal Law Publishing Co., New Delhi, 2012).
127. *State Bank of India* v. *Collector of Customs*, (2000) 1 SCC 727: [2000] 1 SCR 137.

The scope of this right also differs. While one can see the term "reproduction" is used in the case of literary, dramatic, musical and artistic works, it is the words "make any copy" and "make any sound recording" that are the terminology used in case of cinematograph film and sound recording to recognize this right. There is no definition for the words "reproduction" or "copy" used in the Act.

Right to store a work in electronic medium is newly recognised economic right of an author under Copyright Act, 1957. The recent technological development like internet, DVD, CD-Rom etc. have enabled the libraries and publishers of newspapers and magazines and so on to store the printed work in electronic medium. A question arises whether the storing in electronic medium is legal under copyright law? The Section 14 of the Act clarifies that for the purpose of storing in electronic medium the libraries and publishers also have to obtain permission from the author. Therefore, the Copyright (Amendment) Act, 1984 amended Section 14(1)(a)(i) which provided "to reproduce the work in any material form including the storing of it in any medium by electronic means."[128]

The Copyright (Amendment) Act, 2012 amended Section 52 of the Act to make the fair use defence available to all works including cinematograph films and sound recordings. The 2012 amendment replaced the words "literary, dramatic, musical or artistic work" used in Section 52(1)(a) and 52(1)(b) with the expression "any work".[129] The amendment provides that the works which are stored in an electronic medium for the purposes of fair use do not constitute infringing copies. To facilitate digitisation of libraries, a new clause (n) has been introduced to Section 52(1) identifying certain acts not to be infringement of copyright to enable the storage of a digital copy of a work if the library possesses a non digital version of it. The newly substituted clause (n) runs thus: "the storing of a work in any medium by electronic means by a non-commercial public library, for preservation if the library already possesses a non-digital copy of the work." It is remarkable to note that through the legal development of copyright law the scope of the right has been expanded and thus right of reproduction of copyright in Internet also been added to, while on the other hand the defence of the fair use has also been expanded. As a result of which ultimate protection of creative works under copyright law became complex and thus real authors are getting nothing. Seeking any relief for copyright infringement is a difficult issue in the contemporary era.

LIABILITY OF INTERNET SERVICE PROVIDER

In *Tata Sky Limited* v. *National Internet Exchange of India*,[130] the Delhi High Court observed that the Government non-profit company has to provide neutral Internet Exchange Point Services in India and to facilitate the handing over of domestic internet traffic between Internet Service Providers (ISPs) in India rather than using servers in United States or elsewhere and thereby saving foreign exchange. Utilising servers routed through and administered by India also reduces chances of Indian Data being intercepted by others. The (ISPs) connect end-users and businesses to the public Internet. They compete with each other on price, performance, reliability, etc. but they also must cooperate with each other to provide global connectivity to

128. Inserted by the Copyright (Amendment) Act, 1994 [w.e.f. 10. 05. 1995] Section 7.
129. Inserted by the Copyright (Amendment) Act, 2012 [w.e.f. 21. 6. 2012] Section 32(i) (a).
130. 2019 IV AD (Delhi) 533: 259 (2019) DLT 468.

all other attachments on the Internet. The cooperation is explicitly stated at demarcation points where they interconnect, called imprecisely "peering points".[131] Thus, in order to connect to the Internet, there is a need of an ISP. It is the company that the user of the Internet pays a monthly fee in order to use the Internet. If user uses a dial-up modem to connect to the ISP, a Point-to-Point Protocol (PPP) connection is established with another modem on the ISP's end. That modem connects to one of the ISP's routers, which routes the user use the Internet "backbone". From there, the user can access information from anywhere around the world.[132]

Copyright is a bundle of rights including, *inter alia*, rights of reproduction, communication to the public, adaptation and translation of the work. Online copyright infringement occurs when a copyrighted work such as a song, movie, or text is copied, modified, displayed, or performed electronically without the copyright owner's authorisation. When a copyright in a work of a person is infringed electronically, it is all the more difficult to find the infringer and to bring him to justice. The courts in the United States of America have examined the issue relating to liability of Internet Service Providers in a number of cases.[133]

In *Playboy Enterprises Inc.* v. *Frena*,[134] the District Court for the Middle District of Florida examined the issue relating to copyright infringement. In this case the defendant George Frena operated a subscription computer bulletin board service, Techs Warehouse BBS ("BBS"). Photographs copyrighted by Plaintiff, Playboy Entertainment, Inc.'s ("PEI") were uploaded onto BBS without permission. Subscribers of BBS were allowed to browse and download the photographs in high quality computerised images which were then stored on the subscriber's home computer. One hundred and seventy of the images that were available on BBS were copies of photographs taken from PEI's copyrighted materials. The defendant Frena claimed to never have uploaded any of PEI's photographs onto BBS and that subscribers to BBS uploaded the photographs. The defendant Frena states that as soon as he was served with a summon and made aware of this matter, he removed the photographs and has since that time monitored BBS to prevent additional photographs of PEI from being uploaded. The court held that the unauthorised use of photographs infringed on copyright. And using magazine's trademark to identify bulletin board files was trademark infringement; and deleting magazine's trademark from photographs and inserting advertisement was unfair competition.

In *Religious Technology Centre* v. *Online Netcom Communication Services*,[135] the issue was whether the operator of a computer Bulletin Board Service (BBS) and Internet access provider that allows that BBS to reach the Internet should be liable for copyright infringement committed by a subscriber of the BBS. The plaintiff Religious Technology Centre (RTC) argued that defendant Netcom was directly, contributorily, and vicariously liable for copyright infringement. The defendant Netcom moved for summary judgment (a judgment without a full trial), disputing RTC's claims and raising a first amendment argument and a fair use defence. The court held that RTC's claims of direct and vicarious infringement failed, but genuine issues of fact precluded summary judgment on contributory liability and fair use.

---

131. Visit: http://cseweb.ucsd.edu/classes/wi01/cse222/papers/norton-isp-draft00.pdf.
132. Visit: http://www.techterms.com/definition/isp.
133. *Sega Enterprises Ltd.* v. *Maphia*, 948 F. Supp. 923 (N.D. Cal. 1996); *Playboy Enterprises Inc.* v. *Webbworld Inc.*, 968 F. Supp. 1171 (N.D. Tex. 1997); *Playboy Enterprises Inc.* v. *Sanfilippo*, 1998 U.S. Dist. LEXIS 5125.
134. 839 F. Supp. 1552 (1993).
135. 907 F. Supp. 1361 (N.D. Cal. 1995).

In India, the debate is whether any liability can be fixed on the Internet service providers (for example, website owners which serves as platform for online publishing of information, e.g. YouTube, Facebook, etc.), and if yes, to what extent can these service providers be held liable for or what shall be their duties or responsibilities? The Information Technology Act, 2000 is the governing law in India which refers to Internet Service Providers as network service provider and defines the same in Section 79(a) as an "intermediary". The intermediary is further defined under Section 2(w) of the Information Technology Act as "intermediary with respect to any particular electronic message means any person who on behalf of another person receives, stores or transmits that message or provides any service with respect to that message".[136] The telecom service providers, Internet service providers, web-hosting service providers, search engines, online payment sites, online auction sites, online market places and cybercafés are examples of intermediaries under the Act.

A question often arises: Is the Internet service provider liable for each and every act of infringement which is taking place in the digital world by using the Internet? Section 51 of the Copyright Act, 1957 expressly provides the circumstances when a work shall be deemed to be infringed. It is a matter of fact that Section 51 of the Act does not expressly cover the liability of the Internet Service Providers whereas the Information Technology Act, 2000 provides the stringent supplementing provisions to the Copyright Act, 1957. The provisions in relation to the Internet service providers are provided under Section 79 of the Information Technology Act, 2000 which limits the liability of the said providers. The Section illustrates, for the removal of doubts, that no person providing any service as a network service provider shall be liable under this Act, rules or regulations made thereunder for any third party information or data made available by him if he proves that the offence or contravention was committed without his knowledge or that he had exercised all due diligence to prevent the commission of such offence or contravention. Here network service provider is referred to intermediary and third party information means any information dealt with as by a network service provider in his capacity as an intermediary. The Section limits the liability of the Internet service providers by two ways:

(i) The Internet service providers have exercised all due diligence to prevent commission of offence, and
(ii) Offence so committed is without the knowledge of the Internet service providers.[137]

The above stated Section 79 of the Act of 2000 provides exemptions from liability of intermediary in certain cases. Section 79 is, thus, meant for all other Internet wrongs wherein intermediaries may be involved including auctioning, networking servicing, news dissemination, uploading of pornographic content but not certainly relating to the copyright infringement or patent infringement which has been specifically excluded by way of proviso to Section 81. According to proviso to Section 81 "nothing contained in this Act shall restrict any person from exercising any right conferred under the Copyright Act, 1957 (14 of 1957) or the Patents Act, 1970 (39 of 1970)."[138]

---

136. *See, Super Cassetes Industries Ltd.* v. *Myspace Inc.*, MIPR 2011 (2) 303: 2011 (48) PTC 49 (Del).
137. *See, Sanjay Kumar Kedia* v. *Narcotics Control Bureau* (2008) 39 OCR 307: (2008) 2 SCC 294.
138. *See, Christian Louboutin SAS* v. *Nakul Bajaj*, 2018 (76) PTC 508 (Del): 253 (2018) DLT 728; *Gagan Harsh Sharma* v. *The State of Maharashtra*, 2019 ALLMR (Cri) 595: 2019 CriLJ 1398; *Sharat Babu Digumarti* v. *Govt. of NCT of Delhi*, AIR 2017 SC 150: (2017) 2 SCC 18.

Section 51 of the Copyright Act, 1957 defines when copyright infringed. Section 51 is a deeming provision which mandates, *inter alia*, that copyright in a work shall be deemed to be infringed, in case, any person without a licence does anything, exclusive right to do which is by this Act conferred upon the owner of the copyright.[139] Further, Section 55 gives the rights to the owner to take the civil remedies for infringement by way of injunction, damages, accounts, etc., infringement is, doing of any act by a person who is not authorised by the owner, which the owner is conferred to do under the provisions of the Act or permitting any place for profit for infringement of the copyright is also an infringement under the Act.[140] These provisions are disjunctive in as much as that there shall be an infringement even if the acts are done which are of the owner or in the alternative the acts of permitting any place for profit. Section 51 reads thus:

51. When copyright infringed—Copyright in a work shall be deemed to be infringed—

(a) When any person, without a licence granted by the owner of the Copyright or the Registrar of Copyrights under this Act or in contravention of the conditions of a licence so granted or of any conditions imposed by a competent authority under this Act—

   (i) does anything, the exclusive right to do which is by this Act conferred upon the owner of the copyright, or

   (ii) permits for profit any place to be used for the communication of the work to the public where such communication constitutes an infringement of the copyright in the work, unless he was not aware and had no reasonable ground for believing that such communication to the public would be an infringement of copyright, or

(b) When any person—

   (i) makes for sale on hire, or sells or lets for hire, or by way of trade displays or offers for sale or hire, or

   (ii) Distributes either for the purposes of trade or to such an extent as to affect prejudicially the owner of the copyright, or

   (iii) By way of trade exhibits in public, or

   (iv) Imports into India, any infringing copies of the work:

   [Provided that nothing in Sub-clause (iv) shall apply to the import of one copy of any work, for the private and domestic use of the importer.

   EXPLANATION—For the purposes of this section, the reproduction of a literary, dramatic, musical or artistic work in the form of a cinematograph film shall be deemed to be an "infringing copy".

In *Super Cassetes Industries Ltd.* v. *Myspace Inc.*,[141] the plaintiff was owner of the copyright in the repertoire of songs, cinematograph films, sound recordings. The defendant was operating a social networking website www. "MySpace.com" which provided users with

---

139. *See*, *Indian Performing Right Society Ltd.* v. *Badal Dhar Chowdhry*, 2012 (129) DRJ 490; *Super Cassettes Industries Limited* v. *Mr. Chintamani Rao*, 2012 (49) PTC 1 (Del).

140. *See*, *Dabur India Limited* v. *Shree Baidyanath Ayurved Bhawan Pvt. Ltd.*, 193 (2012) DLT 558: 2012 (51) PTC 441 (Del).

141. MIPR 2011 (2) 303: 2011 (48) PTC 49 (Del).

the facility to upload videos and pictures including material not yet released and infringing material. Defendant authorised free uploading and distribution of content through downloading and streaming. The plaintiff issued a legal notice to the defendant to remove infringing material from its website. The court determined the scope of "permitting any place for profit" used in Section 51(a)(ii) and held that "any place" would include a common public place which may be a physical place or place on the Internet or webspace. The words can be given a wider connotation so as to include the place on the Internet and not merely confining it to a place of entertainment. Since the defendants in this case were earning profits or gains and were not doing acts bona fide or mistakenly without notice, there was certainly a complete element of commerce attached to it, and therefore, they were held liable for infringement of copyright of plaintiff. The court further observed:

> The provision of Section 51(a)(i) and Section 51(a)(ii) of the Act are disjunctive in nature in as much as the word "or" between the two makes it clear that even on satisfaction of one provision, there would be an infringement of copyright. The infringement by way of authorization would fall within Section 51(a)(1) read with Section 14 of the Act as against the act of permitting the place for profit which is separately provided under Section 51(a)(ii) of the Act.
>
> There is a distinction between the concept of authorization as well as the concept of permitting the place for profit and the essential ingredients for establishing the same are also different. The acts of the defendants whereby they are offering the space over the internet, getting the works uploaded through users, thereafter saving in their own database with the limited licence to add, amend, or delete the content and thereafter communicating the said work to the public by providing some advertisements alongside the work or in the alternative gaining advertisements or sponsorships on the said basis thereafter would prima facie tantamounts to permitting the place for profit for infringement as envisaged under Section 51(a)(ii) of the Act.

It is a well settled principle that when there are new technological inventions or change in circumstances which was not in contemplation at the time when the statute was enacted, the said invention or technological advancement may be included in the same enactment if they are falling within the same genus provided in the existing enactment. When a change in social conditions produces a novel situation which was not in contemplation at the time when a statute is first enacted, there can be no a priori assumption that the enactment does not apply to the new circumstances. If the language of the enactment is wide enough to extend to those circumstances, there is no reason why it should not apply.[142] Thus, general words are construed as to include new inventions and technological advances not known at the time when the act was passed. In *Gambart* v. *Ball*,[143] the photograph copy is held to be a copy under the Engraving Copyright Act, 1734. Similarly, telephone was not invented in 1869, even then the telephone was held to be a telegraph under the provisions of Telegraphs Act, 1863.[144] Thus, in *Super Cassettes Industries Ltd.* v. *Myspace Inc.*,[145] the Delhi High Court observed:

142. *Comdel Commodities Ltd.* v. *Siporex Trade SA* (1990) 2 All ER 552.
143. (1863) 32 LJCP 166.
144. *A.G.* v. *Edison Telephone Co. of London* (1880) 6 QBD 244. *See also*, *Senior Electric Inspector* v. *Laxminarayan Chopra*, AIR 1962 SC 159: [1962] 3 SCR 146; *State of Maharashtra* v. *Praful B. Desai*, AIR 2003 SC 2053: (2003) 4 SCC 601.
145. MIPR 2011 (2) 303: 2011 (48) PTC 49 (Del).

> The provision provides under Section 51 of the Copyright Act, 1957 for permitting "any place" which itself is loosely worded and is unfettered by any qualification, the said words "any place" have to be construed widely so as to include the place at the web space or internet in order to give effect to the provision to be operative in cases of newer kind of the infringements being caused at the web space.

Fair use provisions of the Copyright Act, 1957 have been extended to the digital environment through the Copyright (Amendment) Act, 2012. Thus, any transient and incidental storage of any work through the process of "caching" has been provided exceptions as per the international practice. Any deliberate storing of such works and unauthorised reproduction and distribution of such works is an infringement under Section 51 of the Copyright Act attracting civil and criminal liability. Exceptions under this Section have been extended to education and research purposes as works are available in digital formats and on the Internet. The scope of these provisions ensures that introduction of new technology will also be covered under this new section. Thus, 2012 amendment has attempted to create a balance between the liabilities attached to publishing the online content along with creating specific provisions relating to voluntary and valid publishing or making available the contents over the Internet. An explanation has been inserted to Clause (1)(a) of Section 52 to clarify that storing of any work in any electronic medium for the specified purposes, including the incidental storage of a computer programme which in itself is not an infringing copy, shall not be an infringement. The newly introduced Section 52(1)(b) states that "the transient and incidental storage of a work or performance purely in the technical process of electronic transmission or communication to the public" would not constitute copyright infringement. Further, Section 52(1)(c), would state that the "transient and incidental storage for the purpose of providing electronic links, access or integration, where such links, access or integration has not been expressly prohibited by the right holder, unless the person responsible is aware or has reasonable grounds for believing that such storage is of an infringing copy" would also not constitute copyright infringement. These provisions have been incorporated keeping in mind the protection of websites like YouTube and yahoo in relation to user generated content uploaded by users such as film songs and other such similar content which are not owned by the uploading website.

JURISDICTIONAL ISSUES IN INTERNET DISPUTES

Concept of Jurisdiction

The word "jurisdiction" is derived from Latin terms "juris" and "dicto" which means "I speak by the law".[146] In *Smt. Ujjam Bai* v. *State of U.P.*,[147] the Supreme Court observed that the question whether a tribunal has jurisdiction depends not on the truth or falsehood of the facts into which it has to enquire, or upon the correctness of its findings on these facts, but upon their nature, and it is determinable at the commencement of the matter. It refers to the right of administering justice by means of law and includes every act from taking cognizance in a matter to the final disposal of a suit. Thus, jurisdiction means the power or authority of a court

146. *See, Nathu* v. *Kamlabai*, 1974 Mh LJ 721.
147. AIR 1962 SC 1621: [1963] 1 SCR 778. *See also, Choube Jagdish Prasad* v. *Ganga Prasad*, AIR 1959 SC 492; *Brij Raj Krishna* v. *Shaw and Bros.*, AIR 1951 SC 115.

to inquire into the facts, to apply the law, and to pronounce a judgment and to carry it into execution.[148] The meaning of the word "jurisdiction" has been well explained in *Halsbury's Laws of England* [149] as follows:

> By jurisdiction is meant authority by which a Court has to decide matters that are litigated before it, or to take cognizance of matters presented in a formal way for its decision. The limits of this authority are imposed by Statute or Charter or Commission under which the Court is constituted and may be extended or restricted by similar means. If no restriction or limitation is imposed, the jurisdiction is said to be unlimited. A limitation may be either as to the kind or nature of the actions or the matters of which a particular Court has cognizance or as to the area over which the jurisdiction extends, or it may partake of both these characteristics.

Thus, the term "jurisdiction" indicates the authority which a Court has to decide matters that are litigated before it or to take cognizance of matters presented in a formal way for its decision.[150] In other words, the term "jurisdiction" determines the power to hear, issues of law and fact, the authority by which the judicial officers take cognizance of and decide causes, the authority to hear and decide a legal controversy, the power to hear and determine the subject matter in controversy between parties to a suit and to adjudicate or exercise any judicial power over them, the power to hear, determine and pronounce judgment on the issues before the Court, the power or authority which is conferred upon a Court by the legislature to hear and determine cause between parties and to carry the judgments into effect, the power to enquire into the facts, to apply the law, to pronounce the judgment and to carry it into execution. Thus, jurisdiction of a court means the extent of the authority of a court to administer justice prescribed with reference to the subject matter, pecuniary value and local limits. Justice Mukherjee, the then Acting C.J. speaking for the Full Bench of the Calcutta High Court in *Hirday Nath Roy* v. *Ram Chandra,*[151] explained what exactly is meant by jurisdiction. Justice Mukherjee observed:

> Before a court can be held to have jurisdiction to decide a particular matter it must not only have jurisdiction to try the suit brought but must also have the authority to pass the orders sought for. It is not sufficient that it has some jurisdiction in relation to the subject-matter of the suit. Its jurisdiction must include the power to hear and decide the questions at issue, the authority to hear and decide the particular controversy that has arisen between the parties.

---

148. See, S.K. Pandit v. Sreekrishna Swamy Devaswom, 2015 (3) KLJ 401: 2015 (3) KLT 628; *S.B.P. and Co.* v. *Patel Engineering Ltd.*, AIR 2006 SC 450: JT 2005 (9) SC 219; *Devender Pal Singh* v. *State,* AIR 2003 SC 886: (2003) 2 SCC 501.
149. Fourth Edition, Vol. 10, paragraph 715.
150. *See*, Jatindra Kumar Das, *Code of Civil Procedure* (PHI Learning Private Ltd., Delhi, 2014) pp. 85–100; *Pankaj Hotel* v. *Bal Mukund*, 2018 (126) ALR 334: 2018 2 AWC2071All; *Babu* v. *Kunjumol Nandiyanathayil*, 2017 (2) KLT 1011: 2017 (2) KLJ 964; *K. Anbazhagan* v. *State of Karnataka*, (2015) 6 SCC 158: 2015 (5) SCALE 577; *Harpal Singh* v. *State of Punjab*, AIR 2008 SC 743: [2007] 12 SCR 830; *A.R. Antulay* v. *R.S. Nayak*, AIR 1988 SC 1531: (1988) 2 SCC 602; *Official Trustee* v. *Sachindra Nath*, AIR 1969 SC 823: [1969] 3 SCR 92; *Raja Soap Factory* v. *S.P. Shantharaj*, AIR 1965 SC 1449: [1965] 2 SCR 800.
151. AIR 1921 Cal 34: ILR 48 Cal 138 (FB). *See also*, *Indian Farmers Fertilizer Co-Operative Limited* v. *Bhadra Products*, AIR 2018 SC 627: (2018) 2 SCC 534; *Begum Sabiha Sultan* v. *Nawab Mohd. Mansur Ali Khan,* AIR 2007 SC 1636: (2007) 4 SCC 343; *T. Arivandandam* v. *T.V. Satyapal,* AIR 1977 SC 2421: (1977) 4 SCC 467; *Official Trustee* v. *Sachindra Nath Chatterjee,* AIR 1969 SC 823: [1969] 3 SCR 92.

In *Begum Sabiha Sultan* v. *Nawab M. Mansur Ali Khan,*[152] the Apex Court approved the expression "jurisdiction" given by Mukherjee, ACJ in the leading case *Hirday Nath Roy*[153] and observed that before a court can be held to have jurisdiction to decide a particular matter it must not only have jurisdiction to try the suit brought but must also have the authority to pass the orders sought for. It is not sufficient that it has some jurisdiction in relation to the subject matter of the suit. Its jurisdiction must include the power to hear and decide the questions at issue, the authority to hear and decide the particular controversy that has arisen between the parties. The essence of the matter is whether the court has power to grant relief prayed by the plaintiff or applicant. If it has not, the order is without jurisdiction and null and void.[154]

Thus, a court must have jurisdiction,[155] venue,[156] and appropriate service of process in order to hear a case and render an effective judgment. Jurisdiction is the power of a court to hear and determine a case. The jurisdiction of the Court may be qualified or restricted by a variety of circumstances. Thus, the jurisdiction may have to be considered with reference to place, value and nature of the subject matter. The power of a Court may be exercised within defined territorial limits. Its cognizance may be restricted to subject matters of prescribed value. It may be competent to deal with controversies of a specified character, for instance, testamentary or matrimonial causes, acquisition of lands for public purposes, record of rights as between landlords and tenants. Besides these classes of jurisdiction, Indian Courts are exercising equitable jurisdiction, inherent jurisdiction as traditional practice. This classification into territorial jurisdiction, pecuniary jurisdiction, jurisdiction of the subject matter, equitable jurisdiction, inherent jurisdiction and personal jurisdiction is obviously of a fundamental character.[157] In the light of the aforementioned discussion, the jurisdiction of a court may be classified under the following categories:

1. Territorial or local jurisdiction.[158]
2. Pecuniary jurisdiction.[159]

---

152. AIR 2007 SC 1636: (2007) 4 SCC 343. *See also*, *Ashok Kumar Kapur* v. *Ashok Khanna*, AIR 1996 SC 987: (1996) 2 SCC 520; *Official Trustee* v. *Sachindra,* AIR 1969 SC 823: [1969] 3 SCR 92.
153. *Hirday Nath Roy* v. *Ram Chandra,* AIR 1921 Cal 34: ILR 48 Cal 138 (FB).
154. *Mukand Ltd.* v. *Mukand Staff and Officers' Association*, AIR 2004 SC 3905: (2004) 10 SCC 460; *Cellular Operators Association* v. *Union of India* (2003) 3 SCC 186: [2002] Supp 5 SCR 222; *Union of India* v. *Tarachand Gupta,* AIR 1971 SC 1558: [1971] 3 SCR 557; *Mathai* v. *Varkey Varkey,* AIR 1964 SC 907: [1964] 1 SCR 495.
155. *See*, Christian M. Rieder, *U.S. Subject Matter Jurisdiction for Copyright Infringements on the Internet* (1988).
156. According to *Black's Law Dictionary* venue is the possible or proper place or places for the trial of a suit, as among several places where jurisdiction could be established. Venue establishes the location where the power of a court should be exercised. It is decided on the basis of convenience and, thus, may be waived by the parties.
157. *See, State of Madhya Pradesh* v. *Dhruv Gurjar*, AIR 2019 SC 1106: (2019) 5 SCC 570; *Chief Engineer, Hydel Project* v. *Ravinder Nath*, AIR 2008 SC 1315: (2008) 2 SCC 350; *Harshad Chiman Lal Modi* v. *DLF Universal*, AIR 2005 SC 4446: (2005) 7 SCC 791.
158. *See, Sneh Lata Goel* v. *Pushplata*, AIR 2019 SC 824: (2019)3SCC594; *A.V.M. Sales Corporation* v. *Anuradha Chemicals Pvt. Ltd.*, 2012 (1) SCALE 349: (2012) 2 SCC 315; *Chief Engineer* v. *Ravinder Nath*, AIR 2008 SC 1315: (2008) 2 SCC 350; *Hasham Abbas* v. *Usman Abbas*, 2006 (14) SCALE 131: (2007) 2 SCC 355; *Harshad Chiman* v. *DLF Universal,* AIR 2005 SC 4446: 2005 (7) SCALE 533.
159. *See, Om Prakash Agarwal* v. *Vishan Dayal Rajpoot*, AIR 2018 SC 5486: 2019 (1) ALJ 337; *Sanjeev Kumar Jai* v. *Raghubir Saran,* 2012 1 AWC (Supp) 408 SC: (2012) 1 SCC 455; *Sri Jeyaram Educational Trust* v. *A.G. Syed Mohideen*, AIR 2010 SC 671: (2010) 2 SCC 513; *Narayanan Rajendran* v. *Lekshmy Sarojini*, 2009 (2) SCALE 414: (2009) 5 SCC 264; *State of West Bengal* v. *Kamal Sengupta,* JT 2008 (8) SC 317: (2008) 8 SCC 612; *Subhash Mahadevasa* v. *Nemasa Ambasa*, AIR 2007 SC 1828: 2007 (5) SCALE 34.

3. Jurisdiction as to subject matter.[160]
4. Original or appellate jurisdiction.[161]
5. Equitable jurisdiction.[162]
6. Inherent jurisdiction.[163]
7. Personal jurisdiction.[164]

Place of Suing in Case of Internet Disputes

The creation of the Internet as a global network has raised significant jurisdictional issues. On the Internet, one can make an unlimited number of copies, virtually instantaneously and without any degradation in quality. These copies can be transmitted to locations around the world in a matter of minutes. The older technologies of photocopying and taping allowed mechanical copying by individual consumers, but in limited quantities, requiring considerable time, and of a lower quantity than the original. Besides, the copies were physically located in the same place as the person making the copy. But in the Internet, the users can access the Internet from almost any place on the earth. Can the traditional rules on jurisdiction, which are geographically orientated and generally rely on the place of performance, apply to the modern Internet disputes?[165] The question of where court proceedings are brought is conceptually distinct from the questions of governing law and the enforcement of a judgment issuing from

---

160. *Sumitomo Corporation* v. *CDC Financial Services,* AIR 2008 SC 1594: (2008) 4 SCC 91; *Hasham Abbas* v. *Usman Abbas*, 2006 (14) SCALE 131: (2007) 2 SCC 355; *Sarwan Kumar* v. *Madan Lal*, AIR 2003 SC 1475: (2003) 4 SCC 147.
161. *See, Mantri Techzone Pvt. Ltd.* v. *Forward Foundation,* 2019 (4) SCALE 218: 2019 (2) Bom CR 901; *Ramesh Gobindram* v. *Sugra Humayun Mirza Wakf,* AIR 2010 SC 2897: 2010 (5) ALT 36 (SC); *Pandey and Co.* v. *State of Bihar,* AIR 2007 SC 465: (2007) 1 SCC 467; *P.S. Sathappan* v. *Andhra Bank*, AIR 2004 SC 5152: (2004) 11 SCC 672.
162. *See, Ram Parshotam Mittal* v. *Hotel Queen Road Pvt. Ltd.*, 2019 (7) SCALE 738: [2019] 154 SCL 147 (SC); *C.K. Sasankan* v. *Dhanalakshmi Bank*, AIR 2009 SC 3171: (2009) 11 SCC 60; *Board of Control* v. *Netaji Cricket Club*, AIR 2005 SC 592: (2005) 4 SCC 741; *Clariant International* v. *Securities and Exchange,* AIR 2004 SC 4236: (2004) 8 SCC 524.
163. *See, Sasikala Pushpa* v. *State of Tamil Nadu*, AIR 2019 SC 2280: (2019) 6 SCC 477; *Competition Commission* v. *Steel Authority of India Ltd.*, JT 2010 (10) SC 26: 2010 (8) UJ 4093 (SC); *Zenit Mataplast* v. *State of Maharashtra*, 2009 (12) SCALE 432: (2009) 10 SCC 388; *Durgesh Sharma* v. *Jayshree*, 2008 (13) SCALE 54: (2008) 9 SCC 648.
164. Personal jurisdiction is simply the competence of the court to determine a case against a particular category of persons. It requires a determination of whether the person is subject to the court in which the case is field. In *Dinesh Singh Thakur* v. *Sonal Thakur* [AIR 2018 SC 2094: 2018 (6) SCALE1] the Supreme Court held that it is a well-settled law that the courts in India have power to issue anti-suit injunction to a party over whom it has personal jurisdiction, in an appropriate case. However, before passing the order of anti-suit injunction, courts should be very cautious and careful, and it should be granted sparingly and not as a matter of routine as such orders involve a court impinging on the jurisdiction of another court, which is not entertained very easily specially when the it restrains the parties from instituting or continuing a case in a foreign court. *See also, Enercon (India) Ltd.* v. *Enercon GMBH*, AIR 2014 SC 3152: (2014) 5 SCC 1; *Modi Entertainment Network* v. *W.S.G. Cricket Pte. Ltd.*, (2003) 4 SCC 341; *Oil and Natural Gas Commission* v. *Western Co. of North America*, 1987 SCR (1) 1024.
165. *See*, Faye Fangfei Wang, "Obstacles and Solutions to Internet Jurisdiction A Comparative Analysis of the EU and US Laws," 3(4) *Journal of International Commercial Law and Technology* (2008) pp. 233–241.

court proceedings. In other words, proceedings may in principle be brought in one jurisdiction and a judgment issuing from those proceedings may be enforced in another.

The whole trouble with the Internet jurisdiction is the presence of multiple parties in various parts of the world who have only a virtual nexus with each other. Then, if one party wants to sue the other, where can he sue? Traditional requirements generally encompass two areas—firstly, the place where the defendant resides, or secondly, where the cause of action arises. However, in the context of the Internet, both these are difficult to establish with any certainty. Even a childishly simple transaction can give rise to a mind-boggling issue of jurisdiction on the Internet. For example, A, in India, decides to download an article from a website, and pays money for it through a credit card, and then is unable to perform the download. He wants to sue the owner of the site. But the owner is in Thailand. The site itself is based on a server in Brazil. Where does the defendant reside? The transaction occurred on the Internet. So was it in India, or in Brazil?[166]

US Legal Position

Traditionally, US courts apply a minimum contacts test to determine whether the exercise of personal jurisdiction[167] is proper.[168] There are generally two standards applied in deciding whether the minimum contacts test has been met. First, the plaintiff must show that "the defendant had the minimum contacts with the forum necessary for the defendant to have reasonably anticipated being held into court there".[169] Second, a court must also inquire whether "the assertion of personal jurisdiction would comport with fair play and substantial justice".[170] In *Cybersell, Inc.* v. *Cybersell, Inc.*,[171] Cybersell, an Arizona corpn. that advertises for commercial services over the Internet, claims that Cybersell, a Florida corpn., that offers web page construction services over the Internet, infringed its federally registered mark and should be amenable to suit in Arizona because cyberspace is without borders and a website which advertises a product or service which is necessarily intended for use on a worldwide basis. Plaintiff argued that the test is met because trademark infringement occurs when the passing off the mark occurs, which in this case, it submitted, happened when the name "Cybersell" was used on the Internet in connection with advertising. Rejecting the plaintiff's argument, the Court observed that it is essential in each case that there be some act by which the defendant purposefully avails itself of the privilege of conducting activities within the forum state, thus invoking the benefits and protections of its laws. Thus, it was held that there was no personal jurisdiction.

---

166. *See*, S.K. Verma and Raman Mittal, *Legal Dimensions of Cyberspace,* Indian Law Institute, New Delhi (2004).
167. In *(India TV) Independent News Service Pvt Limited* v. *India Broadcast Live LLC* [MIPR 2007 (2) 396: 2007 (35) PTC 177 (Del)] the Delhi High Court held that personal jurisdiction is the power which a court has over a person as opposed to jurisdiction over property, etc. Similarly, in *Pennoyer* v. *Neff* [95 U.S. 714: 24 L.Ed. 565] the US court held that a court which lacks personal jurisdiction is without power to issue an in personam judgment.
168. *Miliken* v. *Meyer*, 311 U.S. 457, 463 (1941); *International Shoe Co.* v. *Washington*, 326 U.S. 310, 316 (1945).
169. *World-Wide Volkswagen Corp.* v. *Woodson*, 444 U.S. 286, 297 (1980).
170. *Burger King* v. *Rudzewicz*, 471 U.S. 463, 476 (1985).
171. 130 F.3d 414 (9th Cir. 1997): 1997 U.S. App. LEXIS 33871.

In *Brown* v. *Geha-Werke GMBH, Shredex, Inc.,*[172] the plaintiff had been injured by a paper shredder manufactured by the defendant. He filed suit in federal court in South Carolina. The manufacturer moved to dismiss the case for lack of personal jurisdiction. In granting the motion, the court held that personal jurisdiction could not be exercised by the South Carolina court because the minimum contacts test had not been met. The plaintiff "failed to submit competent evidence that the German company had engaged in additional conduct beyond simply placing the product in the stream of commerce." Citing *Zippo*, the court emphasised that the Geha-Werke website only advertises its products and provides an e-mail address, thus placing it in the passive website category. This would preclude the assertion of personal jurisdiction based on the fact that the site could be reached in the state. The court then noted that "merely categorizing a Web site as interactive or passive is not conclusive of the jurisdictional issue.... The critical issue for the court to analyze is the nature and quality of commercial activity conducted by an entity over the Internet in the forum state."

Indian Legal Position

In India, for the purpose of determining the issue relating to infringement of copyright the remedies are conferred under the special statute of Copyright Act, 1957. The suit for infringement of copyright can be filed and initiated at the place wherein the plaintiff carries on business, or personally works for gain, etc. This is by virtue of non-obstante clause provided under Section 62(2) of the Act. According to Section 62(1) of the Act, every suit or other civil proceeding arising under this Chapter in respect of the infringement of copyright in any work or the infringement of any other right conferred by this Act shall be instituted in the district court having jurisdiction.[173] By mere reading of the provision of Section 62(2) of the Act, it becomes amply clear that the suit for infringement can be filed at the forum where the plaintiff resides or carries on business. The opening words of the provision provides: "Notwithstanding anything contained in the code of civil procedure" which means that the said provision will operate in addition to what has been provided in the Code of Civil Procedure. Thus, in *Ferani Hotels Pvt. Ltd.* v. *State Information Commissioner,*[174] the Supreme Court held that the aforesaid provision would not imply that a disclosure permissible under the Copyright Act, 1957 is taken away under the provisions of the said Act, but rather, if a disclosure is prescribed under any other Act, the provisions of the said Act would have an overriding effect.

In Indian *Performing Rights Society Ltd.* v. *Sanjay Dalia,*[175] considering the very language of Section 62 of the Copyright Act, the Apex Court held that the Section 62 provides an additional forum by including a District Court within whose limits the Plaintiff actually and voluntarily resides or carries on business or personally works for gain. The object of the provisions was to enable the Plaintiff to institute a suit at a place where he or they resided or carried on business, not to enable them to drag Defendant further away from such a place also as is being done in the instant cases. Thus the Court held that the expression "notwithstanding anything contained in the Code of Civil Procedure" does not oust the applicability of the

---

172. 69 F.Supp.2d 770 (D.S.C. 1999).
173. *See, Apex Laboratories Pvt. Ltd.* v. *Ajaat Shatru*, 2019 (77) PTC 436 (Mad).
174. 2018 (13) SCALE 672: 2018 (5) CHN (SC) 238.
175. AIR 2015 SC 3479: (2015) 10 SCC 161.

provisions of Section 20 of the CPC and it is clear that additional remedy has been provided to the Plaintiff so as to file a suit where he is residing or carrying on business etc., as the case may be. Section 20 of the CPC enables a plaintiff to file a suit where the defendant resides or where cause of action arose. Section 20(a) and Section 20(b) usually provides the venue where the defendant or any of them resides, carries on business or personally works for gain. Section 20 (c) of the CPC enables a plaintiff to institute a suit, in a place, where the cause of action wholly or in part has been arises. The Explanation to Section of the 20 CPC has been added to the effect that Corporation shall be deemed to carry on business at its sole or principal office in India or in respect of any cause of action arising at any place where it has subordinate office at such place.

In *Achla Sabharwal* v. *A. Saptrishi Films*,[176] the Delhi High Court examined the scope and ambit of Section 62 of the Copyright Act and prescribes an additional ground for attracting the jurisdiction of a court over and above the "normal" grounds as laid down in Section 20 of the Code of Civil Procedure. Thus, where more than one Court has jurisdiction to adjudicate the subject matter, the parties can legally confer jurisdiction on any one Court having jurisdiction to the exclusion of the other Courts. Thus, the parties can confer exclusive jurisdiction on any one Court having jurisdiction and oust the jurisdiction of the other Courts. The Section 62 (2) only gives the right to the plaintiff to sue on the basis of his residence or carrying business contrary to the provisions of Section 20 of the CPC whereby jurisdiction should be based on the residence or the business of the defendant or cause of action. Thus, if there is an agreement conferring exclusive jurisdiction will not be in violation of Section 28 of the Indian Contract Act, 1872 or Section 62 of the Copyright Act, 1957. The only condition that is to be seen is whether such an agreement is clear and unambiguous and the intention of the parties to submit to one court having jurisdiction to adjudicate the subject matter while excluding the jurisdiction of another is clearly discernible from the agreement itself.

Further, in *Paragon Rubber Industries* v. *Pragati Rubber Mills*,[177] the issue was whether composite suit claiming relief under Copyright Act 1957 and Trade and Merchandise Marks Act, 1958 would be maintainable? The Supreme Court held that such a suit would not be maintainable unless the Court has jurisdiction to entertain the suit in relation to the entire cause of action and the entire relief. For the purpose of invoking the jurisdiction of the Court in a composite suit, both the causes of action must arise within the jurisdiction of the Court which otherwise had the necessary jurisdiction to decide all the issues. However, the jurisdiction cannot be conferred by joining two causes of action in the same suit when the Court has jurisdiction to try the suit only in respect of one cause of action and not the other.

Thus, Section 62 of the Copyright Act enables the suit to be filed at the place of the plaintiff which is the additional ground for attracting the jurisdiction of the court.[178] It is, therefore, clear that the object and reason for the introduction of Sub-section (2) of Section 62

176. 258 (2019) DLT 663: 2019(78) PTC 437 (Del). *See also, Saregama India Limited* v. *Eros Digital FZ LLC*, 246 (2018) DLT 138: MIPR 2017 (3) 323; *Nariman Films* v. *Dilip R. Mehta*, 2005 (31) PTC 571 (Del): (2005) 124 DLT 506; *Exphar Sa* v. *Eupharma Laboratories Ltd.*, AIR 2004 SC 1682: (2004) 3 SCC 688; *A.B.C. Laminart (P) Ltd.* v. *A.P. Agencies*, AIR 1989 SC 1239: (1989) 2 SCC 163.
177. (2014) 14 SCC 762: 2013 (14) SCALE 273.
178. *See, Exphar SA* v. *Eupharma Laboratories Ltd.* (2004) 3 SCC 688. *See also, Bristol Myers Squibb Company* v. *V.C. Bhutada*, 2013 (56) PTC 268 (Del).

of the Act was not to restrict the owners of the copyright to exercise their rights but to remove any impediment from their doing so. Section 62(2) cannot be read as limiting the jurisdiction of the District Court only to cases where the person instituting the suit or other proceeding, or where there are more than one such persons, any of them actually and voluntarily resides or carries on business or presently works for gain. It prescribes an additional ground for attracting the jurisdiction of a Court over and above the "normal" grounds as laid down in Section 20 of the Code of Civil Procedure, 1908.[179]

In *Phonographic Performance Limited* v. *Spring Club*,[180] plaintiff instituted suit for infringement of copyright. On the issue of jurisdiction, the court held: "Jurisdiction to try a civil Suit is conferred on a court by Sections 15 to 20 of the Code of Civil Procedure. Under Sections 15 to 20 of the Code a civil suit can be filed at a place where the subject matter is situated, where the defendants reside or where the cause of action has arisen. Section 62 of the Copyright Act additionally confers jurisdiction on a Court within the local limit of which the plaintiff actually and voluntarily resides or carries on business or personally works for gain."

In *Kapoor Saws Manufacturing Company* v. *Crown Saw Blades Mfg. Co.,*[181] the Court exercised jurisdiction under Section 62(2) of the Copyright Act, 1957 as the plaintiff has a branch office at New Delhi and its goods are extensively sold in Delhi. The court held that to enable the plaintiff to institute any suit or proceedings in the District Court having jurisdiction over the territories where it "actually and voluntarily resides or carries business or personally works for gain". This is also what is postulated by Section 62(2) of the CA 1957. So far as the violation of copyright is concerned, it could not be disputed that under Section 62(2) of the CA 1957, it is where the plaintiff resides/or carries on business, such Court would have territorial jurisdiction. The appellants/plaintiffs carry on business in Delhi as per the case of the appellants in the plaint and therefore, even qua the cause of action of infringement of copyright, the civil courts at Delhi have territorial jurisdiction.[182]

In *Super Cassettes Industries Ltd.* v. *Myspace Inc.*,[183] the website of the defendant was found to be "engaged in the online business of providing and exhibiting the songs and cinematograph films worldwide including India". The Court further noted "the said website is usually accessed by Indians for downloading the songs of upcoming movies from the website

---

179. Section 20 of the Code of Civil Procedure, 1908 provides that all suits (other than those covered by Sections 15 to 19 of the Code) may be instituted at the option of the plaintiff in any of the following courts: (a) the Court of the place where the defendant resides or carries on business, or personally works for gain; (b) where there are two or more defendants, the Court of the place where any one of them resides or carries on business or personally works for gain, provided that in such case either the leave of the Court is taken or the defendants who do not reside, or carry on business or personally work for gain, at the place, acquiesce in such institution; (c) the Court of the place where the cause of action arises either wholly or in part. *See*, Jatindra Kumar Das, *Code of Civil Procedure* (PHI Learning Pvt. Ltd., Delhi, 2014) pp. 2011–2020.
180. 2014 (209) DLT 584: 2014 (59) PTC 182.
181. 2013 (53) PTC 506: 2012 LawSuit (Del) 4765.
182. *See also*, *MVF 3 APS* v. *M. Sivasamy*, 2012 (193) DLT 352: 2012 LawSuit (Del) 2314; *Pfizer Enterprises Sarl* v. *Cipla Ltd.*, 2009 39 PTC 358; *Dabur India* v. *K.R. Industries*, 2008 37 PTC 332; *Boston Scientific International B.V.* v. *Metro Hospital*, 2007 136 DLT 278; *Pfizer Products Inc.* v. *Rajesh Chopra*, 2006 32 PTC 301; *Liverpool* v. *M.V. Sea Success*, 2004 9 SCC 512.
183. 2011 (47) PTC 49: 2011 LawSuit(Del) 2453.

of the defendants". Also the Court noted that the plaintiff has substantiated the cause of action by showing some instances of infringements which has been caused in relation to the specific works. Thus, the said commission of the tort has occurred or occurs in India wherein the Indian user goes to the website, the defendants through its search engine exhibits the said works and the work is communicated to the public by sending the work to him and facilitating downloading or reaching to the computer of Indian user. The Court held that the said actions are sufficient to constitute part of cause of action under Section 20(c) of the Code of Civil Procedure.

In *Oil and Natural Gas Commission* v. *Utpal Kumar Basu*,[184] the Apex Court examine the issue relating to cyberspace. In this case, the issue was whether any part of the cause of action for filing the petition had arisen within the jurisdiction of the Calcutta Court to entitle it to entertain, hear and decide the said petition? The Court held that the jurisdiction of Calcutta High Court could not have been invoked because of an advertisement which appeared in "Times of India" at Calcutta seeking bid of the tenders and in response to the advertisements tendered were submitted from Calcutta office in respect of the revised rates. The Court further observed:

> Merely because it read the advertisement at Calcutta and submitted the offer from Calcutta and made representations from Calcutta would not, in our opinion, constitute facts forming an integral part of the cause of action. So also the mere fact that it sent fax messages from Calcutta and received a reply thereto at Calcutta would not constitute an integral part of the cause of action.

Thus, in *Dhodha House* v. *S.K. Maingi*,[185] the Apex Court observed that Sub-section (2) of Section 62 of the Copyright Act provides for a non-obstante clause conferring jurisdiction upon the district court within the local limits of whose jurisdiction, at the time of the institution of the suit or other proceeding, the persons instituting the suit or other proceedings, have been residing. In terms of sub-section (1) of Section 62, suit can be instituted and the proceedings can be initiated in respect of matters arising under the said Chapter for infringement of the copyright in any work or the infringement of any other right conferred thereunder. In *Varehouse Infotech Ceebros Arcade* v. *SAP Aktiengesellschaft*,[186] the Delhi High Court held that the jurisdiction for the purposes of Section 62 is wider than that of the court as prescribed under the Code of Civil Procedure, 1908. The introduction of Section 62(2) was not intended to restrict the owners of copyright from exercising their rights "but to remove any impediment from their doing so. The word "include" in Section 62(2) shows that the jurisdiction for the purposes of Section 62 is wider than that of the Court as prescribed under the Code of Civil Procedure, 1908. The relevant extract of the report of the Joint Committee published in the Gazette of India dated November 23, 1956 laid the foundation for Section 62(2) thus:

> In the opinion of the Committee many authors are deterred from instituting infringement proceedings because the court in which such proceedings are to be instituted is situated at a considerable distance from the place of their ordinary residence. The Committee feels that this impediment should be removed and the new Sub-clause (2) accordingly provides

184. 1994 (3) SCALE 90: (1994) 4 SCC 711.
185. AIR 2006 SC 730: 2006 (32) PTC 1 (SC). *See also*, *Arun Colour Chem* v. *Mithumal Essance Mart*, 2010 (43) PTC 668 (Del).
186. 2010 (115) DRJ 697: 2010 (42) PTC 650 (Del).

that infringement proceedings may be instituted in the district court within the local limits of whose jurisdiction the person instituting the proceedings ordinarily resides, carries on business etc.[187]

In *Banyan Tree Holdings Limited* v. *M. Murali Krishna Reddy,*[188] defendant's "residence" was not in territorial jurisdiction of court. It did not also have any branch or other offices in Delhi. Slender thread relied on by plaintiff was website of defendant, and "trap transaction" whereby brochure was ordered by it, from defendant, and received in New Delhi. Website, screen shots of which had been reproduced, revealed that defendant had disclosed its activities. It contained web pages eliciting a feedback, and link to an "E-Brochure". Defendant had "banyan tree" retreated in Hyderabad at three locales. Defendant did not have any application form, which could be used by potential customer. Even brochure produced by plaintiff, along with the documents, mentioned booking amount for a unit. Further, the Parliament wanted to redefine issue of jurisdiction, it did so, in terms of Section 134(2) of the Trademarks Act, 1999 and 62(2) of the Copyright Act, 1957. Therefore, Internet based activity or behaviour could in some circumstances, clothed Court with jurisdiction, it would be appropriate to indicate standards, which could be applied with some constancy.

It is true that the owner of the copyright has a right to protect his interests and initiate proceedings against any infringement irrespective of where the infringing activities take place.[189] However, in *Blueberry Books* v. *Google India Pvt. Ltd.*,[190] the Court opined that while Section 62(2) of the Copyright Act is a long-arm provision, the Act itself operates only through the territory of India. For the infringing activity to constitute a cause of action, it must be shown to have taken place in the territory of India. Thus, in *Banyan Tree* v. *A. Murali Krishna Reddy,*[191] the Court held that a passive website would not by itself vest the forum court with jurisdiction. A commercial transaction should be shown to have been concluded using the website within the jurisdiction of the forum court.

In *P.T. Djarum* v. *Chander Sheikhar Marwah,*[192] the plaintiff company is based in Indonesia and was founded in the year 1951. The defendants filed a preliminary objection as to the territorial jurisdiction of the Court to entertain the suit. The court held that one invoice from a "pan shop" in Delhi produced by the plaintiff is insufficient to show that the defendants have any outlet or branch office of their own within the local jurisdiction of the Court. The court further held that the report of the Local Commissioners makes it clear that defendant No. 4 was selling in Delhi not only the impugned goods of the defendants 2 and 3, but also the plaintiff's products. For the purposes of Section 62, this by itself is sufficient to show that the plaintiff is carrying on business within the jurisdiction of the Delhi Court. Thus, the Court restrained the defendants, their servants, agents, employees, stockists, dealers, partners from

187. *See*, *Varehouse Infotech Ceebros Arcade* v. *SAP Aktiengesellschaft,* 2010 (115) DRJ 697: 2010 (42) PTC 650 (Del); *The Indian Performing Right Society Ltd.* v. *Sanjay Dalia*, MIPR 2007 (3) 204; *Shree Rajmoti Industries* v. *Rajmoti Oil Mill Pvt. Ltd.,* 115 (2004) DLT 212: 2005 (30) PTC 38 (Del); *Exphar SA* v. *Eupharma Laboratories Ltd.,* AIR 2004 SC 1682: 2004 (28) PTC 251 (SC).

188. 2008 (38) PTC 288 (Del).

189. *See*, *Consim Info Pvt. Ltd.* v. *Google India Pvt. Ltd.*, 2011 (45) PTC 575; *Super Cassettes Industries Ltd.* v. *Myspace Inc.*, 2011 (47) PTC 49; *Dhodha House* v. *S.K. Maingi*, (2006) 9 SCC 41; *Exphar SA* v. *Eupharma Laboratories Ltd.*, (2004) 3 SCC 688.

190. 2014 (58) PTC 62: 2013 (205) DLT 228.

191. 2010 (42) PTC 361.

192. 2014 (58) PTC 302: 2013 LawSuit (Del) 3086.

reproducing, printing or publishing any label or packaging, including cartons and boxes, which are a colourable imitation or substantive reproduction of the plaintiff's trademark "DJARUM BLACK". For the purpose of testing the jurisdiction of the court in the civil suit on the basis of the objection which has been taken on demurer, the court should see the averments made in the plaint and the same must be assumed to be correct. In *Exphar S.A.* v. *Eupharma Laboratories Ltd.*,[193] speaking for the Apex Court Ruma Pal J. observed:

> Besides when an objection to jurisdiction is raised by way of demurrer and not at the trial, the objection must proceed on the basis that the facts as pleaded by the initiator of the impugned proceedings are true. The submission in order to succeed must show that given those facts the Court does not have jurisdiction as a matter of law.

In *SmithKline Beecham Plc.* v. *Sunil Singhi*,[194] the Court in the context of Section 62(2) of the Copyright Act held that the defendant ought to be shown to be carrying on its local business activities within India. Thus, the Court accepted the plea and observed that "Perhaps, the policies are trimmed by the subsidiaries in different jurisdictions, depending upon the local laws. But, ultimately, it is the holding company which owns the search engine." Thus, it is necessary to allow the application of the plaintiff seeking the impleadment of Google Inc. The stand taken by Google India Pvt. Ltd. in its counter affidavit that "it is a wholly owned subsidiary of Google Inc., USA and that Google Inc. is the owner of the search engine".

In *Blueberry Books* v. *Google India Pvt. Ltd.*,[195] the plaintiffs published a series of books under the name "Moral Stories". The plaintiffs have downloads of the impugned apps from the app store provided on the iTunes platform. Thus, Section 14 of the Copyright Act was violated as Apple India facilitated the download of iTunes. It was further referred to the documents filed by the plaintiff which included the print out of the website and referred to the web address which showed that the stories were downloadable from the web address iTunes. apple.com/in/app/storie-della-buona-notte and pointed out that the contact address for Apple was Apple India. Consequently, the Court was unable to accept the plea of the applicant that Apple India is neither a necessary nor a proper party in the suit. While an issue will be framed on this question, the Court is not persuaded to strike off Apple India from the array of parties at this stage.

In *Super Cassettes Industries Ltd.* v. *Shreya Broadcasting Pvt. Ltd.*,[196] the issue was whether the suit is maintainable under Section 61 of the Copyright Act? Section 61(1) of the Copyright Act is applicable to a licensee of the copyright and has no application to an assignee of the copyright who on assignment becomes the owner of the copyright work. Learned counsel for the plaintiff submits that in view of the assignment in favour of the plaintiff, the plaintiff is not obliged to implead the owner of the copyright as part of the proceedings. The Court held that in view of the detailed assignment in favour of the plaintiff, the plaintiff is the deemed owner of the copyright work with the right to grant licenses. Thus, thus an assignee qua the copyrights mentioned in these assignment deeds and not a licensee, thus not required to implead the original owner of the copyright work as a defendant. The suit cannot be therefore dismissed for non compliance of Section 61 Copyright Act.

---

193. (2004) 3 SCC 688.
194. 2001 (21) PTC 321.
195. 2014 (58) PTC 62: 2013 (205) DLT 228.
196. 258 (2019) DLT 116: 2019 III AD (Delhi) 552.

9

Infringement of Copyright and Defences of Copyright Liability

ABSTRACT

Infringement of copyright is an often phenomena in the contemporary era. In determining copyright infringement a number of doctrines and criteria have been introduced by the judiciary. While copyright provides a bundle of rights but these rights are not an absolute right of the owner. Hence, a number of defences are available in case of copyright infringement. The doctrine of "fair dealing" is used as an affirmative defence in case of infringement of copyright. The 2012 amendment to the Copyright Act, 1957 has widened the scope and ambit of "fair dealing" provisions. These dichotomous issues are the subject matter of this chapter.

INTRODUCTION

Law relating to copyright recognises interest of authors or creators of a work form the foundation on which the "legal rights" of authors rest under the copyright law. An author produces a literary, artistic, scientific or dramatic work or a cinematograph film or a sound recording with various aims and objectives. These aims and objectives can be termed as his "interests".[1] Thus the copyright owner has the exclusive right to: (i) copy the work, (ii) issue copies of the work to the public, (iii) rent or lend the work to the public, (iv) broadcast the work or include it in a cable programme, (v) perform shows or play the work in public, (vi) make an adaptation of the work or do any of the above in relation to an adaptation. These exclusive rights comprised in the copyright in the different classes of protected works are spelt out by Section 14 of the Copyright Act, 1957.

The copyright subsisting in a work is infringed by any person who does or authorises another to do any of these acts restricted by copyright without the licence (that is, without

1. *See,* J.K. Das, "Examination of Contemporary Status of Fair Dealing in Copyright Law in India", 7 *Vidhik Chetana: A Research Journal of Juridical Science* (2014) pp. 43–63; *See also,* Sabine Jacques, "Are the New 'Fair Dealing' Provisions an Improvement on The Previous UK Law, and Why?" 10(9) *Journal of Intellectual Property Law and Practice* (2015) pp. 699–706; Ayush Sharma, "Indian Perspective of Fair Dealing under Copyright Law: Lex Late or Lex Ferenda? 14 Journal of Intellectual Property Rights (2009) pp. 523–531; Sneha Jha and Samar Jha, "An Analysis of the Theory of Contributory Infringement," 11 *Journal of Intellectual Property Rights* (2006) pp. 318–325; Veerendra Tulzapurkar, "Remix and Copyright Law" 10 *Journal of Intellectual Property Rights* (2005) pp. 106–111.

permission, contractual or otherwise) of the copyright owner under Section 51 of the Act. Under the Act, both civil and criminal remedies are available to prevent infringement of copyright. To sustain a criminal proceeding under the Act, the knowledge of the infringing party to infringe the rights shall be proved beyond doubt. While civil remedies compensate the owner, the criminal remedies act as a deterrent against infringing activities. The general defences of copyright infringement are set out by Section 52 of the Act (commonly known as "fair dealing" provisions).[2] The various issues relating to infringement of copyright and defences of copyright liability need detail deliberation.

INFRINGEMENT OF COPYRIGHT

When Copyright is Deemed to be Infringed?

According to Section 51 of the Copyright Act, 1957, a person is deemed to have infringed copyright only if he acts: (i) in contravention of a licence granted by the copyright owner or the Registrar of Copyrights; (ii) without a licence granted by the copyright owner or the Registrar of Copyrights provided such use was also not allowed under Section 52 of the Act.[3] It is a criminal offence to knowingly infringe a copyright. Also, civil proceedings can be initiated against an infringer. Infringing copies of works and plates used to produce them are deemed to belong to the copyright owner. In *L.B. (Plastics)* v. *Swish Products*,[4] the English court held that in order to succeed in a copyright action a plaintiff must prove that the defendant has directly or indirectly made an unlawful use of the plaintiff's copyright. It is not necessary to show that the defendant has copied from the plaintiff's work. As a matter of fact, the plaintiff has to establish and prove that copying has taken place. The beginning of the necessary proof normally lies in the establishment of similarity combined with proof access to the plaintiff's production. A similarity or even identity, if it were conceivable, between two works due to coincidence does not constitute an infringement by the second of the first.[5] However, in *R.C.A. Corporation* v. *Custom Cleared Sales,*[6] the court held that innocence is not a defence in an action for infringement.

The Kerala High Court in *Cherian P. Joseph* v. *Prabhakaran*,[7] held that a person cannot be held liable for infringement of copyright in a work if he has taken only the essential idea of the work, even if it is highly original, provided he gives expression to that idea in his own

---

2. *See,* Binu Poornamodan Cholayil, "Digital Rights Management and Fair Use in Copyright Law" 33(1–2) *Cochin University Law Review* (2009) p. 166; Mishita Jethi, "Dealing 'Fairly' with Software in India", 16 *Journal of Intellectual Property Rights* (2011) p. 313. In *Ravinder Singh and Sons* v. *Evergreen Publications (India) Ltd.* [MANU/DE/5012/2018.] the Delhi High Court observed "It is impossible to define what is "fair dealing". It must be a question of degree. You must consider first the number and extent of the quotations and extracts. Are they altogether too many and too long to be fair? If they are used as a basis for comment, criticism or review, that may be fair dealing."
3. *See, Super Cassettes Industries Ltd.* v. *Shreya Broadcasting Pvt. Ltd.*, 258 (2019) DLT 116: 2019 III AD (Delhi) 552.
4. (1979) RPC 551.
5. *See, Halsbury's Laws of England,* 4th ed., Vol. 9, para. 911 at p. 585.
6. [1978] FSR 576.
7. AIR 1967 Ker 234.

way. In *Pepsi Co. Inc.* v. *Hindustan Coca Cola*,[8] the defendant's use of "Yeh Dil Mange More" used by the plaintiffs in their advertisement was not in relation to their products. It was used in a mocking manner only in the course of comparative advertising. This itself would not *prima facie* amount to infringement of copyright. In an action for infringement of copyright in *Ziff-Davis Inc.* v. *Dr. D.K. Jain*,[9] defendants were licencees of the title "P.C. Magazine" of a publication. Plaintiffs were the owners of the copyright in the name (logo) "P.C. Magazine" etc., written in a stylist form. On the expiry of the licence the defendants continued to use the name for their publication. In this case, injunction was granted in respect of the stylised logo of "P.C. Magazine", computer shopper, internet user and P.C. week.

In *Fateh Singh Mehta* v. *O.P. Singhal*,[10] the Rajasthan High Court observed that copyright in a work is deemed to be infringed when any person, without a licence granted by the owner of the copyright does anything, which is the exclusive right to do conferred by the Act upon the owner of the copyright. Where a person has copyright in a literary work, any other person produces the work or any substantial part thereof in any material form, he is committing an infringement of copyright. The Bombay High Court in *Lallubhai* v. *Laxmi Shankar*,[11] on the question of infringement of copyright observed that the piracy in an alleged infringing work may be detected by making a careful examination of it to see whether any of the deviations and mistakes, which licence permits, in the original has been reproduced into the alleged infringing copy. The Apex Court in *R.G. Anand* v. *Delux Film*,[12] held that it is not necessary that the alleged infringement should be an exact or verbatim copy of the original but its resemblance with the original in a large measure is sufficient to indicate that it is a copy.

Further, in *Penguin Books* v. *India Book Distributors*,[13] the Delhi High Court observed that if any person without the licence of the copyright owner, imports into India for the purpose of selling or distributing for the purposes of trade a literary work the copyright is infringed if the work was lawfully published by the owner of the copyright or the exclusive licencee in the country from which it has been imported. This is clear from the definition of infringing copy in Section 2(m) read with Sections 51 and 53(1). It is also an infringement of copyright knowingly to import into India for sale or hire infringing copies of a work without the consent of the owner of the copyright though they may have been made by or with the consent of the owner of the copyright in the place where they were made. Section 51 of the Copyright Act, 1957 defines the varieties of acts which infringe copyright and all other rights created by the Act.[14] According to Section 51, copyright in a work shall be deemed to be infringed—

(a) when any person, without a licence granted by the owner of the copyright or the Registrar of Copyrights under this Act or in contravention of the conditions of a licence so granted or of any condition imposed by a competent authority under this

8. 2001 AIPC 240 (Del).
9. (2000) AIPC 330 (Del).
10. AIR 1990 Raj 8.
11. AIR 1945 Bom 51: 1946 Bom LR 697.
12. AIR 1978 SC 1613.
13. AIR 1985 Del 29.
14. *See, Lyca Productions* v. *J. Manimaran*, 2018 (73) PTC 525 (Mad): 2018 (3) CTC 605; *Indusind Media and Communications Limited* v. *State of Gujarat*, (2018) 2 GLR 1151: 2017 (71) PTC 60 (Guj).

Act—

(i) does anything, the exclusive right to do which is by this Act conferred upon the owner of the copyright, or

(ii) permits for profit any place to be used for the communication of the work to the public where such communication constitutes an infringement of the copyright in the work, unless he was not aware and had no reasonable ground for believing that such communication to the public would be an infringement of copyright; or

(b) when any person—

(i) makes for sale or hire, or sells or lets for hire, or by way of trade displays or offers for sale or hire, or

(ii) distributes either for the purpose of trade or to such an extent as to affect prejudicially the owner of the copyright, or

(iii) by way of trade exhibits in public, or

(iv) imports into India, any infringing copies of the work

Provided that nothing in sub-clause (iv) shall apply to the import of one copy of any work for the private and domestic use of the importer.

Explanation—For the purposes of this section, the reproduction of a literary, dramatic, musical or artistic work in the form of a cinematograph film shall be deemed to be an "infringing copy".

Thus, under Section 51 of the Copyright Act, 1957, copyright of a work shall be infringed when any person without a proper licence from the owner: (a) does anything, the exclusive right to do which is conferred upon the owner by the Act; (b) permits to use any place for the performance of a copyrighted work in public for profit, unless he was not aware or had no reasonable grounds for believing that such performance would be an infringement of copyright; (c) makes infringing copies for sale or hire, or selling or letting them for hire; (d) distributes infringing copies either for the purposes of trade or to such an extent as to affect prejudicially, the owner of copyright; (e) by way of trade exhibits in public; (f) imports infringing copies, except for the private and domestic use of the importer. In *Koninlijke Philips N.V.* v. *Amazestore*,[15] the Delhi High Court held that as the Plaintiffs are entitled to sole and exclusive rights to reproduce the said works in terms of Sections 13 and 14 of the Copyright Act, 1957. The Defendants' unauthorised and brazen reproduction of the Plaintiffs' literary and artistic work amounts to infringement of copyright in terms of Section 51 of the Copyright Act, 1957.

The explanation to Section 51 of the Copyright Act, 1951 further provides that the reproduction of dramatic, literary or musical works in the form of cinematograph film shall be deemed to be an "infringing copy". Thus when any person carries on any activity which contravenes any rights afforded to the owner of copyright in a work, permits any place for the public performance of the work, makes infringing copies of the work for sale of hire, distributes, exhibits or imports wringing copies of the work for the purposes of trade or

15. 2019 (78) PTC 618 (Del): 260 (2019) DLT 135.

so as to prejudicially affect the owner of copyright in the work, infringes copyright. Any dealing in infringing copies too amounts to an infringement. A reproduction of a literary, dramatic, musical or artistic work in the form of a cinematograph film is also deemed to be an infringing copy. In *Wiley Eastern Ltd.* v. *Indian Institute of Management*,[16] the court held that Section 51 of the Act speaks of what is infringement of copyright. If a particular act is not an infringement falling within any of clauses of Section 51, then the act cannot be an infringement. Section 51 being exhaustive as to what is infringement of copyright. In *Gurukrupa Mech Tech Pvt. Ltd.* v. *State of Gujarat*,[17] the Gujarat High Court held that very act of reproduction of an artistic work would constitute an infringement under Section 51 of the Copyright Act, 1957, while deciding whether the photocopies of course packs extracted from the copyrighted books would constitute infringement, as they would fall within the ambit of reproduction. The Court observed:

> "It is noteworthy that Section 14(a)(i) constitutes right to reproduce literary work per se as copyright and Section 51(a)(i) constitutes such reproduction per se as infringement of copyright and Section 2(m) constitutes the copy so reproduced as infringing copy. Infringement is complete on reproduction of the work. To constitute infringement, it is not necessary that the person who has so reproduced the work, should put it to any use or should distribute or sell the same to others. However Section 14(a)(ii) also vests the exclusive right to issue copies of the work to the public not being copies already in circulation, in the owner of the copyright and constitutes the same as copyright. Thus the action of issuing copies of the work to public would also constitute infringement of copyright under Section 51. Neither Section 14(a) (ii) nor Section 51(a)(i) require such issuance of copies to be for consideration or to make profit. Issuance of copies even if without any charge thus constitutes infringement of copyright."

A question may arise whether a police officer register FIR under Section 51(b)(i) and 63(a) of Copyright Act 1957? In *Sivaji Hi-Tec Foods Pvt. Ltd.* v. State,[18] the FIR has been registered for the offence under Section 51(b)(i) and 63(a) of Copyright Act 1957, as against four persons, in which the petitioner is arraigned. The question is when the offence registered in the FIR itself is non cognizable, whether the police has power to seal the premises or not? The Court is of the view that the offence punishable under Section 63(a) of the Copyright Act is non cognizable offence by virtue of Part II of Schedule I of Cr. P. C., since it carries imprisonment which can be extended up to three years and therefore as per Section 155 of Cr. P. C., no police officer can investigate a non cognizable offence without an order of a Magistrate. Citing the judgment of the Apex Court in *Rajeev Chaudhary* v. *State (N.C.T.) of Delhi*,[19] the Madras High Court held that the expression imprisonment for terms which may extend up to three years would not come within expression of "imprisonment of three years onwards". Therefore, the offence under Section 63(a) of Copyright Act cannot be considered as cognizable offence and the police officer has no power to register a case.

In *Bagga* v. *All India Reporter*,[20] the Bombay High Court held that an advertisement in journals or newspapers published or circulated at a place of infringing copies of a work

16. 61 (1996) DLT 281 (DB).
17. (2018) 4 GLR 3324.
18. 2019 (2) MLJ (Crl) 313.
19. AIR 2001 SC 2369 : 2001 Cri LJ 2941.
20. AIR 1969 Bom 302.

amounts to offer of sale and consequently infringement of copyright. However, in *Watson* v. *Coupland*,[21] it was observed that an agreement to sell or let for hire by itself does not amount to infringement. In *Thankappan* v. *Vidyarambham Press*,[22] the Kerala High Court observed that publishing of work of an author in another person's name without the consent of the author constitutes infringement of copyright. In *Romesh* v. *Ali Mohammad*,[23] it was observed that if an author permits his book to be published by a University as part of its syllabus, the book goes into the public domain and no copyright remains with the author. However, in *Sarma* v. *Ganesan*,[24] the court held that where an artist supplies prints of his painting of a deity to temples for installation, that does not amount to installation in a public place and the prints do not come into the public domain. In *Steelbird Hi-Tech India Ltd* v. *S.P.S. Gambhir*,[25] the Delhi High Court held that in order to succeed in an infringement of copyright, a party has to show that he is the originator of the work in the sense that the concept emanated from him. In *Vior (International) Ltd.* v. *Maxycon Health Care Private Limited*,[26] it was held that a conjoint reading of Section 51 of the Copyright Act, 1957 along with Section 14 of the Act would confer exclusive rights upon the owner of the copyright and any person or entity reproducing the work in any material form would be liable for the act of copyright infringement.

Test for Determining Infringement

The definition clause of the Copyright Act, 1957 (Section 2) does not define infringement as such; but the definition of an "infringing copy" in Section 2(m) provides some standards and criteria for the determination that an infringement has occurred.[27] Accordingly, it means: (i) in relation to a literary, dramatic, musical or artistic work, a reproduction thereof otherwise than in the form of a cinematograph film, (ii) in relation to a cinematograph film, a copy of the film made on any medium by any means; (iii) in relation to a sound recording, any other recording embodying the same sound recording, made by any means; (iv) in relation to a programme or performance in which such a broadcast reproduction right or a performer right subsists under the Act, the sound recording or a cinematograph film of such performance; if such reproduction, copy or sound recording is made or imported in contravention of the provision of the Act. The Copyright Act, 1957 confers upon the owner of the work a bundle of exclusive rights in respect of the reproduction of the work and other acts which enables the owner to get financial benefits by exercising such rights. If any of these acts relating to the work is carried out by a person other than the owner without a licence from the owner or a competent authority under the act, it constitutes infringement of copyright in the work. In *Gurukrupa Mech Tech Pvt. Ltd.* v. *State of Gujarat*,[28] it was held that a machine would

21. (1945) 1 All ER 217.
22. 1968 Ker LJ 440.
23. AIR 1965 J & K 101.
24. 1972 Cr LJ 1098.
25. 2014 (1) MPR 277: 2014 (58) PTC 428. *See also*, *Prem Singh* v. *Ceeam Auto Industries*, AIR 1990 Del 233.
26. 2018 (74) PTC 87 (Del).
27. *See*, *Maroti* v. *The State of Maharashtra*, 2018 ALLMR (Cri) 4460.
28. (2018) 4 GLR 3324.

not fall within the ambit of an "infringing copy" and thus would not fall within the array of "infringement of copyright." The Court further observed:

> So far as an artistic work is concerned any reproduction, except in the form of a cinematograph film, is deemed to be an infringing copy. Furthermore, the right of reproduction in material form, which includes the right to reproduce a two-dimensional work in a three-dimensional form, is an exclusive right vested with the owner of the copyright. Therefore, it substantiates the premise that any reproduction of a copyrighted design like a sketch or a drawing to a material/tangible form, like a machine, will be termed as an infringing copy as it is in violation of the exclusive statutory right of the lawful owner of the work constituting an offence under section 51 of the Act.

In *B.O. Morris Ltd.* v. *F. Gilman,*[29] the court observed that copying may be infringed by reproducing the work, directly from the copyright work or from memory, or from an intervening copying whether protected or unprotected. It is immaterial whether the infringing article is derived directly or indirectly from the original one. In *Gamme* v. *Relaxateze Upholstery,*[30] the court held that for establishing infringement of copyright, there must be conscious or unconscious copying by the alleged infringer. There should be a casual connection between the plaintiff's design and the alleged infringing article. Further, in *John Richardson* v. *Flanders,*[31] the court held that subconscious copying is sufficient to constitute infringement of copyright provided familiarity with the work alleged to be copied is shown.

In *Performing Rights Society* v. *Urban District Council,*[32] the Privy Council held that innocence is not a defence in an action for copyright infringement. In *RCA Corporation* v. *Custom Cleared Sales,*[33] the court laid down the rule that the knowledge of infringement means actual knowledge and not constructive. Thus, in order to determine the question of infringement the following factors are considered: (i) direct copying[34]—(a) casual connection, (b) subconscious copying, (c) direct copying, (d) indirect copying;[35] (ii) substantial taking—(a) unaltered copying, (b) extent of defendant's alteration, (c) character of plaintiff's and defendant's works, (d) nature of plaintiff's effort, (e) extent of plaintiff's effort, (f) manner in which defendant has taken advantage of plaintiff's work, (g) extent of interference with plaintiff's exploitation by defendant's acts, (g) reproduction by the original author.[36]

In *Glyn* v. *Weston,*[37] the English court held that no infringement of the plaintiffs' rights takes place where a defendant has bestowed such mental labour upon what he has taken and has subjected it to such revision and alteration as to produce an original result. But the ultimate test is: "has there been a reproduction in the defendant's work of a substantial part of the

29. [1936] 1 All ER 409.
30. [1976] RPC 377.
31. [1993] FSR 497.
32. AIR 1930 PC 314.
33. [1978] FSR 576.
34. *See, Star India Private Ltd.* v. *Leo Burnett (India) Pvt. Ltd.* (2003) 27 PTC 81 (Bom); *Norowzian* v. *Arkas Limited and Others,* [1996] FSR 394; *CBS Australia Limited and Others* v. *Telmak Teleproducts (Aust) Pvt. Ltd.* [1987] 9 IPR 440; *Telmak Teleproducts (Aust) Pvt. Ltd.* v. *Bond International,* [1985] 5 IPR 203; *Ladbroke* v. *William Hill,* [1964] 1 WLR 273.
35. *See, Zee Telefilms Limited* v. *Sundial Communications Pvt. Ltd.* (2003) 27 PTC 457 (Bom); *Mahendra Chandra Nath Ghosh* v. *Emperor,* AIR 1928 Cal 359; *Coreilli* v. *Gray,* [1913] 29 TLR 570.
36. *See,* W.R. Cornish, *Intellectual Property* (5th edition) paras. 11.03 to 11.17.
37. [1916] 1 Ch. 262.

plaintiff's work".[38] Thus, in *Williamson* v. *Pearson*,[39] the plaintiff's song began with the line, "We got sunlight on the sand". The defendant's song began with the words "We got coffee, we got tea". In this case, interim injunction was granted. However, to constitute infringement, the verbatim copy or an exact reproduction or dealing with the work is not necessary. A resemblance with the original in a large measure is sufficient. It is the degree of resemblance, which makes the infringing work a mere slavish copy of the original.[40] A literal imitation with mirror variations undoubtedly constitutes infringement.[41] Thus, in *Sillitoe* v. *McGraw Hill*,[42] the English court held that reproduction for the purpose of copyright embraces colourable imitation. Explaining the concept "colourable imitation" the Calcutta High Court in *Mohini Mohan Singh* v. *Sita Nath Basak*,[43] observed that whether a work is a colourable imitation of another must necessarily be a question of fact. Similarity is a point to be considered in this connection but mere similarity is not enough as it may be due to any one of the four causes, namely: (i) to mere chance, (ii) to both works being taken from a common source, (iii) to plaintiff's work being taken from the defendants' and (iv) defendants' work being taken from the plaintiffs. Each case must depend upon its own circumstances. It is only in the last case there is infringement. A copyright get infringed if a substantial part of it is copied. But to determine this substantiality component in the different categories of work is not an easy task. It is judged from case to case. It is here that the judiciary assumes a significant role.

Can a substantial difference between two works be a ground in determining infringement of copyright in design was examined by the Delhi High Court in *V2 Corp* v. *Innovative Techpack Limited*.[44] Citing a large number of cases,[45] the court observed that what a substantial difference is, is a question upon which no general principle can be laid down at all; it must depend on the particular facts in each case. In one case a quite small variation in the details of a design may be enough to make the design something quite different from an existing design. On the other hand, there are cases even where quite large alterations in detail leave two designs for all practical purposes the same. The Court has to consider and look at the design in question with an instructed eye and say whether there is or is not such a substantial difference between that which had been published previously and the registered design as to entitle the proprietor of the registered design to say that at the date of registration that was a new or original design and therefore properly registered.

The judiciary through various decisions has laid down certain guiding principles in this regard. To determine infringement one has to see whether the impugned rework is slavish imitation and copy of another persons work or it bears the impress of the authors' own labour and originality. The piracy in an alleged infringing copy can also be detected by making a careful examination to see whether any of the deviations and mistakes, in the original has been

38. *See, Nethaji* v. *The State*, 2015-1-LW (Crl) 300: 2015-1-LW764.
39. [1987] FSR 97.
40. *Cuniah* v. *Balraj*, AIR 1961 Mad 111.
41. V. *Govindam* v. *E.M. Gopalakrishna Kone*, AIR 1955 Mad. 391.
42. [1983] FSR 545.
43. AIR 1931 Cal 233.
44. 2014 LawSuit (Del) 3928.
45. *See, Pilot Pen Company (India) Private Ltd.* v. *Gujarat Industries Private Ltd.*, 1967 AIR (Mad) 215; *Bahkhshi* v. *Ghulam Mohammad*, AIR 1934 (Lah) 709; *Ram Sahai* v. *Angnoo*, AIR 1922 All 496.

reproduced into the alleged infringing copy.[46] The Apex Court in *R.G. Anand* v. *Delux Film*,[47] held that one of the surest and the safest test to determine whether or not there has been an infringement of copyright is to see if the reader, the spectator or the viewer after having read or seen both the works is clearly of the opinion and gets an unmistakable impression that the subsequent work appears to be a copy of the original. Thus, in *Associated Electronic and Electrical Industries* v. *Sharp Tools*,[48] the Karnataka High Court observed:

> One of the surest test to determine whether or not there has been a violation of copyright is to see if the reader, spectator, or the viewer after having read or seen both the works would be clearly of the opinion and get an unmistakable impression that the subsequent work appears to be a copy of the first. In other words, dealing with the question of infringement of copyright of the applicant's work by the respondent's work, the court is to test on the visual appearance of the object and drawing, design, or artistic work in question and by applying the test, viz., 'lay observer test' whether to persons who are not experts in relation to objects of that description, the object appears to be a reproduction. If to the 'lay observer', it would not appear to be reproduction, there is no infringement of the artistic copyright in the work.[49]

Thus, one of the surest test to determine whether or not there has been a copyright violation had been given in 1991 by the Karnataka High Court in above case where the "lay observer test" was laid down, here the lay reader, the viewer or the spectator after reading or viewing the works would be clearly of the opinion and get an unmistakable impression that the subsequent work appears to be a copy/reproduction of the first. However, it is important to state that copyright subsists in expression, not in ideas. Idea is not a subject matter of copyright.[50] Explaining the "lay observer test" in *Mother Dairy Fruit* v. *Mallikarjuna Dairy Products Pvt. Ltd.*,[51] it was held that the degree of resemblance between two works must be such that it suggests an impression, in the mind of the observer, that the work of the defendant is, in fact, the work of the plaintiff. The test called the "lay observer test" applies to find out whether the object of the defendant appears to be the object of the plaintiff.[52] Thus, in *Hindustan Lever Ltd.* v. *Rameshwar Mundia*,[53] the Court observed: "The law is that while dealing with the question of infringement of copyright of an artistic work, the Court is to test on the visual appearance of the object and drawing; design of the artistic work in question and by applying the test viz. 'the lay observer test' whether to persons who are not experts in relation to objects of that description, the object appears to be a reproduction. If to the lay observe it would not appear to be a reproduction, there is no infringement of the artistic copyright in the work." In *Francis Day and Hunter* v. *Bron*,[54] the following principles were

---

46. *Lallubhai* v. *Laxmi Shankar,* AIR 1945 Bom 51.
47. AIR 1978 SC 1613.
48. AIR 1991 Kant 406: 1991 (1) Kar LJ 482.
49. *See also, M. Radhakrishnan v. Surabhi Publications*, 2016 (3) KLJ 321: MIPR 2017 (1) 125; *Nethaji v. State*, 2015 (1) MLJ (Crl) 450.
50. *See, Harnam Pictures NV* v. *Osborne* (1967) 1 WLR 723; *Donoghue* v. *Allied Newspaper Ltd.* (1937) 3 Ch. D 503; *Hollinrake* v. *Truswell* (1894) Ch. 420.
51. 2012 (49) PTC 346 (Del).
52. *See Also, Societe Des Produits Nestle* v. *Continental Coffee Ltd.*, 2012 (49) PTC 46 (Del): MIPR 2012 (1) 135.
53. 2009 (39) PTC 570 (Del).
54. (1963) Ch. D. 587.

laid down by Wilmer, L.J. to consider whether the acts of defendant constituted reproduction of plaintiff's work:

1. There must be sufficient degree of objective similarity between the two works and there should be some casual connection between the plaintiff's and the defendant's work.
2. Whether the defendant was or not consciously aware of such casual connection is quite irrelevant. Where there is objective degree of substantial similarity, this of itself will afford *prima facie* evidence to show that there is a casual connection between the plaintiff's and the defendant's work; at least, it is a circumstance from which the inference may be drawn.
3. The fact that the defendant denies that he consciously copied affords some evidence to rebut the inference of casual connection arising from the objective similarity, but is in no way conclusive.
4. If, however, the defendant is liable to show that the work were created indecently by him, there would be no infringement of plaintiff's right of reproduction.

In *Sitanath Basak* v. *Mohini Mohan Singh,*[55] it was held that mere resemblance of a work by itself is not an evidence of piracy, when the subject matter dealt with is common. This case was an appeal against the order of the trial court injuncting the appellants from publishing a book, which allegedly infringed the copyright of the defendant's book. The appellant claimed that the similarity in the contents is only due to the commonality in the subject matter dealt with in both the books. Even though the Court acknowledged that similarities are bound to occur when a common subject matter is dealt with, it also looked into the degree of similarities and dissimilarities and concluded that the appellant has not only copied the ideas in the defendants book, but also the form and manner of expression of ideas, thus infringing the copyright of the defendant. However, the criteria for determination of infringement are different in respect of each genre of protected work. But the plaintiff must establish that the defendant "reproduced" the entire work or any substantial part thereof in order to succeed in a copyright action. It is very difficult at times to produce the direct evidence of reproduction of work by the defendant. The question of infringement is resolved by comparing the two works. In India the "lay observer test" was successfully used in post *R.G. Anand* v. *Delux Film,*[56] cases of copyright infringement. The *R.G. Anand* case is the first case which applied "lay observer test" to determine copyright infringement. It laid a seven step guideline:

1. There can be no copyright in an idea, subject matter, themes, plots, or historical or legendary facts and violation of the copyright in such cases is, confined to the form, manner and arrangement and expression of the idea by the author of the copyrighted work.[57]

---

55. AIR 1931 Cal. 233.
56. AIR 1978 SC 1613. The "lay observer test" has been used in *See, M. Radhakrishnan* v. *Surabhi Publications*, 2016 (3) KLJ 321: MIPR 2017 (1) 125; *Societe Des Produits Nestle* v. *Continental Coffee Ltd.*, 2012 (49) PTC 46 (Del): MIPR 2012 (1) 135; *Zee Telefilms* v. *Sundial Communications* (2003) 27 PTC 457 (Bom.); *Anil Gupta* v. *Kunal Dasgupta* (2002) 25 PTC 1; *Associated Industries* v. *Sharp Tools,* AIR 1991 Kant 406; *R. Madhavab* v. *S.K. Nayar,* AIR 1988 Ker 39.
57. *See, Pranda Jewelry Pvt. Ltd.* v. *Aarya 24 kt*, AIR 2015 Bom 157: 2015 (62) PTC 254 (Bom).

2. Where the same idea is being developed in a different manner, it is manifest that the source being common, similarities are bound to occur. In such a case, the courts should determine whether the similarities are on fundamental or substantial aspects of the mode of expression adopted in the copyrighted work. If the defendant's work is nothing but a literal imitation of the copyrighted work with some variations here and there, it would amount to violation of the copyright. In other words, in order to be actionable, the copy must be substantial and material one which at once leads to the conclusion that the defendant is guilty of an act of piracy.[58]
3. One of the surest and safest tests to determine whether there has been a violation of copyright is to see if, the reader, the spectator or the viewer after having read or seen both the works is clearly of the opinion and gets an unmistakable impression that the subsequent work appears to be a copy of the original.[59]
4. Where the theme is the same but is presented and treated differently so that the subsequent work becomes a completely new work, no question of violation of copyright arises.[60]
5. Where, however, apart from the similarity appearing in the two works there are also material and broad dissimilarities which negative the intention to copy the original and the coincidences appearing in the two works are clearly incidental, no infringement of the copyright comes into existence.[61]
6. As a violation of copyright amounts to an act of piracy it must be proved by clear and cogent evidence after applying the various tests laid down by the case law.[62]
7. Where the question is of the violation of the copyright of stage play by a film producer or a director, the task of the plaintiff becomes more difficult to prove piracy. It is manifest that unlike a stage play a film has a much broader perspective, wider field and a bigger background where the defendants can by introducing a variety of incidents give a colour and complexion different from the manner in which the copyright work has expressed the idea. Even so if the viewer after seeing the film gets a totality of impression that the film is by and large a copy of the original play, violation of the copyright may be said to be proved.[63]

In *Barbara Taylor Bradford* v. *Sahara Media Entertainment Ltd.*,[64] the Calcutta High Court examined the issue of copyright infringement where Barbara Taylor Bradford alleged that Sahara has copied her novel "A woman of substance" to make a 300 episode TV serial titled "Karishma—A miracle of destiny". The court had ruled that the law protected originality of expression and not originality of the central idea due to the balancing of two conflicting

58. *See, Roderick John Andrew Mackenzie v. Himalayan Heli Services Pvt. Ltd.*, 2019 (77) PTC 379 (Del).
59. *See, Dabur India Ltd.* v. *Vaidya Nandram Gigraj Chamria*, 2018 (75) PTC 38 (Del): MIPR 2018 (3) 112.
60. *See, Khaidem Jacko Meitei* v. *Union of India*, 2018 (4) GLT 107.
61. *See, Zee Entertainment Enterprises Ltd.* v. *Sony Pictures Networks India Pvt. Ltd.*, AIR 2017 Bom 221: 2017 (70) PTC 300 (Bom).
62. *See, M. Radhakrishnan* v. *Surabhi Publications*, 2016 (3) KLJ 321: MIPR 2017 (1) 125.
63. *See, Sanjay Kumar Gupta* v. *Sony Pictures Networks India P. Ltd.*, AIR 2018 Delhi 169: 2018 (75) PTC 562 (Del).
64. (2004) 28 PTC 474 (Cal.).

policies. The first policy was that the law must protect originality of work, thereby allowing the authors to reap the fruits of their labour and stopping unscrupulous pirates from enjoying those fruits. The second policy was that the protection must not become an over protection, thus, curbing future creativity. If mere plots and characters were to be protected by copyright, all authors could not write anything "original" at all, on a similar plot or on similar characters. However, in *Star India* v. *Leo Burnett,*[65] the Bombay High Court had given a different interpretation to the word "copy" where the court observed that making of another film, even though it resembles another film, does not infringe the copyright in the later, provided that it has not been made by a process of duplication, i.e., by using mechanical contrivance. Thus if a film is shot separately by different persons and it still resembles the earlier film, the subsequent film is not a copy of the first film and does not amount to infringement. A narrow copyright protection is accorded to cinematograph film as the requirements of originality is absent for claiming copyright in films. But this approach of "mechanical duplication test" has not been taken up by any other High Court.

In *Super Cassettes Industries* v. *Myspace Inc.*,[66] the plaintiff was the owner of copyright in repertoire of songs, cinematograph films and sound recordings. The defendant was a social networking and entertainment website which offers a variety of entertainment applications including sharing, viewing of music, images, cinematograph works having its base in the United States of America. The website provided country specific content. The plaintiff alleged that the defendant's website myspace.com provides country specific content and is one of the most popular social networking and content sharing websites in the world violating copyright as they had not taken licence to exhibit the material. The plaintiff contends that the defendants' basic point of attraction in running this website is to make available the multimedia content including songs, pictures, clips which can be seen and shared by the user over the Internet space. The said website includes not only recently released infringing material but also the material which has not yet been released or is authorised for broadcast through the authorized distribution channels. MySpace argued that no liability could accrue to it on two counts. The first was that it had no actual or direct knowledge or role in the selection of the content, while the second was that no control was exercised, or was exercisable over the uploading of the content. Additionally, there was no possible means by which it could have identified the offending content and segregated it from lawful content, or monitored all of the content that it serves as a platform for.

Thus, the court observed that the acts of defendants of providing the space on internet or webspace for profit are *prima facie* infringing in nature. The reasons given by the court were: firstly, the provision of Section 51(a)(i) and Section 51(a)(ii) of the Act are disjunctive in nature in as much as the word "or" between the two makes it clear that even on satisfaction of one provision, there would be an infringement of copyright; secondly, the infringement by way of authorisation would fall within Section 51(a)(1) read with Section 14 of the Act as against the act of permitting the place for profit which is separately provided under Section 51(a)(ii) of the Act; thirdly, the said acts of the defendants are certainly falling within the realm of an infringement under Section 51(a)(ii) of the Act. This is due to the reason that the

65. (2003) 27 PTC 81.
66. 2011 (47) PTC 49 (Del.).

defendants are permitting the place which is placed at webspace to the users at large. Thus, the court concluded that infringement in terms of Section 51(a)(ii) had occurred in this case, since web space is a "place" in the terms required by the Section and there were monetary gains in the form of ad revenue. The argument as to a lack of knowledge of infringement was also rejected on the ground that MySpace's provision for safeguards against infringement clearly established a reason to believe that infringement will occur. Also referenced as evidence of knowledge, or at least a reason to believe infringement would occur, is the fact that MySpace modifies the format of the content before making it available on its website. It also tested for infringement by authorisation in terms of Section 14 read with Section 51(a)(i), but concluded that this did not arise here. Thus, *in Chancellor Masters* v. *Narendera Publishing House*,[67] it was held that whenever it is found that the defendants work is nothing but a colourable imitation of the plaintiffs work, then it would amount to infringement. But, where the theme is the same but is presented and treated differently so that the subsequent work becomes a completely new work, no question of violation of copyright arises.

Infringement of Copyright in Different Kinds of Works

Infringement of Literary, Dramatic, Musical and Artistic Works

Reproduction Test of Infringement

Before examining the reproduction test it is essential to examine the issue: who can file a suit for infringement of literary, dramatic, musical and artistic works? In *Novex Communication Pvt. Ltd.* v. *Lemon Tree Hotels Ltd.*,[68] it was held that Section 51 of the Copyright Act 1957 prescribes as to when a copyright is infringed. Obviously, the use of a copyright work, without a license or without the permission of the owner of the copyright or any other person who is entitled to give such license or permission, would be infringement of the copyright. The Section 55 of the Act is very relevant for the purpose of the present judgment and discussion because the Section 55 provides that only an owner of a copyright can institute a suit or legal proceedings with respect to the infringement of a copyright. It is required to be noted that there is no provision in the Act, which entitles a copyright society to sue for infringement of the copyright. Thus, only an owner of a copyright can sue for infringement of the copyright.

In *Gramophone Company of India Ltd.* v. *D.B. Pandey*,[69] the Apex Court held that: "An artistic, literary, dramatic or musical work is the brainchild of an author, the fruit of his labour and, so, considered to be his property." In this way, highly is it prized by all civilised nations that it is thought worthy of protection by national laws and international conventions relating to copyright. According to Section 2(m)(i) of the Copyright Act, 1957 infringing copy in relation to a literary, dramatic, musical or artistic work, a reproduction thereof otherwise than in the form of a cinematographic film made in contravention of the provision of the Act. This includes a reproduction imported in contravention of the Act. Thus, reproduction is an important test to determine the infringement of literary, dramatic, musical and artistic works.

---

67. 2008 (38) PTC 385 (Del): 2008 (106) DRJ 482.
68. 2019 II AD (Delhi) 644.
69. (1984) 2 SCC 534.

In order to succeed in a copyright action the plaintiff must establish that the defendant "reproduced" the entire work or any substantial part thereof. There is no copyright in an idea. Therefore, anyone can make use of an existing idea in creating his "original" work. The Delhi High Court in *Mother Dairy Fruit and Vegetable Pvt. Ltd.* v. *Mallikarjuna Dairy Products Pvt. Ltd.*[70] held that the defendant has every right to use the basic idea involved in the work of the plaintiff, but, he is not permitted to express that idea in the same form and the same manner in which it has been done by the plaintiff.

According to Section 14 of the Copyright Act the copyright is given to a "work" or "any substantial part thereof" in "any material form". Thus, the reproduction of a literary, dramatic, musical or artistic work can be in "any material form" and so is not limited to "carbon copies" of the copyrighted work. In *Public Trust of India Ltd.* v. *Navbharat Press (Bhopal Pvt.)*,[71] the plaintiff was a premier news agency, which provided national and international news content to various newspapers, television or websites and others subscribing to its service. Defendants published verbatim copies and/or colourable imitation of works or news copyright in which vested with the plaintiff. The court held that the acts of defendants constituted infringement of copyright under Section 14(a)(i) read with Section 51.

It is to be noted that a literal imitation of the copyrighted work with some variations here and there would undoubtedly constitute infringement. In other words, the number of words, paragraphs or pages copied is not decisive; even a small amount of reproduction may infringe copyright.[72] In *Frank Educational Aids (P) Ltd.* v. *Fair Deal Marketing*,[73] the plaintiff were exclusive licences for producing an artistic work broad game called "Whatever Next" of a British company who were copyright owners of the broad game. Defendants produced a similar product under the name "Funster". Interim injunction restraining copyright infringement and passing off as plaintiff prior users was granted. In determining the infringement criteria in *Burroughs Welcome* v. *Uni-Sole*,[74] the court held that the test of actual reproduction of the artistic work is not the criteria, substantial similarity is sufficient. In this connection, minor variations are of no consequence. Some decisions apply the criterion of "external" features ("get up and the overall scope of publication") and "internal" features ("the general layout", "the manner of treatment" of subject matter, and "the amount of material contained in the book in question") as relevant to determination of infringement. The criterion of "colourable imitation" or "colourable variation" is also often used. In *Francis Day and Hunter* v. *Bron*,[75] the English court held that in order to constitute infringement of copyright in any literary, dramatic or musical work, it is well established that two elements must be present: first, there must be sufficient objective similarity between the infringing work and the copyright work, or a substantial part thereof, for the former to be properly described, not necessarily as identical with, but as a reproduction or adaption of the latter; secondly, the copyright work must be the source from which the infringing work is derived, but it need not be the direct source.

---

70. 2012 (49) PTC 346 (Del).
71. 2012 (50) PTC 316 (Del).
72. *S.K. Dutta* v. *Law Book Co.,* AIR 1954 All 570.
73. (1998) AIPC 169 (Del).
74. (1999) PTC 188 (Mum).
75. [1963] Ch. D 587.

In *Warwick Film Production Ltd.* v. *Eisinger*,[76] it was held that to constitute infringement the defendant must have reproduced a substantial part of the plaintiffs work. Now the question arises what constitute reproduction? What is relevant to consider constituting reproduction has been stated in *Gleeson* v. *Denne*,[77] thus:

1. In order to constitute reproduction within the meaning of the Act, there must be (a) a sufficient degree of objective similarity between the two works, and (b) some casual connection between the plaintiffs' and the defendants' work.[78]
2. It is quite irrelevant to inquiry whether the defendant was or was not consciously aware of such casual connection.
3. Where there is a substantial degree of objective similarity, this of itself will afford *prima facie* evidence to show that there is a casual connection between the plaintiffs and defendants works; at least it is a circumstance from which the reference may be drawn.[79]
4. The fact that the defendant denies that he consciously copied affords some evidence to rebut the inference of casual connection arising from the objective similarity but is in no way conclusive.[80]

In *Raj Video Vision* v. *K. Mohanakrishnan*,[81] the Madras High Court held that in order to constitute infringement of copyright two elements must be present: (i) there must be sufficient objective similarity between the infringing work and the copyright work, and (ii) the copyright work must be the source from which the infringing work is derived, but, it need not be the direct source. In *William Hill (Football)* v. *Ladbroke (Football)*,[82] the court observed: "If you take a short poem out of an entire volume, you may be infringing copyright, or if you take only 28 bars out of a piece of music, you may do so." However, the reproduction of a part which by itself has no originality will not normally be considered as a substantial part. In *Jarraold* v. *Heywood*,[83] the court held that if any part of a work complained a script of another or with colourable additions and variations and prepared without any real independent literary labour such portion of the work is piratical. But it is impossible to establish a charge of piracy when it is necessary to track many passages and lines through hundreds of pages or when the authors of a work challenged piratical have honestly applied their labour to various sources of infringement available. This principle was followed by the Madhya Pradesh High Court in *Mishra Bandhu Karyalaya* v. *Shivaratanlal*.[84] There is no copyright so far as the general plan, style and arrangement of a book are concerned. Thus, the Madras High Court

76. [1967] 3 All ER 367. *See also*, *Joy Music* v. *Sunday Pictorial Newspapers* [1960] 2 QB 60.
77. [175] RPC 471.
78. *See*, *Chancellor* v. *Rameshwari Photocopy Services*, 2017 (69) PTC 123 (Del): 235 (2016) DLT 409; *Twentieth Century for Film Corporation* v. *Sohail Maklai Entertainment Pvt. Ltd.*, 2010 (44) PTC 647 (Bom): 2010 (112) Bom LR 4216.
79. *See*, *Dart Industries Inc.* v. *Techno Plast*, 2007 (35) PTC 285 (Del).
80. *Garapati Prasada Rao* v. *Parnandi Saroja*, AIR 1992 AP 230: 992 Cri LJ 2561.
81. AIR 1998 Mad 294: 1999 (19) PTC 110 (Mad).
82. [1980] RPC 539.
83. [1870] 18 WR 279.
84. AIR 1970 MP 261.

in *Forster* v. *Parasuram*[85] held that under the guise of copyright, a plan cannot ask the court to close all the avenues of research and scholarship and all frontiers of human knowledge. Where the similarities and identities are due to coincidence and the necessities of the case (e.g. dictionaries, calendars, railway timetables, logarithmic tables, etc.) the question of copyright will not arise.

It emerges from the above discussion that over time the courts have developed certain test to determine what exactly might be covered by "reproduction". Thus, courts have held that there will be infringement if the extracts comprise a "substantial part" of the work. Although Section 14 of the Copyright Act, 1957 used the word "substantial part", but the phrase is not defined in the Act. In *Catnic Components Ltd.* v. *Hill and Smith Ltd.*,[86] the court held that substantial relates not only to the quantity of the work but also its quality. Explaining the concept the court further observed that whenever a person photocopying one page from a report running into a hundred pages has not taken a "substantial part" of the report. But if he copies one page of recommendations and suggestions of the report then it would certainly comprise a "substantial part" of the work. Sometimes the courts have also applied "totality of impression test" in determining copyright infringement. In *Civic Chandaran* v. *Ammini Amma,* the Kerala High Court observed that the "totality of impression test"[87] is satisfied when the reader, spectator or the viewer after having read or seen both works is clearly of the opinion and gets an unmistakable impression that the subsequent work appears to be a reproduction of the original.

Infringement of Literary Work

Although copyright subsists in original literary work under Section 13 of the Copyright Act, 1957, the infringement of literary work is to be examined in the light of Section 51 of the Act. In common parlance, the term "literary work" means any work written or printed in any language such as novels, poetry, history or books on any subject whatsoever.[88] Following the principle laid down by the Allahabad High Court in *Shyam Lal* v. *Gaya Prasad,*[89] the Madras High Court in *Sulamangalam R. Jayalakshmi* v. *Meta Musicals*[90] held that the expression "literary work" not only means such work which deals with any particular aspect of literature in prose and poetry but also indicates a work which is literature, i.e., anything in writing which could be said to come within the ambit of literary work. Further, Section 2(o) of the Act provides that "literary work" includes computer programmes, tables and compilations

85. AIR 1964 Mad 331. *See also, Ramesh Chowdhury* v. *Ali Mohammad Nawsheri*, AIR 1965 J&K 101; *Dutt* v. *Law Book Co.,* AIR 1954 All 570; *Kartar Singh* v. *Ladha Singh*, AIR 1934 Lah 777; *Macmillan Co.* v. *Cooper*, AIR 1924 PC 75.
86. (1982) RPC 183.
87. *See, Hindustan Unilever Limited* v. *Reckitt Benckiser India Limited*, 2014 (57) PTC 495 (Del): 207 (2014) DLT 713; *Reckitt Benckiser India Limited* v. *Naga Ltd.*, 2003 (26) PTC 535 (Del): 104 (2003) DLT 490.
88. *See, Mohanlal Gupta* v. *Board of School Education, Haryana* (1978) IPLR 83; *Agarwala Publishing House, Khurja* v. *Board of High School and Intermediate Education*, AIR 1967 All 91; *Jagdish Prasad Gupta* v. *Parmeshwar Prasad Singh*, AIR 1966 Pat 33.
89. AIR 1971 All 192.
90. AIR 2000 Mad 454: (2000) PTC 681 (Mad).

including computer databases. In *Pearson India Education Service Pvt. Ltd.* v. *New Rubric Solutions LLP*,[91] it was held that even a computer work or chart or tables and compilations can constitute literary work. In the instant case, the chart prepared and the presentation made as referred to in the body of the order under challenge prima facie shows that it falls within the definition of the term "literary work."

In *Burlington Home Shopping Pvt. Ltd.* v. *Rajnish Chibber*,[92] the Delhi High Court held that compilation of list of clients/customers developed by a person by devotion time, money and labour is a literary work having copyright. Thus, it is well settled that even where the source of information used in a book is something common and is such which is available to all even then a compilation which has been brought out as a result of labour and industry put by a person, then in such a case he can claim a copyright in the publication brought out by him. The right which a person acquires in a work which is the result of his intellectual labour is called his copyright. The primary function of copyright law is to protect the fruits of a man's work, labour, skill or test from annexation by other people.

However, in *Rai Toys Industries* v. *Munir Printing Press*,[93] the Delhi High Court held that the commonplace matter of the tables left no room for test or judgment and their selection did not constitute an original literary work and no copyright subsisted in the diary. Thus, pocket diaries which contained, apart from usual pages, information of the kind usually founding diaries a calendar for the year, postal information, a selection of days and dates for the year, tables of weights and measures, etc. are not original literary work therefore the question of infringement of copyright does not arise. In *Rupendra Kashyap* v. *Jivan Publishing House*,[94] it was held that papers set for examinations are literary work within the meaning of Copyright Act, 1957 and the person who sets these questions is the author of the copyright therein. Hence, infringement act lies.

The meaning given to the term "literary work" under Section 2(o) of the Copyright Act, 1957 through the Copyright (Amendment) Act, 1999 is not limited to such work but much wider scope has been provided by the amendment. Thus, according to Section 2(o) "literary work" includes computer programs, tables and compilations including computer literary data bases. Section 2(ffb) of the Act provides that "computer" includes any electronic or similar device having information processing capabilities. Further, Section 2(ffc) provides that "computer programme" means a set of instructions expressed in words, codes, schemes or in any other form, including a machine readable medium, capable of causing a computer to perform a particular task or achieve a particular result. In *Cantor Fitzgerald International* v. *Tradition*,[95] the court held that the architecture of a computer program (which might be either the overall structure of the system at programmes) was capable of protection if a substantial part of the programmer's skill, labour and judgement had gone into it. Again, in *John Richerdson* v. *Flanders*,[96] the court held that where two programmes produced similar screen displays does not necessarily prove similarity in the programmes.

---

91. AIR 2016 Kant 25: ILR 2016 KARNATAKA 2766.
92. (1995) PTC 278 (Del).
93. (1982) PTC 85 (Del). *See also*, *Deepak Printers* v. *Forward Stationery Mart* (1981) PTC 186 (Guj).
94. (1996) PTC 439 (Del): 1996 (38) DIR 81.
95. [2000] RPC 95.
96. [1993] FSR 497.

In *Adobe Systems Inc.* v. *Sachin Naik,*[97] the plaintiffs filed suit for permanent injunction restraining infringement of copyright, rendition of accounts, damages and delivery of plaintiffs' unlicensed software. The Court also appointed a Local Commissioner, who in her report, has stated that thirty-three computer software by the defendants were installed with pirated software of plaintiffs. The Court by an ad-interim ex parte order restrained the defendants, its employees, agents, servants, etc. from using the plaintiffs' unlicensed software. In its reasoning, the court observed that the software programmes as developed and marketed by the plaintiffs are a "computer programme" within the meaning of Section 2(ffc) of the Copyright Act, 1957 and also included in the definition of a literary work as per Section 2(o) of the Act. The plaintiffs' works are also protected in India under Section 40 of the Act read with the International Copyright Order, 1999 as the rights of authors of member countries of the Berne and Universal Copyright Conventions are protected under Indian copyright law. India is the signatory to both the Universal Copyright Convention and the Berne Convention.

The issue regarding the infringement of computer data bases was examined in *Burlington* v. *Rajnish.*[98] The court held that seizing of defendants database stored in floppy disc and getting the contents compared with the contents of plaintiffs' floppy discs by an expert commissioner is necessary to find whether there has been copying. In *Microsoft Corporation* v. *Rajendra Pawar,*[99] the plaintiff was the owner of the copyright in its computer program within the meaning of Section 2(ffc) of the Copyright Act and owner of the registered trademark "Microsoft". The defendants were preloading various software of the plaintiff, without any authorisation or licence from them on to the hard disk of the computers that were being assembled and sold by them. The court Delhi High Court held that this amount to infringement. In *Microsoft Corporation* v. *Nimesh,*[100] defendants were loading software programs of Microsoft on the branded computers without taking any authorisation from them and selling the computers with the unauthorised computer programs to the customer. The court held that the rights of the plaintiff were protected under Section 40 of the Copyright Act and defendants infringed rights of owners of copyright under Section 14(a)(i) and 51.

In *Blackwood* v. *Parsuraman,*[101] the Madras High Court held that a translation of a literary work is itself a literary work and is entitled to copyright protection, if it is original and the author has expended sufficient labour and skill on it. The reproduction or publication of the translation without the consent or licence of the owner of the copyright in the original will constitute infringement. The Bombay High Court in *Reghunathan* v. *All India Reporter Ltd.*[102] held that the head notes of judgments contain in clear and concise language the principle of law to be deduced from the decision to which it is prefixed or the facts and circumstances which bring the case in hand within some principle or rule of law or of practice. The preparation of such a head note or the side or marginal note of a report of a judgment requires the exercise

97. AIR 2013 Del 80: 2013 (54) PTC 443. *See also*, *Microsoft Corporation* v. *S. Sarkar*, 2013 LawSuit (Del) 376: 2013 (2) AD (Del) 625.
98. (1995) PTC 278.
99. 2008 (36) PTC 697 (Del).
100. 2012 (51) PTC 205 (Del).
101. AIR 1959 Mad 410.
102. AIR 1971 Bom 48: (1982) PTC 342. *See also*, *Jogesh Chandra Chaudhuri* v. *Mohim Chandra Rai*, AIR 1915 Cal 112: (1914) CWN 1078.

of skill and thought. The head notes of law reports are therefore original literary work which is entitled to copyright protection. A genuine abridgement of judgment of the court is an original work and can be the subject matter of infringement of a copyright, even if the amount of originality is very small. However, the Delhi High Court in *Eastern Book Company* v. *Navin J. Desai*[103] held that in case the head notes are verbatim extracts from the judgments of the court there is no amount of skill or labour involved in preparing the head notes and no person can claim a copyright therein. Hence, in such a case the question of infringement of copyright does not arise.

The Bombay High Court in *Ganga Vishnu Shrikisondas* v. *Moreshwar Bapuji Hegishte*,[104] the plaintiff brought out a new and noted edition of an old Sanskrit work incorporating extracts from other works with footnotes. In this case, the defendant's work which was closely similar to plaintiff's work with same extracts and footnotes. The court held that defendant infringed plaintiff's copyright. In *Mohini Mohan Singh* v. *Sita Nath Basak*,[105] the Calcutta High Court held that in certain categories of works similarity to a large extent is inevitable and each one of the points of similarity may not be worth anything, but a conglomeration of too many points of similarity may constitute a strange coincidence, which may point to the defendant having copied from the plaintiff's book. Allahabad High Court in *S.K. Dutta* v. *Law Book Co.*,[106] observed that the infringement comes in when it can be shown that someone has instead of utilising available sources to originate his works appropriated the labours of another by resorting to a slavish copy or more colourable imitation thereof. Thus, the court observed:

> Decision reported in law reports are 'common property' for commentators on the law, and they must per necessity have to have recourse to them because without reference to them no commentator can give his readers a correct idea of the law.

Further, in *Shyamlal* v. *Gaya Prasad*,[107] also the Allahabad High Court held that in determining the infringement of copyright one must see whether the impugned work is a slavish imitation and copy of another person's work or it bears the impress of the author's own labour, expert and originality. Thus, a work of compilation of nature similar to that of another will not by itself constitute infringement of the copyright of another person's work written in similar pattern. In *Fateh Singh Mehta* v. *Singhal*,[108] the court held that copyright subsists in a research thesis or dissertation. Unauthorised copying of a student's thesis for muster's degree by his guide for obtaining Ph.D. degree is an infringement of the copyright in the thesis. In *Blackwood* v. *Parasuraman*,[109] the question was whether a student's guide written in respect of a text book is an infringement of the copyright in the textbook will depend upon the particular facts of the case. If the guide reproduces the whole of the work so as that it may serve as a reproduction of or a substitute for the original in addition to being a guide it may be considered as infringement.

---

103. (2001) PTC 75 (Del).
104. (1889) ILR 13 Bom 358.
105. AIR 1931 Cal 233.
106. AIR 1954 All 570.
107. AIR 1971 All 192.
108. (1990) IPLR 69.
109. AIR 1959 Mad 410.

In *J.N. Bagga* v. *AIR Ltd.,*[110] the Bombay High Court has examined the issue of interpretation concerning infringement of copyright in a book by virtue of Section 51(b)(1) of the Copyright Act, 1957 making display "by way of trade" or offer to sell copyrighted work. The accused advertised in a law journal a list of books, including a book published by the complainants which was allegedly an infringing copy. The question arose whether the words "any person ... offers to sell" should be construed in a generic or restricted sense. The generic view would compel the conclusion that "offer to sell" means a proposal for sale; it is a way of soliciting orders for the publication. The restricted view would treat an "offer for sale" through an advertisement as "merely an invitation of an offer or invitation of a proposal", and not as "offer" itself. An advertisement in a newspaper or a law journal, on this view, "never becomes an offer for sale". The High Court preferred the generic construction on the ground that the makers of the 1957 Act had before them the provisions of the *Indian Contract Act* which treat such offers as invitation for proposals rather than an "offer". Moreover, the history of the legislation, both in contract and copyright, was known to the *Indian Parliament*; and yet it elected to define the relevant term without any reference to the law of contract. Above all the legislative intention to "guard the copyright" was decisive for judicial interpretation; accordingly, it was held that the expression "offers for sale by way of trade" or "offering for sale" must "include the newspaper advertisement where the traders merely solicit customers...". This decision is also notable for its approach which in effect maintains that Indian copyright law must be construed in Indian terms.

In *John Wiley and Sons Inc.* v. *Prabhat Chander Kumar Jain,*[111] the Delhi High Court examined the issue relating to copyright infringement of books. In this case, the plaintiffs were publishers in USA. The grievance of the plaintiffs begins with the rampant problem of the export of books which are reprint editions meant for the Indian and neighbouring territories to the western countries which not only causes copyright infringement but also leads to royalty losses of the plaintiffs who are the owners of the respective copyrights. The defendants contended that the export of books did not amount to infringement of copyright. They also relied upon the rule of "exhaustion of rights" whereby the rights of the copyright holder were lost once the first sale of the article was affected. The court, after discussing Sections 13, 14, 30, 51 and 54 of the Copyright Act, 1957 laid down the following propositions:

> That the rights of the owner may be broader than the limited rights of the exclusive licencee, although the exclusive licencee has the independent right to sue for infringement of the copyright.
>
> The rights of the owner and exclusive licencee may not be the same and the rights of the exclusive licensee shall also be subject CS (OS) No. 1960/2008 Page 36 of 57 to the fetters imposed by the agreement between the licensor and licencee.

Applying the above principles, the court held that the representation to the customers by the defendants that the books advertised by them are international editions with content identical to the USA edition is itself evident of the fact that the defendants are aware that the books which are sold in the USA are not the same as those sold by them. The said acts of the defendants are also causing royalty losses to the plaintiffs. Thus, the said acts of the

110. AIR 1969 Bom. 302.
111. 2010 (44) PTC 675 (Del).

defendants are intentional acts and are *prima facie* infringing by way of contravention of the conditions of licensing rights which the defendants have attained by way of purchase with notice. Hence, seen either from the perspective of the rights of the owner or from the position of the licensee, the acts of CS (OS) No. 1960/2008, Page 42 of 57 the defendants are *prima facie* acts of infringement within the meaning of Section 51(a) of the Copyright Act 1957.

Infringement of Dramatic Work

Section 2(h) of the Copyright Act 1957 provides that "dramatic work" includes any piece for recitation, choreographic work or entertainment in dumb show, the scenic arrangement or acting, form of which is fixed in writing or otherwise but does not include a cinematograph film.[112] In *Institute for Inner Studies* v. *Charlotte Anderson*,[113] the Delhi High Court held that the definition of the dramatic work is inclusive one and therefore may include the works of the nature prescribe under the provisions of the Act. The consequence of the said inclusive definition would result that the Asanas of Yoga or Pranic Healing is akin to choreography if the same is written in the form of script and thus if there is no voice or song along with the dance, it is may similar to that of Pantomime or dance. The Asanas of Yoga or Pranic Healing if written may be included within the realm of the dramatic work. On a careful understanding of the concept of the dramatic work as to what sort of the works are protected within the ambit of the dramatic work and after studying the pre-requisite requirements for calling any work as dramatic work, it may be concluded that the arts and exercises like Yoga, Pranic Healing Technique or daily routine exercises though appear to be choreographic work but they are as a matter of fact not a choreographic work.

In *Lyca Productions* v. *J. Manimaran*,[114] the Madras High Court observed that the Sections 13 and 16 of the Copyright Act makes it clear that what is protected under the Copyright Act is the work which is relatable to the visual recording, including sound recording, produced by process analogous to cinematography. The title, which may be a commonly used word, cannot be protected under the law of copyright. Section 13 makes it clear that there is no copyright in a title, it is the entire work which is protected by copyright. The Section 13 shows that copyright subsists in, inter alia, original works including original literary, dramatic and artistic works and cinematograph films. A title is not an original literary work. Hence, a title does not qualify for being described as work.[115] The acts constituting infringement of a dramatic work are the same as those for literary works. According to Section 2(h) of the Copyright Act, 1957.

In *Fortune Films International* v. *Dev Anand*,[116] the Bombay High Court held that under the definition to be found in Section 2(h) only for a dramatic work of any of the three types specified, viz., (i) piece for recitation, (ii) choreographic work, or (iii) entertainment in dumb show would be included, and then further only where the scenic arrangement or acting form of which (in the three types) is fixed in writing or otherwise. When this requirement

---

112. *See, Novex Communication Pvt. Ltd.* v. *Lemon Tree Hotels Ltd.*, 2019 II AD (Delhi) 644.
113. 2014 (57) PTC 228 (Del): MIPR 2014 (1) 129.
114. 2018 (73) PTC 525 (Mad): 2018 (3) CTC 605.
115. *See, Krishika Lulla* v. *Shyam Vithalrao Devkatta*, 2015 (10) SCALE 718: (2016) 2 SCC 521.
116. AIR 1979 Bom 17.

is satisfied, then the work under the consideration will amount to a "dramatic work" which will be protected by the provisions contained in the Copyright Act. In *Green* v. *Broadcasting Corporation of New Zealand*,[117] the format of a Television Programme (talent quest programme) its title "Opportunity Knocks" and various catch phrases used in the programme were held not to constitute a dramatic or literary work to be entitled to copyright protection and consequently copying of these features did not constitute infringement of copyright.

In *Norowzian* v. *Arkas Ltd.*,[118] the question as to whether a short film called "joy" consisting of a man dancing to music was infringed by another film called "anticipation". In both films, the visual impact was produced by an editing technique known as "jump cutting". Both were advertising films. It was held by the court of appeal that (i) since "joy" was a work of action capable of being performed before an audience it was a dramatic work, (ii) "joy" was not a recording of a dramatic work, (iii) "anticipation" was not a copy of a substantial part of "joy". Thus, the film was not a recording of anything that could be performed or danced by anyone. Hence, the action was dismissed.

The question has persisted time and again whether adaptation in relation to a dramatic work is an infringement. According to Section 2(a) of the Copyright Act, 1957, adaptation in relation to a dramatic work means: (i) the conversion of the work into a non-dramatic work, (ii) abridgement of the work or any version of the work in which the story or action is conveyed wholly or mainly by means of pictures in a form suitable for reproduction in a book, or in a newspaper, magazine or similar periodical. Thus, the form, manner or arrangement of a drama and movie are materially different from a newspaper article and by the very nature of the media there is fundamental and substantial dissimilarity in the mode of expression of the idea in a newspaper article and in a stage play or in a movie. Under Section 2(a)(v) of the Act adaptation in relation to any work includes any use of such work involving its rearrangement or alteration, which will obviously apply to dramatic work as well. Thus, copyright subsists not only in the actual words of the work but in the dramatic incidents created, so that if these are taken there may be an infringement although no wards are copied. In *Indian Express* v. *Jagmohan*,[119] the defendants made a stage play and a movie based on the central theme of certain articles published by the plaintiff, purchase of women by name Kamala by a journalist to highlight the flesh trade flourishing in some parts of the country. The article published contained an autobiographical account of the part actually played by the author in the affair and he had presented the whole affair in his own style. In the drama and movie, the emphasis was on human bondage, particularly of Indian women. It was held that the stage play or the movie was not an infringement of the copyright. The court further held that there is no copyright in an event which has actually taken place.

Infringement of Musical Work

Copyright subsists in original musical work and the acts constituting infringement of a musical work are the same as those for literary and dramatic works. However, there are some special features of musical work. According to Section 2(p) of the Copyright Act, 1957, "musical

117. [1989] RPC 469.
118. [2000] FSR 363 (CA).
119. AIR 1958 Bom 229.

work" means a work consisting of music and includes any graphical notation of such work but does not include any words or any action intended to be sung, spoken or performed with the music.[120] In *Gramophone Company of India Ltd.* v. *Super Cassettes Industries Ltd.*,[121] one of the issues that came up for consideration was the definition of the term musical work. After referring to Section 2(p) of the Act the court observed:

> "Musical work" is not merely a combination of melody and harmony or either of them. It must necessarily also have been "printed, reduced to writing or otherwise graphically produced or reproduced". As we know figurations, progressions and rhythmic patterns are sometimes used in creation of melodies. Every musical composition has a structure, or shape, that is, the arrangement of individual elements so as to constitute a whole and that musical notation means a visual record of musical sound (heard or imagined) or a set of visual instructions for performance of music. Its main elements are pitch (location of musical sound on the scale), duration, timbre, and volume. There are various systems of notation like verbal, alphabetical, numerical, graphic and tablatures. The words printed, reduced writing or otherwise graphically produced or reproduced are thus not an empty formality.

According to the definition under Section 2(p) of the Copyright Act, protection of copyright will be given to musical work which has been reduced to any material form. Thus, "musical work" is not merely a combination of melody and harmony or either of them. It must necessarily also have been "printed, reduced to writing or otherwise graphically produced or reproduced". This appears to be permissible under Article 2(2) read with Article 2(1) of the Bern Convention. The definition of composer under the Act is in comfort with this concept. According to Section 2(ffa), "composer", in relation to a musical work, means the person who composes the music regardless of whether he records it in any form of graphical notation. Section 2(d) further provides that author in relation to a musical work is the only composer and Section 16 confirms copyright to these works which are recognised by the Act. The Supreme Court in *Indian Performing Rights Society* v. *Eastern Indian Motion Pictures Association*[122] held that the composer alone has copyright in a musical work. The singer has none, although the major attraction which lends monetary value to a musical performance is not the music maker, so much as the musician. The definition of adaptation, however, differs. According to Section 2(a)(iv) of the Copyright Act, adaptation in relation to a musical work means any arrangement or transcription of the work.

The infringement of copyright in a musical work is not to be determined by a note for note comparison but should be determined by the ear as well by the eye. Applying the test of reproduction in *Joy Music Ltd.* v. *Sunday Pictorial Newspapers*,[123] the court observed that the defendant's work had its original in plaintiff's work but it was produced by sufficient independent new work by the defendant that it to be not a reproduction of the plaintiff's work. In *Francis Day and Hunter* v. *Born*,[124] the defendants' work may be identical to the plaintiff's work in every respect, but if it is created independently it is not infringement. The question whether the defendant has copied the plaintiff's work depends to a large extent on the judge's

120. *See, Indian Performing Right Society Ltd.* v. *Vodafone Idea Ltd.*, (2019) 2 CALLT 436 (HC).
121. 1996 (16) PTC 252 (Del): 58 (1995) DLT 99.
122. AIR 1977 SC 1443.
123. [1960] 1 All ER 703.
124. [1963] 2 All ER 16.

own impression and on expert evidence. The defendant may make use of plaintiffs work but if he has not copied a substantial part of the plaintiffs work or if he has altered it substantially it may not constitute infringement.

In *Gramophone Company of India Ltd.* v. *Super Cassettes Industries Ltd.*,[125] the contention raised by the plaintiff was that the defendant by creating the version record infringed the copyright of the musical work in the film. In this case Rajeshree Production Pvt. Ltd. who produced the film "*Hum Aapke Hain Kaun*" owned the copyright to the songs and musical work incorporated in the film. They assigned the copyright in the songs to the plaintiff to produce sound records. The plaintiff produced and sold about 55 lakhs of audio records and 40,000 CDs with the title "*Hum Aapke Hain Kaun*" and was expecting to sell an equal number in the future. The defendant launched a version record with the same title, get up, etc. The present suit is for infringement of copyright by the defendant. After considering the fact that the plaintiff made the records from the plates given by the owner of the film and examining the definitions of cinematograph film, sound track and infringing copy of the film in the Copyright Act, the court held:

> The plaintiff nowhere claims that the records made by the defendants "embody" the recording in any part of the soundtrack associated with the film. Rather, the records so made by the defendants are only a version recording by using another voice or voices and with different musicians and arrangers. In short the records in question embody no part of the soundtrack of the film. Thus the records so made do not *prima facie* fall within the definition of "infringing copy".

Thus, the court observed that what is surprising is that the defendants have nowhere claimed that the combination of melody and harmony which one finds in the records made by the plaintiff as well as the defendants had ever been printed, reduced to writing or otherwise graphically produced or reproduced. What is more surprising is that the plaintiff too nowhere pleads the record made by it as being a combination of such melody and harmony or either of them which had been printed, reduced to writing or graphically produced or reproduced. The result is that the record made by the plaintiff cannot be claimed to be of a "musical work" both by the plaintiff and by the defendant. In *Sulamangalam R. Jayalakshmi* v. *Meta Musicals*,[126] the defendants copied the musical work composed by the plaintiff and sung and recorded in cassettes. The copyright in which was owned by the plaintiff was infringed by the defendants by reproducing the recorded music from the cassettes. In this case interim injunction was granted.

Infringement of Artistic Work

According to Section 2(c) of the Copyright Act, 1957, an "artistic work" means painting, a sculpture, a drawing (including a diagram, map, chart or plan), an engraving or a photograph, work of architecture; and any other work of artistic craftsmanship. In *IPEG Inc.* v. *Kay Bee Engineers*,[127] it was held that the definition of "artistic work" has a very wide connotation as it is not circumscribed by any limitation of the work possessing any artistic quality. Even

125. 1996 (16) PTC 252 (Del): 58 (1995) DLT 99.
126. AIR 2000 Mad 454: (2000) PTC 681 (Mad).
127. AIR 2016 Guj 104: 2016 (66) PTC 305 (Guj).

an abstract work, such as a few lines or curves arbitrarily drawn would qualify as an artistic work. It may be two dimensional or three dimensional. The artistic work may or may not have visual appeal. However, the design may or may not enjoy a copyright protection under the Copyright Act depending on whether it is an "original artistic work" or not.[128] In *Midas Hygiene Industries Pvt. Ltd.* v. *Sudhir Bhatia*,[129] it was held that Section 2 (c) (iii) of the Copyright Act brings within its purview "any other work of artistic craftsmanship." Evidently, the distinctively written words "Krazy Lines" and "Laxman Rekha" could be understood, within the language of the Act, as a diagrammatic drawing, or alternatively, as an engraving; the innovative representation of the insecticide products are covered by the expression "work of artistic craftsmanship" of the Act.

In *Lallubhai* v. *Laxmi Shankar*,[130] the Bombay High Court held that in case of artistic work, e.g., picture of a deity, there is no better way of detecting the piracy in an alleged infringing work than by making a careful examination of it to see whether any of the deviations and mistakes which artistic licence permits in the original have been reproduced into the alleged infringing copy. Thus, infringement of a painting or a picture may be detected by a close comparison of the two works to see whether minute details in the original work have been reproduced in their alleged infringing copy. In *Surya Roshni Ltd.* v. *Metalman Industries Ltd.*,[131] the plaintiffs claimed ownership of double coloured bands on pipes. The use of colour bands on pipes was prescribed by Indian Standard Institute to indicate quality. Accordingly, there could be no infringement of the use of colours on pipes. Hence, ex-parte injunction granted vacated. But in *Hygienic Research Institute* v. *Shobhan Lal Jain*,[132] plaintiff's product "Super Vasmol-33" hair dye was sold in Cartons in which copyright subsisted in the artistic work. Defendants almost entirely copied this artistic work for their product "Super Vasmol-33". Hence, permanent injunction for copyright was granted.

In *Sarma* v. *Ganesan*,[133] it was held that copyright in a painting is infringed when a person copies the original painting or picture of the painting. But, reproduction of a work in the public domain can be made by anybody. In *Daily Calendar Supplying Bureau* v. *United Concer*,[134] the defendants had reproduced certain substantial details in the original including certain measurements which were mathematically extracted amounting to conscious copying and infringement. Applying the test "a copy is that which comes near to the mind of every person seeing it" in *Cunnaiah* v. *Balraj*,[135] the Madras High Court held that where the question is whether the defendants' picture is a copy of colourable imitation of the plaintiffs' picture the degree of resemblance between the two pictures which is to be judged by eye, must get the suggestion that it is the plaintiff's picture. One picture said to be a copy of another picture finds a place in the reproduction. This principle was also applied by the Karnataka High Court in *Association of Electronics* v. *Sharp Tools*.[136] The issue relating to infringement of

---

128. *See, Ritika Private Limited* v. *Biba Apparels Private Limited*, 230 (2016) DLT 109: MIPR 2016 (2) 166.
129. 2015 (64) PTC 366 (Del): 225 (2015) DLT 178.
130. AIR 1945 Bom 51.
131. (2001) PTC 777 (Del).
132. (2001) PTC 855 (Del). *See, Castrol Ltd.* v. *V.O. Muralidhar Reddy* (2001) PTC 137 (Mad).
133. 1972 Cr LJ 1098.
134. AIR 1967 Mad 381.
135. AIR 1961 Mad 111.
136. AIR 1991 Kant 406: (1992) IPLR 96.

copyright in a picture was examined in *K.R. Venugopala Sarma* v. *Sangu Ganesan,*[137] where the reproduction was not exact but the effect on the mind by a study of the two pictures was that the respondent's picture was nothing but a copy of the plaintiff's picture. The court observed:

> Applying this test, the degree of resemblance between the two pictures, which is to be judged by the eye must be such that the person looking at the respondents' pictures must get the suggestion that it is the appellant's picture. In this sense, the points of resemblance and dissimilarity in the picture assume some importance in finding out whether taken as a whole the respondents' pictures produce the impression in the mind of any observer, which amounts to a suggestion of the appellant's picture. One picture can be said to be a copy of another picture only if a substantial part of the former picture finds place in the reproduction.

In *Coca Cola Company* v. *K.M. Salim,*[138] the court applied the principle of colourable and slavish reproduction. In this case it was alleged that as an artistic work the defendant's labels are the reproduction of the plaintiff's well-known trademarks SPRITE and FANTA. Thus, the defendant has copied the plaintiff's artistic work relating to the manner in which it represents its trademarks SPRITE (label) and FANTA (label) which is nothing but a colourable and slavish reproduction.

A drawing including a diagram, map, chart or plan comes within the definition of artistic work under Section 2(c) of the Copyright Act, 1957 and copyright subsists in it if it is "original" according to Section 13 of the Act. The drawing need not possess any artistic quality. It therefore follows that copyright subsists in original industrial drawings of machines or machine parts or any drawing on the basis of which objects are made. In fact, all mechanical solid products of industry are based on some drawings. In *Action Construction Equipment (P) Ltd.* v. *Escorts Construction Equipment Ltd.*,[139] where a plaintiff complains of infringement of copyright in industrial drawing/drawings. The court held that the defendants cannot be restrained from manufacturing and selling his product unless the plaintiff produces the industrial drawings alleged to have been copied. However, in *Puneet Industrial Controls* v. *Aditya Enterprises,*[140] the court observed that failure to show that manufacturing of product was possible without designs may lead to grant of interim injunction against sale of goods. In *Dray Air India (P) Ltd.* v. *Western Engineering Co.*,[141] it was alleged that the drawing was adopted by breach of confidentiality. But it was shown that the information was widely circulated. Hence, the interim injunction was refused. But in *Escorts Construction Equipment Ltd.* v. *Action Construction Equipment (P) Ltd.*,[142] the interim injunction was granted on the ground that "Pick-N-Carry Mobile Cranes" manufactured by defendant were infringement of plaintiff's industrial designs. On the appeal it was held that unless the industrial designs have been produced, direction to stop manufacture or sale cannot be issued. Defendants directed to maintain record of manufacturing and sale of cranes along with technical drawings and file the same in court. On the question of criteria for infringement of copyright of industrial drawings,

137. 1972 Cr LJ 1098 (Mad).
138. 2014 (1) MIPR 217: 2014 (208) DLT 432.
139. (1999) PTC 369 (Del) (DB).
140. (1999) PTC 311 (Del).
141. (1999) PTC 408 (Del).
142. (1999) PTC 36 (Del).

the Delhi High Court in *Brady* v. *Chemical Process Equipment*[143] held that infringement has to be tested on visual appearance of the drawing and the object in question.

According to Proviso (b) of Section 17 of the Copyright Act, 1957 in the case of a photograph taken, or a painting or portrait drawn, or an engraving or a cinematograph film made, for valuable consideration at the instance of any person, such person shall, in the absence of any agreement to the contrary, be the first owner of the copyright therein.

Thus, the publication of the photograph or its exhibition at any place including the photographer's shop window would constitute infringement of that copyright. Clarifying the law in *Kesari Maratha Trust* v. *Devidas Tularam Bagul,*[144] the Bombay High Court held that publishing a photograph without the permission of the photographer, a photo taken by him by copying it from another published material is infringement of copyright in the photograph. In this case, the claim of copyright in photograph published in a newspaper came for consideration. The plaintiff took the photo of a well-known author in an artistic manner and the same was first published with the permission of the plaintiff in the cover of the Book "Rang Maza Vegale". The name of the plaintiff was also mentioned at the bottom of the photo. The defendant published the same photograph without the permission of the plaintiff in the newspaper. The plaintiff, the photographer sent a notice to the defendant claiming copyright on the photograph and requested them to tender an apology for using it without his consent and publishing the same in the newspaper. On refusal of the request, the plaintiff filed the present suit for injunction and nominal damages of one rupee and the same was granted by the trial court. On appeal it was argued that the photographer had no copyright in the photograph since it was taken at an award function and even if there was copyright, the defendants had not infringed it since there was no notice of copyright and the use was a fair use. Rejecting these arguments, the high court concluded that the photographer had copyright since it was taken by the plaintiff with the permission of the author. On the question of notice of copyright, the court observed, thus:

> This is a case in which the appearance of the plaintiff's name below the photograph was a sufficient notice to the defendants. As per law the plaintiff is admittedly, the author of the copyright in the photograph.... The ignorance of legal aspect of the matter by the defendants that copyright did not exist and it belonged to the author of the photograph is no excuse for them to infringe the copyright.

The Andhra Pradesh High Court in *Ushodaya Enterprises Ltd.* v. *T.V. Venugopal*[145] examined the question of infringement of copyright in the artistic work of the word "EENADU". The plaintiff since 1974 was using the word EENADU for newspaper. TV broadcast, food, chit fund, hotel, etc. without registration. In 1995, the defendants started using the same words with different artistic background for selling *agarbathi.* On receipt of notice from the plaintiff, they stopped using it for some time but obtained copyright registration of the artistic work in EENADU and started selling *agarbathi.* After this the plaintiff also obtained copyright registration of their artistic work in EENADU. The present suit was filed alleging infringement of copyright and trademark of this artistic work. The trial court decreed the suit granting a

143. AIR 1987 Del 372.
144. 1999 IPLR 71 (Bom) *See also, Frito-Lay India* v. *Uncle Chipps Private Ltd.,* 2000 PTC 341 (DB Del); *Sulamangalam R. Jayalakshmi* v. *Meta Musicals,* AIR 2000 Mad 454.
145. 2001 PTC 727 (AP).

limited injunction on the ground of passing off and infringement of copyright in the Telegu letters and the single judge of the high court reversed that decision. On appeal regarding infringement of copyright the division bench made the following observation.

> There is no doubt in our mind to hold that the plaintiff is the owner of the artistic work EENADU as it has been using the same as a Masthead of the newspaper right from the year 1974 and it owns the copyright throughout India. Any attempt made by the defendant with slightly changed version suffixing and affixing anything to the EENADU artistically created word which resembles the plaintiffs artistic work cannot ensure to the benefit of the defendant and the defendant cannot lay a claim for ownership of the said artistic work. As held by the Supreme Court in *Cadila's* case, if the court comes to the conclusion that there is a similarity between the marks of both the plaintiff and defendant, the dissimilarities assume insignificance. As indicated above, though there are dissimilarities between Ex. A8 and A59, but phonetically and visually the inscription EENADU artistic work is one and the same. Thus, having regard to these facts and in the light of the decision of the Supreme Court in *Cadila's case*, the plaintiff is entitled to claim that the defendant has infringed his copyright.

The Indian courts have recognised copyright protection for different persons for pictures—artistic work—of Gods and other personalities like Mahatma Gandhi. Thus, it is the mechanical reproduction of artistic work without the application of knowledge, labour, judgment, skill or taste that is prohibited under copyright law.[146] In *Association of Electronics* v. *Sharp Tools,*[147] the Madras High Court observed that while dealing with the question of infringement of copyright of the applicant's work by the respondent's work the court is to test on the visual appearance of the test, viz. "lay observer test" whether to persons who are not experts in relation to objects of that description, the object appears to be a reproduction. If to the "lay observer", it would not appear to be a reproduction, there is no infringement of the artistic copyright in the work. Further, the Karnataka High Court in *Association of Electronics and Electricals* v. *Sharp Tools*[148] held that there can be copyright in artistic manner in which a word is represented. In such a case the reproduction of the work in ordinary types will not be an infringement of copyright in artistic work. Regarding identical artistic work, the Goa High Court in *Hindustan Pencils Ltd.* v. *Alpana Cottage Industries*,[149] held that similarities between the artistic works of the petitioner and respondent were of fundamental and substantial aspects of the mode of expression which established beyond doubt that it is a copy of the petitioner's work. Petition for rectification allowed with coasts. But in determining infringement of artistic work whether "similarities" will be given priority over dissimilarities? In *S.M. Dyechem Limited* v. *M/s. Cadbury (India) Limited,*[150] the Apex Court held that in determining the essential features, dissimilarities take priority over similarities. An overall comparison of the artistic work, one would come to inescapable conclusion that dissimilarities are in abundance.

"Feeling and artistic character test" is applied for ascertaining sufficient similarity in case of artistic work using the idea of appeal to the viewer's eye. In *Raja Pocket Books* v. *Radha*

146. *See, Camlin Private Ltd.* v. *M/s. National Pencil Industries,* AIR 1986 Del. 444.
147. AIR 1991 Mad 406: (1992) IPLR 96.
148. (1993) PTC 85 (Kant).
149. 2001 PTC (CB) (Goa).
150. AIR 2000 SC 2114.

Pocket Books,[151] the plaintiff owned the copyright in a cartoon in Punch, "Dropping the Pilot" some actors enacted the cartoon on stage by dressing up and posing to look like the original. The court held that this constitute three-dimensional reproduction of the two-dimensional work as both the works gave a feeling that they were same. Section 14(c)(i) of the Copyright Act, 1957 specifically gives the copyright owner the right to convert two-dimensional work into three-dimensional. In *K.S. Gita* v. *Vision Time India Pvt. Ltd.*,[152] the plaintiff alleged that the defendant by telecasting the serial "Thangam" infringing the plaintiff's copyright in the literary work "Thangam/Bangaram/Ganga". The plaintiff alleged that the defendants should be restrain from telecasting the said serial and also defendants should be directed to pay a sum of ₹10,00,000/- per episode from 30 June 2009 towards royalty to the plaintiff for exploiting the copyright. The court held that there is no clear proof of violation. Hence, if it is restrained from being screened at this stage, neither of the parties can have the benefit out of the same, and the balance of convenience, under the stated circumstances, will not be in restraining the mega serial. The question of the violation of the copyright of stage play by a film producer or a director the task of the plaintiff becomes more difficult to prove piracy. It is manifest that unlike a stage play a film has a much broader prospective, wider field and a bigger background where the defendants can by introducing a variety of incidents give a colour and complexion different from the manner in which the copyrighted work has expressed the idea. Even so, if the viewer after seeing the film gets a totality of impression that the film is by and large a copy of the original play, violation of the copyright may be said to be proved. The court further observed:

> The violation of the copyright might be taken as proved if after seeing the serial, the viewer gets a totality of impression that the serial was by and large a copy of the original script. Hence it would not be possible to make a comparison or find out whether there are any similarities, or whether the mega serial now being screened by the respondents 1 to 4 has emanated from the said script of D5 as alleged by her. It is admitted even by the plaintiff that the mega serial has crossed more than 100 episodes for the past one year.

Infringement of Cinematograph Films

A cinematograph film itself is recognised as a separate subject matter for copyright protection under Section 13(1)(b) of the Copyright Act 1957. In *Aamir Khan Productions Private Limited* v. *Union of India,*[153] it was held that Section 13(1)(b) of the Copyright Act, 1956 confers copyright in cinematograph films and Section 14(1)(d)(ii) provides that copyright means the exclusive right to do or authorise the doing or to authorise to sell or give on hire or offer for sale or hire any copy of the film. The producer of the film has exclusive right to decide as to whom he shall sell or give on hire any copy of the film for communicating the film to the public. The controversial question is what is the real test to determine the infringement of a cinemato-graph film? In *Hanfstaengl* v. *Raines,*[154] Lord Herschel, L.C. while dealing with that fact that there can be no test to decide what a substantial part of the picture is. One useful test which has been followed in several decisions of court, the court held: "... it depends really,

---

151. 1997 PTC 84 (Del).
152. 2011 (45) PTC 393 (Mad).
153. 2010 (112) Bom LR 3778: 2010 Comp LR 105 (Bombay).
154. 1895 AC 20 (25).

on the effect produced upon the mind by a study of the picture and of that which is alleged to be a copy of it, or at least of its design."

According to Section 2(f) of the Copyright Act, 1957, "cinematograph film" means any work of visual recording on any medium produced through a process from which a moving image may be produced by any means and includes a sound recording accompanying such visual recording and "cinematograph" shall be construed as including any work produced by any process analogous to cinematography including video films.[155] For the purpose of Section 2(f) "video films" should be deemed to be work produced by a process analogous to cinematograph. Thus, in *Cine India* v. *Muthu Enterprises*,[156] the court held that the author of cinematograph film is the producer under Section 2(d)(v) of the Copyright Act, 1957. Video films are deemed to be work produced by a process analogous to cinematography. The cinematograph film therefore includes "video films" and video taping of cinematograph film will constitute infringement of the copyright in the film.[157]

In *Indian Performing Right Society* v. *Eastern India Motion Picture Association*,[158] the Apex Court held that Section 2(f) of the Act shows that the term "cinematograph film" includes a sound track associated with the film, that is, the sounds embodied in a sound track which is associated with the film. A cinematograph film is ordinarily based on literary, dramatic, musical or artistic work in which copyright may subsists. The question of infringement of a film has to be considered in the context of the nature of the exclusive rights conferred on it. One of the exclusive rights conferred on the owner of the copyright in a cinematograph film is the right to make a copy of the film.

In *Garware Plastics and Polyester* v. *Telelink*,[159] the Bombay High Court examined the issue whether by showing the video films over cable T.V. network infringes the copyright of the plaintiff? To determine the issue, the court framed three sub-issues: (i) the character of audience and whether it can be described as a private or domestic audience consisting of family members or members of the household?; (ii) whether the audience in relation to the owner of the copyright can be so considered? And; (iii) whether permitting such performance would in any way whittle down the protection given to the author of a copyright under the Copyright Act resulting in the owner being deprived of monetary gains out of the intellectual property? After examining all these three sub-issues, the court held that showing the video films over cable T.V. network to the subscribers, amounts to infringement of copyright in the film by broadcasting or communicating it to a section of the public. Justifying its decision the court observed:

---

155. Substituted by the Copyright (Amendment) Act, 1994.
156. (1992) 1 LW 74
157. In *Entertaining Enterprises* v. *State of Tamil Nadu* [AIR 1984 Mad. 278] the court held that as a result of the inclusive definition of "cinematograph film" under Section 2(f) of the Copyright Act, 1957 including any work produced by any process analogous to cinematograph, the exhibition of film in a television through video tapes in which a cinematograph film is recorded, will also fall within the definition of cinematograph film. *See also*, *Venkatesan* v. *Dy. General Manager, Telecom* (1991) 1 LW 465 (Mad); *Tulsidas* v. *Vasantha Kumari* (1991) 1 LW (Mad) 2020; *Dinesh Kumar Hanuman Prasad Tiware* v. *State of Maharashtra*, AIR 1984 Bom 34; *Balvinder Singh* v. *Delhi Administration*, AIR 1984 Del 379; *Restaurant Lee* v. *State of Madhya Pradesh*, AIR 1983 MP 146.
158. AIR 1977 SC 1443.
159. AIR 1989 Bom 331: 1989 (2) Bom CR 433. *See also*, *Indian Performing Right Society Ltd.* v. *Aditya Pandey*, 2011 (47) PTC 392: 2011 LawSuit (Del) 2520.

> The last test which has been applied in such cases is the test of ascertaining the character of the audience in view of the purpose of the Copyright Act. The Copyright Act is meant to protect the owner of the copyright against unauthorised performances of his work, thereby entitling him to earn monetary gain from his intellectual property. The audience which watches such video films would have otherwise paid for watching the film. In fact, the audience does pay the defendants for watching the film. The author of the copyright is, therefore, directly affected as he is deprived of earnings from his intellectual property. What is more, an audience which pays for watching the film cannot be considered as a domestic audience of the person broadcasting the film.

Section 52A(2)[160] of the Copyright Act, 1957 provides that "no person shall publish a video film in respect of any work unless the following particulars are displayed in the video film". In *State of Andhra Pradesh* v. *Nagoti Venkataramanna*,[161] the Apex Court held that if the particulars on "video films", etc. as mandated under Section 52A(2) do not find place, it would be infringement of copyright in the original cinematograph film. It would therefore be unnecessary for the prosecution to track on and trace out the owner of the copyright to come and adduce evidence of infringement of copyright. The absence thereof also does not constitute lack of essential element of infringement of copyright.

In *Super Cassettes Industries Ltd.* v. *Board of Film Certification*,[162] the question involved was whether the DVDs and VCDs labelled as "only for private viewing" which the petitioners sold in the market required certification by Central Board of Film Certification (CBFC). In this case police seized above DVDs and VCDs from shops and started prosecution against them under Section 52A(2) of Copyright Act, 1957. The argument of the petitioner was that the certificate of public exhibition issued by CBFC was required to be displayed only when the video film was publicly exhibited and not for VCDs and DVDs meant for "Private viewing". The Delhi High court analysed the provisions of the Cinematograph Act, 1952 read with Copyright Act, 1957 and laid down the following conclusions:

1. Once a film is made or produced in a DVD or VCD or any other format and is made available or distributed to the public or offered for sale to the public, it will amount to publication of such film within the meaning of Section 52A(2) of Copyright Act.
2. In the context of the present petitions, at the point where a member of the public, to whom the petitioners' films on DVD or VCD is made available, plays it on an equipment and views such films, whether in the confines of a private space or otherwise, prior certification of that film in terms of Section 5A of Cinematograph Act, would become necessary, since for the purposes of Section 52A(2) of Copyright Act, the film is exhibited.
3. The maker or distributor of a film made available to the public by sale or otherwise is expected to anticipate the exhibition of such film by such member of the public subsequently and to ensure, therefore, that the film bears a certificate under Section 5A of Cinematograph Act.
4. Whether such film, if it contains purely religious or devotional songs, should be exempted from the certificate is made for the Government of India to take a decision

160. *See, Uma Shankar Gupta* v. *State of Jharkhand*, 2013 CriLJ 243: 2012 (3) JCR 633(Jhr).
161. 1996 PTC 634 (SC).
162. 2011 (46) PTC 1 (Del).

in exercise of its powers under Section 9 of Cinematograph Act. However, in the absence or such exemption under this Section 9, it must be held that the films being produced and manufactured by the petitioners, even if they contain purely religious or devotional songs as claimed by them, would require prior certification by the Central Board of Film Certification under Section 5A of Cinematograph Act.[163] The absence of such certificate in the film itself when it is exhibited will attract the violation of Section 52A(2) of Copyright Act.

In *Ambience Space Sellers Ltd.* v. *Asia Industrial Technology*,[164] the Bombay High Court held that in a broadcast of programme by TV channels, the blanking out of a portion of a programme by cable TV network operators and substituting their own advertisement during the time amounts to conversion this is also a breach of contract. In *Vicco Laboratories* v. *Art Commercial Advertising (Pvt) Ltd.*,[165] the Apex Court examined the issue relating to right to TV serial episodes. In this case the court held that where the serial is not produced by the respondents as agents of appellants claim under Section 17 of the Copyright act, 1957 is liable to be dismissed. Similarly, in *Zee Telefilm Ltd.* v. *Asia Producers*,[166] interim injunction restraining the telecast of TV serials by the producers was refused. In this case, in an agreement of assignment of copyright in a TV serial "India Most Wanted" comprising episodes already produced and further episodes yet to be produced the agreement was held to be incapable of performance for want of definite or specific details of scripts, concept or story given in the agreement.

In *Twentieth Century for Film Corporation* v. *Sohail Maklai Entertainment Pvt. Ltd.*,[167] the plaintiff claims copyright in the literary and artistic work being the script and screenplay of its film "Phone Booth" assigned to the Plaintiff under certain agreements. Plaintiff claimed that the defendants have infringed its copyright in their film "Knock Out" and claimed for granting injunction restraining the defendants from releasing its film "Knock Out" in theatres or broadcasting or otherwise communicating it to the public in any manner or exporting its copies so as to infringe the script, screen, storyline and dialogues in its copyrighted work or so as to pass off the said film as and for the plaintiff's film as an Indian version thereof. In this case, the issues were for determination:

(i) whether there is no copyright in an idea?
(ii) whether the defendant's film was a copy of the plaintiff's film?

So far as the first issue is concerned, the court held that an idea cannot be owned by a person. An idea, which is available in the world, cannot be the monopoly of anyone. This essentially relates to an idea which is already available and not a theme which is a first time production. Monopoly and consequently the copyright in an idea, which was never available or shown earlier is an original work, would be implicit in such original work. Hence copyright

163. For the commentaries on the Section 5A of Cinematograph Act 1952, *see, Raghu Nath Pandey* v. *Bobby Bedi*, (2006) ILR 1 Delhi 927: 2006 (89) DRJ 40; *Shyam Narayan Chouksey* v. *Union of India*, AIR 2003 MP 233: 2003 (2) MPJR 323.
164. (1998) PTC 232 (Bom).
165. 2001 PTC 687 (SC).
166. (2000) PTC 382 (Bom).
167. 2010 (44) PTC 647 (Bom): 2011 (1) Bom. C.R. 750.

is contained in the original expression of the idea. It is expressed in the frame of the product. Hence whilst the idea may not be unique to the author, the image portrayed or the expression made is essentially unique to the author. If such an expression in the shots of a film is copied, lifted from an earlier film, the infringement is complete. In connection to the second issue the court observed that test of concluding whether the second work is a pirated copy is the impression of the average viewer. Other test is that if those parts were removed from the copied work whether the remainder would become meaningless and hence what must be seen is the substance, the foundation, the kernel and the copied work and to see if the rest can stand without it. In the present case, original novel expression of the idea in both the films of the plaintiff and the defendants relate to a man held hostage in a telephone booth by a sniper. Consequently, the injunction as prayed for granted. Thus the court held that the defendant hall not exhibit, release for exhibition or broadcast their film "Knock Out" in any jurisdiction in the present form so as to infringe the plaintiff's copyright in the script, screenplay, story and dialogues so as to pass off the suit film as that of the plaintiff's film "Phone Booth" without the consent of the film.

However, Section 52 of the Copyright Act, 1957 enlists certain acts not to be infringement of copyright. One has to see whether the film infringes the copyright in other works in the context of the exception to infringements listed in Section 52(1). Thus, if the use of the copyright work in the film is only for fare dealing for the purpose of research or private study or criticism or review, or for reporting current events, it will not constitute infringement.[168] Again the inclusion in a film of any artistic work permanently situated in a public place or any premises to which the public has access is permitted if such inclusion is only by way of background or otherwise incidental to the film.[169]

Infringement of Sound Recording

Copyright subsists in a sound recording as established in Section 13(1) Copyright Act, 1957. Sound recordings protect recorded sounds, both musical and non-musical and include recorded music, songs, audio-books, sound efforts, audio recordings of speeches and interviews, audio products, sounds tracts, etc.[170] Sound recording means a recording of sounds from which such sounds may be produced regardless of the medium on which such recording is the method by which such sounds are produced.[171] In *Saregama Ltd.* v. *The New Digital Media*,[172] the Calcutta High Court held that a sound recording has a "unitary" nature wherein the individual constituents are complete in themselves which enjoy independent copyrights. However, the vesting of such independent copyrights in such ingredients does not affect the unitary nature of a sound recording or its unitary use. Only when the use is not unitary, it results in the infringement of copyrights in underlying works/ingredients. A sound recording may be of a literary work spoken or recited, the spoken dialogue of a dramatic work or of a sound. There may be copyright subsisting in the subject-matter recorded. Since making of a sound

168. *See,* Copyright Act, 1957, Section 52(1)(a).
169. *Ibid.*, Section 52(1)(u).
170. *See,* Daksh Mitra and Aayush Modi, "Pay 'n' Play: Public Performance of Sound Recording *vis-à-vis* Copyright Infringement" 18 *Journal of Intellectual Property Rights* (2013) pp. 123–133.
171. Copyright Act, 1957, Section 2(xx).
172. 2018 (73) PTC 329 (Cal): (2018) 1 WBLR (Cal) 329.

recording of a literary, dramatic or musical work constitutes infringement of that work, a sound recording made without the licence of the owner of the copyright in that work will constitute infringement of that work.[173] In *Shumita Deb* v. *Saregama India Limited*,[174] it was observed that with regard to cover version the Section 31C of the Copyright Act applies to third parties who want to make a sound recording.

In *Vinod Kumar Gupta* v. *State of U.P.*,[175] it was held that to attract an infringement or abetting the infringement of the copyright it should relate to a class of work such as original literary work, dramatic, musical and artistic work; cinematograph film and sound recording. Besides this, everybroadcasting organisation shall have a special right to be known as "broadcast reproduction right" in respect of its broadcasts.[176] During the continuance of a broadcast reproduction right in relation to any broadcast, any person who without the licence of the owner of the right does any of the following acts of the broadcast or any substantial part thereof: (i) makes any sound recording or visual recording of the broadcast; or (ii) makes any reproduction of such sound recording; or (ii) sells or hires to the public, or offers for such sale or hire, any such sound recording, shall, be deemed to have infringed the broadcast reproduction right.[177]

In *Indian Performing Rights Society* v. *Aditya Pandey*,[178] the Delhi High Court held that the Copyright Act, 1957 recognised only three classes of work, viz., (i) literary, dramatic, musical or artistic work, (ii) cinematograph films and (iii) sound recordings. Each class is independent of each other. Each class of work gives a bundle of rights to the owner thereof, which are independent of other works. The owner of a sound recording has, *inter alia*, the exclusive right of communicating the sound recording to the public. Though the exercise of such right has the effect of communicating the underlying work, viz., musical or literary to the public such communication of underlying works being a part of sound recording does not amount to infringement of copyright of communicating to the public, the underlying works. The owner of a sound recording has an exclusive right to communicate the sound recording in any form and such communication in exercise of right under Section 14(1)(e)(111) cannot amount to infringement of any underlying work. Once a sound recording is made, it is only the producer, as the owner thereof, who can exploit it exclusively in the manner provided in Section 14(1)(e). However, those rights are confirmed to that particular sound recording and sound recording alone. The owner of the sound recording can communicate to the public, *inter alia*, by broadcasting it or playing it in the public place.

In case of sound recording, the doing or authorising the doing of any of the following acts by utilising the sound recording without the consent or licence of the copyright owner constitutes infringement of the copyright in that sound recording:[179]

1. to make any other sound recording embodying it.
2. to sell or give on hire, or offer for sale or hire any infringing copy of the sound

---

173. *Ibid.*, Section 14(a)(iv) read with Section 51.
174. 2019 (2) KCCR 1838: 2019 (1) AKR 485.
175. 2019 (106) ACC 378.
176. *See*, *Star India Private Limited* v. *Department of Industrial Policy*, (2019) 2 SCC 104: 2018 (14) SCALE 651.
177. *See*, Copyright Act, 1957, Section 37.
178. 2011 (47) PTC 392 (Del).
179. Copyright Act, 1957, Section 51 read with Section 14(e).

recording regardless of whether such copy has been sold or given on hire on earlier occasions.

3. to communicate the sound recording to the public.
4. to permit for profit any place to be used for the communication of the work to the public where such communication constitutes an infringement of the copyright in the sound recording unless he was not aware and had no reasonable ground for believing that such communication to the public would be an infringement of copyright.
5. to make infringing copies for sale or hire, or to sell or let for hire, or by way of trade displays or to offer for sale or hire.
6. to distribute either for the purpose of trade or to such an extent as to affect prejudicially the owner of the copyright.
7. to exhibit in public by way of trade.
8. to import into India any infringing copy. However, the import of one copy of sound recording for the private and domestic use of the importer is permitted.

According to Section 52A(1) of the Copyright Act, 1957 to deter people from making unauthorised reproduction of copyright of sound recording, it is now mandatory that the following particulars must be displayed on the sound recording and on any container thereof when the sound recording is published, namely (i) the name and address of the person who has made the sound recording (ii) the name and address of the owner of the copyright in such work and the year of its first publication. Contravention of these requirements is made punishable with imprisonment of up to three year and with a fine. In *CBS Inc.* v. *Ames Records & Tapes Ltd.*,[180] the English court held that a record library that lent out records and, relevantly, also sold blank tapes at a discount did not authorise the infringement of copyright in those records. On a common sense view of the facts, Whitford, J. held that plainly: "An act is not authorised by somebody who merely enables or possibly assists or even encourages another to do that act, but does not purport to have any authority which he can grant to justify the doing of the act."

In *Super Cassettes Industries* v. *Myspace Inc.*,[181] the plaintiff was the owner of copyright in repertoire of songs, cinematograph films and sound recording. The defendant was a social networking and entertainment website which offered a variety of entertainment applications including sharing, viewing of music, images and cinematograph films having its base in USA. The website provided country specific content. The plaintiff alleged that free sharing and films provide by myspace.com effected the business of plaintiff and also resulted in the violation of their copyright as they had not taken licence to exhibit the infringing material on their website from the plaintiff. The plaintiff further contended that the acts of providing the space over the Internet and thereafter continuously doing the same even after coming to know about the plaintiff's proprietary interests amounted to "authorization" as the defendants were aware that the space was going to be used for infringement purposes. The court held that the acts of defendants of providing the space on the Internet or webspace for profit are *prima facie* infringing in nature. The court reiterate three proposition: (1) the provision of Section 51(a)(i) and Section 51(a)(ii) of the Copyright Act, 1957 are disjunctive in nature in as much as the

180. [1982] Ch 91: [1981] 2 All ER 812.
181. 2011 (48) PTC 49 (Del).

word "or" between the two makes it clear that even on satisfaction of one provision, there would be an infringement of copyright; (2) the infringement by way of authorisation would fall within Section 51(a)(1) read with Section 14 of the Act as against the act of permitting the place for profit which is separately provided under Section 51(a)(ii) of the Act; (3) there is a distinction between the concept of authorisation and the concept of permitting the place for profit and the essential ingredients for establishing the same are also different. Keeping these three propositions, the court observed that the acts of the defendants whereby they are offering the space over the Internet, getting the works uploaded through users, thereafter saving in their own database with the limited licence to add, amend, or delete the content and thereafter communicating the said work to the public by providing some advertisements alongside the work or in the alternative gaining advertisements or sponsorships on the said basis thereafter would *prima facie* tantamounts to permitting the place for profit for infringement as envisaged under Section 51(a)(ii) of the Act.[182]

However, in *Gramophone Company* v. *Mars Recording (P) Ltd.*,[183] the Karnataka High Court held that a version recording is a sound recording made of an already published song by using another voice or voices and with different musicians and arrangers. Version recording is thus neither copying nor reproduction of the original recording. The record so made does not fall within the definition of infringing copy. It is relevant to mention that Section 52 of the Copyright Act, 1957 enlists certain acts that while appearing as a violation of copyright, do not constitute infringement. Those acts of public performance of sound recordings do not constitute infringement. Section 52(1)(k) is an exception in respect of sound recordings in some circumstances. By virtue of this clause, copyright is not infringed by causing a recording to be heard in public by utilising it: (i) in an enclosed room or hall meant for the common use of residents in any residential premises (not being a hotel or similar commercial establishment) as part of the amenities provided exclusively or mainly for residents therein; or (ii) as part of the activities of a club or similar organisation which is not established or conducted for profit.

It is relevant to note that copyright will subsist in a sound recording only if it is lawfully made. Thus, in *Wellington Cinema Co.* v. *Performing Rights Society*,[184] the Bombay High Court held that copyright will not subsist in any sound recording made in respect of literary, dramatic or musical work, if in making the sound recording, copyright in such work has been infringed.

Infringement of Copyright by Broadcast

Infringement of copyright by broadcast has been a controversial issue in England as well as in India overtime. In England, difficulties in interpretation have arisen as a result of the language used in the Copyright Act, 1911 where the broadcast was not directly protected. What was protected was performance of the work in public. The phrase "performance in public" is vaguely suggestive of the place where the performance takes place. In the case of a

182. *See, Myspace Inc.* v. *Super Cassettes Industries Ltd.*, 2017 (69) PTC 1 (Del): 236 (2017) DLT 478; *Consim Info Pvt. Ltd.* v. *Google India Pvt. Ltd.*, 2013 (54) PTC 578 (Mad); *Super Cassetes Industries Ltd.* v. *Myspace Inc.*, 2011 (48) PTC 49 (Del): MIPR 2011 (2) 303.
183. (2000) PTC 117 (Knt).
184. AIR 1937 Bom 472.

theatrical production or a music recital, the performance takes place, where the artists perform. A broadcast, however, posed problems.[185]

In *Messager* v. *British Broadcasting Company Ltd.*,[186] the plaintiff was a composer of a comic opera, namely, "The Little Michus" who gave to a theatrical producer the right to perform the opera. The theatrical producer in turn gave a licence to the British Broadcasting Company Ltd. (BBC) to broadcast the performance. The plaintiff sued the BBC for an infringement of his copyright in the opera. The BBC in its defence argued that the broadcast was not a performance in public within the meaning of the copyright Act, 1911. It contended that the performance was in the private studio of the BBC were not "public". By mechanical and electrical devices, the performance was heard by the public who possessed radios. The court, however, refused to admit the contention. It said that to broadcast an opera by wireless telephony was to "perform" it "in public" within the meaning of the English Copyright Act, 1911. It said that whether a performance is in public or not must depend upon the circumstance of each case, will not amount to an infringement of copyright. It said that by broadcasting the opera, the defendants clearly gave a public performance.

Subsequently, in *Ernest Turner Electrical Instruments Ltd.* v. *Performance Right Society Ltd.*,[187] the English court observed that the music which was broadcast to employees during work was considered as performance in public. The court applied the following three tests in determining the issue, namely:

1. the character of audience whether it could be considered as purely domestic,
2. the relationship between the owner of the copyright and the audience, and
3. the impact of the performance on the value of copyright or the loss of profit which would otherwise have accrued to the owner if the same audience had watched the performance on payment.

Under the Copyright Act, 1957, a broadcast to the public is expressly covered. According to Section 2(dd)[188] of the Copyright Act, 1957, "broadcast" means communication to the public—(i) by any means of wireless diffusion, whether in any one or more of the forms of signs, sounds or visual images; or (ii) by wire, and includes a rebroadcast. This mode or medium of transmission is at the core of the definition of "broadcast". There are different modes by which content can be broadcasted. And it is the right of the author to have his work broadcasted by any mode he chooses. These different means of broadcasting must be treated differently. The Bombay High Court has recognised this point in *Video Masters* v. *Nishi Productions.*[189] In this case, the plaintiff claimed that he had bought the sole and exclusive video rights of a copyrighted film from the defendant and that the defendant gave away the cable TV rights to another person. The court made a clear distinction between the satellite rights and cable TV rights and held that both rights can exist with different persons at the same time, and that would not amount to infringement of the plaintiff's rights. The Court

---

185. For a critical view, see, Shyamkrishna Balganesh, "The Social Costs of Property Rights in Broadcast (and Cable) Signals," 22 *Berkeley Technology Law Journal* (2008) pp. 1304–1387.
186. (1927) 2 KB 543.
187. (1943) 1 Ch 167.
188. Inserted by the Copyright (Amendment) Act, 1983, Section 3 [w.e.f. 9-8-1994].
189. (1998) 2 Mah JL 81 (Bom): (1998) 23 IPLR 388.

further held that the activity of cable TV operators of receiving signals on dish antenna and thereafter transmitting it by cables to view either at a cost or otherwise, amounts to copyright infringement.

In *Video Master* v. *Nishi Productions*,[190] in which the Bombay High Court held that theatrical rights include the right to exhibit the cinematograph film in theatres, terrestrial rights is the right to exhibit the film on Doordarshan and satellite broadcasting rights is the right to exhibit/communicate the film by satellite signals to public with or without cable and through the satellite medium. The cable TV right is right to exhibit a film by cable originated programme. It is true that in the agreement it has not specifically been mentioned that the rights exclude the cable television or any other satellite rights but the intention of the parties can easily be inferred from the nature of the transaction that had been arrived at.[191]

In *Garware Plastics and Polyester Ltd.* v. *Telelink*,[192] where the court held that broadcasting of content through cable channels to various households, etc. amount to public performance was cited and the plaintiff parlayed that a similar analogy could be drawn in the present case. The English judgment in *Performing Right Society Ltd.* v. *Hammond's Branford Brewery Co. Ltd.*,[193] too was relied on where the plaintiff had, *inter alia*, granted a licence to the British Broadcasting Corporation (BBC) to broadcast their works for domestic and private use only. The defendant company, who owned a hotel, used a receiving set and loudspeakers to reproduce the broadcast by the BBC for customers in their hotel by the hotel owners. This was considered as a performance in public. It should be noted that the BBC did not infinite the copyright by broadcasting. The owner of the hotel, however, was held to have infringed the copyright by receiving the broadcast and relaying it over loudspeakers to his customers.While holding that the hotel was liable for infringement of copyright, Lawrence, J. held as thus:

> The question therefore resolves itself into whether the defendants, by operating their wireless set, were causing an acoustic representation of the works to be given at their hotel. In my judgment that question must be answered in the affirmative. The wireless receiving set by means of which alone the sounds were produced at the hotel belonged to and was under the control of the defendants, who operated it for the purpose of giving to their customers at the hotel an acoustic representation of the musical works being performed at Hammersmith; but for the defendants having put their wireless set into operation there would have been no acoustic representation of the works at the hotel at all, I find it impossible to escape from the conclusion that the owner of a receiving set who puts it into operation cause an acoustic representation of a musical work which is being broadcast to be given at the place where the receiving set is installed and is therefore himself performing or authorizing the performance of the musical work within the meaning of the Copyright Act, 1911.[194]

In *K.A. Abbas* v. *Union of India*,[195] has already held that motion pictures, and print and electronic media are covered with the protection of fundamental right under Article 19(1)(a) of

190. 1998 PTC (18) 117.
191. See also, *Asianet Communications (P) Ltd.* v. *Surya T.V.*, 2016 (1) CTC 493: 2015-4-LW595.
192. AIR 1989 Bom 331: 1989 (2) Bom CR 433.
193. (1933) All ER Rep 270: (1934) Ch. 121. *See also*, *Performing Right Society Ltd.* v. *Camelo* (1936) 3 All ER 557.
194. For the commentaries on Copyright Act 1914, *see*, *Anand Bhushan* v. *Union of India*, 2018 (75) PTC 106 (Del): 2018 VI AD (Delhi) 153; *Super Cassettes Industries Private Limited* v. *HRCN Cable Network*, 2017 (72) PTC 556 (Del): 244 (2017) DLT 350; *Kamal Kishor* v. *State of MP*, 2016 (I) MPJR 301: 2016 CriLJ 1640; *New Central Book Agency Pvt. Ltd.* v. *Madhusri Konar*, 2016 (2) CHN (CAL) 52.
195. (1970) 2 SCC 161.

the Constitution of India. Again, a person has a right to express opinion as well as to impart information, and the right includes the right to express his/her own opinion as well as opinion of others. The latter right is, of course, subject to constrain of the law of copyright. In this connection the *Secretary, Ministry of Information and Broadcasting* v. *Cricket Association of Bengal,*[196] is another landmark judgment pronounced by the Apex Court. The court held that the freedom of speech and expression includes the right to acquire information and to disseminate it. Freedom of speech and expression is necessary, for self-expression which is an important means of free conscience and self-fulfilment. The right to communicate includes right to communicate through any media that is available whether print or electronic or audio-visual. This freedom includes the freedom to communicate or circulate one's opinion without interference to as large a population in the country as well as abroad as is possible to reach. This fundamental right can be limited only by reasonable restrictions under a law made for the purposes mentioned in Article 19(2) of the Constitution. In the context of television, the Apex Court stated:

> The broadcasting media should be under the control of the public as distinct from Government. This is the command implicit in Article 19(1)(a). It should be operated by a public statutory corporation whose composition must be such as to ensure its impartiality in political, economic and social matters and on all other public issues.... Airwaves being public property, it is the duty of the State to see that airwaves are so utilised as to advance the free speech right of the citizens which is served by ensuring plurality and diversity of views, opinions and ideas. This is imperative in every democracy where freedom of speech is assured.

Infringement of copyright by broadcast in the hotel was the contentious issue in the Delhi High Court in *Super Cassettes Industries* v. *Nirulas Corner House (P) Ltd.*[197] The plaintiff in this case was a copyright holder of certain literary and musical works, sound recordings, music videos and cinematograph films. The defendants were engaged in the business of hotels/restaurants in New Delhi. The plaintiff found that few audio clippings of songs in which the plaintiff owned copyright were being played on the television in rooms of the defendant's hotel. Plaintiff alleged that such transmission of works, without a licence amounts to infringement of the copyright as the defendants communicates the works to the public and prayed for injunction against the defendants restraining it from alleged public performance and damages. The court held that plaintiff has been able to show that the defendant is using cable connection and extending facilities of television to their patrons in the hotel rooms. *Prima facie*, the content of songs and videos broadcast are communications to the public. Thus, the plaintiff has established a strong *prima facie* case of infringement. The court in its reasoning observed that according to Section 2(ff) of the Copyright Act, 1957, broadcast is deemed to be communication to the public.[198] Under Section 51(ii) infringement occurs, if anyone permits

196. AIR 1995 SC 1236: (1995) 2 SCC 161. *See also, Express Newspapers (Private) Ltd.* v. *The Union of India*, AIR 1958 SC 578.
197. 2008 (37) PTC 237 (Del.).
198. Section 2(ff) of the Copyright Act, 1957 reads: "communication to the public" means making any work available for being seen or heard or otherwise enjoyed by the public directly or by any means of display or diffusion other than by issuing copies of such work regardless of whether any member of the public actually sees, hears or otherwise enjoys the work so made available. *See, Institute for Inner Studies* v. *Charlotte Anderson*, 2014 (57) PTC 228 (Del): MIPR 2014 (1) 129.

for profit, any place to be used for the communication of the work to the public where such communication constitutes an infringement of the copyright in the work, unless he was not aware and had no reasonable ground for believing that such communication to the public would be an infringement of copyright. The exception to this definition of infringement is contained in terms of Section 52(1)(k) which states that the causing of a recording to be heard in an enclosed room or hall meant for the common use of residents in any residential premises (not being a hotel or similar commercial establishment) as part of the amenities provided exclusively or mainly for residents is not deemed an infringement. Exception is the guiding light to the legislative intent of treating use of televisions and sound recordings, in hotels as communications to the public.

In *NEO Sports Broadcast Pvt. Ltd.* v. *New Sanjay Cable Network*,[199] the plaintiff was a broadcaster having copyright over broadcasting of live test matches between India and other countries pursuant to an agreement entered into between the plaintiff and Board of Control for Cricket in India (BCCI). The defendant was in a hotel which was broadcasting, telecasting, distributing and transmitting television programmes on the Neo Sports and Neo Cricket to its clients. The plaintiff has drawn attention of the court to Section 2(dd) and (ff) read with Sections 30 and 37 of the Copyright Act, 1957 and also plaintiff claims that its broadcast reputation rights embodied in Section 37 so far as the telecast of the live events are concerned, and the copyrights subsisting by virtue of Section 14(1)(c), are infringed. The materials on record, particularly the Local Commissioner's report indicates that the defendants were causing live broadcasts in the NEO Sports and NEO Cricket to be viewed by their clients. The court held that the defendants, to the extent of placing a television set and making available the sports channels for viewing to its customers/clientele does infringe the copyright. The court observed:

> By virtue of Section 51(a), when anyone, without a license granted by the owner of the copyright or in contravention of conditions of license or of any license imposed by competent authority, does anything the exclusive right to which is conferred on the copyright owner, it amounts to infringement.

In *Star India Pvt. Ltd.* v. *Piyush Agarwal*,[200] whereby the Court jointly disposed of three cases filed by Star India Pvt. Ltd. (petitioner) against Piyush Agarwal (Cricbuzz), Mobile Global Ltd., Idea Cellular (respondents). The dispute arose on the issue that the respondents were sending instant cricket score updates by way of text messages to their customers. The petitioner filed the case against the respondents claiming exclusive media rights over all the matches organised by the Board of Control for Cricket in India (BCCI). The BCCI was arrayed as a common defendant in the case but it supported petitioner in claiming its rights against the respondents. The media rights, including "mobile activation rights" and "mobile rights", were entrusted to Star India exclusively for a 72-hour period by virtue of an agreement dated 10 August 2012 entered into between Star India and BCCI. Star India contested that the respondents were infringing these rights by sending live score updates through text messages. Thus, the issues before the court were: (i) Whether a specific right to monetise the information emanating from a cricket match can be created considering there is a specific bar contained

---

199. 2011 (45) PTC 402 (Del).
200. 2013 (54) PTC 222 (Del): MIPR 2013 (1) 201.

in Section 16 of the Copyright Act, 1957? (ii) Whether the respondents are free-riding on the efforts of the BCCI (unjust commercial enrichment)? (iii) Whether the respondents have freedom under Article 19(1)(a) of the Constitution to disseminate contemporaneous match information? The Delhi High Court observed in the instant case that Star India was not seeking for creation of copyright and was merely claiming a remedy under the common law against the tort of unjust commercial enrichment. Therefore, the point that the right to give live score updates cannot be recognised as a separate copyright under Section 16 of Copyright Act is considered not to be relevant. While deciding on the issue of unjust commercial enrichment, the Court held the respondents were enriching themselves at the cost of Star India. The Court observed that all information relating to a cricket match constitutes "news", and would be protected under Article 19. It was further observed that minute-by-minute updates cannot be protected under Article 19 as it would cause huge monetary loss to Star India. In order to strike fair balance between the provisions of Article 19 and the rights of Star India, the Court banned the respondents from giving out live score updates. However, it was held that the respondents can give the score updates after a time lag of 15 minutes by way of text messages. Subsequently, the Court has explained the "mobile rights" thus:

> Mobile Rights means the Mobile Activation Rights and the right to deliver or provide access to the Feed or Footage, and Audio Feed, any Unilateral Commentary and Unilateral Coverages in the Territory during the Rights Period, for reception and viewing in an intelligible form on a Mobile Device where the communication link(s) used in such delivery comprises, at least in part, Mobile Communications Technology and/or Mobile Broadcast Technology but excluding Television delivery and Internet Delivery.[201]

Infringement of Copyright by Film Producers

According to Section 17 of the Copyright Act 1957 the Author is the first owner of copyright, while in relation to a cinematograph film the author is producer as provided under Section 2(d)(v) of the Act. The asymmetry between film producers and authors of other protected works becomes accentuated when the author of dramatic or literary work has established infringement. This is so also because of the fact that "a film has a much broader perspective, wider field and bigger background"[202] and it is always possible for the film maker to give "a colour and complexion" which distinguishes in many ways the story or dramatic theme from the film.[203] The Supreme Court of India, testify to the considerable difficulties in this area, however, adopted in *R.G. Anand* v. *Delux Films* In *Garapati Prasada Rao* v. *Parnandi Saroja*,[204] the Andhra Pradesh High Court held that in a cinematograph film, if a substantial part of the film either of its expression or theme, incidents, treatment, sequences etc. or their treatment or manner are adopted or reproduced from the original copyrighted work, it would be a piracy infringing the copyright of the owner thereof. The Supreme Court of India, testify to the considerable

201. *See, Star India Pvt. Ltd.* v. *Piyush Agarwal*, 2014 (58) PTC 169 (Del).
202. *See, Zee Entertainment Enterprises Ltd.* v. *Sony Pictures Networks India Pvt. Ltd.*, AIR 2017 Bom 221: 2017 (70) PTC 300 (Bom).; *M. Radhakrishnan* v. *Surabhi Publications*, MIPR 2017 (1) 125: 2016 (3) KLJ 321; *Bablu Alam* v. *State of Chhattisgarh*, 2014 CriLJ 4835.
203. *See*, Hariqbal Basi, "Indianizing Hollywood: The Debate Over Copyright Infringement By Bollywood," 18 *UCLA Entertainment Law Review* (2011) pp. 33–74.
204. AIR 1992 AP 230: 1992 CriLJ 2561.

difficulties in this area, however, adopted in *R.G. Anand* v. *Delux Films*[205] the doctrine of "dominant impact" even as regards this question. The test was formulated thus: "If the viewer after seeing the film gets a total impression that the film is by and large a copy of the original play, violation of copyright may be said to have been proved."[206] There were a large number of similarities between the play and the film but the court held that similarities do not constitute infringement. As regards themes, the court found that the film dealt with the themes of provincialism, evils of a caste-ridden society and the evils of dowry whereas the play only dealt with the first theme. The court which heard the script of the play and saw the movie came to the conclusion that "from scene to scene, situation to situation, in climax and anticlimax, pathos and bathos, in texture and treatment and purpose and presentation is materially different from the play".[207]

However, the decision in *R.G. Anand* v. *Delux Films*[208] was not entirely unanimous. Justice Pathak (as he then was) did not think that there was any need for the court to examine "all the several themes embraced within the plot of the film" to decide infringement if "the treatment of the theme in the stage play has been made the basis of one of the themes in the film story and the essential structure of that treatment is clearly and distinctly identifiable in the film story". The private can appropriate the labours of another by ensuring that "his own product ... covers a wider field than the area included within the scope of the earlier product" and in "the common area covered by two productions to introduce changes in order to disguise the attempt at plagiarism".[209] Thus, in *Kapil Chopra* v. *Kunal Deshmukh,*[210] the Bombay High Court held that in the said judgment (*R.G. Anand* v. *Delux Films*), Justice R. S. Pathak (as His Lordship then was) while coming to a conclusion that the judgment of the High Court in that case was not to be interfered with as the Apex Court does not normally interfere with the concurrent finding of facts, went on to sound a note of caution as under:

> In another, and perhaps a clearer case, it may be necessary for this Court to interfere and remove the impression which may have gained ground that the copyright belonging to an author can be readily infringed by making immaterial changes, introducing insubstantial differences, and enlarging the scope of the original theme so that a veil of apparent dissimilarity is cast around the work now produced. The Court will look strictly at not only blatant examples of copying but also at reprehensible attempts at colourable imitation.[211]

The aforementioned formulation of Justice Pathak really deserves to become operative law—a point that those engaged in the revision of copyright law ought to bear in mind. But for the present, it would appear that film producers are virtually immune from the discipline of copyright law, as is poignantly illustrated by the decision we now examine. The *A.L.S.*

---

205. AIR 1978 SC 1613: (1978) 4 SCC 118.
206. *See, Anand* v. *Delux Films*, AIR 1978 SC 1613: (1978) 4 SCC 118 (pp. 631–1632, AIR).
207. *Ibid.*, pp. 1633–1634 (AIR).
208. AIR 1978 SC 1613: (1978) 4 SCC 118.
209. *Ibid.*, pp. 1633–1634 (AIR).
210. 2013 (53) PTC 58 (Bom): 2013 (2) Bom CR 815.
211. *See, Gramophone Company of India Ltd.* v. *Super Cassette Industries Ltd.*, 2010 (44) PTC 541 (Del): MIPR 2010 (2) 349; *NRI Film Production Associates (P) Ltd.* v. *Twentieth Century Fox Film Corporation*, 2005 (1) KCCR 126: ILR 2004 KARNATAKA 4530; *Super Cassette Industries Limited* v. *Bathla Cassette Industries Pvt. Limited*, 2003 (27) PTC 280 (Del): 107 (2003) DLT 91; *Fateh Singh Mehta* v. *O.P. Singhal*, AIR 1990 Raj 8: RLW 1989 (1) Raj 409; *R. Madhavan* v. *S.K. Nayar*, AIR 1988 Ker 39: 1987 KLJ 942.

Productions v. *K. Jayalakshmi*,[212] shows that even if an author of literary or dramatic work can successfully prove infringement, it may be very difficult for the author to get any of the effective civil remedies provided by the Act. The trial court had in this case awarded the author all available reliefs: first, the possession of infringing copies; second, damages for infringement; third, decree for proportion of profits earned by the film; and finally, a preventive injunction. The High Court reversed all the three first reliefs on grounds which betray not even a marginal sensitivity to copyright justice. Section 58 provides that the author shall be the owner of all infringing copies. But Section 2(m) excludes the reproduction of literary, dramatic, musical works in form of cinematograph films from its definition of infringing copies.[213] The High Court conceded that the author of a literary work also had the right to make a cinema film under Section 14(a)(iv)[214]; and that the film owner had clearly plagiarised a key dramatic sub-plot in the literary work. But it took the view that Section 2(m) prevented it from ordering relief under Section 58.

The decision may appear technically correct but can be assailed on both exegetical and policy grounds. The definition and interpretation clause begins; typically, that the works defined therein shall have the meaning assigned to them "unless the context requires otherwise". Section 58 in terms applies to "all infringing copies of any work in which copyright subsists".[215] The question then is for the purposes of Section 58: Is there any work in which copyright subsists and is infringed? If the answer is in the affirmative, the context requires that the term "infringing copy" be so interpreted as a copy that violates the subsisting copyright. Section 2(m) definition is not designed to frustrate the few effective remedies available for infringement of copyright; Section 58 provides one such remedy. If the definition is very strictly construed, even for purposes of a remedial or regressive section like Section 58, the result would be that the violator of valid copyright would remain the proprietor of works which violate copyright. And the author of a literary, dramatic and artistic work will never be in a position to take ownership of films which violate his copyright. Such result is not intended by the Act in view of explanation to Section 51 which clearly provides that for the purposes of the Section the reproduction of literary, dramatic, musical or artistic works in the form of a film shall be deemed an infringing copy. Given the approach of the Madras High Court in this very case, the only remedy would be a preventive injunction against exhibition, which may not be much of a remedy given the long delays in disposal of cases.

Of course, it is possible on a similar strict construction to argue that under Section (2)(m)(ii) the owner of copyright in a cinematograph work can also not avail of Section 58 remedy because an infringing copy of the film means only copy of the film or recording of its soundtrack.[216] But if literary, dramatic or artistic works were made in a manner infringing

---

212. (1972) 85 Mad. L.W. 58: 1972—LW (Crl) 156.

213. Section 2(m) of the Copyright Act 1957 provides that "infringing copy" means in relation to a cinematograph film a copy of the film made on any medium by any means. *See, Nagpur Distilleries Pvt. Ltd.* v. *Karmaveer Shankarrao Kale*, 2017(5) ABR 140.

214. The right to make a cinematograph film (a right under Section 14(a)(iv) of the Copyright Act 1957). See, *Indian Performing Right Society Ltd.* v. *Aditya Pandey*, 2011 (47) PTC 392 (Del): MIPR 2011 (3)19.

215. *See, Birendra Bahadur Pandey* v. *Gramophone Co. of India Ltd.*, AIR 1984 Cal 69: 1984 (4) PTC 183 (Cal).

216. The Section (2)(m)(ii) of the Copyright Act 1957 defines "infringing copy" to mean, in relation to cinematographic film, a copy of the film made on any medium by any means. *See, Gurukrupa Mech Tech Pvt. Ltd.* v. *State of Gujarat*, (2018) 4 GLR 3324.

the copyright of the film manner (owner), she too cannot effectively urge that she is the owner of infringing copies. In practice, it is more likely that the film maker will plagiarise from other *genres* of work rather than *vice versa.* But in theory, the process of Section 58 would remain applicable only to the same classes of work but not across different classes of work provided by the statute. Notionally, and in reality, this limitation of Section 58 remedy, which enhances inhibition against easy infringement, should remain available in all situations.

The decision of the Bombay High Court in *Indian Express Newspapers Ltd.* v. *Jagmohan*[217] seems to have continued this trend. The case is unusual both for its facts and the law it seems to have generated. In late April, early May of 1981, the *Indian Express* carried a series of shocking stories concerning flesh trade in the state of Madhya Pradesh; its team of reporters actually bought a young girl named *Kamala* on payment of ₹2,300 for "half the price one pays for a buffalo in Punjab". Vijaj Tendulkar, among India's foremost playwrights, adopted the story in a play which was staged "about 150 times in 32 cities in 7 languages". The script of the play was published in book form and was on sale. Apart from the issue of libel successfully urged by the plaintiffs against the film maker, it appears that the case raised a question of, as it were, double infringement of the copyright of the newspaper. Interestingly, the playwright denied having read the articles in the Indian Express but acknowledged having read similar stories in a leading fortnightly India Today; the film maker admitted having read the newspaper articles but claimed that the film was an adaptation of the play. Did then the play infringe the "copyright" of the newspaper and the film infringe that of the playwright? The court ruled, following *R.G. Anand* case, on the one hand that there cannot subsist any copyright in "ideas, information, natural phenomena and events" which are common property and on the other that the film significantly differs (as it almost always does) from the newspaper articles, assuming that these provided "the materials on which one claiming the copyright has worked".[218] On the first proposition, one well-settled in copyright jurisprudence, there is, of course, not much room for criticism. But on the second, the formulation for holding infringement of copyright as "misconceived" does afford plenty of room for anxiety. For, the learned single judge holds, in so many words, that:

> The form, manner or arrangement of a drama and movie are materially different from a newspaper article and by very nature of the media there is a fundamental and substantial dissimilarity in the mode of expression of the idea in a newspaper article and in a state play or in a movie.[219]

This "nature of media test", if one may so call it, makes it virtually impossible the task of proving what the court earlier calls the distinction between "the materials upon which one claiming copyright has worked and the product of the application of his skill, judgement and labour and literary talent to these materials".[220] If it is the nature of the media which determines the *prima facie* claim of validity of the plea of infringement no further enquiry into similarities or dissimilarities is relevant. Indeed, given this orientation, any purported enquiry would, as happens in Indian decisions, simply end up in a massive demonstration of dissimilarities.

---

217. AIR 1985 1985 Bom. 229.
218. *Ibid.*, at p. 233.
219. *Ibid.*
220. *Ibid. See also, Zee Telefilms Ltd.* v. *Sundial Communications Pvt. Ltd.*, 2003 (27) PTC 457 (Bom): 2003 (105(3)) BomLR 678; *Michael Heath Nathan Johnson* v. *Subhash Chandra*, 1995 (15) PTC 300 (Del): 60 (1995) DLT 757; *Macmillan and Company* v. *K. and J. Cooper*, AIR 1924 PC 75: 1924 MWN 308.

Infringement of Copyright by Importation

The Copyright (Amendment) Act, 2012[221] has substituted new Section 53 dealing with importation of infringing copies has been substituted with a new section providing detailed border measures to strengthen enforcement of rights by making provision to control import of infringing copies by the Customs Department, disposal of infringing copies and presumption of authorship under civil remedies. The new Section 53 provides that the owner of copyright of any work or any performance embodied in such work, or his duly authorised agent, may give notice in writing to the Commissioner of Customs, or to any other officer authorised on this behalf by the Central Board of Excise and Customs requesting the Commissioner for a period specified in the notice, not exceeding one year, to treat infringing copies of the work as prohibited goods, and that infringing copies of the work are expected to arrive in India at a time and a place specified in the notice.[222] After examination of evidence so furnished, the Commissioner may pass an order treating the infringing goods as prohibited goods.[223] When any such goods are detained, the customs officer shall inform the importer as well as the person who gave notice of the detention of such goods within forty-eight hours of their detention.[224] The customs officer shall release the goods, and they shall no longer be treated as prohibited goods, if the person who gave notice does not produce any order from a court having jurisdiction as to the temporary or permanent disposal of such goods within fourteen days from the date of their detention.[225]

Infringing copy means in this context a copy or reproduction of the work made or imported in contravention of the provisions of the Act. In *Gramophone Company of India Ltd.* v. *Birendra Bahadur Pandey,*[226] the Apex Court held that the word "import" in Sections 51 and 53 of the Act means bringing into India from outside India; and it is not limited to importation for commerce only, but includes importation for transit across the country. The question that can arise, and has in the past in fact arisen, is: can an exclusive licencee for publishing a copyright work in India prevent import of copies of the work lawfully made in any other country, say, by the owner of the copyright himself or by his assignee or licencee,

---

221. Substituted by the Copyright (Amendment) Act, 2012, Section 34 for Section 53 [w.e.f. 21-6-2012]. Section 53, before substitution by Act 27 of 2012, stood as: "Section-53: Importation of infringing copies—(1) The Registrar of Copyrights, on application by the owner of the copyright in any work or by his duly authorised agent and on payment of the prescribed fee, may, after making such inquiry as he deems fit, order that copies made out of India of the work which if made in India would infringe copyright shall not be imported. (2) Subject to any rules made under this Act, the Registrar of Copyrights or any person authorised by him in this behalf may enter any ship, dock or premises where any such copies as are referred to in sub-section (1) may be found and may examine such copies. (3) All copies to which any order made under Sub-section (1) applies shall be deemed to be goods of which the import had been prohibited or restricted 1[under section 11 of the Customs Act, 1962 (51 of 1962),] and all the provisions of the Act shall have effect accordingly: Provided that all such copies confiscated under the provisions of the said Act shall not vest in the Government but shall be delivered to the owner of the copyright in the work." See, *Indusind Media and Communications Limited* v. *State of Gujarat*, 2017(71) PTC60(Guj): (2018)2GLR1151.
222. Copyright Act 1957, Section 53(1).
223. Copyright Act 1957, Section 53(2).
224. Copyright Act 1957, Section 53(3).
225. Copyright Act 1957, Section 53(4).
226. AIR 1984 SC 667: (1984) 2 SCC 534.

on the ground that such importation would amount to an infringement of the copyright of the work? Does such import constitute an import of an "infringing copy" and, as such, an infringement by importation? These questions have been answered in the affirmative by the Delhi High Court in *Penguin Books Ltd. England* v. *M/s. India Book Distributors*,[227] while allowing an appeal from an interlocutory order denying interim injunction. This decision of the Delhi High Court accords with the Australian and English decisions in similar cases, though the language of the Indian statute is not on all fours with the copyright statutes of those countries. It has been opined that the question of parallel imports has to be viewed from the perspective of our national self-interest and when so viewed this judgement is not in the interest of Indian reader who must get books at lower prices. This question must be considered by experts and a policy decision reached.

In connection to the importation of infringing copy in *Gramophone Company of India Ltd.* v. *Birendra Bahadur Pandey*,[228] the Supreme Court held that copies made out of India of any work which if made in India would infringe Copyright, shall not be imported. In *Penguin Books Ltd.* v. *India Book Distributors*,[229] the Delhi High Court held that importation of books which are "infringing copies of the work" is an infringement. So is the sale thereof. If any person, without the license of the copyright owner, imports into India for the purpose of selling or distributing for purposes of trade the literary work the copyright is infringed. Any importation of infringing copies is therefore an infringement unless it is for the importer's own use.[230] American books may be lawfully published in America, but when the copies of those publications are imported into this country, an action for infringement would lie in this country against the importer in respect of those copies. An action would also lie against any person who for instance sold or distributed such copies here. Because the books have been imported and sold without the license of the owner of the copyright or his exclusive licensee. As most infringements of copyrights consist of a continuous process of successive infringing acts such as importation of "infringing copies" as in this case the most important remedy and in many case the only effective one is the injunction.[231] Thus once the infringement and its continuance is proved the plaintiff will usually be entitled to an injunction, but the injunction would not be granted if the damage caused to the defendant by granting the injunction would be out of all proportion to the seriousness of the infringement or to the possible damage to the plaintiff.[232]

In *State of Andhra Pradesh* v. *Nagoti Venkataraman*,[233] the Supreme Court held that keeping in view the object underlying Sections 52A and 68A of the Act, it would be infringement of copyright, if the particulars on video films, etc. as mandated under Section 52A are missing. The absence of the evidence of the owner of the copyright does not constitute lack of

---

227. AIR 1985 Delhi 29: 1984 (4) PTC 285 (Del).
228. AIR 1984 SC 667: (1984) 2 SCC 534.
229. AIR 1985 Delhi 29: 1984 (4) PTC 285 (Del).
230. *See, Eurokids International Pvt. Ltd.* v. *India Book Distributors Egmont Books Ltd.*, 2005 (6) Bom CR 198.
231. *See, Proctor and Gamble Company* v. *Christian Hoden (India) Private Ltd.*, (1989) 1 MLJ 36: 1989-1-LW54.
232. *See, Deccan Bottling and Distilling Industries Pvt. Ltd.* v. *Brihan Maharashtra Sugar Syndicate Ltd*, 2008 (110) Bom LR 3175: 2009 (1) Bom CR 862.
233. (1996) 6 SCC 409.

essential elements of copyright. However, in the instant case, the Supreme Court after holding the accused guilty changed the sentence of six months imprisonment and fine of rupees three thousand imposed by the trial court as upheld by the sessions court to only fine of rupees ten thousand, as it felt that the punishment by way of fine only would meet the ends of justice.

DEFENCES OF COPYRIGHT LIABILITY: CERTAIN ACTS NOT TO BE INFRINGEMENT OF COPYRIGHT

Legislative Scheme

Section 52 of the Copyright Act, 1957 contains some express defences of copyright infringement known as "acts not to be infringement of copyright".[234] The defences as available for an action alleging infringement of copyright as are specified in Section 52 of the Copyright Act, 1957.[235] Section 52 describes these acts in bewildering details; it lists a number of act descriptions [clauses 1(a) to (zc)] with numerous sub-clauses, explanations and provisos. These provisions are popularly known as "fair dealing" provisions or "fair use" provisions.[236] The reason for having provisions relating to "fair dealing" in the Copyright Act is to strike a balance between the interest of the copyright owner, and the interests of the society at large.[237] The principle of balancing exclusive rights of the author/publisher in the work with the public interest in the free dissemination of all works got expressly recognised by the English judgment in *Donaldson* v. *Beckett*, of 1774.[238] Since then, the common law countries including India have adhered to this principle of balance between exclusive rights of copyright owners and interests of the society at large.

In *Wiley Eastern Ltd.* v. *Indian Institute of Management*,[239] the Delhi High Court observed that the basic purpose of Section 52 of the Copyright Act, 1957 is to protect the freedom of expression under Article 19(1) of CS(OS) 1889/2009 & 1889/2009, Page 27 of 32 the Constitution of India so that the research, private study, criticism or review or reporting of current events could be protected. The court further held that the Section 52 of the Act gives examples of fair dealing with regard to literary, dramatic, musical or artistic work for the purposes of research or private study, or for purposes of criticism or review, or a fair dealing for purpose of reporting current events in a newspaper, magazine or periodical or by broadcast or in a cinematograph film. These are constituted as not amounting to infringement of copyright.

---

234. *See*, *Maroti* v. *State of Maharashtra*, 2018 ALLMR (Cri) 4460; *Myspace Inc.* v. *Super Cassettes Industries Ltd.*, 2017 (69) PTC 1 (Del): 236 (2017) DLT 478.
235. *See*, *Brihan Karan Sugar Syndicate Pvt. Ltd.* v. *Karmaveer Shankarrao Kale*, 2018(73)PTC576(Bom): 2018 (5) Bom CR 778; *Mahadevaiah* v. *The Registrar*, 2017 (3) Kar LJ 697: 2017 (3) AKR 731; *Gurukul Books* v. *Evergreen Publications*, 2017 (72) PTC 489 (Del): 2016 XAD (Delhi) 34.
236. For commentaries on "fair dealing", *see*, Mishita Jethi, "Dealing 'Fairly' with Software in India" 16 *Journal of Intellectual Property Rights* (2011) pp. 313–320.
237. *See*, *Institute for Inner Studies* v. *Charlotte Anderson*, 2014 (57) PTC 228 (Del): MIPR 2014 (1) 129.
238. (1774) 4 Burr 2408. *See*, *Beloff* v. *Pressdran Ltd.*, [1973] 1 All ER 241; *Times Incorportion* v. *Bernard Gees Association*, 1968 F. 293 Supp 130; *Rosemant Enterprises Incorporation* v. *Random House Incorporation*, 1966 IInd Cir F 366, 2 ND 303; *Akuate Internet Services Pvt. Ltd.* v. *Star India Pvt. Ltd.*, MIPR 2013 (3) 1.
239. 61 (1996) DLT 281 (DB).

However, in the context of purposes set out in Section 52 if use made by the infringer is not fair, it would not *ipso facto* fall under Section 51 and whenever the use made by the infringer amounts to defamation, the remedy of the person may be in the form of damages. In *Institute of Chartered Accountants of India* v. *Shaunak H. Satya*,[240] the Apex Court held that the words "infringement of copyright" have a specific connotation. Section 51 of the Copyright Act, 1957 provides when a copyright in a work shall be deemed to be infringed, while Section 52 of the Act enumerates the acts which are not infringement of a copyright. A combined reading of Sections 51 and 52(1)(a) of copyright Act shows that furnishing of information by an examining body, in response to a query under the Right to Information Act, 2005 may not be termed as an infringement of copyright.

Section 52 of the Copyright Act, 1957 provides for approximately forty actions which shall not constitute an infringement of copyright. Section 52(1) provides that a fair dealing with a literary, dramatic, musical, or artistic work for the following purposes does not constitute infringement: (i) research or private study, (ii) criticism or review, whether of that work or of any other work, (iii) reporting current events in a newspaper, magazine or similar periodical, or by broadcast or in a cinematograph film or by means of photographs. The explanation to Section 52(1) stipulates that the publication of a compilation of addresses or speeches delivered in public is not a fair dealing of such work. In the case of items (ii) and (iii) the criticism or review or newspaper reporting must be accompanied by an acknowledgment identifying the work by its title or other description and identifying the author unless the work is anonymous, or the author of the work has previously agreed or required that no acknowledgment of his name should be made. Further the above provisions also apply to the translation of a literary, dramatic or musical work or the adoption of a literary, dramatic, musical or artistic work as they apply in relation to the work itself.[241]

Article 9(2) of the Berne Convention[242] authorises a national legislation to permit the reproduction of protected works "in certain special case provided two cumulative conditions are fulfilled: (a) the reproduction does not conflict with the normal exploitation of the work, and (b) such reproduction does not unreasonably prejudice the legitimate interests of the author. These exceptions were conceived mainly with manuscript or typewritten copies in mind, but modern technology have provided new tools which produced major challenges to the right of reproduction. Hence, a debate is centred on the proposition that the Internet and the World Wide Web have upset the sensitive balance between authors and users. Copyright owners claim that unless copyright law is strengthened, contents will not be made available on the Internet and the network will fail. Internet users claim that if their current practices

240. AIR 2011 SC 3336: 2011 (8) SCC 781.

241. Explanation to Section 52(1)(a) of the reads: "Explanation-The storing of any work in any electronic medium for the purposes mentioned in this clause, including the incidental storage of any computer programme which is not itself an infringing copy for the said purposes, shall not constitute infringement of copyright." *See*, *Super Cassettes Industries Ltd.* v. *Shreya Broadcasting Pvt. Ltd.*, 2019 III AD (Delhi) 552: 258(2019) DLT 116.

242. Berne Convention for the Protection of Literary and Artistic Works, Berne, September 9, 1886, came into force on December 5, 1887. India ratified on April 1, 1928. For the text of the Convention, *see*, Alfredo Ilardiand and Michael Blakency, *International Encyclopaedia of Intellectual Property Treaties.* Oxford University Press (2004). *See also*, Shahid Alikhan, "Role of the Berne Convention in the Promotion of Cultural Creativity and Development: Recent Copyright Legislation in Developing Countries", 28 *Journal of the Indian Law Institute,* 1986 pp. 424–440.

are restricted, the Internet will fail to live up to its potential as a democratic, interactive medium of communications and social interaction. The Copyright (Amendment Act) 2012 has been enacted bringing changes to the Copyright Act, 1957. The amendments make Indian copyright law compliant with the Internet Treaties, WIPO Copyright Treaty (WCT) and WIPO Performances and Phonograms Treaty (WPPT). While introducing technological protection measures by the amendments, the law ensures that fair use survives in the digital era by providing special fair use provisions.[243] Thus, under the Copyright Act certain acts can be performed without attracting liability for copyright infringement, but this is without prejudice to other legal rights or obligations. We may classify the defences of copyright liability under Section 52 in Table 9.1:

Table 9.1 Defences of Copyright Liability

Sl. No.	*Description of acts*	*Relevant clauses of Section 52(1) of the Act*
1.	Fair dealing use	(a), (b), (c), (aa), (ab), (ac), (ad), (p), (zb)
2.	Educational uses	(g), (h), (i)
3.	Media reporting uses	(b), (m), (n)
4.	Uses of state produced materials	(c), (d), (e), (g), (r)
5.	Making of records of literary, dramatic, or musical works	(i)
6.	Performance of such works	(f), (k), (l)
7.	Use by public libraries	(o)
8.	Use of engraving, etc.	(s), (t), (x)
9.	Cinematograph films—uses by makers, and exhibitor	(u), (y)
10.	Uses relating to artistic works	(v), (w)
11	Permitted reproduction	(e), (f), (m), (p), (q), (zc)

Thus, a copyrighted work can be used without the consent of the copyright holder to facilitate education, research, dissemination of knowledge and information for promotion of economy and culture of a society, etc., as per the exceptions provided under Section 52 and it can be used generally for public purposes.

In *Tekla Corporation* v. *Suvro Ghosh*,[244] the court held that Clauses (a) to (zc) of sub-section (1) of Section 52 describe in detail the acts which shall not constitute an infringement of copyright. Clauses (a), (aa), (ab), (ac), (ad) thereof *inter alia* exempt fair use as described therein of copyrighted works. Similarly, Clause (p) thereof provides that reproduction for the purpose of research or private study to be not amounting to infringement of copyright therein. Thus, Section 52 is exhaustive as well as inflexible. The main issues under Section 52 can be discussed under the following two broad headings: (ii) fair dealing in certain kinds of works; and (ii) permitted reproduction in certain kinds of works.

---

243. For detail discussions, *see*, S. Sivakumar and Lisa P. Lukose, *Broadcasting Reproduction Right in India: Copyright and Neighboring Rights Issues,* Indian Law Institute, New Delhi (2013); Zakir Thomas, "Overview of Changes to the Indian Copyright Law" 17 *Journal of Intellectual Property Rights* (2012) pp. 324–334.

244. 2014 (2) MIPR 264: 2014 (59) PTC 323.

Fair Dealing in Certain Kinds of Works

Concept of Fair Dealing

The Section 52 of the Copyright Act 1957 provides that "a fair dealing with any work" not being a computer programme, for the purpose of reporting of current events and current affairs, shall not constitute an infringement. Therefore, the legislature while recognizing copyright as statutory right has permitted use of the work of another person for limited purposes, provided that such use does not travel beyond the fair dealing with the work.[245] However, the expression "fair dealing" or "fair use" has not been defined anywhere in the Act. The courts also find it difficult to lay down precise standards. In *Civic Chandran* v. *C. Ammini Amma*,[246] the Kerala High Court observed that it is impossible to define what is "fair dealing." It must be a question of degree. You must consider first the number and extent of the quotations and extracts. Are they altogether too many and too long to be fair? Then you must consider the use made of them. If they are used as a basis for comment, criticism or review, that may be fair dealing.

The Supreme Court of the United States in *Harper and Row* v. *Nation Enterprises*,[247] has explained the breadth of the fair use doctrine where the Court noted that there are four factors relevant in determining whether the use was fair: (i) the purpose and character of the use; (ii) the nature of the copyrighted work; (iii) the substantiality of the portion used in relation to the copyrighted work as a whole; (iv) the effect on the potential market for or value of the copyrighted work and proceeded to test the facts on each of these grounds.[248] Further, in *Dellar* v. *Samuel Goldwyn, Inc.*,[249] the court described the "fair use" doctrine as "the most

---

245. *See, Super Cassettes Industries Ltd.* v. *Shreya Broadcasting Pvt. Ltd.*, 258 (2019)DLT 116: 2019 III AD (Delhi) 552; *ICC Development (International) Ltd.* v. *New Delhi Television Ltd.*, 2012 (132) DRJ 291: 193 (2012) DLT 279; *Dhiraj Dharamdas Dewani* v. *Sonal Info Systems Pvt. Ltd.*, 2012 (52) PTC 458 (Bom): 2012 (2) Bom CR 842.
246. 1996 (16) PTC 670 (Ker).
247. 471 US 539 (1985).
248. Section 107 of the US Copyright Act 1976 deals with the doctrine of "fair use". According to Section 107 the fair use of a copy righted work, including such use by reproduction in copies or phonorecords or by any other means specified by that section, for purposes such as criticism, comment, news reporting, teaching (including multiple copies for classroom use), scholarship, or research, is not an infringement of copyright. In determining whether the use made of a work in any particular case is a fair use the factors to be considered shall include—(1) the purpose and character of the use, including whether such use is of a commercial nature or is for nonprofit educational purposes; (2) the nature of the copyrighted work; (3) the amount and substantiality of the portion used in relation to the copyrighted work as a whole; and (4) the effect of the use upon the potential market for or value of the copyrighted work. The fact that a work is unpublished shall not itself bar a finding of fair use if such finding is made upon consideration of all the above factors. For the various aspect of the doctrine of "fair use", *see, Compare Universal City Studios, Inc.* v. *Sony Corp. of America*, 480 F. Supp. 429 (C.D. Cal. 1979); *Henry Holt & Co.* v. *Liggett & Myers Tobacco Co.*, 23 F. Supp. 302 (E.D. Pa. 1938); *Williams & Wilkins* v. *United States*, 487 F. 2d 1345 (Ct. Cl. 1973) *Universal City Studios, Inc.* v. *Sony Corp. of America*, 480 f. Supp. 429, 453–454 (D.C. Cal 1979); *Encyclopaedia Britannica Educational Corp.* v. *Crooks*, 447 F. Supp. 243 (W.D.N.Y. 1978). *See also*, Wendy. J. Gordon, "Fair use as Market Failure: A Structural and Economic Analysis of Betamax Case and its Predecessors", 82 *Columbia Law Review* (1982) at p. 1600; A.O. Rurke Maureen, "Toward A Doctrine of Fair Use in Patent Law", 100 *Columbia Law Review* (2000) at p. 1177.
249. 104 F. 2d 661 (2d. Cir. 1939).

troublesome in the whole law of copyright". The doctrine of "fair dealing" or "fair use" is used as an affirmative defence and is applied once it is established that the defendant's work is, in fact, substantially similar to the plaintiff's work. It is an extraordinary flexible doctrine in the sense that its application typically turns on the particular facts in issue.

The question often arises that what is the criteria for determination of applicability of the defence of "fair dealing" under Section 52? The Section covers a number of acts descriptions. Hence the problem lies in the determination of the relative thresholds of substantiality and the permitted act in question.

In *Copyright Agency* v. *Haines,*[250] Whitford J. said that in the case of copyright infringement if the part taken is not substantial, there is no infringement and the defence is irrelevant, but if the part taken is substantial then the defence will rarely excuse the defendant's use of the work. It is respectfully submitted that this is wrong and that while the purpose of the defence provisions is to permit, in appropriate circumstances, the taking of a substantial part of a copyrighted work. It is, however, difficult to say where the boundaries circumscribing substantiality and defence lie.

Lord Denning gave a good description of the scope of defence for the purposes of criticism or review in *Hubbard* v. *Vosper,*[251] where he said: "You must first consider the number and extent of the question ... Then you must consider the use made of them." Apart from the purpose of the inclusion of copyright materials, their overall promotion to the while must be considered. Although substantiality is determined by a qualitative test, it appears from Lord Denning's description that the scope of this particular permitted act is determined at least partly by means of a quantitative test. Hence, the difficulty experienced. However, in some circumstances the defence may allow the copying of an entire work. The only thing that can be said with any degree of certainty is that whether a particular act falls within the meaning of "fair dealing" depends very much upon the circumstances surrounding the act. Only sometimes will the factors identified below be said to be conclusive one way or the other and in most cases it will be a matter of combining and weighting the factors:

1. **Proportion:** within a particular form of fair dealing, proportion might be important, for example, it may be fair dealing for the purposes of criticism or review to take 5 per cent of a work, but not to take 40 per cent.[252] Thus, one must consider the proportions of the alleged work. To take long extracts and attach short comments may be unfair. But, short extracts and long comments may be fair.[253]

2. **Purpose:** conceivably, it might be fair dealing to take a copy of an entire work, such a journal article, for the purposes of research or private study. But it will not normally be fair dealing to take a large amount of another's work for the purposes of criticism or review.[254]

---

250. (1982) FSR 331.
251. (1972) 2 QB 84 at p. 94.
252. *Walter* v. *Steinkopff* (1892) 3 Ch. 489.
253. *Super Cassettes Industries Ltd.* v. *Hamar Television Network Pvt. Ltd.*, 2010 LawSuit (Del) 1272: 2011 (45) PTC 70.
254. *Super Cassettes Industries Limited* v. *Chintamani Rao*, 2011 LawSuit (Del) 3245: 2012 (49) PTC 1.

3. **Motive:** if the motive for the act was to compete with the other work, this is unlikely to be fair dealing.[255]
4. **Status of other work:** that is whether confidential or published. It is unlikely to be fair dealing if the work taken has not been published, or in the case of a leak.[256]

While no definition of "fair dealing" or "fair use" is found under the 1957 Act, Indian courts have relied on the English decision in *Hubbard* v. *Vosper*,[257] which held that although "it is impossible to define what is fair dealing" but "fair dealing" is inevitably a matter of degree. The court further observed: "If they are used as a basis for comment, criticism or review, that may be fair dealing. If they are used to convey the same information as the author, for a rival purpose, that may be unfair. Next, you must consider the proportions. To take long extracts and attach short comments may be unfair. But, short extracts and long comments may be fair. Other considerations may come to mind also. But, after all is said and done, it must be a matter of impression. As with fair comment in the law of libel, so with fair dealing in the law of copyright."[258]

In *Eastern Book Company* v. *D.B. Modak,*[259] the Apex Court examined the claim copyright in copy-edited versions of the judgments delivered by the Supreme Court. The Court held that copyright protection is based on fair play. A person is not permitted to make a profit out of the skill and labour of the original author. Copyright law presents a balance between the interests and rights of the author and that of the public in protecting the public domain, or to claim the copyright and protect it under the copyright statute. There is no copyright in facts as facts are not created nor have they originated with the author of any work which embodies these facts. The issue of copyright is closely connected to that of commercial viability, and commercial consequences and implications.

Now question arises: is there any relation between the concept of "fair dealing"/"fair use" and the concept of "public domain"? The Delhi High Court in *Syndicate of the Press of the University of Cambridge on Behalf of the Chancellor* v. *B.D. Bhandari,*[260]explain the concept of "fair dealing"/"fair use" and its relation with the concept of "public domain". The court observed that doctrine of fair dealing/fair use is a limitation and exception to the exclusive right granted by copyright law to the author of a creative work and it allows limited use of copyrighted material without acquiring permission from the rights holders. Quoting the *Black's Law Dictionary*[261] the court defines "fair use" as a reasonable and limited use of a copyrighted work without the author's permission, such as quoting from a book in a book review or using parts of it in a parody. Thus use of a work, RFA (OS) No. 21 of 2009 and FAO (OS) No. 458 of 2008, Page 28 of 89 without any prior permission of the author of that

255. *Wealtheryby* v. *International Horse Agency and Exchange Ltd.* (1910) 2 Ch. 297.
256. *British Oxygen Co. Ltd.* v. *Liquid Air Ltd.* (1925) Ch 383.
257. (1972) 1 All ER 1023: [1972] 2 QB 84.
258. This English principle has been followed in Indian courts in *Syndicate* v. *B.D. Bhandari*, 2011 (47) PTC 244 (Del): 185 (2011) DLT 346; *Super Cassettes Industries Ltd.* v. *Hamar Television Network Pvt. Ltd.*, 2011 (45) PTC 70 (Del): (2010) ILR 6 Delhi 230; *Espn Star Sports* v. *Global Broadcast News Ltd.*, 2008 (38) PTC 477 (Del): MIPR 2008 (3) 257; *ESPN Stars Sports* v. *Global Broadcast News Ltd.*, 2008 (36) PTC 492 (Del): MIPR 2008 (2) 75.
259. AIR 2008 SC 809: (2008) 1 SCC 1.
260. 2011 (47) PTC 244 (Del). 185 (2011) DLT 346.
261. 7th Edition.

work, does not amount to infringement of copyright if the said use can be encapsulated within the ambit of the doctrine of fair use. There are four non-exclusive factors that determine whether any particular use counts as fair use or an infringement. These four factors are (i) the purpose and character of the copyright use, including whether such use is of a commercial nature or is largely for non-profit educational purposes; (ii) the nature of the copyrighted work itself; (iii) the substantiality of the portion used in relation to the copyrighted work as a whole; and (iv) the effect of the use upon the potential market value of the copyrighted work. A court examines these factors in judging the assertion of infringement by the copyright owner on the one hand and the assertion of fair use by the alleged infringer on the other.

In *Syndicate* v. *B.D. Bhandari*,[262] the Court observed:

> The term "public domain" and "fair use" are distinct from each other and once a work comes within the ambit of "public domain" then there is no question of involvement of the fair use doctrine because the term "public domain" means there is no copyright protection is available at all to the concerned work.
>
> What follows form the above is that the two concepts, viz., "public domain" and "fair use" work in altogether different fields. When the defence is taken that a particular work is in public domain, the question for consideration would arise as to whether the appellants enjoys copyright therein or not. On the other hands, when plea of fair use under Section 52 of the Copyright Act is adopted by the respondents what is expected from the Court on the application of the provisions of Section 52 of the Act is not to examine whether the activity is infringement is not, but to examine whether the conditions stated in a particular clause of Section 52 of the Act invoked by the respondents is satisfied or not.

The concept of "public domain" and "fair use" work is applied in altogether different fields. Thus, the court held that the two concepts are distinct from each other and once a work comes within the scope and ambit of "public domain", then there is no question of involvement of the "fair use" doctrine because the term "public domain" means that there is no copyright protection available to the concerned work. There are three common ways under which a work can be attributed as a work in "public domain": (i) copyright law does not protect this kind of work as it does not fall under Section 13 Copyright Act, 1957 (the Act);[263] (ii) the owner of a work may deliberately relinquish his copyright by Section 21 of the Act;[264] and (iii) the term of copyright in the work as provided by the Act has expired.[265]

In *Ram Sampath* v. *Rajesh Roshan*,[266] the Bombay High Court examined the scope of fair dealing of musical works. Plaintiff was the owner of the musical composition entitled "THUMP" created for use in advertisement. The defendant used small portion (six seconds) of the same composition (tune) in the songs for the film "KRAZZY". In a suit for infringement, it was, *inter alia,* contended by the defendant that since the portion copied is very small it falls within Section 52 and not an infringement of the copyright in the musical work. After examining the provisions, the court spelled out the following factors to determine the fair dealing of musical work:

---

262. 2011 (47) PTC 244 (Del): 185 (2011) DLT 346.
263. *See, Gurukrupa Mech Tech Pvt. Ltd.* v. *State of Gujarat*, (2018) 4 GLR 3324.
264. *See, Holland Company LP* v. *S.P. Industries*, 2017 (71) PTC 630 (Del): MIPR 2017 (3) 237.
265. *See, Music Broadcast Limited* v. *Axis Bank*, 2016 (67) PTC 638 (Del); *Dart Industries Inc.* v. *Techno Plast*, 2016 (67) PTC 457 (Del): 233 (2016) DLT 1.
266. 2009 (40) PTC 78 (Bom).

> In my view for considering whether a copy of a part of the former musical work into the latter musical work amounts to an actionable infringement, the following factors would be required to be taken into consideration. First is to identify the similarities and differences between the two works. Second is to find out whether the latter would meaningfully exist without the copied part. It may be necessary to find the soul of a musical work. The soul cannot be determined merely by comparing the length of the part copied but whether the part copied is an essential part of a musical work. Though a musical work may have a length of several minutes, the listener often remembers a "catch part" to which he is immediately hooked on. It is necessary to look for such "catch part" or the "hook part". If the "catch part" or "hook part", however small, is copied the whole of the latter work would amount to actionable infringement. It is necessary to remind oneself that the desire of an infringer is necessarily to copy "the attractive", "the catchy", "the grain" and leave the chaff, for he would attract the audience only by the attractive, and not by the ordinary. These factors are only illustrative and there would be many other factors which may be required to be looked into depending on the factors and circumstances of each case.

The defence of "fair dealing" or "fair use" is analogous to privilege in tort law and, just as tort privileges are determined and justified by broad notions of policy rather than by strict statutory law definitions. It is akin to a privilege because it is essentially a defence to a charge of infringement. As with a defence of privilege in a tort action, the defence of fair use acknowledges the elements of the tort but affirmatively raises other important issues and policies. However, in *Institute for Inner Studies* v. *Charlotte Anderson*,[267] it has been clearly laid down that commercial exploitation of works protected by intellectual property rights will take the matter outside the ambit of "fair use".[268] In determining whether the activity is covered under the fair use or not the court has to consider four factors: (i) the purpose and character of the use, including whether such use is of commercial nature or it is for non-profit educational purposes, (ii) the nature of copyrighted work, (iii) the amount and substantiality of the portion used in relation to copyrighted work as a whole, (iv) the effect of the use upon the potential market for or the value of the copyrighted work.

Thus, a fair dealing with a literary, dramatic, musical or artistic work for the purposes of: "(i) "private or personal use, including research"; (ii) "criticism or review, whether of that work or of any other work"[269] shall not constitute an infringement of copyright if the work is not used for commercial exploitation. Similarly, a fair dealing with a literary, dramatic, musical or artistic work for the purpose of reporting current events—(i) in a newspaper, magazine or similar periodical; or (ii) by broadcast or in a cinematograph film or by means of photographs shall not constitute an infringement of copyright.[270] However, the publication of a compilation of addresses or speeches delivered in public is not a fair dealing of such work.[271] The Copyright (Amendment) Act, 2012 has introduced special provisions for access to the person with disabled and their fair use rights under Section 31B read with clause (zb) of sub-section (1) of Section 52 of the Copyright Act, 1957. Thus, the Copyright Act recognises private or personal use, including research, criticism or review, reporting current events, etc.

---

267. 2014 (1) MIPR 129: 2014 (57) PTC 228.
268. *See also, Super Cassettes Industries* v. *Hamar Television Network*, 2011 (45) PTC 70; *University of Cambridge* v. *B.D. Bhandari*, 2009 (39) PTC 642.
269. Copyright Act, 1957, Section 52(1)(a).
270. *Ibid.*, Section 52(1)(b).
271. *Ibid.*, Section 52(1)(c), Explanation.

as defences of copyright liability under the category of "fair dealing". In this connection in *Super Cassettes Industries Limited* v. *Chintamani Rao*,[272] the Court observed:

> What Section 52(1)(a) permits is that the literary, dramatic, musical or artistic work may be reproduced without fear of infringement of copyright in such works, if such reproduction is a fair dealing of the copyright work in question, for the purpose of criticism or review whether of that work or any other work. Therefore, firstly it has to be "fair dealing" of the work in question. This means that the dealing with the copyrighted work is not an unfair dealing.

Private or Personal use including Research

Under Section 52(1)(i) of the Copyright Act, 1957, the defence of fair dealing for "private or personal use, including research" is available in relation to literary, dramatic, musical or artistic work.[273] However, it is not fair dealing to perform the acts permitted in relation to computer programs under Section 52(1)(aa) Act. As per Section 52(1)(aa), the making of copies or adaptation of a computer program by the lawful possessor of a copy of such computer program from such copy: (i) in order to utilise the computer program for the purpose for which it was supplied; or (ii) to make back-up copies purely as a temporary protection against loss, destruction or damage in order only to utilise the computer program for the purpose for which it was supplied shall not constitute infringement of copyright. Now question arises what should be the formula to determine "private or personal use, including research"?

The terms "research" and "study" has not been defined in the Act. The Oxford English Dictionary defines "research" as a search or investigation directed to the discovery of some fact by careful consideration or study of a subject; a course of critical or scientific enquiry. "Study" is defined as to apply the mind to the acquisition of learning, whether by means of books, observation, or experiment. The relationship between research and study is a close one. "Study" merely refers to the application of the mind to the acquisition of knowledge with a view to the discovery of some fact. In other words, "study" involves understanding and committing to memory existing information, whereas "research" requires the student to discern new and unstated information.[274] "Research" and "study" have been defined by the Federal Court of Australia in *De Garis* v. *Neville Jeffress Pidler Pvt. Ltd.*[275] The question for determination before the Court was whether a "nursing audit committee" was relevantly a "research group"? Answering affirmatively the question, the court defined "research" as the diligent and systematic enquiry or investigation into a subject in order to discover facts or principles and "study" as the application of the mind to the acquisition of knowledge; as by reading, investigation or reflection; a particular course of effort to acquire knowledge; a thorough examination and analysis of a particular subject.

---

272. 2012(49)PTC1(Del). *See also, Super Cassettes Industries Limited* v. *Chintamani Rao*, 2012 (49) PTC 1 (Del); *Academy of General Edu., Manipal* v. *B. Malini Mallya*, AIR 2009 SC 1982: (2009) 4 SCC 256; *Civic Chandran* v. *C. Ammini Amma*, 1996 (16) PTC 670 (Ker); *Romesh Chowdhry* v. *Ali Mohamad Nowsheri*, AIR 1965 J&K 101.
273. *See, Super Cassettes Industries Ltd.* v. *Shreya Broadcasting Pvt. Ltd.*, 258 (2019) DLT 116: 2019 III AD (Delhi) 552; *Chancellor* v. *Rameshwari Photocopy Services*, 2017 (69) PTC 123 (Del): 235 (2016) DLT 409.
274. *See,* Daniel Seng Kiat Boon, "Reviewing the Defence of Fair Dealing for Research or Private Study" *Singapore Journal of Legal Studies* (1996) p. 156.
275. (1990) 18 IPR 291: [1990] FCA 218.

In *Independent Television Publications Ltd.* v. *Time Out Ltd.*[276] the defendant copied details of forthcoming television programmes from the *TV Times* and the *Radio Times*. The defence of fair dealing (in this case under the head of fair dealing for criticism and review) failed because the purpose was to provide a television programme listing service and had nothing to do with research or private study. The financial motive behind making a copy of a work or part of a work for research or private study surely must be considered in determining whether or not it falls within the scope of fair dealing. To this end one can add other factors such as the nature of the research or study and the funds available to the researcher or student. Questions such as whether the person concerned is copying simply to save himself the expense of buying a copy of the work, or whether it is reasonable to expect a copy to be purchased, are important. Take, for example, a postgraduate research student. He will need to refer to hundreds of different journals, articles and books. The student will not be able to purchase more than a handful of these; he will have to be selective. The student may decide to purchase those materials which he will need to use over and over again during the research. But many of the articles and books will be used less frequently and only small portions will be referred to. It would not be realistic to expect the student to purchase a book when he wants to refer to only a small part of it. The role of this defence is particularly important in the field of education.

Is there any limit of fair dealing for private study or research? It is well recognised that copying the whole of one article from an academic journal would be fair dealing, or the copying of part of a book, say, no more than one chapter. Any more would not be fair dealing. In *Sillitoe* v. *McGraw Hill Book Co. (UK) Ltd.*,[277] the defendant had published "study notes" intended to assist students taking examinations in literature, and had reproduced a substantial part of the claimant's works in the study notes. The defendant contended, *inter alia,* that the study notes fell within the fair dealing provisions that is fair dealing for the purposes of research or private study. This submission failed to find favour, as the defendant was not engaged in research or private study, but was merely facilitating this for others, that is the students purchasing copies of the study notes.

In *Rupendra Kashyap* v. *Jiwan Publishing House*,[278] the court considered two issues: (i) the first issue was that the defence of "fair dealing" raised by the defendants on the ground that they were dealing with literary work for the purposes of "research" or "private studies", and (ii) the second issue was that the denial of right to the contesting defendants to publish examination papers would create a monopoly in favour of the plaintiff and hence, would not be in public interest. The court in respect of the defence of fair dealing applied the test of "commercial exploitation" and held that if a CS (OS) 1889/2009 & 1889/2009, Page 26 of 32 publisher commercially exploits the original work and in doing so infringes the copyright, the defence of fair dealing would not be available to such a publisher even if the book published by him is used or meant to be used for research or private study. As regards the second issue, the court held that the argument of public interest was not tenable as it was not as if the examination papers of the past years were not in public domain. The plaintiff, being the

276. (1984) FSR 64.
277. (1983) FSR 545.
278. (1996) PTC 439 (Del): 1996 (38) DRJ 81.

exclusive licencee, had in the past by publishing the papers, put them in the public domain on payment of royalty to Central Board of Secondary Education. The court observed:

> Moreover, the law as to copyright in India is governed by a statute which does not provide for defence in the name of public interest. An infringement of copyright cannot be permitted merely because it is claimed to be in public interest to infringe a copyright.[279]

It may be humbly submitted that the court in above case failed to understand the basic idea behind the copyright law. It is a recognised principle of copyright law that it as a branch of intellectual property law which is the breeding ground of a system that seeks to balance between two conflicting interests of the private creator and the public. While the copyright provides a bundle of rights which are recognised under any contemporary copyright statute, the concept "public domain" balances between two conflicting interests of the creator and the public.

Criticism or Review

The defence of fair dealing for the purpose of criticism or review applies to any form of work or a performance of a work that does not infringe copyright provided a sufficient acknowledgement is given.[280] Thus, in *Kartar Singh Giani* v. *Ladha Singh*,[281] the Lahore High Court held that in the guise of copyright law the plaintiff cannot ask the courts to close all the avenues of research, scholarship and all frontiers of human knowledge. The court found that the guide did not constitute an infringement and therefore, did not go into the question of fair dealing.

However, the question is: what is the nature and scope of "criticism or review" recognised under the "fair dealing" provisions? In *Pro Sieben Media AG* v. *Carlton UK Television Ltd.*,[282] the court held that "criticism or review" is expressions of wide and indefinite scope. Any attempt to plot their precise boundaries is doomed to failure. They are expressions which should be interpreted liberally, but … derive little assistance from comparisons with other expressions such as "current affairs" or "news". Thus, a criticism or a review can be scathing and can involve a substantial part of another work, and yet still be fair dealing. In *Hubbard* v. *Vosper*,[283] the defendant had been a member of the Church of Scientology for some 14 years. After leaving, he wrote a book which was highly critical of the cult of Scientology and used in this book substantial extracts from books, bulletins and letters, some of which were confidential, written by the claimant. The defence of fair dealing for the purposes of criticism and review was successfully raised as regards the copyright issues. The court held that the criticism or review may concern the ideas expressed as well as the mode

---

279. *See also, Super Cassettes Industries Ltd.* v. *Hamar Television Network Pvt. Ltd.*, (2010) ILR 6 Delhi 230: 2011 (45) PTC 70 (Del); *Super Cassettes Industries Limited* v. *Chintamani Rao*, 2012 (49) PTC 1 (Del).
280. *See, Academy of General Edu., Manipal* v. *B. Malini Mallya*, AIR 2009 SC 1982: (2009) 4 SCC 256; *ESPN Stars Sports* v. *Global Broadcast News Ltd.*, 2008 (36) PTC 492 (Del): MIPR 2008 (2) 75; *Blackwood and Sons Ltd.* v. *A.N. Parasuraman*, AIR 1959 Mad 410; *Messes Macmillan and Company Ltd.* v. *The Little Flower Company*, (1959) ILR Madras 484.
281. AIR 1934 Lah 777.
282. (1999) FSR 610.
283. (1972) 2 QB 84.

of expression. However, the court will not permit wholesale borrowing to be dressed up as critical question. *Lord Denning J.* remarks stressing that fair dealing is inevitably a matter of degree can usefully be applied not only to this head but in spirit equally to the other two:

> You must consider first the number and extent of the quotations and extracts. Are they altogether too many and too long to be fair? Then you must consider the use made of them. If they are used as a basis for comment, criticism or review, that may be a fair dealing. If they are used to convey the same information as the author, for a rival purpose, they may be unfair. Next, you must consider the proportions. To take long extracts and attach short comments may be unfair. But short extracts and long comments may be fair. Other considerations may come to mind also. But, after all is said and done, it must be a matte of impression.[284]

In *E.M. Forster and Another* v. *A.N. Parasuram,*[285] the Madras High Court examined the applicability of the defence of "criticism or review" as "fair use". In this case the appellant published a book, namely, *A Passage to India* in 1924. Certain exclusive rights of publication in this work were assigned by appellant to Edward Arnold (Publishers) Ltd. In 1955–1956, the University of Madras prescribed *A Passage to India* as a textbook for the students taking B.A. degree. The respondents published a guide book for the students to the novel *A Passage to India.* The Single Judge found that there was no such infringement by substantial reproduction of the original novel and that the guide book of respondent amounted to an independent literary effort on his part and disposed of the two suits. Dismissing the appeal, a Division Bench held that the objective of respondent was not to express his appreciation of the novel, or his enjoyment of it, or even to make a contribution towards literary criticism. He was concerned to aid the students taking the B.A. degree in answering several questions that would no doubt be set for them, upon the novel in the examination papers for that degree. He might well have been guided by considerable experience, in framing his studies in the manner that he has done and even in the language, he had employed. Either upon the principle of substantial reproduction, or even qualitative reproduction, as far as the verbal expression of the original work goes, there has been no infringement. It is well known that in literary reviews, a very small proportion of verbatim quotation from an original work is always permitted, is the intent of fair criticism. Even taking the guide book of the respondent in its entirety, it can by no means be said that such a proportion has been exceeded.

In *Chancellor Masters and Scholars of the University of Oxford* v. *Narendera Publishing House,*[286] the court in a lucid discussion of the law on the subject of infringement of copyright relied upon the "transformative work" test to determine as to whether there was fair use of the copyrighted work in Section 52(1)(a) with reference to use of questions in one work to produce a guide with answers to those questions. The plaintiff claimed copyright in the book "Oxford Mathematics Part-A and Part-B" prepared by A.K. Roy based on the syllabus for XI of J&K State Board of School Education. It was alleged that the defendants infringed the copyright in the book by copying all the questions at the end of each chapter to prepare a guide solving the questions by providing step-by-step approach to finding the answer. The

---

284. *See also, Super Cassettes Industries Ltd.* v. *Hamar Television Network Pvt. Ltd.*, 2011 (45) PTC 70 (Del): (2010) ILR 6 Delhi 230.
285. AIR 1964 Mad 331.
286. (2008) 38 PTC 385.

defendant claimed exemption under Section 52(1)(a) of the Act copying the work as "fair dealing" for "review" of the book. After examining the object of the Section 52, the Court applied the "fair dealing" provisions in this case and observed:

> The doctrine of fair use then, legitimizes the reproduction of a copyrightable work. Coupled with a limited copyright term, it guarantees not only a public pool of ideas and information, but also a vibrant public domain in expression, from which an individual can draw as well as replenish. Fair use provisions, then must be interpreted so as to strike a balance between the exclusive rights granted to the copyright holder, and the often competing interest of enriching the public domain. Section 52 therefore cannot be interpreted to stifle creativity, and the same time must discourage blatant plagiarism. It, therefore, must receive a liberal construction in harmony with the objectives of copyright law. Section 52 of the Act only details the broad heads, use under which would not amount to infringement. Resort, must, therefore be made to the principles enunciated by the courts to identify fair use.[287]

Thus the court recognises the equally compelling need to promote creative activity and ensure that the privileges granted by copyright do not stifle dissemination of information. Copyright law is premised on the promotion of creativity through sufficient protection. All creativity is in part derivative, in that, no creativity is completely original. Most important areas of intellectual creativity like philosophy, literature and sciences are referential, and require continuous re-examination of existing work. The court gave emphasis to the "transformative character of the work" in finding out fare use. Thus, the court held: "If the work is transformative, then it might not matter that the copying is whole or substantial. Again, if it is transformative, it may not act as a market substitute and consequently, will not affect the market share of the prior work." Applying this principle on the present case, the court held that the defendants' use is of "fair dealing" for "review" and stated thus:

> The purpose and manner of use of the questions found in the plaintiff's textbooks, by the defendants is thus different; additionally, in their books, missing in the plaintiff's works are the steps or process of problem solving. Thus, the defendants' works can be said to be "transformative", amounting to "review" under Section 52(1)(a)(ii) of the Act. Here, the term "review" has to be interpreted in the context. The plaintiffs claim to copyright is premised the work being a "literary "one. The review—or commentary, of a part of such mathematical work too would have to be seen in the background of this claim.
>
> "Review" according to the Shorter Oxford Dictionary (Fifth edition) means "view", inspect or examine a second time or again. In the context of a mathematical work a review could involve re-examination or a treatise on the subject. In that sense, the defendants' revisiting the questions, and assisting the students to solve then, by providing the step by step reasoning prima facie amounts to a "review", thus falling within the "fair dealing" provision of Section 52(1)(a)(ii) of the Act.

In *Civic Chandran* v. *Ammini Amma*,[288] the question of fair dealing came up for consideration. In this case the defendants had published a play, viz., "Ningal Are Communistakki", which was intended to be a critique of a famous play, viz., "Ningal Enna Communistakki". The court referred to *Hubbard* v. *Vosper*,[289] and *R.G. Anand* v. *Delux Films*,[290] and concluded that the play was meant to be a critique and therefore, constituted

287. *See also, Super Cassettes Industries Limited* v. *Chintamani Rao,* 2012 (49) PTC 1 (Del); R.G. *Anand* v. M/s. *Deluxe Films*, 1978 (4) SCC 118.

288. 1996 (16) PTC 670.

289. (1972) 2 WLR 389.

290. *R.G. Anand* v. *Delux Films* (1978) 4 SCC 118.

fair dealing under Section 52(1)(a) of the Copyright Act, 1957. The court further observed that the latter work was not market competitor to the prior work, and by itself constituted a literary work with some amount of originality. Moreover, the Court held that the nature of the work, that is to criticise the social structures in Kerala, by itself meant that certain sequences, events and incidents would be common to both the prior and the subsequent work, and that the latter was not meant to imitate the former.

Reporting Current Events

"Fair dealing" for the purpose of reporting current events shall not constitute an infringement of copyright. Therefore, it is common practice for newspapers, magazines or periodicals to copy extracts from the stories in other newspapers. For example, one newspaper, magazine or periodical may have an "exclusive" in its early morning issue and other newspapers carry the story in their later editions giving sufficient acknowledgement. However, this defence shall not apply in the case of a photograph. In *Benier* v. *News Group Newspaper Ltd.*,[291] the court confirmed that the practice of newspapers of copying a photograph from another newspaper with the intention of obtaining a licence retrospectively was clearly unlawful. Nor could such use of a photograph be considered to be fair dealing for criticism or review, such a photograph being described as totally unreal.

In *Indian Express Newspaper (Bombay) Pvt. Ltd.* v. *Jagmohan*,[292] the Bombay High Court has emphatically stated that there is no copyright for happenings and events which could be news stories, and reporter cannot claim any copyright over such events because he has reported it for the first time. The Court permitted a film producer copying it and changing its form into a movie and make money not minding the hard work, labour and investigative skills put in by the enterprising journalist. It is agreeable that like an idea, an unexpressed event cannot be copyrighted. But when a creative expression involving lot of original work and mental exercise is used to present the event, like the idea being expressed is a pertinent form, such an expression of event should be protected. This another is of the opinion that this decision is against the spirit of the protection of creative expression of abstract idea, as envisaged by the Copyright Act. The Court held in this case that there is no copyright in any event that actually take place. The Bombay High Court said that the ideas, information, natural phenomena; and events on which an author expends this skill, labour, capital, judgment and literary talents are common property and are not the subject of copyright. Hence, there is no copyright in news or information itself. However, copyright may be obtained for the form in which they are expressed, because of the skill and labour that goes into the writing of stories or features and in the selection and arrangement of the material. In this case a journalist *Ashwini Sarin* investigated into the flesh trade in Madhya Pradesh and purchased a woman *Kamala* for ₹2,300 to establish the trafficking in women, in Shivpuri village. The journalist then wrote a series of articles exposing the prostitution trade and involvement of bigwigs in politics and police, on 27th, 29th, and 30th April 1981 and 2nd May 1981. *Mr. Vijay Tendulkar* scripted a play by name *Kamala* based totally on the Indian Express exposure, and staged the play for 150 times in 32 cities and in seven languages. *Jogmohan Mundhara*, a film

291. (1997) FSR 812.
292. AIR 1985 Bom 229.

producer, planned to produce a film on the same theme from the same writer *Vijay Tendulkar*. Journalist *Ashwini Sarin* and the *Indian Express Newspaper* complained that their copyright was infringed by *Jagmohan* and *Vijay*. The Bombay High Court held that there could not be any copyright in an event that has actually taken place. The Court observed:

> There is distinction between the materials upon which one claiming copyright has worked and the product of the application of his skill, judgment, labours and literary talent to these materials. The ideas, information, national phenomena and events on which an author expends his skill labour, capital, judgment and literary talent are common property and are not the subject of the copyright.[293]

This judgment ignored the skill, capital, talent and labour invested by the journalist and simply termed the incident as national phenomena and finally refused the copyright to journalists. The Court should have recognised the way the national phenomena or tragic happening in society was creatively reported by the journalist alerting the authorities. The justice could be ordering *Vijay Tendulkar* and *Jagmohan* to acknowledge the efforts and risk of journalist and secure his permission on token payment of a share in their proceeds. If not, it would amount to permitting a theatre and cinema person to commercially exploit and expression of idea which is not their own, which is against the spirit of copyright regulation.

In *Super Cassettes Industries* v. *Hamar Television Network Pvt. Ltd.*,[294] the plaintiff, Super Cassettes Industries Limited, which operates under the brand T-Series, sought an injunction against infringement of its copyright in cinematographic and musical works, by the defendants, Hamar TV, a television network which primarily caters to Bhojpuri audiences and runs a series of entertainment and news channels, including "Focus TV". The defendants were broadcasting the plaintiff's copyrighted works without a licence. Specific instances of infringement include the use of clips from the movies *Ghajini*, *Main Aisa Hi Hoon* and *Slumdog Millionaire,* as part of its programme. Defendant sought the defence relies upon the judgment in *ESPN Star Sports* v. *Global Broadcast News Ltd.*,[295] *inter alia*, to invoke the test of "fair dealing" to decide as to whether the alleged broadcast would amount to violation of the copyright. In support of its defence based on the principle of "fair dealing" it relied upon the provisions of Section 52(1)(a)(i) and (ii) to contend that the alleged broadcast were in the nature of "review", "preview", "news", "special programmes" and "interviews" and for reporting "current events" under Section 52(b) and Section 39(b) of the Copyright Act, 1957.[296] The court after examining all judgments summarised the broad principles of law which were enunciated in the judgments cited before the court on the aspect of "fair dealing". The judgment also laid down the principles for determining when a substantial part of the work is said to be reproduced by a defendant. In this case the plaintiff, who carries on business under T-Series brand of music cassettes sought an injunction against the defendant, a Bhojpuri channel restraining it from broadcasting copyrighted works of the plaintiff.

It has been pointed out for a long time that a broadcast in the reporting of current events is not an infringement of the broadcasters reproduction right under clause (b) of

---

293. *See, Indian Express Newspaper (Bombay) Pvt. Ltd.* v. *Dr. Jagmohan Mundhara*, AIR 1985 Bom 229.
294. 2011 (45) PTC 70 (Del).
295. 2008 (38) PTC 477 (Del).
296. Defendant also relies upon—*BDA Private Limited* v. *Paul P. John*, 2008 (37) PTC 569 (Del.); *Pro Sieben Media AG* v. *Carlton UK Television Ltd.* (1999) FSR 610; *Hubbard* v. *Vosper* (1972) 2 QB 84.

Section 39 of the Copyright Act 1957[297] and as per Section 52(1)(a)(iii) a fair dealing of a work while the reporting of current events and current affairs do not constitute an infringement of a copyright. Thus, citing *New Delhi Television Ltd.* v. *ICC Development (International) Ltd.*,[298] the Delhi High Court in *Star India Pvt. Ltd.* v. *Piyush Agarwal*[299] observed that with reference to Clause (b) of Section 39, it has to be kept in mind that while reporting current events use, consistent with fair dealing, of excerpts of a performance or of a broadcast do not constitute infringement of the broadcast reproduction right or the performers' right. Similarly, with reference to Section 52(1)(a)(iii), the reporting of current events and current affairs but as fair dealing do not constitute an infringement of the copyright held by the broadcaster or a performer. Thus, one has to first determine: whether the offending activity is by way of reporting or otherwise. For if the offending activity is not reporting, that would be the end of the matter.

Use in Educational Institutions and Public Libraries

Education is treated as a special case by copyright law and, therefore, there are several exceptions to infringement contained in the Copyright Act, 1957. The Act provides that publication in a collection, mainly composed of non-copyright matter *bona fide* intended for the use of educational institutions and so described in the title and in any advertisement issued by or on behalf of the publisher or short passages from published literary or dramatic works, not themselves published for the use of educational institutions, in which copyright subsists shall not constitute an infringement of copyright.[300] In the case of a joint authorship, reference to passages from works shall include reference to passage from works by any one or more of the authors of those passages or by any one or more of those authors in collaboration with any other person.[301] Similarly, the reproduction of a literary, dramatic, musical or artistic work: (i) by a teacher or a pupil in the course of instruction; or (ii) as part of the questions to be answered in an examination, or (iii) in answers, to such questions shall not constitute an infringement of copyright.[302]

Educational institutions are allowed for multiple copying of copyrighted works when done for classroom use under certain conditions. The exact scope of this permissible copying is not defined in the Copyright Act. However, the Act implicitly recognises the right of others

297. According to Section 39(b): "the use, consistent with fair dealing, of excerpts of a performance or of a broadcast in the reporting of current events or for *bona fide* review, teaching or research," no broadcast reproduction right or performer's right shall be deemed to be infringed. *See, Star India Pvt. Ltd.* v. *Piyush Agarwal*, 2014 (58) PTC 169 (Del).
298. 2013 (1) MIPR 118: 2013 (53) PTC 71.
299. 2014 (58) PTC (Del) 169.
300. Copyright Act 1957, Section 52(1)(g). *See*, T.C. James, "Copyright Law of India and the Academic Community" 9 *Journal of Intellectual Property Rights* (2004) pp. 207–225; Denis de Freitas, "The Main Features of Copyright Protection in the Various Legal Systems" 28 *Journal of the Indian Law Institute* (1986) pp. 441–449.
301. Copyright Act 1957, Explanation to Section 52(1)(g).
302. *Ibid.*, Section 52(1)(h). As per Section 52(1)(j) "the performance, in the course of the activities of an educational institution, of a literary, dramatic or musical work by the staff and student of the institution, or of a cinematograph film or a sound recording, if the audience is limited to such staff and students, the parents or guardians of the students and persons directly connected with the activities of the institution or the communication to such an audience of a cinematograph film or sound recording."

to make photocopies in libraries having photocopying machines and immunises libraries from any copyright liability if certain notices are posted. Photocopying is thus to some extent a recognised exception to copyright. Similarly, copying in the course of instruction or in preparation for instruction of a literary, dramatic, musical or artistic work is permitted as long as the copying is done by the person giving or receiving the instruction, for example, the teacher or the pupil, and the copying is not by a reprographic process.[303] For example, it is permissible for a teacher to ask a pupil to write out by hand a substantial extract from a work of literature. Another example is where a teacher reproduces an artistic work on a blackboard in a classroom for the purpose of instruction.

The making of not more than three copies of a book (including pamphlet, sheet of music, map, chart or plan) by or under the direction of the person in charge of a public library for the use of the library if such book is not available for sale in India shall not constitute an infringement of copyright.[304] In such cases, a librarian may rely on a signed declaration by a person requesting a copy of part or whole of a work in which copyright subsists, unless he is aware that the declaration is false in a material particular. A signed declaration will usually contain a statement to the effect that the copy is required for the purpose of research of private study and that the person requesting the copy has not previously been supplied with a copy from the same work. If a signed declaration is false in a material particular, the copy supplied is considered to be an infringing copy and the person requesting the copy is liable for infringement of copyright as if he made the copy himself.

Section 52(1)(j) of the Copyright Act, 1957 provides exception to copyright infringement if performance is made in the course of activities of an educational institution. This position was also elucidated by the Supreme Court of India in the matter of *Academy of General Education, Manipal* v. *B. Manini Mallya.*[305] The dispute related to the infringement of the respondent's copyright by the appellant institute in a new form of "Yakshagana" ballet. In this case the court examined the scope of "fair dealing" works by educational institutions and held that when a fair dealing is made, *inter alia*, of a literary or dramatic work for the purpose of private or personal use, including research and criticism or review, whether of that work or of any other work, such dealing does not constitute an infringement of copyright. The appellant being an educational institution, if the dance is performed within the meaning of provisions of clause (j) of sub-section (1) of Section 52 of the Act such performance does not amount to infringement of copyright. Further, if such performance is conducted before a non-paying audience by the appellant, which is an institution the same would not constitute would not constitute an infringement of copyright therein and an order of injunction cannot be made restraining such performance. However, the appellant argued that the performance was covered under the exemption provided in Section 52 for the performance of the work by an educational institution. After examining various aspects spelt out in Section 52 on fair dealing the Apex Court observed:

> Section 52 of the Act provides for certain acts which would not constitute an infringement of copyright. When a fair dealing is made, *inter alia*, of a literary or dramatic work for the purpose of private use including research and criticism or review, whether of that work or

---

303. *Longman* v. *Carrington* (1993)2 EIPR 67.
304. Copyright Act 1957, Section 52(1)(o).
305. AIR 2009 SC 1982: 2009 (39) PTC 393 (SC).

of any other work, the right in terms of the provisions of the said Act cannot be claimed. Thus, if some performance or dance is carried out within the purview of the said clause, the order of injunction shall not be applicable.[306]

Fair Dealing in Cinematograph Films

According to Section 52(1)(u) of the Copyright Act, 1957, the inclusion in a cinematograph film of (i) any artistic work permanently situate in a public place or any premises to which the public has access; or (ii) any other artistic work, if such inclusion is only by way of background or is otherwise incidental to the principal matters represented in the film shall not constitute an infringement of copyright. This provision provides exemption to film makers in case of copyright infringement.[307] Thus, in the *Gramophone Company of India Ltd.* v. *Super Cassette Industries Ltd.*[308] the Court observed:

> What does not constitute infringement of copyright in the course of making a cinematograph film is the inclusion in the cinematograph film of an artistic work which is permanently situated in a public place or in premises to which the public has access, or the inclusion in the cinematograph film of any other artistic work, if such inclusion is only by way of background, or is otherwise incidental to the principal matters represented in the film. Pertinently, literary, dramatic or musical works or the sound recordings made in respect thereof cannot be incorporated in a cinematograph film without prior licence or consent from the owners of such works, as there is no saving clause in Section 52 in respect of such works being utilized in the making of a cinematograph film.

Similar provisions are also found in statutes of various countries such as New Zealand, Australia, Ireland and Pakistan apart from UK and India. Thus, in *Amsinck* v. *Columbia Pictures Industries Inc.*,[309] the defendants released a film containing about 1 minute 36 seconds of a mobile containing the Plaintiff's copyrighted artwork consisting of pastel-coloured teddy bears, called the "Baby Bears Artwork". The American Court held that such use does not amount to copying as: (i) it is not meant to supplant demand for the copyrighted work, (ii) does not diminish interest in the work, (iii) it is not mechanical, and (iv) it is fleeting and impermanent, (v) the plaintiff had not suffered any demonstrable harm from the defendant's use of the work; and (vi) the film does not pose a threat for future licensing of work or sales to other motion pictures. Again, in *Mura* v. *Columbia Broadcasting System Inc.*,[310] concerned copyrights covering three hand puppets, which were allegedly displayed by the defendants on its show. The court held that the defendant's use did not amount to infringement and observed that (i) any use of the plaintiff's puppets was only to portray music in an incidental manner or tell a story within the programme; and (ii) the electronic image produced is not permanent.

The Delhi High Court has also examined a critical issue relating to use of dress in a cinematograph film in *Suneet Varma Design Pvt. Ltd.* v. *Jas Kirat Singh Narula*.[311] In this

306. *See also, Periyar Self Respect Propaganda Institution* v. *Periyar Dravidar Kazhagam*, 2009 (41) PTC 448 (Mad): 2010 (2) CTC 365.
307. *See, Suneet Varma Design Pvt. Ltd.* v. *Jas Kirat Singh Narula*, 2007 (34) PTC 81 (Del): MIPR 2007 (1) 175.
308. 2010 (44) PTC 541 (Del): ILR (2010) Supp. (5) Delhi 656.
309. 33 USPQ 2d 1131.
310. (1965) 245 F. Supp. 587.
311. 2007 (34) PTC 81.

case the dress in question was an original and distinctive creation of the plaintiffs. Hence, they alleged that without obtaining any permission or consent of the plaintiffs, the said dress is used by the defendant in his film "Bunty Aur Bubli" which is an infringement of copyright. The plaintiffs pointed out that the defendant not only has used the infringing dress as part of the cinematographic film but also has reproduced the artistic work relating thereto in the form of inlay cards used for audio/videos cassettes, CDs, DVDs posters, promotional material of the film, etc. Thus, the court examined the issue whether provisions of Section 52(1)(u)(ii) of the Copyright Act, 1957 are applicable in this case and whether the wearing of the dress in question in the film is by way of background or merely incidental or it played prominent role to depict the character of the film? The court observed that the words "incidental to the principal matters" under Section 52(1)(u)(ii) could be interpreted to mean incidental to the character if the artistic work in question is in respect of dress. The artistic works of other nature like cartoons, puppets, photographs and objects at public place, may be used as incidental to the principal story line of film but the dress of an artist cannot be incidental to the film or subject matter thereof. For example, if a cinematographic film is based on historical or mythological events, the dress of ancient time may in some circumstances be considered to be incidental to the principal matters or characters of the film. In the epic of Tipu Sultan, Ramayana or Mahabharta or a film showing tribal characters, the dress which is incidental to the character may in some cases fall within the purview of Section 52(1)(u)(ii). However, the infringing dress used by defendant as part of the cinematographic film "Bunti Aur Babli" can, by no stretch of imagination, be described as the artistic work incidental to the character and thereby to the principal matters represented in the film.

Performance or Communication in the Course of a Religious Ceremony

Section 52(1)(za) [312] of the Copyright Act, 1957 makes an exception for performance in the course of religious ceremony under certain conditions. According to this clause, the performance of a literary, dramatic or musical work or the communication to the public of such work or of a sound recording in the course of any (i) *bona fide* religious ceremony, or (ii) official ceremony provided such official ceremony has been held by (a) the Central Government, or (b) the State Government, or (iii) local authority does not constitute infringement. It has been clarified in the explanation that religious ceremony would include a marriage procession and other social festivities associated with marriage. But, in *Phonographic Performance Limited* v. *State of Punjab through Secretary,*[313] the Punjab and Haryana High Court observed: "A sound reproduction by a DJ performing at such an event is surely a function that is connected to marriage. It is not as if a DJ's performance amounts to conducting the marriage. Marriage is definitely different from the functions connected to the marriage and the tariff regime applies to performances at such functions even if it has a religious overtone." Also, the activity of cable TV operators of receiving signals on dish antenna and therefore transmitting it by cables to views either at a coast or otherwise, amounts to copyright infringement.

312. Inserted by the Copyright (Amendment) Act, 1994, Section 17 [w.e.f. 10-5-1995].
313. (2011) 164 PLR 519.

Special Provisions for Access to the Persons with Disabilities and their Fair Dealing Rights

Under Copyright (Amendment) Act, 2012, a two-pronged approach has been adopted to facilitate access to the disabled. A fair use provision has been added in Section 52 to provide exemption from copyright for preparation of work in special formats such as Braille. A compulsory licence has been provided for creation of work in such formats by business entities to whom the exemption under Section 52 may not apply. A new Section 31B[314] has been introduced to provide compulsory licence in works for the benefit of the disabled. Any person working for the benefit of persons with disability on a profit basis or for business may apply to the Copyright Board (Appellate Board)[315] for a compulsory licence to publish any work in which copyright subsists for the benefit of such persons. The section further clarifies that the licence is available only in a case to which clause (zb) of sub-section (1) of Section 52 does not apply and the Copyright Board shall dispose of such application within a period of two months from the date of receipt of the application. Every compulsory licence issued under this section shall specify the means and format of publication, the period during which the compulsory licence may be exercised and the number of copies that may be issued including the rate or royalty.

By the Copyright (Amendment) Act, 2012, a new clause (zb)[316] has been added to Section 52(1) of the Copyright Act, 1957 providing for fair use of the work for the benefit of the disabled. The clause provides for the adaptation, reproduction, issue of copies or communication to the public of any work in any accessible format, to facilitate persons with disability to access works including sharing with any person with disability, for private or personal use, educational purpose or research. These rights are available to any person or organisation working for the benefit of the persons with disabilities. The proviso to the clause mandates that the copies of the works in such accessible format are made available to the persons with disabilities on a non-profit basis and only the cost of production could be recovered from them. Such organisation shall ensure that the copies of works in such accessible format are used only by persons with disabilities and should take reasonable steps to prevent their entry into ordinary channels of business.

Fair Dealing in Digital Works

By the Copyright (Amendment) Act, 2012, fair dealing provisions have been extended to the digital environment.[317] Any transient and incidental storage of any work through the process of "caching" has been provided exceptions as per the international practice. Any deliberate storing of such works and unauthorised reproduction and distribution of such works is an infringement under Section 51 of the Act attracting civil and criminal liability. Exceptions under

---

314. *See,* Copyright (Amendment) Act, 2012, Section 18 [w.e.f. 10-5-2012].
315. Substituted by the Finance Act 2017 (7 of 2017), Section 160(a) for "Copyright Board," [w.e.f. 26 May, 2017].
316. *See,* Copyright (Amendment) Act, 2012, Section 17 [w.e.f. 10-5-2012].
317. *See,* Binu Poornamodan Cholayil, "Digital Rights Management and Fair Use in Copyright Law" 33 (1–2) *Cochin University Law Review* (2009) p. 166; Nandan Kamat, *Law Relating to Computers Internet and E-Commerce* (Universal Law Publishing Co., New Delhi, 2012).

this section have been extended to education and research purposes as works are available in digital formats and on the Internet. The scope of these provisions ensures that introduction of new technology will also be covered under this new section. An explanation has been inserted to Clause (1)(a) of Section 52 to clarify that storing of any work in any electronic medium for the specified purposes, including the incidental storage of a computer program which in itself is not an infringing copy, shall not be an infringement. The explanation reads thus:

> EXPLANATION—The storing of any work in any electronic medium for the purposes mentioned in this clause, including the incidental storage of any computer program which is not itself an infringing copy for the said purposes, shall not constitute infringement of copyright.[318]

A new Clause (b) in Section 52 seeks to provide that transient and incidental storage of a work or performance purely in the technical process of electronic transmission or communication to the public shall not constitute an infringement of copyright. Similarly, Clause (c) provides that transient and incidental storage of a work or performance for the purposes of providing electronic links, access or integration, where such links, access or integration has not been expressly prohibited by the right holder, shall not constitute infringement. To facilitate digitisation of libraries, a new Clause (n) has been introduced to enable the storage of a digital copy of a work if the library possesses a non-digital version of it. The unauthorised use of copyright work over the Internet leads to suspension of the service provider's activity. The new Clause (c) of Section 52 while providing for fair use exemption for transient or incidental storage of works, also provides for the Internet service provider's liability when read with the addition of rights of storage and definition of infringement. A proviso has been added to this clause to provide a safe harbour as per international norms to Internet service providers, as they are merely carriers of information provided by others. This is generally referred to as "notice and take down procedure". If the person responsible for the storage of the copy has received a written complaint from the owner of copyright in the work, that the transient or incidental storage is an infringement, such person responsible for the storage shall refrain from facilitating such access for a period of twenty-one days or till he receives an order from the competent court refraining from facilitating access. In case no such order is received before the expiry of such period of twenty-one days, he may continue to provide the facility of such access.

In *Suneet Verma Design Pvt. Ltd.* v. *Jas Kirat Singh Narula,*[319] the Delhi High Court examined the scope and application of the exception under section 52(1)(u)[320] of the Copyright Act. In this case the plaintiff, a renowned designer of international repute, designed a dress for women consisting of blue poncho and heavily embroidered trousers. The blue poncho and trousers consist of specific fabric cuts and original artistic embroidery. This design was presented in many fashion shows. The plaintiff noticed that this dress was used by the heroin of the film "Bunty Aur Bubli" and her picture wearing this dress was used in the advertisements

318. *See*, Copyright (Amendment) Act, 2012, Section 32 [w.e.f. 10-5-2012]. *See also, Super Cassettes Industries Ltd.* v. *Shreya Broadcasting Pvt. Ltd.*, 2019 III AD (Delhi) 552: 258 (2019) DLT 116
319. 2007 (34) PTC 81 (Del).
320. Section 52(1)(u) read: "the inclusion in a cinematograph film of—(i) any artistic work permanently situate in a public place or any premises to which the public has access; or (ii) any other artistic work, if such inclusion is only by way of background or is otherwise incidental to the principal matters represented in the film".

of the film, the cover page of the CD and cassette of the songs, etc. The plaintiff filed the present suit against the dress designer and the producer of the film alleging infringement of her copyright in the said design. The present petition was filed by the producer of the film requesting the court to remove his name from the list of defendants on the ground that he had not violated the copyright of the plaintiff. It was contended by him that he engaged one of the defendants to design/identify suitable dress for the film and he purchased the alleged dress from a shop in Mumbai. It was also contended that the use of the dress in the film was not a violation of the copyright of the plaintiff since this was permissible under Section 52(1)(u)(ii) of the Copyright Act. While rejecting the petition and declaring that the defendant was a necessary party to the suit, the court examined the scope of the exception provided under this section. Rejecting the argument of the defendant that the use of the dress in the film by the heroin was incidental to the film and not a violation of the copyright the court observed:[321]

> ... Many times, for a particular role to be played by an actor in a film, the costumes are designed in such a way as to bring out the character that particular actor is to play. The styling of the movie, therefore, is becoming as important as dialogue, screenplay or music. The audience look at an actor in the move and then notice what he/she is wearing. To promote particular dress used in a film, actors have started walking on the ramp-way during fashion shows. Bollywood has become integral to Indian fashion. In fact, in the award ceremonies, there are specific awards for best costumes in a film. Therefore, it cannot be presumed, *per se,* that for all kinds of clothes worn by the actors in film provisions of Section 52(1)(u)(ii) of the Copyright Act would be applicable. Maybe, this argument would be relevant for most of the dresses worn in a film, however, whether a particular dress/ costume in a film was only by way of background or incidental to the principal matter represented in the film will have to be viewed after the evidence is led.

Whether a Slogan is Entitled for Fair Dealing Defence

It has been reported that a in a large number of cases the issue was whether "Slogan" is original literary/artistic work and if so whether it is entitled for "fair dealing" defence under Section 52 of the Copyright Act, 1957. In *Godfrey Phillips India Ltd.* v. *Dharampal Satyapal Ltd.*,[322] the defendants started using a slogan "Swad Badi Cheez Hai", which is imitation of the plaintiff's slogan and campaign. The plaintiff alleges that the slogan "Shauq Badi Cheez Hai", is original literary work of the plaintiff which was created through an advertisement agency, thus, plaintiff is entitled to copyright protection and no third party has a right to use the same. Plaintiff also enjoys the statutory trademark rights as well as the common law rights in the slogan. In this case, the defendants have only replaced the word "Shauq" with "Swad" while retaining the slogan. The Court examined the issue whether using the "Slogan" with this replacement is the infringement of copyright? The court held that the slogan "Shauq Badi Cheez Hai", being combination of common words, would not fall within the scope of "artistic/literary work" under the Copyright Act, 1957. Slogan "Shauq Badi Cheez Hai" does not appear to be an outcome of great skill, in as much as, it uses the short stereo type combination of words. In fact, both the slogans, that is, "Shauq Badi Cheez Hai" and "Swad

321. *See, Suneet Verma Design Pvt. Ltd.* v. *Jas Kirat Singh Narula*, 2007 (34) PTC 81.
322. 2012 (51) PTC 251: 2012 (191) DLT 109. *See also, Alkem Laboratories Limited* v. *Elnova Pharma*, 2015 (62) PTC 465.

Badi Cheez Hai" are commonly spoken in Hindi language in day-to-day life. Thus the court held that slogans are not copyrightable.

Section 2(c) and (o) of the Copyright Act, 1957 define "artistic work" and "literary work", respectively. A perusal of these definitions creates a serious doubt about slogans being covered under the said definitions. Thus, in *Khemraj Shrikrishnadass* v. *Garg and Co.*,[323] the Court observed: "it is difficult to say that there is any original literary work in the formation of one or two words into a title and that the words or phrase chosen may be original in their application to the subject matter of the work to which they are applied." In *Pepsi Company Inc.* v. *Hindustan Coca Cola*,[324] the single Judge of the Delhi High Court held that advertisement slogans are, *prima facie*, not applicable under the Copyright Act and they may be protected under the law of passing off. An appeal was filed before the Division Bench against the said order, which has been disposed of in *Pepsi Company, Inc.* v. *Hindustan Coca Cola Ltd.*,[325] wherein, the view taken by the single Judge that the advertisement slogans are, *prima facie,* not applicable under the Act has not been reversed. Thus, advertisement slogans are not protectable under the Copyright Act therefore the question of application of the doctrine of "fair dealing" does not arise in slogans.

Fair Dealing Defence of Common Source

It is a debatable issue whether "common source" can be used as a fair dealing defence of copyright infringement as Section 52 of the Copyright Act, 1957 is silent on the point? In *Shyam Lal Paharia* v. *Gaya Prasad Gupta*,[326] the Court held that a compilation derived from a "common source" falls within the ambit of literary work. Again, under Section 13 of the Copyright Act, 1957, copyright shall subsist in literary, dramatic, musical, artistic work, cinematograph film and sound recording. Therefore, defence of "common source" can be claimed by the defendant in case of infringement of copyrighted work subject to certain conditions. Explaining the reason for recognising this defence in *Krisarts* v. *Briarfine*,[327] the English court observed that where two authors use a common source for creating a literary work or artistic work, one is bound to see some similarities. But this does not mean that one is an infringement of the other.

Thus, in *Pee Pee Publisher and Distributors (P) Ltd.* v. *Neena Khanna*,[328] it was held that in a copyright infringement dispute, the defendant can contend that the plaintiff is himself not the owner of the copyright and the said work is taken from a "common source". The said factor is a relevant consideration for the grant or non-grant of the injunction in the copyright dispute.[329] In *Rediff Com India Ltd.* v. *E-Eighteen Com Ltd.*,[330] the Delhi High Court further observed that the defence of "common source" is frequently made where the new publication

323. AIR 1975 Del 130.
324. 2001 94 DLT 30.
325. 2003 27 PTC 305 Del (DB).
326. AIR 1971 All 192.
327. [1977] FSR 557.
328. 2010 LawSuit (Del) 4161.
329. *See also*, *Prem Singh* v. *Ceeam Auto Industries,* 1990 AIR (Del) 233: 1990 (42) DLT 548; *Gentry Traders* v. *Roshan Lal Duggar*, AIR 1978 Delhi 250; *Corn Products Refining Co.* v. *Shangrila Food Products Ltd.*, AIR 1960 SC 142.
330. 2013 (55) PTC 294: 2013 (202) DLT 657.

is alleged to constitute an infringement of an earlier one. As an example, the Court held that in law books there is very little amount of originality but the same is protected by law and no man is entitled to steal or appropriate for himself the result of another's brain, skill or labour even in such works. The court further observed:

> The alleged virtual analogue representation of a Dial is a mechanically reproduced version of a statistical pie chart containing generic features, having been derived from common material source existing in the public domain, which has been, and is being used, for centuries in different industrial/mechanical/graphical appliances. The plaintiff, by claiming copyright on the same, is trying to usurp the proprietary right in an idea which has been a common source of inspiration to people from different streams. This cannot be permitted in public interest.

Thus, in *R.G. Anand* v. *Delux Films*,[331] the Apex Court held that similarity of the alleged infringing work does not itself establish copyright infringement, if the similarity results from the fact that both works deal with the same subject or have the same "common source". However, in *Shyam Lal Paharia* v. *Gaya Prasad Gupta*,[332] the mistakes appearing in the plaintiff's book were also appearing in the defendants book and commenting on that aspect of the case, it was held that it was true that the mere fact that the defendant had the plaintiff's book with him will not by itself lead to an irresistible inference that he had copied the calculations from the plaintiff's work. But from the fact that the mistakes committed by the plaintiff in certain calculations in his book were found in defendants' book in similar calculations, it must be held that the defendants had copied the calculations from the plaintiff's book and must be deemed to have infringed the copyright of the plaintiff with regard to such calculations. In *Feist Publications Inc*. v. *Rural Telephone Service Co. Inc*.,[333] the United States Supreme Court held that a subsequent compiler was not entitled to take one word of information previously published, but rather had to independently work out the matter for himself, so as to arrive at the same result from the same common sources of information.

Further, in *V. Govindan* v. *E.M. Gopalakrishna Kone*,[334] the Madras High Court clarified that where there is a "common source", the person relying on it must prove that he actually went to the common source from where he borrowed, employing his own skill, labour and brains and that he did not merely copy. Again, in *Eastern Book Company* v. *D.B. Modak*,[335] the Apex Court observed that the common source from where the defendant borrowed the material, embodying his own skill, labour and brain and he did not copy it, he must prove. In court judgments, the principle is inapplicable, as much as, there is no copyright in them, unless, so made by the court itself. In *S.K. Dutt* v. *Law Book Company*,[336] the Allahabad High Court held that an author of a law commentary cannot claim that once he quoted a passage in his book from either a decided case or a standard work then no one else has any right again to quote that passage. Otherwise the defence of "common source" can never be available to anyone. Therefore, it cannot be contended that by quoting a passage from a decision or from another work, he was in effect selecting the passage and since the copyright law protects selection, he was protected and nobody else can thereafter make the same selection.

331. 1978 (4) SCC 118: AIR 1978 SC 1613.
332. AIR 1971 All 192.
333. 18 USPQ 2d. 1275.
334. 1955 AIR (Mad.) 391.
335. AIR 2008 SC 809: (2008) 1 SCC 1.
336. AIR 1954 All 570.

Permitted Reproduction in Certain Kinds of Works

Section 52 of the Copyright Act, 1957 recognises certain kinds of reproductions of work that can be reproduced without the authorisation of copyright holder. These kinds of reproductions of work are called "permitted reproduction". Section 52(1)(e)[337] provides that the reproduction or publication of any work prepared by the Secretariat of a Legislature or, where the Legislature consists of two Houses, by the Secretariat of either House of the Legislature, exclusively for the use of the members of that Legislature and reproduction of the work are permitted. Further, under Section 52(1)(f)[338] the reproduction of any work in a certified copy made or supplied is in accordance with any law for the time being in force. In such a case reproductions of work without the authorisation of copyright are not infringement. In *Ferani Hotels Pvt. Ltd.* v. *The State Information Commissioner*,[339] the Supreme Court of India held that insofar as the intellectual property is concerned, the preparation of the plan and its designs may give rise to the copyright in favour of a particular person, but the disclosure of that work would not amount to an infringement and, in fact, Section 52(1)(f) of the Copyright Act 1957 specifically provides that there would be no such infringement if there is reproduction of any work in a certified copy made or supplied in accordance with any law for the time being in force. Similarly, under Section 52(1)(i)[340] the reproduction of any work—(i) by a teacher or a pupil in the course of instruction; or (ii) as part of the questions to be answered in an examination; or (iii) in answers to such questions are not infringement.

According to Section 52(1)(m), the reproduction in a newspaper, magazine or other periodical of an article on current economic, political, social or religious topics, unless the author of such article has expressly reserved to himself the right of such reproduction. In *Periyar Self Respect Propaganda Institution* v. *Periyar Dravidar Kazhagam*,[341] the Madras High Court examined the scope and applicability in the context of republication of the articles of *Periyar* published in "Kudiyarasu". Erode Venkatanaickar Ramasamy, popularly known as *Periyar*, published a number of articles related to economic, political, social issues in the newspaper "Kudiyarasu". The society of the plaintiff was started by *Periyar* in 1952 and he assigned all his "movable property" to the society. The society re-published some of his works earlier. The plaintiff asserted that since the society was started by *Periyar* and he assigned all his movable property to it, all his writings also are property of the society. The defendant who was a member of the society left it, and started a new society to promote the ideology of self-respect proclaimed by *Periyar*. The announcement of the publication of the compilation of "Kudiyarasu" of 26 years by the defendant resulted in the present litigation. According to the defendant, since *Periyar* died intestate in 1973 and there was no clear assignment of the copyright in his work, the plaintiff could not object to the publication of his works. It was also contended that since the works of *Periyar* were based on social, political and religious themes published in newspaper, there was no copyright in the same and hence it could be republished as per Clause (m) of sub-section (1) of Section 52. Regarding the ownership of copyright of

337. Inserted by the Copyright (Amendment) Act, 2012, Section 32 [w.e.f. 10-5-2012].
338. Inserted by the Copyright (Amendment) Act, 2012, Section 32 [w.e.f. 10-5-2012].
339. 2018 (5) CHN (SC) 238: 2018 (13) SCALE 672.
340. Inserted by the Copyright (Amendment) Act, 2012, Section 32 [w.e.f. 10-5-2012].
341. 2010 (2) CTC 365: 2009 (41) PTC 448 (Mad).

the works, the court, after examining Sections 18 and 19 of the Copyright Act dealing with assignment, concluded that there were no documents to show proper assignment of copyright as mandated by the Act. As per Section 17, author of the literary work is the first owner of copyright and it is automatic as soon as it is created. Hence, the law is that *Periyar* being the owner of the copyright in all his literary works published in *Kudiyarasu* which cannot be published without permission. To justify the publication by the defendant, the court relied on clause (m) of sub-section (1) of Section 52 and the public interest in copyright law projected by the Supreme Court[342] and opined:[343]

> In the present case, it has been made clear that the author of Kudiyarasu, i.e., late Periyar, was the owner and the articles published in the newspapers mostly related to the then existed economical, political and religious topics. Therefore, unless the author has expressly reserved his right of reproduction, no copyright will vest with anyone as reproduction of such articles cannot constitute an infringement of copyright as per section 52(1)(m) set out above.

According to Section 52(1)(p) of the Copyright Act, 1952 the reproduction, for the purpose of research or private study or with a view to publication, of an unpublished literary, dramatic or musical work kept in a library, museum or other institution to which the public has access shall not constitute an infringement of copyright. Further, Section 52(1)(q) of the Act provides that the reproduction or publication of—(i) any matter which has been published in any Official Gazette except an Act of a Legislature; (ii) any Act of a Legislature subject to the condition that such Act is reproduced or published together with any commentary thereon or any other original matter; (iii) the report of any committee, commission, council, board or other like body appointed by the Government if such report has been laid on the Table of the Legislature, unless the reproduction or publication of such report is prohibited by the Government; (iv) any judgement or order of a court, tribunal or other judicial authority, unless the reproduction or publication of such judgment or order is prohibited by the court, the tribunal or other judicial authority, as the case may be, shall not constitute an infringement of copyright.[344] According to Section 52(1)(zc), the importation of copies of any literary or artistic work, such as labels, company logos or promotional or promotional or explanatory material, that is purely incidental to other goods or products being imported lawfully shall not constitute an infringement of copyright. Section 52(2) of the Act further provides that the provisions of sub-section (1) of Section 52 shall apply to the doing of any act in relation to the translation of a literary, dramatic or musical work or the adaptation of a literary, dramatic, musical or artistic work as they apply in relation to the work itself.[345]

---

342. Relied on *Entertainment Network* v. *Super Cassettes,* 2008 (37) PTC 253 and *Academy of General Education Manipal* v. *B. Malini Mallya* (2009) 4 SCC 256.
343. *Periyar Self Respect Propaganda Institution* v. *Periyar Dravidar Kazhagam*, 2009 (41) PTC 448.
344. *See, Eastern Book Company* v. *D.B. Modak*, 2002 (25) PTC 641 (Del): 101 (2002) DLT 205.
345. *See, Pandurangan* v. *Govinda Iyer*, 1971 Cri LJ 1399.

10

Enforcement of Copyright

ABSTRACT

Enforcement of copyright in India became more controversial especially since the time of adoption of TRIPS Agreement in 1994. Part III of the TRIPS Agreement provides for "Enforcement of Intellectual Property Rights." Comparing provisions of the TRIPS Agreement, this chapter discusses administrative remedies such as border measures as well as the role of the Copyright Society, Office and Board in enforcing copyright in India. So far as the judicial remedies are concerned, both civil and criminal remedies are available for infringement of copyright. Thus, the judiciary has developed a strict framework of theories for providing remedies in case of infringement of copyright. Injunction, damagses, accounts of profits are some traditional remedies that are available for this purpose. The TRIPS Agreement introduced a number of new doctrines like Anton Piller Order, John Doe Order for providing judicial remedies. These remedies are also available in India.

BACKGROUND

Law relating to copyright provides rights as well as remedies for enforcement in case of infringement of substantive copyright. The Supreme Court in *Eastern Book Company* v. *D.B. Modak*,[1] observed that Copyright Act, 1957 gives to the authors certain exclusive rights in relation to the certain work referred in the Act. The object of the Act is to protect the author of the copyright work from an unlawful reproduction or exploitation of his work by others. The remedies for infringement of copyright deal with a variety of procedural factors. Law of procedure plays a crucial and determining role in expediting the adjudication of disputes. Thus, the law of procedure is an adjunct or an accessory to substantive right. The two branches of law (procedural and substantive) are complementary to each other and interdependent and

1. (2008) 1 SCC 115: [2007] 1 SCR 1018. *See also*, *UTV Software Communication Ltd.* v. *1337X*, 2019 (78) PTC 375 (Del); *Roderick John Andrew Mackenzie* v. *Himalayan Heli Services Pvt. Ltd.*, 2019(77) PTC379(Del); Vior (International) Ltd. v. Maxycon Health Care Private Ltd., 2018 (74) PTC 87 (Del); *Hotel Swagath* v. *Hotel Swagath East Court*, 2018 (73) PTC 51: 2018 (2) ALD 267; *Rediff.Com India Ltd.* v. *E-Eighteen.Com Ltd.*, MIPR 2013 (2) 333: 2013 (55) PTC 294 (Del).

the interplay between them often conceals that which is substantive law and that which is procedural law. The right to secure protection in case of violation of substantive right is a statutory right. Thus, the right to secure protection in case of infringement of copyright is a statutory right. It is a well known principle of law that "where there is a right, there is a remedy" derived from the maxim "*ubi jus ibi remedium.*"[2]

Explaining the aforementioned doctrine the Apex Court in *Bhagwati Developers* v. *The Peerless*,[3] observed:

> if a man has a right, he must have the means to vindicate and maintain it, and also a remedy, if he is injured in the exercise and enjoyment of the said right, and that it is indeed, a vain thing to imagine a right without a remedy, for the want of a right and the want of a remedy, are reciprocal.

In *Blueberry Books* v. *Google India Pvt. Ltd.*,[4] the Delhi High Court observed that under Section 14 of the Copyright Act, 1957, the owner of the copyright has a right to protect his interests and initiate proceedings against any infringement irrespective of where the infringing activities take place. Under the Copyright Act, 1957, the owner of copyright has two kinds of remedies available for enforcement of the copyright: (i) administrative remedies and (ii) judicial remedies. Administrative remedies consisting of remedies followed by the Registrar of Copyright, the Appellate Board and the Custom Authorities under the Customs Act, 1962. Judicial remedies provide civil remedies under Chapter XII (Sections 54–62) and criminal remedies under Chapter XIII (Sections 63–70) of the Copyright Act, 1957. The copyright owner can decide which remedy he wants to use. It is relevant to mention here that the TRIPS Agreement (Agreement on Trade-Related Aspects of Intellectual Property Rights)[5] has influenced to modify the copyright remedies in India. The TRIPS Agreement is one of the most important commercial treaties in the modern history which provides remedies for

---

2. *See, Band Box Pvt. Ltd.* v. *Estate Officer,* 2019 (1) RCR (Rent) 82: 2018 (172) DRJ 519; State of Karnataka v. State of Tamil Nadu, (2017) 3 SCC 362: 2016 (12) SCALE 679; *Re Special Reference No. 1 of 2012,* 2012 (9) SCALE 310: (2012) 10 SCC 1; *Dayaram* v. *Sudhir Batham,* 2011 (11) SCALE 448: (2012) 1 SCC 333; *Pazhassi Raja Charitable Trust* v. *Union of India,* AIR 2010 SC 310: (2010) 13 SCC 285; *Sardar Associates* v. *Punjab and Sind Bank,* AIR 2010 SC 218: (2009) 8 SCC 257; *Rajasthan State Road Transport Corporation* v. *Bal Mukund Bairwa* (2009) 4 SCC 299: [2009] 2 SCR 161; *Atma Linga Reddy* v. *Union of India,* 2008 (9) SCALE 745: (2008) 7 SCC 788; *Arunima Baruah* v. *Union of India,* [2007] 5 SCR 904: (2007) 6 SCC 120; *Swamy Atmananda* v. *Sri Ramakrishna Tapovanam,* AIR 2005 SC 2392: [2005] 10 SCC 51.
3. AIR 2013 SC 1690: (2013) 5 SCC 455. *See also, Santosh Popat Chavan v. Sulochana Rajiv,* AIR 2016 Bom 29: 2015 (5) ALLMR 604; *Dhannalal* v. *Kalawatibai,* AIR 2002 SC 2572: (2002) 6 SCC 16; *Smt. Ganga Bai* v. *Vijay Kumar,* AIR 1974 SC 1126: (1974) 2 SCC 393.
4. 2016 (67) PTC 1 (Del): 230 (2016) DLT 615. *See also, Huntsman International* v. *Abiss Textile Solutions,* MIPR 2018 (2) 39; *See, Consim Info Pvt. Ltd.* v. *Google India Pvt. Ltd.*, 2011 (45) PTC 575; *Super Cassettes Industries Ltd.* v. *Myspace Inc.*, 2011 (47) PTC 49 (Del); *Dhodha House* v. *S.K. Maingi,* AIR 2006 SC 730: (2006) 9 SCC 41; *Exphar SA* v. *Eupharma Laboratories Ltd.*, AIR 2004 SC 1682: (2004) 3 SCC 688.
5. *See*, Carlos M. Correa, *Trade Related Aspects of Intellectual Property Rights* (OUP, 2007).

enforcement of intellectual property rights including copyright.[6] Therefore, before discussing aforesaid two kinds of remedies (administrative and judicial) it is essential to discuss the TRIPS Agreement mandate on enforcement of intellectual property rights as India is a party to the Agreement.

TRIPS AGREEMENT MANDATE ON ENFORCEMENT

When the General Agreement on Tariffs and Trade (GATT) was negotiated in 1986, one of the principal concerns of industrialised countries in the matter of intellectual property was to stop piracy and counterfeiting of intellectual property goods, which were alleged to be taking place at a large scale in developing and newly industrialized countries. The agenda set for negotiations of intellectual property rights (IPRs) gave enough vent to this concern and aimed at not only to set new rules on IPRs but also to ensure that they are enforced. The lack of enforcement powers in the WIPO (World Intellectual Property Organisation) conventions, however, was considered to be the main reason behind the United State efforts in GATT-related solution. On enforcement, it pinpointed five areas of insufficient activity in developing countries: inadequate police support and insufficient possibilities of border seizure; obstacles to access to courts and authorities; stringent rules of evidence; lack of preliminary protection and insufficient deterrent criminal law provisions.

Consequently, when the negotiations went underway, emphasis was two-pronged: (i) to lay down the norms of substantive protection and (ii) to prescribe rules on the enforcement of those rights. The final version of the Agreement on Trade-Related Intellectual Property Rights (TRIPS Agreement) thus carried both of these aspects along. Whereas Parts I and II contain norms of substantive protection, Part III (and to some extent Part IV) incorporates provisions on enforcement. The aim of the provisions on enforcement is to ensure the undisturbed exercise of the IPRs, which find their place in the substantive provisions. All TRIPS members (i.e., WTO members) are required to give effect to these provisions under their national laws. The TRIPS Agreement has, thus, harmonised the law on the protection and enforcement of IPRs. As in the case of substantive standards, the United State's standards were made on the basis of enforcement measures.[7]

---

6. TRIPS Agreement came into force with effect from 1st January 1995. For various issues on TRIPS Agreement, *see*, J.K. Das, "TRIPS Agreement and Intellectual Property Rights: An Indian Perspective" 6 *International Trade Law & Regulation*, Sweet and Maxwell, London, (2010) pp. 165–173; J.K. Das, *Intellectual Property Rights*, Kamal Law House, Kolkata (2008); S.K. Verma , "Enforcement of Intellectual Property Rights: TRIPS Procedure and India", 46 *Journal of Indian Law Institute* (2004) pp. 183–206; C. Niranjan Rao, "Patents for Biotechnology Inventions in TRIPS", 37 *Economic and Political Weekly* (2002), pp. 2126–2129; Sudip Chaudhury, "TRIPS Agreement and Amendment of Patents Act in India", 37 *Economic and Political Weekly* (2002) pp. 3354–3360; Nilima Chandiramani, "Legal Factors in TRIPS" 37 *Economic and Political Weekly* (2002) pp. 200–203; M.D. Nair, "TRIPS and Public Health: The Doha Declaration" 7(3) *Journal of Intellectual Property Rights* (2002) pp. 241–244; T. Ramappa, *Intellectual Property Rights under WTO: Tasks Before India,* Wheeler Publishing, New Delhi (2000); V.K. Ahuja, "GATT, TRIPS and India", 50 *India Quarterly* (1994) pp. 1–14; Suman Sahai, "Indian Patent A ct and TRIPS", 28 *Economic and Political Weekly* (1993) pp. 1495–1497; S.R. Sen, "Innovation , TRIPS and Future Trends", 28 *Economic and Political Weekly* (1993) pp. 1918–1919.
7. *See*, J.K. Das, New Dimensions of Intellectual Property Rights in India" 3(2) *Pragyaan: Journal of Law* (2013) pp. 11–33 at p. 26.

Part III of the TRIPS Agreement on "Enforcement of Intellectual Property Rights" contains a total of 21 Articles (Article 41-61), divided into five sections: General Obligations (Article 41); Civil and Administrative Procedures and Remedies (Articles 42–49); Provisional Measures (Article 50); Special Requirements Related to Border Measures (Article 51–60); and Criminal Procedures (Article 61). Together these provisions are aimed at first, on the measures that the holders of IPRs may require from the judicial, administrative and customs authorities to take against infringements and threatened infringements of their rights, and second, the procedures by which such measures may be obtained. These measures may be civil as well as criminal in nature to terminate and restrain infringements of IPRs. Different provisions of the TRIPS Agreement, detail these procedures and measures.[8]

General Obligations on Members

Article 41 of the TRIPS Agreement sets out the general obligations of WTO members with regard to the domestic enforcement of IPRs. Paragraph 1 of the Article 41 reads: "Members shall ensure that enforcement procedures as specified in this Part are available under their national laws so as to permit effective action against any act of infringement of intellectual property rights covered by this Agreement, including expeditious remedies to prevent infringements and remedies which constitute a deterrent to further infringements. These procedures shall be applied in such a manner as to avoid the creation of barriers to legitimate trade and to provide for safeguards against their abuse."[9]

This provision lays down that WTO members have to ensure that enforcement procedures as specified in this part are available under their law so as to permit effective action against any of infringement of intellectual property rights covered by this agreement. It is up to the members to decide about the exact measures and to ensure their effectiveness in practice.

8. The mandate for negotiations on Trade-Related Intellectual Property Rights (TRIPS) including Trade in Counterfeiting Goods in the Punta del Este Declaration in 1986 was: "[T]o reduce the distortions and impediments to international trade, and taking into account the need to promote effective and adequate protection of intellectual property rights, and to ensure that measures and procedures to enforce intellectual property rights, do not themselves become barriers to legitimate trade, the negotiations shall aim to clarify GATT provisions and elaborate, as appropriate new rules and disciplines. Negotiations shall aim to develop a multilateral framework of principles, rules and disciplines dealing with international trade in counterfeit goods…." For the text of the *Punta de Este Declaration, see,* 25 *International Legal Material* 1623 at 1626 (1986). On the definition of piracy, *see*, J.H. Reichman, "Intellectual Property in International Trade: Opportunities and Risks of a GATT Connection" 22 *Vanderbilt Journal of International Law* 747 (4: 1989). *See also*, D. Peter Harvey, "Efforts Under GATT, WIPO and Other Multinational Organizations Against Trade Mark Counterfeiting" 12 *EIPR* 446 (1993); L.T.C. Harms, *The Enforcement of Intellectual Property Rights: A Case Book* (World Intellectual Property Organization); T. Ramappa, *Intellectual Property Rights under WTO* (Wheeler, New Delhi, 2000); Jayshree Watal, *Intellectual Rights in the WTO and Developing Countries* (Oxford University Press, Watal, 2001); M.D. Nair, "TRIPS, WTO and IPR: Recent Happenings in WTO", 16 *Journal of Intellectual Property Rights* (2011) pp. 267–269.
9. The two copyright treaties concluded by WIPO on 20 December 1996 provide the similar provisions: WIPO Copyright Treaty Article 14, and WIPO Performances and Phonograms Treaty Article 23. For more on these treaties, *see*, Jorg Reinbothe, Maria Martin-Prat & Slike von Lewinski, "The New WIPO Treaties: A First Resume" 4 *EIPR* 171 (1997); Christopher Arup, The World Trade Organization Knowledge Agreements (Cambridge University Press, 2008).

Moreover, in giving effect to these procedures, the members are not obliged "to put in place a judicial system for the enforcement of intellectual property rights distinct from that for the enforcement of laws in general", neither should it affect their capacity to enforce their laws in general.[10] They need not to specifically allocate the resources for the enforcement of IPRs. This provision, thus, accepts the different legal systems for enforcement among the members, which also finds its mention in the preamble to the TRIPs. Hence, the effectiveness of the enforcement measures depends to a large extent on national legislature and practice that should not be subjected to pressure from outside.

The enforcement procedure as prescribed under the TRIPS Agreement should be "fair and equitable", "not unnecessarily complicated or costly, or entail unreasonable time limits or unwarranted delays".[11] Further provisions have tried to give content to these terms. Accordingly, decisions on the merits of the case should preferably be in writing and reasoned[12] and be made available to the parties without delay. The courts must base their decision on evidence only in respect of which parties were offered the opportunity to be heard. There should be an opportunity for review by a judicial authority of final administrative decisions, and subject to the jurisdictional provisions in national laws.[13]

Civil and Administrative Procedures

As stated above, Paragraph 2 of Article 41 of the TRIPS Agreement requires that enforcement procedures be fair and equitable. This principle has been detailed in Section 2 (Articles 42–49) of Part III of the TRIPS Agreement. The fair and equitable procedures, in accordance with Article 42, must provide the holders an access to civil judicial procedures to enforce their IPRs. Defendants should have the right to written notice, which is timely and contains sufficient details, including the basis of the claims. The parties must allowed to be represented by independent legal counsel and overly burdensome requirements concerning mandatory personal appearances must not be imposed. All parties to such procedures should be entitled to substantiate their claims and present all relevant evidence; the opposite party must be required to produce evidence, which are in its possession.[14] There is also the obligation "to identify and protect" confidential information in accordance with the relevant constitutional provisions.[15] Where a party to the proceeding "without any goods reason refuses access to, or otherwise does not provide necessary information within a reasonable period, or significantly impedes a procedure relating to an enforcement action," the judicial authorities may be empowered to make a preliminary or a final determination in the matter on the basis of information available, subject to allowing the parties to be heard on the allegations or evidence.[16] Thus, the members have the discretion to give effect to this provision. Articles 44, 45 and 46 deal with injunctions, damages and other remedies, that should be made available to an aggrieved party are as follows:

10. TRIPS Agreement, Paragraph 5 of the Article 41.
11. *Ibid.*, Paragraph 2.
12. *Ibid.*, Paragraph 3.
13. *Ibid.*, Paragraph 4.
14. *Ibid.*, Article 43.
15. *Ibid.*, Article 42.
16. *Ibid.*, Article 43(2).

1. Injunction as a first measure, the judicial authorities shall issue an injunction order to restrain a party from an infringing activity. But where the party has indulged in the infringing activity, without the knowledge of infringement, the members are not obliged to provide for injunction. However, the members are free to restrict the rights of the right-holder in cases in which the government or a third party, authorised by the government, uses the protected subject matter of the right without the consent of the right-holder, to payment of an appropriate remuneration in accordance with Article 31(h).[17] In all other cases, declaratory judgments and adequate compensation shall be available.[18]
2. Damages where the infringer "knew or had reasonable grounds to know that he was engaged in infringing activity" and thus proves the *mala fide,* the judicial authorities shall award adequate damages to compensate the right-holder for the injury suffered by him, and in appropriate cases, may order for the refund of cost of the proceedings, including attorney's fees. It also means that if the complainant loses the case, then the defendant will also be entitled to attorney's fees, particularly where the right-holder had abused the legal procedure and restrained the defendant from enjoying his lawful right.[19] Where the infringer did not know or had no reasonable grounds to know that he was engaged in infringing activity, the order for recovery of profits and/or payment of pre-established damages may be passed.[20]
3. Other remedies the judicial authorities shall further be empowered to order that infringing goods must be disposed off outside the channels of commerce, or be destroyed in accordance with the law. The materials and implements, which were "predominantly" used in the creation of the infringing goods, must be ordered to be removed from the channels of commerce without any kind of compensation. In giving such order, however, the interests of the third parties should be taken into account.[21]

The above stated civil remedies are novel because for the first time an international convention on IPRs provides rules on compensation and other sanction. However, to provide remedies of injunction and pre-determined damages to the aggrieved party is not mandatory on the member states. Members may (at their discretion) authorise the judicial authorities to seek information from the infringer about the identity of third parties involved in the production and distribution of the infringing goods or services and their channels of distribution.[22] If civil remedies are provided through administrative procedures (rather than judicial), they should be in conformity with the Articles 42 to 48.[23]

---

17. Where the government issues a compulsory license, Article 31(h) states that "right holder shall be paid adequate remuneration in the circumstances of each case, taking into account the economic value of the authorization."
18. TRIPS Agreement, Article 44. *See also, Telefonaktiebolaget LM Ericsson* v. *Competition Commission of India*, 2016 (66 PTC 58 (Del): (2016) 4 Comp LJ 122 (Del); *Natco Pharma Limited* v. *Bayer Corporation*, 2012 (50) PTC 244.
19. *Ibid.*, Article 48(1).
20. *Ibid.*, Article 45.
21. *Ibid.*, Article 46.
22. *Ibid.*, Article 47 (Right of Information).
23. *Ibid.*, Article 49 (Administrative Procedures).

Provisional Measures

Article 50 of TRIPS agreement lays down the provisional measures in order to provide an immediate relief to the right holder against an infringing act. This Article outlines the minimum requirements to be adhered by the TRIPS member in the proceedings for provisional protection of IPRs. Accordingly, Article 50 provides the following measures:

1. The judicial authorities should be empowered to order measures for the preservation of relevant evidence regarding the alleged infringement.[24] In order to satisfy themselves "with a sufficient degree of certainty" about the right-holder's claim about his right being infringed or infringement is imminent, the judicial authorities shall have the authority to "require the applicant to provide any reasonably available evidence" in support of his claim and "any other information necessary for the identification of the goods concerned". On the other hand, in order to check the abuse of provisional measures and to protect the interests of the defendant, the applicant may be asked to provide a neither security nor equivalent assurance.[25]
2. The judicial authorities must be empowered, where appropriate, to adopt provisional measures without the defendant being heard (*inaudita altera parte*), in particular, where delay is likely to cause irreparable damage to the right-holder or where there is a demonstrable risk of evidence being destroyed.[26] This is similar to *Anton Piller* order followed in the United Kingdom and other commonwealth countries, whose purpose is to preserve the evidence by preventing the destruction or concealment of evidence by an alleged wrongdoer.[27]
3. The affected party must be informed without delay after such measures have been executed. After being informed, the defendant may request a review of the measures, including the right to be head, in order to decide whether these measures should be modified, revoked or confirmed. Review must take place within a reasonable period after the notification of the measures.[28]
4. The provisional measures shall be revoked on the request of the defendant or otherwise ceases to have effect if the proceedings concerning the merits of the case are not initiated within a reasonable period of time as determined by the judicial authorities, and in the absence of such a determination, within twenty working days or thirty-one calendar days (whichever is longer).[29] In such a case, and in case the provisional measures are revoked, or where the applicant's action remains unsuccessful, the defendant may be entitled to appropriate compensation from the complainant.[30]

---

24. *Ibid.*, Paragraph 1 of Article 50.
25. *Ibid.*, Paragraph 3 and 5 of Article 50.
26. *Ibid.*, Paragraph 2 of Article 50.
27. *Anton Piller* order, named after the case of *Anton Piller KG* v. *Manufacturing Processes Ltd.* [1976] 1 Ch. 55, is the order of the competent court permitting the complainant party to enter the premises of an alleged wrongdoer and remove material which is evidentially important.
28. TRIPS Agreement, Paragraph 4 of Article 50.
29. *Ibid.*, Paragraph 6.
30. *Ibid.*, Paragraph 7. *See*, Micheal Blackeney (Ed.), *Border Control of Intellectual Property Rights* (Sweet and Maxwell, London, 2004).

Provisional measures ordered through administrative procedures must also conform to the above-said provisional measures.[31]

Border Measures

Articles 51 to 60 of the TRIPS Agreement deal with the boarder measures against infringing goods which have been given an elaborate treatment because of the developed countries' special emphasis to check product piracy in trademark and copyright work. Specific obligations have been imposed on members to institute and enforce boarder measures to prevent infringement of IPRs. These provisions on border measures hold special key in the case of importation of counterfeit trademark or pirated copyright goods, but the members have the discretion to follow these measures for other IPRs as well. Similarly, these measures are made applicable to importation, and not to exportation, though a member can do so for exportation also. The border measures, which the members are required to take, are specified as under:

1. If the right-holder has valid grounds for suspecting the importation of infringing goods, he must request the competent authorities to order for the suspension of the release of those goods.[32]
2. The right-holder, while making such a request, must present adequate evidence which should *prima facie* establish his claim, and to supply a sufficiently detailed description of his goods to make them readily recognisable by the customs authorities. Upon the request of the applicant, the competent authorities shall inform the applicant, within a reasonable period of time that whether they have accepted the application, and the length of time for which the requested measure will remain in force.[33]
3. The competent authorities shall have the authority to order the applicant to provide a security or equivalent assurance, in order to protect the defendant and prevent any abuse of these measures, but such security or assurance should not unreasonably deter applicant to have recourse to border seizure procedures.[34]
4. Where the release of the goods has been suspended, both importer and the applicant must be informed promptly.[35] The right-holder and the importer should be given sufficient opportunity to inspect the detained goods, subject to the protection of confidential information. Where a positive decision on merits has been made in favour of the right-holder, the competent authorities may be empowered to inform the right-holder the names and addresses of the consignor, the importer and the consignee and the quantity of the goods in question.[36]
5. The period of suspension of the goods in question shall not exceed ten working days, which is extendable by a further period of ten working days "in appropriate cases", after service of the notice of suspension to the applicant, unless the customs authorities are informed that a case on merits has been initiated by someone

31. *Ibid.*, Paragraph 8.
32. *Ibid.*, Article 51.
33. *Ibid.*, Article 52.
34. *Ibid.*, Article 53(1).
35. *Ibid.*, Article 54.
36. *Ibid.*, Article 57.

other than the defendant, or the competent authority has provisionally prolonged the suspension, failing which the goods will be released, provided that all other requirements relating to importation have been fulfilled. In the proceedings on merits, the defendant will have the right to be heard and seek a review, within a reasonable time, of the decision on the border measures—to modify, confirm or revoke these measures. But if the suspension is carried out as a part of provisional judicial measure, that will be governed by Article 50(6) on provisional measures.[37]

6. If the suspension is found to be wrongful in the decision on merits, relevant authorities may grant the importer, the consignee and the owner of the goods, the appropriate compensation for the injury suffered by them through the wrongful suspension.[38]
7. The members may also empower the competent authorities to act *ex officio,* i.e., on their own initiative and suspend the release of goods where there is *prima facie* evidence of infringement of IPRs. In such cases, the authorities may, at any time, seek relevant information from the right-holder; the right-holder and the importer will be promptly notified about the suspension. If the importer lodges an appeal against the suspension, it shall be subject to the rules laid down in Article 55.[39] The public authorities and the officials shall be exempted from all liability for the *ex officio* action where the action was taken or intended in good faith.
8. Infringing goods, which are not released, may be destroyed or disposed of in accordance with the principles of Article 46. The defendant, however, may seek review of such measures by a judicial authority. But counterfeit trademark goods shall not be allowed to be re-exported in an unaltered state or subjected to a different customs procedure, except in exceptional circumstances.[40]
9. Border measures[41] in the matter of other IPRs goods have been treated differently. Where goods involving industrial designs, patents, layout-designs or undisclosed information have been suspended on the basis of an application, and the period provided for suspension in Article 55 has expired (ten days, extendable by further ten days) without grant of any provisional relief for prolonging the suspension and on the fulfillment of all conditions regarding importation, the importer, owner or consignee may demand the release of such goods on depositing the sufficient security, even where the applicant initiates the proceedings. If the right-holder does not initiate the proceedings to pursue his right within a reasonable time, the security will also be released. The right-holder has to deposit the security while making application for border measures.[42]

---

37. *Ibid.*, Article 55.
38. *Ibid.*, Article 56.
39. *Ibid.*, Article 58.
40. *Ibid.*, Article 59.
41. The Articles 51 to 60 of the TRIPS dealing with border measures are restricted to Copyright and Trade Marks infringement only. *See*, *LG Electronics India Pvt Ltd* v. *Bharat Bhogilal Patel*, 2012 (51) PTC 513 (Del); *Telefonaktiebolaget LM Ericsson* v. *Union of India*, 2012 (52) PTC 494 (Del): 194 (2012) DLT 248; *LG Electronics India Pvt. Ltd.* v. *Bharat Bhogilal Patel*, 2012 (49) PTC 170 (Del): 2012 (127) DRJ 87.
42. *Ibid.*, Article 53.

It is however, very clear that border measures for other IPRs, than counterfeited trademark and pirated copyrights goods, are discretionary with the members.

Criminal Procedures

Article 61 of the TRIPS Agreement deals with criminal procedures and emphasises on trademark counterfeiting and copyright piracy, if done willfully and on a commercial scale. In the matter of patents and other IPRs, members have the discretion, and may provide criminal procedures and penalties if their infringement is also committed willfully and on commercial scale. The sanctions provided in criminal procedures should be "effective" deterrent against infringement, which shall include imprisonment and/or monetary fines. Other sanctions may include seizure, forfeiture and destruction of the infringing goods and of any materials and implements predominantly used in the commission of the offence.

The TRIPS Agreement, for the first time, creates a multilateral framework for the enforcement of all IPRs, which was so far left to the nation-states to carry out at their discretion under their national laws. It incorporates a minimum set of basic procedural regulations to achieve "effectiveness" in the enforcement of these rights.[43] This has created considerable differences in practice regarding numerous aspects of implantation at the national level. The TRIPS Agreement, by "taking into account differences in national legal systems" has sought uniformity on the rules of enforcement. But, whereas the objective is to achieve sufficiently effective protection through these rules, it is also the aim of the TRIPS that they should not become the barriers to free flow of goods and services (preamble). Thus, it leaves a considerable freedom to the members to give effect to these provisions under their national laws. The provisions on enforcement, however, uses certain very vague terms as "effective", "reasonable", "undue", "fair and equitable", "unwarranted" and "not … necessarily complicated or costly," which, though leave substantial freedom to the members in giving effect to these provisions, create lot of confusion and leave unsettled the implementation as required by the system created by the TRIPS Agreement. However, ever since the negotiations of the TRIPS Agreement started, the efforts were initiated to take "effective" measures for enforcement of IPRs. Thus, the TRIPS Agreement balances the interests of the right holders with those of wrongfully accused infringers so as not to cause obstacles to legitimate trade. The TRIPS Agreement also takes into account the limited resources available with the governments of developing countries to enforce IPRs law, emphasising that IPRs are private rights and action for their enforcement has to be taken by the rights holders themselves.

---

43. Apart from these specific provisions on enforcement, Part IV (Article 62) of the TRIPS Agreement provides for the administrative and judicial procedures for the acquisition and the maintenance of IPRs and related *inter-parte* procedures at the discretion of the members. These procedures, such as opposition, revocation and cancellation, if provided under the national law, shall be governed by the procedural regulations of Article 41(2) and (3). Final administrative decisions on these matters shall be subject to review by "a judicial or quasi judicial authority", but this does not apply to a case of unsuccessful opposition or administrative revocation procedures, but the grounds for such procedures may constitute the subject of invalidation proceedings (Article 62).

ADMINISTRATIVE REMEDIES IN INDIA

The Barne Convention, the TRIPS Agreement and the Copyright Act, 1957 provide a special administrative remedy for arresting imports at their point of entry into India. The copyright owner may notify the Commissioners of Customs and Excise of his right and request that they treat certain imports as prohibited. The imports in question, in the case of copyright, must be infringing copies of literary, dramatic or musical copyright work (in print), or of copyright, sound recordings or films. The Commissioners will then exclude such goods as they can identify. But the copyright owner must indemnify them against any liability and expense. It seems that the system is little used.[44] In order to give effect to the TRIPS Agreement provisions on border measures, no new legislation has been enacted nor has any substantial change been made to the existing laws. However, the different provisions of the Copyright Act and Custom Act have bearing on the border control of copyright.

Border Measures and Customs Act, 1962

An Overview

One of the major concerns of copyright owners has been the trans-border movement of infringing material. Thus, the most important law on the issue is the Customs Act, 1962, which is a complete code in itself.[45] The Customs Officers have been clothed with the powers of police officers under the Act. It does not, therefore, deal only with a matter of imposition of penalty or an order of confiscation of the properties under the Act but also with the offences having serious consequences.[46] In *Noor Aga* v. *State of Punjab*,[47] the Supreme Court observed:

> "Section 53 of the Custom Act 1962 empowers the customs officers with the powers of the Station House Officers. An officer invested with the power of a police officer by reason of a special statute in terms of Sub-section (2) of Section 53 would, thus, be deemed to be police officers and for the said purposes of Section 25 of the Act shall be applicable."

The Customs Act also creates a liability for violation of its provisions on intellectual property rights and provides the complete machinery for obtaining redress against any import or export

44. *See,* W.R. Cornish, *Intellectual Property,* (Universal Law Publishing Co. Pvt. Ltd., Delhi, 2001) at p. 53.
45. The Customs Act, 1962 (Act 52 of 1962). The Act came into force on 13th December 1962. The Act is the successor to the Sea Customs Act, 1878, the Land Customs Act, 1925 and the Inland Bonded Warehouses Act, 1896. It also place Section 16 of the Aircrafts Act, 1934. The new Act was extended to Sikkim with effect from 1-10-1979 by notification no. 185/79—Cus, dated 1-9-1979. This is a consolidating Act, which contains entire law relating to Customs duty and mattes related thereto. The Act has been extended to designated areas in Continental Shelf and Exclusive Economic Zones of India by notifications of Ministry of External Affairs. Notification Nos. S.O. 429(E), dated 18-7-1986 and 643(E), dated 19-9-1996, as notified by customs notification no. 11/87—Cus, dated 14-11-1987 and 64/87-Cus (NT), dated 1-12-1997. *See, Tamil Nadu Pollution Control Board* v. *Sterlite Industries (I) Ltd.*, AIR 2019 SC 1074: 2019 (3) SCALE 721. *Institute of Chartered Accountants of India* v. *Vimal Kumar Surana,* 2010 (12) SCALE 667: (2011) 1 SCC 534; *Atul Commodities Pvt. Ltd.* v. *Commissioner of Customs* (2009) 5 SCC 46: (2009) 3 SCR 589; *Kothari Filaments* v. *Commissioner of Customs,* 2009 (1) SCALE 117: (2009) 2 SCC 192.
46. *Noor Aga* v. *State of Punjab*, 2008 (56) BLJR 2254; *Union of India* v. *Solar Pesticide Pvt. Ltd.,* AIR 2000 SC 862: (2000) 2 SCC 705.
47. (2008)16SCC417: JT 2008 (7) SC 409.

in breach of the law. After the coming into force of the TRIPS Agreement, the Customs Act has not been amended but the Act, along with different intellectual property Acts, lays down the framework for border measures against intellectual property violations. Pirated works, infringing copyright or goods bearing false trademarks or false trade description are prohibited from being imported into India under the Customs Act and when imported are liable to detention or confiscation. There has not been much case law on border measures on IPRS and the Customs Act, 1962 acts as umbrella legislation in this regard. Regarding the importance of the TRIPS Agreement to provide border measures, in *LG Electronics India Pvt Ltd* v. *Bharat Bhogilal Patel*,[48] the Delhi High Court observed:

> The reading of TRIPS Agreement reveals that world over, the underlying intention and the purpose of the countries signatories to TRIPS Agreement to provide border measures for the enforcement of the intellectual properties and to provide the safeguard to the right holder in a limited sense by treating the custom officials either as an implementing authorities under the orders of the court or otherwise giving the powers of temporary suspension so as to enable the right holder to approach the civil court within the time prescribed.

The Government of India under Section 11 of the Customs Act to prohibit importation or exportation of goods either absolutely or subject to conditions as specified in the notification, the import or export of the goods of any specified description.[49] The section, among others, empowers the government to prohibit the import or export of goods for "the protection of patents, trademarks and copyrights" [clause (2)(n)], and for "the implementation of any treaty, agreement or convention with any Country" [clause (2)(r)]. Together, sub-clause (n) and (r) cover within their ambit all forms of intellectual property covered under the TRIPS Agreement. Under Section 11 (n), the government issues notifications from time to time prohibit the imports of goods for the protection of patents, trademarks and copyrights. In accordance with this provision, the Central Government has prohibited the imports of certain right-related goods into India.

The goods imported in contravention of the provisions of the Customs Act or any other law for the time being in force are liable to be confiscated [Section 111 (d)].[50] *Gramophone Company of India Ltd.* v. *Birendra Bahadur Pandey*[51] is the only case so far having direct bearing on IPRS. In this case, Section 53 of the Copyright Act was made to run with Section 11 of the Customs Act. The case was related to the importation of pirated audio cassettes from Singapore designed for Kathmandu. Nepal (a land-locked state), which landed at Calcutta port and were awaiting dispatch to Nepal when it was found by the customs authorities that a substantial number of cassettes were "pirated works". This fact came to light through the broken condition of the consignment, which was lying in the Calcutta Docks. On an application by the appellant to the registrar of copyrights under Section 53 of the Copyright

48. 2012 (51) PTC 513 (Del).
49. *See, Department of Customs* v. *Sharad Gandhi*, 2019 (3) SCALE 447: 2019 (2) Bom CR 517; *Commissioner of Customs* v. *Sayed Ali,* JT 2011 (2) SC 360: (2011) 3 SCC 537; *Gurcharan Singh* v. *Directorate of Revenue Intelligence*, JT 2008 (4) SC 383: 2008 (4) SCALE 403; *Commissioner of Custom, New Delhi* v. *Brooks International*, 2007 (8) SCALE 373: (2007) 10 SCC 396.
50. *Jayantilal K. Katakia* v. *P. Govindan Nair*, AIR 1981 SC 1196: (1981) 2 SCC 423.
51. AIR 1984 SC 667: (1984) 2 SCC 534.

Act and Section 11 of the Customs Act, cassettes were confiscated. The appellant company brought the case to restrain their onward transmission to Nepal. Defendants contended among others, that there was no infringement of Copyright Act, because there was no importation in the local market, as envisaged in the Act. The court gave liberal interpretation to Section 53 of the Copyright Act, which it read with Section 11 of the Customs Act. Section 2(23) of the Customs Act defines the word "import" which means "bringing into India from a place outside India".[52] The court observed, "the language of Section 53 does not justify reading the words 'Imported for commerce' for the words 'imported".[53]

In the case of trademarks, if the Chief Customs Officer, upon representation made to him in respect of any goods imported into India, has reasons to believe that the goods bear a false trademark, he may require the importer of goods or his agent to produce any documents in his possession relating to the goods and also to furnish information as to the name and address of the person by whom the goods were sent in India.[54] Once the registrar of copyrights takes a decision that the work is prohibited, the relevant provisions of the Customs Act are to apply, with the difference that confiscated copies under the Copyright Act shall not vest in the government, but shall be delivered to the owner of the copyright.[55] The registrar is not bound to make an order under Section 53 of the act as soon as the owner of the copyright presents an application to him. He has to consider the context of the mischief sought to be prevented. He must consider whether the copies would infringe the copyright if the copies were made in India and whether the applicant owns the copyright or is the duly authorised agent of the copyright owner. He must follow the principles of natural justice by providing proper hearing to affected parties. In these hearings, all the legitimate defenses are available to the parties. One fundamental difference between the nature of a notification under Section 11 of the Customs Act (by the Customs Officer) and an order made under Section 53 of the Copyright Act (by the registrar of copyright) is that the former is quasi-legislative in character, while the latter is quasi-judicial in nature. The quasi-judicial nature of the order made under Section 53 is emphasised further by the fact that an appeal is provided to the appellate board against the order of the registrar under Section 72 of the Copyright Act. The effect of an order under Section 53 of the Copyright Act is not as portentous as a notification under Section 11 of the Customs Act.

---

52. *See*, *Dhamra Port Company Ltd.* v. *Union of India*, 2018 (362) ELT 41 (Ori.); *State of Kerala* v. *Fr. William Fernandez*, [2018] 57 GSTR 6 (SC): 2017 (12) SCALE 463; *Maharashtra Heavy Vehicle* v. *Union of India*, II (2018) BC 33 (Bom.); *Commissioner of Customs* v. *Aban Loyd Chiles Offshore Ltd.*, 2017 (2) SCALE 183: (2017) 3 SCC 211; *Jindal Stainless Ltd.* v. *State of Haryana*, AIR 2016 SC 5617: (2017) 12 SCC 1.
53. The cases of relevance where it was laid down that the importation was complete as soon as the customs barrier was crossed are: *Warner Bros. Entertainment Inc.* v. *Santosh V.G.*, MIPR 2009 (2) 175; *M.S. Shawhney, Asstt. Collector of Customs* v. *Sylvania and Laxman Limited*, 1988 (19) ECR 192 (Bom): 1987 (30) ELT 126 (Bom); *Radha Kishan* v. *Union of India*, AIR 1965 SC 1072: (1965) 2 SCR 213; and *Bernado* v. *Collector of Customs*, AIR 1960 Ker 170. These cases were brought under the Customs Act and not under the Copyright Act.
54. Section 140(1) of the Trademarks Act, 1999.
55. Section 53 of the Copyright Act, 1957. *See also*, *Jindal Stainless Ltd.* v. *State of Haryana*, AIR 2016 SC 5617: (2017) 12 SCC 1; *Gramophone Company of India Ltd.* v. *Birendra Bahadur Pandey*, AIR 1984 SC 667: (1984) 2 SCC 534.

To stop the import of infringing copyright work, an application has to be made by the owner of any work or by his duly authorised agent to the registrar of copyright, along with the prescribed fee.[56] Section 140 of the Trademarks Act, 1999 provides that "(t) the proprietor or a licensee of a registered trademark may give notice in writing to the collector of customs to prohibit the importation of any goods if the imports of the said goods constitute infringement". On the basis of the application by the right-holder under these relevant laws, the competent authorities initiate further action.

If there are imports of infringing intellectual property works, a complaint from the right holder or his authorised agent/licencee to the registrar of copyrights in the case of infringed copyright work, and to the Chief Customs Officer in the case of trademark falsification, enables the goods to be confiscated under Section 111(d). Where the goods are seized, a notice in respect thereof is required to be given under Section 124 of the Customs Act within six months of the seizure of the goods.[57] The commissioner of customs on sufficient ground can further extend this period for a period of six months.[58] If no notice is served within the stipulated period, the seized goods shall be returned to the person from whose possession they were seized.[59] Under Section 124 of the Customs Act, it is provided further that no order confiscating any goods or imposing any penalty shall be made on any person unless the owner of the goods or such person; (i) is given a notice in wiring; and (ii) is given an opportunity to make a representation in writing. Section 153 lays down the manner to effect the notice.[60]

It is significant to note that neither the Customs Act nor the Copyright or Trademarks Acts have any specific provisions on the indemnification of the importer and of the owner of the goods confiscated by the customs authorities. There are cases under the Customs Act, however, where the release of seized goods was obtained after depositing securities with the government in terms of the mutual consent agreement, the goods were thus out of the purview of Section 110(2) as the consent agreement acted as a waiver of any notice.[61]

The Customs Act, 1962 does not have any specific provision on inspection and information. The Copyright Act, in Section 53, however, empowers the registrar to inspect the goods and for the purpose he can enter any ship, dock or premises.[62] The new Trademarks Act is more comprehensive and empowers the commissioner of customs to require the importer of the goods or his agent to produce any documents in his possession relating to the goods and also to furnish information as to the name and address of the person to whom the goods were

---

56. Customs Act 1962, Section 53(1).
57. *See, Vijender Singh* v. *Commissioner of Customs*, 2019 (365) ELT 717 (Del.); *Regional Deputy Director* v. *Zavaray S. Poonawala*, (2015) 7 SCC 347: 2015 (5) SCALE 184.
58. Section 110(2). Section 110 deals with seizure of goods, documents and things.
59. *See, R. Rajesh Naykar* v. *Commissioner of Customs*, 2019 (1) GLT 360; *R. Sundar* v. *Deputy Collector of Customs, Tuticorin*, 1996 (82) ELT 451 (Mad); *Assistant Collector of Customs* v. *Charan Das Malhotra*, AIR 1972 SC 689: (1971) 1 SCC 697.
60. *See, R.K. Impex* v. *Union of India*, 2018 (171) DRJ 622: 2018 (362) ELT 5 (Del.); *Atul Commodities Pvt. Ltd.* v. *Commissioner of Customs* (2009) 5 SCC 46: (2009) 3 SCR 589; *Andromeda Foundation India P. Ltd.* v. *D.G.H.S.*, 2008 (9) SCALE 405: (2008) 12 SCC 640; *Relax Safety Industries, Mumbai* v. *Commissioner of Customs,* 2007 (7) SCALE 4: (2007) 5 SCC 759.
61. *See, Principal Commissioner of Customs* v. *Santosh Handloom*, 2016 (337) ELT 44 (Del.); *Ravi Crop Science* v. *UOI*, (2014) 43 GST 92 (Delhi): 2014 (201) ECR 327 (Delhi); *Lokenath Tolaram* v. *B.N. Rangwani,* AIR 1974 SC 150: (1974) 3 SCC 575.
62. Customs Act 1962, Section 53(2).

sent in India.[63] The importer of his agent has to comply with this requirement within 14 days. Any information thus obtained from the importer may be communicated by the Chief Customs Officer to the registered proprietor or the registered user of the trademark, which is alleged to have been used as a false trademark.[64] Although Section 140 only refers to a registered trademark, the Customs Officer is not prohibited from communicating the information to the proprietor of registered trademark. The information furnished will enable the owner of the mark to take action against the offender. The Customs Act authorises a Customs Officer to seize any document of things which, in his opinion, will be useful for, or relevant to, any proceeding under the Act[65] [Section 110(3)].

Appeals against order of the Customs Officer (lower than a commissioner of customs) may go to the collector of customs within three months from the date of the communication of such order.[66] An appeal against the order of the collector can be made to the appellate tribunal.[67] There is no specific provision in the Customs Act for the *de minimis* exclusion, but the baggage provision and the rules framed thereunder allow imports of goods if they form part of the baggage of a person entering the country. The important provisions of the Act are 77 and 79. "Baggage" means such articles of necessity, or personal convenience, as are usually carried by passengers for their personal use. Section 2(3) of the Act merely provides an inclusive definition of "baggage" to the effect that "baggage includes unaccompanied baggage but does not include motor vehicles". Section 77 provides "The owner of any baggage shall, for the purpose of clearing of it, make a declaration of its contents to the proper officer" at the port of entry.[68] A person coming to India needs to fill in a baggage declaration form by way of a statement about the baggage.[69] *Bona fide* baggage is exempted from duty under Section 79.[70]

Border Measures and Section 53 of the Copyright Act

Position Prior to 2012 Amendment

Section 53 of the Copyright Act, 1957 provides the measure relating to importation of infringing copies has been substituted with a new section providing detailed border measures

63. Customs Act 1962, Section 140(1).
64. Customs Act 1962, Section 140(3).
65. *See, Customs* Act 1962, Section 140(3). *See, Inspector of Customs, Akhnoor J and K* v. *Yash Pal*, 2009 (3) SCALE 590: (2009) 4 SCC 769.
66. *See*, Customs Act 1962, Section 128. *See also, Commissioner of Customs & Central Excise* v. *M.P. Steel Corporation*, 2003 (88) ECC 11: 2003 (154) ELT 12 (SC); *Todi Industries Ltd.* v. *Union of India*, (1999) 9 SCC 230: 1999 (65) ECC 6.
67. *See*, Customs Act 1962, Section 129A. *See also, Northern Plastics Ltd.* v. *Hindustan Photo Films Mfg. Co. Ltd.*, 1997 (2) SCALE 263: (1997) 4 SCC 452.
68. *See, Malabar Diamond Gallery Pvt. Ltd.* v. *Additional Director General*, 2016 (341) ELT 65 (Mad.): (2016) 8 MLJ 460; Aliyar *Syed Thaha Mohamed Jalal* v. *Department of Revenue*, 2015 (325) ELT2 96 (Mad.); *Naresh Lokumal Serai* v. *Commissioner of Customs (Export)*, 2006 (203) ELT 580: 2006 (137) ECR 263.
69. *See, In Re: Vinay Kumar*, 2016 (343) ELT 861; *Pooja Batra* v. *Union of India*, AIR 2009 SC 2256: (2009) 5 SCC 296; *Gurcharan Singh* v. *Directorate of Revenue Intelligence*, JT 2008 (4) SC 383: 2008 (4) SCALE 403; *Rib Tapes (India) Pvt. Ltd.* v. *Union of India*, AIR 1986, SC 2014: (1986) 4 SCC 185.
70. *Anirudh Singh Katoch* v. *Union of India*, 2010 (5) SCALE 7: (2010) 12 SCC 368.

to strengthen enforcement of rights by making provision to control import of infringing copies by the Customs Department, disposal of infringing copies and presumption of authorship under civil remedies. Prior to the 2012 amendment to the Copyright Act, 1957,[71] Section 53 had to read with Section 11 of the Customs Act, 1962. The Section 53 was thus:

> 53. Importation of infringing copies—(1) The Registrar of Copyrights, on application by the owner of the copyright in any work or by his duly authorized agent and on payment of the prescribed fee, may, after making such inquiry as he deems fit, order that copies made out of India of the work, which if made in India, would infringe copyright shall not be imported.
>
> (2) Subject to any rules made under this Act the Registrar of Copyrights or any person authorised by him in this behalf may inter any ship, dock or premises where any such copies as arc refined to in subsection (1) may be found and may examine such copies.
>
> (3) All copies to which any order made under Sub-section (1) applies shall be deemed to be good of which the import has been prohibited or restriction under Section 11 of the Customs Act, 1962 and all the provisions of the Act shall have effect accordingly.
>
> Provided that all such copies confiscated under the provisions of the said Act shall not vest in the Government but shall be delivered to the owner of the copyright in the work."

There is a difference between notification under Section 11 of the Customs Act and an order made under Section 53 of the Copyright Act is that the former is quasi-legislative in character, while the latter is quasi-judicial in character. The quasi-judicial nature of the order made under Section 53 is further emphasised by the fact that appeal is provided to the Appellate Board against the order of the Registrar under Section 72 of the Copyright Act.[72] In *Warner Bros. Entertainment Inc.* v. *Mr. Santosh, V.G.*,[73] the Delhi High Court held that Section 53 empowers the Register of Copyrights to make an order that copies made out of India of any work which if made in India would infringe copyright, shall not be imported. This the Registrar may do on the application of the owner of the copyright in that work or by his duly authorised agent on payment of the prescribed fee and after making such enquiry, as he deems fit. The effect of such an order by the Registrar is to deem all copies to which the order applies to be goods of which the import has been prohibited or restricted under Section 11 of the Customs Act, 1962, and to attract all the provisions of the Customs Act on that basis, including the liability to be confiscated, with the slight modification that copies confiscated under the provisions of that Act shall not vest in the Government, but shall be delivered to the owner of the copyright.

The question is—What does the word "import" mean in Section 53 of the Copyright Act? The word "import" is not defined in the Copyright Act though it is defined in the Customs Act. But the same word may mean different things in different enactments and in different contexts. It may even mean different things at different places in the same statute. It all depends on the sense of the provisions where it occurs. Reference to dictionaries, it is hardly of any avail, particularly in the case of words of ordinary parlance with a variety

---

71. *See, Indusind Media* and *Communications Ltd.* v. *State of Gujarat*, (2018) 2 GLR 1151: 2017 (71) PTC 60 (Guj); *Warner Bros. Entertainment Inc.* v. *Santosh V.G.*, MIPR 2009 (2) 175; *Penguin Books Ltd.* v. *India Book Distributors,* AIR 1985, Delhi 29: 26 (1984) DLT 316.
72. *Gramophone Company of India Ltd.* v. *Birendra Bahadur Pandey,* AIR 1984 SC 667: (1984) 2 SCC 534.
73. MIPR 2009 (2) 175.

of well-known meanings. Such words take colour from the context.[74] In *Commissioner of Sales Tax* v. *Radhasons International*,[75] the Bombay High Court held that the word "import" means bringing into India from a place outside India. But "import" cannot be said to be even "technically complete" bereft of there being "clearance" by the customs authorities. Merely unloading of the imported goods at a port does not complete an act of import, without the customs authorities granting the necessary statutory clearances for bringing the goods beyond the customs area.[76] Explaining the term "import" in *CMS Info Systems Ltd.* v. *Union of India*,[77] it was held that imported goods mean any goods brought into India from a place outside India but does not include goods which have been cleared for home consumption. Hidayatullah, J. in *Burmah Shell* v. *Commercial Tax Officer*[78] has illustrated how the contextual meanings of the very words "import" and "export" may vary. He said:

> We may look at Section 53, rather than elsewhere to discover the meaning of the word 'import'. We find that the meaning is stated in that provision itself. If we ask what is not to be imported, we find answer is copies made out of India would infringe copyright. So it follows that 'import' in the provision means bringing into India from out of India. That, we see is precisely how import is defined under the Customs Act. Section 2(23) of the Customs Act, 1962 defines the word in this manner: "Import, with its grammatical variation and cognate expression means bringing into India from a place outside India." But we do not propose to have recourse to Customs Act to interpret expressions in the Copyright Act even if it is permissible to do so because Section 53 of the Copyright Act is made to run with Section 11 of the Customs Act.

Post 2012 Amendment Position

As stated above, Section 53 of the Copyright Act, 1957 was replaced by the Copyright (Amendment) Act, 2012.[79] The New Section 53[80] has brought four significant changes: (i) Section 53 is not applicable to goods in transit; (ii) the person giving notice has to produce an order from a court having jurisdiction as to the temporary or permanent disposal of such goods within fourteen days from the date of their detention; (iii) the owner of the work has to deposit some amount as security having regard to the likely expenses on demurrage, cost of storages and compensation to the importer, in case it is found that the works are not infringing copies; and (iv) the custom authorities are not required to collaborate with the Registrar of Copyright before taking any action. The New Section 53 reads as follows:

> 53. (1) The owner of any right conferred by this Act in respect of any work or any performance embodied in such work, or his duly authorised agent, may give notice in writing to the Commissioner of Customs, or to any other officer authorised in this behalf by the Central Board of Excise and Customs,—

---

74. *Gramophone Company of India Ltd.* v. *Birendra Bahadur Pandey*, AIR 1984 SC 667: (1984) 2 SCC 534.
75. [2019] 64 GSTR 404 (Bom). *See also*, *Laxmi Cranes and Trailers (P) Ltd.* v. *Union of India*, ILR 2017 (4) Kerala 383: 2017 (3) KLT 1077; *Commissioner of Customs, Mumbai* v. *Aban Loyd Chiles Offshore Ltd.*, (2017) 3 SCC 211: 2017 (6) SCJ 696.
76. *See*, *Dhamra Port Company Ltd.* v. *Union of India*, 2018 (362) ELT 41 (Ori.).
77. (2017) 61 GST 33 (Bombay): 2017 (349) ELT 236 (Bom.).
78. AIR 1961 SC 315: [1961] 1 SCR 902.
79. Act No. 27 of 2012. Came into force on 21-6-2012, *vide* S.O. 1393(E), dated 20th June, 2012, published in the Gazette of India, Extra., II, Section 3(ii), No. 1164, 20th June, 2012.
80. Inserted by the Copyright (Amendment) Act, 2012 [w.e.f. 21-6-2012], Section 34.

(a) that he is the owner of the said right, with proof thereof; and

(b) that he requests the Commissioner for a period specified in the notice, which shall not exceed one year, to treat infringing copies of the work as prohibited goods, and that infringing copies of the work are expected to arrive in India at a time and a place specified in the notice.

(2) The Commissioner, after scrutiny of the evidence furnished by the owner of the right and on being satisfied may, subject to the provisions of sub-section (3), treat infringing copies of the work as prohibited goods that have been imported into India, excluding goods in transit:

Provided that the owner of the work deposits such amount as the Commissioner may require as security having regard to the likely expenses on demurrage, cost of storage and compensation to the importer in case it is found that the works are not infringing copies.

(3) When any goods treated as prohibited under sub-section (2) have been detained, the Customs Officer detaining them shall inform the importer as well as the person who gave notice under sub-section (1) of the detention of such goods within forty-eight hours of their detention.

(4) The Customs Officer shall release the goods, and they shall no longer be treated as prohibited goods, if the person who gave notice under sub-section (1) does not produce any order from a court having jurisdiction as to the temporary or permanent disposal of such goods within fourteen days from the date of their detention.

Thus, the new Section 53 provides that the owner of copyright of any work or any performance embodied in such work, or his duly authorised agent, may give notice in writing to the Commissioner of Customs, or to any other officer authorised in this behalf by the Central Board of Excise and Customs requesting the Commissioner for a period specified in the notice, not exceeding one year, to treat infringing copies of the work as prohibited goods, and that infringing copies of the work are expected to arrive in India at a time and a place specified in the notice. After examination of evidence so furnished, the Commissioner may pass an order treating the infringing goods as prohibited goods. When any such goods are detained, the Customs Officer shall inform the importer as well as the person who gave notice of the detention of such goods within forty-eight hours of their detention. The Customs Officer shall release the goods, and they shall no longer be treated as prohibited goods, if the person who gave notice does not produce any order from a court having jurisdiction as to the temporary or permanent disposal of such goods within fourteen days from the date of their detention.

Constitution of Copyright Society, Office and Appellate Board

The Copyright society, office and Appellate Board[81] are playing an important role to protect, maintain and administer the rights of authors.[82] Sections 9 to 11 (Chapter II) of the Copyright

81. Substituted by the Finance Act 2017 (7 of 2017), Section 160(a) for "Copyright Board," [w.e.f. 26 May, 2017].
82. *See*, *Novex Communication Pvt. Ltd.* v. *Lemon Tree Hotels Ltd.*, 2019 II AD (Delhi) 644; *Indian Performing Right Society Ltd.* v. *Vodafone Idea Ltd.*, (2019) 2 CALLT 436 (HC); *Anand Bhushan* v. *Union of India*, 2018 (75) PTC 106 (Del): 2018 VI AD (Delhi) 153; *Saregama Ltd.* v. *New Digital Media*, 2018 (73) PTC 329 (Cal): (2018) 1 WBLR (Cal) 329; *Super Cassettes Industries Ltd.* v. *Music Broadcast Pvt. Ltd.*, AIR 2012 SC 2144: 2012 (50) PTC 225 (SC); *Indian Performing Right Society Ltd.* v. *Debashis Patnaik*, MIPR 2007 (1) 323: 2007 (34) PTC 201 (Del).

Act, 1957 provide for Copyright Office and Appellate Board.[83] By virtue of Section 19(a) of the Act, disputes with respect to assignment of copyright are to be referred to the Appellate Board.[84] Sections 33 to 36A (Chapter VII) of the Act provide for copyright societies. In *Event and Entertainment* v. *Union of India,*[85] the Delhi High Court while apprising statutory scheme (Section 33–36A) of the Act held that copyright societies are controlled by and are accountable to the owners of the copyrights. Central government has supervisory control over them. The legislature requires the copyright society to fix traffics subject to approval of the owners of rights. The statutory provisions are supplemented by rules.

Section 33 deals with the registration of copyright society. Registration of such copyright society is mandatory in character. Sub-section (2) of Section 33 provides for that any association of persons who fulfils such conditions as may be prescribed may apply for permission to do the business specified in Sub-section (1) to the Registrar of Copyrights who shall submit the application to the Central Government. Sub-section (3) of Section 33 empowers the Central Government to grant a licence having regard to the interest of the authors and other owners of rights under the Act, the interest and convenience of the public and in particular of the groups of persons who are most likely to seek licences in respect of the relevant rights and the ability and professional competence of the applicants, register such association. Section 34 provides for administration of rights of owner by copyright society. The proviso appended thereto prohibits any discrimination in regard to the terms of licence or the distribution of fees collected between rights in Indian and other works. The concept of copyright society appears to be that the interest of the copyright holder can be protected by the said society while granting licence so as to enable all players to have the benefit of a single window.

Ordinarily the authors of creative works are not business minded and they have seldom the financial resources or the business skill to exploit their work by themselves. For example, in the case of a literary, dramatic, musical or artistic work, one of the ways in which the owner of the right can get monetary benefit is by issuing copies, of the work to the public on a sufficiently large scale. The best way to do this is to licence a publisher to publish the work on a royalty basis. In the case of dramatic and musical works, the owner can derive monetary benefit by licencing its performance in public or communicating the work to the public for a fee. Further, it is extremely difficult for the owner of the work to prevent infringement of the work any where in India or abroad. To overcome this difficulty, owners of copyright works have formed societies to licence their works for performance or communication to the public or issue copies of the work. The copyright societies are formed to protect the interest of copyright owner. Certain administrative powers have been given up on copyright office. Similarly the appellate board discharges some judicial functions.

83. Substituted by the Finance Act 2017 (7 of 2017), Section 160(a) for "Copyright Board," [w.e.f. 26 May, 2017].
84. Substituted by the Finance Act 2017 (7 of 2017), Section 160(a) for "Copyright Board," [w.e.f. 26 May, 2017].
85. 2011(46) PTC 405 (Del). The Court relied upon the judgment in *Indian Performing Right Society* v. *Eastern Indian Motion Pictures Association* [(1977) 2 SCC 820] as well as the observations in *Entertainment Network (India) Limited* v. *Super Cassettes Industries Limited* [(2008) 13 SCC 30].

Constitution of Copyright Societies

The Object of Copyright Societies

The Chapter VII of the Copyright Act, 1957, entitled "Copyright Societies" was substituted by the Copyright (Amendment) Act, 1994. Consequently, the Sections 33–36A of the principal Act provides for establishment of copyright societies.[86] Prior to the Copyright (Amendment) Act, 1994, the Act dealt with only performing right societies,[87] which carried on the business of issuing or granting licences for the performance in India of any work in which copyright subsisted. But the Amendment Act, 1994 has introduced copyright societies and extended the operation of the legal provisions to the business of issuing or granting licences in respect of all rights relating to any class of work in which copyright subsists under the Act.

In *Event and Entertainment Management Association* v. *Union of India*,[88] it was held that copyright societies are controlled by and are accountable to the owners of the copyrights. Central Government has supervisory control over them. The central government can, in the interests of the owners of copyrights, suspend the registration of a copyright society pending inquiry for such period not exceeding one year. Under Section 33 of the Act, the central government can cancel the registration of a copyright society after inquiry "if it is satisfied that the copyright society is being managed in a manner detrimental to the interests of the owners of rights concerned". Further, the administration of rights of owners by a copyright society is provided in Section 34 of the Act. The control over the copyright society by the owner of rights is specified under Section 35 and there is an obligation of the copyright society to submit returns and reports under Section 36 of the Act. The legislature requires the copyright society to fix tariffs subject to approval of the owners of rights. The statutory provisions are supplemented by rules. It followed the decision of the division bench in Federation of *Hotels and Restaurants Association of India* v. *Union of India*,[89] where it was held that the legislative provisions are constitutionally valid and not suffering from the vice of the excessive delegation.

The owner of copyright in any work can derive monetary benefit only by exercising some or all of the rights conferred under Section 14. Either he has to exercise these rights himself or he will have to assign or licence his rights to third parties. Ordinarily, authors of creative works seldom have the financial resources or business skill to exploit their works themselves. Further it is extremely difficult for the author to prevent infringement of the work all around the world. So they are forced to assign or licence their right to capable third parties, who often exploit this weak position of the author. It was in order to overcome this difficulty that the concept of Copyright Societies arose, whereby the author assigns his rights to a society and the society in turn collects licence fee from persons interested in exploiting the work. The accrued licence fee is then distributed proportionately among the various authors who have

86. Chapter VII (Sections 33 to 36A, Copyright Societies) was substituted by the Copyright (Amendment) Act, 1994 (Act 38 of 1994), Section 11 [w.e.f. 10-5-1995].
87. The performing right society could collect fees, charges or royalties for the grant of licences for performances in public in India of the copyright musical works in its repertoire. *See, Eastern India Motion Pictures* v. *Performing Right Society Ltd.*, AIR 1978 Cal 477.
88. MIPR 2011 (2) 107: 2011 (46) PTC 405 (Del).
89. MIPR 2011 (2) 1: 2011 (46) PTC 169 (Del).

assigned their rights to the society. The society also watches cut against infringement activities and take appropriate action against them. Thus, the Copyright Societies are registered as under Section 33 of the Copyright Act, 1957 to monitor, protect and enforce the rights, interest and privileges of its members comprising of authors, composers and publishers of literary or musical works, etc.[90]

The right of the author of a copyright *vis-a-vis* the Society, thus, may be exercised in almost all walks of life from the "Radio Stations" to a small "Hairdressing Salon". In the context of the Statement of Objects and Reasons for amending the said Act where it is clearly stated that one such object is "to deal more effectively with the infringement of copyright and related rights". The Statement of Objects and Reasons of the 1994 amendment would show that the new provisions of Chapter VII providing for such Copyright Societies were incorporated with various objectives and one such objective was to improve the enforcement of Copyright with benefits both to the holders of the right and to the general public. The Statement of Objects and Reasons of the 1994 amendment is as follows:

> Clause 11—This Clause seeks to substitute new provisions for Chapter VII to make provision for copyright societies in respect of any kind of right (and not merely "performer's rights") and to make adequate general provision for the registration and management of such societies in the interests both of authors and of other copyright owners for whom it would be impracticable or uneconomical to license the use of their work individually to all users, or to collect fees from them, and also in the interests of the general public and particularly of users of rights who may not conveniently be able to obtain licenses from individual authors or copyright holders; and thus to improve the enforcement of copyright with benefits both to the holders of rights and to the general public.[91]

Thus, for all intents and purports, the Copyright Society steps into the shoes of the author. The Society grants licences on behalf of the author, it files litigation on his behalf, both for the purpose of enforcement as also protection of enforcement of his rights. Section 34 of the Copyright Act, 1957 creates a virtual agency for all intents and purports so as to enable the Society to act on behalf of the owner. The civil remedy for infringement of copyright as envisaged under Section 55 can also be enforced by the Society. In *Anand Bhushan* v. *Union of India*,[92] the Delhi High Court citing the Supreme Court judgement in *Entertainment Network (India) Ltd.* v. *Super Cassette Industries Ltd.*,[93] observed:

> Chapter VII deals with copyright society, the concept whereof was incorporated in the Act so as to enable an author to commercially exploit his intellectual property by a widespread dispersal in a regulated manner. It for all intent and purport steps into the shoes of the author. The society grants licence on behalf of the author, it files litigation on his behalf, both for the purpose of enforcement as also protection of the enforcement of his right. It not only pays royalty to the author but is entitled to distribute the amount collected by it amongst its members. Section 34 providing for administration of rights of owners by a copyright society for all intent and purport creates a virtual agency so as to enable the society to act on behalf of the owner.[94]

---

90. *See*, *Indian Performing Right Society Ltd.* v. *Gauhati Town Club*, 2013 III AD (Delhi) 333: 2013 (134) DRJ 732.
91. *See*, *Phonographic Performance Limited* v. *Lizard Lounge*, (2009) ILR 2 Delhi 726.
92. 2018 (75) PTC 106 (Del): 2018 VI AD (Delhi) 153.
93. 2008 (9) SCALE 69: 2008 (13) SCC 30.
94. *See also*, *Phonographic Performance Ltd.* v. *Lizard Lounge*, (2009) ILR 2 Delhi 726.

Registration of Copyright Society

The Section 33 of the Copyright Act 1957 deals with the registration of copyright society. Registration of such copyright society is mandatory in character. Sub-section (2) of Section 33 provides for that any association of persons who fulfils such conditions as may be prescribed may apply for permission to do the business specified in Sub-section (1) to the Registrar of Copyrights who shall submit the application to the Central Government. Sub-section (3) of Section 33 empowers the Central Government to grant a licence having regard to the interest of the authors and other owners of rights under the Act, the interest and convenience of the public and in particular of the groups of persons who are most likely to seek licences in respect of the relevant rights and the ability and professional competence of the applicants, register such association. Section 34 provides for administration of rights of owner by copyright society. The proviso appended thereto prohibits any discrimination in regard to the terms of licence or the distribution of fees collected between rights in Indian and other works. The concept of copyright society appears to be that the interest of the copyright holder can be protected by the said society while granting licence so as to enable all players to have the benefit of a single window.[95]

Thus, the Section 33 of the Copyright Act 1957 deals with the existence of a copyright society, the registration thereof, rights of such a copyright society, the requirements it should fulfill for registration etc. Section 33(1) of the Act clarifies that no person or association is entitled to grant license unless such a person is a registered copyright society under Section 33 of the Act. The first Proviso to Section 33(1) of the Act, however clarifies and makes it clear that an owner of a copyright in his individual capacity will continue to have the right to grant licenses in respect of his own works i.e. works owned by the individual person, subject to and consistent with the obligation of such an owner as a member of the copyright society. The second Proviso to Section 33(1) talks of issuing or granting of license with respect to the musical work in sound recordings, it is only for the musical work in the sound recording and not the sound recording itself. In *Novex Communication Pvt. Ltd.*[96] v. *Lemon Tree Hotels Ltd.*, the Delhi High Court observed:

> The first Proviso to Section 33(1) of the Act whereby it is stated that if an individual owner gives such a right to the copyright society that the individual owner though the owner of the copyright, he will not license the copyright works owned by him except to the copyright society, only in such a case would the individual owner of the copyright work not have a right to grant further license, but if the owner of the copyright work has retained with himself the right to give license, although the license is also granted to the copyright society, then such an individual owner despite having granted license to the copyright society can further keep granting licenses with respect to the copyright works owned by the individual owner. [97]

---

95. *See, Novex Communication Pvt. Ltd.* v. *Lemon Tree Hotels Ltd.*, 2019 II AD (Delhi) 644; *Indian Performing Right Society Ltd.* v. *Vodafone Idea Ltd.*, (2019) 2 CALLT 436 (HC); *Super Cassettes Industries Ltd.* v. *Darsh Digital Network Pvt. Ltd.*, 248 (2018) DLT 760: 2018 VIAD (Delhi) 597; *Phonographic Performance Ltd.* v. *Ministry of Human Resources Development*, 2017 (72) PTC 544 (Del): 243 (2017) DLT 342; *Universal Music India Ltd.* v. *Union of India*, [2008] 87 SCL 51 (Delhi); *Bennett Coleman and Co. Ltd.* v. *Phonographic Performance Ltd.*, 2004 (2) CHN 595.
96. 2019 II AD (Delhi) 644.
97. *See also, K.M. Raju* v. *Deputy Director*, MANU/ KE/ 2773/ 2018; *Super Audio Madras Private Limited* v. *Entertainment Network India Private Limited*, 2011-1-LW611; *Phonographic Performance Ltd.* v. *Hotel Gold Regency*, AIR 2009 Delhi 11: 2008 (37) PTC 587 (Del).

> The second Proviso to Section 33(1) provides that with respect to a literary work, dramatic work, musical work or artistic work, as embedded in a cinematographic work or sound recording, with respect to such basic works being a literary work, dramatic work, musical work or artistic work, the business of issuing or granting of license would vest only with a copyright society. The literary work or dramatic work or musical work or artistic work incorporated and embedded in a cinematograph film results in a copyright work, being a cinematograph film as a whole, yet the fact that the cinematograph film contains the basic copyright works, there will continue to exist such independent copyright that will not destroy the copyright in the literary work and/or dramatic work, and/or artistic work which is used to make the cinematograph film. This interpretation applies mutatis mutandis to the sound recording because a sound recording will, besides having an independent copyright, embody in its copyright, literary work and musical work.[98]

Section 33 of the Act permits only Societies registered with the Central Government to carry on the business of issuing or granting licences of any copyright subsisting in any work. Therefore, "No person or association persons shall, after coming into force of the Copyright (Amendment) Act, 1994 commence or, carry on the business of issuing or granting licences in respect of any work in which copyright subsist or in respect of any other rights conferred by this Act..."[99] except under a registration granted under the Act. The procedure for registration of any "association of persons" as copyright society is that such interested society may apply for permission to do the business to the Registrar of copyrights.[100] The Central Government may, having regard to the interests of the authors or other owners of rights under this Act, the interest and convenience of the public and in particular of the groups of persons who are most likely to seek licences in respect of the relevant rights and the ability and professional competence of the applicants, register such association of persons as a copyright society. Ordinarily, more than one copyright society shall not be registered to do business in respect of the same class of works.[101]

In *IPRS* v. *Muthoot Finance Private Limited*,[102] IPRS filed a suit seeking an order of temporary injunction restraining the respondents and their agents from in any manner communicating any of the musical and literary works of its members in form of broadcast on their private FM Radio stations. The members of IPRS had executed deeds of assignment assigning their public performing rights in respect of their music to IPRS. The respondent contended that it had acquired licence from another registered society, namely, phonographic performance limited registered under Section 33(3) of the Copyright Act, 1957 for issuing licences with respect to sound recordings.

However, if any registered copyright society is being managed in a manner detrimental to the interests of the owners of rights concerned, the Central Government shall cancel the registration of such society after proper enquiry.[103] The performing rights society functioning in accordance with the provisions of Section 3 on the date immediately before the coming into

---

98. *See also, Star India Private Limited* v. *Department of Industrial Policy and Promotion*, (2019) 2 SCC 104: 2018 (14) SCALE 651.
99. Copyright Act, 1957, Section 33(1). *See, Indian Performing Right Society Ltd.* v. *Gauhati Town Club*, 2013 III AD (Delhi) 333: 2013 (134) DRJ 732; *Event and Entertainment Management Association* v. *Union of India*, 2012 (52) PTC 380 (Del).
100. *Ibid.*, Section 33(2).
101. *Ibid.*, Section 33(3). *See, Entertainment Network (India) Ltd.* v. *Super Cassettes Industries Ltd.*, MIPR 2008 (2) 129: 2008 (37) PTC 353 (SC).
102. 2010 (42) PTC 752 (Mad).
103. *Ibid.*, Section 33(4).

force of the Copyright (Amendment) Act, 1994 shall be deemed to be a copyright society.[104] The creation of copyright society will not affect any rights or liabilities in any work in connection with performing rights society which has accrued or where incurred on or before the day prior to the commencement of the Copyright (Amendment) Act, 1994 or any legal proceedings in respect of rights or liabilities on that day.[105]

Activities of a Copyright Society

Section 34 of the Copyright Act 1957 provides for the administration of the rights of the owner by copyright society. In *Novex Communication Pvt. Ltd.* v. *Lemon Tree Hotels Ltd.*,[106] the Delhi High Court held that the Section 34 provides for the administration of the rights of the owner by copyright society, and it is relevant to note in this regard that in Section 34(1)(a) there is an expression "exclusive authorisation" and this expression shows that there need not be exclusive authorisation given by the owner of the copyright to give further licenses to the copyright society. The functioning the copyright societies are controlled by and are accountable to the owners of the copyrights. There is also an overall supervisory control by the central government.[107] The Section 34 reads thus:

> "34. Administration of rights of owner by copyright society.—(1) Subject to such conditions as may be prescribed,—(a) a copyright society may accept from an **[authors and other owners of right]**[108] exclusive authorisation to administer any right in any work by issue of licences or collection of licence fees or both; and (b) an author and other owners of right shall have the right to withdraw such authorisation without prejudice to the rights of the copyright society under any contract. (2) It shall be competent for a copyright society to enter into agreement with any foreign society or organisation administering rights corresponding to rights under this Act, to entrust to such foreign society or organisation the administration in any foreign country of rights administered by the said copyright society in India, or for administering in India the rights administered in a foreign country by such foreign society or organisation: Provided that no such society or organisation shall permit any discrimination in regard to the terms of licence or the distribution of fees collected between rights in Indian and other works. (3) Subject to such conditions as may be prescribed, a copyright society may—(i) issue licences under section 30 in respect of any rights under this Act; (ii) collect fees in pursuance of such licences; (iii) distribute such fees among **[authors and other owners of right]**[109] after making deductions for its own expenses; (iv) perform any other functions consistent with the provisions of section 35."[110]

Explaining Section 34 of the Copyright Act in *Entertainment Network (India) Ltd.* v. *Super Cassette Industries Ltd.*,[111] the Supreme Court held that the Section 34 provides for

104. *Ibid.*, Section 33(1) proviso.
105. *Ibid.*, Section 36A.
106. 2019 II AD (Delhi) 644.
107. *See, Event and Entertainment Management Association* v. *Union of India*, 2011 (46) PTC 405 (Del): 182 (2011) DLT 100; *Super Audio Madras Private Ltd.* v. *Entertainment Network India Private Ltd.*, 2011-1-LW611.
108. Inserted by the Copyright (Amendment) Act, 2012 (Act 27 of 2012), Section 19(iii), for "owners of rights" [w.e.f. 21-6-2012].
109. Inserted by the Copyright (Amendment) Act, 2012 (Act 27 of 2012), Section 19(iii), for "owners of rights" [w.e.f. 21-6-2012].
110. *See, Lahari Recording Company Private Limited* v. *Sourabh Marketing and Agencies Private Limited*, ILR 2000 KARNATAKA 5057: 2001 (4) Kar LJ 78.
111. (2008) 13 SCC 30: 2008 (9) SCALE 69.

administration of rights of owner by copyright society. The proviso appended thereto prohibit any discrimination in regard to the terms of licence or the distribution of fees collected between rights in Indian and other works. The concept of copyright society appears to be that the interest of the copyright holder can be protected by the said society while granting licence so as to enable all players to have the benefit of a single window; as such a society is entitled to: (i) issue licences under Section 30 in respect of any rights under this Act; (ii) collect fees in pursuance of such licences; (iii) distribute such fees among owners of rights after making deductions for its own expenses; (iv) perform any other functions consistent with the provisions of Section 35.

Thus, the Section 34 of the Act stipulates the activities to be performed by a copyright society. As per the Section, a copyright society may accept from an owner of rights exclusive authorisation to administer any right in any work by issue of licences or collection of licence fees or both. However, an owner of rights has the right to withdraw such authorisation. The authorised copyright society may enter into an agreement with any foreign society or organisation administering rights corresponding to the rights under the Act to entrust to such society or organisation the administration in any foreign country of rights administered by the said copyright society in India and *vice versa*. Besides the activities as stated above a copyright society enjoys the following powers: (a) to issue licences in respect of any rights under the Act; (b) to collect the fees in pursuance of such licences; (c) to distribute such fees among owners of rights after making deductions for its expenses; (d) to perform any other functions regarding control over copyright society by the owner of rights.[112]

A question arose in *Phonographic Performance Ltd.* v. *Hotel Gold Regency,*[113] whether a copyright society registered under the Act has the right to file civil suit on behalf of the owner for infringement of copyright. In this case, the owners of copyright in sound records licenced their work to the Copyright Society, the plaintiff. The licence agreement also authorised the plaintiff to file infringement suit in case of violation of rights. The present suit was filed by the plaintiff against the defendants for copyright violation. It was contended by the defendant that the plaintiff had no right to file the suit as per the Act since they were not the exclusive licensee of the work. It was argued by the defendant that since Section 34 empowered the society to have exclusive authorisation for licensing the work they must be treated as exclusive licencee under the Act for the purpose of filing the suit. Rejecting the argument the court reasoned thus:

> I have already indicated above that Section 34 of the Act only permits the grant of exclusive authorization by the owners to the copyright society for grant of licence, collection of fees and distribution thereof amongst the owners. The Act does not permit the grant of any authorization by the owners to the Copyright Society to sue for infringement of copyright and seek injunction, damages, account or other civil remedies as provided in Section 55 thereof. The parties can agree to do what the law permits them to do. If they agree on something which is not permissible under law, such an agreement to that extend would not be enforceable.[114]

---

112. *Ibid.*, Section 34(3). *See, Indian Performing Right Society* v. *Adventure Communication India Private Limited* (2012) ILR 6 Delhi 426: MIPR 2013 (1) 48.
113. MIPR 2008 (2) 451: 2008 (37) PTC 587 (Del).
114. *See, Phonographic Performance Ltd.* v. *Hotel Gold Regency*, 2008 (37) PTC 587 (Del) at 596.

The court refused to consider the society as exclusive licencee under Section 61 since it did not consider them to have that power under Section 34. This is a restrictive interpretation of the provisions of the Act defeating the very purpose for which copyright societies are formed. It is true that there is no express provision in Section 34 authorising the society to take action. But the intention of recognising copyright societies is to facilitate collective management of rights by owners since it is difficult for individual owners to enjoy the rights by licensing and effective enforcement. It is not only for licensing, collection of royalties and its distribution but also for effective enforcement of the rights, the societies are formed and registered. It is also the practice that the societies file suits to enforce the rights on behalf of the owners. Keeping this objective in mind, the court should have interpreted the word "exclusive authorisation"[115] in Section 34 to mean exclusive licensing of the rights of owners and treated the society as exclusive licencee and recognised their right to file civil suit following the mandate in Section 61.

Indian Reprographic Rights Organisation and Constitutional Validity of Sections 33 and 34

Reproduction by the use of modern equipment like duplicating machines is called reprography. The term is currently used to cover reproduction by light processes, laser techniques, holographic reproduction, and the use of computers for reproduction. Reproduction with the help of tape recording is called "home page". Duplicating machines are generally used for reproduction of literary work, documents and drawings. Tape records are mainly used for reproducing music and videogames used for reproducing films.[116] Section 33 of the Copyright Act, 1957 provides provisions for registration of copyright society. Thus, Section 33(3) of the Act provides for registration of copyright societies for carrying on business of issuing or granting licences in respect of any work in which copyright subsists. Further, Section 34 of the Act imposes a responsibility upon the copyright society for administration of rights of copyright owner. Indian Reprographic Rights Organisation (IRRO) was registered in the year 2000 for granting reprographic and digital licences on behalf of its members namely, authors and publishers. Rules of IRRO mandate all corporate bodies, reprography shops, libraries, educational institutions, etc., to take "reprographic usage" licences from IRRO on payment of prescribed tariff. IRRO provides for two kinds of licences, blanket and transactional. The IRRO remained dormant and inoperative since its inception in the year 2000. Various institutions were, therefore, not taking any licence from IRRO for carrying out reproduction or copy of the copyright material. The Secretary General of IRRO in fact commented on August, 2012, after the raid in the Delhi University: "We have been giving licences for the last two months but, not a single University or college has taken a licence so far. Only a few corporate houses have. Last week, we asked all universities to take licence so that students and Photostat vendors don't face problems".[117]

---

115. *See*, *Phonographic Performance Ltd.* v. *HT Media Ltd.*, 2017 (70) PTC 211 (Del); *Aamir Khan Productions Private Limited* v. *Union of India*, 2010 Comp LR 105 (Bombay): (2010) 4 Comp LJ 580 (Bom).
116. *See*, *Halsbury's Law of England*, 4th ed., Vol. 8, para. 912.
117. Alka Chawla, "Photostatting in Institutions of the Higher Education-Cure for Copyright Owners or a Boon for the Researchers" 54(4) *Journal of the Indian Law Institute* (2012) pp. 520–538.

The Constitutional validity of Sections 33(3) and 34 of the Copyright Act, 1957 was challenged in the Delhi High Court in *Federation of Hotels and Restaurant Association of India* v. *Union of India.*[118] The petitioners alleged that there were no guidelines to regulate copyright societies and that tariff schemes and licensing rates that were being charged by IRRO and Phonogram Producers Limited (PPL) and IPRS were exorbitant and that there were no means of verifying or checking the reasonableness of licence fees fixed by Copyright Societies. The petitioner further sought cancellation of registration of IRRO and PPL as copyright societies. Dismissing the petition, the Court observed that in a laissez faire economy, such as what exists in India today, every person is entitled to claim any price for utilisation of rights or services. The court went on to add that they were not dealing with essential commodities. If the Government is of the opinion that the public at large is being exploited, appropriate legislation shall, no doubt, be passed. Again in *Event and Entertainment Management Association* v. *Union of India,*[119] the Delhi High Court reiterated that the legislative provisions are constitutional and not suffering from the vice of executive delegation.

Control over the Copyright Society

Section 35 of the Copyright Act, 1957 ensures that the society remains under the collective control of different copyright owners. As per Section 35, every copyright society will be subject to the collective control of the owner of rights whose rights it administered in India. Foreign societies are exempted from this power. Thus, a copyright society shall act in such manner as may be prescribed: (a) obtain the approval of such owners of rights for its procedures of collection and distribution of fees; (b) obtain their approval for the utilisation of any amounts collected as fees for any purpose other than distribution to the owner of rights; and (c) provide to such owners regular full and detailed information concerning all its activities, in relation to the administration of their rights. All fees distributed among the owners of rights shall be, as far as may be, distributed in proportion to the actual use of their works.

In *Phonographic Performance Ltd.* v. *Hotel Gold Regency,*[120] the Court observed that Section 35(2) stipulates that all fees distributed among the owners of the rights shall, as far as may be, be distributed in proportion to the actual use of their works. Section 35 does not, in any way, amplify the authority granted to a copyright society under Section 34. On the other hand, Section 35 clearly stipulates that the copyright society would be under the collective control of the owners of the rights and would have to obtain approvals from them as well as provide full information to them. In *Anand Bhushan* v. *Union of India,*[121] the court further observed:

> We would record that sub-section (4) to Section 35 provides that all members of the Copyright Society shall enjoy equal membership rights and there shall be no discrimination between authors and owners of right in the distribution of royalties. However, our attention is drawn to sub Section (2) to Section 35 which states that the fees distributed among the authors and other owners of right as far as may be in proportion to usage of their works. This, in no way, conflicts with universal and equal voting right envisaged

---

118. 2011 (46) PTC 169 (Del).
119. 2011 (46) PTC 450 (Del.).
120. AIR 2009 Delhi 11: 2008 (37) PTC 587 (Del).
121. 2018 (75) PTC 106 (Del): 2018 VI AD (Delhi) 153.

> and provided under sub-rule (5) to Rule 61. Sub-rule (5) to Rule 61 stipulates that every member of the Society shall have equal voting rights in the General Body meetings. The said sub-rule does not state that the fee distributed and paid amongst the authors shall not be proportionate to actual usage of their works. It only applies to General Body meetings and voting either for the election by the General Body to the Governing Council. Each member of the Copyright Society has equal voting rights. This is clearly the mandate and is so postulated in Section 35 of the Act. In a way sub-rule (6) to Rule 61 is a reflection and concords with sub-section (4) to Section 35 of the Act.

Every copyright society should submit to the Registrar of Copyright such returns as may be prescribed. Any office duly authorised by the Central Government in this behalf may call for any report and also any records of any copyright society for seeing that the fees collected are being utilised or distributed in accordance with the provision of the Act.[122] Now question arises which court has the jurisdiction to decide the competency of authority of a copyright society? This issue was decided by the Calcutta High Court in *Eastern India Motion Picture* v. *Performing Right Society Ltd. and Others.*[123] On February 13, 1971, an advertisement was published in the Gazette of India to the following effect: "Tariffs for India". The following is notified for general information: "Revision of Tariff". The Performing Right Society's Tariff (Statement of Fees, Charges or Royalties) Relating to Cinema has been revised. The Society proposes to collect, until further notice fees, charges or royalties for the grant of licences for performances in public in India of the copyright musical works in its repertoire. The tariff of 1947, was allowed to go on till 31 March, 1969, on 28 June, 1969, a fresh tariff was published whereby the minimum annual licence fee for a cinema was raised from ₹40 to ₹100. Against the said tariff, objections were filed on 7 February, 1971. The society withdrew the said tariff and used the revised tariff published in the Gazette of India dated 13 February, 1971. The society addressed a letter to Copyright Board, New Delhi stating that the Board had notified of the amendments of two tariffs, one of which was the tariffs for cinema. Since the society has promulgated a revised tariff for cinema, it would be pointless to pursue the proceedings. The Copyright Board/Appellate Board[124] declined to revise the tariff as published in the Gazette of India dated 13 February, 1971. The court held that if the authority of the society to grant licence or to fix rates in challenged, the Board had jurisdiction to decide the question of authority of the society concerned.

Constitution of Copyright Office

Under Section 9 of the Copyright Act 1957 a copyright office has also been constituted to administer certain provisions.[125] The Office is under the immediate control of the Registrar of Copyright, who is to act under the superintendence and direction of the Central Government.

---

122. Copyright Act, 1957, Section 36. *See, Event and Entertainment Management Association* v. *Union of India*, MIPR 2011 (2) 107: 2011 (46) PTC 405 (Del).
123. AIR 1978 Cal 477.
124. Substituted by the Finance Act 2017 (7 of 2017), Section 160(a) for "Copyright Board," [w.e.f. 26 May, 2017].
125. Section 9 of the Copyright Act, 1957 constitutes Copyright Office. Section 9 reads: "Copyright Office—(1) There shall be established for the purposes of this Act an office to be called the Copyright Office. (2) The Copyright Office shall be under the immediate control of the Registrar of Copyrights who shall act under the superintendence and direction of the Central Government. (3) There shall be a seal for the Copyright Office".

He is also assisted by a Deputy Registrar of Copyright.[126] The office is located in New Delhi under the Department of Education, Ministry of Human Resource Development Government of India. The Copyright Office also maintains a Register of Copyright containing the names or titles of works and the names and address of authors, publishers and owners of copyright and other particulars as may be prescribed. Any author, publisher, owners of copyright or other interested person can get his right entered in the Copyright Register by making an application along with the prescribed fee to the Registrar of Copyright. However, registration of copyright is not mandatory for either acquiring copyright or enforcing copyright by an infringement suit.[127] It only raises a presumption that the person shown in the register is the actual owner of copyright in the work. But Section 48 of the Act provides that registration of Copyright shall he accepted as *prima facie*, evidence before any court of law regarding title to copyright without further proof or production of the original.

Constitution of Appellate Board

According to Section 11 of the Copyright Act 1957 the Appellate Board established under Section 83 of the Trade Marks Act 1999 (47 of 1999) shall, on and from the commencement of Part XIV of Chapter VI of the Finance Act, 2017, be the Appellate Board for the purposes of this Act and the said Appellate Board shall exercise the jurisdiction, powers and authority conferred on it by or under this Act.[128] Thus, in *Radio Next Webcastion Pvt. Ltd.* v. *Union of India*,[129] the Delhi High Court held that a conjoint reading of Section 11 of the Copyright Act and Section 83 of the Trade Marks Act clearly indicates that the Appellate Board as constituted under Section 83 of the Trade Marks Act would also have the jurisdiction to perform the functions under the Copyright Act as well. There is no dispute that an Appellate Board has been validly constituted in terms of Section 84 of the Trade Marks Act and is now functional. Thus, the Appellate Board also required to exercise the jurisdiction, powers and authority conferred on it by or under the Copyright Act.[130] In terms of Section 11 of the

---

126. Section 10 of the Copyright Act, 1957 reads: "Registrar and Deputy Registrars of Copyrights—(1) The Central Government shall appoint a Registrar of Copyrights and may appoint one or more Deputy Registrars of Copyrights. (2) A Deputy Registrar of Copyrights shall discharge under the superintendence and direction of the Registrar of Copyrights such functions of the Registrar under this Act as the Registrar may, from time to time, assign to him; and any reference in this Act to the Registrar of Copyrights shall include a reference to a Deputy Registrar of Copyrights when so discharging any such functions".
127. *See, Navsafitya Prakash* v. *Anand Kumar,* AIR 1981 All 200.
128. Substituted by the Finance Act 2017 (7 of 2017), Section 160(a) for "Copyright Board," [w.e.f. 26 May, 2017]. The Section 11, before substitution by the Finance Act, 2017, stood as under:
"11. Copyright Board—(1) As soon as may be after the commencement of this Act, the Central Government shall constitute a Board to be called the Copyright Board which shall consist of a Chairman and two other members. (2) The salaries and allowances payable to and the other terms and conditions of service of the Chairman and other members of the Copyright Board shall be such as may be prescribed: Provided that neither the salary and allowances nor the other terms and conditions of service of the Chairman or any other member shall be varied to his disadvantage after appointment. (3) The Chairman of the Copyright Board shall be a person who is, or has been, a Judge of a High Court or is qualified for appointment as a Judge of a High Court. (4) The Central Government may after consultation with the Chairman of the Copyright Board appoint a Secretary to the Copyright Board and such other officer and employees as may be considered necessary for the efficient discharge of the functions of the Copyright Board."
129. (2018) 254 DLT 660.
130. *Radio Next Webcastion Pvt. Ltd.* v. *Union of India*, 254 (2018) DLT 660.

Copyright Act 1957, the Appellate Board established under Section 83 of the Trademarks Act, 1999 is the Appellate Board for the purposes of the copyright matters.[131] Similarly, the Appellate Board established under Section 83 of the Trade Marks Act, 1999, shall be the Appellate Board for the purposes of the Patent Act, 1970.[132]

Composition of Appellate Board

The Appellate Board was created as there was a need for an expert body to adjudicate issues that are technical in nature with respect to trademarks, copyright and patents. According to Section 84 of the Trade Marks Act 1999 the Appellate Board shall consist of a Chairman, Vice-Chairman and such number of other Members, as the Central Government may, deem fit and, subject to the other provisions of this Act, the jurisdiction, powers and authority of the Appellate Board may be exercised by Benches thereof.[133] Besides this, a Bench shall consist of one Judicial Member and one Technical Member and shall sit at such place as the Central Government may, by notification in the Official Gazette, specify.[134] The Chairman: (a) may, in addition to discharging the functions of the Judicial Member or Technical Member of the Bench to which he is appointed, discharge the functions of the Judicial Member or, as the case may be, the Technical Member, of any other Bench; (b) may transfer a Member from one Bench to another Bench; (c) may authorise the Vice-Chairman, the Judicial Member or the Technical Member appointed to one Bench to discharge also the functions of the Judicial Member or the Technical member, as the case may be, of another Bench.[135] Where any Benches are constituted, the Central Government may, from time to time, by notification, make provisions as to the distribution of the business of the Appellate Board amongst the Benches and specify the matters which may be dealt with by each Bench.[136] If any question arises as to whether any matter falls within the purview of the business allocated to a Bench, the decision of the Chairman shall be final. Explanation: For the removal of doubts, it is hereby declared that the expression matter" includes an appeal under section 91.[137] If the Members of a Bench differ in opinion on any point, they shall state the point or points on which they differ, and make a reference to the Chairman who shall either hear the point or points himself or refer the case for hearing on such point or points by one or more of the other Members and such point or points shall be decided according to the opinion of the majority of the Members who have heard the case, including those who first heard it.[138]

Powers, Functions and Procedure of Appellate Board

The powers, functions and procedure of the Appellate Board have been provided in various

131. *See, Saregama India Ltd.* v. *Union of India*, MANU/DE/0664/2018.
132. See, *Aloys Wobben* v. *Intellectual Property Appellate Board, Enercon (India) Limited*, 2014 (57) PTC 107 (Mad): MIPR 2013 (3) 135.
133. Trade Marks Act 1999, Sectiion 84 (1). *See, Radio Next Webcastion Pvt. Ltd.* v. *Union of India*, 254 (2018) DLT 660; *Parthasarathy Seniammal Educational Trust* v. *V. Rangasamy*, AIR 2018 Mad 267.
134. *Ibid.*, Section 84 (2).
135. *Ibid.*, Section 84 (3).
136. *Ibid.*, Section 84 (4).
137. *Ibid.*, Section 84 (5).
138. *Ibid.*, Section 84 (6).

provisions of the Copyright Act 1957. The Section 12 of the Act deals with the powers and procedure of the Appellate Board. Though the proviso to Section 12 speaks about reference by the Chairman to a Special Bench of five members, it is conceded by the respondents that the constitution is only the Chairman and two members.[139] The Appellate Board has been empowered to regulate its own procedure.[140] It may exercise and discharge its powers and functions through Benches constituted by its Chairman from amongst its members, each Bench consisting of not less than three members. If there is a difference of opinion among the members of the Board or any Bench thereof in respect of any matter coming before it for decision under this Act, the opinion of the majority shall prevail and whereas there is no such majority, the opinion of the Chairman shall prevail.[141] The Board shall be deemed to be a Civil Court for the purpose of Sections 345 and 346 of the Code of Criminal Procedure and its proceedings before the Board shall be deemed to be judicial proceedings within the meaning of Sections 193 and 228 of the Indian Penal Code.[142] The Section 12 reads thus:

> "12. Powers and procedure of [Appellate Board][143] —(1) The [Appellate Board][144] shall, subject to any rules that may be made under this Act, have power to regulate its own procedure, including the fixing of places and times of its sittings:
>
> Provided that the [Appellate Board][145] shall ordinarily hear any proceeding instituted before it under this Act within the zone in which, at the time of the institution of the proceeding, the person instituting the proceeding actually and voluntarily resides or carries on business or personally works for gain.
>
> Explanation—In this sub-section "zone" means a zone specified in section 15 of the States Reorganisation Act, 1956.
>
> (2) The [Appellate Board][146] may exercise and discharge its powers and functions through Benches constituted by the Chairman of the [Appellate Board][147] from amongst its members.
>
> [Provided that, if the Chairman is of opinion that any matter of importance is required to be heard by a larger bench, he may refer the matter to a special bench consisting of five members.][148]
>
> [***] [149]

---

139. *See, South Indian Music Companies Association* v. *Union of India*, 2016 (67) PTC 99 (Mad): (2016) 3 MLJ 647.
140. *See, Super Cassettes Industries Ltd.* v. *Music Broadcast Pvt. Ltd.*, AIR 2012 SC 2144: (2012)5 SCC 488.
141. *See, Music Choice India Private Limited* v. *Phonographic Performance Limited*, 2010 (44) PTC 171 (Bom): 2010 (112) Bom LR 470.
142. *See, Lahari Recording Company Pvt. Ltd.* v. *Sourabh Marketing and Agencies Pvt. Ltd.*, ILR 2000 KARNATAKA 5057: 2001 (4) Kar LJ 78.
143. Substituted by the Finance Act 2017 (7 of 2017), Section 160(a) for "Copyright Board," [w.e.f. 26 May, 2017].
144. Substituted by the Finance Act 2017 (7 of 2017), Section 160(a) for "Copyright Board," [w.e.f. 26 May, 2017].
145. Substituted by the Finance Act 2017 (7 of 2017), Section 160(a) for "Copyright Board," [w.e.f. 26 May, 2017].
146. Substituted by the Finance Act 2017 (7 of 2017), Section 160(a) for "Copyright Board," [w.e.f. 26 May, 2017].
147. Substituted by the Finance Act 2017 (7 of 2017), Section 160(a) for "Copyright Board," [w.e.f. 26 May, 2017].
148. Substituted by the Copyright (Amendment) Act, 1994 (Act 38 of 1994), Section 6 [w.e.f. 10-5-1995].
149. Subsection (3) and (4) was omitted by the Finance Act 2017 (7 of 2017), Section 160(d) [w.e.f. 26 May, 2017].

(5) No member of the [Appellate Board][150] shall take part in any proceedings before the Board in respect of any matter in which he has a personal interest.

(6) No act done or proceeding taken by the [Appellate Board][151] under this Act shall be questioned on the ground merely of the existence of any vacancy in, or defect in the constitution of, the Board.

(7) The [Appellate Board][152] shall be deemed to be a civil court for the purposes of [sections 345 and 346 of the Code of Criminal Procedure, 1973][153] and all proceedings before the Board shall be deemed to be judicial proceedings within the meaning of sections 193 and 228 of the Indian Penal Code, 1860 (45 of 1860)."

The main powers and functions of the Copyright Boards are (i) to regulate its own procedure including the fixing of places and times of its sittings; (ii) to decide questions upon publication of work; (iii) to settle disputes arising in respect of assignment and licensing of copyright; (iv) to grant compulsory licences with respect to works withheld from public, to publish unpublished works, to publish translations, etc; (v) rectification of entries made in the Register of Copyright.[154]

The Section 6 of the Copyright Act deals with a reference to be made to the Appellate Board qua certain disputes. The Section 6 of the Act provides that if any question arises,—(a) whether a work has been published or as to the date on which a work was published for the purposes of Chapter V, or (b) whether the term of copyright for any work is shorter in any other country than that provided in respect of that work under this Act, it shall be referred to the Appellate Board. In *Lahari Recording Company Pvt. Ltd.* v. *Sourabh Marketing*,[155] it was held that the provisions of Sections 3 to 6 of the Copyright Act make it clear that the question of controversy, if any, referred to in Section 6 pertains to the "term" i.e., "duration" of a copyright in respect of a published work within the confines of Chapter V which deals with the terms of copyright in various works, and that these terms are created by this statute. Since the question stipulated in Section 6 merely relates to the term of copyright in a published work within the meaning of Sections 3 to 5, the legislature thought it proper to invest the Board exclusively with the powers to adjudicate such questions. The Section 6 further enables the Board to decide disputes regarding "term of copyright and international copyright." It also hears matters relating to rectification of Register involving disputes between private parties under Section 50. Under Section 19A also, the Board hears disputes regarding assignment of copyright, which once again would encompass a private dispute between the parties.[156]

---

150. Substituted by the Finance Act 2017 (7 of 2017), Section 160(a) for "Copyright Board," [w.e.f. 26 May, 2017].
151. Substituted by the Finance Act 2017 (7 of 2017), Section 160(a) for "Copyright Board," [w.e.f. 26 May, 2017].
152. Substituted by the Finance Act 2017 (7 of 2017), Section 160(a) for "Copyright Board," [w.e.f. 26 May, 2017].
153. Substituted by the Copyright (Amendment) Act, 1983 (Act 23 of 1983), Section 6, for "section 480 and 482 of the Code of Criminal Procedure, 1898 (5 of 1898)" [w.e.f. 9-8-1984].
154. *See, Super Cassettes Industries Ltd.* v. *Music Broadcast Pvt. Ltd.*, AIR 2012 SC 2144: 2012 (50) PTC 225 (SC); *Super Cassettes Industries Limited* v. *Entertainment Network (India) Ltd.*, AIR 2004 (Del.) 326.
155. ILR 2000 KARNATAKA 5057: 2001 (4) Ka rLJ 78.
156. *See, South Indian Music Companies Association* v. *Union of India*, 2016 (67) PTC 99 (Mad): (2016) 3 MLJ 647.,

The power of Appellate Board to issue compulsory licence is recognised under Sections 12 and 31 of the Copyright Act, 1957. According to Section 31 if at any time during the term of copyright in [any work][157] which has been published or performed in public, a complaint is made to the [Appellate Board],[158] that the owner of copyright in the work—(a) has refused to republish or allow the republication of the work or has refused to allow the performance in public of the work, and by reason of such refusal the work is withheld from the public; or[159] (b) has refused to allow communication to the public by [broadcast],[160] of such work or in the case of [sound recording][161] the work recorded in such [sound recording],[162] on terms which the complainant considers reasonable;[163] after giving to the owner of the copyright in the work a reasonable opportunity of being heard and after holding such inquiry as it may deem necessary, may, if it is satisfied that the grounds for such refusal are not reasonable, direct the Registrar of Copyrights to grant to the complainant a licence to republish the work, perform the work in public or communicate the work to the public by [broadcast],[164] as the case may be, subject to payment to the owner of the copyright of such compensation and subject to such other terms and conditions as the [Appellate Board][165] may determine; and thereupon the Registrar of Copyrights shall grant the licence to the complainant in accordance with the directions of the [Appellate Board][166], on payment of such fee as may be prescribed.

In *Music Broadcast Limited* v. *Axis Bank*,[167] the Copyright Board/[Appellate Board][168] at New Delhi passed an order in exercise of the powers conferred under Section 31 (1) (b) of the Copyright Act, 1957 directing the Registrar of Copyrights to grant to the complainants (which includes the appellant herein) separate licences for communicating the work recorded in sound recordings in the repertoire, present and future, of the respondent No. 2 to the public by broadcast on revenue sharing basis subject to certain terms and conditions. However, these licences do not contain any exclusive jurisdiction clause and, therefore, it has to be seen as to where the cause of action accrued. The Court held that the exclusive jurisdiction clause in the voluntary licence agreement, does not come into play. In *South Indian Music Companies*

---

157. Substituted by the Copyright (Amendment) Act, 2012 (Act 27 of 2012), Section 16, for "any Indian work" [w.e.f. 21-6-2012].
158. Substituted by the Finance Act 2017 (7 of 2017), Section 160(a) for "Copyright Board," [w.e.f. 26 May, 2017].
159. *See,* Copyright Act 1957, Section 31(1)(a).
160. Substituted by the Copyright (Amendment) Act, 1983 (Act 23 of 1983), Section 2, for "radio diffusion" [w.e.f. 9-8-1984].
161. Substituted by the Copyright (Amendment) Act, 1984 (Act 65 of 1984), Section 2, for "record" [w.e.f. 8-10-1984].
162. Substituted by the Copyright (Amendment) Act, 1984 (Act 65 of 1984), Section 2, for "record" [w.e.f. 8-10-1984].
163. *See,* Copyright Act 1957, Section 31(1)(b).
164. Substituted by the Copyright (Amendment) Act, 1983 (Act 23 of 1983), Section 2, for "radio diffusion" [w.e.f. 9-8-1984].
165. Substituted by the Finance Act 2017 (7 of 2017), Section 160(a) for "Copyright Board," [w.e.f. 26 May, 2017].
166. Substituted by the Finance Act 2017 (7 of 2017), Section 160(a) for "Copyright Board," [w.e.f. 26 May, 2017].
167. 2016 (67) PTC 638 (Del).
168. Substituted by the Finance Act 2017 (7 of 2017), Section 160(a) for "Copyright Board," [w.e.f. 26 May, 2017].,

Association v. *Union of India*,[169] it was held that the functions of the Board are predominantly judicial. Section 31 of the Act deals with granting of compulsory licence in works withheld from public. Such a work ought to have been published or performed in public. Thus, it must have come into the public domain. The Madras High Court further observed:

> A complaint can be made to the Board when the owner of copyright has refused to republish or allow the republication of the work or has refused to allow the performance in public of the work, and by reason of such refusal the work is withheld from the public and similarly when such a owner has refused to allow communication to the public by (broadcast) of such work or in the case of a (sound recording) the work recorded in such (sound recording) on terms which the complainant considers reasonable. When such a complaint is made, the Board after giving to the owner a reasonable opportunity of being heard and after holding such an enquiry, which is required, if it is satisfied that the grounds of such refusal are not reasonable, then direct the Registrar of Copyrights to grant the complainant a licence to republish the work, perform the work in public or communicate the work to the public by (broadcast), as the case may be, subject to adequate payment to the owner of the copyright by way of compensation.
>
> Therefore, once a Copyright is taken in public domain, then it becomes a commercial right. It is not as if the complainant is entitled to succeed in all cases of refusal to grant licence, but only when the Board is satisfied on the grounds being not reasonable. Therefore, the said provision makes a delicate balance between private and public interest.[170]

In *Phonographic Performance Ltd.* v. *Radio Mid Day (West) India Ltd.*,[171] the Delhi High Court held that the jurisdiction of the Appellate Board can be invoked under Section 31(1)(b) of the Copyright Act by a complainant who considers that the owner of a copyright has offered unreasonable terms for the broadcast of a sound recording. When that happens, the Board is required to give the copyright owner a reasonable opportunity of being heard before directing the complainant to pay compensation to him (and determining other terms and conditions) for the broadcast. As a part of the "reasonable opportunity of being heard" the Board may hold such inquiry as it deems necessary. In *Music Choice India Pvt. Ltd.* v. *Phonographic Performance Ltd.*,[172] grant of relief of compulsory license in respect works withheld from public is exclusively vested with the Copyright Board [Appellate Board][173] and such a relief cannot be granted by the Civil Court.

In *Phonographic Performance Ltd* v. *Music Broadcast (P) Ltd.*,[174] the Bombay High Court had an occasion to examine the scheme of the Act and on the interpretation of Section 31 of the Copyright Act, 1957. The Court observed that the perusal of the provisions of Sub-section (1) of Section 31 shows that the complainant in relation to cases covered by both Clauses (a) and (b) of Sub-section (1) of Section 31 is required to first approach the holder of the copyright for permission to republish or rebroadcast the work and offer terms which he considers reasonable and if the permission is refused by the copyright holder, he

169. 2016 (67) PTC 99 (Mad): (2016) 3 MLJ 647.
170. *See, South Indian Music Companies Association* v. *Union of India,* 2016 (67) PTC 99 (Mad): (2016) 3 MLJ 647.
171. 2010 (43) PTC 377 (Del): (2010) ILR 4 Delhi 603.
172. 2010 (44) PTC 171 (Bom): 2010 (112) Bom LR4 70.
173. Substituted by the Finance Act 2017 (7 of 2017), Section 160(a) for "Copyright Board," [w.e.f. 26 May, 2017].
174. 2 2004 (3) ALLMR 196: 2004(29) PTC 282 (Bom).

can approach the Board. The Board then holds an inquiry to find out whether the grounds on which the copyright holder has refused permission are reasonable or not and if the Board finds that the reasons for refusal given by the copyright holder are not reasonable, then, it can decide to grant a license to the complainant. It is thereafter, that the question of determination of compensation arises and then the Board has to hold an inquiry as to what should be the amount of compensation payable by the complainant to the copyright holder as also other terms and conditions on which the license is to be granted.

The Supreme Court in *Entertainment Network (India) Ltd.* v. *Super Cassettes Industries Ltd.*,[175] examined the power of the Board to issue compulsory licence to FM Radio stations to play music and set at rest the conflicting interpretation given by different high courts. Appellants in this case used the songs owned by the respondents without authorisation after they failed in their attempt to negotiate reasonable royalty for use of songs. The appellants then approached the Board for grant of compulsory licence and the same was issued after fixing the royalty rates. It was contended by the respondent that the power under Section 31 is limited only to cases where the work is not available to the public. In the present case, it was argued that since the songs are already available to the public through broadcast from other broadcasting organisations (All India Radio), the Board has no power to issue compulsory licence under this section. The appellants argued that the above interpretation of the section is applicable only for republication of the work under Section 31(1)(a) and not for broadcasting of the work under Section 31(l)(b). According to the appellants, Section 31(1)(b) envisages more than one organisation broadcasting works and denial of licence on reasonable terms by the owner enables the Board to issue compulsory licence on reasonable terms. After examining the wording of the provisions and the international obligations, the court interpreted the provision thus:

> Significantly, in between the clauses (a) and (b), the word "or" has been used. It must be read disjunctively and not conjunctively. Even otherwise, reading the said provision conjunctively is not possible. Clause (a) refers to republication or allowing republication of the works, etc., clause (b) refers to refusal to allow communication to the public in the case of broadcast or in case of sound recording.

JUDICIAL REMEDIES IN INDIA: CIVIL AND CRIMINAL

Civil Remedies: Sections 54–62

The Sections 54 to 62 (Chapter-XII) of the Copyright Act, 1957 provide for civil remedies. Civil remedies are available against infringement of copyright which include injunction, either damages or account of profits and the delivery of the infringing articles for erasure or destruction.[176] A common feature of many intellectual property actions is that speed is of the essence. The claimant's aim is generally to stop a threatened or an on-going infringement

---

175. 2008 (37) PTC 353 (SC).

176. *See*, Copyright Act, 1957, Section 55 (1). *See also*, *Carlsberg Breweries* v. *Som Distilleries and Breweries Ltd.*, AIR 2019 Delhi 23: 2019 (77) PTC 1 (Del); *Gulf DTH FZ LLC* v. *Dishtv India Limited*, 2016 VIII AD (Delhi) 266;

of his rights by obtaining an injunction against the alleged infringer's future activities. Furthermore, once a claimant obtains an interim (or pre-trial) injunction, the defendant may have little incentive to contest the action further.

Apart from injunctions, the main remedies in copyright cases are delivery up, damages and an account of profits. For the reasons stated above, the later two remedies are comparatively underused in copyright actions. In most copyright actions, liability is determined first. Where the claimant chooses to continue, damages are usually determined or an account made at a separate hearing. The third remedy, delivery up of infringing articles, is particularly appropriate where the copyright is embodied in a material form, and may accompany the other two.[177]

According to Section 55 of the Copyright Act in the case of infringement of copyright "the owner of the copyright shall, except as otherwise provided by this Act, be entitled to all such remedies by way of injunction, damages, accounts and otherwise as are or may be conferred by law for the infringement of a right". In *Inception Media LLP* v. *Star India Pvt. Ltd.*,[178] it was held that a suit such as this one can only be brought by the "owner of copyright". This is defined in Section 54 of the Copyright Act, and the civil remedies of such an owner are set out in Section 55. The former says that the owner of a copyright includes an exclusive licensee.

Thus, an owner of Copyright[179] is entitled for all such civil remedies like injunction, damages, accounts and other remedy conferred by law. In *P.K. Sen* v. *Exxon Mobile Corporation*,[180] the Court observed:

> Section 55 of the Copyright Act 1957 provides for civil remedies for infringement of copyright. As per this section, where copyright in any work has been infringed, the owner of the copyright shall, except as otherwise provided by this Act, be entitled to all such remedies by way of injunction, damages, accounts and otherwise as are or may be conferred by law.[181]

Injunctions as Civil Remedies

The main remedy sought in most Copyright suits is an injunction to restrain the defendant from continuing to do acts which constitute infringement.[182] It is the only remedy available against a defendant who proves that at the date of the infringement he was not aware and had no reasonable grounds for believing that copyright subsisted in the work

177. *See, Shuddhananda Yoga Samaj* v. *Rajeswari Book Shop*, 2018 (75) PTC 25 (Mad): 2018 (4) CTC 276.
178. 2016 (65) PTC 149 (Bom): 2016 (5) Bom CR 309.
179. According to Section 54 of the Copyright Act, 1957, the expression "owner of copyright" shall include—
    (a) an exclusive licensee;
    (b) in the case of an anonymous or pseudonymous literary, dramatic, musical or artistic work, the publisher of the work, until the identity of the author or, in the case of an anonymous work of joint authorship, or a work of joint authorship published under names all of which are pseudonyms, the identity of any of the authors, is disclosed publicly by the author and the publisher or is otherwise established to the satisfaction of the Copyright Board by that author or his legal representatives.
180. 2018 (73) PTC 304 (Del): 2017 (69) PTC 271 (Del). *See also, Parul Library Private Ltd.* v. *Sreepati Saha*, AIR 2016 Tripura 10: (2015) 2 TLR 1048.
181. *See also, Maddock Films Private Limited* v. *Shiboprasad Mukherjee*, 2017(4) CHN (CAL) 614.
182. Copyright Act 1957, Section 55(1).

(the innocent infringer).[183] Injunctions are designed to restrain threatened breaches of the defendant's rights. The law of injunctions is beset with over-general propositions that require qualification in particular areas of application. In *M/s. Jawahar Engineering Company* v. *Jawahar Engineers Pvt. Ltd.*,[184] the Division Bench of the Delhi High Court explained thus:

> When an injunction is sought, it is not necessary that the threat should have become a reality before the injunction and it can even be sought for a threat that is still to materialize. An injunction being prohibitive in nature is intended to prevent something that is likely to happen.[185]

In the field of intellectual property an injunction is almost always prohibitory (as opposed to mandatory) since it enjoins the threatened commission or continuance of wrongful acts. It can be granted after a trial establishing infringement of the plaintiff's rights, when it is called "final" or "perpetual." But it may also be sought in "interlocutory" or "interim" form, not to enforce an established right, but to maintain the status quo until a trial of the merits can take place. Injunctions are of several categories: (i) interlocutory or interim injunction,[186] (ii) Anton Piller order,[187] (iii) Mareva injunction,[188] (iv) injunction for groundless threat of legal proceedings,[189] (v) John Doe injunction,[190] and (vi) final or perpetual injunction.[191] These six categories of injunctions need detail deliberation.

Interlocutory or Interim Injunction

An interlocutory or interim injunction protects the plaintiff against injury by violation of his rights for which he could not adequately be compensated in damages recoverable in the action if the uncertainty were resolved in his favour at the trial.[192] Thus, an interlocutory or interim injunction, ordering the defendant not to continue or not to embark upon a course of action until trial of the issue with the plaintiff, is a rapid and relatively cheaper way of procuring

183. *Ibid.*, Proviso to Section 55(1) which reads: "Provided that if the defendant proves that at the date of the infringement he was not aware and had no reasonable ground for believing that copyright subsisted in the work, the plaintiff shall not be entitled to any remedy other than an injunction in respect of the infringement and a decree for the whole or part of the profits made by the defendant by the sale of the infringing copies as the court may in the circumstances deem reasonable." *See, DKT India* v. *HLL Lifecare Ltd.*, 2015 (62) PTC 402 (Del).
184. AIR 1984 Delhi 166: 24 (1983) DLT 129.
185. *See also, Eurobond Industries Pvt. Ltd.* v. *Euro Panel Products Pvt. Ltd.*, 2019 (77) PTC 465 (Bom): 2019 (1) ABR 568; *Lupin Ltd.* v. *Johnson and Johnson*, AIR 2015 Bom 50: 2015(1) Mh LJ 501; *Simla Chemicals Pvt. Ltd.* v. *Sun Soap Industries*, MIPR 2012 (3) 170: 2012 (51) PTC 570 (Del); *LG Electronics India Pvt. Ltd.* v. *Bharat Bhogilal Patel*, 2012 (51) PTC 513 (Del); *South African Breweries International* v. *Mohan Goldwater Breweries Ltd.*, 184 (2011) DLT 252: 2011 (48) PTC 380 (Del); *K. Narayanan* v. *S. Murali, AIR* 2008 SC 3216: (2008) 10 SCC 479.
186. *See, Paramount Surgimed Ltd.* v. *Paramount Bed India*, 2017 (71) PTC 365 (Del): 241 (2017) DLT 319.
187. *See, Foundry Visionmongers* v. *Parish Tekri*, 2017 (69) PTC 360 (Bom).
188. *See, Mohit Bhargava* v. *Bharat Bhushan Bhargava*, AIR 2007 SC 1717: 2007(4) SCC 795.
189. *See, International Association of Lions Clubs* v. *Association of Lions India*, 2009 (40) PTC 346 (Bom).
190. *See, Essel Vision Productions Ltd.* v. *Bharat Sanchar Nigam Ltd.*, MIPR 2018 (1) 323.
191. *See, Tea Board, India* v. *ITC Limited*, (2019) 1 CALLT 538 (HC).
192. *See, Crocs Inc. USA* v. *Bata India Ltd.*, 2019 (78) PTC 1 (Del); *Colgate Palmolive (India) Ltd.* v. *Hindustan Lever Ltd.*, AIR 1999 SC 3105: 1999 (7) SCC 1; *Wander* v. *Antox*, 1990 Supp (1)SCC 727: (1990) Suppl. SCC 727.

temporary redress. In *Alkem Laboratories Limited* v. *Elnova Pharma*,[193] the Himachal Pradesh High Court held that insofar as the claim of the applicant regarding use of its slogan "GEM OF A CALCIUM" and restraining the respondents from using their slogan "PEARL OF CALCIUM", I do not find any merit or substance in such allegation. Both the slogans convey a different meaning making less chances of confusion in the minds of consumers of the product. Both the slogans are at distinct making no possibility of confusion in the minds of the consumers. Thus, regarding grant of interim injunction for restraining the respondents, their directors, licensees, franchisees, subsidiary/affiliated group companies, representatives, distributors, agents, contract manufacturers, employees, from using the slogan "PEARL OF CALCIUM", is dismissed.

An interim/interlocutory injunction order is passed on the basis of *prima facie* findings, which are tentative. Such order is passed as a temporary arrangement to preserve the status quo till the matter is decided finally, to ensure that the matter does not become either in fructuous or a *fait accompli* before the final hearing.[194] Its effect against a business competitor may be to cut off for good the road to commercial success. Even without this, businessmen frequently treat the outcome of the interlocutory proceedings as settling the matter in dispute. Whether such an injunction will be granted has always been a matter of discretion. Grant of an interim relief in regard to the nature and extent thereof depends upon the facts and circumstances of each case as no straitjacket formula can be laid down. There may be a situation where in the respondent may use the suit property in such a manner that the situation becomes irretrievable. In such a situation, interim relief should be granted.[195]

Certain criteria are used by the courts in determining whether or not to grant an interim/ interlocutory injunction. Grant of temporary injunction is governed by three basic principles, i.e., *prima facie* case; balance of convenience; and irreparable injury, which are required to be considered in a proper perspective in the facts and circumstances of a particular case. But it may not be appropriate for any court to hold a mini-trial at the stage of grant of temporary injunction.[196] In *American Cynamid Co.* v. *Ethicon Ltd.*,[197] a case concerning an alleged infringement of the intellectual property rights, the basis for granting an interim injunction was discussed. Lord Diplock J. said:

> The object of an interlocutory injunction is to protect the claimant against injury by violation of his right for which he could not be adequately compensated in damages recoverable in the action if the uncertainty were resolved in his favour at the trial; but the claimant's need for such protection must be weighed against the corresponding need of the defendant to be protected against injury resulting from his having been prevented from exercising his own legal rights for which he would not be adequately compensated under the plaintiff's

---

193. 2015 (62) PTC 465.
194. *See, Beyond Dreams Entertainment Pvt. Ltd.* v. *Zee Entertainment Enterprises Ltd.*, 2015 (62) PTC 241 (Bom): 2016 (5) Bom CR 266; *State of Assam* v. *Barak Upatyaka D.U. Karmachari Sanstha*, AIR 2009 SC 2249: (2009) 5 SCC 694).
195. *See, LA Opala R.G. Ltd.* v. *Cello Plast*, 2018 (76) PTC 309 (Cal): (2018) 4 CALLT 553 (HC); *Turning Point* v. *Turning Point Institute*, 2018 (75) PTC 417 (Del): 251(2018)DLT563; *Shridevi* v. *Muralidhar* (2007) 14 SCC 721; *M. Gurudas* v. *Rasaranjan* (2006) 8 SCC 367.
196. *S.M. Dyechem Ltd.* v. *Cadbury (India) Ltd.* (2000) 5 SCC 573.
197. (1975) AC 396. *See also, Cadila Healthcare Ltd.* v. *Gujarat Co-operative Milk Marketing Federation Ltd.*, MIPR 2007 (3) 497: 2008 (36) PTC 168 (Del).

understanding in damages if the uncertainty were resolved in the defendant's favour at the trial. The court must weigh one need against another and determine whether in 'balance of convenience' lies.[198]

Similarly, in *Zenit Mataplast P. Ltd.* v. *State of Maharashtra,*[199] the Apex Court held that the object of an interlocutory injunction is to protect the plaintiff against injury by violation of his right for which he could not be adequately compensated in damages recoverable in the action if the uncertainty were resolved in his favour at the trial. In *Las Vegas Sands Corp.* v. *Bhasin Infotech & Infrastructure Pvt. Ltd.*,[200] the Delhi High Court held that as the power to grant or refuse an *ad interim* injunction is discretionary, the Court must weigh one need against another and determine where the "balance of convenience lies". In *Wander Ltd.* v. *Antox India (P) Ltd.,*[201] the Apex Court has held that the interlocutory remedy is intended to preserve in *status quo*, the rights of parties which may appear on a *prima facie*. The Court also, in restraining a defendant from exercising what he considers his legal right but what the plaintiff would like to be prevented, puts into the scales, as a relevant consideration whether the defendant has yet to commence his enterprise or whether he has already been doing so in which latter case considerations somewhat different from those that apply to a case where the defendant is yet to commence his enterprise, are attracted. In the issue whether court should grant an interlocutory or not, the court must be satisfied that there is a serious issue to be tried. If there is, the need the court must weigh the claimant's and the defendant's needs in the balance of convenience.

Laddie J. in *Series 5 Software Ltd.* v. *Philip Clarke*[202] said that when deciding whether to grant interim relief, the court should bear the following matters in mind: (i) the grant of an interim injunction was a matter of discretion and depended on all the facts of the case;[203]

---

198. *See also, Lindsay International Pvt. Ltd.* v. *Laxmi Niwas Mittal*, (2017) 3 CALLT 214 (HC): 2018 (1) CHN (CAL) 732; *Sandeep Jaidka* v. *Mukesh Mittal*, 2014 (59) PTC 234 (Del): 211 (2014) DLT 401; *Bilcare Limited* v. *The Supreme Industries Ltd.*, 2007 (34) PTC 444 (Del): MIPR 2007 (2) 13; *Giridhari Balaram Radhakrishnani* v. *Mahisa Electronics*, ILR 1995 KAR 2010; *Dalpat Kumar* v. *Prahlad Singh*, AIR 1993 SC 276.
199. (2009) 10 SCC 388: [2009] 1 5SCR 403. *See also, M.P. Housing Board* v. *Anil Kumar Khiwani*, AIR 2005 SC 1863: (2005) 10 SCC 796; *Anand Prasad Agarwalla* v. *Tarkeshwar Prasad*, AIR 2001 SC 2367: (2001) 5 SCC 568. *Gujarat Bottling Co. Ltd.* v. *Coca Cola Co.*, AIR 1995 SC 2372.
200. MIPR 2012 (2) 359: 2012 (51) PTC 260 (Del). *See also, Mohammed Azharuddin* v. *G. Vivekanand*, 2018 (4) ALT 226: 2018(5)ALD51; *Eveready Industries India Ltd.* v. *Sanjay Chadha,* MIPR 2011 (1) 34: 2011 (45) PTC 22 (Del); *Pine Labs Pvt. Ltd.* v. *Gemalto Terminals India Pvt. Ltd.*, 2010 (42) PTC 229 (Del); *Unistal System Pvt. Ltd.* v. *Prodata Doctor Pvt. Ltd.*, (2010) ILR 1 Delhi 545: 2009 (41) PTC 626 (Del); *Mirabai Films Pvt. Ltd.* v. *Siti Cable Network,* 2003 (26) PTC 473 (Del); *Power Control Appliances* v. *Sumeet Machines Pvt. Ltd.* (1994) 2 SCC 448: [1994] 1 SCR 708.
201. 1990 (Supp) SCC 727: 1991 (11) PTC 1. *See also, SVF Entertainment Pvt. Ltd.* v. *Anupriyo Sengupta*, 2018(4) CHN (CAL) 620: (2018) 3 CALLT 115 (HC); *President D.A.V College Managing Committee* v. *Poonam Mahajan*, 2018 (2) JKJ 414 [NULL]; *Dabur India Limited* v. *Shree Baidyanath Ayurved Bhawan Pvt. Ltd.*, 193 (2012) DLT 558: 2012 (51) PTC 441 (Del); *Mr. Anil Gupta* v. *Mr. Kunal Dasgupta*, 2002(25) PTC 1 (Del); *Gujrat Bottling Co. Ltd.* v. *Coca Cola Co.*, AIR 1995 SC 2372: (1995) 5 SCC 545; *Power Control Appliances* v. *Sumeet Machines Pvt. Ltd.* (1994) 2 SCC 448: [1994] 1 SCR 708; *Rampal Singh* v. *Rias Ahmed Ansari* (1990) Supp. 727.
202. (1996) FSR 273.
203. *Glaxo Smithkline Consumer Healthcare Gmbh and Co. KG* v. *Amigo Brushes Private Limited*, 109 (2004) DLT 41: 2004 (28) PTC 1 (Del).

(ii) there were no fixed rules; (iii) the court should rarely attempt to resolve complex issues of disputed fact or law; (iv) major factors to be taken into account are: (a) the extent to which damages would be likely to be an adequate remedy and the ability of the other party to pay, (b) the balance of convenience, (c) the maintenance of the *status quo,* and (d) any clear view the court may reach as to the relative strength of the parties' cases.[204] The Delhi High Court in *Cable News Network L.P.* v. *Cam News Network Limited,*[205] has succinctly extrapolated the principles determining the grant of interlocutory relief as under:

1. Applications for interlocutory injunctions should be decided primarily on the balance of convenience, in the wider sense of that phrase, rather than on the relative strength of the parties substantive cases as they may then appear;
2. There is no rule of law that the court may consider the balance of convenience only if satisfied that the plaintiff has made out a *prima facie* case;[206]
3. The court must, however, satisfy itself that there is a serious question to be tried;
4. An interlocutory injunction should be refused if damages awarded at trial would adequately compensate the plaintiff and the defendant will be able to pay;
5. But should be granted if the plaintiff's cross-undertaking in damages would adequately compensate the defendant if successful at trial, and the plaintiff would be able to pay;
6. If, as will normally be the case, damages would not fully compensate either party, then the issue depends on the balance of convenience;[207]
7. If other factors are finely balanced, the *status quo* should be maintained;
8. If the balance of convenience favours neither party, then the relative strengths of the parties' respective cases on the merits may be taken into account if one case is disproportionately stronger.

An interim injunction prohibits the defendant from carrying out the allegedly infringing act until trial. Although an interim injunction precedes a finding of liability, its effect is frequently to bring the matter to a close. Issuance of injunction is always at the discretion of the court, therefore, it cannot be demanded as a matter of right. However, such issuance must be guided by some legal principles which cannot be arbitrary, vague and fanciful. Interlocutory injunction is granted under Rules 1 and 2 of Order 39 of the Code of Civil Procedure, 1908. Rule 1, Order 39 of the Code makes a provision for the issue and enforcement of temporary injunctions including *ex parte* orders in a pending suit. Injunction and more so the temporary is an extraordinary remedy and ought to be limited to those cases where it must be granted with a view to prevent a legal injury causing irreparable injury.[208] The applicant

204. *See also, EMAP Publications Ltd.* v. *Security Publications Ltd.* (1997) FSR 891; *Entec Pollution Control Ltd.* v. *Abacus Mouldings* (1992) FSR 332; *Security of State for the Home Development* v. *Central Broadcasting Ltd., The Times*, 28 January 1993.
205. MIPR 2008 (1) 113: 2008 (36) PTC 255 (Del).
206. *See, Advance Magazine Publishers Inc.* v. *Bombay Rayon Fashions Ltd.*, 2017 (72) PTC 124 (Del): 242 (2017) DLT 722.
207. *See, A.S. Hameed* v. *P. Maharajan*, 2019 (77) PTC 556 (Mad): (2019) 3 MLJ 52; *Varsha Polymers* v. *Vajra Plastics Industry*, 2018 (5) KHC 861; *Syed Mohamed Salahuddin* v. *Ahmed Abdulla Ahmed Al Ghurair*, (2018)6MLJ257: 2018 (5) CTC 291.
208. *See, Ashok Kumar* v. *State of Uttarakhand,* 2012 (12) SCALE 338: (2013) 3 SCC 366.

for an interlocutory injunction must satisfy the court that (i) it is a *prima facie* case of legal injury; (ii) it would cause irreparable injury and there is no other way of preventing it; and (iii) the balance of convenience rests in granting the same.[209] The Supreme Court in *Makers Development Services Pvt. Ltd.* v. *M.V. Industrial Research,*[210] observed:

> It is settled law that while passing an interim order of injunction under Rules 1 and 2, Order 39 of the Code, the Court is required to consider three basic principles, namely, (a) *prima facie* case, (b) balance of convenience and inconvenience, and (c) irreparable loss and injury. In addition to the above mentioned three basic principles, a court, while granting injunction must also take into consideration the conduct of the parties. It is also established law that the Court should not interfere only because the property is a very valuable one. Grant or refusal of injunction has serious consequences depending upon the nature thereof and in dealing with such matters the court must make all endeavours to protect the interest of the parties.[211]

The essentials are sound in principle and long established but in actual practice one would find them being ignored by the trial courts which seem to have fallen into the habit of granting *ex parte* temporary injunction for the mere asking after the suit has been filed.[212] The higher courts ought to be vigilant and take a strict view of the matter in the interest of justice. According to Rule 1, wherein a suit it is proved by affidavit or otherwise that: (a) any property in dispute in the suit is in danger of being wasted, damaged or alienated by a party to the suit or wrongfully sold in execution of a decree; and (b) the defendant threatens or intends to remove or dispose of his property with a view to defrauding his creditors; (c) the defendant threatens to disposes the plaintiff or otherwise causes injury to the plaintiff in relation to the property in dispute in the suit. The court may grant a temporary injunction to retrain such act or make such other order for the purpose of staying and preventing the wasting, damaging, alienation, sale, removal or disposition of the property or dispossession of the plaintiff or otherwise causing injury to the plaintiff in relation to any property in dispute in the suit as it thinks fit until the disposal of the suit or until further orders.

Section 55 of the Copyright Act, 1957 provides the remedy of injunction against the infringement of copyright. In *Wander Ltd.* v. *Antox India P. Ltd.*[213] a bench of three learned Judges in the Supreme Court considered the question of grant of interlocutory injunction under Order 39 Rule 1 Code of Civil Procedure in a case under Section 55 of the Copyright Act, 1957 and held that the prayer for grant of an interlocutory injunction is at a stage when the existence of the legal right asserted by the plaintiff and its alleged violation are both

---

209. *See, Ramrameshwari Devi* v. *Nirmala Devi,* 2011 (6) SCALE 677: (2011) 8 SCC 249; *Automobile Products India Ltd.* v. *Das John Peter,* [2010] 8 SCR 764: (2010) 12 SCC 593; *Narendra Kant* v. *Anuradha Kante,* (2010) 2 SCC 77: [2009] 16 SCR 491.

210. AIR 2012 SC 107: (2012) 1 SCC 735.

211. *See also, Pushpavathi N.* v. *Anand A.N.*, 2018(4) AKR 79; *Gorrepati Vijaya Lakshmi* v. *Gorrepati Prabhakara Lakshmi*, 2015 (6) ALD 208; *Sagar Chand Nayyar* v. *Manuj Nayyar*, 2014 (2) Shim LC 609; *Bheru Lal* v. *Addl. Distt. Judge*, AIR 2013 Raj 166: 2013 (4) CDR 1841 (Raj); *Makers Development Services* v. *M. Visvesvaraya Industrial Research*, AIR 2012 SC 437: (2012)1 SCC 735.

212. *See, Anil Kumar Singh* v. *Vijay Pal Singh, AIR 2017 SC 5587*: (2018) 12 SCC 584; *Ramnivas Vyas* v. *H. Srinivasa Bhati*, (2013) 15 SCC 198; *Allahabad Bank, Calcutta* v. *Radha Krishna Maity,* AIR 1999 SC 3426: (1999) 6 SCC 755; *Industrial Credit* v. *Grapco Industries Ltd.,* AIR 1999 SC 1975: (1999) 4 SCC 710.

213. 1990 (Supp) SCC 727: 1991 (11) PTC 1 (SC). *See also, Mahendra and Mahendra Paper Mills Ltd.* v. *Mahindra and Mahindra Ltd.*, AIR 2002 SC 117: (2002) 2 SCC 147.

contested and uncertain and remain uncertain till they are established at the trial on evidence. The court, at this stage, acts on certain well settled principles of administration of this form of interlocutory remedy which is both temporary and discretionary. Thus, in *Raja Pocket Books* v. *Radha Pocket Books*,[214] the plaintiff sought injunction against defendant for infringement of copyright. In this case, the plaintiff was a registered owner of copyright of its artistic snake like comic character "NAGRAJ" and its comic series closely resembling title and Nagraj like character "NAGESH". Defendant publishing comic series under similar title "Radha Comics" depicting similar snake like comic character with same artistic manner which infringed the copyright of the plaintiff as the plaintiff being the registered proprietor of artistic character "Nagraj" in the comic series. The Delhi High Court allowed plaintiff's application and restrained the defendant by way of granting injunction. In *Super Cassettes Industries Ltd.* v. *People Infocom Pvt. Ltd.*,[215] the plaintiff applied for grant of an injunction for restraining the defendant from infringing copyright rights of plaintiff. It was held that court is required to consider *prima facie* case, balance of convenience and irreparable loss to other parties to the suit while deciding an application for grant of an injunction unlike a mandamus which is a strict legal remedy in law.[216]

It is interesting to note that in *Novartis AG* v. *Mehar Pharma*,[217] the Bombay High Court refused to grant interim injunction relying on the decision of the Allahabad High Court in *Mohd. Abdul Karim* v. *Mohd. Yasin*,[218] to the effect that "an interlocutory injunction will not normally be granted where damages will provide an adequate remedy should the claim succeed". The court in this case criticised the Madras High Court[219] in granting interim injunction in a similar situation for not correctly appreciating and applying the settled relating to interim injunction.[220] Another interesting and welcome approach taken by the judiciary in this case is the concern shown on the public interest in deciding cases. The Bombay High Court in *N.T. Raghunathan* v. *All India Reporter*,[221] and the Delhi High Court in *Penguin Book Ltd.* v. *India Book Distributors*,[222] laid down the process through which the Court should go before granting an interlocutory or interim injunction:

1. Is there a serious issue to be tried? If there is not, no injunction will be issued. If there is, then the court moves to the second question;
2. If the plaintiff can be adequately compensated by damages at trial no injunction will be issued. If the defendant can be adequately compensated at trial by the plaintiff's undertaking to pay the defendant his damages, then an injunction should be ordered.
3. If there is no clear answer to either question, then the court should attempt to determine whether the defendant would suffer greater inconvenience if the injunction

214. 1997 (40) DRJ 791.
215. 2007 (34) PTC 273 (Del).
216. *See*, *Shuddhananda Yoga Samaj* v. *Rajeswari Book Shop*, 2018 (75) PTC 25 (Mad): 218 (4) CTC 276.
217. (2005) 30 PTC 160 (Bom.).
218. AIR 1934 All 789 (DB).
219. *Novartis AG* v. *Adarsh Pharma* (2004) (3) CTC 95: (2004) (29) PTC 108 (Mad.).
220. *Novartis AG* v. *Mehar Pharma* (2005) 30 PTC 160 (Bom.): (2005) (3) Bom CR 191.
221. AIR 1971 Bom. 48.
222. AIR 1985 Delhi 29: 26 (1984) DLT 316.

were granted, or the plaintiff if it is not granted. This is known as the balance, of convenience test.

4. It is only if the "balance of convenience" test does not resolve the matter that the court should look at the relative strength of the parties' case as revealed by their affidavit evidence.

Thus, in *UTV Software Communication Ltd.* v. *1337X*,[223] the Delhi High Court held that the Section 55 of the Copyright Act provides civil remedies to the rights holders which includes entitlement to an injunction order on approaching the Court. Consequently, the Court has ample inherent powers to mould the relief to ensure that the plaintiffs' rights as copyright owners are adequately protected.

Anton Piller Order: An Ex Parte Interlocutory or Interim Injunction

Anton Piller orders (*ex parte ad* interim order) became part of the Indian intellectual property rights jurisprudence after the entry into force of the Agreement on Trade Related Aspects of Intellectual Property Rights (TRIPS Agreement). Concrete evidence is vital to substantiate one's claim and obtain relief in any case, including those revolving round infringement of intellectual property rights. To prevent situations where the defendants might destroy the evidences on being aware of the impending legal actions, the English Courts devised a new strategy—an *ex parte* interlocutory injunction which enables the plaintiffs' solicitors to enter the defendants' premises and obtain the offending materials or documents to produce them at the trial—called the *Anton Piller* order.[224]

The *Anton Piller* order is a particularly dramatic example of the courts' recent adaptation of the injunction to provide remedies for plaintiffs in new situations. However, due to its enormous power, if not used sparingly, the *Anton Piller* order can be abused to a large extent. The application of *Anton Piller* order in India is still in nascent stage and lot many questions are still left unanswered. In the following, pages an attempt has been made to discuss the evolution, scope and ambit of *Anton Piller* order, its position in Trademarks law, Code of Civil Procedure and Copyright law, its reasonableness and proper guidelines for application as well as its binding nature.[225]

Anton Piller Order: The Evolution

The first use of *Anton Piller order* was made by Templemen J. in *EMI* v. *Pandit*,[226] to prevent the offending evidences from being destroyed. However, it was only after the case of *Anton Piller K.G.* v. *Manufacturing Processes Ltd.*,[227] that it gained recognition and popularity.

---

223. 2019 (78) PTC 375 (Del).

224. *See*, J.K. Das, "New Dimensions of Intellectual Property Rights in India" 3(2) *Pragyaan: Journal of Law* (2013) pp. 11–33 at p. 26.

225. *See*, *Foundry Visionmongers* v. *Parish Tekriwal*, 2017 (69) PTC 360 (Bom); *Mohit Bhargava* v. *Bharatbhushan Bhargava*, AIR 2007 SC 1717: (2007) 4 SCC 795; *Ganesan* v. *M. Sundararaja Thevar*, (2000) 1 MLJ 121: 2000 (1) CTC 545.

226. (1975) 1 All ER 481.

227. (1976) 1 All ER 776: (1976) Ch. 55: (1976) RPC 719 (In short "*Anton Piller* order").

The purpose of the order was explained in *Yousuf* v. *Salamon*,[228] where Lord Denning observed that the order intends to prevent the danger of destruction of evidence.[229]

Thus, in England, the High Court has jurisdiction on an application made to the court by a plaintiff *ex parte* and in *camera* to make a mandatory order requiring a defendant to permit the plaintiff and his representative to enter the defendant's premises, as specified in the order, to inspect articles and documents relevant to the proceedings and to remove them or take copies of them and even to take proceeds of the infringing articles.[230] This form of an order made under the court's inherent jurisdiction by Lord Denning in *Anton Piller K.G.* v. *Manufacturing Processes Ltd.*,[231] has received recognition in the TRIPS Agreement (Paragraph 2 of Article 50). The order is not a search warrant. It has repeatedly been clarified by Lord Denning in *Anton Piller K.G.* that the order is not a research warrant; the order only authorises an inspection by permission of the defendant. Entry without his permission would be a trespass. The defendant is, however, ordered by the court in *personam* to give his permission with the result that, if he does not do so, he is in contempt of court, but the plaintiff is still not entitled to enter in the absence of permission.

The *Anton Piller* order is only to be made in the most extreme circumstances for the form of the order is drastic and its aftereffects are far reaching. It involves serious inroads on the principles of personal freedom, such as presumption of innocence, the right not to be condemned unheard, protection against arbitrary searches and seizure, and privacy. It is at the extremity of the court's powers and is frequently accompanied by a *Mareva Injunction*[232] which prevents a defendant from taking action, such as disposal of assets, designed to frustrate subsequent orders of the court in favour of the plaintiff. As in the case of *Anton Piller* orders, there are now standard forms of *Mareva Injunction* for use in the Queen's bench and Chancery divisions of the High Courts. The combination of the *Anton Piller* order and *Mareva Injunction* has the effect of destroying a defendant's business without the defendant being in a position to set the order aside before it is executed.[233] They have become the ultimate weapons to combat copyright piracy. The justification for the exercise of this exceptional jurisdiction is that on the facts of the particular case, it is essential that the plaintiff should have inspection, so that justice can be done between the parties where there is a grave danger, that if a defendant is forewarned, he may destroy evidence of vital importance in the litigation, or conceal from the court and from the plaintiff such evidence, or that the evidence may be lost or taken out of the jurisdiction, depriving the plaintiff of his remedy and thereby defeating the ends of justice. The following three conditions must be satisfied before the court will make an order:

---

228. (1980) 3 All ER 405 at p. 406.
229. *See*, Souvik Bhadra and Arka Majumdar, "Anton Piller Order in UK and Its Possible Implications in India." 12 *Journal of Intellectual Property Rights* (2007) pp. 488–426; Frank Carrigan, "The Political Economy of Anton Filler Orders," 11 *Australian Journal of Law and Society* (1995) pp. 33–65; J. Berryman, "Anton Piller Orders: A Canadian Common Law Approach," 34(1) *University of Toronto Law Journal* (1984) pp. 1–25.
230. *C.B.S. United Kingdom Ltd.* v. *Lambert and Another* (1983) Ch. 37.
231. (1976) 1 All ER 776: (1976) Ch. 55: (1976) RPC 719 (In short "*Anton Piller* order").
232. *Mareva Compania Naviera* v. *International Bulk Carriers, SA* (1980) 1 All ER 213.
233. *See*, Jonathon Rayner James and Gillian Davies (Ed.), *Copinger and Skone James on Copyright* (Vol. 1), Sweet and Maxwell, London (1999) at p. 1040.

(i) The plaintiff must show that there is an extremely strong *prima facie* case against the respondent.

(ii) The damage, potential or actual, must be very serious for the applicant.

(iii) There must be clear evidence that the respondents have in their possession relevant documents or things and that there is a real possibility that they may destroy such material before an *inter partes* application can be made on notice.[234]

The court proceeds on the basis that the overwhelming majority of people will comply with its order as to production and delivery of documents. In order to safeguard the defendant, the order expressly limits the persons who are entitled to inspect, defines the premises which can be inspected and specifies the purposes for which the inspection is allowed. For example, the order provides that it is to be served and carried out in the presence of a supervisory solicitor who is experienced in the working of *Anton Piller* order and who is wholly independent of the plaintiff and his solicitor. It is the supervising solicitor's duty to ensure that the order is carried out with meticulous care and he can give reliable evidence on what happens on execution of the order.[235] He should identify the other representatives of the plaintiff and his solicitors to the defendant and must give the defendant an opportunity of considering the order, consulting his own solicitor and applying to the court to vary or discharge the order. He should prepare a full report on what took place and send a copy to the plaintiff's solicitors and to the judge who made the order for the purposes of the court file. Further safeguards for the defendants are set out in the practice directions and can be seen in the body of the draft order prescribed by the court.

Prior to the new form of *Anton Piller* order, the position was that while the order stood, a defendant who refused access to his premises was in default of the order and ran the risk of committal to prison, even if his refusal of consent was his intention to apply to have the order discharged.[236] However, if that party succeeded in getting the order discharged, it was unlikely that he would be held guilty for any breach of the order while it subsisted. The new form of order now provides for the position to be held while an application is made for discharge of variation and a defendant who simply refuses access without availing himself of those provisions is likely to face severe penalties for contempt, even if he manages to persuade the court that he intended to apply to set aside the order. The court may be persuaded to discharge an *Anton Piller* order on the grounds of non-disclosure and order costs to be awarded on an indemnity basis with immediate taxation. The court will be within its right to consider the following, amongst other, relevant factors, while considering an application for discharge: (i) Whether an injustice has been caused to the defendant; (ii) In considering the question the court should have regard to all the evidence on the application to discharge, including the result of the execution of the orders.[237] The TRIPS Agreement contains a similar provision to *Anton Piller* order under Paragraph 1 and 2 of Article 50.

---

234. *Anton Piller K.G.* v. *Manufacturing Processes Limited* (1976) Ch. 55: (1976) RPC 719.
235. *Ibid.*
236. *Ibid.*
237. *Ibid.*

Anton Piller Order: Scope and Ambit

According to the Paragraph 2 of Article 50 of the TRIPS Agreement, the judicial authorities must be empowered, where appropriate, to adopt provisional measures without the defendant being heard (*inaudita altera perte*), in particular where delay is likely to cause irreparable damage to the right holder or where there is a demonstrable risk of evidence being destroyed. The Paragraph 2 of Article 50 of the TRIPS Agreement reads Thus:

> "The judicial authorities shall have the authority to adopt provisional measures inaudita altera parte where appropriate, in particular where any delay is likely to cause irreparable harm to the right holder, or where there is a demonstrable risk of evidence being destroyed."

Besides this, the Paragraph 1 of Article 50 of the TRIPS Agreement provides that "The judicial authorities shall have the authority to order prompt and effective provisional measures: (a) to prevent an infringement of any intellectual property right from occurring, and in particular to prevent the entry into the channels of commerce in their jurisdiction of goods, including imported goods immediately after customs clearance; (b) to preserve relevant evidence in regard to the alleged infringement."[238] These Paragraphs 1 and 2 of Article 50 is similar to *Anton Piller* order followed in the United Kingdom and other commonwealth countries, whose purpose is to preserve the evidence by preventing the destruction or concealment of evidence by an alleged wrong doer. The owners of the protected works in India too, more particularly in cinematograph films and sound recordings, have been seeking orders similar to *Anton Piller* orders against proprietors in "sound recordings", "cinematograph films" and "video recordings". In view of rampant video and record piracy in India, it is necessary to statutorily provide for these powerful procedural weapons in the armoury for copyright protection. The *Anton Piller* order is similar to the *ex parte* interlocutory order/injunction to take an inventory of the articles, etc. passed in an ordinary suit.

In *Gujarat Bottling Co. Ltd.* v. *Coca Cola Company*,[239] the Supreme Court held that the grant of an interlocutory injunction during the pendency of legal proceedings is a matter requiring the exercise of discretion of the court. While exercising the discretion the court applies the following tests: (i) whether the plaintiff has a *prima facie* case; (ii) whether the balance of convenience is in favour of the plaintiff; and (iii) whether the plaintiff would suffer an irreparable injury if his request for an interlocutory injunction were disallowed. It further held that the decision of whether to grant an interlocutory injunction should be taken at a time when the existence of the legal right assailed by the plaintiff and its alleged violation is contested and uncertain. Relief by way of interlocutory injunction is granted to the plaintiff in order to mitigate the risk of injustice during the period before the uncertainty can be resolved (i.e., at the full hearing). The court held that:

---

238. This provision has been applied by the Delhi High Court in *Samsung Electronics Company Ltd.* v. *G. Choudhary*, 2006 (33) PTC 425 (Del): 136 (2007) DLT 605.

239. AIR 1995 SC 2372: (1995) 5 SCC 545. *See also*, *Breach Candy Swimming Bath Trust* v. *Dipesh Mehta*, 2015 (6) ABR 709; *Zenit Mataplast P. Ltd.* v. *State of Maharashtra and Ors*., 2009 (12) SCALE 432: (2009) 10 SCC 388; *M. Gurudas* v. *Rasaranjan*, AIR 2006 SC 3275: 2006 (9) SCALE 275; *Ramdev Food Products Pvt. Ltd.* v. *Arvindbhai Rambhai Patel and Ors.*, AIR 2006 SC 3304: (2006) 8 SCC 726; *M.P. Housing Board* v. *Anil Kumar Khiwani*, AIR 2005 SC 1863: (2005) 10 SCC 796; *M.P. Housing Board* v. *Anil Kumar Khiwani*, AIR 2005 SC 1863: (2005) 10 SCC 796; *Hindustan Petroleum Corporation Ltd.* v. *Sri Sriman Narayan*, AIR 2002 SC 2598: (2002) 5 SCC 760.

> The object of the interlocutory injunction is to protect the plaintiff against injury by violation of his right for which he could not be adequately compensated in damages recoverable in the action if the uncertainty were resolved in his favour at the trial. The need for such protection has, however, to be weighed against the corresponding need of the defendant to be protected against injury resulting from his having been prevented from exercising his own legal rights for which he could not be adequately compensated. The court must weigh one need against another and determine where the 'balance of convenience' lies. In order to protect the defendant while granting an interlocutory injunction in his favour the court can require the plaintiff to furnish an undertaking so that the defendant can be adequately compensated if the uncertainty were resolved in his favour at the trial.[240]

The court passes *ex parte* interlocutory injunction in the form of *Anton Piller* orders in suitable cases.[241] Proceeding on the same lines, the Kerela High Court in *National Garments* v. *National Apparels*[242] held that for an interlocutory injunction to restrain the defendant, until the hearing of the action, the principle applicable is slightly different from the principle applicable in ordinary cases. For a temporary order in an action for passing off, the plaintiff need not in general show a strong *prima facie* case. However, the *prima facie* case that is required to be shown must be something more than a case that will avoid the action being struck out as frivolous or vexatious. Generally stated "even if the chance of success at the trial are only 20 per cent", the interim relief sought for is required to be granted. There is another reason for the grant of the interlocutory injunction under such circumstances. Such an order would stop the infringement without delay. Not only have that from experience it is cleared that a successful motion for interlocutory injunction "normally puts an end to the litigation and the infringement, with a great saving in expense compared with a full trial" and that is the reason why the law insists upon a hearing of such a motion in every case. It is also clear from the treatise of *Kerly*[243] that:

> in extremely urgent cases an *ex parte* injunction may be obtained before the full hearing of the motion or an *Anton Piller* order, for inspection of the defendant's premises without prior warning and discovery of his records, may be obtainable.

In *Buegrus Europe Limited* v. *Vwean Industries Eng. Co.,*[244] the Calcutta High Court examined the scope and validity of the *Anton Piller*[245] type *ex parte* orders issued in India. The plaintiff filed a suit for infringement of the copyright in his artistic design and requested for *ex parte* temporary injunction and recovery of records. This was refused by the lower court and on appeal the single bench of the High Court passed an interim *ex parte* injunction. The

240. *See, Breach Candy Swimming Bath Trust* v. *Dipesh Mehta*, 2015 (6) ABR 709; *State of Assam* v. *Barak Upatyaka D.U. Karmachari Sanstha*, AIR 2009 SC 2249: (2009) 5 SCC 694; *Adhunik Steels Ltd.* v. *Orissa Manganese and Minerals Pvt. Ltd.*, AIR 2007 SC 2563: (2007) 7 SCC 125; *Mahendra & Mahendra Paper Mills Ltd.* v. *Mahindra & Mahindra Ltd.*, AIR 2002 SC 117: (2002) 2 SCC 147; *Colgate Palmolive (India) Ltd.* v. *Hindustan Lever Ltd.*, AIR 1999 SC 3105: (1999) 7 SCC 1; *Power Control Appliances* v. *Sumeet Machines Pvt. Ltd.*, 1994 (1) SCALE 446: (1994) 2 SCC 448.
241. *Ganesan* v. *M. Sundararaja Thevar*, 2000 (1) CTC 545: (2000) 1 MLJ 121.
242. AIR 1990 Ker 119.
243. David Kitchn (Ed.), *Kerly's Law of Trademarks and Trade Names*, Sweet and Maxwell, London (2011) at paras. 15–66.
244. 2005 (1) CHN 106: 2005 (30) PTC 279 (Cal) 2005. *See also, CISOCO Technologies* v. *Shrikanth,* 2005 (31) PTC 538 (Del.).
245. *Anton Piller KG* v. *Manufacturing Process Ltd.* (1976) Ch. 55: (1976) RPC 719.

court also appointed a special officer of the court authorising him to enter into the premises of the defendant as mentioned in the cause title and any other premises within the power and control of the defendant and to inspect the same and seize all goods, papers, documents, challans and invoices showing orders of the products. The period of the order was for 14 days and the court directed the plaintiff to issue notice to the defendant. It was contended by the defendant that the order was obtained by misrepresentation since the design was registered and the cancellation proceedings is pending. It was also contended that the design was in practice for a period of ten years. According to the defendant as per Section 15 of the Copyright Act, once the design was registered there was no protection for the same under the Copyright Act and in this context the order of search issued for violation of copyright needed to be cancelled. The plaintiff relied on *Anton Piller* orders and argued for the continuation of the orders. After examining various cases[246] based on *Anton Piller* orders the court concluded:

> Going by the aforesaid well-settled principles this court holds that there was lack of *bona fides* and good faith in the pleadings on the basis of which an *ex parte* order of injunction on the line of *Anton Piller* was obtained from this Court. From the discussion made in the earlier part of this judgement it is clear that utmost good faith of the plaintiff is the condition precedent from granting an injunction on the lines of *Anton Piller*. Admittedly good faith on the part of the plaintiff is lacking. The Court at an *ex parte* stage accepted the pleading to be true and correct and passed the order. But if there had been a full disclosure of facts, the Court might not have passed the order. That the pendency of cancellation is a relevant fact and cannot possibly be disputed.[247]

The court refused the injunction and directed the plaintiff to pay a cost to the Calcutta High Court Legal Services Authority. This case clearly indicates the possibility of the abuse of the *Anton Piller* type orders in India. It is important to note that in England the courts had a tough time and finally the legislature intervene to regulate the abuse of the order by the plaintiff. In the context of increasing demand to use *Anton Piller* type orders in India, it is important that the Indian courts keep these developments in mind and issue orders only in clear cases that too with sufficient preconditions to protect the interest of the defendants so that abuse of the order could be limited. However, the High Court finds that in the instant case from the report of Special Officer it is clear that the defendant after taking legal advice allowed inspection to some extent and has not complained of any non-cooperation on the part of the defendant. On the other hand, the Special Officer said that the parties cooperated with him. On a proper appreciation of the ratio in *Anton Piller* order, the High Court finds that such an order can be passed in the following five situations: (i) where the plaintiff has an extremely strong *prima facie* case; (ii) where the actual potential damage of the plaintiff is very serious; (iii) where it was clear that the defendant possessed vital evidence; (iv) there was a real possibility the defendant might destroy or dispose of such material so as to defeat the ends of justice; (v) the purpose of *Anton Pillor* order is the preservation of evidence.

Before passing an *Anton Piller* order, some safeguards are also to overlook like asking the plaintiff to give an undertaking in damages in case of plaintiff is wrong if the defendant suffers damage as a result of execution of the order. However, before the court will grant an *Anton Piller* order, the plaintiff must be able to convince the Court that he has a strong case

246. *Systematic Ltd.* v. *London Computer Centre Ltd.* (1983) F.S.R. 313. *See also*, *British North Rop Ltd.* v. *Blackburn Ltd.* (1974) RPC 57 was referred to.

247. *Buergrus Europe Limited* v. *Vwean Industries Engg. Co.*, 2005 (1) CHN 106: 2005 (30) PTC 279 (Cal).

and that the order is indeed essential to the ends of justice. In *Mohit Bhargava* v. *Bharat Bhushan Bhargava*,[248] there were two orders dated 19-3-2003 and 7-7-2003. By order dated 19-3-2003 what the executing court did was, to direct a third party, who had subsequently acceded to the jurisdiction of the executing court. It is seen that the third person submitted to the jurisdiction of the court and surrendered the documents in his possession to the executing court and prayed to that court that he be relieved from the responsibility of managing the property in the circumstances stated by him in his application. It was in that context that the executing court passed another order dated 7-7-2003 that the documents produced by the third party are kept in safe custody of the court. The Supreme Court further observed:

> These two orders are certainly within the jurisdiction of the court which passed the decree since they are only orders of restraint being issued to a person from handing over a property in his possession to the judgment debtor along with the concerned documents and keeping the documents in safe custody. They are in the nature of a "*Freezing Order*"[249] or a "*Mareva Injunction*"[250] and an order akin to an "*Anton Piller Order*"[251] orders that can be issued even if the property or the person concerned is outside the jurisdiction of the court.

Refreshingly, the Delhi High Court has been a bastion of intellectual property protection and has built up a strong *ex parte* philosophy. It has granted *Anton Piller* orders under which court commissioners have been appointed to search and seize infringing goods such as computers and CDs. It has also extended *John Doe* or roving orders to counterfeit cigarettes and granted *Mareva* injunctions. The Delhi High Court in *Hindustan Pencils (P) Ltd.* v. *India Stationery Products Co.*,[252] observed that in cases involving infringement of intellectual property rights, considerable importance is attached to the decision of the application for the grant of interim relief. Filing of such an application has been commented upon by the Court in this case as follows: "The plaintiff in an infringement or 'passing-off' action may move, as soon as the action is commenced, for an interlocutor in junction to restrain the defendant, until the hearing of the action or further order, from continuing or committing the infringement or deceptive conduct of which he complains. Quite apart from the advantages of stopping the Infringement without delay, experience shows that a successful motion for interlocutory injunction normally puts an end—to the litigation and the infringement with a great saving in expense compared with a full trial. Accordingly such a motion should be considered in every case—and accordingly, proprietors of trademarks should make it a rule to take action upon every instance of infringement with the necessary speed to enable such a motion to be launched. In extremely urgent cases an *ex parte* injunction may be obtained before the full hearing of the emption or an *Anton Piller* order for inspection the defendant's premises without prior warning and discovery of his records, may be obtainable.

---

248. AIR 2007 SC 1717: (2007) 4 SCC 795. *See also*, *Indian Oil Corporation Ltd.* v. *Iranian Offshore Engineering and Construction Company*, MANU/DE/2390/2009; *M.V. Al Quamar* v. *Tsavliris Salvage*, AIR 2000 SC 2826: (2000) 8 SCC 278; *Sundaram Finance Ltd.* v. *NEPC India Ltd.*, AIR 1999 SC 565: (1999) 2 SCC 479; *Firm Madanlal Roshanlal Mahajan* v. *Hukumchand Mills Ltd.*, AIR 1967 SC 1030: (1967) 1 SCR 105.
249. *See*, *Vijay Mallya* v. *State Bank of India*, AIR 2019 Kant 23: 2019 (1) Kar LJ 195; *Shantai Industries Limited* v. *Union of India*, 2018 [17] G.S.T.L. 198.
250. *See*, *SE Investments Ltd.* v. *Arch Pharmalabs Ltd.*, 2018 (1) ALLMR 158: 2017 (4) ABR 317.
251. *See*, *Foundry Visionmongers* v. *Parish Tekriwal*, 2017 (69) PTC 360 (Bom).
252. AIR 1990 Delhi 19: 38 (1989) DLT 54.

Anton Piller Order in Trademarks Law

The Indian Trademarks Act, 1999 contains remedy similar to *Anton Piller* order. However, it is unfortunate to mention that Indian Courts hardly refer or interpret these provisions while issuing orders for search and seizure of the materials. As discussed above the *Anton Piller* order is a pre-judgment order which directs a defendant to permit representatives of the plaintiff to the defendant's premises without alerting him. This is for the purpose of searching for evidence which is vital to the plaintiff's case where there is a danger that the evidence will be destroyed. Though it was insisted by courts that the order was introduced to deal with exceptional and emergency cases within few years of its conception the order was in daily use.[253] It is important to note that Section 135(2) of the Trademarks Act, 1999 envisages *Anton Piller* like remedy. The Section 135(2) of the Trademarks Act, 1999 read:

> The order of injunction under sub-section (1) may include an *ex parte* injunction or any interlocutory order for any of the following matters, namely: (a) for discovery of documents; (b) preserving of infringing goods, documents or other evidence which are related to the subject-matter of the suit; (c) restraining the defendant from disposing of or dealing with his assets in a manner which may adversely affect plaintiff's ability to recover damages, costs or other pecuniary remedies which may be finally awarded to the plaintiff.

Anton Piller Order and Code of Civil Procedure

Anton Piller order has also provides a civil remedy of general application to plaintiffs who wish to acquire further and better evidence. It enabled the plaintiff to search and seize the property of a defendant and freeze his assets until judgment. Rule 7, Order 39 of the Indian Code of Civil Procedure (CPC), 1908 could be interpreted and be used to achieve the same purpose in a meaningful way. The Rule 7, Order 39, CPC read:

> (1) The court may, on the application of any party to a suit, and on such terms as it thinks fit—(a) make an order for the detention, preservation or inspection of any property which is the subject-matter of such suit, or as to which any question may arise therein; (b) for all or any of the purposes aforesaid authorize any person to enter upon or into any land or building in the possession of any other party to such suit; and (c) for all or any of the purposes aforesaid authorize any samples to be taken, or any observation to be made or experiment to be tried, which may seem necessary or experiment for the purpose of obtaining full information or evidence. (2) The provisions as to execution of process shall apply *mutatis mutandis,* to persons authorize to enter under this rule.

Thus under the Rule 7, Order 39, CPC court can order for detention, preservation or inspection of any property which is the subject-matter of such suit, or as to which any question may arise therein. For that purpose, it can authorize any person to enter upon or into any land or building in the possession of any other party to such suit or authorize any samples to be taken or observation to be made or experiment to be tried for the purpose of obtaining full information.[254] Rule 8, Order 39, CPC provides that before making such orders, the court shall give notice to the opposite party except where it appears that the object of making such orders would be defeated by the delay. According to Rule 8, Order 39, CPC where the suit land is liable to payment of revenue to government or a tenure liable to sale and the party in

253. *E.M.I. Ltd.* v. *Pandit* (1975) 1 WLR 302.
254. *See,* Jatindra Kumar Das, *Code of Civil Procedure* (PHI Learning Private Limited, Delhi, 2014).

possession of such land or tenure neglects to pay revenue or rent, any other party to the suit claiming an interest in such land or tenure may, on payment of the revenue or rent due, be put in immediate possession of the property. The court may award in the decree, the amount so paid with interest thereon against the defaulter. Where the subject-matter of a suit is money or some other thing capable of delivery and a party to a suit admits that he holds such money or thing as a trustee for another party or that it belongs or is due to that party, the court may order it to be deposited in court or delivered to that party with or without security.[255]

Is Search and Seizure by an Anton Piller Order Unreasonable?

A question often arises: Whether search and seizure by an *Anton Piller* order is unreasonable? The interrelationship between the "right against self-incrimination"[256] and the "right to fair trial"[257] has been recognised in most jurisdictions as well as international human rights instruments. For example, the Constitution of the United States of American incorporates the "privilege against self-incrimination" in the text of its Fifth Amendment. The meaning and scope of this privilege has been judicially moulded by recognising it's interrelationship with other constitutional rights such as the protection against "unreasonable search and seizure" (Fourth amendment) and the guarantee of "due process of law" (Fourteenth amendment).[258] The Canadian Charter of Rights and Freedoms declares: "Everyone has the right to be secure against unreasonable search and seizure." The New Zealand Bill of Rights declares in Section 21 that "everyone has the right to be secure against unreasonable search or seizure, whether of the person, property or correspondence or otherwise".[259] In the International Covenant on Civil and Political Rights (ICCPR), Article 14(3)(g) enumerates the minimum guarantees that are to be accorded during a trial and states that everyone has a right not to be compelled to testify against himself or to confess guilt. In the European Convention for the Protection of Human Rights and Fundamental Freedoms, Article 6(1) states that every person charged with an offence has a right to a fair trial and Article 6(2) provides that "Everybody charged with a criminal offence shall be presumed innocent until proved guilty according to law."

The Supreme Court in *Smt. Selvi* v. *State of Karnataka,*[260] observed that the guarantee of "presumption of innocence" bears a direct link to the "right against self-incrimination"

---

255. Rule 10, Order 39, CPC. *See also, Karam Kapahi* v. *Lal Chand Public Charitable Trust* (2010) 4 SCC 753: 2010 (4) UJ 1783 (SC); *Surya Dev Rai* v. *Ram Chander Rai*, AIR 2003 SC 3044: (2003) 6 SCC 675; *Sushila Devi* v. *Ramanand Prasad*, AIR 1976 SC 117: (1976) 1 SCC 361.
256. *See, Ashish Jain* v. *Makrand Singh*, AIR 2019 SC 546: (2019) 3 SCC 770; *Selvi* v. *State of Karnataka*, AIR 2010 SC 1974: (2010) 7 SCC 263; *Standard Chartered Bank and Ors.* v. *Directorate of Enforcement and Ors.*, AIR 2006 SC 1301: (2006) 4 SCC 278; *State (N.C.T. of Delhi)* v. *Navjot Sandhu*, AIR 2005 SC 3820: (2005) 11 SCC 600; *Nandini Satpathy* v. *P.L. Dani*, AIR 1978 SC 1025: (1978) 2 SCC 424.
257. *See, Accused 'X'* v. *State of Maharashtra*, 2019 (3) RCR (Criminal) 18: 2019 (6) SCALE 407; *Mazdoor Kisan Shakti Sangathan* v. *The Union of India*, AIR 2018 SC 3476: 2018 (10) SCJ 685; *Asha Ranjan* v. *State of Bihar*, AIR 2017 SC 1079: (2017) 4 SCC 397; *G. Someshwar Rao* v. *Samineni Nageshwar Rao*, 2009 (10) SCALE 268: (2009) 14 SCC 677; *T. Nagappa* v. *Y.R. Muralidhar*, AIR 2008 SC 2010: 2008 (6) SCALE 642; *Bhajan Lal, Chief Minister, Haryana* v. *Jindal Strips Ltd.*, 1994 (3) SCALE 703: (1994) 6 SCC 19; *Varkey Joseph* v. *State of Kerala*, AIR 1993 SC 1892: 1993 (2) SCALE 709.
258. *State (N.C.T. of Delhi)* v. *Navjot Sandhu*, AIR 2005 SC 3820: (2005) 11 SCC 600.
259. *Distt. Registrar and Collector, Hyderabad* v. *Canara Bank*, AIR 2005 SC 186: (2005) 1 SCC 496.
260. AIR 2010 SC 1974: (2010) 7 SCC 263.

since compelling the accused person to testify would place the burden of proving innocence on the accused instead of requiring the prosecution to prove guilt. In the Indian context, Article 20(3) of the Constitution of India should be construed with due regard for the inter-relationship between rights, since this approach was recognised in *Maneka Gandhi's*[261] case. Hence, we must examine the "right against self-incrimination" in respect of its relationship with the multiple dimensions of "personal liberty" under Article 21 of the Constitution of India, which include guarantees such as the "right to fair trial" and "substantive due process".[262] It must also be emphasised that Articles 20 and 21 have a non-derogable status within Part III of the Constitution of India because the Constitution (Fourty-Fourth Amendment) Act, 1978 mandated that the right to move any court for the enforcement of these rights cannot be suspended even during the operation of a proclamation of emergency.

The earliest case in India to deal with "privacy" and "search and seizure" was *M.P. Sharma* v. *Satish Chandra,*[263] in the context of Article 19(1)(f) and Article 20(3) of the Constitution of India. The contention that search and seizure violated Article 19(1)(f) was rejected, the Court holding that a mere search by itself did not affect any right to property, and though seizure affected it, such effect was only temporary and was a reasonable restriction on the right. The question whether search warrants for the seizure of documents from the accused were unconstitutional was not gone into. The Court, after referring to American authorities, observed that in, because of the language in the Fourth Amendment of the Constitution, there was a distinction between legal and illegal searches and seizures and that such a distinction need not be imported into our Constitution. The Court opined that a search warrant was addressed to an officer and not to the accused and did not violate Article 20(3) of the Constitution of India. However, the law as to "privacy" was developed in latter cases by spelling it out from the right to freedom of speech and expression in Article 19(1)(a) and the right to "life" in Article 21 of the Constitution of India.

In *Kharak Singh* v. *State of UP*,[264] the Supreme Court held that though the Constitution of India did not refer to the right to privacy expressly, still it can be traced from the right to "life" in Article 21. In *Govind* v. *State of Madhya Pradesh,*[265] Mathew, J. developed the law as to privacy. In this case, the learned Judge referred to *Griswold* v. *Connecticut*[266] where Douglas, J. referred to the theory of penumbras and peripheral rights and had stated that

261. *Maneka Gandhi* v. *Union of India*, AIR 1978 SC 597: (1978) 1 SCC 248.
262. *See, Joseph Shine* v. *Union of India*, AIR 2018 SC 4898: (2019) 3 SCC 39; *Rajbala* v. *State of Haryana*, AIR 2016 SC 33: (2016) 2 SCC 445; *Siddharam Satlingappa Mhetre* v. *State of Maharashtra and Ors.*, AIR 2011 SC 312: (2011) 1 SCC 694; *V. Laxminarasamm* v. *A. Yadaiah*, 2009 (3) SCALE 685: (2009) 12 SCC 544; *Dalmia Cement (Bharat) Ltd.* v. *Union of India and Ors.*, 1996 (4) SCALE 14: (1996) 10 SCC 104; *Charan Lal Sahu* v. *Union of India*, AIR 1990 SC 1480: (1990) 1 SCC 613; *Tinsukhia Electric Supply Co. Ltd.* v. *State of Assam*, AIR 1990 SC 123: (1989) 3 SCC 709; *Charan Lal Sahu* v. *Union of India,* AIR 1990 SC 1480: (1990) 1 SCC 613.
263. AIR 1954 SC 300: (1954) 1SCR 1077. *See also*, *State of Himachal Pradesh* v. *Pawan Kumar*, AIR 2005 SC 2265: (2005) 4 SCC 350; *State and Ors.* v. *N.M.T. Joy Immaculate*, AIR 2004 SC 2282: (2004) 5 SCC 729; *Sharda* v. *Dharampal*, AIR 2003 SC 3450: (2003) 4 SCC 493; *State of Punjab* v. *Baldev Singh,* AIR 1999 SC 2378: (1999) 3 SCC 977.
264. AIR 1963 SC 1295: (1964) 1 SCR 332. *See also, Registrar and Collector, Hyderabad* v. *Canara Bank,* AIR 2005 SC 186: (2005) 1 SCC 496.
265. AIR 1975 SC 1378: (1975) 2 SCC 148.
266. (1965) 381 US 479.

the right to privacy was implied in the right to free speech and could be gathered from the entirety of fundamental rights in the constitutional scheme, for, without it, these rights could not be enjoyed meaningfully. Mathew, J. also referred to *Jane Roe* v. *Henry Wade*[267] where it was pointed out that though the right to privacy was not specifically referred to in the Constitution of the United States of American, the right did exist and "roots of that right may be found in the First, Fourth and Fifth Amendments, in the penumbras of the Bill of rights, in the Ninth Amendment, and in the concept of liberty guaranteed by the first section of the Fourteenth Amendment". Mathew, J. stated that, however, the "right to privacy was not absolute" and that the makers of the Constitution of India wanted to ensure conditions favourable to the pursuit of happiness as explained in *Olmstead* v. *United States*;[268] the privacy right can be denied only when an important countervailing interest is shown to be superior, or where a compelling State interest was shown. Mathew, J. left open the issue whether moral interests could be relied upon by the State as compelling interests. Any right to privacy, the learned Judge said, must encompass and protect the personal intimacies of the home, the family, marriage, motherhood, procreation and child bearing. This list was, however, not exhaustive.

Keeping in view the law on search and seizure as discussed above, there is every possibility that *Anton Piller* orders may be abused by unreasonable search and seizure which may cause the violation of the Constitutional right against self-incrimination, right to life, right to privacy as well as right to fair trial.

Guidelines for Issue of Anton Piller Order

The Courts in the United Kingdom (UK) faced a problem where *Anton Piller* orders have been abused. For instance, one may peruse the case of *Universal Thermosensors Ltd.* v. *Hibben and Ors.*[269] This case deals with the issue of *Anton Piller* abuses where *Anton Piller* orders have been abused leading to great hardships to the defendant. In this case, the Court's order was abused to the extent that a woman alone in her house with her children was confronted by a man she did not know, claiming that he had a right to enter her house, and that she could not contact anyone except her lawyer (who at that time of the day was not available). The Court came up with 7 specific guidelines/safeguards in order to check such abuses. The Court observed that: (i) *Anton Piller* orders must be executed only on the working days in office hours when a solicitor is expected to be available; (ii) In general, *Anton Piller* orders should generally provide that, unless this is seriously impracticable, a detailed list of the items being removed must be prepared at the premises before they are removed and that the defendant should be given an opportunity to check this list at the time; (iii) The scope of *Anton Piller* orders must be limited in a manner to ensure that the plaintiff must not be allowed access to all the defendant's documents/materials (especially if the defendant is a competitor company) and the Court observed that certain means need to be devised to avoid certain situations; (iv) The Court further suggested that judges should ensure through suitable undertakings that the order is served and its execution supervised by a solicitor other than a member of the firm

---

267. (1973) 410 US 113.
268. (1927) 277 US 438.
269. (1992) F.S.R. 361.

acting for the plaintiff and that such solicitor must have experience (and is familiar) with the working of *Anton Piller* orders. Further, the Court recommended that a report be prepared by the solicitor recounting the events of the execution and that such copy of the report be served on the defendants and be presented to the Court at an interpreters hearing within a short period of time; (v) *Anton Piller* orders must not be executed at business premises save in the presence of a responsible officer or representative of the company or trader in the presence of a responsible officer or representative of the company or trader in question; (vi) The defendant must not be restrained from informing others about the existence of the order for an unreasonable period; (vii) If the order is to be executed at a private house, and it is at all likely that a woman may be in the house alone, the solicitor serving the order must be, or must be accompanied by, a woman.

Similarly, in *Columbia Picture Industries* v. *Robinson*,[270] the Court sought to make the following general comments regarding *Anton Piller* orders: (i) *Anton Piller* order must be drawn so as to extend to the minimum extent necessary and to achieve the purpose for which they are granted, i.e., to ensure preservation of evidence, which is likely to be destroyed or concealed. (ii) A detailed record of the material taken should always be required to be made by the solicitors executing the order. (iii) The plaintiff (and his solicitors) must be permitted to remove only those materials/documents from the defendant's premises if they are clearly covered by the order. The Court particularly admonished the practice wherein material not covered by the order is removed after the defendant is procured and his consent is taken. (iv) The Court further recommended that the seized material must be returned to the defendants or else, if ends of justice demand, a neutral officer of the court must be charged with the custody of the material. (v) *Anton Piller* orders further require that the plaintiffs must disclose all relevant facts and the affidavits in support of the applications must err on the side of excessive disclosure.

It is relevant to note that, the above stated guidelines/safeguards, if adopted by the Indian Courts (and more importantly, if their breach is appropriately acted against), would provide solutions to most of the issues raised in the ghost blog and would appropriately safeguard the interests of the defendant. Issue of *ex parte* injunction along with appointment of local commissioner to collect evidence has become a routine matter in the Delhi High Court. Popularly known as *Anton Piller* like order, this was initially issued in software infringement cases but is now granted in almost all intellectual property matters resulting in abuse and attracting criticism. This seems to be the reason for the division bench of the Delhi High Court in *Autodesk Inc.* v. *A.V.T. Shankardass*,[271] issuing guidelines for the issue of this type of orders in case of software infringement. In this case, the single bench though issued an *ex parte* injunction order refused to appoint the local commissioner for collection of evidence. On appeal, the division bench appointed a local commissioner and the parties filed a compromise petition. While disposing of the case, the parties insisted the court to lay down guidelines for issue of such orders. The court formulated the following guidelines in case of software infringement:

---

270. (1986) F.S.R. 367.

271. AIR 2008 Delhi 167: 2008 (37) PTC 581 (Del). *See also*, *Microsoft Corporation* v. *Dhiren Gopal*, MIPR 2010 (1) 85: 2010 (42) PTC 1 (Del); Souvik Bhadra and Arka Majumdar, "Anton Pillar Order and Its Possible Implication in India", 12 *Journal of Intellectual Property Rights* (2007) pp. 488–496.

1. The object of appointment of Local Commissioner in software piracy matters is not, as much to collect evidence but to preserve and protect the infringing evidence. The pirated software or incriminating evidence can only be obtained from the premises of the opposite party alone and in the absence of an *ex parte* appointment of a Local Commissioner there is likelihood that such evidence may be lost, removed or destroyed;
2. Request for *ex parte* appointment of a Local Commissioner in such matters is usual and in fact is intended to sub-serve the ends of justice as it is imperative to have an element of surprise so that the actual position is not altered;
3. The test of reasonable and credible information regarding the existence of pirated software or incriminating evidence should not be subjected to strict proof or the requirement to demonstrate or produce part of the pirated software/incriminating evidence at the initial stage itself. It has to be tested on the touchstone of pragmatism and the natural and normal course of conduct and practice of trade;
4. It may not always be possible for a plaintiff to obtain any admission by employing decoy customers and gaining access to the defendant's premises. Any such attempt also inheres in it the possibility of disappearance of the pirated software/ incriminating evidence in case the decoy customer is exposed. Accordingly, visit by decoy customer or investigator is not to be insisted upon as per condition. A report of private investigator need not be disregarded or rejected simply because of his engagement by the plaintiff. The information provided by the private investigator should receive objective evaluation;
5. In cases where certain and definite information with regard to the existence of pirated software or incriminating evidence is not available or where the court may nurture some element of doubt, it may consider asking the plaintiff to deposit cost in court so that in case pirated software or incriminating evidence is not found then the defendant can be suitably compensated for the obstruction in his work or privacy.[272]

It is evident from the above guidelines that these are meant to ensure that the court issue orders to the plaintiff when it is asked for. In *Pepsico Inc.* v. *Dugar Spices and Eatables (P) Ltd.*,[273] the plaintiffs urged that the cost in terms of appointment of Local Commissioner be awarded. However, since the two Local Commissioners were appointed to inspect the premises of defendant Nos. 1, 6 and 7 only and the matter has been settled by the plaintiffs with the aforesaid defendants, no decree can be passed for cost of execution of Local Commission. In *Sap Aktiengesellschaft* v. *Rohit Sharma*,[274] on an application for appointment of local commissioner filed by the plaintiff, a local commissioner was appointed. The Delhi High Court based on the report of the Local Commissioner and the investigator, leaves no room for doubt that the computers were installed at the premises of the defendants with the SAP Software, various students were enrolled and fees were being charged from them. This is a fit

272. For Indian example, *see*, *Marina Food Products Pvt. Ltd.* v. *Britannia Industries Ltd.*, 2018 (74) PTC 499 (Del): 247 (2018) DLT 485; *SAP AG* v. *Jayanth Kumar*, 2015 (61) PTC 474 (Del); *Microsoft Corporation* v. *Prithviraj*, AIR 2015 Delhi 10; *Pepsico, Inc* v. *PSI Ganesh Marketing*, 2014 (59) PTC 275 (Del): MIPR 2014 (2) 240.
273. MANU/DE/2141/2017.
274. MANU/DE/4057/2014.

case where the plaintiff is entitled to damages of ₹ 5.00 lakhs. Thus, it is important in such cases are the protection of the materials of the defendant in the computer and privacy of the defendant who is not before the court. These orders are used to disrupt the regular work of the defendant and also use it to discredit his reputation. It is unfortunate to note that the court refused to lay down any guidelines to protect the interest of the defendant so that a balance is maintained in achieving the ends of justice. This seems to be the reason for the parties requesting the court to include the suggestion of taking ghost copies and not to remove the computer, hard disk, etc. The court left these issues to be dealt with the court issuing the orders. It is disappointing to note that there is no attempt by any court to issue direction as to the manner in which the visit has to be conducted and evidence collected protecting the genuine business interest of the defendant. It is always the small and medium size industries which are normally affected by such orders and the difficulties of the legal system in defending such cases which compel such parties to agree for compromise. It is evident from this case itself that the order is used by the parties to get compromise without any further proceeding. It is time for the court to have a revisit on such orders and issue directions to protect the business interest of the defendants while meeting the ends of justice.

Contempt of Court in Case of Refusal to Obey Anton Piller Orders

In *Dart Industries Inc.* v. *Techno Plast,*[275] the Delhi High Court directed initiation of contempt of court proceedings against the defendant for obstructing the court commissioner from executing the *ex parte* injunction and visit of the commissioner for search and seizure. The allegation that the defendant obstructed the commissioner, questioned the authenticity of the order, used political pressure, etc., was denied by the defendant. Rejecting this, the court reasoned:

> It is not necessary for me to go into the details inasmuch as if the version of the Court Commissioner and the applicant is correct, it amounts to criminal contempt as obstruction in the working of the Court Commissioner amount to obstruction in the administration of justice. Court Commissioner is the officer of the Court who has given the report, which is to be acted upon for taking *prima facie* view in the matter, subject to such defence that may be available to the respondent/contemners at the appropriate stage.

The court is correct in making the above observation based on the law in India. But from the limited facts available from the report it appears that the order issued by the court is the so called "*Anton Piller Order*" based on the judgment of the English Court in *Anton Piller K.G.* v. *Manufacturing Process Ltd.*[276] If so, it is interesting to examine whether the defendant has the right to object to the inspection of his premise by the Court Officer as per this decision if he is convinced that the order is obtained improperly. It is also interesting to find out the circumstance in which the defendant could be subjected to contempt procedure for refusal to permit inspection. A plain reading of the *Anton Piller* judgment makes it clear that the defendant has the right to object entry into the premises. The following observation of Lord Denning is pertinent:[277]

---

275. 2007 (35) PTC 285 (Del).
276. (1976)1 All ER 779 (CA).
277. *Anton Piller K.G.* v. *Manufacturing Process Ltd.* (1976)1 All ER 779 (CA) at 783.

> Nevertheless, in the enforcement of this order, the plaintiffs must act with due circumspection. On the service of it, the plaintiffs should be attended by their solicitor, who is an officer of the court. They should give the defendants an opportunity of considering it and of consulting their own solicitor. If the defendants wish to apply to discharge the order as having been improperly obtained, they must be allowed to do so. If the defendants refused permission to enter or to inspect, the plaintiff must not force their way in. They must accept the refusal, and bring it to the notice of the court afterwards, if need be on application to commit.

It was made clear by the Court of Appeal that refusal to give permission is at his peril. In this context, the clarification given by Ormrod, L.J. is significant:[278]

> The form of the order makes it plain that the court is not ordering or granting anything equivalent to a search warrant. The order is an order on the defendant in *personam* to permit inspection. It is therefore open to him to refuse to comply with such an order, but at his peril either of further proceedings for contempt of Court in which case, of course the Court will have the widest discretion as to how to deal with it, and if it turns out the order was made improperly in the first place the contempt will be dealt with accordingly—but more important, of course, the refusal to comply may be the most damaging evidence against the defendant at the subsequent trial.

It is interesting to find out whether the mere fact of objecting entry could make the defendant liable for contempt even if it is proved that the order was obtained improperly and was discharged on petition by the defendant. There are conflicting decisions in England in this regard. The passing observation of the Court of Appeal in *Hallmark Cards Inc.* v. *Image Arts Ltd.*,[279] is worth quoting.[280]

> While the order stands, the party who refuses access to his premises is in default of the order. But if the party against whom the order is made were to succeed in getting the order discharged, I cannot conceive that party would be liable to any penalties for any breach of the order of which he may have been guild while it subsisted, for if the order is discharged upon the footing that it ought not to have been made, then the contempt is in truth no contempt, although technically no doubt there is contempt because the order, until discharged, is an operative order and the party who refuses access is acting in disobedience of the order. But if the application to discharge proved to be successful, then it seems to me that the party against whom the order has been made will not turn out really to have been in jeopardy meanwhile.

But the Chancery Division in *Wardle Fabrics Ltd.* v. *G. Myristis Ltd.*,[281] after reviewing the cases including the Court of Appeal decisions took a different stand and observed:

> Having reviewed that body of authority as best I can, it seems to me that what I would have wished to decide on principle is in accordance with the law as it stands, that an order—and I am not speaking of an order which for want of jurisdiction is a nullity *ab initio* but an order of the court made within its jurisdiction—must be obeyed on pain of contempt penalties while it stands. The fact that it is subsequently discharged is no automatic answer to proceedings for contempt, although the circumstances are appropriate to be considered when the court has to decide on penalties.[282]

---

278. *Anton Piller K.G.* v. *Manufacturing Process Ltd.* (1976)1 All ER 779 (CA) at 784.
279. (1977) FSR 150. In this case the defendant refused to give access and moved the court to discharge the order. The order was suspended. The plaintiff appealed to the Court of Appeal on ground of procedural error is suspending the order.
280. *Hallmark Cards Inc.* v. *Image Arts Ltd.* (1977) FSR 150 at 153 (per Buckley L.J).
281. (1984) FSR 263 (Ch. D). In this case the defendant refused permission and the court subsequently discharged the order. The plaintiff filed the contempt petition for not permitting entry.
282. *Wardle Fabrics Ltd.* v. *G. Myristis Ltd.* (1984) FSR 263 (Ch. D) at 275.

It is the need to obey the court order to maintain the status of administration of justice that prompted the judge to come to this conclusion. The remedy in such cases for the defendant seems to be the award of damages. It is important to note that the courts in England take adequate precaution before such orders are issued though there are allegations of its rampant abuse.[283] In this context, it appears that the reasoning of the Chancery Division in *Wardle case* needs reconsideration giving more credit to the passing observation of the Court of Appeal in *Hallmark case.* It is noticed that *Anton Piller* like order is issued by the Delhi High Court as a matter of routine without even taking adequate precautions. One needs to wait and watch how the Indian Courts are going to address the issue of contempt in case the order is obtained improperly.

Mareva Injunction

Mareva injunction restrains the defendant from disposing of assets which may be required to satisfy the plaintiff's claim or removing them from the jurisdiction of the court. The "Mareva injunction" is now an established feather of English Law which could be granted where it appears likely that the plaintiff will recover judgment against the defendant for a certain or approximate sum and there are reasons to believe that the defendant has assets within the jurisdiction to meet the judgment, wholly or in part, but may deal with them, whether by removal out of the jurisdiction or disposing of them within the jurisdiction so that they are not available or traceable when the judgment is given against him.[284] The name "Mareva injunction" came from the case of *Mareva* v. *International Bulk Carriers,*[285] wherein the Court of Appeal in England had approved of the making of an injunction restraining the defendants from removing or disposing out of the jurisdiction monies standing to the credit of the defendants at a London Bank until trial of the action or further order. The plaintiffs were ship owners and the defendants voyage charterers; they had received payment for the freight into that account but had not paid the hire due to the plaintiffs. The scope of this remedy has since been widened and this remedy by way of injunction may be granted to a plaintiff with a proper claim in any case where there are grounds for fearing that the defendant may defeat justice by transferring assets abroad or by concealing them in that country.

Although the "mareva injunction" is originated in England, it can be granted in suitable cases in India.[286] The attachment before judgment is one of the known concepts. In civil law, this jurisdiction is quite familiar and the procedure is known as *saisie conservatoire* whereby the assets of a debtor may be impounded before a judgment, and orders commonly known as "mareva injunction".[287] The "mareva injunction" are made in exercise of admiralty jurisdiction, which is in rem, unlike the jurisdiction in personam in suits inter-parties. The order of interim injunction can, at the most, bind the defendant, but cannot bind the transferee

---

283. For details *see*, Kern Alexander, "The Mareva Injunction and Anton Piller Order: The Nuclear Weapons of English Commercial Litigation" 2 *Florida Journal of International Law,* 487 (1997); Susan Hall, "Anton Piller Orders: A Doorstep Too Far?", 17 *European Intellectual Property Review* (1995) 50.
284. *Formosa Plastic Corporation Ltd.* v. *Ashok Chauhan,* 19991 AD (Delhi) 392: 76 (1998) DLT 817.
285. 1980 (1) All ER 213.
286. *See, Santosh Promoters Pvt. Ltd.* v. *Intrasoft Technologies Ltd.*, 2017 (1) CHN (CAL) 189.
287. *See, Oriental Insurance Company Ltd.* v. *Deputy Commissioner of Income Tax,* [2017] 248 TAXMAN 61 (Delhi): [2017] 394 ITR 58 (Delhi).

pendent lite.[288] The obvious reason is that the Order 39 Rule 1(b) of the Civil Procedure Code which authorizes the civil court to pass an order of temporary injunction for restraining the defendant from transferring any property which the defendant intends to transfer to defraud his creditors during the pendency of the suit for realization of money, even though the property in respect of which an order in the form of injunction is sought for, is not directly and/or indirectly involved in the suit. A decree-holder is entitled to a "mareva injunction" in respect of assets outside as such an injunction is not a form of attachment but is a relief in personam and operates against the persons.[289]

In *Prakash Gobindram Ahuja* v. *Ganesh Pandharinath Dhonde*,[290] the Bombay High Court held that the concept of the "mareva injunction", as operating in rem,. It operates so as to attach any effects of the defendant, whether money or goods, to be found within the jurisdiction of the Court. The reason is because a "mareva injunction" is a method of attaching the asset itself. It operates in rem just as the arrest of a ship does. Just as a debtor gets the ship released on giving security, so does the debtor get an aircraft released. In *Mohit Bhargava* v. *Bharat Bhushan Bhargava*, the Supreme Court of India observed that it was within the jurisdiction of the court which passed the decree to issue orders of restraint to a person from handing over a property in his possession to the judgment debtor along with the documents concerned and to direct keeping the documents in safe custody. Such orders were in the nature of a "freezing order" or a "Mareva injunction" and an order akin to an *Anton Piller* Order, orders that could be issued even if the property or the person concerned was outside the jurisdiction of the courts. In *New Horizons Limited* v. *Union of India*, it was held that where the court considers it appropriate to issue a Mareva injunction the court will use its power to pierce the corporate veil if it is necessary to achieve justice irrespective of the legal efficacy of the corporate situation under consideration.

Similarly, in *Rite Approach Group Ltd.* v. *Rosoboronexport*,[291] the Delhi High Court held that Mareva or freezing injunction is passed when there is evidence or material to show that the debtor is acting in a manner or is likely to act in a manner to frustrate subsequent order/decree of the court or tribunal. The Court, therefore, freezes the assets of the debtor to prevent the assets from being dissipated, to prevent irreparable harm to the creditor. It prevents a foreign defendant from removing his assets from the jurisdiction of the court. It is like and akin to "attachment before judgment" and conditions mentioned in the said provision should be satisfied before freezing junction order is passed.[292]

Injunction for Groundless Threat

Under Section 60 of the Copyright Act 1957 one can obtain injunction in the case of groundless threat of legal proceedings. The Section 60 reads: "Where any person claiming to be the

---

288. *See, Prakash Gobindram Ahuja* v. *Ganesh Pandharinath Dhonde*, 2016 (6) Bom CR 262: 2016 (6) ABR 745.
289. *See, Steel Authority of India* v. *Ram Krishan Kulwant Rai*, 2014(1) CHN (CAL) 493.
290. 2013 (7) Bom CR 595.
291. AIR 2007 Delhi 145: 139 (2007) DLT 55.
292. *Uppal Engg. Co. (P) Ltd.* v. *Cimmco Birla Ltd.*, 121 (2005) DLT (539): [2006] 132 Comp Cas 4 (Delhi); *Formosa Plastic Corporation Ltd.* v. *Ashok Chauhan*, 76 (1998) DLT 817.

owner of copyright in any work, by circulars, advertisements or otherwise, threatens any other person with any legal proceedings or liability in respect of an alleged infringement of the copyright, any person aggrieved thereby may, notwithstanding anything contained [in section 34 of the Specific Relief Act, 1963(47 of 1963)][293] institute a declaratory suit that the alleged infringement to which the threats related was not in fact an infringement of any legal rights of the person making such threats and may in any such suit—(a) obtain an injunction against the continuance of such threats; and (b) recover such damages, if any, as he has sustained by reason of such threats. Provided that this section shall not apply if the person making such threats, with due diligence, commences and prosecutes an action for infringement of the copyright claimed by him."

In *Zee Entertainment Enterprises Ltd.* v. *Saregama India Ltd.*,[294] the Court observed that the juridical philosophy behind Section 60 of the Copyright Act is obvious. If a person issues a legal notice to a party alleging violation of a copyrightable work, the party to whom the notice is served would have to engage the services of a lawyer to respond to the notice, for the reason a non-traverse of the claim in the notice would be held against the recipient of the notice. In this manner a party can be unnecessarily harassed. Therefore, if a party issuing a notice continues with the threat and as a result the sword of domiciles continues to hang over the head of the noticee, the noticee may seek a declaration. But where the person alleging violation commences prosecution with due diligence, of an action for infringement, the proviso to Section 60 would come into play. In *Vortex Engineering Pvt. Ltd.* v. *NCR Financial Solutions Group Ltd.*,[295] the Court held that it is settled law that issuance of legal notice to threaten proceedings against a party amounts to groundless threat, as envisaged under Section 60 of the Copyrights Act. In *Metro Tyres Ltd.* v. *Advertising Standards Council of India*,[296] it was held that the Proviso to the Section 60 is clear to the effect that if an infringement action is filed, Section 60 would not apply. In *Super Cassette Industries Ltd.* v. *Bathla Cassettes India (P) Ltd.*,[297] the Delhi High Court observed:

> The provisions of Section 60 make it clear that if a person is threatened with any alleged infringement of copyright and if, in fact, the actions of the persons threatened do not constitute any infringement of the legal rights of the person who makes such threats, he can file a declaratory suit and obtain an injunction against the continuance of such threats. He can also obtain damages which he may have sustained by reason of such threats. These provisions are designed to protect a person against any wrongful threats relating to infringement of copyright and the only relief which can be asked for is an injunction against the continuance of such threats and damages occasioned by reason of such threats. The proviso to this Section makes this position amply clear because it provides that this section will have no application if a person, who has made such threats, commences and prosecutes with due diligence an action for infringement of the copyright claimed by him. Once a suit is filed for infringement of the copyright by the person who has given the threat, the suit under Section 60 becomes infructuous as the Section ceases to apply in such a situation.

---

293. Substituted by the Copyright (Amendment) Act, 1983 (Act 23 of 1983), Section 21, for "in Section 42 of the Specific Relief Act, 1877 (1 of 1877)" [w.e.f. 9-8-1984].
294. 2017 (70) PTC 209 (Del).
295. 2013 (54) PTC 196 (Mad).
296. 2017 (70) PTC 394 (Del): 240 (2017) DLT 119.
297. AIR 1994 Delhi 237: 1993 (25) DRJ 410.

In *QD Seatamon Designs Private Limited* v. *P. Suresh*,[298] the plaintiff prayed for injunctive relief qua suit copyright, damages for alleged mental agony owing to alleged infringement of suit copyright, for delivery of offending material and costs. The moot question is when an action of infringement of copyright is commenced against an entity/person after such entity/person files a case of groundless threat of legal proceedings, will such commencement of action for infringement of copyright render the groundless threat suit infructuous? Respondent argued that once a suit for infringement has been filed, the previous pending suit with respect to groundless threat under section 60 of the Copyright Act will become infructuous.[299] The word "due diligence" occurring in proviso to section 60 only refers to a point in time, meaning that the plaintiff in the suit for infringement must institute the infringement suit, without any delay. The suit for infringement must be instituted within reasonable time.[300] The Court dismissed the suit as infructuous.

John Doe Injunction

The term "John Doe Injunction" (or John Doe Order) is used to be described as an injunction sought against someone whose identity is not known at the time of filing of the suit.[301] It is basically a simple *ex parte* interim injunction with the added benefit that the plaintiff is given liberty to add to the array of parties, infringers who have been identified after the filing of the suit. These orders are an exception the general rule which requires the defendant to be identified prior to the filing of a law-suit.[302] The *ex parte* interim injunction then applies against even the later defendants. The original version of the "John Doe" order was usually combined with an "Anton Piller" order which used to allow for the seizure of any infringing material.[303]

> The concept of the "John Doe" order evolved to overcome difficulties copyright owners encountered in ascertaining specific defendants, enabling them to institute *ex parte* infringement suits against unknown persons belonging to an identifiable class who upon identification would be impleaded and presented with the opportunity to defend themselves analogues to any civil proceedings,[304] while the "Anton Piller" order is a form of discovery preservation granted on an *ex parte* application.[305]

The "John Doe" orders are granted by English, American, Canadian and Australian Courts frequently. "John Doe" orders enabling the order to be served upon persons whose identity is

---

298. (2019) 1 MLJ 163.
299. The respondent relied on *Music India Ltd.* v. *Super Cassettes Industrial Pvt. Ltd.*, 1987 (7) PTC 83 (Bom).
300. The respondent relied on *Mehta Unani Pharmacy* v. *Amrutanjan Limited*, 2002 (25) PTC 475: LNIND 2002 MAD 298: (2002) 2 MLJ 494.
301. *EMI Records Ltd.* v. *Kudhail* (1985) FSR 36: (1983) Com LR 280.
302. *See*, J.K. Das, New Dimensions of Intellectual Property Rights in India" 3(2) *Pragyaan: Journal of Law* (2013) pp. 11–33 at p. 29.
303. *See*, Hayhurst Gordon W., "Ex parte Anton Piller Orders with John Doe Defendents", 9(9) *European Intellectual Property Review* (1989) 257.
304. *See*, Juhi Gupta, "John Doe Copyright Injunction in India", 18 *Journal of Intellectual Property Rights* (2013), pp. 351–359.
305. *See*, Souvik Bhadra and Arka Majumdar, "Anton Piller Order in UK and Its Possible Implications in India, 12 *Journal of Intellectual Property Rights*, (2007) pp. 488–496.

unknown to the plaintiff at the time the action was commenced, but whose activity falls within the scope of the action. This form of naming a party is considered a mere "misnomer", and as long as the "litigating finger" is pointed at such person then the misnomer is not fatal.[306] The origin of the "John Doe" orders, can be traced way back to the reign of England's King Edward III, when such orders were used to refer to unidentifiable defendants.[307] Thereafter, "John Doe" orders were granted mainly by US and Canadian Courts. Recently, India has started using this unique concept under the alias "John Doe/Ashok Kumar" orders to punish class of unknown infringers.

The first "John Doe" copyright injunction in UK was *EMI Records Ltd.* v. *Kudhail.*[308] In this case, the plaintiff alleged that copyright infringement of certain cassette tapes by street traders, very few of whose names could be found, and thus sought a "John Doe" order against all members of an identifiable class (defined as traders selling goods bearing the pirate brad name "Oak records") to restrain them from engaging in the counterfeiting. The Court held that the plaintiffs have been able to establish the existence of a group sharing a common interest, although the individual members are unidentifiable due to the groups secrecy, justifying the grant of an *ex parte* relief. Thus, *prima facie* "John Doe" orders can be safely regarded as an ingenious and judicious approach to copyright protection. It balances interest of copyright owners and potential infringers since it acts as a shield providing preventive and expeditious remedy to the former which is only enforceable against the letter upon acts of infringement actually being perpetrated and the owner having ascertained identity of the respective John Doe. Initially, "John Doe" orders were primarily used by broadcasters to protect their copyrights from infringement by known and unknown cable operators during sporting events. The orders were enforced through the issuance of blanket search and seizure directives and /or appointment of policemen to assist broadcasters. The test adopted in UK to grant "John Doe" copyright injunction as laid down in *Bloomsbury Publishing Plc* v. *Newsgroup Newspapers Ltd.,*[309] is as follows:

1. The plaintiff must show a good, arguable case;
2. The order must clearly indicate what the defendant/s can and/or cannot do;
3. The order must identify the defendant/s against whom it is made with respect to their works or an identifiable class;
4. The injunction will only be enforceable against a person who once made aware of the order, understands that it applies to him.

In US, the first case in which a "John Doe" copyright injunction was granted was *Billy Joel et al.* v. *Various John Doe.*[310] In this case, a "John Doe" order was granted to prevent the unauthorised sales of merchandise bearing Billy Joel's name outside the venues where he was to conduct his concerts which were negatively impacting revenue generation from sales by authorised vendors inside the concert venues. The court held that notwithstanding

306. *Jackson* v. *Bubels,* 28 (1972) DLT. 500 (B.C.C.A.); *Dukoff* v. *Toronto General Hospital* (1986) 54 O.R. 50 (H.C.).
307. Merriam-Webster, *What's In A Name?* (1996).
308. [1985] F.S.R. 36.
309. [2003] EWHC 1087 Ch.
310. 499 F. Supp. 791 (1980).

the general inability to grant an injunction against unknown persons, the plaintiff has satisfied that court that such an injunction is needed in the given facts and circumstances. In order to ascertain the identities of the unauthorised vendors, the court directed that copies of the restraining order where to be served on all those whose merchandise was seized, such persons reveal their names in order to be added as parties to the suit and appear in court to contest the action. John Doe orders are used in Canada by owners of intellectual property rights to preserve evidence against infringers. Additionally, the rise of the Internet has also brought an explosion of "John Doe" lawsuits.[311] The nature of the unique orders has been summarised by Reed J. in *Fila Canada Inc.* v. *Doe,*[312] as follows:

> The order, which is sought, is what is known as a "rolling" *Anton Piller* order. As is obvious from the style of cause, when these orders are obtained from the Court neither the identity nor the address of the persons against whom they will be executed are known. On some occasions one or two persons may be identified as named defendants but they will have no necessary connection to the Jane and John Doe against whom the order will be executed. The known defendants are allegedly infringing intellectual property rights belonging to the plaintiff but in different places, at different times and in different circumstances. These "rolling" orders can be distinguished from defendant-specific *Anton Piller* orders. While defendant-specific *Anton Piller* orders may also include Jane and John Doe defendants, in general, the latter will be connected to the named defendants....

Drawing the inspirations from the foreign jurisdiction, the "John Doe" order was recognised in *Taj Television* v. *Rajan Mandal*[313] case in India. In this case, the plaintiff owned the ten sports channel and the broadcasting rights to some of the major global sporting events, including the matches of the football World Cup. The plaintiff had entered into agreements with various cable operators in the country to transmit the channel but there were a large number of unlicenced cable operators who were wrongfully transmitted the channel, some of whom had been identified. Accordingly, at the time of the World Cup, the plaintiff instituted a suit to obtained *ex parte* relief against named and unnamed cable operators to restrain them from infringing the plaintiff's broadcasting rights under Section 37 of the Copyright Act, 1957. Under Rule 1, Order 39 of the Code of Civil Procedure, 1908 *prima facie* case,[314] balance of convenience[315] and possibility of irreparable injury[316] are requirements of *ex parte*

---

311. Jeff Berryman, "Thirty Years After: Anton Piller Orders and the Supreme and Federal Courts of Canada", (2) 3 *Journal of International Commercial Law and Technology* (2007) pp. 128–140.
312. [1996] 3 F.C. 493 (T.D.).
313. [2003] F.S.R. 22.
314. For the concept of "prima facie case", *see*, *Kalyan Singh Chouhan* v. *C.P. Joshi*, 2011 (1) SCALE 718: 2011 (1) UJ 453 (SC); *Skyline Education Institute (Pvt.) Ltd.* v. *S.L. Vaswani*, AIR 2010 SC 3221: (2010) 2 SCC 142; *Athar Hussain* v. *Syed Siraj Ahmed*, AIR 2010 SC 1414: 2010 (1) SCALE 95; *Kashi Math Samsthan* v. *Srimad Sudhindra Thirtha Swamy,* AIR 2010 SC 296: (2010) 1 SCC 689; *Zenit Mataplast P. Ltd.* v. *State of Maharashtra*, 2009 (12) SCALE 432: (2009) 10 SCC 388.
315. For the concept of "balance of convenience" *see*, *Bhiaru Ram* v. *Central Bureau of Investigation,* 2010 (7) SCALE 718: [2010] 9 SCR 554; *Sonu Babu Bhambid* v. *Dream Developers*, JT 2009 (13) SC 397: [2009] 11 SCR 1176; *Mandali Rangunna* v. *T. Ramachandra,* AIR 2008 SC 2291: (2008) 11 SCC 1; *Ramdev Food Products Pvt. Ltd.* v. *Arvindbhai Rambhai Patel*, AIR 2006 SC 3304: (2006) 8 SCC 726.
316. For elaborate discussion on "irreparable injury" *see*, *Chhattisgarh State Electricity Board* v. *Central Electricity Regulatory Commission*, [2010] 4 SCR 680: 2010 (4) UJ 1755 (SC); *Jaswant Kaur* v. *Subhash Paliwal*, 2009 (14) SCALE 695: (2010) 2 SCC 124; *Shridevi* v. *Muralidhar*, 2007 (12) SCALE 234: [2007] 11 SCR 375; *M. Gurudas* v. *Rasaranjan*, AIR 2006 SC 3275: (2006) 8 SCC 367.

temporary injunction. Besides, Section 151 of the Code provides that unless specifically prohibited, the Civil Court has inherent power to make such orders as may be necessary for the ends of justice or to prevent abuse of the process of the Court. Therefore, the plaintiff in *Taj Television* case relied upon the Supreme Court decision in *Manohar Lal Chopra* v. *Rai Bahadur Rao Raja Seth Hiralal*,[317] to justify the use of the court's inherent powers in the interest of the justice as powers which are complementary to those provided for in the Code and which can be used as long as they not detract from the Code's provisions and the legislative intent. Thus, the *Taj Television* decision entrenched the dubious legal foundation upon which such orders are granted, a legislative manipulation involving a conjoint reading of the provisions prescribing temporary injunctions and inherent powers under the Code as well as the broadcasting reproduction right under Section 37 of the Copyright Act, 1957.

Similarly, in *Rohit Shekhar* v. *Narayan Dutt Tiwari*,[318] the Delhi High Court relied on "John Doe" orders which are implementable against unknown persons also and where the Commissioners are authorised to visit places of unnamed defendants and wherefrom the infringing goods may be found. In *Ardath Tobacco Company Ltd.* v. *Mr. Munna Bhai*,[319] the Court on the basis of "John Doe" order appointed two court commissioners, one for visiting the premises of the defendants 4 to 6 at Delhi and the other for visiting the premises of the defendants 1 to 3 at Calcutta as well as any other premises where the impugned goods were suspected to be stocked. The Court Commissioner appointed at Calcutta had found infringing goods in the premises of the defendant no. 1. Therefore, plaintiff entitled to permanent injunction and decree for recovery of damages. However, in *Indian Performing Right Society Ltd.* v. *Mr. Badal Dhar Chowdhry*,[320] the plaintiff is unable to identify the works in which it has rights and with respect whereto the defendants are sought to be restrained. In this case, the Court observed that though there is precedent for injuncting others than those impleaded in the suit and who may be found violating the rights, in the field of copyright and what has commonly come to be known as "John Doe" orders, but in that case also, the work with respect where to injunction is issued is identified. The suit was, therefore, failed and dismissed.

In *ESPN Software India Private Ltd.* v. *Tudu Enterprise*,[321] the defendants had without entering into contracts either with distributor of plaintiff or with plaintiff itself transmitted networks channels of plaintiff and showed events to their subscribers and thus violated plaintiff's broadcast reproduction right. In this case, the Delhi High Court examined the issue whether defendant's act of unauthorised transmitting networks channels of plaintiff was justified? In this case, the plaintiff's channels were paid channels and viewed by persons who were subscribers through authorised cable operators and defendants were both known as uncertain. In these circumstances, reliance was placed on the internationally adopted "John Doe" practice as well as India's obligation under the TRIPS Agreement to effectively enforce intellectual property rights. The Court held that the plaintiff has made out a *prima facie* case for grant of *ad interim* orders. Grave and irreparable loss and damages would ensure to the plaintiff in case interim protection is not granted. Balance of convenience and interest of

317. AIR 1962 SC 527: [1962] Supp 1 SCR 450.
318. AIR 2012 Delhi 151: 189 (2012) DLT 105.
319. MIPR 2009 (1) 165: 2009 (39) PTC 208 (Del).
320. 2010 (43) PTC 332 (Del).
321. MANU/DE/1061/2011.

justice are in favour of the plaintiff and against the defendants. Thus, the Court directed as follows:

1. The defendants/their agents, representatives, franchisees, sub-operators, head ends and/or anyone claiming under them are hereby restrained from distributing, telecasting and broadcasting/rebroadcasting or in any other manner communicating to the viewing public/subscribers either by means of wireless diffusion or by wire or in any other manner the ICC Cricket World Cup, 2011 being telecast on the STAR Cricket, ESPN and Star Sports channels and/or in any other manner infringing the copyright/re-broadcast right of the plaintiff by downloading any other channels not registered under the down linking guidelines till further orders.
2. It is further directed that till the present order is vacated or modified, the direction shall operate against the defendants, their agents, representatives, franchises, sub-operators or any person claiming under them an injunction.
3. Further, injunction in terms of serial no. (i) above is passed against un-named and undisclosed persons who may be likewise committing breach of the rights of the plaintiff by resorting to illegal tapping of DTH (Direct to Home) connections by linking the same to the distribution networks.
4. The superintendent of the concerned police station(s) are directed to render assistance to the plaintiff should any be required for purposes of enforcement of the present order as it the obligation of the police authorities and the state to enforce judicial orders passed.
5. The plaintiff shall comply with the provisions of the proviso to Rule 3 of Order 39 of the Code of Civil Procedure, 1908 within a period of one week from today.[322]

Final or Perpetual Injunction

Besides the interlocutory or interim injunction, there are various other civil remedies available for infringement of copyright. One of the important remedies is final or perpetual injunction which is available for copyright owner. The perpetual injunction is granted in order to prevent any further repetition of the infringing action. The perpetual injunction restrains the defendants from taking any other or further coercive steps against the plaintiff.[323] In general, once liability has been established in a copyright action, the claimant may expect to be awarded a final injunction. Exceptions may arise where there has been a long delay in bringing the action or the court has taken the view that there is no likelihood of a repetition of the infringing act, but examples are few. If the plaintiff succeeds at the trial in establishing infringement of copyright, he will normally be entitled to a permanent injunction to restrain future infringements. This injunction will operate only during the unexpired term of the copyright.

In *Mallcom (India) Limited* v. *Rakesh Kumar*,[324] the plaintiff constituted an "artistic work" within the meaning of Section 2(c) of the Copyright Act, 1957 and has also obtained

322. *See, Morgan Stanley Mutual Fund* v. *Kartick Das*, (1994) 4 SCC 225: 1994 (2) SCALE 1121.
323. *See, V.S.G. Lungi Company* v. *Jayam Texti*, 2019 (77) PTC 277 (Mad): MIPR 2018 (3) 295.
324. 259 (2019) DLT 1: 2019 (78) PTC 201 (Del). *See also Reddy Pharmaceuticals Ltd.* v. *Dr. Reddy's Laboratories*, MIPR 2007 (3) 389: 2007 (99) DRJ 331; *Dr. Reddy's Laboratories Ltd.* v. *Reddy Pharmaceuticals Ltd.*, 2004 (29) PTC 435 (Del): (2004) 113 DLT 363; *Info Edge (India) Pvt. Ltd.* v. *Shailesh Gupta*, (2002) ILR 1 Delhi 220: (2002) 98 DLT 499.

a copyright registration for the artistic work. The plaintiffs, in the suit have claimed relief of permanent injunction restraining infringement of design. The Delhi High Court held that the plaintiffs entitled to summary judgment, insofar as the claim of the plaintiffs for permanent injunction restraining infringement of trade mark, passing off. The defendants have not pleaded, if not under the subject mark, under what mark are the plaintiffs marketing their shoes. Thus, the plea of the defendants, of the plaintiffs not using the subject mark, is found to be without any substance and not a material plea on which even an issue would be framed. The defendants, being in the same trade as the plaintiffs, are deemed to be aware of the admitted prior use by the plaintiffs of the mark "TIGER" and for this reason, the adoption cannot be said to be honest or bona fide. The plaintiffs are thus found entitled to summary judgment for the reliefs of permanent injunction restraining infringement of trade mark, copyright and passing off.

In *Hira Sweets* v. *Hira Confectioners*,[325] the plaintiff filed the suit for permanent injunction restraining infringement and passing off of trademark, copyright, damages, delivery up etc. It is stated in the plaint that the plaintiffs through their predecessor are the original conceiver, adopter and users of the artistic work HIRA SWEETS and the same is original artistic work within the meaning of Section 2(c) of the Copyright Act, 1957 having unique colour combination layout lettering style in relation to the aforesaid goods since 1960. The defendant adopted and started using the impugned trade mark/label HIRA CONFECTIONERS in respect of impugned goods and business with a view to take advantage and trade upon the reputation and goodwill of the plaintiff and further with a view to create confusion to pass off its impugned goods and business as those of the plaintiffs. The Court held that the triple identity test is also satisfied as the defendant has made use of an identical/deceptively similar trademark in relation to identical goods having an identical trade channel.

In an interesting decision, *Microsoft Corporation* v. *Plato Technology Ltd.*,[326] the court questioned the appropriateness of final injunctions in copyright actions which are characteristically broadly drawn to restrain all future infringements of the claimant's rights by the defendant. The court suggested instead that in certain cases a "narrow form" injunction which restrains the repetition only of the infringing act for which the defendant has been found liable, might be more appropriate. The latter approach has the advantage of certainty for the defendant, particularly in actions, where the scope of the protected copyrighted works may not always be entirely clear. A broad approach was taken by the court and granted an injunction to restrain the defendant from reproducing a substantial part of any operating system software in which the plaintiff had copyright (not just the software they had already infringed), because the court took the view that the defendants were interested in copying whatever operating systems software was currently saleable. The problem is faced in those cases where only a part of the work in which copyright subsists has been duplicated in the alleged infringing work.

325. 2019 II AD (Delhi) 661.
326. (1999) FSR 834. *See also*, *Microsoft Corporation* v. *Kiran*, 2007 (35) PTC7 48 (Del): ILR (2007) Supp. (5) Delhi 200; *Microsoft Corporation* v. *Deepak Raval*, 2006 (33) PTC 122 (Del): MIPR 2007 (1) 72.

In *Super Cassettes Industries* v. *M/s. Rachana Television Pvt. Ltd.*,[327] the court examined the issue whether suit for permanent injunction for infringement of copyright, damages, delivery was justified or not under Section 55 of the Copyright Act, 1955? The court held that it was not only Plaintiff, who had suffered on account of infringement of its trademark and Magazine design but large number of readers of Defendants' Magazine "TIME ASIA SANSKARAN" had suffered by purchasing defendants' magazines under an impression that same were from reputed publishing house of plaintiff company. The Court further held that the defendant has infringed the plaintiff's rights under Sections 14(a)(iii), 14a(iv), 14(d)(iii) and 14(e)(iii) read with Section 51 of the Copyright Act, 1957 and consequently, plaintiff is entitled to remedies as provided under Section 55 of the Copyright Act, 1957.

In *Hawkins Cookers Ltd.* v. *Magi Cook Appliances Co.*,[328] the issue was also the granting of permanent injunction. In this case, the Court held that the main objective of the Copyright Act, 1957 to give protection to the owner of the copyright from the dishonest manufacturers, who tries to confuse public and make them believe that the infringed products are the products of the owner. Similarly, the Act also wants to discourage the dishonest manufacturers from encashing the goodwill of the owner of the copyright, who has established itself in the market with its own efforts. Thus, the court discussed the grant of permanent injunction to the plaintiff for restraining the defendant from using a label for pressure cookers, which was deceptively similar to the registered trademark HAWKINS of the plaintiff. On non-appearance of the plaintiff, an *ex-parte* order was passed and it was ruled that, the unjust enrichment by the infringing party, was a mischief and the plaintiff was to be protected from it as per Section 55 of the Copyright Act, 1957. Hence permanent injunction was granted.

In *Sanofi* v. *Faisal Mushtaq*,[329] the suit has been filed for permanent injunction, restraining infringement and dilution of trademark, trade name, domain name, passing off, infringement of copyright, damages, delivery-up etc. The Court identified that the plaintiffs' "Bird of Hope" logo constitutes an original artistic work within the meaning of Section 2(c) of the Copyright Act, 1957 and the plaintiffs' tag-line "A global healthcare leader focused on patients' needs" comprises literary work within the meaning of Section 2(o) of the Copyright Act, 1957 and both are entitled to protection under Section 17 of the Copyright Act, 1957. Thus, the Court identified it is a case of trade mark infringement, copyright infringement and passing off is made out. The triple identity test is satisfied as the defendant has made use of identical trademark and trade name in relation to identical products. The Court further is of the view that the plaintiff is entitled to a decree.

Damages as Civil Remedies: Actual and Punitive

Actual Damages

The damages are important remedy available to a copyright owner. The object of an award of damages to a copyright owner is to restore the copyright owner to the position he would have

---

327. 201 (2013) DLT 329: 2013 (55) PTC 122 (Del). *See also*, *M/s. WD-40 Manufacturing Company* v. *M/s. Khemchand Enterprises*, 186 (2012) DLT 672: 2013 (53) PTC 523 (Del); *Klas Tape Company* v. *Vinod Hardware Store*, 2010 (44) PTC 39 (Del); *ESPN Star Sports* v. *Global Broadcast News Ltd.*, MIPR 2008 (3) 257: 2008 (38) PTC 477 (Del).
328. AIR (2003) Delhi 191: 100 (2002) DLT 698.
329. 254 (2018) DLT 597.

been had his copyright not been infringed. This also includes violation in cases of published as well as unpublished work though the quantum of damages in both the cases may be different. Under Sections 55 and 58 of the Copyright Act, 1955, a person complaining of infringement of his copyright is entitled to the remedy for damages except when he could prove lack of awareness of existence of copyright in which case the remedy available are injunction and a decree for whole or part of the profits made by the defendant by sale of the infringing copies. However, the right to recover damages provided under Sections 55 and 58 are not mutually exclusive, but cumulative. One being for infringement and the other for conversation.[330]

Thus, in *Palakurthu Laxmi Ganapathi Rao* v. *Manisha Video Vision*,[331] it was held that the infringement of copyright is established and thus the damages should be incurred. In *Pillalamarri Lakshmikantham* v. *Ramakrishna Pictures*,[332] on the facts of the case the court held that since the publishers were accorded the relief of damages, they cannot lay claim to the relief of accounts. In this case it was it is argued that the damages in ₹ 3,000 was not adequately quantified and a large number of authorities have been cited to show that no method was adopted in quantification of damages by the lower Court. But the Court was satisfied that the decree for damages as not "arbitrary" or "unreasonable." Hence, the Court considered that damages of ₹ 3,000 would be just.

Though ordinarily exemplary damages are not awarded, however, the courts have a tendency to award exemplary damages.[333] Damages in copyright actions are assessed following the same principles as other torts. The victim should be restored to the same position he would have been in if no wrong has been done. Furthermore, the victim should only recover loss which is caused by the defendant's wrongful act and is a reasonably foreseeable result of it. In the case of damages then, the court will look to see how the claimant would have profited without the defendant's infringing acts, rather than, as with an account of profits, looking to the infringer's profit. While the imposition of damages is not intended to punish the defendant, nonetheless "the defendants being wrongdoer", damages should be liberally assessed. The onus is on the claimant to prove the extent of his loss.[334]

The two most obvious ways a claimant may profit from his copyright are that he may exploit it himself or the way licence it to others. The question as to what damages should be attributed to the infringement of copyright also arises. Thus, the calculation of damages can give rise to complex considerations. The formula for calculation of damages in cases where the copyright work is not priced and the award of exemplary damages came for consideration in *P.N. Krishnan Murthy* v. *Co-operative for American Relief Everywhere.*[335] In this case, the plaintiff-appellant is the author of the story *Lakshman Kills a Tiger* and the registered owner

330. *Caxton Publishing Co. Ltd.* v. *Sutherland Publishing Co. Ltd.* (1938) 4 All ER 389: 1939 AC 178.
331. 2007 (34) PTC 33.
332. AIR 1981 AP 224.
333. *Rookes* v. *Barnard,* 1964 AC 264: [1964] 1 All ER 367. *See also, Whatman International* v. *P. Mehta,* 2019 (78) PTC 51 (Del): 257 (2019) DLT 472; *Inter Ikea Systems BV* v. *Imtiaz Ahamed*, 237 (2017) DLT 247, Cartier International AG v. Gaurav Bhatia, 226 (2016) DLT 662; *Jokey International Inc.* v. *R. Chandra Mohan*, 2014 (211) DLT 757; *Lachhman Das Behari Lal* v. *Ghanshyam Das Jetha Nand*, 2007 (35) PTC 693 (Del).
334. *See, General Tire & Rubber Co.* v. *Firestone Tyre & Rubber Co. Ltd.* (1975) RPC 203; *Gerber Garment Technology Inc.* v. *Leetra Systems Ltd.* (1995) RPC 383.
335. AIR 2001 (Del) 258. 2000(20)PTC658(Del).

of copyright from 1969. Under licence, the story was converted into a comic booklet by *Care* for children in many languages and published through CAP a publication unit owned by the plaintiff. In 1970, *Care* under licence from the plaintiff contracted CAP for the publication of 15 lakh copies of the same story in Malayalam. But CAP terminated this contract because of difference of opinion. *Care* with the help of another publisher published the book and circulated it free to the children in Kerala. The plaintiff filed the present suit for infringement of copyright in 1971. Though the trial started in 1972 and the plaintiff completed his evidence in 1973, it took many years for the defendant to complete the evidence. The defendant could not produce any evidence regarding the accounts and the records available at New York were reported to have been destroyed. The District Court finally in 1998 (after 27 years) found that there was infringement of copyright granted injunction and awarded 17.50 per cent of the cost of the publication of one copy of the book, i.e., a total of ₹2,31,000/- with 18 per cent interest from the date of suit for damages. Both the parties appealed to the High Court. The defendants contended that there was no copyright violation since the work was created under employment. Since there was no evidence produced by *Care* to show that there was a valid assignment of right for the translation of the work in Malayalam and based on the evidence on record, the High Court concluded that there was copyright infringement. Regarding the contention of the plaintiff on the calculation of damages, the court after considering the fact that the book was not priced or sold in the market but freely distributed in Kerala State and also that the plaintiff could not prove his actual loss of profit, accepted the formula adopted by the trial court and observed:

> The trial court has taken the cost of publication of the book at ₹1/- and has awarded 17.50% of the same to the plaintiff.... We are conscious of the argument of the plaintiff that 17.50% of this cost which is taken as the basis by the trial court was the amount which the plaintiff would have received had there been printing and publication of the book in question by the plaintiff as per the contract dated 15th September, 1970 and the plaintiff is not claiming the said cost but is claiming damages on account of infringement. However, the absence of any other yardstick, even for the purpose of damages we consider 17.50% of the cost as reasonable particularly when the book is not a priced one and royalty in the normal course would be attracted on the basis of the price of the book. Therefore, we feel that if the plaintiff is given 17.50% of the cost and if the cost of printing and publication of the book is taken as ₹1/- that would be an adequate compensation to the plaintiff.

The court found that 9,847 million copies of the book were published and circulated. Based on this, the court calculated ₹16,92,950/- as damages. It was also contended by the plaintiff that the defendant deliberately delayed the suit at the trial court for a period of more than 25 years and on that ground claimed for exemplary damages. Rejecting this the court opined:

> No doubt conduct of the *Care* during the proceedings before the trial court has not been proper. However, one has to keep in mind that the project in question for which the book was to be distributed and in fact distributed to the poor children was a benevolent project of public service. The books were distributed free of cost to the children and therefore, we do not deem it fit to grant any exemplary damages against the defendants.[336]

---

336. *See, P.N. Krishnan Murthy* v. *Co-operative for American Relief Everywhere*, AIR 2001 (Del) 258: 2000(20)PTC658(Del).

The court seems to be benevolent to an intentional organisation who has not only deliberately violated the copyright of an author but also with all its financial might fought the case at the lower court for a period of 27 years harassing the author monetarily and mentally. This seems to be a fit case to award exemplary damages to send a clear message that be it for charitable purpose or not the parties that too financially sound should not abuse the process of law that too in case of intellectual property infringement. The basic principle for calculation of damages was stated by *Lord Wilberforce* in *General Tire and Rubber Co* v. *Firestone Type & Rubber Co. Ltd.*[337] in the following terms:

> As in the case of any other tort ... the object of damages is to compensate for loss or injury. The general rule at any rate in relation to 'economic' torts is that the measure of damages is to be, so far as possible, that sum of money which will put the injured party in the same position as he would have been in if he had no sustained the wrong.

Thus, in the aforesaid case, it was held that if the proprietor has been exploiting the patent by granting licences to others in return for royalties, then his loss is the capitalised value of the royalties that the infringer would have paid had he taken a licence. Alternatively, the royalty may be calculated as a percentage of the net sale price of the articles where the infringer has been selling them at a lower price than legitimate licencees. The royalty method of calculation falls down altogether if the proprietor does not grant licences but works the patent himself. In this case, it is a question of the profits lost as a result of the infringer's activities. Here, many factors may be relevant, including the effect on the market place of the infringement. Particular issues include:

1. whether every sale of an infringing article represents a lost sale for the proprietor;
2. whether the proprietor would have sold other articles along with those lost sales (for example, the buyer may have also purchased non-patented articles in addition to the patented article)—these damages are often referred to as parasitic damages;
3. whether the infringer had generated additional interest in the patented article through his marketing efforts;
4. what the effect on the market was by changing a monopoly into a duopoly (for example, did the proprietor have to reduce his prices to compete with the infringer);
5. typical profit margins for the category of article concerned;
6. whether the infringer had deliberately undercut the proprietor's sale price.

In US, the copyright owner is entitled to recover the actual damages suffered by him or her as a result of the infringement, and any profits of the infringer that are attributable to the infringement and are not taken into account in computing the actual damages.

Additional Damages including Punitive Damages

Both in the United Kingdom and the United States of America, there are provisions for additional damages in case of flagrant infringement of copyright. Similarly, in India additional damages including punitive damages are recognised. In *Time Incorporated* v. *Lokesh Srivastava*,[338] the

337. (1975) RPC 203.
338. (2005) 30 PTC 3 (Del). *See also, Louis Vuitton Malletier* v. *Iqbal Singh*, 2019 (78) PTC 315 (Del): 258 (2019) DLT 760.

court has recognised third type of damages as punitive damages apart from compensatory and nominal damages. In *Microsoft Corporation* v. *Deepak Raval*,[339] justification given by the Court for award of compulsory damages was to make up for the loss suffered by the plaintiff and deter a wrong doer and like-minded from indulging in such unlawful activities. In *Sap Aktiengesellschaft* v. *Rohit Sharma*,[340] based on the report of the Local Commissioner and the investigator the court held that the computers were installed at the premises of the defendants with the SAP Software, various students were enrolled and fees were being charged from them. This is a fit case where the plaintiff is entitled to damages of ₹5.00 lakh.

In *Mathias* v. *Accor Economy Lodging Inc.*,[341] the US Court examined the underlying factors to grant of punitive damages. Relying on the US case, the Delhi High Court in *Microsoft Corporation* v. *Ganesh Wakode*, [342] observed that the award of punitive damages serves the "additional purpose of limiting the defendant's ability to profit from its fraud by escaping detection and (private) prosecution." If a tortfeasor is "caught" only half the time he commits torts, then when he is caught he should be punished twice as heavily in order to make up for the times he gets away. Thus, the punitive damages should be really punitive and not flee bite and quantum thereof should depend upon the flagrancy of infringement. The court further observed:

> The practice of grant of punitive damages needs to be strengthened particularly in those cases where flagrant infringement is found. Such an exercise of power is not to be fettered by any requirement that the plaintiff must show some particular benefit which has accrued to the defendant or that the plaintiff must satisfy the court by leading evidence that he has suffered actual loss. In a case where the plaintiff proves such actual loss, he would be entitled to the same. However, even without such a proof, in case of flagrant infringement, the court has the complete discretion to make such award of damages as may seem appropriate to the circumstances, so that it acts as deterrent. In some cases, it is not possible to prove the actual damages, namely, that there is a normal rate of profit or that there is a normal or establish licensed royalty. Yet, clearly, the damages have to be assessed.[343]

In *Microsoft Corporation* v. *Indus Valley Partners (India) Pvt. Ltd.*,[344] plaintiffs seeking order of permanent injunction restraining the defendants from infringing the copyright of the plaintiffs as subsisting in their software programs by directly or indirectly copying, reproducing, storing, installing and/or using pirated/unlicenced software programs of the plaintiffs and for ancillary reliefs of delivery-up, rendition of accounts and damages. To find out the reality of the matter, Commissioners have been appointed by the Court. Commissioners in the reports submitted have reported large scale piracy by the defendants. However, in terms of the compromise under which the defendants therein paid a sum of ₹2,00,000/- to the plaintiffs. The court observed that the award of punitive damages in the sum of ₹2,00,000/- is appropriate. In

---

339. MIPR 2007 (1) 72. *See also, Lokesh Srivastava and Microsoft Corporation* v. *Yogesh Papat*, 2005 (30) PTC 245 (Del).
340. 2014 LawSuit (Del) 4002. *See also, Hindustan Unilever Limited* v. *Reckitt Benckiser India Limited*, 2014 (57) PTC 495.
341. 347 F. 3d 672 (7th Cir. 2003).
342. 2013 LawSuit (Del) 638. *See also, HSIL Limited* v. *Gujrat Ceramic Industries*, 2019 IV AD (Delhi) 332: 257 (2019) DLT 706; *Autodesk, Inc* v. *Prashant Deshmukh*, 2011 (46) PTC 38: 2011 (183) DLT 411.
343. *See, Whatman International Limited* v. *P. Mehta*, 257 (2019) DLT 472.
344. 2014 (2) MIPR 373: 2014 (143) DRJ 191.

a similar circumstances, the court in 2005 in *Time Incorporated* v. *Lokesh Srivastava*,[345] and in *Adobe Systems, Inc.* v. *P. Bhoominathan*,[346] has besides the compensatory damages also been awarded punitive damages. The principle of additional damages was followed by the Delhi High Court in *Microsoft Corporation* v. *Deepak Raval*.[347] The court observed:

> It becomes manifest that the Courts in India have treated the same path and applied the same principles as applied by the US, UK and Australian Courts in awarding the damages and have recognised that compensatory as well as punitive damages are to be awarded. The justification for award of compensatory damages is to make up for the loss suffered by the plaintiff and the rationale behind granting punitive damages is to deter a wrong doer and the like-minded from indulging in such unlawful activities. This is more so when an action has criminal propensity. Thus, while awarding punitive damages Courts have taken into consideration the conduct of the defendants which has "wilfully calculated to exploit the advantage of an established mark" (expression used by US Courts), which may also be termed as "flagrancy of the defendant's conduct" (test adopted by Australian Courts). The English Courts have, adopting the same nature of test, have used the test of "dishonest trader", who deals in products knowing that they are counterfeit or "recklessly indifferent" as to whether or not they are.

Punitive damages sometimes called compensatory damages are damages intended to punish and deter similar wrongful conduct rather than merely compensate for losses suffered by the plaintiff. Punitive damages are authorised when the defendant acted with recklessness, malice, or deceit. As for the amount of punitive damages awardable, the US Supreme Court in *BMW of North America, Inc.* v. *Gore*,[348] held that three guidelines help determine whether a punitive-damages award violates constitutional due process: (i) the reprehensibility of the conduct being punished; (ii) the reasonableness of the relationship between the harm and the award; and (iii) the difference between the award and the civil penalties authorised in comparable cases.

The punitive damages to a plaintiff is aimed at compensating him for the loss suffered by him whereas punitive damages are aimed at deterring a wrong doer and the like-minded from indulging in such unlawful activities as has been held by the Delhi High Court in *Times Incorporated* v. *Lokesh Srivastava*.[349] The punitive damages are founded on the philosophy of corrective justice.[350] The time has come while the Courts dealing actions for infringement of copyright it not only grants compensatory damages but awards punitive damages also with a view to discouraging dishearten law breakers who indulge in violations with impunity out of lust for money so that they realise that in case they are caught, they would be liable not only to reimburse the aggrieved party but would be liable to pay punitive damages also, which may spell financial disaster for them. The Court is of the view that the punitive damages should be really punitive and not flee bite and quantum thereof should depend upon the flagrancy of infringement.[351]

---

345. 2005 30 PTC 3.
346. 2009 39 PTC 658.
347. MIPR 2007 (1) 72: 2006 (33) PTC 122 (Del.).
348. 517 U.S. 559: 116 S. Ct. 1589 (1996).
349. 2005 (30) PTC 3 (Del): 116 (2005) DLT 599. *See also*, *Super Cassettes Industries* v. *M/s. Rachana Television Pvt. Ltd.*, 201 (2013) DLT 329: 2013 (55) PTC 122 (Del).
350. *Living Media India Ltd.* v. *M. Hussain*, 202 (2013) DLT 39: 2013 (55) PTC 548 (Del).
351. *Hero Honda Motors Ltd.* v. *Shree Assuramji Scooters*, 2006 (86) DRJ 113: 2006 (32) PTC 117 (Del).

Explaining the factors underlying the grant of punitive damages, the US Court in *Mathias* v. *Accordingly Economy Lodging, Inc.*,[352] observed that one function of punitive damages is to relieve the pressure on an overloaded system of criminal justice by providing a civil alternative to criminal prosecution of minor crimes. It was further observed that the award of punitive damages serves the additional purpose of limiting the defendant's ability to profit from its fraud by escaping detection and prosecution. If a tortfeasor is caught only half the time he commits torts, then when he is caught he should be punished twice as heavily in order to make up for the times he gets away. This Court feels that this approach is necessitated further for the reason that it is very difficult for a plaintiff to give proof of actual damages suffered by him as the defendants who indulge in such activities never maintain proper accounts of their transactions since they know that the same are objectionable and unlawful. In *C.M. Agarwalla* v. *Halar Salt and Chemical Works*,[353] the Calcutta High Court observed:

> Damages are deemed as the pecuniary compensation which the law awards to a person for the injury he has sustained by reason of the act or default of another whether the act is a breach of contract or a tort ... damages are the recompense given by process of law to a person for the wrong that another has done to him. Punitive damages are intended to be *in solatium* to the plaintiff and *in terrorem* to the public.

In *Time Incorporated* v. *Lokesh Srivastava*,[354] the Delhi High Court observed that punitive damages are founded upon the philosophy of corrective justice and as such, these must be awarded in appropriate cases to give a signal to the wrong doer that the law does not take a breach merely as a matter between rival parties but also feels concerned for those who may not be party to the *lis* but suffer on account of the breach. In *Hero Honda Motors Ltd.* v. *Shree Assuramji Scooters*,[355] noticing that the defendant chose to stay away from the proceedings of the Court, the Court felt that punitive damages were required to be made, since otherwise, the defendant who appears in the Court and submits account books would be liable for damages whereas a party that chooses to stay away would escape liability on account of failure of the availability of account books.

In *Microsoft Corporation* v. *Ms. K. Mayuri,*[356] the Delhi High Court emphasised the need to award punitive damages in case of blatant infringement of copyright. In an *ex parte* final order preventing the defendants from the unauthorised loading of MS Windows and MS Office, the court reasoned thus:

> This Court has no hesitation in saying that time has come when the Courts dealing with actions for infringement of trade name, copyright, patents, etc. should not only grant compensatory damages but award punitive damages also with a view to discourage and dishearten law breakers who indulge in violations with impunity out of lust for money so that they realize that in case they are caught, they would be liable not only to reimburse the aggrieved party but would be liable to pay punitive damages also, which may spell financial disaster for them.

---

352. 347 F. 3d 672 (7th Cir. 2003). *See also, M/s. Kee Pharma Limited* v. *M/s. Big M Healthcare*, MIPR 2012 (2) 78: 2012 (50) PTC 501 (Del).
353. AIR 1977 Cal 356.
354. 116 (2005) DLT 599: 2005 (30) PTC 3 (Del).
355. 125 (2005) DLT 504: 2006 (32) PTC 117 (Del).
356. 2007 (35) PTC 415 (Del). *See also, Microsoft Corporation* v. *Kiron,* 2007 (35) PTC 748 (Del).

In this case, the court awarded rupees five lakh as compensatory damages against a claim of ₹26.72 lakh by the plaintiff and another rupees five lakh as punitive damages. Though the reasoning is a welcome move, one wonders whether the amount of rupees five lakh spells "financial disaster" to the defendant who made a profit of ₹26.72 lakh. In *Microsoft Corporation* v. *Deepak Raval,*[357] the Court observed that Courts in India have become sensitive to the growing menace of piracy and have started granting punitive damages even in cases where due to absence of the defendant, the exact figures of sale made under the infringing copyright and/or trademark were not available. The justification given by the Court for award of compulsory damages was to make up for the loss suffered by the plaintiff and deter a wrongdoer from indulging in such unlawful activities. In *Larsen* v. *Chagan Bhai Patel,*[358] the Court observed that it would be encouraging the violators of intellectual property, if the defendants, notwithstanding that they did not contest the suit, are not burdened with punitive damages.

Account of Profits as Civil Remedies

The damages are a matter of right while account of profits is an equitable remedy and the court may or may not grant the latter relief. It is for this reason the claimant is given an option to claim either damages or profits.[359] The claims for damages and/or account of profits are based on common law principle applicable in torts. The plaintiff can claim relief either for damages or relief for account of profits. Also both the reliefs can be claimed in the alternative with right to the plaintiff to make an informed election between damages and profits in the course of trial in the light of information revealed on discovery and the evidence at the trial.[360] In a civil action for infringement of copyright (other than injunction) a claimant must choose between damages or an account of profits. In order to assist in making the election, a claimant is entitled to the disclosure of relevant information by the defendants, such as financial records.[361] It is relatively unusual for a claimant to opt for an account of profits, not least because the process of reckoning may be complex and the outcome uncertain. Furthermore, in copyright cases, where a claimant opts for an account of profits, he cannot then seek exemplary damages.[362] Now question arises what the utility of an actions of account of profit is? An account of profits may be a useful alternative for the claimant in that the infringer may have made a profit from his actions which exceeds in value what would be the normal award of damages. The purpose of the remedy is to prevent *unjust enrichment* of the defendant.[363] The quantum of an account is the profit, that is the gain, made by the defendant attributable to the infringement and not the wholesale or retail value of the offending articles or materials.[364]

---

357. MIPR 2007 (1) 72.
358. MIPR 2009 (1) 194: 2009 (39) PTC 538 (Del).
359. *Titan Industries* v. *Nitin P. Jain*, 126 (2006) DLT 132: 2006 (32) PTC 95 (Del).
360. 2006 (32) PTC 95 (Del): 126 (2006) DLT 132. *See also*, *Reddys Laboratories Limited* v. *Laborate Pharmaceuticals India Ltd.*, 260 (2019) DLT 273.
361. *Island Records Inc.* v. *Tring International* (1995) FSR 560.
362. *Redrow Homes Ltd.* v. *Betts Brothers* (1997) FSR 828.
363. *Indian Performing Right Society Ltd.* v. *Debashis Patnaik,* MIPR 2007 (1) 323: 2007 (34) PTC 201 (Del).
364. *Potton Ltd.* v. *Yorkclose Ltd.* (1994) FSR 567.

The purpose of an account of profits is not to punish the defendant but to prevent his *unjust enrichment.* There has been debate as to whether profits should be assessed incrementally (by looking at the difference between actual profits and those which would have been made without infringement) or alternatively whether they should be apportioned, that is paid only from that part of the defendant's business which is infringing. In *Celanese International Corp.* v. *B.P. Chemicals Ltd. Celanese,*[365] the issue was concerned with intellectual property rights infringement. In this case, the issue although useful was "small" and contributed less than 20% of the profits. The result was that the defendant was ordered to pay a sum less than it had already admitted as being appropriate based on an incremental approach. Some of the principles applicable to an account of profits were set out by Laddie J. in this case as follows:

1. Although an account of profits may produce a figure very different to an assessment of damages, both proceeded on the basis of legal causation.
2. Where the defendant carries on several businesses or sells different products and only one infringes, he has to account only for the profits made by the infringements.
3. There can be no reduction if the defendant could have made some of the profits by non-infringing means if he actually used infringing means.
4. The claimant must take the defendant as he finds him and the claimant cannot ask for an increase in the amount awarded on the basis that the defendant should have generated higher profits.
5. Where only part of a product infringes, the claimant is entitled only to the profit earned by virtue of the use of his invention.
6. An apportionment approach is suitable where, for example, there are three stages to making a product, each of which is protected by a patent. The total profit has to be divided between the three stages.
7. The court should not engage in a substantial rounding up as a way of making the defendant pay punitive damages and, if insufficient information was available, it was not justifiable to pluck a figure out of the air that for little relationship to any of the relevant facts.
8. Accounting principles afforded a useful guide and it was reasonable to assume, unless there was some special reason otherwise, that the profits made on different stages of a project were in proportion to the costs and expenses attributable to those proportions.
9. Acceptable deduction from the total figure were allowable costs, costs of research and development (unless there was a massive imbalance), financing costs, taxes paid.[366]

In the remedy of accounts of profit, the defendant is asked to account to the plaintiff for profits made from wrong doing such as infringement of intellectual property rights. This remedy prevents the defendants from being unjustly enrich at the cost of the plaintiff. An award of account of profits implies an investigation of actual accounts of the profits made by the defendant as a result of the infringement. It is a laborious and expansive procedure

365. *Celanese International Corp.* v. *B.P. Chemicals Ltd.* (1999) RPC 203.
366. *See also, Pan Manufacturing Corp.* v. *Corsets Silhouette Ltd.* (1963) RPC 45.

and is infrequently resorted to. It is usually believed that the plaintiff is entitled only to either of the remedies of damages or accounts of profits.[367] The remedies of damages and accounts of profits are remedies in the alternative for it has been held the two reliefs are incompatible. Damages are a matter of right; the account of profits is an equitable remedy and the court has a discretion whether or not to grant it. Accordingly, a successful claimant in an infringement action is entitled to an inquiry as to damages (at his own risk as to costs) in any case where there is a prospect that the inquiry would reach a positive result; whilst only in certain cases will the court grant an account of profits. In these cases, the claimant has an option (exercisable at the conclusion of the hearing of the case) to claim either damages or profits; he cannot have both. Accordingly, it is usual in particulars of claim to ask for the two in the alternative. This proposition of law was well settled in *Caxon Publishing Co. Ltd.* v. *Sutherland Publishing Co. Ltd.*[368] In the context of the award of the damages and accounts of profits in *Neilson* v. *Betts*,[369] it was observed that "two things are hardly reconcilable, for if you take an account of profits you condone the infringement". Thus, in *P. Lakshmikantham* v. *Ramkrishna Pictures*,[370] the Andhra Pradesh High Court held that the remedy of injunction can be joined either with that of the damage or accounts, but the remedies of accounts and damages can in no case be joined.

In *Ellora Industries* v. *Banarsi Das Goela*,[371] the court held that account of profits is an equitable remedy and the court has a discretion whether or not to grant it. Only in certain cases will the court grant an account of profits. Thus, in this case, the courts order an account of profits on the theory that the defendant was constructively an agent of the plaintiff in disposing of goods in a manner infringing the plaintiff's rights. The principle upon which a court grants account of profits has been explained by the Delhi High Court in *Titan Industries* v. *Nitin P. Jain*,[372] thus:

> The principle upon which the court grants an account of profits is that where one party owes a duty to another, the person to whom the duty is owed is entitled to recover from the other party every benefit which that other party has received by virtue of his fiduciary position if in fact he has obtained it without the knowledge or consent of the party to whom he owed the duty. An account is generally refused if the defendant had no knowledge of the claimant's mark and, when ordered, is limited to the period during which such knowledge had existed; whilst knowledge or absence of knowledge does not affect the right to damages.

In the above case, the issue was whether the plaintiff could claim both the relief, that is, for damages and for rendition of accounts together. The court held that claimant was given an option to claim either damages or profits and such an option was exercisable at the conclusion of hearing of the case. Both the reliefs could be claimed in the alternative with right to the plaintiff to make an informed election between damages and profits in the course of trial.

---

367. N.S. Gopalakrishnan and T.G. Agitha, *Principles of Intellectual Property*, Eastern Book Company, Lucknow (2009) at p. 577.
368. (1938) 4 All ER 389: 1939 AC 178.
369. (1870) 6 HL 1, at p. 22. *See also*, *De Vitre* v. *Betts* (1873) 6 HL 319; *Island Records Limited* v. *Tring International PLC* (1995) FSR 560.
370. AIR 1981 AP 224.
371. AIR 1980 Delhi 254: (1979) ILR 2 Delhi 481.
372. 126 (2006) DLT 132: 2006 (32) PTC 95 (Del).

Jurisdiction of Court in Civil Remedies: Section 62

A civil suit is normally instituted for infringement of copyright by way of filing of a plaint in the District Court or High Court as the case may be. According to Section 62 of the Copyright Act, 1957, every suit or other civil proceedings under the Act shall be instituted in the district courts having jurisdiction and the district court has been defined as the court within the local limits of whose jurisdiction, at the time of the institution of the suit or civil proceedings, the person instituting the suit or civil proceedings actually and voluntarily resides or carries on business.[373] The Section 62 of the Copyright Act[374] reads:

> "62. Jurisdiction of court over matters arising under this Chapter—(1) Every suit or other civil proceeding arising under this Chapter in respect of the infringement of copyright in any work or the infringement of any other right conferred by this Act shall be instituted in the district court having jurisdiction.
>
> (2) For the purpose of Sub-section (1), a "district court having jurisdiction" shall notwithstanding anything contained in the Code of Civil Procedure, 1908 (5 of 1908), or any other law for the time being in force, include a district court within the local limits of whose jurisdiction, at the time of the institution of the suit or other proceeding, the person instituting the suit or other proceeding or, where there are more than one such persons, any of them actually and voluntarily resides or carries on business or personal works for gain."

Thus, in *Foundry Visionmongers Ltd.* v. *Satyanarayana Reddy S*,[375] it was held that the territorial jurisdiction of a court in case of infringement of copyright exists either by virtue of the Section 62 of the Copyright Act or on account of the Section 20 of the Code of Civil Procedure. Under Section 62 of the Copyright Act a suit for the infringement of copyright is to be instituted in the district court having jurisdiction. The Section 20 of the Code contains provisions with respect to institution of suits. It stipulates that every suit shall be instituted in a court with the local limits of whose jurisdiction the defendant or any of the defendants. If there are more than one, resides or cause of action, wholly or in part arises. But, as far as the copyright and trade mark disputes are concerned, Section 62 of the Copyright Act 1957 and Section 143 of the Trade Marks Act 1999, respectively, provide an additional forum by including a district court within whose limits the plaintiff actually and voluntarily resides or carries on business or personally works for gain. Both these provisions, which are identical, contain non-obstante clauses that notwithstanding anything contain in the Code, these provisions would take effect. In *Dhodha House* v. *S.K. Maingi*,[376] the Supreme Court

---

373. *See, Piruz Khambatta* v. *Rajmohan Rupaji Modi*, MIPR 2017 (2) 111; *Manugraph India Limited* v. *Simarq Technologies Pvt. Ltd.*, AIR 2016 Bom 217: 2016 (67) PTC 254 (Bom); *Emergent Genetics India Pvt. Ltd.* v. *Shailendra Shivam*, 2011 (125) DRJ 173: 2011 (47) PTC 494 (Del); *Dashmesh Mechanical Works* v. *Hari Singh*, 2010 (42) PTC 288 (Del); *Banyan Tree Holding (P) Limited* v. *A. Murali Krishna Reddy*, MIPR 2009 (3) 247: 2010 (42) PTC 361 (Del); *Titan Industries* v. *Nitin P. Jain*, 126 (2006) DLT 132: 2006 (32) PTC 95 (Del).
374. For general commentaries on Section 62 of the Copyright Act, 1957, *see, Gulf DTH FZ LLC* v. *Dishtv India Limited*, 2016 VIII AD (Delhi) 266; *Nagpur Distillers Pvt. Ltd.* v. *Kopargaon Sahakari Sakhar Karkhana Limited*, 2013 (4) ABR 639; *M/s. Lakhan Pal Shyam Kumar* v. *M/s. Ram Prasad Gupta*, 190 (2012) DLT 659: 2012 (51) PTC 141 (Del); *Super Cassettes Industries Ltd.* v. *Myspace Inc.*, MIPR 2011 (2) 303: 2011 (48) PTC 49 (Del); *Varehouse Infotech Ceebros Arcade* v. *SAP Aktiengesellschaft*, 2010 (115) DRJ 697: 2010 (42) PTC 650 (Del).
375. 2015 (64) PTC 108 (Del): MIPR 2015 (3) 68.
376. AIR 2006 SC 730: (2006) 9 SCC 41.

held that Section 62 of the Copyright Act allows the plaintiff to file a suit where the plaintiff was carrying on business. A corporation in view of Explanation appended to Section 20 of the Code would be deemed to be carrying on business inter alia at a place where it has a subordinate office. Only because, its goods are being sold at a place would thus evidently not mean that it carries a business at that place. Thus, a plaintiff could file a suit where it carried on business in infringement cases under Copyright Act, but when a plaintiff was a company, carrying on business by a company could only be where the plaintiff company had an office and it was only through office being the principal office or sole office or registered office or subordinate office that, company could be said to carry on business, i.e. a company carrying of business was not seen independently of existence of an office and merely selling of goods by a company without office at place where goods were sold would not mean that the company was said to be "carrying on business" simply because of selling of goods. The Apex Court has also explained the meaning of "carrying on business" thus:

> The expression "carries on business" and the expression "personally works for gain" connotes two different meanings. For the purpose of carrying on business only presence of a man at a place is not necessary. Such business may be carried at a place through an agent or a manager or through a servant. The owner may not event visit that place. The phrase "carries on business" at a certain place would, therefore, mean having an interest in a business at that place, a voice in what is done, a share in the gain or loss and some control there over.

The question as to whether the expression "notwithstanding anything contained in the Code of Civil Procedure," in both Section 62 of the Copyright Act and Section 143 of the Trade Marks Act, out set the applicability of Section 20 came up for the consideration of the Supreme Court in *Indian Performing Rights Society* v. *Sanjay Dalia*.[377] The Apex Court answered the question in the negative and observed that the very language of Section 62 of the Copyright Act and Section 134 of the Trade Marks Act, an additional forum has been provided by including a District Court within whose limits the Plaintiff actually and voluntarily resides or carries on business or personally works for gain. The expression "notwithstanding anything contained in the Code of Civil Procedure" does not oust the applicability of the provisions of Section 20 of the Code of Civil Procedure and it is clear that additional remedy has been provided to the Plaintiff so as to file a suit where he is residing or carrying on business etc., as the case may be. The Court further observed:

> The object with which the latter provisions have been enacted, it is clear that if a cause of action has arisen wholly or in part, where the Plaintiff is residing or having its principal office/carries on business or personally works for gain, the suit can be filed at such place/s. Plaintiff (s) can also institute a suit at a place where he is residing, carrying on business or personally works for gain de hors the fact that the cause of action has not arisen at a place where he/they are residing or any one of them is residing, carries on business or personally works for gain. However, this right to institute suit at such a place has to be read subject to certain restrictions, such as in case Plaintiff is residing or carrying on business at a particular place/having its head office and at such place cause of action has also arisen wholly or in part, Plaintiff cannot ignore such a place under the guise that he is carrying on business at other far flung places also. The very intendment of the insertion of provision in the Copyright Act and Trade Marks Act is the convenience of the Plaintiff. The rule of

377. AIR 2015 SC 3479: (2015) 10 SCC 161.

> convenience of the parties has been given a statutory expression in Section 20 of the Code of Civil Procedure as well. The interpretation of provisions has to be such which prevents the mischief of causing inconvenience to parties.[378]

In *Achla Sabharwal* v. *A. Saptrishi Films*,[379] the Delhi High Court held that the jurisdiction of the Court over the civil remedies has been laid down in Section 62 of the Copyright Act, 1957. Besides this, an additional ground for attracting the jurisdiction of a court over and above the "normal" grounds as laid down in Section 20 of the Code of Civil Procedure. Thus, in *Amilal Ramkishan Dass* v. *Ashok Kumar Sethi*,[380] the Madras High Court held that the jurisdiction of the Court to entertain one cause of action, i.e., cause of action regarding infringement in the light of Section 62(2) of the Copyright Act. Equally, if it is a suit for passing off qua suit of Copyright Act alone, the benefit of Section 62(2) may not be available. But, if it had been filed in the Court, Section 20 of the Code also will not be available in the light of Section 20. As per Section 62(1) of the Copyright Act every suit or civil proceeding arising in respect of the infringement of the copyright in any work, it shall be instituted in the District Court having jurisdiction. Thus, the District Court is having jurisdiction in the matter when there is infringement of copyright, therefore, the writ petition is not maintainable on the ground of availability of the alternate remedy.[381]

In *Ritika Limited* v. *Pramod Kanodia*,[382] the court held that Section 62 of the Copyright Act is more or less a self contained code so far as jurisdiction in relation to matters arising under the Act is concerned. In *Smithkline Beecham Plc* v. Sunil Singhi,[383] the court observed that Section 62 of the Act makes an obvious and significant departure from the norm that the choice of jurisdiction should primarily be governed by the convenience of the defendant. This shift is with considerable wisdom, since the violation of the statutorily protected rights expose the transgressor/pirate with inconvenience rather than compelling the sufferer to chase after the former. It is the general principle of law that Court shall not pass any order without proper jurisdiction.[384] The law on the subject has been well thrashed out in *Dabur India Ltd.* v. *K.R. Industries*.[385] In this case, rejection of the plaint on the ground of lack of territorial jurisdiction was in issue.[386] However, the Court has jurisdiction to entertain and try the present suit by virtue of the provisions of the Section 62 of the Copyright Act, 1957 as the plaintiff carries on its business activities in Delhi. The defendant is also selling its goods in Delhi, i.e., within the territorial jurisdiction of the Court.

In *Sulochana* v. *Rajinder Singh*,[387] the Apex Court has also dealt with the question whether the composite suit for passing off and copyright infringement can be filed at a place where the plaintiff resides or carries on business, etc., in terms of Section 62(2) of the

378. *See, Indian Performing Rights Society* v. *Sanjay Dalia*, AIR 2015 SC 3479: (2015) 10 SCC 161 (at para. 17).
379. 2019 (78) PTC 437 (Del): 258 (2019) DLT 663.
380. 2019 (77) PTC 296 (Mad): (2018) 8 MLJ 160.
381. *See, P.K. Sen* v. *Exxon Mobile Corporation*, 2018 (73) PTC 304 (Del): 236 (2017) DLT 333.
382. 97 (2002) DLT 221: 2002 (24) PTC 572 (Del).
383. 91 (2001) DLT 461: 2001 PTC 321 (Del).
384. *Banyan Tree Holdings (P) Limited* v. *M. Murali Krishna Reddy*, 2008 (38) PTC 288 (Del).
385. AIR 2008 SC 3123: 2008(37) PTC 332 SC. *See also, Dabur India Limited* v. *K.R. Industries*, 2006 (33) PTC 107 (Del).
386. *See, Conzerv Systems P. Ltd.* v. *T.K. Babu*, 2009 (40) PTC 255 (Del).
387. 2008 (8) SCALE 304: (2008) 15 SCC 538.

Copyright Act, 1957. Clause (2) of Section 62 of the Copyright Act provides for an additional forum to file suit for copyright infringement. It authorises a person to institute suit or other proceedings in the court within the local limits of whose jurisdiction the person instituting the suit or other proceedings or, where there are more than one such persons, any of them actually and voluntarily resides or carries on business or personally works for gain as well. It is provided in addition to what is provided under Section 20 of the Code of Civil Procedure. In *Dhodha House* v. *S.K. Maingi*,[388] the Apex Court further held:

> The provisions contained in Section 62(2) of the 1957 Act have been specially designed to confer an extra benefit upon the parties who were not in a position to initiate copyright proceedings in two different courts. In other words, it prescribes an additional ground for attracting the jurisdiction of the court over and above the normal grounds as laid down in Section 20 of the Code of Civil Procedure, 1908.

Clarifying the propositions of composite suit in *Paragon Rubber Industries* v. *Pragati Rubber Mills*,[389] the Apex Court held that for the purpose of invoking the jurisdiction of the court in a composite suit, both the causes of action must arise within the jurisdiction of the court which otherwise had the necessary jurisdiction to decide all the issues. However, the jurisdiction cannot be conferred by joining two causes of action in the same suit when the court has jurisdiction to try the suit only in respect of one cause of action and not the other. In *Carlsberg Breweries* v. *Som Distilleries and Breweries Ltd.*,[390] the issue was whether a composite suit can be used as a ploy to confer jurisdiction on a Court which has jurisdiction to try only the suit in respect of one cause of action and not the other? The Court held that Section 62(2) of the Copyright Act, 1957 which is specially designed to provide an additional forum enabling the author to file a suit who may not otherwise be in a position to file a suit at different places where his copyright was violated has not been incorporated into the Designs Act, 2000. Therefore, akin to a passing off action, a design infringement suit has to be instituted in a jurisdiction where the defendant is located. Consequently, a composite suit in relation to infringement of a design with a passing off should be maintainable as on the same cause of action against the same defendants, territorial jurisdiction made by the plaintiff on one cause of action, would be sufficient for the other.

While Section 62(2) of the Copyright Act, 1957 is a long-arm provision, the Act itself operates only through the territory of India. For the infringing activity to constitute a cause of action, it must be shown to have taken place in the territory of India. In *Banyan Tree* v. *A. Murali Krishna Reddy*,[391] the Court held that a passive website would not by itself vest the forum court with jurisdiction. A commercial transaction should be shown to have been concluded using the website within the jurisdiction of the forum court. In *Smith Kline Beecham Plc* v. *Sunil Singhi*,[392] the Delhi Court in the context of Section 62(2) of the Copyright Act, 1957 held that the defendant ought to be shown to be carrying on its local business activities within India. In the *Indian Performing Right Society Ltd.* v. *Gauhati Town Club*,[393] it was

388. AIR 2006 SC 730: (2006) 9 SCC 41.
389. 2013 (14) SCALE 273: (2013) 8 MLJ 761.
390. AIR 2019 Delhi 23: 2019 (77) PTC 1 (Del).
391. MIPR 2009 (3) 247: 2010 (42) PTC 361 (Del).
392. 2001 PTC 321(Del).
393. 2013 III AD (Delhi) 333: 2013 (134) DRJ 732. *See also*, *P.M. Diesel Ltd.* v. *Patel Field Marshall Industries* (2009) ILR 1 Delhi 674: 2008 (38) PTC 69 (Del).

observed that as far as the aspect of territorial jurisdiction is concerned, Section 62(2) of the Copyright Act permits action for infringement of copyright to be instituted in the Court within whose jurisdiction the plaintiff carries on business. The suit is undoubtedly in respect of infringement of copyright of the plaintiff. Hence, the court has the jurisdiction. The scope and ambit of Section 62(2) was also clarified in *Caterpillar Inc.* v. *Kailash Nichani.*[394] In this case, the court held that particularly Sub-section (2) of Section 62 of the Copyright Act was a significant departure from Section 20 of the Code of Civil Procedure inasmuch as in respect of violation of Copyright the suit could be filed even at a place where the person instituting the suit actually and voluntarily (i.e., the plaintiff) resides or carries on business or personally works for gain as opposed to Section 20 where suit could be filed at a place where the defendant actually and voluntarily resides or carries on business or personally works for gain.

In *Dhodha House* v. *S.K. Maingi,*[395] the Apex Court observed that Sub-section (2) of Section 62 of the Copyright Act provides for a non-obstante clause conferring jurisdiction upon the district court within the local limits of whose jurisdiction, at the time of the institution of the suit or other proceeding, the persons instituting the suit or other proceedings, have been residing. In terms of sub-section (1) of Section 62, suit can be instituted and the proceedings can be initiated in respect of matters arising under the said Chapter for infringement of the copyright in any work or the infringement of any other right conferred thereunder. In *Varehouse Infotech Ceebros Arcade* v. *SAP Aktiengesellschaft,*[396] the Delhi High Court held that the jurisdiction for the purposes of Section 62 is wider than that of the court as prescribed under the Code of Civil Procedure, 1908. The introduction of Section 62(2) was not intended to restrict the owners of copyright from exercising their rights "but to remove any impediment from their doing so. The word "include" in Section 62(2) shows that the jurisdiction for the purposes of Section 62 is wider than that of the Court as prescribed under the Code of Civil Procedure, 1908. The relevant extract of the report of the Joint Committee published in the Gazette of India dated 23 November, 1956 laid the foundation for Section 62(2) thus:

> In the opinion of the Committee many authors are deterred from instituting infringement proceedings because the court in which such proceedings are to be instituted is situated at a considerable distance from the place of their ordinary residence. The Committee feels that this impediment should be removed and the new Sub-clause (2) accordingly provides that infringement proceedings may be instituted in the district court within the local limits of whose jurisdiction the person instituting the proceedings ordinarily resides, carries on business, etc.[397]

In *Exphar SA* v. *Eupharma Laboratories Ltd.,*[398] the Apex Court held that the object and reason for the introduction of Sub-section (2) of Section 62 was not to restrict the owners of the copyright to exercise their rights but to remove any impediment from their doing so.

---

394. 97 (2002) DLT 304: 2002 (24) PTC 405 (Del).
395. AIR 2006 SC 730: 2006 (32) PTC 1 (SC). *See also, Arun Colour Chem* v. *Mithumal Essance Mart,* 2010 (43) PTC 668 (Del).
396. 2010 (115) DRJ 697: 2010 (42) PTC 650 (Del).
397. *See, Varehouse Infotech Ceebros Arcade* v. *SAP Aktiengesellschaft,* 2010 (115) DRJ 697: 2010 (42) PTC 650 (Del); *The Indian Performing Right Society Ltd.* v. *Sanjay Dalia,* MIPR 2007 (3) 204; *Shree Rajmoti Industries* v. *Rajmoti Oil Mill Pvt. Ltd.,* 115 (2004) DLT 212: 2005 (30) PTC 38 (Del); *Exphar SA* v. *Eupharma Laboratories Ltd.,* AIR 2004 SC 1682: 2004 (28) PTC 251 (SC).
398. AIR 2004 SC 1682: 2004 (28) PTC 251 (SC).

Section 62(2) cannot be read as limiting the jurisdiction of the District Court only to cases where the person instituting the suit or other proceeding, or where there are more than one such persons, any of them actually and voluntarily resides or carries on business or presently works for gain. It prescribes an additional ground for attracting the jurisdiction of a Court over and above the "normal" grounds as laid down in Section 20 of the Code. Thus, in *Mitaso Appliances Ltd.* v. *Mehta Zina Bhai Bhimji Bhai*,[399] it was held that the suit for infringement of copyright is maintainable at a place where the plaintiff resides or carries on business. Similarly, in *Exphar SA* v. *Bharat Shah*,[400] it was held that a suit in case of infringement of copyright may be instituted in Court within whose jurisdiction, a person filing suit actually or voluntarily resides or carries on business or personally works for gain.

In *Time Warner Entertainment Co. L.P.* v. *R.P.G. Netcom Ltd.*,[401] jurisdiction of Delhi Court challenged on ground that none of parties used to reside in Delhi as per Section 62(2) of the Copyright Act suit can be file in Court in whose jurisdiction either of party was carrying on business. In the present case, the plaintiff was carrying on business in Delhi, therefore, it was held that the Delhi Court had territorial jurisdiction to try suit. In *Wiley Eastern Ltd.* v. *Indian Institute of Management*,[402] the court observed that if the allegations in the case make out a case for infringement of copyright, the plaintiff can file the suit within the local limits of the Court where he resides. But where there are two forums available to the plaintiff, the plaintiff has to file the suit at the Court of the lowest grade. This was held in *Wockhardt Veterinary Ltd.* v. *M/s. Raj Medicos*.[403] The meaning of the words "any of the plaintiff" under Section 62 of the Copyright Act, 1957 debated in the Delhi High Court in *Smith Kline Beecham Plc* v. *Mr. Sunil Singhi*.[404] In this case, it was argued that Section 62(2) of the Copyright Act, 1957 did not permit the dispute to be adjudicated in Delhi especially since the plaintiffs have no business activity in this city. The territorial jurisdiction could only be invoked if the cause of action had arisen in Delhi. The Plaint should have specifically stated that the Defendants are manufacturing the offending drug in Mumbai. A reading of Sub-section (2) of Section 62 of the Act would dispel any doubt that the Act has no extra territorial application. Thus, if the cause of action did not arise in India, the Plaint called to be returned to the plaintiffs for filing in a court of competent jurisdiction. The court held that the same should not be given the restricted application.

In *Brooke Bond India Ltd.* v. *Balaji Tea (India) Pvt. Ltd.*,[405] the Madras High Court expressed the view that although Section 62(2) of the Copyright Act entitles that plaintiff to file a suit in the District Court having jurisdiction at the place of the business of the plaintiff, yet this provision should be sparingly resorted so that a small trader is not put to unnecessary hardship and disadvantage by being dragged to a distant place. In the said case, the defendant was resident of Raipur. In *M/s. Ruchi Pvt. Ltd.* v. *M/s Indian Flame Enterprises*,[406] the Delhi High Court held that the jurisdiction of the Court depended on the allegation in the plaint

399. 61 (1996) DLT 593: 1995 (35) DRJ 299.
400. 2003 (26) PTC 461 (Del).
401. 2003 (27) PTC 452 (Del)
402. 61 (1996) DLT 281: 1995 (35) DRJ 522.
403. 1998 RLR 353.
404. 91 (2001) DLT 461: 2001 (2) RAJ 446.
405. 1990 (2) ALR 35.
406. 94 (2001) DLT 796.

and not on the taken defence. The court found that jurisdiction was to be invoked on three grounds, firstly; Section 62 of the Copyright Act, secondly, the defendant mark for gain in Delhi, thirdly, the registration of the trademark sought by the defendant for sale in Delhi and goods of defendant sold in Delhi. Thus, the court ruled that the Delhi Court had the territorial jurisdiction to decide the case. Thus, in *P.M. Diesels Ltd.* v. *Patel Field Marshal Industries*,[407] it was observed that plaintiff failing to aver in the plaint that he voluntarily resides or carries on business or personally works for gain within the territorial jurisdiction of the court under Section 62 of the Copyright Act. Thus, prima facie the court has no territorial jurisdiction. The court observed:

> Reverting now to the main question in respect of territorial jurisdiction, it may be noticed that the plaintiff has claimed that Delhi High Court has jurisdiction on three counts. Firstly, in view of Section 62 of the Copyright Act, 1957. Secondly, in view of the fact that the defendants had sought registration of trademark for sale at Delhi as well as, therefore, the plaintiffs entitled to restrain the threatened sale by defendants at Delhi. Thirdly, it has been claimed that the goods under the impugned mark have been sold at Delhi and the plaintiff's rights violated at Delhi. On the other hand, the defendants claim that Delhi Court has no jurisdiction as plaintiff and defendants, have been residing at Rajkot and both the parties have also been ordinarily working for gain at Rajkot and that no sale has been effected by defendants within the territorial jurisdiction of this Court.

In *Microsoft Corporation* v. *Dhiren Gopal*,[408] it was observed that Section 62(2) was introduced in Copyright Act to protect and see that the authors of original works should not be made to run from one court to other court wherever the infringement of their copyright takes place in order to initiate proceedings against the infringements and that they should be able to initiate such proceedings before the District Court where they live. However, in *Caterpillar Inc.* v. *Kailash Nichani*,[409] the court held that the provisions of Section 62 of the Copyright Act provided for the choice of the jurisdiction to be governed by the convenience of the defendant and the same was clearly opposite the norms set out under Section 20 of the Civil Procedure Code, 1908. Thus, the suit of the plaintiff could not have been dismissed under Rule 11 of Order 7 of the Code, for want of jurisdiction under the provisions of Section 62 of the Copyright Act. In *Smithkline Beecham Plc* v. Sunil Singhi,[410] it was observed that Section 62 of the Copyright Act makes an obvious and significant departure from the norm that the choice of jurisdiction should primarily be governed by the convenience of the defendant. This shift is with considerable wisdom, since the violation of the statutorily protected rights exposes the transgressor/pirate with inconvenience rather than compelling the sufferer to chase after the former. In *Brooke Bond India Ltd.* v. *Balaji Tea India Pvt. Ltd.*,[411] the Madras High Court held:

> Sub-section (2) of Section 62 of the Copyright Act, 1957 makes a departure from the normal law that a suit should be instituted at the place where the defendant resides or carries on business or personally works for gain. The language of Sub-section (2) is also significant.

---

407. AIR 1998 Delhi 225: (1998) ILR 1 Delhi 205. *See also, M/s. Ruchi Pvt. Ltd.* v. *M/s. Indian Flame Enterprises*, 94 (2001) DLT 796.
408. MIPR 2010 (1) 85: 2010 (42) PTC 1 (Del).
409. 97 (2002) DLT 304: 2002 (24) PTC 405 (Del).
410. 2001 PTC 321.
411. 1993 (18) IPLR 14.

> The sub-section only includes a Court within whose jurisdiction the plaintiff resides or carries on business, etc. It is very clear that the plaintiff is given a choice of forum and he can institute the suit either in the District Court of the place where the defendant resides or carries on business according to general law or at the place where he himself resides or carries on business.

In *Tata Oil Mills Co. Ltd.* v. *Hansa Chemical Pharmacy*,[412] the issue of pecuniary jurisdiction of copyright infringement was examined by the Delhi High Court. In this case, it was held in respect of the Union Territory of Delhi, the High Court of Delhi has the civil original jurisdiction in every suit value of which exceeds the amount mentioned in the Delhi High Court Act and as such it is the principal civil court of original jurisdiction with respect to every suit above the specified value and as such is the District Court within the meaning of Section 62 of the Copyright Act. It was also held that the suit in respect of infringement of copyright shall be filed in the court where the plaintiff resides or carries on business. Thus, in *Nirex Industries Ltd.* v. *Manchanra Footwear*,[413] it was held that since the plaintiffs were claiming the reliefs for injunction of copyright, the Delhi High Court will have the jurisdiction in view of the provisions of Sections 62 of the Copyright Act. Further, in *Glaxo Operations U.K. Ltd.* v. *Samrat Pharmaceuticals*,[414] it was held that a suit for infringement of copyright by the plaintiff company in the Delhi High Court will be maintainable if it carries on business in Delhi.

In *Royal Biscuits Pvt. Ltd.* v. *Sethi Bakers and Confectioners*,[415] the territorial jurisdiction of the Court under Section 62(2) of the Copyright Act, 1957 was debated. It was held that the provision gave a right to the plaintiff to institute the suit where the plaintiff carried on his business. Hence, it was held that the Delhi Courts had territorial jurisdiction to try the suit. In *Syndet & Chemical Industries Ltd.* v. *Mr. Kishan Aggarwal*,[416] the issue was relating to territorial jurisdiction of the Court under Section 62(2) of the Copyright Act, 1957. While in trying the suit for permanent injunction and rendition of account, the court found that the business was carried out by the plaintiff and its products were sold by the defendant in the territorial jurisdiction of the Court. It was ruled that the Court had jurisdiction for trying the same under Section 62(2) of the Copyright Act, 1957, as the plaintiff is carrying on business at Delhi. Further the goods of the defendants are also being sold in the impugned packaging at Delhi and, therefore, the cause of action has also arisen at Delhi. According to Section 62(1) of the Copyright Act, 1957, every suit of the infringement of copyright shall be instituted in the District Court having jurisdiction. Further, Section 62(2) provides that the person instituting the suit for infringement of copyright or, where there are more than one such person, any of them actually and voluntarily resides or carries on business or personally works for gain. In this case, it was found that the business was carried out by the plaintiff and its products were sold by the defendant in the territorial jurisdiction of the Court. However, in *Lok Nath Prasad Gupta* v. *Bijay Kumar Gupta*,[417] neither of the parties to the suit either "actually

412. 1986 (2) ARBLR 303 (Delhi): (1979) ILR Delhi 236.
413. 1984 IPLR 70.
414. AIR 1984 Delhi 265: 1984 RLR 291.
415. 1993 (1) ARBLR 13 (Delhi): 48 (1992) DLT 9.
416. MANU/DE/0651/1998.
417. 1995 (32) DRJ 350.

and voluntarily residing" or "carries on business" or "personally works for gain" within the territorial jurisdiction of Delhi High Court. Therefore, the suit was held not maintainable.

In *Matrumal Dhannalal Oil Mill* v. *Abhishek Enterprises*,[418] the issue was whether mere registration of copyright would confer territorial jurisdiction on the Court? In this case, the defendant filed application seeking dismissal of the suit for infringement on ground that there is a lack of territorial jurisdiction of Court to entertain the said suit. The court held that mere registration of the copyright at Delhi does not confer territorial jurisdiction on the Delhi Court. To vest territorial jurisdiction in the Delhi Court, plaintiff is required to specifically plead if defendant has infringed his copyright while passing off his goods as that of plaintiff at Delhi. In the instant case, plaintiff has failed to show that it carries on its business at Delhi or that defendant has been selling his goods at Delhi and passing off as that of the plaintiff. Therefore, averments made in the plaint have failed to confer any territorial jurisdiction on the Delhi Court. In the *Indian Performing Right Society Ltd.* v. *Mr. Badal Dhar Chowdhry*,[419] the issue was also whether the Court had territorial jurisdiction to entertain suit. In this case, the plaintiff had instituted suit at Delhi Court for injunction against the defendants from using musical works in which plaintiff Society had a copyright. But the court held that the Delhi Court had not territorial jurisdiction to entertain suit or to injunct defendants. The reason was explained by the court that the plaintiff society had its registered office at Mumbai and all defendants were based at Calcutta but injunction claimed against them was with respect to infringement of copyright of plaintiff occurring at Calcutta. This was neither in conformity with Section 62 of the Copyright Act nor with Section 20 of the Code of Civil Procedure.

In *Caterpillar Inc.* v. *Kailash Nichani*,[420] the issue was whether the suit filed by the plaintiff for infringement of copyright under Sections 51 and 55 of the Copyright Act, 1957, could be dismissed for lack of the territorial jurisdiction under the provisions of Section 62 of the Act? In this case, it was argued that under Section 20 of the Civil Procedure Code, 1908, it is the place where the defendant resides that gives jurisdiction to the Court but Section 62(2) of Copyright Act alters this principle and defines the place where the plaintiff resides or carries on business as the place where the suit has to be filed. It is only for this reason Section 62(2) of the Copyright Act uses non-obstante clause but in other aspects, it is the Code which is applicable. It was also argued that the object of territorial jurisdiction under Section 20 of the Code was that justice should be brought as near as possible to everyman's hearthstone and the defendant is not to be put to the trouble and expose to travel long distance to defend himself in cases where he is involved. It was held that the provisions of Section 62 of the Act had provided for the choice of the jurisdiction to be governed by the convenience of the defendant and the same was clearly opposite the norms set out under Section 20 of the Code. Thus, the suit of the plaintiff could not have been dismissed under Rule 11 of Order 7 of the Code, for want of jurisdiction under the provisions of Section 62 of the Act.

The concept actually resides or works for gain under Section 62 of the Copyright Act has been clarified by the court in *Amar Soap Factory* v. *Public Gram Udyog Samiti*.[421] In this

418. MIPR 2010 (2) 207: 2010 (43) PTC 26 (Del).
419. 2010 (43) PTC 332 (Del).
420. 97 (2002) DLT 304: 2002 (24) PTC 405 (Del).
421. (1985) ILR Delhi 960. *See also, Intas Pharmaceuticals Limited* v. *Allergan Inc.*, AIR 2007 Delhi 108: 2006 (32) PTC 272 (Del).

case, the court held that as per the provisions of Section 20 of the Code of Civil Procedure, every suit has to be instituted in a court within the local limits of whose jurisdiction the defendant at the time of commencement of the suit actually or voluntarily resides or carries on business. However, Section 62 of the Copyright Act is an exception. This provisions alter the principles as laid down under Section 20 of the Code and defines the place where the plaintiff resides or carries on business, as the place where the suit has to be filed. It is enough if the plaintiff actually resides or works for gain within the jurisdiction of the court which is approached and it is not necessary for his residence to be a permanent one. Thus, the court held that for the application of Section 62 of the Copyright Act, it is enough if the plaintiff actually resides or works for gain within the jurisdiction of the court and it is not necessary for his residence to be a permanent one.

The relation between Section 20 of the Code of Civil Procedure, 1908 and Section 62(2) of the Copyright Act, 1957 and combined effect of both provisions of law has been explained by the Delhi High Court in *Pfizer Enterprises* v. *Dr. H.R. Manchanda*.[422] In this case, the court laid down the rule to determine the place of suing in case of copyright infringement. The court held: First, the place at which the defendant actually and voluntarily resides or carries on business. Second, the place at which the cause of action, wholly or in part arises. Lastly, the suit can be instituted at the place where the plaintiff resides and carries on business. The explanation to Section 20 of the Code makes it clear that the place at which a corporate entity carries on business is either the place at which it has its sole or principle office or where it has a subordinate office. In *Indian Performing Rights Society* v. *Sanjay Dalia*,[423] the Court held that the expression "carries on business" in Section 62 of the Copyright Act has the same meaning as in Section 20 of the Code. It was further held that the mere existence of a branch office in Delhi would not mean that the plaintiff carries on business in Delhi. The plaintiff would be deemed to carry on business at a branch office only if a cause of action had arisen in Delhi. A well-established principle of law is that to amount "to carrying on business" in a certain place, the essential part of the business must take place in that place.[424]

In *M/s. Lakhan Pal Shyam Kumar* v. *M/s. Ram Prasad Gupta*,[425] the issue was whether the Court had territorial jurisdiction to entertain present suit under Section 62 of Copyright Act, 1957. The court held that Section 62 of the Act which was available to plaintiff for filing a suit wherein he actually or voluntarily resided or carried on business or personally works for gain was a forum in addition to forum prescribed under Section 20 of the Code of Civil Procedure. The court held that the cause of action was a bundle of facts which were necessary to be proved in a given case and if cause of action arose within jurisdiction of Court concerned, it empowered Court to entertain same. To decide whether or not cause of action had arisen within jurisdiction of present Court, only pleadings in plaint had to be looked at and nothing more. Bald averments in plaint, not based on any cogent material could not form basis to raise a presumption of jurisdiction by present Court, which it otherwise did

422. 2009 (39) PTC 114 (Del).
423. 143 (2007) DLT 617. *See also on Loknath Prasad Gupta* v. *Bijay Kumar Gupta*, 57 (1995) DLT 502.
424. *Dhodha House* v. *S.K. Maingi*, AIR 2006 SC 730: 2006 (32) PTC 1 (SC); *Nedungadi Bank* v. *Central Bank of India*, AIR 1961 Ker 50: AIR 2006 SC 730; *Bharat Insurance Co.* v. *Vasudev*, AIR 1956 Nag 203.
425. 190 (2012) DLT 659: 2012 (51) PTC 141 (Del).

not have. If issue about jurisdiction was a mixed question of law and fact requiring recording of evidence, then same could not be tried as a preliminary issue. In present case, issue of jurisdiction was a pure question of law and thus could be decided as a preliminary issue. None of the causes of action arose within jurisdiction of present Court. Hence, the present Court did not have territorial jurisdiction to try and entertain present suit. Thus, the suit was dismissed due to lack of territorial jurisdiction of present Court.

In *Deep Chand Arya Industries* v. *Kiran Soap Works*,[426] the court examined two issues, one relating to jurisdiction of court and another relating to conditions for granting injunction in case of infringement of the trademark and infringement of the copyright. In this case, the plaintiff and defendants who are in the business of manufacture and sale of soap adopted the trademark "SINAULA" and "SINDRELA" in 1976 and 1979, respectively. On the ground that the trademark adopted by the defendants was deceptively similar to that of the plaintiff and that it amounted to an infringement, the plaintiff filed the present suit and injunction application for restraining the defendant from using the trademark "SINDRELA". The court held that the plaintiff resides and carries on business in Delhi. Section 62 of the Copyright Act gives jurisdiction to the Delhi High Court. There is no misguide of causes of action. The two causes of action, namely, the infringement of the trademark and infringement of the copyright are inter-linked and they can be tried together in one suit. The court further held that the grant of an injunction is a discretionary relief and the factors which lead to the grant of an injunction are, the proof of a *prima facie* case, balance of convenience and whether the interim injunction if not granted will cause irreparable injury to the plaintiff. In the present case, the above conditions exist and therefore the injunction must be granted.

In *John Richard Brady* v. *Chemical Process Equipments P. Ltd.*,[427] the plaintiffs have invoked jurisdiction of this Court under Section 62(2) of the Copyright Act, 1957 on the plea that the plaintiffs carry on business in Delhi, within the local limits of the jurisdiction of the Court. This fact was denied by the defendants. The court held that this is a mixed question of facts and law. It cannot be decided at this stage. Only averments made in the plaint can be seen at this stage. The plaintiffs have pleaded the necessary facts in the plaint to invoke territorial jurisdiction of this Court and also the plaintiff had made out strong prima facie case of infringement of copyright. Accordingly, the injunction was granted by the court. In *Shree Rajmoti Industries* v. *Rajmoti Oil Mill Pvt. Ltd.*,[428] application sought rejection of plaint on plea of want of territorial jurisdiction of Court allegedly that unless there is office of plaintiff situated in Delhi it cannot be said to have been carrying on business in Delhi party can carry on business even without having office. But the plaintiff averred in plaint that it carries on business in Delhi and referred its distributors. The said averment amounts to sufficient compliance with Sections 62(2). However, in *Dabur India Ltd.* v. *K.R. Industries*,[429] it was held that a composite suit would not entitle a Court to entertain a suit in respect whereof it has no jurisdiction, territorial or otherwise. A composite suit within the provisions of the Copyright Act, 1957 would mean the suit which is founded on infringement of a copyright and wherein the incidental power of the Court is required to be invoked.

426. (1980) ILR Delhi 1605.
427. AIR 1987 Delhi 372.
428. 115 (2004) DLT 212: 2005 (30) PTC 38 (Del).
429. AIR 2008 SC 3123: 2008 (37) PTC 332 (SC).

In *M/s. Kapoor Saws Manufacturing Company* v. *M/s. Crown Saw Blades Mfg. Co.*,[430] the issue was whether the Civil Courts at Delhi had territorial jurisdiction to examine the infringement of copyright? The Court held that so far as the infringement of copyright is concerned, it could not be disputed that under Section 62(2) of the Copyright Act, 1957, it is where the plaintiff resides or carries on business, such Court would have territorial jurisdiction. In this case, the plaintiffs carried on business in Delhi as per the plaint and therefore, even qua the cause of action of infringement of copyright, the Civil Courts at Delhi have territorial jurisdiction. It was further held that the Civil Courts at Delhi would have territorial jurisdiction at this stage of pleadings, i.e., nothing contained in present judgment was a final expression of opinion on merits of the issue of territorial jurisdiction and the said issue would be decided after evidence was led by both the parties, i.e., at the stage of final arguments. Hence, the appeal was allowed and disposed of in terms of leaving the parties to bear their own costs.

In *Surendra Kumar Maingi* v. *M/s. Dodha House*,[431] a suit for infringement of trademark and copyright of the mark Maingi's Dodha with the label and wrapper of the plaintiff by the defendant was filed in Ghaziabad where the plaintiff carried on business. The jurisdiction of the Ghaziabad Court was challenged on the basis of Section 105 of the *Trade & Merchandise Mark Act*, 1958 by the defendant since he was carrying on business in Faridkot and not in Ghaziabad. It was contended by the plaintiff that since the suit was also for infringement of copyright, the Ghaziabad Court had jurisdiction under Section 62 of the Copyright Act. This contention was rejected by the court after relying upon the judgments of the Punjab & Haryana High Court and Delhi High Court in *H.P. Marketing and Processing Corporation* v. *M.M. Breweries*[432] and *C.B. Dembla Trading* v. *Bharat Sewing Machine Co.*,[433] respectively where a common view was taken by both courts that for joinder of suits the court must have jurisdiction to try both cases. However, thereafter Delhi High Court has taken a contrary view in *P.H. Diesels Ltd.* v. *M/s. Patel Field Marshal Industries*,[434] where the court held that the joinder of suit was necessary to avoid conflicts of decisions, even though the court had no jurisdiction in one case. The question remained open whether the plaintiff should be extended the benefit of Section 62(1), when his action is at the core to enforce his trademark rights. However, the new provision in the Trademark Act, 1999 has resolved this conflict.

In *Arte Indiana* v. *Mittulaul Lalah*,[435] the division bench of the Bombay High Court examined the question whether actual infringement must take place within India for a court to invoke jurisdiction for copyright infringement. In this case, the plaintiff field a letters patent appeal to invoke the original jurisdiction of the court to jointly sue the defendant for copyright and trademark violation. The defendant was exporting from Madras to Kuwait products violating the copyright and trademark of the plaintiff. The plaintiff staying in Mumbai filed the suit under Section 62 of the Copyright Act at the Mumbai Court. It was argued that since the infringement was taking place at Kuwait and not within the jurisdiction of any court in India, the Mumbai Court had no original jurisdiction as per the provisions of the letters patent. Since

---

430. MIPR 2012 (2) 372: 2013 (53) PTC 506 (Del).
431. AIR 1998 All 43.
432. AIR 1981 P & H 117.
433. AIR 1982 Del 230.
434. AIR 1998 Del 225.
435. 1999 (103) 3 BLR 188 : 2000 PTC (20) 140(Bom).

copyright and the jurisdiction to file infringement suit at the place of residence of the plaintiff are creation of separate statutes, the single bench held that to invoke original jurisdiction there must be actual infringement within the jurisdiction of the court.[436] On appeal, the division bench referring to Clause 14 of letter patent reversed this and observed:

> A bare reading of the aforesaid clause shows that the accrual of the cause of action within the territorial jurisdiction of this Court is not contemplated to permit jointer of cause of action. Clause 14 only contemplates that this Court shall have original jurisdiction in respect of one of such causes of action to permit two separate cause of action being combined together in one suit.[437]

Criminal Remedies: Sections 63–70

The Statutory Scheme

The Copyright Act, 1957 provides criminal remedies against infringement of copyright besides civil remedies. Sections 63 to 70 of the Act deal with the criminal remedies. The Act under Section 63 makes infringement of copyright as an offence for any person knowingly to infringe (a) the copyright in a work or (b) any other right conferred by the Act (e.g., broadcast reproduction right; author's special rights), or knowingly to abate such infringement. It is, however, clarified that the construction of a building or other structural work which infringes or which, if completed would infringe the copyright in some other work is not an offence under the Explanation to Section 63 of Act. The Act under Section 63 now provides for minimum punishment, though the court is given power to impose a lesser punishment for adequate and special reasons to be mentioned in the judgment. The punishment increases for the second or further conviction. Further, it is an offence knowingly to make, or be in possession of any "plate" for the purpose of making "infringing copies" of any work in which copyright subsists. Clear and cogent proof of knowledge is necessary to establish the commission of the offence.[438] In case of criminal remedies of copyright infringement, civil remedies can be provided simultaneously. Although civil and criminal remedies are not mutually exclusive yet both are clearly co-extensive and quite different in content and consequence.[439] Thus, a criminal complaint cannot be dismissed on the ground that the dispute is civil in character.[440]

The Copyright (Amendment) Act, 1984 has also widened the powers of the police under Section 63B of the Copyright Act, 1957.[441] It empowers any police officer, not below the rank of a sub-inspector, if he is satisfied that an offence of infringement of copyright in

---

436. *See, Arte Indiana* v. *Mittulaul Lalah*, at p. 146. (at p. 146).
437. *See, Arte Indiana* v. *Mittulaul Lalah*, at p. 146. (at p. 167). *See also, P.M. Diesels Ltd.* v. *M/s. Patel Field Marshal Industries*, AIR 1988 Del 225; *Wiley Eastern Ltd.* v. *Indian Institute of Management*, 1995 PTR 53 (Del).
438. *See, Noor Fathima* v. *State of Karnataka*, 2019 (2) AKR 555; *Gurukrupa Mech Tech Pvt. Ltd.* v. *State of Gujarat*, (2018) 4 GLR 3324; *Krishna Lulla* v. *Shyam Vithalrao Devkatta*, (2016) 2 SCC 521: (2016) 2 SCC 521; *Cherian P. Joseph* v. *K. Prabhakaran Nair*, AIR 1967 Ker 234; *S.R. Upadhyaya* v. *G.C. Nepali*, AIR 1985 All 275.
439. *Sumeet Machines* v. *Sumeet Research and Holding*, 1993 PTC 75 (Mad.).
440. *V.S. Sharma* v. *Dharma Rao*, AIR 1942 Mad. 124.
441. Inserted by the Copyright (Amendment) Act, 1994 (Act 38 of 1994), Section 23 (Act 38 of 1994), [w.e.f. 10-5-1994].

any work "has been, is being, or is likely to be" committed, to seize without warrant, all infringing copies of the work "wherever found". According to Section 64, he is thereupon required to produce before a magistrate all copies and plates so seized as soon as practicable. Section 65 provides for possession of plates. The court trying the offence is empowered to order, whether the accused is convicted or not, that all copies of the work or all plates in the possession of the accused, which appear to the court to be infringing copies or plates for making infringing copies, be delivered up to the owner of the copyright under Section 66. The Copyright (Amendment) Act, 2012 has inserted new Sections 65A and 65B to the Copyright Act, 1957 for strengthening enforcement of copyright and protecting against internet piracy.[442]

The Copyright (Amendment) Act, 2012 has also amended Section 66 of the Copyright Act for the purpose of disposal of infringing copies or plates.[443] Section 66 relates to disposal of infringing copies by a court of law. The existing provision mandates the courts to deliver the infringing copies to the owner of copyright. A welcome amendment has been made in this section enabling the courts to make order regarding disposal of such copies. The reason is that in many cases owners of copyrights lose interest in obtaining the copies and in such situations courts will have to make appropriate orders relating to disposal of the infringing copies. Sections 67 and 68 of the Act also provides for offences in relation to the register of copyrights kept under the Act and for false representations made for the purpose of deceiving or influencing any authority of officer. Section 69 deals with offences by companies.

Section 70 of the Copyright Act provides for taking cognizance of an offence. There is no specific provision in the Copyright Act with regard to the place of trial. Hence, place of trial is to be determined in accordance with the provisions contained in Sections 177 to 188 of the Code of Criminal Procedure (Cr.P.C.). In *Amarnath Vyas* v. *State of A.P.*,[444] the Andhra Pradesh High Court held that the offence is obviously, as can be seen from Section 70 of the Act, cognizable and triable by a Court, which is not inferior to that of a Metropolitan Magistrate or a Judicial Magistrate of First Class. Therefore, there has been no provision in the Act which makes offence clearly a "non-bailable" one. Undoubtedly, the offence punishable under Section 63 of the Act is triable by a criminal Court of Judicial Magistrate of First Class or Metropolitan Magistrate adopting the procedure envisaged under the provisions of the Cr.P.C. The Cr.P.C. applies *proprio vigore* for the trial of an offence under the Act. In the absence of any specific provision, under the Act, making the offence "non-bailable", one has to fall back upon the Schedule-I appended to the Cr.P.C. Part-II classifies the offences against other laws, which are laws other than the various categories of crimes enumerated in the Indian Penal Code, 1860.

Offence of Infringement of Copyright: Section 63

Chapter XIII of the Copyright Act, 1957 deals with the offences relating to infringement of copyright. Section 63 of the Copyright Act, 1957 provides for offence of infringement of

442. Sections 65A and 65B have been inserted by the Copyright (Amendment) Act, 2012 (Act 27 of 2012), Section 37, [w.e.f. 21-6-2012].
443. Inserted by the Copyright (Amendment) Act, 2012 (Act 27 of 2012), Section 38, [w.e.f. 21-6-2012].
444. 2007 (1) ALD (Cri) 898: 2007 Cri LJ 2025.

copyright or other rights conferred by the Act.[445] Section 63 makes it an offence for a person to knowingly infringe or abate the infringement of (i) the copyright in a work, or (ii) any other right conferred by this Act, except the right conferred by Section 53A. Further, Explanation to Section 63 of the Copyright Act clarifies that construction of a building or other structure which infringes or which, if completed, would infringe the copyright in some other work shall not be an offence under this Section. According to Section 63, the accused shall be punishable with imprisonment for a term which shall not be less than six months but which may extend to three years and with fine which shall not be less than fifty thousand rupees but which may extend to two lakh rupees. However, the proviso to Section 63 provides that the court may, for adequate and special reasons to be mentioned in the judgment, impose a sentence of imprisonment for a term of less than six months or a fine of less than fifty thousand rupees. Thus, the proviso gives the Courts discretion to impose a sentence of imprisonment. The discretion is not arbitrary and fanciful, therefore, the court has to mention in the judgment adequate and special reasons for doing so. In *Vinod Kumar Gupta* v. *State of U.P.*,[446] it was held that the Section 63 relates to an offence of infringement of "copyright" and provides that any person who knowingly infringes or abets the infringement of the copyright in any work, shall be punishable with an imprisonment for a term which shall not be less than 6 months but it may extend to 3 years and with fine which shall be not less than ₹ 50,000 but it may extend to ₹ 2 lakhs. In *Indusind Media and Communications Limited* v. *State of Gujarat*,[447] the Gujarat High Court observed:

> In reference to Section 63 of the Copyright Act pertaining to offence of infringement of copyright or other rights conferred by this Act, 1984 by way of Copyright (Amendment) Act, 1994. In the Act, originally the words used "shall be punishable with imprisonment which may extend to one year, or with fine, or with both" are substituted with the words "shall be punishable with imprisonment for a term which shall not be less than six months, but which may extend to three years and with fine, which shall not be less than ₹ 25,000/-, but which may extend to ₹ 2 lacs."

In *State of Madhya Pradesh* v. *Santosh Kumar*,[448] the Apex court observed that in order to exercise the discretion of reducing the sentence, the statutory requirement is that the Court has to record "adequate and special reasons"[449] in the judgment and not fanciful reasons which would permit the Court to impose a sentence less than the prescribed minimum. The reason has not only to be adequate but also special. What is adequate and special would depend upon

445. *See*, *Entertainment Network (India) Ltd.* v. *Super Cassettes Industries Ltd.*, MIPR 2008 (2) 129: 2008 (37) PTC 353 (SC); *State of A.P.* v. *Nagoti Venkataramana* (1996) 6 SCC 409: [1996] Supp 4 SCR 812; *Ghurey Lal* v. *State*, AIR 1965 All 206.

446. 2019 (106) ACC 378.

447. (2018) 2 GLR 1151: 2017 (71) PTC 60 (Guj).

448. AIR 2006 SC 2648: (2006) 6 SCC 1. *See also*, *Gopal Madhukar Bombatkar* v. *The State of Maharashtra*, 2014 (3) Bom CR (Cri)248: 2014 ALLMR (Cri) 2390; *State of M.P.* v. *Basodi*, AIR 2009 SC 3081: (2009) 12 SCC 318; *State of Madhya Pradesh* v. *Sheikh Shahid*, AIR 2009 SC 2951: (2009) 12 SCC 715; *State of Punjab* v. *Rakesh Kumar*, JT 2008 (9) SC 424: 2008 (12) SCALE 95; *Bhupinder Sharma* v. *State of Himachal Pradesh*; AIR 2003 SC 4684: (2003) 8 SCC 551.

449. For the doctrine of "adequate and special reasons," *see*, *Thongam Tarun Singh* v. *The State of Manipur*, AIR 2019 SC 2456: 2019 (7) SCALE 435; *State* v. *Manimaran*, AIR 2019 SC 655: 2018 (15) SCALE 416; *State of Madhya Pradesh* v. *Preetam*, AIR 2018 SC 4212: 2018 (11) SCALE 120; *Harpreet Singh* v. *State of Himachal Pradesh*, 2017 (3) Crimes 154 (SC): 2017 (3) RCR (Criminal) 727; *State of Rajasthan* v. *Harkesh*, 2016 (2) RCR (Criminal) 273: II (2016) CCR 2 (SC).

several factors and no strait-jacket formula can be indicated. What is applicable to trial Courts regarding recording reasons for a departure from minimum sentence is equally applicable to the High Court. Thus, in *Pramod Mahto* v. *State of Bihar*,[450] the Apex court held that the Court has the discretion to impose a sentence of imprisonment less than the prescribed minimum for adequate and special reasons. If the Court does not mention such reasons in the judgment, there is no scope for awarding a sentence lesser than the prescribed minimum. In *State of M.P.* v. *Babbu Barkare*,[451] the Apex court held that if the Court does not mention such reasons in the judgment, there is no scope for awarding a sentence lesser than the prescribed minimum.

According to the Copyright Act, 1957, the copyright owner have the right to use and reproduce the copyrighted work in any material form. Thus, *Pernod Ricard* v. *Real House Distillery Pvt. Ltd.*,[452] the court held that any colourable imitation or substantial reproduction of essential features thereof by unauthorised persons would be a civil wrong as well as a criminal wrong, being infringement of copyright under Sections 63 of the Copyright Act. In *Event and Entertainment Management Association* v. *Union of India*,[453] the court observed that while Section 55 of the Copyright Act deals with the civil remedies, the criminal remedies are provided under Sections 63 and 64 of the Act. Section 63 postulates filing of the criminal case before a criminal court followed by a trial and resultant punishment, if any. Section 64 empowers the Police to seize infringing copies which are then produced before a Magistrate.

In *Dabur India Limited* v. *Shree Baidyanath Ayurved Bhawan Pvt. Ltd.*,[454] the court rightly stated that being the commissioned work, the plaintiff is the owner of the copyright therein under the provisions of the Copyright Act, 1957 having exclusive right to use or reproduce features thereof in any material form. Any unauthorised copying, imitation and colourable reproduction thereof by any unauthorised person would constitute infringement of copyright of plaintiff therein under Section 51A of the Act which is not only liable to be injuncted but also constitutes a cognizable offence under Sections 63 and 64 of the Act. In *State Govt. of NCT of Delhi* v. *Naresh Kumar Garg*,[455] the issue was whether offence punishable under Section 63 of the Act was bailable or non-bailable? The court held that it would be fruitful to refer to provision of Section 64 of the Act which empowered a police officer not below rank of sub-inspector to seize infringing copies of any work. If offence had been cognizable and non-bailable, there was no necessity to specifically authorise police officer with power of seizure.

The wording of Sections 16 and 63 of the Copyright Act, 1957 refer to "other rights". By Section 16, "copyright or any similar right" (in a work) apart from what is created by the Act is precluded. No doubt, the expression "work" limits the exclusion. However, equally, while the text of the Copyright Act does not prescribe what the rights referred to in the words "other similar rights" other than copyright are, this must necessarily allude to, *inter alia*, broadcasting rights. Section 63 which creates offences (and yet is not included in Section 39A as applicable to broadcasting rights) states that infringement of (a) copyright in a work, or

---

450. 1989 ACR 622 (SC): AIR 1989 SC 1475: *See also*, *State of M.P.* v. *Babbu Barkare*, AIR 2005 SC 2846: (2005) 5 SCC 413.
451. AIR 2005 SC 2846: (2005) 5 SCC 413.
452. MIPR 2010 (1) 340: 2010 (42) PTC 342 (Del).
453. 2012 (52) PTC 380 (Del).
454. 193 (2012) DLT 558: 2012 (51) PTC 441 (Del).
455. 2013 (2) JCC 1063.

(b) "any other right created by this Act" would be punishable with imprisonment. Similarly, expressions which are not defined by Chapter VIII are used; their meaning (i.e., words such as sound recording, visual recording, fair dealing, etc.) can be only construed with reference to other provisions of the Copyright Act. In other words, though there is no express reference to Section 16 in Section 39A, its underlying premise, i.e., preclusion of rights other than those spelt out in Chapter VIII, by common law, would apply. In *ESPN Star Sports* v. *Global Broadcast News Ltd.*,[456] the Division Bench of the Delhi High Court while holding that the express omission of Section 61 in Section 39A did not render that suit fatal, held that broadcasting rights are "akin" to copyrights.

In *Houghton Mifflin Company* v. *Rajinder Kumar Arya*,[457] the court held that where party's right to enforce its legal remedies pertaining to offences relating to Section 63 of the Copyright Act are legitimate it is possible that the plaintiff could succeed in such proceedings. Equally, it could be possible that the defendant may be held guilty or may choose to compound the offence, if permitted in law. Yet, the fluidity of the circumstance persuades the Court to conclude that the mere filing of a complaint cannot in any circumstances be said to result in an actionable claim against the plaintiff. Any other opinion would virtually amount to penalising a litigant who seeks recourse to the law in the assertion of his legitimate rights. In *Pachranga Syndicate Pvt. Ltd.* v. *Som Nath*,[458] the plaintiff filed a complaint under Sections 63 and 65 of the Copyright Act, 1957 read with Section 420 and Section 34 of the Indian Penal Code, 1860. The grievance of the plaintiff was that the plaintiff became aware of the identical labels used by the defendants in respect of pickles being sold under the brand name Garden Fresh. The complaint was filed for infringement of copyright as the defendants were found to be violating the rights of the plaintiff. The court held that as no registration certificates had been filed by the plaintiff, therefore, in view of dismissal of earlier suit on merit, an order of injunction could not be passed against defendants unless the *prima facie* case was made out.

There have been very few prosecutions under the Copyright Act and the cases that have gone to appellate courts show that the High Courts do not view criminal prosecution for infringement of copyright. The case of *Siaram Silk Mills* v. *State,*[459] of the Delhi High Court was based on the complaint of the owner of the copyright a prosecution was initiated for copyright infringement under Section 63 of the Copyright Act and the trademark infringement under Sections 78 and 79 of the Trademarks Act, 1958 read with Sections 420, 489 and 486 of Indian Penal Code. A search was conducted in pursuance of the directions of the magistrate and infringing goods were seized. The magistrate also took cognizance of the offence. However, a petition was filed before the High Court under Section 482 of Cr.P.C. for compromise of the criminal case. The court after identifying the party's role observed thus:

> In view of the above no useful purpose would be served by permitting the above complaint and proceedings to continue. Accordingly, the petition is allowed. The above noted FIR and the proceedings emanating there from are quashed, subject to the payment of ₹10,000/- as costs to the Legal Aid and Advice Board, Patiala House. Petition stands disposed of.[460]

---

456. MIPR 2008 (3) 257: 2008 (38) PTC 477 (Del).
457. 171 (2010) DLT 211: 2010 (44) PTC 240 (Del).
458. 168 (2010) DLT 395: 2010 (42) PTC 253 (Del).
459. (2001) PTC (21) 600 (Del).
460. (2001) PTC (21) 600 (Del).

The offence under Section 63 being one punishable with a maximum of three years imprisonment and a fine of ₹2 lakh, with a minimum of six months imprisonment and a fine of ₹50,000/-, the order seems not proper exercise of the power under Section 482 of the Code of Criminal Procedure. Such approach on the part of the court defeats the intention underlying the amended provisions of 1984 which were intended to make it clear that the infringement of copyright is a serious offence and needs to be dealt with sternly. This only shows that the attitude of the court still is to treat copyright infringement a civil wrong rather than a serious offence. In *Gulfam Exports* v. *Sayed Hamid,*[461] the Bombay High Court was also reluctant to invoke criminal jurisdiction while a civil suit was pending. In this case, the respondent, the owner of copyright, filed a private complaint in the court of the magistrate in 1991 alleging violation of copyright and after enquiry by the police, process, was issued to the petitioner. The petitioner filed petition for quashing of the process on the ground that the copyright was not registered and a civil suit was pending. Even after repeated notice, the respondent did not appear in the matter. The court after hearing the petitioner concluded that the complaint must be quashed since the copyright was not registered and the civil suit was pending and that there was delay in filing the criminal case. The unusual reasons given by the court were:

> The complainant had already gone to the Civil Court and the matter is pending at appellate stage in this Court. The interim order of injunction was already running against the petitioners when the matter was in the trial court and the suit was already decided in favour of the complainant in the Civil Court and the petitioners are still debarred from using the disputed trademark ... In the context of aforesaid facts I am of the view that, it would be in the interest of justice that the complaint should be quashed and set aside.

It seems the court did not correctly appreciate the scheme underlying the provisions of the Copyright Act regarding registration and that the legislature in its wisdom has treated infringement of copyright not only a civil wrong but also a serious criminal wrong. As explained earlier, registration is not mandatory for claiming copyright protection under the Act and the existence of civil remedies is not a bar for criminal prosecution. The offences under the Copyright Act are cognizable offences and, therefore, need to be sternly dealt with.

In *State of Andhra Pradesh* v. *Nagoti Venkataramana,*[462] the Supreme Court examined the need to identify the owner and prove the ownership of copyright before convicting the accused for an offence under the Copyright Act. The inspector of police Tenali, Guntur district of Andhra Pradesh, in one of his regular raids, seizes 90 video cassettes of various films in Telugu, Hindi and English from the video library of the accused and charged him for an offence under Section 52A read with Section 63 of the Copyright Act. He was convicted by the lower courts. On appeal, the High Court acquitted him on the ground that the owners of the film were not identified and the prosecution failed to adduce evidence to prove the ownership of the film. The Supreme Court on appeal examined the question whether the identification of the owner of the copyright was a precondition for the conviction of an offence under the Act. The court after examining various provisions in the Act dealing with punishment found that the objective of introducing Section 52A was to prevent piracy of cinematograph film and sound records and protect the interest of the owner of copyright and the public. The Act mandates the punishment of the accused in case of violation of the provisions. In this context, the court

---

461. 2000 (20) PTC 496 (Bom).
462. 22 1PLR 123 (1979).

rejecting the contention that the identification of the owner of copyright was a precondition for conviction under the Act observed thus:

> In view of the finding of the courts below, the offence would fall under Section 68A of the Act. It would, therefore, be unnecessary for the prosecution to track on and trace out the owner of the copyright to come and adduce evidence of infringement of copyright. The absence thereof does not constitute lack of essential elements of infringement of copyright. If the particulars on video films, etc., as mandated under Section 52A do not find a place, it would be infringement of copyright.

The court is correct in its conclusion. If one examines the scheme of criminal law, it is clear that anyone can initiate a criminal prosecution and in case of serious offences, the police officer is duty bound to investigate the crime. Even in the offences like theft, trespass, etc., on property under the Indian Penal Code, 1960, it is the possession and not ownership of property that is important. In *Vishvajeet Sharma* v. *State*,[463] a petition was filed under Section 482 (inherent power of the High Court) of the Code of Criminal Procedure, 1973 and Section 63 of the Copyright Act, 1957 for quashing of Complaint and FIR registered against petitioner. The court held that at the time when complaint was filed, respondent had not obtained registrations in respect of its trademarks. After filing of complaint respondent claimed that he has already obtained registrations for its trademarks and three further copyright registrations. Therefore, for any act of infringement after date of charge sheet, not forming part of FIR, it would be open to respondent to seek appropriate remedies available to it in law. Thus, the Court held that in this circumstance criminal proceedings cannot be initiated against petitioner.

In *A.K. Mukherjee* v. *State*,[464] an application was filed under Section 319 (power of the court to proceed against persons appearing to be guilty of an offence) of the Criminal Procedure Code, 1973, for summoning the full time directors regarding the infringement of the Copyright Act. It was found that no allegation was made in the complaint that the directors being the in-charge of affairs of the company, were responsible for the offence. Therefore, it was held that summoning the directors was rightly disallowed by the magistrate. Section 19A of the Copyright Act, 1957 covers only disputes which arise with regard to the assignment of a "Copyright" or the terms of an assignment of a "Copyright" only. Thus, where petitioner filed complaint before Metropolitan Magistrate alleging that respondents infringed copyright in book authored by him, the petition will be dismissed on ground of non-maintainability under Section 19A. In such a case, board not justified in going into question whether infringement of copyright done, the issue is beyond scope of Section 19A. According to Section 63, knowledge on part of accused that infringement was done, such evidence led to prove that accused had knowledge of infringement. In *Sri Gopal* v. *Radha Binode Mondal*,[465] the Calcutta High Court observed that the Copyright Board [Appellate Board][466] gave a finding on an unnecessary or irrelevant issue, an issue into which neither it could go nor there was any necessity for it to go.

---

463. 2009 (41) PTC 484 (Del).
464. 50 (1993) DLT 169: 1993 RLR 255.
465. AIR 1925 Cal 996. *See also*, *Issazt-un-Nissa* v. *Kaniz Fatima*, AIR 1916 Oudh 6.
466. Substituted by the Finance Act 2017 (7 of 2017), Section 160(a) for "Copyright Board," [w.e.f. 26 May, 2017].

Further, in *Nana Tukaram* v. *Sonabai*,[467] the Bombay High Court held that the finding in question of the Copyright Board [Appellate Board][468] cannot be said to be final, inasmuch as there could be no appeal against it by the respondents, the decree (if at all it was one) being in favour of the party against whom the finding was recorded. A bare perusal of the provision of Section 63 of the Copyright Act, 1957 would go to show that emphasis is on the words "knowingly infringes ... the Copyright in a work". These words clearly postulate a knowledge on the part of the accused that he was infringing the Copyright in a work. Mere possibility of his having known it would not suffice. There has to be clear and conclusive proof of the requisite knowledge. Even the existence of reasonable means of knowing would not be enough. Thus, the use of the word "knowingly" in the provision results in requiring "mens read in the full sense". This in short, being the legal requirement under Section 63 of the Copyright Board [Appellate Board][469], evidence shall have to be led to bring home the required guilty knowledge.

In *Sunil Kumar Gupta* v. *State*,[470] the complainant was the proprietor/owner of two registered copyright having particular design, used by them in connection with their products, industrial or commercial. In this case, the issue was relating to quashing of proceedings sought on the ground that the trial did not commence even after five years of taking of cognizance. Allegation of cheating the public at large also made against the accused persons. The offence also falling within the category of economic offence. The intention of the petitioner apparently is to derive economic benefit to himself and at the same time, he is making a false representation about the source or origin of the product and thereby is deceiving the public at large who may buy his product by using the infringing design of the copyright of the complainant. This necessarily will result in wrongful gain to him and wrongful loss to the complainant and amounts to cheating. The court held that the proceedings cannot be quashed.

In *Chitra Narain* v. *NDTV*,[471] petitioner who was the Chief Producer of All India Radio filed a complaint under Sections 51, 52A, 63, 69 of the Copyright Act of 1957 against M/s. NDTV and other respondents on the allegations that they have infringed and usurped her copyright over the feature entitled "A National Anthem Born and Exile" which was researched, written and produced by her and broadcast on the National Network of All India Radio on 23 January 1980. According to her, the feature produced by the petitioner and broadcast on AIR by her sheer labour and skill was an Original Work and she had used her ingenuity and innovative traits in making the research (for over 3 years), selection and compilation of this feature. This feature was widely hailed by the Press. Thus, according to the petitioner, the respondents, thus, clearly infringed and usurped upon the copyright of the petitioner by telecasting the said feature and committed the offences punishable under Sections 51, 52A, 63 and 69 of the Copyright Act, 1957. The complaint was registered and the learned Chief Metropolitan Magistrate asked the complainant to lead evidence for inquiry under Sections

467. AIR 1982 Bom 437: 1982 Mh LJ 538. *See also*, *Madras Corporation* v. *P.R. Ramachandriah*, AIR 1977 Mad 35; *Latchayya* v. *Katamma*, AIR 1925 Mad 264; *Jamaitun-Nissa* v. *Lutfun Nissa* (1885) 7 All 606.
468. Substituted by the Finance Act 2017 (7 of 2017), Section 160(a) for "Copyright Board," [w.e.f. 26 May, 2017].
469. Substituted by the Finance Act 2017 (7 of 2017), Section 160(a) for "Copyright Board," [w.e.f. 26 May, 2017].
470. 74 (1998) DLT 838: 1998 (46) DR J702.
471. (2003) ILR 2 Delhi 646: 2004 (28) PTC 238 (Del).

200 and 202 of the Cr.P.C. The court held that an inquiry under Section 202 is not in the nature of a trial for there can be in law only one trial in respect of any offence and that trial can commence only after process is issued against the accused as prior to this stage, the said proceedings are not strictly proceedings between the complainant and the accused. A person against whom a complaint is filed does not become an accused until the Court decides to issue process against him. Even if he participates in the proceedings under Section 202 he does so not as an accused but as a member of the public. The object of the inquiry under Section 202 is the ascertainment of the fact whether the complaint has any valid foundation calling for the issue of process to the person complained against or whether it is a baseless one on which no action need be taken. The section does not require any adjudication to be made about the guilt or otherwise of the person against whom the complaint is filed.

In *R.K. Mehra* v. *State*,[472] the court examined the issue relating to offence committed punishable under Section 63 of the Copyright Act, 1957 and Sections 420 (cheating and dishonestly inducing delivery of property) and 120B (punishment of criminal conspiracy) of the Indian Penal Code, 1860. It also appeared that trial Court had given reasons which were cogent for acquitting accused persons and Trial Court had at length dealt with evidence of PW-3, PW-4 as also PW-5 to arrive at a conclusion. However, offence for which accused persons were charged was not made out. No reason found to interfere with judgment. Therefore, the High Court dismissed the petition.

Similarly, in *Pankaj Kumar Jain* v. *State of Delhi*,[473] on the basis of complaint under Section 200 (examination of complaint) of the Code of Criminal Procedure, initiated by Macmillan India Ltd. alleging commission of offences punishable under Section 63 of the Copyright Act read with Sections 420 and 485 (counterfeiting a property mark) of the Indian Penal Code search investigations were ordered; search and seizure warrants too were issued. As a result of the investigation and raids conducted, allegedly pirated copies of the book "YOU CAN WIN", originally published by the complainant were recovered/seized from five, different places. The Court held that a magistrate is not denuded of power to summon an accused, merely because he issues an order summoning some accused. If, during the course of proceedings, it appears, on the basis of existing materials, that some others have to be summoned, he can do so. Here, the materials in the form of the seizure memo, the report disclosing the name of the petitioner, his status as owner of the shop, and other statements existed. The magistrate exercised his discretion, on application of mind. In these circumstances, The Delhi High Court find no infirmity with the procedure adopted by the Magistrate. As far as other submissions, i.e., the nature of evidence, irregularity of procedure alleged by the petitioner, in regard to the seizure, etc. are concerned, they are not such fatal or grave infirmities as would compel the exercise of jurisdiction of the court under Section 482 of the Indian Penal Code, which has to necessarily be to secure the ends of justice.

In *Ajay Raj Pal* v. *State*,[474] the issue was relating to Sections 173(8), 190 (cognizance of offence), 468 and 482 of the Code of Criminal Procedure, 1973 read with Sections 63 and 68A of the Copyright Act, 1957. In this case, the accused Mukesh was arrested being found in possession of pirated CDs, VCDs, in lay cards, cell phones and blue films from

472. 123 (2005) DLT 355: 2005 (31) PTC 241 (Del).
473. (2007) ILR 1 Delhi 99.
474. (2007) ILR 1 Delhi 889.

the shop owned by the petitioner. Petitioner claimed to have given the shop to the accused Mukesh as per an agreement, to manage the shop, on payment of 2% of the sale by him. Trial court took cognizance on the charge sheet being filed, hence APP moved an application for summoning the petitioner. Trial Court directed further investigation. Petitioner summoned by the trial Court after supplementary charge sheet filed. Revision petition filed by the petitioner dismissed by Sessions Court. Petitioner challenged the order of issuance of summons and the order dismissing his revision petition. Summoning order assailed on the ground of limitation and of not taking cognizance against the petitioner initially. Pleaded that the petitioner had no covert or overt role in the offence. Rejecting the argument, the court held that taking cognizance implies application of mind to the materials on record and proceeding to issue process. Mere absence of the term "cognizance" in the trial Court order could not have taken away the basic import. In regard to the plea of limitation it was held that the court should, in given cases, take a liberal approach and not stifle the prosecution on that ground.

It is a general question of law whether search warrant under Section 63 of the Copyright Act, 1957 can be issued against "unknown offenders"? The practice of filing the criminal complaint against "unknown offenders" in the context of Section 93 of the Code of Criminal Procedure has been examined by the Delhi High Court in a number of cases. In similar circumstances, in *Shri Churiaram Aggarwal* v. *M/s. Aggarwal Sweet Corner*,[475] the Court held that it is no doubt true that Magistrate takes cognizance of an offence and not of the offenders but where the offenders are known, the complaint must be filed against known offenders. Under Section 93 of the Code of Criminal Procedure where the Court considers that the purpose of enquiry trial or other proceedings under the Code would be served by a general search or inspection, it may issue a search warrant and that issuance of a search warrant is a serious matter and being in the discretion of the court, it would be reasonable to expect the Court to give reasons which swayed its discretion in favour of granting their request. Keeping in view the peculiar facts of the said case, the Court held that investigation in offences like those under Copyright Act as well as Trade and Merchandise Marks Act could not be effectively carried out without the assistance of the police force and Magistrate has got to take into account the nature and character of the offences alleged to have been committed and to see as to whether without police assistance he can enquire into such offences and enable the complainant to bring the offenders to book.

Thus, in *Venus Industries* v. *State,*[476] the court held that a similar general search warrant was quashed. Similarly, in *Pramod Kumar Bhandari* v. *State,*[477] the general search warrant against the unknown persons was quashed by the Court. In *P.K. Bagla* v. *State*,[478] looking into the facts and circumstances of the case, the court held that despite knowing fully well who the offenders according to the complainant were, the complaint was filed against "unknown persons" and a search warrant was issued in the name of the petitioner. In view of the settled law, the court concluded that the search warrant is unsustainable in law and was hereby quashed. However, in *New Hariom Industries* v. *Dandi Salt P. Ltd.*,[479] the court examined the

---

475. (1990) ILR 1 Delhi 274: 1990 PTC 175. *See*, *Microfibres Inc.* v. *Girdhar*, MIPR 2009 (2) 229: 2009 (40) PTC 519 (Del).
476. 95 (2002) DLT 348: 2002 (24) PTC 422 (Del).
477. 64 (1996) DLT 732: 1996 PTC (16).
478. ILR (2008) Supp. (6) Delhi 26.
479. 2011 IXAD (Delhi) 33: 2011 (48) PTC 231 (Del).

petition for praying to quash FIR registered under Section 63 of the Copyright Act, 1957. In this case, the court held that goods were lying unidentified at railway yard and thus respondent was justified in taking search warrants against unknown persons. Further even assuming the search warrants were illegally obtained, it is well-settled that evidence collected pursuant to an illegal search does not become inadmissible in evidence during trial. Thus, FIR could not be quashed.

In *Coca-Cola Company* v. *K.M. Salim*,[480] it was held that by reproducing the manner in which the plaintiff represents its trademarks, the defendant has infringed the plaintiff's copyright in the artistic works. In these circumstances, the plaintiffs are entitled to a perpetual order of injunction of the Court restraining the defendant by himself, its servants, dealers and agents from infringing the plaintiff's copyrights in its artistic works by reproducing it or any substantial part thereof in any material form and/or by using its impugned work in any manner, whatsoever. Apart from being a civil violation, the impugned use, imitation and reproduction also constitute a cognizable criminal offence under the provisions of Sections 63 and 64 of the Copyright Act, 1957, punishable with imprisonment up to three years and penalty up to ₹2 lakh.

Infringement of Copyright in Computer Programs: Section 63B

Section 63B of the Copyright Act, 1957 was inserted by the Copyright (Amendment) Act, 2012[481] which provides that if a person knowingly makes use on a computer of an infringing copy of a computer program shall be punishable with imprisonment for a term which shall not be less than seven days but which may extend to three years and with fine which shall not be less than fifty thousand rupees but which may extend to two lakh rupees. However, where the computer program has not been used for gain or in the course of trade or business, the court may for adequate and special reasons to be mentioned in the judgment, not impose any sentence of imprisonment and may impose a fine which may extend to fifty thousand rupees.

In *Tarun Tyagi* v. *Central Bureau of Investigation*,[482] the Supreme Court examined the scope and ambit of Sections 63 and 63B of the Copyright Act 1957. In this case the CBI took up the investigation and seized certain documents and material from the office premises of the Appellant. The trial court took cognizance of offence Under Section 381 of the Indian Penal Code, 1860, Section 66 of the Information Technology Act, 2000 and Sections 63 and 63B of the Copyright Act, 1957. The High Court of Delhi set aside that order and restored the application for release with direction to the concerned Magistrate to deal with the application afresh. The Apex Court observed that in a case like this, at the time of trial, the attempt on the part of the prosecution would be to show that the seized material, which contains the source code, was the property of the complainant. On the other hand, the Appellant will try to demonstrate otherwise and his attempt would be to show that the source code contained in those CDs is different from the source code of the complainant and the seized material contained the source code developed by the Appellant. It was but obvious that in order to prove his defence, the copies of the seized CDs need to be supplied to the Appellant. The

480. 2014 (1) MIPR 217: 2014 (208) DLT 432.
481. Inserted by the Copyright (Amendment) Act, 2012 (Act 27 of 2012), Section 37, [w.e.f. 21-6-2012].
482. Inserted by the Copyright (Amendment) Act, 2012 (Act 27 of 2012), Section 37, [w.e.f. 21-6-2012].

right to get these copies is statutorily recognised under Section 207 of the Indian Penal Code, which is the hallmark of a fair trial that every document relied upon by the prosecution has to be supplied to the defence or accused at the time of supply of the charge sheet to enable such an accused to demonstrate that no case is made out against him and also to enable him to prepare his cross-examination and defence strategy. The Court further clarified thus:

> In order to comply with the provision of Section 207 of the Code, the hard disks marked Q-2, 9 and 20 be supplied to the Appellant subject to the conditions. Before supplying the said CDs, the contents thereof shall be recorded in the Court, in the presence of complainant as well as the Appellant and both of them shall attest the veracity thereof by putting their signatures so that there is no dispute about these contents later thereby removing the possibility of tempering thereof by the Appellant. The Appellant shall not make use of the source code contained in the said CDs or misuse the same in any manner and give an affidavit of undertaking to this effect in the trial court.

Power of Police to Seize Infringing Copies: Section 64

Section 64 of the Copyright Act, 1957 empowers the police to seize infringing copies which are to be produced before a Magistrate. Section 64(1) of the Act provides that where a police officer not below the rank of a sub-inspector of police is satisfied that an infringement or an abatement of infringement of copyright in any work has been or is likely to be committed, he may seize without any warrant all copies of the work and all plates used for the purpose of making infringing copies of the work, wherever found and all copies and plates so seize shall, as soon as practicable, should be produced before magistrate. The power vested in the Police officer under Section 64(1) to seize without warrant all copies of a work in respect of which infringement of copyright is being or is likely to be committed has to be based on a *prima facie* satisfaction that there is such infringement. It cannot be a mechanical exercise based only on the written complaint of the owner of a copyright. Regarding the scope of the Section 64 in *Kamal Kishor* v. *State of MP*,[483] the Madhya Pradesh High Court observed:

> Section 64 of the Copyright Act 1957, in no uncertain terms, makes it clear that any police officer not below the rank of Sub-Inspector can seize copy of the work or plate if he is satisfied that an offence under section 63 in respect of infringement of copyright in any work is made out. Thus, before exercising the power of seizure, there has to be a satisfaction that an offence under section 63 is made out. The Section 63 of the Act itself has no application relating to a duplicate spark plug. Hence, the power under section 64 could not have been exercised. In other words, the satisfaction of police officer about applicability of section 63 is sine qua non for exercising the power under section 64. Unless the Section 63 is not attracted, the exercise of power under section 64 is without authority of law.

In *Event and Entertainment Management Association* v. *Union of India*,[484] the court held that in order that the power to seize in terms of Section 64 of the Copyright Act is not exercised in an arbitrary and whimsical manner, it has to be hedged in with certain implied safeguards that constitute a check on such power. Consequently, prior to exercising the power of seizure under Section 64(1) of the Act, the police officer concerned has to necessarily be *prima facie* satisfied that there is an infringement of copyright in the manner complained of.

---

483. 2016 Cri LJ 1640: 2016 (I) MPJR 301.
484. 2012 (52) PTC 380 (Del).

In other words, merely on the receipt of the information or a complaint from the owner of a copyright about the infringement of the copyrighted work, the police is not expected to straightway effect seizure.

In terms of Section 64(2) of the Copyright Act, 1957, a person having an interest in any copy of the work so seized, may within 15 days of such seizure make an application to a Magistrate for restoration to him of such copies. Upon such application, the Magistrate is required to hear the application and the complainant and make such further inquiry before passing any order on the application. In *Girish Gandhi* v. *Union of India*,[485] it was held that Section 64(2) provides safeguards when the person aggrieved can make an application to the Magistrate within 15 days of such seizure by the police officer for restoring the seized copies to him. It does not permit or facilitate infringement of any of the rights of the person alleged to have committed infringement. In this case, the constitutional validity of Section 64 of the Copyright Act authorising the police officer to conduct search without warrant was challenged. According to the petitioner since no procedure was laid down in the section, the power granted under the Section was arbitrary and hence violative of the constitutional right. Rejecting this, the court observed:

> Section 64 clearly mentions that police officers is to seize the material, if he is so satisfied. But what does the word "satisfaction" mean. It is inborn that police officer will not act until and unless he has got some type of information on which information he is satisfied and his satisfaction shall be objective. It cannot be imagined that only because, Section 64 empowers the police officer to seize the material to his satisfaction, that he would act *mala fide* or arbitrary. If he does so, there is ample remedies available in the appropriate courts and the aggrieved person is always free to safeguard his interest in this respect by resorting to the legal remedies. The power given to the police officer is not at all arbitrary....

In *Lakshmi Narain Mehta* v. *Gramophone Co. of India Ltd.*,[486] two complainants had filed against unknown persons under Section 64 of the Copyright Act, 1957. Those two complaints were later consolidated but the learned magistrate refused to issue a general search warrant. However, the magistrate permitted the police under Section 64 of the Act to search all susceptive places. Raids were organised and a number of infringing articles were recovered from two firms. The inspector of crime branch submitted a report that during the raids conducted on five shops, there was some confrontation between certain persons of the companies and the shopkeepers and the raids had to be abandoned. The High Court observed that issuance of a search warrant is a serious matter and it would be advisable not to dispose of an application for search warrant in a mechanical way by a laconic order. Issue of search warrant being in the discretion of the Magistrate, it would be reasonable to expect of the Magistrate to give reasons which swayed his discretion in favour of granting the request. A clear application of mind by the learned Magistrate must be discernible in the order granting the search warrant.

In *State Government of NCT of Delhi* v. *Naresh Kumar Garg*,[487] the issue was whether offence punishable under Section 63 of the Act was bailable or non-bailable. The court held

---

485. AIR 1997 Raj 78.
486. 24 (1983) DLT 246. *See also*, *Premwati Bansal* v. *M/s. Shri Ganpati International*, 1999 VI AD (Delhi) 687: 82 (1999) DLT 398; *P.K. Bagla* v. *State*, ILR (2008) Supp. (6) Delhi 26.
487. 2013 (2) JCC 1063.

that it would be fruitful to refer to the provision of Section 64 of the Copyright Act, 1957 which empowers a police officer not below the rank of sub-inspector to seize the infringing copies of any work. If the offence had been cognizable and non-bailable, there was no necessity to specifically authorise the police officer with the power of seizure.

Protection of Technological Measures: Section 65A

Section 65A of the Copyright Act, 1957 has been inserted by the Copyright (Amendment) Act, 2012. This new Section emanated from Article 11 of WIPO Copyright Treaty (WCT) and Article 18 of WIPO Performances and Phonograms Treaty (WPPT). The rationale is to prevent the possibility of high rate of infringement (digital piracy) in the digital media. Digital locks (technological protection measures, popularly known as TPMs) were invented to prevent infringement of works. At the same time, circumvention, technologies to overcome the TPMs were also developed to unlock the digital locks used by owners of copyright to prevent infringement. Section 65A(1) makes such circumvention a criminal offence punishable with imprisonment. The use of TPM had a significant impact on users since the freedom to use the work (fair use of works) permitted by law was considerably regulated through these measures. In the absence of the owner of the works providing the key to enjoy fair use, the only option was to circumvent the technology to enjoy fair use of works. The major problem of use of law in preventing circumvention was the impact on public interest on access to work facilitated by the copyright laws. This is the logic of Section 65A(2) permitting circumvention for the specified uses. The Standing Committee of the Parliament which examined the legislation in its report stated that many terms in this section have been consciously left undefined, given the complexities faced in defining these terms in the laws of developed countries. It also stated that the approach enshrined in Section 65A is to give limited legislative guidelines and allow the judiciary to evolve the law based on practical situations, keeping in mind the larger public interest of facilitating access to work by the public.

The new Section 65A[488] of the Copyright Act, 1957 provides as follows:

(1) Any person who circumvents an effective technological measure applied for the purpose of protecting any of the rights conferred by this Act, with the intention of infringing such rights, shall be punishable with imprisonment, which may extend to two years and shall also be liable to fine.

(2) Nothing in Sub-section (1) shall prevent any person from:

(a) doing anything referred to therein for a purpose not expressly prohibited by this Act:

Provided that any person facilitating circumvention by another person of a technological measure for such a purpose shall maintain a complete record of such other person including his name, address, and all relevant particulars necessary to identify him and the purpose for which he has been facilitated; or

(b) doing anything necessary to conduct encryption research using a lawfully obtained encrypted; or

488. Sections 65A and 65B inserted by the Copyright (Amendment) Act, 2012 (Act 27 of 2012), Section 37, [w.e.f. 21-6-2012].

(c) conducting any lawful investigation; or

(d) doing anything necessary for the purpose of testing the security of a computer system or a system or a computer network with the authorisation of its owner; or

(e) operator; or

(f) doing anything necessary to circumvent technological measures intended for identification or surveillance of a user; or

(g) taking measures necessary in the interest of national security.

Thus, the new Section 65A of the Copyright Act, 1957 has been introduced to provide for protection of technological measures used by a copyright owner to protect his rights on the work. According to Section 65A(1), any person who circumvents an effective technological measure applied for the protecting any of the rights, with the intention of infringing such rights, shall be punishable with imprisonment which may extend to two years and shall also be liable to fine. Section 65A(2) of the Copyright Act, 1957 provides for some exceptions. According to Section 65A(2), the prohibition shall not prevent doing anything for a purpose not expressly prohibited by the Act (thus enabling enjoyment of fair use provisions). However, any person facilitating circumvention by another person of a technological measure for such a purpose shall maintain a complete record of such other person including his name, address and all relevant particulars necessary to identify him and the purpose for which he has been facilitated. Exception is available for doing anything necessary to conduct encryption research or conducting any lawful investigation; or doing anything necessary for the purpose of testing the security of a computer system or a computer network with the authorisation of its owner or operator; or doing anything necessary to circumvent technological measures intended for identification or surveillance of a user; or taking measures necessary in the interest of national security.

Protection of Rights Management Information: Section 65B

By the Copyright (Amendment) Act, 2012, a new Section 65B[489] has been introduced to the Copyright Act, 1957 to provide protection of rights management information.[490] The introduction of this new Section 65B is expected to help the film, music and publishing industry in fighting piracy. The Section 65B(1) provides: "Any person, who knowingly (i) removes or alters any rights management information without authority, or (ii) distributes, imports for distribution, broadcasts or communicates to the public, without authority, copies of any work, or performance knowing that electronic rights management information has been removed or altered without authority, shall be punishable with imprisonment which may extend to two years and shall also be liable to fine". The proviso to the Clause (ii) of Section 65B states that if the rights management information has been tampered within any work, the owner of copyright in such work may also avail of civil remedies against the persons indulging in such acts.

---

489. Sections 65A and 65B inserted by the Copyright (Amendment) Act, 2012 (Act 27 of 2012), Section 37, [w.e.f. 21-6-2012].

490. For commentaries, *See,* J.K. Das, *Intellectual Property Rights* (Kamal Law House, Kolkata, 2008) at p. 124.

The 2012 amendment conforms to Article 12 of WIPO Copyright Treaty (WCT) and Article 19 of the WIPO Performances and Phonograms Treaty (WPPT) relating to rights management information. The rationale of the protection emanates from the practice in the digital world to manage the rights through online contracts governing the terms and conditions of use. However, these can be removed. The amendment is intended to prevent the removal of the rights management information without authority and distributing any work, fixed performance or phonogram, after removal of rights management information. It provides for punishment for such acts. The protection of technological measures and rights management information were introduced in WCT and WPPT as effective measures to prevent infringement of copyright in digital environment.

Disposal of Infringing Copies: Section 66

The Court while trying any offence under this act may deliver the infringing copies to the owner of the copy right or may make such order as it deems fit under Section 66 of the Copyright Act 1957. Such order as it deems fit does not mean that it can release the property to the accused himself that would defeat the very purpose of the Act and would have effect of facilitating the accused to perpetrate the very same offence he is accused of.[491] The Section 66 comes into play once the trial is concluded.[492] The Section 66 of the Act is as follows:

> The court trying any offence under this Act may, whether the alleged offender is convicted or not, order that all copies of the work or all plates in the possession of the alleged offender, which appear to it to be infringing copies, or plates for the purpose of making infringing copies, be delivered up to the owner of the copyright [or may make such order as it may deem tit regarding the disposal of such copies or plates].[493]

In *Flower Tobacco Company* v. *State*,[494] the Delhi High Court observed that if on trial it was held that the accused had infringed the copyright of the complainant, the containers containing the tobacco were liable to be delivered to the complainant. In *Gemini Industrial Corporation* v. *Surinder P. Jain*,[495] the Bombay High Court held that under the of the provision of Section 66 of the Copyright Act there is a right to get the infringed copies and has also a right to be handed over infringing copies. In *Screen Craft* v. *State of Karnataka*,[496] referring to Section 66 of the Copyright Act, 1957 the Karnataka High Court held that the infringed copies and other infringed material shall be delivered to the owner of the copyright.

There is an inherent relation between Sections 63, 64, 65 and the Section 66 of the Copyright Act 1957. In *Ghurey Lal* v. *State*,[497] the Allahabad High Court held that Section 64 of the Copyright Act provides that where a magistrate has taken cognizance of any offence under Section 63 in respect of the infringement of copyright in any work, it shall be lawful for a Sub-Inspector to seize all copies of the work wherever found, which appear to be infringing copies. The infringing copies so seized shall as soon as practicable be produced before the

---

491. *See, Madhu Products* v. *Sundaram Files*, MANU/ KA/ 1667/ 2019.
492. *See, Gurukrupa Mech Tech Pvt. Ltd.* v. *State of Gujarat*, (2018) 4 GLR 3324.
493. Inserted by the Copyright (Amendment) Act, 2012 (Act 27 of 2012), Section 38, [w.e.f. 21-6-2012].
494. 1986 (6) PTC 352 (Del): 30 (1986) DLT 158.
495. 1993 (13) PTC 188 (Bom).
496. 2008 (36) PTC 626 (Karn).
497. AIR 1965 All 206.

magistrate. This is a mandatory provision of law and makes the production of the infringing copies necessary before the magistrate trying the case. Section 66 of the Act further provides that the Court trying any offence under the Act may, whether the alleged offender Is convicted or not, order that all copies of the work in possession of the alleged offender, which appear to be infringing copies be delivered up to the owner of the copyright. Therefore, the production before the trying magistrate of the alleged infringing copies recovered from the possession of the accused at Hathras would also be necessary, so that he might deliver the same to the complainant, if he considers it expedient to do so.

In *Gurukrupa Mech Tech Pvt. Ltd.* v. *State of Gujarat*,[498] the Gujarat High Court observed that reading of Section 66 of the Copyright Act 1966 along with Sections 2(m), 2(t) and 2(y) makes it clear that the machine which was seized by the police as a muddamal in the present case, is neither a literary, a dramatic, a musical or an artistic work. The machine in question cannot be called an 'infringing copy' and therefore, is not covered under Section 66 of the Copyright Act. According to him, even otherwise, the application under Section 66 would come into play only after a full-fledged adjudication of the issue i.e. whether manufacturing of a machine can be said to be an infringement of a copyright. In the absence of any adjudication, an application under Section 66 is premature in nature. Thus, the Court while trying any offence under this act may deliver the infringing copies to the owner of the copy right or may make such order as it deems fit. Such order as it deems fit does not mean that it can release the property to the accused himself. Such an order would defeat the very purpose of the Act and would have effect of facilitating the accused to perpetrate the very same offence he is accused of. Therefore, the question of releasing the goods to the accused during the pendency of the trial would be opposed to Section 66 of Copyright Act.[499]

Penalty for Possession of Infringing Plates and Making False Entries in Registrar: Sections 65 and 67

The Section 65 of the Copyright Act, 1957 provides that any person who knowingly makes, or has in his possession, any plate for the purpose of making infringing copies of any work in which copyright subsists shall be punishable with imprisonment which may extend to two years and shall also be liable to fine.[500] Thus, the offence falling under Section 65 is punishable with imprisonment which may extend to two years.[501] In *Vinod Kumar Gupta* v. *State of U.P.*,[502] it was held that there was no case of violation of Section 65 of the copyright Act is made out as there was no recovery of any plate for making infringing copies of any work in which copyright subsisted.

The Section 67 of the Act further provides that any person who makes or causes to be made a false entry in the Register of Copyright kept under this Act, or makes or causes to be made a writing falsely purporting to be a copy of any entry in such register, or produces or tenders or causes to be produced or tendered as evidence any such entry or writing, knowing

---

498. (2018) 4 GLR 3324.
499. *See, Puneet Kumar Grover* v. *State*, 2008 (36) PTC 474 (Del).
500. Substituted by the Copyright (Amendment) Act, 1984 (Act 23 of 1984), Section 8, for "one year, or with fine, or with both" [w.e.f. 8-10-1984].
501. MANU/ RH/ 0427/ 2017.
502. 2019 (106) ACC 378.

the same to be false, shall be punishable with imprisonment which may extend to one year, or with fine, or with both.[503]

Penalty for Making False Statements: Section 68

Section 68 of the Copyright Act, 1957 provides that any person who with a view to deceiving any authority or officer in the execution of the provisions of this Act, or with a view to procuring or influencing the doing or omission of anything in relation to this Act or any matter thereunder, makes a false statement or representation knowing the same to be false, shall be punishable with imprisonment which may extend to one year, or with fine, or with both.[504] Explaining Section 68 of the Act in *Ghurey Lal* v. *State*,[505] the Allahabad High Court held that the Court trying any offence under the Act may, whether the alleged offender is convicted or not, order that all copies of the work in possession of the alleged offender, which appear to be infringing copies be delivered up to the owner of the copyright. Therefore, the production before the trying magistrate of the alleged infringing copies recovered from the possession of the accused would also be necessary, so that he might deliver the same to the complainant, if he considers it expedient to do so. In *Ankit* v. *State of Rajasthan*,[506] the Rajas High Court observed that from a perusal of the Section 68 of the Copyright Act, it becomes apparent that before the person can be prosecuted for infringement of Copyright Act, there has to be material available on the record of the case to show that the accused was infringing the copyright held by some other person. In *Balbir Singh Walia* v. *State of Punjab*,[507] the Punjab and Haryana High Court Observed:

> The offence under Section 63 of the Copyright Act 1957 is punishable up to 3 years and a fine of ₹ 50000/- which can be extended up to two lacs, whereas the offence under Section 65 of the Act is punishable up to 2 years and a fine, whereas offence under Section 68 of the Act is also punishable for one year or with fine or with both.

Penalty for Contravention of Section 52A: Section 68A

Section 68A was inserted to the Copyright Act, 1957 through the Copyright (Amendment) Act, 1984.[508] Section 52A makes it mandatory to give certain information on the sound recordings or video films, regarding the name and address of the person who makes such sound recording or the video films and the name and address of the owner of the copyright in such works, etc. Further, Section 68A provides that any person who publishes a sound recording or a video film in contravention of the provisions of Section 52A shall be punishable with imprisonment which may extend to three years and shall also be liable to fine.[509] Thus, Section 68A provides for penalty for contravention of Section 52A. It provides that any person who publishes a

503. *See*, *Microfibres Inc.* v. *Girdhar and Co.*, MIPR 2009 (2) 229: 2009 (40) PTC 519 (Del).
504. *See*, *SAP India Pvt. Ltd.* v. *M/s. Zenith Software Ltd.*, 201 (2013) DLT 108; *Dabur India Limited* v. *Shree Baidyanath Ayurved Bhawan Pvt. Ltd.*, 193 (2012) DLT 558: 2012 (51) PTC 441 (Del); *Frito-Lay India* v. *Radesh Foods*, MIPR 2009 (3) 525: 2009 (40) PTC 37 (Del).
505. 1965 Cri LJ 530.
506. 2013 (2) Crimes 675 (Raj.).
507. 2009 (1) RCR (Criminal) 76.
508. Inserted by the Copyright (Amendment) Act, 1984 (Act 23 of 1984), Section 9, [w.e.f. 8-10-1984].
509. *See*, *Manpreet Singh* v. *State*, 2013 (139) DRJ 277: 2013 (56) PTC 488 (Del).

sound recording or a video film in contravention of the provisions of Section 52-A, shall be punishable with imprisonment which may extend to three years and shall also be liable to fine.[510] The Section 63 provides for offence of copyright, while 65 provides punishment for possession of infringing copies. In *Pintu Dey* v. *State of Rajasthan*,[511] the Rajasthan High Court observed:

> As per Section 63 of the Copyright Act 1957, the offence under the said Act is punishable with imprisonment for a terms which shall not be less than six months but which may extend to three years and with fine. The offence falling under Section 65 of the Act of 1957 is punishable with imprisonment which may extend to two years and an offence falling under Section 68A of the Act of 1957 shall punishable with imprisonment, which may extend to three years. The expression "imprisonment for a term which may extend up to 3 years" would not come within the expression "imprisonment for 3 years and upwards." Therefore, the offence punishable under Sections 63 and 68A of the Act of 1957 cannot be considered as cognizable offence.

In *Warner Bros. Entertainment Inc.* v. *Mr. Santosh V.G.*,[512] the plaintiffs argued that Section 52A(2)(a) of the Copyright Act, 1957 bars person from publishing a video film without an appropriate censor certificate. According to Section 3 of the Act, publication means "making a work available to the public by issues of copies to the public". All films imported and made available to the public by the defendant, therefore, violate this provision, since they do not possess the censor certificate. It is also argued that likewise, Section 52A(2)(b) will also have to be viewed from an Indian context and none of the films can have such a declaration. The court clarified that violation of Section 52A makes the defendant liable under Section 68A. In *State of A.P.* v. *Nagoti Venkataramana*,[513] the Apex Court examined the issue relating to Sections 52A, 63 and 68A of Copyright Act, 1957. In this case, the respondent exhibiting cinematograph films in his shop for hire or sale of cassettes to public do not contain particulars envisaged under Section 52A. In this case, no specific charge under Section 52A was framed but the charge was framed under Section 51 read with Section 63. The court held that offence would fall under Section 68A, therefore the conviction and sentence ordered by Appellate Court modified to one conviction under Section 68A.

In *Mr. Kiran Jogani* v. *George V. Records*,[514] the court held that the object of Section 52A of the Copyright Act, 1957 is to prevent piracy and counterfeiting. The most material aspect is that the penalty for contravention of Section 52A of the Act is provided under Section 68A of the Act of imprisonment extending up to 3 years and fine. Appellate court should not substitute its own discretion with the exercise of discretion by the trial court except where the discretion has been shown to be exercised arbitrarily, capriciously and perversely. If there is no publication in India so as to infringe the provisions of Section 52A of the Act, then prosecution under the said Section cannot be upheld.

In *Balwinder Singh* v. *Delhi Administration*,[515] a Division Bench of the Delhi High Court had also held that both video and television are cinematographs. Licences for giving their

510. *See*, *Bablu Alam* v. *State of Chhattisgarh*, 2014 Cri LJ 4835.
511. 2015 (2) WLN 404 (Raj.).
512. MIPR 2009 (2) 175.
513. 1996 (6) SCALE 417: (1996) 6 SCC 409.
514. MIPR 2009 (1) 398: 2009 (39) PTC 69 (Del).
515. AIR 1984 Delhi 379: (1984) ILR 2 Delhi 845.

public exhibition is necessary under the Cinematograph Act in spite of their having commercial licences under the Telegraphs Act. Thus, in *State of A.P.* v. *Nagoti Venkataramana*,[516] the Apex Court observed that it is true that there is no specific charge under Section 52A of the Copyright Act, 1957. The charge was under Section 51 read with Section 63 of the Act. In view of the above finding (in *Nagoti Venkataramana*) and in view of the findings of the courts below that the respondent was exhibiting the cinematograph films in his Video City for hire or for sale of the cassettes to the public which do not contain the particulars envisaged under Section 52A of the Act, the infringement falls under Section 51(2)(ii) or Section 52A of the Act. The former is punishable under Section 63 and the latter is punishable under Section 68A of the Act. In view of the above findings of the courts below, the offence would fall under Section 68A of the Act. It would, therefore, be unnecessary for the prosecution to track on and trace out the owner of the copyright to come and adduce evidence of infringement of copyright. The absence thereof does not constitute lack of essential element of infringement of copyright. If the particulars on video films, etc., as mandated under Section 52A do not find place, it would be infringement of copyright.

In *Ajay Raj Pal* v. *State*,[517] the accused Mukesh was arrested being found in possession of pirated CDs, VCDs, in lay cards, cell phones and blue films from the shop owned by the petitioner. Petitioner claimed to have given the shop to the accused Mukesh as per an agreement, to manage the shop, on payment of 2% of the sale by him. Trial court took cognizance on the charge sheet being filed on which an application for summoning the petitioner was filed. Trial Court directed further investigation. Petitioner was summoned by the trial Court after supplementary charge sheet filed. Revision petition filed by the petitioner was dismissed by Sessions Court. Petitioner challenged the order of issuance of summons and the order dismissing his revision petition. Summoning order assailed on the ground of limitation and of not taking cognizance against the petitioner initially. It was argued that the petitioner had no covert or overt role in the offence. Ejecting the plea, the Court held that taking cognizance implies application of mind to the materials on record and proceeding to issue process. Mere absence of the term "cognizance" in the trial Court order could not have taken away the basic import. In regard to the plea of limitation, it was also held that the court should, in given cases, take a liberal approach and not stifle the prosecution on that ground.

Offences by Companies: Section 69

Section 69 of the Copyright Act, 1957 provides for the offence being committed by a company. It is interesting to note that Section 69 consisting with two Sub-sections. Besides the main body of these Sub-sections [Section 69(1) and Section 69(2)] there is an Explanation added to Section 69. While the main body of these Sub-sections deals with a company and the liability of directors and others in management of the company, the Explanation equates a firm or association of persons with a company, and a partner of a firm with a director of the company. According to Section 69(1), when a company commits an offence under the Copyright Act, every person, who at the time the offence was committed was in charge of, and was responsible to the company for, the conduct of the business of the company, as

516. 1996 (6) SCALE 417: (1996) 6 SCC 409.
517. (2007) ILR 1 Delhi 889.

well as the company, shall be deemed to be guilty of such offence and shall be liable to be proceeded against and punished accordingly. The proviso to Section 69(1) further states that a person who proves that the offence was committed without his knowledge or that he exercised due diligence to prevent the commission of the offence will not be punished. This proviso merely points out the defence that can be available to be borne by the persons in management in certain circumstances. Thus, in *Mohammedkutty* v. *State of Kerala*,[518] the Kerala High Court held that the Section 69 of the Copyright Act that when the offender is a company, every person, who at the time the offence was committed was in-charge of and was responsible for the conduct of business of the company as well as the company shall be deemed to be guilty of such offence.

Section 69(2) provides that if an offence is committed under the Act by a company and it is proved that the offence was committed with the consent of or convenience of or can be attributed to the negligence of a director, manager, secretary or other officer of the company, the said person will be held guilty of the offence and liable to be proceeded against and punished accordingly. In *Indu Jain* v. *State of Karnataka*,[519] the Karnataka High Court held that Section 69(2) cannot be considered as a deeming provision to fasten vicarious criminal liability on the Managing Director and Directors of the Company, in the absence of averments in terms of Section 69(1) of the Act. Thus, the Magistrate should have considered the complaint to find out whether averments therein would constitute the alleged offences when the offences alleged to have been committed by the company, the learned Magistrate should have considered the averment of complaint with reference to Section 69 of the Act.

Explanation to Section 69 of the Copyright Act of 1957 provides that for the purposes of this Section "company" means anybody corporate and includes a firm or other association of persons and "director" in relation to a firm means a partner in the firm. Thus, in *J.N. Bagga* v. *All India Reporter Ltd.*,[520] the Bombay High Court held that according to the explanation added to Section 69 of the Copyright Act, 1957, the word "company" is used in this Section in a special sense, and includes a partnership firm or other association of persons. So, like a company, a firm is criminally liable in its own name apart from the parents thereof. The partners are also liable as being in the position of the directors of the company, though the proviso to Section 69(1) will also be available to the partners in a given set of circumstances. The proviso being an exception and the liability of a company being the normal incident.

In *Chitra Narain* v. *NDTV*,[521] the petitioner who was the chief producer of All India Radio filed a complaint under Sections 51, 52A, 63, 69 of the Copyright Act, 1957 against M/s. NDTV and other respondents on the allegations that they have infringed and usurped her copyright over the feature entitled "A National Anthem Born and Exile" which was researched, written and produced by her and broadcast on the national network of All India Radio. Thus, according to the petitioner, the respondents thus clearly infringed and usurped upon the copyright of the petitioner by telecasting the said feature and committed the offences punishable under Sections 51, 52A, 63 and 69 of the Copyright Act, 1957. The complaint was registered and the learned Chief Metropolitan Magistrate asked the complainant to lead

518. MANU/ KE/ 1503/ 2014.
519. 2008 (36) PTC 553 (Karn).
520. AIR 1969 1969 Bom 320: 1971 Bom LR 409.
521. 109 (2004) DLT 394: 2004 (28) PTC 238 (Del).

evidence for inquiry under Sections 200 and 202 of the Criminal Procedure Code, 1973. The Court held that an inquiry under Section 202 is not in the nature of a trial for there can be in law only one trial in respect of any offence and that trial can commence only after process is issued against the accused as prior to this stage, said proceedings are not strictly proceedings between the complainant and the accused. A person against whom a complaint is filed does not become an accused until the Court decides to issue process against him.[522] Thus, no adjudication is to be made about guilt or otherwise of person against whom the complaint is filed.

In *Anuradha Paudwal* v. *Brij Mohan Bhardwaj*,[523] the High Court of Punjab and Haryana examined the issue relating to offence committed punishable under Section 467, 468, 471 and 420 of the Indian Penal Code, 1860 and Sections 61, 63, 65 and 69 of Copyright Act, 1957. The court held that, order of Magistrate, summoning accused must reflect that he had applied his mind to facts of case and law applicable thereto. He had to examine the nature of complaint and evidence both oral and documentary in support thereof, relatable to relevant provisions of offences and that would be sufficient for complainant to succeed in bringing charge home to accused. It was not that Magistrate was a silent spectator at time of preliminary evidence. Thus, the impugned summoning order was quashed.

522. *See*, *Dr. S.S. Khanna* v. *Chief Secretary*, AIR 1983 SC 595: [1983] 2 SCR 724; *Mrs. Chitra Narain* v. *NDTV*, 2004 Cri LJ 2618.

523. 2012 (2) Crimes 448: 2012 (1) RCR (Criminal) 861.

Copyright Act, 1957

[14 of 1957]

[4th June, 1957]

An Act to amend and consolidate the law relating to copyright.

Be it enacted by the Parliament in the Eighth Year of the Republic of India as follows:

Chapter I

PRELIMINARY

1. **Short title, extent and commencement**—(1) This Act may be called the Copyright Act, 1957.

(2) It extends to the whole of India.

(3) It shall come into force on such date[1] as the Central Government may, by notification in the Official Gazette, appoint.

2. **Interpretation**—In this Act, unless the context otherwise requires,—

(a) "adaptation" means,—

(i) in relation to a dramatic work, the conversion of the work into a non-dramatic work;

(ii) in relation to a literary work or an artistic work, the conversion of the work into a dramatic work by way of performance in public or otherwise;

(iii) in relation to a literary or dramatic work, any abridgement of the work or any version of the work in which the story or action is conveyed wholly or mainly by means of pictures in a form suitable for re-production in a book, or in a newspaper, magazine or similar periodical; [***][2]

(iv) in relation to a musical work, any arrangement or transcription of the work; [and][3]

[(v) in relation to any work, any use of such work involving its rearrangement or alteration;][4]

---

1. Came into force on 21 January 1958, *vide*, S.R.O. 269, dated 21st January, 1958, published in the Gazette of India, Extra., Part-II, Section 3, p. 167.
2. The word "and" omitted by the Copyright (Amendment) Act, 1994 (Act 38 of 1994), Section 2 [w.e.f. 10-5-1995].
3. Inserted by the Copyright (Amendment) Act, 1994 (Act 38 of 1994), Section 2 [w.e.f. 10-5-1995].
4. Inserted by the Copyright (Amendment) Act, 1994 (Act 38 of 1994), Section 2 [w.e.f. 10-5-1995].

(b) ["work of architecture"][5] means any building or structure having an artistic character or design, or any model for such building or structure;

(c) "artistic work" means,—

(i) a painting, a sculpture, a drawing (including a diagram, map, chart or plan), an engraving or a photograph, whether or not any such work possesses artistic quality;

(ii) a [work of architecture];[6] and

(iii) any other work of artistic craftsmanship;

(d) "author" means,—

(i) in relation to a literary or dramatic work, the author of the work;

(ii) in relation to a musical work, the composer;

(iii) in relation to an artistic work other than a photograph, the artist;

(iv) in relation to a photograph, the person taking the photograph;

[(v) in relation to a cinematograph or sound recording the producer; and

(vi) in relation to any literary, dramatic, musical or artistic work which is computer generated, the person who causes the work to be created;][7]

[(dd) "broadcast" means communication to the public—

(i) by any means of wireless diffusion, whether in any one or more of the forms of signs, sounds or visual images; or

(ii) by wire, and includes a rebroadcast;][8]

(e) "calendar year" means the year commencing on the 1st day of January;

[(f) "cinematograph film" means any work of visual recording [***][9] and includes a sound recording accompanying such visual recording and "cinematograph" shall be construed as including any work produced by any process analogous to cinematography including video films;][10]

[(fa) "commercial rental" does not include the rental, lease or lending of a lawfully acquired copy of a computer programme, sound recording, visual recording or cinematograph film for non-profit purposes by a non-profit library or non-profit educational institution;

Explanation—For the purposes of this clause, a "non-profit library or non-profit educational institution" means a library or an educational institution which receives grants from the Government or exempted from payment of tax under the Income-tax Act, 1961.][11]

---

5. Substituted by the Copyright (Amendment) Act, 1994 (Act 38 of 1994), Section 2, for "architectural work of art" [w.e.f. 10-5-1995].
6. Substituted by the Copyright (Amendment) Act, 1994 (Act 38 of 1994), Section 2, for "architectural work of art" [w.e.f. 10-5-1995].
7. Substituted by the Copyright (Amendment) Act, 1994 (Act 38 of 1994), Section 2, for sub-clauses (v) and (vi) [w.e.f. 10-5-1995].
8. Inserted by the Copyright (Amendment) Act, 1983 (Act 23 of 1983), Section 3 [w.e.f. 9-8-1984].
9. The words "on any medium produced through a process from which a moving image may be produced by any means" omitted by the Copyright (Amendment) Act, 2012, Section 2(i) [w.e.f. 21-6-2012].
10. Substituted by the Copyright (Amendment) Act, 1994 (Act 38 of 1994), Section 2, for clause (f) [w.e.f. 10-5-1995].
11. Inserted by the Copyright (Amendment) Act, 2012 (Act 27 of 2012), Section 2(ii) [w.e.f. 21-6-2012].

[(ff) "communication to the public" means making any work or performance available for being seen or heard or otherwise enjoyed by the public directly or by any means of display or diffusion other than by issuing physical copies of it, whether simultaneously or at places and times chosen individually, regardless of whether any member of the public actually sees, hears or otherwise enjoys the work or performance so made available.

EXPLANATION—For the purposes of this clause, communication through satellite or cable or any other means of simultaneous communication to more than one household or place of residence including residential rooms of any hotel or hostel shall he deemed to be communication to the public;][12]

[(ffa) "composer", in relation to a musical work, means the person who composes the music regardless of whether he records it in any form of graphical notation;

(ffb) "computer" includes any electronic or similar device having information processing capabilities;

(ffc) "computer programme" means a set of instructions expressed in words, codes, schemes or in any other form, including a machine-readable medium, capable of causing a computer to perform a particular task or achieve a particular result;

(ffd) "copyright society" means a society registered under sub-section (3) of section 33;][13]

(g) "delivery", in relation to a lecture, includes delivery by means of any mechanical instrument or [broadcast][14] by;

(h) "dramatic work" includes any piece for recitation, choreographic work or entertainment in dumb show, the scenic arrangement or acting form of which is fixed in writing or otherwise but does not include a cinematograph film;

[(hh) "duplicating equipment" means any mechanical contrivance or device used or intended to be used for making copies of any work;][15]

(i) "engravings" include etchings, lithographs, wood-cuts, prints and other similar works, not being photographs;

(j) "exclusive licence" means a licence which confers on the licensee or on the licensee and persons authorised by him, to the exclusion of all other persons (including the owner of the copyright), any right comprised in the copyright in a work, and "exclusive licensee" shall be construed accordingly;

(k) "Government work" means a work which is made or published by or under the direction or control of—

(i) the Government or any department of the Government;

(ii) any Legislature in India;

(iii) any court, tribunal or other judicial authority in India;

---

12. Substituted by the Copyright (Amendment) Act, 2012 (Amendment) Act, 2012 (Act 27 of 2012), Section 2(iii) [w.e.f. 21-6-2012].
13. Substituted by the Copyright (Amendment) Act, 1994 (Act 38 of 1994), Section 2 [w.e.f. 10-5-1995].
14. Substituted by the Copyright (Amendment) Act, 1983 (Act 23 of 1983), Section 2, for "radio-diffusion" [w.e.f. 9-8-1984].
15. Inserted by the Copyright (Amendment) Act, 1994 (Act 38 of 1994), Section 2 [w.e.f. 10-5-1995].

[(l) "Indian work" means a literary, dramatic or musical work,—

(i) the author of which is a citizen of India; or

(ii) which is first published in India; or

(iii) the author of which, in the case of an unpublished work, is, at the time of the making of the work, a citizen of India;][16]

[(m) "infringing copy" means,—

(i) in relation to a literary, dramatic, musical or artistic work, a reproduction thereof otherwise than in the form of a cinematographic film;

(ii) in relation to a cinematographic film, a copy of the film made on any medium by any means;

(iii) in relation to a sound recording, any other recording embodying the same sound recording, made by any means;

(iv) in relation to a programme or performance in which such a broadcast reproduction right or a performer's right subsists under the provisions of this Act, the sound recording or a cinematographic film of such programme or performance, if such reproduction, copy or sound recording is made or imported in contravention of the provisions of this Act;][17]

(n) "lecture" includes address, speech and sermon;

[(o) "literary work" includes computer programmes, tables and compilations including computer (databases);[18]

(p) "musical work" means a work consisting of music and includes any graphical notation of such work but does not include any words or any action intended to be sung, spoken or performed with the music;

(q) "performance", in relation to performer's right, means any visual or acoustic presentation made live by one or more performers;

(qq) "performer" includes an actor, singer, musician, dancer, acrobat, juggler, conjurer, snake charmer, a person delivering a lecture or any other person who makes a performance;][19]

[Provided that in a cinematograph film—a person whose performance is casual or incidental in nature and, in the normal course of the practice of the industry, is not acknowledged anywhere including in the credits of the film shall not be treated as a performer except for the purpose of clause (b) of section 38B;][20]

[***][21]

---

16. Substituted by the Copyright (Amendment) Act, 1983 (Act 23 of 1983), Section 3, for clause (1) [w.e.f. 9-8-1984].
17. Substituted by the Copyright (Amendment) Act, 1994 (Act 38 of 1994), Section 2, for clause (m) [w.e.f. 10-5-1995].
18. Substituted by the Copyright (Amendment) Act, 1999 (Act 49 of 1999) Section 2, for "data basis" [w.e.f. 15-1-2000].
19. Substituted by the Copyright (Amendment) Act, 1994 (Act 38 of 1994), Section 2 [w.e.f. 10-5-1995].
20. Inserted by the Copyright (Amendment) Act, 2012 (Act 27 of 2012), Section 2(iv) [w.e.f. 21-6-2012].
21. Clause (r) omitted by the Copyright (Amendment) Act, 1994 (Act 38 of 1994), Section 2 [w.e.f. 10-5-1995].

(s) "photograph" includes photo-lithograph and any work produced by any process analogous to photography but does not include any part of a cinematograph film;

(t) "plate" includes any stereotype or other plate, stone, block, mould, matrix, transfer, negative, [duplicating equipment][22] or other device used or intended to be used for printing or reproducing copies of any work, and any matrix or other appliance by which [sound recording][23] for the acoustic presentation of the work are or are intended to be made;

(u) "prescribed" means prescribed by rules made under this Act;

[(uu) "producer", in relation to a cinematograph film or sound recording, means a person who takes the initiative and responsibility for making the work;][24]

[***][25]

[***][26]

[(x) "reprography" means the making of copies of a work, by photocopying or similar means;][27]

[(xa) "Rights Management Information" means,—

(a) the tide or other information identifying the work or performance;

(b) the name of the author or performer;

(c) the name and address of the owner of rights;

(d) the terms and conditions regarding the use of the rights; and

(e) any member or code that represents the information referred to in sub-clauses (a) to (d),

but does not include any device or procedure intended to identify the user][28]

[(xx) "sound recording" means a recording of sounds from which such sounds may be produced regardless of the medium on which such recording is made or the method by which the sounds are produced;][29]

[(xxa) "visual recording" means the recording in any medium, by any method including the storing of it by any electronic means, of moving images or of the representations thereof; from which they can be perceived, reproduced or communicated by any method;][30]

(y) "work" means any of the following works, namely,—

(i) a literary, dramatic, musical or artistic work;

22. Inserted by the Copyright (Amendment) Act, 1984 (Act 38 of 1994), Section 2 [w.e.f. 8-10-1984].
23. Substituted by the Copyright (Amendment) Act, 1994 (Act 38 of 1994), Section 2, for "record" [w.e.f. 10-5-1995].
24. Inserted by the Copyright (Amendment) Act, 1994 (Act 38 of 1994), Section 2 [w.e.f. 10-5-1995].
25. Clause (v) omitted by the Copyright (Amendment) Act, 1983 (Act 23 of 1983), Section 3 [w.e.f. 9-8-1984].
26. Clause (w) omitted by the Copyright (Amendment) Act, 1994 (Act 38 of 1994), Section 2 [w.e.f. 10-5-1995].
27. Substituted by the Copyright (Amendment) Act, 1994 (Act 38 of 1994), Section 2 [w.e.f. 10-5-1995].
28. Inserted by the Copyright (Amendment) Act, 2012 (Act 27 of 2012), Section 2 [w.e.f. 21-6-2012].
29. Inserted by the Copyright (Amendment) Act, 1994 (Act 38 of 1994), Section 2 [w.e.f. 10-5-1995].
30. Inserted by the Copyright (Amendment) Act, 2012 (Act 27 of 2012), Section 2(vi) [w.e.f. 21-6-2012].

(ii) a cinematograph film;

(iii) a [sound recording];[31]

(z) "work of joint authorship" means a work produced by the collaboration of two or more authors in which the contribution of one author is not distinct from the contribution of the other author or authors;

(za) "work of sculpture" includes casts and models.

[3. **Meaning of publication**—For the purposes of this Act, "publication" means making a work available to the public by issue of copies or by communicating the work to the public.][32]

4. **When work not deemed to be published or performed in public**—Except in relation to infringement of copyright, a work shall not be deemed to be published or performed in public, if published, or performed in public, without the licence of the owner of the copyright.

5. **When work deemed to be first published in India**—For the purposes of this Act, a work published in India shall be deemed to be first published in India, notwithstanding that it has been published simultaneously in some other country, unless such other country provides a shorter term of copyright for such work; and a work shall be deemed to be published simultaneously in India and in another country if the time between the publication in India and the publication in such other country does not exceed thirty days or such other period as the Central Government may, in relation to any specified country, determine.

[6. **Certain disputes to be decided by [Appellate Board][33]**—If any question arises,—

(a) whether a work has been published or as to the date on which a work was published for the purposes of Chapter V, or

(b) whether the term of copyright for any work is shorter in any other country than that provided in respect of that work under this Act,

it shall be referred to the [Appellate Board][34] constituted under Section 11 whose decision thereon shall be final:

Provided that if in the opinion of the [Appellate Board][35], the issue of copies or communication to the public referred to in section 3 was of an insignificant nature it shall not be deemed to be publication for the purposes of that section.][36]

7. **Nationality of author where the making of unpublished work is extended over considerable period**—Where, in the case of an unpublished work, the making of

31. Substituted by the Copyright (Amendment) Act, 1994 (Act 38 of 1994), Section 2 [w.e.f. 10-5-1995].
32. Substituted by the Copyright (Amendment) Act, 1994 (Act 38 of 1994), Section 3 [w.e.f. 10-5-1995].
33. Substituted by the Finance Act 2017 (7 of 2017), Section 160(a) for "Copyright Board," [w.e.f. 26 May, 2017].
34. Substituted by the Finance Act 2017 (7 of 2017), Section 160(a) for "Copyright Board," [w.e.f. 26 May, 2017].
35. Substituted by the Finance Act 2017 (7 of 2017), Section 160(a) for "Copyright Board," [w.e.f. 26 May, 2017].
36. Substituted by the Copyright (Amendment) Act, 1994 (Act 38 of 1994), Section 4, for Section 6 [w.e.f. 10-5-1995].

the work is extended over a considerable period, the author of the work shall, for the purposes of this Act, be deemed to be a citizen of, or domiciled in, that country of which he was a citizen or wherein he was domiciled during any substantial part of that period.

8. **Domicile of corporations**—For the purposes of this Act, a body corporate shall be deemed to be domiciled in India if it is incorporated under any law in force in India.

Chapter II

COPYRIGHT OFFICE AND [APPELLATE BOARD][37]

9. **Copyright Office**—(1) There shall be established for the purposes of this Act an office to be called the Copyright Office.

   (2) The Copyright Office shall be under the immediate control of the Registrar of Copyrights who shall act under the superintendence and direction of the Central Government.

   (3) There shall be a seal for the Copyright Office.

10. **Registrar and Deputy Registrars of Copyrights**—(1) The Central Government shall appoint a Registrar of Copyrights and may appoint one or more Deputy Registrars of Copyrights.

    (2) A Deputy Registrar of Copyrights shall discharge under the superintendence and direction of the Registrar of Copyrights such functions of the Registrar under this Act as the Registrar may, from time to time, assign to him; and any reference in this Act to the Registrar of Copyrights shall include a reference to a Deputy Registrar of Copyrights when so discharging any such functions.

11. **Appellate Board**—(1) The Appellate Board established under Section 83 of the Trade Marks Act 1999 (47 of 1999) shall, on and from the commencement of Part XIV of Chapter VI of the Finance Act, 2017, be the Appellate Board for the purposes of this Act and the said Appellate Board shall exercise the jurisdiction, powers and authority conferred on it by or under this Act.][38]

---

37. Substituted by the Finance Act 2017 (7 of 2017), Section 160(a) for "Copyright Board," [w.e.f. 26 May, 2017].

38. Substituted by the Finance Act 2017 (7 of 2017), Section 160(a) for "Copyright Board," [w.e.f. 26 May, 2017]. The Section 11, before substitution by the Finance Act, 2017, stood as under:
    Copyright Board—(1) As soon as may be after the commencement of this Act, the Central Government shall constitute a Board to be called the Copyright Board which shall consist of a Chairman and [two other members]. [(2) The salaries and allowances payable to and the other terms and conditions of service of the Chairman and other members of the Copyright Board shall be such as may be prescribed: Provided that neither the salary and allowances nor the other terms and conditions of service of the Chairman or any other member shall be varied to his disadvantage after appointment.] (3) The Chairman of the Copyright Board shall be a person who is, or has been, a Judge of a High Court or is qualified for appointment as a Judge of a High Court. [(4) The Central Government may after consultation with the Chairman of the Copyright Board appoint a Secretary to the Copyright Board and such other officer and employees as may be considered necessary for the efficient discharge of the functions of the Copyright Board.]

12. Powers and procedure of Appellate Board[39]—(1) The Appellate Board[40] shall, subject to any rules that may be made under this Act, have power to regulate its own procedure, including the fixing of places and times of its sittings:

Provided that the Appellate Board[41] shall ordinarily hear any proceeding instituted before it under this Act within the zone in which, at the time of the institution of the proceeding, the person instituting the proceeding actually and voluntarily resides or carries on business or personally works for gain.

EXPLANATION—In this sub-section "zone" means a zone specified in section 15 of the States Reorganisation Act, 1956.

(2) The Appellate Board[42] may exercise and discharge its powers and functions through Benches constituted by the Chairman of the Appellate Board[43] from amongst its members, each Bench consisting of not less than three members.

[Provided that, if the Chairman is of opinion that any matter of importance is required to be heard by a larger bench, he may refer the matter to a special bench consisting of five members.][44]

[***][45]

(5) No member of the Appellate Board[46] shall take part in any proceedings before the Board in respect of any matter in which he has a personal interest.

(6) No act done or proceeding taken by the Appellate Board[47] under this Act shall be questioned on the ground merely of the existence of any vacancy in, or defect in the constitution of, the Board.

(7) The Appellate Board[48] shall be deemed to be a civil court for the purposes of 41 [sections 345 and 346 of the Code of Criminal Procedure, 1973][49] and all proceedings before the Board shall be deemed to be judicial proceedings within the meaning of sections 193 and 228 of the Indian Penal Code.

---

39. Substituted by the Finance Act 2017 (7 of 2017), Section 160(a) for "Copyright Board," [w.e.f. 26 May, 2017].
40. Substituted by the Finance Act 2017 (7 of 2017), Section 160(a) for "Copyright Board," [w.e.f. 26 May, 2017].
41. Substituted by the Finance Act 2017 (7 of 2017), Section 160(a) for "Copyright Board," [w.e.f. 26 May, 2017].
42. Substituted by the Finance Act 2017 (7 of 2017), Section 160(a) for "Copyright Board," [w.e.f. 26 May, 2017].
43. Substituted by the Finance Act 2017 (7 of 2017), Section 160(a) for "Copyright Board," [w.e.f. 26 May, 2017].
44. Substituted by the Copyright (Amendment) Act, 1994 (Act 38 of 1994), Section 6 [w.e.f. 10-5-1995].
45. Subsection (3) and (4) was omitted by the Finance Act 2017 (7 of 2017), Section 160(d) [w.e.f. 26 May, 2017].
46. Substituted by the Finance Act 2017 (7 of 2017), Section 160(a) for "Copyright Board," [w.e.f. 26 May, 2017].
47. Substituted by the Finance Act 2017 (7 of 2017), Section 160(a) for "Copyright Board," [w.e.f. 26 May, 2017].
48. Substituted by the Finance Act 2017 (7 of 2017), Section 160(a) for "Copyright Board," [w.e.f. 26 May, 2017].
49. Substituted by the Copyright (Amendment) Act, 1983 (Act 23 of 1983), Section 6, for "section 480 and 482 of the Code of Criminal Procedure, 1898 (5 of 1898)" [w.e.f. 9-8-1984].

Chapter III

COPYRIGHT

13. Works in which copyright subsists—(1) Subject to the provisions of this section and the other provisions of this Act, copyright shall subsist throughout India in the following classes of works, that is to say,—

(a) original literary, dramatic, musical and artistic works;

(b) cinematograph films; and

(c) [sound recordings;][50]

(2) Copyright shall not subsist in any work specified in sub-section (1), other than a work to which the provisions of section 40 or section 41 apply, unless,—

(i) in the case of a published work, the work is first published in India, or where the work is first published outside India, the author is at the date of such publication, or in a case where the author was dead at that date, was at the time of his death, a citizen of India;

(ii) in the case of an unpublished work other than a [work of architecture][51] the author is at the date of the making of the work a citizen of India or domiciled in India; and

(iii) in the case of [work of architecture][52] the work is located in India.

EXPLANATION—In the case of a work of joint authorship, the conditions conferring copyright specified in this sub-section shall be satisfied by all the authors of the work.

(3) Copyright shall not subsist—

(a) in any cinematograph film a substantial part of the film is an infringement of the copyright in any other work;

(b) in any [sound recording][53] made in respect of a literary, dramatic or musical work, if in making the [sound recording][54] copyright in such work has been infringed.

(4) The copyright in a cinematograph film or a [sound recording][55] shall not affect the separate copyright in any work in respect of which or a substantial part of which, the film, or as the case may be, the [sound recording][56] is made.

---

50. Substituted by the Copyright (Amendment) Act, 1994 (Act 38 of 1994), Section 2, for "record" [w.e.f. 10-5-1995].
51. Substituted by the Copyright (Amendment) Act, 1994 (Act 38 of 1994), Section 2, for "architectural work of art" [w.e.f. 10-5-1995].
52. Substituted by the Copyright (Amendment) Act, 1994 (Act 38 of 1994), Section 2, for "architectural work of art" [w.e.f. 10-5-1995].
53. Substituted by the Copyright (Amendment) Act, 1994 (Act 38 of 1994), Section 2, for "record" [w.e.f. 10-5-1995].
54. Substituted by the Copyright (Amendment) Act, 1994 (Act 38 of 1994), Section 2, for "record" [w.e.f. 10-5-1995].
55. Substituted by the Copyright (Amendment) Act, 1994 (Act 38 of 1994), Section 2, for "record" [w.e.f. 10-5-1995].
56. Substituted by the Copyright (Amendment) Act, 1994 (Act 38 of 1994), Section 2, for "record" [w.e.f. 10-5-1995].

(5) In the case of a [work of architecture][57] copyright shall subsist only in the artistic character and design and shall not extent to processes or methods of construction.

[14. **Meaning of copyright**—For the purposes of this Act, "copyright" means the exclusive right subject to the provisions of this Act, to do or authorise the doing of any of the following acts in respect of a work or any substantial part thereof, namely,—

(a) in the case of a literary, dramatic or musical work, not being a computer programme,—

(i) to reproduce the work in any material form including the storing of it in any medium by electronic means;

(ii) to issue copies of the work to the public not being copies already in circulation;

(iii) to perform the work in public, or communicate it to the public;

(iv) to make any cinematograph film or sound recording in respect of the work;

(v) to make any translation of the work;

(vi) to make any adaptation of the work;

(vii) to do, in relation to a translation or an adaptation of the work, any of the acts specified in relation to the work in sub-clauses (i) to (vi);

(b) in the case of a computer programme,—

(i) to do any of the acts specified in clause (a)]; [58]

(ii) to sell or give on commercial rental or offer for sale or for commercial rental any copy of the computer programme:

Provided that such commercial rental does not apply in respect of computer programmes where the programme itself is not the essential object of the rental.][59]

(c) in the case of an artistic work,—

[(i) to reproduce the work in any material form including—

(A) the storing of it in any medium by electronic or other means; or

(B) depiction in three-dimensions of a two-dimensional work; or

(C) depiction in two-dimensions of a three-dimensional work;][60]

(ii) to communicate the work to the public;

(iii) to issue copies of the work to the public not being copies already in circulation;

---

57. Substituted by the Copyright (Amendment) Act, 1994 (Act 38 of 1994), Section 2, for "architectural work of art" [w.e.f. 10-5-1995].
58. Substituted by the Copyright (Amendment) Act, 1994 (Act 38 of 1994), Section 7, for Section 14 [w.e.f. 10-5-1995].
59. Substituted by the Copyright (Amendment) Act, 1999 (Act 49 of 1999) Section 3, for sub-clause (ii) [w.e.f. 15-1-2000].
60. Substituted by the Copyright (Amendment) Act, 2012 (Act 27 of 2012), Section 5(i), for sub-clause (i) [w.e.f. 21-6-2012].

(iv) to include the work in any cinematograph film;

(v) to make any adaptation of the work;

(vi) to do in relation to an adaptation of the work any of the acts specified in relation to the work in sub-clauses (i) to (iv);

(d) In the case of cinematograph film,—

[(i) to make a copy of the film, including—

(A) a photograph of any image forming pan thereof; or

(B) storing of it in any medium by electronic or other means;

(ii) to sell or give on commercial rental or offer for sale or for such rental, any copy of the film;][61]

(iii) to communicate the film to the public;

(e) In the case of sound recording,—

(i) to make any other sound recording embodying it [including storing of it in any medium by electronic or other means];[62]

[(ii) to sell or give on commercial rental or offer for sale or for such rental, any copy of the sound recording;][63]

(iii) to communicate the sound recording to the public.

EXPLANATION—For the purposes of this section, a copy which has been sold once shall be deemed to be a copy already in circulation.

15. Special provision regarding copyright in designs registered or capable of being registered under the [***][64] [Designs Act, 2000 (16 of 2000)][65]—(1) Copyright shall not subsist under this Act in any design which is registered under the [***][66] [Designs Act, 2000 (16 of 2000)].[67]

(2) Copyright in any design, which is capable of being registered under the [***][68] [Designs Act, 2000 (16 of 2000)],[69] but which has not been so registered, shall

61. Substituted by the Copyright (Amendment) Act, 2012 (Act 27 of 2012), Section 5(i)(a) and (b), for sub-clause (i) [w.e.f. 21-6-2012].
62. Inserted by the Copyright (Amendment) Act, 2012 (Act 27 of 2012), Section 5(i), for sub-clause (i) [w.e.f. 21-6-2012].
63. Substituted by the Copyright (Amendment) Act, 2012 (Act 27 of 2012), Section 5(iii)(a), for sub-clause (2) [w.e.f. 21-6-2012].
64. The words "Indian Patents and" omitted by the Copyright (Amendment) Act, 1983 (Act 23 of 1983), Section 7 [w.e.f. 9-8-1984].
65. Substituted by the Copyright (Amendment) Act, 2012 (Act 27 of 2012), Section 6, for Designs Act, 1911 (2 of 1911) [w.e.f. 21-6-2012].
66. The words "Indian Patents and" omitted by the Copyright (Amendment) Act, 1983 (Act 23 of 1983), Section 7 [w.e.f. 9-8-1984].
67. Substituted by the Copyright (Amendment) Act, 2012 (Act 27 of 2012), Section 6, for Designs Act, 1911 (2 of 1911) [w.e.f. 21-6-2012].
68. The words "Indian Patents and" omitted by the Copyright (Amendment) Act, 1983 (Act 23 of 1983), Section 7 [w.e.f. 9-8-1984].
69. Substituted by the Copyright (Amendment) Act, 2012 (Act 27 of 2012), Section 6, for Designs Act, 1911 (2 of 1911) [w.e.f. 21-6-2012].

cease as soon as any article to which the design has been applied has been reproduced more than fifty times by an industrial process by the owner of the copyright or, with his license, by any other person.

16. No copyright except as provided in this Act—No person shall be entitled to copyright or any similar right in any work, whether published or unpublished, otherwise than under and in accordance with the provisions of this Act or any other law for the time being in force, but nothing in this section shall be constructed as abrogating any right or jurisdiction to restrain a breach of trust or confidence.

Chapter IV

OWNERSHIP OF COPYRIGHT AND THE RIGHTS OF THE OWNER

17. First owner of copyright—Subject to the provisions of this Act, the author of a work shall be the first owner of the copyright therein:

Provided that—

(a) in the case of a literary, dramatic or artistic work made by the author in the course of his employment by the proprietor of a newspaper, magazine or similar periodical under a contract of service or apprenticeship, for the purpose of publication in a newspaper, magazine or similar periodical, the said proprietor shall, in the absence of any agreement to the contrary, be the first owner of the copyright in the work in so far as the copyright relates to the publication of the work in any newspaper, magazine or similar periodical, or to the reproduction of the work for the purpose of its being so published, but in all other respects the author shall be the first owner of the copyright in the work;

(b) subject to the provisions of clause (a), in the case of a photograph taken, or a painting or portrait drawn, or an engraving or a cinematograph film made, for valuable consideration at the instance of any person, such person shall, in the absence of any agreement to the contrary, be the first owner of the copyright therein;

(c) in the case of a work made in the course of the author's employment under a contract of service or apprenticeship, to which clause (a) or clause (b) does not apply, the employer shall, in the absence of any agreement to the contrary, be the first owner of the copyright therein;

[(cc) 52 in the case of any address or speech delivered in public, the person who has delivered such address or speech or if such person has delivered such address or speech on behalf of any other person, such other person shall be the first owner of the copyright therein notwithstanding that the person who delivers such address or speech, or, as the case may be, the person on whose behalf such address or speech is delivered, is employed by any other person who arranges such address or speech or on whose behalf or premises such address or speech is delivered;][70]

70. Inserted by the Copyright (Amendment) Act, 1984 (Act 23 of 1984), Section 8(a) [w.e.f. 8-10-1984].

(d) in the case of a Government work, Government shall, in the absence of any agreement to the contrary, be the first owner of the copyright therein;

[(dd) 53 in the case of a work made or first published by or under the direction or control of any public undertaking, such public undertaking shall, in the absence of any agreement to the contrary, be the first owner of the copyright therein.

EXPLANATION—For the purposes of this clause and section 28A, "public undertaking" means—

(i) an undertaking owned or controlled by Government; or

(ii) a Government company as defined in section 617 of the Companies Act, 1956; or

(iii) a body corporate established by or under any Central, Provincial or State Act;][71]

(e) in the case of a work to which the provisions of section 41 apply, the international organisation concerned shall be the first owner of the copyright therein:

[Provided that in case of any work incorporated in a cinematograph work, nothing contained in clauses (b) and (c) shall affect the right of the author in the work referred to in clause (a) of sub-section (1) of section 13.][72]

18. Assignment of copyright—(1) The owner of the copyright in an existing work or the prospective owner of the copyright in a future work may assign to any person the copyright either wholly or partially and either generally or subject to limitations and either for the whole term of the copyright or any part thereof:

Provided that in the case of the assignment of copyright in any future work, the assignment shall take effect only when the work comes into existence:

[Provided further that no such assignment shall be applied to any medium or mode of exploitation of the work which did not exist or was not in commercial use at the time when the assignment was made, unless the assignment specifically referred to such medium or mode of exploitation of the work:

Provided also that the another of the literary or musical work included in a cinematograph film shall not assign or waive the right to receive royalties to be shared on an equal basis with the assignee of copyright for the utilisation of such work in any form other than for the communication to the public of the work along with the cinematograph film in a cinema hall, except to the legal heirs of the authors or to a copyright society for collection and distribution and any agreement to contrary shall be void:

Provided also that the author of the literary or musical work included in the sound recording but nut forming part of any cinematograph film shall not assign or waive the right to receive royalties to be shared on an equal basis with the assignee of copyright for any utilisation of such work except to the legal heirs of the authors or to a collecting society for collection and distribution and any assignment to the contrary shall be void.][73]

71. Inserted by the Copyright (Amendment) Act, 1984 (Act 23 of 1984), Section 8(b) [w.e.f. 8-10-1984].
72. Inserted by the Copyright (Amendment) Act, 2012 (Act 27 of 2012), Section 7 [w.e.f. 21-6-2012].
73. Inserted by the Copyright (Amendment) Act, 2012 (Act 27 of 2012), Section 8 [w.e.f. 21-6-2012].

(2) Where the assignee of a copyright becomes entitled to any right comprised in the copyright, the assignee as respects the rights so assigned, and the assignor as respects the rights not assigned, shall be treated for the purposes of this Act as the owner of copyright and the provisions of this Act shall have effect accordingly.

(3) In this section, the expression "assignee" as respects the assignment of the copyright in any future work includes the legal representatives of the assignee, if the assignee dies before the work comes into existence.

19. Mode of assignment—[(1)][74] No assignment of the copyright in any work shall be valid unless it is in writing signed by the assignor or by his duly authorised agent.

[(2) The assignment of copyright in any work shall identify such work, and shall specify the rights assigned and the duration and territorial extent of such assignment.

(3) The assignment of copyright in any work shall also specify the amount of (royalty and any other consideration payable)[75] to the author or his legal heirs during the currency of the assignment and the assignment shall be subject to revision, extension or termination on terms mutually agreed upon by the parties.

(4) Where the assignee does not exercise the rights assigned to him under any of the other subsections of this section within a period of one year from the date of assignment, the assignment in respect of such rights shall be deemed to have lapsed after the expiry of the said period unless otherwise specified in the assignment.

(5) If the period of assignment is not stated, it shall be deemed to be five years from the date of assignment.

(6) If the territorial extent of assignment of the rights is not specified, it shall be presumed to extend within India.

(7) Nothing in sub-section (2) or sub-section (3) or sub-section (4) or sub-section (5) or sub-section (6) shall be applicable to assignments made before the coming into force of the Copyright (Amendment) Act, 1994.][76]

[(8) The assignment of copyright in any work contrary to the terms and conditions of the rights already assigned to a copyright society in which the author of the work is a member shall be void.

(9) No assignment of copyright in any work to make a cinematograph film shall affect the right of the author of the work to claim an equal share of royalties and consideration payable in case of utilisation of the work in any form other than for the communication to the public of the work, along with the cinematograph film in a cinema hall.

---

74. Section 19 re-numbered as sub-section (1) thereof, by the Copyright (Amendment) Act, 1983 (Act 23 of 1983), Section 9 [w.e.f. 9-8-1984].
75. Substituted by the Copyright (Amendment) Act, 2012 (Act 27 of 2012), Section 9(i), for "royalty payable, if any" [w.e.f. 21-6-2012].
76. Substituted by the Copyright (Amendment) Act, 1994 (Act 38 of 1994), Section 8, for sub-section (2) [w.e.f. 10-9-1995].

(10) No assignment of the copyright in any work to make a sound recording which does not form part of any cinematograph film shall affect the right of the author of the work to claim an equal share of royalties and consideration payable for any utilisation of such work in any form.][77]

[19A. Disputes with respect to assignment of copyright—(1) If an assignee fails to make sufficient exercise of the rights assigned to him, and such failure is not attributable to any act or omission of the assignor, then, the Appellate Board[78] may, on receipt of a complaint from the assignor and after holding such inquiry as it may deem necessary, revoke such assignment.

(2) If any dispute arises with respect to the assignment of any copyright the Appellate Board[79] may, on receipt of a complaint from the aggrieved party and after holding such inquiry as it considers necessary, pass such order as it may deem fit including an order for the recovery of any royalty payable:

Provided that the Appellate Board[80] shall not pass any order under this sub-section to revoke the assignment unless it is satisfied that the terms of assignment are harsh to the assignor in case the assignor is also the author:][81]

[Provided further that, pending the disposal of an application for revocation of assignment under this sub-section, the Appellate Board[82] may pass such order, as it deems fit regarding implementation of the terms and conditions of assignment including any consideration to be paid for the enjoyment of the rights assigned:

Provided also that][83] [no order of revocation of assignment under this sub-section, be made within a period of five years from the date of such assignment.][84]

[(3) Every complaint received under sub-section (2) shall be dealt with by the Appellate Board[85] as far as possible and efforts shall be made to pass the final order in the matter within a period of six months from the date of receipt of the complaint and any delay in compliance of the same, the Appellate Board[86] shall record the reasons thereof.][87]

---

77. Inserted by the Copyright (Amendment) Act, 2012 (Act 27 of 2012), Section 9(ii) [w.e.f. 21-6-2012].
78. Substituted by the Finance Act 2017 (7 of 2017), Section 160(a) for "Copyright Board," [w.e.f. 26 May, 2017].
79. Substituted by the Finance Act 2017 (7 of 2017), Section 160(a) for "Copyright Board," [w.e.f. 26 May, 2017].
80. Substituted by the Finance Act 2017 (7 of 2017), Section 160(a) for "Copyright Board," [w.e.f. 26 May, 2017].
81. Inserted by the Copyright (Amendment) Act, 1994 (Act 38 of 1994), Section 9, for Section 19A [w.e.f. 10-5-1995].
82. Substituted by the Finance Act 2017 (7 of 2017), Section 160(a) for "Copyright Board," [w.e.f. 26 May, 2017].
83. Substituted by the Copyright (Amendment) Act, 2012 (Act 27 of 2012), Section 10(i) [w.e.f. 21-6-2012].
84. Inserted by the Copyright (Amendment) Act, 1994 (Act 38 of 1994), Section 9 [w.e.f. 10-5-1995].
85. Substituted by the Finance Act 2017 (7 of 2017), Section 160(a) for "Copyright Board," [w.e.f. 26 May, 2017].
86. Substituted by the Finance Act 2017 (7 of 2017), Section 160(a) for "Copyright Board," [w.e.f. 26 May, 2017].
87. Substituted by the Copyright (Amendment) Act, 2012 (Act 27 of 2012), Section 10(ii) [w.e.f. 21-6-2012].

20. Transmission of copyright in manuscript by testamentary disposition—Where under a bequest a person is entitled to the manuscript of a literary, dramatic or musical work, or to an artistic work, and the work was not published before the death of the testator, the bequest shall, unless the contrary intention is indicated in the testator's will or any codicil thereto, be construed as including the copyright in the work in so far as the testator was the owner of the copyright immediately before his death.

EXPLANATION—In this section, the expression "manuscript" means the original document embodying the work, whether written by hand or not.

21. Right of author to relinquish copyright—(1) The author of a work may relinquish all or any of the rights comprised in the copyright in the work by giving notice in the prescribed form to [the Registrar of Copyrights or by way of public notice] and thereupon such rights shall, subject to the provisions of sub-section (3), cease to exist from the date of the notice.

(2) On receipt of a notice under sub-section (1), the Registrar of Copyrights shall cause it to be published in the Official Gazette and in such other manner as he may deem fit.

[(2A) The Registrar of Copyrights—within fourteen days from the publication of the notice in the Official Gazette, post the notice on the official website of the Copyright Office so as to remain in the public domain for a period of not less than three years.][88]

(3) The relinquishment of all or any of the rights comprised in the copyright in a work shall not affect any rights subsisting in favour of any person on the date of the notice referred to in sub-section (1).

Chapter V

TERM OF COPYRIGHT

22. Term of copyright in published literary, dramatic, musical and artistic works—Except as otherwise hereinafter provided, copyright shall subsist in any literary, dramatic, musical or artistic work [***][89] published within the lifetime of the author until [sixty][90] years from the beginning of the calendar year next following the year in which the author dies.

EXPLANATION—In this section the reference to the author shall, in the case of a work of joint authorship, be construed as a reference to the author who dies last.

23. Term of copyright in anonymous and pseudonymous works—(1) In the case of a literary, dramatic, musical or artistic work (other than a photograph), which is

88. Substituted by the Copyright (Amendment) Act, 2012 (Act 27 of 2012), Section 11(ii) [w.e.f. 21-6-2012].
89. The words "other than a photograph" omitted by the Copyright (Amendment) Act, 2012 (Act 27 of 2012), Section 12 [w.e.f. 21-6-2012].
90. Substituted by the Copyright (Amendment) Act, 1992 (Act 13 of 1992), Section 2, for "fifty years" [w.e.f. 28-12-1991].

published anonymously or pseudonymously, copyright shall subsist until [sixty][91] years from the beginning of the calendar year next following the year in which the work is first published:

Provided that where the identity of the author is disclosed before the expiry of the said period, copyright shall subsist until [sixty][92] years from the beginning of the calendar year next following the year in which the author dies.

(2) In sub-section (1), references to the author shall, in the case of an anónymous work of joint authorship, be construed,—

(a) where the identity of one of the authors is disclosed, as references to that author;

(b) where the identity of more authors than one is disclosed, as references to the author who dies last from amongst such authors.

(3) In sub-section (1) references to the author shall, in the case of a pseudonymous work of joint authorship, be construed,—

(a) where the names of one or more (but not all) of the authors are pseudonymous and his or their identity is not disclosed, as references to the author whose name is not a pseudonym, or, if the names of two or more of the authors are not pseudonyms, as references to such of those authors who dies last;

(b) where the names of one or more (but not all) of the authors are pseudonyms and the identity of one or more of them is disclosed, as references to the author who dies last from amongst the authors whose names are not pseudonyms and the authors whose names are pseudonyms and are disclosed; and

(c) where the names of all the authors are pseudonyms and the identity of one of them is disclosed, as references to the author whose identity is disclosed or if the identity of two or more of such authors is disclosed, as references to such of those authors who dies last.

EXPLANATION—For the purposes of this section, the identity of an author shall be deemed to have been disclosed, if either identity of the author is disclosed publicly by both the author and the publisher or is otherwise established to the satisfaction of the Appellate Board[93] by that author.

24. Term of copyright in the posthumous work—(1) In the case of a literary, dramatic or musical work or an engraving, in which copyright subsists at the date of the death of the author or, in the case of any such work of joint authorship, at or immediately before the date of the death of the author who dies last, but which, or any adaptation of which, has not been published before that date, copyright shall subsist until

---

91. Substituted by the Copyright (Amendment) Act, 1992 (Act 13 of 1992), Section 2, for "fifty years" [w.e.f. 28-12-1991].

92. Substituted by the Copyright (Amendment) Act, 1992 (Act 13 of 1992), Section 2, for "fifty years" [w.e.f. 28-12-1991].

93. Substituted by the Finance Act 2017 (7 of 2017), Section 160(a) for "Copyright Board," [w.e.f. 26 May, 2017].

[sixty][94] years from the beginning of the calendar year next following the year in which the work is first published or, where an adaptation of the work is published in any earlier year, from the beginning of the calendar year next following that year.

(2) For the purposes of this section a literary, dramatic or musical work or an adaptation of any such work shall be deemed to have been published, if it has been performed in public or if any records made in respect of the work have been sold to the public or have been offered for sale to the public.

[***][95]

26. Term of copyright in cinematograph films—In the case of a cinematograph film, copyright shall subsist until [sixty][96] years from the beginning of the calendar year next following the year in which the film is published.

27. Term of copyright in [sound recording][97]—In the case of a [sound recording],[98] copyright shall subsist until [sixty][99] years from the beginning of the calendar year next following the year in which the [sound recording][100] is published.

28. Term of copyright in Government work—In the case of Government work, where Government is the first owner of the copyright therein, copyright shall subsist until [sixty][101] years from the beginning of the calendar year next following the year in which the work is first published.

Chapter VI

LICENCES

30. Licences by owners of copyright—The owner of the copyright in any existing work or the prospective owner of the copyright in any future work may grant any interest in the right by licence in [writing by him][102] or by his duly authorised agent:

Provided that in the case of a licence relating to copyright in any future work, the licence shall take effect only when the work comes into existence.

94. Substituted by the Copyright (Amendment) Act, 1992 (Act 13 of 1992), Section 2, for "fifty years" [w.e.f. 28-12-1991].
95. Section 15 omitted by the Copyright (Amendment) Act, 2012, Section 13 [w.e.f. 21-6-2012].
96. Substituted by the Copyright (Amendment) Act, 1992 (Act 13 of 1992), Section 2, for "fifty years" [w.e.f. 28-12-1991].
97. Substituted by the Copyright (Amendment) Act, 1992 (Act 13 of 1992), Section 2, for "fifty years" [w.e.f. 28-12-1991].
98. Substituted by the Copyright (Amendment) Act, 1992 (Act 13 of 1992), Section 2, for "fifty years" [w.e.f. 28-12-1991].
99. Substituted by the Copyright (Amendment) Act, 1992 (Act 13 of 1992), Section 2, for "fifty years" [w.e.f. 28-12-1991].
100. Substituted by the Copyright (Amendment) Act, 1984 (Act 38 of 1994), Section 2, for "record" [w.e.f. 8-10-1984].
101. Substituted by the Copyright (Amendment) Act, 1992 (Act 13 of 1992), Section 2, for "fifty years" [w.e.f. 28-12-1991].
102. Substituted by the Copyright (Amendment) Act, 2012, Section 2, for "writing signed by him" [w.e.f. 21-6-2012].

Explanation—Where a person to whom a licence relating to copyright in any future work is granted under this section dies before the work comes into existence, his legal representatives shall, in the absence of any provision to the contrary in the licence, be entitled to the benefit of the licence.

[30A. Application of [section 19][103]—The provisions of [section 19][104] shall, with any necessary adaptations and modifications, apply in relation to a licence under Section 30 as they apply in relation to assignment of copyright in a work.][105]

31. Compulsory licence in works withheld from public—(1) If at any time during the term of copyright in [any work][106] which has been published or performed in public, a complaint is made to the Appellate Board[107] that the owner of copyright in the work—

(a) has refused to republish or allow the republication of the work or has refused to allow the performance in public of the work, and by reason of such refusal the work is withheld from the public; or

(b) has refused to allow communication to the public by [broadcast],[108] of such work or in the case of [sound recording][109] the work recorded in such [sound recording],[110] on terms which the complainant considers reasonable; the Appellate Board,[111] after giving to the owner of the copyright in the work a reasonable opportunity of being heard and after holding such inquiry as it may deem necessary, may, if it is satisfied that the grounds for such refusal are not reasonable, direct the Registrar of Copyrights to grant to the complainant a licence to republish the work, perform the work in public or communicate the work to the public by [broadcast],[112] as the case may be, subject to payment to the owner of the copyright of such compensation and subject to such other terms and conditions as the Appellate Board[113] may determine; and thereupon the

---

103. Substituted by the Copyright (Amendment) Act, 2012 (Act 27 of 2012), Section 15, for "sections 19 and 19A [w.e.f. 21-6-2012].
104. Substituted by the Copyright (Amendment) Act, 2012 (Act 27 of 2012), Section 15, for "sections 19 and 19A [w.e.f. 21-6-2012].
105. Inserted by the Copyright (Amendment) Act, 1994 (Act 38 of 1994), Section 10 [w.e.f. 10-5-1995].
106. Substituted by the Copyright (Amendment) Act, 2012 (Act 27 of 2012), Section 16, for "any Indian work" [w.e.f. 21-6-2012].
107. Substituted by the Finance Act, 2017 (7 of 2017), Section 160(a) for "Copyright Board," [w.e.f. 26 May, 2017].
108. Substituted by the Copyright (Amendment) Act, 1983 (Act 23 of 1983), Section 2, for "radio diffusion" [w.e.f. 9-8-1984].
109. Substituted by the Copyright (Amendment) Act, 1984 (Act 65 of 1984), Section 2, for "record" [w.e.f. 8-10-1984].
110. Substituted by the Copyright (Amendment) Act, 1984 (Act 65 of 1984), Section 2, for "record" [w.e.f. 8-10-1984].
111. Substituted by the Finance Act 2017 (7 of 2017), Section 160(a) for "Copyright Board," [w.e.f. 26 May, 2017].
112. Substituted by the Copyright (Amendment) Act, 1983 (Act 23 of 1983), Section 2, for "radio diffusion" [w.e.f. 9-8-1984].
113. Substituted by the Finance Act 2017 (7 of 2017), Section 160(a) for "Copyright Board," [w.e.f. 26 May, 2017].

Registrar of Copyrights shall grant the licence to the complainant in accordance with the directions of the Appellate Board,[114] on payment of such fee as may be prescribed.

[***][115]

[***][116]

[31A. Compulsory licence in unpublished (or published work)[117]—(1) (Where, in the case of any unpublished work or any work published or communicated to the public and the work is withheld from the public in India, the author is dead or unknown or cannot be traced, or the owner of the copyright in such work cannot be found, any person may apply to the Appellate Board[118] for a licence to publish or communicate to the public such work or a translation thereof in any language.)[119]

(2) Before making an application under sub-section (1), the applicant shall publish his proposal in one issue of a daily newspaper in the English language having circulation in the major part of the country and where the application is for the publication of a translation in any language, also in one issue of any daily newspaper in that language.

(3) Every such application shall be made in such form as may be prescribed and shall be accompanied with a copy of the advertisement issued under sub-section (2) and such fee as may be prescribed.

(4) Where an application is made to the Appellate Board[120] under this section, it may, after holding such inquiry as may be prescribed, direct the Registrar of Copyrights to grant to the applicant a licence to publish the work or a translation thereof in the language mentioned in the application subject to the payment of such royalty and subject to such other terms and conditions as the Appellate Board[121] may determine, and thereupon the Registrar of Copyrights shall grant the licence to the applicant in accordance with the direction of the Appellate Board.[122]

---

114. Substituted by the Finance Act 2017 (7 of 2017), Section 160(a) for "Copyright Board," [w.e.f. 26 May, 2017].
115. Explanation omitted by the Copyright (Amendment) Act, 2012 (Act 27 of 2012), Section 16(i)(c), [w.e.f. 21-6-2012].
116. Sub-section (2) omitted by the Copyright (Amendment) Act, 2012 (Act 27 of 2012), Section 16(i)(c), [w.e.f. 21-6-2012].
117. Substituted by the Copyright (Amendment) Act, 2012 (Act 27 of 2012), Section 17(i), for "Indian work" [w.e.f. 21-6-2012].
118. Substituted by the Finance Act 2017 (7 of 2017), Section 160(a) for "Copyright Board," [w.e.f. 26 May, 2017].
119. Substituted by the Copyright (Amendment) Act, 2012 (Act 27 of 2012), Section 17(ii), for "Indian work" [w.e.f. 21-6-2012].
120. Substituted by the Finance Act 2017 (7 of 2017), Section 160(a) for "Copyright Board," [w.e.f. 26 May, 2017].
121. Substituted by the Finance Act 2017 (7 of 2017), Section 160(a) for "Copyright Board," [w.e.f. 26 May, 2017].
122. Substituted by the Finance Act 2017 (7 of 2017), Section 160(a) for "Copyright Board," [w.e.f. 26 May, 2017].

(5) Where a licence is granted under this section, the Registrar of Copyrights may, by order, direct the applicant to deposit the amount of the royalty determined by the Appellate Board[123] in the public account of India or in any other account specified by the Appellate Board[124] so as to enable the owner of the copyright or, as the case may be, his heirs, executors or the legal representatives to claim such royalty at any time.

(6) Without prejudice to the foregoing provisions of this section, in the case of a work referred to in sub-section (1), if the original author is dead, the Central Government may, if it considers that the publication of the work is desirable in the national interest, require the heirs, executors or legal representatives of the author to publish such work within such period as may be specified by it.

(7) Where any work is not published within the period specified by the Central Government under sub-section (6), the Appellate Board[125] may, on an application made by any person for permission to publish the work and after hearing the parties concerned, permit such publication on payment of such royalty as the Appellate Board[126] may, in the circumstances of such case, determine in the prescribed manner.][127]

[31B. Compulsory licence for benefit of disabled—(1) Any person working for the benefit of persons with disability on a profit basis or for business may apply to the Appellate Board,[128] in such form and manner and accompanied by such 1ie as may be prescribed, for a compulsory licence to publish any work in which copyright subsists for the benefit of such persons, in a case to which clause (zb) of sub-section (1) of section 52 does not apply and the Appellate Board[129] shall dispose of such application as expeditiously as possible and endeavour shall be made to dispose of such application within a period of two months from the date of receipt of the application.

(2) The Appellate Board[130] may, on receipt of an application under sub-section (1), inquire, or direct such inquiry as it considers necessary to establish the credentials of the applicant and satisfied itself that the application has been made in good faith.

---

123. Substituted by the Finance Act 2017 (7 of 2017), Section 160(a) for "Copyright Board," [w.e.f. 26 May, 2017].
124. Substituted by the Finance Act 2017 (7 of 2017), Section 160(a) for "Copyright Board," [w.e.f. 26 May, 2017].
125. Substituted by the Finance Act 2017 (7 of 2017), Section 160(a) for "Copyright Board," [w.e.f. 26 May, 2017].
126. Substituted by the Finance Act 2017 (7 of 2017), Section 160(a) for "Copyright Board," [w.e.f. 26 May, 2017].
127. Inserted by the Copyright (Amendment) Act, 1983 (Act 23 of 1983), Section 12 [w.e.f. 9-8-1984].
128. Substituted by the Finance Act 2017 (7 of 2017), Section 160(a) for "Copyright Board," [w.e.f. 26 May, 2017].
129. Substituted by the Finance Act 2017 (7 of 2017), Section 160(a) for "Copyright Board," [w.e.f. 26 May, 2017].
130. Substituted by the Finance Act 2017 (7 of 2017), Section 160(a) for "Copyright Board," [w.e.f. 26 May, 2017].

(3) If the Appellate Board[131] is satisfied, after giving to the owners of rights in the work a reasonable opportunity of being beard and after holding such inquiry as it may deem necessary, that a compulsory licence needs to be issued to make the work available to the disabled, it may direct the Registrar of Copyrights to grant to the applicant such a licence to publish the work.

(4) Every compulsory licence issued under this section shall specify the means and format of publication, the period during which the compulsory licence may be exercised and, in the case of issue of copies, the number of copies that may be issued including the rate or royalty:

Provided that where the Appellate Board[132] has issued such a compulsory licence it may, on a further application and after giving reasonable opportunity to the owners of rights, extend the period of such compulsory licence and allow the issue of more copies as it may deem fit.][133]

[31C. **Statutory licence for cover versions**—(1) Any person desirous of making a cover version, being a sound recording in respect of any literary, dramatic or musical work, where sound recordings of that work have been made by or with the licence or consent of the owner of the right in the work, may do so subject to the provisions of this section:

Provided that such sound recordings shall be in the same medium as the last recording, unless the medium of the last recording is no longer in current commercial use.

(2) The person making the sound recordings shall give prior notice of his intention to make the sound recordings in the manner as may be prescribed, and provide in advance copies of all covers or labels with which the sound recordings are to be sold, and pay in advance, to the owner of rights in each work royalties in respect of all copies to be made by him, at the rate fixed by the Appellate Board[134] in this behalf.

Provided that such sound recordings shall not be sold or issued in any form of packaging or with any cover or label which is likely to mislead or confuse the public as to their identity, and in particular shall not contain the name or depict in any way any performer of an earlier sound recording of the same work or any cinematograph film in which such sound recording was incorporated and, further, shall state on the cover that it is a cover version made under this section.

(3) The person making such sound recordings shall not make any alteration in the literary or musical work which has not been made previously by or with the consent of the owner of rights, or which is not technically necessary for the purpose of making the sound recordings:

---

131. Substituted by the Finance Act 2017 (7 of 2017), Section 160(a) for "Copyright Board," [w.e.f. 26 May, 2017].
132. Substituted by the Finance Act 2017 (7 of 2017), Section 160(a) for "Copyright Board," [w.e.f. 26 May, 2017].
133. Inserted by the Copyright (Amendment) Act, 2012 (Act 27 of 2012), Section 18 [w.e.f. 21-6-2012].
134. Substituted by the Finance Act 2017 (7 of 2017), Section 160(a) for "Copyright Board," [w.e.f. 26 May, 2017].

Provided that such sound recordings shall not be made until the expiration of five calendar years after the end of the year in which the first sound recordings of the work was made.

(4) One royalty in respect of such sound recordings shall be paid for a minimum of fifty thousand copies of each wade during each calendar year in which copies of it are made:

Provided that the Appellate Board[135] may, by general order, fix a lower minimum in respect of walks in a particular language or dialect having regard to the potential circulation of such walks.

(5) The person making such sound recordings shall maintain such registers and books of account in respect thereof; including full details of existing stock as may be prescribed and shall allow the owner of rights or his duly authorised agent or representative to inspect all records and books of account relating to such sound recording:

Provided that if on a complaint brought before the Appellate Board[136] to the effect that the owner of rights has not been paid in full for any sound recordings purporting to be made in pursuance of this section, the Appellate Board[137] is, *prima facie,* satisfied that the complaint is genuine, it may pass an order *ex parte* directing the person making the sound recording to cease from making further copies and, after holding such inquiry as it considers necessary, make such further order as it may deem fit, including an order for payment of royalty.

EXPLANATION—For the purposes of this action "cover version" means a sound recording made in accordance with this section.][138]

[31D. Statutory licence for broadcasting of literary and musical works and sound recording—(1) Any broadcasting organisation desirous of communicating to the public by way of a broadcast or by way of performance of a literary or musical work and sound recording which has already been published may do so subject to the provisions of this section.

(2) The broadcasting organisation shall give prior notice, in such manner as may be prescribed, of its intention to broadcast the work stating the duration and territorial coverage of the broadcast, and shall pay to the owner of rights in each work royalties in the manner and at the rate fixed by the Appellate Board.[139]

(3) The rates of royalty for radio broadcasting shall be different from television

135. Substituted by the Finance Act 2017 (7 of 2017), Section 160(a) for "Copyright Board," [w.e.f. 26 May, 2017].

136. Substituted by the Finance Act 2017 (7 of 2017), Section 160(a) for "Copyright Board," [w.e.f. 26 May, 2017].

137. Substituted by the Finance Act 2017 (7 of 2017), Section 160(a) for "Copyright Board," [w.e.f. 26 May, 2017].

138. Inserted by the Copyright (Amendment) Act, 2012 (Act 27 of 2012), Section 18 [w.e.f. 21-6-2012].

139. Substituted by the Finance Act 2017 (7 of 2017), Section 160(a) for "Copyright Board," [w.e.f. 26 May, 2017].

broadcasting and the Appellate Board[140] shall fix separate rates for radio broadcasting and television broadcasting.

(4) In fixing the manner and the rate of royalty under sub-section (2), the Appellate Board[141] may require the broadcasting organisation to pay an advance to the owners of rights.

(5) The names of the authors and the principal performers of the work shall, except in case of the broadcasting organisation communicating such work by way of performance, be announced with the broadcast.

(6) No fresh alteration to any literary or musical work, which is not technically necessary for the purpose of broadcasting, other than shortening the work for convenience of broadcast, shall be made without the consent of the owners of rights.

(7) The broadcasting organisation shall—

(a) maintain such records and books of account, and render to the owners of rights such reports and accounts; and

(b) allow the owner of rights or his duly authorised agent or representative to inspect all records and books of account relating to such broadcast, in such manner as may be prescribed.

(8) Nothing in this section shall affect the operation of any licence issued or any agreement entered into before the commencement of the Copyright (Amendment) Act, 2012.][142]

32. Licence to produce and publish translations—(1) Any person may apply to the Appellate Board[143] for a licence to produce and publish a translation of a literary or dramatic work in any language [after a period of seven years from the first publication of the work].[144]

[(1A) Notwithstanding anything contained in sub-section (1), any person may apply to the Appellate Board[145] for a licence to produce and publish a translation, in printed or analogous forms of reproduction, of a literary or dramatic work, other than an Indian work, in any language in general use in India after a period of three years from the publication of such work, if such translation is required for the purposes of teaching, scholarship or research:

Provided that where such translation is in a language not in general use in any developed country, such application may be made after a period of one year from such publications.][146]

---

140. Substituted by the Finance Act 2017 (7 of 2017), Section 160(a) for "Copyright Board," [w.e.f. 26 May, 2017].
141. Substituted by the Finance Act 2017 (7 of 2017), Section 160(a) for "Copyright Board," [w.e.f. 26 May, 2017].
142. Inserted by the Copyright (Amendment) Act, 2012 (Act 27 of 2012), Section 18 [w.e.f. 21-6-2012].
143. Substituted by the Finance Act 2017 (7 of 2017), Section 160(a) for "Copyright Board," [w.e.f. 26 May, 2017].
144. Inserted by the Copyright (Amendment) Act, 1983 (Act 23 of 1983), Section 13 [w.e.f. 09-8-1984].
145. Substituted by the Finance Act 2017 (7 of 2017), Section 160(a) for "Copyright Board," [w.e.f. 26 May, 2017].
146. Inserted by the Copyright (Amendment) Act, 1983 (Act 23 of 1983), Section 13 [w.e.f. 9-8-1984].

(2) Every [application under this section][147] shall be made in such form as may be prescribed and shall state the proposed retail price of a copy of the translation of the work.

(3) Every applicant for a licence under this section shall, along with his application, deposit with the Registrar of Copyrights such fee as may be prescribed.

(4) Where an application is made to the Appellate Board[148] under this section, it may, after holding such inquiry as may be prescribed, grant to the applicant a licence, not being an exclusive licence, to produce and publish a translation of the work in the language mentioned in [the application—

(i) subject to the condition that the applicant shall pay to the owner of the copyright in the work royalties in respect of copies of the translation of the work sold to the public, calculated at such rate as the Appellate Board[149] may, in the circumstances of each case, determine in the prescribed manner; and

(ii) where such licence is granted on an application under sub-section (1A), subject also to the condition that the licence shall not extend to the export of copies of the translation of the work outside India and every copy of such translation shall contain a notice in the language of such translation that the copy is available for distribution only in India:

Provided that nothing in clause (ii) shall apply to the export by Government or any authority under the Government of copies of such translation in a language other than English, French or Spanish to any country if—

(1) such copies are sent to citizens of India residing outside India or to any association of such citizens outside India; or

(2) such copies are meant to be used for purposes of teaching, scholarship or research and not for any commercial purpose; and

(3) in either case, the permission for such export has been given by the Government of that country][150]

[Provided further that no licence under this section][151] shall be granted, unless—

(a) a translation of the work in the language mentioned in the application has not been published by the owner of the copyright in the work or any person authorised by him, [within seven years or three years or one year, as the

147. Substituted by the Copyright (Amendment) Act, 1983 (Act 23 of 1983), Section 13, for "such application" [w.e.f. 9-8-1984].

148. Substituted by the Finance Act 2017 (7 of 2017), Section 160(a) for "Copyright Board," [w.e.f. 26 May, 2017].

149. Substituted by the Finance Act 2017 (7 of 2017), Section 160(a) for "Copyright Board," [w.e.f. 26 May, 2017].

150. Substituted by the Copyright (Amendment) Act, 1983 (Act 23 of 1983), Section 13, for certain works [w.e.f. 9-8-1984].

151. Substituted by the Copyright (Amendment) Act, 1983 (Act 23 of 1983), Section 13, for "Provided that no such licence" [w.e.f. 9-8-1984].

case may be, of the first publication of the work][152] or if a translation has been so published, it has been out of print;

(b) the applicant has proved to the satisfaction of the Appellate Board[153] that he had requested and had been denied authorisation by the owner of the copyright to produce and publish such translation, or that [he was, after due diligence on his part, unable to find][154] the owner of the copyright;

(c) where the applicant was unable to find the owner of the copyright, he had sent a copy of his request for [such authorisation by registered air mail post to the publisher whose name appears from the work, and in the case of an application for a licence under sub-section (1)],[155] not less than two months before [such application];[156]

[(cc) a period of six months in the case of an application under sub-section (1A) (not being an application under the proviso thereto), or nine months in the case of an application under the proviso to that sub-section, has elapsed from the date of making the request under clause (b) of this proviso, or where a copy of the request has been sent under clause (c) of this proviso, from the date of sending of such copy, and the translation of the work in the language mentioned in the application has not been published by the owner of the copyright in the work or any person authorised by him within the said period of six months or nine months, as the case may be;

(ccc) in the case of any application made under sub-section (1A),—

(i) the name of the author and the title of the particular edition of the work proposed to be translated are printed on all the copies of the translation;

(ii) if the work is composed mainly of illustrations, the provisions of section 32A are also complied with;][157]

(d) the Appellate Board[158] is satisfied that the applicant is competent to produce and publish a correct translation of the work and possesses the means to pay to the owner of the copyright the royalties payable to him under this section;

(e) the author has not withdrawn from circulation copies of the work; and

---

152. Substituted by the Copyright (Amendment) Act, 1983 (Act 23 of 1983), Section 13, for "within seven years of the first publication of the work" [w.e.f. 9-8-1984].
153. Substituted by the Finance Act 2017 (7 of 2017), Section 160(a) for "Copyright Board," [w.e.f. 26 May, 2017].
154. Substituted by the Copyright (Amendment) Act, 1983 (Act 23 of 1983), Section 13, for "he was unable to find" [w.e.f. 9-8-1984].
155. Substituted by the Copyright (Amendment) Act, 1983 (Act 23 of 1983), Section 13, for "such authorisation to the publisher whose name appears from the work" [w.e.f. 9-8-1984].
156. Substituted by the Copyright (Amendment) Act, 1983 (Act 23 of 1983), Section 13, for "the application for the licence" [w.e.f. 9-8-1984].
157. Substituted by the Copyright (Amendment) Act, 1983 (Act 23 of 1983), Section 13 [w.e.f. 9-8-1984].
158. Substituted by the Finance Act 2017 (7 of 2017), Section 160(a) for "Copyright Board," [w.e.f. 26 May, 2017].

(f) an opportunity of being heard is given, wherever practicable, to the owner of the copyright in the work.

[(5) Any broadcasting authority may apply to the Appellate Board[159] for a licence to produce and publish the translation of—

(a) a work referred to in sub-section (1A) and published in printed or analogous forms of reproduction; or

(b) any text incorporated in audio-visual fixations prepared had published solely for the purpose of systematic instructional activities, for broadcasting such translation for the purposes of teaching or for the dissemination of the results of specialised, technical or scientific research to the experts in any particular field.

(6) The provisions of sub-sections (2) to (4) in so far as they are relatable to an application under sub-section (1A), shall, with the necessary modifications, apply to the grant of a licence under sub-section (5) and such licence shall not also be granted unless—

(a) the translation is made from a work lawfully acquired;

(b) the broadcast is made through the medium of sound and visual recordings;

(c) such recording has been lawfully and exclusively made for the purpose of broadcasting in India by the applicant or by any other broadcasting agency; and

(d) the translation and the broadcasting of such translation are not used for any commercial purposes.

EXPLANATION—For the purposes of this section,—

(a) "developed country" means a country which is not a developing country;

(b) "developing country" means a country which is for the time being regarded as such in conformity with the practice of the General Assembly of the United Nations;

(c) "purposes of research" does not include purposes of industrial research, or purposes of research by bodies corporate (not being bodies corporate owned or controlled by Government) or other associations or body of persons for commercial purposes;

(d) "purposes of teaching, research or scholarship" includes—

(i) purposes of instructional activity at all levels in educational institutions, including schools, colleges, universities and tutorial institutions; and

(ii) purposes of all other types of organised educational activity.][160]

[32A. Licence to reproduce and publish works for certain purposes—(1) Where, after the expiration of the relevant period from the date of the first publication of an edition of a literary, scientific or artistic work,—

159. Substituted by the Finance Act 2017 (7 of 2017), Section 160(a) for "Copyright Board," [w.e.f. 26 May, 2017].

160. Substituted by the Copyright (Amendment) Act, 1983 (Act 23 of 1983), Section 13 [w.e.f. 9-8-1984].

(a) the copies of such edition are not made available in India; or

(b) such copies have not been put on sale in India for a period of six months to the general public, or in connection with systematic instructional activities at a price reasonably related to that normally charged in India for comparable works by the owner of the right of reproduction or by any person authorised by him in this behalf, any person may apply to the Appellate Board[161] for a licence to reproduce and publish such work in printed or analogous forms of reproduction at the price at which such edition is sold or a lower price for the purposes of systematic instructional activities.

(2) Every such application shall be made in such form as may be prescribed and shall state the proposed retail price of a copy of the work to be reproduced.

(3) Every applicant for a licence under this section shall, along with his application, deposit with the Registrar of Copyrights such fee as may be prescribed.

(4) Where an application is made to the Appellate Board[162] under this section, it may, after holding such inquiry as may be prescribed, grant to the applicant a licence, not being an exclusive licence, to produce and publish a reproduction of the work mentioned in the application subject to the conditions that,—

(i) the applicant shall pay to the owner of the copyright in the work royalties in respect of copies of the reproduction of the work sold to the public, calculated at such rate as the Appellate Board[163] may, in the circumstances of each case, determine in the prescribed manner;

(ii) a licence granted under this section shall not extend to the export of copies of the reproduction of the work outside India and every copy of such reproduction shall contain a notice that the copy is available for distribution only in India:

Provided that no such licence shall be granted unless—

(a) the applicant has proved to the satisfaction of the Appellate Board[164] that he had requested and had been denied authorisation by the owner of the copyright in the work to reproduce and publish such work or that he was, after due diligence on his part, unable to find such owner;

(b) where the applicant was unable to find the owner of the copyright, he had sent a copy of his request for such authorisation by registered airmail post to the publisher whose name appears from the work not less than three months before the application for the licence;

---

161. Substituted by the Finance Act 2017 (7 of 2017), Section 160(a) for "Copyright Board," [w.e.f. 26 May, 2017].
162. Substituted by the Finance Act 2017 (7 of 2017), Section 160(a) for "Copyright Board," [w.e.f. 26 May, 2017].
163. Substituted by the Finance Act 2017 (7 of 2017), Section 160(a) for "Copyright Board," [w.e.f. 26 May, 2017].
164. Substituted by the Finance Act 2017 (7 of 2017), Section 160(a) for "Copyright Board," [w.e.f. 26 May, 2017].

(c) the Appellate Board[165] is satisfied that the applicant is competent to reproduce and publish an accurate reproduction of the work and possesses the means to pay to the owner of the copyright the royalties payable to him under this section;

(d) the applicant undertakes to reproduce and publish the work at such price as may be fixed by the Appellate Board,[166] being a price reasonably related to the price normally charged in India for works of the same standard on the same or similar subjects;

(e) a period of six months in the case of application for the reproduction and publication of any work of natural science, physical science, mathematics or technology, or a period of three months in the case of an application for the reproduction and publication of any other work, has elapsed from the date of making the request under clause (a), or where a copy of the request has been sent under clause (b), from the date of sending of a copy, and a reproduction of the work has not been published by the owner of the copyright in the work or any person authorised by him within the said period of six months or, three months, as the case may be;

(f) the name of the author and the title of the particular edition of the work proposed to be reproduced are printed on all the copies of the reproduction;

(g) the author has not withdrawn from circulation copies of the work; and

(h) an opportunity of being heard is given, wherever practicable, to the owner of the copyright in the work.

(5) No licence to reproduce and publish the translation of a work shall be granted under this section unless such translation has been published by the owner of the right of translation or any person authorised by him and the translation is not in a language in general use in India.

(6) The provisions of this section shall also apply to the reproduction and publication, or translation into a language in general use in India, of any text incorporated in audio-visual fixations prepared and published solely for the purpose of systematic instructional activities.

EXPLANATION—For the purposes of this section, "relevant period", in relation to any work, means a period of—

(a) seven years from the date of the first publication of that work, where the application is for the reproduction and publication of any work of, or relating to, fiction, poetry, drama, music or art;

(b) three years from the date of the first publication of that work, where the

165. Substituted by the Finance Act 2017 (7 of 2017), Section 160(a) for "Copyright Board," [w.e.f. 26 May, 2017].

166. Substituted by the Finance Act 2017 (7 of 2017), Section 160(a) for "Copyright Board," [w.e.f. 26 May, 2017].

application is for the reproduction and publication of any work of, or relating to, natural science, physical science, mathematics or technology; and

(c) five years from the date of the first publication of that work, in any other case.

32B. Termination of licences issued under this chapter—(1) If, at any time after the granting of a licence to produce and publish the translation of a work in any language under sub-section (1A) of section 32 (hereafter in this sub-section referred to as the licensed work), the owner of the copyright in the work or any person authorised by him publishes a translation of such work in the same language and which is substantially the same in content at a price reasonably related to the price normally charged in India for the translation of works of the same standard on the same or similar subject, the licence so granted shall be terminated:

Provided that no such termination shall take effect until after the expiry of a period of three months from the date of service of a notice in the prescribed manner on the person holding such licence by the owner of the right of translation intimating the publication of the translation as aforesaid:

Provided further that copies of the licensed work produced and published by the person holding such licence before the termination of the licence takes effect may continue to be sold or distributed until the copies already produced and published are exhausted.

(2) If, at any time after the granting of a licence to produce and publish the reproduction or translation of any work under section 32A, the owner of the right of reproduction or any person authorised by him sells or distributes copies of such work or a translation thereof, as the case may be, in the same language and which is substantially the same in content at a price reasonably related to the price normally charged in India for work of the same standard on the same or similar subject, the licence so granted shall be terminated:

Provided that no such termination shall take effect until after the expiry of a period of three months from the date of service of a notice in the prescribed manner on the person holding the licence by the owner of the right of reproduction intimating the sale or distribution of the copies of the editions of work as aforesaid:

Provided further that any copies already reproduced by the licensee before such termination takes effect may continue to be sold or distributed until the copies already produced are exhausted.][167]

Chapter VII[168]

COPYRIGHT SOCIETIES

33. Registration of Copyright Society—(1) No person or association of persons shall,

167. Inserted by the Copyright (Amendment) Act, 1983 (Act 23 of 1983), Section 14 [w.e.f. 9-8-1984].

168. Chapter VII was substituted by the Copyright (Amendment) Act, 1994 (Act 38 of 1994), Section 11 [w.e.f. 10-5-1995].

after coming into force of the Copyright (Amendment) Act, 1994 commence or, carry on the business of issuing or granting licences in respect of any work in which copyright subsists on respect or in respect of any other rights conferred by this Act except under or in accordance with the registration granted under sub-section (3):

Provided that owner of copyright shall, in his individual capacity, continue to have the right to grant licences in respect of his own works consistent with his obligations as a member of the registered copyright society:

[Provided further that the business of issuing or granting license in respect of literary, dramatic, musical and artistic works incorporated in a cinematograph films or sound recordings shall be carried out only through a copyright society duly registered under this Act:

Provided also][169] that the performing rights society functioning in accordance with the provisions of section 33 on the date immediately before the coming into force of the Copyright (Amendment) Act, 1994 shall be deemed to be a copyright society for the purposes of this Chapter and every such society shall get itself registered within a period of one year from the date of commencement of the Copyright (Amendment Act, 1994.

(2) Any association of persons who fulfils such conditions as may be prescribed may apply for permission to do the business specified in sub-section (1) to the Registrar of Copyrights who shall submit the application to the Central Government.

(3) The Central Government may, having regard to the interests of the authors and other owners of rights under this Act, the interest and convenience of the public and in particular of the groups of persons who are most likely to seek licences in respect of the relevant rights and the ability and professional competence of the applicants, register such association of persons as a copyright society subject to such conditions as may be prescribed:

Provided that the Central Government shall not ordinarily register more than one copyright society to do business in respect of the same class of works.

[(3A) The registration granted to a copyright society under sub-section (3) shall be for a period of live years and may be renewed from time to time before the end of every five years on a request in the prescribed form and the Central Government may renew the registration after considering the report of Registrar of Copyrights on the working of the copyright society under section 36:

Provided that the renewal of the registration of a copyright society shall be subject to the continued collective control of the copyright society being shared with the authors of works in their capacity as owners of copyright or of the right to receive royalty:

Provided further that every copyright society already registered before the coming into force of the copyright (Amendment) Act, 2012 shall get itself registered under this Chapter within a period of one year from the date of commencement of the Copyright (Amendment) Act, 2012.][170]

169. Inserted by the Copyright (Amendment) Act, 1983 (Act 23 of 1983), Section 14 [w.e.f. 9-8-1984].
170. Inserted by the Copyright (Amendment) Act, 2012 (Act 27 of 2012), Section 19(ii) [w.e.f. 21-6-2012].

(4) The Central Government may, if it is satisfied that a copyright society is being managed in a manner detrimental to the interests of the [authors and other owners of right][171] concerned, cancel the registration of such society after such inquiry as may be prescribed.

(5) If the Central Government is of the opinion that in the interest of the [authors and other owners of right][172] concerned, ["or for non-compliance of sections 33A, sub-section (1) of section 35 and section 36 or any change carried out in the instrument by which the copyright society is established or incorporated and registered by the Central Government without prior notice to it][173] it is necessary so to do, it may, by order, suspend the registration of such society pending inquiry for such period not exceeding one year as may be specified in such order under sub-section (4) and that Government shall appoint an administrator to discharge the functions of the copyright society.

[33A. **Tariff Scheme by copyright societies**—(1) Every copyright society shall publish its tariff scheme in such manner as may be prescribed.

(2) Any person who is aggrieved by the tariff scheme may appeal to the Appellate Board[174] and the Board may, if satisfied after holding such inquiry as it may consider necessary, make such orders as necessary be required to remove any unreasonable element, anomaly or inconsistency therein:

Provided that the aggrieved person shall pay to the copyright society any fee as may be prescribed that has fallen due before making an appeal to the Appellate Board[175] and shall continue to pay such fee until the appeal is decided, and the Board shall not issue any order staying the collection of such fee pending disposal of the appeal:

Provided further that the Appellate Board[176] may after hearing the parties fix an interim tariff and direct the aggrieved parties to make the payment accordingly pending disposal of the appeal.][177]

34. Administration of rights of owner by copyright society—(1) Subject to such conditions as may be prescribed,—

(a) a copyright society may accept from an [authors and other owners of right][178] exclusive authorisation to administer any right in any work by issue of licences or collection of licence fees or both; and

---

171. Inserted by the Copyright (Amendment) Act, 2012 (Act 27 of 2012), Section 19(iii), for "owners of rights" [w.e.f. 21-6-2012].
172. Inserted by the Copyright (Amendment) Act, 2012 (Act 27 of 2012), Section 19(iii), for "owners of rights" [w.e.f. 21-6-2012].
173. Inserted by the Copyright (Amendment) Act, 2012 (Act 27 of 2012), Section 19(iv) [w.e.f. 21-6-2012].
174. Substituted by the Finance Act 2017 (7 of 2017), Section 160(a) for "Copyright Board," [w.e.f. 26 May, 2017].
175. Substituted by the Finance Act 2017 (7 of 2017), Section 160(a) for "Copyright Board," [w.e.f. 26 May, 2017].
176. Substituted by the Finance Act 2017 (7 of 2017), Section 160(a) for "Copyright Board," [w.e.f. 26 May, 2017].
177. Inserted by the Copyright (Amendment) Act, 2012 (Act 27 of 2012), Section 20 [w.e.f. 21-6-2012].
178. Inserted by the Copyright (Amendment) Act, 2012 (Act 27 of 2012), Section 19(iii), for "owners of rights" [w.e.f. 21-6-2012].

(b) an owner of rights shall have the right to withdraw such authorisation without prejudice to the rights of the copyright society under any contract.

(2) It shall be competent for a copyright society to enter into agreement with any foreign society or organisation administering rights corresponding to rights under this Act, to entrust to such foreign society or organisation the administration in any foreign country of rights administered by the said copyright society in India, or for administering in India the rights administered in a foreign country by such foreign society or organisation:

Provided that no such society or organisation shall permit any discrimination in regard to the terms of licence or the distribution of fees collected between rights in Indian and other works.

(3) Subject to such conditions as may be prescribed, a copyright society may—

(i) issue licences under section 30 in respect of any rights under this Act;

(ii) collect fees in pursuance of such licences;

(iii) distribute such fees among owners of rights][179] after making deductions for its own expenses;

(iv) perform any other functions consistent which the provisions of section 35.

[***][180]

35. Control over the copyright society by the [authors and other owners of right][181]—(1) Every copyright society shall be subject to the collective control of the [authors and other owners of right][182] under this Act whose rights it administers [not being (authors and other owners of right)[183] under this Act administered by a foreign society or organisation referred to in sub-section (2) of section 34] and shall, in such manner as may be prescribed,—

(a) obtain the approval of such [authors and other owners of right][184] for its procedures of collection and distribution of fees;

(b) obtain their approval for the utilisation of any amounts collected as fees for any purpose other than distribution to the owner of rights; and

(c) provide to such owners regular, full and detailed information concerning all its activities, in relation to the administration of their rights.

---

179. Inserted by the Copyright (Amendment) Act, 2012 (Act 27 of 2012), Section 19(iii), for "owners of rights" [w.e.f. 21-6-2012].

180. Section 34A was omitted by the Copyright (Amendment) Act, 2012 (Act 27 of 2012), Section 22 [w.e.f. 21-6-2012].

181. Inserted by the Copyright (Amendment) Act, 2012 (Act 27 of 2012), Section 23(a), for "owners of rights" [w.e.f. 21-6-2012].

182. Inserted by the Copyright (Amendment) Act, 2012 (Act 27 of 2012), Section 23(a), for "owners of rights" [w.e.f. 21-6-2012].

183. Inserted by the Copyright (Amendment) Act, 2012 (Act 27 of 2012), Section 23(a), for "owners of rights" [w.e.f. 21-6-2012].

184. Inserted by the Copyright (Amendment) Act, 2012 (Act 27 of 2012), Section 23(a), for "owners of rights" [w.e.f. 21-6-2012].

(2) All fees distributed among the [authors and other owners of right][185] shall, as far as may be, be distributed in proportion to the actual use of their works.

[(3) Every copyright society shall have a governing body with such number of persons elected from among the members of the society consisting of equal number of authors and owners of work for the purpose of the administration of the society as may be specified.

(4) All members of copyrights society shall enjoy equal membership rights and there shall be no discrimination between authors and owners of rights in the distribution of royalties.][186]

36. Submission of returns and reports—(1) Every copyright society shall submit to the Registrar of Copyrights such returns as may be prescribed.

(2) Any officer duly authorised by the Central Government in this behalf may call for any report and also call for any records of any copyright society for the purpose of satisfying himself that the fees collected by the society in respect of rights administered by it are being utilised or distributed in accordance with the provisions of this Act.

[36A. Rights and liabilities of performing rights societies—Nothing in this chapter shall affect any rights or liabilities in any work in connection with a [copyright society][187] which had accrued or were incurred on or before the day prior to the commencement of [the Copyright (Amendment) Act, 2012],[188] or any legal proceedings in respect of any such rights or liabilities pending on that day.][189]

Chapter VIII

[RIGHTS OF BROADCASTING ORGANISATION AND OF PERFORMERS][190]

[37. Broadcast reproduction right—(1) Every broadcasting organisation shall have a special right to be known as "broadcast reproduction right" in respect of its broadcasts.

(2) The broadcast reproduction right shall subsist until twenty-five years from the beginning of the calendar year next following the year in which the broadcast is made.

---

185. Inserted by the Copyright (Amendment) Act, 2012 (Act 27 of 2012), Section 23(a), for "owners of rights" [w.e.f. 21-6-2012].
186. Inserted by the Copyright (Amendment) Act, 2012 (Act 27 of 2012), Section 23(b), [w.e.f. 21-6-2012].
187. Substituted by the Copyright (Amendment) Act, 2012 (Act 27 of 2012), Section 24(a), for "performing rights society" [w.e.f. 21-6-2012].
188. Substituted by the Copyright (Amendment) Act, 2012 (Act 27 of 2012), Section 24(a), for "the Copyright (Amendment) Act, 1994" [w.e.f. 21-6-2012].
189. Substituted by the Copyright (Amendment) Act, 1994 (Act 38 of 1994), Section 11 [w.e.f. 10-5-1995].
190. Substituted by the Copyright (Amendment) Act, 1994 (Act 38 of 1994), Section 12, for "Rights of Broadcasting Authorities" [w.e.f. 10-5-1995].

(3) During the continuance of a broadcast reproduction right in relation to any broadcast, any person who, without the licence of the owner of the right does any of the following acts of the broadcast or any substantial part thereof,—

(a) re-broadcasts the broadcast; or

(b) causes the broadcast to be heard or seen by the public on payment of any charges; or

(c) makes any sound recording or visual recording of the broadcast; or

(d) makes any reproduction of such sound recording or visual recording where such initial recording was done without licence or, where it was licensed, for any purpose not envisaged by such licence; or][191]

[(e) sells or gives on commercial rental or offer for sale or for such rental, any such sound recording or visual recording referred to in clause (c) or clause (d).][192]

[shall, subject to the provisions of section 39, be deemed to have infringed the broadcast reproduction right.][193]

[38. **Performer's right**—(1) Where any performer appears or engages in any performance, he shall have a special right to be known as the "performer's right" in relation to such performance.

(2) The performer's right shall subsist until (fifty years)[194] from the beginning of the calendar year next following the year in which the performance is made.][195]

[***][196]

[38A. **Exclusive right of performers**—

(1) Without prejudice to the rights conferred on authors, the performer's right which is an exclusive right subject to the provisions of this Act to do or authorise for doing any of the following acts in respect of the performance or any substantial part thereof, namely,—

(a) to make a sound recording or a visual recording of the performance, including—

(i) reproduction of it in any material form including the storing of it in any medium by electronic or any other means;

---

191. Substituted by the Copyright (Amendment) Act, 1994 (Act 38 of 1994), Section 13, for section 37 [w.e.f. 10-5-1995].
192. Substituted by the Copyright (Amendment) Act, 2012 (Act 27 of 2012), Section 25, for clause (e) [w.e.f. 21-6-2012].
193. Substituted by the Copyright (Amendment) Act, 1994 (Act 38 of 1994), Section 13, for section 37 [w.e.f. 10-5-1995].
194. Substituted by the Copyright (Amendment) Act, 1999 (Act 49 of 1999), Section 4, for "twenty-five years" [w.e.f. 15-1-2000].
195. Substituted by the Copyright (Amendment) Act, 1994 (Act 38 of 1994), Section 14, for section 38 [w.e.f. 10-5-1995].
196. Sub-section (3) and sub-section (4) were omitted by the Copyright (Amendment) Act, 2012 (Act 27 of 2012), Section 26 [w.e.f. 21-6-2012].

(ii) issuance of copies of it to the public not being copies already in circulation;

(iii) communication of it to the public;

(iv) selling or giving it on commercial rental or offer for sale or for commercial rental any copy of the recording;

(b) to broadcast or communicate the performance to the public except where the performance is already broadcast.

(2) Once a performer has, by written agreement, consented to the incorporation of his performance in a cinematograph film he shall not, in the absence of any contract to the contrary, object to the enjoyment by the producer of the film of the performer's right in the same film:

Provided that, notwithstanding anything contained in this sub-section, the performer shall be entitled for royalties in case of making of the performances for commercial use.][197]

[38B. Moral rights of the performer—

The performer of a performance shall, independently of his right after assignment, either wholly or partially of his right, have the right,—

(a) to claim to be identified as the performer of his performance except where omission is dictated by the manner of the use of the performance; and

(b) to restrain or claim damages in respect of any distortion, mutilation or other modification of his performance that would be prejudicial to his reputation.

EXPLANATION—For the purposes of this clause, it is hereby clarified that mere removal of any portion of a performance for the purpose of editing, or to fit the recording within a limited duration, or any other modification required for purely technical reasons shall not be deemed to be prejudicial to the performer's reputation.][198]

[39. Acts not infringing broadcast reproduction right or performer's right—No broadcast reproduction right or performer's right shall be deemed to be infringed by—

(a) the making of any sound recording or visual recording for the private use of the person making such recording, or solely for purposes of *bona fide* teaching or research; or

(b) the use, consistent with fair dealing, of excerpts of a performance or of a broadcast in the reporting of current events or for *bona fide* review, teaching or research; or

(c) such order acts, with any necessary adaptations and modifications, which do not constitute infringement of copyright under section 52.][199]

[39A. Certain provisions to apply in case of broadcast reproduction right and Performer's rights—(1) Sections 18, 19, 30, 30A, 33, 33A, 34, 35, 36, 53, 55, 58,

---

197. Inserted by the Copyright (Amendment) Act, 2012 (Act 27 of 2012), Section 27 [w.e.f. 21-6-2012].
198. Inserted by the Copyright (Amendment) Act, 2012 (Act 27 of 2012), Section 27 [w.e.f. 21-6-2012].
199. Substituted by the Copyright (Amendment) Act, 1994 (Act 38 of 1994), Section 15, for Section 39 [w.e.f. 10-5-1995].

63, 64, 65, 65A, 65B and 66 shall, with necessary adaptations and modifications, apply in relation to the broadcast reproduction right in any broadcast and the performer's right in any performance as they apply in relation to copyright in a work:

Provided that where copyright or performer's right subsists in respect of any work or performance that has been broadcast, no licence to reproduce such broadcast, shall be given without the consent of the owner of right or performer, as the case may be, or both of them:

Provided further that the broadcast reproduction right or performer's right shall not subsist in any broadcast or performance if that broadcast or performance is an infringement of the copyright in any work.

(2) The broadcast reproduction right or the performer's right shall not affect the separate copyright in any work in respect of which, the broadcast or the performance, as the case may be, is made.][200]

Chapter IX

INTERNATIONAL COPYRIGHT

40. Power to extend copyright to foreign works—The Central Government may, by order published in the Official Gazette, direct that all or any provisions of this Act shall apply—

(a) to work first published in any class territory outside India to which the order relates in like manner as if they were first published within India;

(b) to unpublished works, or any class thereof, the authors whereof were at the time of the making of the work, subjects or citizens of a foreign country to which the order relates, in like manner as if the authors were citizens of India;

(c) in respect of domicile in any territory outside India to which the order relates in like manner as if such domicile were in India;

(d) to any work of which the author was at the date of the first publication thereof, or, in a case where the author was dead at that date, was at the time of his death, a subject or citizen of a foreign country to which the order relates in like manner as if the author was a citizen of India at that date or time; and thereupon, subject to the provisions of this Chapter and of the order, this Act shall apply accordingly:

Provided that—

(i) before making an order under this section in respect of any foreign country (other than a country with which India has entered into a treaty or which is a party to a convention relating to copyright to which India is also a party), the Central Government shall be satisfied that foreign country has made, or has undertaken to make, such provisions if any, as it appears to the Central Government expedient to require for the protection in that country of works entitled to copyright under the provisions of this Act;

---

200. Substituted by the Copyright (Amendment) Act, 2012 (Act 27 of 2012), Section 28 [w.e.f. 21-6-2012].

(ii) the order may provide that the provisions of this Act shall apply either generally or in relation to such classes of works or such classes of cases as may be specified in the order;

(iii) the order may provide that the term of copyright in India shall not exceed that conferred by the law of the country to which the order relates[but such a term of copyright shall not exceed the term of copyright provided under this Act];[201]

(iv) the order may provide that the enjoyment of the rights conferred by this Act shall be subject to the accomplishment of such conditions and formalities, if any, as may be prescribed by the order;

(v) in applying the provisions of this Act as to ownership of copyright, the order may make such exceptions and modifications as appear necessary, having regard to the law of the foreign country;

(vi) the order may provide that this Act or any part thereof shall not apply to works made before the commencement of the order or that this Act or any part thereof small not apply to works first published before the commencement of the order.

[40A. Power of Central Government to apply Chapter VII to broadcasting organisations and performers in certain other countries—(1) If the Central Government is satisfied that a foreign country (other than a country with which India has entered into a treaty or which is a party to a convention relating to rights of broadcasting organisations and performers to which India is also a party) has made or has undertaken to make such provisions, if any, as it appears to the Central Government expedient to require, for the protection in that foreign country, of the rights of broadcasting organisations and performers as is available under this Act, it may, by order published in the Official Gazette, direct that the provisions of Chapter VIII shall apply—

(a) to broadcasting organisations whose headquarters is situated in a country to which the order relates or, the broadcast was transmitted from a transmitter situated in a country to which the order relates as if the headquarters of such organisation were situated in India or such broadcast were made from India;

(b) to performances that took place outside India to which the order relates in like manner as if they took place in India;

(c) to performances that are incorporated in a sound recording published in a country to which the order relates as if it was published in India;

(d) to performances not fixed on a sound recording broadcast by a broadcasting organisation the headquarters of which is located in a country to which the order relates or where the broadcast is transmitted from a transmitter which is situated in a country to which the order relates as if the headquarters of such organisation were situated in India or such broadcast were made from India.

201. Inserted by the Copyright (Amendment) Act, 2012 (Act 27 of 2012), Section 29 [w.e.f. 21-6-2012].

(2) Every order made under sub-section (1) may provide that—

(i) the provisions of Chapter VIII shall apply either generally or in relation to such class or classes of broadcasts or performances or such other class or classes of cases as may be specified in the order;

(ii) the term of the rights of broadcasting organisations and performers in India shall not exceed such term as is conferred by the law of the country to which the order relates;][202]

[Provided that it does not exceed the period provided under this Act;][203]

[(iii) the enjoyment of the rights conferred by Chapter VIII shall be subject to the accomplishment of such conditions and formalities, if any, as may be specified in that order;

(iv) Chapter VIII or any part thereof shall not apply to broadcast and performances made before the commencement of the order or that Chapter VIII or any part thereof shall not apply to broadcasts and performances broadcast or performed before the commencement of the order;

(v) in case of ownership of rights of broadcasting organisations and performers, the provisions of Chapter VIII shall apply with such exceptions and modifications as the Central Government may, having regard to the law of the foreign country, consider necessary.][204]

41. Provisions as to works of certain international organisations—(1) Where—

(a) any work is made or first published by or under the direction or control of any organisation to which this section applies, and

(b) there would, apart from this section, be no copyright in the work in India at the time of the making or, as the case may be, of the first publication thereof, and

(c) either—

(i) the work is published as aforesaid in pursuance of an agreement in that behalf with the author, being an agreement which does not reserve to the author the copyright, if any, in the work, or

(ii) under section 17 any copyright in the work would belong to the organisation; there shall, by virtue of this section, be copyright in the work throughout India.

(2) Any organisation to which this section applies which at the material time had not the legal capacity of a body corporate shall have and be deemed at all material times to have had the legal capacity of a body corporate for the purpose of holding, dealing with, and enforcing copyright and in connection with all legal proceedings relating to copyright.

---

202. Inserted by the Copyright (Amendment) Act, 1999 (Act 49 of 1999), Section 5 [w.e.f. 15-1-2000].
203. Inserted by the Copyright (Amendment) Act, 2012 (Act 27 of 2012), Section 30 [w.e.f. 21-6-2012].
204. Inserted by the Copyright (Amendment) Act, 1999 (Act 49 of 1999), Section 5 [w.e.f. 15-1-2000].

(3) The organisation to which this section applies are such organisations as the Central Government may, by order published in the Official Gazette, declare to be organisations of which one or more sovereign powers or the Government or Governments thereof are members to which it is expedient that this section shall apply.

42. Power to restrict rights in works of foreign authors first published in India—If it appears to the Central Government that a foreign country does not give or has not undertaken to give adequate protection to the works of Indian authors, the Central Government may, by order published in the Official Gazette, direct that such of the provisions of this Act as confer copyright on works first published in India shall not apply to works, published after the date specified in the order, the authors whereof are subjects or citizens of such foreign country and are not domiciled in India, and thereupon those provisions shall not apply to such works.

[**42A. Power to restrict rights in works of foreign authors first published in India**—If it appears to the Central Government that a foreign country does not give or has not undertaken to give adequate protection to rights of broadcasting organisations or performers, the Central Government may, by order published in the Official Gazette, direct that such of the provisions of this Act as confer right to broadcasting organisations or performers, as the case may be, shall not apply to broadcasting organisations or performers whereof are based on incorporated in such foreign country or are subjects or citizens of such foreign country and are not incorporated or domiciled in India, and thereupon those provisions shall not apply to such broadcasting organisations or performers.][205]

43. Orders under this Chapter to be laid before Parliament—Every order made by the Central Government under this Chapter shall, as soon as may be after it is made, be laid before both Houses of Parliament and shall be subject to such modifications as Parliament may make during the session in which it is so laid or the session immediately following.

Chapter X

REGISTRATION OF COPYRIGHT

44. Register of Copyrights—There shall be kept at the Copyright Office a register in the prescribed form to be called the Register of Copyrights in which may be entered the names or titles of works and the names and addresses of authors, publishers and owners of copyright and such other particulars as may be prescribed.

45. Entries in register of Copyrights—(1) The author or publisher of, or the owner of or other person interested in the copyright in, any work may make an application in the prescribed form accompanied by the prescribed fee to the Registrar of Copyrights for entering particulars of the work in the Register of Copyrights:

---

205. Inserted by the Copyright (Amendment) Act, 1999 (Act 49 of 1999), Section 6 [w.e.f. 15-1-2000].

[Provided that in respect of an artistic work which is used or is capable of being used in (relation to any goods or services),[206] the application shall include a statement to that effect and shall be accompanied by a certificate from the Registrar of Trade Marks referred to in (section 3 of the Trade Marks Act, 1999),[207] to the effect that no trade mark identical with or deceptively similar to such artistic work has been registered under that Act in the name of, or that no application has been made under that Act for such registration by, any person other than the applicant.][208]

(2) On receipt of an application in respect of any work under sub-section (1), the Registrar of Copyrights may, after holding such inquiry as he may deem fit, enter the particulars of the work in the Register of Copyrights.

46. Indexes—There shall be also kept at the Copyright Office such indexes of the Register of Copyrights as may be prescribed.

47. Forms and inspection of register—The Register of Copyrights and indexes thereof kept under this Act shall at all reasonable times be open to inspection, and any person shall be entitled to take copies of, or make extracts from, such register or indexes on payment of such fee and subject to such conditions as may be prescribed.

48. Register of Copyrights to be *prima facie* evidence of particulars entered therein—The Register of Copyrights shall be *prima facie* evidence of the particulars entered therein and documents purporting to be copies of any entries therein, or extracts therefrom certified by the Registrar of Copyrights and sealed with the seal of the Copyright Office shall be admissible in evidence in all courts without further proof or production of the original.

49. Correction of entries in the Register of Copyrights—The Registrar of Copyrights may, in the prescribed cases and subject to the prescribed conditions, amend or alter the Register of Copyrights by—

(a) correcting any error in any name, address or particulars; or

(b) correcting any other error which may have arisen therein by accidental slip or omission.

50. Rectification of Register by Appellate Board[209]—The Appellate Board,[210] on application of the Registrar of Copyrights or of any person aggrieved, shall order the rectification of the Register of Copyrights by—

(a) the making of any entry wrongly omitted to be made in the register, or

(b) the expunging of any entry wrongly made in, or remaining on, the register, or

(c) the correction of any error or defect in the register.

---

206. Substituted by the Copyright (Amendment) Act, 2012 (Act 27 of 2012), Section 31(i), for "relation to any goods" [w.e.f. 21-6-2012].

207. Substituted by the Copyright (Amendment) Act, 2012 (Act 27 of 2012), Section 31(ii), for "section 4 of the Trade and Merchandise Marks Act, 1958" [w.e.f. 21-6-2012].

208. Inserted by the Copyright (Amendment) Act, 1983 (Act 23 of 1983), Section 16 [w.e.f. 9-8-1984].

209. Substituted by the Finance Act 2017 (7 of 2017), Section 160(a) for "Copyright Board," [w.e.f. 26 May, 2017].

210. Substituted by the Finance Act 2017 (7 of 2017), Section 160(a) for "Copyright Board," [w.e.f. 26 May, 2017].

[**50A. Entries in the Register of Copyrights, etc., to be published**—Every entry made in the Register of Copyrights or the particulars of any work entered under section 45, the correction of every entry made in such register under section 49, and every rectification ordered under section 50, shall be published by the Registrar of Copyrights in the Official Gazette or in such other manner as he may deem fit.][211]

Chapter XI

INFRINGEMENT OF COPYRIGHT

51. When copyright infringed—Copyright in a work shall be deemed to be infringed—

(a) when any person, without a licence granted by the owner of the copyright or the Registrar of Copyrights under this Act or in contravention of the conditions of a licence so granted or of any condition imposed by a competent authority under this Act—

(i) does anything, the exclusive right to do which is by this Act conferred upon the owner of the copyright, or

[(ii) permits for profit any place to be used for the communication of the work to the public where such communication constitutes an infringement of the copyright in the work, unless he was not aware and had no reasonable ground for believing that such communication to the public would be an infringement of copyright; or][212]

(b) when any person—

(i) makes for sale or hire, or sells or lets for hire, or by way of trade displays or offers for sale or hire, or

(ii) distributes either for the purpose of trade or to such an extent as to affect prejudicially the owner of the copyright, or

(iii) by way of trade exhibits in public, or

(iv) imports [***][213] into India,

any infringing copies of the work:

[Provided that nothing in sub-clause (iv) shall apply to the import of one copy of any work for the private and domestic use of the importer.][214]

EXPLANATION—For the purposes of this section, the reproduction of a literary, dramatic, musical or artistic work in the form of a cinematograph film shall be deemed to be an "infringing copy".

211. Inserted by the Copyright (Amendment) Act, 1983 (Act 23 of 1983), Section 17 [w.e.f. 9-8-1984].

212. Substituted by the Copyright (Amendment) Act, 1994 (Act 38 of 1994), Section 16, for sub-clause (ii) [w.e.f. 10-5-1995].

213. The words "(except for the private and domestic use of the importer)" was omitted by the Copyright (Amendment) Act, 1984 (Act 23 of 1984), Section 3 [w.e.f. 8-10-1984].

214. Substituted by the Copyright (Amendment) Act, 1994 (Act 38 of 1994), Section 16, for the proviso [w.e.f. 10-5-1995].

52. Certain acts not to be infringement of copyright—(1) The following acts shall not constitute an infringement of copyright, namely:

[(a) a fair dealing with any work, not being a computer programme, for the purposes of—

(i) private or personal use, including research;

(ii) criticism or review, whether of that work or of any other work;

(iii) the reporting of current events and current affairs, including the reporting of a lecture delivered in public.

EXPLANATION—The storing of any work in any electronic medium for the purposes mentioned in this clause, including the incidental storage of any computer programme which is not itself an infringing copy for the said purposes, shall not constitute infringement of copyright.][215]

[(aa) the making of copies or adaptation of a computer programme by the lawful possessor of a copy of such computer programme, from such copy—

(i) in order to utilise the computer programme for the purposes for which it was supplied; or

(ii) to make back-up copies purely as a temporary protection against loss, destruction or damage in order only to utilise the computer programme for the purpose for which it was supplied;][216]

[(ab) the doing of any act necessary to obtain information essential for operating inter operability of an independently created computer programme with other programmes by a lawful possessor of a computer programme provided that such information is not otherwise readily available;

(ac) the observation, study or test of functioning of the computer programme in order to determine the ideas and principles which underline any elements of the programme while performing such acts necessary for the functions for which the computer programme was supplied;

(ad) the making of copies or adaptation of the computer programme from a personally legally obtained copy for non-commercial personal use;][217]

[(b) the transient or incidental storage of a work or performance purely in the technical process of electronic transmission or Communication to the public;

(c) transient or incidental storage of a work or performance for the purpose of providing electronic links, access or integration, where such links, access or integration has not been expressly prohibited by the right holder, unless the person responsible is aware or has reasonable grounds for believing that such storage is of an infringing copy:

---

215. Substituted by the Copyright (Amendment) Act, 2012 (Act 27 of 2012), Section 32(i), for clause (a) [w.e.f. 21-6-2012].

216. Inserted by the Copyright (Amendment) Act, 1994 (Act 38 of 1994), Section 17, [w.e.f. 10-9-1994].

217. Inserted by the Copyright (Amendment) Act, 1999 (Act 49 of 1999), Section 7 [w.e.f. 15-1-2000].

Provided that if the person responsible for the storage of the copy has received a written complaint from the owner of copyright in the work, complaining that such transient or incidental storage is an infringement, such person responsible for the storage shall refrain from facilitating such access for a period of twenty-one days or till he receives an order from the competent court refraining from facilitating access and in ease no such order is received before the expiry of such period of twenty-one days, he may continue to provide the facility of such access;

(d) the reproduction of any work for the purpose of a judicial proceeding or for the purpose of a report of a judicial proceedings;

(e) the reproduction or publication of any work prepared by the Secretariat of a Legislature or, where the Legislature consists of two Houses, by the Secretariat of either House of the Legislature, exclusively for the use of the members of that Legislature;

(f) the reproduction of any work in a certified copy made or supplied in accordance with any law for the time being in force;

(g) the reading or recitation in public of reasonable extracts from a published literary or dramatic work;

(h) the publication in a collection, mainly composed of non-copyright matter, *bona fide,* intended for instructional use, and so described in the title and in any advertisement issued by or on behalf of tire publisher, of short passages from published literary or dramatic works, not themselves published for such use in which copyright subsists:

Provided that not more than two such passages from works by the same author are published by the same publisher during any period of five years.

Explanation—In the case of a work of joint authorship, references in this clause to passages from works shall include references to passages from works by any one or more of the authors of those passages or by any one or more of those authors in collaboration with any other person;

(i) the reproduction of any work—

(i) by a teacher or a pupil in the course of instruction; or

(ii) as part of tire questions to be answered in an examination; or

(iii) in answers to such questions;

(j) the performance, in the course of the activities of an educational institution, of a literary, dramatic or musical work by tire staff and students of the institution, or of a cinematograph film or a sound recording if the audience is limited to such staff and students, the parents and guardians of the students and person connected with the activities of the institution or the communication to such an audience of a cinematograph film or sound recording;][218]

218. Substituted by the Copyright (Amendment) Act, 2012 (Act 27 of 2012), Section 32(ii), for clauses (b), (c), (d), (e), (f), (g), (h), (i) and (j) [w.e.f. 21-6-2012].

(k) the causing of a recording to be heard in public by utilising it,—

(i) in an enclosed room or hall meant for the common use of residents in any residential premises (not being a hotel or similar commercial establishment) as part of the amenities provided exclusively or mainly for residents therein; or

(ii) as part of the activities of a club or similar organisation which is not established or conducted for profit;

(iii) as part of the activities of a club, society or other organisation which is not established or conducted for profit;

(l) the performance of a literary, dramatic or musical work by an amateur club or society, if the performance is given to a non-paying audience, or for the benefit of a religious institution;

(m) the reproduction in a newspaper, magazine or other periodical of an article on current economic, political, social or religious topics, unless the author of such article has expressly reserved to himself the right of such reproduction;

[(n) the storing of a work in any medium by electronic means by a non-commercial public library, for preservation if the library already possesses a non-digital copy of the work;][219]

(o) the making of not more than three copies of a book (including a pamphlet, sheet of music, map, chart or plan) by or under the direction of the person in charge of a[non-commercial public library][220] for the use of the library if such book is not available for sale in India;

(p) the reproduction, for the purpose of research or private study or with a view to publication, of an unpublished literary, dramatic or musical work kept in a library, museum or other institution to which the public has access:

Provided that where the identity of the author of any such work or, in the case of a work of joint authorship, of any of the authors is known to the library, museum or other institution, as the case may be, the provisions of this clause shall apply only if such reproduction is made at a time more than [sixty years][221] from the date of the death of the author or, in the case of a work of joint authorship, from the death of the author whose identity is known or, if the identity of more authors than one is known from the death of such of those authors who dies last;

(q) the reproduction or publication of—

(i) any matter which has been published in any Official Gazette except an Act of a Legislature;

---

219. Substituted by the Copyright (Amendment) Act, 2012 (Act 27 of 2012), Section 32(iii), for clause (n) [w.e.f. 21-6-2012].

220. Substituted by the Copyright (Amendment) Act, 2012 (Act 27 of 2012), Section 32(iv), for "public library" [w.e.f. 21-6-2012].

221. Substituted by the Copyright (Amendment) Act, 1999 (Act 49 of 1999), Section 7, for "fifty years" [w.e.f. 15-1-2000].

(ii) any Act of a Legislature subject to the condition that such Act is reproduced or published together with any commentary thereon or any other original matter;

(iii) the report of any committee, commission, council, board or other like body appointed by the Government if such report has been laid on the Table of the Legislature, unless the reproduction or publication of such report is prohibited by the Government;

(iv) any judgment or order of a court, tribunal or other judicial authority, unless the reproduction or publication of such judgment or order is prohibited by the court, the tribunal or other judicial authority, as the case may be;

(r) the production or publication of a translation in any Indian language of an Act of a Legislature and of any rules or orders made thereunder—

(i) if no translation of such Act or rules or orders in that language has previously been produced or published by the Government; or

(ii) where a translation of such Act or rules or orders in that language has been produced or published by the Government, if the translation is not available for sale to the public:

Provided that such translation contains a statement at a prominent place to the effect that the translation has not been authorised or accepted as authentic by the Government;

[(s) the making or publishing of a painting, drawing, engraving or photograph of a work of architecture or the display of a work of architecture;][222]

(t) the making or publishing of a painting, drawing, engraving or photograph of a sculpture, or other artistic work failing under sub-clause (iii) of clause (c) of section 2, if such work is permanently situate in a public place or any premises to which the public has access;

(u) the inclusion in a cinematograph film of—

(i) any artistic work permanently situate in a public place or any premises to which the public has access; or

(ii) any other artistic work, if such inclusion is only by way of background or is otherwise incidental to the principal matters represented in the film;

(v) the use by the author of an artistic work, where the author of such work is not the owner of the copyright therein, of any mould, cast, sketch, plan, model or study made by him for the purpose of the work:

Provided that he does not thereby repeat or imitate the main design of the work;

[(w) the making of a three-dimensional object from a two-dimensional artistic work, such as a technical drawing, for the purposes of industrial application of any purely functional part of a useful device;][223]

---

222. Inserted by the Copyright (Amendment) Act, 1994 (Act 38 of 1994), Section 17, for clause (s) [w.e.f. 10-9-1994].

223. Inserted by the Copyright (Amendment) Act, 2012 (Act 27 of 2012), Section 32(v) [w.e.f. 21-6-2012]. Earlier clause (w) was omitted by the Copyright (Amendment) Act, 1994 (Act 38 of 1994), Section 17 [w.e.f. 10-9-1994].

(x) the reconstruction of a building or structure in accordance with the architectural drawings or plans by reference to which the building or structure was originally constructed:

Provided that the original construction was made with the consent or licence of the owner of the copyright in such drawings and plans;

(y) in relation to a literary, [dramatic or artistic or][224] musical work recorded or reproduced in any cinematograph film the exhibition of such film after the expiration of the term of copyright therein:

Provided that the provisions of sub-clause (ii) of clause (a), sub-clause (a) of clause (b) and clauses (d), (f), (g), (m) and (p) shall not apply as respects any act unless that act is accompanied by an acknowledgment—

(i) identifying the work by its title or other description; and

(ii) unless the work is anonymous or the author of the work has previously agreed or required that no acknowledgement of his name should be made, also identifying the author.

[(z) the making of an ephemeral recording, by a broadcasting organisation using its own facilities for its own broadcast by a broadcasting organisation of a work which it has the right to broadcast; and the retention of such recording for archival purposes on the ground of its exceptional documentary character;

(za) the performance of a literary, dramatic or musical work or the communication to the public of such work or of a sound recording in the course of any *bona fide* religious ceremony or an official ceremony held by the Central Government or the State Government or any local authority.

Explanation—For the purpose of this clause, religious ceremony including a marriage procession and other social festivities associated with a marriage.][225]

[(zb) the adaptation, reproduction, issue of copies or communication to the public of any work in any accessible format, by—

(i) any person to facilitate persons with disability to access to works including sharing with any person with disability of such accessible format for private or personal use, educational purpose or research; or

(ii) any organisation working for the benefit of the persons with disabilities in case the normal format prevents the enjoyment of such works by such persons:

Provided that the copies of the works in such accessible format are made available to the persons with disabilities on a non-profit basis but to recover only the cost of production:

Provided further that the organization shall ensure that the copies of works in such accessible format are used only by persons with disabilities and takes reasonable steps to prevent its entry into ordinary channels of business.

224. Substituted by the Copyright (Amendment) Act, 2012 (Act 27 of 2012), Section 32(vi), for "dramatic or" [w.e.f. 21-6-2012].

225. Inserted by the Copyright (Amendment) Act, 1994 (Act 38 of 1994), Section 17 [w.e.f. 10-9-1994].

EXPLANATION—For the purposes of this sub-clause, "any organisation" includes and organisation registered under section 12A of the Income-tax Act, 1961 (43 of 1961) and working for the benefit of persons with disability or recognised under Chapter X of the Persons with Disabilities (Equal Opportunities, Protection or Rights and full Participation) Act, 1995 (1 of 1996) or receiving grants from the government for facilitating access to persons with disabilities or an educational institution or library or archives recognised by the Government.

(zc) the importation of copies of any literary or artistic work, such as labels, company logos or promotional or promotional or explanatory material, that is purely incidental to other goods or products being imported lawfully.][226]

(2) The provisions of sub-section (1) shall apply to the doing of any act in relation to the translation of a literary, dramatic or musical work or the adaptation of a literary, dramatic, musical or artistic work as they apply in relation to the work itself.

[52A. **Particulars to be included in [sound recording][227] and video films**—(1) No person shall publish a [sound recording][228] in respect of any work unless the following particulars are displayed on the [sound recording][229] and on any container thereof, namely,—

(a) the name and address of the person who has made the [sound recording];[230]

(b) the name and address of the owner of the copyright in such work; and

(c) the year of its first publication.

(2) No person shall publish a video film in respect of any work unless the following particulars are displayed in the video film, when exhibited, and on the video cassette or other container thereof, namely,—

(a) if such work is a cinematograph film required to be certified for exhibition under the provisions of the Cinematograph Act, 1952, a copy of the certificate granted by the Broad of Film Certification under section 5A of that Act in respect of such work;

(b) the name and address of the person who has made the video film and a declaration by him that he has obtained the necessary licence or consent from the owner of the copyright in such work for making such video film; and

(c) the name and address of the owner of the copyright in such work.][231]

[***][232]

---

226. Inserted by the Copyright (Amendment) Act, 2012 (Act 27 of 2012), Section 32(vii) [w.e.f. 21-6-2012].
227. Substituted by the Copyright (Amendment) Act, 1994 (Act 38 of 1994), Section 2, for "record" [w.e.f. 10-5-1995].
228. Substituted by the Copyright (Amendment) Act, 1994 (Act 38 of 1994), Section 2, for "record" [w.e.f. 10-5-1995].
229. Substituted by the Copyright (Amendment) Act, 1994 (Act 38 of 1994), Section 2, for "record" [w.e.f. 10-5-1995].
230. Substituted by the Copyright (Amendment) Act, 1994 (Act 38 of 1994), Section 2, for "record" [w.e.f. 10-5-1995].
231. Inserted by the Copyright (Amendment) Act, 1994 (Act 38 of 1994), Section 4 [w.e.f. 10-9-1994].
232. Section 52B was omitted by the Copyright (Amendment) Act, 2012 (Act 27 of 2012), Section 33 [w.e.f. 21-6-2012].

[53. Importation of infringing copies—(1) The owner of any right conferred by this Act in respect of any work or any performance embodied in such work, or his duly authorised agent, may give notice in writing to the Commissioner of Customs, or to any other officer authorised in this behalf by the Central Board of Excise and Customs,—

(a) that he is the owner of the said right, with proof thereof; and

(b) that he requests the Commissioner for a period specified in the notice,

which shall not exceed one year, to treat infringing copies of the work as prohibited goods, and that infringing copies of the work are expected to arrive in India at a time and a place specified in the notice.

(2) The Commissioner, after scrutiny of the evidence furnished by the owner of the right and on being satisfied may, subject to the provisions of sub-section (3), treat infringing copies of the work as prohibited goods that have been imported into India, excluding goods in transit:

Provided that the owner of the work deposits such amount as the Commissioner may require as security having regard to the likely expenses on demurrage, cost of storage and compensation to the importer in case it is found that the words are not infringing copies.

(3) When any goods treated as prohibited under sub-section (2) have been detained, the Customs Officer detaining them shall inform the importer as well as the person who gave notice under sub-section (1) of the detention of such goods within forty-eight hours of their detention.

(4) The Customs Officer shall release the goods, and they shall no longer be treated as prohibited goods, if the person who gave notice under sub-section (1) does not produce any order from a court having jurisdiction as to the temporary or permanent disposal of such goods within fourteen days from the date of their detention.][233]

[53A. Resale share right in original copies—121(1) In the case of resale for a price exceeding ten thousand rupees, of the original copy of a painting, sculpture or drawing, or of the original manuscript of a literary or dramatic work or musical work, the author of such work if he was the first owner of rights under section 17 or his legal heirs shall, notwithstanding any assignment of copyright in such work, have a right to share in the resale-price of such original copy or manuscript in accordance with the provisions of this section:

Provided that such right shall cease to exist on the expiration of the term of copyright in the work.

(2) The share referred to in sub-section (1) shall be such as the Appellate Board[234] may fix and the decision of the Appellate Board[235] in this behalf shall be final:

233. Substituted by the Copyright (Amendment) Act, 2012 (Act 27 of 2012), Section 34, for Section 53 [w.e.f. 21-6-2012].

234. Substituted by the Finance Act 2017 (7 of 2017), Section 160(a) for "Copyright Board," [w.e.f. 26 May, 2017].

235. Substituted by the Finance Act 2017 (7 of 2017), Section 160(a) for "Copyright Board," [w.e.f. 26 May, 2017].

Provided that the Appellate Board[236] may fix different shares for different classes of work:

Provided further that in no case shall the share exceed ten per cent of the resale price.

(3) If any dispute arises regarding the right conferred by this section, it shall be referred to the Appellate Board[237] whose decision shall be final.][238]

Chapter XII

CIVIL REMEDIES

54. Definition—For the purposes of this Chapter, unless the context otherwise requires, the expression "owner of copyright" shall include—

(a) an exclusive licensee;

(b) in the case of an anonymous or pseudonymous literary, dramatic, musical or artistic work, the publisher of the work, until the identity of the author or, in the case of an anonymous work of joint authorship, or a work of joint authorship published under names all of which are pseudonyms, the identity of any of the authors, is disclosed publicly by the author and the publisher or is otherwise established to the satisfaction of the Appellate Board[239] by that author or his legal representatives.

55. Civil remedies for infringement of copyright—(1) Where copyright in any work has been infringed, the owner of the copyright shall, except as otherwise provided by this Act, be entitled to all such remedies by way of injunction, damages, accounts and otherwise as are or may be conferred by law for the infringement of a right:

Provided that if the defendant proves that at the date of the infringement he was not aware and had no reasonable ground for believing that copyright subsisted in the work, the plaintiff shall not be entitled to any remedy other than an injunction in respect of the infringement and a decree for the whole or part of the profits made by the defendant by the sale of the infringing copies as the court may in the circumstances deem reasonable.

(2) Where, in the case of a literary, dramatic, musical or artistic work, [or, subject to the provisions of sub-section (3) of section 13, a cinematograph film or sound recording, a name purporting to be that of the author, or the publisher, as the case may be, of that work, appears][240] on copies of the work as published, or,

236. Substituted by the Finance Act 2017 (7 of 2017), Section 160(a) for "Copyright Board," [w.e.f. 26 May, 2017].

237. Substituted by the Finance Act 2017 (7 of 2017), Section 160(a) for "Copyright Board," [w.e.f. 26 May, 2017].

238. Inserted by the Copyright (Amendment) Act, 1994 (Act 38 of 1994), Section 19 [w.e.f. 10-9-1994].

239. Substituted by the Finance Act 2017 (7 of 2017), Section 160(a) for "Copyright Board," [w.e.f. 26 May, 2017].

240. Substituted by the Copyright (Amendment) Act, 2012 (Act 27 of 2012), Section 35, for "a name purporting to be that of the author or the publisher, as the case may be, appears" [w.e.f. 21-6-2012].

in the case of an artistic work, appeared on the work when it was made, the person whose name so appears or appeared shall, in any proceeding in respect of infringement of copyright in such work, be presumed, unless the contrary is proved, to be the author or the publisher of the work, as the case may be.

(3) The costs of all parties in any proceedings in respect of the infringement of copyright shall be in the discretion of the court.

56. Protection of separate rights—Subject to the provisions of this Act, where the several rights comprising the copyright in any work are owned by different persons, the owner of any such right shall, to the extent of that right be entitled to the remedies provided by this Act and may individually enforce such right by means of any suit, action or other proceeding without making the owner of any other right a party to such suit, action or proceeding.

57. [**Author's special rights**—(1) Independently of the author's copyright and even after the assignment either wholly or partially of the said copyright, the author of a work shall have the right—

(a) to claim authorship of the work; and

(b) to restrain or claim damages in respect of any distortion, mutilation, modification or other act in relation to the said work [***][241] if such distortion, mutilation, modification or other act would be prejudicial to his honour or reputation:

Provided that the author shall not have any right to restrain or claim damages in respect of any adaptation of a computer programme to which clause (aa) of sub-section (1) of section 52 applies.

Explanation—Failure to display a work or to display it to the satisfaction of the author shall not be deemed to be an infringement of the rights conferred by this section.][242]

(2) The right conferred upon an author of a work by sub-section (1), [***][243] may be exercised by the legal representatives of the author.

58. Rights of owner against persons possessing or dealing with infringing copies—All infringing copies of any work in which copyright subsists, and all plates used or intended to be used for the production of such infringing copies, shall be deemed to be the property of the owner of the copyright, who accordingly may take proceedings for the recovery of possession thereof or in respect of the conversion thereof:

Provided that the owner of the copyright shall not be entitled to any remedy in respect of the conversion of any infringing copies, if the opponent proves—

(a) that he was not aware and had no reasonable ground to believe that copyright subsisted in the work of which such copies are alleged to be infringing copies;

---

241. The words "which is done before the expiration of the term of copyright" have been omitted by the Copyright (Amendment) Act, 2012 (Amendment) Act, 2012 (Act 27 of 2012), Section 36(i) [w.e.f. 21-6-2012].

242. Substituted by the Copyright (Amendment) Act, 1994 (Act 38 of 1994), Section 20 [w.e.f. 10-9-1994].

243. The words "other than the right to claim authorship of the work" have been omitted by the Copyright (Amendment) Act, 2012 (Amendment) Act, 2012 (Act 27 of 2012), Section 36(ii) [w.e.f. 21-6-2012].

or

(b) that he had reasonable grounds for believing that such copies or plates do not—involve infringement of the copyright in any work.

59. Restriction on remedies in the case of works of architecture—(1) Notwithstanding anything contained in [the Specific Relief Act, 1963 (47 of 1963)],[244] where the construction of a building or other structure which infringes or which, if completed, would infringe the copyright in some other work has been commenced, the owner of the copyright shall not be entitled to obtain an injunction to restrain the construction of such building or structure or to order its demolition.

(2) Nothing in section 58 shall apply in respect of the construction of a building or other structure which infringes or which, if completed, would infringe the copyright in some other work.

60. Remedy in the case of groundless threat of legal proceedings—Where any person claiming to be the owner of copyright in any work, by circulars, advertisements or otherwise, threatens any other person with any legal proceedings or liability in respect of an alleged infringement of the copyright, any person aggrieved thereby may, notwithstanding anything contained [in section 34 of the Specific Relief Act, 1963(47 of 1963)][245] institute a declaratory suit that the alleged infringement to which the threats related was not in fact an infringement of any legal rights of the person making such threats and may in any such suit—

(a) obtain an injunction against the continuance of such threats; and

(b) recover such damages, if any, as he has sustained by reason of such threats.

Provided that this section shall not apply if the person making such threats, with due diligence, commences and prosecutes an action for infringement of the copyright claimed by him.

61. Owners of copyright to be party to the proceeding—(1) In every civil suit or other proceeding regarding infringement of copyright instituted by an exclusive licensee, the owner of the copyright shall, unless the court otherwise directs, be made a defendant and where such owner is made a defendant, he shall have the right to dispute the claim of the exclusive licensee.

(2) Where any civil suit or other proceeding regarding infringement of copyright instituted by an exclusive licensee is successful, no fresh suit or other proceeding in respect of the same cause of action shall lie at the instance of the owner of the copyright.

62. Jurisdiction of court over matters arising under this Chapter—(1) Every suit or other civil proceeding arising under this Chapter in respect of the infringement of copyright in any work or the infringement of any other right conferred by this Act shall be instituted in the district court having jurisdiction.

---

244. Substituted by the Copyright (Amendment) Act, 1983 (Act 23 of 1983), Section 20, for "the Specific Relief Act, 1877 (1 of 1877)" [w.e.f. 9-8-1984].

245. Substituted by the Copyright (Amendment) Act, 1983 (Act 23 of 1983), Section 21, for "in Section 42 of the Specific Relief Act, 1877 (1 of 1877)" [w.e.f. 9-8-1984].

(2) For the purpose of sub-section (1), and "district court having jurisdiction" shall, notwithstanding anything contained in the Code of Civil Procedure, 1908, or any other law for the time being in force, include a district court within the local limits of whose jurisdiction, at the time of the institution of the suit or other proceeding, the person instituting the suit or other proceeding or, where there are more than one such persons, any of them actually and voluntarily resides or carries on business or personally works for gain.

Chapter XIII

OFFENCES

63. Offence of infringement of copyright or other rights conferred by this Act—Any person who knowingly infringes or abets the infringement of—

(a) the copyright in a work, or

(b) any other right conferred by this Act, 125[except the right conferred by section 53A][246]

[shall be punishable with imprisonment for a term which shall not be less than six months but which may extend to three years and with fine which shall not be less than fifty thousand rupees but which may extend to two lakh rupees:

Provided that (where the infringement has not been made for gain in the course of trade or Business)[247]the court may, for adequate and special reasons to be mentioned in the judgement, impose a sentence of imprisonment for a term of less than six months or a fine of less than fifty thousand rupees.][248]

Explanation—Construction of a building or other structure which infringes or which, if completed, would infringe the copyright in some other work shall not be an offence under this section.

[63A. Enhanced penalty on second and subsequent convictions—Whoever having already been convicted of an offence under section 63 is again convicted of any such offence shall be punishable for the second and for every subsequent offence, with imprisonment for a term which shall not be less than one year but which may extend to three years and with fine which shall not be less than one lakh rupees but which may extend to two lakh rupees:

Provided that (where the infringement has not been made for gain in the course of trade or business)[249] the court may, for adequate and special reasons to be mentioned in the judgment impose a sentence of imprisonment for a term of less than one year or a fine of less than one lakh rupees:

---

246. Inserted by the Copyright (Amendment) Act, 1994 (Act 38 of 1994), Section 21, [w.e.f. 10-9-1994]
247. Inserted by the Copyright (Amendment) Act, 1994 (Act 38 of 1994), Section 21, [w.e.f. 10-9-1994].
248. Substituted by the Copyright (Amendment) Act, 1984 (Act 23 of 1984), Section 2, [w.e.f. 8-10-1984].
249. Inserted by the Copyright (Amendment) Act, 1994 (Act 38 of 1994), Section 22 (Act 38 of 1994), [w.e.f. 10-5-1994].

Provided further that for the purposes of this section, no cognizance shall be taken of any conviction made before the commencement of the Copyright (Amendment) Act, 1984.][250]

[63B. Knowing use of infringing copy of computer programme to be an offence—Any person who knowingly makes use on a computer of an infringing copy of a computer programme shall be punishable with imprisonment for a term which shall not be less than seven days but which may extend to three years and with fine which shall not be less than fifty thousand rupees but which may extend to two lakh rupees:

Provided that where the computer programme has not been used for gain or in the course of trade or business, the court may, for adequate and special reasons to be mentioned in the judgment, not impose any sentence of imprisonment and may impose a fine which may extend to fifty thousand rupees.][251]

64. Power of police to seize infringing copies—[(1) Any police officer, not below the rank of a sub-inspector, may, if he is satisfied that an offence under section 63 in respect of the infringement of copyright in any work has been, is being, or is likely to be, committed, seize without warrant, all copies of the work, and all plates used for the purpose of making infringing copies of the work, wherever found, and all copies and plates so seized shall, as soon as practicable, be produced before a Magistrate.][252]

(2) Any person having an interest in any copies of a work [or plates][253] seized under sub-section (1) may, within fifteen days of such seizure, make an application to the Magistrate for such [or plates][254] being restored to him and the Magistrate, after hearing the applicant and the complainant and making such further inquiry as may be necessary, shall make such order on the application as he may deem fit.

65. Possession of plates for purpose of making infringing copies—Any person who knowingly makes, or has in his possession, any plate for the purpose of making infringing copies of any work in which copyright subsists shall be punishable with imprisonment which may extend to [two years and shall also be liable to fine].[255]

[65A. Protection of technological measure—(1) Any person who circumvents an effective technological measure applied for the purpose of protecting any of the rights conferred by this Act, with the intention of infringing such rights, shall be punishable with imprisonment which may extend to two years and shall also be liable to fine.

---

250. Inserted by the Copyright (Amendment) Act, 1984 (Act 65 of 1984), Section 6, [w.e.f. 8-10-1984].
251. Inserted by the Copyright (Amendment) Act, 1994 (Act 38 of 1994), Section 23 (Act 38 of 1994), [w.e.f. 10-5-1994].
252. Substituted by the Copyright (Amendment) Act, 1994 (Act 65 of 1984), Section 7, for sub-section (1) [w.e.f. 8-10-1984].
253. Inserted by the Copyright (Amendment) Act, 1994 (Act 65 of 1984), Section 7, [w.e.f. 8-10-1984].
254. Inserted by the Copyright (Amendment) Act, 1984 (Act 23 of 1984), Section 7, [w.e.f. 8-10-1984].
255. Substituted by the Copyright (Amendment) Act, 1984 (Act 23 of 1984), Section 8, for "one year, or with fine, or with both" [w.e.f. 8-10-1984].

(2) Nothing in sub-section (1) shall prevent any person from,—

(a) doing anything referred to therein for a purpose not expressly prohibited by this Act:

Provided that any person facilitating circumvention by another person of a technological measure for such a purpose shall maintain a complete record of such other person including his name, address and all relevant particulars necessary to identify him and the purpose for which he has been facilitated; or

(b) doing anything necessary to conduct encryption research using a lawfully obtained encrypted copy; or

(c) conducting any lawful investigation; or

(d) doing anything necessary for the purpose of testing the security of a computer system or a computer network with the authorisation of its owner; or

(e) operator; or

(f) doing anything necessary to circumvent technological measures intended for identification or surveillance of a user; or

(g) taking measures necessary in the interest of national security.

65B. Protection of rights management information—Any person, who knowingly,—

(i) removes or alters any rights management information without authority, or

(ii) distributes, imports for distribution, broadcasts or communicates to the public without authority, copies of any work, or performance knowing that electronic rights management information has been removed or altered without authority,

shall be punishable with imprisonment which may extend to two years and shall also be liable to fine:

Provided that if the rights management information has been tampered with in any work, the owner of copyright in such work may also avail of civil remedies provided under Chapter XII against the persons indulging in such acts.][256]

66. Disposal of infringing copies or plates for purpose of making infringing copies—The court trying any offence under this Act may, whether the alleged offender is convicted or not, order that all copies of the work or all plates in the possession of the alleged offender, which appear to it to be infringing copies, or plates for the purpose of making infringing copies, be delivered up to the owner of the copyright [or may make such order as it may deem tit regarding the disposal of such copies or plates].[257]

67. Penalty for making false entries in register, etc., for producing or tendering false entries—Any person who,—

---

256. Sections 65A and 65B inserted by the Copyright (Amendment) Act, 2012 (Act 27 of 2012), Section 37, [w.e.f. 21-6-2012].

257. Inserted by the Copyright (Amendment) Act, 2012 (Act 27 of 2012), Section 38, [w.e.f. 21-6-2012].

(a) makes or causes to be made a false entry in the Register of Copyrights kept under this Act, or

(b) makes or causes to be made a writing falsely purporting to be a copy of any entry in such register, or

(c) produces or tenders or causes to be produced or tendered as evidence any such entry or writing, knowing the same to be false,

shall be punishable with imprisonment which may extend to one year, or with fine, or with both.

68. Penalty for making false statements for the purpose of deceiving or influencing any authority or officer—Any person who,—

(a) with a view to deceiving any authority or officer in the execution provisions of this Act, or

(b) with a view to procuring or influencing the doing or omission of anything relation to this Act or any matter thereunder,

makes a false statement or representation knowing the same to be false, shall be punishable with imprisonment which may extend to one year, or with fine, or with both.

[**68A. Penalty for contravention of section 52A**—Any person who publishes a (sound recording)[258] or a video film in contravention of the provisions of section 52A shall be punishable with imprisonment which may extend to three years and shall also be liable to fine.][259]

69. Offences by companies—(1) Where any offence under this Act has been committed by a company, every person who at the time the offence was committed was in charge of, and was responsible to the company for, the conduct of the business of the company, as well as the company shall be deemed to be guilty of such offence and shall be liable to be proceeded against and punished accordingly:

Provided that nothing contained in this sub-section shall render any person liable to any punishment, if he proves that the offence was committed without his knowledge or that he exercised all due diligence to prevent the commission of such offence.

(2) Notwithstanding anything contained in sub-section (1), where an offence under this Act has been committed by a company, and it is proved that the offence was committed with the consent or connivance of, or is attributable to any negligence on the part of, any director, manager, secretary or other officer of the company, such director, manager, secretary or other officer shall also be deemed to be guilty of that offence and shall be liable to be proceeded against and punished accordingly.

EXPLANATION—For the purposes of this section—

(a) "company" means anybody corporate and includes a firm or other association of persons; and

(b) "director" in relation to a firm means a partner in the firm.

---

258. Substituted by the Copyright (Amendment) Act, 1994 (Act 38 of 1994), Section 2, for "record" [w.e.f. 10-9-1994].

259. Inserted by the Copyright (Amendment) Act, 1984 (Act 23 of 1984), Section 9, [w.e.f. 8-10-1984].

70. Cognizance of offences—No court inferior to that of [a Metropolitan Magistrate or a Judicial Magistrate of the first class][260] shall try any offence under this Act.

Chapter XIV
APPEALS

71. Appeals against certain orders of Magistrate—Any person aggrieved by an order made under sub-section (2) of section 64 or section 66 may, within thirty days of the date of such order, appeal to the court to which appeals from the court making the order ordinarily lie, and such appellate court may direct that execution of the order be stayed pending disposal of the appeal.

72. Appeals against orders of Registrar of Copyrights and Appellate Board[261]—(1) Any person aggrieved by any final decision or order of the Registrar of Copyrights may, within three months from the date of the order or decision, appeal to the Appellate Board.[262]

(2) Any person aggrieved by any final decision or order of the Appellate Board,[263] not being a decision or order made in an appeal under sub-section (1), may, within three months from the date of such decision or order, appeal to the High Court within whose jurisdiction the appellant actually and voluntarily resides or carries on business or personally works for gain:

Provided that no such appeal shall lie against a decision of the Appellate Board[264] under section 6.

(3) In calculating the period of three months provided for an appeal under this section, the time taken in granting a certified copy of the order or record of the decision appealed against shall be excluded.

73. Procedure for appeals—The High Court may make rules consistent with this Act as to the procedure to be followed in respect of appeals made to it under section 72.

Chapter XV
MISCELLANEOUS

74. Registrar of Copyrights and Appellate Board[265] to possess certain powers of

260. Substituted by the Copyright (Amendment) Act, 1983 (Act 23 of 1983), Section 22, for "a Presidency Magistrate or a Magistrate of the first class [w.e.f. 9-8-1984].
261. Substituted by the Finance Act 2017 (7 of 2017), Section 160(a) for "Copyright Board," [w.e.f. 26 May, 2017].
262. Substituted by the Finance Act 2017 (7 of 2017), Section 160(a) for "Copyright Board," [w.e.f. 26 May, 2017].
263. Substituted by the Finance Act 2017 (7 of 2017), Section 160(a) for "Copyright Board," [w.e.f. 26 May, 2017].
264. Substituted by the Finance Act 2017 (7 of 2017), Section 160(a) for "Copyright Board," [w.e.f. 26 May, 2017].
265. Substituted by the Finance Act 2017 (7 of 2017), Section 160(a) for "Copyright Board," [w.e.f. 26 May, 2017].

civil courts—The Registrar of Copyrights and the Appellate Board[266] shall have the powers of a civil court when trying a suit under the Code of Civil Procedure, 1908, in respect of the following matters, namely,—

(a) summoning and enforcing the attendance of any person and examining him on oath;

(b) requiring the discovery and production of any document;

(c) receiving evidence on affidavits;

(d) issuing commissions for the examination of witnesses or documents;

(e) requisitioning any public record or copy thereof from any court or office;

(f) any other matter which may be prescribed.

EXPLANATION—For the purpose of enforcing the attendance of witnesses, the local limits of the jurisdiction of the Registrar of Copyrights or the Appellate Board,[267] as the case may be, shall be limits of the territory of India.

75. Orders for payment of money passed by Registrar of Copyrights and Appellate Board[268] to be executable as a decree—Every order made by the Registrar of Copyrights or the Appellate Board[269] under this Act for the payment of any money or by the High Court in any appeal against any such order of the Appellate Board[270] shall, on a certificate issued by the Registrar of Copyrights, the Appellate Board[271] or the Registrar of the High Court, as the case may be, be deemed to be a decree of a civil court and shall be executable in the same manner as a decree of such court.

76. Protection of action taken in good faith—No suit or other legal proceeding shall lie against any person in respect of anything which is in good faith done or intended to be done in pursuance of this Act.

77. Certain persons to be public servants—Every officer appointed under this Act and every member of the Appellate Board[272] shall be deemed to be a public servant within the meaning of section 21 of the Indian Penal Code.

78. Power to make rules—(1) The Central Government may, by notification in the Official Gazette, make rules for carrying out the purposes of this Act.

(2) In particular, and without prejudice to the generality of the foregoing power, the

266. Substituted by the Finance Act 2017 (7 of 2017), Section 160(a) for "Copyright Board," [w.e.f. 26 May, 2017].
267. Substituted by the Finance Act 2017 (7 of 2017), Section 160(a) for "Copyright Board," [w.e.f. 26 May, 2017].
268. Substituted by the Finance Act 2017 (7 of 2017), Section 160(a) for "Copyright Board," [w.e.f. 26 May, 2017].
269. Substituted by the Finance Act 2017 (7 of 2017), Section 160(a) for "Copyright Board," [w.e.f. 26 May, 2017].
270. Substituted by the Finance Act 2017 (7 of 2017), Section 160(a) for "Copyright Board," [w.e.f. 26 May, 2017].
271. Substituted by the Finance Act 2017 (7 of 2017), Section 160(a) for "Copyright Board," [w.e.f. 26 May, 2017].
272. Substituted by the Finance Act 2017 (7 of 2017), Section 160(a) for "Copyright Board," [w.e.f. 26 May, 2017].

Central Government may make rules[273] to provide for all or any of the following matters, namely,—

[(a) the salaries and allowances payable to and the other terms and conditions of service of the chairman and other members of the Appellate Board[274] under sub-section (2) of section 11;][275]

(b) the form of complaints and applications to be made, and the licences to be granted, under this Act;

(c) the procedure to be followed in connection with any proceeding before the Registrar of Copyrights;

[(cA) the form and manner in which an Organisation may apply to the Appellate Board[276] for compulsory licence for disabled and the fee which may accompany such application under sub-section (1) of section 31B;

(cB) the manner in which a person making sound recording may give prior notice of his intention to make sound recording under sob-section (2) of section 31C;

(cC) the register and books of account and the details of existing stock which a person making sound recording may maintain under sub-section (5) of section 31C;

(cD) the manner in which prior notice may be given by a broadcasting organisation under sub-section (2) of section 31D;

(cE) the reports and accounts which may he maintained under clause (a), and the inspection of records and books of account which may be made under clause (b) of sub-section (7) of section 31D;][277]

[(ca) the conditions for submission of application under sub-section (2) of section 33;

(cb) the conditions subject to which a copyright society may be registered under sub-section (3) of section 33;

(cc) the inquiry for cancellation of registration under sub-section (4) of section 33;][278]

[(ccA) the manner in which a copyright society may publish its Tariff Scheme under sub-section (1) of section 33A;

(ccB) the fee which is to be paid before filing an appeal to the Appellate Board[279] under sub-section (2) of section 33A;

---

273. *See*, the Copyrights Rules, 1958.
274. Substituted by the Finance Act 2017 (7 of 2017), Section 160(a) for "Copyright Board," [w.e.f. 26 May, 2017].
275. Substituted by the Copyright (Amendment) Act, 2012 (Act 27 of 2012), Section 39(i), [w.e.f. 21-6-2012].
276. Substituted by the Finance Act 2017 (7 of 2017), Section 160(a) for "Copyright Board," [w.e.f. 26 May, 2017].
277. Clauses (cA) to (cE) inserted by the Copyright (Amendment) Act, 2012, (Act 27 of 2012), Section 39(ii), [w.e.f. 21-6-2012].
278. Inserted by the Copyright (Amendment) Act, 1994 (Act 38 of 1994), Section 24, [w.e.f. 10-9-1994].
279. Substituted by the Finance Act 2017 (7 of 2017), Section 160(a) for "Copyright Board," [w.e.f. 26 May, 2017].

(ccC) the form of application for renewal of registration of a copyright society and the fee which may accompany such application under sub-section (3A) of section 33;][280]

[(cd) the conditions subject to which the copyright society may accept authorisation under clause (a) of sub-section (1) of section 34 and the conditions subject to which owners of rights have right to withdraw such authorisation under clause (b) of that sub-section;

(ce) the conditions subject to which a copyright society may issue licences, collect fees and distribute such fees amongst owners of rights under sub-section (3) of section 34;

(cf) the manner in which the approval of the owners of rights regarding collection and distribution of fees, approval for utilisation of any amount collected as fees and to provide to such owners information concerning activities in relation to the administration of their rights under sub-section (1) of section 35;

(cg) the returns to be filed by copyright societies to the Registrar of Copyrights under sub-section (1) of section 36;

(d) the manner of determining any royalties payable under this Act, and the security to be taken for the payment of such royalties;

(da) the manner of payment of royalty under clause (j) of sub-section (1) of section 52;][281]

[***][282]

(e) the form of Register of Copyrights to be kept under this Act and the particulars to be entered therein;

(f) the matter in respect of which the Registrar of Copyrights and the Appellate Board[283] shall have powers of a civil court;

(g) the fees which may be payable under this Act;

(h) the regulation of business of the Copyright Office and of all things by this Act placed under the direction or control of the Registrar of Copyrights.

[(3) Every rule made under this section shall be laid, as soon as may be after it is made, before each House of Parliament, while it is in session, for a total period of thirty days which may be comprised in one session or in two or more successive sessions, and if, before the expiry of the session immediately following the session or the successive sessions aforesaid, both Houses agree in making any modification in the rule or both Houses agree that the rule should not be made, the rule shall thereafter have effect only in such modified form or

---

280. Clauses (ccA) to (ccC) inserted by the Copyright (Amendment) Act, 2012, (Act 27 of 2012), Section 39(iii), [w.e.f. 21-6-2012].

281. Clauses (cd) to (da) inserted by the Copyright (Amendment) Act, 1994 (Act 38 of 1994), Section 24, [w.e.f. 10-9-1994].

282. Clause (db) omitted by the Copyright (Amendment) Act, 2012 (Act 27 of 2012), Section 39(iv), [w.e.f. 21-6-2012].

283. Substituted by the Finance Act 2017 (7 of 2017), Section 160(a) for "Copyright Board," [w.e.f. 26 May, 2017].

be of no effect, as the case may be; so, however, that any such modification or annulment shall be without prejudice to the validity of anything previously done under that rule.][284]

79. Repeals, savings and transitional provisions—(1) The Indian Copyright Act, 1914, and the Copyright Act of 1911 (3 of 1914) passed by the Parliament of the United Kingdom as modified in its application to India by the Indian Copyright Act, 1914 (3 of 1914), are hereby repealed.

(2) Where any person has, before the commencement of this Act, taken any action whereby he has incurred any expenditure or liabilities in connection with the reproduction or performance of any work in a manner which at the time was lawful or for the purpose of or with a view to the reproduction or performance of a work at a time when such reproduction or performance would, but for the coming into force of this Act, have been lawful, nothing in this section shall diminish or prejudice any rights or interests arising from or in connection with such action which are subsisting and valuable at the said date, unless the person who, by virtue of this Act, becomes entitled to restrain such reproduction or performance agrees to pay such compensation as, failing agreement, may be determined by the Appellate Board.[285]

(3) Copyright shall not subsist by virtue of this Act in any work in which copyright did not subsist immediately before the commencement of this Act under any Act repealed by sub-section (1).

(4) Where copyright subsisted in any work immediately before the commencement of this Act, the rights comprising such copyright shall, as from the date of such commencement, be the rights specified in section 14 in relation to the class of works to which such work belongs, and where any new rights are conferred by that section, the owner of such rights shall be—

(a) in any case where copyright in the work was wholly assigned before the commencement of this Act, the assignee or his successor-in-interest;

(b) in any other case, the person who was the first owner of the copyright in the work under any Act repealed by sub-section (1) or his legal representatives.

(5) Except as otherwise provided in this Act, where any person is entitled immediately before the commencement of this Act to copyright in any work or any right in such copyright or to an interest in any such right, he shall continue to be entitled to such right or interest for the period for which he would have been entitled thereto if this Act had not come into force.

(6) Nothing contained in this Act shall be deemed to render any act done before its commencement an infringement of copyright if that act would not otherwise have constituted such an infringement.

(7) Save as otherwise provided in this section, nothing in this section shall be deemed to affect the application of the General Clauses Act, 1897, with respect to the effect of repeals.

---

284. Substituted by the Copyright (Amendment) Act (Act 23 of 1983), 1983, Section 2, [w.e.f. 9-8-1984].

285. Substituted by the Finance Act 2017 (7 of 2017), Section 160(a) for "Copyright Board," [w.e.f. 26 May, 2017].

Bibliography

Adams, J., *Merchandising Intellectual Property*, Butterworths, London, 1987.

Adelman, M., "Constructed Languages and Copyright: A Brief History and Proposal for Divorce", *Harvard Journal of Law and Technology,* 27(2), (2014), pp. 544–562.

Ahuja, V.K., "GATT, TRIPS and India", *India Quarterly,* 50, (1994), pp. 1–14.

Alexander, G.S., *Commodity and Propriety*, University of Chicago Press, 1997.

Alexander, K., "The Mareva Injunction and Anton Piller Order: The Nuclear Weapons of English Commercial Litigation", *Florida Journal of International Law,* 2, (1997), p. 487.

Ashoke, A., "Technology Protection Measures and the Indian Copyright (Amendment) Act, 2012: A Comment", *Journal of Intellectual Property Rights,* 17, (2012), pp. 521–531.

Astbury, R., "The Renewal of the Licensing Act in 1693 and Its Lapse in 1695", *The Library,* 33, (5th Series, 1978), pp. 296–322.

Ayyar, R.V.V., "Interest or Right? The Process and Politics of a Diplomatic Conference on Copyright", *Journal of World Intellectual Property,* 1(1), (1998), pp. 3–35.

_____, "The Process and Politics of a Diplomatic Conference on Copyright", *Journal of World Intellectual Property*, 1(1), (1998), pp. 3–35.

Bagley, C.E. and Clarkson, G., "Adverse Possession for Intellectual Property: Adapting an Ancient Concept to Resolve Conflicts Between Antitrust and Intellectual Property Laws in the Information Age", *Harvard Journal of Law and Technology,* 16, (2003), pp. 227–393.

Bainbridge, D., *Intellectual Property Law: Cases and Materials*, Pitman Publishing, London, 1995.

_____, *Intellectual Property*, Pearson Education, New Delhi, 2002.

_____, *Software Copyright Law*, Butterworths Tolley (1996).

Balganesh, S., "The Obligatory Structure of Copyright Law: Unbundling the Wrong of Copying", *Harvard Law Review,* 125, (2012), pp. 1664–1690.

Banerjee, A. and Agrawal, A.D., "Morality of Copyright: A Critique in View of the '3 Idiots' Controversy", *Journal of Intellectual Property Rights,* 16(5), (2011), pp. 394–401.

Baron, J.B., "Rescuing the Bundle of Rights Metaphor in Property Law", *University of Cincinnati Law Review,* 82, (2014), pp. 57–45.

Barzel, Y., *Economic Analysis of Property Rights*, Cambridge University Press, 1997.

Baxi, U., "Copyright Law and Justice in India" *Journal of the Indian Law Institute,* 28, (1986), pp. 497–540.

Beebe, B., "Intellectual Property Law and the Sumptuary Code", *Harvard Law Review,* 123(4), (2010), pp. 809–889.

Benkler, Y., "Free as the Air to Common Use: First Amendment Constraints on Enclosure of the Public Domain", *New York University Law Review,* 74, (1999), pp 354–446.

Bently, L. and Sherman, B., *The Making of Intellectual Property: The British Experience*, Cambridge University Press, 1999.

Berryman, J., "Thirty Years After: Anton Piller Orders and the Supreme and Federal Courts of Canada", *Journal of International Commercial Law and Technology,* 3(2), (2007), pp. 128–140.

Beunen, A., *Protection for Databases: The European Database Directive and its Effects in Netherlands, France and United Kingdom*, Wolf Legal Publishers, Leiden, 2007.

Bhadra, S. and Majumdar, A., "Anton Piller Order in UK and Its Possible Implications in India", *Journal of Intellectual Property Rights,* 12, (2007), pp. 488–426.

Birrell, A., *Seven Essays on the Law and History of Copyright in Books*, Cassell and Company Limited, London, 1899.

Blackeney, M. (Ed.), *Border Control of Intellectual Property Rights*, Sweet and Maxwell, London, 2004.

Blagden, C., *The Stationers' Company: A History*, Stanford University Press, Stanford, 1977.

Blakeney, M., *Trade Related Aspects of Intellectual Property Rights*, Sweet and Maxwell, London, 1996.

Bogsch, A., *The Law of Copyright and the Universal Convention*, Sijthoff Leyden Bowker, 1972.

Boon, D.S.K., "Reviewing the Defence of Fair Dealing for Research or Private Study", *Singapore Journal of Legal Studies* (1996).

Bowker, R.R., *Copyright: Its History and Its Law,* Houghton Mifflin Company, Boston and New York, 1912.

Bowrey, K., "Art, Craft, Good Taste and Manufacturing: The Development of Intellectual Property Laws", *Law in Context*, 15(1), (1997), pp. 78–104.

Boyle, J. *The Public Domain*, Yale University Press, 2008.

Bracha, O., "The Adventures of the Statute of Anne in the Land of Unlimited Possibilities: The Life of a Legal Transplant", *Berkeley Technology Law Journal,* 25, (2010), pp. 1427–1473.

_____, *Owning Ideas: A History of Anglo-American Intellectual Property*, Harvard Law School, 2005, pp. 12–129.

Breyer, S., "Copyright: A Rejoinder", *UCLA Law Review*, 20, (1972), pp. 75–83.

_____, "The Uneasy Case for Copyright: A Study of Copyright in Books, Photocopies, and Computer Programs", *Harvard Law Review,* 84, (1970), pp. 281–351.

Carty, H. and Hodkinson, K., "Copyright, Designs and Patents Act 1988", *The Modern Law Review,* 52(3), (1989), pp. 369–379.

Cayne, B.S. (Ed.), *The New Lexicon Webster's Dictionary of the English Language*, Lexicon Publication, New York, 1987.

Chander, A. and Sunder, M., "The Romance of the Public Domain", *California Law Review,* 92, (2004), pp. 1331–1373.

Chandiramani, N., "Legal Factors in TRIPS", *Economic and Political Weekly,* 37, (2002), pp. 200–203.

Chaudhury, S., "TRIPS Agreement and Amendment of Patents Act in India", *Economic and Political Weekly,* 37, (2002), pp. 3354–3356.

Chawhan, D.C., "Intellectual Property Rights have Assumed a Significant Importance", *Indian Bar Review,* 27 (2 and 3), (2001), pp. 61–72.

Cholayil, B.P., "Digital Rights Management and Fair Use in Copyright Law", *Cochin University Law Review*, 33(1–2), (2009), p. 166.

Ciolino, D.S., "Why Copyrights are Not Community Property?" *The ICFAI Journal of Intellectual Property Rights,* 1, (2002), pp. 45–66.

Clement, P., Dinh, V. and Harris, J., *The Constitutional and Historical Foundations of Copyright Protection* (Center for Individual Freedom, Alexandria, 2012).

Cohen, J.E., "Copyright as Property in the Post-Industrial Economy: A Research Agenda", *Wisconsin Law Review* (2011), pp. 141–165.

_____, "Copyright, Commodification and Culture: Locating the Public Domain" in Lucie Guibault and P. Bernt Hugenholtz (Ed.), *The Future of The Public Domain* (2006), p. 121.

_____, "Copyright's Public Private Distinction", *Case Western Reserve Law Review,* 55, (2005), pp. 963–970.

Copinger and Skone James (Eds.), *Copyright* (Sweet and Maxwell, London, 1999), pp. 573–574.

Cornish, W.R., *Intellectual Property,* Universal Law Publishing Co., New Delhi, 2001.

_____, *Intellectual Property*: *Cases and Materials,* Sweet and Maxwell, London, 1999.

_____, *Intellectual Property: Patent, Copyright, Trademark and Allied Rights*, Second Indian Reprint, 2003.

_____, *Intellectual Property: Patents, Copyright, Trademarks and Allied Rights*, Sweet and Maxwell, London, 1995.

Correa, C.M., *Trade Related Aspects of Intellectual Property Rights*, Oxford University Press, Oxford, 2007.

Current, R.N. (Ed.), *The Political Thought of Abraham Lincoln*, Bobbs-Merrill, Indianapolis, 1967.

D. Harvey, P., "Efforts Under GATT, WIPO and Other Multinational Organizations Against Trademark Counterfeiting", *European Intellectual Property Review*, 15 (1993), pp. 446–451.

Dahiya, K., "Cinematographic Lyricists Right to Royalty: Myth or Reality?" *Journal of Intellectual Property Rights,* 16, (2011), pp. 335–340.

Das, J.K., "Copyright Protection for Computer Softwares and Databases: From Sweat of the Brow to Modicum of Creativity", *Indian Journal of Law and Justice,* 3(2), (2012), pp. 57–80.

_____, "Examination of Contemporary Status of Fair Dealing in Copyright Law in India", 7, *Vidhik Chetana: A Research Journal of Juridical Science* (2014), pp. 43–63.

_____, "Legal Framework for Copyright Protection: Its Philosophical Justifications and Practical Implications on Indigenous Peoples", *Banaras Law Journal,* 33–34, (2003–04), pp. 157–180.

_____, "Legal Protection of Creativity under Copyright Law: An Overview", in Shiv Sahai Singh (Ed.), *The Law of Intellectual Property Rights*, Deep and Deep Publications Pvt. Ltd., New Delhi, (2004), pp. 224–235.

_____, "New Dimensions of Intellectual Property Rights in India", *Pragyaan: Journal of Law,* 3(2), (2013), pp. 11–33.

Das, J.K., "TRIPS Agreement and Intellectual Property Rights: An Indian Perspective", 6 *International Trade Law and Regulation*, Thomson Reuters (Legal) Limited, London, (2010), pp. 165–173.

_____, *Code of Civil Procedure*, PHI Learning Private Limited, Delhi, 2014.

_____, *Intellectual Property Rights*, Kamal Law House, Kolkata, 2008.

Davison, M.J., *The Legal Protection of Databases*, Cambridge University Press, Cambridge, 2003.

Deazley, R., "The Myth of Copyright at Common Law", *Cambridge Law Journal,* 62, (2003), pp. 106–133.

_____, *On the Origin of the Right to Copy*, Hart Publishing, Portland, 2004.

_____, *Rethinking Copyright: History, Theory, Language*, Edward Elgar Publishing Ltd., Oxford, 2008.

Dhar, P.M., "Intellectual Property in Computer Programs: Weakness of the Indian Copyright Act, 1957", *Journal of the Indian Law Institute,* 28, (1986), pp. 487–496.

Douglas, S. and McFarlane, B., "Defining Property Rights" in James Penner and Henry E. Smith (Ed.), *Philosophical Foundations of Property Law*, Oxford University Press, Oxford, 2013.

Drahos, P., *A Philosophy of Intellectual Property,* Dartmouth Publications, Aldershot, 1996.

Ellickson, R.C., "Property in Land", *Yale Law Journal,* 102, (1993), pp. 1315–1400.

Epstein, R.A., "Unifying Copyright: An Instrumentalist's Response to Shyamkrishna Balganesh", *Harvard Law Review,* 125, (2012), pp. 120–132.

Epstein, R., "Past and Future: The Temporal Dimension in the Law of Property", *Washington University Law Quarterly,* 64, (1986), pp. 667–722.

_____, "Possession as the Root of Title", *Georgia Law Review,* 85, (1979), pp. 1221–1243.

Feather, J., *A History of British Publishing*, Routledge, London, 1988, pp. 74–75.

Fisher, W.W., "Theories of Intellectual Property", *Chinese Intellectual Property Review,* 1, (2002).

Fitzpatirick, S., "Copyright Imbalance: US and Australian Response to the WIPO Digital Copyright Treaty", *European Intellectual Property Review,* 22, (2000), pp. 214–228.

Françon, A., "Should the Rome Convention on Neighboring Rights be Revised?" *Copyright Bulletin,* 25, (1991), pp. 20–24.

Franklin, J., *International Intellectual Property Law*, American Society of International Law, 2013.

Freitas, de D., "The Main Features of Copyright Protection in the Various Legal Systems", *Journal of the Indian Law Institute,* 28, (1986), pp. 441–449.

Galbraith, C.D., "Remembering the Public Domain", *Denver University Law Review,* 84(1), (2006), pp. 135–142.

Geiger, C., Gervais, D. and Senftleben, M., "The Three-Step Test Revisited: How to Use the Test's Flexibility in National Copyright Law", *Program on Information Justice and Intellectual Property,* 12, (2013), pp. 1–44.

Geist, M. (Ed.), *The Copyright Pentalogy*, University of Ottawa Press, 2013.

Geller, P.A., "Copyright Protection in Barne Union: Analyzing the Issues", *Columbia Law Journal,* 13, (1989), pp. 435–476.

Gervais, D., *The TRIPS Agreement Drafting History and Analysis*, Sweet and Maxwell, London, 2003.

Gleicher, N.J., "John Doe Subpoenas: Toward a Consistent Legal Standard", *Yale Law Journal,* 118, (2008), pp. 320–368.

Gold, A.S., "A Moral Rights Theory of Private Law", *William and Mary Law Review,* 52, (2011), pp. 1873–1931.

Goldberg, J.C.P., "Introduction: Pragmatism and Private Law", *Harvard Law Review,* 125, (2012), pp. 1640–1663.

Goldstein, P., *International Copyright: Principles, Law, and Practice*, Oxford University Press, New York, 2001.

Gopalakrishnan, N.S. and Agitha, T.G., *Principles of Intellectual Property*, Eastern Book Company, Lucknow, 2009.

Gopalakrishnan, N.S., *Intellectual Property and Criminal Law*, National Law School of India University, Bangalore, 1994.

Gordon, W.J., "Fair Use as Market Failure: A Structural and Economic Analysis of Betamex case and its Predecessors", *Columbia Law Review,* 82, (1982), pp. 1600–1657.

Grahm, J.H.S., *Internet Law and Regulation*, Sweet and Maxwell, London, 2002.

Green, T.H., *Lectures on the Principles of Political Obligation*, University of Michigan Press, 1967.

Gubin, R., "Borrowing Privileges: How Does (or Should) Copyright Law Define a Derivative Work?" Visited on January 3, 2015 http://cyber.law.harvard.edu/archivedcontent/events/SignalNoiseBBFINAL.pdf.

Gupta, J., "John Doe Copyright Injunctions in India", *Journal of Intellectual Property Rights,* 18, (2013), pp. 351–359.

Hall, S., "Anton Piller Orders: A Doorstep Too Far?" *European Intellectual Property Review,* 17, (1995), p. 50.

Hamilton, M.A., "Computer Science Concepts in Copyright Cases: The Path to a Coherent Law", *Harvard Journal of Law and Technology,* 10(2), (1997), pp. 2040–2280.

Harms, L.T.C., *The Enforcement of Intellectual Property Rights: A Case Book*, World Intellectual Property Organization, Geneva, 2005.

Harris, D.P., "TRIPS' Rebound: An Historical Analysis of How the TRIPS Agreement Can Ricochet back against the United States", *Northwestern Journal of International Law and Business,* 25, (2004–2005), pp. 99–164.

Haskin, F.J., "First Use of Anesthetics", *Salt Lake Tribune*, Newspaper, Utah, April 19, 1926, p. 6.

Hayhurst, G.W., "Ex parte Anton Piller Orders with John Doe Defendents", *European Intellectual Property Review,* 9(9), (1989), p. 257.

Hegel, G.W.F., *Philosophy of Right*, Batoche Books, Kitchener, 2001.

Holyook and Torremans, *Intellectual Property Law,* Butterworths, London, 1995.

Horowitz, S.J., "Designing the Public Domain", *Harvard Law Review,* 122(5), (2009), pp. 1489–1510.

Howe, H. (Ed.), *Concepts of Property in Intellectual Property Law*, Cambridge University Press, 2013.

Hughes, G.L. (Ed.), *Essays in Copyright Law*, Longman Professional, Melbourne, 1990.

Hughes, J., "A Short History of Intellectual Property in Relation to Copyright", *Cardozo Law Review,* 33, (2012), pp. 1293–1340.

_____, "The Philosophy of Intellectual Property", *Georgetown Law Journal,* 77(2), (1988), pp. 287–366.

_____, *Fair Use Across Time, UCLA Law Review*, 50, (2003), pp. 775–800.

Hunter, D., "Copyright Protection for Engravings and Maps in Eighteenth-Century Britain", *The Library,* 9, (1987), pp. 128-47.

Ilardi, A. and Blakency, M., *International Encyclopedia of Intellectual Property Treaties*, Oxford University Press, Oxford, 2004.

Irvin, S., *Authors, Intentions and Literary Meaning*, Blackwell Publishing, Malden, 2006.

James, J.R. and Davies, G. (Ed.), *Copinger and Skone James on Copyright,* Sweet and Maxwell, London, 1999.

James, T.C., "Copyright Law of India and the Academic Community", *Journal of Intellectual Property Rights,* 9, (2004), pp. 207–225.

_____, "Indian Copyright Law and Digital Technology", *Journal of Intellectual Property Rights,* 7, (2002), pp. 423–435.

Jethi, M., "Dealing 'Fairly' with Software in India", *Journal of Intellectual Property Rights,* 16, (2011), pp. 313–320.

Jha, S. and Jha, S., "An Analysis of the Theory of Contributory Infringement", *Journal of Intellectual Property Rights,* 11, (2006), pp. 318–325.

Johnson, D.R., "Reflections on the Bundle of Rights", *Vermont Law Review,* 32, (2007), pp. 247–272.

Jones, H.W., "Law and Morality in the Perspective of Legal Realism", *Columbia Law Review,* 61, (1961), pp. 799–809.

Julia-Barcelo, R., "On-line Internationally Liability Issues: Comparing US and EU Legal Frameworks", *European Intellectual Property Review,* 22, (2000), pp. 105–112.

Kala, T., *How Copyright Works in Practice*, N.M. Tripathi, Bombay, 1996.

Kamat, N., *Law Relating to Computers Internet and E-Commerce,* Universal Law Publishing Co., New Delhi, 2012.

Kamina, P., "Authorship of Films and Implementation of the Term Directive: The Dramatic Tale of the Two Copyrights", *European Intellectual Property Review,* 16, (1994).

Kant, I., Essays and Treatises on Moral, Political and Various Philosophical Subjects (1798), pp. 229–230.

_____, "Of the Injustice of Counterfeiting Books", in *Essays and Treatises on Moral, Political and Various Philosophical Subjects* (Richardson ed., 1798), pp. 229–230.

Katyal, N.K., "Criminal Law in Cyber-space", *University of Pennsylvania Law Review,* 149, (2001), pp. 1006–1013.

Keller and Cunard, *Copyright Law: A Practitioner's Guide* (Practicing Law Institute, 2005).

Kerever, A., "Should the Rome Convention be Revised and if so, is this the Right Moment?" *Copyright Bulletin,* 25, (1991), pp. 5–16.

Khan, S.A., "Role of the Berne Convention in the Promotion of Cultural Creativity and Development: Recent Copyright Legislation in Developing Countries", 28, *Journal of the Indian Law Institute* (1986), pp. 424–440.

_____, *Socio-Economic Benefits of Intellectual Property Protection in Developing Countries*, WIPO, Geneva, 2000.

Khong, D.W.K., "The Historical Law and Economics of the First Copyright Act", *Erasmus Law and Economics Review,* 2(1), (2006), pp. 35–69.

Kitchn, D. (Ed.), *Kerly's Law of Trade Marks and Trade Names*, Sweet and Maxwell, London, 2011.

Kumar, K., *Cyber Laws Intellectual Property and E-Commerce Security*, Dominant Publishers and Distributors, New Delhi, 2001, p. 69.

Kumar, S., "Economic and Moral Rights of the Copyright Holder under Digital Environment: An Analysis", 1 *Rajiv Gandhi National University of Law Review* (2011).

Labra, V.B., "The Rome Convention: A Three-Cornered Marriage (a love triangle)?" *Copyright Bulletin,* 25, (1991), pp. 17–19.

Laddie, P. and Vitoria, *The Modern Law of Copyright*, Butterworths, London (1980).

Lakshmanan, A.R., *Wharton's Law Dictionary*, Universal Law Publishing Co., New Delhi, 2013.

Landes W.M. and Posner, R.A., *The Economic Structure of Intellectual Property Law,* Harvard University Press, 2003.

_____, "An Economic Analysis of Copyright Law", *Journal of Legal Studies,* 18(2), (1989), pp. 325–363.

Lemley, M.A., "Dealing with Overlapping Copyrights on the Internet", *Dayton Law Review,* 224, (1997), pp. 547–555.

_____, "Property, Intellectual Property and Free Riding", *Texas Law Review,* 83, (2005), pp. 1031–1075.

Leval, P.N., "Toward a Fair Use Standard", *Harvard Law Review,* 103 (1990), pp. 1105–1136.

Lipton, J.D., "Solving the Digital Piracy Puzzle: Disaggregating Fair Use from the DMCA's Anti-Device Provisions", *Harvard Journal of Law and Technology,* 19(1), (2005), pp. 111–160.

Litman, J., "The Public Domain", *Emory Law Journal,* 39(4), (1990), pp. 965–1023.

Liu, J.P., "Copyright and Time: A Proposal", *Michigan Law Review,* 101, (2002), pp. 409–481.

Locke, J., *Liberty of the Press*, Cambridge University Press, 1695, Reprint in 1997.

_____, *Two Treatises of Government* (Churchill, 1698).

Lord Macaulay, *The History of England from the Accession of James II*, Charles H. Firth ed., 1913.

Loren, L.P., "The Pope's Copyright? Aligning Incentives with Reality by Using Creative Motivation to Shape Copyright Protection", *Louisiana Law Review,* 69(1), (2008), pp. 1–41.

Mackaay, E. (Ed.), *The Electronic Superhighway: The Shape of Technology and Law to Come*, Kluwer Law International, 1995.

Maredia, M.K., "Application of Intellectual Property Rights in Developing Countries: Implications for Public Policy and Agricultural Research Institutes", WTO, Geneva, 2001.

Mason, R.L. and Ganz, R.E., "Columbia Broadcasting: Public Access to the Media Denied", *Catholic University Law Review,* 23(2), (1973), pp. 339–358.

Maurke, A.O.R., "Toward a Doctrine of Fair Use in Patent Law", *Columbia Law Review* (2000), 100, pp. 1177–1250.

Merges, R.P., Menell, P.S. and Lemley, M.A., *Intellectual Property in the New Technological Age*, Aspen Publishers, New York, 2000.

Miceli, T., *Economics of the Law: Torts, Contracts, Property, Litigation*, Oxford University Press, New York, 1997.

Miller, A.R. and Davis, M.H., *Intellectual Property Patents, Trademarks, and Copyright: In a Nutshell*, West Publishing Co., Minnesota, 1983.

Mitra D. and Modi, A., "Pay 'n' Play: Public Performance of Sound Recording *vis-à-vis* Copyright Infringement", *Journal of Intellectual Property Rights,* 18, (2013), pp. 133–132.

Monotti, A., "Nature and Basis of Crown Copyright in Official Publications", *European Intellectual Property Review,* 14, (1992), p. 305.

Nair, M.D., "TRIPS and Public Health: The Doha Declaration", *Journal of Intellectual Property Rights,* 7(3), (2002), pp. 241–244.

Narayana, P., *Intellectual Property Law*, Eastern Law House, Kolkata, 2001.

Nessen, P.V., "Law Reporting: Case for Deregulation", 48(4) *Modern Law Review* (1985), Copinger and Skone James (Ed.), *Copyright* , 412–433, (Sweet and Maxwell, London, 1999), pp. 573–574.

Nimmer, M.B. and Geller, P.E., *International Copyright Law and Practice*, Matthew Bender, 1988.

Nordemann, W., *International Copyright and Neighbouring Rights Law*, Aspen Publishers, 1990.

Ochoa, T.T., "Origins and Meanings of the Public Domain", *University of Dayton Law Review,* 28, (2003), pp. 215–267.

Pandey, S., "Neighbouring Rights Protection in India", 9, *Journal of Intellectual Property Rights* (2004), pp. 356–370.

Patterson, L.R. and Lindberg, S.W., *The Nature of Copyright: A Law of Users' Rights*, University of Georgia Press, Athens, 1991.

Patterson, L.R., *Copyright in Historic Perspective—Overview*, Vanderbilt University, 1968.

Pearson, H.E. and Miller, C.G., *Commercial Exploitation of Intellectual Property*, Blackstone Press, 1990.

Pillai, K.N.C., "Copyrightability of Supreme Court Judgment", *Journal of the Indian Law Institute,* 50, (2008), pp. 94–97.

Ponnuswami, K., "Performing Right of the Intellectual Worker: Judicial Annihilation", *Journal of the Indian Law Institute,* 28, (1986), pp. 470–486.

Posner, R.A., *Law and Literature: A Misunderstood Relation*, Harvard University Press, Cambridge, Massachusetts, 1988.

Radin, M.J., *Reinterpreting Property*, University of Chicago Press, 1993.

Ralston, R., Fellenstein, C. and Vassallo, J. (Ed.), *Patents, Copyrights, and Trademarks: A Look Back The History of Copyrights*, Pearson, London, 2005.

Ramappa, T., *Intellectual Property Rights under WTO: Tasks Before India*, Wheeler Publishing, New Delhi, 2000.

Rao, C.N., "Patents for Biotechnology Inventions in TRIPS", *Economic and Political Weekly,* 37, (2002), pp. 2126–2129.

Reichman, J.H., "Intellectual Property in International Trade: Opportunities and Risks of a GATT Connection", *Vanderbilt Journal of International Law,* 22(4), (1989), pp. 747–891.

Reinbothe, J., Martin-Prat, M. and Lewinski, S.V., "The New WIPO Treaties: A First Resume", *European Intellectual Property Review,* 19, (1997), pp. 171–176.

Rembe, R., "Time for a Performer's Convention", *Copyright Bulletin,* 25, (1991), pp. 25–31.

Ricketon, S., *The Berne Convention for the Protection of Literary and Artistic Works: 1886–1986*, University of London, 1987.

Ricketson, S. and Ginsburg, J., *International Copyright and Neighbouring Rights: The Berne Convention and Beyond*, Oxford University Press, 2006.

Rieder, C.M., U.S. Subject Matter Jurisdiction for Copyright Infringements on the Internet, *Computer Law Review and Technology Journal* (1988), p. 23.

Rigamonti, C.P., "Deconstructing Moral Rights" *Harvard International Law Journal,* 47(2), (2006), pp. 353–412.

Robilant, A.D., "Property: A Bundle of Sticks or a Tree?" *Vanderbilt Law Review,* 66(3), (2013), pp. 869–932.

Roeder, M.A., "The Doctrine of Moral Right: A Study in the Law of Artists, Authors and Creators", *Harvard Law Review,* 53, (1940), pp. 554–578.

Rose, C.M., "Possession as the Origin of Property", *University of Chicago Law Review,* 53, (1985), pp. 73–88.

_____, *Property and Persuasion*, Westview Press, Boulder, 1994.

_____, *Authors and Owners: The Invention of Copyright*, Harvard University Press, 1993.

Rosenzweig, S.A., "Don't Put My Article Online: Existing Copyright's New-use Doctrine to the Electronic Publishing Media and Beyond", *University of Pennsylvania Law Review*, 143, (1994–1995), p. 639.

Rumphorst, W., "Neighbouring Rights Protection of Broadcasting Organizations", *European Intellectual Property Review,* 10, (1992), pp. 339–342.

Ryder, R.D., *Intellectual Property and the Internet*, LexisNexis Butterworths, 2002.

Sagar, J., "Entertainment Media and IP Rights: An Indian Perspective", in S.K. Verma and Raman Mittal, *Intellectual property Rights: A Global Version,* Indian Law Institute, New Delhi (2004).

Saha, T.K., "Copyright Law in Changing World", *Journal of Intellectual Property Rights,* 8, (2003), pp. 23–31.

Sahai, S., "Indian Patent Act and TRIPS", *Economic and Political Weekly,* 28, (1993), pp. 1495–1497.

Samuels, E., *The Illustrated Story of Copyright*, St. Martin's Press, New York, 2000.

Sarraute, R., "Current Theory on the Moral Right of Authors and Artists Under French Law", *American Journal of Comparative Law,* 16, (1968).

Sasan, N.K., "Rights of the Author: Possible Extensions under Copyright Law in India", 2(2), *International Journal of Innovation and Applied Studies* (2013), pp. 104–112.

Sehgal, D. and Mathur, S., "Rights and Duties of Broadcasting Organizations: Analysis of WIPO Treaty on the Protection of Broadcasting Organizations", *Journal of Intellectual Property Rights,* 16(5), (2011).

Sen, S.R., "Innovation, TRIPS and Future Trends", *Economic and Political Weekly,* 28, (1993), pp. 1918–1919.

Sengar, D.S., "Protection of Trade Secrets and Undisclosed Information: Law and Litigation", *Journal of the Indian Law Institute,* 53, (2011), pp. 254–274.

Sherman, B. and Bently, L., *The Making of Modern Intellectual Property Law*, Cambridge University Press, 2004.

Singh, S.S., "Privacy and Data Protection in India: A Critical Assessment", *Journal of the Indian Law Institute,* 53, (2011), pp. 663–667.

Sir Jennings. R. and Sir Watts, A. (Ed.), *Oppenheim's International Law*, Pearson Education, New Delhi, 1996.

Sivakumar, S. and Lukose, L.P., *Broadcasting Reproduction Right in India: Copyright and Neighbouring Rights Issues*, Indian Law Institute, New Delhi, 2013, pp. 64–65.

Smith, H.E. "Property as the Law of Things", *Harvard Law Review,* 125, (2012), pp. 1691–1726.

_____, "Intellectual Property as Property: Delineating Entitlements in Information", *Yale Law Journal,* 116(8), (2007), pp. 1742–1822.

_____, "Property Is Not Just a Bundle of Rights", *Econ Journal Watch,* 8(3), (2011), pp. 279–291.

Solum, L.B., "Congress's Power to Promote the Progress of Science: Eldred V. Ashcroft", *Loyola of Los Angeles Law Review,* 36, (2002), pp. 1–82.

Thomas, I.D., "Revision of the Rome Convention: Is it Necessary and Timely?" *Copyright Bulletin,* 25, (1991), pp. 32–35.

Thomas, Z., "Overview of Changes to the Indian Copyright Law", *Journal of Intellectual Property Rights,* 17, (2012), pp. 324–334.

Tier, A.M., "Rights Conferred by Sudanese Copyright Protection Act, 1974", *Journal of Indian Law Institute,* 38, (1996), pp. 331–347.

Tiwari, A. and Rajan, S., "Proprietary Rights or Common Property?—The Dilemmas of Copyright Protection of Case—Law Reporters", *Journal of Intellectual Property Rights,* 11, (2006), pp. 33–42.

Tulzapurkar, V., "Remix and Copyright Law", *Journal of Intellectual Property Rights,* 10, (2005), pp. 106–111.

Tyerman, "The Economic Rationable for Published Books: A Reply to Professor Breyer", *UCLA Law Review*, 18, (1971), pp. 1100–1125.

Vaidhyanathan, S., *Copyrights and Copywrongs: The Rise of Intellectual Property and How It Threatens Creativity*, New York University Press, New York, 2001.

Verma, S.K. and Mittal, R. (Ed.), *Intellectual Property Rights: A Global Vision*, Indian Law Institute, New Delhi, 2004.

Verma, S.K., "Enforcement of Intellectual Property Rights: TRIPS Procedure and India", *Journal of Indian Law Institute,* 46, (2004), pp. 183–206.

_____, "IP Protection of Software and Software Contracts in India: A Legal Quagmire", *Journal of Intellectual Property Rights,* 17, (2012), pp. 284–295.

Waldron, J., "From Authors to Copiers: Individual Rights and Social Values in Intellectual Property", *Chicago Kent Law Review,* 68, (1992), pp. 841–887.

_____, *The Right to Private Property*, Harvard University Press, 1978.

Wang, F.F., "Obstacles and Solutions to Internet Jurisdiction A Comparative Analysis of the EU and US Laws", *Journal of International Commercial Law and Technology,* 3(4), (2008), pp. 233–241.

Watal, J., *Intellectual Property Rights in the WTO and Developing Countries,* (Oxford University Press, New York, 2001).

WIPO, "Protection of Neighbouring Right's (Rights of Performers, Producers of Phonograms and Broadcasting Organisations): International Conventions in the Field of Neighbouring Rights", *Journal of the Indian Law Institute,* 28, (1986), pp. 450–469.

_____, *Intellectual Property Reading Material,* Indiana University, Bloomington, London, 1995.

Yen, A., "Restoring the Natural Law: Copyright as Labor and Possession", *Ohio State Law Journal,* 51, (1990), pp. 517–559.

Zemer, L., "The Making of A New Copyright Lockean", *Harvard Journal of Law and Public Policy*, 29(3), (2006), pp. 891–947.

_____, *The Idea of Authorship in Copyright*, Ashgate Publishing Ltd., London, 2007.

Index